Children and Youth in America

Children and Youth in America

A Documentary History

VOLUME II: 1866–1932

Parts One through Six

EDITOR
Robert H. Bremner

ASSOCIATE EDITORS
John Barnard, Tamara K. Hareven,
Robert M. Mennel

Harvard University Press

Cambridge, Massachusetts   1971

© 1971 by The American Public Health Association

Distributed in Great Britain by Oxford University Press, London

Library of Congress Catalog Card Number 74–115473

SBN 674–11612–7

Printed in the United States of America

Foreword

By Martha M. Eliot, M.D., and William M. Schmidt, M.D.

The roots of many current issues in the welfare, education, and health of children and youth in the United States can be traced to developments in the late nineteenth and early twentieth centuries. This documentary survey of public provisions for young Americans from the end of the Civil War to the start of the New Deal, with its breadth of coverage and wealth of detail, should be of particular value and interest to students of history and also to practitioners, administrators, and others concerned with effective services for today's children and youth.

Volume II of *Children and Youth in America* has been prepared under the auspices of the American Public Health Association and with the financial support of the Children's Bureau and Maternal and Child Health Service of the Department of Health, Education and Welfare. The circumstances of the work's preparation have been outlined in the Foreword to Volume I. Collection and editing of the documents and the interpretive introductions are again the work of Mr. Bremner and his staff. In Volume II, Mr. Bremner assumed responsibility for Parts One, Two, Three, and Six. Mr. Barnard prepared Part Eight and assisted Mr. Bremner with Part Two. Miss Hareven assisted Mr. Bremner in the preparation of Part One and was responsible for Part Five. Mr. Mennel prepared Part Four and, with the assistance of Manfred Waserman, Part Seven.

The editors' aim has been to let the documents speak for themselves with such explanatory comments as seemed necessary. Introductions have been supplied to the parts of the volume and, in Part Eight, to individual chapters. The documents have been selected and organized by the editors with the assistance of consultants chosen for their competence in the fields of health, education, family law, delinquency, dependency, and child labor. Despite the length of the volume, the editors have attempted to keep the reader in mind, retaining material deemed essential to an understanding of the particular issues while excising that which seemed extraneous or marginal to the work. As noted in Volume I, therefore, readers requiring the complete texts of the documents should consult the indicated sources.

Harvard School of Public Health
Boston, Massachusetts

Editor's Preface

As recorded in census returns, the number of people in the United States who were under twenty years of age rose from 17 million in 1860 to 47.6 million in 1930. In percentage of total population, however, the below-twenty population declined sharply in the seventy years after 1860. In 1860, 51 per cent of the total population of the United States was under twenty years of age; by 1900 the figure had dropped to 43 per cent and by 1930 to 38 per cent.[1] The declining proportion of children and youths to elders did not lessen concern for their welfare. On the contrary, the gradual and comparative aging of the total population, a development which began to manifest itself early in the nineteenth century, meant that an increasing share of the American people were available for maintaining and rearing the young. As children became relatively less numerous, they became more visible and the particular needs of their condition were more easily recognized. So too youth became more self-conscious, more easily identified and more demanding of attention as a separate category in the total population.[2]

The years covered in this volume were rich in innovations which, even though incompletely realized, represented substantial advances in the welfare, education, and health of children. Much of the philanthropic energy of the late nineteenth and early twentieth centuries went into the provision of special facilities for children formerly treated in the same way as adults. Special hospitals were organized for the reception and treatment of foundlings and sick and crippled children, and new methods of instruction were devised for the handicapped. Public and private institutions intended exclusively for the care of dependent children replaced or at least supplemented almshouse care for dependent children and these institutions came under closer and more stringent state supervision. Reform schools increased in size and number to receive delinquents who would otherwise have been sent to jails and prisons. The juvenile court movement introduced significant differences between the trials of youthful and adult offenders.

State, and in some cases, federal legislation attempted to safeguard children against premature, excessive, and dangerous labor; sought to protect them against abuse, neglect, immorality, disease, and insanitary surroundings; and compelled them to spend more time in school. These laws, intended to secure better treatment and wider opportunities for all children, advanced governmental authority and diminished the power of parents and guardians. Usually sponsored by reformers who represented the views of the dominant American upper and middle classes, the reforms sometimes met opposition from economic, ethnic, and religious groups who adhered to more traditional points of view toward parental authority and the place of young people in society. Such attitudes manifested themselves in resistance to educational

1. Conrad and Irene B. Taeuber, *The Changing Population of the United States* (New York: John Wiley and Sons, Inc., 1958), p. 28.

2. Subject to qualifications which will appear in the documents, we are adopting fourteen to sixteen years of age as the division between "childhood" and "youth." We have not attempted to assign an upper age limit to youth, but it would be no lower than twenty-one.

reforms, opposition to regulation of child labor, and hostility to public supervision of charitable institutions.

Delegates to the first White House Conference on the Care of Dependent and Neglected Children, convened by Theodore Roosevelt in 1909, voiced a long-established sentiment when they declared that home life represented the highest and finest product of civilization. In the foster home versus institutional care controversy of the late nineteenth century, the belief had often been expressed that the poorest home was superior to the best institution. Nevertheless, child welfare and protection agencies had not hesitated to remove children from homes deemed unfit according to their own moral and economic standards. It was not until the 1909 conference that informed welfare workers affirmed that poverty alone was not sufficient cause for removing children from the care of their parents. The mothers' aid or pension movement of the early twentieth century, although still adhering to the "suitable home" concept and limited mainly to whites, had made such progress by 1930 that about as many needy children were being cared for at home as in institutions. Meanwhile, improved casework services were being developed for all categories of children requiring special care.

The single most important development in public provision for children during the early twentieth century was the establishment of the United States Children's Bureau. The founding of this agency in 1912 signified acceptance by the federal government of responsibility for promoting health and welfare of the young. The bureau was organized as a research and information center and did not initially perform any child welfare services. Its function was to investigate and report upon "all matters pertaining to the welfare of children and child life among all classes of our people," including "questions of infant mortality, the birth rate, orphanage, juvenile courts, desertion, dangerous occupations, accidents and diseases of children, employment, and legislation affecting children in the several States and Territories." [3] Subsequently, the bureau was also charged with administering the first federal child labor laws and grants in aid to states for maternal and child health. Under the brilliant leadership of Julia Lathrop and Grace Abbott, and in spite of the meager financial support provided by congressional appropriations, the Children's Bureau amply fulfilled Miss Lathrop's prophecy that it would become "the nation's greatest aid" in effecting justice for all children. [4]

Well before 1929 the principle was widely accepted that the well-being of children could best be achieved by fostering the economic security of the family through assured compensation for industrial accidents and diseases, unemployment and health insurance, and improved housing. Implementation of most of these programs, however, was still to be achieved when the Great Depression struck. It remained for later generations to attack and to correct problems of poverty and racial discrimination which destroy family life for both adults and children.

3. See below Part Six, Chap. I, sec. A, "The struggle for passage of the Children's Bureau bill, 1909–12," doc. 6.

4. Julia C. Lathrop, "The Children's Bureau," *Proceedings* of the National Conference of Charities and Correction, 1912, p. 33.

Acknowledgments

For direction, administration, and support of the Child and State project, the editors wish to acknowledge their continuing indebtedness to Martha M. Eliot and William M. Schmidt of the Harvard School of Public Health, Berwyn F. Mattison, Thomas R. Hood, and Carroll E. Cary of the American Public Health Association, and Charles Gershenson, Hyman Goldstein, and Gloria Wackernah of the Children's Bureau. Oscar Handlin, director of the Charles Warren Center for Studies in American History, Harvard University, and Harry L. Coles and Charles Morley of the Department of History, Ohio State University, graciously provided facilities and services for the editors and their staff during the preparation of Volume II.

In this volume, even more than in the preceding one, the editors are indebted to Grace Abbott and her work, *The Child and the State* (Chicago 1938). None of the editors possesses the fund of practical and theoretical knowledge of child welfare administration Miss Abbott brought to her magisterial introductions to sections of *The Child and the State*. We have not hesitated to take advantage of Miss Abbott's expertise, and the utilization of her text, in the introduction to Part Six, is intended to suggest the guidance we have derived from her work in preparing numerous portions of this volume.

In addition to the advisers and consultants listed in Volume I, we wish to express our deep appreciation to Dorothy Bradbury of the Children's Bureau, Jane Smith and Joseph Howerton of the National Archives, and to numerous librarians and archivists in university and public libraries and state depositories. We also wish to thank Susannah Adams, Paula Cronin, Robert Demorest, Gultekin Ludden, Leslie Rosenfeld, Manfred Waserman, Patricia Grace Zelman, and all the research and editorial assistants who contributed to the volume. During the critical period of final revision, proofreading and indexing, Elaine Bialczak, Richard Friedman, Nicholas Nelson, Esther Pepple, Donald B. Schewe, Cheryl Wilson, and Roy Wortman gave cheerful and invaluable assistance.

Contents

Illustrations

The Skokie School, Winnetka, Illinois. Reproduced from *Educational Buildings by Perkins, Fellows and Hamilton, Architects, Chicago* (Chicago: Perkins, Fellows and Hamilton, 1925), p. 36.

The Free Kindergarten of the Society for Ethical Culture, 1879. Museum of the City of New York.

Following p. 1154

The American Common School. Drawing by C. S. Reinhart in *Harper's Weekly*, XVI (Dec. 14, 1872), 976.

Snap the Whip. By Winslow Homer. *Harper's Weekly* (Sept. 20, 1873), pp. 824–825.

The New School-Mistress. Drawing by Jeannie Brouincombe in *Harper's Weekly*, XVII (Sept. 20, 1873), 817.

Educating the Freedman. *Harper's Weekly*, II (May 25, 1867), 321.

Following p. 1282

The Colored Douglass High School, Baltimore, Md. ca. 1926. *The Crisis*, XXX (December 1926), p. 86.

Negro Common Schools, Mississippi, ca. 1926. *The Crisis*, XXX (December 1926), p. 93.

School erected with the assistance of the Julius Rosenwald Fund, Goodman, Mississippi, ca. 1926. *The Crisis*, XXX (December 1926), p. 95.

School erected with the assistance of the Julius Rosenwald Fund, Canton, Mississippi, ca. 1926. *The Crisis*, XXX (December 1926), p. 95.

Negro School, Holly Springs, Mississippi, ca. 1926. *The Crisis*, XXX (December 1926), p. 97.

White School, Holly Springs, Mississippi, ca. 1926. *The Crisis*, XXX (December 1926), p. 97.

Above: Negro School, Jackson, Mississippi. Below: White School, Jackson, Mississippi. *The Crisis*, XXX (December 1926), p. 101.

Following p. 1314

Eleventh Ward Industrial School. *Frank Leslie's Illustrated Newspaper*, XXIX (March 5, 1870), 413.

Washing Day at the Whittier, Hampton Normal and Agricultural Institute, ca. 1906. Social Ethics Collection, Harvard University.

"To learn to think, we must exercise our limbs." Francis Parker School, Chicago.

Reproduced from John Dewey and Evelyn Dewey, *Schools of Tomorrow* (New York: E. P. Dutton & Company, 1915), facing p. 15.

Winning competitive design for a Carnegie library, 1902. Joseph Wheeler and Alfred Githens, *The American Public Library Building*, (New York: Charles Scribner's Sons, 1941), p. 7.

Part One   The Social and Cultural Background

It is not the purpose in Part One to recite the familiar catalog of urbanization, industrialization, immigration, and the other broad social forces which reshaped American life in the six decades following the Civil War. Instead, we have focused on individual children and on family experiences in an attempt to suggest the many different conditions of childhood. Limitation of space necessitates that this survey be made in an impressionistic way. We have also attempted to show some of the concerns of youth in the early twentieth century as well as adult attitudes and interpretations of these problems. Again, our aim has been to show the dimensions of the subject rather than to deal with it comprehensively.

I The Setting

A. HOMES

"By Census definition in 1900, a dwelling is a place in which, at the time of the census, one or more persons regularly sleep." [1]

Wilmington, Delaware, ca. 1890

Henry Seidel Canby, *The Age of Confidence: Life in the Nineties* (New York: Farrar & Rinehart, 1934), pp. 7–12, 51–54, 65–66. By permission of Holt, Rinehart & Winston, Inc.

Canby (1878–1961), author and critic, was editor of the *Saturday Review of Literature,* 1924–1936.

In my youth it was still a red-brick town with streets of cobble, through which horse cars bumped and rattled. Along one creek shore railroads and factories covered the old marshes and meadows, with here and there a fine gable of a settler's house unnoticed in the dirt and smoke. As the town grew it climbed. Walking uphill on Market Street was a progress through the history of American architec-

1. *A Century of Population Growth*, by W. S. Rossiter, U.S. Bureau of the Census, (Washington, D.C., 1909), p. 101. At the time of the first census of 1790 the average number of occupants per dwelling was 7. In 1900 the estimated number of persons per dwelling in the states and territories that had been enumerated in 1790 was 5.7.

ture, past dilapidated Colonial houses and really lovely banks and markets of the beginning of the century, to the Second Empire of the Grand Opera House, and the shapeless severity of the library and the one big hotel.

From the ballroom at the top of the Opera House where we went for dancing school there was a view of the whole town at once; and it always surprised me to see how deeply its criss-cross of streets was buried in foliage. The factory districts below were grimy and bare, but to the north and the west the roofs were hid in a forest with only a "mansion" here and there or a church steeple projecting.

Beyond the business and shopping section, and toward the hill tops, were tight little streets, heavily shaded and walled with red-brick fronts built cheek to cheek, with decent chins of white marble steps, and alley archways for ears. Here the well-to-do had lived when the city was still a little town, and had been content to hide their arbored side porches and deep if narrow gardens from the street.

The industrial prosperity of the eighties had ended this Quaker restraint. In my day those who could afford it lived further westward in houses that sprawled in ample yards, thickset with trees and shrubbery behind iron or wooden fences. Here was a God's plenty of architecture. Brick boxes of the seventies, with cupolas or mansard roofs, and porches screened with graceful scrolls of iron work were set in old-fashioned contrast beside new contraptions, some of green serpentine, but the latest of brick pseudo-Gothic, with turrets, pointed towers,

3

and Egyptian ornaments of wood. And a little off line with the right-angle streets were still to be seen a few old farm houses of weathered Brandywine granite as colorful as a slice of plum cake, so severe and pure in line that they made the neighboring mansions seem opulent and vulgar, as indeed many of them were.

The main streets were cobble, too rough for our hard-tired bicycles which had to keep to the brick sidewalks, rutty with the roots of the many trees. Side streets were bedded with yellow clay, morasses in the spring and most of the winter and impassable then except on stepping stones. Two-wheeled carts dragged through them and sometimes stuck fast. Every house of any pretentions had its iron hitching post and marble landing block on which fastidious feet could step from the carriages. There were iron stags on the lawns, but our specialty was iron dogs, especially greyhounds, which crouched on either side of the steps. It was a comfortable region of homes, never quite beautiful, nor ugly, certainly not monotonous, and entirely innocent of those period houses out of magazines, with their shrubbery by the local dealer, which are the current ideal of the American home.

To the southward of the hilltops lived the "plain people" by thousands in rows of brick houses with identical windows and doors, no more differentiation in homes than in their lives; and below them again, reaching down into the factories were the slums, where congestion was painful, dirty water ran over broken pavements, and the yards behind were reduced to a dump heap. Here the decent order of our town broke into shrill voices, fighting, smells, and drunkenness.

Each street had its character for us, at least in those neighborhoods where we felt at home. There were subtle social distinctions which by no means ran with size or elegance of dwelling. The town indeed was divided into neighborhoods, so that the division by streets was as artificial as the division of the Union into States. Nothing of this, however, showed geographically. There was only a progression from older to newer as the prosperous American felt for

elbow room. Zoning of course was rudimentary. Each neighborhood outside the slums was a little town in itself, with a store or two, a livery stable, wooden houses tucked in behind for the darkies, vacant lots held for speculation, solid dwellings of the quality, raw built mansions of the new rich, and rows of little houses for the "plain people."

It all began to seem very ugly when the change of taste came in the early nineteen hundreds, yet, looking back now, it begins to have a quiet beauty of its own. There were so many trees, so much variety, such individualism manifest. Homes then did represent some quality of the owner, for the architects, having no style of their own, gave the buyer what he wanted: the nouveaux riches got exactly the parapets and ornamental porches and zig-zag sky line they longed for, simple people had simple houses, solid folk solid brick with plate glass windows and heavy metal roofs, and transients, who stayed a year or so and then moved on, precisely the thrown-together houses they deserved. As the Scotch or English farmer was known by the name of his farm, so when I think of many of our citizens I see their homes before I can recall their faces.

. . . . . .

In our town, and I think in the American nineties generally, home was the most impressive experience in life. Our most sensitive and our most relaxed hours were spent in it. We left home or its immediate environment chiefly to work, and neither radio nor phonograph brought the outer world into its precincts. Time moved more slowly there, as it always does when there is a familiar routine with a deep background of memory. Evening seemed spacious then, with hour upon hour in which innumerable intimate details of picture, carpet, wall paper, or well-known pointing shadow were printed upon consciousness. When bicycles came in and flocks of young people wheeled through twilight streets past and past again the porches where the elders were sitting, it was the first breakaway from home, a warning of the new age, but then more like a flight of May flies round and round their hatching place.

The home came first in our consciousness and thus in our culture, clubs, civic life, business, schools, society being secondary, and success there, except in money making, a work of supererogatory virtue. The woman who could not make a home, like the man who could not support one, was condemned, and not tacitly. Not size, nor luxury, nor cheerfulness, nor hospitality made a home. The ideal was subtler. It must be a house where the family wished to live even when they disliked each other, it must take on a kind of corporate life and become a suitable environment for its diverse inhabitants. Hence a common tragedy in our town, often noted, though seldom traced to its causes, was the slow crushing of a family by its home. The sprawling house, such as they built in the early eighties, grew and grew until parents, aunts, grandparents, children all had their districts and retiring places in its wings and stories. Though the family might quarrel and nag the home held them all, protecting them against the outside world and each other. Deaths came, children migrated, taxes went up, repairs became numerous, yet still the shrinking remnant of the family held on from use and wont, or deep affection, until in a final scene of depleted capital or broken health, the hollow shell of the home collapsed on a ruined estate and fiercely quarreling heirs.

So often tragedy at the end, the home of the nineties was quite as often idyllic, if not ideal, in its best years. It had a quality which we have lost. We complain today of the routine of mechanical processes, yet routine in itself is very persuasive to the spirit, and has attributes of both a tonic and a drug. There was a rhythm in the pre-automobile home that is entirely broken now, and whose loss is perhaps the exactest index of the decline of confidence in our environment. Life seems to be sustained by rhythm, upset by its changes, weakened by its loss. An apartment house with a car at the door, though comfort summarized, has no rhythm, except for a broken, excited syncopation, or the spondaic movement of boredom.

. . . . . .

Confidence is a habit which must be acquired young and from an environment that is constant and rhythmically continuous. The kaleidoscopic patterns of life today are more exciting and probably liberate the intelligence when there is an intelligence to be liberated; but the pattern they make is seldom realized by youth which turns and twists and darts in an environment which to its seeing never once makes a whole. Home life in the nineties could be very sweet, and often profoundly dull, and sometimes an oppressive weight of routine inescapable; security was often bought at a ruinous price; yet what conditioned reflexes it set up! The peace movement of the early nineteen hundreds, naively confident amidst a world in arms, was an attempt to make that world our home, our American home. Nor was heaven exempt from the home-making activities of the American family. We sang lustily in church —

> There we shall rest,
> There we shall rest,
> In Our Father's House,
> In Our Father's House.

The Age of Confidence got the habit of security in its homes.

New England

___

1. Rural New England

Alvan F. Sanborn, "The Future of Rural New England," *Atlantic Monthly,* LXXX (1897), 74–79.

Sanborn (b. 1866), a journalist and author, was resident worker at South End House, Boston, 1892–1896. He attributed the decline of rural New England to depopulation resulting from the California gold rush, the Civil War, emigration to the West, cities, and manufacturing towns, and the feeling of isolation and lack of opportunity resulting from this emigration.

The township of Dickerman, in the interior of one of the New England States, has a large area, with a scattered population of about fifteen hundred souls. Farming is the only industry of the people. The roads, bad at all seasons, and in the spring almost impassable, are so encroached upon by untrimmed brush that wagons have much ado to pass one another. Such guide-boards as are not prone and crumbling are battered and illegible. The mail-boxes at the crossroads are as untrustworthy as worn-out pockets. The orchards are exceptionally picturesque, but they owe their picturesqueness to the unpruned, scraggly, hollow-trunked condition of the trees. The fields wear a disappointed, discouraged air, and the stone walls and rail fences which outline them — they cannot by any stretch of the imagination be said to inclose them — sag at all possible angles, uncertain in their courses as drunken men without guides. Piles of magnificent logs, valuable even where lumber is cheap, are rotting by the roadsides, and stacks of cord-wood, long ready to be transported, stand in the forests.

Many of the farmhouses have been tenant-less for years. Many of the occupied houses are so gray, moss-grown, and dilapidated that they are only a trifle less ghastly than the tenantless ones. They are so weather-beaten as to retain only the faintest traces of the paint that once brightened them. Their windows have the traditional stuffed panes, and the blinds — when there are any — have broken slats. The chimneys, ragged of outline and almost mortarless, threaten to topple over in the first high wind. The outbuildings are flanked by fence-rail buttresses, lest they fall over or break apart. The door-yards are overgrown with rank weeds and overrun with pigs and poultry; the few flowers, which fidelity to country tradition has planted there, being forced to seek refuge behind screens of rusty wire netting or palisades of unsightly sticks. The barn-yards are littered, miry, and foul-smelling, and the stock within them — with the exception of the pigs, which thrive — are lean and hungry.

Even the few houses that have not been allowed to fall into disrepair have a sullen, forbidding appearance. The blinds are closed or the curtains are drawn at all but the kitchen windows. Seen for the first time, they suggest a recent death and an approaching funeral. Every day, however, year in and year out, it is the same with them; they are perpetually funereal. Spick-and-spanness they have, but without brightness, and thrift, but without hospitality.

Dickerman is traversed by a railway, with a station at the "Corners," as that section of the township is called which contains the post-office, the town-house, two stores, two churches, and a squalid hotel, and which therefore comes a little nearer than any other part to being the village proper. Here are also a deserted store, abandoned saw and grist mills, a long-disused academy, a neglected cemetery, and rather more than a due proportion of empty and dilapidated dwellings. The deserted store has never been deprived of its fittings; the dust-coated shelves, counters, and glass showcases, the rust-incrusted scales, the centre stove and the circle of armchairs about it, all remaining in their places, as any one may see who takes the pains to clean a spot for peering through one of the bedaubed windows.

It is more than twenty years since the wheel of the village mill stopped because of the death of its owner, who left no children. The mill is a sad ruin now, almost roofless, two of its side-walls prone on the ground, its machinery oxidizing and falling to pieces, and the piles of sawed and unsawed lumber decomposing around it. It is longer still — more than thirty years — since the academy closed its doors to pupils. The academy building was used for a variety of purposes afterwards — even as a dwelling — before the ultimate and complete desertion that is now its lot. Its sign has remained in place through all its vicissitudes, and, though badly weather-beaten, would still be legible to an expert decipherer of inscriptions.

There are Catholic communities, both in America and in the Old World, where an extreme wretchedness in the dwellings is at once partially explained by the richness and beauty of the churches. But not so in Dickerman. On the contrary, both the Dickerman churches are of a piece with their surroundings. The Congregational Church, more than a century old ("Orthodox" is the name it still goes by), was a worthy structure in its day, and would be so yet had it been kept in good repair. Alas, it is only the ghost of its former pretentious self! Its sills are badly rotted. Its spire and belfry have been shattered by lightning, and imperfectly restored. Its roof is leaky, the clapboards of its walls are warped and blistered, and its heavy bell, once sweet of tone, is cracked and dissonant. The Baptist Church, built only a few years ago, mainly at the expense of a church building society, is one of the shoddily constructed, many-gabled atrocities due to the malign influence of the so-called Queen Anne restoration. Its original coat of paint of many colors has mostly soaked into the surrounding soil. Its panes of stained glass, as they have been broken from time to time, have been replaced by ordinary window-glass, with piebald, uncanny results. The present town-house (the original town-house was burned several years ago), the only public building in the place, comports well with the churches, being a square, squat, unpainted thing, with so striking a resemblance to a barn that it would surely be taken for one, were it not for its lack of barn doors, its isolated and honorable position in the centre of the village common, and its adornment by a bulletin-board thickly plastered with lists of voters, town-meeting warrants, and legal notices in large variety.

In a word, a stranger entering Dickerman for the first time could not fail to be astounded by the marks of desolation and decay on every hand. To him, the most conspicuous evidence that it was or had been a populated town would be the closeness of the gravestones in the graveyard; the best evidence of business enterprise, a freshly painted undertaker's sign, bearing the brisk announcement that coffins, caskets, and burial-robes are always ready; the one touch of beauty, a magnificent double row of aged elms leading up to the forsaken academy; and the one patch of warm color visible, the flaming circus posters with which both the outside and the inside of the Orthodox Church sheds perennially bloom.

When first I saw the crumbling crofters' huts of the Scottish Highlands, I felt that I could never see anything sadder. I had not then seen the deserted farms of my own New England hills. When I visited them, I recognized instantly a sadder sight than the crofters' huts; decay in a new country being as much more appalling than decay in an old country as the loss of faculties in youth is more appalling than the loss of them in age.

What Dickerman is in appearance, a desolate, destitute community, that it is in reality. To begin with homely and material conditions, even at the risk of seeming pettiness, a word must be said regarding the food of its inhabitants. The Dickerman diet is the most unwholesome possible. Pork in one form or another is its staple, — "meat" and pork, "hearty food" and pork, are used as synonyms; and pork is supplemented mainly with hot cream-of-tartar and saleratus biscuit, doughnuts, and pies. The sanitary, not to mention the epicurean possibilities of the meats, vegetables, mushrooms, and fruits within easy reach, either are not known or are ignored. The results are just what might be expected. The men are listless, sullen, stolid. Chronic dyspepsia and other internal disorders are common. That their constitutions are not completely undermined is due largely to the power of resistance that life in the open air gives them. The women, who have not the advantage of outdoor living, who indeed are by necessity or choice quite as much confined within doors as their sisters of the cities, suffer frightfully. They take refuge (as men would turn to drink) in floods of unwholesome patent medicine, and in the nostrums of quacks who appear at regular intervals in the village, only to make a bad state of health a worse one. Small wonder that as a class they are pale, haggard, prematurely old, shrill, ill-tempered, untidy, and inefficient in their housekeeping. To the physical and sensuous delights of the country — a little fishing and hunting on the part of the men excepted — one sex is as indifferent as the other.

The social life is pinched and bare. The only organizations are the churches and a moribund lodge of Good Templars. Of neighborliness there is little, and that little consumes itself so entirely in the retailing of petty scandal that there is nothing left for beneficence. To the sights and sounds of nature — the spring flowers, the summer insects, the autumn foliage, the winter chiaroscuro, the chants of birds, brooks, and woodlands — the people are deaf and blind. The freshness of the morning and the glowing colors of the sunset stir no more emotion in them than in their kine.

The schools are held in poorly equipped buildings, taught by girls without training or enthusiasm, and attended by children devoid of ambition. One might almost say they are as bad as they could be. The Sunday-schools are even worse.

.   .   .   .   .

One is not surprised to find a dearth of public spirit. The civic sense of Dickerman manifests itself once a year only, at town-meeting, chiefly in reducing the regular and necessary appropriations to the lowest possible limit, in protesting against innovations on the ground of burdensome taxes, and in quarreling over trifles. In fact, were it not for the fears of each of the several sections of the township that it would get less than its share of the public moneys, and for the widespread desire to hold office, which finds profit in encouraging these petty sectional jealousies, there would hardly be any public appropriations whatever in Dickerman. Civic honesty, naturally enough, is at the same low ebb as civic spirit. The buying and selling of votes has been in vogue for years, and has not been as much lessened by the introduction of the secret ballot as in larger communities, where secrecy of any sort is more practicable. Only lately, the chairman of the board of selectmen was kept from foreclosing a mortgage solely by the threat of his mortgagee to make public the amounts that he and others had received from the official for their votes in the preceding election. Liquor-selling under a state prohibitory law is condoned by the selectmen for pecuniary considerations, these being tacitly understood to be legitimate perquisites of the office of selectman.

The two churches of Dickerman are not the dispensing centres of sweetness and light that we would fain believe all religious organizations to be. The Orthodox Church, as immutable in its methods as in its doctrines, is cold, unaggressive, self-righteous, and contemptuous of everything religious or anti-religious that is not part and parcel of its tradition. The Baptist Church, equally conservative in matters of doctrine, is nevertheless committed to sensationalism of method, and it is a poor year indeed when it does not manage to produce at least one genuine excitement. It indulges in fierce and frequent tirades against free-thinking, worldly amusements, and Sabbath-breaking, and, for purposes of edification, imports evangelists, Bible readers, leaders of praying bands, total abstinence apostles, refugee Armenians, anti-Catholic agitators, educated freedmen, and converted Jews. The churchgoers, while they are sadly lacking in the positive virtues of honesty, generosity, and brotherly love, are as a class fairly faithful to the code of a conventional negative morality that makes it incumbent upon them to be temperate and orderly, at least in public. The churches are thus a valuable restraining force. Furthermore, they discharge an important social function in bringing together, regularly, people who would otherwise not be brought together at all in an organized way. Barren, then, as the life of Dickerman is with its churches, it would be still more barren without them. The social immorality of rural New England is a subject that does not fall directly in our way, but it ought to be said that the good people who take it for granted that country life develops social purity probably do not know the true condition of country life anywhere; certainly they do not know it in New England. If the whole truth were told about the people of Dickerman in this respect, it would be sad truth. An eminent American has recently been urging the protection of the morals of the city against the country. Novel as the argument seems, it is none the less a sound one.

The foregoing description of life in Dickerman is not exaggerated. Its outward dilapidation and the emptiness of its inner life could not be exaggerated.

. . . . .

There was once a saying current to the effect that as soon as a boy was able to walk, he walked away from Maine. So it came to be at Dickerman, and has been ever since: as soon as a boy has become able to walk, he has walked away from Dickerman. And, pray, why not? What inducement could he have to remain? Instead of leaving a good place to live in for one that might or might not be better, as the first emigrants did, he was merely leaving a bad place to live in for a place that could not possibly be worse.

2. Beacon Street, Boston

George Santayana, *Persons and Places* (New York: Charles Scribner's Sons, 1944), pp. 140, 142–144. Reprinted by permission.

Santayana (1863–1952) was born in Madrid. His mother, an American, returned to the United States when he was a small boy and he remained in Spain with his father. At the age of eight Santayana joined his mother

and older brothers and sisters in Boston. For more of his observations on American life see Part Eight, Chap. I, sec. C, The disengagement of school and child, doc. 4.

The house to which Robert had guided us, although the most commonplace of houses and meanly built for speculation, is perhaps worth describing. We passed the next nine years in it — all the later years of my boyhood; and its character and the life we led there are indelible not only in my memory but no doubt in my character and sentiment. I was unhappy there. At school nothing was imposed on me that I could complain of; there were no grinding tasks and no punishments; but until the last two or three years, when I formed close friendships and awoke to literature, it was all dead routine, and insufficient. A great void remained, which nothing at home could fill. The family was deeply disunited, and each member unhappy for a different reason. One of the boys at school, Davis, who had once come to lunch with us, said afterwards that we seemed to live as if in a boarding house. This was not true at bottom, or at first, because on our Spanish side we formed a true family; but life in America gradually dispersed our interests and our affections. . . .

Our house was, at that time, one of the last on the waterside of Beacon Street, and there was still many a vacant lot east of it, where on passing in sharp wintry weather it was prudent to turn up one's coat collar against the icy blast from the river; as also, for the matter of that, at every cross-street. On the opposite side there were straggling groups of houses running further west along the Mill Dam, under which, at some points, the tide flowed in and out from the Back Bay, the shallow lagoon that originally extended to Boston Neck, turning the town almost into an island. The water in 1872 still came up to Dartmouth Street and to what is now Copley Square. Among the provisional features of this quarter were the frequent empty lots, ten or fifteen feet below the level of the street. These lots were usually enclosed by rough open fences, often broken down at the corners, from which a short cut could be made diagonally to the next street; and by this we schoolboys were quick to profit, for a free run on rough ground amid weeds and heaps of rubbish. The architecture of these half-built streets was conventional and commercial; no house of more than five stories, no apartment houses, no fanciful architectural styles, only two or three churches, closed except at the hour for services on Sundays. To go to Mass we had to walk over the Dartmouth Street railway bridge and some distance beyond, into the South End. I liked the spire at the corner of Newbury and Berkeley Street, and often walked that way in order to see it . . .

Ours was one of two houses exactly alike; yet as they were only two, we could distinguish ours without looking at the number displayed in large figures on the semicircular glass panel over the front door: for ours was the house to the left, not the one to the right. The pair were a product of that "producer's economy," then beginning to prevail in America, which first creates articles and then attempts to create a demand for them; . . . This view of a vast expanse of water reflecting the sky was unmistakably impressive, especially when the summer sunset lit up the scene, and darkness added to distance made the shabby bank opposite inoffensive. Gorgeous these sunsets often were; more gorgeous, good Bostonians believed, than any sunsets anywhere else in the world; and my limited experience does not belie them. The illumination often had a kaleidoscopic quality, with fiery reds and yellows; but at other hours the seasons and aerial effects of the Charles River Basin were not remarkable. Moreover, the grand attraction of the water view was marred by two countereffects discovered eventually by enthusiastic purchasers. One was the immediate foreground, modified but not removed afterwards, when the embankment was added. Under your nose was a mean backyard, unpaved, with clothes or at least clotheslines stretched across it; and mean plank fences divided it from other backyards of the same

description, with an occasional shed or stable to vary the prospect. Under your nose too — and this was the second counter-effect — rose now and then the stench from mudflats and sewage that the sluggish current of the Charles and the sluggish tides that penetrated to the Basin did not avail to drain properly. However, this was chiefly noticeable in summer, when Beacon Street people were expected to be out of town; they made no loud complaints; and the democracy in general was not yet aroused to the importance of town planning for its own sake. The age was still enamored of *laissez-faire*; and its advantages were indeed undeniable.

·   ·   ·   ·   ·

But we happened to be a family of five, demanding five separate rooms. Entertaining of any description was out of the question for us, apart from the expense, since our mother didn't pay visits or go anywhere, or wish for any society; and at that moment she possessed neither the objects nor the money necessary to furnish decently those superfluous reception rooms. She therefore turned the front parlor into a bedroom for herself, while my sisters occupied the two good rooms on the second floor, and Robert, the cook, the housemaid and I had the four small cubicles in the mansard or French roof. At least, this was the ultimate and normal arrangement; but when my father and I arrived, the family prejudice against doubling up had to be overcome for the time being. Not, however, in the case of my father and mother; for she resigned the front parlor to him and moved to one of the rooms above, the two girls being crowded into the other, while I was tucked, as a waif new to the New World, not only into Robert's room but into his bed, which happened incongruously to be a large double one. My mother had taken on her furniture from previous tenants or from "Aunt Lizzie"; and the double beds, not being wanted, had a tendency to pass out of sight into the upper regions; one falling in this way to Robert's lot. But this cohabitation with my elder brother didn't last long; it was contrary to my mother's instinct and habits; and soon a small bed was provided for me and I was moved into the adjoining little room, as into my own castle.

On the prairies

---

1. Dust and drudgery, ca. 1875

Hamlin Garland, *A Son of the Middle Border* (New York, 1927), pp. 128–130; first published in 1917. Reprinted with permission of The Macmillan Company. Copyright 1917 by Hamlin Garland, renewed 1945 by Mary I. Lord and Constance G. Williams. © by The Macmillan Company 1962.

Garland (1860–1940) was born in West Salem, Wisconsin. In 1869 his family moved to Osage, Iowa, and, in 1881, to Ordway, South Dakota.

One day, just as the early sown wheat was beginning to throw a tinge of green over the brown earth, a tremendous wind arose from the southwest and blew with such devastating fury that the soil, caught up from the field, formed a cloud, hundreds of feet high, — a cloud which darkened the sky, turning noon into dusk and sending us all to shelter. All the forenoon this blizzard of loam raged, filling the house with dust, almost smothering the cattle in the stable. Work was impossible, even for the men. The growing grain, its roots exposed to the air, withered and died. Many of the smaller plants were carried bodily away.

As the day wore on father fell into dumb, despairing rage. His rigid face and smoldering eyes, his grim lips, terrified us all. It seemed to him (as to us), that the entire farm was about to take flight and the bitterest part of the tragic circumstance lay in the reflection that our loss (which was much greater than any of our neighbors) was due to the extra care with which we had pulverized the ground.

．　　．　　．　　．　　．

Most authors in writing of "the merry merry farmer" leave out experiences like this — they omit the mud and the dust and the grime, they forget the army worm, the flies, the heat, as well as the smells and drudgery of the barns. Milking the cows is spoken of in the traditional fashion as a lovely pastoral recreation, when as a matter of fact it is a tedious job. We all hated it. We saw no poetry in it. We hated it in summer when the mosquitoes bit and the cows slashed us with their tails, and we hated it still more in the winter time when they stood in crowded malodorous stalls.

In summer when the flies were particularly savage we had a way of jamming our heads into the cows' flanks to prevent them from kicking into the pail, and sometimes we tied their tails to their legs so that they could not lash our ears . . .

No, no, it won't do to talk to me of "the sweet breath of kine." I know them too well — and calves are not "the lovely, fawn-like creatures" they are supposed to be. To the boy who is teaching them to drink out of a pail they are nasty brutes — quite unlike fawns. They have a way of filling their nostrils with milk and blowing it all over their nurse. They are greedy, noisy, ill-smelling and stupid. They look well when running with their mothers in the pasture, but as soon as they are weaned they lose all their charm — for me.

Attendance on swine was less humiliating for the reason that we could keep them at arm's length, but we didn't enjoy that. We liked teaming and pitching hay and harvesting and making fence, and we did not greatly resent plowing or husking corn but we did hate the smell, the filth of the cow-yard. Even hostling had its "outs," especially in spring when the horses were shedding their hair. I never fully enjoyed the taste of equine dandruff, and the eternal smell of manure irked me, especially at the table.

Clearing out from behind the animals was one of our never ending jobs, and hauling the compost out on the fields was one of the tasks which, as my father grimly said, "We always put off till it rains so hard we can't work out doors." This was no joke to us, for not only did we work out doors, we worked while standing ankle deep in the slime of the yard, getting full benefit of the drizzle. Our new land did not need the fertilizer, but we were forced to haul it away or move the barn. Some folks moved the barn. But then my father was an idealist.

---

2. The dreariness of farm life

E. V. Smalley, "The Isolation of Life on Prairie Farms," *Atlantic Monthly,* LXXII (1893), 379–380.

If there be any region in the world where the natural gregarious instinct of mankind should assert itself, that region is our Northwestern prairies, where a short hot summer is followed by a long cold winter, and where there is little in the aspect of nature to furnish food for thought. On every hand the treeless plain stretches away to the horizon line. In summer, it is checkered with grain fields or carpeted with grass and flowers, and it is inspiring in its color and vastness; but one mile of it is almost exactly like another, save where some watercourse nurtures a fringe of willows and cottonwoods. When the snow covers the ground the prospect is bleak and dispiriting. No brooks babble under icy armor. There is no bird life after the wild geese and ducks have passed on their way south. The silence of death rests on the vast landscape, save when it is swept by cruel winds that search out every chink and cranny of the buildings, and drive through each unguarded aperture the dry, powdery snow. In such a region, you would expect the dwellings to be of substantial construction, but they are not. The new settler is too poor to build of brick or stone. He hauls a few loads of lumber from the nearest railway station, and puts up a frail little house of two, three, or four rooms that looks as though the prairie winds would blow it away. Were it not for the invention of tarred building-paper, the flimsy walls would not keep out the wind and snow. With this paper the walls are sheathed under the weatherboards. The barn is often a nondescript affair of sod walls and straw roof. Lumber is much too dear to be used for dooryard fences, and there is no inclosure about the house. A barbed-wire fence surrounds the barnyard. Rarely are there any trees, for on the prairies trees grow very slowly, and must be nursed with care to get a start. There is a saying that you must first get the Indian out of the soil before a tree will grow at all; which means that some savage quality must be taken from the ground by cultivation.

In this cramped abode, from the windows of which there is nothing more cheerful in sight than the distant houses of other settlers, just as ugly and lonely, and stacks of straw and unthreshed grain, the farmer's family must live. In the summer there is a school for the children, one, two, or three miles away; but in winter the distances across the snow-covered plains are too great for them to travel in severe weather; the schoolhouse is closed, and there is nothing for them to do but to house themselves and long for spring. Each family must live mainly to itself, and life, shut up in the little wooden farmhouses, cannot well be very cheerful. A drive to the nearest town is almost the only diversion. There the farmers and their wives gather in the stores and manage to enjoy a little sociability. The big coal stove gives out a greatful warmth, and there is a pleasant odor of dried codfish, groceries, and ready-made clothing. The women look at the display of thick cloths and garments, and wish the crop had been better, so that they could buy some of the things of which they are badly in need. The men smoke corncob pipes and talk politics. It is a cold drive home across the windswept prairies, but at least they have had a glimpse of a little broader and more comfortable life than that of the isolated farm.

Family Group, Missouri, ca. 1896.

McKee's Rocks, Pennsylvania. Photograph by Lewis W. Hine.

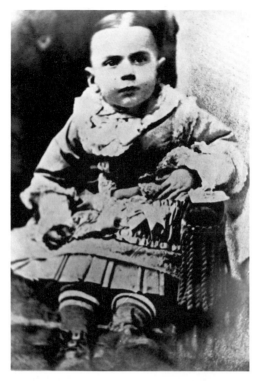

Grace Abbott, Grand Island, Nebraska, ca. 1880.

Little Girls Playing with Their Dolls, ca. 1880.

There are few social events in the life of these prairie farmers to enliven the monotony of the long winter evenings; no singing-schools, spelling-schools, debating clubs, or church gatherings. Neighborly calls are infrequent, because of the long distances which separate the farmhouses, and because, too, of the lack of homogeneity of the people. They have no common past to talk about. They were strangers to one another when they arrived in this new land, and their work and ways have not thrown them much together. Often the strangeness is intensified by differences of national origin. There are Swedes, Norwegians, Germans, French Canadians, and perhaps even such peculiar people as Finns and Icelanders, among the settlers, and the Americans come from many different States. It is hard to establish any social bond in such a mixed population, yet one and all need social intercourse, as the thing most essential to pleasant living, after food, fuel, shelter, and clothing. An alarming amount of insanity occurs in the new prairie States among farmers and their wives. In proportion to their numbers, the Scandinavian settlers furnish the largest contingent to the asylums. The reason is not far to seek. These people came from cheery little farm villages. Life in the fatherland was hard and toilsome, but it was not lonesome. Think for a moment how great the change must be from the white-walled, red-roofed village on a Norway fiord, with its church and schoolhouse, its fishing-boats on the blue inlet, and its green mountain walls towering aloft to snow fields, to an isolated cabin on a Dakota prairie, and say if it is any wonder that so many Scandinavians lose their mental balance.

Mexicans and Indians

1. New Mexico, 1895

Aurthur Goss, *Dietary Studies in New Mexico in 1895,* U.S. Department of Agriculture, Office of Experiment Stations, Bulletin No. 40 (Washington, D.C., 1895), pp. 5–7.

The Mexican or native population of New Mexico and the Southwest in general may, for convenience, be divided into well-to-do people, those in moderate circumstances, and the very poor. The people who have some considerable property and who live and dress very much as do those in similar circumstances in the East are comparatively few. By far the greater number of Mexicans are poor and live in a very primitive manner. There are, of course, people between these extremes. They are somewhat more numerous than the former, but less numerous than the latter.

One of the families selected for this investigation was in moderate circumstances and lived in the town of Las Cruces. The other two families were poor people and lived on a ranch some 4 miles south of Las Cruces.

The poorer class Mexicans, who live out of town, are usually in groups of from two or three to twenty or more families. They cultivate the adjacent land, which they sometimes own, but more often rent, paying grain. As the only arable land to speak of in the arid region is along the water courses, the people are found living along the streams.

MEXICAN HOUSES

Nearly all the Mexicans and many of the Americans in this region live in thick-walled, flat-roofed houses made of large sun-dried bricks or "adobes."

In the case of the poorer class of Mexicans, one family, often large, usually occupies but a single room of less than 20 by 30 feet. This room has but a single door, and one or possibly two openings in the wall to admit light. These "windows" have no glass, and are guarded by wooden slats set into the wall a few inches apart. The floors of the houses are simply the bare ground, and the roofs are made of poles covered with brush, or some similar material, on top of which is spread a liberal coating of

adobe mud. This constitutes the only protection against rain, which, however, seldom falls. The flat-roofed houses, made of earth, present a very peculiar, box-like, and unprepossessing appearance. They are, however, about the most comfortable residence for this country, the thick walls serving to equalize the temperature.

Mexicans of the poorer class raise the greater part of their food, which is almost entirely of vegetable origin. Flour and corn are used, the relative amounts depending upon the amount of money available. If it is necessary to reduce the cost of living to the minimum, as is often the case, more corn and less flour is used.

Probably the next article in amount, and a very important one, is the native bean or "frijole" . . . which, together with peas and lentils, is used to supply the protein necessary in the absence of meats and other nitrogenous foods of animal origin.

Another universal article in the Mexican diet is red pepper, or "chili," which, while it constitutes comparatively a rather small proportion by weight of the total food, is still consumed in enormous quantities as compared with the use of such material by the people of the Eastern States. Chili is probably used more for its stimulating effect on the digestive organs than for the actual amount of nutrients which it furnishes. It or some similar substance is said to be almost essential in the diet of people living in warm countries, who depend almost entirely upon vegetable matter for their food.

In point of cost probably the most important article used by the Mexicans, not home produced, is coffee. This is used almost universally and in large quantities, and is usually purchased unroasted. In the dietary studies here reported the amount paid for coffee varied from 15 to 19 per cent of the total cost of the food used. Lard is another very important article which is usually purchased, and which is used in considerable quantities. As the vegetable foods used contain very little fat, it is necessary to increase the amount of this substance by addition from outside sources, usually either lard compound or beef tallow, which are the cheapest forms of fat in this region.

PREPARATION OF FOOD

In the houses of the poorer class the cooking is done in an open fireplace, usually located in one corner of the room.

The "tortillas," or cakes made of flour or ground corn, are one of the most generally and extensively used foods. When the tortillas are made from corn, the kernels are first boiled with lime, which softens them. The skin is then usually though not always removed, and the grain is ground in a crude stone grinding apparatus or "metate," consisting of a concave slab of stone and a smaller convex piece, which is held in the hands and which serves as a pestle. The grinding is not rotary, however, as in an ordinary mortar, but up and down, toward and from the body. The corn used is usually a small blue kind, rather soft, which seems to contain somewhat more then the average amount of fat. After the corn has been ground into a mush on the metate it is patted out in the hands into the tortillas. Corn tortillas are never rolled, as is the case with those made from flour. If flour is used, it is mixed into a dough with water and the cake rolled out from it. The flour used is not ground in the metate, but in the ordinary flouring mills. It is usually of poor quality, coarse and dark colored. After being worked into the proper form, the tortilla is baked on a flat piece of iron, supported directly over the fire in the open fireplace, the iron being first greased with lard. As soon as it is done on one side the tortilla is turned by pressing the moistened fingers against the upper side of it, thus causing it to adhere to the fingers, whereupon it is deftly turned and the opposite side is browned.

The frijoles or beans are cooked in small homemade earthenware pots, and are almost invariably combined with a very liberal proportion of chili and also considerable lard.

The chili is cooked alone, and also with various other articles of food. It is prepared by

first removing the stems and seeds of the pods, which constitute somewhat more than half of the total weight, after which it is sometimes ground in the metate, but is usually soaked in water and the inner or edible portion separated from the outer skin by squeezing in the hands. Owing to the extremely strong irritating effect on the hands, this operation can not be performed by an amateur. The Mexican women, however, become so accustomed to it that it seems to have no effect on them.

Among the poor families the meals are served on the floor in the middle of the room, the family sitting on the ground around the food and eating without knives, forks, or plates.

MISCELLANEOUS

The houses of the poor people are usually supplied with skins of sheep and other animals, which serve both as chairs and beds for the children. When grinding corn and other articles in the metate and doing other kinds of housework, the women usually sit on the floor on these skins.

A very peculiar feature found in most of these houses is the swallows' nests attached to the ceiling. The swallows continually flitting in and out of the door feeding their young seem to be entirely at home among the dogs and children.

The water supply for a group of families is usually an open well, centrally located, and used by all alike.

In passing from the poor to the well-to-do classes, and from the country to the towns, the manners and customs become more and more Americanized, until finally there is little difference in these respects between Americans and Mexicans. In the families of people in moderate circumstances living in the towns the stove and table make their appearance, and the meals are cooked and served more nearly in the American manner. A greater variety of food is also used, including some meats and other animal foods. The frijoles and chili,

however, are never discarded from the Mexican diet, no matter how high the station in life.

---

2. Living conditions of Indians, 1928

Lewis Meriam, *The Problem of Indian Administration* (Baltimore, 1928), pp. 3–4.

Meriam (b. 1883) was technical director of the Survey Staff of the Institute for Government Research, Brookings Institution. His survey, covering all aspects of the work of the Indian Service, was conducted at the request of the secretary of the interior.

An overwhelming majority of the Indians are poor, even extremely poor, and they are not adjusted to the economic and social system of the dominant white civilization.

The poverty of the Indians and their lack of adjustment to the dominant economic and social systems produce the vicious circle ordinarily found among any people under such circumstances. Because of interrelationships, causes cannot be differentiated from effects. The only course is to state briefly the conditions found that are part of this vicious circle of poverty and maladjustment.

Health. The health of the Indians as compared with that of the general population is bad. Although accurate mortality and morbidity statistics are commonly lacking, the existing evidence warrants the statement that both the general death rate and the infant mortality rate are high. Tuberculosis is extremely prevalent. Trachoma, a communicable disease which produces blindness, is a major problem because of its great prevalence and the danger of its spreading among both the Indians and the whites.

Living Conditions. The prevailing living conditions among the great majority of the Indians are conducive to the development and spread of disease. With comparatively few exceptions the diet of the Indians is bad. It is generally insufficient in quantity, lacking in variety, and poorly prepared. The two great preventive elements in diet, milk, and fruits and green vegetables, are notably absent. Most tribes use fruits and vegetables in season, but even then the supply is ordinarily insufficient. The use of milk is rare, and it is generally not available even for infants. Babies, when weaned, are ordinarily put on substantially the same diet as older children and adults, a diet consisting mainly of meats and starches.

The housing conditions are likewise conducive to bad health. Both in the primitive dwellings and in the majority of more or less permanent homes which in some cases have replaced them, there is great overcrowding, so that all members of the family are exposed to any disease that develops, and it is virtually impossible in any way even partially to isolate a person suffering from a communicable disease. In certain jurisdictions, notably the Osage and the Kiowa, the government has stimulated the building of modern homes, bungalows, or even more pretentious dwellings, but most of the permanent houses that have replaced primitive dwellings are small shacks with few rooms and with inadequate provision for ventilation. Education in housekeeping and sanitation has not proceeded far enough so that the Indians living in these more or less permanent shacks practice ventilation and domestic cleanliness. From the standpoint of health it is probably true that the temporary, primitive dwellings that were not fairly air-tight and were frequently abandoned were more sanitary than the permanent homes that have replaced them. The furnishing of the primitive dwellings and of the shacks is limited. Although many of them still have very primitive arrangements for cooking and heating, the use of modern cook stoves and utensils is far more general than the use of beds, and the use of beds in turn is far

more common than the use of any kind of easily washable bed covering.

Sanitary facilities are generally lacking. Except among the relatively few well-to-do Indians the houses seldom have a private water supply or any toilet facilities whatever. Even privies are exceptional. Water is ordinarily carried considerable distances from natural springs or streams, or occasionally from wells. In many sections the supply is inadequate, although in some jurisdictions, notably in the desert country of the Southwest, the government has materially improved the situation, an activity that is appreciated by the Indians.

New York City

1. Hell's Kitchen, 1902

S. Josephine Baker, *Fighting for Life* (New York: Macmillan, 1939), pp. 57–60.

Dr. Baker (1873–1945) received an M.D. from Women's Medical College, New York Infirmary in 1898. In 1902 she became a medical inspector for the New York City Department of Health and in 1908 was appointed director of the Bureau of Hygiene. For her work in the latter position see Part Seven, Chap. II, sec. B, Introduction of complete physical examinations for school children, doc. 1.

This time I had let myself in for a really gruelling ordeal. Summer anywhere in New York City is pretty bad. In my district, the heart of old Hell's Kitchen on the west side, the heat, the smells, the squalor made it something not to be believed. Its residents were largely Irish, incredibly shiftless, altogether charming in their abject helplessness, wholly lacking in any ambition and dirty to an unbelievable degree. At the upper edge of Hell's Kitchen, just above Fifty-ninth Street, was the then largest colored district in town. Both races live well below any decent level of subsistence. My job was to start in this district every morning at seven o'clock, work until eleven, then return for two hours more — from four to six. I climbed stair after stair, knocked on door after door, met drunk after drunk, filthy mother after filthy mother and dying baby after dying baby. It was the hardest physical labor I ever did in my life: just backache and perspiration and disgust and discouragement and aching feet day in and day out.

I worked out one minor way to save myself by going up the long flights of stairs to the roof of one tenement and then climbing the dividing wall to go down the stairs of the next. Trailing street-sweeping skirts were not much of a help. There was no dodging the hopelessness of it all. It was an appalling summer too, with an average of fifteen hundred babies dying each week in the city; lean, miserable, wailing little souls carried off wholesale by dysentery. Even New York's worst slums have now forgotten what dysentery epidemics were like. But we knew thirty years ago. The babies' mothers could not afford doctors and seemed too lackadaisical to carry their babies to the nearby clinics and too lazy or too indifferent to carry out the instructions you might give them. I do not mean that they were callous when their babies died. Then they cried like mothers, for a change. They were just horribly fatalistic about it while it was going on. Babies always died in summer and there was no point in trying to do anything about it. It depressed me so that I branched out and went looking for healthy babies too and tried to tell their mothers how to care for them. But they were not interested. I might as well have been trying to tell them how to keep it from raining.

.   .   .   .   .

Why I stayed on that job is another mystery. But I actually refused my regular summer

laboratory work at the Dansville Sanitarium in order to stay with this brutal punishment. Perhaps the sight of such sluggish, crawling misery fascinated me. You could not say that I was sentimental about these people. I had a sincere conviction that they would all be better off dead than so degradingly alive. But they apparently had an instinct for life and I had to go through the motions of helping them. It did seem pretty futile. One could hardly walk a block in any tenement district in the city without meeting a "Little White Funeral." Dead horses (there were horses then) were a common sight in almost every street. Pasteurization of the milk supply was just beginning to be urged by that great philanthropist, Nathan Straus, but the bulk of the milk supply that these babies were fed on was drawn from rusty cans and the milk was dotted with flies as well as full of bacteria. One could do so little at best. In my mind was a vague idea that something could and must be done; what it might be I did not yet know, but I did know that it was infamous to let these things go on. I have heard out-of-towners ask the reason for Hell's Kitchen having that picturesque name. I could give them a good reason and it would not have anything to do with gangsters either.

Presently I was in such a frame of mind that no horror could be really disturbing. That was the summer of the General Slocum disaster, when an excursion boat filled with women and children on a picnic party burned in the East River and hundreds were drowned or burned. All of the Health Department inspectors were summoned by telephone to rush to North Brother Island, where bodies were being washed ashore from the burning vessel. There was precious little to do by the time we got there; it was just a question of getting the bodies out of the water and ranging them in long rows on the shore, dead woman after dead woman, dead child after dead child, all huddled and wet and still. It was fearful, I suppose, but you cannot realize things wholesale that way, any more than you could psychologically afford to realize the mass of misery in my Hell's Kitchen slum.

---

2. Tenements for Negroes, 1905

Mary White Ovington, "The Negro Home in New York," *Charities,* XV (October 7, 1905), 25–26.

Miss Ovington (1865–1951), one of the founders of the National Association for the Advancement of Colored People, was author of *Half a Man: The Status of the Negro in New York* (New York, 1911).

Like all the New York poor the Negro lives in a tenement. The lower East Side, famed for its overcrowding, does not know him. His quarters are west, but there he finds conditions that are often quite as bad as those among the Italians or the Jews. In the most thickly segregated Negro section, that between West Fifty-ninth and West Sixty-fourth streets and Tenth and West End avenues, the tenements are of the old double-decker and dumb-bell types with no through ventilation and with twenty and twenty-two families to a house. The air-shafts in these tenements are so small as to be only "culture tubes" except on the top story, where the rooms gain something of air and light. In the lower part of town, about the Thirties, we still find a number of rear tenements occupied by the colored race. The sunlight enters these houses, but they are very old, impossible to keep clean, and dangerous because of their distance from the open street. Again, still further south, about Cornelia street, the race lives in dilapidated former dwelling-houses. These West Side districts have little of the picturesqueness of the lower East Side, and have been more or less neglected by those interested in the moral and civil welfare of the community.

Rents are high for everyone in New York, but the Negroes pay more and get less for their money than any other tenants. Every week in the warm weather hundreds of them come from the South. They must find shelter, and the places that they may rent are few, and those not tenements of the better sort. The many attractive and healthful houses that have been built since the creation of the Tenement House Department are not open to them. They are confined to certain localities, and usually to only a few houses in each block. Forced to crowd into small and uncomfortable rooms, their opportunities for making a home what it should be are much restricted.

.   .   .   .   .

Study closely the tenants in any of these streets and you will find every grade of social life. Their difficulty in procuring a place to live compels the colored people to dwell good and bad together. Ten families of pure and upright lives may be forced to rent rooms in a house where there are other ten families who are rough and noisy, often immoral. This is true of all overcrowded districts, but it is especially true in the Negro quarters; for the landlord of a colored tenement rarely makes any attempt to discriminate among his applicants, but takes in anyone who will pay his rent. Complaints against objectionable tenants are unheeded, and the mother and father in the respectable home have the difficult problem of rearing children in a few rooms from which there is no escape save to a stairway and street where undesirable companions are numerous. Lines need to be drawn very sharply by such parents, and factions arise among the children that are the despair of the club worker who gathers in her boys and girls, believing that propinquity makes a harmonious group.

This decided difference in the standing and character of the Negroes in a tenement block makes it impossible to describe a typical home; but there are a few facts that may be noted as characteristic of perhaps all but the lowest people in the district. Many of the colored women in New York have at one time or another been engaged in domestic service. In such positions they have received many presents, and their homes are likely to be filled with cheap pictures, photographs, cards, vases, little ornaments that the doctor or nurse longs to see thrown away, but that nevertheless give an air of homelikeness to the place. The Negroes' homes are often sadly cluttered, but they are rarely bare and ugly. With this love of pretty things goes a desire to live with something of form in the arrangement of the rooms and in the ordering of the meals. When breakfast or dinner comes you will almost always find the table set. The unappetizing tenement meal, eaten out of a paper bag without the setting of the table or the gathering together of the family, is unusual in the colored district. I have been surprised to find in the most modest homes that the meal carried with it the air of a social function; the mother would use many dishes though she must take the time from her laundry work to wash them.

The Negro home is a generous and hospitable one. Pushed aside by the rest of the community, these folk gather the more closely together, and while this carries with it the cliques and gossipings of a village life, it also strengthens and develops a willingness to help those who are in need. Considering his poverty very little relief is given to the Negro in New York. This is partly because he does not understand how to use the charity that the institutions for relief provide, but it is also because he cares for his own. The colored churches do much for their poor, and nearly all the colored people belong to sick benefit societies, but their frequent kindnesses one to another are their most constant charity. They adopt the child that has been deserted, and they feed the next-door neighbor though they have little themselves. Their hospitality is sometimes almost too overflowing. "Five frens jus' come up f'om de Souf," one woman said to me in excusing the disorderly appearance of her five rooms. Her regular family consisted of nine. "I jes' had t' tek' 'em in," she added, and I could not gainsay her though I thought more than she did of the unhealthfulness and discomfort of fourteen people in one small flat.

---

3. Brownsville

Alfred Kazin, *A Walker in the City* (New York: Harcourt, Brace & World, Inc., 1951), pp. 11–12, 65–66.[1]

Alfred Kazin was born in Brownsville, a section of Brooklyn, in 1915.

We were of the city, but somehow not in it. Whenever I went off on my favorite walk to Highland Park in the "American" district to the north, on the border of Queens, and climbed the hill to the old reservoir from which I could look straight across to the skyscrapers of Manhattan, I saw New York as a foreign city. There, brilliant and unreal, the city had its life, as Brownsville was ours. That the two were joined in me I never knew then — not even on those glorious summer nights of my last weeks in high school when, with what an ache, I would come back into Brownsville along Liberty Avenue, and, as soon as I could see blocks ahead of me the Labor Lyceum, the malted milk and Fatima signs over the candy stores, the old women in their housedresses sitting in front of the tenements like priestesses of an ancient cult, knew I was home.

We were the end of the line. We were the children of the immigrants who had camped at the city's back door, in New York's rawest, remotest, cheapest ghetto, enclosed on one side by the Canarsie flats and on the other by the hallowed middle-class districts that showed the way to New York. "New York" was what we put last on our address, but first in thinking of

1. From *A Walker in the City,* Copyright 1951 by Alfred Kazin. Reprinted by permission of Harcourt, Brace & World, Inc.

the others around us. *They* were New York, the Gentiles, America; we were Brownsville — *Brunzvil,* as the old folks said — the dust of the earth to all Jews with money, and notoriously a place that measured all success by our skill in getting away from it. So that when poor Jews left, *even* Negroes, as we said, found it easy to settle on the margins of Brownsville, and with the coming of spring, bands of Gypsies, who would rent empty stores, hang their rugs around them like a desert tent, and bring a dusty and faintly sinister air of carnival into our neighborhood.

.　　.　　.　　.　　.

The kitchen held our lives together. My mother worked in it all day long, we ate in it almost all meals except the Passover *seder,* I did my homework and first writing at the kitchen table, and in winter I often had a bed made up for me on three kitchen chairs near the stove. On the wall just over the table hung a long horizontal mirror that sloped to a ship's prow at each end and was lined in cherry wood. It took up the whole wall, and drew every object in the kitchen to itself. The walls were a fiercely stippled whitewash, so often rewhitened by my father in slack seasons that the paint looked as if it had been squeezed and cracked into the walls. A large electric bulb hung down the center of the kitchen at the end of a chain that had been hooked into the ceiling; the old gas ring and key still jutted out of the wall like antlers. In the corner next to the toilet was the sink at which we washed, and the square tub in which my mother did our clothes. Above it, tacked to the shelf on which were pleasantly ranged square, blue-bordered white sugar and spice jars, hung calendars from the Public National Bank on Pitkin Avenue and the Minsker Progressive Branch of the Workman's Circle; receipts for the payment of insurance premiums, and household bills on a spindle; two little boxes engraved with Hebrew letters. One of these was for the poor, the other to buy back the Land of Israel . . .

Appalachians

1. Hill Country, Kentucky, 1920

Lydia Roberts, *The Nutrition and Care of Children in a Mountain County of Kentucky,* United States Children's Bureau, Pub. No. 107 (Washington, D.C., 1922), pp. 2–3, 39–41.

The county in which the area studied is located contains within its borders extremes of richness and of poverty of soil. The greater part of the county is in the blue-grass section where the soil is of great fertility, but a small portion of it extends into "the knobs," or "the mountains," as the rocky cone-shaped hills are called, where the soil is for the most part exceedingly poor. It was this small, mountainous part which constituted the area studied.

.　　.　　.　　.　　.

The 123 families visited in this survey were all native white and with very few exceptions were of mountain stock. Poor roads had tended to isolate them, although they lived within a few miles of a small town with railroad and educational advantages, which no doubt had influenced them to a certain extent. Their natural shyness and reserve, a heritage from many generations of mountain ancestors, has made them slow in responding to outside influences.

A visitor to the mountains never fails to be impressed by the premature ageing of the majority of the people, particularly the women. The early age at which the women marry and assume the cares of a home and family doubtless offers a partial explanation of this fact.

.　　.　　.　　.　　.

This study of a small mountain section of Kentucky included 123 families in which lived

256 children from 2 to 11 years of age. The heads of households in 103 families were farmers, but only 59 were occupied in farming alone, while 44 supplemented work on their farms by some other occupation.

A total of 149 children were given physical examinations. Half this number had enlarged or diseased tonsils; more than a fourth showed symptoms of adenoids; over three-fourths had carious teeth. Only 7 per cent of the children were ranked excellent in nutrition; 18 per cent, good; 35 per cent, fair; 34 per cent, poor; and 6 per cent, very poor.

The income in the homes of 42 children was considered adequate; in the homes of 95, its adequacy was doubtful; 119 children, or 47 per cent, were living in homes clearly incapable of providing the essentials of a simple standard of living. Sanitary facilities were poor; 56 per cent of the families had no toilet. More than half the families (55 per cent) depended for their water supply upon a spring, stream, open well, or other source which might suffer pollution.

The family food supply was restricted both in kind and amount and the family diet was in consequence monotonous and sometimes so limited as not to furnish all the elements necessary. Milk and whole corn meal were the redeeming features of the diet, but in many homes even the supply of milk was too limited, especially at certain periods, to insure an adequate diet, though 80 per cent of all the families kept one or more cows.

Only 28 per cent of the children were having a diet which probably included all the constituents necessary to nourish their bodies, provided enough was eaten and the body was able to utilize it. The diets of 27 per cent were clearly inadequate for the needs of growing children. In other words, nearly three-fourths of the children were living on diets of either doubtful adequacy or certain inadequacy.

Fruit and vegetables occupied a minor place in the children's dietary; beans were the predominating vegetable; wild blackberries were practically the only fruit, either fresh or canned, 54 per cent of the children had. Eggs were almost entirely absent from the winter diet and even at the time of greatest yield were eaten by only 62 per cent of the children as often as twice a week. Seventy-seven per cent of the children had meat daily or oftener, but since meat in this community was usually fat salt meat it made a very questionable contribution to the protein in the dietary. It was estimated that 72 per cent of the children had at least a pint of milk daily; 70 per cent had corn bread made of whole corn meal or biscuits made of bolted white flour. Coffee was used by 55 per cent of the children, though only 34 per cent drank it four or more times a week. Eating between meals was indulged in by 43 per cent to such an extent as probably to be harmful.

.   .   .   .   .

Chiefly because of the early rising hour, but 45 per cent of the children were having sufficient hours of sleep. Only a little more than a fourth of the children had clothing which could be considered sufficient to furnish adequate protection from the elements. Care of the teeth was very generally neglected.

---

2. A mining patch in West Virginia, ca. 1930

Statement of Clarence E. Pickett, March 31, 1938, U.S. Congress, Senate Special Committee to Investigate Unemployment and Relief, *Hearings . . . Pursuant to S. Res. 36,* 75 Cong., 3 Sess. (1938), II, 1623.

Pickett was executive secretary of the American Friends Service Committee which conducted relief and rehabilitation projects in the bituminous coal areas.

. . . The Delbos family live at the end of a

hollow in West Virginia. For 20 years Anton Delbos mined coal and lived in a little company house, supporting his large family. Then came decrease in the market for coal, the declining width of the seam where he was at work, and the final collapse of the company that owned this mine. But it had operated for 20 years and certainly it would open again. Days and weeks passed by, and Anton saw his very meager savings that he had laid by gradually exhausted. He scratched the side of the hill — all too steep for cultivation — and began growing a few scrawny vegetables. But that didn't help much. The children began to be droopy at school and to fail in their school work. John, the boy of 13, had to have glasses, but couldn't afford them. Finally a little relief came through the Red Cross, and the visitor from the Salvation Army gave some encouragement. The church in the larger town nearby

started a little mission, and the good women of the city church sent out their second-hand clothes. The Delbos family gradually learned to eke out an existence from this kind of help. Then came the cataclysm of 1929, which reached its depth in 1931–32. There were so many calls for relief that the Delbos family, at the top of the run, were neglected worse than ever. They had by this time lost all sense of shame at begging and stealing. They had gradually given up trying to be decent and respectable. This had come about partly because the Delbos family did not stand alone in their tragedy. Their whole little mining patch of 82 families had fallen to the same level. Losing hope and interest, dejected and disappointed, Mr. Delbos took to the road and left his wife and children to shift for themselves. This was in 1931. It represents about a hundred thousand of the miners at that time.

B. FAMILIES

According to the census of 1900 there were almost 16 million families in the United States. The average size was 4.6 persons, a decrease of about one person since the first census of 1790 when the average number of persons per family was 5.7.[1]

Old Americans

1. The McAdoos and the Floyds

William G. McAdoo, *Crowded Years* (Boston and New York: Houghton Mifflin Company, 1931), pp. 1–16.[2]

1. W. S. Rossiter, *A Century of Population Growth,* p. 97.
2. Reprinted by permission of the publisher, Houghton Mifflin Company.

McAdoo (1863–1941) was secretary of the treasury, 1913–1918, and senator from California, 1933–1939.

My father kept a diary. Year after year he recorded the events of his life in a row of thin brown volumes. There one may read of the ups and downs of his law practice, of his deep devotion to his wife, of the books he bought, and his comments on current events. He was an industrious diary-keeper, painstaking and meticulous, and apparently did not omit very much. Sometimes he would set down the price of a pair of shoes and a record of the fees he had received on the same page with the first draft of a sonnet and the strange Latin names of the flowers that he had come across in his daily walk.

I handle the volumes of his diary with a delicate touch. Their pages are old and tired.

They are brittle with too much time, and if I should let them have their way, they would fall apart and disintegrate. Curious to learn of my own coming into the world, I turn to an entry written in pale, home-made Confederate ink at Marietta, Georgia, on October 31, 1863.

"Today, about thirty minutes after noon, Mary gave birth to a son weighing nearly eleven pounds, with long black hair. He bawled lustily, showing a fine pair of lungs, is voracious, and seems to have a vigorous constitution. My darling wife went through the terrible ordeal bravely, and appears to be doing well tonight."

Though I was born at Marietta — a town about twenty miles north of Atlanta — my parents had lived for many years in Knoxville, Tennessee. Both of them were well acquainted with Marietta and its people, although they did not consider themselves permanent residents. Before the Civil War it was a summer resort, and my father had met my mother there.

The McAdoos belonged to eastern Tennessee. They had lived among its hazy blue mountains for many years; for so many years, indeed, that the story of their coming and their settlement on the new Tennessee land — as I have heard my elders tell it — is mingled with stouthearted tales of Indians and camp-fires. These early McAdoos were bearded, vigorous men of Scotch descent, pioneers by instinct, rough and hearty, living close to the soil, and making their own way without seeking help or guidance. They were all Bible-reading Presbyterians who believed in Judgment Day and the efficacy of shotguns.

My father, whose name was William Gibbs McAdoo, the same as mine, was born in 1820, about the time when schooling and book-learning were beginning to get a toe-hold in that pioneer country. He was the first McAdoo who ever went to college, so far as I know. In 1842, he entered the East Tennessee University, at Knoxville, and graduated in 1845. Before going to the University, he had taught school for several years. The citizens of his country must have had a high opinion of him, for he was

elected a member of the legislature of Tennessee on the day before his graduation.

Soon afterward — that is, in 1846 — the Mexican War began, and a company of volunteers was enrolled at Knoxville. My father was the chief organizer of the company, which consisted of about a hundred raw-boned, stalwart country youths eager for adventure. In the course of their progress toward Mexico, my father, who began as the company's first lieutenant, eventually became its captain.

The company, with its arms and supplies, embarked on flat-boats at Knoxville and drifted down the Tennessee River as far as Muscle Shoals. There the original flat-boats were abandoned and they proceeded to the bottom of the rapids and built another fleet of boats. That task was a mere nothing; those husky boys were all handy with the axe and the plane. Within a week their new boats were completed. They piled in their belongings, their banjos and their dogs and pet raccoons, and started for New Orleans. It took a long time to float down the Tennessee, Ohio, and Mississippi Rivers to New Orleans.

Eventually they were sent to Vera Cruz in a seasick little ship that capered and jumped over the waves. For a day or two the farmer boys were too ill to quarrel. Then they got their sea-legs, and — for some reason that is not clear to me — they announced their intention of throwing the captain of the ship overboard. It seems to have taken a good deal of my father's Tennessee oratory to keep them from actually doing it. They were, I fancy, an unruly lot.

They reached Vera Cruz after a while and aided in the capture of the city. Then, with the rest of General Scott's army, they fought their way — disillusioned and very tired — up the steep mountain roads to the City of Mexico. On the way, my father and his company distinguished themselves at the battle of Cerro Gordo.

After the Mexican War was over, my father studied law, was admitted to the bar, and in time was elected to the position of district attorney-general — or prosecuting attorney — for the Knoxville circuit, which included a number of counties in eastern Tennessee.

As attorney-general he gained a reputation for ability and fearlessness which survived long after he had become only a memory in the Tennessee courts. This distinction was probably magnified and colored by time and much re-telling, but from my knowledge of his character I should say that not a great deal of it was fiction. I never knew him to be afraid of anything or anybody.

.　　.　　.　　.　　.

When the Unionists got control at Knoxville, and became the virtual rulers of eastern Tennessee, my father felt that existence there was no longer possible for him. He wound up his affairs, said good-bye to his friends, and started southward with his family, to a region where there were no Unionists except a few who had been put in jail for their own protection.

My mother, who was a Floyd of Georgia, owned an extensive plantation on the Georgia coast, near Darien. I use the word 'extensive' in a geographical, instead of an economic, sense. Although the plantation was many-acred, widespreading, and probably of fertile soil, it was lean in profits. The slaves that lived on it consumed about all they produced. My father and his famliy started from Knoxville with the intention of going to "Bellevue," as this plantation was called. He was to leave my mother and the children at the plantation while he went into military service.

On the way they changed their minds. They came to the conclusion that the climate of the lowlands would not do for the young children — I had a brother and two sisters living at the time — and they decided to remain in Marietta among the north Georgia hills. A few miles from the town a house was for sale, and they bought it.

This Marietta house was a large, airy place, with a wide, white-columned verandah in front. It stood on elevated, red-clay land with a vista of green valleys and smoky-hued Kenesaw Mountain in the distance. The house, with its grounds, was called "Melora" in the high-toned fashion of the old South, where everything in the shape of a mansion had to have a name. That is how I happened to be born in Georgia instead of Tennessee on the last day of October, in the year 1863.

.　　.　　.　　.

I have no personal memory of living at "Melora." When I was about six months old, my family moved to Milledgeville, in the central portion of the state. Milledgeville was then the capital of Georgia.

There was an immense difficulty in getting moved, as I see from my father's diary. This was in 1864; the Southern Confederacy, reeling and staggering, was bled white of men and resources. Affairs were in such hopeless confusion that few people dared to travel, except on military business. The railroads, all of them controlled by the Confederate government, were hardly more than streaks of rust. The weary, scrap-iron locomotives had to stop for breath on every heavy grade.

Nearly every freight car still capable of running on wheels was in the government service. After besieging everyone within reach who had anything to do with the management of the Western and Atlantic Railroad, my father was finally promised a freight car to move his household goods, and was told that it would be left at Marietta on a certain day. Empty promise. The day came and went with the Marietta siding blank and vacant.

One day, while he was wondering what he would do, he saw a gaunt, weather-beaten wreck of a freight car standing on a spur track near the station. It had holes in it large enough for a man to walk through, and part of its roof was gone. He hurried to the railroad station to see the agent, who told him that he could have the car if he would nail boards over the holes. The agent remarked that the car had been abandoned as unsafe. My father and a negro spent the next day repairing this vehicle; then he went home and dismantled the house as quickly as possible, so as to get his belongings into the car before dark.

As they came in sight of the station with the two wagonloads of furniture, they saw a government train standing there. The officer in charge was looking over the battered car and evidently contemplating its seizure.

My father hurried up and explained his desperate plight. The officer was very agreeable. He said he had intended to attach the car to his train, which was taking munitions to the front, but he would always defer to a family in distress. With a polite gesture he turned over the battered car to the McAdoos. There were many bows and courteous remarks on both sides.

.   .   .   .   .   .

Not long afterward the passenger train that my father intended the family to take stopped at the station, but he made up his mind not to leave until he had seen his furniture start on its way, so we remained overnight at a neighbor's house. Next morning our car was no longer there; the station agent declared that a freight train had arrived and departed during the night, and that the car had gone on to Milledgeville. My father doubted his word; gloom spreads over the diary. But nothing could be done about it. In those perilous times men and women lived in a sort of quiet desperation.

When the morning train, due at nine-thirty in the forenoon, rattled up to the Marietta station at three in the afternoon, the McAdoo family, including four or five negro household servants — slaves — climbed aboard. Before the train started, the conductor came into the car.

"Do you-all count on takin' them niggers in these kyars?" he asked my father, as he pointed at the shrinking darkies.

"Why, I thought so," my father replied. "I've bought tickets for them."

"Well," the conductor went on amiably, "it's a rule that niggers ain't allowed on passenger kyars. I reckon you can't take 'em."

"Then what am I to do about them?"

"They'll have to go by express," the conductor announced.

Then followed a long and lazy argument in the Southern style, over this point, while the wheezing locomotive, with its string of ramshackle cars, waited like a tired and wounded animal. In the end the conductor won. The negroes were sent by express, with destination tags strung around their necks. All but one. The conductor was prevailed upon to allow Sukey, a fifteen-year-old girl, to accompany the family. Sukey was needed as a nurse; she carried me in her arms.

When we arrived at Milledgeville, my father records, there stood our freight car, with its bright red seals, on the side track at the station. Everything was intact.

The negroes did not get there for a week. They were never able to tell where they had been, except that they had stayed for two days in the depot of a place where there were a lot of houses. The Southern Express Company had given them regular meals, they said.

We did not live in the town of Milledgeville at first. The house which my father rented was at Midway, a suburb, about two miles from the central square of the town. It was an ordinary frame building, undistinguished in appearance, that had been used as a small hotel before the war. It had many rooms, some of them not needed at first, but after a time our family grew up to the house's large proportions.

There were shady, pleasant woods all around; the sunlight filtered through the leaves and laid a flickering, checkered pattern on the ground. At one side of the house there was an old rose garden. One of my earliest memories is of rain falling on this garden. I stood at the window and watched the huddled roses, beaten by the storm, bend and bow their heads. I felt sorry for them and I fancied that they would like to run away, if they could.

The coziest place in the house was my father's library. It was well-stocked, for he was the kind of man who would save a book from a burning house before he would even think of saving a bed. On chilly winter evenings the library was bright and pleasant, with a crackling pine-wood fire on the hearth. There was a warm leathery smell of imprisoned books, and on the walls the firelight gleamed cheerfully and made amusing shadows.

.   .   .   .   .

When I think of my father there comes into my mind the idea of stature, poise, and courage. He was an unusually tall man. I am six feet one myself, and my father topped me by three inches. Quiet-speaking, gracious in manner, and highly spirited, he possessed a good deal of that stoic dignity that is ascribed to the classical Greeks.

For two or three years after the war he was disfranchised — was not allowed to vote because he had been an officer of rank in the Confederate service. This kept him from practicing law, which was the only way he knew of earning a living.

It was a hard time for us. We had undoubtedly much difficulty in keeping alive and clothed, yet I must say that, as I look back upon those thin years, I remember them without any recollection of unusual privation. The sense of poverty is often the effect of contrast. Everybody in Milledgeville was poor; everybody had fought and lost; everybody had seen better days. The community felt the comradeship and solidarity that come from a common disaster. All had trod, in blood and tears, the road of defeat.

I shall not describe the straitened circumstances of our life as graphically as I might, for such stories bore me, and I have no sympathy with those who lean upon a poverty-bitten youth as a claim to applause and preferment.

Early experiences have much to do with shaping a man's life; of that I am entirely convinced. But it is a false assumption that these moulding experiences can be so largely expressed in terms of poverty or wealth. One's real inspiration is generally far too subtle to be defined in such crude terms. Therefore, as I

touch upon the makeshifts and expedients of our life at Milledgeville, I hope my readers will understand that I am not laying the ground for a philosophy of personal evolution, but merely painting a picture.

Within the frame of that picture I must include my mother, bent over her sewing, striving with needle and thread to keep us all from nakedness. She would cut down my father's old clothes to make suits for the boys, and her own dresses were fixed up in some way for the girls. My mother was not an expert tailor, and one may readily imagine that we all looked a little grotesque in our made-over clothes. Yet we did not feel grotesque at all. On the contrary, I felt perfectly grand. My clothes did not fit — but what of it? All the boys with whom I played were in the same fix.

The "Bellevue" plantation, according to every reasonable expectation, should have kept us all in comfort, but in that era in the South nothing was reasonable, or turned out the way it should have. It was a nightmare of misgovernment, carpet-baggers, unheard-of taxes, swarms of idle negroes and discouraged white men. The land was filled with low rascals, who had come from the North to make their fortunes. They wallowed over the dead Confederacy like vultures wallowing over a dead lion. The condition of public affairs affected the personal condition of every man in the South. The old economic order had been torn up by the roots too violently, and it was many years before the people could adjust themselves to the new state of things.

The end of the war found "Bellevue" overrun with weeds. Its buildings had been burned by one of Sherman's raiding parties, or by some band of irregular troops. Its livestock was dispersed; its fences were in decay. My father made strenuous efforts to put the place in working order, but very little could be accomplished on account of the uncertainty of negro labor. The freed slaves had a notion that their new freedom, which had come to them without effort on their part, meant a perpetual license for idleness. They could not understand any kind of freedom that involved work. They had always been made to work; now, if work was still to continue, of what use was this talk of freedom and other devices of the Yankees?

After a year or so of loss and discouragement, my father made no further effort to cultivate "Bellevue." He rented portions of it in small patches to white farmers with the idea of getting enough income from the place to pay its taxes and have a little left over. So far as I know the net result was trifling; we got a few barrels of potatoes and rice each year, and occasionally a wagon-load of vegetables. My parents, in their deep necessity, would have sold the land, I am sure, if a purchaser could have been found. A long time afterward, when I was a young lawyer, my father sold a large tract of pine lands — about three thousand acres — for one dollar an acre. A ridiculously low price; the timber on the land was worth many times that amount. It was sold through necessity for whatever it would bring. This tract of land is now owned by Howard E. Coffin, the well-known automobile engineer, and is used by him as a hunting preserve.

As soon as my father's political disabilities were removed by a special grant of amnesty from President Andrew Johnson, he began the practice of law in Milledgeville. It was the poorest place imaginable for anybody who hoped to make a living at the bar. The capital of the state had recently been moved to Atlanta, and nothing of importance was left in Milledgeville but an insane asylum and the state penitentiary. The town had a dejected, grass-grown appearance. In its center stood the abandoned capitol building, a solemn, owl-like structure. Its steps were littered with trash, and many of its windows were broken.

In the dusty streets men pitched horseshoes and talked of the past. Nailed on the doorways were the signs of innumerable lawyers who had done very well while Milledgeville contained the authority and prestige of the state. Now that the capital was gone, they fluttered like dying leaves.

My father's genuine legal ability was wasted.

He knew the origin and history of law, and was familiar with the mass of curious subtleties and impressive dicta that constitute the corpus juris of our race, but he did not know much about getting ahead in the world. If he had been a practical man, he would have left Milledgeville.

As time passed, our family increased in size. My parents had seven children. Caroline, John Floyd, and Rosalie were older than I; Malcolm Ross, Nona, and Laura were younger. When I was a boy of ten the house was full of children. There was a perpetual running to and fro; the long bare rooms resounded with stir and movement.

My mother's maiden name was Mary Faith Floyd. Her grandfather was General John Floyd, who was a figure of distinction in Georgia a hundred years ago. He was an intrepid soldier and a friend of Andrew Jackson, whom he resembled in mind and character. During the War of 1812, General John Floyd was associated with General Jackson in command of the expedition that destroyed the power of the Creek Indians.

General John Floyd had a son named Charles — and Charles Floyd was my grandfather. He might have been created by Sir Walter Scott, as a character in a romantic novel, and someimes I think he was. There is nobody in either Scott or Dumas that excelled Charles Floyd in a hardriding, fox-hunting, gallant, dueling career.

Charles Floyd entered West Point at the age of nineteen. He soon got into a series of strange adventures. When he had been at the Academy about a year, a rule was announced to the effect that every cadet had to set down in a register the name of his parent or guardian.

Cadet Floyd refused, and was summoned before the Commandant. "Have you no parent or guardian?" the Commandant inquired.

"Yes, I have," said Cadet Floyd, "but what business is it of yours? I am here to receive instruction — such as you can give me — so why should I write down in a book such personal matters as the names of my parents?"

Then, while the Commandant was staring dumbly at him, he saluted and walked out of the room. He was promptly dismissed from the Academy for insubordination.

Mounting his fine Georgia horse, Charles Floyd proceeded to ride home with leisurely interludes. Somewhere around Baltimore he had an encounter with a stranger. That evening he wrote to his father that he had encountered 'a puppy on a horse in the road.' The man blocked the bridle-path and did not get out of the way when Charles asked him courteously to stand to one side. Thereupon Charles struck him with his riding-whip. He rode on to a near-by inn for the night. Next morning, upon making inquiries, he learned that the man he had struck was not a puppy at all, but a well-known gentleman of the neighborhood. He called for ink and paper and wrote the gentleman a letter in which he said among other things: "When I struck you with a whip yesterday afternoon I did not know that you have the rank of gentleman, or I would have taken different measures. But your being a gentleman makes your discourtesy even greater than it appeared at first. I anticipate your desire for redress and will therefore await your pleasure. Any friends of yours will find me here. Your humble servitor, Charles Floyd."

The gentleman sent a friend with a challenge. They met at dawn next day, and at the first fire Floyd shot his opponent in the hip. He was filled with remorse for fear that he had killed him, so he remained in the neighborhood for a couple of weeks, inquiring daily as to his late adversary's condition. The gentleman got well promptly, and Floyd sent him a polite note of good wishes. The two met, clasped hands, drank a bottle of wine together, and the gentleman had Floyd come up to the house and meet his family. He stayed there a few days as a guest, spending his time in festivities and fox-hunting. Then he mounted his horse and rode away, while good-byes were waved from the piazza. He had met a puppy, learned that he was not a puppy, had shot him, had feasted with him, and had made a friend. That was the old South.

. . . . .

One might think with reason that the fiery spirit of Charles Rinaldo Floyd could lead only to disaster. But it did not; life is full of paradoxes. Charles Floyd either went through a profound spiritual change, or grew out of his youthful impetuosities — I don't know which; but the family chronicles say that in middle life he was a high-minded although spirited man — a careful planter, a generous friend, a kind neighbor. At the age of twenty-nine, he was appointed Brigadier General of the Georgia Militia.

. . . . .

I never knew Charles Floyd. He died at the age of forty-four while my mother — his daughter — was still a young girl.

By descent I am a McAdoo and a Floyd. Many years of observation of men and women have pretty nearly convinced me that there is not much in heredity, so far as human personality is concerned. But if the conventionally accepted laws of heredity are valid, then I must say that the poise of the McAdoos has beneficially tempered, in my case, the impetuosity of the Floyds. Some deep-lying instinct has kept me outside of the hot and desperate entanglements of the spirit. I have seldom had an impulse to do anything which had no practical justification. The windmills of Don Quixote are far beyond my horizon. I have ideals — have always had them — but I do not nourish ideals which represent the unattainable. Nor do I hold a personal resentment against any man because his opinions differ from my own.

---

2. The Steffens family, ca. 1872

Lincoln Steffens, *The Autobiography of Lincoln Steffens* (New York, 1931), pp.

Steffens (1866–1936) was the only son and the eldest of four children of Joseph and Elizabeth Symes Steffens.

I was well-born. My mother, Elizabeth Louisa Symes, was an English girl who came from New York via the Isthmus of Panama to San Francisco in the sixties to get married. It was rumored about the east that the gold rush of '49 had filled California with men — self-selected, venturesome, strong young fellows who were finding there gold, silver, and everything else that they sought, excepting only wives. There was a shortage of women of the marriageable sort. My mother had highly developed the woman's gift of straight-seeing, practical intelligence which makes for direct action. She not only knew that she, like all girls, wanted a husband; she acknowledged it to herself and took steps to find one. There was no chance for her in the crowded east; competition was too sharp for the daughters of a poor family like hers. She would go west. A seamstress, she could always earn a living there or anywhere. She took one of her sisters, Emma, and they went to the easiest man-market in the world at that time, and there, in San Francisco, they promptly married two young men chums whom they met at their first boarding-house. They paired off, and each married the other's beau; otherwise it turned out just as these two wise maidens had planned. This on the authority of my father, who loved and laughed to tell it thus when my mother was there to hear; it annoyed and pleased her so. She was an amiable, teasable wife. He was a teasing, jesting father with a working theory that a fact is a joke.

My father was one of the sixteen or seventeen children of a pioneer farmer of eastern Canada, who drove west with his wife in a wagon to Illinois, where he bought, cleared, and worked his piece of wilderness, raised his big herd of tall boys and strong girls, and, finally, died in 1881, eighty-one years of age. He was a character, this grandfather of mine. I saw him once. My mother took me and my sister to visit him when we were very small, and I remember how, bent with age and brooding, he gradually looked up, saw us, said "Humph," and went back into himself and his silence. He came to life only one other time for me. I was looking at a duster made of horsehairs that was stuck in a knot-hole on a board fence. It looked just like a horse's tail, and I was peering through a crack to see the horse. My grandfather, watching me, said, "The horse was cut off the tail." I wondered, but he did not laugh, so I believed him.

Besides farming and breeding, my grandfather did some preaching, and when there was no regular teacher he taught the school. Also he raced horses and betted on them. Once, on a wager, he preached on the track between heats a sermon which was remembered long enough for me to hear of it. A favorite indoor winter sport of his was to gather the family around the fireplace and set my grandmother telling a story of some terrible night fight with the Indians. She described the approach of the savages so well that you felt the shivers creeping like Indians up your back, and at the attack, when the varmints broke out of the darkness with their tomahawks raised and ready, when the terror-stricken children turned to see the savages crash at them, a yell ripped the silence — my grandfather's. He chose the moment which he knew — which they all knew — "Mother" was working up to, and springing from his seat he shrieked, as he could shriek, the tearing war-whoop of the wild west. And my father said that though his father and mother played the game over and over, and always in the same way, so that the children not only knew what was going to happen, but were sure they could sit through it, the old folks collaborated so perfectly that, when the yell went up, they all were lifted by fright to their feet to fight, till the war-whoop turned into a laugh. It must have been thrilling; my father could not describe it without some of the old fear in his eyes, the terror which carried over to me, a little boy.

Because my father, the last child of the first "worn-out wife," was small and not strong, his father called him "the scrub" and told him that he probably would not live; and when he did live, the old man said that, anyhow, he was no use on a farm. He let him, therefore, do what he wanted to do: go to town, take a job in a store and courses in two commercial colleges. Working by day and studying at night, my father got his education and saved up enough money to go west. Horace Greeley had been preaching that to the young men of the east, but the old New York *Tribune* was read in the west also, and many a western boy grew up, as my father did, determined to go west.

My father traveled de luxe, for that day: on horseback. He joined a wagon train, led by Col. Levi Carter, and he and a chum of his, likewise mounted, served as scouts. They rode ahead or off on the flanks of the ox-and-horse train to look out for Indians. They saw some. There were several skirmishes and one attack which became a pitched battle. When it was over, my father found his chum dead with an arrow in his breast. That arrow was kept along the front of a shelf in the bookcase of our home, and whenever it was referred to, my father would lay down his newspaper, describe that old fight, and show us the blood-stains on the arrow. If we would let him he would tell the whole tale of the long march across the plains, around the edge of the desert up through the Sierras, down into the Valley of the Sacramento River.

.   .   .   .   .

When the wagon train broke up and scattered, he went on to San Francisco. He was not seeking gold or land but a start in business, and in San Francisco he found it (Sept. 1862) as bookkeeper in the firm of Fuller and Heather, importers and dealers in paints, oils, and glass. That was his job when he married and I was born. But soon thereafter he was offered a quarter interest in a branch store which the firm was establishing in Sacramento. He went there, and that is where my conscious life began.

.   .   .   .   .

Horses, real horses, played a leading part in my boyhood; I seem always to have wanted one. A chair would do on a rainy day, but at other times I preferred to escape into the street and ask drivers to "please, mister, gimme a ride." Sometimes they would. I was a pretty boy with lovely long blond curls. This I know well because it kept me from playing with the other fellows of my age. They jeered at my curls and called me a girl or a "sissy boy" and were surprised when I answered with a blow. They were taken off their guard by my attack, but they recovered and charged in mass upon me, sending me home scratched, bleeding, torn, to my mother, to beg her to cut my hair. She would not. My father had to do it. One day when the gang had caught me, thrown me down, and stuffed horse-droppings into my mouth, he privately promised me relief, and the next morning he took me downtown and had his barber cut off my curls, which he wrapped up in a paper as a gift for my mother. How she wept over them! How I rejoiced over them!

No more fighting by day, no more crying by night. The other boys accepted me as a regular fellow, but I got fewer free rides. I have no doubt the drivers liked my angelic locks. Anyway, before they were cut off, drivers used often to take me up in their seats with them and let me hold the reins back of where they held them and so drive real horses. My poor mother suffered so much from these disappearances that the sport was forbidden me: in vain. I went right on driving. I did it with a heavy sense of doing wrong, but I couldn't help going whenever a driver would take me. Once, when I was sitting alone holding the reins to let a team drink at a trough (the driver stood away off at the horses' heads), I saw my father come around the corner after me. I dropped the reins and climbed down off the wagon. My father took my hand and, without a word, led me home. There, at the door, my mother caught me up away from my stern father and, carrying me off into the parlor, laid me across her knees and gave me a spanking, my first. My mother! I had expected punishment, but from my father, not from her; I felt saved when she rescued me from him. And then she did it — hard.

This turned out to be one of the lasting sorrows, not of my life, but of hers. She told it many, many times. She said that my father stood at the door, watching her till she was done with me, and then he asked her why she did it.

"I did it," she said, "to keep you from doing it. You are so hard."

"But," he answered, "I wasn't going to spank him for that. He was having such a good time, he looked so proud up there on that old manure wagon, and when he saw me, he came right down, put his hand in mine, and came straight home, trembling with fear. I couldn't have spanked him. And you — Why did you do it? And why so hard?"

My mother cried more than I did at the time, and she always wept a little when she told it, explaining to the end of her days that she did it so hard just to show that he need not ever spank me, that she could do it quite enough. "And then," she'd break, "to think he wasn't going to do it at all!"

---

3. The money measure of life

Frederic C. Howe, *Confessions of a Reformer* (New York: C. Scribner's Sons, 1925), pp. 13–14. By permission of Charles Scribner's Sons.

Howe (1897–1940), lawyer, author, and public official, spent his boyhood and youth in Meadville, Pennsylvania.

I remember my boyhood through a haze, as of a tranquil, bright September day. There was no sharpness, no struggle, little reproof. My mother kept a large house immaculate, entertained guests, raised her children and saw them with unremitting care through school and college. Her anxieties were all for us. The family worries had to do largely with money. Although my father's furniture store and factory were prosperous when I was a lad, there never seemed to be money enough to go around, and the weekly budgetary discussions on Saturday night were distressing times. My mother kept house on a very small allowance, but there was minute examination at the supper-table of the next week's necessary outlay. She put off as long as possible the moment of asking for her housekeeping money, and approached the subject nervously. There was no friction and no quarrelling, but a sharp line was drawn between necessary and unnecessary expenditures. I learned that extravagance was a cardinal sin and that money was not to be spent lightly. Small monetary units and a low scale of expenditure were early established for me. "Take care of the pennies and the dollars will take care of themselves" was a maxim far more deeply ingrained in my mind than any of the Ten Commandments. *Poor Richard's Almanac* was a much-quoted guide, and the end dramatically held before a spendthrift child was the poorhouse. My mind got a pattern of life from these Saturday-night talks. Right living was living carefully, avoiding debts of any kind, and husbanding for some distant future when sickness and old age would overtake one. My sisters and I got the pleasures we wanted if they could be provided, but we felt the sacrifices involved in them. We got a money measure of life and a fear of prodigality from which I, for one, have never escaped.

---

4. The Hapgoods

Hutchins Hapgood, *A Victorian in the Modern World* (New York: Harcourt, Brace and

Company, 1939), pp. 15–17, 21–23. Reprinted with permission of Charles H. Hapgood.

Hutchins Hapgood (1869–1944), journalist and writer, was born in Chicago and grew up in Alton, Illinois.

I do not now care for the so-called "manly" activities to the same degree as when I was a boy. Then they were to me everything. That was in part due to my father, who was not only all Puritan in blood, but had also undergone in his early manhood the reactions from religious bigotry in somewhat the same form as expressed by Robert Ingersoll. Human honesty, courage, and decency were advocated by him for their own sake and not because of any supernatural command. He early removed from us the fear of theological punishment. "There is no hell," he said, simply, and we all readily believed him. This was to spare his children the fears of his boyhood; the positive aspect of religion he did not touch upon. I realized that the subject did not interest him and I became a skeptic at an early age. For my father's word to me was law. He was all flame and nerve, of the best of the Puritan stock before degeneration sets in, unsparing of himself, vigorous and devoted to duty. His was that racy breeding which is especially effective with boys, who love almost exclusively the manly qualities.

In my earliest childhood I had emotions which were probably of a religious character. I had natural respect and piety, and was often overcome by a poignant sense of sin. I often felt myself to be in the presence of my Maker. A dream that recurred frequently seems to indicate a nature needing religious expression, but handicapped through lack of an historical symbolism. It was a dream difficult to describe, for nothing happened, in spite of its vividness and intense sense of reality. I felt myself in a Presence that had an attitude towards me of terrifying disapproval. I always awoke from this dream in a state of the utmost fear and remorse.

But these early instincts gradually disappeared, probably through lack of nourishment. My father discouraged Church, fairy-tales, and dancing; not that he prohibited them, but he referred to them, if at all, with a certain dry irony. He was a strong man, with an exaggerated feeling of the difficulty of life, a tender sympathy for all things that had the hard fact of life thrust upon them. Life to him was something undesirable, to be endured with stoical courage. He felt that religion and poetry and dancing expressed pathetically the illusions of suffering mortals, were great deceivers, confidence men, held forth futile dreams from which there must be a severe awakening. He planted his feet firmly on self-denying skepticism and on unwavering determination to do his duty as he saw it.

In my childhood I knew nothing of the Bible, nor of any other religious classic. I had nothing on which to frame my natural mystical awe and my desire for emotional rhythm. My father helped me to a vivid regard for honesty, industry, exactness, and punctuality, which to this day have for me esthetic value, but as I grew older I constantly missed what was not given me in my childhood. My religious and imaginative impulses, largely shut up within me, turned inward in the shape of questioning remorse and unhappy doubt. No external forms were given them upon which they could take purifying shape. I probably had greater need of religion than most children, for in my nature were rank emotional growths which for many years made my boyhood, active and well cared for physically as it was, the most unhappy period of my life.

When I was about eight years old I killed a wren. I had been trying for days to prove my skill with the "flipper," a sort of slingshot which threw stones with great force. Finally, I was successful, and brought one of the little birds to the ground. For a moment my joy was unbounded. I had succeeded in my undertaking. But the next moment I was overcome with pity and remorse and burst into a flood of repentant tears. The noises made by the locusts and the soughing of the wind in the trees increased my agony, for it gave me a miserable sense of Nature's reproach. I feared for a time to be alone, and took the wren to my mother, whose sympathy and gentleness and sweetness I was always sure of. Afterwards, I buried the little corpse with great circumstance and pomp; inviting several of my little playfellows to attend the funeral. I was continually conscious during this entire episode of an external invisible Reproach, and that Reproach followed me to my dreams at night. In its vagueness and awfulness and invisible externality this experience seems certainly to have touched upon the religious.

I could not, while the thought of the dead wren was upon me, bear to be alone. Painful consciousness was then too intense. Not only, indeed, at moments when my thoughts brought self-reproach and remorse did I fear solitude, but in solitude then and always since have come my most passionate experiences. The madness of joy and the turmoil of distress come to me at their most tumultous point when alone. In the midst of Nature I become excitedly conscious of my nature and of all being. And this consciousness is not calming. Quiet, breathing solitude, instead of soothing, distracts and harasses me, sometimes with a sense of disturbing beauty, sometimes with a sense of terror and impending awfulness. . . .

.   .   .   .   .

I had as a child great respect for rules and laws but found it very difficult to obey them. I never violated rules because they were rules, but always because I wanted to do something the doing of which involved, quite incidentally, the breaking of the rules. This is the case with all normal criminals.

Continually, I attempted to lead my older brother[1] from the path of virtue; but he would always obey the law, apparently without emotion, simply because it was the law. This, to me, has always seemed inexplicable. Even at that early age he, too, proved himself the father of the man, for he not only walked the straight

1. Norman Hapgood (1868–1937), editor of *Collier's Weekly* and *Harper's Weekly*.

and narrow path himself, but he tried to make me do so, too, just as in his manhood, he showed the way to all. If, notwithstanding, I went my sinful way alone, he would sometimes report me to the authorities — my parents — as a good boy-citizen should.

.   .   .   .   .

As a child I violated all kinds of rules and regulations and laws, and yet everyone who knew me saw that my intentions were good. I was very mischievous but seldom cruel or malicious. The sense of adventure rather than the desire to hurt led to my innumerable fights. My parents early understood my character in this respect, and to me were always extremely lenient. My father, to be sure, as I have said, tried repeatedly to develop in me the ability to do the things I did not want to do. I would try faithfully but generally fail, and my father came philosophically to see that this was inevitable, and to recognize how integral a part of my character was this lack of ability, this lack of cleverness, whenever my emotions were not aroused. His forceful and willful character was in this respect very different from my own and, therefore, his understanding of my nature has always made me wonder. It showed what experience and love could do.

---

5. Noblesse oblige

Eleanor Roosevelt, *This Is My Story* (New York: Harper & Brothers, 1937), pp. 27–29. By permission of Harper and Row, Publishers, Inc.

Eleanor Roosevelt (1884–1962) was eight years old when her mother died; her father, the younger brother of Theodore Roosevelt, died two years later. Eleanor and her younger brother then went to live with their maternal grandmother, Mary Livingston Ludlow Hall.

Very early I became conscious of the fact that there were men and women and children around me who suffered in one way or another. I think I was five or six when my father took me for the first time to help serve Thanksgiving Day dinner in one of the newsboys' clubhouses which my grandfather, Theodore Roosevelt, had started. He was also a Trustee of the Children's Aid Society for many years. I was tremendously interested in all these ragged little boys and in the fact, which my father explained, that many of them had no homes and lived in little wooden shanties in empty lots, or slept in vestibules of houses or public buildings or any place where they could be moderately warm. Yet they were independent and earned their own livings.

A few of them had homes, but then they usually had added cares, a mother and little brothers and sisters to help. The boys' clubhouse was their only place for recreation, often their only chance of education. The men who went there were their friends and advisers.

After dinner was over the boys themselves put on an entertainment and as I remember it, if I hadn't been so sleepy I would have enjoyed it, but I am afraid I disgraced myself by placidly going to sleep!

Every Christmas I was taken by my grandmother to help dress the Christmas tree for the babies' ward in the Post Graduate Hospital. She was particularly interested in this charity.

My father's aunt Annie, Mrs. James King Gracie, whom we children called "Auntie Gracie," took us to the Orthopædic Hospital which my Grandfather Roosevelt had been instrumental in helping Dr. Newton Shaffer to start and in which the family was all deeply interested. There I saw innumerable little children in casts and splints. Some of them lay patiently for months in strange and curious positions.

Perhaps I was particularly interested in them because I had a curvature myself and wore for some time a steel brace which was vastly uncomfortable and prevented my bending over.

Even my Uncle Vallie, who at this time was in business in New York, a champion tennis player and a very popular young man in society, helped along my education in human suffering and want.

. . . He took me to help dress a Christmas tree for a group of children in a part of New York City which was called "Hell's Kitchen." This was for many years one of New York's poorest and worst sections. I also went with Maude and Pussie to sing at the Bowery Mission, so I was not in ignorance that there were sharp contrasts, even though our lives were blessed with plenty.

---

6. Daughters

Paul de Rousiers, *American Life* (New York, 1892), pp. 265–269.

Rousiers (1857–1934) subsequently wrote on international economic problems for the League of Nations.

This breath of independence which moves throughout American society stirs in the feeble sex also, and their education is, perhaps, the most original of all. If we Europeans are astonished by the little boys brought up on the other side of the Atlantic, we must be still more surprised at the little girls. This ought to happen at any rate, for we know how much a French woman, for instance, finds herself exiled and ill at ease in the environment we are describing.]

The first impression of the stranger is that there are no sexes in the United States. Girls and boys walk to school side by side, they sit on the same benches, they have the same lessons, and go about the streets alone. So much for their earlier years. Girls of twenty are found in the factories, in the halls of great hotels, where they act as clerks to anybody, for they know shorthand and typewriting; in the primary schools, where they teach; in the lecture-room, where they study medicine; in the streets, where they preach; in charitable institutions, which they manage, and sometimes, as in Kansas, for instance, even in the polling-booths, at the head of municipalities, etc.

How is this strange and complex being brought up? For what ends and duties is she trained? A moment's reflection is needed before answering.

Perhaps Americans do not know very well themselves, for in reading a newspaper I came across the notice of a very curious competition: "$20 prize to the person who sends the best answer to the question, 'What Shall We Do with Our Girls?' " The competitors were divided into two groups: some wished girls to be brought up so as to be able to earn their own living. . . . The other insisted more on domestic virtues, on household duties — cooking, washing, etc.

These two tendencies are well marked in society, and correspond to the two different situations a woman may fill. If she remains unmarried she must struggle for life like the men with whom she competes, and the best education for a spinster is a virile, practical training for that struggle. If she marry, her husband assumes all responsibility of supplying daily bread, and her part is to look after and bring up the children and manage the house.

But it is impossible to know which will be the lot of a little girl of ten, and the problem is what sort of a training to give her?

Americans usually act as if their daughters would never have a husband, and bring them up as they do the boys, letting them have as much liberty as possible, for in this difficulty of telling what will be the future they prefer to give them the means of making their way in life alone. If a companion offers to give one of them his arm and walk along with her, so much the better; but it is well to be prepared for the worst in order to avoid disagreeable surprises.

It would seem that there must be equality among the boys and girls, but this equality, of which I have spoken, is balanced by a great inequality which custom determines and the law supports.

In order that a girl may have complete liberty in American society she must be protected by its conventions as much as the strict family supervision does with us. An old French gentleman said to me: "You can send your daughter from North to South and from East to West of the States without fearing either any unpleasantness or adventure. That is because there are so few women in the West, and in earlier times there were very few everywhere; so the Americans look up to them as goddesses." Since then I have often heard and been much amused by this reason of the old gentleman. Just think of a young woman lost among two hundred Frenchmen? Do you imagine they would honor her as a divinity? Well, perhaps like some pagan goddess. The fewness of the women has little to do with the respect of the people for them. This respect is an outcome of the constitution of their society, and to understand it we must consider its origin.

However mixed may be the origin of citizens of the Union, we have shown several times that the immigrants from Northern Europe take the first place in American society. They founded the mother-colonies of New England and of Pennsylvania, and they are to be found in the West to-day, coming straight from the plains of Saxony, the British Islands and Scandinavia. There is no need to insist on this idea, which has been expounded here several times already.

But we know, for instance in the case of England, that girls of this race are protected by a strong moral and legal barrier, and they are allowed a liberty which seems strange to us and would bring about grave inconveniences in our country.

The Americans are thus predisposed in favor of such an education, but the peculiar nature of the surroundings accentuates this, and it often happens there that girls settle far away in situations where there are many risks — on a ranch lost in the Far West, or in some rising town. It is impossible to be too well prepared for so stirring and uncertain a life; hence fathers give their daughters much more liberty than in England, and raise a still higher moral barrier around them.

So one sees young people of both sexes living on terms of intimacy without any bad results. I know that everybody does not admit this, and that some French authors consider mixed schools to be sources of great mischief. However, everybody I asked about it unanimously testified to the contrary. A Catholic priest, who had been stationed in the States for many years, said to me: "I live quite close to a high-school, where boys and girls of eighteen both go. I often see them pass the windows when the classes are dismissed, and I can assure you, that I have on no occasion noticed the least impropriety of bearing or of conversation." Yet he was right in the middle of a big town.

In addition to this, ask the mothers and they will tell you that their daughters go out at any hour of day or night, either alone or with their friends, and nobody is the least surprised. If you have been presented in any house, you may ask a young lady to go to the theatre with you; and, if that young lady be hungry at 11 o'clock at night, you may take her to sup at a restaurant, and then conduct her home. All that is perfectly allowable. Your discretion and good-breeding are trusted; and should you be indiscrete, the law courts will make you follow the path of duty; and the courts are by no means tender. An innkeeper in Pittsburg lately surprised a pretty Irish girl by embracing her, and had to pay her $1,000 damages. Another man in the same town was fined $2,000 for kissing the wrinkled skin of an old woman of sixty. Of course, the penalty is proportionate to the position of the offender, rather than to the charms of the victim. Punishments of this sort are needed to remind people who have no sense of propriety nor any respect for woman, that such things are expected from them. Such penalties are enforced only in societies where such sentiments and respect exist.

There, as elsewhere, public opinion backs up the law.

Moral mixed schools do not surprise me any more than respectable streets and decent suppers, and, in general, the propriety of the relations between American young men and women left to themselves. The decency of American manners is incontestable, and the best proof is that this liberty given to girls would be disastrous in France, for instance; everybody feels and understands this. It follows that manners must be better in the United States, otherwise the system would be broken up by the abuses which would result.

As it exists, this state of things brings about two characteristic advantages. Unmarried women can get respectable situations; and the future mothers of families gain experience and are able to choose their husbands with some knowledge of what they are about. Marriage does not wear the aspect of an escape from family subjection, but appears a serious step whose consequences and burdens are realized.

---

7. The care of babies

Mrs. Max West, *Infant Care,* United States Children's Bureau, Pub. No. 8 (Washington, D.C., 1914), pp. 59–63.

This pamphlet sold for twenty-five cents. Frequently revised and reissued, it became the best-selling publication of the Government Printing Office.

HABITS, TRAINING, and DISCIPLINE

Habits are the result of repeated actions. A properly trained baby is not allowed to learn bad habits which must be unlearned later at great cost of time and patience to both mother and babe. The wise mother strives to start the baby right.

Systematic Care

In order to establish good habits in the baby, the mother must first be aware what they are, and then how to induce them. Perhaps the first and most essential good habit is that of regularity. This begins at birth, and applies to all the physical functions of the baby — eating, sleeping, and bowel movements. The care of a baby is readily reduced to a system unless he is sick. Such a system is not only one of the greatest factors in keeping the baby well and in training him in a way which will be of value to him all through life, but reduces the work of the mother to the minimum and provides for her certain assured periods of rest and recreation.

As a sample of what is meant by a system in baby care the following plan is suggested, which may be variously modified to suit particular cases:

6 a.m., baby's first nursing.
Family breakfast; children off to school.
9 a.m., baby's bath, followed by second nursing.
Baby sleeps until noon.
12 to 12.30, baby's noon meal.
Out-of-door airing and nap.
3 to 3.30 p.m., afternoon nursing.
Period of waking.
6 to 7 p.m., baby's supper and bed.

It is quite feasible to have the baby's night meal at 11.30 or 12 o'clock, in order to give the mother a chance to spend an occasional evening in pleasant recreation.

Playing with the Baby

The rule that parents should not play with the baby may seem hard, but it is without doubt a safe one. A young, delicate, or nervous baby especially needs rest and quiet, and however robust the child much of the play that is indulged in is more or less harmful. It is a great pleasure to hear the baby laugh and crow in apparent delight, but often the means used to produce the laughter, such as tickling, punching, or tossing makes him irritable and restless.

It is a regrettable fact that the few minutes of play that the father has when he gets home at night, which is often almost the only time he has with the child, may result in nervous disturbance of the baby and upset his regular habits.

The mother should not kiss the baby directly on the mouth, nor permit others to do so, as infections of various kinds are spread in this way. She needs also to be cautioned about rocking the baby, jumping him up and down on her knee, tossing him, shaking his bed or carriage, and, in general, keeping him in constant motion. All these things disturb the baby's nerves and make him more and more dependent upon these attentions. But this is not to say that the baby should be left alone too completely. All babies need "mothering," and should have plenty of it. When the young baby is awake he should frequently be taken up and held quietly in the mother's arms, in a variety of positions, so that no one set of muscles may become overtired. An older child should be taught to sit on the floor or in his pen or crib during part of his waking hours, or he will be very likely to make too great demands upon the mother's strength. No one who has not tried it realizes how much nervous energy can be consumed in "minding" a baby who can creep or walk about, and who must be continually watched and diverted, and the mother who is taking the baby through this period of his life will need to conserve all her strength, and not waste it in useless forms of activity.

.   .   .   .   .

Early Training

The training in the use of individual judgment can be begun even in infancy; a child should early be taught to choose certain paths of action for himself; and if he is continually and absolutely forbidden to do this or that he is sometimes seriously handicapped later, because he does not know how to use his own reasoning faculties in making these choices. On the other hand, obedience is one of the most necessary lessons for children to learn. A wise mother will not abuse her privilege in this respect by a too-exacting practice. For the most part she can exert her control otherwise than by commands, and if she does so her authority when exercised will have greater force and instant obedience will be more readily given.

Most of the naughtiness of infancy can be traced to physical causes. Babies who are fussy, restless, and fretful are usually either uncomfortable in some way because they have not been properly fed and taken care of, are sick or ailing, or have been indulged too much. On the other hand, babies who are properly fed, who are kept clean, and have plenty of sleep and fresh air, and who have been trained in regular habits of life, have no cause for being "bad" and are therefore "good."

It must not be forgotten that the period of infancy is a period of education often of greater consequence than any other two years of life. Not only are all the organs and functions given their primary education, but the faculties of the mind as well receive those initial impulses that determine very largely their direction and efficiency through life. The first nervous impulse which passes through the baby's eyes, ears, fingers, or mouth to the tender brain makes a pathway for itself; the next time another impulse travels over the same path it deepens the impression of the first. It is because the brain is so sensitive to these impressions in childhood that we remember throughout life things that have happened in our early years while nearer events are entirely forgotten. If, therefore, these early stimuli are sent in orderly fashion, the habits thus established and also the tendency to form such habits will persist throughout life.

Negro families

1. Family relationships among emancipated blacks, Sea Islands, Georgia, 1862–1865

William C. Gannett, "The Freedmen at Port Royal," *North American Review,* CI (1865), 5–7.

Gannett, a theological student from Boston, taught in the freedmen's schools in the Sea Islands, 1862–1865. For Gannett's discussion of his educational experiences see Part Eight, Chap. II, sec. A, On the Sea Islands of South Carolina, doc. 3.

Contrary to our expectation, we have never seen parents more apathetic. Certainly the expression of affection is rare to any children who are old enough to get out of the way. But this is not strange. From the example hitherto always before them, their only theory of management is that of threat and force. Formerly many husbands seem to have transferred in miniature to their wives, and both parents to their children, the blows they themselves received from their masters. Wife-beating is now infrequent, but the children are not spared the most terrific language; the whippings, as they usually involve a chase and are often given on the run, perhaps inflict less pain than the usual New England chastisement. Moreover, child-bearing was systematically encouraged by the owner, and a child who is simply "one more little nigger for Massa," and procures a yearly exemption of a month's field-work for the mother, is a very different thing from one's own son or daughter, the child of suffering and sacrifice. The women are proud of a numerous offspring; but in the ten to twenty names which many middle-aged women will count off to you, they usually include as many dead as living. Either from their constant labor almost to the day of confinement, or from subsequent ignorance and carelessness, a vast number of infants perish before they are three years old. And this doubtless strengthens the feeling that their children are hardly their own. We have rarely seen tears shed at a funeral, and never any of the prostrating grief which a mother usually feels. The rough pressure of slavery tends especially to crush the tender expression of feeling. The daily task must be finished, and whatever sorrow exists is locked under dumb lips. The family separations — those buryings alive of slavery — may be, at the time, as heartrending as they seem to us. But whether the sense of loss continues keen may be doubted. Of the refugees, many have left a husband or wife in slavery; yet probably the majority have again married since gaining their freedom. It is not uncommon to form a second marriage within a few weeks after death has severed the first. It should be remembered, however, that, among people of their condition in life, marriage is as much a matter of convenience and necessity as of affection. Yet with all this the duties of family relationship are admirably observed. To the negro the plantation is his country, and "the fam'ly" his state; but the latter is as broad in its meaning as in its pronunciation, for on many estates the whole population consists of but two or three distinct families. Every one is aunt or uncle or cousin to every one else. The latter titles are so common that abbreviations are necessary; at " 'Cl' Arklis!" Uncle Hercules will turn his head; and even in a quarrel with "Co' Ranty," the cousinship is not denied. Hospitality, which is ever ready, may be taxed as a right by all the kin. We have seen a strapping young fellow fighting off a band of devoted relatives, who wished to tie and whip him because he would not hoe his corn; they feared that they would have to support him the next winter. Orphans are at once adopted by connections, and the sick are well nursed by their friends. The old are treated with great reverence, and often exercise a kind of patriarchal authority. Children are carefully taught "manners," and the common address to each other, as well as to the "buckra people," is marked by extreme courtesy.

Washington (1865–1915) was born in Franklin County, Virginia. After emancipation he and his mother moved to Malden, West Virginia. A portion of his autobiography is printed in Part Eight, Chap. II, sec. B, Training hand and mind together, doc. 1.

. . . The negro has not had time enough to collect the broken and scattered members of his family. For the sake of illustration, and to employ a personal reference, I do not know who my own father was; I have no idea who my grandmother was; I have or had uncles, aunts and cousins, but I have no knowledge as to where most of them now are. My case will illustrate that of hundreds of thousands of black people in every part of our country. Perhaps those who direct attention to the negro's moral weakness, and compare his moral progress with that of the whites, do not consider the influence of the memories which cling about the old family homestead upon the character and aspirations of individuals. The very fact that the white boy is conscious that, if he fails in life, he will disgrace the whole family record, extending back through many generations, is of tremendous value in helping him to resist temptations. On the other hand, the fact that the individual has behind him and surrounding him proud family history and connections serves as a stimulus to make him overcome obstacles, when striving for success. All this should be taken into consideration, to say nothing of the physical, mental and moral training which individuals of the white race receive in their homes. We must not pay judgment upon the negro too soon. It requires centuries for the influence of home, school, church and public contact to permeate the mass of millions of people, so that the upward tendency may be apparent to the casual observer.

2. "I do not know who my own father was"

Booker T. Washington, "Education Will Solve the Race Problem. A Reply," *North American Review,* CLXXI (1900), 223.

3. "Black Code" of South Carolina, 1865

"An Act to Establish and Regulate the Domestic Relations of Persons of

Color . . . ," *Statutes at Large of South Carolina,* XIII (Columbia, 1866), 291–295.

After abolition of slavery, South Carolina and other former slave states found it necessary to enact laws establishing the legal status of freedmen and regulating domestic relations among them.[1] For apprenticeship of children under the Black Codes, see below, Part Five, Chap. I, sec. A, Kinds and conditions of child labor, doc. 1.

I. The relation of husband and wife amongst persons of color is established.

II. Those who now live as such, are declared to be husband and wife.

III. In case of one man having two or more reputed wives, or one woman two or more reputed husbands, the man shall, by the first day of April next, select one of his reputed wives, or the woman one of her reputed husbands; and the ceremony of marriage, between this man or woman, and the person so selected, shall be performed.

IV. Every colored child, heretofore born, is declared to be the legitimate child of his mother, and also of his colored father, if he is acknowledged by such a father.

.   .   .   .   .

X. A husband shall not, for any cause, abandon or turn away his wife, nor a wife her husband. Either of them that abandons or turns away the other may be prosecuted for a misdemeanor; and upon conviction thereof, before a District Judge, may be punished by fine and corporal punishment, duly apportioned to the circumstances of aggravation or mitigation. A husband not disabled, who has been thus convicted of having abandoned or turned away his wife, or who has been shown to fail in maintaining his wife and children, may be bound to service by the District Judge from year to year, and so much of the profits of his labor as may be requisite, be applied to the maintenance of his wife and children; the distribution between them being made according to their respective merits and necessities. In like manner, a wife not disabled, who has been thus convicted, may be bound, and the proceeds of her labor applied to the maintenance of her children. In either case, any surplus profit shall go to the person bound. At the end of any year for which he was bound, the husband shall have the right to return to, or receive back, his wife, and thereupon shall be discharged, upon condition of his afterwards maintaining his wife and children. A like right a wife shall have, at the end of a year for which she was bound, on condition of her making future exertions to maintain her family.

.   .   .   .   .

XII. The relation of parent and child, amongst persons of color, is recognized, confers all the rights and remedies, civil and criminal, and imposes all the duties that are incident thereto by law, unless the same are modified by this Act, or some legislation connected herewith.

XIII. The father shall support and maintain his children under fifteen years of age, whether they be born of one of his reputed wives or of any other woman.

XIV. The relation of guardian and ward, as it now exists in this State, with all the rights and duties incident thereto, is extended to persons of color, with the modifications made by this Act.

---

1. For provisions of the Black Codes of other states see "Laws in Relation to Freedmen Compiled by Command of Major General O. O. Howard, Commissioner, Bureau of Refugees, Freedmen and Abandoned Lands" in U.S. Senate, *Executive Document No. 6.* 39 Cong. 2 Sess. (Washington, 1867), pp. 170–229.

---

4. Country and village Negroes, Georgia, 1899

W. E. B. Du Bois, *The Negro in the Black Belt: Some Social Sketches,* U.S. Department of Labor Bulletin 22 (Washington, D.C., 1899), pp. 401–405.

When this study was published Du Bois (1868–1963) was professor of economics and history at Atlanta University.

A COUNTRY DISTRICT IN DEKALB COUNTY, GEORGIA

Seventeen miles east of Atlanta is a small village of less than 500 persons called Dora-ville; 21 miles southeast is a bit of country without a special name. There are in these two localities between 60 and 75 Negro families, of whom 11 fairly representative ones have been chosen for this study.

In general these Negroes are a degraded set. Except in two families, whisky, tobacco, and snuff are used to excess, even when there is a scarcity of bread. In other respects also the low moral condition of these people is manifest, and in the main there is no attempt at social distinctions among them.

In these 11 families there are 131 individuals, an average of nearly 12 persons to a family. . . .

The fecundity of this population is astonishing. Here is one family with 19 children — 14 girls and 5 boys, ranging in age from 6 to 25 years. Another family has one set of triplets, two sets of twins, and 4 single children. The girls of the present generation, however, are not marrying as early as their mothers did. Once in a while a girl of 12 or 13 runs off and marries, but this does not often happen. Probably the families of the next generation will be smaller.

Four of the 11 heads of families can read and write. Of their children, a majority, possibly two-thirds, can read and write a little. Five of the families own their homes. The farms vary from 1 to 11 acres in extent, and are worth from $100 to $400. Two of these farms are heavily mortgaged. Six families rent farms on shares, paying one-half the crop. They clear from $5 to $10 in cash at the end of a year's work. They usually own a mule or two and sometimes a cow.

Nearly all the workers are farm hands, women and girls as well as men being employed in the fields. Children as young as 6 are given light tasks, such as dropping seed and bringing water. The families rise early, often before daylight, working until breakfast time and returning again after the meal. One of the men is a stonecutter. He earns $1.50 a day, owns a neat little home, and lives comfortably. Most of the houses are rudely constructed of logs or boards, with one large and one small room. There is usually no glass in the openings which serve as windows. They are closed by wooden shutters. The large room always contains several beds and homemade furniture, consisting of tables, chairs, and chests. A few homes had three rooms, and one or two families had sewing machines, which, however, were not yet paid for.

These families raise nearly all that they eat — corn, wheat, pork, and molasses. Chickens and eggs are used as currency at the country store to purchase cloth, tobacco, coffee, etc. The character of the home life varies with the different families. The family of 21 is a poverty-stricken, reckless, dirty set. The children are stupid and repulsive, and fight for their food at the table. They are poorly dressed, sickly, and cross. The table dishes stand from one meal to another unwashed, and the house is in perpetual disorder. Now and then the father and mother engage in a hand-to-hand fight.

In some respects this family is exceptionally bad, but several others are nearly as barbarous. A few were much better, and in the stonecutter's five-room house one can find clean, decent family life, with neatly dressed children and many signs of aspiration. The average of the communities, however, was nearer the condition of the family first described than that of the latter one.

.   .   .   .   .

On the whole, a stay in this community has a distinctly depressing effect. There are a few indications of progress, but those of listlessness and stagnation seem more powerful.

A SMALL VILLAGE: LITHONIA, DEKALB COUNTY, GA.

Lithonia is 24 miles east of Atlanta, and has a population of perhaps 800. There are in the town two dry goods stores, a drug store, three grocery stores, a barber shop, and a millinery shop conducted by white persons, and a blacksmith shop and a barber shop conducted by Negroes. Nearly all the workingmen of the town are employed in the three rock quarries, which furnish the chief business of the village. The Negro stonecutters here used to earn from $10 to $14 a week, but now they receive from $5 to $8.50 a week. There are many "scabbers" outside the union who work for still less. They now include the majority of the Negro laborers. Some Negroes are also employed in domestic service and at the large boarding house.

Less than a dozen homes are owned by the Negroes; they rent for the most part small, two-room tenements, at $4 a month. The whites have a private and a public school, giving them a term of 8 or 9 months. The Negro schools are divided into a Methodist and a Baptist school, each of which has a term of 3 months. The school buildings are old and dilapidated and scarcely fit to teach in; they will not accommodate nearly all the Negro children of school age.

•   •   •   •   •

The morals of the colored people in the town are decidedly low. They dress and live better than the country Negroes, however, and sent their children more regularly to school. The union stonecutters are nearly all members of a local branch of the Odd Fellows. The women have a beneficial society. There are three churches — two Baptist and one Methodist — whose pastors are fairly intelligent.

•   •   •   •   •

Between 250 and 300 Negro families live in the town, representing all conditions. From these have been chosen 50 families for the purposes of this investigation. These families represent the better class of Negroes, and are rather above the average for the town. Their condition shows the general development of the more favorably situated Negroes in a thriving country town. At the same time some notice of general conditions has been taken. The 50 families, according to size, are as follows:

	Families
2 persons	15
3 persons	12
4 persons	9
5 persons	10
7 persons	1
9 persons	1
10 persons	2
Total	50

The total number of members of these families was 188, making the average size of the families 3.76 members. In the following table is shown the number of members of these families, by age and sex:

Number of persons in 50 selected families of Covington, Ga., by age and sex

Age	Male	Females	Total
Under 15 years	31	40	71
15 to 40 years	35	37	72
40 years or over	19	26	45
Total	85	103	188

---

5. Life in Washington, D.C. 1901

Alice Dunbar, Washington, D.C. to Mrs. Matilda Dunbar, Nov. 1, 1901, Dunbar Papers, Ohio Historical Society, Columbus, Ohio.

Alice was the wife of the poet Paul Lawrence Dunbar (1872–1906); Matilda was Alice's mother-in-law.

---

321 Spruce St., N. W. Washington, D.C.,
Nov. 1, 1901,

Dear Mother,

Your letter came several days ago, but I thought I would wait a day or two before I answered. I suppose by this time you have Paul's special letter enclosing the postal from your niece. I hope Aunt Rebecca is better. Paul was wondering if you wanted to go to Dayton to see her.

No, it is all too true about my sister's husband leaving her. He has gone, absquatulated, and taken all the money he could get his hands on with him. Poor Mrs. Smith, his partner, is penniless, as he took all the money he could collect from the business and left it in debt. Also he mortgaged Leila's house for two thousand dollars and I suppose she will be turned out when the mortgage falls due, as I know she can't raise the money to pay it. She is expecting her baby this week or next, and writes me that she is unable to do much or to find out a great deal until after the baby comes. I know it is wicked in me to say so, but I do hope the poor little thing won't live, for it seems awful for a lone woman to have four babies to raise, the eldest four years old. I have been very much upset, as I don't know how she and mama will get on.

You know Mrs. Moore, Professor Moore's wife? Well, we were all much shocked to hear of her death Tuesday. She died in childbirth, and it is her third child, too. It was quite a shock to every one. She is such a young woman too, I don't think more than twenty-five or twenty-six, although, as you know, she looked much older. George Cook's wife is quite ill. She has been in bed for a month, unable to put her feet to the floor. She is expecting her stranger at any time, and grave doubts are expressed as to whether she will live through it or not, as she is much too old to be having her first child. Mrs. Hilyer was dreadfully upset about Mrs. Moore's death. You know how Mrs. Hilyer is. Her sister is expecting very soon, and Mrs. Hilyer was positive then that she was going to die too.

Mr. Toomey is home from the hospital, much better. Mabel Turner has surprised us all by getting better, and now it is hoped that she will live, after all. She is doing real well.

Noah Thompson marries in Baltimore Wednesday. I had intended going and having a new dress for it, had engaged Mrs. Kelly to make it for me, but after I heard of Leila's trouble, I didn't feel that I wanted to be running around to weddings, buying new dresses and all that, so I gave up the idea of going. Paul is going over with Dr. Curtis and a number of other young men here. They are going to have a big stag in Baltimore Monday night, and I suppose they will have a great time, but I am going to stay right here. Dr. Warfield married last night in Baltimore, and will bring his bride here to live in the house he bought on Eleventh street.

Last night being Hallowe'en, a number of the girls met at Hattie Curtis' and had a vaudeville show all to themselves. It was very funny. Each girl took some character, and some of them went as men. Hattie was a shirt waist man, and she did look too funny in trousers. Mame Shepard also was a man, and Lulu Love. I was an old maid chaperon. I just took one of my old dresses, with a tight funny evening waist and fixed it up too ridiculous, with a lot of artificial flowers, fur and brass breastpins, and beads and truck. Paul made me a fake necklace of twine and bangles. I curled my hair in old fashioned curls all over my head. I had on mitts and about five pairs of brass bracelets. I had on white slippers and red stockings, one slipper had a big blue bow on it and the other slipper had on a yellow bow. Around my waist I had a[n] old velvet collar with cheap lace, and for a sash I had about twenty pieces of ribbon tied together, all different colors. It was killing. When all the girls got down stairs in the parlor, I cam[e] in very gravely with a big dry goods box, put it in the middle of the floor, put a stool in the box and sat down. It was an opera box, you know. Then I took out opera glasses and began to look at the performance. After each turn, I'd get up in the box and applaud, and wave a very torn handkerchief at the girls. Paul put a sign on the box[.] "This is the Chaperon. Lord Help Her!" I gave Lou Smallwood a feather duster tied with red ribbon for a bouquet. The fellows tried to get in the house, and rang the bell and scared us several times. But all the windows were closed and stuffed with paper so they could not peep, and finally when a number of them, with Paul and Dr. Curtis came in about twelve o'clock to try to scare us again, we had all changed our dresses, and all the boys were girls again, and they didn't see a thing but a lot of shirt waists and skirts.

I have made my Christmas fruit cake, and it certainly is fine. The quantity that the recipe called for made three cakes. The big cake pan, the smaller one, and one of the bread pans. Of course, I had to cut the loaf cake to see how it tasted, but I didn't use it all. My cakes are all wrapped up in much paper and put carefully away until Christmas. What do you think, I used some of the cherry wine to make the cake. We have a beautiful new latrobe in the parlor, and I have had the parlor carpet made into a rug, so that now there are polished floors all over. I did my curtains Wednesday. Margery Smith helped me put them on the frames. They look fine.

How did I and your Uncle Lou get so thick? I don't know. It was all on account of my policeman, I guess. Everybody got so mad because the policeman cracked my head that they forgot personal animosities and went to work and commiserated with me. Mrs. Fraser is in town, but I haven't been over to see her yet. I've been intending to go, but you know how long it takes me to get around to anything.

Let me hear from you soon. I hope Alice Madigan is better. It is very foolish in her to try to spend a winter in Chicago. Give them all my best love. Also all the folks, babies and yourself. Paul weighs one hundred and forty-seven pounds and a half. What do you think of that?

Lovingly your daughter,
Alice.

---

6. New York City, 1905

Ovington, "The Negro Home in New York," pp. 26–27.

The standard of manners, save among the very rough and uncultivated, is high for New York, where the tenement dweller must live largely in the street. This may be because the Negro is not a New Yorker, or is so in very few cases, but a Southerner. The pleasant voice and courteous ways of his old home remain with him. Some of his children after a time learn to adopt the rude standard of the street, but their shortcomings do not mean that they are without home training. I remember one little girl in a club of which I had charge. When I expostulated with her on her rudeness in interrupting me and ended by saying that perhaps in this case she did not know what good manners were she told me emphatically: "Yes, we knows what good manners are, our mothers learn us. It's we that's bold."

.   .   .   .   .

The Negro children are seldom offenders against the law; in the records last year at the juvenile court few serious cases were brought up against them. Nineteen children were accused of petit larceny and eight of grand larceny. On this last charge only two were found guilty and convicted, and but four in the petit larceny cases. This would seem to show little theft, much less than among the Jewish and Italian children of the lower East Side. The Negro boys and girls, however, are often truants, and this is partly because they do not have the same regular home care that is given to most of the children of the tenement.

For there is another aspect of the Negro home that is of great importance, the presence of the mother as a wage-earner. Sometimes the woman of the household earns more money than the man; often she earns as much. Her most profitable employment is domestic service, but this takes her away from her home for eight or ten, even for fourteen hours of the day. Many a mother, feeling that she cannot leave her children for the most of their waking hours, engages in the chief home industry of the colored woman, washing. In this she is an expert and her laundry commands good prices; but it turns her home into a workshop, and makes her few rooms hotter, more cluttered, more unhealthful. There is no space for the little children to play, and they are taught when very young to be of help. The work is unendingly wearying, lasting often into the night, and it results in a smaller wage than can be obtained with less expenditure of time in a workshop.

The colored men who work on the railroads and on the boats, or who go as waiters to the large hotels, are absent from their families for much of the year. They have little part in the care and rearing of their children. Others, such as the night watchmen and the hotel men, have some of their leisure in the daytime and can give more attention to their children than is possible with many fathers. Parental feeling is often strong among the Negro men and it is not difficult to find Dunbar's father holding his "little brown baby wif sparklin' eyes."

It may be said, however, with some certainty, that the economic situation of the New York Negro does not lead to a strengthening of the home life and of the marriage tie. The economic independence of the woman and the frequent absence from home of the man lead to desertions and separations. The attractive woman who is able to care for herself may grow to resent the presence of a husband whose support she does not need, and the lazy man may find another woman than his wife to support him. The presence of lodgers, necessitated by a high rent, is also a cause of loose family life. That there are many separated families among the poorer class of colored people all charitable workers know, and the woman's economic independence coupled with the man's inability to earn a good wage does something to promote such a condition.

7. Father and son in the Atlanta race riot, 1906

Walter White, *A Man Called White. The Auto-*

biography of Walter White (New York: The Viking Press, Inc., 1948), pp. 5–6, 10–12.[1]

Twelve years after the incident here described White (1893–1955) became assistant secretary of the NAACP. He was national secretary from 1929 until his death.

On a day in September 1906, when I was thirteen, we were taught that there is no isolation from life. The unseasonably oppressive heat of an Indian summer day hung like a steaming blanket over Atlanta. My sisters and I had casually commented upon the unusual quietness. It seemed to stay Mother's volubility and reduced Father, who was more taciturn, to monosyllables. But, as I remember it, no other sense of impending trouble impinged upon our consciousness.

Father was a mail collector. His tour of duty was from three to eleven P.M. He made his rounds in a little cart into which one climbed from a step in the rear. I used to drive the cart for him from two until seven, leaving him at the point nearest our home on Houston Street, to return home either for study or sleep. That day Father decided that I should not go with him. I appealed to Mother, who thought it might be all right, provided Father sent me home before dark because, she said, "I don't think they would dare start anything before nightfall." Father told me as we made the rounds that ominous rumors of a race riot that night were sweeping the town. But I was too young that morning to understand the background of the riot. I became much older during the next thirty-six hours, under circumstances which I now recognize as the inevitable outcome of what had preceded.

Late in the afternoon friends of my father's came to warn of more trouble that night. They

1. Copyright 1948 by Walter White. Reprinted by permission of The Viking Press, Inc.

told us that plans had been perfected for a mob to form on Peachtree Street just after nightfall to march down Houston Street to what the white people called "Darktown," three blocks or so below our house, to "clean out the niggers." There had never been a firearm in our house before that day. Father was reluctant even in those circumstances to violate the law, but he at last gave in at Mother's insistence.

We turned out the lights early, as did all our neighbors. No one removed his clothes or thought of sleep. Apprehension was tangible. We could almost touch its cold and clammy surface. Toward midnight the unnatural quiet was broken by a roar that grew steadily in volume. Even today I grow tense in remembering it.

Father told Mother to take my sisters, the youngest of them only six, to the rear of the house, which offered more protection from stones and bullets. My brother George was away, so Father and I, the only males in the house, took our places at the front windows of the parlor. The windows opened on a porch along the front side of the house, which in turn gave onto a narrow lawn that sloped down to the street and a picket fence. There was a crash as Negroes smashed the street lamp at the corner of Houston and Piedmont Avenue down the street. In a very few minutes the vanguard of the mob, some of them bearing torches, appeared. A voice which we recognized as that of the son of the grocer with whom we had traded for many years yelled, "That's where that nigger mail carrier lives! Let's burn it down! It's too nice for a nigger to live in!" In the eerie light Father turned his drawn face toward me. In a voice as quiet as though he were asking me to pass him the sugar at the breakfast table, he said, "Son, don't shoot until the first man puts his foot on the lawn and then — don't you miss!"

In the flickering light the mob swayed, paused, and began to flow toward us. In that instant there opened up within me a great awareness; I knew then who I was. I was a Negro, a human being with an invisible pigmentation which marked me a person to be hunted, hanged, abused, discriminated against, kept in poverty and ignorance, in order that those whose skin was white would have readily at hand a proof of their superiority, a proof patent and inclusive, accessible to the moron and the idiot as well as to the wise man and the genius.

.   .   .   .   .

Yet as a boy there in the darkness amid the tightening fright, I knew the inexplicable thing — that my skin was as white as the skin of those who were coming at me.

The mob moved toward the lawn. I tried to aim my gun, wondering what it would feel like to kill a man. Suddenly there was a volley of shots. The mob hesitated, stopped. Some friends of my father's had barricaded themselves in a two-story brick building just below our house. It was they who had fired. Some of the mobsmen, still bloodthirsty, shouted, "Let's go get the nigger." Others, afraid now for their safety, held back. Our friends, noting the hesitation, fired another volley. The mob broke and retreated up Houston Street.

In the quiet that followed I put my gun aside and tried to relax. But a tension different from anything I had ever known possessed me. I was gripped by the knowledge of my identity, and in the depths of my soul I was vaguely aware that I was glad of it. I was sick with loathing for the hatred which had flared before me that night and come so close to making me a killer; but I was glad I was not one of those who hated; I was glad I was not one of those made sick and murderous by pride. I was glad I was not one of those whose story is in the history of the world, a record of bloodshed, rapine, and pillage. I was glad my mind and spirit were part of the races that had not fully awakened, and who therefore had still before them the opportunity to write a record of virtue as a memorandum to Armageddon.

It was all just a feeling then, inarticulate and

Shanty Dwellers, Washington, D.C. Photograph by Charles F. Weller.

At Home, Pittsburgh, 1909.
Photograph by Lewis W. Hine.

Chiricahua Medicine Man and Family.

Apache Indian Scout and Family at Home.

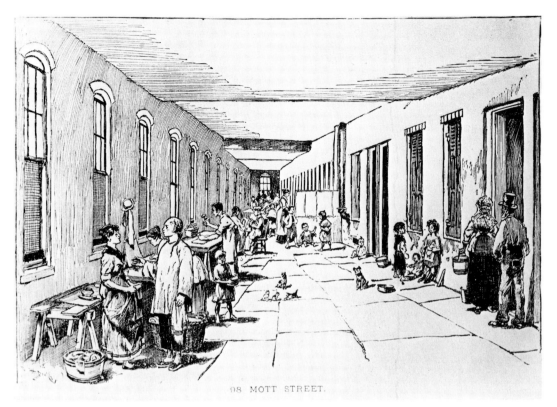

98 MOTT STREET.

The Big Flat, New York City, ca. 1875. This building, known as
"The Big Flat," was erected as a model tenement in 1855 and for many
years was the largest multiple dwelling in New York City. The
apartments opened off a public hall which ran the length of each floor.
The building was demolished in the late 1880's.

Playing Hose on Children during Heat Wave, Mulberry Bend Park, New York City.

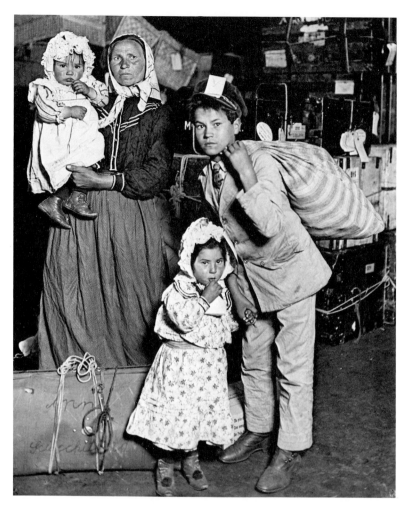

New Immigrants Searching
for Their Luggage, Ellis
Island, 1905. Photograph by
Lewis W. Hine.

In Front of the Joss House, San Francisco, ca. 1900. Photograph by
Arnold Genthe.

melancholy, yet reassuring in the way that death and sleep are reassuring, and I have clung to it now for nearly half a century.

---

8. Hunger, ca. 1914

Richard Wright, *Black Boy* (New York: Harper & Brothers, 1945), pp. 13–14. By permission of Harper & Row, Publishers, Inc.

Wright (1908–1960), author of *Native Son* (New York, 1940), was born near Natchez, Mississippi. His father deserted the family when Richard was six years old.

Hunger stole upon me so slowly that at first I was not aware of what hunger really meant. Hunger had always been more or less at my elbow when I played, but now I began to wake up at night to find hunger standing at my bedside, staring at me gauntly. The hunger I had known before this had been no grim, hostile stranger; it had been a normal hunger that had made me beg constantly for bread, and when I ate a crust or two I was satisfied. But this new hunger baffled me, scared me, made me angry and insistent. Whenever I begged for food now my mother would pour me a cup of tea which would still the clamor in my stomach for a moment or two; but a little later I would feel hunger nudging my ribs, twisting my empty guts until they ached. I would grow dizzy and my vision would dim. I became less active in my play, and for the first time in my life I had to pause and think of what was happening to me.

"Mama, I'm hungry," I complained one afternoon.

"Jump up and catch a kungry," she said, trying to make me laugh and forget.

"What's a kungry?"

"It's what little boys eat when they get hungry," she said.

"What does it taste like?"

"I don't know."

"Then why do you tell me to catch one?"

"Because you said that you were hungry," she said, smiling.

I sensed that she was teasing me and it made me angry.

"But I'm hungry. I want to eat."

"You'll have to wait."

"But I want to eat now."

"But there's nothing to eat," she told me.

"Why?"

"Just because there's none," she explained.

"But I want to eat," I said, beginning to cry.

"You'll just have to wait," she said again.

"But why?"

"For God to send some food."

"When is He going to send it?"

"I don't know."

"But I'm hungry!"

She was ironing and she paused and looked at me with tears in her eyes.

"Where's your father?" she asked me.

I stared in bewilderment. Yes, it was true that my father had not come home to sleep for many days now and I could make as much noise as I wanted. Though I had not known why he was absent, I had been glad that he was not there to shout his restrictions at me. But it had never occurred to me that his absence would mean that there would be no food.

"I don't know," I said.

"Who brings food into the house?" my mother asked me.

"Papa," I said. "He always brought food."

"Well, your father isn't here now," she said.

"Where is he?"

"I don't know," she said.

"But I'm hungry," I whimpered, stomping my feet.

"You'll have to wait until I get a job and buy food," she said.

As the days slid past the image of my father became associated with my pangs of hunger, and whenever I felt hunger I thought of him with a deep biological bitterness.

Indian families

1. Boyhood of a Hopi

Leo W. Simmons, ed., *Sun Chief: The Autobiography of a Hopi Indian* (New Haven: Yale University Press, 1942), pp. 51–53, 56, 60–61, 66–71. By permission of Yale University Press.

Don C. Talayesva, a Hopi Indian, told his life history to the staff of the Institute of Human Relations at Yale University. Talayesva was born in 1890 in Oraibi, Arizona, one hundred miles east of the Grand Canyon.

I was my grandfather's favorite. As soon as I was old enough to take advice, he taught me that it was a great disgrace to be called kahopi (not Hopi, not peaceable). He said, "My grandson, old people are important. They know a lot and don't lie. Listen to them, obey your parents, work hard, treat everyone right. Then people will say, 'That boy Chuka is a good child. Let's be kind to him.' If you do these things, you will live to be an old man yourself and pass away in sleep without pain. This is the trail that every good Hopi follows. Children who ignore these teachings don't live long."

He told me that I was a boy after his own heart and that he could look into my life and see that I would become an important man, perhaps a leader of the people. I wanted to be a medicine man as he was, but he told me that I could not be a very good healer because I was not a member of the Badger Clan, nor even of the Snake Clan. They made the best doctors, but he thought I might become a Special Officer in the ceremonies. He advised me to keep bad thoughts out of my mind, to face the east, look to the bright side of life, and learn to show a shining face, even when unhappy.

While I was still sleeping with him he taught me to get up before sunrise, bathe and exercise my body, and look around for useful work to do. He said, "Work means life. No one loves a lazybones."

Learning to work was like play. We children tagged around with our elders and copied what they did. We followed our fathers to the fields and helped plant and weed. The old men took us for walks and taught us the use of plants and how to collect them. We joined the women in gathering rabbitweed for baskets, and went with them to dig clay for pots. We would taste this clay as the women did to test it. We watched the fields to drive out the birds and rodents, helped pick peaches to dry in the sun, and gather melons to lug up the mesa. We rode the burros to harvest corn, gather fuel, or herd sheep. In house-building we helped a little by bringing up dirt to cover the roofs. In this way we grew up doing things. All the old people said that it was a disgrace to be idle and that a lazy boy should be whipped.

The importance of food was a lesson I learned early. My mother taught me never to waste it or play with it carelessly. Corn seemed to be the most important. A common saying was, "Corn is life, and piki is the perfect food." My mother-corn ears, which had been placed by my side at birth and used in my naming ceremony, were regarded as sacred and were kept a long time, but finally they were ground into meal and used for food before bugs got into them. Every family tried to keep a full year's supply of corn on hand and used it sparingly. There was always a pile of it in our house, neatly stacked in rows. A small supply of corn in a dry season was viewed with alarm, for to be without corn was a calamity. Whenever we shelled it we were careful to pick up every grain.

.   .   .   .   .

We were taught that whenever anyone came to our house we should sweep a clean place on the floor, set out the food, and invite him to eat. It was only after the company had eaten that my father ever asked, "What can I do for you?" My grandfather said that we must always observe this rule and feed visitors first, even when we were hungry or unhappy. I noticed that my mother and father stopped quarreling whenever company came. At mealtime we children were permitted to eat all that we wanted, but were told to behave and not to be greedy. It was no disgrace to break wind at mealtime or to laugh when someone else did. Whenever we went to a neighbor's house, we were told that we should eat their food to make them happy. It was proper to eat a little even when we were already full up to the neck. On a dance day we often ate ten or fifteen times.

.   .   .   .   .

While I was learning the importance of food and trying to recognize the different things that were fit to eat, I kept going to my mother for milk and was still nursing at six. Whenever we boys set out to hunt kangaroo rats or other small game, I ran first to my mother, placed my bow and arrows on the floor, sat beside her, and drank from her breasts. The other fellows would say, "Come Chuka, come, or we will be late." "Wait, wait," I replied between draughts. But on account of their teasing, I finally gave up the breast in embarrassment. My mother did not wean me; I just decided to let her alone.

.   .   .   .   .

Most of my time was spent in play. We shot arrows at targets, played old Hopi checkers, and pushed feather-edged sticks into corncobs and threw them at rolling hoops of cornhusks. We wrestled, ran races, played tag, kickball, stick throwing, and shinny. We spun tops with whips and made string figures on our fingers. I was poor at races but good at string figures. Another game I liked was making Hopi firecrackers. I mixed burro and horse dung, burned a lump of it into a red glow, placed the coal on a flat rock, and hit it with a cow horn dipped in urine. It went "bang" like a gun.

We hunted rabbits, kangaroo rats, and mice to feed to hawks and eagles. We also waged little wars with children of unfriendly families who were most opposed to the Whites. They criticized us for accepting gifts from white people and we called them Hostiles. Their children would upset our traps for turtledoves and try to torment us in every way. We had many fights with them, and my brother and I fought a great deal, even throwing stones at each other.

.   .   .   .   .

In winter we played in the kivas and listened to the long stories which the men told while they worked at spinning, weaving, and other jobs. They often picked out a boy to take messages and trade for them from kiva to kiva, and frequently I was chosen. The men would collect the things that they wished to exchange — wool, yarn, pieces of calico, leggings, and perhaps a sheep. Since a trader boy naturally could not carry a large animal, the owner would tie some wool from a sheep, or the hair of a horse or burro, on a stick to represent the animal. I would go from kiva to kiva showing the objects of trade. If a man wanted to purchase an animal or other large objects represented by a stick, he would make the trade and take the stick as proof of payment. Of course I had to remember the value of these objects and know exactly what the owner would take in exchange. It was great fun, and it also taught me to measure and to count.

I learned to count up to twenty with my fingers and toes. That was as high as we went. If, for example, we wanted to indicate forty-four, we would say "two twenties and four." Four was a lucky number, but we had no unlucky numbers. In measurement we said "one finger wide" for about one inch, "from the reach of the thumb to the middle finger" for about six inches, and "one foot" for the length from heel to toe. For long distances we counted in steps. I did not learn much about the weight of things at this time. Morning and afternoon were determined by the direction of the shadows, and we told time at night by the position of the moon and stars. Promises to pay at a future date were expressed in number of days, the state of the moon, or the number of moons.

.   .   .   .   .

As soon as I was old enough to wander about the village my grandfather suggested that I go out to the Antelope shrine and look for my deer people who were invisible to ordinary human beings. Sometimes I thought I could see antelopes who changed into people. Whenever I dreamed of antelopes in the village, my parents would say, "That is to be expected, for you are an antelope child." Then when I was perhaps five I would wander off a mile or two from the village to a place where sunflowers grew and where it was known that the spirits of deer and antelope gathered to give birth to their young and to feed on the sunflowers. It was a miracle that I could see these deer while others could not. I would return home with a bunch of sunflowers and with the juice of the sunflowers spread around my mouth. My grandfather or parents would remark that I had been feasting with my relatives and would probably use my special power soon to heal some poor person who was sick and unable to urinate.

I had also learned to pick out the people whom I could trust. My own mother still stood at the head of the list. She was my best friend. Though always busy, she was ready to help any person who came to her. My father also was a good friend and taught me how to do many things with my hands. I liked him, except on a few occasions when he punished me. He worked hard in his fields and with his herd, and was one of the best weavers in Oraibi. He traded the garments that he wove for things for his family to eat and wear. My grandfather, who lived in the house with us, liked me best and spent most time in teaching me. I knew I could count on him. My uncle Naquima and my sister Tuvamainim were good pals to me, but my brother Namostewa was not much of a friend.

Outside of our household, Masenimka, my aunt and godmother who named me, was perhaps the most important. She often kept me at her house, but was hot-tempered and sometimes treated me unfairly. I liked to go to her place, nevertheless, because she fed me the white-flour food. Her family was rich; she owned turkeys and her husband owned the first wagon and team in Oraibi.

.   .   .   .   .

By the time I was six, therefore, I had learned to find my way about the mesa and to avoid graves, shrines, and harmful plants, to size up people, and to watch out for witches. I was above average height and in good health. My hair was clipped just above my eyes, but left long in back and tied in a knot at the nape of my neck. I had almost lost one eye. I wore silver earrings, a missionary shirt or one made of a flour sack, and was always bare-legged, except for a blanket in cold weather. When no Whites were present, I went naked. I slept out on the housetop in summer and sometimes in the kiva with other boys in winter. I could help plant and weed, went out herding with my father, and was a kiva trader. I owned a dog and a cat, a small bow made by my father, and a few good arrows. Sometimes I carried stolen matches tucked in the hem of my shirt collar. I could ride a tame burro, kill a kangaroo rat, and catch small birds, but I could not make fire with a drill and I was not a good runner like the other fellows. At the races people teased me and said that my feet turned out so far that I pinched my anus as I ran. But I had made a name for myself by healing people; and I had almost stopped running after my mother for her milk.

I was full of mischief and hard to manage. Therefore I was scolded, doused with cold water, rolled in the snow, and teased terribly. But we children were never denied food, locked in a dark room, slapped on our faces, or stood up in a corner — those are not Hopi ways . . .

I also learned early to mark the people who

could punish me. My parents whipped me some and so did my grandfather, Homikniwa — at least twice . . .

There was a time when my father and mother said that I needed a spanking daily, but they could not make me behave. Since blows seemed useless, one day they put some coals in a broken dish, covered them with cedar boughs, and held me under a blanket in the smoke. When I cried, smoke entered my throat and nearly choked me. They finally let me go but said, "The next time you get into mischief we will punish you the same way, but worse." It seemed to me that this was the worst punishment a child could get. When I warned my playmates to be careful and avoid a smoking, some listened and some laughed.

Sometimes my father said to his brother, "My boy pays no attention to my blows; you whip him." He would do a thorough job of it . . .

---

2. Making the Indian family self-reliant, 1903

Department of the Interior, *Annual Report: Indian Affairs,* Part I, "Report of the Commissioner for 1903" (Washington, D.C., 1904), pp. 4–5.

THROWING THE INDIAN ON
HIS OWN RESOURCES

It is easy to point out difficulties, but it is not so easy to overcome them. Nevertheless, an attempt will now be made to indicate a policy which, if steadfastly adhered to, will not only relieve the Government of an enormous burden, but, it is believed, will practically settle the entire Indian question within the space usually allotted to a generation. Certainly it is time to make a move toward terminating the guardianship which has so long been exercised over the Indians and putting them upon equal footing with the white man so far as their relations with the Government are concerned. Under the present system the Indian ward never attains his majority. The guardianship goes on in an unbroken line from father to son, and generation after generation the Indian lives and dies a ward.

To begin at the beginning, then, it is freely admitted that education is essential. But it must be remembered that there is a vital difference between white and Indian education. When a white youth goes away to school or college his moral character and habits are already formed and well defined. In his home, at his mother's knee, from his earliest moments he has imbibed those elements of civilization which developing as he grows up distinguish him from the savage. He goes to school not to acquire a moral character, but to prepare himself for some business or profession by which he can make his way in after life.

With the Indian youth it is quite different. Born a savage and raised in an atmosphere of superstition and ignorance, he lacks at the outset those advantages which are inherited by his white brother and enjoyed from the cradle. His moral character has yet to be formed. If he is to rise from his low estate the germs of a nobler existence must be implanted in him and cultivated. He must be taught to lay aside his savage customs like a garment and take upon himself the habits of civilized life.

In a word, the primary object of a white school is to educate the mind; the primary essential of Indian education is to enlighten the soul. Under our system of government the latter is not the function of the state.

What, then, is the function of the state? Briefly this: To see that the Indian has the opportunity for self-support, and that he is afforded the same protection of his person and property as is given to others. That being done, he should be thrown entirely upon his own resources to become a useful member of the community in which he lives, or not, according as he exerts himself or fails to make an effort. He should be located where the conditions are such that by the exercise of ordinary industry and prudence he can support himself and family. He must be made to realize that in the sweat of his face he shall eat his bread. He must be brought to recognize the dignity of labor and the importance of building and maintaining a home. He must understand that the more useful he is there the more useful he will be to society. It is there he must find the incentive to work, and from it must come the uplifting of his race.

As has been said before, in the beginning of his undertaking he should have aid and instruction. He is entitled to that. Necessaries of life also will doubtless have to be furnished him for a time, at least until his labor becomes productive. More than this, so long as the Indians are wards of the General Government and until they have been absorbed by and become a part of the community in which they live, day schools should be established at convenient places where they may learn enough to transact the ordinary business of life. Beyond this in the way of schools it is not necessary to go — beyond this it is a detriment to go. The key to the whole situation is the home. Improvement must begin there. The first and most important object to be attained is the elevation of the domestic life. Until that is accomplished it is futile to talk of higher education.

This is a mere outline. There are many details to be considered and some difficulties to overcome. Of course it can not all be done at once. Different conditions prevail in different sections of the country. In some places the conditions are already ripe for the surrender of Government control; in others the natural conditions are such and the Indians are so situated that if protected in their rights they should soon be ready for independence. But in other places the question assumes a more serious aspect. Located in an arid region, upon unproductive reservations, often in a rigorous climate, there is no chance for the Indian to make a living,

even if he would. The larger and more powerful tribes are so situated. So long as this state of things exists the ration system with all its evils must continue. There can be little or no further reduction in that direction than that already made without violating the dictates of humanity. Already in several quarters there is suffering and want. In these cases something should be done toward placing such Indians in a position where they can support themselves, and that something should be done quickly.

But whatever the condition of the Indian may be, he should be removed from a state of dependence to one of independence. . . .

3. Weakening of family and community life, 1928

Meriam, *The Problem of Indian Administration,* pp. 15, 547–548, 573–575.

Family and Community Development. The Indian Service has not appreciated the fundamental importance of family life and community activities in the social and economic development of a people. The tendency has been rather toward weakening Indian family life and community activities than toward strengthening them. The long continued policy of removing Indian children from the home and placing them for years in boarding school largely disintegrates the family and interferes with developing normal family life. The belief has apparently been that the shortest road to civilization is to take children away from their parents and insofar as possible to stamp out the old Indian life. The Indian community activities particularly have often been opposed if not suppressed. The fact has been appreciated that both the family life and the community activities have many objectionable features, but the action taken has often been the radical one of attempting to destroy rather than the educational process of gradual modification and development.

. . . . .

A relatively small number of Indians make the transition from primitive to civilized life successfully; the great majority tend to shift from primitive ways to the ways of the poorest and least enterprising of the white population.

. . . . .

Indian social structure tends to break down instead of adapting itself to the conditions of civilized life. That the family is unstable is not surprising, for it has been subjected to severe strains. Indian families like white families suffer the disintegrating effects of poverty, illness, ignorance, and inability to adjust themselves to an industrial world. Among the Indians these strains are peculiarly great because the race is undergoing a shift from primitive to modern life. They are further intensified by the condition of perpetual childhood in which the Indians have been held, for both the system of education and the type of control exercised by the government over tribal and personal property have tended to loosen family ties. So far no program of the Indian Office has included constructive work with families by workers specially trained to deal with the problems involved in family disintegration. Some work of this kind is necessary to the success of any social program for the Indians.

The fundamental importance of community life, like that of family life, has apparently never been recognized by the government in the treatment of the Indians. Communities have never been organized for the ends the government seeks to attain. Government control has, moreover, operated to break down native forms of organization. The forcible removal of whole tribes to very different physical environments resulting in the disruption of economic life, the detention of large groups as prisoners of war for long periods, the common discouragement of Indian leadership on the reservations and in the government schools, the disrespect of white employees for native customs and ceremonies, and the assumption on the part of teachers and others in the schools that all Indian ways are bad ways, have tended to break down native social structure. Primitive organization gradually gives way in the face of white civilization and nothing takes its place. As a rule those forms of community activity have persisted that least serve the real interests of the Indians. The habit of wandering, in particular, persists, although it interferes seriously with economic prosperity and the stability of home life.

. . . . .

Strains Imposed by the System of Education. Indian families are subjected to peculiar strains growing out of their relation to the government. Some of the projects of the government, notably the appointment of field workers to deal with home conditions, have tended to strengthen family bonds. But on the whole government practices may be said to have operated against the development of wholesome family life.

Chief of these is the long continued policy of educating the children in boarding schools far from their homes, taking them from their parents when small and keeping them away until parents and children become strangers to each other. The theory was once held that the problem of the race could be solved by educating the children, not to return to the reservation, but to be absorbed one by one into the white population. This plan involved the permanent breaking of family ties, but provided for the children a substitute for their own family life by placing them in good homes of whites for vacations and sometimes longer, the so-called "outing system." The plan failed, partly because it was weak on the vocational side, but largely by reason of its artificiality. Nevertheless, this worst of its features still persists, and many children today have not seen their parents or brothers and sisters in years. A Hopi boy describing his home says:

We used to have lots of fun when we were

little fellows. Of course we sometimes get into fight, but since then I never have seen my sisters for seven years, they both away from home like me, so I hope we will all see each other some day.

A Navajo mother said: "I hated to send this boy to school. I knew I was saying goodbye. He would come back a stranger."

But parents know a worse fear than this. On many reservations there is distress because children die away at school. An Apache voiced the general sentiment in a speech in council:

I know the results of the reservation school but when we send our children to non-reservation schools we do not see these children for a long time, and sometimes they die. The reservation school is what we want.

A Hopi, speaking in council, said:

I wish to speak about students educated in non-reservation schools. In the matter of transfer of pupils to other schools, climatic conditions are often different and the child gets sick and yet parents are not notified. We all have children, as you may have, and we are all interested in these children. If a child is taken sick and brought home dead we feel very bad. Often in the case of sickness parents watch closely. If notified the child might be saved. Parents know the health conditions of the child. We all want our children educated, every one of us, but health comes first. I hope if the child gets sick in a different climate he may be returned home. I wonder if the grades may not be made higher at the day school, for such cases of sick children who have been sent home.

A Ute girl in one of the larger schools writes of conditions on her reservation as follows:

A lot of the young Ute girls that went away to school have gone home and died and the old Ute Indians don't want for us to go away to school and are having trouble about it, most of the girls died from T. B. and there are hardly any young girls on the Ute reservation and old people, they think that soon their will be hardly any more of this tribe and I think one of the nicest things to be done would be for them to have a hospital around Ignacio to care for the sick so they could get well.

Sometimes of course it is the parents or brothers or sisters who die, as in the case described by a girl of the Aricari and Pawnee tribes:

My mother died while I was away at school. Three of my other sisters died with flue that same winter. And so there was just my father and a little sister two years old and a little brother five years old, left at home. When vacation time came I went home to see the folks that remained. But I could not stand to stay at this home. I was always lonely without my mother and the three sisters, and every time I went from one room into another I thought of them and it made me more lonesome than ever.

The real tragedy, however, is not loss by death but the disruption of family life and its effect on the character of both parents and children. The personal care of helpless offspring is the natural expression of affection no less among Indians than among parents of other races. No observer can doubt that Indian parents are very fond of their children, and though the care that they give may be from the point of view of white parents far from adequate, yet the emotional needs of both parents and children are satisfied.

Effects of the System upon Parents. A normal emotional life is essential to the development of parents to full adult responsibility. In relieving them of the care of their children the government robs them of one of the strongest and most fundamental of the economic motives, thereby keeping them in the state of childhood. One of the most common remarks to be heard in the Indian Service is that the Indians are like children. Certainly most of them retain their primitive characteristics of improvidence. Since the avowed purpose of the government has been to develop the race to the point of full adult competence, it seems strange that the greatest incentive to industry and to provision for the future should have been overlooked. Evidences are not lacking that many tribes are today less industrious, less able to fit themselves to their environment than they were fifty years ago; that they were in some ways better off in their primitive state. Insofar as the government has sacrificed real and vital adult education to the formal education of children in institutions it has handicapped a primitive people in their development, and the Indians have little to show to repay them for the sorrows of broken homes. The loss of children tends still further to disrupt the family through the loosening of marital ties. Normally husband and wife have a strong bond in their common responsibility for children. To take away this responsibility is to encourage a series of unions with all the bad social consequences that accompany impermanence of marital relations.

Effects of the System upon Children. The effects of early deprivation of family life are apparent in the children. They too are the victims of an arrested development. The experience of the white race abundantly demonstrates that institutional children, even with the best of care, have greater health and personality difficulties than children in families. Affection of an intimate sort is essential to normal development. Recognizing this fact the better societies for the care of dependent white children have for many years been placing their wards out in families as rapidly as the very delicate adjustment involved can be made. Even in institutions for the care of dependent white children the children are there because they have no homes or because normal home life is impossible, and very few are taken forcibly from their parents. But many children are in Indian schools as the result of coercion of one kind or another and they suffer under a sense of separation from home and parents. Since initiative and independence are not developed under the rigid routine of the school, the whole system increases the child's sentiment for dependence on parental decisions and children in their teens go back to their mother with a six-year old's feeling for her.

Under normal conditions the experience of family life is of itself a preparation of the children for future parenthood. Without this experience of the parent-child relation throughout the developmental period Indian young people must suffer under a serious disability in their relations with their own children. No kind of formal training can possibly make up for this lack, nor can the outing system when the child is half grown supplement what he has missed in his own family and with his own race in earlier years.

Cross currents of immigrant life

1. An Italian boy's image of America

Constantine M. Panunzio, *The Soul of an Immigrant* (New York: Macmillan, 1921), pp. 58–65.

Panunzio, born in Molfetta, Italy, in 1884, came to the United States at the age of eighteen. He graduated from Wesleyan University in 1911 and in 1925 received a Ph.D. in sociology from Brookings Graduate School.

Of course, like every Italian boy, I had heard from earliest childhood of America, the continent which "Colombo," one of our countrymen, had long ago discovered. However, my idea of America was as misty as that of the Old World on the day when Columbus returned from his famous voyage . . .

. . . to me there was no distinction between North and South America. There was but one America. I had read something of Boston and New York, but the words brought only a vague and indefinite idea to my mind. Even Montevideo and Buenos Ayres, of which I had heard much, were far from definite and concrete realities. Two things alone I seemed able to picture; the vast stretches of virgin lands and the great, winding rivers. I had read something of the Indians, who were very much like the cannibals of my childhood stories. The uncle to whom I have already referred would often recount stories of his voyages to America, but these presented vague pictures and were invariably connected with thrilling experiences with pirates which he had had off the coast of that continent . . .

I knew of only one person who had gone from our small city to North America. He came to visit Molfetta when I was a small boy, and his visit left certain distinct impressions upon my mind. He had lived in America for several years. From what I recall, it seems that he had changed his name while living in America, and therefore his family had lost all trace of him, and considered him dead. They were friends of our family, and when he finally came back for a visit, I was much impressed. I remember him as clearly as if it were to-day. He could not speak our dialect any more. What little of the language he spoke was the pure Italian, which he had learned in America. I recall also his purple, showy necktie, and a stickpin with brilliants. What impressed me most of all was the white collar which he wore. These things were great luxuries in our town, worn only by the well-to-do, and not by "la gente," or common folks, to which he belonged.

Another close-up view of America which I got in my childhood was that of what I thought were American sailors on board an American steamer, which chanced to come to Molfetta. This was such a rare happening that of course I learned of it, and taking a special leave of absence from school, I went to call upon the honorable gentlemen, the American sailors. For all I know they may have been Chinese coolies, but as long as they were on board an American steamer, to me they were Americans. There were several interesting and peculiar things about these American sailors. For one thing, they were very paragons of filth. I liked to hear them speak their foreign, and to me, "barbarian" language. I can recall to-day their shouts as they unloaded the coal. And most interesting of all was the sight of them drunk on the streets of our little Molfetta, where drunken persons were never seen. They had gone ashore, and taking advantage of the inexpensiveness of our good Molfettese wine, they had laid in a goodly provision of it, and from the way they staggered about the streets,

it was evident that they had stored away within their bodily cellars slightly more than they could carry well. We boys followed them from street to street, and made sport of them in order to hear their funny jabbering.

Another glimpse of America, strangely contradictory to the one I have just related, came through a ship builder who lived in Molfetta. This man was quite well-to-do, and greatly respected in our town. He had been in America several years, had made money and returned to our city, where he had established a shipbuilding business of his own. He was, however, considered one of the queerest and most extraordinary members of our little society, for the reason that he did not drink wine or liquors of any kind . . .

Still another view of America had come to me through the eyes of a blind man. In my boyhood, he was a man of about fifty years of age; stone blind, and led about the streets by a small boy. The story was that he had been in America, where he had worked "in campagna" — in the country — and that the climate was so hot that he had lost his eyesight by sunstroke. He had been back in Molfetta for some twenty years. Apparently he had made some money before his return, for he did not seem to be a mendicant like most of the blind people of the town. To me the most striking thing about this man was that he was the only person in Molfetta who could speak English, and he always acted as interpreter when English or American vessels chanced to come to the city. It was this man who first awakened in me a desire to learn the English language. I used to think that if I could learn English and become an "interrupter" myself, I would be in the height of my glory.

From some source I got the idea that America was a continent of great forests, and that the trees when cut grew again, not new trees, but that they grew up again from the stumps, and that by this method of growth America was always covered with great stretches of forests.

Now it does not require a great artist nor a

great stretch of the imagination to piece together these various fragments and create a picture of America as I saw it when I turned my steps westward; it was a great country, vast in its proportions, vaguely beautiful, covered with forests, leisurely-winding rivers and great stretches of farm lands. There were some large cities like Montevideo or Boston, a little larger perhaps than Genoa, or Naples, and all belonging to the same country. It was so hot that persons working in the fields became blind from sunstroke. In that country lived many pirates who attacked passing ships; dirty drunken sailors who spoke a barbarian tongue; the Indians, who were a sort of wild creatures on the order of cannibals. People from Molfetta went there and made much money. Some of them acquired strange habits, like not drinking wine or not speaking our dialect any more, wearing white collars and purple neckties when they belonged to the "gente."

---

2. The arrival

Mary Antin, *The Promised Land* (Boston, 1912), pp. 185–186.

Miss Antin (1881–1949) emigrated to Boston from Polotzk, Russia, in 1894.

Our initiation into American ways began with the first step on the new soil. My father found occasion to instruct or correct us even on the way from the pier to Wall Street, which journey we made crowded together in a rickety cab. He told us not to lean out of the windows, not to point, and explained the word "greenhorn." We did not want to be "greenhorns," and gave the strictest attention to my father's instructions. I do not know when my parents found opportunity to review together the history of Polotzk in the three years past,

for we children had no patience with the subject; my mother's narrative was constantly interrupted by irrelevant questions, interjections, and explanations.

The first meal was an object lesson of much variety. My father produced several kinds of food, ready to eat, without any cooking, from little tin cans that had printing all over them. He attempted to introduce us to a queer, slippery kind of fruit, which he called "banana," but had to give it up for the time being. After the meal, he had better luck with a curious piece of furniture on runners, which he called "rocking-chair." There were five of us newcomers, and we found five different ways of getting into the American machine of perpetual motion, and as many ways of getting out of it. One born and bred to the use of a rocking-chair cannot imagine how ludicrous people can make themselves when attempting to use it for the first time. We laughed immoderately over our various experiments with the novelty, which was a wholesome way of letting off steam after the unusual excitement of the day.

In our flat we did not think of such a thing as storing the coal in the bathtub. There was no bathtub. So in the evening of the first day my father conducted us to the public baths. As we moved along in a little procession, I was delighted with the illumination of the streets. So many lamps, and they burned until morning, my father said, and so people did not need to carry lanterns. In America, then, everything was free, as we had heard in Russia. Light was free; the streets were as bright as a synagogue on a holy day. Music was free; we had been serenaded, to our gaping delight, by a brass band of many pieces, soon after our installation on Union Place.

Education was free. That subject my father had written about repeatedly, as comprising his chief hope for us children, the essence of American opportunity, the treasure that no thief could touch, not even misfortune or poverty. It was the one thing that he was able to promise us when he sent for us; surer, safer than bread or shelter . . .

3. Saluting the flag

Jacob Riis, "The Children of the Poor," in Robert Woods *et al., The Poor in Great Cities* (New York, 1895), pp. 110–114.

. . . Very lately a unique exercise has been added to the course in the schools, that lays hold of the very marrow of the problem with which they deal. It is called "saluting the flag," and originated with Colonel George T. Balch, of the Board of Education, who conceived the idea of instilling patriotism into the little future citizens of the Republic in doses to suit their childish minds. To talk about the Union, of which most of them had but the vaguest notion, or of the duty of the citizen, of which they had no notion at all, was nonsense. In the flag it was all found embodied in a central idea which they could grasp. In the morning the star-spangled banner was brought into the school, and the children were taught to salute it with patriotic words. Then the best scholar of the day before was called out of the ranks, and it was given to him or her to keep for the day. The thing took at once and was a tremendous success.

Then was evolved the plan of letting the children decide for themselves whether or not they would so salute the flag as a voluntary offering, while incidentally instructing them in the duties of the voter at a time when voting was the one topic of general interest. Ballot-boxes were set up in the schools on the day before the last general election. The children had been furnished with ballots for and against the flag the week before, and told to take them home to their parents and talk it over with them. On Monday they cast their votes with all the solemnity of a regular election, and with as much of its simple machinery as was practicable. As was expected, only very few votes against the flag were recorded. One little Irishman in the Mott Street school came without his ballot. "The old man tore it up," he reported. In the East Seventy-third Street school five

Bohemians of tender years set themselves down as opposed to the scheme of making Americans of them. Only one, a little girl, gave her reason. She brought her own flag to school: "I vote for that," she said, sturdily, and the teacher wisely recorded her vote and let her keep the banner.

. . . . . .

The first patriotic election in the Fifth Ward Industrial School was held on historic ground. The house it occupies was John Ericsson's until his death, and there he planned nearly all his great inventions, among them one that helped save the flag for which the children voted that day. The children have lived faithfully up to their pledge. Every morning sees the flag carried to the principal's desk and all the little ones, rising at the stroke of the bell, say with one voice, "We turn to our flag as the sunflower turns to the sun!" One bell, and every brown right fist is raised to the brow, as in military salute: "We give our heads!" Another stroke, and the grimy little hands are laid on as many hearts: "And our hearts!" Then with a shout that can be heard around the corner: " — to our country! One country, one language, one flag!" No one can hear it and doubt that the children mean every word, and will not be apt to forget that lesson soon.

Immigrants and their children

1. What's in a name, ca. 1896

Leonard Covello with Guido D'Agostino, *The Heart Is the Teacher* (New York, 1958), pp. 21–22, 29–31. Copyright © 1958 by Leonard Covello, used with permission of McGraw-Hill Book Company.

Leonard Covello, principal of the Benjamin Franklin High School in East Harlem, 1934–1957, and leader in immigrant education, was born in Avigliano, Italy, in 1887. His father migrated in 1891 and sent for his family five years later.

Our first home in America was a tenement flat near the East River at 112th Street on the site of what is now Jefferson Park. The sunlight and fresh air of our mountain home in Lucania were replaced by four walls and people over and under and on all sides of us, until it seemed that humanity from all corners of the world had congregated in this section of New York City known as East Harlem.

The cobbled streets. The endless, monotonous rows of tenement buildings that shut out the sky. The traffic of wagons and carts and carriages and the clopping of horses' hoofs which struck sparks in the night. The smell of the river at ebb tide. The moaning of fog horns. The clanging of bells and the screeching of sirens as a fire broke out somewhere in the neighborhood. Dank hallways. Long flights of wooden stairs and the toilet in the hall. And the water, which to my mother was one of the great wonders of America — water with just the twist of a handle, and only a few paces from the kitchen. It took her a long time to get used to this luxury. Water and a few other conveniences were the compensations the New World had to offer.

"With the Aviglianese you are always safe," my father would say. "They are your countrymen, *paesani*. They will always stand by you."

The idea of family and clan was carried from Avigliano in southern Italy to East Harlem. From the River to First Avenue, 112th Street was the Aviglianese Colony in New York City and closest to us were the Accurso and Salvatore families. My father had lived with the Accursos during the six years he was trying to save enough for a little place to live and the money for l'umbarco. In fact, it was Carmela, wife of his friend Vito Accurso and mother of the girl who met us at the boat, who saved his money for him, until the needed amount had accumulated. It was Carmela Accurso who made ready the tenement flat and arranged the

welcoming party with relatives and friends to greet us upon our arrival. During this celebration my mother sat dazed, unable to realize that at last the torment of the trip was over and that here was America. It was Mrs. Accurso who put her arm comfortingly about my mother's shoulder and led her away from the party and into the hall and showed her the water faucet. "Courage! You will get used to it here. See! Isn't it wonderful how the water comes out?"

Through her tears my mother managed a smile.

. . . . .

One day I came home from the Soup School [1] with a report card for my father to sign. It was during one of these particularly bleak periods. I remember that my friend Vito Salvatore happened to be there, and Mary Accurso had stopped in for a moment to see my mother. With a weary expression my father glanced over the marks on the report card and was about to sign it. However, he paused with the pen in his hand.

"What is this?" he said. "Leonard Covello! What happened to the *i* in Coviello?"

My mother paused in her mending. Vito and I just looked at each other.

"Well?" my father insisted.

"Maybe the teacher just forgot to put it in," Mary suggested. "It can happen." She was going to high school now and spoke with an air of authority, and people always listened to her. This time, however, my father didn't even hear her.

"From Leonardo to Leonard I can follow," he said, "a perfectly natural process. In America anything can happen and does happen. But you don't change a family name. A name is a name. What happened to the *i*?"

"Mrs. Cutter took it out," I explained. "Every time she pronounced Coviello it came

1. On the Soup School see below Part Eight, Chap. IV, sec. B., School experiences of immigrant children, doc. 3.

out Covello. So she took out the *i*. That way it's easier for everybody."

My father thumped Columbus on the head with his fist. "And what has this Mrs. Cutter got to do with my name?"

"What difference does it make?" I said. "It's more American. The *i* doesn't help anything." It was one of the very few times that I dared oppose my father. But even at that age I was beginning to feel that anything that made a name less foreign was an improvement.

Vito came to my rescue. "My name is Victor — Vic. That's what everybody calls me now."

"Vica. Sticka. Nicka. You crazy in the head!" my father yelled at him.

For a moment my father sat there, bitter rebellion building in him. Then with a shrug of resignation, he signed the report card and shoved it over to me. My mother now suddenly entered the argument. "How is it possible to do this to a name? Why did you sign the card? Narduccio, you will have to tell your teacher that a name cannot be changed just like that. . . ."

"Mamma, you don't understand."

"What is there to understand? A person's life and his honor is in his name. He never changes it. A name is not a shirt or a piece of underwear."

My father got up from the table, lighted the twisted stump of a Toscano cigar and moved out of the argument. "Honor!" he muttered to himself.

"You must explain this to your teacher," my mother insisted. "It was a mistake. She will know. She will not let it happen again. You will see."

"It was no mistake. On purpose. The *i* is out and Mrs. Cutter made it Covello. You just don't understand!"

"Will you stop saying that!" my mother insisted. "I don't understand. I don't understand. What is there to understand? Now that you have become Americanized you understand everything and I understand nothing."

With her in this mood I dared make no answer. Mary went over and put her hand on my mother's shoulder. I beckoned to Vito and together we walked out of the flat and downstairs into the street.

"She just doesn't understand," I kept saying.

"I'm gonna take the *e* off the end of my name and make it just Salvator," Vito said. "After all, we're not in Italy now."

Vito and I were standing dejectedly under the gas light on the corner, watching the lamplighter moving from post to post along the cobblestone street and then disappearing around the corner on First Avenue. Somehow or other the joy of childhood had seeped out of our lives. We were only boys, but a sadness that we could not explain pressed down upon us. Mary came and joined us. She had a book under her arm. She stood there for a moment, while her dark eyes surveyed us questioningly.

"But they don't understand!" I insisted.

Mary smiled. "Maybe some day, you will realize that *you* are the one who does not understand."

---

2. *Amerikane kinder*

Hutchins Hapgood, *The Spirit of the Ghetto,* 2nd ed. (New York, 1909), pp. 23–28.

The Spirit of the Ghetto originally appeared as a series of articles in *Atlantic Monthly,* 1898–1902. Hapgood was then a reporter for the (New York) *Commerical Advertiser,* which was edited by Lincoln Steffens.

With his entrance into the public school the little fellow runs . . . against a system of education and a set of influences which are at total variance with those traditional to his race and with his home life. The religious element is entirely lacking. The educational system of the public schools is heterogeneous and worldly. The boy becomes acquainted in the school reader with fragments of writings on all subjects, with a little mathematics, a little history. His instruction, in the interests of a liberal nonsectarianism, is entirely secular. English becomes his most familiar language. He achieves a growing comprehension and sympathy with the independent, free, rather sceptical spirit of the American boy; he rapidly imbibes ideas about social equality and contempt for authority, and tends to prefer Sherlock Holmes to Abraham as a hero.

The orthodox Jewish influences, still at work upon him, are rapidly weakened. He grows to look upon the ceremonial life at home as rather ridiculous. His old parents, who speak no English, he regards as "greenhorns." English becomes his habitual tongue, even at home, and Yiddish he begins to forget. He still goes to "chaider," but under conditions exceedingly different from those obtaining in Russia, where there are no public schools, and where the boy is consequently shut up within the confines of Hebraic education. In America, the "chaider" assumes a position entirely subordinate. Compelled by law to go to the American public school, the boy can attend "chaider" only before the public school opens in the morning or after it closes in the afternoon. At such times the Hebrew teacher, who dresses in a long black coat, outlandish tall hat, and commonly speaks no English, visits the boy at home, or the boy goes to a neighboring "chaider."

Contempt for the "chaider's" teaching comes the more easily because the boy rarely understands his Hebrew lessons to the full. His real language is English, the teacher's is commonly the Yiddish jargon, and the language to be learned is Hebrew. The problem before him is consequently the strangely difficult one of learning Hebrew, a tongue unknown to him, through a translation into Yiddish, a language of growing unfamiliarity, which, on account of its poor dialectic character, is an inadequate vehicle of thought.

The orthodox parents begin to see that the boy, in order to "get along" in the New World, must receive a Gentile training. Instead of hoping to make a rabbi of him, they reluctantly consent to his becoming an American business man, or, still better, an American doctor or lawyer. The Hebrew teacher, less convinced of the usefulness and importance of his work, is in this country more simply commercial and less disinterested than abroad; a man generally, too, of less scholarship as well as of less devotion.

The growing sense of superiority on the part of the boy to the Hebraic part of his environment extends itself soon to the home. He learns to feel that his parents, too, are "greenhorns." In the struggle between the two sets of influences that of the home becomes less and less effective. He runs away from the supper table to join his gang on the Bowery, where he is quick to pick up the very latest slang; where his talent for caricature is developed often at the expense of his parents, his race, and all "foreigners"; for he is an American, he is "the people," and like his glorious countrymen in general, he is quick to ridicule the stranger. He laughs at the foreign Jew with as much heartiness as at the "dago"; for he feels that he himself is almost as remote from the one as from the other.

"Why don't you say your evening prayer, my son?" asks his mother in Yiddish.

"Ah, what yer givin' us!" replies, in English, the little American-Israelite as he makes a bee-line for the street.

The boys not only talk together of picnics, of the crimes of which they read in the English newspapers, of prize-fights, of budding business propositions, but they gradually quit going to synagogue, give up "chaider" promptly when they are thirteen years old, avoid the Yiddish theatres, seek the up-town places of amusement, dress in the latest American fashion, and have a keen eye for the right thing in neckties. They even refuse sometimes to be present at supper on Friday evenings. Then, indeed, the sway of the old people is broken.

"Amerikane Kinder, Amerikane Kinder!" wails the old father, shaking his head. The trend of things is indeed too strong for the old man of the eternal Talmud and ceremony.

An important circumstance in helping to determine the boy's attitude toward his father is the tendency to reverse the ordinary and normal educational and economical relations existing between father and son. In Russia the father gives the son an education and supports him until his marriage, and often afterward, until the young man is able to take care of his wife and children. The father is, therefore, the head of the house in reality. But in the New World the boy contributes very early to the family's support. The father is in this country less able to make an economic place for himself than is the son. The little fellow sells papers, black boots, and becomes a street merchant on a small scale. As he speaks English, and his parents do not, he is commonly the interpreter in business transactions, and tends generally to take things into his own hands. There is a tendency, therefore, for the father to respect the son.

---

3. The breach between the new and the old, ca. 1910

Mary McDowell, "The American Citizen in the Making," ca. 1910, Folder 12,
Mary McDowell Papers, Chicago Historical Society.

Miss McDowell (1859–1936), a former resident of Hull House, established the University of Chicago Settlement in the Packington district of Chicago in 1894.

A baby born back of the Yards is a very common occurrence, yet even when there are seventy-five in one block, each new comer is loved and is an ever new object of interest.

It was in a typical long frame tenement of two stories and a basement that this new baby had come to live or to die. The home of the parents was in a basement below the level of the city street. The father worked in the Stockyards as an unskilled laborer, receiving $1.65 a day. As the rent of the four rooms was ten dollars a month, and as the expenses of the wedding and the journey from Galicia had just been paid for, this new family imitated their neighbors by taking boarders to help carry their economic burden.

The Settlement nurse had been consulted before the birth, so when at last the little one came, the father hurried to this wise friend who knew what was needed for a newly arrived American citizen. She carried with her some modern, simple and hygienic clothes — the first step into a life beset with all kinds of unsanitary dangers. While she was performing these first rites of citizenship, the boarders, large Polish men, filled the room about the nurse and baby. She had finished the washing, and was putting on the American clothes, when one of the interested on-lookers remarked in broken English: "Little American baby now," and another continued: "Baby got citizen papers?" Then all laughed at the joke, the nurse joining in.

.　　.　　.　　.　　.

This break between the past of the parents and the future of the child in the foreigner's home starts our young American without that cultural advantage that an historic perspective gives to those of us of many generations in America. It is a great waste not to conserve to this first generation all that is best in their families' past. These new comers are not without beautiful traditions, good, simple manners and ideals that our forefathers held dear. Those who in the old land read at all knew Geo. Washington and Abraham Lincoln. They to them embodied American ideals, and great numbers came to America hoping to see realized their dreams of democracy.

.　　.　　.　　.　　.

It is said that the criminals of the cities come from the ranks of the children of the immigrants, not from the immigrants themselves. Those who live near these transplanted people tell us of the struggle in the family life between the standards of the old country father and mother and those of the children who have learned the language and caught the spirit of the new country, and have become the important factor in the family life.

The child stands between the new life and its strange customs; he is the interpreter; he often is the first breadwinner; he becomes the authority in the family.

The parents are displaced because they are helpless, and must trust the children. This superficial, though very practical superiority forces the children and parents into a false position with relation to each other and towards the outside world. The parents have religious and social ideals, and an impassioned faith that in America is to be found liberty and independence. The children's ideals are formed by the teachers, the politicians and often the saloonkeepers. The parents' ideals are discredited; they are old fashioned; in some way the children enter into their parents' vague desire for freedom, but it becomes to them such freedom as is hurriedly realized in a do-as-you please philosophy. They have lost the restraints of an old community feeling that surrounded the parents in their old home and have not yet become rooted in the new. They are even yet held by the restraints of the public opinion of a neighborhood they do not know. The parent's values are belittled and their loyalties scorned. "Shut up talking about Bohemia," said a boy to his mother who was shedding homesick tears as she spoke of the beauties of her old home. "We are going to live in America, not in Bohemia." She had a vision of beauty, while she was living in the sordid ugliness of the stockyards district of Chicago, while her boy could never have her vision and was losing something in this change that nothing in America could supply.

The children are determined to drop the mother tongue, and they very soon learn English, while the parents are past the age when it is easy to acquire a new language. One often hears of children refusing to answer in the language of the family. Everything seems to be done to develop and educate the children, forgetting that this cannot be done for the child independently of the family or the community. The school, the church, the social settlement all emphasize the child's importance. The parents are ignored, left behind and the breach between the new and the old in the family is not spanned as yet by any of the agencies in the community.

4. The dual life of children of oriental parentage, 1926

William C. Smith, *The Second Generation Oriental in America* (Honolulu, 1927), pp. 8, 10, 12, 13. Reprinted with permission of *Pacific Affairs.*

These interviews were part of a study of American-born children of Oriental parentage conducted in 1926 by the staff of the Survey of Race Relations on the Pacific Coast of North America.

I can never forget the feeling of adventure and strangeness and quaintness I felt as I walked through the streets of Yokohama from the steamer to the hotel. Everything impressed me as being funny; the super-dignified, stern, little policeman who courteously but haughtily directed the way, the small telephone poles, the traffic keeping to the left, the rickshaw men jogging along at a funny trot, numerous servants at the hotel who bowed ceremoniously at every turn. We soon went to Tokyo and saw the sights. The modernness of the capital surprised me, but like a true Angeleno, I compared everything I saw with some corresponding thing in Los Angeles, and said to myself: "We can beat that in Los Angeles." Then we went to the home of my uncle in Kobe, who is a professor in a college there. When I went there I spoke so much about Southern California that he could not show me anything in Japan to beat my stories of California, so he tried to beat my stories by telling me of Scotland, where he had studied at the University of Glasgow . . . I grudgingly admitted that Japan was an interesting country to see, but I maintained that Southern California was the only place in the world to live. I converted one of my cousins, and now he wants to come to America to study. I was glad when I got back to America. The country seemed to be so much more open, and quiet and freer, and natural. I felt as if I had at last reached home when the train came into the warm Southern California sunshine, passing through the dry, barren, brown, hay stubble-covered hills near Santa Barbara. At Santa Barbara I bought a Los Angeles newspaper, the *Examiner,* and I turned first to the sports page and saw that my old high school had won another football game, and I felt happy. It takes a Hearst paper to make me feel at home.

.   .   .   .   .   .

I was born in America, but was raised in Oriental fashion. My mother died while I was quite young and I was raised by my grandmother. My father was dominated by the Chinese idea that the man was the head of the family and that the children were to be entirely submerged in the family — we were not considered as having any individuality of our own. When I was in school I was told that my position was a subordinate one, even in cases where I had more information than father on account of my school work, but he would never admit anything like that. I was kept closely at home and restrained until I began to revolt against this situation. I saw the freedom of the American children and saw that some of the other Chinese children had more freedom than I had. I have noticed a great deal of change in my father's home since I was a child, however. The younger children now do

not obey him as I had to do. One day I said to my half-brother that they had a chance to attend school and should make the most of their opportunities so they would be able to take care of father in his old age. One of them spoke up and said, "I'll have all I can do to take care of myself." In China such an expression would be considered disgraceful, because the children take care of their aged parents.

.   .   .   .   .   .

To meet the situation we children of Oriental parentage try to live a dual life. At home we try to act and speak like typical Japanese. Outside of the home we try to act and speak like "Old Americans." Whenever possible we of the second generation try to live a dual life. We are criticized by our parents for speaking an imperfect Japanese; we are also criticized by the Americans. Despite these criticisms, in general, we are facing the situation and doing a pretty good job of it. We are being Americanized gradually; we do not wish to throw away entirely our old traditions and customs. We realize that sudden changes are very harmful to any group of people. What we need is sympathy from the "Old Americans." Time only will solve this problem. Therefore, let us be patient and try to understand each other.

.   .   .   .   .   .

The children here have no respect for the old people. It is not so in China; there they respect them. But here, if you are old, they think you ought to die. When the boy is twenty-one, he says, "I am twenty-one and I will do as I please." When the girl is eighteen she says, "I am eighteen and I can do as I please." The father will want to advise them and will say, "I think it is better this way," but the young people will reply, "We want to do this way and we are going to do this way." I see this so often in families. I believe in liberty, but I think in some ways there is too much among the young people.

Workers

1. Vices and virtues of a working-class family, ca. 1880

William Graham Sumner, "A Parable," in *Essays of William Graham Sumner,* ed. Albert Galloway Keller and Maurice R. Davie, (New Haven: Yale University Press, 1934), I, 497–499. By permission of Yale University Press.

Sumner (1840–1910) was professor of political and social science at Yale. He wrote "A Parable" in the 1880's.

A PARABLE

A certain respectable man had three sons, who grew up, lived, and died in the same city.

The oldest one turned his back at an early age on study. Being eager to earn something at once, he obtained employment driving a grocer's delivery wagon. He never acquired a trade, but was a teamster or driver all his life. In his youth he spent all his spare time with idle companions and devoted his earnings to beer, tobacco, and amusement. At twenty-two he fell in love and married. He had six children who scrambled part way through the public grammar school after a negligent fashion, but cost as much money and more of the teachers' time than if they had been regular and studious. This son never earned over two dollars a day except on election day, when he earned five or more, according to circumstances. He never had ten dollars in his possession over and above his debts.

The second son was the scholar of the family. By energy, perseverance, and self-denial he managed to get a professional education. He married at thirty, being in the receipt of an adequate income from his profession, but not yet having accumulated any capital. He had three children who were all educated in the public grammar and high schools, and his son went to the university, which was a state institution supported by taxation. His wife had strong social ambition, and, although he had early trained himself in habits of frugality and prudence, he found himself forced to enlarge his expenditures quite as rapidly as his income increased; so that, although he earned at last several thousand dollars a year, he left no property when he died.

The third son had no taste for professional study, but he had good sense and industry. He was apprenticed to a carpenter. He spent his leisure time in reading and formed no expensive habits. As soon as he began to receive wages he began to save. On account of his care, diligence, and good behavior, he was made an under-foreman. The highest earnings he ever obtained were $1,500 per year. At thirty years of age he had saved $2,000. He then married. He invested his savings in a homestead, but was obliged to incur a debt which it took him years of patient struggle to pay. He had three children who went through the public grammar school, but he was not able to support them through the high school and college. When he died he left the homestead clear of debt and nothing more.

The oldest son never paid a cent of local or direct tax in his life. The second son never paid any. The third paid taxes from the time he was twenty-two, when he first began to save, and while the mortgage rested on his homestead, he paid taxes on his debt as well as on his property. The taxes which he paid went to pay for police, lights, sewers, public schools, public charity, state university, public prison, public park, and public library, and also for soldiers' monuments, public celebrations, and all forms of occasional public expenditure. His brothers and his brothers' children all enjoyed these things as much as, or, as we have seen, more than he and his children.

The oldest brother borrowed constantly of the two others, and he and his children availed themselves freely of the privileges of relationship. Inasmuch as the second brother, in spite of his large income, was constantly in pecuniary straits, it was the youngest who was the largest creditor of the oldest. The oldest was an earnest greenbacker with socialistic tendencies, and the only payment he ever made to the youngest was in the way of lectures on the crimes of capital, the meanness of capitalists, and the equality of all men. The oldest died first. Two of his children were still small and the older ones were a cause of anxiety to their relatives on account of careless habits and unformed character. The second son, or to be more accurate, his wife, would not, for social reasons, take charge of the orphans, and they fell to the care of the youngest brother, although the second, while he lived, contributed to their maintenance.

The neighbors differed greatly in their views of this family. Some called the oldest poor and the other two rich. Some called the two oldest poor and the other rich. Some called the oldest and youngest poor and the second rich. As the facts were all known throughout the neighborhood, it was found to be a very interesting and inexhaustible subject of debate. Some people compared the first and second and moralized on the inequality of the distribution of wealth — one living in poverty and the other in luxury. This state of things was generally regarded as very "unjust" to the oldest brother. He was fond of demonstrating that it was so to anyone who would listen. Nobody ever was known to refer to the youngest brother as the victim of any injustice. The oldest brother was liked and pitied by everybody. The second was very popular in his circle. The third was not very well known and was not popular with anybody.

---

2. A textile worker, Fall River, Massachusetts, 1893

Testimony of Thomas O'Donnell, Boston, Oct. 18, 1883, in U.S. Senate, Committee on Education and Labor, *The Relations Between Labor and Capital,* 48 Cong., 1 Sess. (1883), pp. 451–457.

Question. Where do you live? — Answer. At Fall River.
Q. How long have you lived in this country? — A. Eleven years.
Q. Where were you born? — A. In Ramsbotham, England.
Q. Have you been naturalized here? — A. No, sir.

LIFE OF A MULE-SPINNER

Q. What is your business? — A. I am a mule-spinner by trade. I have worked at it since I have been in this country — eleven years.
Q. Are you a married man? — A. Yes, sir; I am a married man; have a wife and two children. I am not very well educated. I went to work when I was young, and have been working ever since in the cotton business; went to work when I was about eight or nine years old. I was going to state how I live. My children get along very well in summer time, on account of not having to buy fuel or shoes or one thing and another. I earn $1.50 a day and can't afford to pay a very big house rent. I pay $1.50 a week for rent, which comes to about $6 a month.
Q. This is, you pay this where you are at Fall River? — A. Yes, sir.
Q. Do you have work right along? — A. No, sir; since that strike we had down in Fall River about three years ago I have not worked much more than half the time, and that has brought my circumstances down very much.
Q. Why have you not worked more than half the time since then? — A. Well, at Fall River if a man has not got a boy to act as "back-boy" it is very hard for him to get along. In a great many cases they discharge men in that work and put in men who have boys.

Q. Men who have boys of their own? — A. Men who have boys of their own capable enough to work in a mill, to earn 30 or 40 cents a day.

CHILD LABOR NECESSARY TO THE EMPLOYMENT OF PARENTS

Q. Is the object of that to enable the boy to earn something for himself? — A. Well, no; the object is this: they are doing away with a great deal of mule-spinning there and putting in ring-spinning, and for that reason it takes a good deal of small help to run this ring work, and it throws the men out of work because they are doing away with the mules[1] and putting these ring-frames in to take their places. For that reason they get all the small help they can to run these ring-frames. There are so many men in the city to work, and whoever has a boy can have work, and whoever has no boy stands no chance. Probably he may have a few months of work in the summer time, but will be discharged in the fall. That is what leaves me in poor circumstances. Our children, of course, are very often sickly from one cause or another, on account of not having sufficient clothes, or shoes, or food, or something. And also my woman; she never did work in a mill; she was a housekeeper, and for that reason she can't help me to anything at present, as many women do help their husbands down there, by working, like themselves. My wife never did work in a mill, and that leaves me to provide for the whole family. I have two children.

HARDSHIP OF UNDERTAKERS' AND DOCTORS' BILLS UPON THE POOR

And another thing that helped to keep me down: A year ago this month I buried the

1. A mule was a heavy machine requiring mechanical skill to operate; ring spinning, a comparatively simple operation, could be performed by women and children.

oldest boy we had, and that brings things very expensive on a poor man. For instance, it will cost there, to bury a body, about $100. Now, we could have that done in England for about £5; that would not amount to much more than about $20, or something in that neighborhood. That makes a good deal of difference. Doctors' bills are very heavy — about $2 a visit; and if a doctor comes once a day for two or three weeks it is quite a pile for a poor man to pay.
Q. Will not the doctor come for a dollar a day? — A. You might get a man sometimes, and you sometimes won't, but they generally charge $2 a day.
Q. To operatives? — A. Oh, all around. You might get one for $1.50 sometimes.
Q. They charge you as much as they charge people of more means? — A. They charge as much as if I was the richest man in the city, except that some of them might be generous once in a while and put it down a little in the end: but the charge generally is $2. That makes it hard.

ONE DOLLAR AND A HALF A DAY FOR NINE MONTHS TO SUPPORT SIX PEOPLE TWELVE MONTHS

I have a brother who has four children, besides his wife and himself. All he earns is $1.50 a day. He works in the iron works at Fall River. He only works about nine months out of twelve. There is generally about three months of stoppage, taking the year right through, and his wife and his family all have to be supported for a year out of the wages of nine months — $1.50 a day for nine months out of the twelve, to support six of them. It does not stand to reason that those children and he himself can have natural food or be naturally dressed. His children are often sick, and he has to call in doctors. That is always hanging over him, and is a great expense to him. And then if he does not pay the bill the trustee law comes on him. That is a thing that is not properly looked after. A man told me the other day that he was trusteed for $1.75, and I understood that there was a law in this State that a man could not be trusteeed for less than $10. It seems to me there is something wrong in the Government somewhere; where it is, I can't tell.

Q. How much money have you got? — A. I have not got a cent in the house; didn't have when I came out this morning.

Q. How much money have you had within three months? — A. I have had about $16 inside of three months.

Q. Is that all you have had within the last three months to live on? — A. Yes; $16.

SUPPORTING A FAMILY ON $133 A YEAR

Q. How much have you within a year? — A. Since Thanksgiving I happened to get work in the Crescent Mill, and worked there exactly thirteen weeks. I got just $1.50 a day, with the exception of a few days that I lost — because in following up mule-spinning you are obliged to lose a day once in a while; you can't follow it up regularly.

Q. Thirteen weeks would be seventy-eight days, and, at $1.50 a day, that would make $117 less whatever time you lost? — A. Yes. I worked thirteen weeks there and ten days in another place, and then there was a dollar I got this week, Wednesday.

Q. Taking a full year back can you tell how much you have had? — A. That would be about fifteen weeks' work. Last winter, as I told you, I got in, and I worked up to about somewhere around Fast Day, or may be New Year's day; anyway, Mr. Howard has it down on his record, if you wish to have an exact answer to that question; he can answer it better than I can, because we have a sort of union there to keep ourselves together.

Q. Do you think you have had $150 within a year? — A. No, sir.

Q. Have you had $125? — A. Well, I could figure it up if I had time. The thirteen weeks is all I have had.

Q. The thirteen weeks and the $16 you have mentioned? — A. Yes, sir.

Q. That would be somewhere about $133, if you had not lost any time? — A. Yes, sir.

Q. That is all you have had? — A. Yes, sir.

Q. To support yourself and wife and two children? — A. Yes, sir.

Q. Have you had any help from outside? — A. No, sir.

Q. Do you mean that yourself and wife and two children have had nothing but that for all this time? — A. That is all. I got a couple dollars' worth of coal last winter, and the wood I picked up myself. I goes around with a shovel and picks up clams and wood.

DIGGING CLAMS TO EKE OUT
AN EXISTENCE

Q. What do you do with the clams? — A. We eat them. I don't get them to sell, but just to eat, for the family. That is the way my brother lives, too, mostly. He lives close by us.

Q. How many live in that way down there? —A. I could not count them, they are so numerous. I suppose there are one thousand down there.

Q. A thousand that live on $150 a year? — A. They live on less.

Q. Less than that? — A. Yes; they live on less than I do.

Q. How long has that been so? — A. Mostly so since I have been married.

Q. How long is that? — A. Six years this month.

Q. Why do you not go West on a farm? — A. How could I go, walk it?

TOO POOR TO GO WEST

Q. Well, I want to know why you do not go out West on a $2,000 farm, or take up a homestead and break it and work it up, and then have it for yourself and family? — A. I can't see how I could get out West. I have got nothing to go with.

Q. It would not cost you over $1,500. — A. Well, I never saw over a $20 bill, and that is when I have been getting a month's pay at once. If some one would give me $1,500 I will go.

Q. Is there any prospect that anybody will do that? — A. I don't know of anybody that would.

Q. You say you think there are a thousand men or so with their families that live in that way in Fall River? — A. Yes, sir; and I know many of them. They are around there by the shore. You can see them every day; and I am sure of it because men tell me.

Q. Are you a good workman? — A. Yes, sir.

Q. Were you ever turned off because of misconduct or incapacity or unfitness for work? — A. No, sir.

Q. Or because you did bad work? — A. No, sir.

Q. Or because you made trouble among the help? — A. No, sir.

Q. Did you ever have any personal trouble with an employer? — A. No, sir.

Q. You have not anything now you say? — A. No, sir.

Q. How old are you? — A. About thirty.

Q. Is your health good? — A. Yes, sir.

Q. What would you work for if you could get work right along; if you could be sure to have it for five years, staying right where you are? — A. Well, if I was where my family could be with me, and I could have work every day I would take $1.50, and be glad to.

Q. One dollar and fifty cents a day, with three hundred days to the year, would make more than you make now in three or four years, would it not?

ONLY A DOLLAR'S WORTH OF COAL IN TEN MONTHS

A. Well, I would have no opportunity then to pick up clams. I have had no coal except one dollar's worth since last Christmas.

Q. When do the clams give out? — A. They give out in winter.

Q. You spoke of fuel — what do you have for fuel? — A. Wood and coal.

Q. Where does the wood come from? — A. I pick it up around the shore — any old pieces I see around that are not good for anything. There are many more that do the same thing.

Q. Do you get meat to live on much? — A. Very seldom.

Q. What kind of meat do you get for your family? — A. Well, once in a while we gets a piece of pork and some clams and make a clam-chowder. That makes a very good meal. We sometimes get a piece of corn beef or something like that.

Q. Have you had any fresh beef [meat] within a month? — A. Yes; we had a piece of pork steak for four of us yesterday.

Q. Have you had any beef within a month? —A. No, sir. I was invited to a man's house on Sunday — he wanted me to go up to his house and we had a dinner of roast pork.

Q. That was an invitation out, but I mean have you had any beefsteak in your own family, of your own purchase, within a month? — A. Yes; there was a half a pound, or a pound one Sunday — I think it was.

Q. Have you had only a pound or a half a pound on Sunday? — A. That is all.

Q. A half pound of pork? — A. Yes. About two pounds of pork I guess we have had in the month, to make clam-chowder with, and sometimes to fry a bit.

Q. And there are four of you in the family? — A. Yes, sir.

Q. How many pounds of beefsteak have you had in your family, that you bought for your own home consumption within this year that we have been speaking of? — A. I don't think there has been five pounds of beefsteak.

Q. You have had a little pork steak? — A. We had a half a pound of pork steak yesterday; I don't know when we had any before.

Q. What other kinds of meat have you had within a year? — A. Well, we have had corn beef twice I think that I can remember this year — on Sunday, for dinner.

Q. Twice is all that you can remember within a year? — A. Yes — and some cabbage.

Q. What have you eaten? — A. Well, bread mostly, when we could get it; we sometimes couldn't make out to get that, and have had to go without a meal.

Q. Has there been any day in the year that you have had to go without anything to eat? — A. Yes, sir, several days.

Q. More than one day at a time? — A. No.

Q. How about the children and your wife — did they go without anything to eat too?

THE CHILDREN CRYING FOR FOOD

A. My wife went out this morning and went to a neighbor's and got a loaf of bread and fetched it home, and when she got home the children were crying for something to eat.

Q. Have the children had anything to eat to-day except that, do you think? — A. They had that loaf of bread — I don't know what they have had since then, if they had anything.

Q. Did you leave any money at home? — A. No, sir.

Q. If that loaf is gone, is there anything in the house? — A. No, sir; unless my wife goes out and gets something; and I don't know who would mind the children while she goes out.

Q. Has she any money to get anything with? — A. No, sir.

Q. Have the children gone without a meal at any time during the year? — A. They have gone without bread some days, but we have sometimes got meal and made porridge of it.

Q. What kind of meal? — A. Sometimes Indian meal, and sometimes oatmeal.

Q. Meal stirred up in hot water? — A. Yes, sir.

Q. Is it cold weather down there now? — A. It is very cold now.

SCANT CLOTHING IN COLD WEATHER

Q. What have the children got on in the way of clothing? — A. They have got along very nicely all summer, but now they are beginning to feel quite sickly. One has one shoe on, a very poor one, and a slipper, that was picked up somewhere. The other has two odd shoes on, with the heel out. He has got cold and is sickly now.

Q. Have they any stockings? — A. He had got stockings, but his feet comes through them, for there is a hole in the bottom of the shoe.

Q. What have they got on the rest of their person? — A. Well, they have a little calico shirt — what should be a shirt; it is sewed up in some shape — and one little petticoat, and a kind of little dress.

Q. How many dresses has your wife got? — A. She has got one since she was married, and she hasn't worn that more than half a dozen times; she has worn it just going to church and coming back. She is very good in going to church, but when she comes back she takes it off, and it is pretty near as good now as when she bought it.

Q. She keeps that dress to go to church in? — A. Yes, sir.

Q. How many dresses aside from that has she? — A. Well, she got one here three months ago.

Q. What did it cost? — A. It cost $1 to make it and I guess about a dollar for the stuff, as near as I can tell.

Q. The dress cost $2? — A. Yes.

Q. What else has she? — A. Well, she has an undershirt that she got given to her, and has an old wrapper, which is about a mile too big for her; somebody gave it to her.

Q. She did not buy it? — A. No. That is all that I know that she has.

Q. Is there anything else that you want to say to the committee? — A. Well, as regards debts; it costs us so much for funeral expenses and doctors' expenses; I wanted to mention that.

The CHAIRMAN.   You have stated that. It is clear that nobody can afford either to get sick or to die there.

The WITNESS.   Well, there are plenty of them down there that are in very poor health, but I am in good health and my children generally are in fair health, but the children can't pick up anything and only get what I bring to them.

Q.   Are you in debt? — A.   Yes, sir.

Q.   How much? — A.   I am in debt for those funeral expenses now $15 — since a year ago.

Q.   Have you paid the rest? — A.   Yes, sir.

Q.   You live in a hired tenement? — A.   Yes; but of course I can't pay a big rent. My rent is $6 a month. The man I am living under would come and put me right out and give me no notice either if I didn't pay my rent. He is a sheriff and auctioneer man. I don't know whether he has any authority to do it or not, but he does it with people.

Q.   Do you see any way out of your troubles — what are you going to do for a living — or do you expect to have to stay right there? — A.   Yes. I can't run around with my family.

Q.   You have nowhere to go to, and no way of getting there if there was any place to go to? — A.   No, sir; I have no means nor anything, so I am obliged to remain there and try to pick up something as I can.

Q.   Do the children go to school? — A.   No, sir; they are not old enough; the oldest child is only three and a half; the youngest one is one and a half years old.

Q.   Is there anything else you wanted to say? —A.   Nothing further, except that I would like some remedy to be got to help us poor people down there in some way. Excepting the Government decides to do something with us we have a poor show. We are all, or mostly all, in good health; that is, as far as the men who are at work go.

Q.   You do not know anything but mule-spinning, I suppose? — A.   That is what I have been doing, but I sometimes do something with pick and shovel. I have worked for a man at that, because I am so put on. I am looking for work in a mill. The way they do there is this: There are about twelve or thirteen men that go into a mill every morning, and they have to stand their chance, looking for work. The man who has a boy with him he stands the best chance, and then, if it is my turn or a neighbor's turn who has no boy, if another man comes in who has a boy he is taken right in, and we are left out. I said to the boss once it was my turn to go in, and now you have taken on that man; what am I to do; I have got two little boys at home, one of them three years and a half and the other one year and a half old, and how am I to find something for them to eat; I can't get my turn when I come here.

He said he could not do anything for me. I says, "Have I got to starve; ain't I to have any work?" They are forcing these young boys into the mills that should not be in mills at all; forcing them in because they are throwing the mules out and putting on ring-frames. They are doing everything of that kind that they possibly can to crush down the poor people — the poor operatives there.

---

3. The unskilled worker and the poverty line, 1904

Robert Hunter, *Poverty* (New York, 1904), pp. 56–59.

Hunter (1874–1942) was head worker at the University Settlement House, New York City.

It can be assumed, therefore, fairly, I think, that the problem of poverty in this country is in ordinary times confined to a certain percentage of the unskilled laborers who have employment, to most unskilled laborers without employment, and to many unemployed skilled workers. In addition to these workers in poverty, there are those who are weak, infirm, unfortunate, the widows, the families of the sick or the injured, and those who are too incompetent, drunken, or vicious, etc., to be reliable workmen. These are, in the main, the classes of persons in poverty in this country.

It is safe to say that a large number of workers, the mass of unskilled and some skilled workmen with their families, fall beneath the poverty line at least three times during their lives, — during childhood, in the prime of life, and at old age. Mr. Rowntree, as a result of his inquiries in York, has made the following diagram which illustrates this fact: —

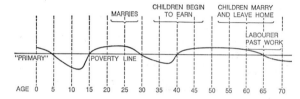

The ordinary increase of family numbers, and the increase or decrease in the family of the capacity for earning, forces the ordinary working-class family above and beneath this line at certain periods, despite their will. Some families may always remain beneath the line by reason of individual or social causes. The curve may at any moment drop to the bottom by reason of unemployment, infirmity, sickness, exhaustion, or accident. There are many observations of fundamental social importance that might be made upon the significance of this diagram. The things of real significance are, however, that the laborer in childhood, when he most needs upbuilding, is in poverty; the wife, when she is bearing children, — a time when she most needs good food and relief from want and worries, — is in poverty; the aged, when they should be in peace and comfort, are in poverty. The reason for this is that the wages of the ordinary unskilled workman are sufficient to support him and his wife, and perhaps one or two children. As more children arrive, the income gradually becomes less and less adequate to meet their needs. The family drops below the poverty line. They are unable to get sufficient necessaries. They drop lower and lower as the children grow and larger supplies of food and clothing and more house-room are needed. Then as the children begin to earn, the family rises out of poverty again, but it remains above the poverty line only until the children leave home or marry, or for some other reason may not continue to aid in the support of the family. At about this time the father's earnings are likely to drop off through age or infirmity, and again the parents are in poverty. In this way laborers of the poorest class pass backward and forward over the poverty line. The coming of children, the leaving of children, the periods of employment and of unemployment, the days of health, the days of sickness, the coming of infirmity, the hour of death, — all of these things either force the workers of this class backward, or carry them forward over the poverty line. A large immigration, insanitary tenements, dangerous trades, industrial changes, panics and bankruptcies — in a word, the slightest economic disturbance or rearrangement — may precipitate them into misery. The margin of life upon which many of them live is so narrow that they must toil every possible hour of working time, and the slightest economic change registers its effect upon this class of workers.

Any one going carefully through the figures which have been given will agree that poverty is widespread in this country. While it is possible that New York State has more poverty than other states, it is doubtful if its poverty is much greater proportionately than that of most of the industrial states. Twelve years ago I made what was practically a personal canvass of the poor in a small town of Indiana. There were no tenements, but the river banks were lined with small cabins and shanties, inhabited by the poorest and most miserable people I have almost ever seen. About the mills and factories were other wretched little communities of working people. All together the distress extended to but slightly less than 14 per cent of the population, and the poverty extended to not less than 20 per cent of the people.

---

4. Homestead, Pennsylvania, 1907

Margaret F. Byington, "The Family in a Typical Mill Town," *American Journal of Sociology,* XIV (1909), 649–657.

Homestead was the site of the main plant of the United States Steel Corporation. Miss Byington was author of *Homestead, The Households of a Mill Town* (New York, 1910), a volume in the Pittsburgh survey, a study of living and working conditions in Allegheny County (Pennsylvania) made in 1907–1908.

From the standpoint of family development probably the most significant fact about the town is that it offers work for men only. Aside from the steel mill and one machine shop, the only work in the town is in providing for the needs of the workers, with but chance work for women. As Pittsburg is a 45 minutes' car ride distant the work it offers is not easily available. The wage in the mill, moreover, though by no means abundant, is fair and steady. The laborer earns at a minimum rate of 16½ cents an hour, $1.65 a day, while the semi-skilled or skilled workers earn from $2.00 to $4.00, and occasionally as high as $5.00 or $6.00 a day.

.   .   .   .   .

As a result of these factors the town in general seems to have adopted the position that the women should stay at home, and, by good housekeeping, make the money go a long way, rather than go out to work and earn a little more. This is shown concretely in the incomes of those families whose budgets were secured for the investigation. Among the English-speaking people the husbands and sons contributed 92.8 per cent. among the native

whites — practically the entire income, and 94.6 per cent. among the English-speaking Europeans. There was no income from the work of women unless one would so consider what was received from lodgers. This constituted 4.6 per cent. of the total income in the European group, and 2.7 per cent. among the native white.

We find, then, that as a result of the kind of work offered the town consists of a group of working-men's families; the man is the breadwinner. The effect of the industrial situation is further shown in the work of the children. The girls show little more tendency than their mothers to become wage-earners. In the thirty-eight English-speaking families there were fifteen girls over fourteen, not one of whom was at work. Four were in the high school, the remainder at home helping with the housework.

.   .   .   .   .

The situation as far as the sons are concerned is somewhat different. Fifteen of the seventeen boys over fourteen were at work contributing among the whites 9.6 per cent., and among the English-speaking Europeans 18 per cent. of the total income. Though the other two boys were still in the high school we find on the whole a marked absence of interest in academic or even in technical training for these sons. As the daughters, instead of learning trades are at home becoming practical housekeepers under their mothers' direction, so the sons following in their fathers' footsteps, are entering directly into the practical work of the mill to get there the training for future success . . . Through the influence of the fathers, the boys sometimes get what are known as pencil jobs, or other places where the work is light and apparently more gentlemanly, but where the pay is seldom so high. Usually, however, they begin in the regular boy's work, as messenger-boys in the yards, or door-openers. Though these give no special training for the future, as the line of promotion is usually open a boy has a good chance of becoming at least a semi-skilled workman on fair pay. Promotion is sometimes unduly rapid, however, so that boys of 16 or 18 are earning men's wages, with little chance of further promotion. One woman who regretted that her son had not learned a trade, said that he was unwilling to go through a long apprenticeship when in the mill he could earn good pay at once. In spite of the fact that because of long hours and the danger from accident, women often wish their sons to take some other work, they usually do go into the mill. This means that as for some years they stay at home and contribute their share to the family income, they create a period of economic prosperity. The family is at this time often able to make extra provision for the future, as, for instance, buying a house.

.   .   .   .   .   .

. . . I will give the average expenses of 40 families with an income of less than $12 a week. Of a total expenditure of $530 a year, $241 goes for food; $103 for rent; $50 for clothing; $18 for furniture; $25 for fuel; $11 for medical care, and $13 for tobacco and liquor. In addition an average of $38 was spent annually for insurance, leaving but $31 a year for amusements of all sorts, church expenses, savings, and the necessary sundries. Now obviously no one of these items is adequate, to say nothing of being superabundant. Rent, for example, at $2 a week provides only a two-room tenement, and that without water or toilet in the house. Food at $4.64 a week would mean for a family of five, only 20 cents a day, two cents a day less than Prof. Chittenden estimates as absolutely essential in New York. Fifty dollars for clothing is just one-half the sum Mr. Chapin gives as necessary. The tobacco and liquor item which is especially large among the Slavs, could, of course, be cut with profit, but in no other way can that pitiably small sum of $31 be increased. Yet from that sum savings must come if there are to be any.

The different nationalities meet this problem in varying ways according to their ideals.

Among the native white families a comfortable home is an essential proof of respectability. Consequently we find that they spend for rent 21.2 per cent. as against 16.4 per cent. among the Slavs. On the other hand, the Slav spends 54.3 per cent. for food, while the native whites spend but 44.7 per cent. That is, the Slavic family will have enough food anyway, while the American demands a big enough house. Inadequate food or bad housing alike endanger physical efficiency, while with overcrowding any semblance of home life becomes impossible. In neither group is there any margin for amusements.

It is not a question of good management. The cleverest housekeeper I know was doing marvelously on $14 a week, and the following statement of her average expenditure for 8 weeks, shows how she did it: Food $7.05; clothing .57; household expenses .59; rent $2.50; insurance and lodge dues .65; church and charity .09; recreation and spending money 0.3; doctor $1.46; sundries .35. Though, as you may see, she was keeping the unessential elements of expenditure at their lowest point, her food-supply was still quite inadequate. I found by a rough estimate that it was deficient about 20 per cent. in both proteida and calories. The budget revealed a wise choice of food aside from a possibly extravagant expenditure for fresh fruit and vegetables. If a skilful woman of Pennsylvania Dutch stock cannot manage on this wage, what can be expected of the average housekeeper?

The necessity of facing these problems three times a day has its effect also on the overtaxed mother. One woman, who on an income of from $2 to $3 a day was providing for five children, had bought a small farm and was carrying heavy insurance. In order to accomplish this, she told me, she must not spend even five cents for a visit to the nickelodeon. When she described to me her hunts for bargains and her long hours of sewing to make her girls presentable, I did not wonder that she had the reputation of being a cranky person.

These two women were Americans, but by

far the largest majority of the laborers are Slavs, and it is among them that we find the worst results of the low wage.

The death-rate among the children is high, twice as high as in the other wards of Homestead. Moreover, training children under these conditions is difficult and a terrible knowledge of evil results from the close mingling of the children with this group of careless, drinking men.

.   .   .   .   .

Summing up the results of indifference on one side and ignorance on the other, we find a high infant death-rate, a knowledge of evil among little children, intolerable sanitary conditions, a low standard of living, a failure of the community to assimilate this new race in its midst.

As we waited in one of the little railroad stations in Homestead, a Slavak came in and sat down next to a woman and her two-year-old child. He began making shy advances to the baby, and coaxing her in a voice of heart-breaking loneliness. But she would not come to him, and finally the two left the room. As they went he turned to the rest of the company, and in a tone of sadness, taking us all into his confidence said simply, "Me wife, me babe Hungar." But were they here it would mean death for one baby in three, it would mean hard work in a dirty, unsanitary house for the wife, it would mean sickness and much evil. With them away, it means for him isolation and loneliness and the abnormal life of the crowded lodging-house.

.   .   .   .   .

By the 12-hour shift as well as by the low wage the mill is affecting thte lives of these families. Though the long hours and hard work may seem to be hardships that only the man would feel, they do react on family life. Not only do his weariness and his irregular hours make him less inclined to enter into the family pleasures, but he also fails to change, through political or other action, the conditions under which

they live. Because of this weariness-induced apathy, a man usually stays at home and smokes his pipe instead of troubling himself with outside affairs. This tendency is doubtless intensified by conditions within the industry . . .

---

5. Effect of father's unemployment on children, 1921–1922

Emma O. Lundberg, *Unemployment and Child Welfare,* United States Children's Bureau Pub. No. 125 (Washington, D.C., 1923), pp. 1–4.

Emma Lundberg (1881–1959) was director of the social service division of the Children's Bureau. The cities studied in the inquiry were Racine, Wisconsin, and Springfield, Massachusetts.

During the industrial depression of 1921 and 1922, the Children's Bureau undertook a careful study of the effect of unemployment upon local problems of child welfare. For this inquiry two cities were selected in which there was successful coordination of the public and private resources and generous expenditure for the mitigation of the hardships incident to that period. They were cities in which the industries required a large percentage of skilled workers and paid wages that permitted a higher standard of living than the workers in many industrial communities enjoy; both had been unusually prosperous during the period immediately preceding the industrial depression.

The families for whom schedules were taken were selected from the lists of the men who were registered in the local employment offices and represented, as nearly as possible, a cross section of families of unemployed men in which there were two or more children under 18 years of age. The evidence shows that their earnings prior to the period of depression had permitted the families of many of these workingmen to begin payments on homes, lay aside money for the education of their children, for possible emergencies and for old age, and that they were at the same time living comfortably. It is probably safe to say that the families of these two cities had resources both in actual savings and in credit which the workers in many communities did not have.

But a long period of unemployment — more than two-thirds of the fathers included in the study had been out of work for more than a year — had gradually exhausted the resources of the families, and recourse to public and private relief as well as great changes in the family life had become necessary.

A large proportion of the men being skilled workers, the incomes in the families had, in normal times, ranged from $75 to more than $200 per month. More than nine-tenths of the men for whom complete information as to income was secured had been earning between $100 and $175 per month. During the period of unemployment, the complete family resources in four-fifths of the families of these same men amounted to between $25 and $100 a month — this, too, when the earnings of the father in such temporary work as could be secured, the wages of the mother and the children, the savings that were taken from the bank, and the loans that were made, the food and other necessaries purchased on credit, and aid from relatives and public and private relief agencies were all included. Half of the families for which there was complete information averaged for their maintenance during unemployment one-half as much as while the father was working.

It is inevitable that there should be a lowering of the standards of family life when the regular income is interrupted. Frugality in food, even to the point of actual privation, a dangerous saving of fuel, economy in clothing and household supplies, reduction of the housing cost through seeking cheaper quarters or crowding the family to secure an income from lodgers, always follows the breadwinner's loss of work, even though the family does not actually have

to seek outside sources of aid. When the father loses his job the mother must secure work if it is possible for her to do so. Approximately one-third of the children included in the study were in families in which the mother did undertake and was engaged in gainful employment either within or outside her home. The evidence indicates that in some of these families the money for the family's food was secured at the cost of permanent injury to the health of the mother and neglect of the children.

The investigation made by the bureau shows that unemployment not only carries with it immediate deprivation and hardship but leaves a burden of debt and discouragement for the years to come. More than two-fifths of the families included in the study had been able to maintain themselves in part during the unemployment period on their savings. In many cases these savings represented years of economizing and of planning for the future. Homes that had been purchased in whole or in part had to be sacrificed by many families.

Over four-fifths of the families were in debt for food, rent, fuel, medical attendance, and other necessities. When the father eventually secures work, those families which lived on credit at the stores, or on borrowed money, will have a burden of debt to meet.

It has been pointed out that the families included in this inquiry represented as nearly as possible a cross section of families of unemployed men in two cities in which wages had been high. It is therefore especially significant to find that over half of them had received charitable aid from public or private agencies during the father's unemployment. In almost three-fourths of the families receiving such aid, the men had been skilled workers, and 42 per cent of the families that had had savings when the father was thrown out of work had been compelled to seek aid from public or private relief agencies after their savings were exhausted.

In addition to the other hardships, almost two-thirds of the families reported the illness or disability of one or more members during the time the father was out of work. Of especial interest in connection with child welfare are the families — almost a fourth of the whole number — in which the mother was pregnant or had been confined during the father's unemployment.

One of the outstanding conditions incident to the industrial depression, and one that on its face would appear to be entirely beneficial, was the shortage of work for children. Many children who had been employed were forced to go back to school, and others who would have tried to eke out the family income while the father was unemployed remained in school because work could not be secured. But this gave no guaranty of permanent educational gains. Savings that would have assured many of the children real educational opportunities had been spent. Many of the children in the families whose future had been burdened by debts would undoubtedly be sent to work just as soon as they could find any kind of a job. Some children during all the time when men and women were so desperately in need of employment left school and secured work.

Thus, the hardships that must be endured by a family when the father is out of work do not end when conditions improve and he again has a steady job. The savings of years have been used up in order to provide maintenance during months of enforced idleness, perhaps the home whose purchase represented the fulfillment of the family's ambitions has been sacrificed. For many months after the father secures work his wages will have to be divided between the purchase of the necessaries of life and the payment of the heavy burden of debt. Many of the fathers interviewed had little hope of successfully taking up again the task of providing a home and comforts for those dependent on them.

Besides the deprivation of material needs, there is the suffering that perhaps can be understood only by those who have themselves been the victims of the dread uncertainty and fear that besets a workingman's family when the father is "laid off." The most important

feature of unemployment is its effect on the family morale — the father idle about the house, unsettled, disheartened; the mother going out to work if she can secure it, and using up every bit of her strength in the double task of providing for the family's maintenance and caring for the household and the children; the children suffering from the depression and uncertainty of what the future may mean, which is even more to be dreaded than the discomforts of the immediate present.

Unemployment, then, because it means lowered family standards, anxiety and dread, the loss of savings, and the mortgaging of the future, has a direct and disastrous effect upon the welfare of children. While communities are usually able to organize their resources so that children are not removed from their own homes because of poverty caused by an industrial crisis, these resources have not been sufficient to prevent very real suffering in family groups stricken with the misfortune of loss of work by the father.

Discards

1. Mrs. Wasilewski and her children

William I. Thomas and Florian Znaniecki, *The Polish Peasant in Europe and America,* V (Boston: Random House, Inc., 1920), 198–202.

This family history was based on the records of the United Charities of Chicago.

Wasilewski Family. Mrs. Wasilewski was born in Galicia. She left home alone at the age of 15 years and it was 8 years before her family heard of her again. Her father had been organist in a church for 20 years and retired to spend his old age on a small four-acre farm. When she did write home to complain of her poverty here her father wrote her that she had made her own choice and he could not help her, that it grieved him to hear of her misfortune and therefore he preferred she would not write at all.

"June 13, 1910, woman in office [of the United Charities] saying she married one year ago. Has a baby [Helen] 5 months old. Man does not want to support her and child . . . Woman had man arrested some time ago, for which he received a 7-months' sentence in Bridewell. Man begged woman to have him released and promised to do better, which woman did. [Man disappeared. Marriage had been a forced one, 3 months before Helen's birth.] . . . She came to office again and again. United Charities proposed different plans but she refused to consider them; she did not want to give up her flat, was very unwilling to go to work and simply wanted money . . . Later her landlord in office . . . Says that woman quarrels with every one. Also that men come to the house; says that she neglects the baby, leaving it sometimes for hours in a swing out in the yard or locked in the house. Says she has a mania for swearing out warrants for people. Says she swore out warrant for her husband because he talked to some girl boarders that she had. She would like to get out of working, if possible . . .

"August 20, 1910, woman in office saying she had no food in home. Gave her grocery order. Refused to take it, saying Damman does not carry the sort of groceries she likes, especially her favorite bread . . . [She put her girl boarders out because she found them having men callers and acting disorderly. One man gave her a black eye.] She said she was ashamed to go to work with the black eye. Asked her why she was not ashamed to come to office with her black eye, to which she answered very impudently. [Continues asking for rent.]

"March 21, 1911. Woman is going from door to door with baby and begging [stating that her husband is dead] . . . Visited . . . found woman living in 3 rooms all very neat and clean. Said she is sick and cannot do hard work . . . Says if she could not get any assistance she would be obliged to take in boarders which would mean that she must live with a man. This she had tried to keep from doing. Asked for shoes for herself and dress [as Easter is coming] . . .

"December 16, 1911. . . . County substation phoned to say that woman is there asking rations and had a doctor's certificate with her saying she is pregnant. [Roy John was born 5 months later. Father was married man with 2 children in Europe. He gave her a little money occasionally and she says he promised to get a divorce and marry her.] . . .

November 21, 1912.

. . . . .

She was committed to Kankakee Insane Asylum upon the finding of a jury composed mostly of Poles who found her quite incapable of caring for herself or using money sensibly. The children were placed in an institution. Mrs. Wasilewski wrote imploring letters to her brother and finally induced him to take her and the children to his home in Minneapolis. The report which the United Charities later received from the Charities of Minneapolis is as follows: "March 7, 1916 . . . her brother . . . has had very little to do with Mrs. Wasilewski for the last 2 years because of her actions since coming here. After he got her out of the Sanatorium at Kankakee he intended to take care of Helen and John so that she could go to work. She would not do this but preferred to run around with other men. An illegitimate child (Victoria) was born in Minneapolis in September, 1914. This child died in infancy . . . After Mrs. Wasilewski came to Minneapolis, Mr. Wasilewski wrote from Texas saying he would return to her if she were leading a better life. They did not remember name of city correspondence came from. She was pregnant at the time and he was not heard from since."

The United Charities learned from other sources that Mrs. Wasilewski had lived with her brother only a month and left to live with

Homestead, Pennsylvania, ca. 1908. Photograph by Lewis W. Hine.

Nickelodeon and Audience, Homestead, Pennsylvania, ca. 1908. Photograph by Lewis W. Hine.

An Unpaved Alley in Homestead, Pa. Photograph by Lewis W. Hine.

a man. She insisted upon having her children. Helen was with her brother who fought for the custody of the child, showing much hard feeling against Mrs. Wasilewski. He had prejudiced the child against her mother so that she was actually afraid of her. John was in a German Catholic Orphan Asylum. Mrs. Wasilewski persuaded the Juvenile Court to place Helen in the orphanage also, because her brother refused to let her see the child. Mrs. Wasilewski paid the children's board regularly for a time until she convinced the judge that she was able to care for the children and entitled to have them with her. She then adopted a different name and continued her old ways of living, receiving assistance from the United Charities who did not connect her story with what they knew of Mrs. Wasilewski. Finally the United Charities procured a warrant against her from the Juvenile Court because she neglected the children. After the summons was served on her she left town to avoid appearing in court and came to Chicago. Here she began begging under still a different name but was discovered and identified by the United Charities.

"February 21, 1916, Mrs. Wasilewski had large, healthy twins at the Chicago Woman's Shelter where she was put temporarily.

"March 3, 1916. . . . Hospital phones they cannot keep woman any longer . . . now that woman is getting up she is very hard to manage; uses vile language too [she was to work when well enough to pay for her back board, but was sent immediately to the poorhouse in Oak Forest. From there she wrote the United Charities] I don't ask you to put me in a poorhouse where I have to cry for my children. I don't ask you to put them in a home and eat somebody's else's bread. You only want people to live like you but I will not listen to you no more . . . I bet some people would have taken me and kept me there for a few days. I can't even live here without Helen and John. I am so sick for them. I listened to you and went to the hospital. I could live at home and spare good eats for them. What good did you give me to send me to the poorhouse. Please

tell me and send me a letter back. For money I could find lots and lots of good places. Thanks Miss Jablowska that you told me of my children. I ask you Miss to send me the address of my children . . . I am a good lady. I live like god gives me living. I want to live like good kind ladies live. I am such a not right lady living without a husband.

"March 20, 1916, Mrs. Wasilewski left Oak Forest during the night and was picked up by the Travelers' Aid Society at the depot and taken to St. Vincent de Paul's, who placed her in St. Joseph's Home. [She was again sent to Oak Forest.]

"March 29, 1916 (Clipping from Chicago *Daily Tribune*): 'Twins offered to Police. Mother brings 2 months old boy and girl to station for adoption . . .' [Mrs. Wasilewski gave an assumed name.]

"April 8, 1916, Home for Friendless phones that Mrs. Wasilewski is there [applying for help] . . . Said she intended to find rooms and support herself and her children by taking in washing and keeping boarders. [After a great deal of trouble Mrs. Wasilewski and the children were sent back to Minneapolis, as the County Agent decided she was not a resident of Cook County and thus not entitled to support in Chicago. To induce him not to send her she showed the $65 she had treasured all the time she had been in Chicago. He took this and used it to pay the carfare of herself and her children back to Minneapolis. The Juvenile Court of the latter place agreed to arrest her on her arrival for not appearing in answer to the summons it had issued before her departure. Her children were unusually attractive, docile and easily managed.]"

---

2. The foundling

Carl Sandburg, "Boy Baby," *American Mercury,* XV (October 1928), 155.

BOY BABY
by Carl Sandburg

The baby picked from an ash-barrel by the night police came to the hospital of the Franciscan brothers in a diaper and a white sheet.

It was a windy night in October, leaves and geese scurrying across the north sky, and the curb pigeons more ravenous than ever for city corn in the cracks of the street stones.

The two policemen who picked the baby from the ash-barrel are grayheads; they talk about going on the pension list soon; they talk about whether the baby, surely a big man now, votes this year for Smith or Hoover.

II Youth in American Society

Adolescence and youth

---

1. G. Stanley Hall

G. Stanley Hall, *Adolescence, Its Psychology and Its Relations to Physiology, Anthropology, Sociology, Sex, Crime, Religion, and Education* (New York, 1904), I, xiii-xviii.

Hall (1844–1924) was professor of psychology and pedagogics at Johns Hopkins University and, from 1889 to 1919, president of Clark University, Worcester, Massachusetts. *Adolescence* was the culmination of more than twenty years of research in child development and education. In 1906, two years after publication, Hall published an abbreviated version of the work under the title *Youth: Its Education, Regimen and Hygiene.*

Adolescence is a new birth, for the higher and more completely human traits are now born. The qualities of body and soul that now emerge are far newer. The child comes from and harks back to a remoter past; the adolescent is neo-atavistic, and in him the later acquisitions of the race slowly become prepotent. Development is less gradual and more saltatory, suggestive of some ancient period of storm and stress when old moorings were broken and a higher level attained. The annual rate of growth in height, weight, and strength is increased and often doubled, and even more. Important functions previously non-existent arise. Growth of parts and organs loses its former proportions, some permanently and some for a season. Some of these are still growing in old age and others are soon arrested and atrophy. The old moduli of dimensions become obsolete and old harmonies are broken. The range of individual differences and average errors in all physical measurements and all psychic tests increases. Some linger long in the childish stage and advance late or slowly, while others push on with a sudden outburst of impulsion to early maturity. Bones and muscles lead all other tissues, as if they vied with each other, and there is frequent flabbiness or tension as one or the other leads. Nature arms youth for conflict with all the resources at her command — speed, power of shoulder, biceps, back, leg, jaw, — strengthens and enlarges skull, thorax, hips, makes man aggressive and prepares woman's frame for maternity. The power of the diseases peculiar to childhood abates, and liability to the far more diseases of maturity begins, so that with liability to both it is not strange that the dawn of the ephebic day is marked at the same time by increased morbidity but diminished rates of mortality. . . .

The momentum of heredity often seems insufficient to enable the child to achieve this great revolution and come to complete maturity, so that every step of the upward way is strewn with wreckage of body, mind, and morals. There is not only arrest, but perversion, at every stage, and hoodlumism, juvenile crime, and secret vice seem not only increasing, but develop in earlier years in every civilized land. Modern life is hard, and in many respects increasingly so, on youth. Home, school, church, fail to recognize its nature and needs and, perhaps most of all, its perils. . . .

The functions of every sense undergo reconstruction, and their relations to other psychic functions change, and new sensations, some of them very intense, arise, and new associations in the sense sphere are formed. Haptic impressions, appetite for food and drink, and smell are most modified. The voice changes, vascular instability, blushing, and flushing are increased. Sex asserts its mastery in field after field, and works its havoc in the form of secret vice, debauch, disease, and enfeebled heredity, cadences the soul to both its normal and abnormal rhythms, and sends many thousand youth a year to quacks, because neither parents, teachers, preachers, or physicians know how to deal with its problems. Thus the foundations of domestic, social, and religious life are oftenest undermined. Between religion and love, God and nature have wrought an indissoluble bond so that neither can attain normality without that of the other. Secondary sexual qualities are shown to have an ever-widening range, and parenthood to mean more with every upward step of development. The youth craves more knowledge of body and mind that can help against besetting temptations, aid in the choice of a profession, and if his intellect is normal he does not vex his soul overmuch about the logical character of the universe or the ultimate sanction of either truth or virtue . . . There are new repulsions felt toward home and school, and truancy and runaways abound. The social instincts undergo sudden unfoldment and the new life of love awakens. It is the age of sentiment and of religion, of rapid fluctuation of mood, and the world seems strange and new. Interest in adult life and in vocations develops. Youth awakes to a new world and understands neither it nor himself. The whole future of life depends on how the new powers now given suddenly and in profusion are husbanded and directed. Char-

acter and personality are taking form, but everything is plastic. Self-feeling and ambition are increased, and every trait and faculty is liable to exaggeration and excess. It is all a marvelous new birth, and those who believe that nothing is so worthy of love, reverance, and service as the body and soul of youth, and who hold that the best test of every human institution is how much it contributes to bring youth to the ever fullest possible development, may well review themselves and the civilization in which we live to see how far it satisfies this supreme test.

Never has youth been exposed to such dangers of both perversion and arrest as in our own land and day. Increasing urban life with its temptations, prematurities, sedentary occupations, and passive stimuli just when an active, objective life is most needed, early emancipation and a lessening sense for both duty and discipline, the haste to know and do all befitting man's estate before its time, the mad rush for sudden wealth and the reckless fashions set by its gilded youth — all these lack some of the regulatives they still have in older lands with more conservative traditions. In a very pregnant psychological sense ours is an unhistoric land. Our very Constitution had a Minerva birth, and was not the slow growth of precedent. Our ideas of freedom were at the outset fevered by the convulsion of the French Revolution. Our literature, customs, fashions, institutions, and legislation were inherited or copied, and our religion was not a gradual indigenous growth, but both its spirit and forms were imported ready-made from Holland, Rome, England, and Palestine. To this extent we are a fiat nation, and in a very significant sense we have had neither childhood nor youth, but have lost touch with these stages of life because we lack a normal development history. It is not merely that we have no antiquity rich in material and spiritual monuments that is the best nursery of patriotism in the young, but our gallery of heroes is largely composed, not of glorious youth but of sages advanced in age or old in wisdom for their years. Our immigrants have often passed the best years of youth or leave it behind when they reach our shores, and their memories of it are in other lands. No country is so precociously old for its years. . . . In this environment our young people leap rather than grow into maturity. . . . We are conquering nature, achieving a magnificent material civilization, leading the world in the applications though not in the creation of science, coming to lead in energy and intense industrial and other activities; our vast and complex business organization that has long since outgrown the comprehension of professional economists, absorbs ever more and earlier the best talent and muscle of youth and now dominates health, time, society, politics, and law-giving, and sets new and ever more pervading fashions in manners, morals, education, and religion; but we are progressively forgetting that for the complete apprenticeship to life, youth needs repose, leisure, art, legends, romance, idealization, and in a word humanism, if it is to enter the kingdom of man well equipped for man's highest work in the world.

2. Youthful ardor as an unused national resource

Jane Addams, *The Spirit of Youth and the City Streets* (New York, 1910), pp. 140–162.

Jane Addams (1860–1935), the founder of Hull House, was the foremost spokesman of youth in the first decade of the twentieth century. She criticized American society for failing to channel youthful enthusiasm into zeal for social betterment.

It may relieve the mind to break forth in moments of irritation against "the folly of the coming generation," but whoso pauses on his plodding way to call even his youngest and rashest brother a fool, ruins thereby the joy of his journey, — for youth is so vivid an element in life that unless it is cherished, all the rest is

spoiled. The most praiseworthy journey grows dull and leaden unless companioned by youth's iridescent dreams. Not only that, but the mature of each generation run a grave risk of putting their efforts in a futile direction, in a blind alley as it were, unless they can keep in touch with the youth of their own day and know at least the trend in which eager dreams are driving them — those dreams that fairly buffet our faces as we walk the city streets.

At times every one possessed with a concern for social progress is discouraged by the formless and unsubdued modern city. . . . When we count over the resources which are at work "to make order out of casualty, beauty out of confusion, justice, kindliness and mercy out of cruelty and inconsiderate pressure," we find ourselves appealing to the confident spirit of youth. We know that it is crude and filled with conflicting hopes, some of them unworthy and most of them doomed to disappointment, yet these young people have the advantage of "morning in their hearts"; they have such power of direct action, such ability to stand free from fear, to break through life's trammelings, that in spite of ourselves we become convinced that

"They to the disappointed earth shall give
The lives we meant to live."

That this solace comes to us only in fugitive moments, and is easily misleading, may be urged as an excuse for our blindness and insensitiveness to the august moral resources which the youth of each city offers to those who are in the midst of the city's turmoil. A further excuse is afforded in the fact that the form of the dreams for beauty and righteousness change with each generation and that while it is always difficult for the fathers to understand the sons, at those periods when the demand of the young is one of social reconstruction, the misunderstanding easily grows into bitterness.

The old desire to achieve, to improve the world, seizes the ardent youth to-day with a stern command to bring about juster social conditions. Youth's divine impatience with the world's inheritance of wrong and injustice makes him scornful of "rose water for the plague" prescriptions, and he insists upon something strenuous and vital.

.   .   .   .   .

Unfortunately, we do little or nothing with this splendid store of youthful ardor and creative enthusiasm. Through its very isolation it tends to intensify and turn in upon itself, and no direct effort is made to moralize it, to discipline it, to make it operative upon the life of the city. And yet it is, perhaps, what American cities need above all else, for it is but too true that Democracy — "a people ruling" . . . no longer stirs the blood of the American youth, and that the real enthusiasm for self-government must be found among the groups of young immigrants who bring over with every ship a new cargo of democratic aspirations. That many of these young men look for a consummation of these aspirations to a social order of the future in which the industrial system as well as government shall embody democratic relations, simply shows that the doctrine of Democracy like any other of the living faiths of men, is so essentially mystical that it continually demands new formulation. To fail to recognize it in a new form, to call it hard names, to refuse to receive it, may mean to reject that which our fathers cherished and handed on as an inheritance not only to be preserved but also to be developed.

.   .   .   .   .

It is difficult to illustrate what might be accomplished by reducing to action the ardor of those youths who so bitterly arraign our present industrial order. While no part of the social system can be changed rapidly, we would all admit that the present industrial arrangements in America might be vastly improved and that we are failing to meet the requirements of our industrial life with courage and success simply because we do not realize that unless we establish that humane legisla-

tion which has its roots in a consideration for human life, our industrialism itself will suffer from inbreeding, growing ever more unrestrained and ruthless. It would seem obvious that in order to secure relief in a community dominated by industrial ideals, an appeal must be made to the old spiritual sanctions for human conduct, that we must reach motives more substantial and enduring than the mere fleeting experiences of one phase of modern industry which vainly imagines that its growth would be curtailed if the welfare of its employees were guarded by the state. It would be an interesting attempt to turn that youthful enthusiasm to the aid of one of the most conservative of the present social efforts, the almost world-wide movement to secure protective legislation for women and children in industry, in which America is so behind the other nations.

.   .   .   .   .

It is because the ardor of youth has not been attracted to the long effort to modify the ruthlessness of industry by humane enactments, that we sadly miss their resourceful enthusiasm and that at the same time groups of young people who hunger and thirst after social righteousness are breaking their hearts because the social reform is so long delayed and an unsympathetic and hardhearted society frustrates all their hopes. And yet these ardent young people who obscure the issue by their crying and striving and looking in the wrong place, might be of inestimable value if so-called political leaders were in any sense social philosophers. To permit these young people to separate themselves from the contemporaneous efforts of ameliorating society and to turn their vague hopes solely toward an ideal commonwealth of the future, is to withdraw from an experimental self-government founded in enthusiasm, the very stores of enthusiasm which are needed to sustain it.

.   .   .   .   .

All of us forget how very early we are in the experiment of founding self-government in this trying climate of America, and that we are making the experiment in the most materialistic period of all history, having as our court of last appeal against that materialism only the wonderful and inexplicable instinct for justice which resides in the hearts of men, — which is never so irresistible as when the heart is young. We may cultivate this most precious possession, or we may disregard it. We may listen to the young voices rising clear above the roar of industrialism and the prudent councils of commerce, or we may become hypnotized by the sudden new emphasis placed upon wealth and power, and forget the supremacy of spiritual forces in men's affairs. It is as if we ignored a wistful, over-confident creature who walked through our city streets calling out, "I am the spirit of Youth! With me, all things are possible!" We fail to understand what he wants or even to see his doings, although his acts are pregnant with meaning, and we may either translate them into a sordid chronicle of petty vice or turn them into a solemn school for civic righteousness.

We may either smother the divine fire of youth or we may feed it. We may either stand stupidly staring as it sinks into a murky fire of crime and flares into the intermittent blaze of folly or we may tend it into a lambent flame with power to make clean and bright our dingy city streets.

---

3. Youth and age, 1912

Randolph S. Bourne, "Youth," *Atlantic Monthly,* CIX (1912), 433–441.

An injury in infancy left Bourne (1886–1918) crippled and deformed. When he entered Columbia University as a freshman in 1909 he was older than many college graduates. This essay, published while Bourne was in college, was incorporated in his collection of essays, *Youth and Life* (New York, 1913).

How shall I describe Youth, the time of contradictions and anomalies? The fiercest radicalisms, the most dogged conservatisms, irrepressible gayety, bitter melancholy, — all these moods are equally part of that showery springtime of life. One thing, at least, it clearly is: a great, rich rush and flood of energy. It is as if the store of life had been accumulating through the slow, placid years of childhood, and suddenly the dam had broken and the waters rushed out, furious and uncontrolled, before settling down into the quieter channels of middle life. The youth is suddenly seized with a poignant consciousness of being alive, which is quite wanting to the naïve unquestioning existence of the child. He finds himself overpoweringly urged toward self-expression. Just as the baby, born into a 'great, blooming, buzzing confusion,' and attracted by every movement, every color, every sound, kicks madly in response in all directions, and only gradually gets his movements coördinated into the orderly and precise movements of his elders, — so the youth suddenly born into a confusion of ideas and appeals and traditions responds in the most chaotic way to this new spiritual world, and only gradually learns to find his way about in it, and get his thoughts and feelings into some kind of order.

. . . . .

This is the great divergence which sets youth not only against old age, but against youth itself: the undying spirit of youth that seems to be fed by an unquenchable fire, that does not burn itself out but seems to grow steadier and steadier as life goes on, against the fragile, quickly tarnished type that passes relentlessly into middle age. At twenty-five I find myself full of the wildest radicalisms, and look with dismay at my childhood friends who are already settled down.

. . . . .

Youth is vulnerable at every point. Prudence is really a hateful thing in youth. A prudent youth is prematurely old. It is infinitely better, I repeat, for a boy to start ahead in life in a spirit of moral adventure, trusting for sustenance to what he may find by the wayside, than to lay in laboriously, before starting, a stock of principles for life, and burden himself so heavily for the journey that he dare not, and indeed cannot, leave his pack unguarded by the roadside to survey the fair prospects on either hand. Youth at its best is this constant susceptibility to the new, this constant eagerness to try experiments.

It is here that youth's quarrel with the elder generation comes in. There is no scorn so fierce as that of youth for the inertia of older men. The lack of adjustment to the ideas of youth's elders and betters, one of the permanent tragedies of life, is certainly the most sensational aspect of youth. That the inertia of the older people is wisdom, and not impotence, is a theory that you will never induce youth to believe for an instant. The stupidity and cruelties of their management of the world fill youth with an intolerant rage . . .

Youth sees with almost a passionate despair its plans and dreams and enthusiasms, that it knows so well to be right and true and noble, brushed calmly aside, not because of any sincere searching into their practicability, but because of the timidity and laziness of the old, who sit in the saddle and ride mankind. And nothing torments youth so much as to have this inertia justified on the ground of experience. For youth thinks that it sees through this sophism of 'experience.' It sees in it an all-inclusive attempt to give the world a character, and excuse the older generation for the mistakes and failures which it has made. What is this experience, youth asks, but a slow accretion of inhibitions, a learning, at its best, not to do again something which ought not to have been done in the first place?

Old men cherish a fond delusion that there is something mystically valuable in mere quantity of experience. Now the fact is, of course, that it is the young people who have all the really valuable experience. It is they who have constantly to face new situations, to react con-stantly to new aspects of life, who are getting the whole beauty and terror and cruelty of the world in its fresh and undiluted purity. It is only the interpretation of this first collision with life that is worth anything. For the weakness of experience is that it so soon gets stereotyped; without new situations and crises it becomes so conventional as to be practically unconscious. Very few people get any really new experience after they are twenty-five, unless there is a real change of environment. Most older men live only in the experience of their youthful years.

.   .   .   .   .

There is no great gulf between youth and middle age, as there is between childhood and youth. Adults are little more than grown-up children. This is what makes their arrogance so insulting, — the assumption that they have acquired any impartiality or objectivity of outlook, and have any better standards for judging life. Their ideas are wrong, and grow progressively more wrong as they become older. Youth, therefore, has no right to be humble. The ideals it forms will be the highest it will ever have, the insight the clearest, the ideas the most stimulating. The best that it can hope to do is to conserve those resources, and keep its flame of imagination and daring bright.

Therefore, it is perhaps unfair to say that the older generation rules the world. Youth rules the world, but only when it is no longer young. It is a tarnished, travestied youth that is in the saddle in the person of middle age. Old age lives in the delusion that it has improved and rationalized its youthful ideas by experience and stored-up wisdom, when all it has done is to damage them more or less — usually more. And the tragedy of life is that the world is run by these damaged ideals. That is why our ideas are always a generation behind our actual social conditions. Press, pulpit, and bar teem with the radicalisms of thirty years ago. The dead hand of opinions formed in their college days clutches our leaders and directs their activities in this new and strangely altered physical and spiritual environment. Hence grievous friction, maladjustment, social war. And the faster society moves, the more terrific is the divergence between what is actually going on and what public opinion thinks is actually going on. It is only the young who are actually contemporaneous; they interpret what they see freshly and without prejudice; their vision is always the truest, and their interpretation always the justest.

Youth does not simply repeat the errors and delusions of the past, as the elder generation with a tolerant cynicism likes to think; it is ever laying the foundations for the future. What it thinks so wildly now will be orthodox gospel thirty years hence. The ideas of the young are the living, the potential ideas; those of the old, the dying, or the already dead. This is why it behooves youth to be not less radical, but even more radical, than it would naturally be. It must be not simply contemporaneous, but a generation ahead of the times, so that when it comes into control of the world, it will be precisely right and coincident with the conditions of the world as it finds them.

.   .   .   .   .   .

It is the glory of the present age that in it one can be young. Our times give no check to the radical tendencies of youth. On the contrary, they give the directest stimulation. A muddle of a world and a wide outlook combine to inspire us to the bravest of radicalisms. Great issues have been born in the last century, and are now loose in the world. There is a radical philosophy that illuminates our environment, gives us terms in which to express what we see, and coördinates our otherwise aimless reactions.

In this country, it is true, where a certain modicum of free institutions, and a certain specious enfranchisement of the human spirit have been achieved, youth may be blinded and drugged into an acquiescence in conditions, and its enthusiasm may easily run into a glorification of the present. In the face of the more urgent ideals that are with us, it may be inspired by vague ideas of 'liberty,' or 'the rights of man,' and fancy it is truly radical when it is but living on the radicalisms of the past. Our political thought moves so slowly here that even our radicalism is traditional. We breathe in with the air about us the belief that we have attained perfection, and we do not examine things with our own eyes.

But more and more of the clearsighted youth are coming to see the appalling array of things that still need to be done. The radical young man of to-day has no excuse for veering round to the conservative standpoint. Cynicism cannot touch him. For it is the beauty of the modern radical philosophy that the worse the world treats a man, the more it convinces him of the truth of his radical interpretation of it. Disillusion comes, not through hard blows, but by the insidious sappings of worldly success. And there never was a time when there were so many radical young people who cared little about that worldly success.

The secret of life is then that this fine youthful spirit should never be lost. Out of the turbulence of youth should come this fine precipitate — a sane, strong, aggressive spirit of daring and doing. It must be a flexible, growing spirit, with a hospitality to new ideas, and a keen insight into experience. To keep one's reactions warm and true, is to have found the secret of perpetual youth, and perpetual youth is salvation.

___

4. Youth rejects American culture, 1921

Harold Stearns, *America and the Young Intellectual* (New York, 1921), p. 159.

Stearns (1891–1943) is best known as editor of *Civilization in the United States* (New York, 1922), a collection of essays critical of most aspects of American life and culture.

___

Something must be radically wrong with a culture and a civilisation when its youth begins to desert it. Youth is the natural time for revolt, for experiment, for a generous idealism that is eager for action. Any civilisation which has the wisdom of self-preservation will allow a certain margin of freedom for the expression of this youthful mood. But the plain, unpalatable fact is that in America to-day that margin of freedom has been reduced to the vanishing point. Rebellious youth is not wanted here. In our environment there is nothing to challenge our young men; there is no flexibility, no colour, no possibility for adventure, no chance to shape events more generously than is permitted under the rules of highly organised looting. All our institutional life combines for the common purpose of blackjacking our youth into the acceptance of the *status quo;* and not acceptance of it merely, but rather its glorification.

---

5. The social aspect of adolescence, 1930

Miriam Van Waters, "Adolescence" in Edwin R. A. Seligman, ed., *Encyclopedia of the Social Sciences,* I (New York: The Macmillan Company, 1930), 455–459.

Miss Van Waters (b. 1887), anthropologist and penologist, was a leading figure in correctional work for delinquent girls and women.

Adolescence literally means growth, but as the term is used in biology and psychology it defines the period of human development from the beginning of puberty to the end of the maturation process. Its physiological characteristics are now well understood. Its chronological boundaries vary with race, climate, nutrition, social status and inheritance, and may include some individuals as young as eight and others as old as twenty-five. . . . There is a growing conviction that the period of infancy and childhood should be surrounded by special immunities and protection, and that its prolong-

ation has significance for the more complete higher evolution of human beings. The status of the child in a given society is therefore held to be an index of social well-being. Undoubtedly the scientific study of child life has had a profound effect upon our modern social organization.

To set forth the position and the influence of the adolescent is a more difficult matter. Physically and mentally the normal adolescent is capable of approximating the adult role, as he frequently does among primitive peoples and pioneer groups. The adolescent can win his bread, produce offspring, fight and participate in social and religious activities. His immaturity comes to light in the more subtle phases of social life. He appears to be an adult yet he is not, and both primitive and civilized peoples have denied him complete political participation and have extended to adolescence some degree of immunity from adult legal and social responsibilities. Scientific evidence to support this "common sense" policy is vague because of a lack of systematic research into the norms of adolescent development. A scientific description of the normal adolescent in society remains to be written.

A study of adolescence has passed through four phases: first, interest in problems of physical growth and anthropometric measurements, which has resulted in the concept of physiological age; second, interest of the psychologist in individual differences and progressive development, leading to the concept of psychological age; third, the interpretation of these findings in terms of evolution, the "recapitulation theory," and the doctrine of adolescence as a "storm and stress" period; fourth, the definition of the problems of the adolescent in terms of the social situation.

.   .   .   .   .

A more recent phase in the study of adolescence is the emphasis on its social aspect. The literature of the child guidance clinics and juvenile court studies points out that maladjustment occurs frequently in infancy and early childhood and is not more characteristic of adolescence than other periods. Where maladjustment is pronounced in the healthy adolescent it is now thought to be due to the social situation. W. I. Thomas gives evidence that when social norms and structures evolve more slowly than activities and inventions the result is a stage of disorganization, apparent alike in personalities and in society. When old habits are no longer adequate they break down, and before new habits are learned there is instability. Thus in the twentieth century youth appears to be in conflict with the standards of behavior in home, school, church and community. To add to the confusion, the dress, habits, activities and mood of youth are copied by adults so that the value of youth appears to have an exaggerated significance in social life, and the young have few recognized goals of maturity to follow. At present infants and preschool and school children are better cared for than in the past with reference to scientific programs of diet, sleep, exercise, physical safety and "chaperonage," while the adolescent is prematurely exposed to self-regulation.

More direct evidence that adolescence in itself is not a period involving special adjustment comes from the study of primitive youth, particularly that undertaken by Margaret Mead. The difficulties which we have ascribed to fundamental human traits are apparently nonexistent among such a group as the Samoans. Civilization imposes restraints on the one hand, and increased stimulation on the other. There is absolutely no evidence that the conflicts and difficulties of adolescence are inevitable. The behavior of adolescents in modern society, the symptoms of unrest and maladjustment, are no proof that these are normal characteristics of the age group.

.   .   .   .   .

Recent neurological studies have indicated that maturation is a subtle process, extending long after gross size and weight have been attained. Lawyers have recognized this and have hesitated to allow young persons the full man-

agement of large estates until they have reached the age of about twenty-five years. Legislation has lagged behind in matters of criminal responsibility, so that we see youthful individuals of fourteen, sixteen or eighteen held completely responsible for their deeds. Strict proof is lacking, but all studies seem to indicate that the integration of the nervous system is not complete until the middle twenties, whereas the conventional view that youth is mature at the time of political majority (twenty-one) prevails to the detriment of the individual adolescent. What we call wisdom and discretion are certainly not to be expected of the normal adolescent in his 'teens.

Among European and American civilized peoples the age of compulsory education has been extended to sixteen or eighteen. The state has definitely undertaken the academic and vocational guidance of adolescents. Youth is now definitely interested in programs of social betterment, war and peace, economic equality and democracy. The social situation is complicated, but youth remains the same — a period of life when physical and mental energy is at its height, when charm dominates, and the adult role is eagerly anticipated, yet when complete social participation is impossible because of fundamental biological immaturity. As long as our social situation is somewhat pathological, youth will remain in conflict with prevailing social standards.

The young American Negro

1. The Negro Youth Movement, 1923

Countee Cullen, "The League of Youth," *The Crisis,* XXVI (1923), 167–168. Republished from THE CRISIS by permission of the Crisis Publishing Company.

Cullen (1903–1946), poet, author, and

teacher, was an undergraduate at New York University when he delivered this address.

Youth the world over is undergoing a spiritual and an intellectual awakening, is looking with new eyes at old customs and institutions, and is finding for them interpretations which its parents passed over. Youth everywhere is mapping out a programme for itself, is banding together in groups whose members have a common interest. In some places these various youth movements, such as the German Youth Movement, are assuming proportions of such extent that they are being viewed with trepidation by those who desire to see things continue in the same rut, who do not wish the "old order to change, yielding place to new."

And so it is not to be wondered at that the young American Negro is having his Youth Movement also. We in America have not yet reached the stage where we can speak of an American Youth Movement, else I had not been asked to speak this afternoon. The American Negro's Youth Movement is less ostentatious than others, perhaps, but it is no less intense. And if there is any group which is both a problem for itself and a problem for others, and which needs a movement for the solving of both it is the American Negro. Details and specific instances of what I mean may be met with daily segregation, discrimination, and just this past week the barring by an American board of a colored girl from entering The Art School at Fontainbleau, France, because her presence *might* be objectionable to certain people who would be along, this supposed objection being based not on character, but on color. Surely where such conditions obtain a movement is needed. I may say that the majority of people, even my own people, do not realize that we are having a Youth Movement at all. It is not crying itself from the house tops. It is a somewhat subsurface affair like a number of small underground currents, each working its individual way along, yet all bound at length to come together.

In the first place the young American Negro is going in strong for education; he realizes its potentialities for combating bigotry and blindness. Those colleges which cater exclusively to our own people are filled to capacity, while the number of Negro students enrolled in other colleges in the country is yearly increasing. Basically it may be that this increased respect for education is selfish in the case of each individual without any concern for the group effect, but that is neither here nor there, the main point to be considered is that it is working a powerful group effect.

Then the New Negro is changing somewhat in his attitude toward the Deity. I would not have you misconstrue this statement. I do not mean that he is becoming less reverent, but that he is becoming less dependent. There is a stereotype by which most of you measure all Negroes. You think of a healthy, hearty fellow, easily provoked to laughter, liking nothing better than to be slapped on the back, and to be called a "good fellow" — and to leave all to God. The young Negro of today while he realizes that religious fervor is a good thing for any people, and while he realizes that it and the Negro are fairly inseparable, also realizes that where it exists in excess it breeds stagnation, and passive acquiescence, where a little active resistance would work better results. The finest of lines divides the phrase "Let God do it," from the phrase "Let George do it." And there are some things which neither George nor God can do. There is such a thing as working out one's own soul's salvation. And that is what the New Negro intends to do.

Finally, if I may consider myself to be fairly representative of the Young American Negro, he feels that the elder generations of both Caucasian and colored Americans have not come to the best mutual understanding. I mean both North and South. For the misunderstanding is not one of sections, but is one of degree. In the South it is more candid and vehement and aboveboard; in the North where it does obtain it is sly and crafty and cloaks itself in the guise of kindness and is therefore more cruel. We have not yet reached the stage where we realize that whether we side with Darwin or with Bryan we all spring from a common progenitor.

There is a story of a little girl of four or five years of age who asked her father, "Daddy, where were you born?" "Why I was born in San Francisco," said her father. "And where was mother born?" "Why in Chicago." "And I, where was I born?" "In New York." The little girl thought this over for a while, then said, "Father was born in San Francisco, Mother in Chicago, and baby in New York. Isn't it wonderful how we all got together?" Wouldn't it be wonderful if we could all get together? The Young Negro feels that understanding means meeting one another half way. This League has taken a splendid forward step. Will it go further?

In the words of a Negro poet, I bring you a challenge:

How would you have us? As we are?
  Or sinking 'neath the load we bear?
Our eyes fixed forward on a star?
  Or gazing empty at despair?

Rising or falling? Men or things?
  With dragging pace or footsteps fleet?
Strong willing sinews in your wings?
  Or tightening chains about your feet?

It is a challenge to be weighed mightily. For we must be one thing or the other, an asset or a liability, the sinew in your wing to help you soar, or the chain to bind you to earth. You cannot go forward unless you take us with you, you cannot push back unless you retrograde as much yourself. Mr. President, I hope his league will accept my challenge and will answer it in the new spirit which seems to be animating youth everywhere — the spirit of what is just and fair and honorable.

---

2. The Negro Renaissance, 1925

Alain Locke, "Negro Youth Speaks," in Alain Locke, ed., *The New Negro* (New York: A. and C. Boni, 1925), pp. 47–53. Reprinted from the Arno Press Edition, 1968, by permission.

In March 1925 Locke (1886–1954), professor of philosophy at Howard University, edited a special Harlem issue of the *Survey Graphic*. Locke incorporated the materials gathered for this issue of the magazine in *The New Negro*, an anthology of poetry, fiction, drama, criticism, and historical and sociological essays dealing with Negro life and culture in America.

The Younger Generation comes, bringing its gifts. They are the first fruits of the Negro Renaissance. Youth speaks, and the voice of the New Negro is heard. What stirs inarticulately in the masses is already vocal upon the lips of the talented few, and the future listens, however the present may shut its ears. Here we have Negro youth, with arresting visions and vibrant prophecies; forecasting in the mirror of art what we must see and recognize in the streets of reality tomorrow, foretelling in new notes and accents the maturing speech of full racial utterance.

Primarily, of course, it is youth that speaks in the voice of Negro youth, but the overtones are distinctive; Negro youth speaks out of an unique experience and with a particular representativeness. All classes of a people under social pressure are permeated with a common experience; they are emotionally welded as others cannot be. With them, even ordinary living has epic depth and lyric intensity, and this, their material handicap, is their spiritual advantage. So, in a day when art has run to classes, cliques and coteries, and life lacks more and more a vital common background, the Negro artist, out of the depths of his group and personal experience, has to his hand almost the conditions of a classical art.

Negro genius to-day relies upon the race-gift as a vast spiritual endowment from which our best developments have come and must come.

Racial expression as a conscious motive, it is true, is fading out of our latest art, but just as surely the age of truer, finer group expression is coming in — for race expression does not need to be deliberate to be vital. Indeed at its best it never is. This was the case with our instinctive and quite matchless folk-art, and begins to be the same again as we approach cultural maturity in a phase of art that promises now to be fully representative. The interval between has been an awkward age, where from the anxious desire and attempt to be representative much that was really unrepresentative has come; we have lately had an art that was stiltedly self-conscious, and racially rhetorical rather than racially expressive. Our poets have now stopped speaking for the Negro — they speak as Negroes. Where formerly they spoke to others and tried to interpret, they now speak to their own and try to express. They have stopped posing, being nearer the attainment of poise.

The younger generation has thus achieved an objective attitude toward life. Race for them is but an idiom of experience, a sort of added enriching adventure and discipline, giving subtler overtones to life, making it more beautiful and interesting, even if more poignantly so. So experienced, it affords a deepening rather than a narrowing of social vision. The artistic problem of the Young Negro has not been so much that of acquiring the outer mastery of form and technique as that of achieving an inner mastery of mood and spirit. That accomplished, there has come the happy release from self-consciousness, rhetoric, bombast, and the hampering habit of setting artistic values with primary regard for moral effect — all those pathetic overcompensations of a group inferiority complex which our social dilemmas inflicted upon several unhappy generations. Our poets no longer have the hard choice between an over-assertive and an appealing attitude. By the same effort they have shaken themselves free from the minstrel tradition and the fowling-nets of dialect, and through acquiring ease and simplicity in serious expression, have carried the folk-gift to the altitudes of art. There they seek and find art's intrinsic values and satisfactions — and if America were deaf, they would still sing.

.   .   .   .   .

Not all the new art is in the field of pure art values. There is poetry of sturdy social protest, and fiction of calm, dispassionate social analysis. But reason and realism have cured us of sentimentality: instead of the wail and appeal, there is challenge and indictment. Satire is just beneath the surface of our latest prose, and tonic irony has come into our poetic wells. These are good medicines for the common mind, for us they are necessary antidotes against social poison. Their influence means that at least for us the worst symptoms of the social distemper are passing. And so the social promise of our recent art is as great as the artistic. It has brought with it, first of all, that wholesome, welcome virtue of finding beauty in oneself; the younger generation can no longer be twitted as "cultural nondescripts" or accused of "being out of love with their own nativity." They have instinctive love and pride of race, and, spiritually compensating for the present lacks of America, ardent respect and love for Africa, the motherland. Gradually too, under some spiritualizing reaction, the brands and wounds of social persecution are becoming the proud stigmata of spiritual immunity and moral victory. Already enough progress has been made in this direction so that it is no longer true that the Negro mind is too engulfed in its own social dilemmas for control of the necessary perspective of art, or too depressed to attain the full horizons of self and social criticism. Indeed, by the evidence and promise of the cultured few, we are at last spiritually free, and offer through art an emancipating vision to America.

---

3. The creed of Negro youth, 1926

Negro Yearbook, 1925–1926 (Tuskegee, Ala.,

1926), pp. 76–77. Reprinted with permission of Tuskegee Institute.

The text was written by William Pickens (1881–1954), college teacher and administrator, field secretary of the N.A.A.C.P., and a prolific writer on Negro history.

CREED
Of American Negro Youth

1. I believe in God as the embodiment and the expression of all the goodness of the universe, material and immaterial.
2. I believe in Youth as the recurrent, perennial, eternal spirit of progress.
3. I believe in Humanity, the humanity that transcends color, feature, geography or social and political organization.
4. I believe in the Negro Race as in any other race, only as an element, and perhaps an episode, of this humanity.
5. I believe therefore in Unsegregated Justice as the only justice, and in Unqualified Equality as the only equality.
6. I believe in Individual Liberty, which is possible only in a society of essential individual equality.
7. I believe in Tolerance which is possible only in a society of liberty.
8. I believe in Eternal Progress, which is possible only in a society of tolerance.
9. I believe in the Divine Destiny of Man, which is thinkable only as the progressive purpose of progress.
10. I believe therefore in the present, as the all Mother of the illimitable Future; in happiness limited only by other happinesses and by the legitimate claims of future happiness. Selah.

B. YOUTH AND WAR

William James proposes conscripting youth for national service, 1910

William James, "The Moral Equivalent of War," *Memories and Studies* (New York, 1911), pp. 286–293.

In the earlier part of this essay (first published in 1910 by the Association for International Conciliation) James describes history as "a bath of blood" and declares: "war-taxes are the only ones men never hesitate to pay."

Having said thus much in preparation, I will now confess my own utopia. I devoutly believe in the reign of peace and in the gradual advent of some sort of a socialistic equilibrium. The fatalistic view of the war-function is to me nonsense, for I know that war-making is due to definite motives and subject to prudential checks and reasonable criticism, just like any other form of enterprise. And when whole nations are the armies, and the science of destruction vies in intellectual refinement with the sciences of production, I see that war becomes absurd and impossible from its own monstrosity. Extravagant ambitions will have to be replaced by reasonable claims, and nations must make common cause against them . . .

. . . I do not believe that peace either ought to be or will be permanent on this globe, unless the states pacifically organized preserve some of the old elements of army-discipline. A permanently successful peace-economy cannot be a simple pleasure-economy. In the more or less socialistic future towards which mankind seems drifting we must still subject ourselves collectively to those severities which answer to our real position upon this only partly hospitable globe. We must make new energies and hardihoods continue the manliness to which the military mind so faithfully clings. Martial virtues must be the enduring cement; intrepidity, contempt of softness, surrender of private interest, obedience to command, must still remain the rock upon which states are built — unless, indeed, we wish for dangerous reactions against commonwealths fit only for contempt, and liable to invite attack whenever a centre of crystallization for military-minded enterprise gets formed anywhere in their neighborhood.

.   .   .   .   .

Let me illustrate my idea more concretely. There is nothing to make one indignant in the mere fact that life is hard, that men should toil and suffer pain. The planetary conditions once for all are such, and we can stand it. But that so many men, by mere accidents of birth and opportunity, should have a life of *nothing else* but toil and pain and hardness and inferiority imposed upon them, should have *no* vacation, while others natively no more deserving never get any taste of this campaigning life at all, — *this* is capable of arousing indignation in reflective minds. It may end by seeming shameful to all of us that some of us have nothing but campaigning, and others nothing but unmanly ease. If now — and this is my idea — there were, instead of military conscription a conscription of the whole youthful population to form for a certain number of years a part of the army enlisted against *Nature,* the injustice would tend to be evened out, and numerous other goods to the commonwealth would follow. The military ideals of hardihood and discipline would be wrought into the growing fibre of the people; no one would remain blind as the luxurious classes now are blind, to man's relations to the globe he lives on, and to the permanently sour and hard foundations of his higher life. To coal and iron mines, to freight trains, to fishing fleets in December, to dishwashing, clothes-washing, and window-washing, to road-building and tunnel-making, to foundries and stoke-holes, and to the frames of skyscrapers, would our gilded youths be drafted off, according to their choice, to get the childishness knocked out of them, and to come back into society with healthier sympathies and soberer ideas. They would have paid their blood-tax, done their own part in the immemorial human warfare against nature; they would tread the earth more proudly, the women would value them more highly, they would be better fathers and teachers of the following generation.

Such a conscription, with the state of public opinion that would have required it, and the many moral fruits it would bear, would preserve in the midst of a pacific civilization the manly virtues which the military party is so afraid of seeing disappear in peace. We should get toughness without callousness, authority with as little criminal cruelty as possible, and painful work done cheerily because the duty is temporary, and threatens not, as now, to degrade the whole remainder of one's life. I spoke of the "moral equivalent" of war. So far, war has been the only force that can discipline a whole community, and until an equivalent discipline is organized, I believe that war must have its way. But I have no serious doubt that the ordinary prides and shames of social man, once developed to a certain intensity, are capable of organizing such a moral equivalent as I have sketched, or some other just as effective for preserving manliness of type. It is but a question of time, of skilful propagandism, and of opinion-making men seizing historic opportunities.

The martial type of character can be bred without war. Strenuous honor and disinterestedness abound elsewhere. Priests and medical men are in a fashion educated to it, and we should all feel some degree of it imperative if we were conscious of our work as an obligatory service to the state. We should be *owned,* as soldiers are by the army, and our pride would rise accordingly. We could be poor, then, without humiliation, as army officers now are. The only thing needed henceforward is to inflame the civic temper as past history has inflamed the military temper.

Advantages of universal military training, 1916

George Creel, "Military Training for Our Youth," *Century Magazine,* XCII (May, 1916), 20–22.

Creel (1876–1953), newspaper editor in Kansas City and Denver, was chairman of the Committee on Public Information, 1917–1919.

Compulsory military training, in its essence, is merely an extension of compulsory education by which the citizen is equipped not only to achieve his very American privilege of fighting for an individual place in the sun to earn a decent living and to strengthen his mental and moral fiber, but also to achieve his equally American duty of fighting to maintain the collective rights of all American citizens.

Education develops individuality; military education develops nationality. In this country to-day it is a menacing fact that the average citizen, while jealous of his prerogatives, has only a vague conception of his duties to his country. — THE EDITOR.

.   .   .   .   .

Is patriotism a duty that must be discharged by all or a favor to be bestowed at will? In the United States, where cities, commonwealths, and nation equally *compel* obedience to a multitude of laws concerned with the general good, is it to be the case that defense shall remain on no firmer base than the differing impulses of individual men?

These are not by any means questions of abstract interest. Mr. Chamberlain, chairman of the senate committee on military affairs, has introduced a bill that provides for universal training, the Chamber of Commerce of the United States stands pledged to this idea, and all over the country there is evidence that the lessons taught by Switzerland and Australia are filling the thought of the great mass of people . . .

The volunteer system is now an obvious and admitted failure, and it is in the light of this breakdown that its hopes and assurances for the future must be viewed. It is on trial in the court of public opinion, and it must make the attempt to justify itself. The organized militia of the United States is naturally the first witness to be called, since it has ever been the choice medium for uncompelled patriotism.

.   .   .   .   .

Universal training means more than national defense and national safety. It means national health, national virility, national progress; for there is not a weakness in American life that it would not strengthen. Stronger bodies, clearer minds, higher civic ideals, a keener sense of the man's obligation to his fellows, his community, and his country, a solution of the immigrant problem, by giving aliens a sense of belonging — all these are only a few of the benefits that might be expected to flow.

Should eighteen-year-olds be drafted?

Congressional Record, 65 Cong., 2 Sess. (1918), LVI, Pt. 8, pp. 8236–8241, 8356, 8411.

The Selective Service Act, passed May 1917, required all men between the ages of twenty-one and thirty to register for military service. In 1918 the Senate debated and eventually adopted an amendment to the Selective Service Act lowering the minimum age to eighteen and raising the maximum to forty-two.

[Senator Albert Fall, New Mexico]

Mr. President, the provision that the boys

under 21 years of age shall not be placed upon the firing line is one which I have said I personally do not favor. The history of our former wars shows that they were won by boys under 23, and that the majority of the soldiers who fought in the Civil War were under 21. Under the provisions of the draft act as it is the law now, the President has the power not only to exempt certain classes, but to summon into the semimilitary service each of the men or classes whom he exempts, if in his judgment he desires to do so.

.   .   .   .   .

The only question meriting discussion, as it appears to me, is the question of decreasing or lowering the age limits. As I have said, in our past history we have started at 18, always. To repeat myself, with reference to practically a million men now in the military service we have started at the age of 18. It is true that it is a hardship upon the mothers to take from them their boys between 18 and 21. It is true, of course, that some of these boys will be taken from their schools if this provision is adopted. Nevertheless, Mr. President, the country is going to be compelled, in my judgment, notwithstanding the good news that we have had in the past two days, to use all its manhood to win this war. We are face to face with the proposition and we might as well settle it. If in the President's discretion he sees fit not to draw the boys from 18 to 21, or if he sees fit to classify them into the third, fourth, or fifth classes, or any other class which he may designate, he has the power to do so. He is not compelled to draft them, to take them away from their farms or their schools or their mothers or their families. He is simply authorized to do so. There is not a direction in this entire bill, in the original draft bill, or in the present bill. There is nothing compelling the President to do anything whatsoever. Authority is simply vested in him, in his discretion, to do certain things in the event he desires to avail himself of such authority.

.   .   .   .   .

[Senator James K. Vardaman, Mississippi]

. . . In the first place, I shall not vote to conscript a man for service at the front who has not reached 21 years of age. That is, I shall not do it at this time. From 18 to 21 years of age is the formative period in a man's life. During those years he lays the foundation of a life's work — builds the substratum upon which character is erected. He is not consulted about the laws of the country; he is not permitted to go to the polls and settle with his Congressman for the blessings or the damage that that Congress man by his vote may have imposed upon him, and since he is not permitted to participate in the affairs of his Government I shall never vote to compel him to render service such as is contemplated in this amendment. There are enough older men who under the draft system can be selected — men capable of rendering efficient service in the Army, who have had their "swing around the circle" — and if they happen to be killed they have not lost as much as a boy who has had no chance at all.

I shall not take by conscription the mother's boy; I shall not break the ties that bind to a mother's heart this child who to her is yet a child until he reaches the age of maturity or manhood. This, Mr. President, is sentimental, it may be said, but the world is controlled by sentiment, and not even the armies, the cannon, the shot, and the shell will contribute more to winning this war than sentiment.

There is another reason why these boys should not be taken as proposed under this amendment. They are needed on the farm and in the industrial pursuits of life. Many of them are the stay and support of the home, and if they are taken and put in training it will materially, I fear, reduce the yield of the farms and the products of the factory which are needed to support our armies, our women and children at home, and our allies abroad. The man above 31 years who will be taken under this draft will not have the home ties and responsibilities which usually devolve upon a boy, especially among the middle or laboring class of people between the years of 18 and 21.

. . . . .

[Senator Knute Nelson, Minnesota]

If you want to carry on this war successfully, why resort to any maudlin sympathy? Make the age limit from 18 to 45, or 35 if you please. If you want good soldiers, take the young men. They are the most effective.

As to this story about taking young men out of school, Mr. President, it was my lot to serve in the Army as an enlisted man, a private, and a noncommissioned officer, and I regard my Army service as the best part of my education. I feel confident I would never have gotten along as well in the world as I did if I had not gotten my diploma as a noncommissioned officer in the Fourth Wisconsin Regiment of the Union Army during the war.

Let our boys go into the Army. It gives them a training, a discipline, which they can get nowhere else.

. . . . .

[Senator George E. Chamberlain, Oregon]

. . . I believe . . . that the age limit ought to be fixed between 18 and 45, because aside from the sentiment which is involved there is no reason in the world why young men between 18 and 21 should not be called upon to serve their country.

I think the records of the Civil War will show that most of the Army on both sides was composed of young men under 21 years of age, and not only between 18 and 21, but they went in from 13 and upward. I know in the neighborhood where I lived young men did not dare to stay at home beyond the age of 16, because if they did they were practically ostracised from the society of all good people. So the Army on both sides was composed of young men between 14 and 21.

But feeling as I do about it, we have got to meet a situation. This war can not be waged, Mr. President, unless we have the sentiment of the country behind us, and I am satisfied from what I have seen that the country will not stand for the drafting of young men into the active service under 21.

. . . . .

Mr. SHIELDS: I was not speaking about raising the age limit. I was speaking about taking the boys who are on the farm, assisting their fathers, as members of his family, in producing crops. I agree with the Senator in raising the age limit to reach men who are just as able-bodied and make as good soldiers as those under 21, say to 35, but it is the question of taking the young boys we are now discussing. They are on the farm, and they are needed there. They are now being educated. They are right in the most important part of their youth in that respect. It would be far better to have men already mature, who are already educated, and who in many cases have left the farms, and allow these young men to stay and be educated and be producers of food, which is indispensable to the winning of this war.

. . . . .

[Senator Henry Cabot Lodge, Massachusetts]

Now, Mr. President, I shall be very brief, but I want to say a word in regard to draft ages.

It is common to speak about 18 to 45 as if those ages rested upon some solid basis of reason. They do not. They are entirely haphazard. We use them for the regular Army, the regular Navy, the regular Marine Corps, and the National Guard. I suppose they rested originally on the somewhat loose theory that a boy of 18 was sufficiently developed physically to go into military service, and that when you reached 45 you reached a point where there was a physical decline sufficient to make the man undesirable for the hardships of a soldier's life. But, Mr. President, both assumptions are unfounded. A boy of 18 is still in the growing stage. He is better material two years or three years later.

.   .   .   .   .

Of course we can imagine the war reaching such a point that, in the conventional phrase, we rob the cradle and the grave. If it is necessary, we will take them of all ages and any age, but we have not reached that point yet; and in fixing these ages it is important, in my opinion, to try to fix them in some way so as to conserve as far as possible the strength of the country. If you go below 21, still more if you go below 20 and take boys of 18, and fill your Army from them, there will be very few exemptions — practically none on account of dependents, or indispensability in any trade; but you take the boy before he is physically at his best, and you cut him off from all education. If we extend the draft down to 18 at this time, I do not hesitate to say it will close practically every college in the country. They are deprived now of more than half, and the half that remains is made up of the younger classes of boys under the draft age.

Harvard College had its commencement the other day. The senior class had entered 700. It graduated 173. They had all gone except the 173. But in the younger years the colleges take the men under the draft age; and we do not want, if we can help it — we may have to come to it, but we do not want deliberately by law, by compulsory service — to take those very young men, mere boys, and create a general illiteracy among the men in whose hands the future of the country rests.

.   .   .   .   .

[Senator John S. Williams, Mississippi]

The cheaper you can fight a war, of course, the better for the Republic. You are not hunting around for the man who has a wife and four or five children; but, if possible, you are hunting for the man who has neither wife nor children, and that is generally the case with a boy under 21. Down South they frequently marry before they are 21, but up in the North

and the East they very seldom do; and out in the West they less frequently do it than they do down South, so that there is every reason in the world why they should be subject to military duty.

I rather resent the idea that a boy owes nothing to his country until he has a right to vote. That seems to be upon a sort of equal footing with the idea that a woman owes nothing to her country unless she has a right to vote. I think that when the laws take care of a fellow personally and protect him in his property, in his liberty, in his limb, in his right to exist, and in his pursuit of happiness, even if he is only 20 years of age, he owes as much to the American Republic as if he were pretty nearly as old as I am . . .

A writer assays the effect of the First World War on Americans of his generation, 1934

Malcolm Cowley, *Exile's Return: A Literary Odyssey of the 1920's* (New York, 1956), pp. 41–42, 46–47. Copyright 1934, copyright © renewed 1962 by Malcolm Cowley, reprinted by permission of The Viking Press, Inc.

Cowley (b. 1898) interrupted his studies at Harvard to serve as an ambulance driver with the French army.

The war created in young men a thirst for abstract danger, not suffered for a cause but courted for itself; if later they believed in the cause, it was partly in recognition of the danger it conferred on them. Danger was a relief from boredom, a stimulus to the emotions, a color mixed with all others to make them brighter. There were moments in France when the senses were immeasurably sharpened by the thought of dying next day, or possibly next week. The trees were green, not like ordinary trees, but like trees in the still moment before a hurricane;

the sky was a special and ineffable blue; the grass smelled of life itself; the image of death at twenty, the image of love, mingled together into a keen, precarious delight. And this perhaps was the greatest of the lessons that the war taught to young writers. It revivified the subjects that had seemed forbidden because they were soiled by many hands and robbed of meaning: danger made it possible to write once more about love, adventure, death. Most of my friends were preparing to follow danger into other branches of the army — of any army — that were richer in fatalities.

. . . . .

. . . School and college had uprooted us in spirit; now we were physically uprooted, hundreds of us, millions, plucked from our own soil as if by a clamshell bucket and dumped, scattered among strange people. All our roots were dead now, even the Anglo-Saxon tradition of our literary ancestors, even the habits of slow thrift that characterized our social class. We were fed, lodged, clothed by strangers, commanded by strangers, infected with the poison of irresponsibility — the poison of travel, too, for we had learned that problems could be left behind us merely by moving elsewhere — and the poison of danger, excitement, that made our old life seem intolerable. Then, as suddenly as it began for us, the war ended.

When we first heard of the Armistice we felt a sense of relief too deep to express, and we all got drunk. We had come through, we were still alive, and nobody at all would be killed tomorrow. The composite fatherland for which we had fought and in which some of us still believed — France, Italy, the Allies, our English homeland, democracy, the self-determination of small nations — had triumphed. We danced in the streets, embraced old women and pretty girls, swore blood brotherhood with soldiers in little bars, drank with our elbows locked in theirs, reeled through the streets with bottles of champagne, fell asleep somewhere. On the next day, after we got over our hangovers, we didn't know what to do, so we got drunk. But slowly,

as the days went by, the intoxication passed, and the tears of joy: it appeared that our composite fatherland was dissolving into quarreling statesmen and oil and steel magnates. Our own nation had passed the Prohibition Amendment as if to publish a bill of separation between itself and ourselves; it wasn't our country any longer. Nevertheless we returned to it: there was nowhere else to go. We returned to New York, appropriately — to the homeland of the uprooted, where everyone you met came from another town and tried to forget it; where nobody seemed to have parents, or a past more distant than last night's swell party, or a future beyond the swell party this evening and the disillusioned book he would write tomorrow.

Physical conditions of young American males as revealed by the draft

Albert G. Love and Charles B. Davenport, *Physical Examination of the First Million Draft Recruits: Methods and Results,* U.S. War Department, Office of the Surgeon General (Washington, D.C., 1919), pp. 15–18.

The initial selective draft of 1917 upon the male population of military age to meet the emergencies of the world war, gave the first opportunity in half a century to make a census of the physical constitution of the people of the United States. Out of approximately 10,-000,000 males registered, ages 21 to 30 years, there were measured and examined physically at local boards about 2,510,000 men, of whom 730,000, or 29.1 per cent, were rejected on physical grounds. After Dec. 15, 3,208,446 were examined physically by local boards up to September 11, 1918. Out of these two groups during the period down to May, 1918, approximately a million men were sent to mobilization camps and any physical defects found in them were recorded. The defects thus recorded, distributed by States and by rural and urban districts, have been made the subject of analysis in the Medical Records Section of the Surgeon General's Office. The results of this examination of the first million men are given in the accompanying report.

.   .   .   .   .

The relative frequency of the different causes of rejection is a matter of perennial interest. From fairly complete returns as to rejections at local boards, at mobilization camps, and of discharges on account of disability in camps, the Provost Marshal General concludes that during the first four months of mobilization about one-third of the men who were physically examined were rejected on physical grounds, and during the following eight months about one-fourth of such men were rejected. The Provost Marshal General's figures indicate that about 22 per cent of the rejections were caused by some mechanical effect in the organism, or rather some defect or disease that would interfere with its mechanical performance, such as defects in the bones and joints, flat-foot, and hernia. An additional 15 per cent were rejected because of imperfections of the sense organs and about 13 per cent for defects in the cardiovascular system. About 12 per cent were rejected on account of nervous and mental troubles, in part due to abnormal thyroid secretions. About 10 per cent were rejected on account of the two communicable disease groups — tuberculosis and severe cases of venereal diseases. About 8½ per cent were rejected because of developmental defects in physique; about 6 per cent on account of troubles in skin and teeth, and about 13½ per cent for other defects.

The rejections at camps following the physical examination of the first million men reveal a different order. Thus, imperfections in the sense organs are the principal defects in this group, amounting to 21 per cent, and the mechanical defects take second place, being 20 per cent of all the rejections. Circulatory defects and diseases come next at 15.7 per cent.

The two great disease groups of tuberculosis and venereal follow at 15 per cent. Then come the skin and teeth (10 per cent); nervous and mental troubles (9 per cent); developmental defects (6 per cent), and "others," at 4 per cent, account for the remainder.

.   .   .   .   .

These facts about the amount and nature of disability have their importance in considering the military power of the United States. Their significance for civil life is less. Because one-third or even one-fourth of males 20 to 30 years of age are physically unfit to fight, it does not follow that so large a proportion are handicapped in appreciable degree for civil life. Combatant forces have to move on their feet often great distances each day and carry a load of 40 pounds or more on the back. A man who weighs only 100 pounds, however healthy and however strong he may be for his size, can rarely do this. But his small size may be even an advantage in civil life.

Again, many a man with tendency toward flat-foot or hernia may do his work in civil life well and always enjoy excellent health and be really unaware of any weakness, but his presence may handicap combatant groups. Defects in sense organs again are less important in civil life than in warfare, and the stress of struggle, work, and excitement on the battlefield requires a degree of perfection in heart action and innervation that is rarely demanded in civil life. On the other hand, nearly all the disabilities found in the nervous and mental group, and also tuberculosis and symptoms of venereal disease, are a handicap in civil life. These considerations reduce to possibly 15 per cent the proportion of males 20 to 30 years old who carry a serious physical handicap against normal activity in civil occupations; that is, about half of the men rejected for general military service were without important physical handicap for activity in civil affairs.

C. YOUTH IN THE POST WORLD WAR ERA

Parents and children

---

1. Changing functions of the family

William F. Ogburn with the assistance of
Clark Tibbit, "The Family and its Functions,"
in President's Research Committee on Social
Trends, *Recent Social Trends* (New York:
McGraw-Hill Book Company, 1933), I,
661–663. Used with permission of
McGraw-Hill Book Company.

Ogburn (1886–1959) was professor of
sociology at Columbia University, 1919–1927,
and at the University of Chicago, 1927–1951.
He was director of research of the
President's Committee on Social Trends.

Two outstanding conclusions are indicated
by the data on changes in family life. One is the
decline of the institutional functions of the family as for example its economic functions. Thus
the family now produces less food and clothing
than it did formerly. The teaching functions of
the family also have been largely shifted to another institution, the school. Industry and the
state have both grown at the family's expense.
The significance of this diminution in the activities of the family as a group is far reaching.

The other outstanding conclusion is the resulting predominant importance of the personality functions of the family — that is, those
which provide for the mutual adjustments
among husbands, wives, parents and children
and for the adaptation of each member of the
family to the outside world. The family has always been responsible to a large degree for
the formation of character. It has furnished
social contacts and group life. With the decline
of its institutional functions these personality
functions have come to be its most important

contribution to society. The chief concern over
the family nowadays is not how strong it may
be as an economic organization but how well it
performs services for the personalities of its
members.

.   .   .   .   .

These historical changes in family functions
have not been accomplished without corresponding changes in structure. The household
of today is about a quarter smaller than that
of the colonial family. Marriage occurs probably somewhat later in life now than in earlier
times, especially for women. There are many
more families without children. The American
home is broken much more frequently by separation and divorce than in colonial times. Children are an economic burden for a longer time
and an economic asset for a shorter time, although in this respect there is still a difference
between the city and the country. Wives, except
when they work outside the home for pay, contribute proportionately less to the family support. The organization of the family is becoming diversified. The rural family differs from
the city family, and the family in the village
from both. Families in cities vary according to
economic level, cultural status and occupation.

The personality functions of the family have
suffered somewhat by the decline in the number of children in the average family and by
the increase in the relative number of families
with no children at all; by the growing demands
of the schools; and perhaps also by the fact
that the modern city makes possible a wider
range of contacts beyond the limits of the family
circle. Men in particular seem less dependent
on the family for social contacts than was formerly the case.

Nevertheless, it may be said that the affectional function is still centered in the family
circle and that no evidence is recorded of any
extensive transfer elsewhere. The evidence of

increased separations and divorces does not prove that husbands and wives now find marriage less agreeable than their ancestors did. It may mean only that certain functions and traditions which once operated to hold even an inharmonious family together have now weakened or disappeared.

If the personality functions have undergone a slight positive decline they have risen in relative importance because of the much greater decline of the institutional functions. To express it differently, the family is thought of much less as an economic institution than as an organization for rearing children and providing happiness . . .

2. Mechanistic and conventional pressures on children

Katharine Anthony, "The Family," in Harold E. Stearns, ed., *Civilization in the United States* (New York: Harcourt, Brace & Co., 1922), pp. 319–336. By permission of Harcourt, Brace and World, Inc.

Miss Anthony (1877–1965), a student of feminism, was the author of biographies of Margaret Fuller and Susan B. Anthony.

The tremendous influence of the family on the individuals, old and young, composing it is not merely a pious belief. We are, alas, what our families make us. This is not a pleasant thought to many individuals who have learned through bitter experience to look on family relationships as a form of soul imprisonment. Yet it seems to be an incontestable fact that personality is first formed — or deformed — in the family constellation. The home really does the job for which the school, the press, the church, and the State later get the credit. It is a smoothly articulated course from the cradle onward, however, in which the subjugated parent produces a sub-jugated child, not so much by the rod of discipline — which figures very little in American family life — but by the more powerful and pervasive force of habit and attitude. Parents allow themselves to be a medium for transmitting the incessant pressure of standards which allow no room for impulse and initiative; they become the willing instrument of a public mania for standardization which tries to make every human soul into the image of a folded pattern. The babe is moulded in his cradle into the man who will drop a sentimental tear, wear a white carnation, and send a telegram on Mother's Day — that travesty of a family festival which shames affection and puts spontaneous feeling to the blush.

As the family itself grows smaller, this pressure of mechanistic and conventional standards encroaches more closely upon the child. A sizeable group of brothers and sisters create for themselves a savage world which is their best protection against the civilization that awaits them. But with one or two children, or a widely scattered series, this natural protection is lost. The youngster is prematurely assimilated to the adult world of parents who are nowadays, owing to later marriage, not even quite so young as formerly they were. It is a peculiarity of parents, especially of mothers, that they never entertain a modest doubt as to whether they might be the best of all possible company for their children. And obviously the tired business man cannot properly substitute in the evenings for a roistering, shouting brother who never came into the world at all; nor can all the concentrated care of the most devoted mother take the place of the companionship and discipline which children get from other children. These considerations deserve more attention than they usually receive in connection with the falling birth-rate. The figures mean that the environment of the young child is being altered in a fundamental respect. Parents of small families need to take effective steps to counteract the loss. Practical things, like nursery schools, would be a help. But, chiefly, if parents will insist on being companions of their children, they need themselves to understand and practise the art of common joy and happiness.

---

3. Child-rearing in Middletown, ca. 1929

Robert S. and Helen M. Lynd, *Middletown* (New York: Harcourt, Brace and Company, 1929), pp. 150–151.[1]

Middletown was a study of the changes wrought by industrialization in Muncie, Indiana, from the 1890's to the mid-1920's.

The attitude that child-rearing is something not to be taken for granted but to be studied appears in parents of both groups. One cannot talk with Middletown mothers without being continually impressed by the eagerness of many to lay hold of every available resource for help in training their children: one business class mother took a course in the Montessori method in a near-by city before the birth of her daughter; another reads regularly the pamphlets of the Massachusetts Society for Mental Hygiene and such books as *A System of Character Training for Children*; a few get informal help from the head of the Home Economics Department of the schools and from occasional state demonstrations on child care; a handful get hold of government bulletins. Some mothers found help in a "mothers' training class" conducted for a time by a minister's wife, and a score of others are enthusiastic over a Mothers' Sunday School Class in another church; a few look to the Mothers' Council, but many of the supporters of these groups say that they get little concrete help from them. Forty mothers, many of them from the working class, paid over forty dollars for an installment set of ten volumes on child-training entitled *Foundation Stones of Success*; with the purchase went membership in a mothers' club where child-training programs were to have been studied, had not the club died after a meeting or two. Some working class mothers receive advice in the physical care of their children from the Visiting Nurses' Association and some through the schools, although the latter, like the medical profession, appear to be chiefly concerned with remedial rather than preventive work. Most important of all new sources of information are the widely-read women's magazines . . .

And yet a prevalent mood among Middletown parents is bewilderment, a feeling that their difficulties outrun their best efforts to cope with them:

"Life was simpler for my mother," said a thoughtful mother. "In those days one did not realize that there was so much to be known about the care of children. I realize that I ought to be half a dozen experts, but I am afraid of making mistakes and usually do not know where to go for advice."

One working class wife, deeply concerned over her oldest boy of eighteen, said, "We thought we'd have an easier time when we moved in from the farm three years ago, but now my husband is laid off and can't get work anywhere. The boy is still working, but we never know anything about him any more; he don't pay any attention to Mom and Pop. He might be better if we had stayed on the farm, but I suppose he'd be in town all the time anyway. I helped him to buy his Ford by not taking board money for three months; we didn't want him to get it, but he was paying out so much on renting cars to go out with parties, it seemed cheaper to let him buy it. Now he wants a Studebaker so he can go seventy-five miles an hour. I told him I'd take in washing if he'd go to our church college, but he wanted to go to work. We wanted him to be a missionary; to run all over the country, that's his mission now! We never were like this when we were young, and we don't know what to do about him."

The following discussion among eighteen

1. From *Middletown* by Robert S. and Helen M. Lynd. Copyright 1929, by Harcourt, Brace and World, Inc.; renewed, 1957, by Robert S. Lynd and Helen M. Lynd. Reprinted by permission of the publishers.

high school boys and girls at a young people's meeting in a leading church on the general topic, "What's Wrong With the Home?" reveals the parents' perplexity as seen by the children:

Boy. "Parents don't know anything about their children and what they're doing."

Girl. "They don't want to know."

Girl. "We won't let them know."

Boy. "Ours is a speedy world and they're old."

Boy. "Parents ought to get together. Usually one is easy and one is hard. They don't stand together."

---

4. Manus and Americans, ca. 1930

Margaret Mead, *Growing Up in New Guinea* (New York, 1930), pp. 211–215, 220–222.[1]

Margaret Mead (b. 1901), assistant curator of ethnology, American Museum of Natural History, studied the Manus during an expedition to the Admiralty Islands in the South West Pacific, 1928–1929.

Because Manus society is so like our own in its aims and values, we may compare its methods of education with ours, put current theories to the test of Manus experience. American children are as a rule very lightly disciplined, given little real respect for their elders. This increasing lack of discipline has been hailed by some enthusiasts as the type of what all education should be. There are theorists to-day who, proceeding upon the assumption that all children are naturally good, kind, intelligent, unselfish and discriminating, deprecate any discipline or direction from adults. Still others base their disapproval of disciplinary measures upon the plea that all discipline inhibits the child, blocks and mars his develop-

ment. All of these educators base their theories on the belief that there is something called Human Nature which would blossom in beauty were it not distorted by the limited points of view of the adults. It is, however, a more tenable attitude to regard human nature as the rawest, most undifferentiated of raw material, which must be moulded into shape by its society, which will have no form worthy of recognition unless it is shaped and formed by cultural tradition. And the child will have as an adult the imprint of his culture upon him whether his society hands him the tradition with a shrug, throws it to him like a bone to a dog, teaches him each item with care and anxiety, or leads him towards manhood as if he were on a sightseeing tour. But which method his society uses will have far-reaching results in the attitudes of the growing child, upon the way he phrases the process of growing up, upon the resentment or enthusiasm with which he meets the inevitable social pressure from the adult world.

The Manus teach their children very young the things which they consider most important — physical skill, prudery and respect for property. They teach them these things firmly, unrelentingly, often severely. But they do not teach them respect for age or for knowledge; they enjoin upon them neither courtesy nor kindness to their elders. They do not teach them to work; they regard it as quite natural if a child refuses to rescue a lost necklace from the sea, or retrieve a drifting canoe. When a new house is thatched the children clamber over the scaffolding, shouting and useless. When they catch fish they do not bring them home to their parents; they eat them themselves. They are fond of young children and enjoy teaching them, but refuse to take any responsibility for them. They are taught to control their bodies but not their appetites, to have steady hands but careless tongues. It is impossible to dose them with medicine for all their lives they have spat out anything which they disliked. They have never learned to submit to any authority, to be influenced by any adult except their beloved but not too respected fathers. In their enforced

---

1. Reprinted by permission of Little, Brown and Company. Copyright, 1930, 1958, 1962 by Margaret Mead.

servitude to their older brothers and uncles, they find neither satisfaction nor pride. They develop from overbearing, undisciplined children, into quarrelsome, overbearing adults who make the lagoon ring with their fits of rage.

It is not a pretty picture. Those things which the children learn young, which they are disciplined into accepting, they learn thoroughly and well. But they are never taught participation in adult life nor made to feel themselves an integral part of adult life. When participation is thrust upon them, they resent it as slavery. They are never taught to respect age or wisdom, so their response to their elders is one of furious inferiority. They have learned no humility while they were younger; they have little dignity when they are older. Manus elders have climbed to a place of authority upon the unwilling shoulders of resentful young men; they strut, but they have no peace there.

In many ways this picture is like our society to-day. Our children are given years of cultural non-participation in which they are permitted to live in a world of their own. They are allowed to say what they like, when they like, how they like, to ignore many of the conventions of their adults. Those who try to stem the tide are derided as "old fogies," "old fashioned," "hide bound" and flee in confusion before these magic words of exorcism. This state of discipline is due to very real causes in American society. In an immigrant country, the children are able to make a much better adjustment than have their parents. The rapid rate of invention and change in the material side of life has also made each generation of children relatively more proficient than their parents. So the last generation use the telephone more easily than their parents; the present generation are more at home in automobiles than are their fathers and mothers. When the grandparent generation has lived through the introduction of the telegraph, telephone, wireless, radio and telephotography, automobiles and aeroplanes, it is not surprising that control should slip through their amazed fingers into the more readily adaptable hands of children. While adults fumbled help-lessly with daylight saving time, missed appointments and were late to dinner, children of six whose ideas of time had not yet become crystallised rapidly assimilated the idea that ten o'clock was not necessarily ten o'clock, but might be nine or eleven. In a country where the most favoured are the ones to take up the newest invention, and old things are in such disrepute that one encounters humourless signs, which advertise, "Antiques old and new" and "Have your wedding ring renovated," the world belongs to the new generation. They can learn the new techniques far more easily than can their more culturally set elders. So the young in America seize their material world, almost from birth, without any practice in humility, and their parade of power becomes a shallow jugglery with things, phrases, catchwords.

·   ·   ·   ·   ·

In modern America, the shift in techniques, the changes in material culture, the great immigrant invasions whose descendants are inevitably better adjusted than were their parents, the emphasis upon the possession and control of a fluid undifferentiated material like money, have all undermined the respect for the aged as such. It would probably be impossible and equally undesirable to return to an attitude which bows to grey hairs and gives deference to parents no matter what their character or just deserts. Once the myth of the innate superiority of age is overthrown, no matter how irrelevant the agents of its downfall — in America these agents have been different language groups, the sudden growth of mechanical invention and the money dictated fluidity of class lines — it cannot easily be reinstated. It is because they do not realise this that parents and teachers who insist upon respect to-day are met with mocking eyes and shrugging shoulders. They insist upon respect given to status and the young people have tested the quality of status based upon the possession of wealth and found it wanting. If we wish to reestablish some sort of discipline which will make it possible for our young people to grow up less ungraciously, we must sacrifice the old insistence upon respect for *all* parents, *all* teachers, *all* guardians. We cannot deceive the perspicacity of present-day youth, but we can utilise it. The acumen which has been displayed in finding out some of its elders, may be turned to honouring others of them if only the elders will change their line of battle. The adult world to-day is like a long and straggling battle line, weekly defended by the advocates of an old fashioned respect for those in authority. The defenders of this line are too few, too scattered. Too many of those who would once have stood beside them have gone over completely to the young invaders, admitting miserably that they have no bulwark worth defending. The remainder stretch their depleted ranks along too long a line, a line the defences of which are all known to the enemy. In defending all the bulwarks they lose the entire battle. It is time to admit the worthlessness of the present claims, to admit that neither age nor status nor authority are capable of commanding real respect unless they are joined with definite qualities worthy of admiration. Then those who have deserted the battle line — in laziness, desperation, or real humility — can return to defend a modified and more exacting dogma of superiority.

In so doing, in rewriting the relationship between youth and age so that some of the aged will always outrank the finest youths, while admitting that many of the aged have earned no guerdon of respect, the elders will serve youth more than themselves. In offering them nothing they do them only injury. If children were moved by great internal drives which drove them into manufacturing a new heaven and a new earth, then the elders might benefit them by standing aside and letting the experiment have free play. But the children have no such creative gift. They have no stuff to build with except tradition. Left to themselves, deprived of their tradition or presented with no tradition which they can respect, they build an empty edifice without content. And come to maturity, they must make terms with the culture of their adults, live on the same premises, abide

by the same values. It is no service to them to so rear them that they take over the adult life sullenly, with dull resentment. The perpetuation of the given culture is the inevitable fate of the majority of any society. We who cannot free them from that fate may at least give them such a phrasing of life that it may seem to them important and dignified. To treat our children as the Manus do, permit them to grow up as the lords of an empty creation, despising the adults who slave for them so devotedly, and then apply the whip of shame to make them fall in line with a course of life which they have never been taught to see as noble or dignified — this is giving a stone to those who have a right to good bread.

Dream and reality in the early depression

1. The Children's Charter, 1930

U.S. Children's Bureau, *The Story of the White House Conferences on Children and Youth* (Washington, 1967), pp. 11–12.

On November 22, 1930, the approximately 3,000 delegates attending the White House Conference on Child Health and Protection adopted the following statement of objectives for American Children.

THE CHILDREN'S CHARTER

PRESIDENT HOOVER'S WHITE HOUSE CONFERENCE ON CHILD HEALTH AND PROTECTION, RECOGNIZING THE RIGHTS OF THE CHILD AS THE FIRST RIGHTS OF CITIZENSHIP, PLEDGES ITSELF TO THESE AIMS FOR THE CHILDREN OF AMERICA

I For every child spiritual and moral training to help him to stand firm under the pressure of life

II For every child understanding and the guarding of his personality as his most precious right

III For every child a home and that love and security which a home provides; and for that child who must receive foster care, the nearest substitute for his own home

IV For every child full preparation for his birth, his mother receiving prenatal, natal, and postnatal care; and the establishment of such protective measures as will make child-bearing safer

V For every child health protection from birth through adolescence, including: periodical health examinations and, where needed, care of specialists and hospital treatment; regular dental examinations and care of the teeth; protective and preventive measures against communicable diseases; the insuring of pure food, pure milk, and pure water

VI For every child from birth through adolescence, promotion of health, including health instruction and a health program, wholesome physical and mental recreation, with teachers and leaders adequately trained

VII For every child a dwelling-place safe, sanitary, and wholesome, with reasonable provisions for privacy; free from conditions which tend to thwart his development; and a home environment harmonious and enriching

VIII For every child a school which is safe from hazards, sanitary, properly equipped, lighted, and ventilated. For younger children nursery schools and kindergartens to supplement home care

IX For every child a community which recognizes and plans for his needs, protects him against physical dangers, moral hazards, and disease; provides him with safe and wholesome places for play and recreation; and makes provision for his cultural and social needs

X For every child an education which, through the discovery and development of his individual abilities, prepares him for life; and through training and vocational guidance prepares him for a living which will yield him the maximum of satisfaction

XI For every child such teaching and training as will prepare him for successful parenthood, home-making, and the rights of citizenship; and, for parents, supplementary training to fit them to deal wisely with the problems of parenthood

XII For every child education for safety and protection against accidents to which modern conditions subject him — those to which he is directly exposed and those which, through loss or maiming of his parents, affect him indirectly

XIII For every child who is blind, deaf, crippled, or otherwise physically handicapped, and for the child who is mentally handicapped, such measures as will early discover and diagnose his handicap, provide care and treatment, and so train him that he may become an asset to society rather than a liability. Expenses of these services should be borne publicly where they cannot be privately met

XIV For every child who is in conflict with society the right to be dealt with intelligently as society's charge, not society's outcast; with the home, the school, the church, the court and the institution when needed, shaped to return him whenever possible to the normal stream of life

XV For every child the right to grow up in a family with an adequate standard of living and the security of a stable income as the surest safeguard against social handicaps

XVI For every child protection against labor that stunts growth, either physical or mental, that limits education, that deprives children of the right of comradeship, of play, and of joy

XVII For every rural child as satisfactory schooling and health services as for the city child, and an extension to rural families of social, recreational, and cultural facilities

XVIII To supplement the home and the school in the training of youth, and to return to them those interests of which modern life tends to cheat children, every stimulation and encouragement should be given to the extension and development of the voluntary youth organizations

XIX To make everywhere available these minimum protections of the health and welfare of children, there should be a district, county, or community organization for health, education, and welfare, with full-time officials, coördinating with a state-wide program which will be responsive to a nationwide service of general information, statistics, and scientific research. This should include:

(*a*) Trained, full-time public health officials, with public health nurses, sanitary inspection, and laboratory workers

(*b*) Available hospital beds

(*c*) Full-time public welfare service for the relief, aid, and guidance of children in special need due to poverty, misfortune, or behavior difficulties, and for the protection of children from abuse, neglect, exploitation, or moral hazard

FOR EVERY CHILD THESE RIGHTS, REGARDLESS OF RACE, OR COLOR, OR SITUATION, WHEREVER HE MAY LIVE UNDER THE PROTECTION OF THE AMERICAN FLAG

---

2. On the road, 1932

"Survey of Transient Boys in the United States," *Monthly Labor Review,* XXXVI (1933), 91–93.

The survey was conducted by Professor A. W. McMillen of the University of Chicago and Miss Mary Skinner of the Children's Bureau.[1]

---

1. For a popularization of the report see Maxine Davis, "200,000 Vagabond Children," *Ladies Home Journal* (September 1932) pp. 8–9, 46, 48, 50. For Professor McMillen's testimony on the subject before a Senate subcommittee see U.S. Congress, Senate, *Congressional Hearings before a Subcommittee of the Committee on Manufactures, on S. 5121,* 72 Cong., 2 Sess. (1933), XCIII, 44–46, 91–92, 96–97.

In the spring of 1932 the United States Children's Bureau undertook a survey of conditions relative to boys under 21 who had taken to the road, either seeking employment which they could not find in their own community, or simply driven forth by the want at home. Lack of time and means prevented a complete statistical study, but the survey brought to light some striking conditions, which have been summarized in a mimeographed memorandum recently issued.

The purpose of the survey was to secure as definite information as possible as to how many boys are leaving their own homes and wandering through the country, what local communities are doing to take care of them, whether local resources are adequate to the demand, and how the boys are actually faring. Material was sought through correspondence with chiefs of police and executives of community chests or councils of social agencies in 25 cities in different parts of the country, and through field visits to certain points in the South and Southwest.

One of the first points noted was the breakdown of the approved method of handling transients, which had been carefully built up through the years preceding the depression. A cardinal point of that method was that each case should receive individual attention, that if the transient had a valid claim on any given community he should, if possible, be returned to that community, and that if he had no such claim or if for any reason he could not be returned, an effort must be made to secure for him a job or the training which would enable him to take a job, and to fit him, as far as possible, into the new environment. Under existing conditions this program has become in many instances impossible.

Communities do not have the funds to pay transportation to the place of established responsibility. Many communities lack even the resources necessary to maintain transients during the period required to make an investigation in a distant area. Hence there has been a widespread relapse into the vicious practice of "passing on," due to the sheer inadequacy of local resources. At the same time social agencies are confronted with a transient problem that transcends anything the country has yet known. The numbers of wandering families, unattached men and women, and boys and girls, vastly exceed those of former years. And the make-up of the groups has changed radically. The traditional single transient of earlier years was the seasonal laborer, the "knight of the road," commonly called the hobo, and the occasional runaway boy or adventurous youth. To-day young men and boys who would normally be at work or in school predominate.

NUMBER OF YOUNG TRANSIENTS

As to the number of such young transients, only indications could be secured. Local observers gave estimates which seemed to show that the problem is more serious than had been supposed.

Men and boys swarm on every freight in such numbers that the railroad police would be helpless to keep them off. Along the route of the Southern Pacific many small towns in Texas, New Mexico, and Arizona reported the daily passing of about 200 men and boys during the winter and spring. The Santa Fe at Albuquerque averaged 75 a day. From September 1, 1931, to April 30, 1932, the Southern Pacific, with 9,130 miles of track, recorded 416,915 trespassers ejected . . . In Kansas City in May the railroad men emphatically stated that a conservative estimate of the men and boys riding the freights through that city at that time was 1,500 per day. In general the estimates as to what proportion of these freight riders are under 21 clustered in the neighborhood of 20 to 25 per cent. This is borne out by sample counts where ages were recorded.

Reports from shelters and other local agencies confirm these estimates. The Volunteers of America in Phoenix, Ariz., fed and lodged 1,529 different boys under 21 during the three and a half months at its soup kitchen from November 1 to March 15, of whom at least one-fifth are estimated to have been under 21. At El Paso, Tex., during April and May, the Salvation Army reports feeding and lodging 9,551 men and boys, of whom 2,059 were under 21.

TYPE OF BOYS ON THE ROAD

There is much teestimony that these boys who come from practically every State in the Union, represent, in the main, substantial American families. High-school students are not uncommon among them, and the class of professional wanderers is not conspicuous.

Social workers, police, and railroad men, who are in constant touch with these boys, assert their belief that the overwhelming majority of them are young men and boys who would normally be in school or at work; that they are "on the road" because there is nothing else to do — sometimes because sheer pride will not permit them to sit idle at home — sometimes because support for the whole family came from a relief agency and was wholly inadequate properly to feed the younger children; that they are, on the whole, not of the habitual hobo or criminal types.

TREATMENT RECEIVED

For the most part the communities through which they pass are too heavily burdened with the care of their own unemployed to be able to give these wanderers intelligent and effective aid.

The local agency charged with service to transients will usually give him lodging for one night and two meals. Then he must move on. In the urban centers the time limit is sometimes a little longer. But in the whole mass of evidence assembled the universality of the policy of keeping these wanderers moving stands out conspicuously. Shelter facilities range all the way from a basement jail devoid of sanitary arrangements or from permission to sleep in the sandhouse on railroad property, where the warmed sand lends some degree of comfort on a frosty night, up to a well-regulated lodging house, with beds equipped with fresh linen, and with bathing arrangements and a place to launder soiled clothing. In cities where conservation of resources is a primary consideration, the food given the transients has sunk to a dead level of monotony. Coffee, bread, beans, and an occasional vegetable stew constitute the menu at station after station. Occasionally persons with imagination and initiative have found ways to vary this diet at little increase in cost. Riding freights and hitch hiking are hard on clothes and shoes. Cities are now providing little help in this line to nonresidents. Medical care for those sick as a result of exposure or hardship is practically not to be had until the sufferer is in an obviously serious condition. Except in a very few of the larger cities no case work, even of the most rudimentary character, is attempted. In most places a simple form of registration, varying greatly from place to place, is all that is undertaken.

The effect of such conditions upon boys, many of them accustomed to decent standards of living, needs no elaboration, and the survey does not labor the point. Instead, it points out briefly the lines along which improvement is needed. Community action, both preventive and protective, is called for. The first object of the preventive program is to induce the boys to stay at home. Where work can not be found, more adequate relief is one measure indicated; others are plans for keeping up the morale of energetic boys in their enforced idleness, such as diversifying and enlarging school curricula, instituting trade courses when possible, asking all the school equipment for recreational and vocational training available for evening use by community groups, opening gymnasiums, athletic fields, and parks to wider use, and establishing special projects suitable to local circumstances. The forestry camps of California are cited as examples of such projects. Along the lines of protective action, it is suggested that each community should plan for more careful

treatment of the youthful transients who are stranded within their bounds. Provision should be made for food and shelter of acceptable standards, for registration and interviewing, and for a training program for those who can not be sent home and who should not be passed on. Not all cities could afford to undertake such a program, but some might, and each center of this kind would help to diminish the proportions of the problem.

---

3. The impact of the depression on children, December 1932

Grace Abbott in *New York Times,* Dec. 18, 1932.

Grace Abbott (1878–1939) was chief of the United States Children's Bureau, 1921–1934.

Letters and personal visits to the Children's Bureau from those who have been placed in a position of community responsibility for the care of children indicate a widespread conviction that children have suffered many serious permanent losses during these years of depression and that the coming winter presents even more serious hazards. While an eager desire that we should not fail in the duty of safeguarding children may have led to an exaggeration of what is in fact happening to children, on the whole there is much evidence that this concern is fully justified.

The economic depression has been and still is so extensive that very few homes have escaped altogether the anxieties which these last three years have brought. We can ignore those in which the only effect has been to lower the degree of affluence. But having done so, we come to those whose lives have been greatly changed, and, except in rare instances, we can only conclude for the worse. We come to acute

Our Gang in "Jubilo, Jr." (1924).

Harlem, 1932.

Coeds, 1927.

Unemployed Youth, ca. 1932.

suffering, both physical and mental, long before we reach that constantly increasing group who have lost their independence and become dependent upon public support.

Even those with little imagination know how no employment or underemployment, the failure of banks and building and loan associations have affected many children whose parents faced the future self-reliant and unafraid a few years ago. In the millions of homes which have escaped the abyss of destitution fear of what may still happen is destroying the sense of security which is considered necessary for the happiness and well-being of children . . .

Great effort has been made to prevent suffering. Last year probably more than a billion dollars was expended by public and private agencies for the relief of the unemployed. Although this is probably some eight times as much as was spent for relief in normal times, no one who has been going in and out of the homes of the unemployed in large urban centres or in the single-industry towns and mining communities has reported that it has been adequate to insure shelter, clothes and reasonably adequate diet for all needy children.

However, instead of discussing expenditure for relief, my subject is: What evidence is there of the effect of the depression upon children? This is not easy to determine. Many of the effects will not be immediately apparent. Malnutrition sufficiently prolonged and widespread will definitely reduce resistance to disease, not necessarily this year but in the future. Some losses cannot be evaluated statistically, and as to others accurate information is not available. But there are facts on which some conclusions can be based.

In the first place, we find that in these years of depression there have been fewer babies born. Like the infant mortality rate, the trend of the birth rate has been downward, particularly during the last decade, when the average annual decline has been 2.5 per cent. But in 1931 there was a decline of 5.8 per cent from the 1930 rate, so that the birth rate was 17.8 per 1,000 (a new low for this country), and

the indications are that it will probably reach 17 in 1932.

Following the depression of 1921 there was also a sharp decline in the birth rate. This decline, as one statistician has said, "can hardly be attributed to any factors other than unfavorable business conditions superimposed on those influences which have caused the general decline in the birth rate."

For the health of children the only general test is the very low one of the numbers who die and those who are sick with communicable diseases. There is no nation-wide reporting as to under-nourishment or deficiency diseases. Although hospitals have reported some deaths due to starvation and others in which malnutrition was a secondary cause of death, such cases are quite unusual. Instead of a higher infant death rate during these years of depression, the general downward trend of the rate has been maintained. During the last ten years what is known as the "United States registration area" has been greatly expanded as the birth and death registration of one after another State has been found sufficiently accurate to be admitted to the registration area by the Vital Statistics Division of the Census Bureau. The infant mortality rate for this expanding registration area of the United States was 68 per 1,000 live births for 1929, 65 for 1930 and 62 (provisional rate) for 1931, according to the bureau.

No causal connection has been established between this lowered death rate and the depression. The generally downward trend of the infant mortality rate over the last twenty years indicates that the low rates in 1930 and 1931 must be ascribed to the cumulative effects of twenty years of educational work with mothers, and the absence of any serious epidemics, together with favorable climatic conditions.

While health officers and social workers have made great efforts to insure the protection of the health of children and of adults during these years, the first cuts in the health budgets have been in the child health and public health nursing divisions. It is impossible to escape the conclusion that under normal economic conditions low rates would have been lower still during these years.

Although the death rate is low, there is much evidence that the health of many children is being adversely affected by the prolonged depression. For example, hospitals and clinics report an increase in rickets among children; in New York City, where relief for the unemployed has probably been more nearly adequate than in any other of the largest cities, the city Health Department reports that 20.5 per cent of the school children examined were suffering from malnutrition in 1932 as compared with 13.6 per cent in 1928 and 13.4 per cent in 1929.

Undernourishment is even more widespread in areas of extreme depression, where the available relief has been quite inadequate, such as the coal-mining communities and "one-industry towns," where there has been little or no work for several years, or in districts where the depression has been added to the economic losses brought by flood and drought.

In a recent report of the Surgeon General of the Public Health Service on the rural health work in the drought-stricken areas in 1931, the reports of the health officers as to health conditions in the counties are summarized. Here one finds the health officers of Alabama and Arkansas, for example, reporting for county after county an increase in pellagra due to inability to purchase the necessary food; and "dietary diseases" and widespread undernourishment were frequently referred to in the reports for these and other States. The bulletin, "Health Briefs," of the Tennessee Health Department for August of this year says that "the increase in deaths from pellagra that has been forecast since the beginning of the reduced economic conditions is now beginning to show on the tally sheets of vital statistics."

The science of nutrition has greatly advanced during recent years, so that we now know with much greater accuracy than ever before what are the necessary protective foods; and where relief funds have been reasonably adequate

and well administered, malnutrition has been controlled in families receiving relief. But one city after another reports reduction of relief budgets because of inadequate relief funds, and trained workers are not available in some places, and in others considered unnecessary, so that the relief funds are not everywhere expended so as to insure the largest possible value to the children.

Recently the director of the Child Hygiene Division of the Children's Bureau was called into conference to discuss how the reduced relief budget should be expended so as to insure the health of the children. Protective foods for children include milk, fruits, some fresh vegetables, and eggs, and the problem was how to purchase these as well as the foods that supply energy for a family of five when the total income is $11 a month. Some families are managing to exist on a smaller per capita than $2 a month, but at the cost of greatly lowered vital capacity and resistance to disease.

It is the future effects of undernourishment among children that are to be feared. As Dr. William H. Welch has put it, "The ground lost by undernourishment in childhood may never be regained." That many children have suffered such losses during the past three years is certain.

After health, one is asked about the conduct of children. Has the depression brought an increase in delinquency? For several years the Children's Bureau has been cooperating with an increasing number of courts in an effort to secure uniform statistics of juvenile delinquency. This is not yet accomplished, but from the courts reporting to the bureau evidence as to the juvenile delinquency rate can be obtained. For the calendar year 1931 reports of cases of children dealt with by the juvenile courts were received from all the courts in Connecticut and Utah, and from seventy-one courts in twenty-one other States and the District of Columbia. Nineteen large courts have reported to the bureau every year since the experiment in developing uniform statistics was begun in 1927.

In these nineteen cities the trend of the delinquency rates for boys from 1927 to 1930 was upward, but in each year of this period the percentage increase was less. Thus the 1928 increase over 1927 amounted to 8 per cent, the 1929 over 1928 to 5 per cent, and the 1930 increase over 1929 to only 1 per cent. This slowing up in the percentage increase to a point where it is negligible between 1929 and 1930 was followed by a definite drop in the rate in 1931, amounting to 8 per cent from the preceding year. In the delinquency rates for girls the same general tendency is apparent. There was an upward trend from 1927 to 1929; the 1930 rate was the same as that of 1929; and the 1931 rate definitely lower than that of 1930.

But while the total numbers indicate that delinquency is on the decline, an analysis of the offenses for which the children are brought to the courts raises grave doubts as to whether conduct problems have not, in fact, been growing more serious.

The most common offense for which boys are brought before the juvenile court is stealing. This is an offense that one would expect to see affected by economic conditions and apparently this has happened, for in the nineteen courts for which comparable figures are available for the three-year period the number of boys' cases brought before the courts for stealing was as follows: 1929, 10,105; 1930, 10,850; 1931, 11,244.

Meanwhile the number of boys and girls before the court for truancy has declined. In the nineteen courts for which reports have been made to the bureau for five years, truancy accounted for 7 per cent of the boys cases brought to court in 1927 and for 5 per cent in 1932.

There has, therefore, been an actual decline either in truancy or in interest in the enforcement of compulsory school laws through the juvenile courts. While school may seem relatively more alluring than in normal times, one suspects that a slackening of efforts to solve the problems which result in truancy is the explanation of this lower rate. The cuts in school budgets which have been so general and so

serious in some communities make it easy to believe that the apparent reduction in juvenile delinquency may reflect only a reduction in the budget of the attendance department. This would mean that by ignoring the causes of truancy, we may be permitting children to drift into more serious delinquency.

There has been much discussion recently of the new and serious problem of the transient boy. It is estimated that there are at least 200,-000 boys who have left home because the family income or the family relief was inadequate for all of them and they were unable to get work. Getting away from the home town seemed to them one way out of it all. With only the most temporary relief available in most communities for non-residents who are without funds, these boys have become wanderers. They have learned how to "get by" in one community after another. They have conquered their repugnance to begging and to unsanitary living conditions.

The potential danger in this situation many communities now appreciate and they are attempting to deal more adequately with the transient during the coming Winter. But the number dependent on relief funds is larger this year than last. Whether we prevent delinquency as well as maintain the health of children will depend upon whether the total of Federal, State and local relief funds will be adequate to meet the needs of the children.

Not only are many boys and young men leaving bad conditions at home for worse conditions on the road but desertion by fathers and husbands is increasing. The newspapers report, for example, that in New York City there were 3,495 arraignments for abandonment in 1931, as compared with 1,488 in 1928. Arraignment statistics represent only a small percentage of the number of abandonments.

Under the circumstances it is not surprising to find that reports from institutions and child-caring agencies show that the number of dependent children being cared for away from their own homes had increased. In the eighteen metropolitan centres reporting regularly to the

Children's Bureau, the number of children cared for in foster-homes has risen steadily until by May, 1932, there was a 25 per cent increase in the number of children who were being provided for away from their own homes. The number cared for in orphanages or institutions also showed an increase, though very slight, during the same period. The Child Welfare League of America reports that among its constituent societies the number of children received as a result of the break-up of homes has increased 48 per cent since July of this year.

While the value of keeping intact the family unit cannot be statistically stated, that it is important and fundamental has been affirmed and reaffirmed by experts. The conferences called to consider the welfare of children, first by President Roosevelt and again by President Wilson and President Hoover, have all pointed out the importance of preventing the break-up of the home on the ground of poverty alone. The so-called "mothers' pensions" or "funds to parents" acts have done much to give reality to these statements of principle, but during the past years, according to the statistics quoted, we have lost ground.

Premature child labor, which in the past has blighted the childhood of considerable numbers, has been reduced by the industrial depression. Reports received by the Children's Bureau as to the numbers of work permits issued each year showed that during the first months of 1929 there was an increase over the previous year in the number of children going to work, but during the last part of that year there was a general decline in applications for work per-mits. Jobs had already become scarce. That general decline has continued as jobs have grown fewer. Nevertheless, the census enumerators reported in 1930 more than 2,000,000 boys and girls between 10 and 18 years of age gainfully employed; 667,000 of them were under 16 years of age and 235,328 under 14.

Even as the census of 1930 showed that considerable numbers of children were employed in spite of the fact that millions of men and women were unable to get work, the annual reports made to the Children's Bureau by the local agencies charged with the responsibility of issuing work permits show that, in 1931, some children were still able to get jobs.

Moreover, many among the unemployed are boys and girls who are only recently out of school. The United States Office of Education reports that 100,000 high school graduates have returned to school this Autumn . . .

These facts about health, delinquency, dependency and child labor give a gloomy picture of the outlook for children. But it is only as dark as we permit it to become. Facts must be faced before a preventive program can be planned. Conditions which appear menacing can, to a very large extent, be brought under community control.

Despair is not the emotion which consideration of the needs of children should create in the United States. We are still the richest country in the world, both actually and potentially. Our affectionate interest in the welfare of children has not changed. Whatever our resources, our capacity for sacrifice is certainly equal to their needs at least.

Part Two   The Legal Status of Children and
            Protection Against Cruelty and
            Immorality

During the nineteenth century the rights of children in relation to parents and to others standing in the place of parents steadily if slowly enlarged. In the United States the legal adjustment between children and parents derived mainly from English common law with some modifications introduced from equity decisions. This relatively stable equilibrium was not static nor were all of its parts consistent with each other. Because of separate state court systems there were bound to be differences in judicial interpretations of the common law and state statutes affecting children's legal rights were not uniform. Although it is difficult to identify a consistent and common trend in the various categories of children's rights, it is possible to note a gradual elevation of the child's status under the protection and patronage of public authority.[1]

A similar tendency was present in other fields of child-parent relationships such as recognition of the child's right to public education and to protection against excessive labor regardless of the parent's wishes. As the state intervened more frequently and effectively in the relations between parent and child in order to protect children against parental mismanagement, the state also forced children to conform to public norms of behavior and obligation. Thus the child did not escape control; rather he experienced a partial exchange of masters in which the ignorance, neglect, and exploitation of some parents were replaced by presumably fair and uniform treatment at the hands of public authorities and agencies. The transfer of responsibilities required an elaboration of administrative and judicial techniques of investigation, decision, and supervision.

1. For comprehensive coverage of children's rights in relation to parents and guardians during the period under consideration in this volume see Chester G. Vernier, *American Family Laws,* IV [*Parent and Child*] (Stanford University, California, 1936).

Protecting children against physical abuse was a particularly difficult problem because administering corporal punishment to minors was one of the best recognized and most widely exercised rights of adults. Under the common law the right of the parent, guardian, or master to chastise children was the corollary of the obligation to support them. The appropriate degree of severity of punishment was ordinarily left to the judgment of the parent or master but, from time to time, adults were prosecuted for mistreating children under their care.

Organized efforts for the protection of children developed as an outgrowth of humane work for animals. Beginning with the founding of the New York Society for the Prevention of Cruelty to Children (S.P.C.C.) in 1874, societies devoted exclusively to child protection or jointly to animal and child protective work increased rapidly. By 1900 the number of such societies exceeded 250. From the start the societies concerned themselves not only with protection of children against physical abuse but also with protection against other forms of cruelty such as exploitation, exposure, and neglect.

The New York S.P.C.C. was not only the oldest but the most powerful and influential of the societies. Despite its name, the New York S.P.C.C. was not as much interested or involved in the prevention of cruelty as in the rescue of children from improper homes, the enforcement of laws, and the punishment of offenders against children. The S.P.C.C. was a private corporation but its agents wore police badges and were duly constituted officers of the law. Enjoying the status of a law-enforcement agency and not subject to supervision by the State Board of Charities, the S.P.C.C. came to exercise a powerful influence on the welfare of poor and immigrant children in New York City. Its influence was usually exerted in support of institutional care for children adjudged neglected or abused.

After the turn of the century some of the anti-cruelty and humane societies began to depart from the law-enforcement aims and police methods which had formerly characterized their work. The Massachusetts S.P.C.C. took the lead in developing case work with families and in emphasizing reform and rehabilitation to permit retention of the child in his own home. Societies in Philadelphia, Newark, Cleveland, Detroit, and Minneapolis also adopted the case work as opposed to punitive approach. After 1912, however, the most important advances in this field came about as a result of the growth of public agencies charged with child protection and with improvement in the administration of child welfare services. These topics are dealt with in Part Six.

The movement for protecting children from immoral influences developed simultaneously with and along lines similiar to the anti-cruelty movement. The New York Society for the Suppression of Vice, founded in 1872 by Anthony Comstock (1844–1915) with the encouragement of the Young Men's Christian Association and the backing of Christian business men, enjoyed the same preeminence in its work as the New York S.P.C.C. Like "the Cruelty," the Vice Society was a private corporation charged with law enforcement duties and armed with police powers. Comstock first directed his energy and zeal to an attack on pornographic books but he soon extended his vigilance to any publications or articles he deemed of an immoral or irreligious character. Thus the federal anti-obscenity act of 1873, popularly known as the Comstock law, prohibited the mailing of contraceptives and birth control information as well as "obscene, lewd, or lascivious" books,

pamphlets, and prints. Always alarmed about the effect of "evil reading" on the minds of children, Comstock also engaged in a forty-year campaign against gambling, abortion, indecent exposure, "the nude in art," "free-love and free-thought traps," and countless other snares of Satan.

Comstock's methods, which verged on entrapment, and his subjective interpretation of obscenity made him the subject of both criticism and derision. The courts, however, upheld his actions in most of the many cases in which he was involved and, in important decisions, defined obscenity broadly as the tendency of a book or picture to deprave or corrupt the morals of the immature. When Comstock died a journalist observed that he had both represented and parodied the moral values of his era.

During the last decade of Comstock's life motion pictures, offering cheap and exciting entertainment to mass audiences, emerged as a new "devil trap" for the young. Parents, educators, and youth workers denounced movie theaters as disreputable resorts, movie-going as a dangerous habit, and motion picture films as tasteless and baneful in influence. These adult considerations seem to have had little impact on the popularity of the movies among young people. Police surveillance of theaters, local and state censorship, and various forms of industry self-regulation were all tried, and federal censorship or licensing proposed, to protect the morals of the sizable proportion of movie audiences who were juveniles. Despite periodic efforts at reform, moving pictures, the great twentieth-century innovation in communication and the arts, continued to serve the interests of commerce and the delectation of youth.

I Rights of Parents and Children

A. RIGHTS AND OBLIGATIONS OF PARENTS

Correction and discipline

---

1. Parental authority must be exercised, "within the bounds of reason and humanity," Illinois, 1869

Fletcher et al. *v.* Illinois, 52 Ill. 395.

This was an indictment against Samuel Fletcher and his wife, Ledicia, for false imprisonment of Samuel Fletcher, junior, the son of Samuel, senior, and step son of Ledicia. The defendants were found guilty, and sentenced to pay a fine of $300 each.

The instructions gave the law correctly to the jury, and so far as relates to Samuel Fletcher, we are of opinion the evidence sustains the verdict. It shows the wanton imprisonment, without a pretense of reasonable cause, of a blind and helpless boy, in a cold and damp cellar without fire, during several days of midwinter. The boy finally escaped and seems to have been taken in charge by the town authorities. The only excuse given by the father to one of the witnesses who remonstrated with him was, that the boy was covered with vermin, and for this the father annointed his body with kerosene. If the boy was in this wretched state, it must have been because he had received no care from those who should have given it. In view of his blind and helpless condition, the case altogether is one of shocking inhumanity.

Counsel urge, that the law gives parents a large discretion in the exercise of authority over their children. This is true, but this authority must be exercised within the bounds of reason and humanity. If the parent commits wanton and needless cruelty upon his child, either by imprisonment of this character or by inhuman beating, the law will punish him . . . It would be monstrous to hold that under the pretense of sustaining parental authority, children must be left, without the protection of the law, at the mercy of depraved men or women, with liberty to inflict any species of barbarity short of the actual taking of life.

---

2. Permanent injury or malice the test of excessive punishment, North Carolina, 1886

State *v.* Jones, 95 N. C. 588.

In this decision the Supreme Court of North Carolina reversed a lower court's conviction of a father for assault and battery against his daughter.

The defendant is charged, in the ordinary form of an indictment, with an assault and battery committed upon the person of Mary C. Jones, who, though not so designated, is his daughter, and was then sixteen years of age. Upon the trial, she testified that the defendant was a man of bad temper and frequently whipped her without any cause; that on one

119

occasion he whipped her at the gate in front of his house, giving her about twenty-five blows with a switch, or small limb, about the size of one's thumb or forefinger, with such force as to raise whelks upon her back, and then going into the house, he soon returned and gave her five blows more with the same switch, choked her, and threw her violently to the ground causing a dislocation of her thumb joint; that she had given him no offence; that she did not know for what she was beaten, nor did he give her any reason for it during the time. No permanent injury was inflicted upon her person. There was other corroborative testimony, and one witness saw her tongue hanging out of her mouth while being choked. The defendant and his wife, stepmother of the girl, swore that she was habitually disobedient, had several times stolen money, and was chastised at the time spoken of for stealing some cents from her father; that he never whipped her except for correction, and this he was often compelled to do for that purpose, and had never administered punishment under the impulse of high temper or from malice.

.   .   .   .   .

Smith, C.J. It will be observed that the test of the defendant's criminal liability is the infliction of a punishment *"cruel and excessive,"* and thus it is left to the jury without the aid of law for their guidance to determine.

It is quite obvious that this would subject every exercise of parental authority in the correction and discipline of children — in other words, domestic government — to the supervision and control of jurors, who might, in a given case, deem the punishment disproportionate to the offence, and unreasonable and excessive. It seems to us, that such a rule would tend, if not to subvert family government, greatly to impair its efficiency, and remove restraints upon the conduct of children. If, whenever parental authority is used in chastising them, it could be a subject of judicial inquiry whether the punishment was cruel and excessive — that is, beyond the demerits of the disobedience

or misconduct, and the father himself exposed to a criminal prosecution at the instance of the child, in defending himself from which he would be compelled to lift the curtain from the scenes of home life, and exhibit a long series of acts of insubordination, disobedience and ill-doing — it would open the door to a flood of irreparable evils far transcending that to be remedied by a public prosecution. Is it consistent with the best interest of society, that an appeal should thus lie to the Court from an act of parental discipline, severe though it may be, and unmerited by the particular offence itself, perhaps, but one of a series evincing stubbornness and incorrigibility in the child, and the father punished because the jurors think it cruel and immoderate?

.   .   .   .

While acts of indiscreet severity are not criminally punishable . . . their check for the good and welfare of society must be found in the promptings of parental affection and a wholesome public opinion, and if these are insufficient, they must be tolerated as an incident to the relation, which human laws cannot wholly remove or redress.

.   .   .   .

The test, then, of criminal responsibility is the infliction of permanent injury by means of the administered punishment, or that it proceeded from malice, and was not in the exercise of a corrective authority. It would be a dangerous innovation, fruitful in mischief, if, in disregard of an established rule assigning limits to parental power, it were to be left to a jury to determine in each case whether a chastisement was excessive and cruel, and to convict when such was their opinion.

We do not propose to palliate or excuse the conduct of the defendant in the present case. The punishment seems to have been needlessly severe, but we refuse to take cognizance of it as a criminal act, because it belongs to the domestic rather than legal power, to a domain into which the penal law is reluctant to enter, unless induced by an imperious necessity.

---

3. A child denied right to recover damages for alleged mistreatment by stepmother, Tennessee, 1903

McKelvey *v*. McKelvey et al., 77 S 664.

This is a suit instituted by a minor child, by next friend, against her father and stepmother, seeking to recover damages for cruel and inhuman treatment alleged to have been inflicted upon her by the latter at the instance and with the consent of the father. Upon demurrer the suit was dismissed, and, the case being properly brought to this court, error is assigned upon this action of the trial judge.

We think there was no error in this dismissal. At common law the right of the father to the control and custody of his infant child grew out of the corresponding duty on his part to maintain, protect, and educate it. These rights could only be forfeited by gross misconduct on his part. The right to control involved the subordinate right to restrain and inflict moderate chastisement upon the child. In case parental power was abused, the child had no civil remedy against the father for the personal injuries inflicted. Whatever redress was afforded in such case was to be found in an appeal to the criminal law and in the remedy furnished by the writ of habeas corpus. So far as we can discover, this rule of the common law has never been questioned in any of the courts of this country, and certainly no such action as the present has been maintained in these courts . . .

The fact that the cruel treatment in this case was inflicted by a stepmother can make no difference, for, whether inflicted in the presence of the father or not, if the action could be maintained at all, he would be responsible for the tort. If inflicted in his presence, he alone would be responsible, nothing appearing to repel the presumption that it was the result of his coercion; if out of his presence, then he and she would be jointly liable for the wrong. So at last it comes back to the question as to the right of a minor child to institute a civil action against the father for wrongs inflicted upon it.

.   .   .   .   .

We think that the circuit judge acted in obedience to a well-settled rule controlling the relation of father and child, and in furtherance of a sound public policy, in sustaining the demurrer to the declaration in this case, and his judgment is affirmed.

---

4. Mistreatment of a child by one acting *in loco parentis,* Wisconsin, 1925

Steber *v*. Norris, 188 Wisc. 366.

The plaintiff in this action at the time of the alleged assault was an eleven-year-old boy, whose parents had sent him to the farm of the defendant in the summer of 1923, and upon request he was permitted to return in 1924 when the mother signed a written statement giving the defendant authority to discipline the plaintiff if and when he broke the rules and regulations enforced upon the farm. The plaintiff was supposed to work at assigned tasks about the farm for six hours a day and for this labor received his board and room.

The undisputed testimony shows that the plaintiff had failed to perform some of the tasks assigned to him and had told several falsehoods, and that upon July 23, 1924, the defendant took the plaintiff to his office and there, after asking him why he had not performed his work and receiving no answer, inflicted corporal punishment by means of a crude rubber whip about thirty inches long. The clothing of the boy had been so removed that the punishment was inflicted upon the nude body of the boy, who swore that he was undressed and stripped by the defendant, though the defendant testified that the plaintiff removed his clothing voluntarily.

The boy testified that while he was being whipped he pleaded to be allowed to go, and cried and promised "not to do it any more"; that he was struck about forty or fifty times. He was required to work overtime for six days after the whipping, and on the seventh day he found a way to escape and went home. The day after the whipping he wrote his mother asking her to write the defendant to let him come home, but at the bottom of the letter the defendant wrote requesting the mother not to comply. The boy's testimony was somewhat confused and not entirely consistent, but he testified that he had much pain and suffering and that his back still pained him at the time of the trial when the weather was damp. He claimed that he was not well upon the days when he did not work. Five or six days after his return home he was examined by two physicians, who testified in substance that there were stripes on his back reaching down to the middle of the thighs; that there were several crusts where abrasions were in the process of healing and scabs on numerous parts of the body; that there were marked swellings and discoloration of the right lumbar region. One of the physicians testified that there were a good many stripes on the back, possibly twenty; there were five other witnesses, mostly members of the plaintiff's family, who gave testimony as to the bruises and contusions and scabs which they found when the boy returned home from the defendant's farm.

The defendant testified that it was brought to his notice that the plaintiff had failed to work as required and had lied upon several occasions; that he claimed the authority to punish the plaintiff by virtue of the card signed by the mother; that he used the whip in question because he expected to find a strap which was missing and the whip was the only thing con-

venient; that he did not count the strokes, but they could not have exceeded ten; giving the boy ten lashes he thought was punishment enough of that kind; that in inflicting the blows there was not more than a three-foot swing. He swore that he inflicted only light punishment; that he struck the lad only with the idea of punishing him for his disobedience and untruthfulness; that the boy proceeded to play with a dog in the yard as soon as he was dismissed from the office; that he showed no marks such as were testified to by the plaintiff's witnesses, and that he slept normally after this whipping.

During the summer of 1924 the defendant had with him between ninety and one hundred boys, who were required to work from 8 to 11:30 and from 1 to 4 o'clock. There were two large farms on which there were many kinds of work to be done. The defendant was an officer of the juvenile court of Milwaukee county, serving without pay, and there was testimony to the effect that the institution is maintained as a charitable one from which no profit is made; on the contrary, it is operated at a loss. Many of the boys were delinquent and sent there by court orders; others, including the plaintiff, were sent there by their parents. In the evening recreation of various kinds was furnished.

The defendant produced one witness, a minister, who examined the plaintiff's back on or about the 9th of August and said that he saw no marks or scars. Three physicians were called by the defendant. One testified that he examined the plaintiff about September 20th, and "at that time Dr. Corcoran called to my attention two or three brown spots which I had noticed over the right hip. Aside from that I could find nothing." Dr. Corcoran, one of the physicians called by the plaintiff, testified that at that time the marks had somewhat disappeared, but that marks were then present although they did not look nearly as bad as on his former examination. The two other physicians called for the defendant testified that on

May 27, 1925, and May 28, 1925, they examined the plaintiff and found no evidence of trouble.

.   .   .   .   .

It may be said to be the general rule that one standing *in loco parentis* has the right to punish a child under his care if the punishment is moderate and reasonable and for the welfare of the child. Necessarily, the propriety of inflicting corporal punishment to a considerable extent rests in the discretion of the person holding such relation. But whether the correction is reasonable and proper or whether it is immoderate or excessive does not rest absolutely in the discretion of the teacher or other person inflicting the punishment. It is a matter for judicial investigation. It is not to be assumed that although a teacher or the defendant in this case stands in the relation of a parent he has the same right to inflict punishment as a parent.

.   .   .   .   .

In determining whether the punishment has been excessive, the conduct of the child, the nature of his misconduct, the nature of the whip or instrument used for punishment, the kind of marks or wounds left on the body, are all subjects to be considered . . .

It is argued by counsel for respondent that there was ample testimony to sustain the verdict and that the plaintiff sustained only nominal damages. It is true there is some conflict in the testimony and it becomes necessary to consider the nature of that conflict. There was a large mass of testimony, part of it by disinterested witnesses, showing a condition of the boy's body one week after the assault which could only have resulted from severe blows. That evidence is undisputed except by the statement of the defendant that he inflicted only a light punishment . . .

We see no reason to doubt the truthfulness of the two experts called by the plaintiff who testified to the condition of the boy's person about one week after the assault. Their testimony and that of other witnesses called by the plaintiff is corroborated by the nature of the lash which was used. It was one bought by the defendant in South America and it does not appear for what general purpose it was used. It was described by the defendant as follows: "The whip was made out of not very well refined rubber and was twisted. The whip was about two feet six or eight inches in length. There was a ring made of the rubber itself at the end of it. The whip varies from about one and one-fourth inch down to about one-fourth of an inch." It is one of the exhibits in the case. Being twisted and rather heavy, it has great possibilities when applied to the bare flesh.

The only misconduct of the boy which was objected to was that he had not worked as directed and that he had lied. Those things deserve correction, but they were not unpardonable sins, nor did they call for such a lashing as left marks, which, according to the almost undisputed testimony, were found on the boy on his return to his home. The jury found the defendant guilty of assault, and we do not see how on the testimony they could avoid so finding. It follows that under the instructions given by the court the jury must have believed that the punishment was excessive, but they measured the excess by the sum of one dollar, although they were given the usual instruction that if they found for the plaintiff they should assess such compensatory damages as they found from the preponderance of the evidence to a reasonable certainty would be required to reasonably compensate the plaintiff for his mental and physical suffering . . .

We are convinced that in this case the jury disregarded both the strongly preponderating and almost undisputed testimony given for the plaintiff on the question of damages and the instruction of the court. We cannot understand how on finding the assault they arrived at their verdict, except as an improper compromise. We appreciate the weight to be given to the finding of a jury on the question of damages, especially when it is approved by the trial judge. We have considered the argument of counsel that in carrying on his farms in the manner he did the defendant was doing a laudable work. But we cannot sanction the view that in this generation it is permissible for a teacher or other person *in loco parentis,* for such misconduct as was proven in this instance, to inflict such blows as were given in this case with such a whip as was used, on the bare body of a child. The verdict of the jury may not have been perverse in the sense that they acted dishonestly or from improper motives. Such action is not an indispensable element in perversity.

.   .   .   .   .

We consider that the jury disregarded the instructions of the court, that the award of damages was grossly inadequate and therefore perverse within the meaning of the decisions, and that the verdict should have been set aside and a new trial granted.

.   .   .   .   .

By the Court. — Judgment reversed, and the cause remanded with directions that a new trial be ordered.

Support

1. The responsibility of a divorced father for the support of his child, Ohio, 1887

Pretzinger *v.* Pretzinger, 45 Ohio St. Rpts. 452.

Izora Pretzinger was divorced from her husband, by reason of his misconduct, and his ill-treatment and neglect of her; and was, in consequence, awarded the custody, nurture, education and care of their minor child, then about eight years of age. The court decreed an allowance to her as alimony, but it does not appear that any allowance was made to compensate her for the expense of her son's maintenance. For several years after the granting of the divorce, she furnished to her son such boarding, clothing, care and attention, as were necessary and appropriate to his comfort and condition in life. When the divorce was granted the father was insolvent, but at the rendition of the judgment in the case at bar, he was solvent and able to support his son.

The duty of the father to provide reasonably for the maintenance of his minor children, if he be of ability, is a principle of natural law. . . . This natural duty is not to be evaded by the husband's so conducting himself, as to render it necessary to dissolve the bonds of matrimony, and give to the mother the custody and care of the infant offspring. It is not the policy of the law to deprive children of their rights on account of the dissensions of their parents, to which they are not parties; or to enable the father to convert his own misconduct into a shield against parental liability. The divorce may deprive him of the custody and services of his children, and of the rights of guardianship against his will; but if by the judgment of the court, and upon competent and sufficient evidence he is found to be an unfit person to exercise parental control, while the mother is in all respects the proper person to be clothed with such authority, he cannot justly complain.

The alimony allowed by the court below is not to be construed into an allowance for the support, also, of the child. Alimony, in its proper signification, is not maintenance to the children, but to the wife; and the fact that there has been a judgment of divorce, with alimony and custody of minor children to the wife, will not of itself operate as a bar to a subsequent claim against the husband for the children's maintenance.

We think it is a sound principle that, if a man abandons his wife and infant children, or forces them from home by severe usage, he becomes liable to the public for their necessaries. . . .

If a minor is forced out into the world by

the cruelty or improper conduct of the parent, and is in want of necessaries, such necessaries may be supplied, and the value thereof collected of the parent, on an implied contract. . . .

There is evidently no satisfactory reason for changing the rule of liability, when, through ill-treatment, or other breach of marital obligation, the husband renders it necessary for a court of justice to divorce the wife, and commit to her the custody of her minor children. If, under such circumstances, upon the allowance of alimony with custody of children, the court omits to make an order for the children's maintenance, the father's natural obligation to support them is of none the less force.

.   .   .   .   .

It is urged that the father is released from obligation to maintain his infant children, when deprived of their society and services against his will. But if voluntary misconduct on his own part leads to the deprivation, he is himself responsible, and not the court which intervenes for the protection of his children. And if the father, as against a stranger, cannot escape liability for necessaries furnished to his minor children, though remaining with their mother after the divorce, the mother will not be barred of an action against her former husband, for the expense of maintaining the children. After a dissolution of the marriage relation by divorce, the parties are henceforth single persons, to all intents and purposes. All marital duties and obligations to each other are at an end, and they become as strangers to each other. Upon the establishment of such new relations, a promise may be implied, on the part of the father, to pay the mother, as well as a third person, who has supplied the necessary wants of his infant child.

---

2. The obligation to support is a duty owed to the public as well as to the child, Iowa, 1890

Porter *v*. Powell, 79 Ia 151, 44 NW 295 (1890)

The circumstances disclosed in this case are these: The defendant's daughter, at the age of 14, went to reside away from her father's house, at a place 30 miles distant, where for three years she contracted for, earned, and controlled her own wages, and provided herself with clothing, her father consenting thereto; he not furnishing, or agreeing to furnish, her with any money, or means of support. That, while thus absent, she was dangerously attacked with typhoid fever, and at her request was attended by the plaintiff, as her physician, from day to day, for a period of 21 days, which services were rendered without the procurement, knowledge, or consent of the defendant. . . . The circumstances disclosed in this case are such as are of frequent occurrence in this country. Parents, either from necessity or from a desire to teach their children to be industrious and self-supporting, emancipate them from service, for a definite or indefinite time, without any intention of thereby releasing their right to exercise care, custody, and control over the child. The obligation of parents to support their minor children does not arise alone out of the duty of the child to serve. If so, those who are unable to render service because of infancy, sickness, or accident — who, most of all others, need support — would not be entitled to it. . . . This obligation to support is not grounded on the duty of the child to serve, but rather upon the inability of the child to care for itself. It is not only a duty to the child, but to the public. The duties extend only to the furnishing of necessaries. What are necessaries must be determined by the facts in each case. The law has fixed the age of majority; and it is until that age is attained that the law presumes the child incapable of taking care of itself, and has conferred upon the parent the right to care, custody, control, and services, with the duty to support.

.   .   .   .   .

The father had a right at any time to require the daughter to return to his home and service; and she had a right at any time to return to his service, and to claim his care, custody, control, and support. There was no such an emancipation as exempted the father from liability for actual necessaries furnished to his daughter. In view of the legal as well as the moral duty of appellant to furnish necessary support to his daughter during minority, and especially when unable, from infancy, disease, or accident, to earn her own necessary support, we think he may well be understood as promising payment to any third person for actual necessaries furnished to her. As already stated, what are necessaries must be determined from the facts of each case. What would be necessary support to a child in sickness would not be necessary in health. The services sued for were evidently necessary for the support and well-being of the defendant's daughter. As we have seen, he had not relieved himself from the duty to furnish her such support, and, from his obligation to do so, may be presumed to have promised payment to any one who did furnish it in his absence. Our conclusion is that the judgment of the district court should be affirmed.

---

3. Support of children after divorce, Oregon, 1918

State *v.* Langford, 90 Ore. 251, 176 Pac. 197 (1918)

Cases concerning the support of children after divorce of the parents may be divided into three classes: (1) Where the decree is silent as to both the custody and the maintenance of the child; (2) where the decree provides for the custody of the child but is silent as to its maintenance; and (3) where the decree not only provides for the custody but also requires the payment of money for the maintenance of the child. In the first class of cases, the general rule is that the obligation of the father is, after divorce, exactly the same as it was before dissolution of the marriage contract . . . In the second class of cases, there is a difference of judicial opinion. One line of authorities proceeds upon the theory that the duty of the father to support the child and the obligation of the latter to serve the former present reciprocal rights and duties, and that therefore to award the custody of the child to the mother is to deprive the father of the child's services, and hence the loss of the right to the services of the child operates as a release from the duty to support; but a majority of the well-considered precedents denounce and condemn this cold and illogical doctrine, which not only ignores the rights and welfare of the child, but also enables an unfaithful husband and unnatural father to compel his wife to divorce him, on account of grievous wrongs done by him, with the assurance given to him in advance that when she does divorce him she will not have lost the maternal instinct, but will cling to the child, and thus enable him further to wrong her by cowardly casting his burden upon her; for the great weight of judicial authority is to the effect that a father is not released from his obligation to support his child by reason of the fact that the mother has secured a divorce and been awarded the custody of the child by a decree which makes no provision for the child's maintenance.

B. THE CUSTODY OF CHILDREN

Establishment of equal custody rights for parents

1. Constitution of Kansas gives women equal rights of custody, 1859

Constitution of the State of Kansas Adopted 1859, (n.p., n.d.), Article 15, Sec. 6, p. 25.

Rights of Women — The legislature shall provide for the protection of the rights of women, in acquiring and possessing property, real, personal and mixed, separate and apart from the husband; and shall also provide for their equal rights in the possession of their children.

2. Equal custody by statute, Oregon, 1880

"An Act to Establish and Protect the Rights of Married Women," *The Laws of Oregon Passed at the Eleventh Regular Session of the Legislative Assembly 1880* (Salem, 1880), p. 7.

Rights of parents equal in control of children. — Henceforth the rights and responsibilities of the parents, in the absence of misconduct, shall be equal, and the mother shall be as fully entitled to the custody and control of the children and their earnings as the father, and in case of the father's death, the mother shall come into as full and complete control of the children and their estate as the father does in case of the mother's death.

3. The age of the child may determine custody, New York, 1905

People *ex rel.* Sinclair *v.* Sinclair, 95 N.Y. Supp. 861.

In this suit the father of a boy regained custody when the child reached the age of five.

At the time when the order, thus affirmed by the Appellate Division, was made, the child, a boy, was three years of age. He is now five years of age, and the respondent moves for an order giving him the custody. So far as the rights and merits of the controversy, which has resulted in the unfortunate estrangement of this husband and wife, are concerned, the situation is the same in all its essential details as it was when the order was originally made giving the custody of the child to the wife; but the sole ground upon which this order was affirmed was that, in view of the tender age of the child, its welfare required that it should receive its mother's care, and that, so far, the paramount right of the father should give way.

While affidavits have been submitted, to some length, by both parties upon the present application, there is no substantial ground for a conclusion that this husband and wife are not equally fit custodians of this child, so far as the matter depends upon their personal qualities, their moral standing, and their ability, financially, to accord to the child all that its welfare would require. The separation has been due to the fact that these parties have been unable to agree in their domestic relations. Whether they will be able to come to better accord in the future is a matter which it is not within the power of the court to forecast, but, treating the matter as it is presented, in view of the existing separation, the age of the child, and the relative fitness of the parents as its custodians, I must hold that the father, by reason of his paramount right in law, is entitled to the custody of the child at this time. A boy of three years of age may properly be deemed to be of such tender age that considerations of his welfare call for his having a mother's care, but the same cannot be said when the child has reached the age of five. The Domestic Relations Law not having effected any substantial change in the husband's paramount right, founded upon his primary duty to support the family, the case of *People ex rel. Barry* v. *Mercein* . . . is an authority directly in point. In that case the court held that the father was entitled to the custody of his child when the child had reached the age of five years, the custody having theretofore been awarded to the mother by reason of the tender age of the child. Other things being equal, I find no escape from the conclusion that the respondent's claim to the possession of this child at its present age must control. If the question of the child's tender years, as bearing upon the necessity of his having a mother's personal care, is not eliminated at the age of five years, it is difficult to see how it would be eliminated at the age of ten years, and I conclude, therefore, that the "changed conditions and lapse of time," referred to by the Appellate Division as affording the respondent the right to interpose for the assertion of his claim to the possession of the child, are sufficiently present to justify the granting of the relief sought.

Motion granted.

---

4. The equal custody rights of parents, Pennsylvania, 1925

Laws of the General Assembly of the Commonwealth of Pennsylvania Passed in 1925 (Harrisburg, 1925), pp. 638–639.

Hereafter a married woman, who is the mother of a minor child (and who contributes by the fruits of her own labor or otherwise toward the support, maintenance and education of her said minor child), shall have the same and equal power, control and authority over her said child and shall have the same and equal right to its custody and services and earnings as is now by law possessed by her husband, who is the father of such minor child: Provided, however, That the mother of such minor child is otherwise qualified as a fit and proper person to have the control and custody of said child. If either the father or the mother desert their child or fail to perform their parental duties the right to the custody, services, and earnings of the child shall belong to the other: Provided, however, That such remaining parent is otherwise qualified as a fit and proper person to have the control and custody of said child. The father and mother shall have a joint right of action for injuries to their minor child, for the loss of its services and expenses incidental thereto, and either the father or mother shall have the right to sue therefor in the name of both. In case the father and mother live apart the action shall be maintained by the parent having the custody of the child and the control of its services.

The child's welfare as the ruling principle in custody disputes

---

1. A mother temporarily denied custody in the interest of the child's welfare, Pennsylvania, 1872

Commonwealth *ex rel.* Goerlitz *v.* Barney, 4 Brewster 408.

A mother's suit for a writ of *habeas corpus* to remove her daughter from the custody of the child's grandmother and restore her to the mother was denied in this decision by the Pennsylvania Court of Common Pleas for the Eleventh Judicial District.

This case, . . . exhibits a daughter in novel antagonism to her mother, the former claiming her own child by virtue of a natural right, the latter withholding it, and basing her claim to its custody, first, on natural love and affection, intensified necessarily by reason of the care and tenderness bestowed by her upon it from its very infancy; further, that the child was the gift of a dying father; and lastly, that the ability of the mother, pecuniary as well as mental, is not such at present as the best interests of the child require.

These natural, but unfortunately conflicting claims, raise an important question, which it becomes our duty to determine. That question is, shall the mother or the grandmother have the custody of the child?

.   .   .   .   .   .

At the time of the marriage of Andrew Goerlitz, now deceased, with the relator, they appear to have been in indigent circumstances. For some months immediately ensuing thereafter they lived at the board of the respondent in Hanover Township, Luzerne County, and there the child, Marion, was born. During the following year they removed to Wilkes-Barre, but the child remained with the respondent, its grandmother. It has so remained ever since, except on occasions when it has visited its parents and its paternal grandparents.

Prosperity never seems to have been the lot of the father and mother. They returned again to the home of the respondent, and domiciled there for many months. Subsequently, they sought new places of habitation. Other children were born to them, and these shared the parental home wherever it chanced to be. But Marion's home remained unchanged. It was the home of the respondent. Later still, severe and dangerous illness smote the mother, and for a time prostrated her physical and mental energies. We find then the whole family, father, mother, and all the children again around the common fireside, at the house of the respondent, in Hanover Township. Civil war was raging in the land. The father went to the battle-fields. At last his duties as a soldier terminated, and he returned, but not to chase again the flying phantom of prosperity. He came home to sicken and to die. The destitution of his family in that hour constituted the great burden that oppressed him; and if we may believe the testimony of his sisters, that burden was greatly lightened by the affectionate assurances of his mother and their own, that his children should be cared for; and if we may believe also the testimony of the respondent, one of his dying requests was, that Marion, now the innocent cause of this unnatural controversy, should be hers, to be nurtured and reared in the future as she had been in the past. At this time the family resided in Wilkes-Barre, and the child, Marion, was also here. She had come to see her father for the last time. He died. Immediately thereafter the relator, with her two other children, became members of the household of the respondent. Marion did not then accompany them. She had been stricken with that scourge of children, scarlet fever, and remained with the paternal grandparents until her recovery was assured. Her return to the house of the respondent was, alas! too soon, for she bore with her the contagion of the disease from which she had recovered, and gave it fatal root in the persons of her little brothers. A few weeks afterwards, and the relator was not only a widow, but childless, save Marion.

From that time until within a few weeks past, mother and child have lived with the respondent. Marion still remains there, but the mother has sought an abode elsewhere. She asks for the custody of her child, and hence this present proceeding.

We learn from the proofs, that a room in the house of the parents of her deceased husband has been assigned to her upon the express condition that the child, Marion, should be removed out of the custody of the respondent. In this room the relator, though in destitute circumstances, and not yet in fully established health, hopes, by the use of her needle, to support herself and her child. We learn further from the proofs, that the respondent, on the other hand, has the immediate pecuniary ability to maintain the child; that she cares for and watches over it with all that tenderness and solicitude peculiar to a grandmother; that she sends it unremittingly both to the common and to the Sabbath-school; that she governs it well, and instructs it in all things best suited for its present needs.

Besides, the wishes of the child herself, now about seven years of age, are not wholly to be overlooked. With an intelligence little less than remarkable in one so young, she communicates her inclinations, and begs that they be not disregarded. In short, she clings to the respondent, her grandmother.

Unless, therefore, we permit our sympathies for the relator, and our appreciation of the promptings of parental love, to block up the path of official duty, we can discover nothing in this case that would justify a conclusion adverse to the respondent having, for the present at least, the custody, care, and oversight of this child. She is at a home in every way comfortable and proper for her, at which, as the proofs indicate, she is well cared for, well treated, and well and tenderly beloved. There, for the present, I propose she shall remain.

But Mrs. Goerlitz, the mother and relator, must not be denied access to her. She must be permitted at all reasonable times to visit her, and on such occasions to have her to herself and by herself, if she shall so desire. And at the end of one year, or whenever the circumstances of the relator shall become so improved that the best interests of the child will not be prejudiced by removing her into maternal custody, this application may be renewed; and if no sufficient cause be shown to the contrary, the legal right of the mother, before referred to, may not further be overridden.

2. Mother granted custody despite the father's

ability and willingness to care for the children, New Jersey, 1880

English *v.* English, 32 N.J. Eq. 738.

The New Jersey Court of Errors and Appeals stated that the interest of the child was superior to the wishes or rights of either parent in determining its custody.

The appeal is from the chancellor's decree disposing of the custody of two infant children of the parties — Richard W. English, aged about eleven years, and Phebe E. English, aged about nine years. The litigants are husband and wife, and, since November, 1875, have lived separate. The wife, on removing from the domicile of her husband, took with her, to her father's house, both children, and has since resided there, retaining their possession. The appellant, in January, 1879, filed his petition with the chancellor, setting forth the wife's removal from his home without just cause; the taking and detention of the children without his consent and against his will; and prayed allowance of a *habeas corpus* to bring them into court, and the award of their custody to him. It is not alleged that the children are there against their will; that they are not properly cared for; or that the mother is an unsuitable person to be entrusted with their care, except in respect to her dereliction in duty to her husband and home.

The respondent, by her return, admitted their custody, and produced them before the court. She alleges, in justification of her removal, abuse, by the husband, of marital rights, and fear of its repetition, if she returned to him, as her reason for continued separation. She charges him with attempts to regain possession of the children by fraud and force; and that, not through regard for them, but for the purpose of distressing her with fears for their safety, and thereby to coerce her to return to his abode. She alleges that the children are properly cared and provided for by her; that it is their desire and for their welfare to remain with her, and she prays that to her their continued custody may be decreed.

The appellant's answer to the return denies any effort by deception, force or violence to regain possession of the children. He avers that the acts with which he is charged with respect to them, are greatly exaggerated, their true character being mere indiscretions in conduct arising out of uncontrolled affection for his children; or, that they were the result of accident. The answer admits that the children are so young that they require the attentions of the mother, yet he insists that they can be better cared for at his home than where they are.

The chancellor, upon the pleadings and proofs, decreed that the mother retain the custody of both children, and from that decree this appeal is taken.

.   .   .   .   .   .

In considering the grounds which should have weight in deciding controversies of this character, while the rights of parents will not be disregarded or their interests overlooked, the court will not be controlled in its decision by the strict rights of either party, but will determine the question of custody mainly upon considerations of advantage to the infant; the cardinal rule of action governing the court being regard to the benefits of the minor, holding its welfare superior to the claims of either parent.

This is a rule in courts of equity, and was declared and applied in this court, in the case last cited, before the passage of the supplement of 1871 to the act concerning divorces. In this respect, that act introduces no new rule; but it embodies a clear declaration of the legislative approval of that which the court had adopted. Under it, in controversies between parents for the custody of their children, there can exist no restraint upon the mind of the court, arising out of the superior rights of the father at common law, but all legitimate force must be accorded to those considerations which touch the well-being of the child.

.   .   .   .   .   .

The faults thus attributed to these litigants, and urged upon the court by the opposite sides, as elements to be considered in reaching a decision, unfortunate as they are in their results upon their own lives and prospects of future happiness, are not of a nature to affect the moral fitness of either of these parents to have the control of the children. The character of the father, in his other relations, appears to be that of a sober, moral and industrious man, and he has pecuniary ability amply to provide for his children. Nothing is alleged or hinted against the moral character of the mother; it is conceded that she is a suitable person for the trust, and that she has done and is doing everything for the care and comfort of the children that one parent can do. The chancellor adjudged rightly in placing their claims upon an equality; either is suitable for the trust, and the welfare of the children remains the sole criterion for determination.

The true interests of these children unquestionably call for the united care of both their parents, but as in the posture which they have assumed, and still maintain toward each other, this cannot be had, I am of opinion that the chancellor, in deciding to leave them for the present where they are, is as nearly right, under all the circumstances, as it is possible to be. In view of their tender years, a mother's care seems to be necessary to both; this is conceded by the appellant's answer. It is certainly so as to the daughter, and they are receiving the kindest maternal care at her hands. Their reasonable wants are supplied, clothing and food are furnished, and the advantages of good schools afforded them.

That the children desire to remain with the mother, although not an infallible test of what will best conduce to their true happiness, is, nevertheless, a circumstance entitled to the court's consideration. I also think it is very desirable that these children should be kept together in personal association, until other and more important considerations shall render a separation necessary. It is neither shown in the case, nor averred, that any influence is exerted over these children by the mother, or others about them, to prejudice their minds against their father. The fear that this may be so, introduces one of the most troublesome elements in this case. One of the objects of the law is to foster and encourage mutual affection between parent and child. An important purpose of education is to train children to the cultivation of filial affection and confidence, and, until it otherwise appears, we must rely upon the good sense and justice of the respondent, that she will not, in this respect, abuse the trust reposed in her, or permit those in whose society these children are, by act or word, to alienate their affections from their father.

The decree settles the present status only of these children, and it invites the father to seek such terms of access to them as may be reasonable in the judgment of the chancellor. Of these he may avail himself if he desires to visit them. Were the son of an age and condition of health to enter upon a course of business training, I should have regarded it as promotive of his interests to be placed under the charge of his father. He is, however, of delicate constitution, and too young, as I think, to have his mind so directed now; yet, the time must soon come when the interests of the son will require that he have the aid and guiding hand of some proper person in fitting him for and directing him in a suitable business pursuit; and this duty no one can so well perform as a father who has experience and possesses, or is worthy of, the affection and confidence of his child. This father, by his own business success, has given the best evidence of his ability and qualification for the discharge of this duty. This office belongs to him as a right as well as a duty. He has done nothing, that I can perceive, to forfeit his right to such control, and when the son arrives at a proper age, if this unfortunate separation continues, it will be difficult, upon any reason that now appears, to offer effectual resistance to his just demand to resume the sole custody of the son. No one can be a safer guide in this respect than a prudent father; no one is likely to feel a stronger interest in the future of

his boy than he; and this father would be unnatural in his feelings and affections, to a degree not proved by anything in this case, if he did not fully equal all others in the desire for the success and prosperity in life of this his only son. For the present, however, I think the children should remain with the mother, and I shall vote to affirm.

---

3. A court of chancery may deny custody to both parents, Kansas, 1881

In re Bort, 25 Kan. 308.

This is a proceeding in *habeas corpus,* brought by Frank B. Bort, the father of Edith M. Bort and Fred Bort, against Medora E. Bort, the mother, for the possession of these children. At the time of the commencement of this proceeding the children lacked a few weeks of being, respectively, four and five years old. The parents were divorced by a decree of the circuit court of Sauk county, Wisconsin, on January 26, 1881.

. . . . .

We understand the law to be, when the custody of children is the question, that the best interest of the children is the paramount fact. Rights of father and mother sink into insignificance before that. Even when father and mother are living together, a court has the power, if the best interests of the child require it, to take it away from both parents and commit the custody to a third person. In other words, a court of chancery stands as a guardian of all children, and may interfere at any time and in any way to protect and advance their welfare and interests . . .

The petitioner is a traveling salesman, away from home a large part of his time. While away, the children would necessarily have to be under the care of his mother — a woman past middle age — or such hired help as he might secure.

On the other hand, Mrs. Bort is now living with her parents, Mr. and Mrs. D. W. Powers, reputable citizens of Leavenworth. They have an elegant home a few miles from the city, and have expressed their desire to have the care and custody of their little grandchildren. Besides these, an unmarried sister and a brother of Mrs. Bort constitute the household. All seem to have the warmest affection for these children. We see no reason to doubt that Mrs. Bort is a loving mother, devoted and faithful to her little ones. Her conduct since she left her husband, and since the divorce, seems to have been without reproach. Whatever may be her faults, it is evident that these children will receive only the kindest care if left in their present home. They are of that tender age when they need a mother's care. No stranger, however kind, can fill her place. We may not ignore these universal laws of our nature, and they compel us to place these children where they will be within the reach of a mother's love and care. At the same time, it would be unjust to have the minds of these children poisoned against their father. He is industrious, energetic, a good salesman, traveling for a reputable house in Chicago, a house which appreciates and has confidence in him. He has a father's love for these little ones, and desires their best welfare. He would not have them alienated from him, and they ought not to be. Without discussing the situation further, the order which will be made is as follows:

The children will be committed to the care and custody of Mrs. Powers, their grandmother, upon her giving a bond to the state of Kansas in the sum of three thousand dollars, with two sufficient sureties, to be approved by the clerk of this court, conditioned that she will keep the children within the jurisdiction of this court, and will produce them in court whenever so required.

Whenever the father desires, he shall, upon giving twenty-four hours notice to Mrs. Powers, be permitted to visit his children at the house of Mrs. Powers, going there alone to be with them there alone; he must be received without insult or injury . . .

4. A father's plea for custody denied, Kansas, 1881

Chapsky v. Wood et al., 26 Kan. 650.

This decision, written by Justice David Josiah Brewer of the Kansas Supreme Court, was frequently cited in later custody cases.

In questions of this kind three interests should be considered: The right of the father must be considered. The right of the one who has filled the parental place for years should be considered. Perhaps it may not be technically correct to speak of that as a right; and yet, they who have for years filled the place of the parent, have discharged all the obligations of care and support, and especially when they have discharged these duties during those years of infancy when the burden is especially heavy, when the labor and care are of a kind whose value cannot be expressed in money — when all these labors have been performed and the child has bloomed into a bright and happy girlhood, it is but fair and proper that their previous faithfulness, and the interest and affection which these labors have created in them, should be respected. Above all things, the paramount consideration is, What will promote the welfare of the child? These, I think, are about all the rules of law applicable to a case of this kind.

Now, passing to the facts, which I shall only outline: Morris A. Chapsky married the mother of this child ten years ago. The marriage was not acceptable to his parents, though for no reason that we are advised of, involving the character of any of the parties. Returning home immediately after his marriage, the father, commenting upon the fact of the marriage, which had been made without his consent, was not satisfied, and bade him start out for himself. . . . He started out . . . and wandered around, as a young man is apt to do, and drifting from place to place, finally came penniless to Kansas City. He struggled for a series of years under pecuniary embarrassment; and during these years this child was born. His wife's health was delicate, and she was obviously unable to discharge ordinary household duties, even without the care of this child; and the respondent, Mrs. Wood, her sister, kindly provided for her during her confinement, and took care of the child. The child was left with her (Mrs. Wood) and from that day to this, a period of about five and one-half years, has been all the time in her custody. During the very early infancy of the child, the question arose as to her custody — Mrs. Wood insisting that the mother should take the child, or that it should be given to her. It is clear that this matter of discussion between the parties lasted for some time, and we are satisfied from the testimony that in fact a gift was made of the child by both mother and father, to Mrs. Wood. The mother's letters exhibit this; and, while the father does not recollect of having made such gift, we are convinced that he did so, and by parol agreement relinquished to the respondents his parental rights. No writing passed between them; but, regarding as we do that a gift is not decisive in the case, unless made in accordance with the statutory form, the want of a writing cuts no figure now. The child was given to Mrs. Wood, and has been in her care for five years and a half — from the date of its birth to the present day. What the future of the child will be is a question of probability. No one is wise enough to forecast, or determine absolutely, what or what would not be best for it; yet we have to act upon these probabilities from the testimony before us, guided by the ordinary laws of human experience. Involved in the question as to what will promote the welfare of the child, are questions of wealth, questions of social position, of health, questions of educational advantages, moral training — of all things, in short, which will tend to develop a little girl into a perfect woman.

And, first, we remark that the child has had, and enjoys today, good advantages, and its welfare has been promoted, and is promoted today. No one has said that this child has lacked anything which a child should have, and the testimony all shows that it has been cared for most patiently and faithfully — as well as it could have been cared for by any one; and to that care the face and appearance of the child abundantly testify. This fact does not rest on probabilities. It is a serious question, always to be considered, whether a change should be advised. "Let well enough alone," is an axiom founded on abundant experience. There is nothing in the present situation of the respondents, their pecuniary condition, the business capacity of the husband, their social position, their affection for this child — absolutely nothing which tends in any way to suggest that the welfare of the child, which has been promoted in the past, would be limited or abridged in the future. What they have done for the child tends to show what they will do through the future years of its girlhood. What that has been is certainly as much, and I think more, than the average child receives.

Again, while there is more wealth on the side of the father, and pecuniary advantages are held out for her future — greater than those, perhaps, which the respondents can present — yet we cannot be insensible to the surroundings under which the child would be placed if committed to its father. The grandfather has been on the stand before us, and not merely from the testimony adduced from his relatives and neighbors, but from his appearance and manner on the stand, evidently he is a gentleman of character and responsibility, not destitute of affection, and one who has provided a comfortable home and is in a position to give to the child all these advantages. Yet the child, if it goes, goes to the care of its father; and while there is no testimony showing that the father is what might be called an unfit person, that his life has not been a moral one, yet we can but think it is developed, both by testimony and his manner and appearance on the stand, that there is a coldness, a lack of energy, and a shiftlessness of disposition, which would not make his personal guardianship of the child the most likely to ripen and develop her character fully. He seems to us like a man still and cold, and a warm-hearted child would shrink and wither under care of such a nature, rather than ripen and develop. These are facts that we can but notice, and they have in them no imputation against the father of an unkind nature or immoral life; but the facts as they impress us are, that the child would not really grow to its fullest promise under the care of such a man.

Again, and lastly, the child has had, and has today, all that a mother's love and care can give. The affection which a mother may have and does have, springing from the fact that a child is her offspring, is an affection which perhaps no other one can really possess; but, so far as it is possible, springing from years of patient care of a little, helpless babe, from association, and as an outgrowth from those little cares and motherly attentions bestowed upon it, an affection for the child is seen in Mrs. Wood that can be found nowhere else. And it is apparent, that so far as a mother's love can be equaled, its foster-mother has that love, and will continue to have it.

On the other hand, if she goes to the house of her father's family, the female inmates are an aunt, just ripening into womanhood, and a grandmother; they have never seen the child; they have no affection for it springing from years of companionship. While she is a child of perhaps a favorite son or brother, she is also the child of a disowned or repudiated daughter-in-law and sister-in-law, and the appeal which the child will make naturally — and the child is one to make a strong appeal to any one — will always be shadowed and clouded by the fact that she comes from one who was not a favorite in that family.

Human impulses are such that doubtless they would form an affection for the child — it is hardly possible to believe otherwise; but to that deep, strong, patient love which springs from either motherhood, or from a patient care during years of helpless babyhood, they will be strangers.

5. Mother who is properly supporting and caring for her children allowed to retain custody despite husband's low social status, Virginia, 1911

Moon et al. *v.* Children's Home Society of Virginia, 72 SE Rep. 707.

In 1901 the Virginia legislature passed a law authorizing the Children's Home Society to take custody of any child under fourteen who was growing up without education or in circumstances conducive to vice. The Society attempted to remove two girls from the home of their mother and stepfather because the latter was of partial Negro ancestry.

The question involved in the case is whether or not, upon the facts before the court, the act authorized it to deprive the mother of the custody of her children.

The evidence as certified by the court and the reason upon which it based its action are as follows:

"Be it remembered that on the trial of this cause the following facts were proven:

"That Lucy Moon, whose maiden name was Lucy May, and who was a granddaughter of George Christopher Gilmer, one of the most prominent citizens of this county, was prior to her marriage to John Moon the widow of one I. B. Grasty, by whom she had two children, the infant defendants, Madeline, being now 12 years of age, and Ruby, 10 years of age; that Mr. Grasty, the former husband of Lucy Moon, died leaving her in destitute circumstances; that she, with her two infant children, was offered a home with her brother, Lee May, who married one Bessie Moon, the sister of her present husband, John Moon; that she continued to live with her brother, and was given no assistance from her parents or husband's people; that, although both she and her husband were residents of this county, they went to Washington, D.C., and were married; that since her marriage to her present husband, John Moon, he has comfortably provided for her and her two children by her former husband; that these two infant defendants are not neglected as far as physical comforts are concerned, and no drunkenness or vice of their adults was proven. It was proven, however, that John Moon has negro blood in his veins; that his mother, Margaret Moon, of whom he is the illegitimate son, has according to her statement one-eighth of colored blood in her veins. The said Margaret Moon appearing upon the witness stand, it was plainly apparent to the court and to counsel and to spectators that she would pass anywhere as a mulatto woman . . .

"It was proven further that Madeline and Ruby Grasty were properly clothed and physically well taken care of; that they had been sent to a public school, but after their mother's marriage with John Moon they left the public school; that since her marriage with the said John Moon the mother applied for the admission of the children at the Miller Manual Labor School in Albemarle county, and in the statement filed with the application for their admission into the school, which is a part of the defense in this case and will be filed with the record, she stated that these children were the children of her husband, the said I. B. Grasty; that after the children had been at school some time she made repeated efforts to get them away from the school, and on being refused finally made an application for their withdrawal in writing, in which she certified that they were not the children of Grasty, but the children of the said John Moon, although they had been born, one during the lifetime of Grasty, and one but a short time after his death; that the children were thereupon surrendered to her by the school — children with colored blood in their veins not being allowed to enter the school and even with the suspicion of such blood their condition would be unendurable at the school; that these two infant children had not been cruelly treated and were controlled and looked after; that there were no dissolute characters permitted at the house of John Moon, nor was

there any drinking or improper conduct there; that the said John Moon was not a man of means, but had a farm and comfortable home, and was able and willing to care for the two infant defendants; that the said children had never attended the public school since their return from the Miller school, but were taught by their mother or some of the Moon connection.

.   .   .   .   .

"After the above facts were proven, the court entered an order giving the custody of the infant defendants to the Children's Home Society of Virginia, stating that it did so because their mother had married a person with colored blood, who was only recognized as a colored man, and that the associations of these children, who were of pure blood and gentle ancestors would be with persons of mixed blood, and that they would be deterred from association with gentle people of white blood."

It is clear from the facts certified that the act of the General Assembly furnished no authority for the action of the court in depriving the mother of the custody and control of her children. The children were not neglected, but were comfortably cared and provided for by their mother and their stepfather. It does not appear that either from neglect or crime, or drunkenness, or other vice of the mother or her husband, the children were growing up without education or salutary control and in circumstances exposing them to a dissolute and vicious life. On the contrary, it appears that dissolute persons were not permitted at their home, and neither drinking nor improper conduct were allowed there. It further appears that, while the children had not gone to the public schools since their return from the Miller school, they were taught by their mother or some of the Moon connection.

The act of assembly furnishes no authority for depriving a mother of the care and custody of her children merely because she has married into a family lower in the social scale than that in which she was reared, even though her husband has negro blood in his veins, unless he has one-fourth or more of such blood and is therefore a "colored person," within the meaning of section 49 of the Code, and prohibited under our laws from intermarrying with a white woman . . . It is not pretended in this case that the stepfather was a colored person within the meaning of our statute, or that he and the mother of the children were guilty of any crime in intermarrying, or were not persons of good character.

The mother, the father of the children being dead, however poor and humble she may be,

being of good moral character and able alone, or with the assistance of their stepfather (also of good moral character), to properly support and care for her children, and who is so supporting and caring for them, cannot be deprived of that privilege by the defendant in error under the provisions of its charter.

We are of opinion, therefore, to reverse the order of the circuit court, and enter such order as it ought to have entered, dismissing the proceeding commenced before the justice of the peace, and restoring the said children to the custody of their mother, the plaintiff in error.

Reversed.

C. ADOPTION

Adoption through statutory requirements and by deed

In 1851 Massachusetts enacted the first state law regulating adoption.[1] During the second half of the nineteenth century most northern and western states passed adoption laws similar to that of Massachusetts. Adoption by deed persisted in the South and in a few northern states such as Pennsylvania and Iowa.

---

1. The New York state adoption law, 1873

"An Act to legalize the Adoption of Minor children by adult persons," 1873 — ch. 830, *Laws of the State of New York Passed at the Ninety-Sixth Session of the Legislature* (Albany, 1873), pp. 1243–1245.

---

1. See *Children and Youth in America*, Vol. I, pp. 369–370.

Section 1. Adoption, as provided for in this act, is the legal act whereby an adult person takes a minor into the relation of child, and thereby acquires the rights and incurs the responsibilities of parent in respect to such minor.

Sec. 2. Any minor child may be adopted by any adult, in the cases and subject to the rules prescribed in this act.

Sec. 3. A married man, not lawfully separated from his wife, cannot adopt a child without the consent of his wife; and a married woman, not lawfully separated from her husband, cannot adopt a child without the consent of her husband.

Sec. 4. The consent of a child, if over the age of twelve years, is necessary to its adoption.

Sec. 5. Except in the cases provided for in the next section, a legitimate child cannot be adopted without the consent of its parents, if living, or the survivor, if one is dead; nor an illegitimate child without the consent of its mother, if she is living.

Sec. 6. The consent provided for by the last section is not necessary from a father or mother deprived of civil rights, or adjudged guilty of adultery or cruelty, and who is, for either cause, divorced; or is adjudged to be an insane person or an habitual drunkard, or is judicially deprived of the custody of the child on account of cruelty or neglect.

Sec. 7. When the child to be adopted has neither father nor mother living, or whose consent, if living, is made unnecessary by the provisions of the last section, such consent must be given by an adult person having the lawful custody of the child.

Sec. 8. The person adopting a child, and the child adopted, and the other persons whose consent is necessary, shall appear before the county judge of the county in which the person adopting resides, and the necessary consent shall thereupon be signed, and an agreement be executed by the person adopting, to the effect that the child shall be adopted and treated, in all respects, as his own lawful child should be treated.

Sec. 9. The judge shall examine all persons appearing before him pursuant to the last section, each separately, and, if satisfied that the moral and temporal interests of the child will be promoted by the adoption, he shall make an order in which shall be set forth, at length, the reasons for such order, directing that the child shall thenceforth be regarded and treated, in all respects, as the child of the person adopting.

Sec. 10. A child, when adopted, shall take the name of the person adopting, and the two thenceforth shall sustain toward each other the legal relation of parent and child, and have all the rights and be subject to all the duties of that relation, excepting the right of inheritance, except that as respects the passing and limitations over of real and personal property, under and by deeds, conveyances, wills, devises and trusts, said child adopted shall not be deemed to sustain the legal relation of child to the person so adopting.

Sec. 11. Whenever a parent has abandoned or shall abandon an infant child such parent shall be deemed to have forfeited all claim that he or she would otherwise have, as to the custody of said child or otherwise, against any person who has taken, adopted and assumed the maintenance of such child; and in such case the person so adopting, taking and assuming the maintenance of such child may adopt it under the provisions of this act, with the same effect as if the consent of such parents had been obtained. In all cases of abandonment after this act takes effect the person adopting shall proceed under the provisions of this act within six months after he or she has assumed the maintenance of such child; in such case of abandonment, the county judge may make the order provided for in this act without the consent of such parent or parents.

Sec. 12. The parents of an adopted child are, from the time of the adoption, relieved from all parental duties toward, and of all responsibility for, the child so adopted, and have no rights over it.

Sec. 13. Nothing herein contained shall prevent proof of the adoption of any child, heretofore made according to any method practiced in this State, from being received in evidence, nor such adoption from having the effect of an adoption hereunder; but no child shall hereafter be adopted except under the provisions of this act, nor shall any child that has been adopted be deprived of the rights of adoption, except upon a proceeding for that purpose, with the like sanction and consent as is required for an act of adoption under the eighth section hereof; and any agreement and consent in respect to such adoption, or abrogation thereof hereafter to be made, shall be in writing, signed by such county judge or a judge of the supreme court, and the same, or a duplicate thereof, shall be filed with the clerk of the county and recorded in the book of miscellaneous records, wherein the same shall be made, and a copy of the same, certified by such clerk, may be used in evidence in all legal proceedings; but nothing in this act contained in regard to such adopted child inheriting from the person adopting shall apply to any devise or trust now made or already created, nor shall this act in any manner change, alter or interfere with such will, devise, or said trust or trusts, and as to any such will, devise or trust said adopted child shall not be deemed an heir so as to alter estates, or trusts, or devises in wills already made or trusts already created.

---

2. Advertisements for adoption, Chicago, 1919, 1921

Chicago Tribune, dates as indicated.

Personal — Wanted to Adopt Baby girl up to 4 years. Will furnish ideal home and best refs. Address M476, Tribune. [December 4, 1921]

Personal — Wanted — Healthy Twins or Baby girl under 6 months, by couple able to give children wonderful home & future. Address KH 385, Tribune. [December 21, 1919]

Personal — Wanted for adoption by wealthy Chicago couple, infant girl or boy. Address KH 386, Tribune. [December 21, 1919]

Personal — Wanted to Adopt Baby month old, by responsible couple; good home. Address B 599, Tribune. [December 21, 1919]

Personal — Want Home. 7 Year old boy, adoption. Call 2932 Indiana Av., Chicago. [December 28, 1919]

---

3. Observations and recommendations, Children's Code Commission, Pennsylvania, 1925

"Study of the Practices of Adoption in Philadelphia County," in *Report of the Commission Appointed to Study and Revise the Statutes of Pensylvania Relating to Children, Part I* (n.p., 1925), pp. 132–134.

---

(1) It is evident that adoptions which expose young children to neglect and hardship and an adverse and unsuitable home life do actually and will continue to take place if the adoption process continues to be unattended by the exercise of judgment and discretion on the part of those in authority to decree adoptions and if adoption by deed continues to be legally authorized. Without certain legally prescribed measures safeguarding the child's welfare, the exercise of discretion on the part of the individual judges and other officials is and will be of an uncertain nature.

(2) As adoption is now handled in the Common Pleas and the Municipal Courts it seems evident that:

(a) It is possible for perjury to go undetected in an adoption proceeding. There is no requirement in the process which challenges any fairly plausible statement which may be made in the petition.

(b) In a large proportion of the cases the statements of affiants for the character of the adopting people are of no value. The statements themselves are so vague, general and conventionalized as to be meaningless for any practical purposes. The people who make the statements are in the vast majority of the cases unknown to the courts in large communities. Sometimes they are obviously relatives of the adopting people and in other cases they obviously have some material interest in getting the adoption decreed . . . Ordinarily they are not accessible to the court for further questioning about their knowledge of the adopting people. In a large proportion of the cases not even their addresses are a part of their affidavits.

(c) The judge frequently seeing none of the parties at interest, has no basis of judgment other than what appears in the petitions and what is said by the attorney for the adopting people unless he especially asks that the parties be present or calls upon some outside agency, public or private, to assist him. This is infrequently done and then not always attended with satisfactory results . . .

(d) The practice of presenting an adoption petition in open court and of filing it where it is accessible to the general public operates to keep at a minimum the amount of information therein contained.

(3) The process of adoption of minors by deed carries no safeguards for the child and seems to have no possibilities, legal or administrative, for the development of such safeguards.

(4) Adoption by court decree has possibilities of development and should be the one process followed in all adoption proceedings of minors.

(5) The Common Pleas and the Civil Division of the Municipal Courts seem not to be parts of the judicial system best adapted to handling the adoption petitions since they are courts with dockets heavily loaded with business which has little or no relation to the problems presented by adoption.

.   .   .   .   .

(7) The proper safeguarding of adoptions necessitates three kinds of measures. Changes of a fundamental nature should be made in the law itself. There should be a development of uniform rules for court procedure. A simple way of enabling judges to secure a clear and minute understanding, on the one hand of the child, his family and their difficulties, and on the other hand, of the conditions of the home into which the child is to be adopted and the motives of the adopting people must be worked out. In the large communities a person in the employ of the court might combine this with other social service duties connected with the court. In small communities the court could in all probability make a suitable arrangement with some social service agency to secure this service.

Even when all of the undesirable adoptions that can be prevented by laws and rules of court, have been thus eliminated, there will still be a considerable margin of cases in which a discerning judge, after careful examination of all the facts, will hesitate to decree an adoption. People of obviously unsuitable temperaments, homes which labor under handicaps of disgrace, of members with physical and mental afflictions, homes of uncertain income, all present serious problems which can be solved only by having a careful and tactful handling of each case on the basis of complete knowledge of all the outstanding circumstances. Where an adoption could hardly be refused outright on any specifically defined legal basis it could be delayed or the would-be adopting parents could be dissuaded by a judge who helps them to analyze their situation and who has a wealth of experience from which to draw in dealing with them and their perplexities. Judges and investigators connected with the court handling adoptions should know thoroughly both the legal technicalities and the social and personal problems which attach to the adoption process and should give the clients the benefit of their advice.

Careful observation and study of adoptions in which there were serious personal or social problems either in the adopting home or where the adopted child comes from defective or diseased parentage should from the basis of an intelligent handling of the adoption work of the community. It seems hardly necessary to add that such observation and study of the problem would require that those responsible for decreeing adoptions should utilize all the resources of the community for securing medical and social information regarding the parties concerned.

----

4. Case studies of abuse in deed adoption, 1925

"Study of the Practice of Adoption in Philadelphia County," in *Report of the Commission Appointed to Study and Revise the Statutes of Pennsylvania Relating to Children, Part I,* pp. 150–152.

ADVERTISING BABIES

It was impossible to get any accurate idea of the amount of advertising carried on throughout the State both of babies for adoption and of requests for children. A survey made of the files of the Pittsburgh newspapers which specialize in "want ads" showed that during a six months period twenty-five babies were advertised for adoption while in ten cases prospective foster parents were advertising for babies.

It is significant that in many of the striking cases of bad adoptions such as the following, the advertisement of the child figured more or less conspicuously. It would seem that an enactment making it illegal either to secure or to dispose of a baby through the medium of the newspapers would be in line with common sense measures of child protection.

Case V.

In 1918 a case was brought against Mrs. D. for assault and battery and neglect of a foster child. In the testimony it was brought out that for hours she would leave the child locked in a room; would neglect to feed it; that she got into a bad temper very easily and would then swear and beat the child. After investigation the court had the child removed from her home.

In August 1920 Mrs. D. answered an advertisement in a newspaper, offering a child for adoption. On January 23, 1922, after seventeen months in the foster home the child was legally adopted by Mrs. D. and her husband. As usual the affidavits testified that the petitioners were "Persons of good moral character." It is known that Mrs. D. is a prostitute. The three affiants were an alderman of rather dubious character, the real estate man from whom the D.'s rented and the child's grandmother who had advertised it for adoption.

Later the grandmother was much upset when she learned that the court had already taken away one child from the D.'s. Apparently she was in ignorance of the "character and respectability" of the petitioners to which she testified in the affidavit. The natural mother of the child, who has been diagnosed as a high grade defective, is now on the waiting list for Laurelion. She is also siphilitic. The chance of the child's securing the necessary observation and care to overcome, so far as can be, the handicaps of its mental and physical inheritance, is not bright.

NEED FOR INVESTIGATION BEFORE ADOPTIONS ARE DECREED, ESPECIALLY IN CERTAIN CLASSES OF CASES.

If the court had some means of having a thorough investigation made by a trained case worker could such an adoption as the following have occurred?

Case VI.

Margaret, aged fifteen and Ethel, aged thirteen, at the time of their adoption in 1923, came from a home with no moral standards nor were they more fortunate in the foster home into which they were adopted. Their family had long been known to various social agencies because of the flagrant immorality of the mother and the poverty and shiftless character of both parents.

In June 1923 the girls disappeared and the Juvenile Court was asked to find them. They were located by the probation officer the following September four days after their adoption had been consummated. The consent to adoption had been given by the natural mother and the overseers of the poor. The whereabouts of the father was unknown as he had deserted some time before. In the petition, however, it was stated that he was dead and the mother unable to support the two girls. The probation officer made an effort to ascertain whether Mr. and Mrs. Y., who were caring for Margaret and Ethel were fit persons to assume the responsibility of adopting parents. The affidavit in the petition to adopt stated that the adopting parents were "persons of industry, good character, and reputation." They were local representatives of a national "rescue" organization.

In answer to a query addressed by the probation officer to this organization, the national director replied that these persons were worthy and should be encouraged in their work.

A few months later the case came into court

when complaints were brought against both man and wife by the children. From evidence given in court it would appear that the children, unaccustomed to decent living standards, were not shocked by the lewd behavior of their foster parents but were merely resentful of their own forced participation in these orgies.

The man was sent to jail for three years, on being convicted of his crime, but he escaped after serving a sentence of a few months.

The special need of investigation by courts of those adoptions in which there has been no participation by a social agency of recognized standing, seems to be obvious. This point of view is not held, however, in all quarters. A director of the poor stated to the investigator that in his county the adoption cases engineered by the directors of the poor and by the Children's Aid Society and other agencies assured the children adequate protection; but with regard to "private adoptions" as he called those falling in Groups III and IV, "they are nobody's business and any mother has a right to give her child to whom she will without interference from others." The question of the rights of the child to protection and to at least a minimum of education and proper nurture seemed not to occur to him. Is the prevention of such cases as the following outside the interest of the public authorities, and when they fail, outside the legitimate range of interest of a private incorporated agency to promote child welfare?

Case VII.

Frances, aged thirteen, recently made a personal application to a social agency stating that her foster father had been having sexual relations with her for the last two years. Upon investigation living conditions were found to be very bad. The foster mother corroborated the child's statements.

Frances had been legally adopted in May 1918. She was sold to her foster parents by her mother for a quart of whiskey.

The adoption of abandoned children

1. Judicial determination of abandonment, California, 1914

In re Kelly, 25 Cal. App. 651.

As a preliminary to adoption, Mr. and Mrs. Kelly asked the court to declare that Mary Louise Donahoo had been abandoned by her parents.

Among other provisions, section 224 [of the California Civil Code] contains the following: "Any child deserted by both parents or left in the care and custody of another by its parent or parents, without any agreement or provision for its support, for the period of one year, is deemed to be an abandoned child within the meaning of this section . . ." It is claimed and the petition avers that the parents of the minor concerned here left said minor in the care and custody of the petitioners, without having made any agreement or provision for its support, for a period of more than one year.

The salient facts upon which this controversy is to be determined are practically undisputed and may be briefly stated as follows:

The minor involved in this controversy is one of twins — a boy and a girl — born to the contestants, Mr. and Mrs. M. J. Donahoo, on the twenty-second day of January, 1909. The mother of the twins was, after the birth thereof, left in such delicate health that she became apprehensive that she could not properly take care of and maintain both the infants, and the parents, therefore, came to the conclusion that the infants would fare the better by placing one in the custody and under the control of a sister of the father of the children, a Mrs. Emma Swanson, then residing in the city of Sonora. To this end, and some three weeks after the birth of the infants, the father and mother completed arrangements whereby Mrs. Swanson

Bond and Free.

Padrone and Children.

The Work of the Children's Aid Society.

took the custody and assumed the responsibility of caring for and maintaining the girl baby.

Shortly after the infant was given into the custody of Mrs. Swanson, and while yet in such custody, the Donahoos departed for Los Angeles, where they took up their residence.

The infant remained with Mrs. Swanson until the month of June, 1912 — a period of over three years — when the latter was taken so seriously ill as to have suffered mental derangement to a degree which required her removal to and, for a brief period, incarceration in the state hospital for the insane at Stockton.

The petitioners were near neighbors of Mrs. Swanson and so became aware of her illness immediately upon the happening thereof. They gave her much attention and did all that lay within their power to make her as comfortable as she could be made under the circumstances. They took charge of and ministered to the wants and necessities of the baby girl during Mrs. Swanson's illness and prior to her removal to the asylum. They communicated the fact of Mrs. Swanson's illness to the Donahoos, and informed them that she was greatly embarrassed financially. Upon receiving that information the father of the child forwarded to the petitioners, for the use and benefit of Mrs. Swanson, the sum of thirty dollars.

After Mrs. Swanson had been committed and taken to the asylum, the petitioner, William P. Kelly, addressed a letter to the parents of the child in which he declared that he and his wife had become greatly attached to the baby, that they had no children of their own and that they desired to adopt the infant. To that proposition no response was made by the Donahoos, so far as the record discloses.

The petitioners retained custody of the child after Mrs. Swanson was sent to the asylum and for over a year cared for and supported her. During that period a number of letters was written by the Donahoos to the petitioners concerning Mrs. Swanson and the child. In one of said letters the father of the baby explained that he had just suffered the loss of several

hundred dollars through the failure of a concern for which he had been working, but that he was then working for another company and that, "as soon as I get a pay day, I will send you more money, and as often as I do get one." He further stated in said letter that "if anything should happen to sister (referring to Mrs. Swanson) we will arrange about Louise," referring to the baby. The other letters above referred to as having been written to the Kellys by the Donahoos disclose a commendable degree of parental solicitude for the child, and, while they contained no direct statements indicative of an intention on the part of the Donahoos to compensate the petitioners for caring for and supporting the baby, the general tenor of their language does not support the conclusion that the parents intended to abandon or relinquish their right to its custody.

It appears that, a few months after being committed to the asylum, Mrs. Swanson sufficiently recovered her physical and mental health to justify her discharge from that institution, and so, in the month of December, 1912, she left the asylum and went to Fresno, where she remained until July, 1913, when, at the request of the Donahoos, she went to Sonora for the purpose of regaining possession of the child. Mrs. Swanson testified in part as follows. . . .

"I came to Sonora about the 10th day of July for the purpose of getting the litle girl, acting in behalf of Mr. and Mrs. Donahoo. I did not know that any proceedings had been commenced at that time to have the child declared an abandoned child. I was informed of such proceedings by Mr. Kelly after I reached Sonora. From my knowledge of the conditions surrounding Mr. and Mrs. Donahoo in this matter I know neither of the parents had any intention at any time of abandoning the little girl. At one time I tried to get the consent of the father and mother to adopt the little girl, but they refused to consider the matter at all. When I came to Sonora in July, 1913, Mr. Kelly told me that Mr. Donahoo had promised to pay for the care of the child, but that he had failed to keep his promise. I have recollections during lucid moments of my sickness in July, 1912, of Mrs. Kelly telling me that she and her husband would care for the child and that Mr. Donahoo had promised to pay for the care of the child. . . ."

M. J. Donahoo testified that, during the time the child was with his sister, Mrs. Swanson, he paid for its support and maintenance and at times paid for the support of Mrs. Swanson. . . .

Both Mr. and Mrs. Kelly testified that when Mrs. Swanson was taken ill, as above explained, they found that the child had been very much neglected; that she was weak and emaciated for want of sufficient food; that she was without proper raiment and unclean of body. They declared that they had never been remunerated by her parents for the care and support they had given the child for a period of over one year, and that no provision had been at any time made by the parents for the child's care and maintenance.

. . . Was the court legally justified in declaring and adjudging upon said facts that the minor involved here was an abandoned child within the meaning of section 224 of the Civil Code?

We cannot persuade ourselves that the conclusion of the learned trial judge is sustainable.

In the first place, it is to be remarked that a statute which authorizes, upon a showing of the existence of certain designated facts or conditions, a court to make a decree or an order whereby the natural relation between parent and child is destroyed, must be strictly construed and is, therefore, to be applied in those cases only in which the precise facts or conditions prescribed by such statute are shown to exist. As is said in the case of *Matter of Cozza,* 163 Cal. 514, 522. ". . . Consent lies at the foundation of statutes of adoption, and under our law this consent is made absolutely essential to confer jurisdiction on the superior court to make an order of adoption, unless the conditions or exceptions exist specially provided by the statute itself and which render such consent

of the parents unnecessary. Unless such consent is given, or, for the exceptional causes expressly enumerated is expressly dispensed with, the court has no jurisdiction in the matter."

. . . . . .

In the second place, we are persuaded to say that the mere failure of the parents of a minor child, in the custody and under the care of a third party, to contribute, while it is in such custody and care, to the support and maintenance of such child for a period of one year, does not itself constitute an abandonment of the minor within the purview of said section of the code. If the rule were otherwise — that is, if an adjudication of abandonment could legally be predicated on the mere failure by the parents to support their minor children — the result, in innumerable instances, would be to work a manifest wrong upon parents. It is not difficult to conceive of circumstances wholly beyond the control of parents having the deepest affection for their children which would render it impossible for them to support their children or care for them in a proper way. It would indeed, be a harsh rule which would, under such circumstances, authorize a judicial determination by which the natural right of the parents to the custody and control of their children would be forever destroyed.

To constitute an abandonment under said section of the code it must appear by clear and indubitable evidence that there has been by the parents a giving up or total desertion of the minor. In other words, there must be shown an absolute relinquishment of the custody and control of the minor and thus the laying aside by the parents all care for it. . . . And abandonment is a question of intention, which must be shown by a clear, unequivocal, and decisive act of the party — an act done that shows a determination not to have the benefit of the right to which he is entitled.

We have been unable to perceive in the evidence adduced at the hearing of this proceeding a single fact which may fairly be said to indicate an intention in the parents of the child concerned here to desert said minor or relinquish their natural right to her custody, care, and control. To the contrary, according to our interpretation of the proofs, the parents not only manifested a desire to perpetuate all the consequences of the natural relation subsisting between them and the infant, but displayed commendable anxiety for its welfare.

.   .   .   .   .

It may be true that the child, now approaching her sixth year, and having been with the Kellys for over a year, has formed a strong attachment for the petitioners, as they no doubt have for the child. It may also be true that the Kellys are better circumstanced than are her parents for bestowing upon her proper care. But, while these considerations might, perhaps, be of more or less importance in disposing of a guardianship proceeding, they cannot, obviously, enter into the determination of the question of adoption against the consent of the parents or of a proceeding, like the present, which, if sustained, would render it legally unnecessary to consult the desires or wishes of the parents in a proceeding looking to the adoption of their minor children by another.

---

2. The rights of the foster parent and of the child following abandonment by the natural parents, Washington, 1915

In re Potter, 85 Wash. 617.

CHADWICK, J. — On the 23d day of November, 1910, one Elsie Potter gave birth to an illegitimate child. Nellie Myers, the petitioner and appellant herein, a caller at the place where the mother was staying, was informed that the mother, a girl only sixteen years old, had given birth to a child. Petitioner talked with the mother, who told her that she wanted her to "take it away and get rid of it. I don't want it and I don't want to see it, and get it away just as quick as you can." Appellant informed the mother that she would be willing to take the child if she would be allowed to adopt it. She was told that she might adopt it as soon as she, the mother, could "get out of town where people did not know her." Within three or four hours after its birth, appellant took the child to her own home. She then lived, and does now, about twenty-five miles from the town of Oroville, where she has been farming land belonging to her mother and brothers. Some days later, appellant returned to Oroville to get something to show a right of adoption. The mother wrote and gave her the following:

"Oroville, Washington, November 23, 1910.
"I hereby turn over my right and title of my baby girl, born November 23, 1910, to Mrs. Nellie Myers, Riverside, Wash. E. N. Potter. Witness — Edith Hayes, R. H. Hayes."

From this time on, the foster mother has been the sole support of the child. She has cared for her as her own, according to the testimony of many neighbors and residents of that county. She has given her a good home, good clothing and good food, and is sincerely attached to it.

In July, 1913, she filed a petition with the court asking for a formal order of adoption. The statutory notice was given. Upon her petition, W. E. Grant, an attorney practicing at the bar of the court in Okanogan county, was appointed the next friend of the child. A trial was had. Many witnesses were called and examined. They were closely and severely cross-examined by Mr. Grant. The proofs were abundant to show that appellant has been a true mother; that she is able to care for, support and educate the child in keeping with its station in life. The proofs show that at no time has the mother ever concerned herself about her offspring, nor has she contributed in any way or in the slightest degree to its support. Her brother, who cared for her at the time of her confinement, testified to the good character of the appellant; to her situation in life; to the condition of the little one, and expressed, in a most positive way, his belief that its interest would be best served by allowing appellant to adopt it. After the trial had been concluded, the judge *pro tempore* who tried the case directed that all papers and proceedings be served upon the mother, who had since married, but who at the time was not living with her husband. She was directed to appear at a certain time and show cause why an order of adoption should not be made. The mother did not appear as directed, but some time thereafter filed an answer or an objection. Neither the mother or the next friend made any appearance in this court. It is impossible for us to determine from the record the character of her appearance in the court below. . . . It is evident, however, that the court treated the objection as indicating that the mother did not intend to abandon her child; that if it appeared in a proceeding of this kind, at any stage, that a parent desired to keep the custody of his child, an order would not be made under the statute, which requires the consent of the parent in an adoption proceeding.

.   .   .   .   .   .

Reference to § 1696 of the code will show that the consent of a parent is not necessary where there has been an abandonment. The trial judge has fallen into error in this: He has treated the filing of the objection by the mother as a fact sufficient in itself, whereas, the question of abandonment should have been determined by reference to all of the facts in the case. When so measured, it is clear to us that the objection should not be allowed to overcome what we may justly term the right of the foster parent and the right of the child.

Abandonment does not necessarily mean that a parent has no interest in a child's welfare. It means rather a withdrawal or neglect of parental duties. It means a withholding of care and protection, of sympathy and affection. When the subsequent conduct of the mother is considered in connection with her expressed dislike for the child and her desire that appellant get rid of it for her, and the giving of the writing which we have quoted, after sufficient time for the mother love to reassert it-

self, we have no hesitation in finding an abandonment . . .

It cannot be said that because a woman has given birth to a child she has a mother love for it. Mother love does not depend upon the pains and perils of childbirth. It is not every child that is welcome. On the other hand, there is an affection that grows from care and association and the tender ministrations which are prompted by a heartfelt sympathy for the weak and helpless. These beget a love as real as the love of a mother, and more, for the one who voluntarily assumes such a privilege must have far deeper maternal instincts than one who is an unwilling mother.

This court has frequently held, in considering cases of this kind, that we will make our first consideration the welfare of the child. It seems to the writer of this opinion that we would not be true to our own expressions if we were to hold that this child had not been abandoned by its parent.

In *In re Fields,* 56 Wash. 259, 105 Pac. 466, we held to the doctrine that abandonment was a question of intent.

.   .   .   .   .   .

Furthermore, we are of the opinion that the writing made by the mother at the time the baby was turned over to appellant is a sufficient evidence of consent to an adoption. It will hardly be denied that, if the proceeding had been had immediately, the paper would have been sufficient, if authenticated and filed, as an exhibit in court.

.   .   .   .   .   .

We hold that the mother abandoned her child at the time she gave it into the keeping of the appellant, and has since continued to abandon it; that the right of the foster mother is paramount to that of the parent, and that the interest of the child will be better served by an order of adoption.

If there were anything in the record to suggest that the objection made by the mother was well founded, or if there was any showing of conduct on her part that could be construed as consistent with her present declarations, we would remand the case for a further hearing. There is not.

The judgment of the lower court will be reversed, with directions to enter an order of adoption.

The role of government in adoption

1. Investigation of adopting parents by the court, Michigan, 1891

"An Act to provide for the adoption and change of name of minors, and for making them heirs at law of the person or persons adopting them . . . ," 1891 — ch. 77, *Public Acts of the Michigan Legislature — Regular Session 1891* (Lansing, 1891), pp. 81–82.

Michigan was the first state to require investigation of the prospective parents of an adopted child.

[The] judge of probate with whom such instrument is filed, shall thereupon make an investigation, and if he shall be satisfied as to the good moral character, and the ability to support and educate such child, and of the suitableness of the home, of the person or persons adopting [said] such child, he shall make an order to be entered on the journal of the probate court that such person or persons do stand in the place of a parent or parents to such child, and that the name of such child be changed to such name as shall be designated in said instrument for that purpose. Whereupon such child shall thereafter be known and called by said new name, and the person or persons so adopting such child, shall thereupon stand in the place of a parent or parents to such child in law, and be liable to all the duties, and en-

titled to all the rights of parents thereto; and such child shall thereupon become and be an heir at law of such person or persons, the same as if he or she were in fact the child of such person or persons.

2. Minnesota requires investigation by the state board of control in adoption proceedings, 1917

"An Act relating to Adoption and change of name . . . ," 1917 — ch. 222, *Session Laws of the State of Minnesota Passed During the Fortieth Session of the State Legislature* (Minneapolis, n.d.), p. 335.

7151. Adoption — petition and consent. — Any *resident* of the state may petition the district court of *the county in which he resides* for leave to adopt any child not his own. If the petitioner be married the spouse shall join in the petition. All petitions for the adoption of a child who is a ward or pupil of the state public school shall be made jointly by the person desiring to adopt such child and the superintendent of the state public school. *The state board of control* may determine by resolution that the joinder of the superintendent in *the* petition shall be its consent to the adoption of *the* ward or pupil, as prayed for in *the* petition. A person of full age may be adopted.

7152. Investigation by board of control. — *Upon the filing of a petition for the adoption of a minor child the court shall notify the state board of control. It shall then be the duty of the board to verify the allegations of the petition; to investigate the condition and antecedents of the child for the purpose of ascertaining whether he is a proper subject for adoption; and to make appropriate inquiry to determine whether the proposed foster home is a suitable home for the child. The board shall as soon as practicable submit to the court a full report in writing, with a recommendation as to the granting of the petition and any other information regarding the child or the proposed home which the court shall require. No petition shall be granted until the child shall have lived for six months in the proposed home. Provided, however, that such investigation and period of residence may be waived by the court upon good cause shown, when satisfied that the proposed home and the child are suited to each other.*

7153. Consent, when necessary. — *Except as herein provided* no adoption of a minor shall be permitted without *the* consent of his parents, but the consent of a parent who has abandoned the child, or who cannot be found, or who is insane or otherwise incapacitated from giving such consent, or who has lost custody of the child through divorce proceedings *or the order of a juvenile court,* may be dispensed with, and consent may be given by the guardian, *if there be one or* if there be no guardian, *by the state board of control.* In case of illegitimacy the consent of the mother alone shall suffice. In all cases where the child is over fourteen years old his own consent must be had also.

---

3. More effective regulation of adoption needed, New York, 1921

Sophie van Senden Theis, "Round Table Conference," in *Proceedings* of the New York State Conference of Charities and Correction (1921), 162–165.

We all know in a general way of the contradictions which exist in the interpretations of laws regulating guardianship and adoption of children, and of the inadequacy of the present law, but we do not realize perhaps unless we are actually doing children's work, to what extent children are suffering because of this situation. Whole groups of children are left without proper legal protection.

Let us take, for example, the children who are advertised in newspapers for adoption and see what happens to them. The advertisements read something like this, "Mother wants to give up baby boy two weeks old," or "For adoption, baby boy two weeks old; full surrender," or "New born, blue-eyed baby girl for adoption." We have been investigating such advertisements as they appear in the New York newspapers during the last three months. There were eighty-two children for whom adoption homes were sought in this way, the term "adoption" being used very loosely, frequently meaning the handing over of a child to another person without any legal procedure. In our investigation we found, furthermore, there were forty-four advertisements by families wishing to adopt children. It was difficult sometimes to get at the facts back of these advertisements, but in general we found it to be true that the babies who were advertised were children of unmarried mothers, that the mothers advertised in this anonymous and secret way to get rid of the baby quickly without being found out. We found in general that it was shame rather than poverty, that made them wish to part with their children. People who wished to take children for adoption were usually families looking for very young infants. From the cases we were able to follow up and from our general experience, we found that it is not unusual for a woman who tries to get a child to palm off on her husband as his own child, to resort to this kind of advertisement. Naturally such advertisements have to be regarded with suspicion.

I shall cite a few cases to show what happened to some of the children who were advertised and were so-called "adopted" by people who answered the advertisements . . .

First case: — Florence Graham when two weeks old, was advertised for adoption by her mother. This mother gave the baby to the first woman who called, without asking a question. In a day Florence was brought back because she cried. Her mother advertised her again and Florence was given away again. The second woman sent word to the mother that she would have to take the baby back because she cried. The mother went to the foster home and was shocked at the uncared for and poverty stricken home. Nevertheless she advertised once more. The baby was placed and returned for the same reason. When the mother called at this home she thought the foster mother was too lazy to care for the baby. This woman refused to return the baby's outfit. This performance was gone through three times more, until the baby had been in six homes in six weeks. One foster mother had a poor, dirty home, another "drank whiskey," and another refused to return the baby's outfit. By that time the baby was in a serious condition from neglect and undernourishment, and it took months of careful nursing to get her into good condition.

Second case: — Edward Andrews was advertised in the newspaper. A Mrs. Robinson, who read the advertisement, arranged by letter to meet the person in charge of the baby at a ferry at a given time. At the appointed time Mrs. Robinson, the prospective foster mother, met at the ferry "a tall woman, stout, dressed in black," who gave her the baby, giving her no information about him. Mrs. Robinson, an ignorant, incompetent woman, destroyed the small amount of correspondence which she had had with the woman in black, and six months later could not give a clue as to the identity of the baby, who had been about ten days old when she took him. Four times had the Robinson family done this same thing, taken in babies in this haphazard way. Their neglect of the children, their filthy home and their notorious reputation, forced an investigation by the children's agent, which resulted in the breaking up of the household and the commitment of the children. By that time all trace of Edward's own family had been lost, and he had had a year and a half of neglect in a beggarly, filthy home.

Third case: — Robert Dunn was a premature baby who lived for nine months in the hospital incubator. When he was ready for discharge his own parents refused to take him. Their marriage had been a forced marriage, but that fact was known only to the girl's mother. They had left New York after the baby's birth and refused to come for him, as they feared a disclosure of their situation. They persuaded a Miss Price, a friend, to board the baby for them and to look for a home of adoption for him. Miss Price worked and had little time to care for the baby. Her mother was partly paralyzed. In desperation they advertised for a home for Robert and a Mrs. Hawkins called at their home. She told them that she owned their home and had $4,000 in the bank. She made a sufficiently good impression on the Prices and they let her take the baby. The only document in the case was a statement signed by the parents authorizing Miss Price to dispose of the baby. Later the Prices became uneasy and made some inquiries about Mrs. Hawkins. Further inquiries were made by an agent of a children's society. The facts concerning Mrs. Hawkins thus discovered were that she was probably not married to Hawkins and had probably been in a house of prostitution before she lived with him; that she had deceived Hawkins into thinking the baby was her own, probably to force him to support her; that she had been carrying on affairs with two young doctors in the town.

I think we should all agree that in order to protect the children from this haphazard way of being passed about, there should be some formal registration of transfer with, perhaps an official Board of Children's Guardians, or perhaps the Court should be made responsible for protecting the child's welfare. It seems clear that no permanent transfer of a child should be made without the approval of some official body and that such a transfer should be properly recorded. I think it is interesting to note that in the matter of transferring property, it would never occur to any one to sell a piece of land without going through elaborate formalities of having deeds drawn up and recorded. It seems to me that we ought to consider children's rights at least as important as a parcel of material property.

---

4. The state cannot encroach upon the rights of parents in making children available for adoption, Wisconsin, 1922

Lacher *v*. Venus, 177 Wisc. 558.

This case raised the issue of the authority of state agencies for the care of dependent children to arrange adoptions without obtaining the consent of natural parents.

The question presented for decision may be stated thus: Can a county court acquire jurisdiction so as to make a valid order of adoption as to an infant under fourteen years of age, then in the custody of the state board of control, where no written consent thereto has been given by the living natural parents of such child or due notice of such hearing served upon them? — the commitment of such child to the state school at Sparta having been made by a juvenile court on findings that the child was dependent and the parents unable then to care for the same, there being no finding to the effect that there has been an abandonment of the child by the natural parents.

We are constrained to answer this question as thus stated No, fully appreciating the possible far-reaching effect of such ruling.

We do not deal with or determine the questions that may arise where a record discloses or determines that there had been an actual and wilful abandonment by the natural parents of their offspring or such a condition of moral depravity on their part as warrants and requires a judicial determination that there is a moral abandonment thereof. We are here only concerned with a situation where sickness, poverty, untoward circumstances, or ill fortune enters a home, and the state, entering also in its eminently proper and beneficent capacity as a guardian and conservator of the life, liberty, and happiness of its citizens, takes the children and supplies for the time that which the natural home cannot furnish them.

We base our conclusion in this case upon the following propositions:

First, the judicial proceedings for the commitment of dependent children to the care of the state . . . and the judicial proceedings for adoption . . . are entirely distinct, separate, and independent.

Second, that except there be an abandonment by the natural parents of the child and such fact of abandonment be found, the written consent of or actual notice to the living natural parents is an essential to jurisdiction of the county court to make a lawful order of adoption for such child.

Third, that notice of an participation in the commitment proceedings by the natural parents cannot be substituted for their required written consent to or notice of subsequently proposed adoption proceedings.

Fourth, that the written consent of the state board of control, or any guardian, cannot be declared to be a legal and sufficient substitute for the written consent of the living natural parents where required in such adoption proceedings.

In the proceedings in juvenile court for the commitment of children to the state school at Sparta or elsewhere . . . the state itself is the principal and moving actor, the immediate welfare of the child the paramount, if not the sole and controlling, consideration. Its fundamental purpose is the conservation of the child as a member of the state, and it extends alike to the child who is then not properly cared for by reason of the misfortune of its parents; is abandoned or neglected by reason of their wilful neglect to perform their parental responsibilities; or, being itself delinquent, needs the supervision and control of the state. Such proceedings, therefore, reach out into at least three separate and distinct fields. The exercise of this broad and generous function of the state has been expressly declared to be based upon the quality of mercy rather than upon the idea of punishment . . . Notice to the natural parents is not a jurisdictional essential for the court to proceed in any one of these several fields. All this has been repeatedly declared by this court . . .

Any judgment or order in such proceeding, whether the parent has notice or knowledge thereof or not, is not conclusive or binding upon the parent. . . .

On the other hand, the proceedings for the

adoption of children are purely statutory, and, affecting as they do substantial rights, there must be substantial compliance with their provisions. . . .

They in a measure involve a human triangle: the child at the apex, the living natural parents and the prospective adoptive parents completing the figure. The moving party here is not the state but the prospective adoptive parents. They can obtain no rights as to the child except through the surrender by or deprivation of substantially the same rights then existing in the living natural parents. Neither statute nor judicial decree attempts to or could give to the new parent anything that is not surrendered by or taken from the natural parent.

Before such extinguishment of the rights of the natural parents and creation of rights in the adoptive parents there must be an abandonment thereof by the natural parents by conduct or written consent, or else due notice to them of the proceedings wherein such transformation is to take place. Such are the clear and explicit directions of the statutes . . . Such would be the result in the absence of statutory provisions. Such are the repeated rulings of this court, from which we have no desire to recede, nor to the vigor with which they are expressed could we add.

.   .   .   .   .

The unit of the state is the individual, its foundation the family. To protect the unit in his constitutionally guaranteed right to form and preserve the family is one of the basic principles for which organized government is established . . .

That natural parenthood implies both substantial responsibilities and gives substantial rights needs no discussion. That wilful neglect to perform the one may properly result in the forfeiture of the other is also not open to debate and not here for consideration.

A natural affection between the parents and offspring, though it may be naught but a refined animal instinct and stronger from the parent down than from the child up, has always been recognized as an inherent, natural right, for the protection of which, just as much as for the protection of the rights of the individual to life, liberty, and the pursuit of happiness, our government is formed. We trust that it will never become the established doctrine that the state shall say to the parents, and particularly to the mother, she who doth travail, and in great pain bring forth her child and after labor doth rejoice that the child is born, that there is but a mere privilege and not a right to the subsequent affection, comfort, and pride of and in such child.

.   .   .   .   .

Undoubtedly many children would be better cared for were the state to shift them to other homes than those nature gave them, and to what extent the state can lawfully go in that field we need not now and do not now venture to suggest; but to transform a temporary separation of the family, incurred by reason of misfortune, into an absolute severance of those ties so interwoven with human hearts, should, and can, be done only under due process of law.

It is suggested that to require notice to be given to the natural parents of any subsequently proposed adoption proceedings after a child has been committed to a state institution will seriously interfere with the obtaining of homes by adoption for such children, and that such or similar considerations based upon the idea of an absolutely primary and paramount interest in the welfare of the child should be sufficient to require the natural parents to forego their rights to be heard on the question of whether such child is to have a new permanent home and as to what the new home shall be. However well founded, as an abstract question, such view may be, we cannot permit it to override constitutional guarantees.

---

5. A survey of state supervision of adoption with recommendations for a model adoption procedure, 1925

United States Children's Bureau, *Adoption Laws in the U.S.,* Pub. No. 148 (Washington, D.C., 1925), pp. 22–26.

Recognition of the advisability of public supervision of adoption is of comparatively recent appearance in adoption legislation. The need of such supervision is suggested by two facts; namely, that the ties created by the process of adoption are not necessarily so strong as those of blood and that complex situations may conceivably arise through the very performance of their functions by agencies and institutions organized for the purpose of placing out children who are homeless or destined to become so. This latter fact rests in turn upon the undeniable truth that there are children born to parents who are unable or unwilling to assume the responsibilities of parenthood.

In addition to an effort to prevent children from being placed out in a temporary or undefined status (especially by persons not directly responsible to public authorities), control has been further attempted by regulation of the child placement which child-caring institutions or organizations undertake to do. The requiring of reports from responsible individuals or organizations is one method of accomplishing supervision. Alabama requires the judges of its probate courts to make monthly reports to the child-welfare department on all adoptions handled during the preceding month.

Most of the statutes attempt to secure supervision at an early stage in the process; that is, at the time when the children are placed in homes for adoption or otherwise. If provision is made that the State board must investigate before a decree is granted, as in Minnesota, North Dakota, Oregon, and Virginia, or when it may be called upon for such investigation, as in Ohio, the State board thus exercises supervision over adoption. Massachusetts secures direct oversight of the adoption of public wards by providing that when a petition is entered in behalf of a child who is a public dependent the court must notify the State department of public welfare or the local authority responsible for the child. Minnesota makes mandatory a report to the State board of control concerning all children placed out by child-caring organizations. North Dakota places the licensing and supervising of child-placing work under the State board of administration and requires that all child-placing agencies report to the board concerning the placing of children. Organizations in Illinois in receipt of public funds must report placements to the State department of public welfare. In Indiana the State board of charities must inspect institutions and homes receiving children on court commitment. In Missouri the State board of charities and corrections licenses boarding homes and institutions, except those under "well-known religious orders." In Georgia child-placing work is under license of the circuit court after investigation and report by the State board of public welfare. In New York it is the policy of the State to maintain with the State board of charities a central confidential registration of children under institutional care or placed out or boarded out by requiring child-caring institutions and agencies to make to that board reports of children whom they receive, place out, or board out. The following paragraph occurs in the standards for child-placing agencies issued by the State Board of Charities and Corrections of California, April 27, 1921: "No agency should consent to the adoption of any of its wards until the child has been in one home under the supervision of the agency for at least six months."

Wisconsin forbids any one other than a parent or guardian to place out any child without license from the State board of control. Massachusetts requires any one receiving an infant under 2 years of age for adoption or for giving it a home, or for procuring a home for adoption for it, to give notice to the State department of public welfare, which may investigate and at any time before adoption may take the child into its own custody. Ohio prohibits giving a child under 2 years of age into the temporary or permanent custody of any person, association, or institution which is not certified by the division of charities (department of public welfare) without the written consent of this division or by commitment of a juvenile court; and provides that records of such temporary and permanent surrenders be kept.

Adoption and child placing effected by maternity homes or by patients in such homes have been placed under supervision by a number of statutes. In Ohio maternity homes must keep a record of children given out for adoption (on the form prescribed by the State board of health); and a copy of this record is sent to the local health board. Although in this State the supervision (and licensing) of maternity homes is a duty of the State board of health any transfer of custody of children (aside from juvenile-court commitment) must be made with the consent of the State department of public welfare. Thus Ohio undertakes to bring the child under the oversight of both health and child-caring authorities. A difficulty in the arrangement which places inspection of maternity homes under only the health department is that the social aspects of the problem, as distinguished from the health aspects, may not always receive adequate consideration. In Virginia, which provides for licensing of maternity homes by the State board of public welfare and for inspection by that board, the State board of public health, and the local board of health, no maternity hospital may engage in child placing. Any child born therein who is destitute must be committed through the proper court to the State board of public welfare or any agency licensed for child placing. In Illinois no child from a maternity hospital may be placed in a family home or adopted until after investigation and approval of the home by the State board of public welfare; and Wyoming forbids private individuals, lying-in homes, hospitals, and "other unqualified institutions" to place out children. Statutory provision for supervision of child-placing or adoption from maternity hospitals, as well as for the granting of licenses to such institutions, occurs in the acts of many States dealing with inspection of child-caring institutions.

Not only has child placing from maternity homes and hospitals frequently taken place without adequate consideration of the welfare of the child and without supervision by any public authority; but it was inevitable that such action should lead to offers of collusion, and to open advertisement of opportunities for such disposal of young children. In this connection a definition of a maternity home may be quoted from a statute embodying a phrase not found in most of the legislation on this subject: "A house or other place maintained or conducted for the care and treatment of women during pregnancy and subsequent to the birth of children, and usually advertised for such work and the disposition of unwanted children."

Recent laws have dealt with the matter of collusion, and especially of advertising, and the problem has also received attention from State boards empowered by statute to regulate such institutions. Thus the Missouri regulations for government of maternity hospitals, adopted June 8, 1922, direct that "No maternity hospital shall be permitted to advertise that it will procure the adoption of children." Prohibitions of such advertising may be observed in the legislation of Georgia, Minnesota, Nebraska, and North Dakota. The laws in Kansas and Ohio seem more far-reaching. Kansas directs that "no personal firm, corporation, or association shall offer to adopt, find a home for, or in any manner offer to dispose of any child as an inducement to a woman to come to his or its place during pregnancy, or at or after delivery; or shall offer such as an inducement to any parent, guardian, or custodian of an infant or child to place such infant or child in his or its home, institution, or establishment." Ohio also uses the phrase "hold out inducements."

The importance and the complexity of the subject of adoption legislation have been indicated in the foregoing pages. The tendency of recent legislation and the standards which are being developed by those engaged in child-welfare work emphasize as the primary consideration the welfare of the child and also provide for safeguarding the rights of all the parties in interest.

The requirement of notice to the State department of public welfare and of investigation and recommendation by the department is a recognition of the State's interest in children placed for adoption and gives the State a method of fulfilling its responsibility toward the children who have been placed. If the jurisdiction is vested in a court equipped to make social investigations the law may properly direct that investigations be made either by the court or by the State department, but in any case the State department should be vested with ample supervisory powers covering all aspects of the placement of children.

.   .   .   .   .   .

In drafting adoption acts the welfare of the child, the rights of the parents and the possibilities of their assuming the care of the child under proper conditions, and the rights of the adopting parents must be borne in mind. Provision for social investigation, for trial period in the home either before petition is filed or before a final decree is granted, and for State supervision will safeguard the interests of all the parties. The investigation should include the fitness of the natural parents to care for the child, the physical and mental condition and the antecedents of the child with a view to determining whether he is a proper subject for adoption, and the financial ability and moral fitness of the adopting parents and general suitability of the proposed home.

Among the items in adoption procedure which are of especial importance with reference to the child's welfare are those providing that if the petitioner is married the spouse shall join in the petition, and those safeguarding records from publicity. The provisions of the statute with reference to the consent of the parents and the conditions under which their consent is dispensed with should be carefully

drawn. Where social investigation is required the provision need not be so specific in its terms as when no such provision is made, but surrender of rights by parents otherwise than through a court proceeding or upon action of a responsible public agency should not be permitted. The law should provide for the consent of the child if he has reached an age at which his judgment is of value (probably 12 or 14 years).

Other important points to be considered in connection with adoption legislation include provision for appeal, for vacation of order or annulment for good cause, and for inheritance rights. The statute should specifically provide that adoption shall establish between the child and the adopting parents the legal relationship existing between parents and their children born in lawful wedlock. Either in the adoption law or in related laws the transfer of parental rights and responsibilities without order or decree of court should be prohibited. Administration of adoption laws for the welfare of the child is to a large extent dependent upon the administration of related laws governing children's institutions and the placing of children in family homes.

The application of the science of child development to adoption

Arnold Gesell, "Psychoclinical Guidance in Child Adoption," in *Foster-Home Care for Dependent Children,* United States Children's Bureau Pub. No. 136 (Washington, D.C., 1926), pp. 196–204.

Dr. Gesell (1880–1961) was the founder and director of the Yale University Clinic of Child Development.

From the standpoint of child adoption . . . the situation involves a paradox which contains an element of hazard as well as of promise. Infancy is the best time for adoption, but in the nature of things it is also the time when developmental prediction is most difficult.

.   .   .   .   .

Infancy is the period of most rapid growth in the whole life cycle, except, of course, the intrauterine period of which it is but an extension. This very fact simplifies, more than it encumbers, the task of developmental diagnosis. The infant to be sure is very immature, which tends to make him inscrutable; but, on the other hand, he matures at an extremely rapid rate, and this tide of maturation brings him more repeatedly and more cogently within the purview of systematic observation.

The changes which the infant undergoes from the age of 4 months to 6 months, from 6 to 9 months, from 9 to 12 months occupy chronologically a short span of time; but from the standpoint of developmental economy they may be equivalent to the progress which in later childhood it will take him a whole decade to accomplish. It is assumed, moreover, that the infant is father of the child, just as the child is father of the man; and that the characteristics of the infant during the heyday of growth have some coherent relation to the characteristics which will emerge in later life. The rate and limits of his growth may also be foreshadowed by the manner and the fullness in which he makes the first stage of his developmental journey, say from 4 months to 12, or 18, or 24 months.

In principle, these considerations have a bearing on the question whether in time the adoption of infants may be brought under more adequate clinical control. The greater speed of growth has very practical diagnostic implications. It means that a probationary year prior to adoption may be made to yield more evidence in infancy than at any later period. In the first year of life four periodic developmental examinations may readily be made to determine the increments of mental growth, whereas a few years would be necessary to observe as many comparable increments in later childhood.

.   .   .   .   .

There is occasional danger that the demand for prediction will be pushed too far by child-placement agencies. It is also true that certain foster parents are unreasonably detailed and exacting in their specifications for their desired adoptee. Such parents should know that adoption must retain some elements of faith, adventure, and sacrifice.

But neither the faith nor the adventure should be blind . . .

The clinical aspects of child adoption can be discussed most briefly and concretely by means of a few illustrative cases. These cases . . . are representative of those situations in which the importance of clinical control asserts itself most clearly; but it must be remembered that so-called exceptional cases can be discovered only by incorporating clinical safeguards as a regular procedure in all instances of adoption. The cases which seem "perfectly all right" in the eyes of all the well-minded adults concerned may be just the cases which need careful investigation and clinical appraisal. Perhaps the first case presented below will illustrate this point.

A BLIND ADOPTION — CHILD A

This child was first examined as a mere infant, at the age of 6 months . . . Although she was poorly nourished, her general appearance was relatively normal. She smiled, cooed, followed moving objects with her eyes, gave transient regard to a dangling ring. But she did not reach for the dangling ring; nor could any object entice her to reach. Her developmental status was estimated to be at the three-month level. A diagnosis of mental deficiency was made, and the agency then supervising the child was notified.

.   .   .   .   .

When 9 months old A was reexamined. She approximated the four-month level of development. Nothing would induce her to reach even now. The dangling ring was attended to with more fixed and prolonged gaze, but there was no other reaction toward it. The diagnosis was confirmed.

At the age of 12 months A was again examined. Now the behavior picture changes. She goes out with avidity to every object in her reach. She grasps the dangling ring; she seizes a piece of writing paper and crumbles it with lusty vigor. She is now in good nutritional trim; she looks attractive; she bears no obvious badge of defect anywhere; and she is so reactive to the play material given to her that she makes an excellent impression. The baby is physically well developed; she evidently has a good disposition; she is alert. Surely she is adoptable! In a sense she is a fine baby — but only in the sense . . . of a 6-month baby. However, she is 12 months old; she is still mentally deficient.

It was at this time that this child was placed under the supervision of a second agency; and it was necessary to make a rather emphatic report concerning her developmental outlook because the plans were to have her adopted.

At 18 months she was reexamined. Her developmental level consistently approximated nine months . . . At 24 months she was examined once more. Her developmental level was clearly 12 months. She behaved very much like a normative 12-month-old baby. The diagnosis of mental deficiency was now confirmed beyond dispute.

And the moral? Well, just before the last examination she went out of the hands of the XYZ agency, and she was adopted very soon by a very excellent and most affectionate foster mother, who does not know what she has done.

BAD BACKGROUND BUT ADOPTABLE — CHILD J

It is not the function of preplacement clinical examination solely to discover the deterrents and to define the hazards of adoption, but to emphasize positive, promising constructive possibilities. A great deal is heard about poor family background in child-placement work. Social workers speak in a vague, foreboding way about the bad background of this and that child. What does the background mean? Alcoholism, abuse, shiftlessness, poverty, neglect, insanity, mental deficiency, illegitimacy, and the like. Often it is gratuitously assumed that in some way or other this background is in the inherent constitution of the child.

This does not always follow. To be sure, long residence in an incompetent home may warp a child and leave a deposit which is part and parcel of his acquired personality. On the other hand, a child may have a feeble-minded mother and still be a relatively safe placement or even adoption prospect.

This morning J, a girl of 20 months, was brought to the clinic. Her mother is so mentally deficient that she (the mother) is about to be committed to a State institution. Her husband does not know the difference between a one-dollar and a five-dollar bill and is thought by the neighbors to be more defective than his wife. The actual paternity of the child is unknown, because the mother has been promiscuous in her sexual relations. It is not known whether the maternal mental defect is definitely transmissible or of a secondary, acquired character. When the child is estimated on her own merits it is necessary to consider her fully normal in her present developmental status. Her personality traits are not only normal but positively favorable. In spite of her forbidding background, she is entitled to more than an indifferent or temporizing placement. She is entitled to a good placement, and she is a safer adoption prospect than many a child with an "excellent background."

The foregoing cases cover some of the more important psychological problems which arise out of the complicated task of child adoption. They demonstrate that this task can not be intrusted altogether to good will or to intuitive impulse, or even to unaided common sense.

There are too many opportunities for error and miscarriage. The combined critical judgment of the social investigator, the court, the physician, and the mental examiner should enter into the regulation of adoption.

The greatest universal safeguard is a period of probation, but this can not be wisely used unless supplemented by clinical determinations of health conditions and development outlook. Mental examinations are particularly necessary to forestall serious errors of selection by oversanguine foster parents. These examinations are also necessary to reduce the number of replacements or uprootings which still figure too frequently in the lives of dependent children.

.   .   .   .   .

Systematic psychoclinical examinations not only will reduce the wastes of error and miscarriage but will serve to reveal children of normal and superior endowment beneath the concealment of neglect, of poverty, or of poor repute.

Clinical safeguards can not solve all the problems of child adoption, but they can steadily improve its methods and make them both more scientific and humane.

D. BIRTH CONTROL AND ABORTION

Margaret Sanger traces the history of the birth control movement

Margaret Sanger, "Birth Control," *Social Work Year Book, 1929* (New York, 1930), pp. 38–40. By permission of the Russell Sage Foundation.

Margaret Sanger (1883–1966) took training as a nurse and through her work among New York's tenement dwellers became aware of the need for contraceptive information among the poor. Her efforts on their behalf launched her into leadership of the birth control movement, as well as into a prolonged effort to repeal the state and federal laws banning the sale and distribution of contraceptives and contraceptive information.

The general aim of the birth control movement is to legitimatize the practice of contraception through scientific and hygienic methods, and to educate the adult public as to its advantages from the personal and social points of view. International in scope, the movement has been known under a number of names; in the British Empire as "neo-malthusianism"; in France as "conscious generation"; and occasionally as "voluntary parenthood."

History and Present Status. In English-speaking countries the present movement derives from Malthus. In the second edition of his famous *Essay on Population,* published in 1803, the English clergyman first enunciated his law of the pressure of population upon the means of subsistence. The only solution he suggested for overpopulation was the practice of celibacy and late marriage. In 1826 Dr. Charles Knowlton, a Boston physician, was prosecuted for publishing a small book, *The Fruits of Philosophy,* advocating mechanical and chemical methods of contraception. In 1876–1877 Charles Bradlaugh and Mrs. Annie Besant were prosecuted and convicted for distributing that book among the working classes of Great Britain. Their conviction led to the foundation of the Malthusian League in 1878 by Dr. Charles Drysdale and his wife, Dr. Alice Vickery Drysdale. A Dutch League was founded in 1881. The neo-malthusians differed from

Malthus in advocating contraception to prevent overpopulation and to reduce birth rate.

The period between 1914 and 1921 in the United States was one of militant agitation and widespread publicity, partly as a result of several convictions of persons active in the movement for challenging federal and state laws. In New York City in 1914 Mrs. Margaret Sanger began to advocate contraception on feministic and libertarian grounds, coining at that time the term "birth control." The interest awakened in the whole question of contraception resulted in 1921 in the foundation of the American Birth Control League and of the Voluntary Parenthood League; also in the publication of a monthy periodical, the *Birth Control Review,* edited by Mrs. Sanger. The two organizations were subsequently combined under the name of the former.

Activities of the second period of the American movement, from 1921 to 1925, included the organization of local leagues, the education of public opinion, and campaigns for the amendment of statutes which class the practice of contraception with obscenity and criminal abortion. During the third period, 1925 to the present, advocates of birth control have concentrated upon the establishment of clinics and research bureaus, and upon enlisting the interest and activities of physicians, biologists, bio-chemists, and social scientists generally. Results of these efforts are seen in the fact that no less than 55 clinics and bureaus are now operating legitimately in the United States (covering 23 cities and 13 states), dispensing contraceptive information to all persons legally permitted to receive it. In New York State it is given to married people for the cure or prevention of disease. In California there are 12 clinics; there is one each in Baltimore, Cincinnati, Cleveland, Denver, Detroit, Newark, New Haven, and Philadelphia; there are six in Chicago; and New York City has eight in hospitals and one operating independently. In addition a branch for colored women has recently been established in the Harlem section of New York City by the Clinical Research Bureau.

The year 1929 was marked by the establishment of 27 new clinics. The successful operation of such clinics and research bureaus, under medical direction, makes possible the scientific analysis of individual cases, and also statistical studies. Through the latter material is being developed for the replacement of untested theory with impartial analysis. Social agencies are beginning to cooperate with such clinics. Owing to the widespread change in public opinion, physicians are more willing to give advice in private practice. Over 10,000 of them have expressed willingness to do so.

The birth control movement is exerting a noticeable influence upon eugenics and giving a new direction to programs for race-betterment; it has resulted in renewed consideration of the problem of legal sterilization of the unfit; and has influenced programs for the control of dependent, delinquent, and defective groups in society. It has been given consideration by many social agencies seeking to decrease maternal and infant mortality rates, particularly by the Committee on Maternal Health of New York City. Financial support of the birth control movement has been from independent and anonymous sources, with the exception of temporary support from the Brush Foundation of Cleveland. During 1929 a study of 10,000 cases was made by the Birth Control Clinical Research Bureau, and a study of fertility and sterility by the Committee on Maternal Health.

Legislation, 1929. No laws on the subject were passed during the year. Bills to amend the laws which prohibit contraceptive instruction were defeated in New York and Connecticut.

The Cummins-Vaile Bill, 1923–1925

A bill sponsored by the Voluntary Parenthood League of America and intended to remove contraceptives and contraceptive information from the list of obscene objects and literature prohibited from the mails by the Comstock Act (See below, Chap. II, sec. B., "Comstockery," doc. 3.) was introduced into Congress by Senator Albert B. Cummins of Iowa (president pro tem of the Senate, 1919–1925) and Representative William N. Vaile of Colorado, first in 1923 and again in 1924. Hearings were held in 1924 but Congress adjourned without action.

---

1. Legislative history of the Cummins-Vaile Bill

Mary Ware Dennett, *Birth Control Laws* (New York: F. H. Hitchcock, 1926), pp. 294–298.

1919. July 24. Began preliminary interviews with Senators and Congressmen with a view to discovering the right sponsor for the bill, and to create a good atmosphere for its introduction.

Sept. 24. Asked Senator France of Maryland to introduce it, he being chairman of the Committee on Public Health, a physician and heartily in favor of the bill. He agreed to consider it.

Oct. 21. Senator France doubted the wisdom of his being sponsor. He suggested Senator Norris of Nebraska.

Oct. 22. Senator Norris was wholly favorable to the measure, but said the prejudice of the Judiciary Committee against other measures for which he stood would hurt his sponsorship and he hadn't the advantage of being a physician.

Oct. 23. As Senator France was most desirable, the sponsorship was again put up to him and he said he would again consider it.

1920. Jan. 19. After nearly three months of prodding by letters and interviews, Senator France wrote that he did not feel ready to shoulder our bill ahead of others to which he was already committed. He did not decline, but thought it unfair to keep us waiting further.

Jan. 21. Took it back to Senator Norris, who agonized over it conscientiously, but decided he had better not. He had sounded Senator Ball, the only other physician in the Senate beside France. Found him rather skeptical. He then suggested asking Senator Nelson, chairman of the Judiciary Committee to do it as proof of his repentance for having been an abusive opponent (one of the very few we have met).

Jan. 22. Senator Nelson's repentance went to the extent of recommending that the bill be referred first to the Committee on Public Health and implied that the Judiciary Committee would concur if the report should be favorable.

During the next few weeks, besides hunting for a sponsor we interviewed the Health Committee. Seven out of eleven were wholly in favor or inclined favorably toward the bill.

Senator Ball was seen several times, in the hope that he would prove to be the right sort for a sponsor. He was slow in coming to a conclusion as to the merits of the bill.

Meanwhile two other Senators were asked.

Jan. 29. Senator Sterling of South Dakota, first. The discussion convinced him as to the merits of the bill, and he finally agreed to consider sponoring it.

Feb. 18. Urged his decision. He did not refuse, but said he would be relieved to be released from consideration. Promised to work for the measure in Committee and on the floor.

Mar. 5. After conferring with Senators France and Norris, whose advice has always been helpful, took the bill to Senator Dillingham of Vermont. He is wholly in favor but considered himself unsuitable sponsor. He is the *only* Senator who has not kept us waiting for his decision. He urged Ball as best sponsor.

Mar. 6. As Senator Ball had announced on February 20th, that he was convinced by our data — on the advice of Dillingham, France and Norris, he was asked by letter to introduce the bill.

Mar. 11. Went to Washington for his decision. Found him; he had not even read the letter carefully enough to realize he was being asked. Said "No." Then reconsidered and agreed to talk it over with France.

Mar. 19. *He promised to sponsor the bill.* He asked for "a few days of grace" before introducing it, to recover from influenza and attend to the suffrage crisis in Delaware.

Apr. 21. Introduction still hanging. Said he "hadn't had time." Meanwhile the comments of the other Senators had begun to disconcert him. He turned us over to Major Parkinson of the bill drafting service to discuss phraseology and work out an opposition-proof bill. Everything was settled to our satisfaction. It was the Senator's next move.

Apr. 24. He "hadn't had time to see Parkinson," and asked for a few days more of patience. We reminded him that we had waited over a month. He said he would surely do it during this session. We insisted on something definite. He finally promised "some day next week" and that he would wire us what day.

May 25. No word, despite letters from our office and many from the supporters of the League.

Letters, telegrams, personal interviews with Senator Ball in Washington were all unavailing. He did nothing but reiterate promises.

June 5. *The Senate adjourned and the bill was not introduced.*

Dec. 6. With the opening of the last session of Congress, we began the sponsor hunt again. Nine Senators in succession have been asked to sponsor the bill, as follows:

Sen. Capper of Kansas. For the bill, but too submerged in his agricultural relief bills to take ours on.

Sen. Townsend of Mich. (Member of Health Com.) Favors the bill, but declined on grounds that he was too ignorant on the data to face debate, and too busy to get primed.

Sen. Kenyon of Iowa. (Had reputation of being chief welfare advocate of Senate.) Too busy with his "packer" bill. Might consider it at next session.

Sen. McCumber of S.D. Admitted merit of bill, but thought he better not imperil his re-election (in 1923) by sponsoring it. Suggested

that it be introduced by Health Com. as a whole, without individual sponsorship, so no one would "be the goat."

Sen. Sheppard of Texas. (Sponsor of Sheppard-Towner Maternity Bill.) Recognized necessity of our bill to complete the service provided by his bill, but could not consider sponsoring ours till next session anyway, and probably not then, as he thinks it should come from a Republican.

Sen. Fletcher of Fla. (Member of Health Com.) Heartily approves bill, but considers himself unsuitable sponsor because he is a Democrat.

Sen. Frelinghuysen of N.J. (Member of Health Com.) Like Senator France, author of bill for Federal Health Dept. — unqualifiedly in favor, but sure bill should not be sponsored from Democratic side.

Dec. 31. Proposed to Senator France that the bill be introduced by the Health Committee without individual sponsorship.

1921. Jan. 5. Senator France declined the proposition on the ground that the burden of the bill would fall on him just the same.

Jan. 13. After thorough consultation with Senator France, took bill back to Senator Sterling.

Jan. 27. Senator Sterling answered that he was "too busy to do it at this session."

Feb. 11. Senator Kenyon was asked to reconsider. He replied, "I'm mighty sorry, but I am just loaded down with bills that are taking every minute of my time, and I must ask you to secure some other Senator to take care of this legislation for you."

Mar. 1. Senator Borah was asked to sponsor the bill. He did not see his way to doing it.

Aug. 19. Post Master General Hays had put himself on record as not believing in the maintenance of Post Office censorship laws. He was accordingly asked to consider recommending to Congress the removal of the censorship law regarding birth control knowledge. He was most hospitable to the suggestion — said it was timely, that he was interested and had about come to the conclusion that he ought to ask Congress to revise all the laws bearing on Post Office censorship power. He asked for a compilation of pertinent data, which was promptly provided. He had the matter under consideration till he resigned office the following March. But he made no recommendation to Congress.

The sponsor hunt began again.

Senator Borah suggested the possibility that he might slip in our bill as an amendment to the bill proposing to extend Post Office censorship to information about race track betting tips, if it was reported out of committee and reached the floor for discussion. The bill was killed in Committee, due in part to Senator Borah's opposition to it.

1922. Dec. Sponsors found in both Houses. Senator Cummins in the Senate, and Congressman John Kissel of New York in the House. The latter responded to a circular letter asking for a volunteer statesman for the task.

1923. Jan. 10. Bill introduced in both Houses.

Jan. 22. Sen. Nelson, Chairman of the Judiciary Committee appointed Sub-Committee of three to consider the bill — Senators Cummins, Colt and Ashurst. Senator Cummins was ill and went to Florida. Committee action was stalled.

Strenuous effort was made to get substitute Chairman so action could proceed. Norris was added to Committee but not as Chairman.

Feb. 6. Sen. Colt declined to act as Chairman.

Feb. 8. Sen. Colt asked to be excused from the Committee.

Feb. 13. Sen. Cummins returned.

Feb. 19. Sen. Cummins tried to get vote of full Judiciary, as conditions had not permitted a Hearing and report from the Sub-Committee. Meeting adjourned without action. They "did not get to the bill."

Feb. 26. Sen. Cummins tried again to get a vote. Announced that he would call for it before adjournment, again. The members slipped out one by one, so no quorum was present. The Senator said, "They just faded away."

1924. Jan. 30. Bill reintroduced by Senator Cummins.

Feb. 1. Bill introduced in House by Congressman William N. Vaile of Colorado.

Mar. 7. Bill referred to Senate Sub-Committee, consisting of Senators Spencer, Norris and Overman.

Mar. 22. Bill referred to House Sub-Committee of seven, Congressmen Yates, Hersey, Perlman, Larson, Thomas, Major and O'Sullivan.

Apr. 8. Joint Hearing held before both Sub-Committees. Ten spoke for the bill and five against.

May 9. Hearing reopened at request of the Catholics.

June 7. Congress adjourned. Neither Committee reported the bill.

1925. Dec. Senator Cummins made Chairman of the Judiciary Committee.

Jan. 20. Senate Sub-Committee unanimously reported Cummins-Vaile Bill "without recommendation."

House Sub-Committee evaded making a report.

Mar. 4. Congress adjourned.

---

2. Pro and con testimony at hearings, April 8 and May 9, 1924

U.S. Congress, The Subcommittee of the Committees on the Judiciary, *Joint Hearings on H.R. 6542 and S. 2290, Cummins-Vaile Bill.* 86 Cong., 1 Sess. (1924), pp. 3–5, 12–13, 17–18, 19, 21.

STATEMENT OF HON. WILLIAM N. VAILE, A REPRESENTATIVE IN CONGRESS FROM THE STATE OF COLORADO

Mr. VAILE. Mr. Chairman and gentlemen, I want to remove a little misapprehension concerning this bill, or these bills, which seems to have been spread about pretty largely. These bills do not propose any new or strange legislation, and these bills themselves do not propose to teach birth control, although, of course, it is hoped and expected by the advocates of this legislation that it will be possible, by legalizing this information, to give it where it may be needed, and it really may be needed, to protect the health of women.

Mr. HERSEY. You said that this is no new matter.

Mr. VAILE. I think I can say to the committee that this is not a new proposition.

Mr. HERSEY. Is there any legislation of this sort which has been passed hitherto?

Mr. VAILE. The legislation on this matter consists of our statute classifying contraceptives as obscene of themselves. We are the only country in the world having this legislation. We did not have it prior to 1873. The bill, therefore, proposes no new or affirmative doctrine. It simply proposes to make lawful what was lawful in the United States prior to 1873, and what is lawful in every other country of the world, so far as I am able to determine; namely, the giving of information under medical supervision concerning methods of preventing conception, and giving the means to do so. It does not propose to do this by any new or affirmative legislation, but by simply striking those provisions from five sections of our Penal Code.

Let me, at the outset, refer to a question which immediately bobs up in the minds of everybody with whom you discuss this subject. They say, "It will promote immorality." Let me ask the committee, in all fairness, if the morality of this country is strikingly superior now to what it was before 1873. You can not pick up a daily paper, you can not go into a church, you can not hear a subject of public morals discussed to any great length by any speaker but what you will be advised that we are at a lower stage of morals than we were 50 years ago. Fifty years ago we did not have such a statute on our books. Certainly the insertion of this proviso in our statutes has not noticeably increased the morality of the United States. It is common knowledge that methods of contraception are used by the educated, the well-to-do classes of the community. Would anybody say that those classes are conspicuously less moral than those who can not obtain this information and have no knowledge of it? I think that would be a great reflection on many people, with certainly a highly developed civic consciousness, people prominent in every good work of the community, all of whom as a matter of common knowledge, of which this committee can take judicial notice, do have and use this information.

Let me ask also if this country is conspicuously more moral or less immoral than other countries of the world? . . .

I submit in all fairness that those who charge that this bill will promote immorality should judge by what has happened.

To summarize, the United States is certainly not conspicuously more moral now than it was 50 years ago. Is church attendance, are divorces, is prevalence of crime any test of public morality? Our church attendance certainly does not exceed that of, we will say, Italy. I will admit birth-control methods are not generally practiced in Italy, but neither are they unlawful in Italy. Our church attendance is not less than it is in Holland or New Zealand. Is prevalence of divorce any index of immorality in America? We have the highest divorce rate in the world. Is crime any index of public immorality? We have the highest record of homicides in the civilized world. And so, I submit, in all fairness, by merely removing the provisions which were put into the code 50 years ago, and which did not exist theretofore, we won't be rushing on a downward path, so far as we can judge by our own experience or that of any other country.

.   .   .   .   .

STATEMENT OF REV. JOHN A. RYAN

Mr. RYAN. My name is John A. Ryan, representing the National Catholic Welfare Conference.

Mr. Chairman and members of the subcommittee, although I have occasionally been accused of being radical in social doctrines and theory, I am old-fashioned enough in this matter to approach the subject with a great deal of reluctance. I feel that this whole subject is one to which the words of St. Paul are still applicable, as being among those things that should not be so much as mentioned among Christians.

However, since the situation is what it is, I want to present the viewpoint, not merely of the National Catholic Welfare Conference, but of the Catholic Church, whose hierarchy directs that organization.

The sections of the Penal Code to which this amendment is proposed include the prohibition of the sending of obscene literature and literature described by other synonymous terms through the mails. It is not proposed by the advocates of this bill to eliminate those sections. In passing, I might say that the argument of the first gentleman about the weakness of human nature, which is assumed by the proponents of this bill, ought to be applied to the obscene literature sections as well, and if he and his friends were consistent, they would say "let us eliminate these prohibitions of obscene literature going through the mails, because our daughters and our sons and all the rest of us are perfectly capable of standing up against all the insinuations and allurements of that kind of literature."

The question was asked here just how information would be given to these persons who are supposed to need it under this proposed change in the law. The answer was, I think, that the information would be got from the physician. The physician can give it now. Some of the States, I believe, prohibit that kind of thing and others do not. In any case the individual is not helped by this bill or by the passage of this bill toward getting the information from physicians. The only access he will get to through the mails, through general information, or information of that sort sent out generally by quacks or anybody else. So it won't be scientific information that he will be getting, necessarily, since he is not getting it from a physician, but will get it from general sources, from anybody who wants to send it out, provided he can get five physicians to sign a statement to the effect that this particular information contains nothing contrary to health. We know there will be no great difficulty in getting five physicians to recommend almost anything. A certain ex-Cabinet member a short time ago, was able to get four physicians to declare that he could not testify before a Senate committee, but the Senate committee got its own physicians who declared that he was able to testify.

So that the so-called scientific guaranties surrounding this amendment amount to nothing at all. It would simply be throwing open the doors to the giving out of information by anybody who wanted to give it, provided he gets the signatures of these five physicians.

The opposition which we have, which I take it the proponents of this bill also have, to the sending of what is ordinarily called obscene literature or pornographic literature through the mails, is applied to the sending of this information concerning the control of birth, and for the same reason, because we regard these practices about which information is proposed to be given as immoral — everlastingly, essentially, fundamentally immoral, quite as immoral as adultery, for instance, or rather a little more so, because adultery, whatever may be its vicious aspects, does not commit any outrage upon nature, nor pervert nature's functions. That is enough of the moral side of it.

.   .   .   .   .

STATEMENT OF DR. LAWRENCE LITCHFIELD, PITTSBURGH, PA.

Doctor LITCHFIELD. I came here simply to speak on the medical aspects of birth control, knowing that this bill is not a bill authorizing birth control or advocating birth control, but it is necessary for all of us who consider the bill to realize what birth control means.

I find myself a little bit in the position of speaking for immorality, on the other side from the previous speaker, who spoke for morality so strongly. I do not pretend to be particularly immoral. My idea of God Almighty's plan is that if he gave certain human beings more intelligence than others they were to use them for the rest. If the terrible toll of suffering which is put upon the women of certain classes is necessary for high moral and Christian development, it is not fair. I do not wish to go further into that argument, but briefly go over the medical aspects of the case.

I have practiced medicine for 36 years. I have been interested in international movements for the control of and the abating of venereal diseases, child labor, and tuberculosis. All of these problems for the benefit of the human race bring us back one after another to the necessity for intelligent birth control. The human race has the same right and need for scientific development that other animals have. We have many laws and many books and many theories that control the breeding of animals, but the breeding of human beings is left entirely to chance.

Senator SPENCER. In what State do you practice?

Doctor LITCHFIELD. Pennsylvania.

Senator SPENCER. Is there any law in Pennsylvania against a physician freely communicating to his patients?

Doctor LITCHFIELD. Yes. If a patient of mine whom I believe would be seriously injured by not having the information to prevent conception, if she wrote me for such information I am legally unable to send it to her. If she comes into my office and the doors are locked, I tell her what I think is wise.

·   ·   ·   ·   ·

STATEMENT OF REV. J. FREDERIC WENCHEL, SECRETARY OF THE EVANGELICAL LUTHERAN SYNODICAL CONFERENCE OF NORTH AMERICA

Senator SPENCER. It would conserve time if those who are opposed to the bill would, among themselves, decide as to who they want to speak, for the hearing will have to close soon.

Mr. WENCHEL. I will only take about five minutes. My name is J. Frederic Wenchel, representing the Evangelical Lutheran Synodical Conference of North America. The officers of my synod have asked me to protest against this birth-control bill. I am not appearing to argue on the bill.

I have listened with a great deal of attention to what has been said here. Neither am I here as a churchman. I am here in the capacity of a citizen. We are not opposing this bill on the grounds of the immorality of birth control. That is the viewpoint of our body of the Lutheran Church.

The great thing that we fear in this bill, as was said by Doctor Ryan, is this, that birth control will get into the hands of those people who do not need it, not only those who do not want it, but the young especially, and we shall find this literature on sale on all the book stands, and that it will do a great deal more harm than good.

·   ·   ·   ·   ·

STATEMENT OF DR. MARGUERITA A. STEWART, REPRESENTING THE NATIONAL CHRISTIAN LEAGUE FOR THE PROMOTION OF PURITY, NEW YORK CITY

Doctor STEWART. Mr. Chairman and gentlemen of the committee, I hope this bill will not be reported for legislative action. Its intent is to give legal sanction to a practice which has been outlawed in this Nation for 50 years. The prevention of conception is a practice which is hoary with age. We can trace it at least as far back as the days of Onan, where we find record of its practice by the man in Genesis, thirty-eighth chapter and ninth verse. It is a practice which is wrong in principle and violates the moral law of the universe. If legalized, it maintains for a man a standard of sex ethics below that of all the nobler species of the animal kingdom. In the animal kingdom below man no noble male approaches the female except at her invitation.

That woman should be driven to protect herself from undesired conceptions by contraceptive methods is degrading to both the man and the woman. (Parenthetically, I may say here that I have been told that modern teachers of this practice put the onus entirely upon the woman by advising her to great secrecy lest the man's moral sense be disturbed.)

Woman is the race carrier, and should be free to conserve to the uttermost her life-giving value to the race. In the periodic functioning of her reproductive organs is written the law of control over that function. Within that law once every month, at her discretion, she may receive the embraces of her man. The woman's control over reproductive functioning would conserve for man the precious vitality of his loins and give to woman her self-respect as a free moral agent in the reproduction of the race. Under these conditions shame would be removed, parentage would become voluntary, and motherhood become the supreme service and joy of woman's life.

To hold up before the young people of our land through legal sanction a standard of sex ethics below that of the nobler beasts of the field would be to debase the character of our Nation and finally disintegrate all morality. And so, gentlemen of the committee, I pray you that this bill may not be reported for legislative action. It would give legal sanction to an unmoral practice which has grown out of woman's age-long sex slavery to man, known in common law as "marital rights."

State laws on birth control, 1926

Dennett, *Birth Control Laws,* pp. 268–270.

Twenty-four States (and Porto Rico) specifically penalize contraceptive knowledge in their obscenity laws.

Twenty-four States (and the District of Columbia, Alaska and Hawaii) have obscenity laws, under which, because of the Federal precedent, contraceptive knowledge may be suppressed as obscene, although it is not specifically mentioned. Obscenity has never been defined in law. This produces a mass of conflicting, inconsistent judicial decision, which would be humorous, if it were not such a mortifying revelation of the limitations and perversions of the human mind.

Twenty-three States make it a crime to publish or advertise contraceptive information. They are as follows: Arizona, California, Colorado, Idaho, Indiana, Iowa, Kansas, Maine, Massachusetts, Minnesota, Mississippi, Missouri, Montana, Nebraska, Nevada, New Jersey, New York, North Dakota, Ohio, Oklahoma, Pennsylvania, Washington, Wyoming; also Porto Rico.

Twenty-two States include in their prohibition drugs and instruments for the prevention of conception. They are as follows: Arizona, California, Colorado, Connecticut, Idaho, Indiana, Iowa, Kansas, Massachusetts, Minnesota, Mississippi, Missouri, Montana, Nebraska, Nevada, New Jersey, New York, Ohio, Oklahoma, Pennsylvania, Washington, Wyoming and Porto Rico.

Eleven States make it a crime to have in one's possession any instruction for contraception. These are: Colorado, Indiana, Iowa, Minnesota, Mississippi, New Jersey, New York, North Dakota, Ohio, Pennsylvania, Wyoming.

Fourteen States make it a crime to tell anyone where or how contraceptive knowledge may be acquired. These are: Colorado, Indiana, Iowa, Massachusetts, Minnesota, Mississippi, Missouri, Montana, Nevada, New Jersey, New York, Pennsylvania, Washington, Wyoming.

Six States prohibit the offer to assist in any method whatever which would lead to knowledge by which contraception might be accomplished. These are: Arizona, California, Idaho, Montana, Nevada, Oklahoma and Porto Rico.

Eight States prohibit depositing in the Post Office any contraceptive information. These are: Colorado, Indiana, Iowa, Minnesota, New York, North Dakota, Ohio, Wyoming.[1]

One State, Colorado, prohibits the bringing into the State of any contraceptive knowledge.

Four States have laws authorizing the search for and seizure of contraceptive instructions, and these are: Colorado, Idaho, Iowa, Oklahoma. In all these States but Idaho, the laws authorize the destruction of the things seized.

Certain exemptions from the penalties of these laws are made by the States for

Medical Colleges	Medical Books	Physicians
Colorado	Colorado	Colorado
Indiana	Indiana	Indiana
Missouri	Kansas	Nevada
Nebraska	Missouri	New York
Ohio	Nebraska	Ohio
Pennsylvania	Ohio	Wyoming
Wyoming	Pennsylvania	
	Wyoming	

Druggists

Colorado, Indiana, Ohio, Wyoming.

Seventeen States prohibit any information which corrupts morals, 12 of them, as starred in the following list, particularly mentioning the morals of the young. This is an interesting point of view of the frequently offered objection to freedom of access to contraceptive knowledge, that it will demoralize the young. These States are: Colorado, Delaware,* Florida,* Iowa,* Maine,* Massachusetts,* Michigan,* Rhode Island, South Carolina, South Dakota, Tennessee, Texas,* Vermont,* Virginia,* West Virginia,* Wisconsin* and Hawaii.

Two States have no obscenity statutes, but police power in these States can suppress contraceptive knowledge as an "Obscenity" or "public nuisance," by virtue of the Federal

1. These States present a knotty legal question as to whether the repeal of the Federal prohibition relating to the mails will automatically make these State laws void. Legal opinion (as expressed by Attorneys Alfred Hayes and James F. Morton, Jr.) seems to agree that the Federal action will probably be effective, but there is authority for the assumption that under the State law police power might withhold such supposedly undesirable mail from the recipient. [Note in Dennett, *Birth Control Laws.*]

precedent. These States are: North Carolina and New Mexico.

The future of birth control, 1932

The Nation, CXXXII (1932), 89.

The Nation for January 27, 1932, was devoted largely to discussion of the birth control controversy.

We have gone out of our way to devote a considerable portion of this unusually large issue of *The Nation* to the subject of birth control because of the overshadowing importance of the question at this grave juncture of the world's economic history. With millions upon millions out of work, on the verge of starvation or actually starving, the question of population becomes of transcendent importance — so much so that H. G. Wells on his recent visit to New York declared that if things continue as they are some 400,000,000 people must needs perish in order to restore the old equilibrium. Fantastic that utterance sounds; exaggerated it indubitably is. Still, the present emergency is too grave and the threat of a long-drawn-out world convalescence too likely, not to call peoples' attention sharply to a reconsideration of the old theory that the larger the nation the better for all its people.

But if there were no economic crisis whatever, we should none the less again be lifting our voice to demand that no limits of any kind be set to the dissemination of facts about birth control and to urge its practice. This is in its essence a question of individual freedom and liberty. Unlike the question of drink or drugs, it connotes, our Catholic friends to the contrary notwithstanding, no injury to public morals or well-being; on the contrary there is no single thing we know of that could bring greater health and happiness and a sounder morality to the masses of the working people, or bring them as quickly. We are especially aiming this issue of *The Nation* at Congress and men in public life, because of the direct efforts now being made to induce Congress and the State legislatures to expunge from the statute books the legislation which makes it criminal to disseminate birth-control information through the mails and to distribute contraceptives. We are in favor of complete repeal of all such laws. In taking this stand we are merely asking that the country revert to its historic position during the first hundred years of its existence, when there were no restrictions whatever, as is pointed out by Morris L. Ernst in his article printed elsewhere in this issue. We are aware, of course, that in asking complete repeal we are asking what is impossible today. So we are quite ready to accept any legislation and to welcome any court decision which will break down any part of the now existing laws. The courts have done excellent work so far and will doubtless continue to do so. But we wish that anti-social legislation entirely repealed before it becomes a dead letter, before it too is nullified by non-enforcement and joins the mass of matter which would be wiped off the statute books if we should ever have a complete elimination of the unenforced and unenforceable laws.

Meanwhile we have this constructive suggestion to make: We urge a Congressional committee on birth control for a complete inquiry into the whole subject by an authoritative body. We would not limit it merely to the question of whether legislation is desirable or not. We would not limit it merely to the pros and cons of a particular bill or bills. We would have it go into such subjects as the extent of the present dissemination of birth-control knowledge and of the existing nullification of the law, whereby, like so many other statutes, it has become a weapon to be used only when, because of pressure from some bigoted or clerical source, the police decide suddenly to move against a particular person or set of persons. Such a committee could discover that in the case of the Lee Rubber Company in the United States Circuit Court of Appeals the evidence indicated that

one particular contraceptive circulated in the mails to the extent of 20,000,000 in a single year. Such a committee might even interest itself in the development of the technique of birth control.

That birth-control advocates are in for a long fight no one can doubt. The ignorance, the cowardice, the prejudices with which they have to contend are sufficient to daunt any hearts less brave than those of Mrs. Sanger, or Mrs. Mary Ware Dennett, or the other pioneers and leaders in this great movement to end unnecessary and unwilling motherhood, to put marriage and the marriage relation where they rightfully belong. In America the chief enemy is, of course, the Catholic church. That that opposition will in time be overcome we do not question; there are too many Catholics themselves profiting by the knowledge of birth control, especially among the rich members of the church, to leave any doubt as to that. The question becomes merely one of obeying the dictates of sound sense, sound morals, and economic wisdom. Today most of our politicians, even those that come from overwhelmingly Protestant districts, are too much afraid to speak out, or to advocate the position some know to be correct. Especially is this true of Congress. But greater odds were faced by Abolitionists and the woman suffragists, who yet lived to see their causes triumph in far shorter time than anyone dreamed to be possible. So will it be with birth control.

Abortion and the question of when life begins

Both the common law and state abortion statutes distinguished between delivery of the embryo in the first stage of pregnancy and the aborting of the fetus after it had quickened in the womb, ordinarily about four months after conception. Since it was assumed that life did not exist prior to the quickening, the former was only an offense against morality while the latter was legally defined as manslaughter and carried harsher penalties. The Connecticut law of 1821, for example, permitted life imprisonment for criminal abortion on a woman "then being quick with child." [1] The Comstock Act of 1873 included abortifacients among obscene objects which could not legally be shipped through the United States mail (see below Chap. II, sec. B., "Comstockery", doc. 3.).

1. The common law on abortion as interpreted by the Supreme Court of Kentucky, 1879

Mitchell *v.* Commonwealth, 78 Ky. 204.

In this criminal prosecution a man was charged with performing an abortion on a woman who had been pregnant about three months. It was not averred that the fetus had quickened. The Kentucky court reviewed earlier decisions and, relying especially on a decision in the Massachusetts courts in 1812, Commonwealth *v.* Bangs, 9 Mass. 387, declared the common law provided no grounds for prosecution.

In the interest of good morals and for the preservation of society, the law should punish abortions and miscarriages, wilfully produced, at any time during the period of gestation. That the child shall be considered in existence from the moment of conception for the protection of its rights of property, and yet not in existence, until four or five months after the inception of its being, to the extent that it is a crime to destroy it, presents an anomaly in the law that ought to be provided against by the law-making department of the government. The limit of our duty is to determine what the law is, and not to enact or declare it as it should be. In the discharge of this duty . . . we are forced to the

1. *The Public Statute Laws of the State of Connecticut, 1821* (Hartford, 1821), p. 152.

conclusion that it never was a punishable offense at common law to produce, with the consent of the mother, an abortion prior to the time when the mother became quick with child.

2. Judicial determination of the beginning of life, Wisconsin, 1923

Foster *v.* State, 182 Wisc. 298.

In this interpretation of Wisconsin laws, the court held that an abortion produced before the embryo had quickened could not be prosecuted as manslaughter. It could, however, be prosecuted as an "offense against . . . morality, and decency," a lesser charge.

Plaintiff in error, hereinafter called the defendant, was prosecuted . . . and convicted of having feloniously produced the death of the child of one Anna Jung. The evidence showed among other things that Miss Jung was advanced in pregnancy from six to eight weeks; that she consulted the defendant; that he made an examination and pronounced her pregnant, and performed a criminal operation upon her resulting in a premature expulsion of the fœtus. He claimed the evidence fails to show that Miss Jung was pregnant; that there is not sufficient proof of his having performed an operation; and that if guilty at all he should have been prosecuted under the provisions of sec. 4583, Stats., relating to producing a miscarriage . . .

.   .   .   .   .

Vinje, C. J. We shall not devote any time to the discussion or recital of the evidence further than to say that it sustains a finding that Miss Jung was pregnant; that the defendant performed a criminal operation upon her by means of which the embryo or fœtus was prematurely expelled; and that there were no prejudicial errors in the trial of the case.

The really serious question in the case is

whether the defendant was prosecuted under the proper section of the statute. Sec. 4352, under which he was prosecuted, reads as follows:

"Any person who shall administer to any woman pregnant with a child any medicine, drug or substance whatever, or shall use or employ any instrument or other means with intent thereby to destroy such child, unless the same shall have been necessary to preserve the life of such mother or shall have been advised by two physicians to be necessary for such purpose, shall, in case the death of such child or of such mother be thereby produced, be deemed guilty of manslaughter in the second degree."

It is found in the chapter relating to "Offenses against Lives and Persons." The penalty for its violation is imprisonment in the state prison from four to seven years.

Sec. 4583 reads as follows:

"Any person who shall administer to any pregnant woman, or prescribe for such woman, or advise or procure any such woman to take any medicine, drug or substance or thing whatever, or shall use or employ any instrument or other means whatever, or advise or procure the same to be used, with intent thereby to procure the miscarriage of any such woman shall be punished by imprisonment in the county jail not more than one year nor less than six months or by fine not exceeding five hundred dollars nor less than two hundred and fifty dollars, or by both such fine and imprisonment in the discretion of the court."

It is found in the chapter entitled "Offenses against Chastity, Morality, and Decency." It is evident that the legislature did not intend to define the same offense in the two sections. In the latter it defines the offense of an act intended to produce miscarriage or one that does produce miscarriage.

.   .   .   .   .

In order to commit such an offense there must be a pregnant woman. A normal pregnancy can exist only where there is embryonic life in the womb of the pregnant woman; therefore, in order to commit the offense of producing a miscarriage, there must be a destruction and expulsion of embryonic life. So we have a statute covering the offense of destroying and expelling from the womb embryonic life. This offense is one not against a person because the law does not recognize a mere embryo as a person or human being, but is an offense against morality because it is against good morals to destroy that which otherwise presumably would develop into a human being. It interferes with the normal functions of nature in the perpetuation of the race.

The offense described in sec. 4352 constitutes manslaughter in the second degree and is by statute included under the denomination of "homicide," which means the killing of a human being . . . Neither in popular nor in scientific language is the embryo in its early stages called a human being. Popularly it is regarded as such, for some purposes, only after it has become "quick," which does not occur till four or five months of pregnancy have elapsed. In contemplation of law, says Blackstone, life begins as soon as an infant is able to stir in its mother's womb . . . It is obvious that no death of a child can be produced where there is no living child. Sec. 4352 requires the existence of a living child and the causing of its death, or that of the mother, before the offense there defined is committed. If pregnancy has not advanced sufficiently so that there is a living child, that is, a quick child, then felonious destruction of the fœtus constitutes a criminal miscarriage only. This construction gives full force and effect to each section as defining a distinct separate offense, is in accordance with the common conception of the beginning of life, and is sustained by authority . . .

.   .   .   .   .

In a strictly scientific and physiological sense there is life in an embryo from the time of conception, and in such sense there is also life in the male and female elements that unite to form the embryo. But law, for obvious reasons, cannot in its classifications follow the latest or ultimate declarations of science. It must for purposes of practical efficiency proceed upon more every-day and popular conceptions, especially as to definitions of crimes that are malum in se. These must be of such a nature that the ordinary normal adult knows it is morally wrong to commit them. That it should be less of an offense to destroy an embryo in a stage where human life in its common acceptance has not yet begun than to destroy a *quick* child, is a conclusion that commends itself to most men. The legislature saw fit to enact sec. 4583, a law making it an offense to produce a criminal miscarriage. It also made it a graver offense by sec. 4352 to produce a criminal abortion re-

sulting in the death of a quick child or of its mother. Both the quick child and the mother are human beings — hence to unlawfully kill either constitutes manslaughter. A two months' embryo is not a human being in the eye of the law and therefore its destruction constitutes an offense against morality and not against lives and persons. Defendant should have been prosecuted under the provisions of sec. 4583. The evidence does not sustain a conviction under sec. 4352.

E. CHILDREN OF UNMARRIED PARENTS

Providing means of support for illegitimate children

1. The putative father must expressly promise to maintain the child, Illinois, 1884

Glidden *v.* Nelson, 15 Ill. App. 297.

This was an action . . . commenced by appellee . . . to recover for the care, nurture and maintenance of the bastard child of the appellee which she claimed was begotten by the appellant, out of wedlock, and while she was an unmarried woman.

It appears from the evidence that some time from 1872 to 1875 the appellee entered service in the family of James Glidden, the father of appellant, as a house servant, and was there in that capacity at various times from that date up to a few months before this suit was brought. During that time James Glidden was absent from home more or less, and appellant, his son, lived at home and had charge in part of the farm and work. The wife of James Glidden, the appellant's mother, was at home nearly all the

time and had charge of the house. The appellant is now thirty years old and was married in 1882. The appellee testifies that the child was three years old July 17, 1883, and that it was begotten by appellant while she was an inmate of his father's family, and that in consequence of her pregnancy in the spring of 1880, she was requested by appellant to go away, and that if she did not go away he would have to leave, and that she accordingly went to the State of Wisconsin, and there, at the home of her sister, Mrs. Mason, gave birth to the child. She afterward returned to Glidden's.

The appellant denies all knowledge of the child until about a month after he was married, and denies having had sexual intercourse with the appellee, and denies any intimacy with her, and his father and mother testify that they never saw appellant have any improper intimacy with her, and the mother saw nothing different between appellant and appellee while at her house from the ordinary way in which an ordinary hired girl is treated, and did not know she was in the family way. Appellee had a husband, but she thinks he was dead and had been dead about ten years at the time she testified — got killed on a railroad. She got a letter from him that he was coming to see her on the train and there was an accident on the train that he was to come on, and she never heard from him after the letter. There was no express promise on the part of appellant to pay for the care and nurture of the child and he never adopted it as his own, and no proceedings in bastardy were ever commenced against him by appellee. There was a recovery of $600 by appellee, which judgment is appealed from. There is the evidence of appellee that appellant promised to send her money to Wisconsin, made just before she left Glidden's, but it clearly appears that this promise referred solely to her wages and nothing more.

.   .   .   .   .

Lacey, J. Three main points are made by appellant as grounds for reversal. First, that there was no sufficient proof that the husband of the appellee was dead at the time of the alleged act of bastardy. Second, that there is no preponderance of proof that the appellant was the father of appellee's child, and thirdly, that under the proof there can be no recovery for want of an express promise on the part of the appellant to pay for the care and nurture of the child. It is claimed that there is not sufficient proof that seven years had elapsed from the time appellee last heard of her husband, to the time of the conception of the child, and hence no proof of the death of the husband; and as to the second point, that the evidence that appellant was the father of the child, rests alone on the testimony of appellee, contradicted by the positive denial of appellant, who, it is claimed, is corroborated by circumstances testified to by the appellant's father and mother, and that this proof is insufficient.

However this may be, we have not deemed it necessary to determine, as the decision of the case must rest on the third point made.

As to the third point, we find no evidence in the record to show that the appellant at any time made any express promise to pay for the care, nurture and expenses attending the birth of the child, or for any other matter concerning the maintenance of it; nor is there any proof

that the appellant ever adopted the child as his own, or that any proceedings in bastardy were ever had against appellant by appellee.

We find upon examination, that the authority cited by counsel for the appellant fully sustains the doctrine contended for, that unless the father voluntarily adopts the child as his own, which he may do with the consent of the mother, he will not become liable for its necessary maintenance. That in other cases he is not liable except on an express promise or an order of affiliation. This is the common law rule on the subject. But upon the strength of the natural or moral obligation arising out of the relation of the putative father to his child, an action at common law lies for its maintenance and support upon an express promise . . . in the absence of statutory regulations, the father is under no legal obligations to support his illegitimate child. The statute prescribes the only legal mode by which this support can be obtained . . .

This being the law, under the proof in this case there could be no cause of action, and the verdict of the jury was entirely without evidence to support it. The judgment will therefore be reversed.

———

2. Undermining the common law doctrine, Kansas, 1923

Doughty v. Engler, 112 Kan. 583.

———

A four-year-old boy, born out of wedlock, brought this action through his mother as his next friend, against one alleged to be his father, to require the defendant to make provision for his support. This appeal is taken from the sustaining of a demurrer to the petition.

At common law the father of an illegitimate child was under no legal duty to support it. In behalf of the plaintiff it is urged that this rule is not sound in reason and not in keeping with modern ideas of natural right, and should not be regarded as remaining in force in aid of our statutes by virtue of the act giving that effect to the common law as modified by "the conditions and wants of the people." . . . The courts of this country apparently in every case in which the question has been raised have held, that without legislation on the subject, the father of an illegitimate child cannot be required to provide for its support . . . In most of these cases, however, the matter has been treated as settled by the mere fact that the common law recognized no such duty on his part, and the question whether the rule is so repugnant to present-day conceptions of social obligations that courts should refuse to follow it has not been extensively discussed.

The common law with almost uniform consistency treated an offspring of parents not married to each other as *nullius filius* —the son of no one — of no father and no mother. That is to say, it closed its eyes to the fact of that relation and in legal aspect ignored its existence. It absolved the mother equally with the father from liability for the support of the child . . . But the common law in failing to require the parent of an illegitimate child to support it did not rest wholly upon the *nullius filius* idea, for as interpreted in England and in some of the American states it imposed no legal obligation in that respect even upon the parents of legitimate children . . . By the great weight of judicial opinion in this country parents are under a legal duty, regardless of any statute, to maintain their legitimate minor children . . . the obligation being sometimes spoken of as one under the common law and sometimes as a matter of natural right and justice, and often accepted as a matter of course without the assignment of any reason.

.   .   .   .   .   .

A sufficient reason for holding parents to be under a legal obligation, apart from any statute, to support their legitimate child while it is too young to care for itself, is that the liability ought to attach as a part of their responsibility for having brought it into being. If that reason is not found convincing, it would be useless to seek others. And it does not in the least depend for its force upon the fact that the parents were married to each other, but is equally persuasive where that is not the case . . .

The courts of some states, in the absence of a statute on the subject, hold the mother of an illegitimate child liable for its support, usually upon the ground that such liability is an incident to her right of custody . . . which is sometimes assumed to exist at common law — a sort of inversion of the process by which a statutory duty of support has been said to carry with it the right of custody . . . This court does not regard the duty of support as dependent upon the right to custody . . .

In a commissioner's opinion in a statutory action to charge the father of an illegitimate child with its support it was said: "Under the law, the mother of an illegitimate child is all the while known, and is at all times, at least during its infancy, liable for its support, while the father of such child is unknown until ascertained by judicial proceedings, unless he acknowledges its paternity; and therefore, he is liable only when the paternity of the child is acknowledged by him, or it is established by judicial inquiry." . . . This was sufficiently accurate for the purposes of the case, the paternity of the child being the matter to be determined. No attempt was there made to state the ground of the mother's liability. As already indicated we place it upon the fact of parentage, and upon that basis it must extend to the father as well. The circumstance of the father's being unknown could not relieve him from the nonstatutory inherent obligation if it exists at all, although the difficulty of ascertaining the paternity might as a matter of policy influence legislation on the subject.

We do not think the legislature should be regarded as intending to relieve the father from this obligation to the child by the enactment of the statute above referred to, which authorizes the mother of an illegitimate child, if she sees fit, to maintain an action for her benefit in the name of the state against the putative father, and provides for the enforcement of a judgment by imprisonment . . . It would obviously be inadequate to cover the entire field of paternal liability, since the mother might not care to institute such a proceeding, or might die without instituting it. The measure is one providing machinery for the enforcement of a duty already existing rather than one creating a new obligation. Parental liability for the support of legitimate children did not originate with the statute of 1911 . . . imposing punishment for a default in that respect.

A rule of the common law may be unadapted to the conditions and unsuitable to the needs of the people of this state, although the change that has taken place is rather in the manner of looking at things — in the standards of obligation and conduct — rather than in more objective matters. Instances in which this court has refused to follow a rule of the common law, for reasons based in a greater or less degree upon its essential unsoundness, are collected in Cooper v. Seaverns, 81 Kan. 267, 105 Pac. 509, where the grounds of such departure are fully discussed.

The right of a child of tender years to look to its father for support being determined, the matter of procedure presents no great difficulty . . . A court of equity in its historical capacity as guardian of infants can readily devise means for its enforcement.

The judgment is reversed and the cause is remanded with directions to overrule the demurrer to the petition.

The illegitimate child's right of inheritance

1. An illegitimate child may inherit from collateral relatives as well as lineal ancestors, Connecticut, 1875

Dickinson's Appeal from Probate, 42 Conn. 491.

The appellants are the grandsons of Mary Cotton, their mother being her illegitimate daughter. Mary Cotton was a sister of the testatrix, Eliza J. Cotton, and it is from the decree of the court of probate approving her last will that this appeal was taken. The mother and grandmother of the appellants had been dead some fifteen years at the time of the death of the testatrix, who was a single woman, having never been married. She left no parents, no brothers or sisters, and no blood relations, unless the appellants are to be so considered, nearer than cousins. In the Superior Court the appellees moved to dismiss the appeal on the ground that the appellants were not heirs at law of the deceased, and had no interest in or title to her estate. The question thus raised is reserved for the advice of this court.

·   ·   ·   ·   ·

The laws of the different states of our Union differ widely as to the rights of illegitimates. Most of the states have passed statutes mitigating more or less the rigors of the common law, and conferring rights which that law denied. The general tendency seems to be one of increasing liberality. In most, if not in all of the states, they inherit from the mother, and the mother from them. In some states they inherit from each other, from collateral kindred, and from the father, when there has been a general, notorious, and mutual recognition. In many of the states subsequent marriage of parents legitimates. Connecticut is one of the very few states, possibly the only one, that has passed no statute defining the rights of bastards.

·   ·   ·   ·   ·

It was at first held that a bastard derived its settlement from its mother, not from its place of birth. This was analogous to an interest derived by inheritance, and recognized the legal relation of parent and child.

It was next held that illegitimate children of

the same mother could inherit from each other. This recognized the relation of brother and sister.

It was then held that an illegitimate child could inherit from its mother; and so the relation of parent and child was most directly recognized, and the reciprocal rights and duties growing out of that relation were thoroughly established.

The learned counsel for the appellees, admitting that a wide difference exists between our law and the English common law as to the rights of illegitimates, still insists that, under our law, their right, and the right of their descendants, is strictly lineal, never collateral; and so the appellants have no rights as heirs at law of the testatrix. In the expressive language of the counsel, though this progeny be grafted on the lineal stock, it has not been grafted on the collateral, and it is urged that this ought not to be done; that it will be taking another and farther departure from the wise principles of the common law, and that it will tend to encourage immorality and impair the sanctity of the marriage relation. These views have been pressed upon us so eloquently and so forcibly that we should regret to be thought insensible to the appeal.

If however we find the law to be in favor of the appellants, whatever we may think of its wisdom or its policy, we must so pronounce it . . .

After as careful a consideration of the question as we have been able to give, we think that the points decided in the cases we have quoted tend strongly to the conclusion that these appellants, by the law of Connecticut, are heirs at law of the testatrix, Eliza J. Cotton.

.   .   .   .   .

Now if there be no obstacle, and we discover none, to having an estate pass from an illegitimate child through its mother to her collateral relations, can there be any obstacle to the passing of an estate from collateral relations, through its mother, to an illegitimate child? If any discrimination is to be made, ought it not to be the reverse of that claimed? Do not reason and justice loudly demand that the disability should fall on the erring parent rather than on the innocent child? . . .

A fair construction of our statute of distributions leads us therefore to the conclusion that these appellants have an interest, as heirs at law, in the estate of the testatrix. Nor does it seem to us that in reaching this result we are making a farther departure than we have already made from the English common law. The cases heretofore decided in this state involve principles which must control this case, and the decision we make is necessary to vindicate those principles and preserve the symmetry of our law.

But the appellees quote to us a number of cases decided in states where, by statute, bastards are authorized to inherit from their mothers, and their mothers from them, and yet all right of inheritance among collaterals is denied.

To these cases we deem it a sufficient answer in the first place to say, that in all those states the doctrine of the common law as to a bastard, that he was *nullius filius,* was considered as established. The statute, being in derogation of the common law, was therefore to be construed strictly. The bastard was to inherit to the extent, and only to the extent, specified in the statute. If the statute gave him a morsel of bread, the common law gave him a stone if he asked to have that morsel of bread enlarged.

In Connecticut, as we have seen again and again, this doctrine of the common law as to bastards never obtained, and so these decisions lack applicability.

.   .   .   .   .

Arriving as we do, unhesitatingly, at the result, both by the common law of this state, and by our statute of distributions, that these appellants are heirs at law of the testatrix, we shall add little, and perhaps should add nothing, as to the character or tendency of the law. The removal of disabilities from illegitimates, so as to leave them capable of inheriting and transmitting inheritances on the part of the mother, collaterally, as well as lineally, like other persons, is sharply denounced. Facts however, we believe, fail to show either the immorality or impolicy of our law. We have been at some pains to examine the statistics on this subject, but have not been able to obtain returns from any of our sister states. We doubt if such returns are generally made. In ten years ending on the 31st day of December, 1874, there were born in this state 137,396 children, of which 1,118 (eighty-one hundredths of one per cent.) were illegitimate; as small a ratio, we venture to assert, as can anywhere be found. In England, for three years prior to and including 1860, the ratio of illegitimate to legitimate births was over 6½ per cent.; and in Scotland, for ten years ending in 1870, it was 9.77 per cent. On the continent, so far as we have had access to the returns, the ratio is, generally, much larger. The number of illegitimates now in England and Wales alone is over one million. Surely it is not beneath the consideration of a wise statesmanship, whether it is just or prudent to cut off so large a portion of the population, who are charged with no crime, from all rights of inheritance, and isolate them almost absolutely from the body politic.

---

2. An illegitimate child who has not been acknowledged according to the laws of the state cannot inherit, Illinois, 1885

Stoltz et al. *v.* Doering, 112 Ill. 234.

This was an action of ejectment, brought by Henry Doering in the circuit court of DeKalb county, against Mary Elizabeth Stoltz, and Jacob Stoltz, her husband, to recover a certain tract of land in DeKalb county, which was owned originally by John Doering, who died intestate, seized of the land, in 1860. The cause was tried, by agreement, before the court, without a jury, and judgment was rendered in favor of the plaintiff, and defendants appealed.

Mary Elizabeth Stoltz, as appears from the evidence, was the daughter and only child of John Doering, who died seized of the land; but she was an illegitimate child, and upon this ground, plaintiff, who was a brother and next of kin of deceased, contends that the daughter can not inherit from the father, and that he, as sole heir of his brother, is entitled to recover. The plaintiff resides in Germany. The defendants were residing in this country at the time John Doering died, and upon his death they went into the possession of the land, and have remained in possession ever since, paying all taxes, and claiming to be the owners.

It appears from the evidence, that in 1831 John Doering, then a young unmarried man, resided in the province of Hesse Darmstadt, Germany; that he became acquainted with a girl residing at the same place, named Mary Webber. These parties became attached to each other, and were engaged to be married, and in April, 1832, Mary Webber gave birth to a female child, — now Mary Elizabeth Stoltz, the defendant in this action. John Doering was the father of the child. He never, however, married Mary Webber, but, in 1834, left Germany and came to this country. He settled in DeKalb county, where, in 1845, he purchased the land in question. It is plain, from the evidence, that Doering always, after the birth of Mary Elizabeth, recognized and treated her as his daughter. In 1849 he had her brought to this country at his own expense, and introduced her to his friends and acquaintances as his child and daughter. Indeed, in the records of births and baptisms of the evangelical diocese of Meichs, in Germany, where Doering and Mary Webber resided, and where the child was born, John Doering acknowledged, in a public manner, in writing, over his own signature, that he was the father of the child.

The public acknowledgment of John Doering, in connection with the action taken in the parochial church by the mother and father of the child, it is contended, gave her the right of inheritance under the laws of the province in

Germany where they resided, and as she became entitled to inherit there, she became the heir of John Doering, and as such entitled to inherit his property wherever situate . . .

At common law a bastard has no right of inheritance. In the eyes of the law, bastards are not regarded as children for civil purposes . . . Under our statute in force at the time of the death of John Doering, a bastard could not inherit from a father unless such father had married the mother of the child, and acknowledged the child as his own. Under section 65, chapter 109, Gross' *Statutes of 1869,* a bastard might inherit from the mother, but this statute confers no right of inheritance from the father.

The first question then to be determined is, whether the rights of the defendant, Mary Elizabeth Stoltz, are to be determined by the laws of the province of Germany, where she was born and baptized, or are those rights to be determined by the laws of this State, where the land involved is located. The general rule in regard to the descent of real estate is, that it is governed by the law of the country where the land is located . . .

If we are correct in our view of the law on this question, then, although the defendant may have been entitled to inherit from her father under the laws of Germany, where she was born, had he died leaving property in that country, it does not follow that the defendant can inherit the property in this State, as real estate situated here must descend in conformity to the laws of our State, and not as provided by the laws of Germany, — a foreign country.

It is also claimed by counsel for appellants, that Mrs. Stoltz is the legitimate child of John Doering, from a common law marriage with Mary Webber *per verba de futuro cum copula.* There is no doubt from the evidence but Doering and Mary Webber had agreed, between themselves, that they would, at some future day, become husband and wife, and while this contract was in existence, sexual intercourse was had and the child begotten; but we do not understand that this constituted a common law marriage . . . The fact that sexual intercourse

occurs after an agreement to marry at some future day, is not of itself sufficient to establish the marriage relation. To be availing, the parties, at the time of *copula,* must *then* accept each other as husband and wife. This was not done here . . .

Judgment affirmed.

---

3. An illegitimate child, though unacknowledged by its father, can inherit if its parents cohabited, Washington, 1894

In re Matthias' Estate, 63 Fed. 523.

This case involves a contest on the part of Rebecca Lena Graham in which she asserts . . . her right as an heir at law of Franklin Matthias, deceased, to receive from the administrator of his estate the residue remaining after the payment of costs and expenses of administration and all indebtedness. She claims to be a daughter and only child of Franklin Matthias. The other parties to the suit, who claim to be the lawful heirs, are collateral heirs; and no one other than Mrs. Graham claims to be a lineal descendant.

The questions in the case are whether Mrs. Graham is in fact the daughter of Franklin Matthias, whether she is his legitimate daughter, and under the laws of this state entitled to inherit his property. A large number of witnesses have been called to testify in support of Mrs. Graham's claim, and to dispute it. I find in the testimony a great deal that is mere surmise, a great deal of gossip, a great deal of rumor, and a great deal that I regard as fiction.

.   .   .   .   .

From consideration of all the evidence, I am well convinced that Matthias and Peggy were never married. I am also convinced that Frank Matthias was the father of this complainant. To entitle her to inherit his estate, being his daughter, it is not absolutely necessary that there should be proof of a marriage between her parents. If they lived together as man and wife during the period of time within which she was born, their so living together would, for the purpose of determining the rights of their child, be equivalent to a marriage, under a statute of Washington territory, enacted at its first session. That is the third section of an act entitled "An act in relation to marriage" . . . which provides that "All children born of marriages declared void by the preceding section, and all children born of persons living and cohabiting together, as man and wife, and all children born out of wedlock whose parents shall intermarry, shall be legitimate." This statute is somewhat peculiar. It is made for the protection and benefit of children. Without attempting to legislate as to the status of the parents, or determining or fixing their rights as married people, it does give rights to the innocent offspring; and, having that object in view, effect should be given to it according to its spirit, because it is a just law. Where children are born under such circumstances as to leave no just ground for doubting their parentage, and where there is no probability of injustice being done by imposing upon a man spurious offspring, it seems to me right that his children should inherit his estate. This law provides not only for the children of void marriages, and children born out of wedlock whose parents afterwards married, but provides specifically for children of unmarried persons who live and cohabit together as man and wife, and declares that such children shall be legitimate. Now, if the testimony of . . . those . . . people to the actual fact that Peggy and Frank Matthias did live together as man and wife, and kept house together before and after the birth of this plaintiff, be true, then, under that law, she is entitled to all the rights of a legitimate child of Frank Matthias.

.   .   .   .   .   .

My conclusion is that there is a fair preponderance of the evidence, in favor of this complainant, to the fact that her mother and Frank Matthias lived together as man and wife before and after the complainant's birth; and, upon that preponderance of evidence, she is entitled to a finding in her favor. The laws of this state in force at the time of the death of Frank Matthias entitle this complainant, as his only lineal descendant, to receive his estate; and I will decree that she is so entitled.

---

4. Equal inheritance for illegitimate children, Arizona, 1921

"An Act declaring every child to be the Legitimate Child of its Natural Parents . . . ," 1921 — ch. 114, *Acts, Resolutions and Memorials of the Regular Session of the Fifth Legislature of the State of Arizona* (Phoenix, 1921), pp. 248–249.

Every child is hereby declared to be the legitimate child of its natural parents and as such is entitled to support and education to the same extent as if it has been born in lawful wedlock. It shall inherit from its natural parents and from their kindred heir lineal and collateral in the same manner as children born in lawful wedlock . . .

This section shall apply to cases where the natural father of any such child is married to one other than the mother of said child, as well as where he is single. Provided, however, this law shall not be so construed as to give to said child the right to dwelling or a residence with the family of its father, if such father be married.

. . . The mother of any child born out of lawful wedlock may within one year after the birth of such child bring a civil action in the superior court to establish the parentage of such child. Such action shall be commenced by complaint filed by the mother as plaintiff against the alleged natural father as defendant, and summons shall be issued and served and the same proceedings had as in other civil cases. In such cases the parentage may be proved like any other fact.

Provided, that the mother of said child shall not be considered a competent witness in any case where the alleged natural father of said child shall be dead at the time of the trial.

Provided further, that a statement in writing may be made by the parents of said child, admitting the parentage thereof, and upon which a judgment may be entered.

Minnesota reforms the treatment of illegitimate children

1. Securing equal treatment for illegitimate children, 1917

"An Act to amend chapter 17, General Statutes, 1913, relating to illegitimate children," 1917 — ch. 210, *Session Laws of the State of Minnesota, 1917* (Minneapolis, 1917), pp. 296–300.

Minnesota was the first state to make radical and comprehensive changes in its laws and administrative procedures to safeguard the rights of illegitimate children and to make their status equal to that of children born of lawful marriage. The reforms were made on the recommendation of the Minnesota Children's Code Committee. (See below Part Six, Chap. II, sec. A, Minnesota revises laws concerning children, 1917, docs. 1 and 2.)

. . . On complaint being made to a justice of the peace or municipal court by any woman who is delivered of an illegitimate child, or pregnant with child which, if born alive, might be illegitimate, accusing any person of being the father of such child, the justice or clerk of

the court shall take the complaint in writing, under her oath, and thereupon shall issue a warrant, directed to the sheriff or any constable of the county commanding him forthwith to bring such accused person before such justice or court to answer such complaint.

.   .   .   .   .

. . . Upon the trial the examination taken before the justice or judge of the municipal court shall in all cases be read to the jury when demanded by the defendant. If he is found guilty, or admits the truth of the accusation, he shall be adjudged to be the father of such child and thenceforth shall be subject to all the obligations for the care, maintenance and education of such child, and to all the penalties for failure to perform the same, which are or shall be imposed by law upon the father of a legitimate child of like age and capacity. Judgment shall also be entered against him for all expenses incurred by the county for the lying-in and support of, and attendance upon the mother during her sickness, and for the care and support of such child prior to said judgment of paternity, the amount of which expenses, if any, shall also be found by the jury if they return a verdict of guilty; together with the costs of prosecution. If the defendant fails to pay the amount of such money judgment forthwith, or during such stay of execution as may be granted by the court, he shall be committed to the county jail, there to remain until he pays the same or is discharged according to law.

.   .   .   .   .

. . . Any person who has been imprisoned ninety days for failure to pay any such money judgment may apply to said court, by petition setting forth his inability to pay the same, and praying to be discharged from imprisonment, and shall attach to such petition a verified statement of all his property, money and effects whether exempt from execution or otherwise . . .

. . . At the hearing the defendant shall be examined on oath in reference to the facts set forth in such petition and his ability to pay such money judgment, and any other legal evidence in reference to such matters may be produced by any of the parties interested. If it appears that the defendant is unable to pay such judgment, the court may direct his discharge from custody, upon his making affidavit that he has not in his own name any property, real or personal, and has no such property conveyed or concealed, or in any manner disposed of with design to secure the same to his use or to avoid in any manner payment of such judgment . . .

. . . If a woman is delivered of an illegitimate child, or is pregnant with a child likely to be illegitimate when born, the county board of the county where she resides, or any member thereof, or the state board of control or any person duly appointed to perform in said county any of the duties of said board relating to the welfare of children, may apply by complaint to a justice of the peace of the county or to a municipal court to inquire into the facts and circumstances of the case . . .

. . . Such justice or the judge of the municipal court may summon the woman to appear before him, and may examine her on oath respecting the father of such child, the time when and place where it was begotten, and any other facts he deems necessary for the discovery of the truth, and thereupon shall issue his warrant to apprehend the putative father. Thereafter the proceedings shall be the same as if the complaint had been made by such woman under the provisions of this chapter, and with like effect, and in all cases the complainant and the accused may require the attendance of such woman as a witness.

. . . . .

. . . The state board of control or the duly appointed guardian of the person of an illegitimate child shall have authority to accept from the duly adjudged or acknowledged father of the child such sum as shall be approved by the court having jurisdiction of proceedings to establish the paternity of the child, in full settlement of all obligations for the care, maintenance and education of such child; and shall hold or dispose of the same as ordered by said court. Such settlement shall discharge the father of all further liability, civil and criminal, on account of such child.

. . . . .

. . . This chapter shall be liberally construed with a view to affecting its purpose, which is primarily to safeguard the interests of illegitimate children and secure for them the nearest possible approximation to the care, support and education that they would be entitled to receive if born of lawful marriage, which purpose is hereby acknowledged and declared to be the duty of the state; and also to secure from the fathers of such children repayment of public moneys necessarily expended in connection with their birth.

. . . All records of court proceedings in cases of alleged illegitimacy shall be withheld from inspection by, and copies thereof shall not be furnished to, persons other than the parties in interest and their attorneys, except upon order of the court.

---

2. Regulation of maternity hospitals, 1919

"An Act defining and regulating maternity hospitals," 1919 — ch. 50, *Session Laws of the State of Minnesota, 1919* (Minneapolis, 1919), pp. 76–79.

The state board of control is hereby empowered to grant a license for one year for the conduct of any maternity hospital that is for the public good and that is conducted by a reputable and responsible person; and it shall be the duty of the board of control to prescribe such general regulations and rules for the conduct of all such hospitals as shall be necessary to effect the purposes of this act and all other laws of the state relating to children so far as the same are applicable and to safeguard the well-being of all infants born therein, and the health, morality and best interests of the parties who are inmates thereof. No maternity hospital shall receive a woman for care therein without first obtaining a license to conduct such hospital from said board of control. No such license shall be issued, unless the premises are in fit sanitary condition. The license shall state the name of the licensee, designate the premises in which the business may be carried on, and the number of women that may be properly treated or cared for therein at any one time. Such license shall be kept posted in a conspicuous place on the licensed premises. No greater number of women shall be kept at any one time on the premises for which the license is issued than is authorized by the license and no woman shall be kept in a building or place not designated in the license. A record of the license so issued shall be kept by the board of control, which shall forthwith give notice to the state board of health and to the local board of health of the city, village or town in which the licensee resides of the granting of such license and the conditions thereof. The license shall be valid for one year from the date of the issuance thereof. The state board of control may, after due notice and hearing, revoke the license in case the person to whom the same is issued violates any of the provisions of this chapter, or when, in the opinion of said board, such maternity hospital is maintained without due regard to sanitation and hygiene, or to the health, comfort or well-being of the inmates or infants born to such inmates or in case of the violation of any law of the state in a manner disclosing moral turpitude or unfitness to maintain such hospital or that any such hospital is conducted by a person of ill repute or bad moral character.

·   ·   ·   ·   ·

. . . No person, as an inducement to a woman to go to any maternity hospital during confinement, shall in any way offer to dispose of any child or advertise that he will give children for adoption or hold himself out as being able to dispose of children in any manner.

·   ·   ·   ·   ·

. . . Every birth occurring in a maternity hospital shall be attended by a legally qualified physician or midwife. The licensee owning or conducting such hospital shall, within twenty-four hours after a birth occurs therein, make a written report thereof to the state board of control, giving the name of the mother, the sex of the child and such additional information as shall be within the knowledge of the licensee and as may be required by the board . . .

. . . The officers and authorized agents of the state board of control, and of the state board of health and the local board of health of the city, village or town in which a licensed maternity hospital is located, may inspect such hospital at any time and examine every part thereof. The officers and agents of the state board of control may call for and examine the records which are required to be kept by the provisions of this act and inquire into all matters concerning such hospital and patients and infants therein; and the said officers and authorized agents of the state board of control shall visit and inspect such hospitals at least once every six months and shall preserve reports of the conditions found therein . . .

---

3. Regulation of Minnesota maternity hospitals by State Board of Control

Grace Abbott, *The Child and the State* (Chicago: University of Chicago Press, 1938), II, 563. No source given.

This policy was adopted in 1928.

Because of the very large death rate among children born out of wedlock the State board of control has declared:

1) That it is the *policy* of the board of control that such illegitimate children should be nursed by their mothers for a period of at least three months and as long thereafter as is advisable:

2) That it is agreed between certain properly equipped and specialized maternity hospitals in the State of Minnesota and the State board of control that such hospitals will receive women for this full term of maternity care and afford the mother and child full protection as well as aid and assistance at a reasonable cost; and

3) That it is the policy of such specialized maternity hospitals and the State board of control that the consent of the mother to remain in such hospital for a period of at least three months after the birth of her baby, should be obtained before her admission thereto.

---

4. Regulation of infant homes, 1919

"An Act defining and regulating infant homes," *Laws of the State of Minnesota, 1919,* Extra Session, Chap. 52, in Abbott, *The Child and the State,* II, 563–567.

. . . Any person who receives for care or treatment or has in his custody at any one time three or more infants under the age of three years, unattended by a parent or guardian, for the purpose of providing them with food, care and lodging, except infants related to him by blood or marriage, shall be deemed to maintain an infants' home . . .

. . . The state board of control is hereby empowered to grant a license for one year for the conduct of any infants' home that is for the public good, and is conducted by a reputable and responsible person; and it shall be the duty of the board to provide such general regulations and rules for the conduct of all such

homes as shall be necessary to effect the purposes of this act and all other laws of the state relating to children so far as the same are applicable, and to safeguard the well-being of all infants, born therein and the health, morality and best interests of the patients who are inmates thereof.

.   .   .   .   .

. . . The officers and authorized agents of the state board of control and of the state board of health and the local board of health of the several cities, villages and towns of the state in which a licensed infants' home is located may inspect such home at any time and examine every part thereof. The officers and agents of the state board of control may call for and examine the records which are required to be kept by the provisions of this act and inquire into all matters concerning such home and the infants therein; and the officers and agents of the state board of control shall visit and inspect such homes at least once in every six months and shall make, and the board shall preserve, reports of the conditions found therein . . .

---

5. An evaluation of the administration of Minnesota's laws for children of illegitimate birth

Unpublished report of the United States Children's Bureau, in Abbott, *Child and State,* II, 567–573.

The responsibility for care of children of illegitimate birth was undertaken as a result of legislation recommended by the Children's Code Committee and passed in 1917. Although the law confers upon the Board of Control neither custody nor guardianship of the child born out of wedlock it makes it "the duty of the board of control when notified of a woman who is delivered of an illegitimate, or pregnant with child, likely to be illegitimate when born, to take care that the interests of the child are safeguarded, that appropriate steps are taken to establish his paternity, and that there is secured for him the nearest possible approximation of the care, support and education that he would be entitled to if born of lawful marriage. For the better accomplishment of these purposes the board may initiate such legal or other action as is deemed necessary; may make such provision for the care, maintenance and education of the child as the best interests of the child may from time to time require, and may offer its aid and protection in such ways as are found wise and expedient to the unmarried mother approaching motherhood."

Satisfactory administration of this provision is dependent upon complete and prompt notification of births. The requirement that maternity hospitals report all admissions of unmarried mothers and births of children born out of wedlock has been useful . . .

Immediately upon receiving notice of the birth or impending birth of a child out of wedlock the Children's Bureau notifies the child welfare board of the county in which the mother is living so that plans for her may be worked out at once. Thereafter the case work with the mother is the responsibility of the child welfare board under the general supervision of the Children's Bureau. A duplicate copy of the child welfare board's contact with the girl is sent to the Children's Bureau where a central file is maintained of all unmarried mothers and their children referred to the Bureau since January 1, 1918.

During the sixteen years of its work for unmarried mothers and their children the Children's Bureau and the State Board of Control have adopted a number of policies which govern the work of the Bureau. The policy with regard to the 3 months' nursing period has already been described. Others are as follows:

1) In order to prevent duplication in work it has been decided that the individual county child welfare boards should assume all responsibility for the care and assistance of unmarried mothers who are residents of the county. The bureau assumes responsibility for intercounty cases presenting special problems, and through its field agents will assist any county in its case work or give any other help that is needed.

2) The responsibility of the State Board of Control for the child born out of wedlock ceases when the child (a) is legitimated through marriage of its parents and a form stating the date and place of this marriage and admitting the paternity of the child is signed by the father and filed with the State Registrar; (b) is adopted; (c) is legally separated from its mother and guardianship has been assumed by an authorized agency caring for children; (d) leaves the State; (e) dies, or is stillborn; (f) is satisfactorily adjusted in his home; is being adequately supported by his mother or relatives, and is at least 8 years of age, and the Bureau has no funds in trust or is receiving no monthly allowance from the father.

3) The bureau has discouraged judgments for a lump sum payment from an adjudged father unless such sum with accrued interest is adequate to support the child until he is 16 years of age. All such payments must be made to the State Board which holds the money in trust for the children. The bureau urges that $1,500 should be considered the minimum amount that should be accepted and that every effort should be made to obtain more. Continuing monthly payments throughout the period required by law (until the child is 16 years of age) are considered more desirable than small lump sum payments.

4) Settlements out of court without an adjudication of paternity shall be discouraged by the Children's Bureau.

5) If a child born out of wedlock is adopted by another person and the mother of the child is thus released from further responsibility, the father is likewise released from further requirement for support.

In a study of the work of 6 child welfare boards, including those of Hennepin and Ramsay Counties, it was found that from one-quarter to one-half of the total number of cases under the care of the individual boards were those of unmarried mothers and their children. A similar condition exists in the State Children's Bureau. Of the 8,084 cases of all kinds reported to the Bureau in 1934, about 39 per cent were those of unmarried mothers. The records of the Bureau showed that from January 1, 1918 to June 30, 1934 a total of 22,636 cases involving illegitimacy had come to the attention of the Bureau, the average number reported each year being about 1,400. It is the opinion of the director of the Bureau that this number represents with fair accuracy the total number of illegitimate births in the State.

Since the Board of Control is specifically charged with the responsibility for initiating action for the establishment of paternity, this problem is given particular attention by the Children's Bureau and the county child welfare boards. The law provides that "a complaint shall be filed and all further proceedings had either in the county where the woman resides or in the county where the alleged father resides, or in the county where the child is found if it is likely to become a public charge upon such county." In practice, action is usually taken in the county where the mother resides. Since it is the State that is interested in determining parentage the county attorney represents the child in these cases and the mother is the complaining witness.

Reports of the Children's Bureau show that, in spite of the efforts to establish paternity, the number of children for which this has been accomplished is not large. For the 6 year period from June 30, 1924 to June 30, 1930, paternity had been established for from one-fifth to one-third of the children coming to the attention of the department.

For the children born 1930–32 an even better record was made as paternity was established in 40.6 per cent of the 3,011 cases reported to the Bureau during this period. In 619 cases paternity was established by court action but in the remainder it was determined (1) through acknowledgment and affidavit, (2) by verbal admissions and (3) by marriage of parents.

Following an establishment of paternity an order is made by the judge of the district court specifying the amount and method of payment of support to be paid by the adjudicated father. The statutes provide that such payments shall be made to the Board of Control, to the county welfare board or to the duly appointed guardian of the child. In practice, practically all payments are ordered made to the county child welfare boards.

In the biennial ended June 30, 1934, a total of $136,699 was collected by the Children's Bureau and the Child Welfare Boards of Hennepin, Ramsey and St. Louis counties for the support of children born out of wedlock. This was less by more than one-quarter of the amount collected in the preceding biennium. Monthly payments are the most usual method of payment and these are usually ordered to continue until the child is 16 years of age. The amounts vary from $5 to $20 a month depending upon the financial circumstances and earning capacity of the father. The usual order at the present time is from $10 to $15 a month. Many of the orders are made "until further order of the court" which makes it possible to adjust the amount to the changing needs of the child and to changes in the financial situation of the father. Confinement expenses are usually included in the court order over and above the monthly payments. Although $1,500 has been considered the minimum amount acceptable in a lump sum it has sometimes been found necessary to accept less than this. Lump sum payments have varied from $100 to $2,500, although very few have been less than $500.

The plan of making the Children's Bureau or the county child welfare boards responsible for the administration of funds paid for the support of children born out of wedlock means that the money will actually be used for the child and not be dissipated by an irresponsible or unreliable mother.

Court action to enforce support of a child for whom paternity has been established may be taken as a contempt of court proceeding or on a warrant issued following a complaint for non-support. The statute provides "If the defendant fails to comply with any order of the court, hereinbefore provided for, he may be summarily dealt with as for contempt of court, and shall likewise be subject to all penalties for failure to care for and support such child, which are or shall be imposed by law upon the father of a legitimate child of like age and capacity, and in case of such failure to abide any order of the court, the defendant shall be fully liable for the support of such child without reference to such order." Legal action on the whole has not been resorted to except in rare instances where it has been felt that the failure to make payments was unjustified. It has been the attitude of the Children's Bureau that a man should be assisted in every way in meeting his obligations before legal pressure is exerted, and that only those cases should be brought before the court in which something can be accomplished by the action.

.   .   .   .   .   .

It has been generally conceded that mortality is much greater among children of illegitimate birth than among legitimate children. Yet it is interesting to see what has happened to such mortality rates since greater protection was thrown about the child of illegitimate birth in Minnesota. In 1915, 13 per cent of the illegitimate children born alive died under the age of 2 years while only 7.8 per cent of the legitimate children died under 2 years of age. In 1925, 7 years after the protective program was put into operation, 10 per cent of the illegitimate children born alive died under the age of 2 years and 6.7 per cent of the legitimate children. In 1929, 7.9 per cent of the illegitimate children born alive died under the age of 2 years and 5.7 per cent of the legitimate children. Thus we find a drop of from 13 per cent to 7.9 per cent in 14 years for the child born out of wedlock and of from 7.8 per cent to 5.7 per cent for the legitimate child. There seems little question but that the safeguards set up in Minnesota through its laws regulating maternity hospitals, infants' homes, boarding homes, as well as those specifically for the welfare of the child born out of wedlock have been worthwhile not only as social measures but also as a means of decreasing the mortality rates for these children.

II Child Protection

A. PROTECTION AGAINST CRUELTY AND NEGLECT

The case of "Little Mary Ellen,"
New York, 1874

---

1. Henry Bergh takes the case to court

New York Times, April 10, 1874

Henry Bergh (1811–1888) was founder (1866) and president of the Society for the Prevention of Cruelty to Animals.

MR. BERGH ENLARGING HIS SPHERE OF USEFULNESS Inhuman Treatment of a Little Waif — Her Treatment — A Mystery To Be Cleared Up

It appears from proceedings had in Supreme Court . . . yesterday, in the case of a child named Mary Ellen, that Mr. Bergh does not confine the humane impulses of his heart to smoothing the pathway of the brute creation toward the grave or elsewhere, but that he embraces within the sphere of his kindly efforts the human species also. On his petition a special warrant was issued by Judge Lawrence, bringing before him yesterday the little girl in question, the object of Mr. Bergh being to have her taken from her present custodians and placed in charge of some person or persons by whom she shall be more kindly treated. In his petition

Mr. Bergh states that about six years since Francis and Mary Connolly, residing at No. 315 West Forty-first street, obtained possession of the child from Mr. Kellock, Superintendent of the Department of Charities; that her parents are unknown; that her present custodians have been in the habit of beating her cruelly, the marks of which are now visible on her person; that her punishment was so cruel and frequent as to attract the attention of the residents in the vicinity of the Connolly's dwelling, through whom information of the fact was conveyed to Mr. Bergh; that her custodians had boasted that they had a good fortune for keeping her; that not only was she cruelly beaten, but rigidly confined, and that there was reason to believe that her keepers were about to remove her out of the jurisdiction of the court and beyond the limits of the State.

Upon this petition, Judge Lawrence issued, not an ordinary writ of habeas corpus, but a special warrant, provided for by section 65 of the Habeas Corpus act, whereby the child was at once taken possession of and brought within the control of the court. Under authority of the warrant thus granted, Officer McDougal took the child into custody, and produced her in court yesterday. She is a bright little girl, with features indicating unusual mental capacity, but with a care-worn, stunted, and prematurely old look. Her apparent condition of health, as well as her scanty wardrobe, indicated that no change of custody or condition could be much for the worse.

In his statement of the case to the court Mr. Elbridge T. Gerry, who appeared as counsel for Mr. Bergh, said the child's condition had been discovered by a lady who had been on an errand of mercy to a dying woman in the house adjoining, the latter asserting that she could not die happy until she had made the child's treatment known; that this statement had been corroborated by several of the neighbors; that the charitable lady who made the discovery of these facts had gone to several institutions in the vain hope of having them take the child under their care; that as a last resort she applied to Mr. Bergh, who, though the case was not within the scope of the special act to prevent cruelty to animals, recognized it as being clearly within the general laws of humanity, and promptly gave it his attention. It was urged by council that if the child was not committed to the custody of some proper person, she should be placed in some charitable institution: as, if she was to be returned to her present custodians, it would probably result in her being beaten to death.

The Connollys made no appearance in court, and on her examination the child made a statement as follows: My father and mother are both dead. I don't know how old I am. I have no recollection of a time when I did not live with the Connollys. I call Mrs. Connolly mamma. I have never had but one pair of shoes, but I cannot recollect when that was. I have had no shoes or stockings on this Winter. I have never been allowed to go out of the room where the Connollys were, except in the night time, and then only in the yard. I have never had on a particle of flannel. My bed at night has been only a piece of carpet stretched on the floor underneath a window, and I sleep in my little under-garments, with a quilt over me. I am never allowed to play with any children, or to have any company whatever. Mamma (Mrs. Connolly) has been in the habit of whipping and beating me almost every day. She used to whip me with a twisted whip — a raw hide. The whip always left a black and blue mark on my body. I have now the black and blue marks on my head which were made by mamma, and also a cut on the left side of my forehead which was made by a pair of scissors. (Scissors produced in court.) She struck me with the scissors and cut me; I have no recollection of ever having been kissed by any one — have never been kissed by mamma. I have never been taken on my mamma's lap and caressed or petted. I never dared to speak to anybody, because if I did I would get whipped. I have never had, to my recollection, any more clothing than I have at present — a calico dress and skirt. I have seen stockings and other clothes in our room, but was not allowed to put them on. Whenever mamma went out I was locked up in the bedroom. I do not know for what I was whipped — mamma never said anything to me when she whipped me. I do not want to go back to live with mamma, because she beats me so. I have no recollection of ever being on the street in my life.

At this point of the investigation, and adjournment was taken until 10 o'clock A.M., to-day.

In addition to the foregoing testimony, Messrs. Gerry and Ambrose Monell, counsel on behalf of the application, stated in court that further evidence would be produced corroborating the statement of the child as to the cruelty and neglect which she has sustained; also, as to the mysterious visits of parties to the house of the Connollys, which, taken together with the intelligent and rather refined appearance of the child, tends to the conclusion that she is the child of parents of some prominence in society, who, for some reason have abandoned her to her present undeserved fate.

Before adjournment the child was removed into the Judge's private room, where, apart from all parties to the proceedings, she corroborated before Judge Lawrence her statement as herein given. Counsel on behalf of Mr. Bergh, in his statement to the court, desired it to be clearly understood that the latter's action in the case has been prompted by his feelings and duty as a humane citizen; that in no sense has he acted in his official capacity as President of the Society for Prevention of Cruelty to Animals, but is none the less determined to avail himself of such means as the laws place within his power, to prevent the too frequent cruelties practiced on children.

In ordering the adjournment, Judge Lawrence said he would direct a subpoena to issue for the woman who has the child in charge, as, he said, he had no doubt she could disclose the names of one or both of the child's parents, and he desired to be informed on that point before making a final disposition of the child's custody.

---

2. How Mrs. Connolly obtained Mary Ellen Wilson

New York Times, April 11, 1874.

THE MISSION OF HUMANITY
Continuation of the Proceedings Instituted by Mr. Bergh on Behalf of the Child, Mary Ellen Wilson

Proceedings in the case of Mary Ellen Wilson, the little girl of eight years, charged to have been cruelly treated by Francis and Mary Connolly, of No. 315 West Forty-first street, an account of which appeared in The Times of yesterday, were continued yesterday, before Judge Lawrence, in Supreme Court, Chambers. Quite a number of persons, including several ladies, were attracted to the court by the publicity which had been given to the proceedings had on the previous day, all of them evidently deeply sympathizing with the little neglected waif, whose cause had been espoused by Mr. Bergh. Ten o'clock in the morning, to which the hearing had been adjourned, found the little girl, Mr. Bergh and his counsel, Messrs. Elbridge T. Gerry and Ambrose Monell, and Mrs.

Connolly, the former custodian of the girl, all present in court. The first witness put upon the stand was Mrs. Connolly, who testified as follows: I was formerly married to Thomas McCormack, and had three children by him, all of whom are dead. After Mr. McCormack's death I married Francis Connolly. Before my first husband died he had told me he had three children by another woman, who was alive, but was a good-for-nothing. I went with McCormack to Mr. Kellock, and got out the child, Mary Ellen, my husband signing the paper.

Here the paper referred to was produced, and which proved to be an "indenture" of the child, Mary Ellen Wilson, aged one year and six months, to Thomas McCormack, butcher, and his wife, Mary, in February, 1866, and whereby they undertook to report once a year the condition of the child to the Commissioners of Charities and Correction. This indenture was indorsed by Commissioner Isaac Bell and Secretary Brown.

Witness continued as follows: I know this was one of my husband's illegitimate children. He selected this one. The mother's name, I suppose, is Wilson, because Mr. Kellock, the Superintendent, had the name down. Mr. Kellock asked no questions about my relation to the child. I told him I wanted this child. My husband never told me where the woman Wilson lived. We got the child out on the 2d of January, without any paper being served or any receipt for the child. This was the only paper we signed, and it was not signed until the 15th of February. Sometimes my husband told me the mother of the child lived down town. I learned from several people who knew my husband that the woman is still alive. I could not tell who they were. They were laborers who came from work with him and stopped there drinking. I have no way of knowing if the woman is still alive, or if she has any relatives. I never received a cent for supporting this child. At the time I took the child we were living at No. 866 Third avenue, and my husband said the mother left it there, and he would take it out until such time as she called for it. I have instructed the child according to the undertaking in the indenture — that there is a God, and what it is to lie. I have not instructed her in "the art and mystery of house-keeping," because she is too young. She had a flannel petticoat when she came to me, and I gave her no others.

At this point the witness grew somewhat excited at Mr. Gerry, the examining counsel, whom she assumed to be ignorant of the difficulties of bringing up and governing children, and concluded her testimony by an admission that on but two occasions had she complied with the conditions of the indenture requiring her to report once a year to the Commissioners of Charities and Correction the condition of the child.

New York Times, April 14, 1874.

Mr. Geo. Kellock, Superintendent of Out-door Poor, testified that a child named Mary Ellen Wilson was indentured from the Department of Charities in 1866, being then eighteen months old; that the records show the same to have been left there on the 21st of May, 1864, by a woman named Mary Score, giving her address as No. 235 Mulberry street, and who swore that until within three weeks of that time she had received $8 per month for the child's support; had no means of knowing who the child's parents were, and nothing was said by either Mr. McCormack or his wife, Mrs. Connolly, at the time, as to any relationship of either of them to the child; the $8 per month had been paid to Mary Score by the parties leaving the child with her, and it was when that payment stopped that she brought the child to his office. Reference was demanded from Mr. and Mrs. McCormack when they took the child, and they gave their family physician, Dr. Laughlin or McLaughlin, whose statement in reference to them was deemed satisfactory, and an order for the delivery of the child was given

accordingly; believes he can find Dr. Laughlin, who lived in the vicinity of Twenty-third street and Third avenue. During the past year about 500 children have passed through the department, and witness has no recollection of this one other than the records of his office record. At this point the further hearing was adjourned to Thursday morning next, at 10 o'clock A.M.

3. Mrs. Connolly found guilty of felonious assault

New York Times, April 22, 1874.

MARY ELLEN WILSON
Mrs. Connolly, the Guardian, Found Guilty, and Sentenced One Year's Imprisonment at Hard Labor

Mary Connolly, the discovery of whose inhuman treatment of the little waif, Mary Ellen Wilson, caused such excitement and indignation in the community, was placed on trial before Recorder Hackett yesterday, in the Court of General Sessions. The prisoner, whose appearance is anything but prepossessing, sat immovable during the proceedings, never lifting her eyes from the ground, except when the child was first placed on the stand. Little Mary Ellen, an interesting-looking child, was neatly dressed in the new clothes provided for her by the humane ladies who have taken an interest in her, and has so much improved since her first appearance in the courts as to be scarcely recognized as the cowering, half-naked child rescued by Mr. Bergh's officers. The child was brought into court in charge of Mrs. Webb, the matron at Police Headquarters. Mr. Bergh occupied a seat beside District Attorney Rollins, and took an active part in the proceedings. There were two indictments against the prisoner, one for feloniously assaulting Mary Ellen Wilson with a pair of scissors on the 7th of April, and the other for a series of assaults committed during the years 1873 and 1874. The trial yesterday was on the indictment charging felonious assault.

The little child was put upon the stand, and having been instructed by Recorder Hackett in the nature and responsibility of an oath, was sworn. At first she answered the questions put to her readily, but soon became frightened and gave way to sobs and tears. She was soon reassured, however, by the kind words of the Recorder and District Attorney Rollins, and intelligently detailed the story of her ill-treatment. The scar on her forehead when taken from Mrs. Connolly's house, had been inflicted, she said, by her "mamma" with a pair of scissors. Her "mamma" as she called Mrs. Connolly, had been ripping a quilt, which she held, and struck her with the scissors because she did not like how the quilt was held. The child stated that she had been repeatedly beaten with a long cane by her "mamma" without having done anything wrong. The general cruelty and neglect of Mrs. Connolly were also testified to by the child, as has already been published in the proceedings of the preliminary examinations. Mrs. Webb, Matron at Police Headquarters, Detective McDougall, Alonzo S. Evans, of Mr. Bergh's society, Mrs. Wheeler of St. Luke's Mission, Mrs. Bingham, from whom the prisoner rented apartments, Mrs. States, and Charles Smith, testified to the bruises and filth on the child's body when rescued from Mrs. Connolly's, and to the instances of ill-treatment which had come to their knowledge. After an able argument from District Attorney Rollins and a charge of characteristics clearness from the Recorder, the jury retired, and after twenty minutes deliberation, returned a verdict of guilty of assault and battery.

Recorder Hackett, addressing the prisoner, said that he had no doubt whatever of her guilt. She had been accorded every opportunity to prove her innocence, and the court was fully satisfied that she had been guilty of gross and wanton cruelty. He would have been satisfied if the jury had found her guilty of the higher offense charged. As a punishment to herself, but more as a warning to others, he would sentence her to the extreme penalty of the law — one year in the Penitentiary at hard labor. The prisoner heard her sentence without moving a muscle, and preserved the same hard, cruel expression of countenance displayed by her during the trial, while being conveyed to the Tombs.

A brother of Mrs. Connolly says that the child was legally adopted by the prisoner, who has the legal proofs in her possession, and will seek to gain the custody of the little one at the expiration of her term of punishment.

---

4. Mary Ellen sent to an asylum

New York Times, Dec. 27, 1875

LITTLE MARY ELLEN FINALLY DISPOSED OF

In the matter of the child Mary Ellen Wilson, rescued from Mary Connolly, and whose grandparents were alleged to be residing in London, Judge Lawrence yesterday decided that the relatives not having been found, the child should be sent to "The Sheltering Arms." It was the case of little Mary Ellen which led to the formation of the Society for the Prevention of Cruelty to Children.

New York Society for the Prevention of Cruelty to Children

---

1. The Society is organized, December, 1874

New York Times, Dec. 17, 1874

Elbridge T. Gerry (1837–1927), lawyer and philanthropist, was legal advisor to the American Society for the Prevention of Cruelty to Animals and served as president of the New York Society for the Prevention of Cruelty to Children from 1879 to 1901.

The apprehension and subsequent conviction of the persecutors of little Mary Ellen, some time since, suggested to Mr. Elbridge T. Gerry, the counsel engaged in the prosecution of the case, the necessity for the existence of an organized society for the prevention of similar acts of atrocity. Upon expressing his views among his friends he found plenty of sympathizers with the movement, but no one sufficiently interested to attempt the formation of such a society. About this time he met Mr. John D. Wright, to whom he stated his plan. The latter at once became warmly interested, and undertook the necessary steps toward effecting an organization. Invitations were extended to a large number of prominent citizens interested in the welfare of children to meet at Association Hall on Tuesday afternoon and many promptly responded. Mr. Gerry defined the object of the meeting which, he said, was to organize a society for the prevention of cruelty to children. There were in existence in this City and State, he said, many excellent institutions, some as charitable corps, and others as State reformatories and asylums, for receiving and caring for little children. Among these ought be cited the Children's Aid Society, Society for the Protection of Destitute Children, etc., and in addition each religious denomination had one or more hospitals and similar institutions devoted to the moral and physical culture of helpless children. These societies, however, only assured the care of their inmates after they had been legally placed in their custody. It was not in the province of these excellent institutions to seek out and rescue from the dens and slums of the City the little unfortunates whose lives were rendered miserable by the system of cruelty and abuse which was constantly practiced upon them by the human brutes who happened to possess the custody or control of them; and this was the defect which it was proposed to remedy by the formation of this society. There were plenty of laws existing on the statute books of the State, which provided for all such cases as had been cited but unfortunately no one had heretofore been held responsible for their enforcement. The Police and prosecuting officers were engaged in the prosecution and conviction of offenses of a graver legal character, and, although they were always ready to aid in enforcing the laws when duly called upon to do so, they could not be expected to discover and prosecute those who claimed the right to illtreat the children over whom they had an apparent legal control. This society proposed to enforce legally, but energetically, the existing laws and to secure the conviction and punishment of every violation of any of those laws. The society would not interfere with the numerous institutions already existing, but would aid them in their work. It did not propose to aid any religious denomination, and would be kept entirely free from any political influences. Its duty toward the children would be discharged when their future custody should be decided by the courts. The counsel for the society volunteers his gratuitous services in the prosecution of cases reported by its officers during the first year. The Secretary will be entitled to a moderate compensation, but no salary will be paid to the remaining officers.

.   .   .   .   .

The Secretary will be provided with a book in which all parties who desire to enroll themselves as members may do so at the office of the society, which will be located temporarily in the office of the Society for the Prevention of Cruelty to Animals, No. 100 East Twenty-second Street. The first annual meeting of the society will be held on December 28, 1875.

New York Times, December 29, 1874.

The Society for the Prevention of Cruelty to Children met yesterday afternoon at No.

100 East Twenty-second street, Mr. John D. Wright presiding. There was a very large attendance, three-fourths of whom were ladies, and all evinced the deepest interest in the proceedings. The Chairman stated briefly the objects of the society, and said that they felt complimented at seeing so many ladies with them, which showed that they felt an interest in the objects of the society. He hoped that all of those present would, in common with the society, interest themselves in the matter, and become co-workers with them. The object was one which had long been overlooked in this City. Children have rights which parents and guardians should respect, and he was sure that the more the society became known the more interest would be felt in it.

Mr. Elbridge T. Gerry, counsel for the society, said that the press throughout the City, with one unimportant exception, had endeavored to do them justice. It was unjustly intimated that the society was got up in favor of the Protestant sects, and that it was to interfere with the religion of Roman Catholic children. The society, he said, had no sectarianism about it, and if the person who found fault with them had read the law on the subject he would not have written as he did. The law provides that the Judge before whom the child is brought shall inquire into its antecedents, and he shall assign it to the care of some person or some institution of the same faith as the child belongs to. He mentioned this to disabuse the minds of Roman Catholics. He, as counsel, would place all Roman Catholic Children in Roman Catholic institutions. When the fact of a child's ill treatment comes to the knowledge of the society they would, without stopping to know the religion of the child have it brought before the court and sent to the proper institution. The society claimed the sympathy of every woman in the community, the co-operation of every married man, and also the assistance of every young man. They had a case now pending where a woman was arrested for placing her own child on a red-hot stove, the result of which was that the child died. He hoped for the sake of humanity that the mother was insane. The law, said Mr. Gerry, does not authorize a brutal father to injure his child, and they would take such measures as would prevent it, if possible, in the future. They proposed to receive complaints from any person, and such complaints will be promptly investigated. He alluded to the case of little Mary Ellen, who was beaten with a raw cow-hide for three months, and he was glad to say that the woman who inflicted the cruelty was sent to the Penitentiary for one year. What the society wanted was to find those persons who are ready to place the facts before them. He predicted that as soon as the habitual abusers of children learn that there is a law to reach them, there will be very few cases like that of Mary Ellen, or the red-hot stove case. He concluded by hoping that various institutions would give the society their aid and co-operation.

.   .   .   .   .

Mr. Henry Bergh said he felt a great interest in the subject. There seemed to him "that there is a providence in the affairs of men, rough hew them as they may." The slaves were first freed from bondage; next came the emancipation of the brute creation, and next the emancipation of the little children was about to take place. He took exception to Mr. Gerry calling a father who ill treated his child a "brute." His (the speaker's) clients never got drunk and did not chastise in that way. While anxious to protect children from undue severity, he said he was in favor of good wholesome flogging, which he often found most efficacious. His connection with the society is only a slender one, the Chairman and Mr. Gerry being the active agents. There was, he said, a serious aspect to the question. These little waifs of society were destined at a future day to become the fathers and mothers of this Republic. If they were neglected the permanent interests of this Republic would be neglected. He drew attention to "baby farming," and said the question would receive the attention of the society. Policemen, too, who used their clubs would not be neglected, and one of these officers was now under arrest for injuring a child. He hoped every man and woman would aid this Christian and civilized work.

.   .   .   .   .

Mr. Bergh said the society should be careful not to interfere in petty cases, as it would ruin their usefulness. It is only the atrociously bad cases that should engage their attention at first.

---

2. Authority of the Society under act of incorporation

"An Act of the incorporation of societies for the prevention of cruelty to children," 1875 — ch. 130. *Laws of New York* (Albany, 1881), p. 114.

Section 1. Any five or more persons of full age, a majority of whom shall be citizens of, and residents within, this State, who shall desire to associate themselves together, for the purpose of preventing cruelty to children may make, sign and acknowledge before any person authorized to take the acknowledgment of deeds in this State, and file in the office of the Secretary of State and also in the office of the clerk of the county in which the business of the society is to be conducted, a certificate in writing, in which shall be stated the name or title by which such society shall be known in law, the particular business and objects of such society, the number of trustees, directors or managers to manage the same, and the names of the trustees, directors or managers of the society, for the first year of its existence; but such certificate shall not be filed, unless the written consent and approbation of one of the justices of the Supreme Court of the district in which the place of business or principal of-fice of such society shall be located, be indorsed on such certificate.

.   .   .   .   .

3. Any society so incorporated may prefer a complaint before any court or magistrate having jurisdiction for the violation of any law relating to or affecting children, and may aid in bringing the facts before such court or magistrate in any proceeding taken.

4. All magistrates, constables, sheriffs and officers of police shall, as occasion may require, aid the society so incorporated, its officers, members and agents in the enforcement of all laws which now are or may hereafter be enacted, relating to or affecting children.

---

3. First year of the Society

William P. Letchworth, *Extract from the Ninth Annual Report of the State Board of Charities of the State of New York, Relating to Orphan Asylums and Other Institutions for the Care of Children.* (Albany, 1876), pp. 306–308.

The Secretary, Mr. E. Fellows Jenkins . . . furnished the following information in regard to the operations of the society:

"We have agents about the city to look after poor children in the streets. In cases where we find children are hired to beg, we arrest the parties who hire them out. This is frequently done by Italian organ-grinders, of whom we arrested quite a number during the past month. The society in all its transactions in reference to children, brings them before the court having jurisdiction in the matter. If a complaint is made to us of any child being ill-used, we send an officer to investigate the case and see what can be done. If the child is very badly abused, we cause it to be taken away and put into an asylum or otherwise properly provided for. Children abandoned in the streets are likewise disposed of. We also give advice and information to all parties asking for it, relating to children, and a great many come to us for this purpose. When there is any offense committed against the child, like that of inducing a young girl to go into a house of ill-fame, we follow the case through to the end. We have caused many children to be sent to Randall's Island, but we do not like to send them there."

During the short time the Society has been in existence it has done a large amount of humane work, a record of which will be found in its first annual report just issued. Seventy-two children have been disposed of at the instance of the Society, as follows:

Homes found or situations obtained for	8
Stolen or lost children returned to parents	11
Sent to the Association for Befriending Children and Young Girls	1
Sent to Commissioners of Charities and Correction	31
Sent to N.Y. Roman Catholic Protectory	11
Sent to N.Y. Infant Asylum	1
Sent to N.Y. Juvenile Asylum	3
Sent to Roman Catholic Orphan Asylum	3
Sent to St. Vincent's Home for Boys	2
Sent to Women's Aid Society and Home for Friendless Girls	1
Total	72

The receipts of the Society have been from donations and dues of members, $5,800; from other sources, $198.24. The expenditures thus far have amounted to $5,077.13.

4. "Prince Leo" is rescued by the Society

Harpers Weekly, Dec. 11, 1875, p. 1009.

In 1876 the Society was instrumental in securing passage of an act to prevent employment of children in "singing, dancing, begging . . . or as a gymnast, rider or acrobat . . . or for any immoral purpose."

LITTLE SLAVES OF THE ARENA

Public indignation is every now and then aroused by some extreme case of cruelty to a child, like the one recently brought to light in this city by the intervention of Mr. Bergh and the Society for the Prevention of Cruelty to Children . . . From the examination of the man who is charged with cruelty toward the little acrobat, "Prince Leo," it appears that he came into possession of the child by means of an advertisement in a Philadelphia paper, and that he had seventeen answers to that advertisement. He was confident that he could have had a thousand children if he had advertised in this city. This man denies that he treated "Prince Leo" with harshness; but he knew a woman in the same line of business who has several young children in training for acrobatic performances, all of whom she treats with great cruelty. It is more than probable that Mr. Bergh's humane efforts and investigations will bring to light other cases of a similar nature. He should have the hearty support not only of the press, but of society, in this philanthropic work. The public should refuse to patronize places of amusement where little children are made to perform difficult and dangerous feats. The victims of the cruel taskmasters of the arena are generally poor little castaways, whom society should protect from a servitude as wretched as slavery itself. They are sometimes picked up in the streets, but more frequently they are purchased of unnatural parents, who are glad to be relieved of their support, and who do not care what becomes of them.

5. Powers of the Society under New York anti-cruelty act, 1881

HARPER'S WEEKLY. [DECEMBER 11, 1875.

INFANT SLAVES OF THE ARENA.—[SEE PAGE 1009.]

MASTER ON THE STAGE RECEIVING HIS SLAVE FROM THE TRAPEZE.
"Bravo, my little Pet! You are the Prince of them all."

MASTER AND SLAVE BEHIND THE SCENES.
"You little Wretch! if you dare to look frightened another time when you are 'on,' I'll break every bone in your body."

"Abandonment and Other Acts of Cruelty to Children," 1881 — ch. 676, *Laws of New York* (Albany, 1881), II, 69–72.

287. A parent, or other person having the care or custody, for nurture or education, of a child under the age of six years, who deserts the child in any place, with intent wholly to abandon it, is punishable by imprisonment in a state prison, for not more than seven years, or in a county jail for not more than one year.

288. A person who willfully omits, without lawful excuse, to perform a duty by law imposed upon him to furnish food, clothing, shelter, or medical attendance to a minor, is guilty of a misdemeanor.

289. A person who, having the care or custody of a minor, either

1. Willfully causes or permits the minor's life to be endangered, or its health to be injured, or its morals to become depraved; or

2. Willfully causes or permits the minor to be placed in such a situation, or to engage in such an occupation, that its life is endangered, or its health is likely to be injured, or its morals likely to be impaired;

Is guilty of a misdemeanor.

290. A person who admits to, or allows to remain in any dance-house, concert saloon, theater or other place of entertainment, owned, kept or managed by him, where wines or spirituous or malt liquors are sold or given away, any child, actually or apparently under the age of fourteen years, unless accompanied by a parent or guardian, is guilty of a misdemeanor.

291. A male child actually or apparently

under the age of sixteen years, or a female child actually or apparently under the age of fourteen years, who is found;

1. Begging or receiving or soliciting alms, in any manner or under any pretense; or

2. Not having any home or other place of abode or proper guardianship; or

3. Destitute of means of support, and being either an orphan, or living or having lived with or in custody of a parent or guardian, who has been sentenced to imprisonment for crime, or who has been convicted of a crime against the person of such child, or has been adjudged an habitual criminal; or

4. Frequenting the company of reputed thieves or prostitutes, or a house of prostitution or assignation, or living in such a house either with or without its parent or guardian, or frequenting concert saloons, dance-houses, theaters or other places of entertainment, or places where wines, malt or spirituous liquors are sold, without being in charge of its parent or guardian; or

5. Coming within any of the descriptions of children mentioned in section 292, must be arrested and brought before a proper court or magistrate, as a vagrant, disorderly, or destitute child. Such court or magistrate may commit the child to any charitable, reformatory or other institution authorized by law to receive and take charge of minors, or may make any disposition of the child such as now is or hereafter may be authorized in the cases of vagrants, truants, paupers, or disorderly persons.

292. A person, who employs or causes to be employed, or who exhibits, uses, or has in custody for the purpose of exhibiting or employing, a female child apparently or actually under the age of fourteen years, or a male child apparently or actually under the age of sixteen years, or who having the care, custody or control of such a child as parent, relative, guardian, employer or otherwise, sells, lets out, gives away or in any way procures or consents to the employment or exhibition of such a child, either

1. As a rope or wire walker, dancer, gymnast, contortionist, rider or acrobat; or

2. In begging or receiving alms, or in any mendicant occupation; or

3. In peddling, singing or playing upon a musical instrument, or in a theatrical exhibition, or in any wandering occupation; or

4. In any indecent or immoral exhibition or practice; or

5. In any practice or exhibition dangerous or injurious to the life, limb, health or morals of the child;

Is guilty of a misdemeanor. But this section does not apply to the employment of any child as a singer or musician in a church, school, or academy, or in teaching or learning the science or practice of music, or as a musician in any concert with the written consent of the mayor of the city, or the president of the board of trustees of the village, where such concert takes place.

293. A constable or police officer must, and any agent or officer of any incorporated Society for the Prevention of Cruelty to Children may, arrest and bring before a court or magistrate having jurisdiction, any person offending against any of the provisions of this chapter, and any minor coming within any of the descriptions of children mentioned in section 291 or in section 292.

Such constable, police officer or agent may interfere to prevent the perpetration in his presence of any act forbidden by this chapter.

A person who obstructs or interferes with any officer or agent of such society in the exercise of his authority under this chapter, is guilty of a misdemeanor.

---

6. The Society to enforce "baby farming" law, 1883

"An act to prevent baby farming," 1883
— ch. 40, *New York Sessions Laws* (Albany, 1883), pp. 30–31.

"Baby farming" was the business of boarding unwanted infants in private homes or institutions until death, adoption, or other disposition.

Section 1. No individual shall receive or board more than two infants under the age of three years in the same place at the same time, unless within two days after the reception of every such infant beyond the first two, a license shall be duly issued by the mayor or board of health of the city or town wherein such infant is so to be received or boarded, specifying the name and age of the child and the name and place of residence of the party so undertaking its care and authorizing the same. Such license shall be revocable at the will of the authority granting it, and every person omitting or refusing to comply with the provisions of this section shall be guilty of a misdemeanor.

2. It shall be lawful for the officers of any incorporated society for the prevention of cruelty to children at all reasonable times to enter and inspect the premises wherein such infants are so boarded, received or kept, and it is hereby made their duty to see that the provisions of this law are duly enforced.

3. This act shall not be construed to prohibit the boarding of infants when accompanied by their parent, relative, or some person entitled to their custody, and shall not apply to corporations incorporated under the laws of the state of New York for the purpose of receiving and caring for foundlings or abandoned or homeless infants.

4. This act shall take effect immediately.

7. Philosophy of the Society, 1882

Elbridge T. Gerry, "The Relation of Societies for the Prevention of Cruelty to Children to Child-Saving Work," *Proceedings* of the National Conference of Charities and Correction (1882), 129–130.

Under our system of government, the enforcement of the laws is usually left to public officials, either elected or appointed by the sovereign people for that purpose. But there are certain branches of the law which seem peculiarly to require the creation of corporations for their enforcement, in order to protect those who are unable to protect themselves; and especially in dealing with offenders who are wealthy, influential and powerful, and who might and do often exert influences which are powerless with a corporation. And this is particularly the reason for the creation of societies for the prevention of cruelty to children. Most of them are based upon the principle that a cohesion of effort insures success; or, to use the aphorism of the wise king of old, that a three-fold cord is not quickly broken. Throughout this great continent there is a net-work of these societies to-day in active operation. They are composed of humane persons of social position, unquestioned integrity and undoubted zeal. They interfere only when the law authorizes their interference for the benefit of the child; and they assert alike in their teaching and in their practice, the existence of the axiom that at the present day in this country, children have *some* rights, which even parents are bound to respect. Their duty is to present the facts which bring the case within the law before the appropriate tribunal; and then to leave the disposition of the case to the officers of the law, who are bound by their oaths and their official position to enforce that law, irrespective of persons. No matter how exalted the offender, the society has the right to confront him with its proofs; no matter how degraded the object of its mercy, the society is bound by its corporate duty to stretch out its hand and rescue from starvation, misery, cruelty and perhaps death, the helpless little child who ought to have a protector, but for some reason, not its fault, has been deprived of that advantage. On the other hand, where the parent properly discharges the parental functions, the society, so far from interfering, frequently and with success aids that parent in the reclamation of the erring, the wilful, and the disobedient child. It is only when the parent exceeds the proper exercise of the parental functions, or omits or refuses to perform those functions, that the society protects the child against the parent . . .

---

8. The Society not a charitable institution, 1900

The People of the State of New York *ex rel.* The State Board of Charities *v.* The New York Society for the Prevention of Cruelty to Children, 161 N.Y. 239–240, 248.

For the circumstances and significance of this decision see below Part Three, Chap. I, sec. D, "State supervision of institutions and home finding agencies," doc. 3 b. The following is an extract from the majority opinion.

The defendant receives under the charter of New York the sum of thirty thousand dollars annually from the city treasury to promote the objects of its organization. But in receiving and disbursing that sum of money, it neither receives nor administers any charity, but is simply allowed something by the city for doing work that otherwise would devolve, as we shall see hereafter, on the police department, and which the society can do better and with much less expense than the police. The fact that the president of this corporation and the then mayor of New York, when commending its work to the public, described it as an institution founded on the broadest principles of charity, has no weight in the determination of the question involved in this appeal. A corporation cannot be classified by what its friends or promoters may say about it, but only from the nature of the powers which it may lawfully exercise and the business in which it is lawfully engaged. It is manifest, therefore, that in any inquiry concerning the nature, character or classification of any particular corporation, the only safe guide is the charter or law of its creation prescribing the powers that it may exercise and defining the nature of the business or the duties for which it was created. The defendant was incorporated under a general law enacted for the express purpose of giving to such societies a corporate organization . . . The certificate of the founders of this corporation was filed April 27, 1875. The name selected was that which the defendant now bears and the objects of the corporation are stated in the following words: "The particular business and objects of this society are the prevention of cruelty to children and the enforcement by all lawful means of the laws relating to or in anywise affecting children."

This corporation was, therefore, created for the purpose of enforcing laws enacted to prevent cruelty to children, and that is the only object or purpose of its existence . . . a corporation, created and existing to aid in the enforcement of the criminal law to prevent cruelty to children, cannot be held to be a charitable institution.

Protecting immigrant children against abuse by padrones

Padrones bought the services of poor Italian children from their parents for an agreed term of years, brought the children to America, put them to work as beggars or street musicians, and pocketed their earnings. During the 1870's both the Italian and the United States governments attempted to suppress the padrone system.

1. Organ grinders' assistants

New York Times, Nov. 20, 1875.

Three Italian organ grinders, all living in Baxter Street, were yesterday arraigned . . .

on charges of employing children to solicit alms. Lucien Baptiste, for so employing Darius Burginone, aged ten, was committed for trial at the Court of General Sessions in default of $500 bail. Marcus Dominick was similarly disposed of, he having in his service, Theresa, aged eleven, a sister of the boy Darius. The mother of the children was paid twenty-five cents per day for the boy and thirty cents for the girl. Francis Bruski who proved that the child he employed was his own daughter, was discharged, and the child was committed to the Catholic Protectory. As the father was leaving the court room the little thing raised such an outcry that the Judge had not the heart to separate them, and the commitment was revoked. An agent of the Society for the Prevention of Cruelty to Children, who was present, was instructed to inquire into the treatment of the child.

---

2. "Twenty ducats a year"

New York Times, Nov. 18, 1879.

Giuseppe Antonio Ancarola, the padrone, was again under examination yesterday, before United States Commissioner Lyman, on the charge of kidnapping and inveigling seven small Italian boys from Italy to this country under contracts of involuntary servitude during which they were to play musical instruments in the streets for Ancarola as their master. Superintendent Jackson, of the Castle Garden Emigrant Depot, testified as to the arrival of the boys with Ancarola on November 3, on the steam-ship *Elysia,* and the fact already published of Ancarola's disappearance from the Garden when he found he was under suspicion. Luigi Corregliano, one of the boys, was next examined, Detective Chiardi acting as interpretor. Luigi testified in effect that his father is in prison and that his mother sailed from Marseilles for Buenos Aires about the time

Luigi left that port for London; that he heard Ancarola at his home in Calvello offer his mother money if she would allow her boy, Luigi, to come to America; his mother said he might come if he wished, and he was quite contented and happy at having the opportunity; his mother was to be paid, he believed, twenty ducats a year for his services, and the written contract hiring Luigi to Ancarola for four years was drawn by a priest, Padre Vincenzo, at the priest's house; Luigi was to play the violin. Officer Chiardi testified to the fact of his arresting Ancarola at No. 87 Crosby street on November 9, and the further hearing was adjourned to tomorrow.

---

3. A padrone convicted under federal statute

United States *v.* Ancarola, 1 Fed. Rep. 676

In this case, decided January 26, 1880, the Circuit Court for the Southern District of New York upheld the conviction of the padrone referred to in the previous document.

Blatchford, J. On the twenty-third of June, 1874, an act was passed by congress (18 U.S. *St. at Large,* 251), entitled "An act to protect persons of foreign birth against forcible constraint or involuntary servitude."

It provides that "whoever shall knowingly and wilfully bring into the United States, or the territories thereof, any person inveigled or forcibly kidnapped in any other country, with intent to hold such person so inveigled or kidnapped in confinement, or to any involuntary service, and whoever shall knowingly and wilfully sell, or cause to be sold, into any condition of involuntary servitude, any other person, for any term whatever, and every person who shall knowingly and wilfully hold to involuntary service any person so sold and bought, shall be deemed guilty of a felony, and on conviction thereof be imprisoned for a term not exceeding five years, and pay a fine not exceeding $5,000."

Under this statute an indictment was found in this court against the defendant, charging . . . that he unlawfully, feloniously, knowingly, and wilfully brought into the United States . . . one Francesco Libonati, a person who had theretofore been inveigled in the kingdom of Italy, with intent to hold said Libonati in confinement, and to an involuntary service of begging and of playing on musical instruments.

.   .   .   .   .

Two other indictments, with the same charges, were found against the defendant, except that one of them related to a person named Michele Quirino, and the other to a person named Giosue Givrieri. The three indictments came on for trial before this court, held by Judge Benedict, and a jury, and were consolidated by the court . . . and one trial was had on them as so consolidated. The jury found the defendant "guilty of the several offences charged in the indictments" . . .

The evidence given on the trial showed these facts: The defendant arrived in the city of New York on the second of November, 1879, in a steamer from Europe, having with him seven boys, of whom the three persons named in the indictment were three. He came on shore with the seven boys. Mr. Jackson, superintendent of the depot at Castle Garden, where he landed, had a conversation with him there immediately after he landed. Mr. Jackson testified: "I asked this man if those children were with him, and he said they were. I then asked his name, and he told me Ancarola. I brought him up to the register's desk, and he registered their names. I asked him where they were going, and he said to Montreal, to their relatives there. I brought them inside then, and he handed me their passage ticket to Montreal, as evidence that they were going there." The children were not allowed to go with him. He was arrested on the eighth of November. At the trial no evidence was introduced by the

defendant. The chief testimony for the government was that of the three boys named in the indictments, Quirino being 13 years old, and Libonati and Givrieri being each 11 years old.

The story of Libonati is this: He was born at Calvello, Italy. His mother is living there. His father is dead. The boy was working in a blacksmith shop for two and a half cents a day, making nails. He had two sisters and a brother in Calvello, and a brother and a cousin in New York. His family were poor. He could not play upon any musical instruments. His father had gone to New York, and had died there. The boy, being at his shop, was sent for by his mother, and went and found with her her brother and the defendant. His mother asked him if he wanted to go to America, and he said "Yes." His uncle said, "Go to America with this man?" and the boy said "Yes." The defendant said to the mother, "Will you give me your son?" and she said "Yes." He also said to her that the boy was to play the harp in Chicago. The boy said that he wantaed to play the violin, but the defendant said that he must play the harp, and the boy then said that he would play the harp. The boy went with his uncle to Naples, thence he went to Marseilles and London with another boy. At London he met the defendant and other boys, and they came from London to New York in the steamer. On the way over the defendant said to the boy, "If we get arrested say we are going to Montreal." The boy had no relations in Montreal.[1]

The story of Quirino was this: His mother is living. His father died in New York. The boy was born in Calvello, Italy, and lived there. He is a relative of the defendant. He has a sister. His family are poor. He did not work at anything, but went to school. The boy and his mother, his uncle and the defendant, being together at Calvello, it was verbally agreed

1. During the trial the *New York Times* reported (Nov. 18, 1879): "Francesco testified that he cried when he came away at the thought of leaving his mother, and that she cried too, and they kissed each other; but that he came away willingly, and expected to go back again at the end of the four years."

between the mother and the defendant that the boy was to be four years and a half with the defendant, in Chicago, and that the defendant was to give the mother 40 ducats. The defendent said: "You live four and a half years with me, and I will teach you the business, and whatever money you make you will give to me." The mother said: "If you want to go, go; I don't want to compel you to the contrary." The uncle said the same. The defendant told the boy he would have to learn the violin, and that he would be clothed and fed. The boy said that he would go. His uncle took him from Calvello to Marseilles. There he met the defendant, who took him to London, and thence to New York in the steamer. On the way over, the defendant told the boy to tell every one that he was going to see his uncle in Montreal. He did not have an uncle in Montreal.

The story of Givrieri is this: His father and mother are living in Calvello, Italy, where he was born. He has a brother and a sister. His mother proposed to the defendant to take the boy to America. The defendant had just returned from there. He said, in the presence of the boy, that America was a good place, and he talked of the "beautiful things of America." He said to the father and mother: "If you let your son go with me he will do very well in America and send you plenty of money bye and bye." He said several times, in the hearing of the boy, that America was a good place, and that they would make plenty of money there, and that they were going to make money for him. The boy was to work, and all the money he was to give to the defendant. The defendant was to take the boy to Chicago and teach him music, and from Chicago he would take him further. This was said in the presence of the parents. They told the defendant not to ill-treat the boy and to feed him properly, and that if they should get a letter from him saying that he was not properly treated they would come and take him away. It was then agreed that the defendant should give the father 80 ducats, and that the boy should go with the defendant for four years and be fed

and clothed by him, and taught music. The boy went to Marseilles, and there the defendant found him. On the way to New York, in the steamer, the defendant said to the boy: "Let us pray to God that we can pass through New York all right. After that I will teach you music." He gave the boy a paper with an address in New York where to go, and told him not to let himself be seen by any officer for they might arrest him, and if any one asked him what he was going to do not to say that he was going with a padrone. He also told him if any one asked what his business was to say that he was a printer, and if they asked where he was going to say that he was going to Montreal, and if they asked to whom, to say that he was going to an uncle. He did not have an uncle in Montreal.

.   .   .   .   .

After charging that it must be "proved that the accused brought the child here with the intent to hold the child when so brought to involuntary service as a begger or as a musician," the court proceeded as follows: "Upon this question the age of the child is important, for, as you know, in regard to some things a child of such tender years is incapable of consent. The nature of the employment to which the accused intended to put the child, the evidence in regard to the arrangement made in Italy, and the ability of the child to labor or play an instrument, are important circumstances in this connection, also, for if you believe from the evidence that the intention of the accused in bringing the child to this country was to employ the child as a beggar or as a street musician, for his own profit, and that such intended employment was one injurious to its morals and inconsistent with its proper care and education, according to its condition, then you will be justified in finding that he intended to hold such child to involuntary service, as charged in the indictment, and this, notwithstanding the fact that the child had consented to the employment in Italy, and that no evidence of a subsequent dissent, while under the control of the accused, has been given."

The foregoing portion of the charge was excepted to by the defendant. The defendant also contends that there was no evidence that any of the children had been inveigled in Italy, and no evidence that the defendant had the intent to hold any of the children to any involuntary service in this country.

"Inveigle," is defined by Worcester thus: "To persuade to something bad, to wheedle, to entice, to seduce, to beguile." He defines "entice" thus: "To allure to ill, to attract, to lure, to draw by blandishments or hopes, to decoy, to tempt, to seduce, to coax." To inveigle or persuade or entice necessarily implies that the person is persuaded or enticed, and yields assent as the result of the persuading or enticing. Yet the statute is founded on the view that the person so assenting and so inveigled may be brought here by one who knows the circumstances of the case, with the intent to hold such person to involuntary service, although the service be the one to which the inveigling related. The arrangement made in Italy was, clearly, a transfer of the children to the service of the defendant to earn money for him as street musicians in Chicago. They were of an age to be able to do so. The influence brought to bear upon them by their parents and uncles, and by the statements of the defendants, to induce them to consent, in view of their condition in life and their ages and their inexperience, was enticement and inveiglement. The charge on this subject was proper and not open to exception. *Moody* v. *The People,* 20 Ill. 315, 319.

In regard to the other portion of the charge, the children, in serving the defendant as street musicians, for his profit, to the injury of their morals, subject to his control, could not properly be considered as rendering him voluntary service. They were incapable of exercising will or choice affirmatively on the subject. They were cast off by their parents, in violation of the law of Italy, and their being in this country at all with the defendant was, on all the facts, really involuntary on their parts, although the

sham form of their consent was gone through with. The charge seems to us entirely correct. *Moody* v. *The People.* 20 Ill. 315, 319; *The State* v. *Rollins,* 8 N.H. 550, 565. The observations already made, taken in connection with the testimony recited, show that there was ample evidence to warrant the jury in finding inveiglement in Italy, and the intent of the defendant, with full knowledge of such inveiglement, to hold the children in this country to involuntary service to him as street musicians.

The motions are denied.

Spread and work of "cruelty" and humane societies, 1875–1900

A quarter century after the founding of the New York Society more than 150 organizations devoted in whole or part to the prevention of cruelty to children were in operation. Most of them, usually called Humane Societies, combined protective work for children and animals. About twenty, patterned after the New York Society, confined their activities to child protection. The societies sought to protect children not only against abuse and neglect but from the moral dangers of certain types of employment.

1. Chicago Society for the Prevention of Cruelty to Animals becomes the Illinois Humane Society, 1877–1881

Oscar L. Dudley, *Saving the Children. Sixteen Years' Work Among the Dependent Youth of Chicago* (Boston, 1893), pp. 6–10.

During the year 1877 complaint was made to the Illinois Society for the Prevention of Cruelty to Animals that a woman residing at No. 171 Randolph Street had beaten a six-year-old boy nearly to death, and that she was in the habit of practising all manner of cruelties upon him. The evidence of the neighbors pointed to so serious a state of affairs that the writer, who represented the Society for the Prevention of Cruelty to Animals at that time, seeing no reason that a child should not be entitled to as much protection under the law as a dumb animal, concluded to investigate the charges, with a view to taking action if they could be substantiated. He found that the woman had for a long time been in the practice of inflicting the most barbarous treatment upon her six-year-old stepson, Harry. The boy was bright and intelligent, but very delicate in health. On examination it was found that his back was one mass of bruised flesh, while on the left shoulder were deep red scars, evidently inflicted with some pointed instrument, although the frightened little fellow, when questioned, said, "The cat did it." His hips were black and blue, the coagulated blood being visible beneath the skin. Both eyes were blackened; and the face, legs, and arms were covered with burns and contusions. The neighbors had heard the woman frequently beating the child, and he had told them that his mother held his hands on the stove until they were blistered. The woman was sent to jail, and the child was taken care of by the Society.

.   .   .   .   .

The work grew on our hands until two-thirds of our time was taken up with the investigation of charges of cruelty to children and the prosecution of offenders. Finally, it became necessary to improve the machinery of operations; and the Board of Directors of the Society for the Prevention of Cruelty to Animals met on Jan. 23, 1881, and adopted the following resolutions, subsequently changing the name of the Society to the Illinois Humane Society. The resolutions read: —

We report that the protection of children of tender years from cruelty, abuse, and criminal neglect, and their rescue from im-

moral surroundings and influences, is, in our opinion, a work not exceeded in importance by any other benevolence among us . . . That it seems at present naturally and legitimately to belong to the work of the Society, aside from which we know of no organization in the State prepared to engage in it. That its prosecution thus far has not lessened nor impaired the efficiency of our animal protection service. That, without our seeking it, the work has come to us, we are now performing it, and the public sentiment demands that we continue to do so. That the creation of a separate branch for this service does not now appear to be necessary. That Chicago has never yet failed to give a generous support to all forms of benevolent work for which a real necessity exists, when honestly and efficiently performed and plainly and fairly presented for support. Therefore,

Resolved, That we will continue to prosecute this work of protecting children, as well as dumb animals, from cruelty, abuse, and criminal neglect, appealing to and relying upon the liberality of all who are in sympathy with our purposes and aims, for the means with which to meet the increased expenses of the work, that it may be carried on efficiently and without embarrassment.

---

2. "Infant prodigies," 1877

Thomas Bailey Aldrich, *A Midnight Fantasy; and The Little Violinist* (Boston, 1877), pp. 72–75.

Aldrich's story, inspired by the death of the young violinist, James Speaight, was sold at the fund-raising fair of the Massachusetts Society for the Prevention of Cruelty to Children in 1880. The Society was organized in 1878.

THE LITTLE VIOLINIST

I have, I trust, great tenderness for all children; but I know I have a special place in my heart for those poor little creatures who figure in circuses and shows, or elsewhere, as "infant prodigies." Heaven help such little folk! It was an unkind fate that did not make them commonplace, stupid, happy girls and boys like our own Fannys and Charleys and Harrys. Poor little waifs, that never know any babyhood or childhood, — sad human midges, that flutter for a moment in the glare of the gaslights, and are gone. Pitiful little children, whose tender limbs and minds are so torn and strained by thoughtless task-masters, that it seems scarcely a regrettable thing when the circus caravan halts awhile on its route to make a little grave by the wayside.

I never witness a performance of child-acrobats, or the exhibition of any forced talent, physical or mental, on the part of children, without protesting, at least in my own mind, against the blindness and cruelty of their parents or guardians, or whoever has care of them.

I saw at the theatre, the other night, two tiny girls, mere babies they were, doing such feats upon a bar of wood suspended from the ceiling, as made my blood run cold. They were twin sisters, these mites, with that old young look on their faces which all such unfortunates have. I hardly dared glance at them, up there in the air, hanging by their feet from the swinging bar, twisting their fragile spines and distorting their poor little bodies, when they ought to have been nestled in soft blankets in a cozy chamber, with the angels that guard the sleep of little children hovering above them. I hope the father of those two babies will read and ponder this page on which I record not alone my individual protest, but the protest of hundreds of men and women who took no pleasure in that performance, but witnessed it with a pang of pity.

There is a noble "Society for the Prevention of Cruelty to Dumb Animals." There ought to be a Society for the Prevention of Cruelty to Little Children; and a certain influential gentleman who does some things well and other things very badly, ought to attend to it. The name of this gentleman is Mr. Public Opinion.

---

3. Specimen cases handled by Massachusetts S.P.C.C., 1881

Massachusetts S.P.C.C., *First Annual Report* (Boston, 1881), pp. 31–33.

1437. Man arrested for incestuous relations with his own daughter, a pretty girl of 12 years of age. Sentenced to five years in State Prison. Girl adopted by a good family.

1928. A young girl enticed into the lodging room of a man who committed a felonious assault upon her. Three years in State Prison.

1841. Sick girl, 9 years old, beaten and abused by drunken father and mother. After child's removal to hospital by friends the parents were arrested on complaint of the Society for assault. Father, six months in House of Correction. Mother, $50 and costs.

1593. Boy, 7. Father dead. Mother died from abuse by second husband. Boy left in charge of a miserable woman. Taken by Society. Step-father in prison, the only relative, consented. Child now well cared for.

1069. Girl, 9. Mother dead. Step-mother had severely whipped the girl. Had scars on head and face; had been placed on hot stove. Left naked in a cold room in winter. Difficult to obtain evidence. Child taught to conceal cruelty. To avoid publicity father gave the child to the Society.

1090. An interesting and amiable girl, 15, living with an aunt, who had overworked her, and abused her by blows on the head, and by striking on neck with hot poker. Girl sought our protection. We obtained guardianship and custody after a long contest.

1676. Three children, 2 to 5 years of age, abandoned by father. Mother very intemperate.

When found the mother was lying drunk and insensible, and the *children all intoxicated.* Mother arrested. Children sent to the Marcella Street Home.

1656.   Five children from 2 to 9 years of age, living in a wretched condition, taught to lie and steal by drunken parents. Children removed to a Home.

1217.   Two children, boy 9, girl 7, terribly beaten with a broomstick. Both children had their eyes blackened by blows, their bodies fearfully bruised, and patches of skin taken from their faces. Father and mother arrested. Fine and costs, $75. Well treated since.

1683.   Girl, 9, taken to New York from wretched home in Boston by a blind peddler, who claimed he had the parents' consent. New York Society rescued her and returned her to us. Father and mother intemperate. The girl, with other children of same family, placed in a Home.

1637.   Boy, 15. Father dead. Abandoned by his mother in the street when 10 years of age. No home or known relatives. At his request Society took guardianship papers, to enable him to enlist in the navy.

1536.   Three children, 16 months to 6 years of age. Mother intemperate and dissolute, wasting her husband's wages in riotous living. Children rescued and placed with a relative, father paying board. Mother leaves the State.

1446.   Girl, 14, seeks our protection from intemperate parents, who abuse her shamefully. Send her to the "dump" to pick coal to be sold for liquor. For refusing to go for liquor is kept out of doors, improperly clad, for two hours in cold weather. Has been dragged by her hair. An elder sister had had same experience. Pending our action for guardianship parents surrender all legal rights to a good family.

1311.   Boy, 2, badly deformed, a cripple, destitute. Removed to hospital. Surgical operation. Entire cure.

1316.   Girl, 16. Long continued overwork by stepmother. Girl diseased and feeble. Guardianship and custody obtained. Placed in a happy home.

1349.   Three children, 3 to 13, dirty, ragged, almost naked. No furniture, no food. Father intemperate and indifferent. Mother dead. Rescued under the "neglect law."

1400.   Six children, from 2 to 16. Father intemperate. Mother dead. Boy, 14, in truant school. Girl, 10, with relative. Girl, 16, having charge, was sick and under hospital treatment. Three younger children placed in a Home for adoption.

1409.   Six children, 4 months to 10 years. Father drunken and ugly, abused wife and children. Case investigated. Arrangements made to send wife and children to relatives in another State. Father repented, promised reform; mother accepted his promises. At last accounts doing well.

1375.   Four children, 5 months to 9 years. Father intemperate, sickly. Mother negligent and dissolute, absenting herself for weeks at a time, abandoning her nursing infant. Under "neglect law" children sent to Marcella Street Home and City Nursery.

Hundreds of cases could be added to the above, but from these the general nature of the work can be appreciated.

---

4. Josef Hofmann plays in Boston, 1887

Massachusetts S.P.C.C. *Seventh Annual Report* (Boston, 1887), pp. 14–15.

The pianist Josef Hofmann (1876–1957) made his American debut in 1887 at the age of eleven. His schedule called for eighty concerts in one season but pressure from anti-cruelty societies caused cancellation of the tour after forty-two concerts.

In the reports of previous years we have spoken of the law forbidding the appearance of children under fifteen years of age upon the stage in dancing, singing or playing on musical instruments. The evil has been much controlled by the statutes, and by our action in warning managers and parents, who would help to maintain themselves at the sacrifice of their children's welfare.

This subject has been prominently before the public, of late, by the appearance of Josef Hoffman, a child of marked musical ability, attracting crowds to be amused, but exciting the sympathy of the public when they saw how he was being overworked. Our Board gave the case early consideration, and would have taken legal action, but were prevented, much to our regret, by the fact that the managers procured a license under the following proviso in the law: "*Provided,* that nothing in this section shall be construed to prevent the education of children in vocal and instrumental music, or their employment as musicians in any church, chapel, school, or school exhibition, or prevent their taking part in any concert or musical exhibition on the *special written permission of the mayor and aldermen of* any city, or the board of selectmen of any town." But it is a healthful indication of public opinion that so many of our citizens have felt the wrong which is being done to the child, and had hoped we could have prevented its continuance.

The problem of "neglect"

1. When may the state rightfully intervene in family affairs?

David Dudley Field, "The Child and the State," *The Forum* I (1886), 106–109.

Field (1805–1894), constitutional and corporation lawyer, led the movement for reform of New York state's penal and civil procedural codes.

In one of the tenement houses of the city, and their number is legion, there is a room, nineteen feet long, fifteen feet broad and and eleven high, where live a man and his wife and eight children. They sleep, dress, wash, cook and eat in this one room. These ten persons have altogether thirty-one hundred and thirty-five cubic feet of air, while the law requires at least six thousand feet — nearly twice as much as they get. From tenement houses like this there flows out daily a stream of children, ragged and dirty, to pick up rags, cigar stumps, and other refuse of the streets, or to pilfer or beg, as best they can. This is not the place to describe the horrors of the tenement house, nor to discuss the duty or failure of duty on the part of the state in respect of its construction and occupation. I ask attention only to the condition of the children, and for illustration take the case of a boy, five years old, who is found, in a chill November day, barefooted, scantily clothed, searching among the rag heaps in the street. He is a well-formed child, his face is fair, and as he turns his bright eyes upon you when you ask him where he lives, you see that he has quick intelligence. Altogether he is such a child as a father should look upon with pride and a true mother would press to her bosom. Yet the parents are miserably poor, the father half the time out of work, and the mother wan with the care of her family. This is not all. Father and mother both drink to excess, and each is intoxicated as often at least as Saturday night comes round.

Has the state any duties toward this little boy, and if so what are they?

All will agree that it has some duty, at least that of protection from personal violence. May it go further, and rescue the child from its loathsome occupation, its contaminating surroundings and its faithless parents? I think that it may, and having the right, that it is charged with the duty of rescuing the child. This is a large subject, larger indeed than can be fully treated in this paper, but some of the reasons for my opinion shall be stated. At the outset, let me say that I am not a believer in the paternal theory of government. The great ends for which men are associated in political communities are mutual protection, and the construction of those public works, of which roads and bridges are examples, for which individuals are not competent. The state should interfere as little as possible with the economy of the family and the liberty of the individual to pursue his own happiness in his own way. And as a general rule parents are the best guardians of their children. The family is the primæval institution of the race. The love of the parent is the strongest of motives for the care of the child. But when parental love fails, and the offspring is either abandoned or educated in vice, the state may rightfully intervene. Its right is derived from its duty to protect itself and to protect all its people.

I am not deducing the right of interference from an impulse of the heart, though that be the foundation on which our hospitals and almshouses are built, but I place it upon the inherent and all-pervading rights of protection and self-defense. Charity is an individual privilege; the impulse is an individual gift from Heaven. The state is not founded for charity, but for protection. The dictate of humanity is without doubt to take a child from an unfaithful parent and give it the training most likely to lead to an honest and industrious life. This is to transfer the child from an unclean home to one that is clean, from indecency to decency, from foul air to pure, from unhealthy food to that which is healthy, from evil ways to good. Who can doubt that the greatest good which can be done to a child neglected by its parent or taught beggary or crime, is to take it from the wicked parent, and give it into the care of one who will teach it not only the rudiments of learning but honest labor. In what other way can we better follow the example of the Divine Master than by caring for these little ones, who are unable to take care of themselves?

Protection, however, is the foundation of the right I am asserting. We must of course have a care that interference for protection be not carried beyond its rightful limits. If any general rule could be laid down for marking these limits it would perhaps be this, that the state should not invade one man's rights in order to protect another's. What the individual can do for himself the state should not undertake. But in the case supposed, the faithless parent has forfeited his right to his child, and the only point to be considered is the relation of the child to the state. This relation involves considerations of economy and of safety, each of which may be considered by itself.

The question of economy has political and social aspects. The prevention of crime and the punishment of the criminal impose upon the state some of its heaviest burdens. The cost of the police, of the courts and the prisons, makes one of the longest items in the roll of public expenditure . . .

It is hard to find out how much the people of this State, in all their municipalities and political divisions, pay for police, courts and prisons. We know that the amount is appalling. Much of this, how much cannot be told, might be saved by fulfilling the scriptural injunction: "Train up a child in the way he should go, and when he is old he will not depart from it."

The question of safety is more vital still. Every one of these boys may be a voter ten or twenty years hence. His vote will then be as potent as yours or mine. In countries where the sovereign is a prince it has ever been thought prudent to bestow special care upon the training of an heir to the throne. Here the people are sovereign, and the little boy, now wandering about the streets, neglected or led astray, is in one sense joint heir to a throne. Every dictate of prudence points to his being fitted to fulfill the duties of his station. Who can say that if duly cared for he may not grow to the stature of a leader of the people ranking with the foremost men of his time, a benefactor of the race, a teacher of great truths, a helper of the helpless, a brave soldier in the "sacramental host of God's elect." If, on the other hand; he is left to himself in the swift current of want and vice, floating in the scum of sewers and the company of thieves, he will prove a scourge to the state, and may bring up in a prison, or perchance on the scaffold.

For this reason, and the one preceding, it should seem to be the duty of the community to look after children whose parents abandon them or lead them into evil ways, or are incapable of taking care of them.

2. The Massachusetts "neglect" law

"An Act relating to indigent and neglected children," 1882 — ch. 181, *Acts and Resolves of Massachusetts* (Boston, 1882), p. 135.

SECTION 3. Whenever it shall be made to appear to any court or magistrate that within his jurisdiction any child under fourteen years of age, by reason of orphanage, or of the neglect, crime, drunkeness or other vice of his parents, is growing up without education or salutary control, and in circumstances exposing him to lead an idle and dissolute life, or is dependent upon public charity, such court or magistrate shall, after notice to thte state board of health, lunacy and charity, commit such child, if he has no known settlement in this Commonwealth, to the custody of said board, and if he has a known settlement then to the overseers of the poor of the city or town in which he has such settlement, except in the city of Boston, and if he has a settlement in said city, then to the directors of public institutions of said city until he arrives at the age of twenty-one years, or for any less time; and the said board, overseers and directors are authorized to make all needful arrangements for the care and maintenance of children so committed in some state, municipal or town institution, or in some respectable family, and to discharge such children from their custody whenever the object of their commitment has been accomplished.

3. Purposes and processes of The Massachusetts S.P.C.C., 1887

Massachusetts S.P.C.C., *Seventh Annual Report,* pp. 11–14.

The report was prepared by Frank B. Fay, general agent of the Society.

PURPOSES

Prevention, Rescue, Punishment, cover the ground of our work.

Prevention is secured by warning, advice, and the enactments of laws, the penalty of which is held over men and women as a check.

Rescue is accomplished by processes to be hereinafter described.

Punishment. — Our human nature prompts us to desire to punish those who neglect or abuse children, but when we can better secure the happiness and welfare of the child by rescue, and allowing the parent to escape, we do so.

In ordinary cases of assault, for example, the parent would be fined, and the child would go back to its home, perhaps to be tortured in many ways which would not be recognized by the law.

In aggravated cases, punishment must follow, and, in such instances, we may be able to convince the court that the child is not "under salutary control," and so take him away under the neglect law. We have no ambition to make an extended prison record of parents, but consider the child as our ward, and his welfare our first care.

PROCESSES

Neglect Law. — We rescue the larger number of children by the neglect law, which authorizes action by the lower courts when "by reason of the neglect, crime, drunkenness or other vice of his parents, a child is growing up without education or salutary control, and in circumstances exposing him to lead an idle and dissolute life."

If the case is made out, the child is committed, during minority, to the town, city or State authorities, according to its legal settlement, who are to educate and care for the child until, in the language of the law, "the object of his commitment has been accomplished." These authorities have the right to discharge the child to the parents or other parties, when they can be shown to be worthy. We regret to say the parents are seldom able to recover their children by showing their fitness to care for them.

We are obliged to notify the Board of State Charities before the trial, in order that they may determine the legal settlement, and act as next friend of the children, in case the parents are not present.

These cases are heard in the Juvenile Court, so that the children are not exposed to the ordinary proceedings in criminal suits.

Our object, in these "neglect cases," is not to show how many we rescue, and we often make repeated appeals and warnings before acting legally, keeping in mind always that the natural place for a child is with its parents.

The children seldom grieve at the transfer from their parents, and the parents drown their grief, if they have any, in the cup that brought about the neglect and destitution.

We never take neglected children by law from their parents, where the neglect arises from honest poverty alone, for we would not thus punish misfortune; but we appeal to public or private organizations, and secure the protection and care of the child in its own or some other home. Nor do we take such children forcibly, when one parent is worthy. We simply insist that the child shall be removed or be better cared for.

Non-Support Law. — The work under this law constantly increases, as more mothers find the power it has over their recreant husbands.

The public little appreciate how many fathers waste their wages, leaving their children to be cared for by the mothers or dependent upon charity.

In most cases, to escape arrest, the father assigns a portion of his wages to the family, or pays it weekly through this office. In many other cases the wife holds the terror of the law over her husband.

Guardianship. — Probate courts are courts of equity, and, in many cases where we might not be able to show actual abuse, the court feels it for the best interests of the child to remove it from its parents, recognizing that the child has some rights over which the parents have not supreme control.

Girls and boys over fourteen, whose wages are wasted by their parents, seek release from parental control by this method, and the law gives such children the right to nominate their own guardian, subject to the approval of the court.

This method of securing custody of children is adopted where one parent has abandoned the children, and the other seeks absolute control to prevent the possible return and interference in the future.

Adoption. — Legal adoption is another method of protecting children, but this requires the consent of the parents, unless they have abandoned the child for two years, or have been convicted of being a common drunkard or a wanton, or are in prison or insane. If no parent is living, next of kin must consent.

If a child has been given to a charitable institution by the parent, the consent of its officers is sufficient to secure adoption.

Various. — Abandoned, runaway, sick, deformed, feeble-minded, blind and deaf and dumb children, not properly cared for, are brought to us, and we seek protection for them in some hospital or other institution.

.   .   .   .   .

Death Rate. — We feel assured that the death rate is lessened by our efforts in transferring children from the homes where we find them to those where they will be properly fed, clothed and cared for.

---

4. A delicate duty, 1893

Frank B. Fay, "The Protection of Neglected and Abused Children," in Anna Gorlin Spencer and Charles Wesley Birtwell, eds., *The Care of Dependent, Neglected and Wayward Children* (Baltimore, 1894), pp. 131–132, 138–139.

Fay's paper was read and discussed at a session of the International Congress of Charities, Correction and Philanthropy held in Chicago in June 1893.

It is a delicate duty to deprive parents of their children, and the work must be done with caution, and only in cases of necessity. The parents thus deprived are not destitute of affection; the liquids they imbibe do not quench parental love; and the tears they shed are as real as those flowing from the eyes of men and women who have had better opportunities in life, or who have better resisted temptation. But our duty demands that, while we appreciate the loss of the parents, we think of the gain to the child. We should strive to be as kind in our action as a just enforcement of the law will permit, having a constant care, in cases of apparent neglect, to distinguish between the poor and destitute and the unworthy and dissolute. But we have a constant duty to remember that these neglected children have more years before them of happiness or misery than their parents, and have not lost their rights by their own bad conduct; so that, if there is to be suffering by the severing of the family tie, the parents should be the sufferers, and the child have the "right to life, liberty, and the pursuit of happiness."

·   ·   ·   ·   ·

DISCUSSION

CHARLES E. FAULKNER, superintendent of the Soldiers' Orphans' Home, Atchison, Kansas . . . I desire to call attention to another point — as to the propriety of the state interfering to take the child away from its parents. That is a delicate point, but everybody must concede the right of the state to interfere. Where the child has a depraved father or mother and is clearly neglected, going the wrong way, the state, in the interest of society, should take possession of the child and see to it that it finds a lodgment in some well-ordered home. Here you strike the keynote to the whole subject.

If a mother is very poor and unable to care for her child, and in consequence has temporarily given up her child, when she gets on her feet again it should be returned to her; but if the mother is unworthy and on that account the child has been taken from her, and she comes and seeks to recover it, then refuse to return the child to her custody and control. Parental authority must be respected so long as the parents are worthy. But if the mother is dissolute and the father depraved, the power of the state should interfere and take the child.

A MEMBER. — Who is to judge?

Mr. FAULKNER. — The judge of the probate court in the county where the parents reside. In Kansas no child can be committed without a finding by the judge of the probate court. If a mother comes and makes a plea of destitution and desires to surrender her child, and the probate court finds that she is absolutely destitute, the judge finds that a case of merit, and the institution takes the child. Cases of neglect and ill-treatment, also, are tried by the judge of the probate court on any complaint properly lodged.

A MEMBER. — Who can complain?

Mr. FAULKNER. — Any citizen of the state.

A MEMBER. — How can a mother get her child back? How can she prove that she is capable of taking care of her child and worthy of having it restored to her?

Mr. FAULKNER. — Certainly a mother residing in the county is capable of furnishing evidence as to her capability of taking care of the child. The trustees are vested with full discretionary power to return any child. We require the same evidence that people require in ordinary business transactions.

A MEMBER. — What can you do with a mother who is not dissolute, but deserted by her husband and herself utterly inefficient?

Mr. FAULKNER. — Our law provides that any child dependent upon the public for support may be sent on the application of the mother. The purpose in having the probate court supervise the proceedings is to prevent the parents from needlessly unloading their children on the state. The tendency on the part of a great many people is to let the state take the children until the parents are ready to take them back again. A careful examination is made as to the merits of each case, and the probate judge makes a certified finding of all his proceedings, and the child can be received into the institution only on a finding of the probate judge.

A MEMBER. — I would like to know whether the probate judges are appointed or elected.

Mr. FAULKNER. — They are elected. There has never been any complaint in Kansas, so far as I know, that the duties of probate judge have been performed in any manner which would indicate political discrimination.

---

5. Hiding Carminella from "The Society"

Edward W. Townsend, *A Daughter of the Tenements* (New York, 1895), pp. 12–13, 25–27.

In Townsend's novel of life in the Mulberry Bend section of New York City Teresa, a dancer, fears that her daughter will be "rescued" by the New York S.P.C.C. while she is hospitalized.

"You must go to the hospital, dear," said the woman who was called Maggie.

"But Carminella!" cried Teresa in sudden anguish. "Who will take care of Carminella?"

"What is it?" asked the doctor.

"Her baby, Carminella," answered Maggie. . . .

Teresa only moaned . . .

The doctor may have guessed a little, for he said kindly: "The Society will look after the child."

"No! no!" shrieked Teresa, and many of the other women looked nearly as frightened as she.

Teresa motioned to Maggie, and as the woman bent over her again, whispered: "Go to my room and take Carminella before they get her. Hide her! Come closer." Maggie put her ear to Teresa's lips: "My keys are in my satchel there, the room key and the trunk key. There's money in the trunk. Take it all. Pay to keep Carminella away from the Society."

Maggie, a handsome Irish girl, one of the four who belonged to Teresa's squad in the burlesque, had the wit to take the keys from the satchel then and there, and say,

"You want me to go to your room, dear, and get the baby and the money?" Teresa nodded, "Yes."

"And it's by legal right, whatever the Society or Hector say?"

Again the injured woman assented, and the other girls of the ballet regarded Maggie with admiring approval for her evidence of profound learning and knowledge of the law.

"She said 'by legal right,'" one whispered. "The Society even can't touch her because we're witness that Teresa said it was by legal right."

"I wonder Maggie wouldn't hurry though," another whispered. "The Society might get there first. I've heard they have spies out."

Teresa caught this last remark and apparently forgot her pain in the overwhelming terror with which she begged her companion to hurry.

.   .   .   .   .

"I'll come to the hospital and let you know when I have the baby safe," whispered the good-hearted Irish girl to Teresa, as she walked by the side of the stretcher to the ambulance.

"To-night?" asked Teresa.

"Sure, to-night, before I go to bed," answered Maggie, and Teresa smiled.

Maggie once proposed to bring the baby to the hospital, but, although the mother's heart choked her at the thought, she said "No." The Society might have heard that she was in the hospital and that the baby had no kin to look after it, and might capture it if it were taken so far away from its friends.

It may be incumbent on me to explain a little this foolish fear of Teresa's about "the Society," as that Society is called which takes the children of the poor, when the poor cannot help themselves. I explain only because it is proper that my readers should have the same sensible ideas about this matter that all other highly respectable and intelligent persons have. Of course, if charitable people will give up their valuable time to having laws passed giving them extraordinary and arbitrary powers over the children of the poor, all reasonable persons are justified in supposing that the poor appreciate the noble and self-sacrificing motive which prompts such efforts. Being poor, they can have no such natural love for their offspring as would prompt resentment against any interference by the Society in their relations with their children. That, I say, is what one would reasonably and properly suppose. But the poor are unreasonable and not infrequently improper, so the rule does not work. They are sometimes so sinfully unreasonable as to love their children, or at least affect to, as much as if they were creatures of refinement and education, and had power enough to take other people's children away from them.

It is really humiliating to know the ingratitude of the poor in this regard. Why, I recall, for instance, the case of that Polish woman who was arrested because she could not make enough money in her little tobacco shop to pay the blackmailing demands of two police officers (she thought they were collectors of legal taxes), and when she was sent to jail to teach her to work harder, "the Society" took her children, and very properly. But when she came from jail and found there was no law by which she could get her children away from the Society, that unreasonable woman went insane. The doctors said she went insane from grief, but I have my own opinion, and that is that she went insane through native, inborn, crass unreasonableness. You see, those stories become known, and foolish and ignorant people like Teresa hear them, and are thus possessed by a wicked prejudice against the Society. Besides, Teresa knew of a woman of her profession who, ignorant of the law, allowed her fourteen-year old daughter to dance on the stage — she had danced at home, and in the tenement courts, and on the streets for years — and the Society got that girl, took her where the wicked mother could not see her, and the wicked mother (in wicked rage, no doubt, but Teresa believed it was in grief), killed herself. I have made this little explanation because I should feel that I had been unjust to Teresa if I had not explained that she had some reasons, false and foolish reasons, to be sure, but she believed them good, for her terror of that most kind, considerate, and at all times reasonable institution, "the Society."

---

6. Neglect cases, Boston, 1901

Massachusetts S.P.C.C., *Twenty-First Annual Report* (Boston, 1901), pp. 23–25.

23705.   Parents and six children, ages from one year to twelve. Both parents drink badly. A girl of four was suffering from an injured knee, and could not leave her bed. The city physician was notified, but was refused admittance by the parents, who were drinking at the time. Our agent visited, and removed the injured child at once to the hospital. The baby, which appeared in a dying condition, was taken by an aunt to her home, also two of the other children. A complaint of nonsupport was made against the father, who was earning an average of $20 per week. He pleaded guilty to the charge, and agreed to pay $8 per week for the children, and was put on probation. A month later both parents were again in court for drinking. The father was again put on probation, and the mother was sent to the House of Correction for six months.

13321. A mother and four children. The youngest, a babe of five months, was found very emaciated and apparently dying from starvation. The mother had offered to give the child to any one who would take it. Its body was completely raw from neglect. A boy of three was nearly naked. A complaint of neglect of the two children was made, and on the evidence given at the hearing both children were committed to the care of the State Board.

15278. Parents, seven children, and an old grandmother constituted the family. The mother enceinte. The case has been known to the society for several years. Repeated warnings have been given the parents that they were in danger of losing their children unless they reformed. The father worked steadily, and yet the house was as desolate as it was possible for a house to be. Filth reigned everywhere. There was but one bed for the entire family. No food in the house, and the father earning eleven or more dollars every week. Neighbors testified that the children were in the habit of eating from their swill barrels. Children were in a terrible condition, — with heads sore from vermin, and with little clothing. A warrant was secured, and the children promptly removed. The family bed was black with dirt, the floors looked as though water had never touched them; and the breakfast table dirty, and with no food, was a sad sight. The court found the children neglected, and they were sent to the Catholic Home, and the case continued to wait the mother's recovery from her sickness. Three months later another child had been born, new furniture had been bought and paid for, new

muslin curtains put at the windows, and a radical change made in the whole house. The parents admitted that formerly all the income went for drink, but not a drop since the children were taken. The parents are hoping to recover the children after a little longer probation.

23152. Parents intemperate. Five children, ages from one to seven years. The father could have steady work, but steals tools, gets drunk, and is arrested. After release the same process occurs again and again. Agent found two dirty rooms, one dirty bed, and a crib for the baby. Parents were warned, and case watched. A few months later the parents deserted, leaving the baby, who was sick, with an old grandmother. Both father and mother had been drinking for a week. The father was under $1,000 bonds for larceny. A complaint of neglect was made of the children, and sustained on a hearing. The children were sent to the Catholic Home, and case continued in the court.

·   ·   ·   ·   ·

20735. Father earning $3 per day, and with his wife and four children living in the utmost condition of filth. But one bed, the children burrowing in a pile of feathers on the floor. They were so foul that, when they went to school, the teacher had to burn sticks to fumigate the room. A complaint of neglect was made.

At the hearing an agent of the Board of Health testified that the place was unfit for habitation, and that he had notified the owner to empty the rooms. The eldest girl was in the habit of sitting up all night to protect her parents from falling on the stove, as they sat by the stove instead of going to bed. The man admitted he drank, claimed his wife and two eldest children were demented. These children were taken as neglected two years ago, but on supposed reform of the parents were returned to them. The court found the children neglected, and they were committed to the trustees for children.

Problems and issues in child protection, ca. 1900–1925

1. A critical look at the New York S.P.C.C., 1902

Homer Folks, *Care of Destitute, Dependent, and Delinquent Children* (New York, 1902), pp. 173–175.

The New York society has had an exceptional history. Its first annual report stated that there were already in existence many institutions and societies for the care of children, but that it was not their business to seek out and to rescue children whose lives were rendered miserable by constant abuse and cruelty. The laws for the prevention of cruelty to children were considered ample, but it was nobody's business to enforce the laws. To this task the new society addressed itself. In addition to seeking to discover cases of cruelty and neglect, it stationed agents in all the magistrates' courts, to investigate all cases involving children, whether for destitution, neglect, cruelty, or waywardness. Through these agents it has advised the magistrates, not only as to whether commitment should be made, but as to what institutions the children should be committed to. Subsequently, the children were placed under the care of the society pending investigation, and the agents of the society were given the powers of police officers. Though the power to discharge the children was vested in the managers of the institutions, they, often regarding the society as the real authority through which the children had been sent to them, usually did not discharge the children either to their parents or by adoption or indenture, without consulting the society, and in some cases took no action in reference to discharge until so requested by the society. This society thus became, by 1890, the factor which actually controlled the reception, care, and disposition of destitute, neglected, and wayward children in New York city, thus practically controlling the lives of an average number of about fifteen thousand children, and an average annual expenditure for their support of more than one and one half million dollars. Its influence has done more to strengthen and perpetuate the subsidy or contract system, as it existed prior to 1894, than any other one factor.

·   ·   ·   ·   ·

The influence of the "cruelty" societies as a whole has been in favor of the care of children in institutions, rather than by placing them in families. So far as known, none of the societies have undertaken the continued care of the children rescued by them, but all have turned them over to the care of institutions or societies incorporated for the care of children. By a vigorous enforcement of the laws authorizing the commitment of vagrant, begging, and various other classes of exposed children, they have very largely increased the numbers of children becoming wards of public or private charity. Usually they have not coöperated to any extent with placing-out societies, perhaps because of being continually engaged in breaking up families of bad character, but have rather become the feeders of institutions, both reformatory and charitable. The New York society during 1900 placed six children in homes or situations; during the same period 2407 children were, upon its recommendation, committed to institutions. Constantly occupied with questions involving the custody of children, they have, not unnaturally, preferred to place the children rescued by them within the walls of institutions, where possession is at least nine points of the law, rather than to trust to a measure of uncertainty necessarily involved in the placing-out system. Without detracting from the great credit due to such societies for the rescue of children from cruel parents or immoral surroundings, it must be said that their influence in the upbuilding of very large institutions, and their very general failure to urge the benefits of adoption for young children, have been unfortunate. Probably their greatest beneficence has been, not to the children who have come under their care, but to the vastly larger number whose parents have restrained angry tempers and vicious impulses through fear of "the Cruelty."

---

2. Divergent trends in child protection, ca. 1910

Roswell C. McCrea, *The Humane Movement, A Descriptive Survey* (New York, 1910), pp. 138–146.

The New York Society for the Prevention of Cruelty to Children stands foremost in the policy of emphasizing child-rescue as a distinct phase of work, and has maintained the policy of aloofness from all other child-helping agencies. The officers of this organization maintain that societies for the prevention of cruelty to children never were created for the purpose of reforming or of educating children, or for transporting them into other homes.[1] Such societies are simply "a hand affixed to the arm of the law by which the body politic reaches out and enforces the law. The arm of the law seizes the child when it is in an atmosphere of impurity, or in the care of those who are not fit to be entrusted with it, wrenches the child out of these surroundings, brings it to the court, and submits it to the decision of the court — unless, on the other hand, it reaches out that arm of the law to the cruellist, seizes him within its grasp, brings him also to the criminal court and insures his prosecution and punishment."[2]

In this view, objects such as these can be assured only by specialization of function, and through an organization dominated by discipline

---

1. In an address at the first international humane conference held in 1910 Elbridge Gerry declared, "*Child rescue* is not *child reformation.*" American Humane Association, *34th Annual Report* (Albany, 1910), p. 12.

2. *31st Annual Report* of American Humane Association, 1907, p. 51. [Notes 2–6 are from McCrea.]

rather than by discretion on the part of workers, by the following of definite legal rules of procedure rather than by the looser adaptation of means to ends in individual cases. The idea of the exclusive nature of child-rescue work was well expressed by Mr. Elbridge T. Gerry at the [1908] annual convention of the New York State Societies for the prevention of cruelty. Among other things he said:

"Year after year there are added to the ranks of philanthropy those who are anxious to benefit the helpless, to devote their time to works of charity and mercy, to aid in the education of the growing children of the great republic and to promote the spread of religion and learning throughout the country; but they draw no practical distinctions in their work. The ancient axiom that it is better to do one thing well than half a dozen imperfectly does not enter their mind.

"If child-rescue is the object, stick to that and that alone. If general philanthropy is the object, leave child-rescue work to those who by devotion to it and exclusion of other subjects have become experts in that work; just as the specialist in disease by exclusion of other subjects stands at the head of his profession in his particular department, and accomplishes marvels in his results. It is so in every science, and in one sense child-rescue is a science, . . . , because its object is not simply a work of mercy, but the saving of a helpless human being from a life of misery, suffering and sin. The very fact that child-rescue work while properly carried on induces outside agencies, reforms and promoters of general scientific charity work to endeavor to utilize its machinery for their own purposes, shows how valuable that machinery is, and that the work, when concentrated on a single subject and conducted without regard to matters which do not belong to it, becomes preeminently successful in its results as a consequence. There is nothing to-day which scientific charity does not seek to appropriate to itself, and when it cannot absorb collateral work it endeavors to obtain possession of the subject of that work and utilize it for its own ends. Our workers should be careful to remember the copy book axiom and mind their own business, politely suggesting the like course to outsiders who endeavor to improve upon it."

It is a practical experience, however, that the line between destitute and neglected children is a very shadowy one. And a society which maintains a policy of absolute aloofness in its attitude toward other local societies is often placed under the necessity of doing "charity" work, or of consigning to forgetfulness and probable neglect cases requiring the friendly handling of some remedial agency. The New York Society has encountered this dilemma. In instances it "has, in its coöperation with the courts, included also the investigation of cases of destitution," [3] and in other instances it has refused to act, on grounds already indicated. Anti-cruelty societies as a rule have followed the lead of the New York organization. By effecting the enforcement of laws providing for the commitment of vagrant, mendicant and other classes of neglected or exposed children, and by refusing ordinarily to coöperate with other child-helping organizations, they have tended to emphasize the separating of children from their families, and their placing in reformatory and charitable institutions. They have had little in common with societies for the placing out of children in families, or with agencies for the reconstruction or maintenance of family ties.

On the other hand, noteworthy exceptions to this rule have developed. A broader interpretation of anti-cruelty work in some instances, and in others a more definite relating of such work to that of other child-caring agencies is becoming noticeable. The Massachusetts Society for the Prevention of Cruelty to Children, for instance, sees in the tendency of anti-cruelty societies to become arms of the police, a dangerous one. The necessity for prosecution is regarded as a diminishing phase of anti-cruelty work. The need for preventive and remedial measures, on the other hand, is viewed as a rapidly growing one. In this view, social work, rather than police activities, should be the aim of such organizations. It is recognized that the sanction of the law must often be invoked to promote the ends of the community, and this is the distinctive function of anti-cruelty organizations; but in addition to the protection of children

from bodily harm by this means and from serious neglect and moral injury, these societies must take upon themselves the work of developing conditions of normal family life. The Massachusetts Society seeks to realize these ends. This represents "a considerable change of emphasis from that of five years ago. Children still need to be protected against the brutality of parents, and offenders need to be prosecuted relentlessly. Children will still need to be rescued from degrading surroundings for many years to come, but the Society recognizes more definitely that it is a preventive agency. It believes that it has a duty toward the children whose circumstances are, each week that the family is left to itself, becoming worse, but which are not yet so bad that court action is advisable or possible. If, by means of its close relation to the courts, it can awaken neglecting parents to a better understanding of their responsibilities before it is too late, and insist on improvement being made, the Society becomes in every sense an agency for preventing cruelty and conserving family life. . . . The Society has, therefore, a threefold task to perform. It must rescue children from degrading conditions, it must avail itself of every reasonable opportunity to try to reconstruct such families as are moving on to inevitable shipwreck, and, while it is working with each individual instance, it must try to seek out the causes, which bring about these bad conditions, so that it may do its part to prevent them." [4]

The Pennsylvania Society is another that has come to share "the modern economic thought that the normal condition of the child is in the home, even though the home be a poor one; the children often help their parents to reform, and the father and mother can in many cases be made to realize and feel . . . that upon them is the burden of responsibility to see that their children do not become in any sense a charge

3. From *The Care of Destitute, Neglected and Delinquent Children,* by Homer Folks, p. 173.

4. *27th Annual Report* of the Massachusetts Society for the Prevention of Cruelty to Children, p. 17. *Cf.* this view with the very similar conclusions of the "White House" Conference on the Care of Dependent Children. *Proceedings,* pp. 8–14.

upon the community. Its belief in this theory is evidenced by the fact that in the year just closed 1,522 cases have been 'passed' over to what is technically known as 'supervision,' cases in which, perhaps on the first visit the breaking up of the family seemed justifiable. Endeavors have, therefore, been made in every case to preserve the family as a whole. The results obtained by the visitors and agents in this work of reconstruction have been beyond belief." [5]

This Society, like the Massachusetts and New York ones and others, maintains a detention home for the temporary care of children. This is regularly regarded as within the proper scope of the activities of such a society, regardless of other differences of view that have arisen. In the disposal of children that have come into a society's care, however, as well as in the degree of coöperation with other child-caring agencies, there is a wide divergence of view and of practice. The New York Society adheres to the policy of exclusiveness. It neither receives cases on the basis of the investigation of any other organization, nor does it refer cases to other societies. Nearly all of its children are sent to institutions where its legal hold on them is strong and its influence large. The Massachusetts Society aims to maintain a well-rounded organization for social work in the children's field. It aims to differentiate its work in independent fashion from that of other organizations in the social field; but its attitude is not exclusive, and every effort is made to come into closer touch with all agencies that aim to improve the conditions in which children live. The Pennsylvania Society has gone further. It has become associated with two other Philadelphia organizations[6] concerned with children's work in forming the Children's Bureau. By means of this commonly supported central agency, a clearing house in children's work has been established. Through this joint application bureau, the needs of any child in distress can be considered. The Bureau aims to make available for such a child the particular agency in the community best fitted to this end. "It is the belief of those who have helped to develop this joint undertaking that the problem of securing proper care for dependent, neglected, deficient and so-called delinquent children is not so much dependent upon the creation of new agencies as upon securing the proper correlation and use of the numerous existing institutions and societies for the care of children." This makes it possible for each organization to perform the work to which it is best adapted. Under these conditions each can "keep within its proper sphere," and at the same time no child need be neglected.

.   .   .   .   .

Of the more than two hundred societies in the United States that aim to protect children from cruelty, the large majority approach more nearly the working plan of the New York Society than they do that of the Massachusetts or Philadelphia organizations. But after all, in the general field of child-helping and child-caring work, organizations and institutions other than those specifically organized for the prevention of cruelty are a largely preponderating element.

------

3. Problems of a combined child — and animal — protection society, Cincinnati, 1921

William J. Shultz, *The Humane Movement in the United States, 1910–1922* (New York: Columbia University Press, 1924), p. 185. Printed by permission of Columbia University Press.

The Ohio Humane Society has several times sought to release itself from the necessity of carrying on animal protection. Despite the fact that there exists in Cincinnati another animal protective society, the Hamilton County

5. *31st Annual Report* of the Pennsylvania Society for the Prevention of Cruelty to Children, p. 12.

6. The Children's Aid Society and the Seybert Institution for Poor Boys and Girls.

S.P.C.A., to which it would gladly turn over its animal work, it has been unable to succeed in doing this without running the risk of forfeiting its charter. Moreover, a share of its income depends upon the maintenance of its activities in behalf of animals, under the provisions of the "Ohio Sheep Fund." This "Sheep Fund" is composed of the registration fees for dogs and dog kennels in each Ohio county. It was originally intended to reimburse sheep owners whose flocks had been attacked by the wild dogs which used to infest the state many years ago. It was provided that whenever there was a surplus of more than $1000 at the end of a year after paying the claims of the sheep owners, it should be transferred to the treasuries of animal protective societies in the country. There are several humane societies in the state of Ohio whose interest is in child welfare rather than in animal protection, but who are forced to engage in a certain minimum of animal protection to receive a part of their income.

---

4. Public agencies for child protection, ca. 1922

Shultz, *The Humane Movement in the United States, 1910–1922*, pp. 223–228. Printed by permission of Columbia University Press.

There are many persons to-day engaged in child protective work who feel that such work can be done better by the State than by private societies. In 1914 the Secretary of the Pennsylvania S.P.C.C. said at the conference of the American Humane Association held in that year: "This thing that we are doing is, after all, the job of the public authorities. The public ought to protect all citizens, including the children, from cruelty and improper care. As speedily as conditions admit, we should turn over to the public the things we are at present doing." [1] The present secretary of the Massachusetts S.P.C.C. has expressed his opinion that the State should take over the agents, the offices, and the organizations of the child societies and carry out their work. He expects that this will eventually develop in some states. The S.P.C.C.s will then turn to educational work in parenthood, sex hygiene, and recreation, and engage in other activities to raise the standard of family life. In addition, there will always be some specialized case work for them to take charge of.

·   ·   ·   ·   ·

The advantages of state administration have been stated: (1) The prestige and power given to the humane officers by state authority, and the cooperation of all legal authorities; (2) the completeness and effectiveness of the work, covering every remote section of the state; (3) the keeping of a permanent record belonging to the state of every child taken by the state; (4) the supplying of sufficient funds by the state to carry on the work without appealing to charity; (5) the avoidance of all conflict between local, city, and county authorities, or societies, in carrying on humane work; (6) the great improvements in methods of humane work resulting from a uniform system, and from the mobilization and organization of all the forces engaged in humane work. [2]

The state bureaus in Colorado, Minnesota, Montana, Washington and Wyoming, and the Wisconsin State Agent, combine child protection with that of animals. In most cases the emphasis is laid on animal protection. During the biennial period from 1920 to 1922, the Colorado Bureau, which has stated as its policy not to expand either branch of work to the detriment of the other, handled cases involving 1,118 children and 5,183 animals.

In West Virginia, the State Board of Children's Guardians was created in 1919 to take

---

1. American Humane Association, *38th Annual Report* (1914), p. 25. [Notes 1–8 are from Shultz.]
2. American Humane Association, *41st Annual Report* (1917), p. 61.

the place of the former Humane Society of the state and to look after the general welfare of the dependent, neglected and homeless normal children of the state. Unlike similar Boards in other states, it is an active prosecuting agency in cases involving cruelty to children and during 1921 and 1922, dealt with 209 such cases. In its protective activities, it operates similarly to the state bureaus already mentioned.[3]

Recently in several states, organization for child protection has been developed along county lines. Emphasis has been placed upon the prevention of child dependency and cruelty rather than upon the prosecution of cruelists, with the avowed purpose of preserving the child's own home wherever possible.[4]

The scope of such work is largely a matter of local expediency. The denser the population, the more opportunity of separating child welfare and adult work. Local resources are also a matter to be considered, and as always, much depends upon the attitude of the executive officer and the adequacy of his assistants. County organization of child welfare has been most highly developed in Minnesota. Here the State Board of Control is the official central agency. It consists of five members, two of whom must be women, with office terms of six years. In 1917 it was authorized to create a children's bureau. This bureau had charge of all fields of child welfare, among others the enforcement of the child-protective laws of the state, and was intended to take the initiative to conserve the interests of children wherever adequate provision had not been already made.

Under its supervision, county boards of child welfare were appointed. By the end of 1921 sixty-nine of the eighty-six counties of the state were so covered. Each county board is composed of from five to seven members, of whom at least two must be women. It is closely affil-iated with the school system of the county — the county school superintendent is always an ex-officio member. It is expected to cooperate with all the private and semi-public agencies for the benefit of children within its jurisdiction.[5] In addition, the Minnesota Society for the Prevention of Cruelty, a state association supported by state funds, operates throughout the state.

North Carolina is beginning a similar system of county boards. In 1917 the State Board of Charities and Public Welfare was created. The statute provided for county organization for child welfare similar to that in Minnesota, permissive but not obligatory. No counties adopted the plan. In 1919 it was made compulsory,[6] and provision was made for cooperation with a state-wide system of juvenile courts.

.   .   .   .   .   .

In Alabama the Board of County Welfare movement has developed along different lines. During the past few years, the advisory committees of the county juvenile courts have exercised the functions of county welfare boards . . . Recent legislation has superseded this rudimentary type of county child-welfare organization by providing for a fully developed system of county boards. Each county board is to be appointed by the judge of the county juvenile court upon resolutions to the effect by the board of county commissioners and the county board of education. It is provided that each board shall have the power to appoint an agent or county superintendent of child welfare.[7]

Pennsylvania has likewise laid the foundation for a system of county welfare boards. The state departments of Health, Labor and Industry, Public Instruction, and Public Welfare have entered into cooperation to further this work. The Commonwealth Committee of six members

3. West Virginia State Board of Children's Guardians, *2nd Biennial Report* (1922), p. 15.

4. Emma O. Lundberg, "Unifying County Work for Child Care and Protection," in U.S. Dept. of Labor, Children's Bureau Publication No. 107, *County Organization for Child Care and Protection* (Washington, 1922), p. 2.

5. William W. Hodson, "Organization and Development of County Child-Welfare Boards in Minnesota," in Children's Bureau pub. no. 107.

6. *N.C. Sess. Laws,* 1919, chap. 46.

7. *Ala. Sess. Laws,* 1923, no. 369.

was organized to serve as a clearing house for public welfare plans. Upon invitation from any responsible group of citizens within a county it undertakes the organization of a county welfare board, whose chairman will be appointed by the Committee.

Finally, there should be noted the rudimentary county organization which has been sponsored in New York by the department of county agencies of the New York State Charities Aid Association. In 1908 the Dutchess County committee of the Association was organized. A trained agent was obtained to undertake welfare work. She found that the protection of the children of the county was an important part of her work. "Unbelievably bad conditions were found in the county, and the most revolting crimes against childhood were discovered." The agent frequently secured evidence and became prosecuting witness in proceedings both to rescue children and to punish adult offenders. In 1917 the Dutchess County committee was constituted by statute the Dutchess County Board of Child Welfare and its activities expanded.[8]

---

5. Child protective agencies in 1924

C. C. Carstens, "The Next Steps in the Work of Child Protection," *Proceedings* of the National Conference of Social Work, 1924, pp. 135–139.

Carstens (1865–1939), formerly secretary of the Massachusetts S.P.C.C., was director of the Child Welfare League of America.

There is a limited group of vigorous children's protective agencies, but the humane movement as a whole is in a strange situation at the present time. By adding to their earlier programs the field of child protection, the humane societies which make up the largest group in the movement obtained a new impetus and new supporters, often men and women of the greatest philanthropic interest of their respective communities. With enthusiasm in many places much active work in child protection was undertaken. But with the new emphasis and the modern methods in children's work which came in the last decade of the nineteenth century and particularly in the first two decades of the twentieth, these societies did not keep pace. In a few instances only have they been leaders in their respective communities in the general development of a program of child protection and care; generally they have been followers, and often they have stood still.

Meanwhile children's protective work has been waiting entirely upon a hope for stimulation into activity of a national children's protective movement to be brought about either by galvanizing the programs of the older agencies into new life, or by starting new children's protective societies. Much children's protective work has been undertaken by the other agencies which had mostly been started since the children's protective agencies were first organized, and this work has become more or less a formal and recognized part of the programs of these agencies. The work is being done in a variety of ways:

First, in many communities children's aid or children's home societies have undertaken children's protective work, often because the children's protective agency could not be depended upon to undertake it, or if it could, it would be a "case-grabber" and not be willing to "play the game" in which each organization would have its part in a well-thought-out program in behalf of the family; sometimes because no children's protective work was organized in that area, and the children's aid was thought to include the children's protective function.

Second, juvenile protective societies have gotten under way in some cities because the children's protective work in at least some of

8. H. Ida Curry, "County Organization for Child-Welfare Work in New York State by the New York State Charities Aid Association," in Children's Bureau Pub. no. 107.

those communities did not extend its programs to include newer menaces to children, and they have in large measure supplanted the older children's protective work in those cities. The most flagrant and most complicated cases in child protection are doubtless those involving assault or rape of young girls and sex practices of or upon young children of either sex. A few communities of the United States have equipped themselves with suitable police and court personnel for these cases, and besides are having their laws so wisely administered that not only the culprits' rights are safeguarded but also the young prosecuting witnesses are protected from humiliation and degradation. All too frequently still the man in a rape case "gets off easily," but the young girl has lost the last shreds of modesty when the case is over. Or else the prosecution is not attempted because of fear of just these consequences. The children's protective work of this nature is on the whole badly done, and mostly for the reason that the punishment of the offender has been the principal consideration and not the safety and well-being of the child. Juvenile protective associations have called attention to a need of protection in these cases and have rendered valuable assistance.

Third, in other places the family welfare society, instead of turning to the humane society which it has tried and found wanting, would undertake family reconstruction and court work itself in cases that it is advantageous to turn over to a children's protective agency when it has a skilled staff.

Fourth, the juvenile court has become the active children's protective agency, even where there is a humane society. The children's protective functions of a juvenile court are inherent in its very structure and organization. In many instances it is doubtless the best instrument to use, and in flagrant instances family reconstruction and child protection are impossible without recourse to some court. There are, however, many instances in which child life is menaced which would either not be reported to a court or which can be adjusted best without a court being drawn in. It is the experience of active children's agencies that to every case requiring court intervention there are four or five that had best not go to court at all.

Fifth, there have also come into existence services which are in the nature of supplements and enrichments of the programs of children's protective societies rather than their substitutes. I refer to the health and recreation agencies. These play a very large part in children's protection in all of our communities, for they may be both preventive and remedial.

Health agencies, public and private, have saved the lives of untold thousands. Likewise, recreation agencies, through group and character-building service, save many thousands from degraded lives because they have provided normal interests that are educational, stimulating, and protective.

In this unsatisfactory stage of the children's protective movement there are certain noticeable trends:

First, the children's protective and children's aid functions are being combined under one society, as for example the Cleveland Humane Society, the Buffalo Children's Aid and Society for the Prevention of Cruelty to Children of Erie County, the New Hampshire Children's Aid and Protective Society, the Minneapolis Children's Protective Society, etc. The last was organized out of a combination of the children's department of the humane society and a juvenile protective society.

Second, public departments have been given the power and to some extent the equipment to take over the whole of the children's protective service, as for example, the provincial boards of Alberta, Saskatchewan, and Manitoba, county child welfare boards of Minnesota, the county boards of public welfare of North Carolina, State Board of Children's Guardians of West Virginia, the Board of Children's Guardians of the District of Columbia, and the county boards of children's guardians of Indiana, etc. In many parts of these states the service is yet quite undeveloped.

Third, juvenile courts have assumed to provide the service both in investigation of complaints and in taking the necessary action, either with or without the use of the court. This service is widespread, but it is "spread thin" and well organized in a few places only.

Fourth, new agencies for child protection have been organized, such as juvenile protective agencies in various cities, that combine the rooting out of bad conditions with the protection of children. An increase in this group may be looked for.

Fifth, the assumption, by agencies having other purposes, of the functions of a children's protective agency without equipping themselves specifically for that purpose, is also observed. Usually this work is incidental to case problems that come up in the regular part of their program, and because of lack of any children's protective agency or any effective work by an existing one, it undertakes the work itself.

Children's aid or children's home societies are most numerous in this group. Inevitably their agents become familiar with the laws relating to children and they render more or less expert service in the children's field. But family welfare societies, health agencies, relief societies, and many other kinds of agencies, and even settlements in flagrant situations take the initiative, largely because the situation is serious, the work needs to be done, and there is no one else to do it.

This raises the question inevitably in many communities whether perhaps it would not be well to have each social agency finding a children's protective task to undertake it instead of turning it over to a specialized agency. This is now the case in some communities where neglect problems come up, especially when they are not very flagrant. Are these agencies satisfied with the results they have attained? Or does it require special skill to sift and marshal evidence, to use the technicalities of the law for a social purpose, to use the knowledge of the domestic relations and children's laws for disciplining neglectful parents and stiffening the fiber of the home life of neglectful families

without recourse to court? These questions can be answered as easily by the citizen who is not a social worker or by the social worker who is not a children's protective worker as by the one that is.

First we are going to assume that there is a special children's protective function, with not much fear of finding it eliminated in the near future.[1]

Second, the combination of children's protective and animal protective work is not economical because it is not effective. The same agents cannot do both well. The functions should be separated.

Third, the humane society should devote its energies to its older program, namely, animal protection. The members of the board of directors rarely are interested in children's work. Animal protection has a separate clientèle and generally obtains ample support.

Fourth, in all but the largest cities the children's work of a humane society should be combined with the work of any other children's agency serving children in their own homes, and this agency might well be called a Children's Aid and Protective Society, so that it may be descriptive of both functions and may add friends of both services to its clientèle.

Fifth, in cities of a half-million or more population the work of a children's protective society is likely to be so extensive as to make a combination with a children's aid society un-

1. Cf. Ray S. Hubbard, "Child Protection" in Fred S. Hall, ed., *Social Work Yearbook, 1933* (New York, 1933), p. 68: "Societies for the prevention of cruelty to children are decreasing, and it is doubtful whether any new ones will be formed. In 1922 there were 57 such societies, while in 1931 there were but 48. Reasons which may be assigned for this decrease are the desire by those promoting the more recently formed protective associations for a name not so associated with compulsory methods, the broadening of operations of children's aid societies and other child-placing agencies to include the care of neglected children, and the growing acceptance by states, counties, and municipalities of the responsibility for protective work. The number of humane societies combining the work for children and animals has been reduced since 1930 from 319 to 307, the change being probably due to the transfer of the children's work to other agencies in the field."

wise. Either one is likely to be an economical unit of service in itself.

Sixth, the services of both are not incompatible. They supplement each other well. The disadvantages which at an earlier stage were believed to arise when court prosecution and children's placement work were combined have in practice not been found to exist in large enough measure to count.

Seventh, every city, county, and state will in the proper development of its service for children require a public agency that shall serve them, as far as these services cannot be provided for by the various private agencies.

Eighth, the children's protective function is a fundamental public service toward its children, and each community should equip itself to serve such as are not properly cared for by their own families or by other agencies. This can be done best through state children's bureaus and county or ctiy units coordinate with it.

Ninth, the relationship of such a public agency toward a private children's protective society is the same as that of a public child-caring agency toward a private children's aid society. The private agency can more easily become an educational, experimental, and flexible agency in its work. The public agency for all the children of the area will be able to render such service as has been recognized as needful by the community.

Tenth, the community in its private capacity is constantly discovering possible new services in child protection which the private agency may try out. It should also seek by educational work to make a community sensitive to all of the needs of its children. And as a fearless but friendly critic it also has work of great importance.

Eleventh, the private children's protective agency should not be deprived of an opportunity to serve the court in cases it may undertake; otherwise much of its usefulness is gone. It should, however, in general, attempt to take up the earlier, less flagrant, and more hopeful cases in the protection of children. The juvenile court is an important adjunct in child protection, but all of the services of a children's protective agency cannot advantageously be left to the court.

Twelfth, a children's protective agency, whether public or private, must so co-ordinate its work with the other social agencies of a community that it can take advantage of the valuable lessons that have been learned in psychiatry and psychology, preventive medicine, habit clinics, adaptive placement, and family rehabilitation, and while finding its special place in the community's plan utilize the many other agencies in the complete protection of children.

B. PROTECTION AGAINST IMMORALITY

"Comstockery"

1. Origin and activity of the New York Society for the Suppression of Vice, 1872–1882

Anthony Comstock, "The Suppression of Vice," *North American Review,* CXXXV (1882), pp. 484–489.

Comstock (1844–1915) was founder and secretary of the New York Society for the Suppression of Vice.

In the year 1872, being then a salesman in a mercantile house, I found that many of my former associates had been morally ruined by demoralizing publications, while others of them had been arrested for peculation from their employers, in order to indulge their passion for gambling. On investigation, the fact was developed that there was a very large and systematic business, of the most nefarious character, carried on to corrupt and destroy the morals of the young. With the first arrests which I caused to be made came strenuous opposition. I soon learned that there were one hundred and sixty-five different books of the vilest kind published in New York and Brooklyn, and four thousand dealers engaged in disseminating this matter all over the country. I had neither money nor influential friends, yet I resolved that "something must be done" to save the youth, and, knowing that the Young Men's Christian Association was founded for the purpose of helping and saving young men, I invoked the powerful aid of that organization. Providentially, as I believe, my letter fell under the eye of Morris K. Jesup, Esq., who personally sought out the writer, and, having acquainted himself with the facts, not only furnished means with which to carry on the work I already had commenced, but also called a meeting of prominent citizens to deliberate upon the questions involved. At this meeting a committee was appointed to direct and supervise the work; but soon it became apparent that the evils to be warred against were of such a magnitude as to demand a more effective organization, and accordingly in the ensuing year the Society for the Suppression of Vice was founded. It was incorporated by the Legislature of the State of New York, May 16, 1873, the incorporators being Morris K. Jesup, William E. Dodge, Jr., Howard Potter, Jacob F. Wyckoff, Charles E. Whitehead, Cephas Brainard, Thatcher M. Adams, William F. Lee, J. Pierpont Morgan, J. M. Cornell, Elbert B. Monroe, George W. Clark, Cornelius R. Agnew, and R. R. McBurney, of New York; and Moses S. Beach and Henry R. Jones, of Brooklyn. Since its organization about two hundred and fifty gentlemen of equal respectability have been added as members.

The title of the society shows its object — the Suppression of Vice — "the enforcement of the laws for the suppression of the trade in, and circulation of, obscene literature and illustrations, advertisements, and articles of indecent and immoral use, as may be forbidden by the laws of the State of New York, or of the United States."

About one-half of all the crimes which it is the province of this society to suppress are perpetrated through the agency of the mails, and consequently, since March, 1873, the chief agent of the society has been commissioned a "special agent," or inspector of the Post-office Department (without compensation), charged with the enforcement of all laws prohibiting the transmission of obscene matter, and the conduct of the business of lotteries and fraudulent schemes, through the mail.

.   .   .   .   .

Our aim has been to procure the enactment of good laws against these crimes, and then vigorously and zealously to enforce them. The question here occurs, Having secured these stringent laws, how have you carried them into effect? We answer, by the same methods which have ever been employed by zealous ministers of the law, and in entire conformity to the lines of procedure approved by the courts long before we came into existence as an organized society. We hold it to be our duty simply to see that the laws are executed, both the State laws which prohibit any person selling, lending, giving away, exhibiting, or having in his possession, for illicit purposes, any obscene book, picture, pamphlet, paper, etc.; and the United States law, which prohibits depositing, or causing to be deposited, such articles in the mails; together with the laws against lotteries and gambling.

The first element in a case under these statutes is information that a crime is being committed. This is found most frequently in the public advertisements in the newspapers, or in printed or written circulars. Often the information is supplied by a citizen, who makes a complaint that some youth has been ruined. Again, a parent or teacher finds some of these obscene publications or other objectionable articles in the possession of his child or pupil, and demands that the vender be prosecuted.

It is not enough that a complaint is lodged against a party that he offers, for a consideration, to supply these illicit wares. The point we have to ascertain is whether the party complained of is actually engaged in conducting any of the schemes which it is our province to suppress. His advertisement says that he is, and we take him at his word; and having ascertained that a party is thus regularly engaged, we seek to obtain legal evidence of the fact. This is done by purchasing the articles which the party advertises to sell (if he does advertise), and in the manner proposed by himself. To illustrate. When we began operations, hundreds of individuals were advertising "Rich, Rare, and Racy Books," and often the titles of these books were given, always in the printed circulars. The advertisement, or the circular, would direct the intending buyer to send the price named, or to call at such a place. This was an invitation to the public to come and buy, and we, or our agents, as a part of the public so invited, did buy these wares, thus procuring for the ministers of the law conclusive evidence that the statutes were being violated. We have not asked the dealer in illicit articles to procure for us a thing that he had not in stock, or that he did not offer for sale, but we have accepted his invitation to come and buy of him the things which we find that he has, the very possession of which is a violation of law. One point I beg the reader specially to note: We do not offer any person any inducement, beyond exact compliance with his own terms, to violate the law; neither do we ask any one to get what he has not, or what he does not deal in; nor do we approach any person unless we have probable cause to believe that he is violating the laws.

A short time ago there was in Broadway a lottery office, which was conducted in the full light of publicity; it has since been suppressed by the society. The managers of this lottery advertised extensively, and, as an inducement to the public to come and buy their tickets at two dollars each, offered prizes of many thousand dollars. A line of ticket-buyers might be seen any day waiting their turn, often attended by uniformed policemen to maintain order. To procure evidence against this concern, one of our men must take his place in line, and do as every one else did, viz.: state the number of tickets he desired, and, when they were handed to him, pay for the same. These instances fairly illustrate our methods for the enforcement of State laws.

Now for the United States laws, and the course of procedure we follow in securing their enforcement. What have we to say of the mode of securing evidence here? How about "decoys," "inducing men to commit crimes," and "tampering with the mails," of which we hear so much?

The offenses which we seek to suppress are brought to our notice either by advertisements in the newspapers, or by written or printed circulars containing the titles and prices of obscene books or other illicit articles, or by getting hold of objectionable material, sent perhaps to some child through the mail. There is no such thing as "tampering with the mails" practiced by this society or its agents, nor has there ever been. Ex-Postmaster-General James, in his address at our last annual meeting, effectively disproved that accusation.

We follow Greenleaf "On Evidence," and Russell "On Crime," in preparing evidence against these criminals. Of course each case stands by itself: there are always peculiar circumstances, which require a more or less different procedure in each. But the general practise of the society is to order the illicit publications and other articles by letter, precisely as the party advertising directs, and then to observe the rules laid down by the jurists just named, in the matter of preserving copies, mailing, etc., so as to make the correspondence strictly legal evidence.

All matter sent sealed through the mails is inviolable. The dealers in illicit wares usually collect names from school and college catalogues, by purchasing old letters from other dealers, or from advertising agents, or by sending out circulars offering prizes for lists of names of young people. They then emit circulars, often in thousands, in sealed envelopes, addressed to these names, offering their prohibited wares. Suppose a girl at school receives one of these circulars; she sends it to her father, who brings it to us. Here is probable cause. Now, suppose we go and find the clerk who wrote the address on this envelope. He, as the custom is, will say that he did not know what inclosure the envelope contained, inasmuch as it was sealed when it came into his hands; but he fully identifies the address. Most people will say, Here you have a perfect case. Yes, if we can bring that innocent girl from her school, and compel her to go into court to testify as to receiving the obscene thing by mail. Again, if we use the envelope thus brought into the case, we must set the name and address in the indictment, and couple the name of this girl with this vile thing so long as the record of the court endures. Who would consent to such an outrage?

We take the child's place, and do just what she has been asked to do, viz.: write to the fictitious address given in the circlular — it is almost a universal practice with these scoundrels to cloak their identity with fictitious names — and send the price of the article advertised, giving the address to which it is to be sent. In so doing we aim to find out, first, whether the articles are illicit, and secondly, whether they are sent by the United States mail. We do not write, "Send by mail"; neither do we ask for anything the party does not offer for sale: we simply write to the fictitious address given in the circulars for just what is advertised in the circulars, and in the precise form there prescribed. We thus secure legal evidence, check the stream of corruption that is flooding the land, and at the same time save the child from disgrace.

To apply these tests, under our oaths of office, is not "decoying," but is "testing" to see if the laws are indeed violated, and, if so, securing, at the same time, the means to check the evil.

The necessity for the existence of this and like societies is found in the hundreds of gambling hells, the defilement of evil reading, and the thousands of influences which threaten the morals of the young. Public sentiment must be aroused against the publication, in the newspapers, of the sickening details of hideous crimes; against the contagion, worse than yellow fever, coming from the weekly illustrated "criminal papers"; against the low and debasing theaters; against the indecencies of the concert dives; against the crime-breeding pestilence of the "half-dime" novel and boys' story-paper; against the blasphemies of infidel publications; against all schemes for corrupting the rising generation, ere the community can call on this society to disband.

What has the society achieved? The plates for printing and illustrating one hundred and sixty-three out of the one hundred and sixty-five obscene books published ten years ago, have been seized and destroyed. The other two works were destroyed by the owner, through fear, as we have ample evidence to believe. More than twenty-five tons of contraband matter have also been seized and destroyed. Every photograph gallery and other establishment where obscene pictures or indecent articles were manufactured has been closed and their stock confiscated. Upward of six hundred and fifty persons have been arrested. Nine lotteries, claiming an aggregate income of ten million dollars per year, have been forced to close their offices in New York City. More than one hundred policy and gambling places have been raided, and their properties seized. Scores of men and boys, who formerly thronged the streets selling obscene and indecent matter, have been driven out of business, while shop-windows have been cleared of many of their objectionable features. Several of the more indecent papers have been suppressed, while nearly all publications have been purged of indecent advertisements. Over sixty abortionists have been arrested, and all but a few convicted and sentenced. We have secured for the public treasury $63,931 in fines, while bail bonds to the amount of $50,900 have been forfeited, up to January 1, 1882. Since January 1st of the present year we have made eighty-seven arrests. All this, and more, has been done, at an expense of only about $7,000 per year, all raised by voluntary contributions. There yet remains much to be done. This society has earned for itself a name, and has made an honorable record. It has shown what can be done, by patient, persistent effort, toward saving the young from contamination. Can philanthropists withhold aid and sympathy from so worthy a cause?

Dangers in half-dime novels and story papers, 1883

Anthony Comstock, *Traps for the Young,* ed. Robert H. Bremner (Cambridge, Mass.: Belknap Press of Harvard University Press, 1967), pp. 21–28, 238–242; first published in 1883. Reprinted by permission of the publishers. © Copyright 1967 by the President and Fellows of Harvard College.

Dime novels were directed mainly toward adult readers, "half-dimes" toward boys. Weekly story papers serialized fiction previously or subsequently issued in dime or half-dime novels.

Satan stirred up certain of his willing tools on earth by the promise of a few paltry dollars to improve greatly on the death-dealing quality of the weekly death-traps, and forthwith came a series of new snares of fascinating construction, small and tempting in price, and baited with high-sounding names. These sure-ruin traps comprise a large variety of half-dime novels, five and ten cent story papers, and low-priced pamphlets for boys and girls.

This class includes the silly, insipid tale, the coarse, slangy story in the dialect of the barroom, the blood-and-thunder romance of border life, and the exaggerated details of crimes, real and imaginary. Some have highly colored sensational reports of real crimes, while others, and by far the larger number, deal with most improbable creations of fiction. The unreal far outstrips the real. Crimes are gilded, and lawlessness is painted to resemble valor, making a bid for bandits, brigands, murderers, thieves, and criminals in general. Who would go to the State prison, the gambling saloon, or the brothel to find a suitable companion for the child? Yet a more insidious foe is selected when these stories are allowed to become associates for the child's mind and to shape and direct the thoughts.

.   .   .   .   .

Again, these stories breed vulgarity, profanity, loose ideas of life, impurity of thought and deed. They render the imagination unclean, destroy domestic peace, desolate homes, cheapen woman's virtue, and make foul-mouthed bullies, cheats, vagabonds, thieves, desperadoes, and libertines. They disparage honest toil, and make real life a drudge and burden. What young man will serve an apprenticeship, working early and late, if his mind is filled with the idea that sudden wealth may be acquired by following the hero of the story? In real life, to begin at the foot of the ladder and work up, step by step, is the rule; but in these stories, inexperienced youth, with no moral character, take the foremost positions, and by trick and device, knife and revolver, bribery and corruption, carry everything before them, lifting themselves in a few short weeks to positions of ease and affluence. Moral courage with such is a thing to be sneered at and despised in many of these stories. If one is asked to drink and refuses, he is set up and twitted till he yields or is compelled to by force. The idea of doing anything from principle is ridiculous in the extreme. As well fill a kerosene-oil lamp with water and expect a brilliant light. And so, in addition to all else, there is early inculcated a distaste for the good, and the piercing blast of ridicule is turned upon the reader to destroy effectually all moral character.

.   .   .   .   .

Satan is more interested in the child than many parents are. Parents do not stop to think or look for their children in these matters, while the arch-enemy is thinking, watching, and plotting continually to effect their ruin.

Thoughtless parents, heedless guardians, negligent teachers, you are each of you just the kind that old Satan delights to see placed over each child. He sets his base traps right in your very presence, captures and ruins your children, and you are each of you criminally responsible.

Take further instances of the effect of this class of publications, and then say if my language is too strong. Does it startle and offend? To startle, to awaken, to put you on your guard, to arouse you to your duty over your own children, is my purpose. *Your child is in danger of having its pure mind cursed for life.*

.   .   .   .   .

From infancy to maturity the pathway of the child is beset with peculiar temptations to do evil. Youth has to contend against great odds. Inherited tendencies to wrong-doing render the young oftentimes open to ever-present seductions. Inherited appetites and passions are secretly fed by artificial means, until they exert a well-nigh irresistible mastery over their victim. The weeds of sin, thus planted in weak human nature, are forced to a rapid growth, choking virtue and truth, and stunting all the higher and holier instincts. Thus many a child of dissolute parents is born with natural desires for strong drink, and early becomes intemperate. In his thoughtful moments he loathes drink, and yet there comes upon him a force he is powerless to resist. So, too, the incontinence of parents brings into the world children inheriting morbidly susceptible natures — natures set like the hair-trigger to a rifle — ready to fall into shame at the slightest temptation.

.   .   .   .   .

We speak of youth as the plastic state — the period of all others when the human soul is most easily moulded and character formed. Youth is the seed-time. Maturity gathers in the crop. Youth is the fountain from which the waters of life flow. *If parents do not train and instruct their children, the devil will.* Whether parents deem it important to watch the child or no, there is one who deems it so important that he keeps a constant watch. *The devil stations a sentry to observe and take advantage of every point open to an evil influence.* He attacks the sensitive parts of our nature. He would destroy the finest and most magnificent portion of our being. The thoughts, imagination, and affections he is most anxious to corrupt, pervert, and destroy.

.   .   .   .   .

I unhesitatingly declare, there is at present no more active agent employed by Satan in civilized communities to ruin the human family and subject the nations to himself than EVIL READING.

.   .   .   .   .

If gambling saloons, concert dives, lottery and policy shops, pool-rooms, low theaters, and rumholes are allowed to be kept open; if obscene books and pictures, foul papers and criminal stories for the young are allowed to go broadcast, then must State Prisons, penitentiaries, workhouses, jails, reformatories, etc. be erected and supported. Expensive courts and high-salaried officials must be employed at the taxpayer's expense, to care for those youths who are ruined, or to protect society against them.

.   .   .   .   .

Parents do not permit their children to make a playhouse of a sewer, nor to breathe its poisoned gasses. It is not popular to set diseased meat before the public in any of our numerous hotels or restaurants. Infected clothing may not be offered for sale, much less hawked about the streets. Yet worse evils than these are tolerated and encouraged, even while they are scattering moral death and physical suffering among those whom it is the especial duty of every civilized government to shield and protect — the young.

---

3. The Comstock law, 1873

U.S. *Statutes at Large,* XVII, 598–600.

Comstock lobbied effectively for the adoption of this law, officially styled "An Act for the Suppression of Trade in, and Circulation of obscene Literature and Articles of immoral Use." The bill was sponsored in the Senate by William Windom (1827–1891) of Minnesota and in the House by Clinton L. Merriam (1824–1900) of New York. The measure, passed without public hearings and with almost no debate, was signed by President Grant on March 1, 1873. On March 5, 1873, Comstock was commissioned special agent of the Post Office Department to enforce the act. He continued to serve in this capacity for the rest of his life.

For the birth control aspects of the act see above Chap. I, sec. D, The Cummins-Vaile Bill, 1923–1925.

Sec. 2. That section one hundred and forty-eight of the act to revise, consolidate, and amend the statutes relating to the Post-office Department, approved June eighth, eighteen hundred and seventy-two, be amended to read as follows:

"Sec. 148. That no obscene, lewd, or lascivious book, pamphlet, picture, paper, print, or other publication of an indecent character, or any article or thing designed or intended for the prevention of conception or procuring of abortion, nor any article or thing intended or adapted for any indecent or immoral use or nature, nor any written or printed card, circular, book, pamphlet, advertisement or notice of any kind giving information, directly or indirectly, where or how, or of whom, or by what means either of the things before mentioned may be obtained or made, nor any letter upon the envelope of which, or postal-card upon which indecent or scurrilous epithets may be written or printed, shall be carried in the mail and any person who shall knowingly deposit, or cause to be deposited, for mailing or delivery, any of the hereinbefore-mentioned articles or things, or any notice, or paper containing any advertisement relating to the aforesaid articles or things, and any person who, in pursuance of any plan or scheme for disposing of any of the hereinbefore-mentioned articles or things, shall take, or cause to be taken, from the mail any such letter or package, shall be deemed guilty of a misdemeanor, and, on conviction thereof, shall, for every offense, be fined not less than one hundred dollars nor more than five thousand dollars, or imprisoned at hard labor not less than one year nor more than ten years, or both, in the discretion of the judge."

Sec. 3. That all persons are prohibited from importing into the United States, from any foreign country, any of the hereinbefore-mentioned articles or things, except the drugs hereinbefore-mentioned when imported in bulk, and not put up for any of the purposes before mentioned; and all such prohibited articles in the course of importation shall be detained by the officer of customs, and proceedings taken against the same under section five of this act.

Sec. 4. That whoever, being an officer, agent, or employee of the government of the United States, shall knowingly aid or abet any person engaged in any violation of this act, shall be deemed guilty of a misdemeanor, and, on conviction thereof, shall, for every offense, be punished as provided in section two of this act.

---

4. A stronger anti-obscenity law based on the federal law adopted in New York, 1873

"An act to amend an act for the suppression

of the traffic in and circulation of obscene literature," 1873 — ch. 777. *Laws of the State of New York, 1873* (Albany, 1873), pp. 1183–1185.

Section 1. The first section of the act for the suppression of the traffic in and circulation of obscene literature, being chapter seven hundred and forty-seven of the laws of eighteen hundred and seventy-two, is hereby amended so as to read as follows:

1. If any person shall sell, or lend, or give away, or in any manner exhibit, or shall offer to sell, or to lend, or to give away, or in any manner to exhibit, or shall otherwise publish or offer to publish in any manner, or shall have in his possession, for any such purpose or purposes, any obscene book, pamphlet, paper, writing, advertisement, circular, print, picture, drawing or other representation, figure or image on or of paper, or other material, or any cast, instrument, or other articles of an indecent or immoral nature, or use, or any drug or medicine, or any article whatever, for the prevention of conception, or for causing unlawful abortion, or shall advertise the same for sale, or shall write or print, or cause to be written or printed, any card, circular, book, pamphlet, advertisement or notice of any kind whatsoever, stating when, where, how, or of whom, or by what means, any of the articles in this section hereinbefore mentioned can be purchased or obtained, or shall manufacture, draw, or print, or in anywise make any of such articles, every such person if of twenty-one years of age or over, shall, on conviction thereof, be imprisoned at hard labor for not less than three months or more than two years, and be fined not less than one hundred dollars or more than five thousand dollars for each offense; but if under twenty-one years of age, shall be imprisoned not more than three months and be fined not more than five hundred dollars, in the discretion of the court, for each offense; one-half of said fine shall be paid to the orphan asylum of the county, and one-half to the school fund of the county in which said conviction is obtained, except that in

the city and county of New York, one-half shall go to the Female Guardian Society in said city and the other half to the Prison Association of New York.

2. All articles of raw materials found in the possession of any person or persons intending to manufacture the same into the articles or things described in the first section of this act and also all tools, machinery, implements, instruments and personal property found in the place or building where the articles described in the first section of this act are found or seized, and used or intended to be used in the manufacture of such articles or things, may be seized and shall be forfeited; and the proceedings to enforce such forfeiture shall be in the nature of a proceeding in rem before the court of record of criminal jurisdiction having jurisdiction of the crime specified in the first section of this act in the city or county wherein the arrest or seizure was made.

3. Nothing in this act shall be construed as repealing section one of the act to which this is amendatory or as affecting any indictments heretofore found for offenses against the same, and such indictments may be prosecuted to judgment and sentence passed upon persons convicted and punishments inflicted as if this act had not been enacted.

4. Section three of said act is hereby amended so as to read as follows:

3. All magistrates are authorized, on due complaint, supported by oath or affirmation, to issue a warrant directed to the sheriff of the county within which such complaint shall be made, or to any constable, marshal, or police officer within said county, directing him, them, or any of them, to search for, seize and take possession of such obscene and indecent books, papers, articles and things, and said magistrate shall transmit, inclosed and under seal, specimens thereof, to the district-attorney of his county, and shall deposit within the county jail of his county or such other secure place as to him shall seem meet, inclosed and under seal, the remainder thereof, and shall, upon the conviction of the person or persons, offending under any of the provisions of this act, forthwith, in the presence of the person or persons upon whose complaint the said seizure or arrest was

made, if he or they shall after notice thereof elect to be present, destroy or cause to be destroyed the remainder thereof so seized as aforesaid, and shall cause to be entered upon the records of his court the fact of such destruction.

5. The words in this act in section one, "articles of indecent or immoral nature or use," shall not be construed as applying to articles or instruments which are used or applied for the cure or prevention of disease.

5. New York law gives power to the New York Society for the Suppression of Vice to make arrests, 1875

"An act for the better suppression of vice and of obscene literature," 1875 — ch. 205. *Laws of the State of New York, 1875* (Albany, 1875), p. 181.

Section 1: Any agent of the New York Society for the Suppression of Vice, upon being designated thereto by the sheriff of any county in this State, may within such county make arrests and bring before any court or magistrate thereof having jurisdiction, offenders found violating the provisions of any law for the suppression of the trade in, and circulation of obscene literature and illustrations, advertisements and articles of indecent and immoral use, as it is or may be forbidden by the law of this State, or of the United States.

6. The test of obscenity, 1878–1879

U.S. *v.* Bennett, 24 Fed. Cas. 1093, 1100, 1102–1105.

In 1878 Comstock, using an assumed name, induced D. M. Bennett to mail him a free-love tract entitled *Cupid's Yokes.*

Bennett was indicted and convicted of violating the federal anti-obscenity law. In charging the jury the trial judge adopted the so-called "Hicklin rule" for determining obscenity. On appeal the U.S. Circuit Court pronounced the test "very sound," thus establishing an important precedent in federal law.

The court then charged the jury as follows:

. . . . .

"The question is, whether this man mailed an obscene book; not why he mailed it. His motive may have been ever so pure; if the book he mailed was obscene, he is guilty. You see, then, that all you are called upon to determine in this case is, whether the marked passages in this book are obscene, lewd or of an indecent character. Now, I give you the test by which you are to determine the question. It is a test which has been often applied, and has passed the examination of many courts, and I repeat it here, as the test to be used by you. You will apply this test to these marked passages, and if, judged by this test, you find any of them to be obscene, or of an indecent character, it will be your duty to find the prisoner guilty. If you do not find them, judged by this test, to be obscene, or of an indecent character, it will be your duty to acquit him. This is the test of obscenity, within the meaning of the statute: It is, whether the tendency of the matter is to deprave and corrupt the morals of those whose minds are open to such influences, and into whose hands a publication of this sort may fall. If you believe such to be the tendency of the matter in these marked passages, you must find the book obscene. If you find that such is not the tendency of the matter in these marked passages, you must find the book not obscene, and acquit the prisoner. The statute uses the word 'lewd,' which means, having a tendency to excite lustful thoughts. It also uses the word 'indecent.' Passages are indecent within the meaning of this act, when they tend to obscenity — that is to say, matter having that form of indecency which is calculated to promote the general corruption of morals. Now, gentlemen, I have given you the test; it is not a question whether it would corrupt the morals, tend to deprave your minds or the minds of every person; it is a question whether it tends to deprave the minds of those open to such influences and into whose hands a publication of this character might come. It is within the law if it would suggest impure and libidinous thoughts in the young and the inexperienced."

.   .   .   .   .

In saying that the "test of obscenity, within the meaning of the statute," is, as to "whether the tendency of the matter is to deprave and corrupt the morals of those whose minds are open to such influences, and into whose hands a publication of this sort may fall," the court substantially said, that the matter must be regarded as obscene, if it would have a tendency to suggest impure and libidinous thoughts in the minds of those open to the influence of such thoughts, and thus deprave and corrupt their morals, if they should read such matter. It was not an erroneous statement of the test of obscenity, nor did the court give an erroneous definition of obscenity, or a definition different from that of the first request to charge. It gave a definition substantially agreeing with that of such request.

In Reg. *v.* Hicklin, L. R. 3 Q. B. 360, the question arose as to what was an "obscene" book, within a statute authorizing the destruction of obscene books. The book in question was, to a considerable extent, an obscene publication, and, by reason of the obscene matter in it, was calculated to produce a pernicious effect, in depraving and debauching the minds of the persons into whose hands it might come. It was contended, however, that, although such was the tendency of the book upon the public mind, yet, as the immediate intention of the person selling it was not so to affect the public mind, but to expose certain alleged practices and errors of a religious system, the book was not obscene. As to this point, Cockburn, C. J.,

said: "I think, that, if there be an infraction of the law, the intention to break the law must be inferred, and the criminal character of the publication is not affected or qualified by there being some ulterior object in view (which is the immediate and primary object of the parties), of a different and an honest character. It is quite clear, that publishing an obscene book is an offence against the law of the land. It is perfectly true . . . that there are a great many publications of high repute in the literary productions of the country, the tendency of which is immodest, and, if you please, immoral, and, possibly, there might have been subject-matter for indictment in many of the works which have been referred to. But it is not to be said, because there are in many standard and established works objectionable passages, that, therefore, the law is not as alleged on the part of this prosecution, namely, that obscene works are the subject-matter of indictment; and I think the test of obscenity is this, whether the tendency of the matter charged as obscenity is to deprave and corrupt those whose minds are open to such immoral influences, and into whose hands a publication of this sort may fall. Now, with regard to this work, it is quite certain that it would suggest to the minds of the young of either sex, or even to persons of more advanced years, thoughts of a most impure and libidinous character." These views seem to us very sound.

.   .   .   .   .

We are of opinion that there was no error in what was charged by the court as to the test of obscenity.

---

7. Expert opinion is not necessary to determine obscenity, 1884

People *v.* Muller, 96 N.Y. 408–412.

Muller, a clerk in an art store, was found guilty of selling photographs of paintings of nude women. He appealed his conviction on the grounds that the trial judge erred in refusing to allow the testimony of an artist and art expert on the distinction between pure and indecent art.

Andrews, J.

.   .   .   .   .

But exceptions were taken by the defendant on the trial which render it necessary to consider to some extent the scope of the statute, the method of trying the issue of obscenity and indecency, and the relevancy of proof of an innocent intent on the part of a defendant charged with a violation of the statute. It is to be observed that the statute does not undertake to define obscene or indecent pictures or publications. But the words used in the statute are themselves descriptive. They are words in common use, and every person of ordinary intelligence understands their meaning, and readily and in most cases accurately applies them to any object or thing brought to his attention which involves a judgment as to the quality indicated. It does not require an expert in art or literature to determine whether a picture is obscene or whether printed words are offensive to decency and good morals. These are matters which fall within the range of ordinary intelligence, and a jury does not require to be informed by an expert before pronouncing upon them.

.   .   .   .   .

The defendant on the trial called as witnesses an artist who had practiced painting for many years, and also a person who had been engaged in the study of art. They were asked by defendant's counsel whether there was a distinguishing line, as understood by artists, between pure art and obscene and indecent art. The question was objected to by the prosecutor and excluded by the court. The issue to be tried was whether the particular photographs in question were obscene or indecent. The defendant was entitled to prove in his defense any facts legitimately bearing upon this issue. The fact that the original pictures of which the photographs were copies had been exhibited in the Salon in Paris was admitted by the prosecution, and it was proved that one of them had been publicly exhibited in Philadelphia. But this did not, as matter of law, exclude a finding by the jury that the photographs were obscene and indecent. It is not impossible certainly that the public exhibition of indecent pictures may have been permitted in Paris or Philadelphia, and the fact that a picture had been publicly exhibited would not necessarily determine its character as decent or indecent. Indeed there is but little scope for proof bearing upon the issue of decency or obscenity, beyond the evidence furnished by the picture itself. The question which was excluded, if intended to bring out the fact that pictures might be either decent or indecent, and that the canons of pure art would accept those of one class and reject those of the other, was properly overruled as an attempt to prove a self-evident proposition. If the question was intended to be followed by proof that, according to the standard of judgment adopted and recognized by artists, the photographs in question were not obscene or indecent, it was properly rejected for the reason that the issue was not whether in the opinion of witnesses, or of a class of people, the photographs were indecent or obscene, but whether they were so in fact, and upon this issue witnesses could neither be permitted to give their own opinions, or to state the aggregate opinion of a particular class or part of the community. To permit such evidence would put the witness in the place of the jury, and the latter would have no function to discharge. The testimony of experts is not admissible upon matters of judgment within the knowledge and experience of ordinary jurymen . . . The question whether a picture or writing is obscene is one of the plainest that can be presented to a jury, and under the guidance of a discreet judge there is little danger of their reaching a wrong conclusion. The opinions of witnesses would not aid the jury in reaching a conclusion, and their admission would contravene the general rule that facts and not opinions are to be given in evidence.

---

8. George Bernard Shaw on "Comstockery," 1905

a. *Current Literature,* XXXIX (1905), 551.

IS BERNARD SHAW A MENACE TO MORALS?

A rather lively discussion on this question has been provoked lately by the action of Prof. A. E. Bostwick, head of the circulating department of the New York Public Library, in placing Shaw's works on the restricted list, on the ground that, while it is all right for people of mature years to read these works, children are better off without them. . .

Professor Bostwick explained the reasons for his action (which, however, was shortly afterward rescinded) in an interview as follows:

"His [Shaw's] attacks on existing social conditions are very radical and are almost certain to be misinterpreted by children. Take 'Man and Superman,' for example. Supposing that play fell into the hands of a little east sider. Do you think it would do him any good to read that the criminal before the bar of justice is no more of a criminal than the Magistrate trying him? Do you think that would tend to lower the statistics of juvenile crime? I believe not, and for that reason have kept 'Man and Superman' off the open shelves. There is no personal motive in my action. I am merely doing what I believe to be right."

---

b. *New York Times,* Sept. 26, 1905.

BERNARD SHAW RESENTS ACTION OF LIBRARIAN

Calls "American Comstockery" World's Standing Joke.

AN ARTIST AND A MORALIST

And as Such He Knows Better Than Our Library Officials What is Proper for People to Read.

Special Cable to *The New York Times.*

LONDON, Sept. 25. — From his country home in Ireland George Bernard Shaw sends me a letter in which he replies to the question:

"What do you think of the action of the public librarian in New York in placing your books upon the restricted list?"

Mr. Shaw writes as follows:

"Dear Sir — Nobody outside of America is likely to be in the least surprised; Comstockery is the world's standing joke at the expense of the United States. Europe likes to hear of such things. It confirms the deep-seated conviction of the Old World that America is a provincial place, a second-rate country-town civilization after all.

"Personally I do not take the matter so lightly. American civilization is enormously interesting and important to me, if only as a colossal social experiment, and I shall make no pretense of treating a public and official insult from the American people with indifference.

"It is true I shall not suffer either in reputation or pocket. Everybody knows I know better than your public library officials what is proper for people to read whether they are young or old. Everybody knows also that if I had the misfortune to be a citizen of the United States I should probably have my property confiscated by some postal official and be myself imprisoned as a writer of 'obscene' literature.

"But as I live in a comparatively free country and my word goes further than that of mere officialdom, these things do not matter. What does matter is that this incident is only a symptom of what is really a moral horror both in America and elsewhere, and that is the secret and intense resolve of the petty domesticity of the world to tolerate no criticism and suffer no invasion.

.   .   .   .   .

"I have honor and humanity on my side, wit in my head, skill in my hand, and a higher life for my aim. Let those who put me on their restricted lists so that they may read me themselves while keeping their children in the dark, acknowledge their allies, state their qualifications, and avow their aims, if they dare.

"I hope the New York press will in common humanity to those who will now for the first time hasten to procure my books and witness the performance of my plays under the impression that they are Alsatian, warn them that nothing but the most extreme tedium and discomfort of conscience can be got by thoughtless people from my sermons, whether on the stage or in the library.

"I hope also that the many decent and honorable citizens who are bewildered and somewhat scandalized by my utterances will allow me to choose my own methods of breaking through the very tough crusts that form on the human conscience in large modern civilizations. Indeed, a man is hardly considered thoroughly respectable until his conscience is all crust and nothing else. The more respectable you are the more you need the pickaxe.

.   .   .   .   .

"Before you undertake to choose between evil and good in a public library or anywhere else, it is desirable that you should first learn to distinguish one from the other. The moment you do that, say, after forty years' study of social problems, you realize that you cannot make omelettes without breaking eggs; that is, you cannot have an advance in morality until you shake the prevailing sense of right and wrong sufficiently to compel a readjustment.

"Now, if you shake the sense of right and wrong you give to every rascal his opportunity and to every fool his excuse. Preaching of Christianity makes some men Doukhobors instead of better citizens. Socialism may become the plea of the Anarchist or the dynamiter, science of the vivisectionist, and Puritanism of the Comstocker; but the nation that will not take these risks will never advance morally.

"I do not say that my books and plays cannot do harm to weak or dishonest people. They can, and probably do. But if the American character cannot stand that fire even at the earliest age at which it is readable or intelligible, there is no future for America.

"Finally, I can promise the Comstockers that, startling as 'Man and Superman' may appear to them, it is the merest Sunday school tract compared with my later play, 'Major Barbara,' with which they will presently be confronted.

"Yours faithfully,
"G. BERNARD SHAW."

Unofficial Censorship of Motion Pictures

In the decade after 1905, as motion pictures grew into a multi-million dollar industry, the moral influence of movies on young people was widely discussed. Exhibitors and producers attempted to maintain patronage and ward off official censorship by policing the industry themselves.

1. "Authorized" films, 1909

Charles V. Tevis, "Censoring the Five-Cent Drama," *The World Today,* XIX (1910), 1132–1138.

All at once the lights went out . . . "The Judgment of the Mighty Deep" was about to be depicted.

The man on the left muttered something about "another sea picture," and one of the ladies exclaimed, "Oh, look at the surf!" . . . The try-out of a new idea, a new story, which was to be told in pictures to hundreds of thousands of people, was in process. And in anything but a grim, condemning mood sat the official censor committee.

It did not take long for the story to be told. The pretty fisher maiden made her choice between two lovers in record-breaking time, and it took about as long for the discarded one to plot dire vengeance and scuttle his rival's boat.

According to melodramatic ethics, the hero was a laggard, so, of course, the heroine took the boat to sea. And, again of course, the villain discovered the result of his work too late and endeavored to make amends, only to accomplish nothing and, perforce, return to the blind father of the girl and confess his evil doing. Thereupon the father did some quick work in the midst of which the life of the villain was choked out. Then the old man groped his way out of the little cabin onto the shore in search of his daughter.

"How in the world will he find her?" some one asked in a loud whisper.

Certainly he did. In a riot of surf on the rocky reef he stumbled across her. How he bore her back to the hut was not shown. The moving-picture audience must be credited with some imagination. There the hero and heroine were reunited and the object-lesson of villainy made plain.

"That's a good picture," one of the audience remarked, as the secretary of the committee passed around the slips for a vote.

·   ·   ·   ·   ·

"These votes," explained one of the committee, "all are collected and counted by the secretary, who then issues a bulletin announcing the result. Sometimes an argument is necessary. Some may believe that the film should be changed; some that it is altogether bad; some that it is worthy. This film is not passed until there is a consensus of opinion one way or another. If the vote is unanimous either for or against, no further action is taken. Our conclusions are then published in a bulletin and circulated over the country among the managers of moving-picture houses. If they want au-

thorized films they order those we have O.K.'d. Otherwise they take chances — not only with their local authorities but with the manufacturers from whom they rent their stock in trade."

"But what of these manufacturers — do they not lose a lot of money in making films which may not get any farther than this judgment chamber?"

"Sometimes — yes," the censor replied. "But that is their lookout. Our committee is their own institution, you know. They want us as a sort of moral certificate of the high character of their product.

·   ·   ·   ·   ·

Since March, 1909, this sort of work has been going on five days in a week, every week in the month. Prior to that date effort had been made by the managers of the show-houses in New York to organize such a committee, but internal dissension among the producers hurt whatever success they might have had. Then the manufacturers of films, trust firms and independents, took the matter up and formed a permanent organization.

Chosen members from fully a score of charitable, religious and educational institutions in the metropolis were sent as delegates to the manufacturers to make up a committee which should sit in judgment on their work. The men and women were from the Young Men's Christian Association, the Young Women's Christian Association, The Children's Aid Society, the People's Institute, the Women's Municipal League, the different branches of the city's associated charities, the Society for the Prevention of Cruelty to Animals, the Purity League, the Women's Christian Temperance Union, a number of denominational societies and many other civic and private organizations. There was no remuneration; the services of the members were donated in the interest of public morals. There was even no law to direct the forming and working of such a body. It existed purely on invitation of the manufacturers. Yet, since its inception, not one verdict of the committee has been set aside.

.   .   .   .   .

Mr. John Collier, the member of the committee representing the People's Institute, who has made several years' study of the matter of moving-picture morals, has expounded some of the unwritten "don'ts" according to the lights of the censors.

"All obscene subjects are strictly taboo. If manufacturers put them out the local boards and police authorities over the country will place the ban on them.

"All crime pictures, showing gruesome details or tending to teach the technique of crime, are voted against. The suggestion is too strong, even where the picture brings out a strong lesson. The minds of the young to-day are too fertile to trust such pictures to. And we believe that the same lessons can be shown as effectively in other ways.

"All suggestive crime, that is, crime like arson or suicide, is taboo. We do not object to a Shakespearean suicide. But we do object to a picture which shows a man or a woman jumping off the Brooklyn Bridge into the East River. That picture would possibly be the cause of several people trying such a leap for themselves.

"Unmitigated sensationalism and malicious mischief we do not believe should be exploited. We are not prudes in this direction, however. We even encourage innocent mischief.

"Nothing that is in any way offensive to any religious sentiment is allowed to pass. Biblical pictures and stories we do not object to, and we do not demand historical accuracy in them. We are not censoring for theological seminaries. And, if they want to make George Washington the discoverer of America, why, as far as we are concerned, they may.

"We discourage pictures dealing with the subject of marital infidelity. But in some cases we do not condemn them. We believe that the problem play is all right, if it is presented in a proper manner.

"Kidnaping pictures we do not like and seldom pass. In New Jersey there is a law against producing them. Also pictures, which show wanton cruelty to animals, even hunting scenes, we cut out, except in remote cases where there is a moral pointed that could not be shown in any other way.

.   .   .   .   .

"As the audiences of the moving-picture shows over the United States are between twenty and twenty-five per cent children, we give special consideration to subjects of interest wholly, or in great part, to the little ones. This phase of our work is most difficult. Herein our responsibility is heavy indeed. We, therefore, do not approve anything which by any chance might be harmful."

The finished film, the one you may see at any moving-picture exhibition, be you in Oshkosh, Wisconsin, or Tallahassee, Florida, really passes through three boards of censor nowadays. Besides the official one, each manufacturer has two and sometimes three of his own. The studio "round table" reviews it first, then the officers of the company, and, after a final revision, the whole staff gives it another inspection. The negative is then sent to the central office and the real censor committee acts upon it.

---

2. Self-regulation under National Board of Censorship of Motion Pictures, 1914

Orrin G. Cocks, "Applying Standards to Motion Picture Films," *The Survey,* XXXII (1914), 337.

Especial interest . . . attaches to a statement recently issued by the National Board of Censorship of Motion Pictures giving its present policy and standards of judgment.

The board is a voluntary self-governing organization working with the manufacturers and importers of motion pictures and in the interests of the public. It was formed by the People's Institute of New York. No member is engaged in any branch of the motion picture business. The thirty-three members of the general committee speak as skilled social workers, representing such agencies as the Y. M. C. A., Charity Organization Society, Children's Aid Association, the churches, settlements, women's clubs, Young Women's Christian Association and People's Institute.

.   .   .   .   .   .

It realizes that pictures stimulating the senses require particular study from the point of view of the adolescent. It, therefore, has adopted standards "curtailing prolonged love scenes which are ardent beyond the strict requirements of the dramatic situation. It believes that it is one of the purposes of censorship to keep out of the mire the great experiences of humanity so that they may not be cheapened to the extent of losing their significance." The board restricts also very carefully the display of clothing and the person in ways to arouse the imagination and suggest immorality and indecency. It also enforces strictly the exclusion of those forms of close dancing which have the same sensuous appeal.

---

3. Industry self regulation, 1922

Will H. Hays, "Improvement of Moving Pictures" in National Educational Association *Addresses and Proceedings,* LX (1922), 254–255.

Will H. Hays, president of the Motion Picture Producers and Distributors of America, was a lawyer from Indiana who had been chairman of the Republican National Committee and postmaster general under President Harding. He was considered an expert in public relations; the motion picture industry hoped his influence would avert federal censorship.

May I refer a minute to this question of censorship, which is an incident in the matter? The people of this country, of course, are against censorship fundamentally — are against censorship of press, against censorship of pulpit, and against censorship of pictures. But just as certainly, my friends, is this country against wrong doing — and the demand for censorship will fail when the reason for the demand is removed. As we move toward the consummation of the objects of our association so in like degree will recede all demands for censorship.

I am against political censorship, of course, because political censorship will not do what is hoped for it in the last analysis. The motion-picture business objects to political censorship for one great reason — because the motion-picture business is an American business. But there is one place and one place only where the evils can be eliminated and the good and great advantage of motion pictures retained, and that is at the point where and when the pictures are made. And it *can* be done then and there, make no mistake about that. There is no twilight zone in the matter. Right is right and wrong is wrong, and men know right from wrong. The corrections *can* be made, real evil can and must be kept out, the highest standards of art, taste, and morals *can* be achieved, and it is primarily the duty of the producers to do it.

---

4. The National Board of Review, 1909–1926

Wilton A. Barrett, "The Work of the National Board of Review," *The Annals* of The American Academy of Political and Social Science, CXXVIII (November, 1926), 175, 177–178, 181.

Barrett was executive secretary of the National Board of Review of Motion Pictures, originally known as the National Board of Censorship.

The National Board of Review of Motion Pictures, 70 Fifth Avenue, New York City, is a trained, volunteer, disinterested citizen organization, composed of upward of three hundred people reviewing films in New York City before they are released for general exhibition to the public, with associate, advisory members and affiliated citizen groups in many localities throughout the country. The National Board is opposed to legal censorship and in favor of the constructive method of selecting the better pictures, publishing classified lists of, and information about them, and building up audiences and support for them through the work of community groups, in order that the producers may be encouraged to make the finest pictures and exhibitors to show them, and the people in general helped to a response to the best that the screen has to offer. This places the emphasis on making the public conscious of its taste in, and giving it a voice in the selection of its entertainment.

.   .   .   .   .   .

Under the name . . . of the National Board of Censorship, the National Board was organized in March, 1909, by the People's Institute of New York City, of which the late Charles Sprague Smith was founder and director.

The local situation, out of which the National Board immediately originated, was one in which the then mayor of New York City, Mayor McClellan, had closed the motion picture theatres of that city because of the alleged conditions in the theatres themselves and the alleged character of some of the films exhibited therein. Both the patrons and, as has been suggested, the exhibitors and leading producers were in a quandary. As a citizen bureau of social research and activity, the People's Institute felt itself justified in trying a solution,

believing as it did that the motion picture was the great, new medium of expression of untold potentialties as a recreative, educational and artistic force, which an increasing number of foresighted people all over the country were declaring it to be, and that it must be protected as such from any ill-advised effort to hamper its growth or smother it before it could confer its benefits on the American people.

The National Board was not created by the motion picture industry, is not and never has been controlled by the motion picture industry, and is distinct in its operation and the conduct of its financial affairs from any organization which at any time has been created by, or has acted for, the industry. On the other hand, the Board has always been willing to co-operate with any agency in or outside of the motion picture industry, holding out possibilities or appearing to be valuable agencies for the proper furtherance of its own work and aims; — namely, those entailed in bringing help, encouragement, and, wherever possible, guidance to the motion picture in developing its possibilities and achieving its future as a great medium of expression.

The group of people organized by the People's Institute was gathered together from among the foremost local leaders in social endeavor of various kinds, representing the various prominent social service organizations in the field with headquarters in New York City. Among this group were people who were interested in the arts and in creative endeavor. Many of this original group are still interested or active in the affairs of the Board . . .

The National Board's first purpose was the pre-publicity inspection of films, which the producers agreed to submit to its members. A mutual agreement was reached that when the Board, as a result of this inspection, asked for changes in part or total condemnation of films, the producers would abide by its decisions, with the right to appeal to the Board's General Committee in cases where they believed the decisions were unjustified, the opinion of this General

Committee to be final and binding on the companies.

.   .   .   .   .

The Review Committee — [is] the large group of two hundred and fifty members carrying on the actual work of reviewing the films. It is divided into sub-groups which meet per schedule during each week, in the projection rooms of the various motion picture companies, to review their product.

All members of the above committees are volunteer, serving without pay and unconnected with the motion picture industry. They are enlisted from all walks of life — professional, avocational, business and private. Most of the members of the General Committee are representatives of large public welfare organizations. About two-thirds of this group are women, one-third men.

The basic work of the National Board is the review of motion pictures which are submitted by the film companies producing and distributing pictures before they are released to the country at large. In this connection it may be mentioned that the Board is reviewing from ninety-eight to 100 per cent of all entertainment films, i.e. drama, comedy, animated cartoons, etc., exclusive of news reels, strictly scenic and educational subjects and industrial films, distributed to the public in the United States. In passing on this product the Board's review groups earnestly endeavor to reflect the attitude of the national mind of the patrons of films as to what is the most desirable type of picture. Regarding the passage of pictures, "Passed by the National Board of Review," does not necessarily mean the Board approves or recommends the picture upon which the legend appears. In all cases it means that in the opinion of the reviewing committee the picture will not have a morally subversive effect upon large numbers of persons in different sections of the country. It further means that the review committee in so passing a film has detected in it, judged in a common sense way by its probable net moral effect on an audience in a motion picture theatre, nothing that violates in part or in whole what amounts to the common law against the publication of the immoral, obscene or anything detrimental to public morality.

Official censorship of motion pictures

1. Ohio movie censorship law, 1913

"An Act providing a board to censor motion picture films and prescribing the duties and powers of the same," 1913. *State of Ohio Legislative Acts,* CIII (Springfield, 1913), 400–401.

Chicago instituted municipal censorship of movies in 1907; Pennsylvania and Ohio were the first states to adopt film censorship laws. By the early 1920's their example had been followed by Kansas, Maryland, New York, Virginia, and Florida.

SECTION 3. It shall be the duty of the board of censors to examine and censor as herein provided, all motion picture films to be publicly exhibited and displayed in the state of Ohio. Such films shall be submitted to the board before they shall be delivered to the exhibitor for exhibition. The board shall charge a fee of one ($1.00) dollar for each reel of film to be censored which does not exceed one thousand (1,000) lineal feet; for any reel of film exceeding one thousand (1,000) lineal feet, the sum of two ($2.00) dollars shall be charged. All moneys so received shall be paid each week into the state treasury to the credit of the general revenue fund.

SECTION 4. Only such films as are in the judgment and discretion of the board of censors of a moral, educational or amusing and harmless character shall be passed and approved by such board. They shall be stamped or designated in an appropriate manner and consecutively numbered. Before any motion picture film shall be publicly exhibited, there shall be projected upon the screen the words "Approved by the Ohio Board of Censors" and the number of the film.

SECTION 5. The board of censors may work in conjunction with any censor board or boards of legal status of other states as a censor congress and the action of such congress in approving or rejecting films shall be considered as the action of the board and all films passed, approved, stamped and numbered by such congress, when the fees therefor have been paid to the Ohio board, shall be considered approved by such board.

SECTION 6. Ninety days after this act shall take effect no films may be publicly shown or exhibited within the state of Ohio unless they have been passed and approved by the board or the censor congress and stamped and numbered by such board, or congress, as provided for herein.

SECTION 7. Any person, firm or corporation who shall publicly exhibit or show any motion picture within the state of Ohio unless it shall have been passed, approved and stamped by the Ohio board of censors or the congress of censors shall upon conviction thereof, be fined not less than twenty-five ($25.00) dollars nor more than three hundred ($300.00) dollars, or imprisoned not less than thirty days nor more than one year, or both, for each offense.

SECTION 8. Any person in interest being dissatisfied with any order of such board shall have the same rights and remedies as to filing a petition for hearing on the reasonableness and lawfulness of any order of such board or to set aside, vacate or amend any order of such board as is provided in the case of persons dissatisfied with the orders of the industrial commission.

2. Federal court upholds constitutionality of Ohio movie censorship law, 1914

Mutual Film Corporation *v.* Industrial Commission of Ohio, 236 U.S. 241–242.

The next contention is that the statute violates the freedom of speech and publication guaranteed by the Ohio constitution. In its discussion counsel have gone into a very elaborate description of moving picture exhibitions and their many useful purposes as graphic expressions of opinion and sentiments, as exponents of policies, as teachers of science and history, as useful, interesting, amusing, educational and moral. And a list of the "campaigns," as counsel call them, which may be carried on is given. We may concede the praise. It is not questioned by the Ohio statute and under its comprehensive description, "campaigns" of an infinite variety may be conducted. Films of a "moral, educational or amusing and harmless character shall be passed and approved" are the words of the statute. No exhibition, therefore, or "campaign" of complainant will be prevented if its pictures have those qualities. Therefore, however missionary of opinion films are or may become, however educational or entertaining, there is no impediment to their value or effect in the Ohio statute. But they may be used for evil, and against that possibility the statute was enacted. Their power of amusement and, it may be, education, the audiences they assemble, not of women alone nor of men alone, but together, not of adults only, but of children, make them the more insidious in corruption by a pretense of worthy purpose or if they should degenerate from worthy purpose. Indeed, we may go beyond that possibility. They take their attraction from the general interest, eager and wholesome it may be, in their subjects, but a prurient interest may be excited and appealed to. Besides, there are some things which should not have pictorial representation in public places and to all audiences. And not only the State of Ohio but other States have considered it to be in the interest of the public morals and welfare to supervise moving picture exhibitions. We would have to shut our eyes to the facts of the world to regard the precaution unreasonable or the legislation to effect it a mere wanton interference with personal liberty.

---

3. Authority of censors restrained, 1918

City of Chicago *et al. v.* Fox Film Corporation, 251 *Fed. Rep.,* 883–884.

BAKER, Circuit Judge. This appeal . . . involves the construction and application of the following provisions of the ordinances of Chicago:

"Sec. 1627. If a picture or series of pictures for the showing or exhibition of which an application for a permit is made, is immoral or obscene, or portrays any riotous, disorderly or other unlawful scene, or has a tendency to disturb the public peace, it shall be the duty of the general superintendent of police to refuse such permit; otherwise it shall be his duty to grant such permit."

Section 1 of amendatory ordinance of July 2, 1914: "That in all cases where a permit for the exhibition of a picture or series of pictures has been refused under the provisions of section 1627 of the Chicago Code of 1911, as amended, because the same tends towards creating a harmful impression on the minds of children where such tendency as to the minds of adults would not exist if exhibited to persons of mature age, the general superintendent of police may grant a special permit limiting the exhibition of such picture or series of pictures to persons over the age of twenty-one years: Provided, such picture or pictures are not of such character as to tend to create contempt or hatred for any class of law-abiding citizens."

Appellants refused to grant a permit under section 1627 for the exhibition of appellee's moving picture, "The Spy," but offered a permit "for adults only" under amendatory section 1.

From the pleadings and affidavits, the following may be accepted as the situation, pending final hearing: The photoplay depicts a young American's efforts to obtain in Germany the list of German spies in America, his capture, torture and death at the hands of a firing squad. There is nothing obscene or immoral; no portrayal of any riotous, disorderly, or other unlawful (*noscitur a sociis*) scene; nothing tending to disturb the public peace; but the action of the play, where great drops of sweat stand out on the face and chest of the hero as he endures torture and faces death, is too harrowing, in the honest judgment of the city's administrators, for the sensibilities of minors; and for that reason, and that alone, the permit under section 1627 was refused.

. . . The only misapprehension we find in the case is that of the city's administrator with respect to the discretion committed to him by the ordinances. Section 1627 sets up a standard, but allows no discretion. If a photoplay conforms to that standard, "it shall be his duty to grant such permit." If it does not, he must refuse the permit. In deciding the question of fact the trier must of course take the viewpoint of old and young, wise and foolish, learned and ignorant; but a picture either is or is not obscene, by the one standard, including all the public. Amendatory section 1 brings in the matter of discretion. If a permit under section 1627 is refused, the administrator nevertheless "may grant a special permit," limiting the exhibition to adults. The discretion goes only to permitting a nonconforming picture to be exhibited to adults on the administrator's belief that such exhibition would not undermine the settled moral and peaceful character of adults. The "harmful impression on the minds of children" must be an impression caused by the obscenity or other forbidden characteristic of the picture — not an impression which the administrator on nonlegislatively defined grounds may deem harmful to them. Since Euripides' time it has been mooted, in the dramatic and other arts, how far the depiction of terror and anguish may properly be employed for the purification of the passions of the observer. If the glycerine tears and beads of sweat of the moving picture art are too horrifying for children, it was not for the administrator of these ordinances to say so; it must first be declared by the lawmaking body — if constitutional restrictions permit.

---

4. Proposed federal censorship laws

Ford H. MacGregor, "Official Censorship Legislation," *The Annals* of the American Academy of Political and Social Science, CXXVIII (November, 1926), 164–166.

A dozen or more bills have been introduced in Congress during the last fifteen years to provide for Federal censorship of motion picture films. With two exceptions, these bills have not received very careful consideration or been taken very seriously.

The first important one was introduced by Congressman D. M. Hughes, of Georgia, December 6, 1915. It provided for the creation of a Federal Motion Picture Commission as a division of the Bureau of Education in the Department of the Interior. The commission was to be composed of five members appointed by the President for terms of six years, the chairman to receive $4000, and the other members $3500 per year. This commission was charged with the duty of examining, censoring and licensing all films before they could be admitted to interstate commerce. The expense of the commission was to be met from fees received for the licenses or certificates issued. It was to have the power to approve films as presented, to approve them with eliminations, or to reject them entirely. No standards were set forth in the bill except the provision that the commission should license every film presented unless it found that such film was

obscene, indecent, immoral, inhuman, or depicts a bull fight, or prize fight, or is of such character that its exhibition would tend to impair the health or corrupt the morals of children or adults, or incite to crime.

This bill attracted great attention throughout the country, particularly among moving picture interests. Extended hearings were held by the Committee on Education, of which Mr. Hughes was chairman, and exhaustive briefs were printed by both sides, but the bill was finally defeated. Several bills have since been introduced embodying the same or similar provisions, conspicuous among which was the one introduced in 1922 by Mr. Appleby of New Jersey.

By far the most comprehensive and radical bill that has been proposed for Federal censorship was that introduced by Congressman Wm. D. Upshaw, of Georgia, in December, 1925. This bill also provided for the creation of a Federal Motion Picture Commission as a division of the Bureau of Education in the Department of the Interior. It was to be composed of seven members, the Commissioner of Education, ex officio, and six commissioners appointed by the Secretary of the Interior from a list of eighteen persons nominated by the Commissioner of Education. Two of the commissioners were to be women. At least two of the commissioners were to be members of the legal profession, two experienced teachers with a knowledge of the psychology of youth, and at least one with experience as a member of a state or municipal board of censors. The chairman of the commission was to receive $10,000, and the other commissioners $9000 per year, and all were to serve during good behavior.

The bill gave the commission power (1) to preview and license motion picture films, (2) to examine and censor scenarios, and (3) to supervise their production in the studios. A license from the commission was made a prerequisite for copyright. The board was given authority to issue permits without inspection for scientific, educational, industrial and religious films, and for news reels, and current events films. No film could be accepted for interstate commerce unless accompanied by a license or permit from the commission. The inspection fees were fixed at $10 per reel for originals and $5 for duplicates, and from the receipts, $1,000,000 was to be appropriated annually to the Bureau of Education. The commission was also given power to inspect and censor posters and advertising material of all kinds.

Any commissioner or deputy was authorized by the bill to view films, but in case he refused a license, the applicant could demand a review by three members of the commission. Final appeal was provided to the Court of Appeals of the District of Columbia. The bill laid down minimum standards for the guidance of the commission. In addition to the general prohibitions, it listed thirteen specific prohibitions. For instance, under the bill no films could be licensed which "emphasize and exaggerate sex," "based upon white slavery," "making prominent an illicit love affair," "exhibit nakedness or persons scantily dressed," "bedroom scenes," "passionate love," "scenes which are vulgar," etc.

But the most radical provisions of the bill were of a regulatory character. It required all persons engaged in any branch of the moving picture industry, whether as producer, distributor, exhibitor, director, actor, artist, photographer, costumer, or in other capacity, to register with the commission, and gave the commission power to cancel registration for violation of its orders or regulations, or the provisions of the law. It forbade unfair and deceptive practices and gave the commission power to investigate such practices and to issue orders with reference to the same. It gave the commission power to fix rentals for films, and to fix the admission rates for theatres. It required trade associations (and trade associations were defined to include any association of members engaged in any branch of the business, or in any contributory industry) to file with the commission statements of their proposed activities, minutes of their meetings, names of officers and members, copies of all resolutions, and all agreements, annual reports, contracts, rates and prices, and any other information which the commission might require, and gave the commission the right to publish any such information and statistics. Finally, it gave the commission the authority, if it deemed wise, to take over as a governmental function the entire distribution of moving picture films in this country.

It is difficult to imagine Congress enacting a law of this kind, but the bill was given very careful consideration, extended hearings were held, and very exhaustive briefs and exhibits were presented to the committee. A determined effort was made to secure its passage, but it was finally defeated, as was also a much simpler bill introduced by Mr. Swope.

There is little question of the constitutional authority of Congress to enact a Federal censorship law. Through its control over interstate commerce and the mail, it has an effective means of enforcing such a law, and undoubtedly future bills will be introduced on the subject. Up to the present time, however, Congress has followed the policy of leaving official censorship of motion pictures to the states and their municipalities.

---

5. Supervision of films for minors in various countries, 1927

League of Nations. Advisory Commission for the Protection and Welfare of Children and Young People, Child Welfare Committee, *The Cinema* (Geneva, 1928), 1–3.

In 1927 the Child Welfare Committee of the League of Nations submitted to forty-seven governments a questionnaire on the cinema in relation to child welfare.

REPLY TO 1927 QUESTIONNAIRE

Only twelve countries have so far replied to the questionnaire drawn up by the Child Welfare Committee at its third session. These are Brazil, Canada, Denmark and Iceland, the Free City of Danzig, Estonia, Latvia, Monaco, Norway, Poland, Sweden, Turkey and the Union of South Africa.

In reply to Point I of the questionnaire, the Governments are mainly in favour of the principle of an exchange between the supervisory authorities in the various countries of lists of films which each of them considers suitable for children and young people.

The Government of the Turkish Republic has communicated the suggestion of the Minister of Education that a permanent bureau should be established, under the supervision of the Child Welfare Committee at Geneva, for the purpose of keeping the Ministers of Education in the participating States regularly informed of the appearance of films considered to be suitable for, or harmful to, children and young people.

Sweden, on the other hand, is doubtful as to the value of such exchanges, as the supervision exercised in Sweden is generally much stricter than elsewhere. Moreover, any considerable divergencies of views and opinions in the matter would, to a large extent, discount the advantages to be derived by the various countries from international agreements to prevent the circulation and exhibition of demoralising films.

· · · · ·

Admission of Minors to Cinematograph Performances

It should be noted that special regulations for the admission of minors and the selection of films to be shown to them have been issued by thirty-one Governments out of the forty-seven given in the list.

In most cases the prohibition applies to only one class of film, and is evidently framed to safeguard the mental and moral well-being of children. It appears that, in the countries which have gone furthest in the matter of such regulations, the age-limit for the admission of minors to all cinematograph performances has been fixed at 18.

In some countries, young children are absolutely prohibited from attending cinematograph performances, mainly on grounds of health. Of the six countries which, to our knowledge, have introduced this measure of complete prohibition, four fix the age-limit at 6, namely, the Free City of Danzig, Germany, Nicaragua and Peru. Hungary has fixed this limit at 5 years and the Republic of Salvador at 3 years.

The legislative provisions of certain countries stipulate that the measures for the control of the admission of minors to cinematograph performances shall not apply when the minor is accompanied by his parents or one of them, his guardian, or some other responsible adult person. Such is, for instance, the case in Canada (in the provinces of Alberta, British Columbia, New Brunswick, Nova Scotia, Ontario, Quebec and Saskatchewan), in Japan, in Spain with reference to evening performances, in Sweden as regards the admission of minors to children's performances finishing after a certain hour, and in certain Swiss cantons.

Measures have been adopted in Belgium, Hungary, Italy, the Grand Duchy of Luxemburg, the Netherlands and Uruguay making it compulsory for cinemas to display a conspicuous notice outside their premises stating whether minors are admitted to the performance or not.

Control of Films

The general regulations fixing the standards adopted for the approval of films suitable for exhibition to minors may be either negative or positive. The following are usually prohibited: films likely to be morally or intellectually injurious to minors or to over-excite their imagination; scenes of seduction and debauchery, and sex or crime films. The following are generally recommended: films of an instructive and educative character, showing works of art, travels, historical scenes, national customs, scientific phenomena and experiments, agricultural work, industrial establishments and processes, etc.

The Netherlands appears to be the only country which, by a provision in the Law of May 14th, 1926, on the Campaign against the Moral and Social Dangers of Cinematograph Performances, has subdivided films suitable for exhibition to minors. This subdivision is as follows:

(*a*) Films for exhibition to children under 14 years of age;
(*b*) Films (including those in (*a*) above) for minors from 14 to 18.

Instructive films or films reproducing ordinary public events are not subject to any censorship or control in certain countries, such as Belgium, Danzig, Germany, the Netherlands, Norway, and Sweden, although police permission is required in some countries. Instructive and educational films are also exempt from any restrictions in certain cases. It likewise appears from the communications received that, in certain countries where there are no special regulations concerning the admission of children to cinematographic performances, the general system of censorship of the films or of the cinematographic performances as a whole provides for certain measures to ensure that no films shall be shown in public likely to be detrimental to the mentality or morals of minors. Annex II mentions seven such cases.

CONTROL OF PUBLICITY IN REGARD TO FILMS

We may mention in passing that a few countries have included provisions of the control of posters and advertisements of films in measures for the protection of children from the demoralising effect of certain cinematograph performances. Such is the case in Germany, in the Free City of Danzig, in the State of Victoria (Australia), in Canada, in the province of Saskatchewan, in Ireland, in the Netherlands and in Peru. We shall not, however, lay any stress on this aspect of the question, which has already been regulated by the International Convention of 1923 for the Suppression of the Circulation of and Traffic in Obscene Publica-

tions. We would recall the fact that this Convention has been ratified by twenty-two countries and signed by forty-three, and that six Governments and forty-three British colonies have acceded to it.

---

6. Proposal for federal licensing of films to be shown to children, 1931

"Gangster Movies and Children," *The Christian Century,* XLVIII (1931), 1015–1016.

Feeling ran high in East Orange, New Jersey, last month over gangster films. Twelve-year-old Winslow Elliott was shot by a playmate, Harold Gamble, of the same age, after the two had seen the movie "The Secret Six." Voicing the public indignation Mayor Charles H. Martens wrote a letter to the Hays office protesting such films. He received a reply from one of Mr. Hays' numerous assistants defending gangster pictures as made under the usual formula on the ground that the moral of all such pictures is that crime does not pay. The assistant concluded his letter with the assertion that the movies "by unanimous scientific judgment" are deterrents of crime. The gangster films, he intimated, are really doing the public a service by exposing the criminals. Just how much comfort the parents of the boys, not to mention the mayor and the other citizens, derived from this response the newspapers do not say. They simply record the facts.

.   .   .   .   .

What then can parents do? They can help their children select the pictures they see. They can organize a local pre-viewing service to see every program about to be presented and endorse only the wholesome ones. They can make these endorsements available through local press, church calendars, and bulletin boards. They can join with other parents throughout America in the effort to bring this industry under federal regulation without censorship. If every picture to be shown to children had first to be licensed by the bureau of education or the children's bureau in Washington local censorship problems would largely vanish.

Part Three   Care of Dependent Children

All children, for longer or shorter periods, are dependent upon adults. We are concerned here, with children who, because of the death, incapacity, or poverty of natural guardians had to look to the community for support, protection, and guidance. In the years immediately following the Civil War the children who seemed most deserving of society's compassion and generosity were orphans of soldiers killed in the war. Discovery that many of them were treated as paupers and confined in almshouses led state governments and private associations to establish special institutions for their shelter and education. Sympathy for war-orphans prompted the broader movement to get all dependent children out of almshouses and into situations better suited to their conditions and needs.[1] While nearly everyone might agree that children should be removed from the demoralizing and pauperizing influence of the almshouse, there was difference of opinion as to the proper method of disposing of them. The alternatives most often proposed were institutional care and placing out in families.

Both children's institutions and home-finding agencies proliferated in the late nineteenth century. In theory they were complementary since institutions had traditionally used indenture, adoption, or other arrangements to place children in homes. In practice the two systems came to be regarded as rivals. Indifference on the part of officials, pride in numbers, difficulty in finding foster homes that were

both suitable and free, and the practice followed in some states and municipalities of using public funds to subsidize private child caring institutions led to prolongation of institutional care. Reformers and child welfare experts, although deploring the haphazard placement methods employed by home-finding agencies, usually took the position that except in unusual circumstances children were better off in foster families than in institutions. Conversely Roman Catholics, Jews, and other religious minorities, championed institutional care as essential to training and retaining children in the faith of their fathers. Debate over the relative merits and defects of institutions and foster homes continued into the 1920's, but after the turn of the century the dispute was muted somewhat by the greater availability of Roman Catholic and Jewish foster homes, development of paid boarding homes, and the spread of mothers' pension systems.

During the first three decades of the twentieth century notable progress was made in bringing institutions and placement agencies under stricter state supervision. The movement encountered resistance from administrators of both public and private agencies and from religious bodies who resented encroachments on their autonomy. Despite such opposition state authorities developed programs for visiting and inspecting institutions and placement agencies and required them to submit regular reports of their operation. Subjecting child welfare agencies and institutions to approval before incorporation and to annual licensing further strengthened public control and raised standards of performance.

The great discovery of the era was that the

---

1. In 1880 approximately 9,000 children under 15 years of age were in almshouses. By 1923 the number had dropped to 1,900. United States Bureau of the Census, *Paupers in Almshouses, 1923* (Washington, D.C., 1925), p. 10.

best place for normal children was in their own homes. This idea conflicted with the widespread dislike of public relief but coincided with the philanthropic desire to preserve the integrity of the family. Delegates to the White House Conference of 1909 went on record as favoring assistance in the form of private charity rather than of public relief. Under the laws adopted in most of the states during the two decades after the White House Conference the assistance took the form neither of private charity nor of public relief, but of a public program administered somewhat in the spirit of private charity. Mothers' Aid or pension laws provided public funds to help "fit" and "proper" mothers maintain their dependent children in "suitable" homes. As early as 1923, although many of the mothers' aid laws were permissive rather than mandatory, and the assistance was rendered in a selective manner, the number of dependent children being maintained in their own homes was approaching the number of those in institutions and far in excess of those in foster homes. This revolutionary shift in methods of care for dependent children was to continue and expand under the aid to dependent children program of the Social Security Act.

I Institutions and Foster Homes

A. PUBLIC INSTITUTIONS

Children in almshouses

---

1. Children in Ohio infirmaries, 1867

Ohio. Board of State Charities, *First Annual Report* (Columbus, 1867), pp. 34–36.

Albert G. Byers was secretary of the Ohio Board of State Charities. In his third annual report (1869) Byers gave the total number of children in the county infirmaries (i.e., poorhouses) as 974.

The especial attention of the Board is also earnestly directed to the number and condition of homeless children.

There have been in thirteen infirmaries during the year . . . an aggregate of two hundred and twenty children, nearly all under 10 years of age. Some of these are of feeble mind, and they, with the idiotic, I doubt not, will soon be permitted to share in the noble provision now being made for such, in our new State Idiotic Asylum. Some are blind, and one, at least, deaf and dumb; many of them as pretty and as smart as little boys and girls can be.

In no less than three different infirmaries, we found little boys confined, for constraint or punishment, with the insane. In one instance, a little deaf and dumb boy was locked in a cell, in the insane department, opposite a cell in which a violently insane woman was con-

fined. This woman had been casting her own filth, through the shattered panels of her door, at this little boy, the door of whose cell was all bespattered. He was crying bitterly, and, on being released, made signs indicating that he was very hungry. He was locked here to prevent him from running off.

This little boy is something over 10 years of age. His father was killed in the war of the rebellion; his mother is an inmate of a lunatic asylum. He (the boy) is of sound body and mind. A gentleman to whom a letter from this office (directed to the Superintendent of the Infirmary) had been referred, in his answer to certain inquiries concerning the boy, says: "If there is a possibility of getting him (the boy) into the Deaf and Dumb Asylum, please use your best endeavors to do so, as the place where he now is is far from being what it should be."

In another infirmary we found quite an interesting little girl, said by the Superintendent to be "remarkably smart," entirely blind. This child is probably 7 or 8 years old; but as we have failed to get answers to letters inquiring into her history, we cannot state more in regard to her, than that she seemed to have won for herself an unusual degree of affection from those who had her in charge, and that they earnestly entreated that some better provision should be made for her than they could possibly make.

In another infirmary we found another blind child. Its parents had sinned; its blindness was the effect of congenital syphilis. As we stood by the rude cradle of this sightless child, in a bare room where it was sole occupant, and where it sat swaying to and fro in its darkness, shrinking from our voice, with its thumbs pressed with nervous twitchings beneath its senseless eyeballs, a half-witted pauper woman thrust her head through the open window of the apartment, and with her finger giving dreadful emphasis, pointing to that little helpless, abandoned waif, demanded to know, of an officer of the institution, whether or not she, in addition to the "milking of four cows," was to "take care of that thing?"

These are sad details, but there are other children, to whom God has given all their senses, and who are fully endowed with the social instincts and mental faculties of our nature, whose condition is not less deplorable than those already mentioned.

Let those who appreciate the importance of early impressions, who acknowledge childhood as the seed-time of life — let such estimate, if they may, what it must be to have these impressions formed by association with the idiotic, the insane, and amid the loathsome moral corruption so common to our poor-houses. Let them calculate the harvest not only to the future individual life of the child, but to the State, which must be gathered sooner or later from such sowing.

2. Children in Westchester County Poorhouse, New York, 1872

State Charities Aid Association, *First Annual Report, 1873* (New York, 1873), pp. 15–17.

The State Charities Aid Association was organized in 1872 by Louisa Lee Schuyler (1837–1926) as a volunteer adjunct of the State Board of Charities. Visiting committees of the Association inspected and publicized conditions in county institutions. The report on the Westchester County poorhouse was written by Miss Schuyler.

The Visiting Committee for the Westchester County Poorhouse was organized on the 9th of January, 1872. The institution, which they proposed to visit fortnightly, is the fourth largest County Poorhouse in the State, containing about three hundred and seventy pauper inmates — men and women, children and old people, the sick, the insane, the blind, deaf-and-dumb, and idiots . . . Having no authority in the management of the affairs of the institution, they assumed none, but hoped to find the Superintendents of the Poor willing to allow them to work in concert with them. With the full knowledge and sanction of the Superintendents they began their work. They took little comforts to the sick, they opened a sewing school for the children, they found places for some of the women who were able to take them. For the sake of ensuring harmony of action, they met the Superintendents once a month at the Poorhouse. So long as the ladies were contented to work themselves, and make no criticism upon the management of the institution, everything worked smoothly. But in the course of visiting they became aware of many things needing immediate reform: an absence of classification which led to gross immorality, a want of enlightened treatment of the insane, no nursing for the sick; the children badly fed, badly clothed, badly taken care of, and exposed to the degrading influence of those in immediate charge of them.

The children, about sixty in number, are in the care of an old pauper woman, whose daughter and whose daughter's child, both born in the poorhouse, make her one of three generations of paupers. The daughter assists in the care of the children. She has a contagious disease of the eyes which is, apparently, communicated to them. The children are neither properly clothed nor fed; but saddest of all is to see the stolid look gradually stealing over the faces of these little ones, as all the joy of their lives is starved out of them — to think what these children must grow up to, what they must become, if they are not soon removed from this atmosphere of vice. Last spring I was much attracted by a little girl in the poorhouse, three years old, whose parents were respectable people. The father had been drowned, the mother had an arm so wasted by rheumatism that she was unable to support herself and child. Notwithstanding the painful surroundings, she being one of three respectable women in a room otherwise filled with women of bad character, the love of the mother and child, the one so tender and patient, the other so clinging and affectionate, brought a redeeming flood of light into the darkened room. Shortly after, the mother died. Last autumn I saw the little girl. In the interval she had changed to stone. Not a smile nor a word could be drawn from her. The bright look had faded utterly. She was now under the care of the old pauper-woman. I had known this old woman for more than a year, and ought not therefore to have been surprised at the change in little Mary, and yet I did not recognize the child at first. I could not believe such a change possible. Since then, through the efforts of one of our Visitors, the child has been adopted into a respectable farmer's family in Dutchess County, and is now well and happy.

A member of our Committee on Children, Mr. Charles L. Brace, when informed of the condition of these children, offered, as Secretary of the Children's Aid Society, to take all these children, including the little babies, free of charge, and provide them with homes in the West. But the Superintendents declined this offer. They wished the children to remain in the county, where, as they said, they could see them themselves, look after them, know what became of them. Alas! we know only too well what becomes of children who live and grow up in the poorhouse.

3. State Charities Aid Association recommends removal of all children from poorhouses, New York, 1874

State Charities Aid Association, *Second Annual Report, 1874* (New York, 1874), pp. 12–14.

1st. *All* children older than infants, whether sick or well, of sound mind or otherwise, should be removed from the Poorhouses, and not be allowed to grow up exposed to the contaminating influences of adult paupers.

2d. Healthy children who are orphans or abandoned, should be placed in families, either by adoption or indenture. There should be intelligent supervision of the children placed in these families, by which it can be ascertained whether the terms of the agreement are carried out, and whether the children are kindly treated.

3d. No healthy child of sound mind should be allowed to remain and grow up in any institution, public or private, however well managed.

We strongly advocate the so-called Family System as opposed to the Institutional System, believing that the former is most conducive to the better development and ultimate welfare of the child.

4th. For sick, crippled, deformed and otherwise physically afflicted children, Hospital homes should be provided. Here they should be tenderly cared for, educated if possible and taught such light trades and household service as their condition permits.

5th. An Asylum for Incurable Idiot children is imperatively needed. The hopeful cases from the State generally are sent to the well-managed State Asylum at Syracuse, those from New York City to the excellent school for Idiots on Randall's Island, but the condition of the more unfortunate little ones left in the County Poor Houses is most pitiable.

Does not the care of this class seem to be

the especial duty of benevolent parents? Can there not be found homes where all of these children can be received as part of the family? There are hardly more than 2500 in all the Poor Houses of the State, and of these not fewer than one-third are babies. How many a home would be brightened by the presence of one of these little ones. How many a child now exposed to almost certain ruin, would become a true man or woman under good domestic influence.

---

4. "What shall be done with pauper children?"

William P. Letchworth, "Report," in New York State Board of Charities, *Eighth Annual Report* (Albany, 1875), pp. 176–178.

Letchworth (1823–1910) accumulated a sizable fortune as a hardware merchant in Buffalo. He retired from business in 1869 and in 1873 accepted an appointment as member of the New York State Board of Charities. A childless bachelor, he devoted his energies to helping and protecting those he called "the children of the state." In 1878 he became chairman of the State Board of Charities.

Persons of experience whose opinions I have obtained seem to have arrived at the conclusion that the first step to be taken in overcoming the great evils herein treated is to promptly remove all healthy and intelligent children from association with adult paupers and from poor-house life and its stigma, and to place them immediately upon their sinking to the line of public dependence and before being stigmatized as paupers, among such surroundings and under such remedial influences as shall be likely to reclaim them. Aside from the moral benefits of such a course, immense pecuniary saving will result to the public.

In a case of acute insanity, the law now requires that superintendents of the poor shall promptly convey the patient to an appropriate lunatic asylum for treatment. This is done in the expectation, based upon medical authority, that the chances for the recovery of the patient are in the ratio of the promptitude of the application of remedies. Would it not be wise to apply the same principle to the case of an unfortunate child who has been thrown upon the public for support, and thus save it from sinking into pauper life? The statute already makes it obligatory upon county officials to transfer every deaf-mute child of a certain age, becoming a dependent, to asylums for instruction. It virtually does the same with certain other defectives.

I beg to ask, whether a statute extending the benefits of this principle to other dependent children would not be desirable — requiring county officials to place in families or fitting asylums all children over two years of age, excepting unteachable idiots and others unfitted for family care, who become dependent, and prohibiting their being hereafter committed to poor houses.

The following reasons may be stated in addition to those already set forth elsewhere in favor of such legislative action:

1st. It appears from results already reached in the inquiry now being conducted by this Board, and which has been completed so far as it relates to pauper children, except in the county of New York, that there are now only about three hundred and twenty-five healthy and intelligent children, over two years of age, in the various poor-houses of the State. The number being now so reduced, the work of transfer, it is believed, will not inconvenience officials nor cause embarrassment otherwise.

2d. Superintendents of the poor in many counties are now embarrassed in their efforts to dispose promptly and humanely of the children under their charge, and keep the poor-house entirely free from them, for lack of some legislative action.

3d. In case of a change of officials and the

multiplicity of cares incident to the closing up of an official term, the work of placing children out is sometimes temporarily suspended by the incumbent in charge of the poor-house, and when the new official has become fairly inaugurated in his position, he finds that a considerable number of children have accumulated in the county-house, and his administration may be near its close before the establishment is again free from them.

4th. It will be seen by the tables herewith submitted that many of the children now in poor-houses were born in them, and have remained there through nearly all their childhood.

5th. There are many mothers now dependents in the poor-houses, who would go out and support themselves if some general regulations were in force, whereby their children would be transferred to places in which they would be properly cared for, and many families that include children would not come under poor-house influences, but for the provision made by the public for rearing children in the county-house.

6th. In a large number of poor-houses in the State there are children that have been committed as truants or vagrants; among these are many girls. Sometimes parents are committed as vagrants, and bring family of children with them. It is clearly apparent that the poor-house is no fit place for this class of children. If such children are bad, they make their associates in the poor-house worse; if they are not vicious, and are committed in consequence of their parents' faults, and are made worse by poor-house associations, then a manifest injustice is done to the children.

7th. In certain poor-houses of the State, there are sons and daughters of soldiers, who died honorable deaths in their country's service. A grateful recognition of the sacrific made by their fathers, should secure to them better advantages than poor-house training for pauper life.

8th. A large number of counties in the state have already, through the action of their several boards of supervisors, virtually closed their poor-houses against children by better providing for them elsewhere. The effect of a general law having the same bearing, would be to prevent the stigma or brand of pauperism from being affixed to many homeless, orphan and destitute children.

---

5. The New York children's law of 1875

"An Act To Provide For the Better Care of Pauper and Destitute Children," 1875 — ch. 173. *Laws of the State of New York, 1875* (New York, 1875), p. 150.

On and after January first, 1876, it shall not be lawful for any justice of the peace, police justice or other magistrate to commit any child, over three and under sixteen years of age, as vagrant, truant or disorderly, to any county poor-house of this State, or for any county superintendent or overseer of the poor, or other officer, to send any such child as a pauper to any such poor-house for support and care, unless such child be an unteachable idiot, an epileptic or paralytic, or be otherwise defective, diseased or deformed, so as to render it unfit for family care; but such justice of the peace, police justice or other magistrate, and also such county superintendent or overseer of the poor, or other officer, shall commit or send such child or children not above exempted to some orphan asylum or other charitable or reformatory institution, as now provided for by law.

It shall be the duty of the county superintendents of the poor, or other proper officers charged with the support and relief of indigent persons of the several counties of this State, in which there are county poor-houses, to cause the removal of all children between the age of three and sixteen years (not exempted by the first section of this act) from their respective poor-houses, on or before the first day of January, eighteen hundred and seventy-six, and also to cause the removal of those who may hereafter come under the care and control, or hereafter be born in such poor-houses, before they shall have arrived at the age of three years, and provide for their support and care in families, orphan asylums or other appropriate institutions as now provided for by law; and the boards of supervisors of the several counties are hereby required to take such action in the matter as may be necessary to carry out the provisions of this act. In placing any such child in any such institution, it shall be the duty of the officer, justice or person placing it there to commit such child to an orphan asylum, charitable or other reformatory institution that is governed or controlled by officers or persons of the same religious faith as the parents of such child, as far as practicable.

---

6. Children left in poorhouses after the Act of 1875

Records of Children in County Poor Houses, Box 47, Mss. and History Section, New York State Board of Charities Records, New York State Library, Albany, N.Y.

By Charles S. Hoyt, Secretary
June 23, 1881.

RECORD of Children between the ages of 2 and 16 years in Poor-Houses and Alms-Houses of the State of New York, 1881. Oneida County Poor House.

Examination No. 2

1. **Name,** William B——
2. **Sex (Male M. Female F.),** Male
3. **Age at last birthday,** 9 years.
4. **Color (White, Black — if mixed, state degree),** White
5. **Birth Place (State or Country, N.Y. County,** Oneida **Town,** City,). (If born in a poor-house or other public institution, state the fact.)

If of foreign birth, how long in the U.S.? how long in this State? at what port landed?

6. **Birth place of Father (State or Country, N.Y. County,** Oneida **Town, City,** .) (If born in a poor-house or other public institution, state the fact.)
7. **Birth place of Mother (State or Country, N.Y. County,** Oneida **Town, City,** .) (If born in a poor-house or other public institution, state the fact.)
8. **At what age did this child become an inmate of a poor-house?** 4 years.
9. **How long an inmate of this poor-house?** 5 years. (If less than one year give the months.)
10. **Has this child been in other poor-houses?** No
11. **If so, how many?**
12. **How long in all has this child been an inmate of poor-houses?** 5 years. (If less than one year give the months.)
13. **Has this child been an inmate of any insane asylum, blind asylum, idiot asylum, deaf and dumb asylum or refuge? (If so, state which, and how long?)** No
14. **Has this child been in Jails or Reformatories? (If so, state which, how long an inmate, and the nature of the offense.)** No
15. **Is this child of legitimate or illegitimate birth? (Write which.)** Legitimate
16. **Is there consanguinity in the parents? (If so, write what degree.)** No
17. **Was the Father temperate or intemperate? (Write which.)** Intemperate
18. **Was the Mother temperate or intemperate? (Write which.)** Temperate

19. **Was the Father immoral, sensual or otherwise debased? (State facts.)** Yes: From intemperate habits

20. **Was the Mother immoral, sensual or otherwise debased? (State facts.)** No

21. **What was the occupation of the Father of this child?** A laborer

22. **Was the Father a pauper** No
    "   Mother   "   No
    "   **Grandfather a pauper?** Unknown
    "   **Grandmother**   "   Unknown
    Were any of the Brothers of this child paupers? No
    Were any of the Sisters of this child paupers? No
    Were any of the Uncles of this child paupers? Unknown
    Were any of the Aunts of this child paupers? Unknown

23. **What is the immediate cause of dependence in the case of this child?** Epilepsy

24. **Is there proof of insanity, epilepsy, paralysis, special feebleness of mind or body, syphilis, or any other entailment of bodily or mental misfortune from parentage in this child's history? (If so note the fact.)** No. Except Drunkenness in the father.

25. **Is this child likely to become self-supporting, or will it probably remain dependent?** No. Entirely hopeless

26. **Has this child Parents or Brothers or Sisters able to provid for its support?** No. Father dead; Mother married second time, but poor.

REMARKS:

The father of this child is said to have been a violent tempered drunkard, who died soon after this child's birth. The mother, a respectable woman is living with a second husband, but is unable to provide for this child. There were no other children in this family. This boy is a violent epileptic, in constant motion, and regarded as dangerous to associate with other children. He is kept on the halls of this asylum, with the insane, and is under the supervision of the attendants. The violence of his convulsions increases each year, and he is regarded as wholly incurable. His presence in the Asylum is a source of annoyance to the insane.

1. **Name,** Joseph B———
2. **Sex (Male M. Female F.),** Male
3. **Age at last birthday,** 4 years.

.   .   .   .   .

REMARKS:

This child is a congenital idiot, and has no use of language. It is noisy, at times filthy, and very troublesome. The father is dead; the mother, said to be a respectable woman, supports herself and three other children, one of whom is a paralytic, by her industry. It is not probable, however, that she will ever be able to provide for this child; indeed, it could not be cared for in a family without an attendant. It may be regarded as wholly unteachable, and a permanent burden upon the public. It is domiciled in the Nursery Ward of the institution.

1. **Name,** Levi S———
2. **Sex (Male M. Female F.),** Male
3. **Age at last birthday,** 11 years.

.   .   .   .   .

REMARKS:

This child was brought, by its mother, with four other children, — one sister and three brothers, — all being congenital idiots — , to this Poor-House some five years ago. The latter have all died in the institution. The Mother is still an inmate. The Child is entirely helpless, has no use of language, and causes great trouble. [The mother's] father was a drunken vagrant, and her mother, is of feeble intellect. She gives no promise of becoming self-supporting, and the child is wholly unteachable.

1. **Name,** Laura S——
2. **Sex (Male M. Female F.),** Female
3. **Age at last birthday,** 3 **years.**

. . . . .

REMARKS:

The mother of this child, about 18 years old, was committed to this Poor-House with it some two months ago. The child is totally blind, the result of inflammation of her Eyes when about six months of age. It appears to be fairly intelligent, and at suitable age should be placed in one of the institutions for the Blind, for instruction. The Mother, a fairly intelligent woman now has its immediate charge. It is in a healthy condition.

1. **Name,** Mary C——
2. **Sex (Male M. Female F.),** Female
3. **Age at last birthday,** Three **years.**

. . . . .

REMARKS:

The Mother has been insane and is not very strong mentally and the father has deserted her and the mother is unable to support herself this child and its little Baby Brother.

1. **Name,** Florence C——
2. **Sex (Male M. Female F.),** Female
3. **Age at last birthday,** Ten **years.**

. . . . .

REMARKS:

The mother of this child in question came to our Poor House with three children; two were idiotic; one died with fits; one is in the Wilbur Inst. and one with us. The one we have also has fits but is improving. The father of these children was own Uncle to their mother and about seventy years of age when the mother was brought to the Poor House. The mother twenty nine. The aunt of this child is a pauper and insane.

7. Progress in removing children from almshouses, 1876–1894

Homer Folks, "The Removal of Children from Almshouses," *Lend a Hand,* XIII (1894), 174–175.

Homer Folks (1867–1963) was secretary of the State Charities Aid Association of New York from 1893 to 1947. This article was originally presented as a paper at a meeting of The National Conference of Charities and Correction in Nashville, Tennessee, in May, 1894.

A law forbidding the sending of children over five and under sixteen years of age to poorhouses, was passed in Wisconsin in 1876. Similar legislation was secured in Massachusetts in 1879. In Indiana and Michigan in 1881; in Ohio and Pennsylvania in 1883; Minnesota and Rhode Island established State Schools for dependent children in 1885; Kansas in 1887. An effort to secure such a law in Illinois in 1893 was unsuccessful, but will be renewed in 1895.

Of these laws, that of New York in its present amended form, is perhaps the most radical, making it unlawful to send any child, between the ages of two and sixteen years, to any poorhouse or almshouse. Pennsylvania exempts feebleminded and other defective children. It does not forbid the sending of children to poorhouses, but commands their removal within sixty days. Massachusetts allows children to remain until four years of age, and if they have mothers in the poor-house able to care for them, until eight years of age. Only within the past year has this law been made to apply to the town almshouses of which there are a large number in the state. In Wisconsin, children under six years of age are exempted from the law as are also defective children.

In regard to such legislation the consensus of opinion among those familiar with the subject, seems to be, I think, that the more radical is the better; that in fact any statute which does not absolutely prohibit the residence of children of sound mind and body, and past two years of age in any almshouse, is seriously defective.

In spite of the unanimity of opinion as to the beneficial effects of such a law and the possibility of its easy enforcement, statutes forbidding the residence of children in poorhouses have been passed in only a few states. The census of 1890 tells us that there are still 4,987 children, between two and sixteen years of age, inclusive, in poorhouses in the United States. No doubt a proportion of these are defective children, who could not ordinarily be placed in families or asylums for normal children, but the fact seems to be indisputable that several thousand children, practically sound in mind and body, still remain in our poor-houses.

I had gained the impression from some source that a large proportion of these children were in the Southern states, and when I began to prepare for this meeting, I supposed that it would probably be our duty to "gently but firmly" remind our friends of the South that this was not creditable. A study of the census figures, however, shows that although children form a larger proportion of the almshouse population in the South than in the North, those states having the largest number of children in poorhouses in proportion to the population of the state, are located without reference to Mason and Dixon's line. The states which have the largest number of children, between two and sixteen years of age, in almshouses in proportion to their total population are as follows: New Hampshire, 46 children in almshouses to every one hundred thousand of the general population; Vermont, 27; West Virginia, 25; New Jersey, 23; Virginia, 19; Maine, 18; Ohio, 17; Rhode Island, 16; Massachusetts, 15; Indiana, 15; Kentucky, 14; Montana, 12; North Carolina, 19; Pennsylvania, 8; Illinois, 8; Tennessee, 8; Delaware, 7; Maryland, 6; Connecticut, 6; Michigan, 6; Missouri, 5; Kansas, 5; Georgia, 4. All other states and territories are reported to have less than four children in almshouses per one hundred thousand population.

---

8. Children in almshouses, 1910

U.S. Bureau of the Census, *Paupers in Almshouses, 1910* (Washington, D.C., 1915), pp. 35–36.

Of the 84,198 paupers enumerated in almshouses on January 1, 1910, 2,486, or 3 per cent, were under 16 years of age, and of the 88,313 paupers admitted during 1910, 6,396, or 7.2 per cent, were in that age group. Of the 2,486 child paupers enumerated, 524 were born in the institution and 869 were born elsewhere, while the place of birth was not reported in 1,093 cases. The figures, though incomplete, indicate that a considerable proportion of the children found in almshouses were born on the premises.

.   .   .   .   .

Of the 2,486 children enumerated in almshouses in 1910 nearly one-half, 1,186 were under 5 years of age, 641 were between 5 and 9 years of age, and 543 were in the age group 10 to 14, which is the age when school attendance is most general. The comparatively large number of young children is probably due to the fact that some are born in the almshouse and that others accompany their mothers when they go to the institution.

Between 1904 and 1910 the number of children enumerated in almshouses decreased in every age period. Among the paupers admitted to almshouses there were fewer in the age groups 5 to 9 and 10 to 14 in 1910 than in 1904, but the number under 5 and the number 15 years of age was greater in 1910 than in 1904.

The following table shows the number and

	Paupers in Almshouses, 1910					
	Enumerated on Jan. 1			Admitted during the year		
		Under 16 years of age			Under 16 years of age	
Division	Total	Number	Per cent	Total	Number	Per cent
United States	84,198	2,486	3.0	88,313	6,396	7.2
New England	11,886	520	4.4	14,716	1,645	11.2
Middle Atlantic	23,772	384	1.6	23,927	1,489	6.2
East North Central	21,358	405	1.9	17,116	982	5.7
West North Central	6,366	143	2.2	4,585	299	6.5
South Atlantic	7,706	470	6.1	7,945	718	9.0
East South Central	4,266	352	8.3	3,086	475	15.4
West South Central	1,630	111	6.8	2,068	167	8.1
Mountain	1,652	34	2.1	3,505	157	4.5
Pacific	5,562	67	1.2	11,365	464	4.1

percentage of paupers who were under 16 years of age, by geographic divisions.[1]

The proportion under 16 years of age is considerably higher among the paupers enumerated in the southern divisions than among those of the North or West. The same is true of the admissions, except that the proportion is higher in New England than in two of the southern divisions. The fact that the Southern states are predominantly rural, and that specialization in the care of dependent children is, as a rule, not as well developed in that section, may be in part responsible for the presence of many children in the almshouses, for the general trend of development is in the direction of keeping children out of the poorhouse and caring for them in special institutions or placing them in families.

.   .   .   .   .

More than one-half of the children under 16 who were enumerated in almshouses on January 1, 1910, and more than three-fifths of those who were admitted during the year (considering only those who have reported as to this question) had both parents living; comparatively few were motherless or were total orphans, while a considerable proportion were fatherless. The figures suggest that children are more likely to be sent to almshouses when their father dies than when they are deprived of their mother. This is natural, as the death of the father usually deprives the home of its chief economic support, and the mother may be forced to go to the poorhouse with her children, or else to place the children there while she herself seeks employment outside.[2]

1. The geographic divisions were: New England: Maine, New Hampshire, Vermont, Massachusetts, Rhode Island, Connecticut; Middle Atlantic: New York, New Jersey, Pennsylvania; East North Central: Ohio, Indiana, Illinois, Michigan, Wisconsin; West North Central: Minnesota, Iowa, Missouri, North Dakota, South Dakota, Nebraska, Kansas; South Atlantic: Deleware, Maryland, District of Columbia, Virginia, West Virginia, North Carolina, South Carolina, Georgia, Florida; East South Central: Kentucky, Tennessee, Alabama, Mississippi; West South Central: Arkansas, Louisiana, Oklahoma, Texas; Mountain: Montana, Idaho, Wyoming, Colorado, New Mexico, Arizona, Utah, Nevada; Pacific: Washington, Oregon, California.

2. As of February 1, 1923, the Census Bureau estimated that the number of children remaining in almshouses was 1992. U.S. Bureau of the Census, *Children Under Institutional Care, 1923* (Washington, D.C., 1927), p. 14.

Soldiers' orphans' homes

Orphans of soldiers and sailors killed in the Civil War were among the first dependent children removed from almshouses and placed in special institutions. At the close of the war Pennsylvania, Illinois, Kansas, Minnesota, Ohio, Indiana; Iowa, and Wisconsin established state orphanages for these children. As the years passed and the number of applicants declined some states abolished the soldiers' orphans' homes; others converted the institutions into state schools for dependent orphan children.

1. Pennsylvania takes the lead in providing "liberally and practically" for soldiers' orphans, 1866

Harrisburg Telegraph, March 20, 1866.

THE ORPHANS OF THE BRAVE WHO PERISHED IN DEFENCE OF THE COUNTRY.

We have already alluded to the presence, in the State Capital, of a portion of the orphans of those Pennsylvania soldiers who perished while battling in defence of the Government. But the subject is worthy of further elaboration. It was no common gathering. A similar spectacle was never beheld in any of the Capitals of the other States of the Union. Indeed, we challenge whether Europe, with all the prudence with which she provides for the humblest of those who go forth to battle for any of her tyrants, ever vouchsafed the same succor, like protection and education for the orphans of dead soldiers. . . . The widows and orphans of the slain European soldiers are left to pro-cure their support as best they can, and are only afforded relief by parishes as paupers.

There is no education provided for the orphans of soldiers, except it is such as is afforded in the workhouse. This is the difference, in the case of its defenders, between Europe and America. And, in fact, there is a difference, on the same score, between the States of the Union. Pennsylvania is the first State, not only in the American Union, but in the world, which provided for the liberal education and support of the orphans of soldiers. This provision means something more than a mere training, for a few months, in a public school. It contemplates the support as well as the education of the orphan — his maintenance, moral training, mental culture and complete fitting of the orphan boy and girl for useful, respectable and profitable lifetime employment. And so singularly successful has this patriotic enterprise become, that application has been made to Governor Curtin, by the Executives of other States, for the plans on which the Soldiers' Orphans' Schools of Pennsylvania are conducted; a fact itself conclusive that the Keystone State is the first to provide liberally and practically for the education of the orphans of her slain heroes.

2. The soldiers' orphans speak, 1866

Ceremonies at the Reception of the Orphan Children of Pennsylvania Soldiers in the State Capital, March 16, 1866 (Harrisburg, 1866), pp. 9, 12–13.

At a reception tendered the soldiers' orphans by the Governor and legislators of Pennsylvania, two students expressed gratitude for the fatherly care extended them by the state.

R. Stanley Booz, of Bristol, Bucks county, Pennsylvania, son of Robert Booz, of the Third Pennsylvania Reserves, now a pupil of the

MOUNT JOY SCHOOL, delivered the following OPENING ADDRESS.

Honorable Senators and Representatives:

We feel very much embarrassed in attempting to speak before so honorable a body of men, and we have to beg your kind indulgence and ask you to overlook our errors, and imperfections.

We did not come up here to parade our abilities, nor to display our learning.

But we came at the order of our noble superintendent, and with your kind permission to let you see how we are dressed, how we look and conduct ourselves, and what kind of boys and girls we are.

We are but destitute orphans whose education had been sadly neglected.

Many of us had not been in school for years before we were sent to the soldiers' orphans' school through your kindness and generosity.

Our fathers had the misfortune to be poor men, and could not afford even to buy books and clothing suitable for us to attend school regularly. But they were patriotic men and sacrificed their lives in defence of their country and its sacred liberties.

This makes us feel that we have a claim upon our nation and to look to it for support, providing above all for a good education.

Having this, we hope to be able to earn our own livelihood, and also to become useful citizens, and honorable members of society.

We have been taught to look upon, and call the State our father. We feel that in it we have a kind father — one that has provided us with good homes, kind teachers and every facility for acquiring a thorough education.

We are receiving not only an intellectual and a physical, but also a moral and religious education. We get moral and religious instructions daily from our teachers, and also frequently from the ministers of the gospel of our place.

We are learning how to farm, to garden and to attend to stock, and to do any kind of work that is done on a farm.

We *like* to *work* as well as to *study*.

Our Creator has given us minds to cultivate and improve; and we feel it to be our solemn duty to become good scholars, so as to be fitted for any position in life.

We return our most hearty thanks to you for the fostering care bestowed on us thus far, and respectfully ask that it may be continued.

We feel ourselves under very great obligations to improve our advantages better than we have hitherto done. We feel very grateful to our excellent Governor, our worthy Legislature and to our kind superintendent for the delightful privilege of visiting the capital of the State, and of seeing so many interesting sights new to most of us, and of occupying seats in this Hall where, through your kind benefience, we may be qualified to sit as you now do.

We sincerely thank you for this opportunity of seeing you here, and shall remember this occasion with pleasure throughout our lives.

·　　·　　·　　·　　·

ORIGINAL ORATION — "OUR FATHERS," *Delivered by Dalsell M. Severns, son of Allen Severns, of the 3d Pennsylvania Reserves, of Bristol, Bucks County, Pennsylvania.*

SENATORS, AND MEMBERS OF THE HOUSE OF REPRESENTATIVES: — In appearing as a speaker before so honorable and intelligent a body as yours, I must confess that I feel a timidity creeping over me that is hard to resist. But having been selected for that purpose I will not *shrink* from the task — arduous as it is — believing, as our *fathers* did, that "when duty calls we must obey."

Our *fathers* did, I say? Ah! where are they? Ask these, my bereaved schoolmates. Go from one to the other and ask "where is your father?" and they will tell you. One will answer *mine* died in camp; another, *mine* was killed at the battle of Fair Oaks; another, *mine* was a color bearer, and was shot through the heart while boldly pressing forward with his country's flag at the "battle of the Wilderness"; in death, he grasped the starry banner as if to die beneath *its* folds were "far more sweet"; another will answer, *mine* fell at the battle of Petersburg; another, *mine* was starved to death in Andersonville prison; and others will answer, *mine* fell at the battle of Gettysburg. Are these sad tales, and do they touch a tender chord in your fatherly bosoms and enlist your sympathies?

Then you may have some faint conception of our condition.

As orphans, made so by the same common cause, we appear before you. As you view us, so fitly brought together as members of one family, we would respectfully ask you to recall the times when the cry was, "We want *men* — we must *have men,* or the rebels will overpower us." And as you review those stirring times, behold our dear fathers — as dear to us as you, gentlemen, are to your children — go forth to the conflict; bidding the last sad farewell to their weeping wives and little ones, to battle for Liberty and the Union of States — sacrificing the comforts and affections of home and families, and giving their lives for the salvation of their country. They are gone! And we *only,* perhaps, *deeply* feel the loss.

But Pennsylvania has been very generous towards the children of her fallen heroes, by kindly making provision for our education. For this we bless *her,* and thank you, her legislators, for the interest you have taken in our welfare; and promise you, that if you continue these favors, we shall make every effort to properly use them by becoming useful members of society; and, though we are averse to war, yet, if needed, we, the soldiers' orphan boys, are willing and ready, *like* our fathers, to rally 'round the flag, and like them — TO DIE FOR OUR COUNTRY.

3. The Indiana Soldiers' Home, 1867

Indiana. General Assembly, "Supplemental Report of the Board of Trustees of the Sol-

diers' Home," Doc. 6, *Documents, 1869* (Indianapolis, 1869), II, 5–7.

In 1867 Indiana passed an act establishing a home for sick and disabled soldiers and seamen and their orphans and widows. In practice widows were not received at the home. In 1872 the soldiers were transferred to The National Asylum at Dayton, Ohio. The superintendent recommended that the name of the institution be changed to The Indiana Soldiers' Orphans' Home and that, if vacancies occurred, destitute children who were not soldiers' orphans should be moved from poor houses to the Home.

Our Home provides for all honorably discharged soldiers of our State, who were disabled in any branch of the government service, either regular, volunteer, or marine, and also those who may have been disabled after their discharge, and who are necessitous at the time of application for admission.

These soldiers enlisted to serve as Indiana soldiers — their attachments are for their own State. They were promised, in hundreds of speeches made to them to enlist, that, should they become disabled, they should be cared for. Will Indiana now turn her back upon these noble veterans? We hope not.

But another and greater reason why this institution should be continued and liberally supported, is the hundreds of helpless, destitute orphans of the hundreds of our brave men who sacrificed their lives upon the altar of their country that it might be saved from destruction, and whose last thoughts, while they lay upon the battle field, mortally wounded, and their life blood slowly ebbing out, or while they lay languishing in prison pens with their lives starving out, or in hospital with disease and death staring them in the face, were, "Who will take care of the little ones at home?"

Indiana stood in the front rank during the war, and yet she is not in the front rank in providing for her destitute soldiers and orphans. We give below a few facts and statistics showing what other States are doing, so far as we have been able to gather them:

.   .   .   .   .

Pennsylvania has now Orphan Homes located in different parts of the State, with about thirty-five hundred soldiers' orphans attending school and receiving their entire support from the State, at an expense of a half million dollars annually. These several institutions are managed, so far as the schools and the general care of the children is concerned, on much the same principle as our orphan department.

Iowa has three Orphan Homes, which are at this time caring for eight hundred and thirty-three orphans of deceased soldiers and seamen, which costs the State about one hundred thousand dollars annually.

Wisconsin maintains a Soldiers' Orphan Home at Madison, at an annual cost of twenty-five thousand dollars.

.   .   .   .   .

With the foregoing facts we leave this subject, and pass to the consideration of our wants.

In making up our estimates of what we want to make the Home what it should be, we asked for thirty thousand dollars for buildings, five thousand dollars for purchase of real estate, and an increase for subsistence of one dollar per week, making two dollars and fifty cents per week for current expenses. If the soldier and the orphan of the State are to be cared for at all, they should be well cared for; in other words, if the institution is to be supported, it should be liberally supported. If it is right to care for part of the orphans it is right to care for all. At the lowest possible estimate there are in this State five hundred totally helpless orphans, who are destitute and have no visible means of support, and who should be in the Orphan Home to-day.

We have now one hundred and eight, with sixty applications pending for admission, making strong appeals to us for a home. We receive, almost daily, letters from different parts of the State, saying: "There are so many chil-

dren here, orphans of soldiers, whose mothers died a few days ago, leaving them perfectly helpless. If you can not take them, they will be compelled to go to the Poor House." The answer goes back to them, "We are full, and can not possibly take any more," thus making the Poor House their inevitable doom.

Now we should by all means erect a building this season, and with an appropriation of thirty thousand dollars for this purpose we could provide for about three hundred, which would greatly relieve the pressing demands upon us. Compared with what other States are doing for their orphans, we think this is not an unreasonable request.

---

4. Soldiers' orphans' homes, 1910

Hastings H. Hart, *Preventive Treatment of Neglected Children* (New York, 1910), pp. 54–55

Although the War of the Rebellion closed forty-five years ago, Soldiers' Orphans' Homes, for the care of orphans of the soldiers of the War of the Rebellion, are still maintained in the states of Maine, Pennsylvania, Ohio, Indiana, Illinois, Iowa and Kansas.

As a matter of fact, these soldiers' orphans' homes have become free boarding schools for the children of indigent soldiers. In most of them there is no adequate system of industrial training, reliance being placed, for the most part, upon the school of letters. As a rule, the children sent to the soldiers' orphans' homes are not taken from the guardianship of their parents, but are received with the consent of their parents, and are restored to their parents upon leaving the school.

In the states of Kansas, Iowa and Illinois, laws have been passed for the admission of dependent children other than the children of soldiers to the soldiers' orphans' homes, with a proviso in each case for the placing of such children in family homes if eligible. These laws have been for the most part inoperative, for the reason that the traditions of the soldiers' orphans' homes have not been favorable to the placing-out method. The practice of allowing the parents to retain guardianship, and to continue in communication with their children, does not work well with the placing-out system, for the reason that the parents, intentionally or otherwise, almost invariably create a divided interest, which is apt to lead sooner or later to the removal of the child from the foster home . . .

The time is rapidly approaching when there will be no legitimate work for the soldiers' orphans' homes to do in behalf of soldiers' orphans. When that time comes, these schools should either be abolished or should be entirely reorganized along the lines of the Michigan and Minnesota schools.

In the state of Maine a law has been passed extending the privileges of the State Military and Naval Orphan Asylum to the grandchildren of soldiers of the War of the Rebellion. A little reflection will make it obvious that this plan is impractical, for the reason that if carried out to its logical conclusion it would mean, after a little, the extension of the public boarding school privilege to a large portion of the juvenile population of the state.

Special institutions for children

1. The Michigan State Public School, 1871–1896

C. D. Randall, "The Michigan System of Child Saving," *The American Journal of Sociology,* I (1896), 710, 716–718.

In 1871 the Michigan legislature authorized the establishment of the "State Public School" as a temporary home for dependent and neg-

lected children. The School, which opened in 1874, received children between the ages of four and sixteen "in suitable condition of body and mind to receive instruction who are neglected and dependent, especially those who are now maintained in the county poor-houses, those who have been abandoned by their parents, or are orphans, or whose parents have been convicted of crime." [1] State Senator C. D. Randall was the principal author of the act establishing the State Public School.

The State Public School has been on trial nearly twenty-two years and can now demonstrate the value of its work for the dependent children of the state. It has more than realized the highest expectations of its friends. It is a state institution, entirely supported and conducted by the state, the expenses being paid with biennial appropriations. Its basic principle is the support and education of all the dependent children of the state of sound mind and body under twelve years of age in a temporary educational home, from whence they are to be placed in approved families as soon as practicable on indenture or by adoption. It has no connection with the penal system of the state and is a part of the educational system, making its reports to the Superintendent of Public Instruction. No taint of crime attaches to any child by reason of its admission. No child is admitted because it has become delinquent. Poverty is the only cause. Michigan radically separates the dependents from the delinquents. It is the first government that ever undertook such a work, and the trial was looked upon with interest in and out of the state, and by some almost with alarm, who feared the expense would be greater than the results would warrant. But it was intended to be helpful to the state as well as to the children and so it has proved.

While admissions to private and sectarian asylums are usually informal, often by direction,

1. "An Act to Establish a State Public School for Dependent and Neglected Children," *Laws of Michigan, 1871* (Lansing, 1871), I, 54–57.

by parents or by town or city officers without form of law, no child is admitted to this state school except on evidence in probate court and on order from the judge after full opportunity has been given the parents or friends of the child to be heard. There is thus a public record of the dependence of the child and a history of where the child comes from and where it has gone to. Even a destitute child has rights and these rights and the rights of its parents are respected. The ease of admission and withdrawal of private charity inmates often induces parents to have their children supported in them for a time. But admission to the State Public School forfeits all parental rights. The parents knowing this make a more serious effort to keep their children and often succeed. This is one important cause of decrease of child dependence. In all cases where parents become able to support their children, and the instances are very few, an effort is made to arrange for the restoration of the child, and this is done at times by consent of the foster parents if the child is on indenture.

The county superintendents of the poor are required to bring all admissible children before the judge of probate to determine their dependence. Notice is served on the parents if they can be found and the case is regularly tried. After admission the children are taught the branches usually taught in the public schools, by the best primary and kindergarten teachers that can be procured. The institution is on the cottage plan, the children living in cottages — about twenty-five in each, supervised by a lady cottage manager, acting in the capacity of mother. The children live and sleep in the cottages, attend school in the schoolhouse, eat in the large general dining room and work in and out of the buildings as their age or ability warrants. They remain in this temporary home on the average less than a year. Some of the younger well fitted for it go almost immediately into homes, while many others need much done for them mentally, morally and physically before going into a respectable home. The indenture provides for good treatment as a mem-

ber of the family, for their attending the public schools and their being taught some useful occupation or trade. A clause in the contract authorizes the board to cancel it if deemed for the best interest of the child. When adopted in the probate court, the child becomes the heir of the foster parents.

The institution is in charge of a board of control of three members, while the more direct management is by the superintendent who resides at the school. The school has a state agent whose duties lie almost entirely outside in visiting the children in families and in finding homes. If he learns that a child is ill treated, he is to remove it and place it in another family or return it to the school. His position requires great zeal, good judgment and delicacy of treatment. His work has very much to do with the success of the school. He visits and reports on all the children once each year, the county agent once, and the foster parents once, such reports as near as may be coming about four months apart. Some cases need more attention and have it from both the state and county agents. Some of the best children in most excellent families need much less supervision. In this way during the minority of the children their interests are watchfully guarded, and whether in families or in the school, in health and in sickness, they have most kind attention. Many never knew kind treatment until they entered the school, and no private charity ever cared for children better than the state has done.

The institution provides for all the admissible dependent children of the state not cared for by private charities. The state in no way restricts the private institutions. There are several laws under which they may be organized and some operate without incorporation. The law does not regulate the manner of admission or discharge. These laws were enacted mainly before the State Public School was established and have been amended from time to time. There never has been any collision between the state and these institutions, the former apparently yielding to private charity all it desired to do. The state school not being sectarian does not seek to place children in families of the religion of the parents but welcomes aid from the churches that desire to do so.

---

2. A state institution for Indian children, New York, 1882

William P. Letchworth, "The Thomas Asylum for Orphan and Destitute Indian Children," in New York State Board of Charities *Fifteenth Annual Report* (Albany, 1882), pp. 173–175.

This institution is located on the Cattaraugus Indian Reservation, about one mile from the village of Versailles . . . The main buildings are of wood, two stories high, with basement, and have pleasant verandas. The nursery and hospital building, for the accommodation of the sick and very young children — which was erected during the past year — is two stories high and has no basement. A corridor, which may be inclosed in winter, connects it with the main group.

In a grove, a few rods from the asylum building, is the school-house for the use of the inmates, the school being under the control and direction of the Department of Public Instruction.

The asylum was incorporated April 10, 1855, and an appropriation toward its support was made by the Legislature in that year. By an act passed April 24, 1875, it was reorganized and became one of the State institutions.

Its affairs are controlled by a board of ten managers, appointed by the Governor, of whom five are Indians . . .

On the first of April last, in consequence of failing health, Mr. B. F. Hall, who had faithfully discharged the duties of superintendent during the previous twenty-three years, resigned his position, and Mr. J. H. Van Valkenburgh was appointed in his place. The salary of the superintendent is fixed at $800 per year. His wife, who acts as matron, receives $400 per annum. The subordinate force consists of a nurse, receiving $4 per week, assistant nurse, $2.50 per week, a laundress, $3 per week, and a farm hand who is paid $20 per month. The physician, A. D. Lake, M.D., who is additionally compensated by the government for medical services to the Indians on this reservation, receives $50 per year.

Orphan and destitute Indian children are received from all the Indian reservations in the State. The average number of inmates during the present year has been one hundred and two. On the first of October, there were fifty-two boys and fifty-six girls.

The object of this institution, is to extend protection to Indian children who would otherwise suffer or perhaps perish, and while imparting a plain, elementary education, also to instruct them in home and domestic industries, thus, not only enabling them to become self-supporting, but to carry with them into Indian families the elements of civilization.

The method of training is indicated by the following daily routine: The rising bell is rung at 5 o'clock, A.M. After washing and dressing, the girls are employed in preparing the breakfast, while the boys do the chores at the barn and about the house. At 6 o'clock the bell rings for morning worship, after which breakfast is eaten, and the boys then take up the unfinished duties of the early morning, as bringing in wood and coal, while the girls clear the table, prepare the vegetables for dinner, sweep, wash in the laundry, etc., until ten minutes before nine, when the bell is again rung to make changes in the toilet for school. During the morning recess, the tables are set and preparations made for dinner. During the noon hour dinner is eaten, dishes washed, house swept, etc. After school the girls devote one and one-half hours to the manufacture of garments, mending, knitting, and to several varieties of fancy work, while the boys spend the same length of time on the farm in summer, and making brooms in the shop in winter. After this, supper is prepared by the girls, while the boys milk and do the evening chores. Supper is served at 6 o'clock, evening exercises and worship are held at 7 o'clock. At 8 o'clock the bell rings for the younger children to retire, after which a variety of exercises are conducted for the benefit of those older. They are taught singing and instrumental music, books are read to them, and every Friday evening the "Band of Hope," a temperance organization, composed of all the older inmates, meets in the assembly-room. Saturday morning, after the usual work is done, the boys work in the shop or on the farm, and work classes for the girls are conducted in the sewing-room. Saturday afternoon is devoted to bathing and recreation. A complete change is made in the routine of employment every month, in order that each may have an opportunity of learning the different kinds of household and farm work.

An appropriation of $3,450 was made by the last Legislature, for the erection of the hospital and nursery building before mentioned, for needed changes to insure health, and for extraordinary repairs. The nursery building, with its connecting corridors, has cost about $2,600. In addition to this, the following changes have been effected, or are now in process of completion. It having been found that the water, supplied from a well by a hydraulic ram, was insufficient to meet the general wants of the institution, or properly to cleanse the closets within the buildings, earth closets have been temporarily substituted . . . The labor of the larger boys of the asylum has been utilized in making these improvements, several having aided in the plain carpenter work, thus considerably lessening the expenditure.

.   .   .   .   .

The farm connected with the institution comprises fifty-six acres. There were raised during the last year 160 bushels of wheat, 500 bushels of oats, 900 bushels of corn, 300 bushels of potatoes and about 200 bushels of apples. About two acres are appropriated to garden culture, for the benefit of the inmates. The farm

stock comprises two horses, six milch cows, six hogs and a flock of poultry.

Two visits have been made by the commissioner of the district to the institution, during the year. Careful inspections were made on the occasions of these visits, resulting in the conclusion, that the ends sought by the managers of the asylum were satisfactorily attained, especially as regards the industrial training and the moral and religious sentiments inculcated, through the medium of sacred song.

---

3. County children's homes in Ohio, 1882

Ohio. Board of State Charities, *Seventh Annual Report* (Columbus, 1883), pp. 31–34.

In 1866 Ohio passed an act authorizing, but not requiring, county commissioners in any county to establish a children's home as an asylum for children under sixteen who had previously been sent to the county infirmary. A decade and a half after the passage of the Children's Home Act only fourteen of the state's eighty-eight counties had established such homes. In a few cases neighboring counties established jointly owned institutions. By 1910 the number of county homes had risen to fifty.

These institutions are slowly multiplying, and the work they have accomplished in removing children from the miserable and degrading surroundings and associations of our county infirmaries; in supplying educational advantages, with social and moral training for these children; in the rescue of other children from the streets or homes of poverty and vice; in tiding over, by temporary care and relief, children of sick and disabled parents, and especially in the accomplishment [of] the one important end contemplated in the organization of these homes, that of placing homeless and dependent children in families; in all these things a great work has been accomplished, and cannot be too highly spoken of.

If all has not been done that would seem possible, or if there are apparent defects in the organization and management of these homes, it should be remembered, that as public institutions these Homes for Children are of recent date. Experience thus far has justified every rightful expectation of success, and would encourage progress, and yet there are serious liabilities involved in the organization and management of such charities, and no small danger that the County Home may be so managed as to become burdensome to the people without accomplishing a corresponding benefit to the children.

. . . . .

A uniform system of keeping expense accounts would contribute greatly to convenience in computing the average cost of maintenance of these homes, and would serve the further purpose of ascertaining the real economy in their equipment and support. For instance, Fairmount Home, under the joint ownership and support of Columbiana and Stark counties, is provided with a farm of one hundred and fifty-four acres, which cost originally $13,770. This institution was organized in 1877, and from that time until the present we have been unable to secure any evaluation of farm products; meanwhile, the per capita cost year by year has been little, if any, below the average.

The Knoop Home, of Miami county, has a farm of one hundred and sixty acres donated to the county. During the past year the per capita cost was, "exclusive of farm products," $141.70; the value of farm products is reported at $1,000, which would add $12.50 per capita to the cost or give us a per capita cost, including farm products, of $154.20.

This wide difference in cost, when the farms are so nearly alike, in the absence of a system of farm accounts, renders the question of large farms for children's homes still unsettled. This is to be regretted, as other counties about to establish homes ought to have better light of experience for their guidance.

The Belmont County Home, with less than half the land of the two mentioned, maintained its children at a per capita cost of $77.06; and the Scioto County Home, with only ten acres, reports a per capita cost of $76.66. These figures would indicate that the large farms add to rather than diminish from the cost of maintenance.

The Lawrence County Home has no premises—scarcely a playground for its children, and the cost per capita was $76.76. This home, it must be remembered, is situated within the corporation of Ironton, and the children attend the public schools, and thereby the salary and boarding of a teacher or teachers is saved.

Some important ends are served by these comparative statements; they indicate the darkness through which we are compelled to grope in seeking to ascertain how best this great public interest may be promoted, and may possibly lead to some study upon the part of those interested of the statistical tables, showing number, classes, etc., of children provided for, and especially to the classified expenditures of the several homes.

To those who may turn to these tables, it may be proper to state that no entreaty could secure the return of the blank sent to Lawrence county, and in reply to our final appeal, the following letter was received:

IRONTON, OHIO, November 21, 1882
A. G. BYERS, ESQ.:

DEAR SIR: Yours of yesterday at hand, and contents noted. I have not been a trustee or manager for some time, and I do not think any one now connected with the home can give you anything more than a guess at the answers to your questions in your printed circulars. We have a cheap home. It don't cost much to run it. The children all keep healthy. We have no deaths. We find homes for a great many children.

Respectfully,
T. J. MURDOCK

4. A children's almshouse, Boston, 1892

Boston. Special Committee to Inspect the Public Institutions, City Doc. 122, *Final Report* (Boston, 1892), pp. 46–48.

The most active member of the Special Committee was Elizabeth Glendower Evans (1856–1937), a trustee of several state institutions for children and a vigorous advocate of boarding children in foster homes.

MARCELLA-STREET HOME

Net cost for 1891 . . . . $42,699.57

Census for March 22, 1892

Children in the institution	250
Children boarding in country . . .	120
Children placed out in free homes . .	442
Officers and employees	36

Marcella-street Home is the almshouse for children — for neglected children who are committed by the courts to the care of the city for minority because abused by their parents, and for pauper children who are received through the admitting agency at No. 14 Beacon street under the plea of inability to support on the part of the parents. It is the wise policy of the Commissioners to give many of these children the advantage of life outside of the institution, and a number of those who have no friends to claim them are placed permanently, when possible, in free homes in the country, and those under five years of age are boarded out near the institution and come and go from it. At present there are 370 children under the charge of the Home, of whom 114 are neglected and 256 are pauper children. In order to understand better just who these children are and the difficult problems which their care involves, your committee has studied the record of each one as shown by the files at the office, has talked with the superintendent, the admission agent, and the placing-out agent; and finds that the greater proportion of them reach the home through the faults rather than the misfortunes of their parents, and that many come from the class of those who people the almshouses and penal institutions under the care of this department . . .

In this school, at this time, is a pathetic group of 104 so-called defective children suffering from distinct physical disabilities. They are lame, blind, dull, feeble-minded, idiotic. They have eczema, scrofula, erysipelas, hip disease, syphilis.

The city has entire control of these children, for a time at least, and true economy, as well as humanity, urge the utmost endeavor to give them a liberal training of mind and body, and to make this home a centre of regenerating influences. Great praise is due the superintendent for the effective efforts he has made in this direction, and the success with which he has fought ophthalmia and other diseases, and it is hoped that the Commissioners will stand behind him in the further improvements he desires to make.

The institution is a large, imposing brick building, standing back from the street, in about four acres of ground, enclosed by a ten-foot fence with locked gates. Close behind it is the city offal-heap, which, though not objectionable in winter, is intolerable in summer, and should be removed.

The house is clean and well ordered. The department for boys is kept quite distinct from that for girls. The girls (143) have three dormitories, two school-rooms, one kindergarten-room, a sewing-room, a cutting-room, a dining-room (with twelve tables), hospital, play-room, and wash-room. The boys (225) have three dormitories, four school-rooms, a shop with knitting-machines, a dining-room, hospital, play-room, and wash-room. There is a library for all, and a nursery in a separate building for children under four who need hospital care. There are playgrounds for both boys and girls.

The large basement serves well for a rainy day play-room for boys, but is not well fitted for a reception-room on visiting day, for which it is also used. Families sit crowded together on long wooden benches, and many mothers and fathers, of doubtful character, are mixed with the rest, and must be seen by all. It may surely be questioned whether justice to the children should not shut some parents away from this privilege of visiting them.

The children rise at 6 and go to bed at 7. They make their beds and do the cleaning. They have 2½ hours of school in the morning, and 2 hours in the afternoon, and they play games for several hours. The little girls have sewing-classes three times a week, and the olders ones twice a week. The boys knit all the stockings of the school on machines. They have sufficient clothing, but the committee would advocate the use of nightgowns, as the children now follow the untidy institution-practice of sleeping in their underclothing.

The food is good, but the supply of milk should be increased.

The children are kindly treated, and are not often punished; but there should be a punishment book to note the real facts.

In spite of the fact that some are boarded, the institution is still very large, and with the best intentions on the part of the superintendent, a big institution affords enormous chances for evil as well as good, and the children must be managed like a little army. They must eat, sleep, and play under rigid rule and necessary surveillance. Natural freedom must be repressed for the sake of order, and free intercourse constantly watched to prevent the spread of bad habits and vulgar ways — a contagion always imminent in such a promiscuous assemblage, and worse, even, than the physical contagion which must also have its constant guards. The lessons of self-help and the need of work to obtain anything worth obtaining are almost a dead letter in a big institution, and to the very children whose whole inheritance inclines them to weakness and moral laziness, and who, more than most children, need personal and individual responsibilities to awaken their invention and stimulate their energy.

B. PRIVATE INSTITUTIONS

Despite the development of public institutions the vast majority — perhaps nine out of ten — children's asylums were established and conducted by religious denominations or non-sectarian private corporations. The extent to which these private institutions deserved support from public funds and the necessary degree and type of public supervision over their operations were subjects of continuing discussion and, on occasion, sharp controversy.

Charitable institutions

1. The Sheltering Arms, New York, 1875
United States Bureau of Education, *Circular of Information No. 6, 1875. Statements Relating to Reformatory, Charitable and Industrial Schools for the Young* (Washington, D.C., 1875), pp. 118–120.

This was the institution in which "Little Mary Ellen" was placed by court order. See above, Part Two, Chap. II, sec. A., "The Case of Little Mary Ellen," doc. 4.

The origin of The Sheltering Arms is best given in the words of its founder and president, Rev. Thomas W. Peters, D.D. We quote from his sermon on "The gradual growth of charities," preached before the Protestant-Episcopal City Mission Society in 1873:

"Ten years ago, two ladies, visiting the Tombs, or city-prison, in concert with the missionary of our City Mission Society, found, from time to time, mothers committed for drunkenness, who were sent to Blackwell's Island. Some of these women had children, who, by the removal of the mother, were deprived of all care. Even in their degradation, these unhappy mothers had some humanity remaining, and were concerned for their children's welfare. 'They literally lay their children at our feet,' said one of the visiting ladies, 'imploring us to find them a home.' At about the same time there was brought to the notice of another lady of the same society a little blind girl, deserted by her parents, without friends, and not of an age to be received at the asylum for the blind. Shortly after, a home was sought by a workingman for an incurable, motherless, crippled boy. As there was no hope of his restoration, no then existing hospital or institution would receive him. Further inquiry resulted in the unexpected discovery that there were in the city of New York, and out of it, large numbers of children, who, though surrounded by many asylums, were yet without a home, because needing some necessary qualification for admission to institutions already established. It was also ascertained, in the course of these inquiries, that there were many cases of neglect of children, owing to the usual requirement of our charitable institutions that their inmates should be formally surrendered to the trustees. There are hundreds of cases in which a family is abandoned by the father, thus throwing the support of the children upon the mother, and obliging her, perhaps, to break up the household and go out herself to service. With the hopefulness of human nature she believes the separation but temporary, and looks for a happy home once more, at no very distant day. If she could place her children for a few months, or a year, in good hands and under christian training, she would gladly do so, provided that, when able, she might claim them again. 'But I cannot,' said one of these deserted mothers, 'sign away my own flesh and blood.'

"There are other cases, also, among the families of the poor, which make necessary a temporary removal of the children from home. The comfort of health gives place to the famine of sickness; the father of a family is disabled, for a time, by accident or disease, and there is no money to buy food; or the mother is the sufferer, and there is no one to do the household-work, or watch over the children during the day, while the father is at his labor. For such as these, there was no place where the children could be left for a time, and claimed in returning prosperity, and without the liability of their being sent or given away beyond the parents' reach. Friends adopted, but too frequently, the unhappy alternative of placing them in wretched, squalid homes, where they were poorly kept, on a promise of future pay, and ranged the streets half clothed, and untaught, because not fitly dressed for school.

"Thus, by the directing hand of God, was indicated another work to be done, other human woes to be healed. With no promise beyond a house free of rent and a few children to inhabit it, it was resolved, in obedience to the divine Guide, to go forward. The distinguishing features of this charity were fixed upon as these: the only qualifications for the admission of a child shall be that it is not entitled to reception elsewhere and that in the institution there is a vacant bed; the children cared for there belong to their parents, not to the institution, and can be claimed by parents at will; by the introduction of the cottage-system, the children are to be distributed into separate families, with a responsible head over each.

"Gifts were soon received to furnish, and multiplying applications of little ones to inhabit, the house, so that, a few months later, on the sixth day of October, 1864, it was opened, with all its forty beds taken up. Such was the commencement of The Sheltering Arms."

Children between the ages of 2 and 10 years are received from the following classes:

1st. The blind and deaf-mutes, until the age

at which they become entitled to admission at the asylums especially devoted to such unfortunates.

2d. Crippled children past hope of cure, and therefore no longer retained in ordinary hospitals.

3d. Children of poor parents, obliged on account of sickness to enter a hospital, and who commit their children for a season to our charge, with the expectation, upon recovery, of reclaiming their own.

4th. Children rendered temporarily homeless by fire or other accident.

5th. Children whose home has been broken up by the intemperance or desertion of father or mother. In such cases, the remaining parent pays, according to ability, a small sum monthly.

6th. Children abandoned by both parents, brought to us by friends or relatives unable to find immediately a proper home, and yet unwilling to lose control of the children or to place them beyond their reach.

Up to January, 1875, six hundred and eighty-two children have been received. The needs of some few were met by one day's hospitality. Others have remained ten years. In every case the child's necessity is the limit of its stay. The cottage-system is carried out as fully as may be, and has proved a valuable aid in the training of the children, affording a good substitute for the home-life from which they are debarred. Each cottage (except the center-house) contains a dormitory, bath-room, play-room, and dining-room for thirty or thirty-five children, besides a convenient sleeping-room for the "mother" of the family. Each family is entirely separate from the others, meeting, however, at church and in school, and occasionally in the play-grounds.

The property now owned and occupied by The Sheltering Arms is situated on the corner of One hundred and twenty-ninth street and Tenth avenue. The principal building is of brick, and contains five cottages under one roof. The center-house, named the Van Horne Cottage, is used for the general purposes of the institution, and contains the office, reception-rooms, linen-rooms, kitchen, laundry, &c. The west wing is devoted to boys, and consists of two cottages, bearing respectively the names of John D. Wolfe and James E. Montgomery. The two cottages of the east wing are named after Mrs. Peter Cooper and "The Ladies' Association of the Sheltering Arms," and are occupied by girls. The school-house is a frame building, at one end of the boys' play-ground. At the end of the girls' play-ground is a brick hospital, entirely detached, and sufficiently large to meet the ordinary needs of the house.

The annual cost of each child, including *all expenses,* varies from $130 to $140. Parents or friends pay, according to their means, from two to ten dollars per month. About seventy children are received on the free list. A subscription of $138 entitles the donor to a year's support for any child of suitable age, &c. Three churches and not less than forty-three charitable persons availed themselves of this provision last year. A gift of $100 constitutes a life-member; of $500, a patron; $1,000 endows a bed, the nomination of the occupant belonging to the donor for life; $2,000 is invested as a permanent endowment of one bed, the nomination of the occupant remaining always with the donor and his heirs; a gift of $5,000 builds a cottage bearing the name of the donor.

---

2. Two asylums in Chicago, 1875

United States Bureau of Education, *Circular of Information No. 6, 1875,* pp. 60–61.

PROTESTANT ORPHAN-ASYLUM, CHICAGO

During its early years the reports were not published very regularly, and more recently some have been destroyed by fire.

The orphan-asylum was rendered necessary by the fearful ravages of the Asiatic cholera, which visited this city in 1849, it proving fatal to many immigrants, thereby leaving their children orphans and destitute.

On the 3d of August, 1849, (a day appointed by the President as a day of fasting and prayer, in view of the spreading epidemic,) a meeting was held for the purpose of affording them a home. A contribution of over $400 was raised and an adjourned meeting appointed for the following Tuesday, when a constitution was adopted and a board of trustees chosen; the 13th of the same month, the board of directresses held their first meeting at the asylum, 13 children having been admitted. Up to the present time, 1,894 children have been cared for at the asylum.

In 1851 the board of trustees (seeing the necessity of a permanent location) purchased two acres of land from the trustees of the Illinois and Michigan Canal, at the first canal-land-sale, for $800, to be paid in annual payments of $200 each. The amount necessary was raised by the ladies from the proceeds of fairs, and the building now occupied was erected in 1853.

In 1870 the location had become so desirable for residences that the trustees built four brick houses, facing on Michigan avenue, two each side of the asylum, which were immediately rented for five years, at $1,000 each. In 1873 four more were built on Wabash avenue, which rent for $1,500 each — $30,000 being still owed for the last set. The rents from the first-named houses are applied towards paying the debt, together with half the rent from the Wabash-avenue houses, the remaining $3,000 being paid for interest on the money borrowed to build the houses. It is hoped that when the debt is all paid the asylum will be nearly self-sustaining. At present it is supported by donations.

The treasury is nearly empty, the panic of last fall causing a marked decrease in the subscriptions, as well as a corresponding increase in the number of children received.

Many of the inmates have one parent, who for various reasons cannot care for children in a home of their own, yet can contribute to their support in the asylum by paying a small amount for board. Frequently these are as evidently cases for the exercise of the charities of the institution as the orphans themselves.

Many vagrant and homeless children have been surrendered to the asylum by the mayor who otherwise would have been sent to penal institutions.

All the children of a suitable age attend school, and one afternoon in each week the girls are instructed in sewing. Much of the light work of the house is done by the larger girls.

CHICAGO NURSERY AND HALF–ORPHAN ASYLUM

The object of this charity is the care and maintenance of the children of poor women, for the purpose of enabling them to find employment; also, the care and maintenance of such children as are deprived by death, or other cause, of either parent.

It was originally established as a nursery, where young children could be cared for during the hours of work, the parents bringing them in the morning and claiming them at night, paying five cents a day for their care.

The circumstances of many of the women made it a kindness to supply lodgings for their children, as well as care through the day, and therefore the plan of the institution was somewhat modified and enlarged to suit the need.

Several changes were made, until, in the spring of 1870, a lot was purchased, and on it was erected a building, commodious, airy, and suitably equipped for carrying out its charitable object, and it is doing among the better class of poor an amount of good that cannot be overestimated.

At the time of the great fire the work was within a few weeks of its completion, and in the distress of that fearful time those interested in it were only too glad of its shelter for themselves and families; thus, for a time, many other children, and even adults, had to be received. And in a building without doors, only partially glazed, and entirely without heating-apparatus, the discomforts and suffering endured can scarcely be exaggerated.

Having struggled through difficulties that can scarcely be appreciated, during a season of exceptionable hardship, the institution is at last in admirable working order.

Special attention is given to vocal music, which is considered one of the most desirable aids to the discipline and happiness of the children.

In connection with the institution there is a day-school, with an average attendance of 86, and the children are making good proficiency in reading, spelling, and arithmetic. A Sunday-school is also well kept up, owing to the kindness and energy of its superintendent, who labors faithfully for its success.

---

3. The San Francisco Ladies' Protection and Relief Society, 1901

Managers of the San Francisco Ladies' Protection and Relief Society, *Forty-Eighth and Forty-Ninth Annual Reports* (San Francisco, 1903), pp. 7–10.

The first year of a new century has passed since we met in annual session, and the time has now come for the forty-eighth yearly report. The little band of "praying women," as our President has called them, sowed in 1853 seed that still "shoots after rainless years, bearing bright leaves." In these forty-eight years charity has become less sentimental and more reflective. We are more scientific in methods without being, I hope and believe, less sympathetic with individual suffering and individual joy. Our belief in the germ theory and sanitary science may be entirely compatible with the truest charity. Turning from abstract to concrete, and looking into the daily life of the Home, we find the view a pleasant one. The year has been rich in experience and events,

many of which must of necessity be omitted from this report. To begin with material things, we have gone on improving our buildings. The preceding year's efforts were all towards the completion and equipment of the new wing. This year the old building, yard, and outbuildings have received much attention.

The most necessary undertaking was the removal of the schoolhouse from the Geary-Street frontage to the back of the lot. The lower part was turned into a gymnasium, and the upper part, at some future time, is to be used for rooms for help. A high fence was erected from this building to Geary Street, in part to create a place where the boys could play ball without endangering the neighbors' windows, and in part to prevent an easy and unceremonious exit from the institution. This work of removing, grading, and fencing cost $729. In connection with it, the sheds and fences received attention. In October and November the old planking, always in need of renewal and repairs, was done away with and the yard bituminized. The hygienic value of this cannot be overestimated, and the money expended, $1,354.08, was cheerfully given, in spite of the fact that our financial condition is somewhat low. Interior improvements in the way of carpets and glass doors for the library were made, but perhaps the most important was with a view to the increased safety of the children in the event of a fire. A member of the Fire Department, at our request, made a thorough examination of the premises. At his suggestion a partition in the boys' dormitory was torn down, hand-rails put on all staircases, "Rex" fire-extinguishers and a fire alarm put in, and a fire drill organized which empties the house in three minutes. The Board then felt that nothing had been left undone to secure the reasonable safety of the children should a fire occur.

.   .   .   .   .

The school has been in the main building this year, with the Misses Moulthrop and Knowlton in charge. Their proven efficiency is too well known for any comments or words of praise. The four children sent out to the public schools in 1893 as an experiment did so well, that by degrees the number has been increased, and now all but the kindergarten children and one Home class attend outside schools.

The children have had many pleasures during the year in the way of excursions and treats. Mr. Goodman, of the S. P. R. R., Mr. Foster, of the N. P. C. R. R., and the Sutter-Street and Geary-Street roads have given free transportation on several occasions. Mr. Vining's generosity gave them a glorious "Fourth" with all the joys of fireworks and an abundance of ice cream. The Park Commissioners twice gave parties of children the freedom of the Park in the way of donkey-rides, merry-go-rounds, ice-cream, and fresh milk. The kindergarten and Home schools were given a party by Mrs. J. A. Robinson, with abundance of good things to eat. A donation of twenty dollars from Mrs. S. Hopkins went in part for pleasure, in part for books for the library. Plymouth Church gave the girls an outing to Mirabel Park, and Miss Beaver took the Girls' Club to the May-day festival and to San Rafael. The Christmas festival was held on Saturday, December 21st, and the merry voices and happy faces testified to the good time they had. Generous donations in the way of money, toys, and good things for the table were received and the holiday season was a happy time to all the inmates of the Home.

The health of the children has been satisfactory. In February there were a few cases of measles, and in May forty-seven cases, with severe complications in many instances. One boy had a severe case of typhoid fever, but owing to the devoted nursing given by our Matron is now well and strong. In April a boy of six years died from measles with complications.

.   .   .   .   .   .

During the year we have cared for 379 children, 7 orphans, 61 half-orphans, 63 for whom a small board was paid, and 32 wholly destitute, besides giving a comfortable home to four aged women. January 1, 1902, we had 245 enrolled — 12 orphans, 116 half-orphans, 18 abandoned, 69 for whom a small board is paid, and 30 wholly destitute.

Subsidized private institutions

---

1. Charles Loring Brace defends the subsidy system, 1872

Charles Loring Brace, *The Dangerous Classes of New York and Twenty Years' Work Among Them* (New York, 1872), pp. 377–381.

One of the main duties of a Legislature is to care for the interests of the poor and criminal. The English system, dating as far back as Henry VIII, has been to leave the charge of the poor and all educational institutions, as much as possible, to counties or local bodies or individuals. It has been, so far as the charge of the poor is concerned, imitated here. But in neither country has it worked well; and the last relic of it will probably soon be removed in this State, by placing the defective persons — the blind and dumb, and insane and idiot, and the orphans — in the several counties in State institutions. The charge of criminals and reformatory institutions are also largely placed under State control and supervision.

The object of a State Legislature in all these matters is *bonum publicum* — the public weal. If they think that a private charity is accomplishing a public work of great value, which is not and perhaps cannot be accomplished by purely public institutions, they apparently have the same right to tax the whole community, or a local community, for its benefit, that they have now to tax it for the support of schools, or Almshouses, or Prisons, or Houses of Refuge. In such a case it need not be a matter of question with the Legislature whether the charity is "sectarian" or not; whether it teaches Roman Catholicism, or Protestantism, or the Jewish faith, or no faith. The only question with the governing power is, "Does it do a work of public value not done by public institutions?" If it does; if, for instance, it is a Roman-Catholic Reformatory, or a Protestant House of Refuge, or Children's Aid Society, the Legislature, knowing that all public and private organizations together cannot fully remedy the tremendous evils arising from a class of neglected and homeless children, is perfectly right in granting aid to such institutions without reference to their "sectarian" character. It reserves to itself the right of inspection, secured in this State by our admirable Board of Inspectors of State Charities; and it can at any time repeal the charters of, or refuse the appropriations to, these private associations. But thus far its uniform practice has been to aid, to a limited degree, private charities of this nature.

This should by no means be considered a ground for demanding similar assistance for "sectarian schools." Education is secured now by public taxation for all; and all can take advantage of it. There is no popular necessity for Church Schools, and the public good is not promoted by them as it is by secular schools. Where there are children too poor to attend the Public Schools, these can be aided by private charitable associations; and of these, only those should be assisted by the State which have no sectarian character.

Charities which are entirely supported by State and permanent endowment are liable, as the experience of England shows, to run into a condition of routine and lifelessness. The old endowments of Great Britain are nests of abuses, and many of them are now being swept away. A State charity has the advantage of greater solidity and more thorough and expensive machinery, and often more careful organization. But, as compared with our private charities, the public institutions of beneficence are dull and lifeless. They have not the individual enthusiasm working through them, with its ardor and power. They are more like machines.

On the other hand, charities supported entirely by individuals will always have but a small scope. The amount of what may be called the "charity fund" of the community is comparatively limited. In years of disaster or war, or where other interests absorb the public, it will dwindle down to a very small sum. It is distributed, too, somewhat capriciously. Sometimes a "sensation" calls it forth bountifully, while more real demands are neglected. An important benevolent association, depending solely on its voluntary contributions from individuals, will always be weak and incomplete in its machinery. The best course for the permanency and efficiency of a charity seems to be, to make it depend in part on the State, that it may have a solid foundation of support, and be under official supervision, and in part on private aid, so that it may feel the enthusiasm and activity and responsibility of individual effort. The "Houses of Refuge" combine public and private assistance in a manner which has proved very beneficial. Their means come from the State, while their governing bodies are private, and independent of politics. The New York "Juvenile Asylum" enjoys both public and private contributions, but has a private board. On the other hand, the "Commissioners of Charities and Correction" are supported entirely by taxation, and, until they had the services of a Board carefully selected, were peculiarly inefficient. Many private benevolent associations in the city could be mentioned which have no solid foundation of public support and are under no public supervision, and, in consequence, are weak and slipshod in all their enterprises. The true policy of the Legislature is to encourage and supplement private activity in charities by moderate public aid, and to organize a strict supervision.

2. New York restricts state subsidies to private institutions, 1873–1874

New York State. Constitutional Commission, 1873, "Report of the Committee on Sectarian Appropriations," *Amendments Proposed to the Constitution of the State of New York* (Albany, 1873), pp. 38–40.

The proposed amendment prohibited state aid to private associations except to institutions for the education and support of the blind, deaf mutes, and juvenile delinquents. The amendment, which was approved in 1874, did not effect the granting of subsidies by city and county officials.

The committee *on sectarian appropriations* beg leave to report the following reasons which governed the Commission in recommending the favorable consideration of a proposed amendment to article eight:

The manner in which moneys have been appropriated by the State for charitable purposes for many years past, excepting those appropriated for State institutions, has been a cause for very general complaint throughout the State.

Without going into the details which may be found in the yearly volumes of the statutes, it is sufficient to say that they have been distributed to classes of the population, in very unjust proportions, and with very little reference, if any, to their respective numbers or wants.

They have also been distributed to the several parts of the State, without any reference to their population or their necessities — giving to some parts of the State, for many years in succession, large sums of money — while other localities have received comparatively little or nothing whatever.

When we reflect that this money is raised by direct taxation on every county in the State in proportion to the assessed value of its property, any such distribution, as above, is most manifestly unsatisfactory and unjust.

The State has been filled with complaints of this injustice, springing from each of these sources for many years.

There is also another ground of objection to this mode of distribution, in this, that the moneys are given to private corporations not owned or controlled by the State, which cannot superintend the expenditure of the money, or even control it, so far as to compel its use for the purposes for which it was appropriated.

Your committee are fully impressed with the belief that the proposed amendment will not seriously interfere with the great good accomplished by the Orphan Asylums, Homes for the Friendless, Hospitals and other charitable institutions, so freely scattered over our State. The Boards of Supervisors of the various counties and the Common Councils of the different cities, have all the power they have heretofore had to pay to each class of said institutions the most liberal compensation for the care and support of the different classes of unfortunates for whom they were designed; and should this source of support be insufficient, they have but to make their appeal to the charitable feelings of the community, and a generous response will always be the result. Such we believe to be the uniform experience of our citizens in every part of the State.

When the State yearly makes appropriations of money, our citizens are but the almoners of the State bounty; there is not only no charity in such expenditure of the money of the State, extracted by force from the unwilling taxpayer, but it has the most direct tendency to extinguish in the human heart those kind and humane feelings which are developed and nourished in the bosom of the free and liberal giver.

We are fully persuaded that under the system which will grow out of this amendment, all our humane and charitable institutions will be as useful as they ever have been in the past, and the charity and liberality of our citizens will be greatly stimulated.

It is true that the amendment proposed by the Commission cuts off all gifts of money and all loaning of the credit of the State to all other asociations, corporations, etc., but they are all subject to the same objection, and appropriations to them of the money of the State are liable to the same abuses. They must all stand or fall together.

All of which is most respectfully submitted, in behalf of the committee.

Albany, March 15, 1873.

E. W. Leavenworth,
Chairman.

---

3. Louisiana prohibits state appropriations for private charities, 1879

Louisiana. Constitution (1879), Article 51.

In 1870 Louisiana granted $98,250 to orphanages, homes for the aged, and benevolent societies. No appropriations were made after 1870.

Art. 51. No money shall ever be taken from the public treasury, direct or indirect, in aid of any church, sect or denomination or religion, or in aid of any priest, preacher, minister or teacher thereof . . . and no preference shall ever be given to, nor any discrimination made against any church, sect or creed, or religion, or any form of religious faith or worship, nor shall any appropriation be made for private, charitable or benevolent purposes to any person or commitee, *provided* this shall not apply to state asylums for the insane, and deaf, dumb and blind, and the county hospitals and public charitable institutions conducted under state authority.

---

4. The subsidy system in California, 1880

California Superintendent of Public Instruction, "Care and Education of Orphans, Half Orphans, and Abandoned Children," *Ninth Report* for the School Year Ending June 30, 1880 (Sacramento, 1880), pp. 47–49.

The new Constitution fortunately made it possible for the Legislature to continue the aid of the State to those denominational and charitable institutions, whose object it is to care for these unfortunate children. They are wards of the State, and it is the duty of the State, in some manner, to provide for them; and this can be done in no way so well, and at the same time so economically, as by legislative appropriation to supplement the private charities, which erect the necessary buildings and bear the larger part of the current expenses of the institutions. The objection that most of these asylums are sectarian institutions, has no weight; for these unfortunate ones being deprived of their natural home and the religious training which our system of public education properly and wisely leaves exclusively to parents and the home, it is but right and proper that, in the home which private and public charity provides, they should be trained in religious faith of their dead parents. This is the plan, I learn, which is followed even in England, where they have an established church. To follow any other course would be taking advantage of their misfortunes in the interest of proselytism.

It is earnestly hoped that the example set by the first Legislature under the new Constitution, in this connection, will be followed by all succeeding Legislatures . . . I would venture but one recommendation, viz: that the maximum age for receiving the pro rata from the State be extended, in the case of *girls,* to sixteen years. Fourteen years is too early an age, in most cases, at which to turn girls, friendless and alone, abroad in any part of the world to do for themselves, and certainly not less so in California. If it be urged that these institutions will not do it, then it is answered that they should no more be charged with the sole cost of supporting and educating these wards of the State, during the later years of their necessary stay in the institutions, than during their early stay.

Following is the section of the Constitution, and the Act of the Legislature, above referred to.

ARTICLE IV

Legislative Department

Section 22. No money shall be drawn from the treasury but in consequence of appropriations made by law, and upon warrants duly drawn thereon by the Controller; and no money shall ever be appropriated or drawn from the State treasury for the use or benefit of any corporation, association, asylum, hospital, or any other institution not under the exclusive management and control of the State as a State institution, nor shall any grant or donation of property ever be made thereto by the State; *provided,* that notwithstanding anything contained in this or any other section of this Constitution, the Legislature shall have the power to grant aid to institutions conducted for the support and maintenance of minor orphans, or half orphans, or abandoned children, or aged persons in indigent circumstances — such aid to be granted by a uniform rule, and proportioned to the number of inmates of such respective institutions; *provided further,* that the State shall have, at any time, the right to inquire into the management of such institution; *provided further,* that whenever any county, or city and county, or city, or town, shall provide for the support of minor orphans, or half orphans, or abandoned children, or aged persons in indigent circumstances, such county, city and county, city, or town, shall be entitled to receive the same pro rata appropriations as may be granted to such institutions under church or other control. An accurate statement of the receipts and expenditures of public moneys shall be attached to and published with the laws at every regular session of the Legislature.

AN ACT

To Appropriate Money for the Support of Orphans, Half Orphans, and Abandoned Children. Approved March 25, 1880.

Section 1. There is hereby appropriated out of any money in the State treasury not otherwise appropriated, to each and every institution in this State, conducted for the support and maintenance of minor orphans, half orphans, or abandoned children, and to each and every county, city and county, city, or town, maintaining such orphans, half orphans, or abandoned children, or any or all of such classes of persons, aid as follows: For each whole orphan supported and maintained in any such institution, the sum of seventy-five dollars per annum; for each abandoned child supported and maintained in any such institution, the sum of seventy-five dollars per annum; *provided,* such abandoned child shall have been an inmate thereof for one year prior to receiving any support as provided in this Act.

.   .   .   .   .

Section 4. The State Board of Examiners are authorized, in behalf of the State, at any time to inquire, either in person or by authorized agent, into the management of any such institution; and any institution refusing, upon due demand, to permit such inquiry, shall not thereafter receive any aid under this Act. All expenses incurred in visiting said asylums shall be audited and allowed by the State Board of Examiners out of the appropriations for the support of orphans, half orphans, and abandoned children.

.   .   .   .   .

Section 7. In order that the provisions of this Act shall not be abused, it is hereby declared:

1. That no institution which has less than twenty inmates of either or all the classes mentioned in section one hereof, shall be deemed an institution for the support and maintenance

of minor orphans, half orphans, or abandoned children, within the intent and meaning of this Act.

2. That no child over the age of fourteen years shall be deemed a minor orphan, half orphan, or abandoned child, within the intent and meaning of this Act.

3. That no child for whose specific support there is paid to any such institution the sum of ten dollars or more per month, shall be deemed a minor orphan, half orphan, or abandoned child, within the intent and meaning of this Act.

Sec. 8. No money appropriated by the State to any institution claiming aid under this Act, shall be expended either in improvements, or in the erection of new buildings by such institutions.

---

5. Subsidized institutions in Wisconsin, California, and District of Columbia, 1879

E. C. Wines, *The State of Prisons and of Child-Saving Institutions in the Civilized World* (Cambridge, Mass., 1880), pp. 186, 215–216.

Wines (1806–1879) completed this work shortly before his death. It is an informative and entertaining compendium of observations and data collected by the author during his service as secretary of the Prison Association of New York (1861–1879) and of the National Prison Association (1870–1877).

There is no State, city, or county orphan asylum in Wisconsin. There are, however, in the city of Milwaukee five orphan asylums,— four under Catholic and one under Protestant control. These are private corporations, organized under special charters. They are supported mainly by voluntary contributions, with occasional grants of money from the State or the county in which they are situated. They contain an aggregate average number of about three hundred inmates. There are also two orphan asylums in the western part of the State, both Catholic,— one at La Crosse, the other at Sparta,— with an aggregate average of sixty to seventy inmates. They take orphan children, feed, clothe, educate, and instruct them in some useful occupation; and then find for them suitable homes. They are doing great good, and are recognized as valuable institutions.

There is also an orphan asylum at Green Bay, under Episcopal control; and one at Racine,— founded by a liberal and wealthy citizen, a Mr. Taylor, in accordance with the provisions of his will,— known as the "Taylor Orphan Asylum." These are both excellent institutions, and well managed.

.   .   .   .   .

California seems well provided with child-saving institutions in the form of orphan asylums and homes for the neglected and exposed waifs of society. The legislature, too, is liberal in its contributions to the support of these institutions. For every orphan by the loss of both parents it allows one hundred dollars a year to the institution having charge of it; and for every orphan by the loss of one parent, seventy-five dollars. Altogether the number of these institutions exceeds twenty, and the number of inmates is over two thousand. Nearly three-fourths of the children are in Catholic, forty-six in Jewish, and the remainder in Protestant asylums. The amount paid by the State for their support is about $150,000; the balance is made up from earnings of the inmates, private contributions, and revenues from endowments. The good accomplished is immeasurable and in manifold directions. It would be interesting to enter into details, but lack of space is an insuperable bar.

.   .   .   .   .

Washington, D.C. appears to be pretty well provided with preventive institutions of one kind or another. It counts three orphan asylums; three industrial schools; two children's hospitals; one infant asylum; one foster home; and one national association for the relief of colored women and children. These are all organized and managed by private citizens or churches, but most of them receive more or less aid from Congress or the District government, or both. Of course it would occupy too much space in a work of this nature to give a detailed account of their several specific aims, labors, and accomplishments. They bring relief and healing, physical and moral, to many hundreds of persons, mostly children; and, large as the volume of crime is, they make it less than it would be without them.

The most important of these establishments, in many respects, appears to be the industrial-home school on Georgetown Heights. Of this it will be proper, as being highly suggestive in several of its details, to give some little sketch. It was organized in 1867, and incorporated in 1872 as a home for destitute and neglected children of both sexes, with a view to make useful men and women of them by providing tuition in the elementary branches of education and instruction in some trade or vocation. To accomplish this, (1) the government of the District has set apart a large building, with seventeen acres of land attached, within the corporate limits of the city, formerly used for the adult poor; (2) the board of trustees of the public schools have opened a school upon the premises, where the children receive primary instruction, while the more advanced inmates can attend the schools of a higher grade in Georgetown; (3) Congress has donated a steam-engine, machinery, and some tools, which have enabled the managers to establish a workshop in which boys have been taught the use of tools and the elements of carpentry, cabinet-making, and lathe-work; the girls being taught household duties and sewing.

The institution has heretofore had a hard struggle to maintain its existence. More recently the District government and Congress, in recognition of its work, have liberally con-tributed towards its support. Its managers, therefore, have in view to erect during the present year (1879) a commodious workshop (the present one being leased and too distant from the house), together with a laundry and spacious school-room. They also propose to have those essential branches of domestic economy, bread-making and laundry-work, thoroughly taught by competent instructors, and shoe-making and tailoring by able foremen; also blacksmithing, gardening, the culture of fruit, the management of a dairy, and in time the art of printing.

A board of managers, serving gratuitously, exercise general control of the institution, employing a superintendent, a matron, a foreman, a seamstress, to instruct both boys and girls in plain sewing and mending, and a cook, with assistants in the laundry. At present the number of inmates is limited to fifty, but arrangements are making to permit a considerable increase of the number, and then the family system will be regularly inaugurated.

---

6. The subsidy system in New York, 1889

Josephine Shaw Lowell in New York State Board of Charities, *Twenty-Third Annual Report* for the year 1889 (Albany, 1890), pp. 180–204.

Omitting the three oldest institutions for children in the city (the Orphan Asylum Society, the Roman Catholic Orphan Asylum and the Protestant Half-Orphan Asylum, supporting 1,250 children) which receive no public money except from the school fund, and which are practically supported by private charity or by invested funds, there remain twenty-five institutions for children in this city which all receive large sums from the public funds. These may be divided into two classes, those which receive less than half their support from this source, and those which receive more than half, many of which last may be said to be supported wholly by public money. In the former class are four Catholic, three Protestant and one Hebrew institution; in the latter class are ten Catholic, five Protestant and two Hebrew institutions.

As appears from the above, there are among these twenty-five institutions fourteen Roman Catholic, eight Protestant or non-sectarian, and three Hebrew. During the year 1888, the Roman Catholic institutions had an average of about 9,200 children to care for and received $951,808 from the city, the Protestant or non-sectarian cared for about 3,000 children and had $420,342 from the city, and the Hebrew received $153,899 from the city for an average of about 1,475 children.

Nine of these twenty-five institutions, seven Roman Catholic with 1,780 children and two Hebrew with 1,252 children, have been established since the passage of chapter 173, *Laws of 1875,* which provides that a dependent child shall be committed to an institution controlled by persons of the same religious faith as the parents of such child, so far as practicable, and that the board of every child so committed shall be paid by the authorities of the county, and there is no doubt that these institutions were established in consequence of the passage of that act, and to take advantage of the facilities granted for the education at public cost of large numbers of children in the Roman Catholic and Hebrew faiths.

This law has also encouraged the increase in the number of children cared for in several other institutions, which prior to its passage were of very moderate size and supported mainly by private contributions. At the time of the passage of that law the city of New York was supporting 9,363 children in private institutions and on Randall's island, at a cost of $757,858. In 1888 it supported 14,939 children in private institutions and 758 on Randall's island, at a cost of $1,526,617 for the children in private institutions, and at a cost of $106,274 for the children on Randall's island, a total of 15,697 dependent children at a cost

of $1,632,891 for one year. This is an increase since 1875 of 6,334 children and $875,033 in cost.

In former reports the attention of the Board has been called to the number and constant increase of the dependent children supported in whole or in part by public money in New York city, and this increase has been ascribed to the "per capita" allowance for the maintenance of children from the city funds, and to that provision of the law of 1875 already quoted, that is, to what has been called the "religious clause." That this law should serve to increase the number of dependent children was to be expected, because it provided exactly the care which parents desired for their children, that of persons of their own religious faith, and supplied ample means for the children's support, while, although the funds were to be derived from public sources, yet since the institutions were to be managed by private persons, the stigma which fortunately attaches to public relief, was removed. Thus every incentive to parents to place their children upon the *public* for support was created by the provisions of the law, and every deterrent was removed, for the law demanded nothing from the parent in return for the support of his child and did not deprive him of any of his rights over the child, although relieving him of every duty towards it. That the causes of the large number of children who are dependent wholly or in part on the public for support in New York have been correctly pointed out, seems to be proved beyond a doubt by the experience of the only other State in the Union, which, so far as I know, has been equally reckless in providing from the public funds for the support of unlimited numbers of dependent children, leaving the selection of the children to the persons who undertake their care and to the parents who desire to be relieved of the expense of supporting them . . .

Despite the different circumstances of the two States of New York and California, the result of mistaken legislation seems to have been almost identical in both. In New York, with an area of 45,658 square miles we have a population of 6,000,000 and about 20,000 children supported by the public—one in every 251 of the population — in California, the population is about 1,250,000, occupying 188,981 square miles, but they have succeeded in tempting parents to abandon their children almost as effectually as we have, for they have 4,300 children supported by the public, one in every 290 of the population.

.   .   .   .   .

Besides the above interesting and suggestive comparison between States, we may find a second and equally useful lesson from the different practice in this matter of various counties in New York, and the results as contrasted with the experience of the city of New York. The city of New York is estimated to have a population of about 1,500,000 — the number of her children who are supported by public funds, as has been said, is 15,697, or one to each 100 of the population. The city of New York is the only community of the State for which the Legislature has passed laws requiring that the public funds (not State funds, but funds raised by local taxation) shall be paid into the hands of private persons for the support of such children as these persons shall consider to be fitting subjects for public support, and, within very wide limits, for such time as these persons shall think well to retain them as public dependents. The rest of the State was, however, equally subject with New York city to the provisions of chapter 173, *Laws of 1875,* by which counties were required to pay the board of all children committed by all magistrates in the county, to institutions controlled by persons of the same religious faith as the parents of the children. Two counties have, since the passage of that law, sought and obtained exemption from some of its provisions. Kings county and Albany county have each secured the passage of a special act, whereby, in the former, the power to commit children to private institutions for destitution was taken from the magistrates, and placed exclusively in the hands of the public officers hav-

ing charge of the other dependent poor of the community, and, in the latter, the action of the superintendent of the poor was rendered necessary to secure payment from the public funds, so that the result was the same . . .

Under this law the Commissioners of Charities and Correction of Kings county have assumed the whole control of the dependent children supported by the county, with the following results: In 1880, with a population of 599,-495, of which the city of Brooklyn contained 566,663, it supported 1,479 dependent children, or one to every 405 of the population. The county is now estimated to have a population of 880,000, and it supported, in 1888, 1,180 dependent children, at an expense of $106,379.75. This is one child to every 745 of the population . . .

Westchester county has probably increased the number of its dependent children more steadily and more in proportion, than any other county since the passage of the children's law. In 1876, with a population of 103,564, there were fifty-two children supported by the county, or one to every 1,991 of the population . . .

.   .   .   .   .

At present, allowing for increase of population, the county probably has one dependent child to every 250 of the population.

It is stated that there are 132 officials in Westchester county authorized to commit children to private institutions at the public expense, and the children are retained by the institutions after commitment at the will of the authorities of the institution . . .

.   .   .   .   .

Is it not time that the interests of the public, and the interests of these 15,000 children [of the city of New York] were intrusted to the care of some responsible man or men, in New York city, to see to it, not only that $1,500,000 of the taxpayer's money is not worse than wasted every year, but to study the whole question, to devise means to save parents from the temptation to desert their children, and to save the children from a life of dependence, not only now, but in the future.

Institutional statistics

1. Cost of institutional care, 1892

Hastings H. Hart, "The Economic Aspect of the Child Problem," *Proceedings* of the National Conference of Charities and Correction (1892), 191–193.

Hart (1851–1932) was secretary of the Minnesota State Board of Corrections and Charities.

The State of California appropriates from $75 to $100 a year for the care of each of four thousand dependent children. In the State of New York the average yearly cost of taking care of children in one hundred and fifty orphan asylums and other children's institutions is officially reported at $130 per year. The estimated cost of caring for children in State institutions for dependent children in Massachusetts, Wisconsin, Michigan, Minnesota, Illinois, and Indiana, is about $160. The average cost of caring for children in reform schools of these States is $145 per capita. This cost does not include any interest on the invested capital or any expenditure for new buildings and permanent improvements. In private families in the Northern United States the cost of food, clothing, medical attendance, and schooling, together with a very moderate allowance for the value of maternal care, will be found to average more than $100 for each child.

. . . . . .

There are in the United States twenty-five million children under the age of sixteen years. Of this number there are, as nearly as can be ascertained, about 100,000 children under public care, or that of charitable agencies, distributed approximately as follows: in orphan asylums, children's homes, almshouses, etc., 74,000; in juvenile reformatories, 15,000; in schools for feeble-minded, 5,000; in schools for deaf, 4,500; in schools for blind, 1,500. Our inquiry has to do with this portion of the children of the State, together with those who are likely, through neglect, homelessness, or disease, to become members of these classes.

The magnitude of the economic problem involved can be seen from a statement of the capital already invested, the amount annually expended, and the number of persons employed. The value of the property invested in institutions for the care of children in the United States may be estimated as follows: —

Orphan asylums, children's homes, and other institutions for dependent children	$40,000,000
Juvenile reformatories	10,000,000
Schools for feeble-minded children	2,500,000
Schools for deaf children	2,000,000
Schools for blind children	1,000,000
Total value of property	$55,500,000

The annual expenditure for the support of children in these institutions may be estimated as follows: —

Care of 74,000 dependent children at $130	$9,500,000
Care of 15,000 delinquent children at $133	2,000,000
Care of 5,000 feeble-minded children at $160	800,000
Care of 4,500 deaf children at $200	900,000
Care of 1,500 blind children at $270	400,000
Total annual expenditure	$13,600,000

The number of persons employed in the immediate care of these 100,000 children may be estimated as follows: —

1 for each 8 dependent children	9,000
1 for each 12 delinquent children	1,200
1 for each 4.5 feeble-minded children	1,100
1 for each 5 deaf children	900
1 for each 3.75 blind children	400
Total estimated number of care-takers	12,600

These estimates are believed to be safely within the actual facts; and they sufficiently indicate the magnitude of the economic problem, though they do not include the unpaid labor of thousands of men and women who act as managers, secretaries, solicitors, etc., nor the labor of those who search out and gather the children who are the objects of this care.

2. 1151 institutions for children, 1910

United States Bureau of the Census, *Benevolent Institutions, 1910* (Washington, D.C., 1913), pp. 26–27.

Census Bureau statistics indicated that at the end of 1910 151,441 children were under the care of institutions. Slightly more than 110,000 children were actually in the institution; approximately 40,000 others, still under the nominal guardianship of institutions, had been placed in families or "elsewhere."

The institutions covered by this classification are those especially designed for children. They include orphanages, children's homes and asylums, receiving homes for societies for the protection and care of children, detention homes connected with juvenile courts, and similar institutions which receive children as resident inmates, sometimes for a very short period, but do not include day nurseries or homes open for only a part of the year.

. . . .

The institutions covered . . . are mostly of the old type, where orphan or dependent children are gathered in a single building under the care of a private association. There are, however, 92 county homes (50 in Ohio, 17 in Indiana, and 7 in Connecticut); 18 state homes, several of these being for the orphans of soldiers or sailors; and 5 municipal homes. There are also 9 detention homes for dependent and delinquent children under the care of the juvenile courts, and a number of receiving homes for societies for the protection and care of children. The cottage system has been adopted by 168 homes.

The total number of homes reported, 1,151, represents an increase of 76 over the number reported in 1904. The following table arranges the states according to the number of institutions reported in 1910:

Institutions for the Care of Children, Distributed by States, 1910

State	Number	State	Number
United States	1,151	Colorado	14
		District of	
New York	154	Columbia	14
Ohio	106	Washington	14
Pennsylvania	105	Rhode Island	13
Illinois	64	Maine	12
California	56	South Carolina	19
New Jersey	50	Arkansas	9
Massachusetts	49	Nebraska	9
Indiana	47	West Virginia	8
Maryland	36	Alabama	7
Missouri	32	Florida	7
Virginia	32	Mississippi	6
Kentucky	25	Oregon	5
Louisiana	24	Delaware	5
Michigan	24	Oklahoma	4
Connecticut	23	Vermont	3
Georgia	22	Montana	3
Texas	20	Utah	2
Wisconsin	19	Arizona	2
Iowa	18	Idaho	2
New Hampshire	17	New Mexico	2
North Carolina	17	North Dakota	2
Kansas	16	South Dakota	1
Minnesota	16	Nevada	1
Tennessee	15	Wyoming	0

The rank of the states, as shown in this table, is determined by varying conditions. The high rank of New York and Pennsylvania is natural, in view of the size and peculiar type of their population; that of Ohio is due chiefly to its system of county homes, which also figures largely in Indiana and Connecticut.

Pacific division
New England division
Middle Atlantic division
East North Central division
South Atlantic division
Mountain division
West North Central division
West South Central division
East South Central division

The following statement showing the number of homes in proportion to the population in the different geographic divisions is of interest, especially as indicating the result of the activities of the charitable organizations on the Pacific coast, which place that division in the lead, above even the New England and Middle Atlantic divisions:

One home to every 55,162 inhabitants
One home to every 55,531 inhabitants
One home to every 62,511 inhabitants
One home to every 70,195 inhabitants
One home to every 80,229 inhabitants
One home to every 94,054 inhabitants
One home to every 122,504 inhabitants
One home to every 151,457 inhabitants
One home to every 152,907 inhabitants

Life in the asylums

---

1. Recollections of asylum life, ca. 1900

Henry W. Thurston, *The Dependent Child* (New York: Columbia University Press, 1930), pp. 70–71, 77–79.

The following statements were prepared in response to Thurston's request for the writers' experiences of and reaction to institutional life. Thurston identified the author of the first statement as "a national figure" who wished to remain anonymous.

Life for the typical boy in an institution at the time when I was in one, meant essentially shelter, the actual necessities in the way of clothes, and food which primarily served the purpose of preventing starvation, rather than scientific or, may I say, common sense nourishment. The attitude of those responsible for the institution was that the boys and girls were unfortunate objects of charity, and therefore should be content with whatever was done for them.

I demonstrated to the satisfaction of the Board of Managers where I was, based upon thirteen years of experience, that aside from the bread and milk bill of the institution it cost more and involved more labor and trouble to prepare the meals for the limited staff of employees than it did for the one hundred and eighty children in the institution. The limited educational program, covering primarily the "three R's," and the unwillingness to accept the opportunities of the public school system of education reflects the institution's attitude of not wanting to be bothered with having the children think too much of their education. While I managed, with the aid of friends from the outside, to break through this tradition and secure for myself and many others the privilege of going through public school from the fifth grade, it so greatly upset the routine of the institution as to make the practice very unpopular and very difficult for the boys and girls who were involved.

Well do I remember the amazement of the matron and the ridicule she heaped upon me when I ventured to urge a plan of giving me an opportunity of entering high school. Her question as to "who had ever heard of an orphan boy having a high school education" reflected the attitude of the institution towards me as an ambitious boy, as well as the others in the institution. For the most part the boys who were in the institution during my experience were indentured out to farmers or mechanics or others, without any obligation of adoption or relationship other than that of apprentice. Fortunately, for me, because of my lameness, I was not eligible, although very definite efforts were made to have me taken by a number of different people. I remember one, a tailor, who was made to believe that I could more than earn my board because of my experience in sewing. In other words, the institution did not mean opportunity to the boys. It did not mean preparing them for life's responsibilities and opportunities. It meant, primarily, treating them as so many paupers dependent upon charity, under conditions which would not tolerate anyone inquiring too closely as to whether everything was being done that should be done for the individual boy. What a difficult time those who indicated such interest had!

I do hope this will not be interpreted as a lack of appreciation for the good intentions of the lady managers and those who contributed to the support of the institution. Bless their souls! Their ignorance of actual conditions because they thought it more charitable to pay their fines rather than visit the institution; the lack of development of standards through conference and exchange of ideas on the part of institutional leaders; and the willingness of the general public to assume what was done in the name of charity is done wisely and scientifically, are some of the contributing causes for the lack of efficiency in the management of the institution, but no one should be permitted to challenge the sincerity and devotion of the good people who served as members of the Board of Lady Managers and those who contributed to the support of such institutions.

.   .   .   .   .

STATEMENT BY AN ORPHAN ASYLUM BOY WHO BECAME A SUPERINTENDENT
E. J. HENRY

When I was about four years old, my father was drowned in the North River, New York City. My mother was not a success in managing her financial affairs and in a short time she had nothing on which to support her family. She had a sister in Cleveland who was a business woman, but no housekeeper. This aunt induced my mother to come to Cleveland and keep house for her, while she looked after the store. My mother accepted and started west. We were soon settled in the new home. I was a normal, healthy boy and full of mischief, and my aunt was not accustomed to children. Naturally, I was in the way. My aunt, unknown to my mother, went to the officials of the institution and found that by paying a nominal sum, they would take care of me. When she first broached the subject my mother absolutely refused to have me go and threatened to take me and go elsewhere, but pressure was brought to bear and she finally consented to place me in the institution temporarily. Of course, after I had been placed, everything went lovely at home and I remained in the institution.

I was very fortunate in this, that the institution in which I was placed was one of the best of its kind, but I will never forget the impression that was made upon me when I entered that large building. It was no "Daddy-Long-Legs" affair, for in those days people had the means to provide only the necessities.

When my mother and I were waiting in the room where they received children, I was frightened, wondering what kind of a place it was, and what they were going to do to me, as I had had the threat held over my head that if I were not a good boy, I would be put in an institution; but to my surprise, the matron was very pleasant and it impressed me that she was interested in me more than she was in my mother, which is a big asset to any matron. After taking my name, my mother's and the address, she told my mother that she could see me once a week and that they expected her to clothe me.

I then went down a long unfurnished hall to a large room, and there I found about twenty-five boys, averaging from six to fourteen years. I was the smallest boy in the department. There were no furnishings in the room, except a small table and chair, in which the governess, as we called her, sat. The floors were of rather rough boards, but very clean. It was the boys' job to do the scrubbing. As I was the smallest boy, no doubt I had the sympathies of the others, so I did not have a very hard time, but my mischievous trend often got me into trouble.

The Board of Managers of the institution were exceptional women; their hearts were in the work and they not only gave financial assistance, but personal service, and it was my very great privilege to get acquainted with them. Being the smallest, they called me the baby of the family.

When night came, we all had to be in our places in the playroom. We took off our shoes and stockings and placed them in front of the bench where we sat, before which we knelt for our devotional exercises. Then we formed in line and marched upstairs to the dormitories.

There were ten iron beds in this dormitory; two boys slept in each bed. The governess in charge had her hands full until all had gone to sleep. This dormitory was a very plain room — no pictures on the walls and no furniture except the beds.

In the morning when the rising bell rang, we all jumped up, dressed and marched downstairs where we washed and combed our hair. The dining room and kitchen were in the basement. We marched down single file, to long, roughly made tables, such as you see on picnic grounds; we had wooden benches to sit on. There was mush and milk for breakfast. At noon we would have soup and bread and water, or once in a while chopped meat made into a gravy to put on our bread. At night we would have bread and milk — and only one helping. We growing boys were never satisfied when the bell tapped to get up from the table — there was no danger of stomach trouble from overeating in those days. I never held this against the management, as I know they were working hard to provide even what we had.

There was about the same number of girls and their ages ranged about the same as the boys'. Very strict discipline was maintained. The girls' playroom was across the hall from the boys' and the playgrounds were separated by a high board fence. Sometimes there would be weeks at a time, when brothers and sisters in the same building would have no chance to talk with each other. This was rather hard on many of the boys and girls, but the management thought that was the way it should be done.

There was no such thing as playground equipment in those days, but when we were turned loose in what we called the play-yard we got busy digging caves, building shacks, and in fact, we constructed our own equipment and it worked . . .

Our institution always believed in the public school. We never had a school in the building or on the grounds. Going to public school gave us a chance to mix with the girls and boys outside, although we always had a feeling that because we were in an institution, we were not entitled to the same privileges as those living in their own homes. I was in the institution about three years. They allowed me to go home to my mother for a couple of days about once in six months, as she was paying the large sum of $1.00 per week for my board. During that time, I saw many boys come and go. Some would come back and tell about the farm, the country, etc., and I thought it would be a wonderful thing if I could go into the country into a home, but my mother would not consent. The superintendent talked to her but she would not allow it, as in those days children were indentured or apprenticed and many of them legally adopted. Finally the superintendent took it up with me, thinking possibly I might have some influence with my mother. They told me of the beauties of the country, about the cows, horses, sheep and chickens, and naturally it "got me" and I coaxed and coaxed and finally persuaded my mother to allow me to go. She consented but with the understanding that I should not be given for adoption. Never will I forget the day I was called into the office and told by the superintendent that he had a very nice home for me in the country, with good religious people, a widow and her grown daughter. They wanted a little boy who could do the errands and small chores around the place and they thought that I was just the boy. It happened that at that time we had in the institution three or four very pretty puppies and one of them was given to me as a pet. I told the superintendent that if I could take my puppy, I would like to go, so he said he would write and ask if I could bring the pup. In a few days he told me that he had just received a letter asking him to send boy and pup. I was then ready to go.

---

2. Saturday at the orphanage, ca. 1910

Rudolph Reeder, *How Two Hundred Children Live and Learn* (New York, 1910), pp. 233–235, 239–247.

Reeder was superintendent of the New York Orphanage, Hastings-on-Hudson, New York. He asked children in the orphanage to write papers on the subject "How I Spent Last Saturday."

In the morning I had to put the breakfast on the table. After breakfast my work was to help in the kitchen until noon, then I helped get dinner. After dinner I washed the dishes and when I had finished that I took a bath. After bathing I made arrangements with William Kidd to go fishing and we went to Harriman's Dock, but we did not catch any fish. We then went to the Amackassin Dock. While there we learned how to catch eels in a different way than the way we had always caught them.

When we returned from fishing I played ball until our supper bell rang and I had to go in and put supper on the table for the boys in our cottage. After supper I washed the dishes quickly and then went out and played ball until the curfew rang. We then all came into the library to read books or magazines. At half past eight we went to bed.

Lawrence Welch
15 years
Rogers Cottage

In the early morning I dressed, went down stairs and moulded the bread I had made the night before into pans, after which I had my breakfast.

About seven o'clock I went over to the Administration Building and cleaned the offices, the Board room and the teachers' room. I finished this cleaning about eleven o'clock, went home and cleaned my own room. It was then time for dinner. After dinner I read to a few of the little children from a book called "Miss Minchin." About two o'clock a few of the girls and myself who sing in the choir went to rehearse some music at the M. E. Church in Yonkers. We arrived home at half past four and I soon became very much interested in watching a ball game played by our boys. At half past five I prepared supper. After supper I worked six arithmetic problems, after which I played games with the girls until it was time for me to go to bed.

Alva Stewart
16 years
Perkins Cottage

. . . . .

Saturday before breakfast I swept the basement and scoured the sink. Then I washed, cleaned my teeth well and went into the dining room where I ate my breakfast. After breakfast I made my bed, after which I went down stairs and emptied the dirt barrel and burned the rubbish. When I had put my barrel away and had finished my work in the cottage I put up a bird house in the bushes next to our cottage. I softened up and made level the dirt on our lawn. After dinner I went out into the pantry and helped wash the dishes. When the dishes were finished I had to go out and work again on the lawn with my pickax and shovel. I worked there until Mr. R——— asked for the horse that was carrying dirt to our cottage, then I was allowed to go out and play ball. When the game was finished I went into the cottage and read until the bell rang for supper. After supper I went out and played tag until the curfew rang when I came in and went to bed.

Albert Roche

12 years

Satterlee Cottage

On Saturday all the boys in our cottage have to work in the morning. After I had finished my regular work which consists in cleaning the matron's room, I waxed the library floor and then went to dinner. After dinner I polished the kitchen stove and helped the kitchen boy. Then I worked in the basement. My work for the day being done I went down in the woods to see how many wild flowers I could find. I found the blue violet, white violet, the May flower, wild geranium and another flower which I did not know. I then went out on the grounds and watched a game of ball between the boys of two of our cottages. Some of the older boys came along and picked sides for another game. I was chosen but happened to be on the losing side. I then went to supper.

After supper I played ball until the curfew rang.

Harry Kohout

14 years

Rogers Cottage

Saturday morning I got up early, prepared the yellow meal and made milk toast for breakfast. In the morning I made a loaf cake, baked bread and made rolls, also stewed fruit, made two loaves of brown bread, prepared the baked beans for the oven and got dinner ready which consisted of creamed codfish, mashed potatoes and bread pudding. In the afternoon Janet and I went to Yonkers to see Tessie. In the evening I played Parchesi and indoor baseball, after which I studied my Sunday School lesson.

Amelia Wingerter

15 years

Perkins Cottage

Before breakfast I dressed, washed and went down stairs. Then Harry Kohout asked me to help him with the library work. I helped him carry out the chairs. After this was done, I put the chairs back on the carpet in their right places. I also dusted the table and put the books on. Then I dusted the windows and the baseboards. Soon the library work was done. While I was putting the magazines and "Boys' Worlds" in order, I saw a nice story called "Where the Sea Flag Floats." I had time to read one chapter before the bell rang.

After breakfast I did my work with Henry Burkle, which was to sweep, polish, dust and put the beds in order. After I had my bath I went down to the basement to skate. Then I took off my skates and went up stairs to read the rest of the story which I had begun before breakfast. I finished that and then drew pictures. The first picture I drew was of a battle between Spain and America. Then the bell rang and I ate my dinner. After dinner I asked my cottage mother for my money to buy oranges. I bought some oranges and then went to the barn to see Rex harness the horses. He asked me if I would hold Harry, the horse, for him. After he hitched the horses to the carriage he asked me if I wanted a ride. After awhile I went over on the toboggin slide. I played there a good while. Then I went in to supper, after supper drew pictures and then went to bed.

John Tonkins

10 years

Rogers Cottage

.   .   .   .   .

In the morning before breakfast I dressed, washed and combed my hair. After breakfast I made my bed, swept and flanneled the floor, dusted the chairs and made the room look tidy. Then I went down stairs, dusted the office and flanneled the floor. I also dusted the chairs and tables and helped polish the floor in the parlor. I cleaned the cottage mother's bath room and washed out the basin and bath tub. After that I helped sweep and flannel the hall. After I had finished my work I went down stairs to the basement, washed and combed my hair and went to sewing class. Here I made a skirt for my doll. After dinner I helped upstairs in the attic and when the work there was finished I played for the rest of the afternoon. After supper I went up stairs, read and then went to bed.

> Ethel Hammonds
> 10 years
> Odell Cottage

In the morning after breakfast I made my bed and did my usual work. When this was finished I took my bath and then helped in the kitchen until dinner. After dinner I swept the dining room floor and set the table. Then I covered the floor of my rabbit cage with wire so if the rabbits burrowed they could not get out. I put in dirt from two to three inches thick. The afternoon passed so quickly that I had no time to play.

> Eugene Gostely
> 12 years
> Rogers Cottage

. . . . . .

We got up at six o'clock and I did my bathroom work before breakfast. At seven we had our breakfast. After breakfast I did my pantry work and when I had finished it I went outside and raked our road. At eleven o'clock I went fishing with one of the boys, but only caught nine fish. At twelve o'clock I went home for dinner. After dinner I did my pantry work again, and went fishing until four o'clock. We caught a hundred and seventeen Tommy Cods, the largest being over nine inches long and weighing about one half pound. At four o'clock I went to Hastings for the mail. On returning

to Bethune I spent the evening reading "Under Drake's Flag."

> Verne Jimmerson
> 15 years
> Bethune Cottage

. . . . . .

After breakfast I did my usual work, which consists of making my bed, scrubbing the basement steps and cleaning the garbage can. Then I got ready and went to the village and got the mail. After it was looked over, I delivered it. At ten o'clock I went to work out in the field, pulling up turnips and rutabagas until noon.

After dinner I helped to clean the store room, and received about a half dozen sweet apples for it. I then played baseball until three o'clock. I saw a wagon going down the hill and after receiving permission from the driver, some other fellows and I tumbled in the back of the wagon. Landing at the bottom of the hill, we jumped out and had a race down to the bathing houses. I came in last. We fished until supper time and caught about fifty fish, which we cleaned that night and had fried for Sunday morning breakfast. After supper I did my school work for Monday.

> Sumner Archer
> 14 years
> Satterlee Cottage

About half past five I awoke and went into the kitchen to prepare breakfast for the girls. The earliest part of the morning was spent in cleaning the kitchen. After dinner I dressed and got ready to take some of the younger girls for a walk. About two o'clock we started and returned home at five. Until supper time I buried my thoughts in the book called, "The Daughter of an Empress." After I had finished my evening work, which is to wash and dry the matron's dishes, I did a little sewing and then prepared my Sunday School lesson for Sunday. We played a few games and then retired.

> Ethel Rainbird
> 16 years
> Perkins Cottage

After finishing my usual work, which consisted of scrubbing and cleaning the kitchen, I went fishing. There were quite a number of boys fishing. I caught ten fish from about one o'clock until half past three. I stopped because when I was throwing out my fishing line one of the hooks caught in my hand and I had a hard time getting it out. I came up home and put a bandage on my hand and went out to play. When the supper bell rang I went into my cottage and helped get supper ready, after which I finished my work and studied some of my lessons.

> Charles Goodman
> 14 years
> Graham Cottage

Last Saturday before breakfast I fed my chickens. After breakfast I swept my cottage mother's rooms and the hall. I then helped her with other work until dinner time. After dinner I dried the dishes and set the table. About three o'clock in the afternoon I bought four oranges. I gave two to my brother and kept the rest for myself. About four o'clock I played ball. After playing for awhile I went to supper. After supper I studied my lessons and went to bed.

> Louis Maurer
> 13 years
> Satterlee Cottage

I picked dandelions and earned three cents. I played in the afternoon. I polished the hall and I slid down the slide.

> Octavius Bruce
> 8 years
> Satterlee Cottage

C. FOSTER HOME CARE

Placing-out vs. *institutions*

---

1. Is a poor home better than the best institution?

Charles L. Brace, "What is the Best Method for the Care of Poor and Vicious Children?" *Journal of Social Science,* II (1880), 93–98.

Brace's paper was read at a meeting of the American Social Science Association in Saratoga, New York, February 12, 1879. At that time the Children's Aid Society of New York City, of which Brace was secretary, had been in operation for twenty-five years and had sent 40,000 homeless or destitute children from New York City to foster homes in the country.

In this country, there was the greatest possible inducement for the "placing out" system, for Reformatories on the family plan, and for Farm Schools. The demand here for children's labor is practically unlimited. A child's place at the table of the farmer is always open; his food and cost to the family are of little account. A widespread spirit of benevolence, too, has inspired all classes — perhaps one of the latest fruits of Christianity — such as opens thousands of homes to the children of the unfortunate. The chances, too, of ill treatment in a new country, where children are petted and favored, and every man's affairs are known to all his neighbors, are far less than in an old. The very constitution, too, of an agricultural and democratic community favors the probability of a poor child's succeeding. When placed in a farmer's family, he grows up as one of their number, and shares in all the social influences of the class. The peculiar temptations to which he has been subject — such, for instance, as stealing and vagrancy — are reduced to a minimum; his self-respect is raised, and the chances of success held out to a laborer in this country, with the influences of school and of religion, soon raise him far above the class from which he sprang.

The cost, too, should have been a powerful inducement. A child's expense in an Asylum, Poor House, or Reformatory for a year, cannot be less than one hundred dollars, and may be much more; the placing out costs but a small sum.

Then, experience has taught that large numbers of poor and neglected children, placed in institutions together, deprave and injure one another. Their virtues, too, have an institutional flavor. They incline to be hypocritical; they lack in independence of character, and are weak under temptation, though outwardly respectable. Being supplied by machinery, they do not learn the small household arts — of making a fire, taking care of lamps, drawing water, cutting wood, and the like — which a poor man is compelled to practice. The most profitable branches of labor in this country for the workingman are agricultural; but the boy of the Asylum and Refuge has usually been trained in the poorest and most simple mechanical trades, such as shoe-pegging and similar occupations, and is comparatively unfitted for farm and garden work.

All these inducements should have led early in this country to the employment of the placing out plan for orphan, homeless and pauper children, and even for those sentenced for trivial offences, such as vagrancy and the like; while for the vicious and those who had committed criminal offences, Farm Schools and Family Reformatories should have taken the place of Congregated Reformatories and large Houses of Refuge.

The great principle at the base of modern criminal reform is *individual influence,* and the nearest approach possible to a natural system. The best influence on a poor child must come from a family life, and no asylum, however well

managed, can approach in healthful natural influences an average farmer's family.

.   .   .   .   .   .

If we . . . endeavor to answer the question, "What is the best method for the care of poor and vicious children," we should say,

(1.) All pauper children should be removed as soon as possible from Almshouses, and placed, if possible, at once in families, subject to a careful visitation and inspection by officials or local committees. The poor-house is no place for a child. Nor is there need of intermediate institutions, except for those of unsound mind and body. Under a good system, any pauper children who are of sound mind, and not defective in body, can be at once well placed in families.

(2.) The orphan, homeless, and street-wandering children of villages and cities should be temporarily gathered in asylums, homes for the friendless, lodging houses, and industrial schools, and, as soon as practicable, be distributed in homes and upon farms. No orphan asylum or home of the friendless should detain their inmates after they are ten or twelve years of age, unless they are of peculiarly unfortunate condition, physical or mental. For the expense of one child kept during a year, seven can be placed out; while the chances for improvement are far greater in the farmer's home than in the asylum . . .

(3.) Children who are habitually vicious or who have inherited very bad tendencies, or have an abnormal constitution, or have committed serious offences, should be placed in Farm Schools, arranged after the family plan. There should be small groups of children, say twenty or twenty-five in number, gathered in cottages, each group under a teacher or superintendent, who could learn the habits and characters of each and exert an individual influence upon them. These children should do all the work of the house, garden, and farm. Their great employments should be in the soil. Those are the labors most healthful, needed most in this country, and which in the long run repay the best . . .

As to the petty criminals among children — those convicted of vagrancy, petty thieving, disobedience of parents, quarreling and like offences — they should also be placed in Family Reformatories; but they need be kept there only for a short time, and then should be carefully distributed in families. This class of children are frequently no worse than the great body of those outside, and turn out very well under family influence. Asylum life (if long continued) only weakens their character. A certain amount, however, of punishment and discipline is very useful to them.

The principle lying at the bottom of all these suggested improvements, it cannot too often be said, is the necessity of *individual influence* on each child to be reformed, and the superiority of family life to any other influence in the improvement and reform of children.

DEBATE ON THE CARE OF CHILDREN

The reading of Mr. Brace's paper was followed by an animated discussion, during which Mr. W. P. Letchworth, President of the New York State Board of Charities, presided. The discussion was opened by Rev. T. K. Fessenden, of Farmington, Conn., who read a paper of some length, describing the Industrial School for Girls, at Middletown, Conn., of which he was one of the founders, and criticising some of the positions taken by Mr. Brace. Mr. Fessenden said that Mr. Brace's paper was of great excellence and showed a thorough acquaintance with the subject, but it did great injustice in some respects. He especially objected to the impression it might create that all institutional life is unnecessary and undesirable; that it is unnecessarily expensive and protracted too long; that institutions are failures and can be dispensed with. Mr. Fessenden's proposition was this: "That for viciously inclined poor children institutional life in properly organized and administered institutions is not only desirable, but absolutely the indispensable essential." He explained, however, that he meant small establishments on the family system, like the school at Middletown, of which he is one of the managers, and concerning which the Superintendent, Mr. Bond, would soon furnish the Department with information . . .

Ex-Governor Bagley, of Michigan, read a strong letter from Mr. L. P. Alden, Principal of the State Public School for Poor Children at the town of Coldwater in Michigan as follows:

MR. ALDEN'S LETTER

COLDWATER, MICH., Sept. 9th, 1879.

F. B. SANBORN, ESQ., Saratoga, N.Y.:

Dear Sir, — Your invitation to discuss the paper of Mr. Charles L. Brace, on "The Care of Poor and Vicious Children," was duly received, and I had hoped either to be present at your meeting or send you a paper embodying my experience in the placing out of children, and my present convictions on this subject. But my duties have been so pressing that, until today, I had forgotten that your Association met so soon. I have, therefore, time merely to outline my views.

1. I think that Mr. Brace has done a great thing for the city of New York in relieving it of so many incipient criminals, for which that city could well afford to erect him a monument. From all the testimony, however, that has reached me, it seems quite improbable that the West, where these children are sent, feels so grateful that it will contribute much towards its erection.

2. Without doubt, many children have been saved to good citizenship, through Mr. Brace's system, who would have grown up in vice and been lost, had they remained in the streets of New York, and certainly none have been made worse by diffusing them through the West.

3. But, nevertheless, I am very certain that a very much larger *percentage* of these children

would have been saved had they been placed in well regulated industrial institutions, where, for a term of months or years, they would have been placed under a course of instruction, training and discipline, such as the average country home cannot possibly secure.

4. I believe this, because I have received into this institution large numbers of children who had been repeatedly placed in homes, where they had failed, before coming to us, and who are now promising children, some of whom, after several years' training in this institution are now doing well in homes. Mr. Wright, of Normal, Ill., who has had twenty years' experience in placing out the children of the New York Juvenile Asylum, and looking after them when so placed, informs me that the children who have had some months or years of training in the institution, do much better as a rule, than those who come directly from the House of Reception, shortly after being taken from the streets . . .

Many of our children, who steadily improved all the time they were with us, and of whom we had high hopes, going out before their principles were confirmed, were not able to withstand the temptations of neighborhood association, and relapsed. If it is replied that the hot-house air of institutional life does not fit the child to endure the temptations of life as it is, I would reply that some plants must be nurtured for a time in the hot-house before they are strong enough to be placed out doors, and that many of these had not thriven in the house where they had been placed before entering our institution.

5. The great majority of even respectable well-to-do families are unfit to train up their *own* children, to say nothing of training up the children of others, many of whom are unattractive in appearance, have unpleasant habits and bad dispositions. If such children are taken by them, they are taken mainly for the labor they will perform, not from love or a high sense of duty towards these poor children; and while they may be kind enough people, and give them enough to eat and wear, they do not understand child-life, how to train and discipline it; and the children placed in such homes are quite likely, in many cases, to retrograde. I do not mean that all homes are such. There are many striking exceptions, but even where the people are fully competent to care for the children, and take them from a high sense of duty, as well as for the assistance they may receive, the neighborhood influences often thwart all their efforts, — often, I say, not always.

6. The difficulty of finding such homes as those spoken of above, where the child shall receive kind, wise, Christian care and instruction, is so great that they cannot be found for *car-loads* at a time. Only now and then one such can be found scattered over a large territory.

7. My experience in placing out children with all the care we can exercise in securing for them good homes, and with the help that the excellent county agency system, which Michigan has established, can give me, has led me to a very different conclusion from that which has generally been arrived at, viz.: that "a poor home is better than the best institution." I *know* that this is not so.

8. Finally, I am led to the conclusion that about twenty per cent. of the children that come to us, who are attractive in appearance, bright and free from bad or vicious habits, and for whom the best class of homes can be found, should be placed in such homes as soon as possible. I believe that they will be taken into the hearts of those who have them, and will be happier and better provided for than in any institution. But the remainder, who are towheaded, freckled-faced, disagreeable in appearance, not very apt to learn, with many bad habits, it may be, should remain for a time, from one to five years, in a good institution, if there is room for them there; and that more of them would be saved if they could be so retained. In a measure we can control this in our institution, and do send the most promising out first, of whom we have about 400 now in families, most of whom are doing fairly or well,

probably as well as those placed out by any other institution.

I have written this in great haste, and shall not even have time to read it over, as the mail is just going out. If you can make any use of this hasty outline, you are at liberty to do so or to destroy it.

Very respectfully,

L. P. ALDEN,
Supt. State Public School.

Governor Bagley, after reading this letter, said that he admired the skill and fidelity with which Mr. Alden managed the school at Cold-water, but dissented entirely from his opinions in regard to institution life for the children of the poor. He described the State institutions of Michigan, several of which, and this Public School in particular, had been built or com-menced while he (Mr. Bagley) was Governor of Michigan; but he thought, good as they were (and they were among the best in the land), that their work should be only temporary. They should prepare their inmates for family life, and should send out the children as soon as possible into good families. It was a poor home that was not better than the best institution. Citizens of the right stamp are not turned out from institutions; the only firm foundation of the Temple of Liberty is the family hearth-stone.

Mrs. Clara T. Leonard, of Springfield, Mass., thought institutions were like medicines, val-uable when there is disease, but not to be ad-ministered all the time. The tendency of late is too much to institutions. The Massachusetts school for poor children at Monson has been a great pauper mill. Reformatories are all more or less vicious, their moral atmosphere low. All persons are more or less controlled by the prevailing public sentiment of their community, and the influence of a home on children is much better than that of any institution. It is hurtful to have so many together who are nearly of an age. Children need association with older and more experienced people whom they can look up to. Local administration is the strength of our government, and each community should look after its poor children. The tendency of institutions is to pile up numbers, and regard that as the test of success. She agreed with Governor Bagley, that it was a very poor home, so far as poverty is concerned, that is not better than any institution.

Prof. Wayland would say amen to all Mrs. Leonard's remarks.

.   .   .   .   .

Mr. Sanborn, referring to a remark made in Mr. Alden's letter that few parents are fit to bring up their own children, inquired, "Who, then, is fit? who is sufficient unto these things?" He thought there was a profound fal-lacy in such remarks. Even a bad family, as we are apt to use the word "bad," is not al-ways the worst place for children; a great many good children have grown up in wretched fam-ilies. A child, upon the whole, gets more good than harm from its parents; if it were not so, how could the world continue to exist? We are not left to the wisdom and goodness of a few great men and saintly women, — the heart and purpose of the human race is really sound. "Everybody is wiser than anybody," says the proverb. He had known many bad people, but few grown persons who would purposely and disinterestedly labor to make a child worse. Yet in great establishments for children there are half-grown boys and girls who exercise a per-verse and depraved ingenuity in corrupting those younger than themselves. This is one of the many insidious perils of large reformatories. They spread a physical and moral contagion; the mortality in large establishments is com-monly greater than elsewhere, and the standard of morality is low. Routine and indifference prevail, and the minds of children become en-feebled and corrupted. He did not think so ill of the State Primary School at Monson as Mrs. Leonard did, but there was an evil tend-ency in all accumulations of poor and vicious children. They should be dispersed rather than congregated, as Dr. Howe and Mr. Letchworth had so well shown in former years.

Miss Elizabeth Peabody, of Concord, Mass., the sister-in-law of Horace Mann, and the patroness of kindergarten schools in America, closed the discussion. She thought nothing so important in education as to put a child on its own responsibility; it must learn not only obedience but independence. We would like to begin our lives over and avoid mistakes, but we cannot. We can, however, help children to avoid them

2. Benefits of asylum training and dangers of over-retention, 1886

Wiliam P. Letchworth, "Children of the State," *Proceedings* of the National Conference of Charities and Correction (1886), 142–145.

In respect to [homeless and destitute children], a difference of opinion exists as to whether they should be placed in families by adoption, indenture, or verbal agreement at once upon becoming dependent, or whether they should be permanently placed in asylums. On one hand, it is asserted that the simple routine of the asylum does not give sufficient variety of mental or manual employment for proper development; and that the children thus become institutionized, and graduate inefficient, lacking confidence in themselves to cope with the world in a struggle for a livelihood. On the other hand, it is as confidently held that, for lack of preparatory training, the children are not accepted in the most desirable homes, and consequently too frequently drift away into the vagrant and criminal classes. Extreme views in either direction I hold to be erroneous.

It seems evident that the family is the natural place for the true development of the child, especially when it is received as a member of the family, and allowed to participate in its industrial, social, and religious life, having its faculties stimulated and its ingenuity taxed by unexpected emergencies, its sympathies awakened by home-life troubles and trials, and its affections deepened through kindness and reciprocal confidence. But homes affording these opportunities, where real safeguards exist, are not always easily found; and when found, if the little applicant is ragged and dirty, ignorant of all decorum and profane in speech, he is not readily admitted, and some preparatory care and training are necessary to make him eligible to a desirable home. The asylum should be so organized as to effect this, and then the child should be given out. Many children do not need this preparation, and can be placed in the family at once.

These institutions for children are generally managed by benevolent ladies who give largely of their time and means. The child, upon entering the asylum, is at once the object of sympathetic interest, which, to a greater or less degree, extends to a protecting and helpful influence through life. All possible means are brought into requisition to improve and develop the little one's character. When ready for the family, great care is taken in making the selection where the proper moral influences will surround it and where it will have reasonable advantages of education. Visitation and inquiry after its welfare follow; and, in a rightly constituted asylum, records of its history are made through succeeding years. These I have found exceedingly interesting.

On one occasion, when, without previous notice, I was inspecting an asylum, in looking over the journal of its personal histories, I came upon the record of three children — a brother and two sisters — who had been placed in charge of the institution by order of the court. One parent was a criminal, the other licentious: both were notoriously dissipated. The boy and the girls had been placed in good families in different parts of the country. After a time, the parents demanded their children, claiming that they were able to support them. This demand was refused, and no information respecting their whereabouts granted; but the assurance was given that they were doing well.

The father and mother were told that, when the managers were convinced that the children would not be dishonored by parental association, then, but not till then, could they be permitted to see them. After I had finished reading the history, the lady secretary, who was showing me the books, turned and introduced an elderly, cleanly dressed, happy-looking couple seated in the office. They were the parents, just returned from the first visit which they had been permitted to make their children, then settled in homes of their own. In referring to the dates, I found that many long years had elapsed since these persons had been brought within the redeeming influences of this society; but all were saved, and a bond of Christian sympathy united parents and children.

However well-intentioned and faithful may be the efforts of a public official, he has not the same experience in the work as ladies connected with asylums. Critically responsible to the tax-payer, he is not so liberal in his expenditure for an outfit for the child, nor do the multiplied duties of his position permit his devoting the necessary time to this important work; and frequent changes in office render it impracticable long to continue visitation of these wards.

But the tendency of all asylums is to retain their children too long. We have examples of institutions that were established under the name of temporary homes, for the sole purpose of effecting a rapid transition from a condition of dependence to family life, which, in a few years, lapsed into inactivity in placing out, and eventually became permanent homes for children. Among the temptations to over-retention is a pride in numbers. After much drilling, the children become proficient in their exercises, and there is a reluctance to be continually breaking up the band that makes the asylum inmates, as a whole, appear attractive; and there are all the while growing personal attachments between the children and those connected with the asylum, which it is hard to sunder. Thus it sometimes happens, that, when the best family homes are open and waiting, the managers resist the attempts to place out their wards. Again, when the payment by municipalities or counties for the child's maintenance is sufficient to meet the entire cost of support, or, as is sometimes the case, afford a small profit, there is a pecuniary inducement to retain children.

There is, however, a class of girls that find their way into the orphan asylums, who, while not feeble-minded, are, nevertheless, so weak in character as to require constant guidance; and it is therefore better they should be retained in an institution until they reach maturity. In some of the asylums, after passing through a course of advanced industrial training, they graduate into the world under the protecting influences of the social organizations that are fostered by sisterhoods engaged in the asylum work.

The result of retaining children so long within the institution is, that the asylums in some of the municipalities have greatly expanded, and their numbers increased to an extent that has caused complaint from tax-payers, as also from the benevolent who contribute to their support. Another serious consequence is that of overcrowding, which, in some of the larger institutions, has resulted in the prevalence of ophthalmia to an alarming extent. Thus there is danger of this otherwise excellent system being crushed by its own weight. It is but just to state, however, that, in very many of the asylums, the population changes upon an average once a year, some of the children being placed out very soon after admission. Where there are so many dependent children needing the very best care and help that can be secured for them, we must see that none are deprived of the benefits of asylum training because of over-retention. It would seem better that ten children should enjoy the privileges of the asylum for one year each than that one child should remain during the period of ten years. Notwithstanding the dangers referred to, in my opinion, as children become dependent, the best course is to place them immediately in charge of benevolent societies organized for their care and protection, and at the same time to bring greater activity into the placing-out branch of asylum work. This activity could be promoted in localities where the institutions are largely supported by appropriations from municipalities and counties, by public authorities offering a moderate premium for every dependent child provided, within a given period, with a good home.

3. "Our experience with farmers has not been satisfactory," 1885

Lyman P. Alden, "The Shady Side of the 'Placing-out System'," *Proceedings* of the National Conference of Charities and Correction (1885), 203–205.

Alden was superintendent of the State Public School, Coldwater, Michigan.

It is well known by all who have had charge of the binding out of children that the great majority of those who apply for children over nine years old are looking for cheap help; and while many, even of this class, treat their apprentices with fairness, and furnish them a comfortable home, a much larger number of applicants do not intend to pay a *quid pro quo,* but expect to make a handsome profit on the child's services, and, if allowed one, will evade, as far as possible, every clause in the contract, — furnishing poor food, shoddy clothing, work the child beyond its strength, send it to school but a few months, and that irregularly, and sometimes treat it with personal cruelty, though this, in a thickly settled country, is not likely to occur so frequently. I could fill this paper with instances in proof of this that have come under my personal observation, in an experience of eight years as superintendent of the Michigan State Public School. These people can always get good indorsements. That my experience may not appear singular, I have taken considerable pains, by correspondence and otherwise, to ascertain the views of old and successful workers in this field, in the East and West; and I find remarkable unanimity of opinion on this point, so far as I have investigated.

Miss Susan Fenimore Cooper, of Cooperstown, N.Y., whose labors for poor children are distinguished, and make her an authority, says:—

Our chief difficulty lies with the families who receive the children when they leave us. In many instances, very respectable people, who have brought the best of references, seem to have no judgment in training children. They are careless of the child's best interests, allow it to associate with evil companions, to run wild, and to read pernicious books and papers.

Mrs. Virginia Ohr, for about fifteen years superintendent of the Illinois Soldiers' and Sailors' Orphans' Home, says: —

Our experience in placing children in homes is very unsatisfactory. I find that the greater number of applicants for children have no other aim in view than to secure cheap help.

Says the committee for placing out children, of the Cleveland Protestant Orphan Asylum, "The larger proportion of homes offered we are compelled to decline." Mrs. Mary E. Cobb, superintendent of the Wisconsin Girls' Industrial School, and one of the most experienced and successful workers in this country, says, "Many more must be rejected than accepted, even when the applications come indorsed according to the strictest rule."

Says A. H. Fetterolf, President of Girard College for Orphan Boys: "Our experience with farmers has not been satisfactory. They are not considerate for the child's welfare, caring only to use him for their profit."

S. W. Pierce, for eighteen years superintendent of the Iowa Soldiers' Orphan Home and Home for Indigent Children, says, "The average family with us wants a child for what they can get out of it in the way of work."

Says Rev. E. Wright, of Normal, Ill., agent for the New York Juvenile Asylum, which during the past thirty years has placed out in Illinois, with the greatest possible care, 4,285 children: —

The beneficence of an apprenticing agency is not attested by the number of children which it disposes of. It is not quantity, but quality, that determines the real excellence of its work. It would be an easy matter for us to place a thousand children annually in homes, in the Western States, if nothing more than that were required. But, of all the outrages that have been perpetrated in the name of Christian charity, none is more reprehensible than that of leaving helpless children without recourse in such situations. That this is not an extravagant assertion could be proved from the experience of this agency during almost any single week of its history.

Now, all this does not prove, nor is it intended to prove, that many good homes cannot be found for children, if proper care is taken. I know that thousands of such homes have been found, where the children are treated with affectionate consideration. But it does prove, I think, that the great majority of those who apply for children should never have them, and that great caution and discrimination should be used in selecting homes. It does prove that, if institutional care for children, where specialists are employed, who are constantly under the eye of the public and of official boards and visiting committees, is not so perfect as it should be, it is still more difficult to secure uniformly wise and kind treatment of children where they are placed in so many different families, scattered, perhaps, all over a State, which, with the best system of supervision practicable, cannot be visited, usually, oftener than once in each year. It does prove that a glamour has been thrown over the work of placing out children, which should be dispelled. It takes something more than a farm of a hundred and sixty acres and well-filled granaries to constitute a good home. There may be all of these, and yet the elements of a good home be entirely wanting. The man may be vulgar, profane, intemperate, penurious, or tyrannical. Or the mistress may be slovenly, sickly, peevish, and an eternal scold. Or, if the parents are all right, there may be disagreeable, overbearing, hateful children; and a child placed in such a home would be living in the antipodes of a heaven on earth, while those who bound it out might complacently imagine that its life was a happy one.

---

4. Institutions praised, placing-out endorsed, 1898–1899

T. M. Mulry, "Report of the Committee on Neglected and Dependent Children," *Proceedings* of the National Conference of Charities and Correction (1899), 167–168.

Thomas Maurice Mulry (1855–1910), a prominent Roman Catholic layman, was active in the Society of St. Vincent de Paul, a member of the New York State Board of Charities, and a founder of the Catholic Home Bureau for Dependent Children. For another section of the report see below Chap. II, sec. A, Philanthropic experiments, doc. 3.

The last [1898] Conference of Charities and Correction held in New York City was probably the most representative, as it certainly was the most fruitful, in results upon the subject of child-saving. While those taking part in the discussions held positive views, there was a spirit of toleration; and the interchange of ideas and the moderate expressions of views proved that the differences of opinion were not so great as had been at first imagined. The preponderance of opinion seemed to be in favor of placing the children in good homes, where such could be found and the circumstances warranted such action being taken.

The good work accomplished by the institutions in the past was fully recognized, as well as the fact that the institution has an important place to fill in the future on the disciplinary and educational lines and the care of those children who are prevented by circumstances from being placed in homes. It was said that many children are kept longer than necessary in the institution, because, having no relatives, there were no persons to claim them; and such children it was thought, might well be placed in good homes, provided the families were of the same religious faith as the child. The earlier they are placed in such families, the better it is for the child, as the motive which induces one to take a child of tender years is apt to be more disinterested than when they are old enough to be utilized as help.

The improvement in the industrial training of the children during the past few years has been of great benefit to the inmates of institutions, and has resulted in sending large numbers of them out into the world well equipped for the battles of life.

The finding of family homes for children has been taken up enthusiastically and with excellent success in many localities. In New York State the Catholic Home Bureau has been recently organized and incorporated. Its object is to place dependent Catholic children in homes. On its board of management are gentlemen connected actively with the different Catholic charitable societies and institutions. The various institutions have shown their interest in the new organization by placing in its possession the names and conditions of the children who are fit subjects for placing in family homes. The cordial support received from them and from the public generally proves the opportuneness of this movement and the material help it will be in solving the problem of how best to care for dependent children.

This assistance and encouragement is by no means confined to Catholics. On the contrary, the help extended and suggestions given by the various societies associated in the same kind of work have been most valuable in advancing the new bureau.

One drawback to the placing-out system in the past was the disregard, in frequent cases, of the religious belief of those placed, which resulted in children being sent to homes of a different religion from that in which they were baptized.

This naturally prevented the unanimous support so essential to the permanent success of every movement, but the difficulty has been overcome in most instances by providing that children be placed in homes of their own religious faith.

The placing-out system needs the most careful supervision; and those interested in the work realize how prone to selfishness people are, and that many wish the children only for the work they can obtain for them. There is generally a demand for boys and girls from twelve to fourteen years of age. The main difficulty is to find homes for children from seven to eleven years of age, and in large communities it will be found difficult to secure desirable homes for all dependent children. This does not, however, mean that any effort should be spared to place as many children as possible in good homes; and this committee is strongly in favor of renewed activity in this direction. It is the opinion of some interested in the work that the payment of board in families would facilitate securing good homes for all children to be placed out.

---

5. Influence of institutional life upon the Negro, 1909

Booker T. Washington, "Destitute colored Children of the South," *Proceedings of the Conference on the Care of Dependent Children Held at Washington, D.C., January 25, 26, 1909* (Washington, D.C., 1909), pp. 114–117.

I heard a gentleman state a few moments ago that the State of Massachusetts alone pays over $600,000 annually toward the care and support of the dependents in that State. Why, my friends, I guarantee that the most careful and rigid examination into the facts would reveal that which I think is true — that that is more money than is spent for the dependent negro children in the whole southern country.

I think you will find that the latest statistics show that in the whole United States there are about 31,000 negro dependent children in institutions of all kinds. The total negro population of Alabama is about 900,000, and out of the total population of 900,000 I find that, according to our most recent reports in Alabama, there are 301 children in institutions for the care of the dependent — 301 out of a total population of about 900,000.

In fact, this subject of the care of dependent children with us who reside in the rural districts of the South is so new and so little discussed that I confess I never looked into it very carefully from your point of view until after I received the invitation to come to this meeting. When I received the invitation I said at once that I would look about me and see what was going on in my own county — in Macon County — which is largely a rural and farming county. On making an examination I found that there were 23,000 people of my race in that county. I went at once to an institution about 9 miles from our institute, for the care of dependents of both races in that county, and I made an examination. I went to the superintendent, who had been in charge of that institution for eight years, and got what information I could from him.

In the first place, I found that during the past four years there had been an average of only six dependents of any age in this institution of my race — only six in four years of any age. I found, when I made my visit last week, that there was not a single negro dependent of any age in that institution.

The county authorities there will admit the members of my race fairly and they will extend to them the same care in Macon County that they will extend to the people of their own race. The dependents of my race are not kept out by reason of any special discrimination

against them or because they are not wanted. I will explain to you later why they are not there.

I found, further, that not only was there not a single dependent there at the present time, but I found by investigating the record that during the past eight years there had been in that institution only one negro child, and the superintendent told me that this child went there because his grandmother was taken there and the little fellow cried and he was humored to the extent of being taken there with her. As soon as his grandmother died the superintendent said that some strange woman came there and begged the privilege of taking that child home and making him a part of her family. Since that time we have not had a negro dependent in that institution. Remember, that is out of a total negro population of 23,000 in our county.

You may suggest that this is an unusual condition, existing perhaps by reason of the influence of the Tuskegee Institute. That may have something to do with it; but very little, I think. I hope that our good friend who is the leader of this movement in Alabama will speak to you about this subject, and I am quite sure that he will bear out the statements I am trying to emphasize.

You will find that in other counties where there is no Tuskegee Institute much the same conditions prevail.

This condition exists because, as you will find, the negro, in some way, has inherited and has had trained into him the idea that he must take care of his own dependents, and he does it to a greater degree than is true, perhaps, of any other race in the same relative stage of civilization. Why, my friends, in our ordinary southern communities we look upon it as a disgrace for an individual to be permitted to be taken from that community to any kind of an institution for dependents. [Applause.]

I do not know of any case in my own experience where the parents of children have died but what within a few hours, almost before the breath has passed from the body of the parent, one neighbor, sometimes two, three, and sometimes half a dozen have appeared on the scene and begged the privilege of taking this child and that child into their own families. You will find the same to be true in reference to sick people and to the unfortunate of all classes. They are cared for by individuals in the community. They are cared for through their churches. We have not got so far along yet in civilization that we do not think it is a part of the duty of the church to take care of the sick people of the community. [Applause.]

.   .   .   .   .   .

It is only as the negro is brought into contact with an artificial civilization and newer surroundings, as he leaves his normal, regular, and best life in the South, in my opinion, and comes into contact with the artificial life of the city and especially with the artificial life of your northern cities, that this condition is changed.

.   .   .   .   .

But, my friends, those of you who have the privilege and opportunity, and many of you will have the privilege and opportunity, of observing my race and the children of my race, I beg of you to exert that influence in keeping the negro on the soil, in keeping him close in touch with Mother Earth, in keeping him out of contact with the temptations and complications and the artificial influences of your large-city life. Just in proportion as that is done you will find that many of these problems you are discussing in such an interesting manner will not disturb you so far as the negro race is concerned.

The very minute a negro leaves the South and comes to a place like Washington, Baltimore, or New York he hears, in some roundabout way, that there is a fund somewhere, which grows in importance and amounts up into the thousands of dollars. He gets the idea that this fund is meant to support all the poor people, and the hard-working people, and every person who gets into trouble, and he

usually gets his part of that fund. He knows how to get it, and in proportion as he is brought into contact with this artificial life, this new life, in that proportion he loses the spirit of simplicity, the spirit of helpfulness which he had before he came into the city environments.

I repeat that, in the negro's present condition of inexperience and lack of strength in many matters, that you should use your influence, wherever you can, to keep him on the soil in the rural districts, and especially in the rural districts of our southern country.

As I have suggested, the negro has been putting into practice the very ideas you have been emphasizing all through this afternoon and evening. He has been putting into practice more largely than any other race in America in the same relative stage of civilization, the principles which you have been talking about to-day.

Now as to the influence of institutional life upon the negro: I strongly advocate, as I have already suggested, the keeping of the individual negro child in the individual family. I have had some experiences in connection with asylums of various kinds and with institutions that are organized for the care of dependent children of my race, and my observation and experience, so far as it concerns my people, is this: I find that in many cases the child would be better off if left to chance to get into some home than he is in the average orphan asylum. We have at Tuskegee many individuals and many students who come to us from the orphan asylums. We used to have more than we have now; but we have learned something in recent years that we did not know then, so that we have still fewer now. We have looked with suspicion upon any boy or girl that comes to us from an orphan asylum. In fact, I happen to know of a case with reference to one of our most widely advertised orphan asylums. One morning, when I happened to be in this institution, I learned that a previous night a number of the boys had got together and broken open the cupboard and got out the pies; the pies had disappeared overnight. The next morning

New Hampshire Orphans' Home, Franklin, New Hampshire, 1903.

Orphan Girl, 1908. Photograph by Lewis W. Hine.

the good woman — she was one of these good-hearted creatures — called these boys in and had special prayer with them. [Laughter.]

The difficulty is that the large proportion of the people who organize these institutions for the care of negro children are wanting in executive business ability. They are good people, sentimental people, and the best people on earth, and they want to do everything for everybody. Those are the people who usually start an orphan asylum first of all. In many other cases I have found that many of these institutions are started, primarily, with a view to finding a job for a superintendent or somebody else, and not with a view to helping the negro child. [Applause.]

And so in this way or that way I have learned, my friends, to become very suspicious of the average orphan asylum, organized and built up for the support of the members of my race. It pays far better to use our time and our influence and our money, if we have it, to keep the negro in the country, in the natural environment, until he gets the strength and experience which has made your race great and strong and useful.

6. The role of personality in institutions and foster homes

Reeder, *How Two Hundred Children Live and Learn,* pp. 194–200.

Of all the working forces which make or mar the child's future well-being, the personality of those in close touch with him far outranks every other influence.

If the placing out system has any great advantage over institutional care, it will be on account of the superior personalities with whom the child comes in contact, or a larger share in association with these personalities than is possible in the institution. On the other hand, if the institution is so managed that the children come into intimate relations with adult characters who are strong, sympathetic, intellectually alert, and socially, morally and spiritually uplifting, it ceases to be a mere abiding place where the creature comforts only are provided, and becomes a school home from which the children go forth better prepared to make their own way in the world than are most of those set adrift from their parental homes at the same age.

Wherever the dependent child is, whether in a foster home or an institution, he will make but little headway if left to himself and his environment. He must have the society, or better, comradeship, as well as the instruction of older people who are interested in him. He must be known and trained according to his personal and individual characteristics and not merely by a name or number. Institutionalism, whether it exists in the form of congregate housing or the cottage system — for it may exist in either — is opposed to this recognition of the child's individuality. It is rote, routine and dead-levelism. It is law, coercion and suppression. It is praying by rote, singing by rote, repeating portions of the Bible by rote. It is walking in silent rows, eating in silent rows, sleeping in silent rows. It is religion without personality, discipline without individuality, and play without initiative.

But it is as easy to find defects in family training as in institutional. The attempt to escape their God-given responsibility by many parents now-a-days is the chief cause for juvenile delinquency, of well-filled protectories, reformatories and so-called "industrial schools."

One parent in a neighboring state gained considerable notoriety through the daily press a short time ago by claiming a new idea for relieving parents of the burden of personally looking after and associating with their children. The plan proposed was the building of a bungalow near the parental home in which the six boys of the family, all under sixteen years of age, were to live. They were not to enter their parents' home except on invitation. Such a scheme implies that the home cannot or will not adapt itself to the needs of the natural boy, or else the natural boy must necessarily make himself a nuisance in the ordinary home. Both of these implications may be true, and probably they are true in many of even our well-to-do homes, where the parents are willing to give their children everything except their greatest gift, and that which the child most needs — themselves.

The deepest meaning of home is associated with children; with their freedom and spontaneity, their sunshine and shadows, their joys and tears; with the roistering, rollicking exuberance of boys, and the gentler play-loving nature of girls. It is these things that enrich and endear home life to both parents and children, taking away from it the boarding-house atmosphere. Children can receive from their parents the heritage of culture to which they are entitled only by living with them. The best that has come to parents and teachers through heredity, education and experience, can be passed on to their children, not by formal instruction, but through comradeship and intimate association with them in all of the relations and interests which enlarge and enrich home life.

The most precious thing you can give a child is yourself. Wise parents will enter into the games and pastimes of their children, will swim and skate and coast with them, will read and stroll and play games with them, will plan and build and sympathize with them in their struggles, in their failures, and in the training of their pets.

But all this means the spending of a great deal of time with one's children. Outside of the time required for providing the means of support for the family, I know of no better way, however, in which parents may employ their time. It is not only the child that is benefited; it builds character in the parents as well, and it keeps them young. The period of childhood is all too short to those parents who enter into the spirit of child life. The time will come too soon when the absence of dolls, toy dogs and tin soldiers, scattered about the room — even the family sitting room — and the barrenness of the corners and closets where bats and balls, rackets and mitts were wont to lie, will bring loneliness to the heart and moisture to the eyes. Our boys and girls are children but once, and childhood days are short.

In both the placing out system and in institutional care of children, too little attention has been paid to the personality of those responsible for them. Those who find homes for children frequently exhibit photographs of the home and its environment, pictures of the child driving a pony cart followed by a pet dog, etc. A photograph of the foster parents accompanied with a character sketch and a report of hours a day or week spent with the child would be worth more than a whole herd of ponies and dogs, dear as these pets may be to the ordinary child. It really makes little difference whether the foster home is a beautiful house surrounded by lawns and gardens with shade trees and piazzas, serpentine walks and rose bushes, or just a plain four-walled structure at the crossroads of a treeless prairie where the monotonous expanse of broad-acred grain fields meet. Love of home, sweetness and light, and the development of character, may go with either, provided, the personalities are there in which these qualities live and grow. Daily association and companionship with a strong, sympathetic and lovable character is a brief but comprehensive description of a happy condition of child life. The child that has such a heritage for his early years needs little else, and he that lacks it will be little the better off for anything else he may have.

Placement procedures of the New York Children's Aid Society

---

1. The work of the society debated, 1879

Proceedings of the National Conference of Charities and Correction (1879), 157–158.

J. W. Skinner, superintendent of industrial schools of the city of New York, reported in reference to the work in the Children's Aid Society in that city. He said that last year Mr. Brace placed out in homes of the West 4,000 children, sheltered 14,234 in lodging-houses, and educated 9,000 in the schools. His assistants went through the city collecting children into schools (giving food and clothes when needed), and six lodging-houses, where food and shelter were furnished at nominal rates to the children engaged in street trades. Mr. Brace long ago organized a system of Western transportation, sending the children at first to Indiana, then to Illinois, and now to Kansas. The boys liked it, and did well. In all, forty-eight thousand children had been sent out from New York. Agents were sent out occasionally to see how these little emigrants were getting on. Every two weeks a party of from fifty to one hundred children left New York for the West. This was checking pauperism and crime. The society was organized in 1853. In 1860 the commitments of youth for vagrancy and small crimes numbered 5,880. The corresponding commitments in 1876 were 1,666. In 1863 1,133 girls were committed for petit larceny, and in 1876 the number was reduced to 496. Local committees were organized in advance in towns where the boys and girls were to be distributed; and this committee attended to sending the children into families, and maintained an oversight over them. Besides, Mr. Fry of Chicago, the general agent of the society, devoted himself to looking after the boys. The children thus sent out were not indentured.

Dr. Byers thought Mr. Brace dumped carloads of children in the West, where the people took them in as a matter of humanity, but without that solicitude for their real welfare that ought to be provided. The reduction of juvenile crime in New York might be attended by an increase of juvenile crime in the West.

Mrs. Louisa Rockwood Wardner said, that in a part of the poorhouses of this State, outside of Chicago, there were over 700 children. In Chicago there were 1,200 children needing immediate attention. She thought the people of the West should find homes for their own poor children before they furnished homes for the 10,000 children sent from New-York City to the State of Illinois. She was satisfied that these children did not stay long in the homes where they were first placed. Many of them became tramps.

2. Evaluation of the Society's work in Minnesota, 1881–1884

Hastings H. Hart, "Placing Out Children in the West," *Proceedings* of the National Conference of Charities and Correction (1884), 143–150.

I am to speak of the work of the most extensive and important children's charity in the United States; namely, that of the Children's Aid Society of New York City. As one branch of its work, it places in homes some 3,500 children annually. I have been asked by the chairman of the Committee on Child-saving work to present to the Conference the results of an inquiry into the placing of children in Minnesota under the auspices of this society . . .

A little more than a year ago, the attention of our board was drawn to the criticisms of the emigration work of the Children's Aid Society, which have arisen at intervals for several years past. Except a small number several years ago, Minnesota has received but 340 of these children, all within three years past. This is a comparaively insignificant number in a great State; but it appears that Michigan, Illinois, and Indiana have received 4,000, 5,000, and 6,000 respectively. Should Minnesota receive as many in proportion to her area as Michigan, she would have 6,000; if as many in proportion as Indiana, 15,000. Five counties in our State have received at the rate of one child for every ninety-three inhabitants. Even with our present sparse population, if the State were colonized at the same rate, it would give us over 10,000. In view of such possibilities, it became a question of vital importance whether the charges brought against this immigration were true. Gentlemen interested in public and private charities in various parts of the West and South have stated that many vicious and depraved children are sent out by the society; that they are hastily placed in homes without proper inquiry, and are often ill-used; that the society, having disposed of the children, leaves them to shift for themselves without further care; and that a large proportion turn out badly, swelling the ranks of pauperism and crime.

Examination of the records did not solve the question. The friends of the society and its critics seemed involved in hopeless contradiction, each party quoting many individual instances in support of their opinions. It did not appear that any comprehensive inquiry had ever been made into the history of the children sent to any one State (at least, of late years). The nearest approach to it was an inquiry, made by agents of the society in Wisconsin in 1882, tracing about 100 out of 1,000 placed in that State. The question naturally arose, What about the other 900? When four or five thousand children are scattered in a State, they soon become so far absorbed in the body politic as to render complete statistics impossible. It was thought, however, that, with so small a number as we have in Minnesota (only 340, all received within three years), information might be gathered sufficiently full to yield valuable figures. The attempt has been made, with only partial success; yet it is hoped that the results are not valueless. Six of the seven counties receiving children were visited by the secretary about a year ago, and four have been revisited within the past few weeks. Lists of the children were obtained, careful inquiry was made as to each case, and a considerable number of the children were visited in their new homes. The results were carefully tabulated, after correspondence with the chairman and most active members of the local committees appointed by the society in the seven counties, and a full correspondence with Secretary Brace and Agent Mathews of the society.

The inquiry will be grouped under four heads: —

First. Is it true that many vicious and depraved children are sent out? A few such were found, but there is no evidence that their selection was intentional. Six are known to have committed offences against the laws, of whom I shall speak later. Nine have been sent back by the local committees as incorrigible; and, in such cases, the society has promptly taken charge of them, paying all expenses. Three or four depraved adults have come to the State under the auspices of the society.

Second. Are children hastily placed in homes without proper inquiry, and are they often ill-used? Some five or six cases of abuse are reported. The society has recently prosecuted one case and is reported to be about to prosecute another. A third case was prosecuted, I believe, by the boy himself. In two or three less glaring instances, the children were transferred to suitable homes. Some false stories of abuse have been traced back to gossips or jealous neighbors.

To the first count of this indictment, however, — namely, the hasty placing of children without proper investigation, — we fear that the society must plead guilty. The plan is as follows: A representative of the society first visits the town where distribution is to be made, and secures three leading citizens to act as a volunteer committee, pass upon applications for children, and take general charge of the matter. A notice is published in local newspapers inviting applications and announcing the day of arrival and distribution. I was myself a witness of the distribution of forty children in Nobles County, Minnesota, by my honored friend, Agent James Mathews, who is a member of this Conference. The children arrived at about half-past three P.M., and were taken directly from the train to the court-house, where a large crowd was gathered. Mr. Mathews set the children, one by one, before the company, and, in his stentorian voice, gave a brief account of each. Applicants for children were then admitted in order behind the railing, and rapidly made their selections. Then, if the child gave assent, the bargain was concluded on the spot. It was a pathetic sight, not soon to be forgotten, to see those children and young people, weary, travel-stained, confused by the excitement and the unwonted surroundings, peering into those strange faces, and trying to choose wisely for themselves. And it was surprising how many happy selections were made under such circumstances. In a little more than three hours, nearly all of those forty children were disposed of. Some who had not previously applied selected children. There was little time for consultation, and refusal would be embarrassing; and I know that the committee consented to some assignments against their better judgment. There was similar speed in Freeborn, Rock, and Watonwan Counties, and, I presume, elsewhere. In Watonwan County, only six days intervened between the published notice and the arrival of the children, leaving no time for investigations by the committee. The committee usually consists of a minister, an editor, and a doctor, a lawyer or a business man. The merchant dislikes to offend a customer, or the doctor a patient; and the minister fears to have it thought that his refusal is because the applicant does not belong to his church. Thus, unsuitable applications sometimes succeed. Committee men and officers of the society alike complain of this difficulty. The evil is aggravated by the fact that, while the younger children are taken from motives of benevolence and uniformly well treated, the older ones are, in the majority of cases, taken from motives of profit, and are expected to earn their way from the start. The farmers in these counties are very poor. I speak within bounds, when I say that not one

in five of those who have taken these children is what would be called, in Ohio or Illinois, well-to-do. To my personal knowledge, some of them were taken by men who lived in shanties and could not clothe their own children decently. A little girl in Rock County was placed in a family living on a dirt floor in filth worthy of an Italian tenement house. A boy in Nobles County was taken by a family whose children had been clothed by ladies of my church, so that they could go to Sunday-school. I have seen other similar instances. Probably as many failures have resulted from unsuitable homes as from the fault of the children. We believe that the society should employ responsible, paid agents to investigate deliberately all applications beforehand.

Third. Does the society, having disposed of the children, leave them to shift for themselves, without further care? No, not in Minnesota. The agents of the society have revisited the counties where children are placed, — most of them repeatedly. These trips, being hurried, have not permitted visits to all of the children, special attention being given to urgent cases. Cases of incorrigibility reported to the society have received prompt attention, — homes being changed or the child removed from the State, as seemed best. Letters of inquiry are sent by the society to the children and employer, and letters addressed to the society are promptly answered. Local committees were judiciously selected, and their (very small) bills of expenses incurred for children have been promptly paid. I am informed by Agent Mathews that the society employed a local agent in Rock County and vicinity during the past year, and paid him for his services.

This supervision is inadequate, for reasons which I will explain. The society expressly withholds guardianship from those taking children, itself retaining it except in a few cases of adoption. Mr. Mathews tells me that the society understands that the committees stand *in loco parentis;* but the committees have no legal guardianship, nor do they usually attempt to exercise it. To avoid mistakes, I quote from

Secretary C. L. Brace's book, *The Dangerous Classes of New York,* p. 243: "The children are not indentured, but are free to leave, if ill-treated or dissatisfied; and the farmers can dismiss them, if they find them useless or otherwise unsuitable. This apparently loose arrangement," he adds, "has worked well." Mr. Brace said before this Conference in 1876 (see *Proceedings,* p. 139): "The employers agree to send the children to school, and, of course, to treat them kindly. Beyond this there is no agreement, and no indenture is made out. The relation is left much to the good feeling of both parties." Agent Trott, in the St. James (Minnesota) *Journal* of Aug. 26, 1882, says: "Applicants are expected to treat the children as their own in the matter of schooling and training. Neither is bound by writing; and the society reserves the right to remove the child, at any time, for what may be considered a just cause." Under these conditions, the present system of supervision works well with young children and tractable older ones; but it fails with the restless and intractable, who need supervision. The employer gives no security for redeeming his promises, and may discharge the child without warning, "if found *useless* or otherwise unsatisfactory." A prosperous farmer in Watonwan County worked a boy all summer, and turned him out ragged just before winter, apparently to save his board. He found him "useless," and there was no remedy. Employers agree to "treat them as their own in the matter of schooling," but many do not send their own to school. On the other hand, "the children are free to leave, if ill-treated or dissatisfied." A bad boy is sure to become dissatisfied, and good boys often do; and most boys feel ill-treated the first time they are punished or even reprimanded. The result is that many boys, from ten to sixteen years old, in Minnesota, have exercised their privilege, and left. Sometimes, they come to the chairman of the local committee. He finds a new home, if possible. If not, he writes the society (the legal guardian) for instructions. But he cannot hold the boy, and often instructions come too late. Thirty per cent of the children brought to Minnesota have gone from the vicinities where placed; and, of these, at least forty have drifted off and been lost sight of in less than three years, for lack of adequate supervision. The agents are efficient men, but they are not omnipresent. We believe that the society should have responsible, paid local agents, to whom legal guardianship should be given. Their duties should be similar to those of the county agents of Michigan.

Fourth. The crucial question is, Does "a large proportion turn out badly, swelling the ranks of pauperism and crime"? Here, I beg leave to submit the following table, showing the condition of the children . . . so far as ascertained: —

	Under thirteen	Per cent	Over thirteen	Per cent	All ages	Per cent
Total number reported	130	100	134	100	264	100
Remaining in vicinity where placed	116	90	70	52	186	70
Gone from vicinity	14	10	64	48	78	30
Doing well	101	78	70	52	171	65
No special complaint	11	4	22	8	33	$12\frac{1}{2}$
Doing badly	9	7	32	24	41	16

Age	1	2	3	4	5	6	7	8	9	10	11
Number received	3	1	3	11	10	23	17	19	17	18	23

Age	12	13	14	15	16	17	18	19	20	Over 21	All ages
Number received	26	31	22	35	22	21	25	2	2	9	340

The above table shows the ages when brought, as nearly as can be ascertained.

Care has been exercised not to report children as doing badly except for sufficient cause. The list of those doing well includes two boys whose employer works on Sundays in busy times; a boy of eleven who is kept at herding seven days in the week, and has never been sent to school; a boy whose employer took him to a saloon and treated him to beer to celebrate their new relation; another who shot a thieving tramp causing the loss of a leg; and a dozen or more of those who are reported as gone to New York or elsewhere, but whose conduct was good while they stayed. I have not reported as doing badly five children, whose mother, a dissolute variety actress, dragged them from their new homes in Cottonwood County and took them back to New York; nor five others whose parents claimed them in Watonwan County, — the whole family became a public charge and were finally sent back to New York by joint public and private charity.

Of those reported doing badly, six have committed offences against law. One is in the Reform School; a second is serving a three years' sentence in the State prison for a felonious attempt upon a little girl; a third was in jail thirty days for assault and battery; a fourth, twenty days for beating a little boy; a fifth stole small articles from his employer, and ran away; a sixth stole $60, and ran away. Besides these, a boy was arrested with some tramps. Another served three years in the Reform School. He was one of those brought several years ago. As I have already said, nine have been returned to the society as incorrigible. A girl of twenty-three, partly deranged, was for a year a charity patient in St. Luke's Hospital, St. Paul. Five, with their parents, became a public charge in the city of Mankato. I estimate the cost to the public of the crime and pauperism above mentioned at about fifteen hundred dollars.

From our experience, we are positive in the opinion that children above the age of twelve years ought not to be sent west by the Children's Aid Society. In this opinion, I understand that the officers of the society concur. Secretary Brace says (*Dangerous Classes of New York,* p. 245), "The emigration plan must be conducted with careful judgement, and be applied, so far as practicable, to children under, say, the age of fourteen years." If the society would adhere to this wise rule, we should have little cause for complaint.

Our examination shows, with reference to the children under thirteen years old, that nine-tenths remain, four-fifths are doing well, and all incorrigibles are cared for by the society. If properly placed and faithfully supervised, we are willing to take our full share of these younger children in Minnesota.

---

3. The Children's Aid Society in Kansas, 1867 and 1884

Francis H. White, "The Placing-out System in the Light of its Results," in Anna Garlin Spencer and Charles Wesley Birtwell, eds., *The Care of Dependent, Neglected and Wayward Children* (Baltimore, 1894), pp. 81–87

The conclusions presented in his paper are founded upon an investigation into the after-life of the children placed in Kansas by the New York Children's Aid Society. The state, as you know, is centrally located, and its people and physical features are fairly typical of the other states in the Mississippi valley where thousands of children have been given homes. My interest in the work dates back to a time when I was superintendent of the Brooklyn Children's Aid Society. Five years ago I accepted a chair in the State Agricultural College of Kansas, a position which has brought me in contact with the class of people among whom most of the children have been placed.

The agencies within the state engaged in placing-out children are a few private institutions, whose work is not extensive, and a state institution, established a few years ago, which receives and trains dependent children, and finds homes for them through the aid and supervision of the county superintendents of public instruction. There is no organized system of boarding-out children such as is practised in some other states.

Two societies having headquarters outside of Kansas are engaged in placing-out children within it. These are the Chicago Children's Home Society and the New York Children's Aid Society. The first has done little in the state, but the second has accomplished a large work, extending over a long period of time. There are other states in which it has operated more extensively than in this, indeed it has placed out over 75,000 children in various parts of the country since 1857. There is good reason to believe that the work done in Kansas is a fair sample of what it has done everywhere.

At my request, an official of the New York Children's Aid Society made a careful examination of their records and vouches for the following general summary: —

The total number of children placed in homes among the residents of Kansas is 960, of whom 13 per cent were girls.

2 per cent are known to be dead.

10 per cent have no records. These were mainly large boys placed early in the history of the society.

3 per cent were returned as not satisfactory because of some mental or physical disability.

10 per cent left their homes within the first few years.

2 per cent have bad records, that is, were guilty of some serious misdemeanor.

7 per cent have poor records.

22 per cent have very fair records.

44 per cent have excellent records.

The average age of the children was 12.3 years.

84 per cent of those under eight years do well.

It will be noticed that only 66 per cent of the whole work is known to be successful. Let us examine somewhat more closely into the history of these children in order to discover the reasons for this rather low percentage.

Two New York Children's Aid Society parties have been selected, the first composed of boys between the ages of fourteen and seventeen, and undoubtedly typical of the methods and results of the early work; the second chiefly made up of children under fourteen. Considerable inquiry has been made by the writer, and the facts collected have been added to the records as they appear on the Society's books. Still, much desirable information is lacking, especially in regard to the party placed in 1867, the first taken to Kansas. Both the boys and the pioneer farmers with whom they were placed have moved frequently, and hence tracing the path of two such erratic bodies has proved quite difficult. In the list numbers have been substituted for names, and only the essential facts are stated.

PARTY PLACED IN KANSAS, 1867

1. Reported a good boy, but no record after first year, though many letters have been sent.

2. Wrote once. No trace of him since.

3. Stayed nine months, then went west and has never been heard from.

4. Remained about two years, then ran away. Some years later served a term in the penitentiary. Afterwards wrote his foster-parent he was employed and doing fairly well.

5. Left after staying a few months.

6. Stayed about a year and a half, then went to Michigan, where he married and still lives.

7. Soon left.

8. Remained in place for several years, then went elsewhere in the neighborhood to work. Not been in the vicinity for many years.

9. No replies to letters sent.

10. Was a good boy, but died in second year.

11. Left the first year.

12. A good boy, but met with accident and went east for treatment. Nothing known of him since.

13. Did well. Is now married; has children of his own, and is living near a large western city, employed as a railroad conductor.

14. Left the first year.

15, 16. Brothers. Placed with same man. No record or replies to seven letters sent.

17. Stayed six months, then went to live with another man in the vicinity. Now has considerable property and is highly respected.

18. No record or replies to letters.

The chairman of the committee that found homes for these boys is still living and is a man of some prominence in the community. He remembers very well the disappointment of the farmers when they found the boys were over fourteen, for they had requested younger children, knowing well they could not induce the older ones to remain. The chairman seemed quite sure that the farmers had no intention of doing a charitable act nor of satisfying their own longing for children, but that they simply wished to obtain cheap labor, as the boys were only to receive board and clothes for their services. He says that when he expressed doubt

as to whether the boys ought to be placed with these men without any written agreement on the part of the latter to take good care of them, the agent laughed and told him not to worry about that; if the homes were not agreeable to them they would soon leave. Not one of this party now resides in the county, and only two are known to live in Kansas. Over half of the persons with whom they were placed are dead or have moved out of the county, and their present address is unknown to former acquaintances.

PARTY PLACED IN KANSAS, 1884

1. Age 6. Visited one year later and found he was doing well and had excellent home; frequent good reports; now working out and earning $10 per month; goes by his foster-parents' name.

2. Age 17. Wrote same year thanking Society for home. In 1891 joined regular army, was assigned to infantry band, and stationed in New Mexico. Has written and published some poems, and now employs leisure time studying Spanish and translating poetry. Reports he is saving money and has joined the church.

3. Age 6. Stayed until man with whom placed moved away, then went to live in town near by and is now doing well.

4. Age 12. Stayed until man moved away, then went to live with excellent family; still there and doing well.

5. Age 9. Stayed until man broke up housekeeping, then went elsewhere, and when last heard from was doing well.

6. Age 12. Visited and found to be doing well; letters confirmed report; died in 1888 of consumption.

7. Age 10. Remained six years, then went to New Mexico; returned, and later reported doing well.

8. Age 14. No replies to letters sent.

9. Age 9. Visited and found to be doing well; remained seven years and then went to

work for himself; now reported to be making a good living.

10. Age 10. Visited and reported as getting along all right and that he had joined the church; stayed three years; is now in neighborhood and said to be succeeding.

11. Age 8. Visited and reported a good boy; remained till 1889, then left and has worked in several places since.

12. Age 12. Remained for several years, was slow and stubborn, but a good worker; went to Colorado and then returned, and is now reported as in the neighborhood, but "doing no good."

13. Age 16. An excellent young woman; married a relative of the man with whom she was placed, and is doing well.

14. Age 6. Visited and found to have a good home, but after three years left it; reported that he lied and stole and could not be managed; brought back, but was dissatisfied, and was transferred to another home, where he did fairly well. Later, taken to New York and placed in the Eye and Ear Infirmary for treatment.

15. Age 5½. Visited and found to be doing well; failing health of his foster-parent made it necessary to give him another home, where he is now living and getting along well; is well liked.

16. Age 6. Visited and found to be doing well; a letter from foster-parent says boy goes by his name; a recent letter, that "he is satisfied with them and they with him."

17. Age 7½. Stayed until foster-parents gave up housekeeping, then went to another home, where she is reported to be contented, giving fair satisfaction, though she is not very intelligent.

18, 19, 20, 21. Ages 15, 13, 12, 11. Brothers and sisters; all doing well at last account; one of them now owns an eighty-acre farm.

.   .   .   .   .

Of the party placed in 1867, composed of boys between the ages of fourteen and seventeen, by far the larger part drifted away or turned out badly; while just the reverse is true of the party placed in 1884, composed of children for the most part twelve years old or under. The histories of other children I have traced confirm me in this opinion. It seems clear that the earlier children are placed, the more likely are the results to be satisfactory.

See, too, the picking and choosing that is necessary in making up a party to go west. From the street, the newsboys' homes, the charitable institutions, come the applicants for western homes, bright, dull, hardened, sad, gay — their natures so different, their friendless and homeless condition so similar. Will the net take all? No! only the gold fish, — the "gilt-edged children," as they are popularly called. This astonishes us at first. Nearly every one pictures the work as an effort to relieve the city of the bad, not the good, dependent children.

Why does the Society refuse to send west the hardened, the incorrigible, the vicious? For two reasons: first, the west would not take them, and second, they could not be induced to remain in the homes provided. The experiment was tried repeatedly in the early history of the work, but almost invariably failed.

Finding homes for children and children for homes

1. National Children's Home Society, New York, 1897

New York. State Board of Charities, *Thirty-first Annual Report, 1897* (New York, 1898), pp. 18–19, 24–34.

In this interrogation the questioner was Enoch Vine Stoddard, M.D., Vice-President of the State Board of Charities. The witness, Rev. W. Jarvis Maybee, continued to place out county charges for several years after 1897.

_____

To illustrate practically, some of the serious abuses of this placing-out work, as carried on by persons prominently engaged in it, and viewed from the Board's standpoint, the following *verbatim* extracts from the testimony of the Rev. W. Jarvis Maybee, agent of the "National Children's Home Society," [1] taken early in the year 1897, by the Board's special committee . . . are presented with the explanatory statement that although this society has been refused incorporation in New York State by the Board, there is no law on the statute book to prevent its alleged agents from carrying on their objectionable trade in this State:

.   .   .   .   .   .

Q. Now, were you paid for taking that child over there; paid for taking the child and putting it in a home, as you call it?

A. I was to receive pay.

Q. Did you receive pay?

A. I received some.

Q. How much?

A. I think I received, I think I was paid $45.

Q. How much was your charge for taking the child?

A. They were to pay $100 for that child.

Q. Can you explain to me who was to pay this amount; you say they were; who was?

A. The mother of the child.

Q. Was she a person of means?

A. Well, she wasn't perhaps; her father was going to pay it and wanted to keep it quiet to screen himself and his child.

Q. How did that child happen to get in the Door of Hope? Was it born there?

A. No, sir.

Q. Did you know where it was taken from?

Was it from Rochester? Was the child born in Rochester?

A. Yes, sir.

Q. So that it is known that in such a case as that application can be made to you and that a child can be taken and disposed of for money under such circumstances; there are other cases that you have done the same thing in; that we understand?

A. Yes, sir.

Q. Now, then, in regard to this child, you say that you took this child here to this person; how long did the child remain there?

A. With them?

Q. Yes, this baby that you took from that Miss B——?

A. It remained with them some time.

Q. About how long do you think it remained there, about how long, one day, or one week, or a month?

A. I should say a few weeks.

Q. What became of it then?

A. It went from there down to the Sanitarium at the beach for a couple of weeks.

Q. Then what became of it?

A. And they brought it back again, and later it died.

A. There was one case where I received $40.

Q. Well, what was your price if you could have got it in that case; in this case your price was $100 and you got $45?

A. I asked them $50.

Q. Where was that case, what part of the State?

A. In this city.

Q. Now the second one; how much did you get for that?

A. One hundred dollars.

Q. And you got the $100?

A. Yes, sir.

Q. Suppose you give us a history of that

1. For an account of the origin and development of this society, which in 1897 was recognized as the Illinois Children's Home and Aid Society, see Thurston, *The Dependent Child*, pp. 140–155.

case; that child was born where, in Syracuse?

A. It was born here in Syracuse, but a short time ago.

Q. But where, I mean?

A. It was born in the Homeopathic Hospital.

Q. Was the mother married?

A. She was not.

Q. How did you hear of that case?

A. A physician reported the case to me.

Q. A physician in Syracuse?

A. Yes, sir?

Q. Who was it?

A. Dr. L——.

Q. And how long before the child was born was the case reported to you by Dr. L——?

A. If I remember, it was inside of a month.

Q. Not to exceed a month; how long was the mother in the Homeopathic Hospital?

A. Well, I don't know, doctor.

Q. Was she a resident of Syracuse?

A. She was not.

Q. Do you know where her home was?

A. Her home was in another State.

Q. Not in New York State?

A. No, sir.

Q. What State was that in and what town?

A. I don't know the town, but from Massachusetts.

Q. How did she happen to come to Syracuse under those circumstances?

A. I think she was sent here by her physician.

Q. In Massachusetts; do you know how she happened to come?

A. That is as near as I know.

Q. Do you know the name of the young woman?

A. I don't know her name.

Q. Did they give you any name at all?

A. No, sir; they didn't give me the name but simply gave me the name of the child as Arthur.

Q. The number?

A. Two hundred and twenty-seven on the record.

Q. And the child was born, ——

A. March 14th.

Q. How old was that child when you took it from the Homeopathic Hospital?

A. I received it the same day.

Q. So, as soon as the child was born you were notified, and took it away?

A. Yes, sir.

A. The physician told me that they were married just about a month; they were respectable people, came from another town and came on their wedding trip this way, and had this child born a month after they were married, and the disgrace of the thing, to cover it up they desired to keep it quiet and to find a home for the child and go home without it; a physician came to me and asked if I could find a home for the child, and I believed their story was true.

Q. And so you took the child in that case, at their request?

A. At their request.

Q. What did you do with the child?

A. I took the child to H——, and the child has been since adopted by a family in H——.

Q. You took that child from those people that you believed to be the parents, according to your statement?

A. Yes, sir.

Q. Did you simply take the child and carry it away, or did they give you some papers that relinquished their claims to the child in every possible way, putting it in your hands?

A. They signed some papers.

Q. I would like to ask you now in regard to what you received from this man and woman for taking that child?

A. Forty dollars.

Q. Was that paid to you in cash in hand?

A. Yes, sir.

Q. At the time that you took the child?

A. Yes, sir; he was to send me $10 more, but never sent it.

Q. So that you agreed to take the child for

$50, and received $40 in cash, and there is $10 still owing?

A. Yes, sir.

Q. Now, that is the only case, then, that you have had in Syracuse?

A. Those two cases.

Q. Now give us another case; what other part of the State; how, as a Christian minister, can you justify yourself in being an accomplice with parents in getting rid of a legitimate child in that way, born after lawful wedlock, how can you justify yourself in doing it?

A. Well, they desired to be screened from the disgrace of having a child born before time and wished to give it up and have it placed in a home.

Q. Do you as a Christian minister, as a teacher of morals, as an example to youth, as a guide to Christian people that you talk so much about, recommend such procedures as that?

A. I don't recommend them, doctor.

Q. Why do you do them?

A. I discourage them in every case I can.

Q. You discourage them by taking money and being an accomplice in it?

A. I talked to them and told them they ought to take care of the child.

Q. Is that the way you stand before the community and teach temperance, chastity and morality?

A. No; but if they will abandon the child and give the child up, we think the best thing is to place the child in a good family.

Q. Now, I want to ask you this about it for my own satisfaction; have you ever heard anything from either of those parents since?

A. Not a word.

Q. Any inquiries ever been made about it?

A. Yes, sir; I wrote the father because he was to give me $10 more, and was to send it when he went home; I wrote him, the address he gave, B———, and the name, but I heard nothing from him; I have never heard anything from him since.

Q. Did they absolutely abandon the child?

A. Yes, sir.

Q. Now, the next case; I want another instance where you have had another case?

A. I don't know of another case.

Q. But you admitted there were other cases in the State; you have already admitted there were several?

A. No; I did not.

Q. Where you have taken infants and put them out in this way for money?

A. Oh, yes.

Q. Give me another one; where did you have another one?

A. That we have taken and received?

Q. That you have taken, just what we have been talking about?

A. I received some from the Door of Hope.

Q. You told me a little while ago that that one was the only one that was taken under such circumstances?

A. That was through a doctor that I meant there, through the physician you were asking.

Q. Well, tell me another child that you have taken from the Door of Hope, in Rochester?

A. Oh, we have received some others from the Door of Hope.

Q. Tell me when you received another one that you received money for, a little infant like this; have you found another one in your records?

A. I have another, Joseph C———.

Q. Where was that, Mr. Maybee?

A. It was at the Door of Hope, in Rochester.

Q. When was that?

A. Born, March 27, 1896.

Q. And how do you know about that child?

A. Well, I think the information came to me through the matron of the Door of Hope.

Q. What was her name?

A. Miss B———.

Q. That is the same person that you have spoken of previously?

A. Yes, sir.

Q. Did she communicate with you personally or by letter?

A. By letter, I think.

Q. Written to you at your home at Syracuse?

A. I think so, I won't speak positively about that.

Q. How long before this child was born did you receive this information?

A. I don't know.

Q. How long after the child was born did you see the child?

A. Did I receive the child; the 25th of April, 1896.

Q. When was the child born?

A. March 27th.

Q. And where did you receive the child?

A. Where; I received it from the Door of Hope.

A. I believe I did.

Q. Did you bring it away from there yourself?

A. I think so.

Q. And where did you take that child?

A. Placed it in a family in the city here.

Q. In Syracuse?

A. Yes, sir.

Q. Now, your attention was called to that child by Miss B—— and was taken from her to Syracuse and put out in a home at I——. Now, how much money did you receive for taking that child from the Door of Hope?

A. I received $50.

Q. Now, in regard to the cases which you take from the Overseers of the Poor of the towns or counties, what arrangements have you for them for taking children?

A. Well, with most of them the arrangement is to receive $50 for settling children, $50 each for settling them in good homes.

Q. So, you have that agreement that for each child you take you receive $50?

A. I have placed some from some of the overseers for less than that.

Q. Why did you place them for less than that? When you receive $50 from some, why not $50 from all?

A. Why, one case, for instance, up in B—— where I received two children, a brother and sister that had been abandoned by the parents, from the Overseer of the Poor at B——, and I took those children and received $50 for the two instead of $50 each.

Q. Where did you put these, in the same home, or in separate homes?

A. They are in separate homes.

Q. Now, you say there are some that you don't receive the full $50 for? Isn't that your price?

A. Yes, sir; that is the regular price.

Q. Do you charge more for taking a little child four or five months old than you do for one ten or twelve?

A. We charge more for little babies because it is harder to get homes for them while they are young; we have to keep them.

Q. I thought your charge was $50 for any child?

A. Those are for county or town children, but illegitimate children, we charge $100 for the little infants if we take them when they are young.

Q. So, if a child is illegitimate, you expect the town or other persons to pay more than if it is legitimate? Why do you do that?

A. We think if you take those children without any pay at all it would encourage immorality.

Q. Why do you charge $50 instead of $100, because the child is illegitimate?

A. Because we think they ought to pay the expenses in connection with the child and securing a home.

Q. If you deal with the parents of the children that want to get rid of the children, you go right in and help them out, but if you go to the Overseer of the Poor, where the children have been left on his hands, illegitimate, then you go and charge double?

A. The Overseer of the Poor, in that case I referred to, he didn't pay that $100; it didn't come from the town, but it came from the individual, from the young man, or the mother of the young man who was responsible for the child, and he paid that $100, or the mother did, and then it was $50 paid back again by the overseer of the town.

Q. That $100 was paid by the young man, the father of the child?

A. Yes, sir.

Q. And you took the $100?

A. Yes, sir.

Q. Then you say you turned around and gave the Overseer of the Poor $50 of that; why did you give it to him?

A. To meet the expenses of the court.

---

2. Children's home societies, 1907

George Harrison Durrand, "The Study of the Child from the Standpoint of the Home-Finding Agency," *Proceedings* of the National Conference of Charities and Correction (1907), 256–258, 261–263.

Between 1883 and 1909 children's home societies were established in twenty-eight states to promote adoption or foster home placement on a state-wide basis. For a review of the work of the societies around 1910 see Hart, *Preventive Treatment of Neglected Children,* pp. 145–193.

In 1883 the Children's Home Society was founded by Rev. M. V. B. Van Arsdale in the State of Illinois. His plan differed from that of the New York [Children's Aid] Society in that he dealt with children singly. He also organized the state into districts, with district superintendents, and established local advisory boards in communities, to assist the agents of the society in their work. The earlier years of the history of the society were fraught with difficulties and shaken by storms, yet the idea of the family home for the homeless child gradually gained ground. It appealed to benevolent people as an economical and practical charity, and as the simple and natural way of providing for homeless children. Two plain facts have always impressed themselves upon promoters and friends of this charity, which they believe to have a strikingly logical connection: First, everywhere little children without homes; secondly, everywhere lonely homes without children. To serve just here as a kind of equalizing providence, helping these two needs to answer each other in mutual benefit — this has been from the beginning the ideal of the National Children's Home Society. It is summed up in their motto: "Two things which should not be; a home without a child and a child without a home."

The plan, as originally put in operation in Illinois, looked to the extension of the work in other states under the control of the parent society, which early assumed the name of the National Children's Home Society. But as the state organizations increased in importance the plan of central control became impracticable, and the state societies proceeded to incorporate under their own state laws and to take up the management of their own affairs. The state societies then united themselves for mutual help and encouragement in the federation, which is the form of organization now existing.

The plan of the work as it stands at the present is briefly as follows:

The national society has headquarters at Chicago. Its list of directors and officers includes the superintendents of a majority of the state societies. It has thus far no endowment or working fund, and it exercises no absolute authority over its constituent societies. Its relation to them is advisory, rather, its meetings and its publications serving as a clearing house of ideas and methods by which the work of the separate societies is benefited. The National Society also has charge of establishing the work in new states where opportunity is found.

It is by the individual state societies that the child-saving work is directly carried on. Each society is composed of benevolent men and women of the state, prominent in social and public life, who give of their money and their time to its support. The immediate working head of each society is the state superintendent. Under him, in all but the newer state societies, are from one to eight assistant superintendents, each having charge of an appointed district. And finally, for the rounding out of the system and keeping watch over every nook and corner of the state, each society is aided by the local advisory boards. These boards are interdenominational in membership, and number from three to a dozen persons. They are organized in communities all over the state, and co-operate with superintendents and assistants, reporting cases of destitute and neglected children, helping to find desirable homes, and assisting to safeguard the welfare of those placed in homes in their locality. Michigan, for example, has two hundred thirty of these local boards; Illinois has six hundred forty; Iowa nearly a thousand.

The societies for the most part are not endowed and do not receive aid from public treasuries but derive their support from voluntary contributions. These contributions are from churches, public schools, Sunday schools, fraternal lodges and societies of various kinds, and also from individuals of every occupation and degree. Large gifts are rare; small gifts are multitudinous. From two to three dollars is perhaps the average size of gifts to the society. The number of persons who actually contributed one dollar or more last year to the Wisconsin society was over 4,300; to the Illinois society was 11,000. An estimate on this point, based upon such records as are available, places the number of persons contributing at present to the federated societies of the National Children's Home Society at not less than 120,000. While some of the states feel strongly the need of endowment in order to give greater stability to their work, yet this feature of contributions from great numbers of small givers is generally regarded by the society as an ideal condition in private benevolence and one of the strongest elements of its system.

.   .   .   .   .

In the large cities the societies are usually in co-operation with other child-helping agencies, to whom they refer cases outside their own proper sphere. The Children's Home Societies, also, in the cities and elsewhere receive into their guardianship children from other charitable societies and from public authorities. Thus, in many states, the societies receive children from orphanages and reformatory institutions, from aid societies and from county and town officers. In most states the societies receive children into their care by commitment of the courts, while in Illinois, Kentucky, Wisconsin and Minnesota they have regular connection with the courts as placing-out agencies for dependent children. For assuming charge of children from public authorities or other agencies, the societies usually receive compensation, although frequently only a nominal amount. But it is the rule of the societies never to refuse to accept (from whatever source) a child needing their care, even if no compensation is offered.

.   .   .   .

A significant fact of recent occurrence was the action of the New York Children's Aid Society in uniting with the National Children's Home Society as one of its constituent societies. This organization, the oldest of its kind in the country, which last year in addition to its aid work cared for six hundred children on the placing-out plan, was the forerunner, as has been said, of the National Children's Home Society. It now joins its strength and experience to the latter organization and becomes a part of it.

---

3. The Delineator campaign, 1907–1911

"The Delineator Child-Rescue Campaign," *The Delineator*, LXX (November 1907), 715–718.

Shortly after assuming editorship of *The Delineator* in 1907, Theodore Dreiser (1871–1945) launched this women's fashion magazine on a campaign to provide homes for dependent children. The campaign continued until February 1911.

In all of the great cities of the United States to-day there are children who have missed their natural birthright . . . Scattered over the land, sometimes in the country, sometimes in the city, are also homes that for one reason or another lack their natural right of a little child. Each needs the other to lead it to the highest happiness.

The Delineator herewith undertakes the mission of bringing them together. For this purpose we begin with this number our Child Rescue Campaign. We intend from time to time to present to you specific cases of children who need homes. They will be children for whom institutions in various parts of the country are trying to find the surroundings of family life. Sometimes they may be orphans. Sometimes they may have fathers and mothers who have neglected them. Always they will have human souls possessed of all the potentiality for making good men and women, provided some one will lend a helping hand along the rough way of life, and through a new, right environment there may be a wonderful development for them in the future.

In telling the histories of these children it is deemed best not to use the child's real name. For some of them are heart-breaking histories which it is better should not follow the child's identity when he or she goes into the new home. So always when we are talking to you about a child it will be under his or her *Delineator* name . . .

All of these children *The Delineator* will offer for you to take into your homes. Among the million subscribers and millions more of readers whom we reach, we are convinced that there will be those eager to avail themselves of this opportunity. We do not ask for homes of wealth for these, our little foster charges. The best that can be given them is homes of comfort, with loving kindness as their richest asset. Wherever there is a white, clean farmhouse with green meadows lying round about, a small neat cottage on a wide village street, or a modest city dwelling with a woman who has room in her heart to let a little stranger in, there we shall welcome an invitation for *The Delineator* child. Fine rich mansions are not necessary, though when they have a need we would not pass them by. But it is a home and family affection that are wanted.

There will be three methods by which you may take a *Delineator* child: by the placing-out system, by indenture and by adoption. By adoption, the child becomes legally yours to be brought up as your own, and, if it is desired, arrangements may be made that the world shall not know otherwise. By indenture, you sign an agreement, definitely binding yourself to give the child a home and clothes and schools. By the placing-out method, the child is given into your care without any written instrument, but those responsible for placing it reserve the privilege of visiting your home from time to time to see that all is well with the child.

It is, of course, necessary to exercise the greatest care that the children reach only good, true homes where they will come to no harm. For this reason, there are certain formalities to be observed and recommendations of character to be furnished. In the large cities there are organized charitable societies that have this work in hand and are thoroughly competent to fulfil all its legal technicalities. To them *The Delineator* will entrust the entire matter of arranging the final details. We will bring the children before you and will tell you how to secure them.

There is one thing more: We believe that all our family of readers will develop a sense of personal kinship to *The Delineator* children, and will want to express their personal interest in a definite way. So we are going to open a bank account in the name of *The Delineator* child. Each of our readers we invite to contribute a postage stamp. Even the little boys and girls can do that. You can send it to us in a letter. And for each stamp that you send *The Delineator* will add another. The money will be used in supplying the child with clothing and other articles that may be needed for its new start in life. And we will tell you all about how it is expended. So soon as one child is comfortably placed the bank account will be at the service of the next. If the account should run low, we will remind you of the fact.

We now await a call from the first home that needs a child. We give you the address of the society having each child in charge to whom you may write, or you may write to us, addressing "The Child Rescue Department" of *The Delineator* . . .

The first *Delineator* child offered for adoption is Evelyn, aged seven, a little girl from Philadelphia . . . According to the regulations of the society having her in charge, she must be placed in a home somewhere in the state of Pennsylvania.

.   .   .   .   .

The Children's Aid Society is paying Evelyn's board in the country. Meantime they are looking for a permanent home for her. By the sacred trust that her mother imposed on them it must be a good, kind home. She is offered for legal adoption. The exact steps to be taken may be learned by writing Edwin D. Solenberger, General Secretary of the Children's Aid Society of Pennsylvania, care of *The Delineator*.

.   .   .   .   .

The second *Delineator* child offered for adoption is Bobby, aged four, an unusually bright little boy from Chicago. The society having him in charge is not limited in its territory and therefore this child is available for a good home in any part of the country.

Bobby is a little boy given to the Illinois Children's Home and Aid Society by his father, who could no longer support him. His task was doubly hard because the home was without a mother.

.   .   .   .   .

Bobby is ready for adoption in any home in the United States. He must be taken on probation first, and if the term proves satisfactory to those concerned, Bobbie's adoption can be carried through according to the law of the State in which the home is found. You may learn all about it by writing to the Reverend Hastings H. Hart, LL.D., Superintendent of the Illinois Children's Home and Aid Society, care of *The Delineator*.

---

4. Catholic Home Bureau for Dependent Children, New York City, 1898–1908

Hart, *Preventive Treatment of Neglected Children,* pp. 171–175.

The Catholic Home Bureau was organized in December [1898]. It was begun as one of the special works of the St. Vincent de Paul Society, under the leadership of its president, Mr. Thos. M. Mulry.

The objects of the bureau are declared in its constitution as follows:

"The particular objects for which the bureau is formed are as follows: To place destitute, dependent or neglected children in family homes, in accordance with the laws of the state of New York, and for that purpose to receive such children by surrender, commitment, or otherwise, or to do such work as may tend to improve the condition of such children."

The early experiences of the bureau are humorously described in the annual report for 1909:

"As the way to place out seemed to be to place out, we began with the simple proposition of accepting every home and taking every child offered. It is, therefore, natural to find that in the early days our efforts were confined principally to securing positions for big boys and girls, who we soon found were men and women quite difficult to manage. Our views, however, very quickly changed. Experience taught us that not every householder looking for a child was actuated by charity, and that many who were charitable, were not wise, or discreet, or careful, or possessed of those qualities which the protector of a child should have. Good judgment was needed on the part of all concerned. But officers and employes could not always be expected to constantly exercise good judgment, therefore checks were invented to protect all in the exercise of judgment. The result of this was the formation of the committee on homes.

"To explain properly the work of this committee it may not be amiss to detail slightly our method of finding homes. In the first place, the machinery of our canvass is such that no time is wasted on obviously unworthy prospective homes, and every effort is given to searching for the openings that exist in very worthy ones. This part of the work is attended to by a traveling canvasser, who puts himself in thorough accord and close touch with the pastors whom he meets in his tours. This agent sends forward to our office as full information about the proffered home as he can get. Every detail is gone into. In addition to the pastor, several other worthy citizens are consulted, and the clerical staff of the office send forward the proper blanks to the references. When these have all been received, it becomes necessary to weigh the statements and correct any errors of judgment that the agent may have fallen into in suggesting a home. This work is the particular duty of the committee on homes. They weigh carefully every statement and accept or reject them or call for further statements or opinions from the agent.

"Later, the desire for the best possible protection of the placed-out child brought about the development of an excellent system of visitations. Agents were sent on tours for this work alone. Routes were changed and no expense considered in cases where reports had indicated that children could be protected from ill-treatment, or even from minor adverse re-

sults from mistakes in placement. We early learned, also, that the office should be developed with as much care, thoroughness and perfection of details and system, as that of the best business house."

The bureau is supported partly by an annual appropriation from the city of New York, amounting to $10,000, partly by appropriations from the St. Vincent de Paul Society, and partly by donations. The expenditures of the bureau for the year 1908 were $13,667.

The bureau acts as the agent of 22 different institutions.

.   .   .   .   .

The bureau has placed children in the states of New York, Pennsylvania, Vermont, New Jersey and Indiana. The rule of the bureau is to visit each child twice a year. The total number of children placed from the beginning is 2035.

.   .   .   .

It is interesting to know that the number of applications for boys over twelve declined from 274 in 1903 to 49 in 1908, and the number of applications for girls over twelve declined from 214 in 1905 to 55 in 1908. This decline is doubtless due to the faithfulness with which the bureau has refused to be an agency for people who desire to secure cheap unpaid servants. There has been a corresponding decrease in the number of girls over twelve placed, from 58 in 1902 to 3 in 1908, and boys from 97 in 1903 to 12 in 1908. In 1901 the placements of children over 12 were 81 per cent of the whole number. In 1908 they were only 5 per cent of the whole number.

During the year 1908 the bureau had under its supervision in family homes 1430 different children, and it reports 2750 visits, an actual average of nearly two visits to every child. The amount of supervision exercised by the Catholic Home Bureau is far in excess of that which is exercised by the average placing-out agency in the United States.

The boarding-out system

1. Massachusetts' experience with boarding-out, 1878–1886

Adelaide A. Calkins, "Boarding Out of Dependent Children in Massachusetts," *Proceedings* of the National Conference of Charities and Correction (1886), 158–161.

In 1868, as an alternative to institutional care and in the absence of free family homes, the Massachusetts Board of State Charities began to pay for the board of children in private family homes.

The observation for ten years of the difficulty, not to say impossibility, of finding homes for a limited number of children from private institutions, led those interested to advocate the boarding-out system, as practised in Great Britain.

With the projectors of this new policy, the prime idea was so to place these children that they should have as nearly as possible an equal chance with the average of children in their new homes, and so be absorbed into respectable communities, and grow up useful citizens, with the least possible chance of lapsing into pauperism. In the spring of 1880, the following act was passed by the legislature: —

Section 1. The trustees of the State Primary and Reform Schools shall have full power to place in charge of suitable persons any of the children of the State Primary School, the power of visitation and final discharge remaining with the State Board of Health, Lunacy, and Charity, as now fixed by law. And said trustees may provide for the maintenance of any child so placed, in whole or part, at a cost to the State not exceeding two dollars per week. The expense of such maintenance shall be paid from the annual appropriation for the current expense of said school.

In December, 1880, the work actually commenced by the placing of four children under eight years of age at board. Further legislation in May, 1882, enabled the Board of Health, Lunacy, and Charity to provide for children in need from three to sixteen years of age at the State Primary School or "elsewhere." By this act, the board were permitted to board out indigent and neglected children *directly*, without passing through the institution.

In connection with the boarding out, upon which the degree of success must depend, is a closely guarded system of visitation by women. Not more than two children are permitted in one family, unless brothers and sisters; and the State permits no children except its wards to be boarded in a family. This is to prevent families from becoming small institutions, and children being taken for profit.

For obvious reasons, the work has proceeded slowly and cautiously. No unfavorable criticisms of the system are anywhere heard. Eight children under eight years of age were placed at board from the School within a year after the law passed. The number boarded from that institution in 1884 was thirty-one. Jan. 1, 1886, forty-eight children under eight years of age had been placed out to board, not including the neglected children boarded by the Board of Health, Lunacy, and Charity . . .

The following extracts from the report of the trustees of the State Primary School for the year ending Oct. 1, 1884, will perhaps give a fair idea of the cost and its practical benefits: —

The average cost per week for each inmate, including expenditures for extraordinary repairs and improvements, was $2.25 4/10, an annual *per capita* cost of $117.89. Including the said extraordinary expenses and improvements, the weekly cost was $2.29.

Each child boarded out in a family under the Act of 1880 costs for board $1.50 per week, and an allowance for clothing of $4 per quarter, a little less than 31 cents per week. An outfit of clothing varying in cost from $12 to $15 is furnished to each one of these children.

If the cost of the outfit be added to the price paid for board and the allowance for clothing, the cost to the State for the first year is slightly above, but for two or more years it is somewhat below, the $2 per week prescribed by the statute.

In occasional and peculiar cases, when circumstances have seemed to require it, the trustees have authorized the payment of bills for medical attendance, and, in one instance, the expense of nursing for boarding-out children.

The boarding out has in some cases resulted in the adoption of the child into the same or some neighboring family, and the State has thus been relieved of the burden of its support.

.   .   .   .   .

The city of Springfield adopted the boarding-out system for its wards under twelve years of age when the law was passed prohibiting children over three years of age from remaining in almshouses. At present, the number boarded is eighteen, rather below the average of other years. The cost *per capita,* including clothing and other necessary expenses, is a little less than $2 per week.

With seven years' experience, the city officials having the work in charge express unqualified satisfaction with the method. Eighty-two individual children have been boarded between the years 1878 and 1886, and the success with which at twelve years of age they pass into satisfactory self-support is reported by the agent of the Overseers of the Poor to be most gratifying.

The visitation of the city's wards is by a system of regular voluntary service of women, as well as by the agent of the Overseers of the Poor.

The comfortable home life now opened to the young dependent children of city and State by the boarding-out system is elevating, and affords the best practical training that can be given. There is little difficulty in securing all the privileges demanded for them by the State.

Their health is protected, attendance at school regular. Being made presentable by suitable dress, they are received pleasantly by the children of the neighborhood at church and social gatherings. All of which is quite unlike the placed-out, self-supporting child, too often overworked, with school and social privileges curtailed to the minimum.

It is accepted as true that a poor home is better for the rearing of a child than an institution; but it is also true that the better the home, the better the chances for the child's future well-being.

To accomplish the best results in preventive work, the fact must not be overlooked that character and habits in the young are not so dependent upon parentage and heredity as upon daily impressions received.

---

2. Rationale of payment for board of children in families, 1893

Homer Folks, "Family Life for Dependent Children," in Spencer and Birtwell, eds., *Care of Dependent, Neglected and Wayward Children,* pp. 75–80.

We have not yet spoken of the terms on which children may be safely and properly entrusted to families — a matter in regard to which there is great diversity both in practice and in opinion. Legal adoption, securing for the child the full standing and rights of an own child, including heirship, is, of course, the ideal; but as a matter of fact it is very rarely secured, except for children placed out under three years of age. The more usual arrangement is that of the indenture, a legal contract, the essential feature being that the child is compelled to remain with the family until he reaches a certain age, if a boy eighteen, if a girl twenty-one. It must be said that the earlier forms of these legal indentures seem to have been drawn with the sole idea of "protecting" the foster parents against the loss of the child's services and afforded little or no safeguard to the child against the possible cupidity or cruelty of the master. The provision for the education of the child was either vague and indefinite or wretchedly inadequate. There stands upon the statute books of New York a law, re-enacted in 1884, which states that in every indenture it shall be provided "that the child shall be instructed to read and write, and, if a male, in the elements of arithmetic, and at the expiration of the indenture shall be given a new Bible"!

While among progressive institutions the terms of indenture have been much modified in the interest of the child, there is a growing feeling that any legal contract compelling a child to serve a master for a certain term of years, mortgaging his future to pay for his present, affects unfavorably the standing of the child in the community and in the mind of the foster parent, degenerating in its worst phases into something little better than slavery. Nor is it apparent that any inflexible contract can meet varying conditions. If the agreement is to be based, as it should be, on equity, it must take into account the age of the child when placed, his physical strength, his previous training, the amount of attendance at school, and many other factors. The Children's Aid Societies of New York, Boston, Pennsylvania, and perhaps others, use no written agreement whatever, but adjust the terms from year to year as the developments of each individual case seem to require, excepting, of course, in cases of legal adoption. This method gives perfect flexibility and is undoubtedly the best plan, provided it is guarded by an ever-vigilant supervision, but is possibly the worst plan of all if not so guarded. It should be stated in this connection that no agreement, written or unwritten, is either just or wise which contemplates conditions for these children any different from the conditions of the other children of the community of like age. Any plan which compels or allows these children to work when the others are at play or in school, or to give services without pay for which

others under like circumstances receive wages, is as unwise as it is unjust, and is a disgrace to the people of any state.

To reject unflinchingly all applications which this sifting process has shown to be undesirable requires courage. Placing out is not easy work. The current statement, "There are always more applications than children," which so generally passes at par value, must be heavily discounted if we mean suitable homes and without payment. It is true as regards healthy infants and, in some seasons of the year, for children evidently able to work. It is not true with regard to ordinary boys from four to eight or ten years of age, it is not true as regards delicate or unattractive children, or children who may be reclaimed by parents. Many advocates of the family plan seem to believe that it is only necessary that the managers of institutions should be willing to place out; that if the doors of the institutions can only be opened, crowds of benevolent people will press in and carry away every child to a happy home. This, alas, is contrary to the general experience. As one has said, "We must go far and wide into the world with lanterns in our hands, looking, like Diogenes, for an honest man and a good woman, and we must look till we find them." Institutions will remain in their present congested condition until their managers are not simply willing to place out but are ready to take active, aggressive measures in finding and using suitable homes.

Even then the institution population will hardly be materially diminished until we add to our plan one more provision, namely, payment for board of children in families when necessary. The family plan as usually understood, that is, without provision for payment for board in special cases, cannot provide for that very large class of dependent children whose parents are living and have not forfeited their natural rights by unnatural neglect or cruelty. It is an injustice to respectable parents to remove their children permanently at the first blow of misfortune, and thoughtful people will not often receive such children into their homes, expecting them to be permanent members of their households, if the whole truth has been told. There is also a large class of children who are unattractive in appearance or who have some slight physical, mental, or moral defect or peculiarity which turns the balance against them when foster parents are making their choice. Even if the defect be successfully concealed and the people take with them an undesirable child, the deception is soon discovered and the child returned, often with exaggerated stories of moral perversity. There is also a large class of children whose early years have not been childhood. Premature burden-bearing has left no place for happy, innocent play, for kindergarten or school. The physical growth and the mental development have been stunted alike. These are the children who, more than any others, need a country home and a mother's love. Yet, without payment for board, they are either retained for years in the institution, or, if placed out in free homes, they are soon returned with the complaint, "so slow and dull." "Slow and dull" indeed! "Weak and untrained" are more often the proper words. Many believe that there is a need for an institution in which such children may be trained a year or two and made "ready for families," that is, serviceable.

Beyond question we have here reached a limitation of the family plan without payment, and it now becomes a choice between an institution and boarding in families. To those who reject boarding in families, an institution becomes at this point a necessity, both in theory and practice. Those, however, who accept the other alternative, namely, the principle of the payment for board of such children in families, argue that the need is not to "make the child ready for family life," but to make the conditions of the family ready for the child; to obviate the demand for services by paying for the child's maintenance in the family, where, they believe, he rightfully belongs. The great majority of children who are returned after being placed in homes are returned not because of moral perversity, but because of their inability to render a certain amount of service which the foster parents rightfully expected. In most cases the

boy was not a bad boy, but a bad bargain. He was a small boy, a weak boy. He was not able to be self-supporting, not ready to face life's battle yet; and the parent, or whoever stood in place of parent, must bear the burden of his support for a year or two longer. The boy did not need special or industrial training; he needed more muscle, more climbing of trees, more running after rabbits, more play, more childhood.

I believe that this issue can and must be met on purely business principles. If we try to get something for which we give no return, we degrade ourselves and our children and find in the end, as all such people do, that we have been chasing an *ignis fatuus*. Two things are needed — good, healthy, average family life for those children who are not especially attractive, are too old for adoption and too young to be serviceable; and, second, special care, wise training, and extra school privileges for those who are old enough but not strong enough to be serviceable or whose earlier education has been neglected. These things we cannot secure, except in very rare cases, without payment for board. That they can be secured by such payment is amply proven by the success of boarding out in Pennsylvania, Massachusetts, Australia, and many European countries. The Children's Aid Societies of Pennsylvania and Boston, which receive and care for dependent children of all ages and conditions, have for them no institution whatever. Whenever the alternative between an institution and payment for board in a private family is presented, the latter is accepted. Their undoubted success proves that the plan is as good in practice as it is in theory.

But philanthropic people ask, "Will not this boarding out break down entirely the system of adoption and free or permanent homes?" If some families are paid for the care of children, will it not discourage other people who might have taken a child without payment and from benevolent motives? The best answer to this objection lies in the fact that where boarding out on this principle, namely, of paying when necessary to secure proper care, has been tried, it has not hindered but has greatly assisted in the finding of free homes, and that there is just as much benevolence, and just as little, in boarding out as in placing in free homes. The reasons for this are not far to seek. The facts in human life which create the demand for children for adoption or free homes are too deep-seated to be affected by the fact that other children are received for payment. I will frankly avow my conviction that, whatever the future may hold in store for dependent children, people do not at present, except in very rare instances, apply for children from a desire to do good, but from a desire to secure for themselves either company or service. The demand is of great value in our system of benevolent work, but is not itself benevolent. I do not mean to suggest that the motives are evil; they are simply neutral. The demand for young children for adoption, legal or otherwise, is simply the expression of that universal desire for the presence and affection of children which is everywhere one of the most constant factors of human life. It is no more benevolent than is the appetite for food. The same desire for the inspiration, cheerfulness, and sunshine which the presence and companionship of a child bring is present in varying degree in many of the applications for older children. In the demand for older children there is also present in varying degree a second element — the desire for service; a perfectly legitimate and a valuable factor, but neither benevolent nor necessarily evil. These two things, the desire for companionship and the desire for service, have actuated the people who come to our placing-out offices to apply for children.

Boarding out, in the sense described above, does not satisfy and hence does not remove either of these demands, insofar as they are legitimate demands. It does not satisfy the desire for companionship, because there is always, so long as a child is boarded, the certainty that sooner or later it will be removed, unless in due time it is kept free of charge by the same family, as so frequently occurs. To those who really wish a child "as their own," present satisfaction is forbidden by the certainty of future separa-

tion. It does not satisfy the desire for services, because while the child is boarded he must be sent to school from September until June and be given more personal attention and care than he can possibly return. He is boarded simply because he cannot with justice to his future be now serviceable. But boarding out does foster both these demands, because it places the young child in the family, where nature can develop an affection which in many cases results in its adoption; the older child it places in a family where in some degree the attachments are also developed, and where the child is under conditions and receiving training which will enable it to be serviceable at the earliest moment. "The family plan," without any provision for payment when necessary, is not the family plan. It is only a part of it, and should be called "the family system, so far as it can be utilized without cost."

---

3. Boarding-out Jewish children, New York City, 1910

Solomon Lowenstein, "A Study of the Problem of Boarding Out Jewish Children and of Pensioning Widowed Mothers," *Proceedings* of the Sixth Biennial Session of the National Conference of Jewish Charities in the United States (1910), 206–211.

Lowenstein was superintendent of the Hebrew Orphan Asylum in New York City. In 1910 the Hebrew Orphan Asylum and the Hebrew Sheltering Guardian Society supported a total of about five hundred children in boarding homes.

It may be in order to state, first, the methods employed in this work. Homes are secured, primarily, in response to advertisements in the daily newspapers — English, German and Yiddish. Families are referred to the institution from various private sources; for example, by lodges, charitable individuals and families already having children in board. All such applications are carefully investigated by a special agent, giving his entire time to this work. This results in the rejection of the overwhelming majority of the applications received. During the past fiscal year 50 of 148 applications were accepted by the Hebrew Sheltering Guardian Society; 80 out of 603 by the Hebrew Orphan Asylum. In addition to the inspection by the institutions, all homes, found satisfactory by them, must be reported to the Board of Health of the City of New York, which rigorously investigates and determines whether the home is satisfactory for the placement of children and, at the same time, limits the number that may be so placed, in accordance with the size of the rooms, sanitary accommodations, number of persons in applicant's family and character of furniture. No children are ever boarded by either institution until the Board of Health permit has been secured. Speaking for the Hebrew Orphan Asylum, I may state, in this connection, that no home, recommended by our inspector, has ever been rejected by the Board of Health, and I am confident that a similar assertion might be made on behalf of the Hebrew Sheltering Guardian Society.

It is required that, in all cases, the family applying shall have sources of income other than that received for the care of children. All applicants must furnish at least five references, not related to them, who must testify in writing, on supplied forms, to a list of questions, designed to secure information as to the financial, social, religious and moral responsibility of the persons applying for the care of children. Children are placed in Jewish families only, and never in families where there are small children who will require the attention of the mother and divert it from the boarded children.

All boarded children attend the public schools, and report cards of their progress must be shown to the investigator of the institution each month, when issued. Children in board are entered at the nearest religious school, when there is one at an accessible distance. In a number of instances special payments are made for this purpose.

The health of the children is carefully supervised by means of regular examinations by the institutional physicians and, in the case of the children placed by the Hebrew Sheltering Guardian Society, by a visiting nurse. All children are regularly weighed and measured and, naturally, receive special treatment in cases of acute illness.

All clothing is furnished by the institutions and, likewise, all incidental expenses, apart from board, are met.

This work is supervised by the State Board of Charities, which, in New York State, is a very efficient body. Boarding homes are visited and office records examined by a special investigator of the State Board of Charities. During the past year the work of both institutions in this department has been placed in Class I, the highest rating of the State Board. In view of the fact that some of the most efficient agencies for placing children have their headquarters in New York City, this rating is a source of just pride to the institutions.

In order that the work of supervision may be thoroughgoing additional investigators are employed for this purpose, who investigate and visit the homes in which children have been placed at least once a month in all cases, and in many cases semi-monthly. The children themselves make frequent visits to the institution for the purposes of obtaining clothing, to have shoes repaired, to visit the physician and to be advised concerning their work in school, when this is necessary. They are thus under constant observation, and are free to report concerning their homes, so that whenever it appears advisable children may be transferred to another home in case the one already found should for any reason prove undesirable.

.   .   .   .   .

During the past year an attack upon the work of boarding out Jewish children in New York City was made by Dr. S. Wolfenstein, of the Cleveland Orphan Asylum, after a visit to

New York and an investigation of a few homes. We believe, with all due respect to Dr. Wolfenstein's judgment, that he was grossly mistaken in his estimate of this work. In connection with this report an independent investigation of homes in which children have been placed by the two institutions was made by Messrs. M. D. Waldman, of the United Hebrew Charities of New York City, and D. M. Bressler, of the Industrial Removal Office. These gentlemen visited homes of their own selection in various parts of the city. No notification of these visits had been given to the boarding mothers, and the homes were visited by them under the same conditions as those in which they were accessible to Dr. Wolfenstein, to whom likewise a full list of the homes of the Hebrew Orphan Asylum had been furnished upon his visit to New York. The writer does not believe that he can enter, with any impartiality, into this discussion, and he prefers, therefore, to leave this matter to be presented to the Conference by the two gentlemen mentioned, as part of the discussion upon this paper.

I would, however, present the following points in resumé of this portion of the topic. The children placed in good boarding homes receive, in general, more individual attention and, in the great majority of cases, more individual affection than is possible in the best institution. They are kept clean, both as regards their bodies and their clothing. They live in a type of home far better, in most instances, than those from which they had been taken, and as good as those occupied by the great majority of the self-respecting, independent working class of New York's Jewish population. They are living, some of them, in the far better neighborhoods of New York; most in the newer parts of the city, and many in houses of a type of construction definitely better than were the homes of New York's Jewish population at a time when the present generation of well-to-do Jews of New York were children. There need be no fear that these children are being placed in improper homes. It is true that, at times, the right personal adjustment is not always secured

at the first placement, and subsequent transfers may be necessary. In other cases women, whose homes have been found satisfactory, have proved unsatisfactory because of personal characteristics, which make them ineligible to continue in charge of children. Such homes must be abandoned, but the percentage of such failures is small and does not militate against the general value of this method of care. But, beyond such general argument in its favor as a means of caring for all kinds of children that come to us, we may definitely assert that it has decided advantages over the institutional method in at least three classes of cases:

First — The child, under seven or eight years of age, really has no proper place in a large congregate institution. Such children thrive much better, both physically and mentally, in the small private home, and should be boarded out, whenever possible.

Second — Every institution has its share of children who are abnormal or atypical, either socially or intellectually. They may be unduly precocious or abnormally dull, without having sunk to the level of feeble-mindedness. They may be unfit, by reason of undue timidity or undue assertiveness, for life in the crowded institutional ranks. The well-selected boarding home is far better than the institution for such cases.

Third — The class of physical defectives; children having heart trouble, crippled children or those suffering from any other physical ailment, requiring hospital treatment, are ineligible for admission to most institutions, but can easily be cared for in a good private home.

For another class the boarding home is often preferable. I refer to those half-orphans, who are motherless. The father is often able and anxious to live with his children, and very often the boarding home provides this means. Often, though the father cannot live in the same home with his children, the boarding home is, in many instances, preferred by him because of the frequency with which he may visit the children and the oversight that he can bestow upon them. The Hebrew Orphan Asylum makes it a rule never to place fatherless half-orphans in board unless the mother is incapable of caring for her own children by reason of physical or moral disqualifications.

The one great question that the boarding-out system has yet to answer and which, at least in the case of the Jewish institution, it cannot yet answer because of its comparative newness, is what effect will it have upon the children as they become older, and what can it give in the way of future training. With regard to the latter, I see no reason why the institution cannot give its boarding-out children the same advantages as it offers to those brought up within its walls. The answer to the former is more dubious, and can be determined only when the future shall have given us more material upon which to base our judgment.

---

4. Status of boarding-out system, 1910

Hart, *Preventive Treatment of Neglected Children,* pp. 225–227.

Children may be placed out in private families on board, the board being paid either by the parents, in whole or in part, or from the public treasury, or from the treasury of some private organization. The boarding-out system is used extensively in the state of Massachusetts, where in 1908 the state board of public charities paid from the public treasury for "the support of state minor wards," $346,000. The city of Boston paid for the board and care of children in the neighborhood of $75,000, and private organizations paid in the neighborhood of $50,000, a total of about $471,000 for the care of children boarded in private family homes.

The boarding-out system is practiced quite extensively in the state of Pennsylvania and the District of Columbia. It is practiced to a considerable extent also in the states of New Jersey and California, and in a lesser degree in the other states of the Union.

In Massachusetts, the tendency has been to substitute the placing-out method for the care of children in institutions. The building of new orphan asylums has practically ceased, and no less than 13 orphan asylums and children's homes have been closed within the last few years, family home care being substituted. Among the institutions closed were: The Massachusetts State School at Monson; the two homes of the Boston Children's Aid Society; the home of the Boston Children's Friend Society; the home of the Boston Children's Mission; the Boston Female Asylum.

The Boston child-helping societies have substituted home care for institutional care, even in cases where the child is only to be under care for a day or two.

The boarding-out plan has not yet made much headway, except on the Atlantic border. In the central states, public sentiment has not yet advanced to the point of providing the necessary financial support for the boarding-out system. It is usually much easier to induce people to contribute toward the support of an institution with visible buildings, grounds and groups of children, than to induce them to contribute toward the support of children scattered in farm and village homes, without any visible institutional signs. Strangely enough, people will cheerfully contribute for the building of expensive institutions, and will contribute in addition full as much for the support of children in these institutions, as they would have to pay for their support in family homes outside of the institutions.

On the other hand, it is always easier to obtain free homes (without the payment of board) for children in new and undeveloped communities, than in old and rich communities. People in primitive communities are apt to be warm-hearted and hospitable. They have no fine furniture and polished floors to be injured, and, on the other hand, they are glad of the contributory services of a growing boy or girl. As a community grows older or richer, and as people accumulate mahogany furniture, fine rugs, polished floors and formal manners, they become less willing to receive a neglected, untaught, dirty and troublesome child.

It is not easy to predict whether the boarding-out system will find favor in the West, but the probability is that it will develop there, as it has in the East. It is probable also that this plan will have to be taken up by the state governments in the West, as has already been done in the East, for the reason that the cost of this method on a large scale is beyond the probable means of the child-helping societies.

D. PROBLEMS OF SUPERVISION

Defects in the indenture system of public institutions

1. Children indentured at Monson Almshouse, Massachusetts, 1865

Franklin B. Sanborn, "The Children Indentured at Monson," in Massachusetts, State Board of Charities, *First Annual Report, 1864* (Boston, 1865), pp. 282–287.

Monson was one of three almshouses maintained by Massachusetts for "state paupers," that is paupers who could not claim legal residence in any of the towns of the state.

Closely connected with the education of the poor children at the Almshouse, is the disposal made of them on leaving it. Of course, the great majority of them are returned to the custody of their parents or other relatives, from whom they are separated in the Almshouse, even if the whole family is there. There have probably been no less than 8,000 children admitted to the Almshouse. The number now remaining is 462; the number who have died is less than 500; number of indentured children is 728; and

enough more have probably been adopted or sent to places without the formality of an indenture, to make up the full number of one thousand. It would appear, then, that no less than 75 per cent of the whole have been discharged without going to service.

Mr. Joseph H. Brewster, the experienced clerk of the Almshouse, has, according to my request, and with considerable pains, collected and furnished the following statement of the localities, age, sex, condition, etc., of the 728 indentured children, which, though far from being complete, will give a comprehensive view of many of the particulars which should be known concerning them: —

Return Concerning Children Indentured by the Inspectors and Superintendent of the State Almshouse, Monson, up to October 1st, 1864

1.	Whole number indentured	728
2.	Number indentured in Massachusetts	580
3.	Whole number of boys	449
4.	Whole number of girls	279
5.	Number known to have died	1
6.	Number known to have absconded	49
7.	Number returned to the Almshouse	138
8.	Number who have enlisted	6
9.	Number known to be married	1
10.	Number supposed to be now with their employers	505

	Girls	Boys	Total
11. Number indentured under 10 years old	116	38	154
12. Number indentured at 10 years old	57	85	142
13. Number indentured at 11 years old	34	126	160
14. Number indentured at 12 years old	35	110	145
15. Number indentured at 13 years old	20	53	73
16. Number indentured at 14 years old	10	23	33
17. Number indentured over 14 years old	7	14	21
Totals	279	449	728

18. Number whose employers have sent
reports the present year — 60
19. Number visited by
Superintendent or Inspectors — Large number
20. Number who have visited the
State Almshouse — Unknown
21. Number heard from in other ways — Unknown
22. Number known to have done well — Unknown
23. Number known to have led vicious
lives — Unknown
24. Number known to have been ill-treated
by their employers — 3
25. Average age of all who have been
Indentured — $11\frac{157}{728}$ years
26. Number taken for adoption — 16
27. Number now out on trial —
Girls, 16; Boys, 17. Total — 33

The number of these indentured children is greater than at both the other Almshouses, although the whole number of children placed out, with or without indentures, is probably greater at the other Almshouses, taken together. At neither of them, however, have I been able to procure statistics so complete as these.

Yet a cursory examination will show how defective these must be. Out of 728 who have been indentured in a period of ten years, only *one* is reported dead and *one* married, and three ill-treated by their employers. A mortality of less than one-seventh of one per cent in ten years is, of course, much too low; and a conjugality at the same rate would threaten the extinction of the human race, if it were not accompanied by so low a rate of mortality. Nor can any one doubt, who knows what human nature is, and what has been the experience of the officers at Westborough and Lancaster, that a considerable number of these children have been ill-treated by their employers. It will be noticed, too, that no record has been made of those who visited the almshouse, or were visited by its officers, or heard from in other ways. The number in each of these classes is known to be large, and if a record had been kept it would have furnished answers in some degree to ques-

tions 22 and 23, which are the most important of all in the list.

It is not to be wondered at that the return is so imperfect, for with all the other duties of the officers at Monson, they cannot be expected to look closely after the children whom they indenture. Yet it is manifest that the duty of the State towards these poor children is not performed, when she has relieved herself of the burden of their support. Massachusetts does not regard their support as a burden; for she can, by assuming it, also secure to them a competent education, placing them at once outside of the class of paupers. But she fails to secure this education when she places them under masters at the age of eleven years, and takes no pains to learn how those masters treat them, how they teach them, or how they protect them. I have already spoken on this subject in treating of the schools at Westborough, Lancaster and Tewksbury, and can here only repeat my former suggestion, that an agent should be employed to visit all the indentured children sent out from all the State institutions, and to have a general oversight of the whole matter of apprenticeship. When I visited the New York City Nurseries on Randall's Island, I found that precisely the same difficulty exists there. That is an institution, as you know, similar to what Monson would have become under the classification law of 1855. It is devoted exclusively to children, and I found nearly 500 of both sexes there at school. While they remain they are well instructed; but they are rapidly sent out to places in various parts of the country, and there is no certainty that they will ever be heard of again. During the administration of Mr. Leonard as one of the board of Ten Governors of the New York City institutions, I was informed that he secured the adoption of precisely such a system as I have recommended, and that it worked well. At the New York House of Refuge, also on Randall's Island, the Chaplain is made the agent to visit apprenticed boys and girls, and to a limited extent, he is able to do so.

It will be noticed, that out of 505 children

supposed to be still with their employers, only 60 have been heard from during the past year, or about one in eight. Of the great majority of the rest, little is really *known*. At the other State Almshouses the provisions requiring masters to report the condition of their apprentices is not in force at all, so that, of all the children annually sent out to places from the three institutions (upwards of a hundred) not more than ten per cent probably have their condition made known to the officers who sent them.

was scarcely an unbruised spot, and around her neck, the well-defined bruised line and abraded surface, made by a rope with which she had been hung. The parties perpetrating these outrages were subsequently arrested and tried, and one of them (the woman) fined.

That there should be some further accountability of infirmary officers and better protection of infirmary children provided for by law, this and other cases that might be cited will indicate.

2. Child placed out without record of transaction, Ohio, ca. 1867

Ohio, State Board of Charities, *Third Annual Report, 1869* (Columbus, 1870), p. 57.

The case is reported by Albert G. Byers, secretary of the State Board of Charities.

. . . an occurrence incident to my visit . . . suggests a matter of importance to a class of infirmary inmates that is constantly increasing, and for whom, as yet, comparatively little interest is shown. Some two years ago, under the management of the Greene County Infirmary . . . a little girl, seven or eight years old, was given out to a family to be "raised." No record was made of the transaction, nor was there anything (so far as shown in the infirmary records) to show that any such child had had an existence. She had been taken away to a remote part of the county, and no remembrance had of her afterwards. On the day of my visit, in June last, the little girl returned to the infirmary, complaining of great cruelty experienced at the hands of the family that had taken her away, and bearing upon her person sad confirmation of her complaint.

God only knows what she had endured during these two years. At the time of her return, her flesh was livid with terrible beating. From her shoulders to her heels, body and limbs, there

3. "Letting out children to all comers," New York, 1874

New York Times, April 14, 1874.

The public will learn with satisfaction that the Grand Jury have found several indictments against the woman Connolly, for her alleged inhuman treatment of the child Mary Ellen Wilson. In the course of yesterday's investigation into the matter, the Superintendent of Outdoor Poor gave some instructive evidence in regard to the mode of disposing of children practiced by the Commissioners of Charities. In the case of little Mary Ellen, a reference from a physician of undetermined status was taken as sufficient guarantee that the child would be properly treated by the persons applying for her custody. There was evidently no attempt made to find out by actual inspection whether Mrs. Connolly's ward received the kind of attention which was contemplated in her "indenture." [1] Under the haphazard operations of such a system, it is not reassuring to hear that, "during the past year 500 children have passed through the department." What guarantee can the Commissioners give that some of these have not been used to swell the ranks of professional beggars, or to become the objects of base and brutal

1. For the indenture of Mary Ellen Wilson to Mrs. Connolly see above Part Two, Chap. II, sec. A, "The Case of Little Mary Ellen," New York, 1874, doc. 2.

usage? This care ought not to be lost sight of till public opinion has compelled the Department of Charities to make provision against the gross abuse of their system of letting out children to all comers.

Responsibility of New York State Board of Charities, 1894–1900

The New York State Board of Charities, created by statute in 1867, received constitutional status in the state Constitution of 1894. Section 11 of Article VIII of the Constitution provided that the State Board should "visit and inspect all institutions, whether State, county, municipal, incorporated or not incorporated, which are of a charitable, eleemosynary, correctional or reformatory character," with the exception of institutions subject to inspection by the State Commission on Lunacy and the State Commission of Prisons. Legislation enacted in 1875 and 1896 strengthened the Board's powers of visitation, inspeciton, and general supervision of charitable institutions.

---

1. Investigation of a subsidized orphan home, New York City, 1896

New York, State Board of Charities, *Report of an Investigation of the Affairs of the Ladies' Deborah Nursery and Child's Protectory by a Special Committee* (Albany, 1896), pp. 9–10.

The special committee included Dr. Stephen Smith and two other commissioners, Mrs. Beekman de Peyster and Tunis G. Bergen. The institution under investigation had been incorporated in 1878 "for the temporary nursing and taking care of such infant children of poor parents, or abandoned children between the age of two years and six years, as the managers may be willing to receive." In 1897, as a result of the investigation, the institution was closed.

The committee find that the Ladies' Deborah Nursery and Child's Protectory of the city of New York is an institution without an endowment fund, receiving no fees and but few donations, and dependent for its existence upon the allowance per capita out of the excise funds of the city of New York; that out of the revenue of more than $40,000 per annum which it receives from the excise funds the Nursery not only supports about 400 children, but also has managed to accumulate substantially all of its property, renting and furnishing buildings, and also purchasing real estate; that for many years its members have paid no fees and the managers have elected themselves; that two or three families with their connections have controlled its affairs; that one of its buildings is rented from its President, who also owns another building, which has been occupied by the suppliers of meat to the Nursery, that another manager, lately the Treasurer, also supplies it with the large items of bread and milk; that the wife of the President is the Chairman of the House Committee and substantially orders all the supplies; that its financial management has been practically in the hands of but three or four persons and that other trustees confess ignorance of its affairs; that many of the old books of account, vouchers, etc., are missing and some of those produced show irregularities in the care and disposition of large funds received from the Comptroller; that the expenditures show large sums paid for salaries, buildings, furniture and improvements and comparatively small sums for the care, clothing, education and general treatment of the children; that carelessness and ignorance are displayed in both the physical and mental treatment of the children; that children are said to be in good health at times when examination shows the prevalence of disease; that complaints about the treatment of children seem to be numerous and the chief managers admit that they have great trouble with their own superintendents; that there is no system of placing out children, and the belief of the chief managers is expressed that they are obliged to keep the children until they are 16 years of age; that the history of the Nursery betrays the desire of the managers to maintain as large a number of children on its rolls as possible in order to become entitled to the per capita allowance from the City funds; that such rolls are not always in good order or accurately kept; that in the year 1892 the Comptroller compelled the Nursery to repay more than $4,600; that, although the Nursery was designed for the care of Hebrew children, it has not the respect of prominent Hebrew philanthropists of the city, is not in good repute with the officers of the United Hebrew Charities, and is not in favor with the Society for the Prevention of Cruelty to Children; that in general the management of this Nursery shows a lack of the proper spirit of charity and philanthropy and is neither careful nor intelligent in the mental or physical development of the children of the poor who are under its control.

Your Committee, therefore, recommend that the State Board of Charities take action to prohibit the further detention of children in the Nursery and to prevent the further payments of money to it by the Comptroller of the City of New York, after consulting with the officers of the United Hebrew Charities and other benevolent Hebrews with the view of properly providing for the care and custody of the children now in the Nursery in other institutions, or of so reorganizing the Nursery as to provide it with proper funds and a new membership with new officers, managers and trustees.

Dated *April* 6th, 1896.

---

2. Jurisdiction of the State Board limited, 1900

The People of the State of New York ex rel. The State Board of Charities v. The New York Society for the Prevention of Cruelty to Children, 161 N.Y. 233, 242–246; 272–274.

In 1898 the New York Society for the Prevention of Cruelty to Children challenged the State Board's supervisory powers by refusing to allow the Board to inspect its temporary quarters for children.[1] Lower courts upheld the Board's authority but in this case the Court of Appeals ruled that the S.P.C.C. was not a charitable institution within the meaning of the Constitution of 1894 and hence was not subject to visitation. The court also ruled that the jurisdiction of the State Board was limited to those charitable institutions which received public funds. The following are excerpts from the majority (O'Brien) and dissenting (Martin) opinions.

O'Brien, J. . . .

In a very broad and general sense it may doubtless be said that any individual or corporation that does anything to avert or alleviate human misery or human suffering in any of their varied forms without gain or reward is engaged in a work of charity. All good works of this description generally proceed from motives of charity, and it is in that sense only that the defendant can with any propriety be called a charitable institution. But it is obvious that upon an inquiry with respect to the true legal meaning of a charitable institution, as that term is used in the Constitution and the statutes, that line of argument is misleading and fallacious, since it proves altogether too much. It would embrace a great variety of corporations that have never been and are not now classed as charitable in any legal sense. It would include all organizations of a religious or benevolent character, all educational institutions and all fraternal societies like the Masons and Odd Fellows, since they all possess some feature that might be called charitable. It would include every society for the prevention of crime, or for the promo-

1. For the opposition of the S.P.C.C. to the founding of the United States Children's Bureau see below Part Six, Chap. I, sec. A, The struggle for passage of the Children's Bureau bill, 1909–1912, doc. 5.

Cincinnati Children's Home Children Depart for Picnic, ca. 1910.

Is the poorest home better than the best institution? "Bandit's Roost," Mulberry Street, New York City, 1888. Photograph by Jacob A. Riis.

tion of temperance, the elevation of the condition of the Indians or the colored people in the south, and even societies formed to mitigate the calamities of war and to promote peace. Surely we cannot impute to the framers of the Constitution and the statute an intention to use terms in such a vague and general sense. . . . The charitable institutions referred to in the Constitution and the statute are those that have long been known and recognized as such by legislators and other officers engaged in the administration of the state government. The visitorial power of the state board of charities over such institutions is not new. It was conferred by the same act which created the board. . . The present Constitution added nothing to these powers, except the right to make rules for the government of such institutions as were subject to visitation. If the defendant is a charitable institution, subject to such visitation, it has been such for nearly a quarter of a century, since the day of its creation.

The powers of the board over charitable institutions originated in the abuses supposed to exist in the appropriation and expenditure of public money for charitable purposes. Therein is to be found the reason of the law, and it is safe enough to assume that a corporation that does not fall within the reason of the enactment is not a charitable institution, even though engaged in a good and laudable work without gain or reward. The board was empowered to deal with charitable institutions, not in the broad and general sense to which I have referred, but in the more limited and restricted sense in which these terms are used in the Constitution and the statute. The scheme of state supervision was not intended to apply to every institution engaged in some good or commendable work for the relief of humanity from some of the various ills with which it is afflicted, but only to those maintained in whole or in part by the state or some of its political divisions through which charity, as such, was dispensed by public authority to those having a claim upon the generosity or bounty of the state. These are the only institutions that are within

the reason or policy of the law, and when thus limited and restricted there is still ample scope for its application. It will apply to all institutions, public or private, that give public pecuniary relief in that form commonly called charity when we refer to the administration of government, and it will exclude only those institutions that ask nothing in the form of charity from the state though they may be engaged in some good work in their own way that might be called charitable in the sense that it is unselfish and voluntarily assumed.

There is such a plain distinction between the charity which the state dispenses by statute, and that which is voluntarily extended by private benevolence, either through individuals or societies with a corporate organization, that there will be little practical difficulty in fixing the limits of supervision by the state board of charities. There are numerous incorporated missionary societies in this state that in a large sense might be called charitable institutions, since the object of their creation and existence is the dissemination of religious ideas, not only at home but throughout the world, even in regions the most remote. They are maintained by private bequests, voluntary donations and collections made in the various churches. They have legal capacity to receive and administer all such gifts, as we know from the very frequent controversies that come before us concerning the validity of such bequests in wills. But no one, I think, will contend that the state board of charities has any right to an inspection of the books and papers of these corporations, or to make rules for the transaction of their business, for the obvious reason that they are not the charitable institutions that come within the purview of the Constitution or the statutes. The charity with which the state is concerned is something quite different. That consists in the distribution of relief or public aid, the fruit of taxation levied alike upon the willing and the unwilling. The right of visitation and regulation applies only to those institutions, public or private, through which the state fulfills this function. They alone are within the reason of the law, and, consequently, within its scope and operation. One of the most familiar rules of statutory construction is that general words must be limited to the particular purpose or end which the lawmakers had in view. They must be understood and applied in the special sense in which they are used by legislators. What may be called governmental charity, or charity based upon public taxation and administered by a system of staute law, is a very different thing from the charity that moved the good samaritan and prompted the widow's mite. The power of visitation and regulation applies to those institutions administering charity of the former kind in whole or in part, but not to those voluntarily engaged in some good work of the latter character. They are left by the state to manage their own affairs in their own way, or, at all events, are not within the jurisdiction of the state board of charities. That jurisdiction can then be defined by the application of a very just and simple test. If the particular institution, whether public or private, receives public money for use or distribution *as charity* and not for some other reason or some other purpose, that institution is subject to visitation by the board, but this system of state supervision does not extend to the efforts of private benevolence. That may flow in various channels not subject to state regulation, since the government is in no way concerned with it.

.   .   .   .   .   .

Martin, J. (dissenting) . . .

After a careful examination of all the questions presented in this case, we are unable to reach any other conclusion than that the defendant is subject to the inspection and visitation of the state board of charities, and that the court below correctly so held.

That those who inaugurated and carried into successful operation, and have maintained this institution which has awakened the interest and aroused to action the charitable and humane everywhere throughout the land, object to the supervision of the state board of charities, is somewhat difficult of explanation. But assuming, as we do, that the reason in no way involves

a lack of integrity or uprightness on the part of those connected with it, still, it in no way changes the duty of the court. It has ever been the theory of our government that the rich and the poor, the powerful and the weak, the high and the low, all stand alike in courts of justice. Therefore, although the reputation of the promoters of the defendant may be a moral assurance that no supervision of the institution is necessary, it is not a legal one. Indeed, one of the greatest difficulties which has been encountered in this case is the unimpeachable and unstained reputation of its promoters. That fact has been kept prominently before us. It is sometimes difficult to divert the mind from accompanying facts and individual friendships, even when a mere principle of law is involved, especially when a situation is disclosed where its application may seem unnecessary or unimportant. That such considerations may sometimes unconsciously warp the judgment and dull the perception of the most upright and independent, cannot be denied. And, yet, it is our imperious duty to close our eyes to questions of policy and personal friendship and simply decide the question before us without any regard to whom it may affect.

An erroneous decision of this case may not be especially important or harmful so far as the mere denial of the right to visit the institution of the defendant is concerned. The injury of such a decision arises from the fact that it practically repeals or substantially ignores the Constitution and statutes by which it was sought to protect the people, the charitable or eleemosynary institutions of the state and the objects of their bounty. This was to be accomplished by a reasonable supervision by a board which, in the language of the defendant's president, is "composed of eminent individuals from different parts of the state," and which is "entirely unsectarian, conservative in its views and firm in its action when abuses present themselves." To again subject those institutions to the negligence or rapacity of careless or unscrupulous officers or employees is to be deplored and, if possible, avoided. Hence this court should hesitate before it disregards the plain and direct mandate of the people and of the legislature, their constitutional representative.

We are of the opinion that the defendant is an institution of a charitable or eleemosynary character, and that under the Constitution and statutes the state board of charities is required to visit and inspect it in the same manner as in case of other institutions of a similar character.

---

3. The effect of the S.P.C.C. decision

William Rhinelander Stewart, "State Inspection of Private Charitable Institutions, Societies or Associations," in New York, State Board of Charities, *Thirty-fourth Annual Report, 1900* (Albany, 1901), I, 219–220.

Stewart (1852–1929) was chairman of the State Board of Charities 1894–1903 and 1907–1923. The Board's authority to visit and inspect private charitable agencies not in receipt of public funds was partially restored in 1931 and finally established by a constitutional amendment in 1938.

The immediate effect of this judgment is to destroy the system of State inspection of all private charitable institutions not in receipt of public money, a system which . . . has been the growth of a generation, built stone by stone in a series of clearly expressed statutes, and capped by the Charities Article of the Constitution and the State Charities Law.

At the close of the year 1899 about 1,200 charitable institutions, societies or associations had been visited and inspected by the State Board, and had reported to it. One thousand and eighty of these are private institutions. Of this latter number 663 are entirely supported from private sources. They include 47 day nurseries, 74 homes for aged persons, 3 homes for the blind, 35 homes for children, 6 homes for women and children, 14 homes for women and

girls, 63 general hospitals, 8 hospitals for convalescents, 1 reformatory for children, 8 reformatories for women and girls, besides a large number of other charitable institutions, societies or associations caring in some manner for the dependent and helpless classes. The inmates of the institutions specially named by classes numbered, during the year 1899, 57,571, and, through the operations of other charitable organizations not specially named, 540,000 indigent persons were relieved.

In obedience to the judgment of the court, the State Board has discontinued inspections of all of these institutions, and of their inmates. It has no further authority to obtain from them reports of their operations, and such other statistical information as has been from time to time published in the Board's reports, and furnished to the Legislature and the public . . .

A directory, with useful statistics, of all the charitable institutions of the State, public or private, was published by the Board for the years 1897 and 1898, and is in preparation for 1899. Further publication of this valuable source of reference must be suspended, the Board possessing no further power to require reports from the 663 private charities receiving no public money.

All of the inmates or beneficiaries of these several hundred institutions are now without the protection which State inspection has afforded them in the past. There is now no regularly constituted department of the State government having authority to visit and inspect any of them, investigate their management where necessary, or, through the order of the Supreme Court, to correct abuses and enforce remedies. Must not this condition be regarded as a public calamity?

.   .   .   .   .

In summing up the legislation and the constitutional provisions . . . may it not be fairly claimed that the State has evidently sought in them to protect two important interests? The greater of these is the life, health, morals and happiness of all its destitute or delinquent citizens who are the care of any organized charitable, eleemosynary, correctional or reformatory institution. The unit here considered is the individual. The lesser interest sought to be protected is the expenditure of public money for their maintenance or relief. The unit here considered is the dollar.

The first of these interests was sought to be protected by section 11 of article 8 of the Constitution, providing for visits and inspections of all institutions of a charitable, eleemosynary, correctional or reformatory character by the State Board of Charities, or the Lunacy or Prison Commissions; the second, by section 14 of the same article, restricting the payments of public money for the inmates of private charitable institutions for such only as were received and retained pursuant to rules established by the State Board of Charities.

The effect of the decision of the Court of Appeals in the case of the New York Society for the Prevention of Cruelty to Children would seem to overlook the greater interest and to pass upon the lesser one alone. The constitution clearly regarded both.

Can it be regarded as settled that the State, in allowing charitable institutions, societies or associations to take temporary charge of some of its people, relinquishes all its rights in or its duties toward them?

Under the law as it now stands, the State Board of Charities is clothed with the responsibility of approving or disapproving the incorporation of the most numerous and useful classes of private charitable institutions. Several of these applications are now pending. In case of approval, the Board on one day legalizes the existence of a charitable institution. If such institution receives no public money, the Board has no power, under the judgment of the Court of Appeals, to visit and inspect it on the next day.

No important question can be regarded as definitely settled in our age and land until it has been settled for the best interests of the people. The hands of the clock may be set back, but this does not stay the flight of time.

The great question of the proper relation of the State to all charitable institutions, societies or associations, and their inmates or beneficiaries, has yet to be tried in the enlightened forum of public opinion, to whose judgment the Legislature, the courts, and all the departments of the State government must bow. This is the tribunal of last resort. To it the destitute, unfortunate and delinquent of our people needing the protection of the State, and all who believe that they are entitled to and should receive it as a matter of right, make appeal.

State supervision of institutions and home finding agencies

1. Massachusetts appoints an agent to visit children in foster homes, 1869

"An Act in addition to an act to establish the Board of State Charities," 1869 — ch. 483, Massachusetts, *Acts and Resolves* (Boston, 1869), pp. 762–764.

The governor, with the advice and consent of the council, shall appoint an agent to visit all children maintained wholly or in part by the Commonwealth, or who have been indentured, given in adoption or placed in the charge of any family or person by the authorities of any state institution, or under any provision of this act.

He shall hold his office for one year, subject to removal by the governor and council, and shall receive an annual salary of twenty-five hundred dollars; and, with the approval of the board of state charities, he may employ such assistants and incur such expenses as may be necessary for the discharge of his official duties.

It shall be his duty to visit the children aforesaid, or cause them to be visited, at least once in three months, to inquire into their treatment, their health and their associations, and especially to ascertain whether their legal rights have been invaded, and whether all contracts or stipulations made in their behalf have been duly observed, and to collect such other information respecting them as the board of state charities may direct; and, for this purpose, he shall have the right to hold private interviews with the children, whenever he may deem it advisable.

All applications to take any of the children above specified, by indenture, adoption or any other method fixed by law, shall be referred to the aforesaid agent, who shall investigate the character of each applicant, and the expediency of so disposing of the child applied for, and report the result to the board or magistrate having jurisdiction over the child, and no such child shall be indentured or otherwise disposed of until such report is received; and in case any child shall be placed in a home which the said agent may deem unsuitable, he shall forthwith report the facts to the board of state charities for their action thereon, and the governor and council may at any time annul any indenture by which such child may be held.

Whenever application is made for the commitment of any child to any reformatory maintained by the Commonwealth, the magistrate before whom the hearing is to be held shall duly notify the visiting agent of the time and place of the hearing, by written notice mailed one week at least before the time of hearing, and directed to said agent at the state house, and the agent shall attend at said hearing in person or by deputy, in behalf of the child; and if it shall appear to the said magistrate that the interests of the child will be promoted by placing him in a suitable family, he may, instead of committing him to a reformatory, authorize the board of charities to indenture the child during the whole or a portion of his minority, or to place him in such family. And the board of state charities is hereby authorized to provide for the maintenance of any child placed in a family as aforesaid at an expense not exceeding the average cost of the support of such child in any of the state reformatories. And it shall be the duty of said agent to seek out families willing and suitable to receive such children, and furnish the names and places of residence of the same to the boards or magistrates who are to provide for the commitment or indenture of a child under this act: provided, that the provisions of this section so far as they require notice to the visiting agent shall not apply to the superior court.

The visiting agent shall make a monthly report to the board of state charities of all his proceedings, especially concerning children placed in families under the fourth section of this act, and any person aggrieved by this action shall have the right of appeal to the board or magistrate having original jurisdiction of the child.

---

2. Why state supervision is needed, 1895

Homer Folks, "State Supervision of Child-Caring Agencies," *Proceedings* of the National Conference of Charities and Correction (1895), 209–212.

The first duty of a State toward its dependent children is to know where they are. For this reason it seems to me that every society, institution, and public official should report to the State concerning each child whom it receives into its charge, stating from whom and why it receives the child, what it does for him, and, finally, what it does with him . . . It is one of the anomalies of child-caring work that, speaking broadly, nobody knows what becomes of the children.

So, too, the State, as the natural guardian of dependent children, should, it seems to me, visit and inspect at regular intervals all institutions and agencies in whose charge such children are placed. In several States the existing State Boards of Charities have authority to visit and inspect all such institutions. But in none, so far as I am aware, are all the institutions visited regularly . . .

A large proportion of the children of the State are not living in institutions, but in families. It is unfortunately the case that in most systems of State supervision and inspection these children seem to be practically lost sight of, and to be regarded as being no longer the wards of the State. The abuses in child-caring work are, however, not limited to institutions; and those who have seen much of placing-out work as it is usually done will, I am sure, agree with me that there is fully as much need that the protecting care of the State should be extended to the children who are in families as to those who are in institutions.

The reports made by institutions, agencies, and public officers to the State should therefore include the names and addresses of persons with whom children are placed, with some statement of the terms of the agreement; and subsequently reports should be made, from time to time, as to the progress and condition of the children who are placed out, and changes of residence should be reported as faithfully as transfers from one institution to another. I would go still further, and insist that the State, through its representatives, should have authority to visit and should visit, in its discretion, all these children placed in families except possibly those placed by legal adoption. In proposing this, I am not unmindful of the delicacy of the relations that frequently exist between the foster-parent and the placing-out agency, and of the danger that too many cooks may spoil the broth. Undoubtedly there might be a few cases of real hardship from such a system of State visitation; but I am convinced that the benefits would far outweigh any evil effects . . .

·   ·   ·   ·   ·

Concerning county, town, and municipal agencies for the care of children, I am of the opinion that the State should exercise large supervisory powers. As a rule, the work of these local agencies is of an inferior character. The contamination of petty politics, the narrow-mindedness of men who deal only with small affairs, and the impossibility of acquiring expert knowledge in the handling of a few cases, all these facts render the town, the county, and in most cases the city, an undesirable unit for performing child-caring services. I would recommend an exclusive State system for the public care of children in the newer States; and I believe that in the older States a State supervisory board should have large powers in compelling these local officers to perform their duties properly. As concerns the internal management of county, town, and municipal institutions for children, this board should, in my opinion, be authorized to issue a formal order to the local officers, containing its recommendations as to the remedy for any existing abuses or defects, and that this order, if approved by a judge of the Supreme Court after a hearing before him, of which the local officers should be informed, and at which they might appear, should have all the force of law, and be capable of being enforced by adequate penalties.

As to children placed in families by such local officers, I am of the opinion that the State supervisory agency should have power to remove them in its discretion, and either to return them to the proper local authorities or to make suitable provision for them at the expense of the county, city, or town.

·   ·   ·   ·   ·

By what machinery shall this State supervision be exercised? Under present political conditions the best results will probably be secured by a staff of paid officials, working under the direction and control of an honorary board of not less than seven members, appointed by the governor, the term of one member expiring each year. As to whether there should be a board devoted exclusively to child-caring agencies, separate and distinct from the ordinary State Board of Charities, I should, so far as all the larger States are concerned, unhesitatingly say yes. The intimate acquaintance with the subject which the performance of such duties presupposes seems to me to be all but incompatible with an equal familiarity with all the other divisions of the great field of charities and correction.

---

3. State supervision discussed and endorsed at first White House Conference, 1909

"Discussion," *Proceedings of the Conference on the Care of Dependent Children, 1909,* pp. 56–70.

For the Conference's resolution of state supervision, see below Chap. II, sec. A, The first White House Conference, 1909, doc. 3.

The secretary read as follows:

Should the State inspect the work of all child-caring agencies, including both institutions and home-finding societies?

. . . . . .

ADDRESS OF MR. AMOS W. BUTLER, OF INDIANAPOLIS, IND., SECRETARY STATE BOARD OF CHARITIES

Mr. BUTLER. Mr. Chairman and friends, I am aware that the subject upon which I am to speak this afternoon is one upon which there may be great difference of opinion, and therefore I have attempted to present the subject as fully as possible, and largely out of experience, or theory that has been enacted into experience, in a western State.

In years past great numbers of dependent children were brought into some of the Western States. While some were placed with care and given supervision, others were not well placed and many became poor citizens or public charges. In consequence, some States have passed laws regulating the bringing of dependent children within their borders. The facts learned regarding these alien children were in part responsible for calling attention more forcibly to the existing local children's agencies.

A study of conditions in my own State has shown what may be true elsewhere, that while we have a number of good institutions for children, none of which are of large size, that are well equipped and carefully administered, there are others which are only nominally homes. In these, children are simply boarded, without proper training or discipline, and from them they are placed out in families without any proper investigation of the home and without after-supervision. In some no records are kept, and it is impossible to tell what became of the children who went forth.

I know a man who says he feels called to care for unforunate children. He has a cottage in the country, containing four rooms and a covered porch. This he calls a children's home. Into it he has gathered, in addition to his own family, from twenty to twenty-five children. They are overcrowded, herded together, without proper attention or oversight. What kind of care and training can they receive? There is no incorporated organization. No public wards are received.

There have been home-finding agencies which for a fixed sum, varying in amount, relieved the county of the support of dependent children. The county authorities were satisfied to be relieved of this expense without ever inquiring what became of their wards. The children disappeared wholly from view.

These things are not all in the past. There has been no accurate information, to say nothing of oversight, of maternity homes, foundling homes, or baby farms. Recent investigation has brought to light the fact that there are in the city of Indianapolis alone 11 institutions that may be classed as maternity homes. Into these come women from other counties and other States and leave their offspring a public burden upon the local community. There are in Indianapolis 28 institutions or homes for foundlings. From these, children are placed out on any terms or no terms at all, simply to get rid of them. In my own State there are maternity homes, homes for foundlings, children's homes, and child-placing agencies. Some are wholly or partly supported from public funds; others are private enterprises. In caring for children all are doing a public service. Some are incorporated, others are not. All organizations or associations that receive any support whatever from the public funds or receive any public wards are under the supervision of the board of state charities. All children in family homes who are public wards are subject to the visitation and oversight of its agents. All articles of incorporation of any organization for the care of dependent children must be approved by it. All institutions that desire to receive wards from the juvenile courts — one of which is authorized in each county — must have its approval. The juvenile court-law gives authority to this board to visit and inspect all institutions, both public and private, that care for dependent children.

It seems to me that where such organizations, institutions, or agencies are engaged in doing a service for the public, and where, as in some cases, they are incorporated and receive thereby a franchise or charter from the State, it is right and desirable that at least certain classes of them should be licensed or certified, and that all of them should be subject to inspection.

I believe it to be desirable for the institution as well as for the child and the State that there should be provision for official inspection of all children's agencies; for licensing such classes of institutions dealing with infants as have been shown to be injurious or destructive to child life or careless or neglectful in the disposition of children; for the visitation of all public wards in foster homes until they are adopted. Possibly with more experience I should be willing to go further.

It should be understood that this inspection, visitation, and licensing should be done by proper persons and in the proper way. I fully realize that it is possible to do these things in such a way as to arouse just criticism. They should be done by qualified persons, in a tactful and helpful manner, with a desire to assist, in every way possible, those who are charged with this important duty to children. No child should

be made a public ward that can be reasonably well cared for by a good parent. Complete records should be kept of the children in institutions, of their antecedents and of their placement. The State is vitally interested in all its children. If they have property, even a small amount, its officers will see that a guardian is appointed therefor; that he gives bond; that he is answerable to the court; that he makes a regular written report. But if it is a child without property that is left, who thinks of having a guardian appointed for it or of having a regular report made to the court as to its condition, its progress and possibilities? Is not a child worth more than its property?

·   ·   ·   ·   ·

ADDRESS OF MR. HUGH F. FOX, PRESIDENT
STATE BOARD OF CHILDREN'S GUARDIANS
OF NEW JERSEY

·   ·   ·   ·   ·

For the past fifteen years people who deal with dependent children have thrashed this question out at the annual meetings of the National Conference of Charities and Correction, and at many of the state and local conferences.

Inspection or supervision is advocated upon the following grounds: The prevention and correction of abuses, the check upon irresponsible power, the need of assurance of fitness for the work involved, the prescribing of rules for the conduct of the work, and the raising of the general standard of efficiency, all of which imply concern for the welfare of the child, rather than concern for the protection of the public against imposition.

The objections to such inspection or supervision are all carefully qualified, and are based upon the fear of the possible political character of the state board charged with such duty, the danger attending the exercise of public authority by erratic individuals, and the fear of official fussiness and red tape.

We are all agreed as to the right and duty of

the State to supervise institutions and societies which are in receipt of public funds. The question as to inspection of private agencies, which are supported entirely by private contributions, seems to resolve itself into one of practical utility. We are all agreed as to the splendid work which has been done by private agencies, such as children's aid societies, societies to prevent cruelty to children, and orphan asylums, but we might draw upon a common fund of experience for hundreds of instances of abuse, both by public and private agencies. It should be remembered that even a private institution, supported entirely by voluntary contributions, is in a certain sense the recipient of public funds. That is to say, if it is a charitable institution, its taxes are remitted, and it receives gratis the service which the rest of us have to buy with our taxes.

.   .   .   .   .

I question the wisdom of handling dependent children through any national agency, or even through an agency which is doing an interstate business, unless it operates under state authority and direction in each State. Take the case of a society which in the course of ten years may scatter several thousand children through a territory covering an area of a thousand miles. Let us suppose that such a society, for financial or other reasons, should be discontinued. What happens to the children? Can it reinsure the human risks for which it is responsible with other agencies? If a receiver was appointed, would the receiver undertake to recognize the claims of these children for protection during their minority at the hands of the parent society? Would it be anybody's business to find out whether records of these children had been kept, and what was their present status? Do you not know of instances of this kind which have really constituted wholesale abandonment of dependent children by benevolent agencies? Or, again, take the case of societies which are organized for the protection of children against cruelty and abuse, and which, according to our careless custom, have been granted extraordinary police powers,

and even magisterial authority. There is no question that such societies have done an enormous amount of good. Can we say that these powers are not at times abused, and should there not be some provision for the instant remedy of such abuse?

I could tell you of cases in which, under the operation of the fee system, agents of such a society have cooperated with a crooked justice of the peace and have made arrests and conducted prosecutions for the sake of the fees involved. Of course, inspection will not entirely prevent such abuses. We know that even in state institutions which are subject to inspection grave evils sometimes occur, but they do not go unchecked and the remedy for them is soon found. I think that a large part of the objections to public inspection of private institutions and agencies could be removed by a careful definition and limitation of the meaning of "inspection." When you talk of inspecting the work of such organizations, it may be interpreted to mean the actual visitation by the State of children who have been placed in families, which seems to me to be most unwise. What the State should do is to make sure that the children who are placed in families are visited and kept track of, so that the particular agency may have a constant record of the condition of each child. In the case of an institution, the inspection should be sufficient to satisfy the State as to the high character and conduct of the institution. The state should make sure that the buildings are sanitary, and that they are provided with proper fire escapes, and that the children are being comfortably fed and clothed, and given instruction in conformity with the school law. Personally, I believe that every child-caring agency should be chartered by the State, and under the terms of their charter the agencies should be required to make an intelligent annual report to the State. The State should have the right to suspend or abolish the charter after thorough investigation and a hearing, and the State should have the right to order such an investigation and compel the attendance and testimony of witnesses. At the same time the State's inspection should be carefully defined and limited, so that the evils and abuses of officialism could be avoided.

I don't think we need waste time in considering the question as to the right of the State to interfere on behalf of the child. The question is one of practical utility. If the advantages of State inspection are thoroughly demonstrated, reputable agencies, whether public or private, will be only too glad to get the benefit of it. After all, it is a case of the end justifying the means.

.   .   .   .   .

The secretary read as follows:

Should the approval of the state board of charities (or other body exercising similar power) be necessary to the incorporation of all child-caring agencies and to an amendment of the charter of an existing benevolent corporation if it is to include child-caring work; and should the care of children by other than incorporated agencies be forbidden?

.   .   .   .   .

ADDRESS OF MR. ROBERT W. HEBBERD, COMMISSIONER OF CHARITIES, NEW YORK CITY

If it is necessary to require the best citizens in our communities to secure charters with the approval of the state authorities to carry on banks and insurance companies having the care of finances, why should it not, in view of the issues involved, be even more important to require a duly approved charter for the care or the placing out of children, whose welfare should be regarded as more important than the care of money.

The principle must be clearly recognized that children bereft of home and parents are the children of the State, and that only through the action of the state legislature in the enactment of general or special laws can the lawful custody of such children be given to artificial parents, whether such parents be individuals or institutions. In other words, the natural rights

which parents have in children can not be transferred, even with the consent of such parents, without such transfer is made in the manner directed by the State through statutory enactments.

This being so, it is clearly the function, and I believe a paramount duty of the state, to see that such children are cared for properly.

These laws have worked well in New York State. The old abuses have substantially disappeared and child-caring work is being carried on, whether it be in the form of institutional activities or in the placing out of children, on a higher plane and in a more progressive manner than ever before in the history of our State. The influence of the state board of charities in this respect has always been, and is now, far-reaching for good.

For these reasons, Mr. President, I am confident that this question should be answered in the affirmative by this conference.

.   .   .   .   .

REMARKS OF MRS. KATE WALLER BARRETT, GENERAL SUPERINTENDENT FLORENCE CRITTENTON MISSION. [ALEXANDRIA, VIRGINIA]

Mrs. BARRETT. I want briefly to say a word in behalf of the inspection of private institutions which have the care of children. I represent 78 private institutions, all of which care for some children. If there is one thing that impresses me in my work with private institutions for caring for children, it is the need of state supervision. [Applause.] I come across the need of it almost every day of my life. Only the other day in a city not far from here, at 10 o'clock at night, the doorbell rang and when I answered it there stood on the step a little colored girl 13 years old. In her hands she held a pasteboard shoe box that contained all her earthly possessions. When I asked the history of the child, she told me that she had been in three private institutions for the care of children in that State. The State has a board of charities, but with no authority over private institutions; I believe not over even those that receive public money. I could not believe the story the child told me. The next morning I started out, with a friend of mine, not known to these various institutions, and I visited the three, and I found that the child's story was true. She had been placed in a half dozen homes. None of those who placed her had taken proper care or supervision of the child, and at the last home into which she was placed the people moved into the country and turned her out into the street, without any place to go, and she came to the Florence Crittenton Mission. I took the child in and we have had her now four or five months. Physically she was in a bad condition, but she has the making of a useful woman in her. All the lack of care and of training that she had had came about because of the inefficiency or the oversight of the institutions that had handled her.

Under proper state supervision I do not believe many such cases as that would be possible, and so I most earnestly plead with every man and woman in this audience — it does not matter how much it may cost you — to use your influence in behalf of state supervision of private institutions, particularly of private institutions that have child caring as their principal work. I want to make that appeal from the very bottom of my heart, because I have had so much experience lately with children who have been placed in homes by indifferent societies and have not had the proper supervision after having been so placed. A private institution has nothing to lose and everything to gain by public investigation. [Applause.]

．　　．　　．　　．　　．

FRANK D. LOOMIS, GENERAL SECRETARY CHILDREN'S BUREAU, NEWARK, N.J.

Mr. LOOMIS. State inspection of child-caring agencies should be made for two reasons: First, in behalf of the welfare of the child who must be cared for, and, second, in behalf of the general social welfare as affected by the work of the child-caring agency.

It has frequently been found that child-caring societies keep children as if they were charitable wards when the parents themselves are abundantly able to provide for them. If such parents pay a dollar or two a month, it is represented that they are paying the board, although the actual cost per month for each child is usually $10 or $12. Thus homes are deliberately broken without justification, while the public pays the cost.

So long as the child remains in his own home the State supervises him in many ways which are discontinued if the child is removed to an institution. For instance, while in the custody of his own natural parents the State requires that the child shall attend school regularly. But if the child is transferred to the custody of a child-caring agency the control of the State in that regard ceases. The institution can maintain almost any kind of a school and send the child according to its own convenience. It reports only to itself. Surely state supervision of the care of children should be exercised as carefully in behalf of the child as when he is in the custody of his own parents and in his natural home.

Moreover, in the placing out of children, children of the age of 10 or 11 years are frequently put in homes where they are never sent to school. In remote rural communities the state laws regarding education are not always enforced, and while a parent may send his own boys to school he keeps the strange boy at home to help with the chores; or girls of tender age have been placed with respected families in the best of cities where they are registered as servants and treated as such. They do not come under the supervision of the truant officer, because he has no way of knowing that they are there.

Certainly the welfare of the child and the welfare of the community are concerned in the inspection of all child-caring agencies. [Applause.]

4. Supervisory and administrative authority of state boards of charity, 1910

U.S. Bureau of the Census,
Benevolent Institutions, 1910, pp. 13–14.

An important factor in the development of benevolent institutions is the changing attitude of the state toward all classes dependents, manifest in the organization of systems of supervision of charitable institutions, and the enactment of laws governing the treatment of dependents, especially children and delinquents. Seldom does a year pass without the enactment by some state of elaborate statutes providing for the better care of orphans and dependents, the establishment of juvenile courts, and the placing of all relief institutions under the general supervision, and sometimes the authority, of a state board. One result has been a new emphasis upon the close relation between the different classes of dependents. In many states children are no longer allowed in almshouses, but must be provided for in benevolent institutions; and juvenile delinquents, pending full trial, are cared for in detention homes, classed as benevolent institutions, and when committed by the courts are, except in cases of serious crime, intrusted to benevolent institutions. Furthermore, the poor officers or other authorities charged with looking after the poor in many states are specially instructed to keep in constant communication with private institutions, not merely that private relief may assist public relief, but that the recipients of relief may receive attention which the public institution could scarcely give.

State boards of charities. — Probably the most powerful influence in this direction has been that exerted through the state boards of charities. Under various names and with differing status these exercise a general supervision over the entire field of charity, often adding to it that of correction. They are generally charged with the duty of immediate inspection of institutions with a view to the prevention of abuses and the adoption of the best methods, but in the later and more elaborate codes they are required to make careful study of the entire problem of the care of the "wards of the state." Originally their duties were simply supervisory and the members gave their services for the public good, although necessary office or traveling expenses were paid. Of late it is becoming the custom to recognize them as an integral part of the state government, and the members are salaried and give their entire time to the work. In the latter case the board generally has administrative as well as supervisory authority and is frequently termed a board of control. In many cases, a supervisory board has a salaried secretary who acts as an executive officer. The following list describes the situation in each state:

Alabama	No state board. Inspector of jails, almshouses, cotton mills, and factories (salaried).
Arizona	Board of Control, supervisory and administrative (salaried).
Arkansas	Board of Trustees for State Charitable Institutions, administrative (unsalaried).
California	State Board of Charities and Corrections, supervisory (unsalaried).
Colorado	State Board of Charities and Corrections, supervisory only (unsalaried).
Connecticut	State Board of Charities, supervisory (unsalaried).
Delaware	No state board.
District of Columbia	Board of Charities, supervisory (unsalaried).
Florida	Board of Commissioners of State Institutions, supervisory; state executive officers (salaried).
Georgia	No state board.
Idaho	No state board.
Illinois	Board of Administration of State Charities (salaried). Charities Commission, supervisory (unsalaried).
Indiana	State Board of Charities, supervisory (unsalaried).
Iowa	Board of Control of State Institutions, administrative and supervisory (salaried).
Kansas	Board of Control of State Charitable Institutions, administrative and supervisory (salaried).

Kentucky	State Board of Contol of Charitable Institutions, administrative and supervisory (salaried).
Louisiana	State Board of Charities and Corrections, supervisory (unsalaried).
Maine	No state board.
Maryland	Board of State Aid and Charities, supervisory (unsalaried).
Massachusetts	State Board of Charity, supervisory (unsalaried).
Michigan	Board of Corrections and Charities, supervisory (unsalaried).
Minnesota	State Board of Control, administrative and supervisory (salaried).
Mississippi	No state board.
Missouri	State Board of Charities and Corrections, supervisory (unsalaried).
Montana	State Board of Charities and Reform, supervisory (unsalaried).
Nebraska	State Board of Charities and Corrections, supervisory (unsalaried).
Nevada	No state board.
New Hampshire	State Board of Charities and Corrections, supervisory (unsalaried).
New Jersey	Commissioner of Charities and Corrections, supervisory (salaried).
New Mexico	No state board.
New York	State Board of Charities, supervisory (unsalaried).
North Carolina	Board of Public Charities, supervisory (unsalaried).
North Dakota	Board of Control of State Institutions, administrative and supervisory (salaried).
Ohio	Board of State Charities, supervisory (unsalaried). Ohio Board of Administration, administrative (salaried).
Oklahoma	State Commissioner of Charities and Corrections, supervisory (salaried).
Oregon	No state board.
Pennsylvania	Board of Public Charities, supervisory (unsalaried).
Rhode Island	Board of State Charities and Corrections, administrative and supervisory (unsalaried).
South Carolina	No state board.
South Dakota	State Board of Charities and Corrections, administrative and supervisory (salaried).
Tennessee	Board of State Charities, supervisory (unsalaried).
Texas	No state board.
Utah	No state board.
Vermont	No state board, except for the insane.
Virginia	Board of Charities and Corrections, supervisory (unsalaried).
Washington	State Board of Control, administrative and supervisory (salaried).
West Virginia	State Board of Control, administrative and supervisory (salaried).
Wisconsin	State Board of Control, administrative and supervisory (salaried).
Wyoming	State Board of Charities and Reform, administrative and supervisory (all salaried executive officers of the state).

As will be seen these boards in most cases include under their supervision poorhouses and general poor relief, hospitals for the insane, reformatories, and not infrequently prisons, as well as what are generally regarded as more properly benevolent or charitable institutions, and this increasingly close interrelation of the different branches of their work will have an undoubted effect upon the development of distinctly charitable or benevolent work.

II Care of Children in Their Own Homes

A. PRESERVATION OF THE HOME

Philanthropic experiments,
1893–1910

---

1. Charity to the widow and her children, 1893

Robert Treat Paine, "Pauperism in Great Cities: Its Four Chief Causes," *Proceedings* of the International Congress of Charities, Corrections, and Philanthropy (1893), 27–30.

Paine (1835–1910) was founder and president of the Associated Charities of Boston.

I wish especially to draw attention to the need of a great development of charity in the treatment of widows with young children.

Large cities are disputing about the comparative merits of systems, all of which are so unworthy of our age, and so cruel to the mother and dangerous to the welfare of the child that the time has come for worthier treatment by the best method science and sympathy can devise.

No one will deny the influence growing out of different systems of dealing with this class of children. The systems in England, New York, and Massachusetts are radically different. No one of them can escape condemnation.

England very largely refuses out-relief to the widow with children, breaks up the family, and sends one or more of the children into the district school or into that department of the almshouse called the Industrial School, usually a vast institution where children are gathered by hundreds. The mother is left with only one or two children whom she may be able to support.

Am I wrong in ranking the English system as least favorable for the happiness of the home or the future welfare of the child, unjust to both mother and child, and not worthy of the Christian philanthropy of the age?

The New York system has no provision of out-door relief for such a family of children, and resembles the English method in that the family must be broken up, but the children instead of being sent to great public institutions, are distributed among private institutions which receive a per capita allowance from the state; tempting them to promote this destruction of family life.

.   .   .   .   .

The Massachusetts system aims to keep families together where there is a not totally unfit home, and if relief is not obtained from some other source, the Overseers of the Poor give, and continue, needed relief to a widow until the children grow to an age when their labor added to their mother's earnings can support the home.

Many competent judges cannot believe that

348

the Massachusetts system works well for the child, though it is certainly more humane for the mother than the system either in England or New York.

The poisonous influence of our out-door pauper relief must be felt upon the child's character in many cases, yet the family is kept together, and the children are brought up under the loving care and influence of their mother, free from the injurious influence of any institution, and especially escaping the almshouse brand.

Critics who urge the total abolition of out-door relief may claim that this system works badly even in this class of cases, and sometimes with justice when pauper relief leaves upon the child a pauper taint.

Do you ask whether in Massachusetts we think our system the best and are resolved to maintain it? I answer frankly, *No.*

Here is a better method which I believe to be the best. Aid the mother to maintain her home, provide adequate relief, but free from any pauper poison. Let it go from her church, from some private society, from some benevolent individual. Let it go as from the hand of a friend, as the circumstances of each special case may suggest to be best to the friendly visitor who undertakes the continuous task. Shame on the charity of any city which shrinks from this duty.

This is the reform which in the judgment of many of us in Massachusetts, should be engrafted upon our public relief system.

This is the class of cases which has always been used most effectively by our Overseers of the Poor in advocating the necessity of out-door relief. Taking from the Overseers this class of cases would greatly facilitate its total abolition, or great reduction.

.   .   .   .   .

A few thousand dollars of benevolent funds would replace out-relief to this class of widows and orphans, and provide for them in the best possible way, by judicious aid from a friendly hand, usually not known either to child or neighbor. How long will it be before Charity fully assumes this loving but imperative duty to the widow with her children?

---

2. The helping hand, 1898

Josephine Shaw Lowell, "Children," in William Rhinelander Stewart, *The Philanthropic Work of Josephine Shaw Lowell* (New York, 1911), pp. 268–276.

Mrs. Lowell (1843–1905) was a member of the New York State Board of Charities from 1876 to 1889, and founder of the New York Charity Organization Society. This address was originally delivered on November 18, 1898, to volunteer workers of the Charity Organization Society.

It is a truism to say that the most important work to be done among the poor is for the children, and I am almost inclined to declare that nothing else is of any importance at all, as compared with it, for every other branch of charitable work produces but small results and for only short periods of time, while what is done for the children may make the difference for each child between a whole long life of virtue or of vice, and may make the difference for the community between a large or a small number of paupers for hundreds of years.

.   .   .   .

I am going to speak today only of what should be done for children arbnormally situated, and of course I want it to be fully understood that I recognize that the training and education of the children of the great mass of the people is to be left to their parents, to the public schools, and to such other agencies as the community may devise to forward their full and well-rounded development in body, mind and soul.

What then can be done by private benevolent societies and by private benevolent individuals for children whose parents are unable to bring them up properly? What can be done which shall be beneficent as well as benevolent? One very natural answer will occur to a great many people — that these children should be taken away from their parents and put with persons who can bring them up properly; and the fact that there are in the old City of New York today eighteen thousand children who have been taken away from their parents and placed with others to be brought up shows how generally this solution of the difficulty is considered the best, and how easy it is supposed to be to find those who can bring children up better than it is possible for their parents to do.

But unhappily the problem is by no means so simple as it appears when first considered, and it is not so easy to decide upon the comparative value of a home and a strange bringing up. To begin with, there is a great variety both in the degree and in the kind of incapacity on the part of the parents. They may only be incapable physically, they may be ill or weak, or the father may be dead and the mother left alone to take the place of both father and mother, and yet they may love their children dearly and be eminently fit to bring them up worthily. Surely in such cases, it cannot be right to tear the children away? They may be foolish, weak and over-indulgent, they may be wicked and cruel, they may degrade and corrupt their children; and while there is no question that children should be saved from parents who will maim them physically or morally, there is a decided question as to whether it is good for them to be taken away from foolish and weak parents, for there is every degree of foolishness and weakness, and it is difficult to decide when the evil of the foolishness and weakness outweighs the good of the unconscious discipline of family life and of family affection.

On the other hand, also, it is necessary to consider what the alternative is. To what influences and training are the children to be subjected? Just as there is a great variety in the character of incompetent parents, so there is a great variety in the methods by which chil-

dren may be educated when taken away from their parents. Children may be put in an institution where there are many hundreds of inmates, where they must live by rule, and in crowds, without personal affection, without natural outlet of any kind, where their health, their feelings, and their minds and souls must be stultified, because the life is absolutely unnatural. They may also be put in an institution where there are only a few children and where, so far as is possible, every effort is made to teach them the ways of family life, from which they go out to the public school and mix with children living in their own homes, and are thus stimulated mentally and morally, and escape some of the very bad results of institution life. They may also not be put in an institution at all, but be boarded out in an everyday decent family, where they will be subjected to all the natural influences, pleasant and unpleasant, of common family life, and so become fitted to take their part in such life in the future. This unconscious education in the little daily duties of life is what no institution can give, and therefore, if children must be taken from their own homes, the best substitute is another home, unless indeed they are abnormal children and need special training or discipline.

But I have only touched on this question of home *vs.* outside training to call attention to the fact that even though children may be poorly placed with their own parents, it is a very serious question whether they should be removed, and also that it is very important to choose wisely the substitute for their homes, if it is necessary to separate them. In deciding the question of removal, it is also necessary to consider not only the direct effect on the child itself, but also upon the parents and upon other children and other parents, and therefore, as I have said, the problem in each case is not simple, but very complicated. But I shall not speak further of the children who have to be taken away from their parents, but rather of the comparatively large class who ought not to be taken away and who yet cannot be properly brought up without outside help; and I will hastily sketch some of the kinds of help they need. Take first the families where there is no moral deficiency, where the sickness or death of the father has removed the natural bread-winner and has made it necessary for the mother to support the family, in whole or in part, besides caring for their daily well-being. Some women can do both, but not the average woman whom we meet. They must be helped . . . and I feel sure that in all such cases the help must be given upon the principles adopted by the first benevolent society established by women in New York one hundred and ten years ago, the Society for the Relief of Poor Widows with Small Children. By that society a regular monthly pension is given, and the family is placed under the care of a special member of the society, and the help is often continued from the time of the death of the father until all the children are over ten years of age. Unhappily, however, the society does not give the help throughout the whole year, and therefore the principle of regular help is not carried out by them; nor do they usually give large enough pensions, so that a family receiving aid from the society has often to get aid from elsewhere also. I fear, too, that often the visitors cannot give as much time and care to the family as is needed. Still these are all failures to live up to their own principles, and the principles are, as I have said, those upon which help to such families should be given. Regular help, friendly supervision, the help to be as much as is needed to supplement the earnings of the mother, and the supervision to be continued until the children have been trained in some means of self-support — these are the essentials, and it takes a great deal of money for each family, at least ten dollars a month, and a fair share of time and trouble; but the results are worth it, and it ought to be considered cruel and wicked to take children away from a decent mother just for want of money to support them and friends to look after them. In these cases the money and the friend are equally necessary, and the work is very simple indeed, requiring only kindness and

perseverance. It is necessary to see that there is money enough, regularly supplied, so that the family does not suffer; that the mother does not overwork herself, but does work so far as she is able; that her work does not prevent her giving the proper care to the children; that the latter go to school and to church regularly; that when old enough, they begin to learn some good trade; that they get work and keep at it; and finally that, as their earnings increase, the money given to the mother diminishes gradually until the family is self-supporting.

This sort of help is not demoralizing nor pauperizing, if properly watched, because it only places the family in a natural position. Women and children ought to be supported, and there is no sense of degradation in receiving support. The woman has plenty to do in caring for her family; and when the duty of supporting them also comes upon her, it is an unnatural strain, and results disastrously unless she can be helped.

With families where there is plenty of earning power and where the deficiencies are moral and not physical, the case is very different; here the friend is of paramount importance and the giving of money is not only unnecessary, but usually very hurtful, and the work is very hard indeed, requiring devotion and consecration. If, however, such work were undertaken by a number of people with conscientious persistent zeal, it would go far to make the next generation very much better than the present one. If for every family where the parents are weak, inefficient, shiftless, improvident, lazy, foolish, in fact everything short of downright vicious, a wise, kind, patient friend could be found, who would undertake the task of seeing that the children were trained so that they should grow up without these faults and the contrary virtues, you can see what a tremendous moral force it would be in the community. Of course to achieve such results requires the charity which beareth all things, endureth all things, hopeth all things; and equally, of course, the moral objects to be attained must be constantly kept in view, and striven for. If people who want to do good would give up some of the many varieties of charities upon which they expend time and strength, and would each concentrate their force upon one family, they would accomplish a great deal more than they can by their present scattering manner of working.

. . . . . .

Whether it would be possible to find friends who could hope against hope in these particular cases and follow the families round as they are dispossessed from one place to another, and whether, if such could be found, they could save these children, are questions which only experience can answer. Naturally one longs to take those poor little children away; but is it right to leave the parents absolutely free to live as they choose by relieving them of the children as fast as they are born, and putting them in institutions at a cost to the taxpayers of New York of one hundred and four dollars a year for each child, and then permitting the parents to take them home again and make slaves of them as soon as they are of an age to earn? Is not such a course as likely as any other to drive the children into early loveless marriages, like those of their parents, just to escape the tyranny at home? The whole problem is one of human weakness and human vice. What is needed is better education of every kind.

I should personally be glad if we could have a law by which, when parents had proved themselves entirely incompetent to care properly for their children, the children might be taken from them and given to other people to bring up, and by which the parents themselves should be subjected to a thorough course of education and not allowed to continue to produce children whom others must care for. I should like to have two large farms bought, one for men and one for women, and on these farms I should like to have such poor creatures as I have depressed you by describing shut up for one, two, five, or ten years, as might prove necessary, to train and fit them for normal life, and when they were prepared for liberty, I would return their children to them, but not before.

I have not kept to my subject, but I hope you will forgive me, and I hope you will feel with me, how great is our responsibility to try to mould the children while we may, and not let them grow up, as we have their parents, without a helping hand to guide them.

---

3. "Alms of good advice," 1899

Thomas Mulry, "Report of the Committee on the Care of Destitute and Neglected Children," *Proceedings* of the National Conference of Charities and Corrections, (1899), 169.

Your committee is emphatically of the opinion that the "ounce of prevention is better than the pound of cure," and it strongly urges upon all charitable people the absolute necessity of preserving the home wherever possible.

Do not be in a hurry to send the children to an institution until you are convinced of the hopelessness of preserving the home. Remember that, when the home is broken up, even temporarily, it is no easy task to bring it together again, and that a few dollars of private charity, a friendly visit, a kind word, and a helping hand will lift up the courage of the deserving poor; and this is half the battle, because discouragement begets carelessness.

Our work should not be done fitfully, but should be continuous, and not cease until all danger of falling back into original conditions is effectually removed.

It is often through mistaken kindness that homes are broken up and children scattered. It is as bad for the parent as for the child. There is something ennobling and soul-inspiring in the spectacle of a good woman working and slaving, if you will, to keep her little family together; and if, instead of turning over such families to relief societies or to the public charge, as is frequently the case, the charitable men and women of this land would take a personal interest in such cases, and each would take under his or her care such a family, help them materially, give them also the "alms of good advice," and kindly listen to the story of bitter struggles which will always be found ready for a sympathetic listener, giving them assistance in a way which will not degrade the beneficiary, much will have been done to advance this great question of the care of dependent children.

---

4. Charity versus "public outdoor relief,"
1898–1901

"Dependent Children in New York City with Special Reference to the Work of the Committee on Dependent Children of the Charity Organization Society," *Charities,* VII (1901), 369–373.

The Committee on Dependent Children in the past three years has developed from an experiment, suggested by unwise legislative proposals at Albany, into a permanent and important department of the work of the Charity Organization Society of New York City.

The immediate occasion of the new movement was Senator Ahearn's proposal (three times embodied in bills and introduced in the Legislature) that the City of New York, instead of supporting children in private institutions should pay to parents the cost of their support and thus prevent the evils of the separation of families and of institution-life for children. The Charity Organization Society, in conjunction with other societies, was obliged to oppose Senator Ahearn's bills, owing to the certainty that great moral injury would be sure to result to the character of the people by this return to "public outdoor relief." Yet the question arose as to whether there was not much truth in the Senator's arraignment of the existing system whereby parents and children were

separated in many instances for years simply because of poverty. It is certainly a hardship to separate children from a mother who is of good character and who is prevented from caring for them only through her inability to earn a living and at the same time give them proper maternal care.

It was to select such cases from the applications at the Department of Charities and in the Magistrates' Courts and to secure for them adequate relief in their homes that the Committee on Dependent Children was organized. The work would have been quite impossible except for the rule of the State Board of Charities that the Department of Charities must accept as a public charge each child committed to a charitable institution before such institution can receive payment for its support from the city, and it would have been equally impossible had not the city been fortunate in having a public-spirited and intelligent Commissioner of Charities, Hon. John W. Keller, who was ready to allow the Society every facility for learning the facts in relation to all applications for the commitment of children at public expense. Whenever it appeared from the facts that the children should be kept at home, a thorough investigation was made, and the Society then offered to take charge of the family, thus making commitment unnecessary. The experiment continued from July 1, 1898, to January 1, 1899; during that time ninety-two families were investigated, involving the commitment of 172 children; of the latter, sixty-eight (belonging to thirty-seven different families) were saved from commitment by the intervention of the Charity Organization Society.

By the report of the Committee on its experimental work the Society was satisfied that the field was one which promised great usefulness both to individuals and to the public, and decided to enter it permanently. Since January 1, 1899, the work has been more and more thoroughly prosecuted.

The method adopted in the work of the Committee is as follows: Each day a representative of the Society calls personally at the Bureau of Dependent Children in the Department of Public Charities and obtains information concerning all of the applications for commitment of children which are under favorable consideration at the Department or which the Department deems it wise to refer to private charity for special reasons. These vary from two to eight or ten in number daily. Each of these families is visited by an agent of the Committee who usually has time to go over the records of the Department and is thus cognizant of the facts obtained by the examiners of the Department in the course of their investigation. If it appears as a result of this examination that private assistance and encouragement will keep the family together and prevent the proposed commitment; that the home conditions are not unfavorable; and the parents or surviving parent is of good character, the superintendent of the Bureau at the Department of Public Charities is so notified and the case is left by him for the time being in the hands of the Committee on Dependent Children. When there is immediate need, assistance is supplied at once from the Provident Relief Fund or some other cooperating relief agency. If it is found that a regular monthly allowance of some kind is essential, it is provided either through newspaper appeal or by the organization of various sources of relief when such are available. Relatives, former employers and others upon whom the family has any claim are expected to contribute their due share, and if the family has any church connection this is also taken into account. In many instances the Society has through newspaper appeal provided for the rent of these families, while other needs which could not be supplied by the work of the members of the family are met by the church or some other local agency. There are at the present time under the care of the Society some 350 families in which there are 800 children who would have been accepted as public charges except for the intervention of the Society in the manner described. The entire number of children in these families is much greater than this as parents usually apply for the commitment of only part of their children, expecting to be able to support the remainder.

In some instances the legal requirement of a residence of one year in the city prevents the commitment of children in cases where assistance is nevertheless greatly needed. Such cases are referred to the Society by the Department of Public Charities. In other instances the only need is for employment of an able-bodied adult, and in still other instances moral oversight and personal interest are required rather than material assistance.

There are, however, many instances in which there is little or no time or opportunity for the mother to undertake any remunerative employment after the children have received the personal attention which she should give them, and in such cases regular, and often long-continued help must be given. Whenever a woman of good character is willing to do her utmost to keep her children with her she should have all the assistance in money and all the help of other kinds that may be necessary to enable her to do it. It is cruel to deprive children of the oversight and parental care which is their birthright merely because of poverty or because of the lack of friends to tide over a period of discouragement and exceptional hardship.

.   .   .   .   .

The following "typical cases" will illustrate the kind of work undertaken by the Committee on Dependent Children:

(1) A widow with six children, two of whom were able to work, applied for the commitment of the three younger children in March, 1901. This woman was trying to earn her living with a push-cart, claiming to be unable to do other work. Aid in rent to the amount of $35 extending over several months was secured. Suitable employment which she still retains was found for her, and also for the girl several times. The boy earned $5 per week for a time but finally his mother turned both him

and the oldest girl out of the house because they would not give her their earnings and were unkind to the younger children. For some time the woman made attempts to commit her children, saying nothing had been done for her, but finally gave up the idea. She and the second girl are working regularly. The two oldest children have returned home and are helping somewhat towards the support of the family. Fresh-air trips have been provided for all.

(2) In July, 1900, this family was dispossessed and the home broken up. The man drank and his work was irregular. His wife with five children was living with her brother who could not continue to keep them. She applied for the commitment of four children. The oldest child was earning $6 per month at service. As the man was very repentant it was thought well to give him another chance. Rooms and necessary furniture were secured at a cost of $19.75, also clothing for the woman and children. Woodyard tickets were supplied to the man until he could secure regular employment. He has had several relapses, but has managed to recover himself and work. In May, 1901, he took the pledge again, and kept it for three months. At present he is working, and keeping sober. The oldest girl is earning $3 per week.

(3) A deserted woman with three children asked for the commitment of two in May, 1901, though she was very anxious to keep her children with her. Five dollars was secured toward the rent for one month, and $4 toward the next. Shoes were provided for one of the children, and a small amount of groceries given. The woman had several days' work each week, and although given an opportunity to go to the Charity Organization Society Laundry or to the Workrooms, was able to get as much work as she was strong enough to do without using this opportunity. In July the man returned, soon secured work, first at $1.50, then at $2.50 a day. He has made and is making a hard struggle to keep away from drink. The family is doing nicely at present. The woman's courage seems to have returned and with it her pride in having a clean, well-kept house and neatly-dressed children.

---

5. Necessity for adequate relief, 1910.

Lowenstein, "A Study of the Problem of Boarding Out Jewish Children and of Pensioning Widowed Mothers," *Proceedings* of the Sixth Biennial Session of the National Conference of Jewish Charities in the United States (1910), 218–219, 229–234.

Given a good mother there is no reason, as has been stated frequently on the platform of this Conference, why she should be compelled to add the distress of breaking up her home to the grief occasioned by the loss of her husband, but, if the community has wisely decided to assist her to do this, it must, at the same time, determine that its support shall be adequate. It must give generously and not with niggardly hand. The mother ought not to be compelled to engage in work that will call her away from her own home, nor be forced, in her own home, to perform so large a quantity of work as to cause her to neglect her children, nor should her work be of such character as to impair her own health or that of her offspring. Above all, the keeping of lodgers, other than those related by blood ties to the family, should be prohibited absolutely. The family should not be allowed to remain in the poorer overcrowded neighborhoods of the city, but inasmuch as, in most cases, the majority of the children are below the legal working age, they should be required to move out into suburban or less closely settled neighborhoods, where the opportunities for fresh air and healthful play are unrestricted. The relief granted should be sufficient to enable the child, in addition to remaining at home, to have at least a fair share of the recreative opportunities that are afforded to his fellow in the institution. But, for the proper working out of this class of cases, a much greater degree of supervision must be provided than is furnished by any of the existing New York agencies. This is not work for the salaried employe. It is pre-eminently the task of the friendly visitor . . . Too often the mother is not competent to spend wisely the amount of money that may be necessary to give her adequate relief. The friendly visitor, sympathetic, tactful, with a knowledge of good housekeeping, can be of invaluable service to her. In addition to assisting in the expenditure of funds and the management of the family budget, she may find work to do in advice concerning the preparation of foods and the foods to be used; the cleanliness of the children, their schooling and amusement. With proper supervision, I believe this kind of work can become extremely valuable; without it, I am convinced that it can result only in failure.

.   .   .   .   .

DISCUSSION

Mr. Saul Drucker, Chicago . . .

I heard a story once of a Jew in Russia, who had a boy about fourteen years of age. The boy's birth was never recorded in the city government, and the father being anxious to have a record made of it asked a friend's advice whether to record the age as sixteen or twelve. The friend said: "Why wouldn't it be more advisable to record fourteen years, the correct age?" The answer was: "This is something I never thought of."

This may serve as an illustration of the various child-caring agencies, which have devised every possible means for the proper caretaking of children, excepting the idea of keeping children with the mother, which, apparently, is something they never thought of.

.   .   .   .   .

Miss Minnie F. Low, Chicago . . .

We have all heard of the unsatisfactory effects of insufficient relief-giving. We give our widows and deserted women a small pension, never enough; a little clothing now and then, never enough; we make of the 365 days of a year a continuous struggle for existence, and yet we expect these women to bring up their children properly, and we expect the children to grow up into the best type of citizenship.

I believe in the home for a child every time, but it must be the right sort of home, and in the right neighborhood. In Chicago we insist that the widows whom we compensate move into the better neighborhoods. We do not give them $15.00 per month, as the relief agencies now give them, but we give them as much as $50.00 per month, the amount depending upon the size of the family. In one case we are allowing a widow with four children $50.00. We saw her last week, and she expressed herself as being "the happiest mother in Chicago." The principal of the school, which the children attend, wrote us a letter, unsolicited, speaking of the splendid condition in which the children are kept, and saying that the Home Finding Society was doing for this family what all the institutions in the world could not do — giving the mother the benefit of her children's love and society, and giving the children a mother's devotion and care.

We do not permit our compensated mothers to go out to work. They can supplement their incomes by doing some work in their homes, especially while the children are at school, but further than this it is a condition imposed upon them that they do not leave the home nor the children to add to their incomes.

We find it is after all not the best plan to separate a mother from her children even temporarily. The mother, being relieved of the care of a home and children grows timid about reassuming the burden and responsibility. One woman, whose children had been in the institution for nearly two years, when told she must remove them and establish a home with compensation of $35.00 per month, said: "I can't take care of my children; I am afraid to try it. If you had offered me this amount when my husband first died, when for days I walked about the building in which my children were put, just to see the place that held them, I would have been a very happy mother, but now my courage is gone." It took weeks of coaxing before this mother made up her mind to take her children.

The first White House Conference, 1909

On December 25, 1908, President Theodore Roosevelt invited 216 child welfare workers to attend a conference on the care of dependent children to be held in Washington. The first of the decennial White House Conferences on Children assembled on January 25 and 26, 1909. The calling of the conference was suggested to President Roosevelt by James E. West (1876–1948), a Washington attorney who subsequently became chief executive of the Boy Scouts of America. On the background of the conference, see Walter Trattner, *Homer Folks; Pioneer in Social Welfare* (New York, 1968), pp. 104–105.

---

1. Request for a national conference

Proceedings of the Conference on the Care of Dependent Children, 1909, pp. 17–18.

December 22, 1908

Hon. Theodore Roosevelt,

President of the United States, Washington, D.C.

Dear Mr. President: In your message to Congress December 6, 1904, urging the estab-

lishment of a juvenile court for the District of Columbia, you said:

No Christian and civilized community can afford to show a happy-go-lucky lack of concern for the youth of to-day; for, if so, the community will have to pay a terrible penalty of financial burden and social degradation in the to-morrow.

Congress promptly responded and enacted an excellent juvenile court law. The wisdom of this step has already been proven by the work of the court.

Generally speaking, the cause of the delinquent child has been well advanced. Juvenile courts have been established in many States; a considerable number of probation officers have been appointed; many of the juvenile reformatories are progressing along well established lines of modern thought and are supported by generous appropriations from the public treasury; detention homes have been opened in many cities to keep children out of jail; parental schools are being established for the training of truants and unruly school children.

The State has dealt generously with her troublesome children; but what is she doing for those who make no trouble but are simply unfortunate? There are a large number of these children for whom there is need of special activity and interest. Some are orphans or half-orphans; some are abandoned by heartless parents; some are victims of cruelty or neglect. They are not delinquents; they are accused of no fault; they are simply destitute or neglected.

Destitute children certainly deserve as much consideration and help as those who, by reason of some alleged delinquency, enforce the attention of the State and become objects of its care; but only a few States have defined responsibility for this class of children. Their care and protection is left in many localities to the fidelity of volunteer agencies without requiring proper standards of method or efficiency and without definite responsibility to the State or the community.

Unfortunately there has not been as frequent interchange of ideas and experiences among the officials of orphan asylums, with consequent progress, as among those who work for delinquents.

These dependent children are cared for in different ways. According to a special bulletin of the United States Census there were in orphan asylums and kindred institutions on December 31, 1904, not less than 92,887 children. In addition to these there were probably some 50,000 dependent children in family homes under supervision.

In many States, however, little or no child-saving work is done, and in many States the organizations are greatly handicapped by the lack of appreciation and of adequate support.

It is of the highest importance to the welfare of this vast number of future citizens that all child-saving work shall be conducted on a high plane of efficiency; that in the placing of children in families the utmost care shall be taken to exclude all undesirable applicants; that every precaution shall be taken in the subsequent supervision of the children to prevent neglect, overwork, insufficient education, or inadequate moral and religious training, of each individual child and to fit it for active and creditable citizenship.

The problem of the dependent child is acute; it is large; it is national. We believe that it is worthy of national consideration. We earnestly hope, therefore, that you will cooperate in an effort to get this problem before the American people.

If a conference could be arranged, under your auspices, in Washington, some time in January, to which leaders of this particular phase of child-caring work could be invited, it would, in our judgment, greatly advance the cause of the dependent child. Such a conference could formulate a plan for your consideration, pointing out ways whereby you could specially help by recommending to Congress certain legislation and in other ways.

Hoping for your favorable consideration of this matter, we are,

Very respectfully,

Homer Folks,
Secretary, New York State Charities Aid Association.

Hastings H. Hart,
*Superintendent Illinois Children's Home and Aid Society,
Chairman, Study of Child Placing,
Russell Sage Foundation.*

John M. Glenn,
Secertary and Director, Russell Sage Foundation.

Thomas M. Mulry,
President, St. Vincent de Paul Society of the United States.

Edward T. Devine,
*Editor Charities and The Commons,
General Secretary, Charity Organizing Society,
Professor of Social Economy, Columbia University.*

Julian W. Mack,
*Judge Circuit Court, of Chicago, Ill.,
Ex-President, National Conference of Jewish Charities.*

Charles W. Birtwell,
General Secretary, Boston Children's Aid Society

Theodore Dreiser,
Editor of the Delineator.

James E. West,
Secretary, National Child-Rescue League.

---

2. Should homes be broken because of poverty?

Proceedings of the Conference on the Care of Dependent Children, 1909, pp. 41–53.

The secretary read as follows:

Should children of parents of worthy character, but suffering from temporary misfortune, and the children of widows of worthy character and reasonable efficiency, be kept with their parents — aid being given the parents to enable them to maintain suitable homes for the rearing of the children? Should the breaking of a home be permitted for reasons of poverty, or only for reasons of inefficiency or immorality?

The CHAIRMAN. The opening speaker will be Mr. Michael J. Scanlan, who was for some years a member of the state board of charities of New York, and who has long been one of the most active members of the Society of St. Vincent de Paul, in that city, and who is the president of the New York Catholic Home Bureau for Dependent Children.

ADDRESS OF MR. MICHAEL J. SCANLAN, PRESIDENT CATHOLIC HOME BUREAU FOR DEPENDENT CHILDREN, NEW YORK

Mr. SCANLAN. Mr. Chairman and ladies and gentlemen, when I first heard this proposition announced, it struck me that there could be no negative to it, and I said as much to the committee; but they assured me that there might be room for a difference of opinion. So I was induced to jot down a few arguments in favor of the maintenance of family relations.

.   .   .   .   .

The question now under discussion, as I apprehend it, is substantially this: Should workers in the field of charity make extraordinary efforts to preserve the family; should the children of those in destitute circumstances be kept with their parents or be taken from them and brought up elsewhere? In other words, should the family of those who have the misfortune to be poor be preserved rather than destroyed?

.   .   .   .   .

For us Catholics there can be no question where we stand. The teaching of our church has always been in favor of the preservation of family ties, and the wisdom of this teaching

has been commended by those separated from her. For us members of the society of St. Vincent de Paul there can likewise be no question as to where we stand. The special object of our society, its fundamental work, is the visiting of the poor at their homes. Our members are exhorted by all means to keep the family together. Funds are distributed liberally for that purpose. Situations are procured if necessary. It is only a very last resort and for very grave reasons and after many trials that a family group is broken up. And if because of the dissipated lives of parents the household is dispersed, our members are keen to discover symptoms of reformation so that they can rehabilitate that household again. By following out these rules we frequently have the happiness and consolation of seeing the children of those who have been on our relief rolls grow up to be respected and useful members of society. The question here discussed could not be the subject of debate at a meeting of the St. Vincent de Paul Society, because the maintenance of the family is so much a part of our creed . . . It should be the cardinal aim of charity workers to keep intact the family circle of the poor. Children should be reared in the family where God Almighty has placed them, and while we know from sad experience that cases will arise where the removal of children from their homes is necessary, it should be done reluctantly and only where proper supervision at home has become impossible. Aid should be given to preserve the home in case of poverty, not public aid but aid such as is given by the St. Vincent de Paul Society; and even where children have the misfortune to have dissipated parents, some attempts at reformation should be made before the home is broken up.

.   .   .   .   .

The CHAIRMAN. Mr. Jackson is at present the executive officer of the Associated Charities of Cleveland. He has had a very wide experience as secretary of the Associated Charities of St. Paul, as secretary of the Minnesota state board of charities, and as secretary of the committee on dependent children of the Charity Organization Society of New York, a committee whose particular object was to assist in aiding in the maintenance of dependent children in their own homes. [Applause.]

ADDRESS OF MR. JAMES F. JACKSON, SUPER-INTENDENT ASSOCIATED CHARITIES, CLEVELAND

Mr. JACKSON. Mr. Chairman, ladies, and gentlemen, it has not always been possible for us to have the agreement of the church and the state relative to the care of children. Today the state and the church have agreed as to what should be done for the child, as far as the question under consideration is concerned, and it simply rests upon laymen—the common, ordinary, every-day laymen in this tremendously democratic country of ours — to say that both the church and the state are just and wise and humane. And there is little more to say.

Civilization demands that a mother shall do more than bring up her child. When an animal is born and anything chances to happen to the mother, if it happens to find a foster mother that animal may grow up; if not, it will have to die. But with the human species, we demand that the mother shall do more than simply bring up animals of the human kind. We demand that they shall educate their offspring; that they shall train them to be good citizens. Morally, mentally, and physically children must be educated. That education chiefly falls to the mother, and therefore it has come about with us that the mother is not expected to become the breadwinner. When anything happens to the breadwinner, if the mother is capable, it seems to be perfectly clear that it is our business, either as a state or as individuals, to see that she has material support. Always there should be individual friendliness as a part of such aid. Either the state or the individual, or the two in cooperation, should see that the mother has the necessities of existence, has the

raw material, we may say, with which to care for the children and provide the home where she may educate them. We make this demand upon her on the assumption that she has the capacity. Should she lack the capacity, if she is inefficient or below the community standard of morality, the mother is thereby unable to rear good men and women. Then we must help substitute capacity for her incapacity, or if that is impossible the children must be rescued from her.

.   .   .   .   .

As Mr. Scanlan has just said, it is up to us as individual societies. It is a work that can not remain entirely with the state; in fact, it is usually better for the state to take no part in the aid. It is the work of individual societies to see that she has a fair chance in the development of her child; that she not only has a fair chance, but has good backing, especially that she has friendship.

It seems to me, when we talk about starvation in this country, we must bear in mind that practically nobody starves in America who can digest food. But thousands are dying every year, morally and physically, from the lack of friendship. The dependent parent or parents are entitled to our friendly aid and our material support until they can prove whether or not they are capable of developing children to good citizenship. If they are incapable, then it is necessary that the children be taken from them.

I think there is one more point that may be fairly made. Whereas I think we all agree that the interests of the child entirely overbalance the interest of the parents, the welfare of the parents should be considered. When we take her children from a mother simply because of poverty, we subject her to temptations which frequently she is not able to bear. The child, in many instances, is the anchor that holds the woman to a good life, and in that good life she will herself bring up good children.

Then the mother has another interest which I think is perfectly fair to be considered; that is, the chance of being cared for in her old age. Every woman makes an investment with each child for care in her old age. If we have taken the child from an efficient mother simply because of poverty, we have robbed her of possible care in old age, and the injustice is as great as in any form of robbery.

Mr. Chairman, I am glad that we are in accord — the state, the church, and the common democracy — in the conclusion that the home should not be broken up simply for reasons of poverty, and that children should be removed only for reasons of inefficiency or immorality. I thank you. [Applause.]

.   .   .   .   .

REMARKS BY MR. W. B. SHERRARD, OF SOUTH DAKOTA, SUPERINTENDANT NATIONAL CHILDREN'S HOME SOCIETY, ETC.

Mr. SHERRARD. Mr. Chairman, among my friends I am looked upon as a radical in regard to the rights of childhood, but I think the question as presented for consideration has only one side to it, namely, that we should help the parents to keep their children, bearing in mind this: That that provision is made conditioned that they are proper people themselves.

In South Dakota it is not the breaking up of homes that we are doing, but it is breaking up bad homes; and the country will not do what it ought to do for the children of the nation until it investigates every disreputable home in the land. I venture the assertion that I could send out half a dozen competent young women in the city of Washington who would find a thousand children in it who will grow up to be immoral or vicious or undesirable citizens if left to themselves. I believe the rights of children demand that they should be surrounded with pure, moral influence.

I want you to bear in mind another thing — that the physical ability to bring a child into the world does not constitute fatherhood and motherhood in the highest sense. There are men and women who have never been privileged to bring an immortal being into existence who in all the higher attributes of motherhood and fatherhood far surpass those who have, by the gratification of their animal passions, brought an immortal being into the world. For this reason I advocate and beg and plead that the children of the nation be surrounded with pure influences. [Applause.]

.   .   .   .   .

REMARKS OF MR. MORNAY WILLIAMS, OF NEW YORK CITY, CHAIRMAN NEW YORK CHILD-LABOR COMMITTEE, ETC.

Mr. WILLIAMS. Mr. President and ladies and gentlemen, I suppose that I am in a minority here to-day because I am not entirely convinced that even in the case of dependent children it is always best to leave them in their own homes. I say that not because I am not interested in the child, but because I am so profoundly interested in the child. I believe that for the child always the best thing should be done, and my own belief is that for the normal boy — not the abnormal boy, but the normal boy — at a certain age the discipline of the school is absolutely essential. My own conviction is that the greatness of England, for instance, is largely to be traced to her great public schools.

.   .   .   .   .

I, at least, stand for the proposition that there are cases, not infrequently, in which the school should be the place in which the boy for a period is reared before he should be returned either to his own home, or, if his own home can not receive him, then to some other home. I speak of that out of the experience I have had with street boys. To my mind — I may be dreaming — the street boy is the great problem of to-day. The President well said that the boys of to-day are the citizens of to-morrow; and, trust me, my friends, the thing that we have to face as citizens here is that we are breeding at home the destroyers of our civilization.

Now, it is not the delinquent child I am speaking about. I am talking about a boy who has just as great capabilities of development as your boy, but who has not, because of the necessary conditions of poverty in which he has been born, learned how to lead life aright, and for him I say that there are very often cases where the good school is better than the home.

For that reason I am not willing to admit the general proposition that the home is always better, even for poor children, than the school. The home ought to have its influence on the school; and when I speak of the school I speak of it as a temporary expedient only. I never wish to institutionalize a boy, and I think in the school it is absolutely essential that you shall bring the conditions under which the boy lives as nearly to home conditions as you can, and then always put him back for a brief term in some home, either his own or another. [Applause.]

.   .   .   .   .   .

REMARKS OF MR. A. W. CLARK, SUPERINTEND-
ENT CHILD SAVING INSTITUTE, OF OMAHA,
NEBR.

Mr. CLARK. Mr. President and ladies and gentlemen, I just want to say a word in favor of keeping parent and children together, growing out of eighteen years of experience and consecutive work for the dependent children.

Fifteen or sixteen years ago it was easy for a poor man or a poor mother in great poverty to persuade me to let her or him sign the papers of relinquishment because of this extreme poverty, and I would receive the child. Now, after placing or directly controlling the placement of nearly 2,000 children, I am convinced that at that time I made some very great mistakes. Fourteen years ago, when I began to realize the necessity, as it seemed to me, of keeping parents and children together,

I began to study the question of going beyond simply the matter of poverty, and when I found inefficiency I began to try to find some way to overcome the inefficiency. I want to say that for the past fourteen years when a case of this sort is brought to me I assume it is possible to overcome inefficiency and to arrange it and make it possible for the child to stay with the parent. Then in the case of immorality it is exactly the same. I began to assume years ago that it might be possible to overcome those conditions that are immoral at the time. I have in mind an instance. Fourteen years ago last month, I think it was, my attention was called to a mother locked up in jail. I went to her and found that there was inefficiency in her past life, that there was immorality. Her little girl was 4 years of age. She wanted to sign the papers of relinquishment. I allowed her to sign them and I took the little girl. Then I said to the mother, "Now, it is possible for you to have this child with you later." I found a position for the mother afterwards, and I expended $500 in the care of that child in private homes and in the Child Saving Institute of which I am superintendent; and at the end of the two years I restored this little girl to her mother, who was in a position, showing that she was a moral, good woman, and from that time to the present she has maintained her position as such, the little girl being in the home, and six months ago she took the silver medal in an oratorical contest which the Woman's Christian Temperance Union gave, a little later the gold medal, and just a few weeks ago the grand gold medal in the oratorical contest. It is a beautiful home.

I had all kinds of chances to place that little girl. One millionaire begged for her, and there were others who wanted her. I said, "No; there is the mother of that child." I want to say further that, growing out of these experiences of eighteen years, I believe that the relationship between a mother and her child is a different relationship than that which ever exists between foster parent and children. It is stronger, it is more vital, and I believe that we are bound to devise ways and means for the keeping of parents and children together when it is possible to do so. [Applause.]

REMARKS OF MR. MAX MITCHELL, OF BOSTON, MASS., SUPERINTENDENT FEDERATED JEWISH CHARITIES

I believe we are fairly agreed that the children of parents who are of worthy character, but suffering from temporary misfortunes, children of widows of good character and reasonable efficiency, when life and conditions of their homes are normal, are best cared for by remaining in the custody of their parents.

.   .   .   .   .

REMARKS OF DR. WILLIAM P. SPRATLING, OF BALTIMORE, MD., EDITOR TRANSACTIONS OF THE NATIONAL ASSOCIATION FOR THE STUDY OF EPILEPSY; FORMERLY MEDICAL SUPERINTENDENT OF THE CRAIG COLONY FOR EPILEPTICS, SONYEA, N.Y.

Doctor SPRATLING. Mr. Chairman, I desire to say only a word, and that is, that my sentiments along this line agree very closely with those expressed by Mr. Mornay Williams. . .

Wherever you find delinquent and dependent children you are almost sure to find chronic disease of some kind or other; and it is not possible to satisfactorily treat or care for children in such homes.

And here is another point that is often as prohibitive of good treatment as it is possible for almost any material factor to be, and that is, the influence of parental sympathy.

Very often parents with the best possible meaning unwittingly set aside all good that is being done the child simply through the display of sympathy; through letting the child do what it wants to do and not what it should do.

In some cases like these kindness can be almost as destructive of good results as harshness, and the only way in which the evil condi-

tion in the child can be successfully combatted is to remove the child from its home and place it in some place that from every point of view is as nearly like the home as possible.

We ought to strive continually to preserve the home, but let us not forget that it is just as important to preserve those who are to live in it; and if the child of to-day is lost through neglect or through bad policy, then we lose the adult, the responsible citizen, of to-morrow.

Where substitutes for home life in the past have fallen short in doing that which we had a right to expect of them has been in the fundamental nature, in the very type of these places. Provide small cottages; furnish them and conduct them like homes — like real homes — and "institutionalism" will lose most of its evil features.

REMARKS OF HON. JULIAN W. MACK, OF CHICAGO, ILL., JUDGE OF CIRCUIT COURT, COOK COUNTY

Judge MACK. Mr. Chairman, as I understand the question that is put, it is not the one touched upon by the last speaker or by Mr. Williams. The sole proposition is, shall parents, merely because of poverty, be deprived of their children? Now, if the child, because of its own delinquency, is to be taken away from home, of course let it be cared for somewhere. The question whether it should be in another home or in an institution is another point of discussion hereafter. But the question before us now is, shall a parent, merely because of poverty, not because of inefficiency, not because of disease of any kind, whether it be that sympathetic disease alluded to or physical or mental disease, be deprived of the care and custody of the child? To that I can see but one answer. That answer of course is in the negative. I can not understand why poverty alone should give anybody the right to deprive that child of that which it needs most in life — its own parents' love and care and sympathy [applause]; to deprive the parent of that which he or she needs most in life, the love and the support of the child, the reciprocal relations between the parent and the child.

In my personal experience I know of nothing sadder than the case of children that were taken away, or the case of the mother who came into the juvenile court ready to give up her child, ready to give it up merely because of poverty. I saw the twofold danger, the danger to the child in losing that mother's love and companionship, no matter how good a substitute we might find in any institution or in any foster home, and I saw again, time after time, the terrible danger that confronted the young mother without proper stay in the world except that child's love, forced to go out and fight the battle alone in the big cities. [Applause.]

We must not look at it solely from the standpoint of the child, although looking at it from that standpoint there can be but one answer to this question; but we must look at it, as one of the former speakers has said, from the standpoint also of the parent, and that brings me to a criticism of the phraseology of this question — "worthy parent." I should include under the word "parent" many a mother of an illegitimate child [applause], because if we stop that mother from giving away her child, and we can stop it in many cases if we will only see that she has work or gets the means of life without going out to work, if she is supplied with the money to keep her child in her own home, it is in that case particularly that we are going to save not only the child but the mother too — the mother possibly from a life of immorality. [Applause.]

.   .   .   .   .

REMARKS OF DR. HASTINGS H. HART, OF CHICAGO, ILL., SUPERINTENDENT CHILDREN'S HOME AND AID SOCIETY OF ILLINOIS

Doctor HART. Mr. Chairman, I have been listening to this matter with a view to getting the consensus of the resolution we are expected to prepare on this matter. I discover only one point that seems to be a point of very sharp difference when we analyze it. The first speaker said he thought the relief to be given to mothers to enable them to keep their own children should be entirely private relief. The second speaker thought it might be either private or public relief.

I wish we could know what is the sentiment of this convention on that question, as to whether private relief should be provided in all these cases, or whether this is an exception to the sentiment that many of us hold against outdoor relief.

The CHAIRMAN. I think the chair would be inclined to rule that out of order, Mr. Hart, because if we go into public outdoor relief versus private relief, we are apart from our general field, and we shall never get through. The question is whether each community, by the methods of relief which it has in that community by its own elected policy, should afford aid, and I think we would get pretty far afield if we should attempt to thrash out the difference between private and public relief.

---

3. "Home life is the highest and finest product of civilization": recommendations of the conference

"Letter to the President of the United States Embodying the Conclusions of the Conference on the Care of Dependent Children," *Proceedings of the Conference on the Care of Dependent Children, 1909,* pp. 192–197.

HON. THEODORE ROOSEVELT,

President of the United States

SIR: Having been invited by you to participate in a conference on the care of dependent children, held at Washington, D.C., January 25–26, 1909, and having considered at the sessions of such conference the various phases of the subject as stated in the memorandum accompanying your letter of invitation, and such others as have been brought before us by the executive committee, we desire to express the very great satisfaction felt by each member of this conference in the deep interest you have taken in the well-being of dependent children. The proper care of destitute children has indeed an important bearing upon the welfare of the nation. We now know so little about them as not even to know their number, but we know that there are in institutions about 93,000, and that many additional thousands are in foster or boarding homes. As a step, therefore, in the conservation of the productive capacity of the people and the preservation of high standards of citizenship, and also because each of these children is entitled to receive humane treatment, adequate care, and proper education, your action in calling this conference, and your participation in its opening and closing sessions, will have, we believe, a profound effect upon the well-being of many thousands of children and upon the nation as a whole.

Concerning the particular objects to which you called attention in the invitation to this conference, and the additional subjects brought before us by the executive committee, our conclusions are as follows:

HOME CARE

1. Home life is the highest and finest product of civilization. It is the great molding force of mind and of character. Children should not be deprived of it except for urgent and compelling reasons. Children of parents of worthy character, suffering from temporary misfortune, and children of reasonably efficient and deserving mothers who are without the support of the normal breadwinner, should as a rule be kept with their parents, such aid being given as may be necessary to maintain suitable homes for the rearing of the children. This aid should be given by such methods and from such sources as may be determined by the general

relief policy of each community, preferably in the form of private charity rather than of public relief. Except in unusual circumstances, the home should not be broken up for reasons of poverty, but only for considerations of inefficiency or immorality.

PREVENTIVE WORK

2. The most important and valuable philanthropic work is not the curative, but the preventive; to check dependency by a thorough study of its causes and by effectively remedying or eradicating them should be the constant aim of society. Along these lines we urge upon all friends of children the promotion of effective measures, including legislation, to prevent blindness, to check tuberculosis and other diseases in dwellings and work places and injuries in hazardous occupations, to secure compensation or insurance so as to provide a family income in case of sickness, accident, death, or invalidism of the breadwinner; to promote child-labor reforms, and generally, to improve the conditions surrounding child life. To secure these ends we urge efficient cooperation with all other agencies for social betterment.

HOME FINDING

3. As to the children who for sufficient reasons must be removed from their own homes, or who have no homes, it is desirable that, if normal in mind and body and not requiring special training, they should be cared for in families whenever practicable. The carefully selected foster home is for the normal child the best substitute for the natural home. Such homes should be selected by a most careful process of investigation, carried on by skilled agents through personal investigation and with due regard to the religious faith of the child. After children are placed in homes, adequate visitation, with careful consideration of the physical, mental, moral, and spiritual training

and development of each child on the part of the responsible home-finding agency, is essential.

It is recognized that for many children foster homes without payment for board are not practicable immediately after the children become dependent, and that for children requiring temporary care only the free home is not available. For the temporary, or more or less permanent, care of such children different methods are in use, notably the plan of placing them in families, paying for their board, and the plan of institutional care. Contact with family life is preferable for these children, as well as for other normal children. It is necessary, however, that a large number of carefully selected boarding homes be found if these children are to be cared for in families. The extent to which such families can be found should be ascertained by careful inquiry and experiment in each locality. Unless and until such homes are found, the use of instituitons is necessary.

COTTAGE SYSTEM

4. So far as it may be found necessary temporarily or permanently to care for certain classes of children in institutions, these institutions should be conducted on the cottage plan, in order that routine and impersonal care may not unduly suppress individuality and initiative. The cottage unit should not be larger than will permit effective personal relations between the adult caretaker or caretakers of each cottage and each child therein. Twenty-five is suggested as a desirable cottage unit, subject to revision in the light of further experience in the management of cottage institutions. The cottage plan is probably somewhat more expensive, both in construction and in maintenance, than the congregate system. It is so, however, only because it secures for the children a larger degree of association with adults and a nearer approach to the conditions of family life, which are required for the proper molding of childhood. These results more than justify the increased outlay, and are truly economical. Child-caring agencies, whether supported by public or private funds, should by all legitimate means press for adequate financial support. Inferior methods should never be accepted by reason of lack of funds without continuing protest. Cheap care of children is ultimately enormously expensive, and is unworthy of a strong community. Existing congregate institutions should so classify their inmates and segregate them into groups as to secure as many of the benefits of the cottage system as possible, and should look forward to the adoption of the cottage type when new buildings are constructed.

The sending of children of any age or class to almshouses is an unqualified evil, and should be forbidden everywhere by law, with suitable penalty for its violation.

INCORPORATION

5. To engage in the work of caring for needy children is to assume a most serious responsibility, and should, therefore, be permitted only to those who are definitely organized for the purpose, who are of suitable character, and possess, or have reasonable assurance of securing, the funds needed for their support. The only practicable plan of securing this end is to require the approval by a state board of charities or other body exercising similar powers, of the incorporation of all child-caring agencies, including the approval of any amendments of the charter of a benevolent corporation, if it is to include child-caring work; and by forbidding other than duly incorporated agencies to engage in the care of needy children.

STATE INSPECTION

6. The proper training of destitute children being essential to the well-being of the State, it is a sound public policy that the State through its duly authorized representative should inspect the work of all agencies which care for de-

pendent children, whether by institutional or by home-finding methods, and whether supported by public or private funds. Such inspection should be made by trained agents, should be thorough, and the results thereof should be reported to the responsible authorities of the institution or agency concerned. The information so secured should be confidential — not to be disclosed except by competent authority.

INSPECTION OF EDUCATIONAL WORK

7. Destitute children at best labor under many disadvantages, and are deprived in greater or less degree of the assistance and guidance which parents afford their own children. It is important, therefore, that such children be given an education which will fit them for self-support and for the duties of citizenship, and the State should provide therefor. In order that this education may be equal to that afforded by the schools attended by the other children of the community, it is desirable that the education of children in orphan asylums and other similar institutions or placed in families should be under the supervision of the educational authorities of the State.

FACTS AND RECORDS

8. The proper care of a child in the custody of a child-caring agency, as well as the wise decision as to the period of his retention and ultimate disposition to be made of him, involve a knowledge of the character and circumstances of his parents, or surviving parent, and near relatives, both before and at the time the child becomes dependent and subsequently. One unfortunate feature of child-caring work hitherto is the scanty information available as to the actual careers of children who have been reared under the care of charitable agencies. This applies both to institutions, which too frequently lose sight of the children soon after they leave their doors, and home-finding agencies, which too frequently have failed to exercise super-

vision adequate to enable them to judge of the real results of their work. It is extremely desirable that, taking all precautions to prevent injury or embarrassment to those who have been the subjects of charitable care, the agencies which have been responsible for the care of children should know to what station in life they attain, and what sort of citizens they become. Only in this manner can they form a correct judgment of the results of their efforts.

We believe, therefore, that every child-caring agency should —

(a) Secure full information concerning the character and circumstances of the parents and near relatives of each child in whose behalf application is made, through personal investigation by its own representative, unless adequate information is supplied by some other reliable agency.

(b) Inform itself by personal investigation at least once each year of the circumstances of the parents of children in its charge, unless the parents have been legally deprived of guardianship, and unless this information is supplied by some other responsible agency.

(c) Exercise supervision over children under their care until such children are legally adopted, are returned to their parents, attain their majority, or are clearly beyond the need of further supervision.

(d) Make a permanent record of all information thus secured.

PHYSICAL CARE

9. The physical condition of children who become the subjects of charitable care has received inadequate consideration. Each child received into the care of such an agency should be carefully examined by a competent physician, especially for the purpose of ascertaining whether such peculiarities, if any, as the child presents may be due to any defect of the sense organs, or to other physical defect. Both institutions and placing-out agencies should take every precaution to secure proper medical and

surgical care of their children and should see that suitable instruction is given them in matters of health and hygiene.

COOPERATION

10. Great benefit can be derived from a close cooperation between the various child-caring agencies, institutional and otherwise, in each locality. It is especially desirable that harmonious relations be established in regard to the classes of children to be received by each agency; the relations of such agencies to the parents of children received; and the subsequent oversight of children passing from the custody of child-caring agencies. The establishment of a joint bureau of investigation and information by all the child-caring agencies of each locality is highly commended, in the absence of any other suitable central agency through which they may all cooperate.

UNDESIRABLE LEGISLATION

11. We greatly deprecate the tendency of legislation in some States to place unnecessary obstacles in the way of placing children in family homes in such States by agencies whose headquarters are elsewhere, in view of the fact that we favor the care of destitute children, normal in mind and body, in families, whenever practicable.

We recognize the right of each State to protect itself from vicious, diseased, or defective children from other States, by the enactment of reasonable protective legislation; but experience proves that the reception of healthy normal children is not only an act of philanthropy, but also secures a valuable increment to the population of the community and an ultimate increase of its wealth.

The people of the more prosperous and less congested districts owe a debt of hospitality to the older communities from which many of them came.

We earnestly protest, therefore, against such legislation as is prohibitive in form or in effect, and urge that where it exists, it be repealed.

PERMANENT ORGANIZATION

12. The care of dependent children is a subject about which nearly every session of the legislature of every State in the Union concerns itself; it is a work in which state and local authorities in many States are engaged, and in which private agencies are active in every State; important decisions are being made constantly by associations, institutions, and public authorities, affecting questions of policy, the type of buildings to be constructed, the establishment of an adequate system of investigating homes and visiting children placed in homes, and scores of important matters affecting the well-being of needy children. Each of these decisions should be made with full knowledge of the experience of other States and agencies, and of the trend of opinion among those most actively engaged in the care of children, and able to speak from wide experience and careful observation. One effective means of securing this result would be the establishment of a permanent organization to undertake, in this field, work comparable to that carried on by the National Playground Association, the National Association for the Study and Prevention of Tuberculosis, the National Child Labor Committee, and other similar organizations in their respective fields. It is our judgment that the establishment of such a permanent voluntary organization, under auspices which would insure a careful consideration of all points of view, broad-mindedness and tolerance, would be desirable and helpful, if reasonably assured of adequate financial support.

FEDERAL CHILDREN'S BUREAU

13. A bill is pending in Congress for the establishment of a federal children's bureau to

collect and disseminate information affecting the welfare of children. In our judgment, the establishment of such a bureau is desirable, and we earnestly recommend the enactment of the pending measure.

SUMMARY

14. The preceding suggestions may be almost completely summarized in this — that the particular condition and needs of each destitute child should be carefully studied and that he should receive that care and treatment which his individual needs require, and which should be as nearly as possible like the life of the other children of the community.

15. We respectfully recommend that you send to Congress a message urging favorable action upon the bill for a federal children's bureau and the enactment of such legislation as will bring the laws and the public administration of the District of Columbia and other federal territory into harmony with the principles and conclusions herein stated, and we further recommend that you cause to be transmitted to the governor of each State of the Union a copy of the proceedings of this conference for the information of the state board of charities or other body exercising similar powers.[1]

By order of the conference:

Yours, very respectfully,

> HASTINGS H. HART,
> EDMOND J. BUTLER,
> JULIAN W. MACK,
> HOMER FOLKS,
> JAMES E. WEST,
> *Committee on Resolutions.*

B. THE MOTHERS' AID MOVEMENT

The question of public assistance to widows, 1911–1914

As indicated in the preceding document delegates to the White House Conference indicated a preference for "private charity rather than public relief" as the means of supporting dependent children in their own homes. This pronouncement was in keeping with the revulsion charity workers generally felt toward public outdoor relief. But as the idea spread that homes should not be broken simply because of poverty, and despite qualms regarding the pauperizing effects of public assistance, state legislatures began to give increasing consideration to the use of public funds to preserve "the highest and finest product of civilization."

1. The first mothers' aid law, Illinois, 1911

"Juvenile Courts — Funds to Parents," *Laws of Illinois,* XLVII (Springfield, 1911), 126–127.

Be it enacted by the People of the State of Illinois, represented in the General Assembly: That section 7 of the Act entitled "An Act relating to children who are now or may hereafter become dependent, neglected or delinquent . . . approved June 4, 1907, be and the same hereby amended so as to read as follows:

1. The President complied with this request in a special message to Congress on February 15, 1909, in which he personally endorsed the conference's conclusions.

If the court shall find any male child under the age of seventeen years or any female child under the age of eighteen years to be dependent or neglected within the meaning of the Act, the court may allow such child to remain at its own home subject to the friendly visitation of a probation officer, and if the parent, parents, guardian or custodian consent thereto . . .

If the parent or parents of such dependent or negelcted child are poor and unable to properly care for the said child, but are otherwise proper guardians and it is for the welfare of such child to remain at home, the court may enter an order finding such facts and fixing the amount of money necessary to enable the parent or parents to properly care for such child, and thereupon it shall be the duty of the county board, through its county agent or otherwise, to pay to such parent or parents, at such times as said order may designate the amount so specified for the care of such dependent or neglected child until the further order of the court.

---

2. Illinois law defended

Merritt W. Pinckney, "Public Pensions to Widows. Experiences and Observations Which Lead Me to Favor Such a Law," *Proceedings* of the National Conference of Charities and Correction (1912), 474–480.

Pinckney, judge of the Cook County Juvenile Court, sponsored the Illinois "Funds to Parents" act of 1911. For Grace Abbott's comments on Judge Pinckney and the Illinois law see below, The spread of mothers' aid, doc. 1.

For four years past I have sat in the Juvenile Court of Chicago and watched with ever increasing interest the steady endless stream of city youth come and go — numbering in that time approximately 15,000 boys and girls, two-fifths of whom were dependents. Naturally in searching for remedies I have come to study and recognize causes and to appreciate the value of preventive measures. You can no more eliminate the dependency and delinquency of children by placing them on probation and by institutional care than you can cure crime by imprisonment and death. And yet, while studying the dependency of children and searching for measures to eradicate the cause and prevent its recurrence, we must not forget the patient nor neglect the curative. Poverty is a cause of dependency and will be until social justice shall prevail throughout the world and the dawn of the millennium breaks upon us. Motherhood, widowhood and poverty combined challenge universal compassion.

THE ADMINISTRATION OF THE LAW

The Act is either the best law for our dependent poor ever enacted, or else it is the worst, depending upon its administration. So far as I am advised, the operation of the law has been confined almost entirely to Cook County, which includes Chicago. On July 1st, 1911, when the law became operative, no funds were available, and from that time until November 30th, 1911, the end of the County's fiscal years, the total funds provided were $2,000. While the sum of one hundred and twenty-five thousand dollars was asked for to provide relief for the ensuing year, beginning December 1st, 1911, the County Board appropriated only $75,000.

The administration of this law by the Juvenile Court was from the very beginning attended with difficulties. The real intent of the law, which was to keep children at home with their parents, who, because of poverty alone, would otherwise be sent to institutions, was apparently lost sight of. A wide-spread publicity fostered by those who either did not understand the real purpose of the legislation, or else, from selfish reasons, did not want to understand, soon flooded the Juvenile Court with applications for relief . . . The absence of adequate help requested of the County Board to meet these new conditions added materially to the work of the Court. Indeed all the evils found by experience to be inherent in any plan for public outdoor relief, together with many unfavorable local conditions seemed to beset at the beginning the successful administration of the Act.

In the absence of willing co-operation by the county officials and their failure to furnish adequate and competent help, it was but natural to turn for assistance to those great charitable, social and civic welfare societies and associations in Chicago which are most active in relief-giving and in advancing the cause of good citizenship and a purer body politic.

. . . After several conferences these societies organized and furnished a committee consisting of five experienced workers to examine and pass upon the applications for relief.

.   .   .   .   .

Of the 1,156 applications investigated and considered by the Conference Group 850 were not recommended for relief. This was about two out of every three cases. The importance of having trained, experienced and intelligent workers to investigate and consider in conference these applications has been clearly demonstrated. The careful, painstaking and efficient work done by the Conference Group is largely responsible for the apparently satisfactory administration of the law to date. The Conference Group chosen by the Advisory Board from the corps of workers in Chicago's great charitable, social and civic welfare societies and associations, represents the best thought of the community on this subject. It would appear to be an ideal co-operation of society and the state in administering a worthy law.

The work of the Juvenile Court and of the Probation Department does not end with the entry of the order for relief, indeed it has only just begun. The Court must be kept constantly advised as to the continued fitness of the parent to whom relief has been granted and as to the wise and proper use of the money paid. Under our present plan the Judge, at the time of granting the relief introduces the mother to the probation officer in the district where the mother resides, and informs her that she will be subject to visitation by the officer and that she will be required to furnish the officer an accurate account of what she does with the money. Up to the present time there has been no opposition to this plan by the recipients of the relief. We hope by a careful and systematic supervision not only to prevent the unwise and wasteful use of the money provided, but also to collect data from which we can eventually determine an adequate standard of relief.

ADEQUACY OF THE RELIEF GRANTED

It will be difficult to standardize the relief. Certainly there can be no rigid and inflexible standard fixed. The circumstances, conditions, needs and resources of every family will, of necessity, differ and must be ascertained by patient and discriminating observation and inquiry. For years, "proper parental care" of the child has been interpreted in the Juvenile Court of Chicago to mean something more than a roof over the head, sufficient food for the stomach and clothes for the back. While avoiding the purely theoretical and ideal we must of necessity consider in administering the relief many conditions of family life other than those of health and physical comfort.

The average relief of $6.33 per month, granted for each child is undoubtedly too low. This low general average per child is in part due to the difficulties besetting the Court when the Act became a law. You will recall that there was available for the first six months the meagre sum of $2,000. We were in the experimental stage of the law's administration. Not a few men and women were prophesying either the early bankruptcy of the County or the repeal of the law. These conditions to a certain extent controlled our early action. As we gain in experience and as the public begins to see the possibility of a successful administration of the law, we shall be able to approach more nearly to a just and adequate standard of relief. In granting the relief, the earning capacity of the family is considered. We seek to supplement the family income with sufficient public funds to meet the family needs, whenever such income is earned without neglect of home and children or the sacrifice of health and strength. The spirit of self-dependence must not be broken down, nor should the effort to accomplish partial self-support be discouraged. We, who believe in the law, believe that, administered along these lines, it can help the dignified self-help of the families which it seeks to benefit and that the children who are brought up under these influences will become American citizens worthy of the name.

PRESENT AND FUTURE ECONOMY OF THE LAW

The Act is economical. The economy of its present practice in Illinois has been clearly demonstrated. Take a widowed mother and her group of six little ones — three girls and three boys. Even after you eliminate the mother and her future welfare from your consideration, you will find that the amount of money demanded by institutions for their care and custody is nearly double that required to rear these children in their own homes. The expense of maintaining the family group of six in institutions is $75 per month. It must be conceded that these children including the mother can be supported at home at a much smaller monthly expenditure.

Then, again, our experience teaches us that many mothers can almost support themselves and their children. When some supplementary relief, fixed and regular, is added to the family income, the problem of support is solved. Why then destroy the home and dismember the family and incur a larger expense when a little relief — a smaller expense — will keep the family together?

.   .   .   .   .

We concede, say the critics, that the relief administered under the Funds to Parents Act and similar laws, costs less than institutional relief. That, they reply, is not the issue. The question arises between so-called public and private outdoor relief. It is impossible, they contend, to honestly, efficiently and economically administer public outdoor relief on account of abuses which necessarily attend the administration. We admit the abuses. Equal candor will compel the critics to admit that the abuses resulting from private charity have often been quite as serious as from public relief. In the final analysis, both private and public relief, when administered without proper inquiry and investigation are harmful and demoralizing. The success of either method is chiefly a matter of administration.

There is a future as well as a present economy of the law. Institutional care has never been adequate. The institutions are too few. Mothers, however worthy, toiling for the bare necessities of life from early morn till late at night are poor guardians of the mental, moral and physical welfare of their offspring. Many of these unfortunate children who never had a decent chance grow up into a depraved manhood and womanhood and drift naturally into that great and ever increasing army of criminals who are a menace to society and to care for and control whom the state spends annually millions of dollars.

We like to think of the state as the *parens patriae* — the ultimate parent of all children. Upon this basic principle the state has fashioned a law and a Court for the child. The state must not stop here. Its duty is to enact and enforce such laws as will raise the standard of its citizenship. When bad conditions over which the individual has no control, stand in the way of this result, it is the duty of the state to remove them. The Funds to Parents Act is the next step forward. Its proper enforcement means normal, healthy, well-trained, properly-clothed and comfortably housed children guarded and protected at home by a mother's care and love, to the end that they become intelligent, industrious and respectable citizens and add to the industrial prosperity of the community.

---

3. Illinois law attacked

C. C. Carstens, "Public Pensions to Widows with Children," *The Survey,* XXIX (1913), 4.

Carstens (1865–1939) was secretary of the Massachusetts Society for the Prevention of Cruelty to Children.

The theory upon which pension legislation was based in this state, as in the others, was that children were being separated from their mothers for reasons of poverty only, and that children were coming before the Juvenile Court for forms of waywardness or delinquency which the court believed were due to the lack of the necessary care which the mother was capable of providing, but which she was prevented from giving because of the necessity of going out to earn the support for herself and her children.

The term "dependent children" does not have the same meaning in every state. In most states, the class of dependent children includes neglected as well as dependent children, and in certain states it includes a considerable number of those that in other states would be classed as wayward. When, therefore, it is stated that children have been committed to institutions, before one can reach a conclusion regarding the number of children that have been taken from homes because of poverty only, it is necessary to separate from this total the number that have been removed because of the neglect, crime, cruelty, drunkenness or other vice of the parents, so that they might have a better home than the parent has been able or willing to provide. We must also deduct the number that were removed because of the children's own waywardness, with which the home was unable to cope.

POVERTY AS A SINGLE FACTOR

This lack of distinction between neglected, wayward and dependent children is at the foundation of much loose thinking on this subject, and at final analysis the number of children who have been removed from their mothers because of poverty alone is found to be only a very small percentage of those in these various institutions. That there are children in institutions or in the care of children's societies because of poverty alone is unquestionably true, but it is essential that one should have a fairly clear idea of their number, so as to determine the advisability of developing an entirely new form of public aid to provide against this evil.

.   .   .   .   .   .

In certain instances the probation officers made an investigation sufficiently complete to answer the question whether a pension should be granted or not, but wholly inadequate for any constructive and supervisory work with the family. It must be conceded that, where an average of $23.28 is provided for each family, temptations come to spend money recklessly or foolishly, even in some of the better families. A pension plan of this sort requires careful following up, so that appropriate suggestions in regard to the health of mother and children, employment of older children, difficulties in discipline, an improved diet, and many other matters that come up in family life, besides advice on expenditures, may be made. The probation officer's investigation, however, seemed to develop into espionage instead of friendly supervision.

By means of a small staff of trained investigators, an inquiry was undertaken by the writer, with the cordial and helpful co-operation of the judge, the chief probation officer, and his deputy. The circumstances of one hundred pensioned families chosen at random were looked into. These families were visited in their own homes and a patient and painstaking statement was had from them regarding their present situation, the health, schooling, and work of the children, the mother's health, work and fitness to care for them, the adequacy of the pension, the items of the budget, and the individual expenditures per week. Inquiry was also made with reference to the family's condition before the death of the breadwinner, and after the breakdown had occurred and before the pension began. In addition, other inquiries were made in verification if it seemed necessary.

.   .   .   .   .

The effect of the pension upon the generosity of relatives, and upon the development of private aid through church, employers, friends or societies is a thing which will be keenly watched by all who are interested in the care of needy families. It is a subject of large concern to know whether, through such a large relief fund as a widows' pension fund, churches, relatives, employers or private societies will become less interested or cease their interest altogether at the point where the pension begins. On this subject 51 per cent of the cases examined show either that less interest began to be felt as a result of a pension plan or that these agencies ceased their interest altogether. In 19 instances there seems to have been no effect, but in some of these no other agencies or individuals were at any time interested. In 30 instances it was impossible to measure just what effect the pension had had. In 34 instances it was believed that the application for the pension was due to the existence

of the pension itself, while 64 applications did not seem to have originated in that way, and 2 were doubtful.

Under these circumstances one would expect that there would be evidence of undue dependence in the families. We find, however, that the number showing this attitude is not as large as the number of applications due to the existence of a pension, for 74 showed no evidence of such dependence. In 26 families, however, the fact that this sum was granted from public funds by the court and called a widows' pension either had not prevented the development of a pauper spirit or had not removed it in instances in which it had previously existed. It is evident that pensions have the same effect as relief . . .

The administrators of pension funds in Chicago, as well as those in the other cities visited, find that in common with administrators of other relief funds they are dealing with at least two types: first, families who, because of their receiving generous aid, rapidly deteriorate, become less energetic, less self-reliant and less moral than before such aid was given; second, families who, because of more generous aid, feel that economic security which becomes for them the basis of family rehabilitation. Most of the families visited are now better off financially than before the pension was granted, and are also better off than during the period preceding the death or last illness of the chief breadwinner, or whatever other cause led to economic breakdown. In some instances the family has never been as prosperous as it is now.

It was interesting to find that in a large majority of the families visited there was no evidence of wanton recklessness, extravagance or foolishness in the expenditures. There are many in the total number who have a large measure of family life and whose care of the children is most excellent, but a few of the mothers were clearly intemperate women, and there was a tendency to keep family groups together that had better be broken up. In one family, for instance, the mother was making capital of her crippled child and was interfering with its proper care. In another a patient in the highly contagious stage of tuberculosis was being kept at home under conditions detrimental to the two children. In another the family was syphilitic. In still others, the moral tone was low and the children unlikely to prosper, no matter how adequately relieved.

.   .   .   .   .

EFFECT ON COMMITMENTS

Those who expected that pensions to mothers with dependent children would reduce the number of commitments to institutions materially are doomed to disappointment, judging from the experience of the cities where pensions are in vogue. The number of children committed because of poverty alone is much smaller than is generally supposed, and only a careful case-by-case examination of the reasons leading to the commitments would bring out the facts. Most of the dependent children committed in Chicago were neglected by their parents and had no homes to which they could safely be returned.

CREATING NEW DEPENDENTS

The passage of new laws for the pensioning of widows with dependent children who are in need will inevitably create a new class of dependents in our communities. Thirty-four of the 100 cases examined in Chicago seem to be due to the fact of the existence of a pension plan. In communities where the forms of cooperation between the juvenile court and the private relief agencies are not as carefully worked out as they are in Chicago, this number will be materially increased. Any legislation that seeks to aid new groups of dependents without at the same time guarding against the creation of such dependents is dangerous.

PREVENTING WIDOWHOOD

The enthusiasm in favor of widows' pensions must not be underestimated and undervalued. It is born of a desire to have justice done to the mother who is attempting to keep her brood of children together under trying circumstances. A number of the states of the Union have, however, begun to meet this question in a more logical way, and are pointing the way to a better solution. They have discovered the causes of some of the deaths which have brought about widowhood, and have passed laws for their prevention. They have discovered that deaths from accident and from industrial and other preventable diseases constitute a considerable porportion of the total number. They have better protected the living so that there might be fewer widows and dependent children. They have passed workmen's compensation and employers' liability laws, so that the industry and the consuming public might carry the expense that comes as a result of the risk involved in the production of goods. They have passed insurance legislation which has decreased premiums and encouraged thrift.

When, in addition to measures that look toward the prevention of accident, disease and death, the community has also recognized the importance of a strict enforcement of legal responsibilities, still less will remain to be done through the pensioning of a new dependent class. There are few states that have laws to deal at all adequately with desertion, bastardy, and support by relatives in line of descent, and where such laws are reasonably adequate their rigid and intelligent enforcement is rare. The enthusiast in favor of widows' pensions is indifferent to the rigid enforcement of responsibilities. He is apt to hold lightly the ties of kinship and of those natural community relations which find their most beautiful expression in the service which one person may render to another in a time of distress. He is apt to turn easily toward the payment of a lump sum from the public treasury as a substitute for family

376] Care of Children in Their Own Homes

and neighborhood responsibility, and as a remedy for all social ills.

---

4. Social worker questions feasibility of public aid to mothers

Frederic Almy, "Public Pensions to Widows. Experiences and Observations Which Lead Me to Oppose Such a Law," *Proceedings* of the National Conference of Charities and Correction (1912), 482–483.

Almy was the secretary of the Buffalo Charity Organization Society.

Why am I opposed to this plan of public pensions for widows? My opposition is not academic. I do not care whether the relief is a public or a private function, or whether it is given by the poor master, or by the Juvenile Court as in Chicago, or by children's guardians, or by a board of home assistance as proposed in New York. I think much, very much, of Thomas Mackay's classic argument that to the imagination of the poor the public treasury is inexhaustible and their right, and that they drop upon it without thrift, as they dare not do on private charity, and this argument is one that cannot be met by any excellence of administration, but I remember too that pauperizing by alms is no worse than pauperizing by neglect. Moreover, Mackay's argument applies mainly to indolence and improvidence, which are voluntary. The poverty of widowhood is not usually due to lack of thrift, and what widow ever became a widow because aid was public rather than private?

The crux of my opposition to public pensions to-day is that the public does not stand for fit salaries for relief. I am an advocate of more adequate relief, but I am an advocate first of more adequate brains and work for the poor. Relief without brains is as bad as medicine

without doctors. I would much rather see doctors without medicine, or salaries without relief, as is the practice of some of the best of our charity organization societies. Like undoctored drugs, untrained relief is poisonous to the poor. Good charity is expensive, and poor charity is worse than none, yet what city would support adequate case work for its public aid?

In Buffalo where we have had organized charity for thirty-five years and for five years much talk and less practice of adequate relief, public opinion supports adequate salaries for a large staff in the charity organization society. Nevertheless, the city poor office has but five investigators, while we have fourteen, of better ability. Moreover, the city investigators merely investigate, while we make plans, find friends and find money from natural sources. Last month the money found by our paid visitors from relatives, employers and friends nearly equalled the total of their salaries, and if we add the wages for work found by them it would have exceeded their salaries. Of course these visitors gave the poor also a service which is worth ten times more than the money they get for them; but I find that the monthly statement of this money got by them for their poor, does much to justify the salaries in the eyes of the public.

Will the voters stand in any city for the salaries without which charity is a pest and curse? Even in Chicago where a bad law in a good cause is redeemed by a good judge, I do not find any indication of adequate case work. Judge Pinckney has voluntarily associated with himself a salaried case committee, paid for by private charities and not from the public treasury; but the record stories, which I have glanced at in the few days since I undertook this paper, would not pass muster for case work in some cities. They show good diagnosis and study of temperament, but I have not noticed in them search for relatives who can give, or attempts to find work or to find better paid work, or official records of the school attendance of children as a condition of aid, or constructive plans for removing poverty. A pension committee needs all of these things for its action. Even under Judge Pinckney, the Chicago relief looks like mere relief, which keeps the family from deteriorating after the bread-winner has gone. Indemnity relief may have no higher function than to prevent deterioration, but charity relief aims to redeem the family. It is not too much to ask that the tax payers' money should be educational and constructive.

---

5. Mothers' aid — a backward step, 1913

Edward T. Devine, "Pensions for Mothers," *American Labor Legislation Review*, III (1913), 193–199.

Devine, secretary of the Charity Organization Society of New Yory City (1896–1917) and director of the New York School of Philanthropy, delivered this paper at a conference on social insurance sponsored by the *American Labor Legislation Review*.

As an advocate . . . of social insurance, I sharply challenge the proposal for weekly or monthly payments to mothers from public funds raised by taxation, as not in harmony with the principles of social insurance; as not being insurance at all, but merely a revamped and in the long run unworkable form of public outdoor relief; as having no claim to the name of pension and no place in a rational scheme of social legislation; as embodying no element of prevention or radical cure for any recognized social evil; as an insidious attack upon the family, inimical to the welfare of children and injurious to the character of parents; as imposing in the form in which it is usually embodied an unjustifiable burden upon the courts at a time when the

courts are having rather more than they can do to discharge their time honored functions to the general satisfaction; as illustrating all that is most objectionable in state Socialism, and failing to represent that ideal of social justice which the Socialist movement, whatever its faults, is constantly bringing nearer.

.   .   .   .   .

Whatever they are called, money payments to mothers from public funds are relief; public charity. No hysterical denunciation or passionate protest will change the bald fact that the transaction is a gift for which the persons at whose expense it is made have received no direct equivalent. Sympathy and not the payment of a financial obligation explains it. Need and not exchange is its basis. The distinction between the new mothers' pensions and the old county relief, in so far as it is not purely one of administration, is purely a subjective difference, a change in the point of view of the observer. This subjective change could just as well have been made, and in fact often is made, without any corresponding change in the procedure to which it refers. The discovery that the mother by bringing children into the world thereby establishes a claim to an allowance from the state could just as well have been applied to the old poor relief as to the new pensions. Whether the man who carries the money is called a county visitor or a probation officer, whether the man who decides on the amount is called a county commissioner or a judge, are surely of no real consequence, either to the mother or to the discriminating student. This being so, the sound policy of reform and progress would seem to lie in the improvement of the administration of public relief where that system prevails, rather than in a process of self-delusion and of solemn pretense that changing the names of things alters their essential character.

The advocacy of mothers' pensions rests in part upon opposition to, dislike of, and prejudice against, private charity, and especially against what is known as organized charity, distinguished by investigation, the keeping of records, discrimination in relief, and the insistence upon the full utilization of personal resources rather than impersonal relief funds. It is true that differences of opinion about the relative merits of private organized charity and public relief funds rest less upon evidence than upon the social philosophy and general point of view of those who differ. It is not too much to hope, however, that the numerous inquiries, official and unofficial, instigated by the present interest in this subject may bring reasonable people to an open-minded examination of the evidence and a willingness at least to take it into account. Such an examination will, I believe, disclose the fact that there is a legitimate place for

(1) Social insurance;

(2) Public institutional relief, and perhaps public outdoor relief also in some communities;

(3) Organized charitable relief of families;

(4) Voluntary neighborly help.

Any one of these four means of supplementing self help and family responsibility, or all of them together, do not compare in importance with what must always be the main reliance, namely the personal responsibility of the individual for his own welfare and for that of those who, in infancy, in sickness, in misfortune or in old age, are naturally dependent upon him. The time has not come — I see no reason why it should ever come — when it is necessary or expedient to seek a substitute for this principle of individual responsibility and of family solidarity. The family for whom provision needs to be made by any kind of public or private relief is and should remain the exceptional family. The ordinary expectation should be that one will provide for himself in sickness and in old age, and upon his death for his widow and orphan children. This is no utopian or antiquated ideal. It is in fact the ordinary and all but universal ideal of American citizens. We who are engaged in relief work or in advocating social schemes of vari-

ous kinds are apt to get very distorted impressions about the importance, in the social economy, of the funds which we are distributing or of the social schemes which we are promoting.

. . . . . .

Children should be protected, as the advocates of mothers' pensions insist, but the giving of a pension by the state to the mother does not constitute such protection, and, in a large majority of instances is not even a substantial contribution to this end. Children need protection very often because of improper guardianship, or because of ignorance and neglect of parents, or because of their own physical defects or mental peculiarities, or because they are hard to manage and discipline and their parents, even if perfectly respectable people, are not good managers and disciplinarians; because of a hundred other reasons which have no earthly relation to income. They need protection sometimes because of poverty alone, but far less frequently than most advocates of mothers' pensions seem to imagine. If the poverty which does lead to a need for protection is due to any insurable risk such as death, sickness, or old age, or even the involuntary unemployment of the bread-winner, then that need should be met by insurance, in the expense of which industry must bear its due burden, the state and the insured also doing their part according to the principles of social insurance as they are being successfully worked out in foreign countries and in some of our states. With what unholy joy will the anti-social type of employer, who now throws his maimed and mangled workers, his exhausted, worn out workers, and the widows and orphans of those whom he has slain, indiscriminately upon the scrap heap of public relief, welcome a movement which, by changing the name of this relief to widows' pensions, makes it more palatable to the widows and to sentimental reformers, and thus gives the exploiters a new strangle-hold on the exemption privileges of which they are about to be deprived. An income for widows, from a state administered fund, raised by the joint contributions of the insured and their employers, the burden lightly felt because widely distributed and borne in part by all of us who purchase the commodities in the manufacture of which the insured was engaged — that is the honorable income which I covet for every mother who is widowed by the death of an industrial worker. In the professions and in agriculture there are obvious analogous means of making similar provision. In the comparatively few instances in which, for any exceptional reason, insurance funds would not be applicable, we would have recourse to public relief, to organized charity and to voluntary individual neighborly help.

.   .   .   .   .

I have no more right than any other to represent philanthropy as it has been understood by our fathers, no mandate to defend its representatives; but I cannot forbear to warn my friends who would lightly discard voluntary charity utterly from human society, that they are building upon the sand; that when they put their reliance entirely upon a self-contained, coercive system in which all the relief funds are raised by taxation and all are distributed arbitrarily on a per capita plan without reference to individual circumstances, without reference to the thrift or efforts of the individual, without reference to the cooperation of relatives, of trade unions, of churches, or neighbors, without reference to any charitable agencies or social sources, they are making a violent break with the historical evolution of human society, they are following a will-o'-the-wisp.

They are just now having a heyday of popularity. Many laws they have secured, and others are on the way.

As a student of social economy I am much interested in these experiments. As a progressive and radical social reformer I deeply regret the painful steps which we shall certainly have to retrace

6. "A step forward," 1914

New York State, *Report of the Commission on Relief for Widowed Mothers,* 1914 (Albany, 1914), pp. 7–10, 114–119, 126–133, 151–152.

The appointment of the New York Commission on Relief for Widowed Mothers was due largely to the efforts of Sophie Irene Loeb (1876–1929), social worker and reporter for the New York *Evening World.* Miss Loeb, herself one of six children of a widow, carried on a vigorous personal campaign to secure aid for mothers of dependent children. After serving on the Commission, and leading a successful drive for the passage of a mothers' pension act in 1915, Miss Loeb was appointed president of the New York Child Welfare Board with responsibility for executing the new law.

BASIC PRINCIPLES

The Commission believes it to be fundamentally true that:

1. The mother is the best guardian of her children.

2. Poverty is too big a problem for private philanthropy.

3. No woman, save in exceptional circumstances, can be both the home-maker and the bread-winner of her family.

4. Preventive work to be successful must concern itself with the child and the home.

5. Normal family life is the foundation of the State, and its conservation an inherent duty of government.

THE GENERAL SITUATION

The Commission finds that:

1. Widowhood is the second greatest cause

of dependency, the first being the incapacity of the bread-winner.

2. The widowed mother is in peculiar need of adequate assistance, and is uniquely open to constructive educational endeavors.

3. Public aid to dependent fatherless children is quite different in theory and effect from "charity" or "outdoor relief."

4. The experience of twenty-one other states in the Union, and of the larger countries of Europe, proves that it is feasible to administer such aid wisely and efficiently by public officials.

5. The experience elsewhere has shown that such aid is the most economical as well as the most socially advanced method of caring for dependent children.

THE SITUATION IN NEW YORK STATE

This Commission finds that:

1. Commitment of Children

Two thousand seven hundred and sixteen children of 1,483 widowed mothers are at present in institutions at public expense, who were committed for destitution only; 933 children of 489 widows are at present in institutions because of illness of the mother, resulting often from overwork and overworry that might easily have been prevented.

2. Self-Support Impossible

a. The unskilled widowed mother is unable to support herself and her family at a reasonable standard of living by taking work into the home or going out into the broader fields of industry.

b. The work available to such women outside of the home inevitably breaks down the physical, mental and moral strength of the family and disrupts the home life through an inadequate standard of living and parental neglect, due to the enforced absence of the mother at the time the children most need her care.

c. The work available in the home results, equally inevitably, in the prevention of normal family life, by causing overwork, congestion, child-labor, contagion, and a dangerously low standard of living.

3. Normal Childlife Impossible

This disruption of the home contributes largely and directly to the backwardness and delinquency of children.

4. Present Sources of Assistance Inadequate

Neither the public outdoor relief system extant in the State, nor the private charities in our larger cities, have sufficient funds to relieve adequately all widows of the grim burden of support so that they might remain at home to take personal care of their dependent children.

5. Present Assistance Wrong in Principle

That neither public outdoor relief nor private charity constitutes the proper method of carrying on the conservation of the good home.

FIRST RECOMMENDATION

With these principles as a basis, and these facts as a reason, the Commission respectfully recommends the immediate enactment into law of the principle of State aid to the dependent children of widowed mothers.

GOVERNMENT AID THE ONLY SOLUTION

Other solutions that have been suggested to and rejected by the Commission are:

1. That all such relief be left in the hands of private charity.

By a review of the work done in individual families, and through the testimony presented by many charity experts, the Commission finds that private charity has not the funds, and cannot, in the future, raise the funds to give adequate relief in the home, nor to administer such funds in the efficient, wise and sympathetic manner which it has itself set up as the ideal.

2. That the State grant aid through the volunteer relief societies or the private child-caring institutions.

The Commission finds that experience in other states demonstrates clearly that public officials can be found who can administer such assistance as wisely and as sympathetically as can private social workers.

3. That this question be left until a complete system of social insurance be adopted in this State.

The Commission finds that no comprehensive system of social insurance, covering all the possible causes of the death of the breadwinner of the family is apt to be adopted in New York State for a great many years to come, and that the social insurance system of Europe, though in certain instances it has been in operation for more than a generation, has not even yet succeeded in making adequate provision for the homecare of widowed mothers. Further, and as a lesson to be drawn from European experience, the Commission believes that a system of direct governmental aid to the widowed mother with children should be considered not as an alternative to, but as a necessary and integral part of social insurance.

.   .   .   .   .

SOCIAL PROGRESS

The Mothers' Assistance Laws in this country are a step forward from and not back to the old "outdoor relief," which has been a failure everywhere. The leaders in private charity in the West fully appreciate this — in fact, it is largely because of this they so unanimously approve of these laws. Our leaders here have as yet been unwilling to face the truth of this and have opposed the principle of government aid because of their fear that

it will mean a return to the disgraceful condition that existed in New York city up to 1878 and that still exists, though in lesser degree, throughout the rest of the State.

The success of the measure elsewhere, the ever advancing standards of all public work should convince all those who are progressive at all that such fears are without foundation.

.   .   .   .   .

We have now shown that the indigent widowed mother cannot by her own efforts earn enough to maintain a standard of home life that is beneficial to her children, and that our present system of relief is totally inadequate to relieve her of enough of her burden to make the load bearable.

Twenty-one States in the Union have faced this same situation and have met this same problem by creating a system of State aid, popularly known as Mothers' Pensions. The development of this system everywhere and its adoption in New York has been vigorously opposed by many of the leading charitable societies throughout the country. More particularly however that opposition has emanated from the charity workers that dominate the New York School of Philanthropy and the Russell Sage Foundation.

In a large measure these organizations lead in the development of philanthropic thought and work in America. In order then fully to understand their opposition and to answer their objections it becomes necessary to discuss more fully the various phases of the philosphy of private philanthropy.

FUNDAMENTAL FLAWS IN THE PHILOSOPHY OF PRIVATE CHARITY

1. Monetary Assistance an Essential

Up to within a few years ago, the nonsectarian charities held as a fundamental principle that financial aid was a very minor, if not a negligible, element of family rehabilitation, counting as infinitely more valuable the ministrative services of their trained district secretaries, and their volunteer friendly visitors.

.   .   .   .   .

The fear of pauperizing the needy by giving them money has proven in most instances without foundation; the dangers of giving inadequate relief have come to be recognized as a far greater evil. But organized charity has been unable to raise funds sufficiently large to permit their meeting this higher standard of adequacy in any appreciable number of families. The rest must be content with aid that is insufficient for their needs, and the widowed mother must supplement it by her own earnings. Thus again she must work either in or out of her house to the detriment of the family's health and well-being.

.   .   .   .   .

Lately, then, there is a tendency to recognize lack of money as one of the fundamental causes of poverty and the supplying of this want at least as important a feature of their work as the friendly advice and educational guidance in the home.

We are just discovering the truth of the words of the Bible:

"What doth it profit my brethren if a brother or sister be naked and destitute of daily food, and one of you say unto them go, depart in peace, be ye warmed and filled; notwithstanding ye give them not those things which are needful to the body; what doth it profit."

That the truth of this was ever doubted is humorous. But when we realize that for years it has been doubted and the doubt carried out in the name of "charity," it becomes tragic.

.   .   .   .   .

Some of the private societies . . . are making special efforts to increase the amount of relief available for the widows in their community and to give adequately for the protection of normal family life . . .

. . . The others, after evading the question of adequacy for a long while, fell back on the old plea that the giving of money was secondary to the counsel of good visitors.

The new note in charitable work was struck by Mr. Cyrus L. Sulzberger, former president and now a trustee of the United Hebrew Charities, when he stated:

"My judgment is that no relief organization is adequately aiding widows at the present time or has been at any time, for as many years as I can recollect. I believe very strongly that there should be all the modern aids to philanthropy that are involved in friendly visiting and in nursing and in all the other aids to charity. But a hungry widow cannot eat a friendly visitor. There are certain elemental needs that must be provided that these aids will not provide. I mean to say there is a certain fundamental amount of money that must be provided before the assistance of the friendly visitor is of any use. The first thing the woman needs is food and a roof over her head, and clothing and fuel. You cannot preach high thinking on such very low living."

.   .   .   .   .

While it is, of course, true that all the relatives of a dependent family should be keenly interested in her welfare, and should give her financial and moral support, reliance upon them as a source of income can easily be pushed to an extreme. In the majority of indigent families the relatives are little better off than the applicant and are having sufficient of a struggle to keep the wolf from their door. The private charities often count upon the assistance of relatives who are not legally bound, or upon those who must be allowed to keep their little money to protect their own interests. Too often also is a charity willing to assume that a relative is granting adequate assistance upon the assurance of a mother that he is "helping her." No careful investigation is made of the actual amount of such assistance.

The average applicant for relief resents bitterly the inquiry from the relatives of her worthiness by the agents of private societies. There is a natural cry that rebels against such an inquiry, particularly when it does not take into account the petty family quarrels and jealousies that mar the friendships of relatives or neighbors.

There are some extreme instances in the family histories reviewed by the sub committee of this Commission which show to what extent this reliance upon relatives has gone.

Sometimes even charitable societies have "closed" a case and refused assistance because the applicants were unwilling to have their troubles aired before distant members of the family.

.   .   .   .   .

One of the favorite arguments against government assistance is the plea that it will break down this family coherence and relieve the relatives of the responsibilities of their relationship.

Mr. Robert W. de Forrest said:

"State pensions for widows would tend to relieve neighbors and relatives from their present sense of responsibility and to cut off supplies from them. Moreover, and this is perhaps a stronger reason, it would tend to cut off widows from the friendly aid and friendly sympathy that usually goes with material aid and which is often of greater importance than the material aid itself. Underlying the idea of widows' pensions seems to be the thought that material aid is everything, or if not everything, the most important thing."

.   .   .   .   .

In all the States visited by our subcommittee the testimony of all who appeared was unanimous in agreeing that the public pension did relieve relatives, not of their interest in but of the burden of support of the mother only in cases where the relief was not only improper but advisable.

Miss Gertrude Vaile, of the Juvenile Court in Denver, Colorado, says:

"There seems no doubt that a system of public pensions must be expected to take over an immense financial burden, now actually being borne by relatives and friends. That may not wholly be an evil. One of our present pensioners was recommended for pension by the school authorities for the sake of her overburdened sister, whose children were being kept out of school to help the widow. We are satisfied that the sister is no less kind and personally helpful now that she is relieved of the financial strain."

Whatever possibility exists of the State's being forced to care for the poor whose relatives can well afford to support them, it is easily safeguarded against and in every State has been successfully guarded against both by the law itself and by its administration.

These laws in other States are based on a new recognition of social responsibility and of democratic interdependence.

The agencies organized for private charity in New York State seem to fear that the public, through their officials, cannot attain the same high order of efficiency which they claim to have reached. This is the most serious of their objections to public allowances to Widowed Mothers.

Mr. Otto T. Bannard expressed his fears quite bluntly:

"Widowed mothers present the strongest sentimental appeal and the very best case for this entering wedge towards State socialism. The battle cry is not alms, but their right to share. The subsequent steps are old age pensions, free food, clothing and coal to the unemployed and the right to be given work. It breeds candidates for alms, multiplies upon itself, represses the desire for self-help, self-respect and independence and inflicts upon its beneficiaries what is termed in England the government stroke of paralysis. It is not American; it is not virile."

This "cultivation of the pauper spirit," this "attitude of the public mind," is, of course, a menace to American civilization. Is it true, however, that such a menace will be fostered by outdoor public relief wisely given and carefully supervised? It has not been the experience in the twenty-one States where pensions are now being paid.

· · · · ·

We have pointed out that the private charities have been short-sighted in their opposition to State aid to the widowed mother because of their own inability to cope with the problems and their own air of superiority over the government.

If we search but a little beyond these objections we find that philanthropy is of itself aristocratic and fashionable.

Inherent in the organizations of private charity is the undemocratic spirit that "noblesse oblige." The theory is accepted that the "fiddler plays the tune" and that he who supports a charity can dictate its policies. This principle is sound, without doubt, if the gift of money is accompanied with the gift of personal service — it is not true otherwise.

There is evident among the larger philanthropists of to-day a feeling that the poor are ordained on earth in order that they — the rich — may develop their pious generosity. Aid is given the good mother with dependent children, not because of her need, not even because of the interdependence of her welfare and that of the State, but because of the aristocratic principle of a social duty to the lower classes. This would, of course, be destroyed if the people themselves undertook to abolish poverty and care for their dependents.

· · · · ·

Mr. Robert de Forrest stated:

"If the duty of helping their less fortunate neighbors were taken off the shoulders of those who are able to help by having the city or State assume that burden, much of the neighborly intercourse between the poorer and the richer would cease. Public outdoor relief makes for a class separation and the enmity of classes.

Private charity makes for brotherhood of men."

Surely we have ceased to believe this. Surely we will all believe that the truth was more clearly expressed by Miss Flaherty of the Church of the Messiah:

"The idea that it is done as a philanthropy, that the relief given to widows is charity, is one of the worst handicaps, I think, because the most self-respecting widows, the widows whom you want most to help, will not accept it, because their children would become dependents on the rich."

Surely all of us, whatever may be our conception of "social justice," believe that the child must not be left to the care of the charitable, but has a right to be protected and cared for by the State. Every stage of progress in child caring has met with this same objection from well-intentioned philanthropists. Public schools, public libraries, public textbooks, public school lunches were all attained over this same sort of opposition. Strange as it seems, we are told that the "brotherhood of man" ceases at the very point when all men as brothers unite democratically to help their children, and is only developed when the few help the many through "charity."

This conception is a relic of the days when to be charitable was a religious duty and when it was sincerely believed that the poor were created that the fortunate might attain holiness by graciously granting relief to their humble brothers.

The spread of mothers' aid, 1911–1931

1. Background and significance of public aid for dependent children

Grace Abbott, *The Child and the State*

(Chicago: University of Chicago Press, 1938)
II, 229–231, 234.

The substitution of workmen's compensation for the uncertainties of employers' liability under the common law and of "mothers' pensions," or, more accurately, public aid for dependent children in their own homes, for the uncertainties and inadequacies of relief under the poor law or care by charitable agencies were the first social-insurance measures to be adopted in the United States. Both were enacted in 1910–11 and were rapidly adopted in the Northern states. Illinois led with "Funds to Parents" Act. In two years twenty states, in ten years forty states, and by 1935 all the states except Georgia and South Carolina had passed some kind of mothers' aid laws.

Their enactment constituted public recognition by the states that the contribution of the unskilled or semiskilled mothers in their own homes exceeded their earnings outside of the homes and that it was in the public interest to conserve their child-caring functions; and as this group of children whose fathers were dead, incapacitated, or had deserted them would need care for a long period, the states recognized that the aid should not be administered in connection with or as part of general relief and must have a different standard of adequacy than emergency relief. This legislation also represented a revolt against the current policy of separating children from their mothers on the ground of poverty alone and caring for them at greater cost in institutions and foster-homes. The decisions of the courts regarding the early laws make it clear that they were child welfare measures and not new poor relief laws.

The storm of controversy that developed among social workers with the passage of the Illinois Act showed how out of line many of them were with current public opinion and how little they appreciated the needs of mothers who were not cared for or were very inadequately cared for by the private charities they administered. The Illinois law was proposed by Judge Merritt W. Pinckney of the Cook County Juvenile Court because he found himself continually asked to take children from poor but competent mothers and commit them to institutions. Public relief in Cook County was at that time limited to grocery and coal orders which the United Charities and other private agencies often supplemented by money for rent, clothes, and types of food not supplied by the County. But such assistance was generally regarded as emergency aid. Usually work was secured for the mother, and sometimes she was persuaded to give up one or two children when it was obvious that she could not hope even with some assistance combined with her meager earnings to care for all her children. At the White House Conference on Dependent Children which President Theodore Roosevelt called in 1909, the first resolution adopted laid great stress on the importance of providing means for keeping children in their own homes, but, reflecting a public opinion which was already in process of change, added that such assistance should be given, "preferably in the form of private charity, rather than public relief." While the charitable agencies usually had some money for pensions for such mothers, very few of them, in Chicago or elsewhere, were given any real security. Indeed, security was not generally considered desirable as it was thought to discourage relatives and friends from giving assistance to the families. Such a program or policy meant all too often that at the end of a period of years the mother broke down under the double burden of wage-earner and housekeeper, and the children were first neglected and then delinquent.

Judge Pinckney was in charge of a publicly supported agency and he properly sought public funds to remedy a need of which he was an almost daily witness. This need the legislators understood because they knew the problems that the widows of workingmen faced, and so, with no estimate of numbers or costs and no discussion of the administrative problems involved, they passed the Funds to Parents Act. Judge Pinckney did not consult the interested social agencies before proposing the law, and it lacked administrative safeguards. But Chicago social workers had great confidence in him and in his objectives, and so the emergency need for an administrative staff was met by the organization of a committee composed of representatives of the leading private social agencies of the city, which undertook to help Judge Pinckney test the value of the law by providing temporarily out of private-agency funds a mothers' pension staff just as they had provided the original probation staff of the court. Their action was much criticized by some leaders in social work on the ground that the whole theory of the law was wrong and it had better be allowed to fail at once.

At that time the opinion was widespread that public relief would never be well administered because of the traditional theory that adequate salaries would not be provided for administration, that there would be political interference, that relief from the public treasury would increase pauperism, and that private charity would and could meet the need if it did not have to compete with public relief. Public relief had been abolished in a number of cities, among them New York, Philadelphia, and Baltimore some thirty years before the mothers' aid movement started, and it was from these centers that criticism by social workers, especially those connected with charity organization societies, was most vehement. Moreover, the statement of the existing need was regarded as a criticism of the adequacy of these agencies, and it was true that among the supporters of mothers' pensions there were some who were critical of the charity organization policies as the report of the commisisons appointed in New York and Massachusetts revealed.

.   .   .   .   .   .

The critics were eventually silenced by the success and popularity of mothers' aid, but some still held to the theory of non-categorical

relief and to their distrust of any form of public aid. The depression finally convinced them of the necessity for public relief, but only after private charity had tried unsuccessfully to meet the mounting needs of millions of unemployed did they abandon the theory that private charity if not forced to compete with public provision could carry the entire relief load.

---

2. An Ohio proposal, 1912

Ohio Commission to Codify and Revise the Laws of Ohio Relative to Children, *Report* ([Columbus], 1912), pp. 27–28.

The commission, appointed by Governor Judson Harmon in 1911 to draw up a Childrens' Code, recommended passage of the following provisions for funds to mothers. The Legislature approved in 1913, adding Ohio to the list of states providing mothers' pensions.[1]

For the partial support of women whose husbands are dead, or become permanently disabled for work by reasons of physical or mental infirmity, or whose husbands are prisoners, when such women are poor, and are the mothers of children under the age of fourteen years, and such mothers and children have a legal residence in any county of the state, the Juvenile Court shall make an allowance to each of such women, as follows: Not to exceed fifteen dollars a month, when she has but one child under the age of fourteen years, and if she has more than one child under the age of fourteen years, it shall not exceed fifteen dollars a month for the first child and seven dollars a month for each of the other children under the age of fourteen years. The order making such allowance shall not be effective for a longer period than six months, but upon the expira-

1. Laws of Ohio, CIII (Springfield, Ohio, 1913), pp. 877–879.

tion of such period, said court may from time to time, extend such allowance for a period of six months, or less, provided the home of such woman has first been visited by a probation officer or other competent person.

AMOUNT OF ALLOWANCE

Such allowance shall be made by the Juvenile Court, only upon the following conditions: First — the child or children for whose benefit the allowance is made, must be living with the mother of such child or children; Second — the allowance shall be made only when in the absence of such allowance, the mother would be required to work regularly away from her home and children, and when by means of such allowance she will be able to remain at home with her children, except that she may be absent not more than one day a week for work; Third — the mother, must in the judgment of the Juvenile Court, be a proper person, morally, physically and mentally, for the bringing up of her children; Fourth — such allowance shall in the judgment of the court be necessary to save the child or children from neglect and to avoid the breaking up of the home of such woman; Fifth — it must appear to be for the benefit of the child to remain with such mother; Sixth — a careful preliminary examination of the home of such mother must first have been made by the probation officer, an associated charities organization, humane society, or such other competent person or agency as the court may direct, and a written report of such examination filed.

AGE LIMIT

Whenever any child shall reach the age of fourteen years, any allowance made to the mother of such child for the benefit of such child shall cease. The Juvenile Court may, in its discretion, at any time before such child reaches the age of fourteen years, discontinue

or modify the allowance to any mother and for any child.

URGENT CASES

Should the fund at the disposal of the court for this purpose be sufficient to permit an allowance to only a part of the persons coming within the provisions of this act, the Juvenile Court shall select those cases in most urgent need of such allowance.

WHEN NO ALLOWANCE ALLOWED

The provisions of this act shall not apply to any woman who, while her husband is imprisoned, receives sufficient of his wages to support the child or children.

PENALTY

Any person or persons attempting to obtain any allowance for a person not entitled thereto, shall be deemed guilty of a misdemeanor and on conviction thereof, shall be punished by a fine of not less than five nor more than fifty dollars, or imprisonment in the county jail, for a period of not less than two months, or both.

RECORDS

In each case where an allowance is made to any women under the provisions of this act, a record shall be kept of the proceedings, and any citizen of the county may, at any time, file a motion to set aside, or vacate or modify such judgment and on such motion said Juvenile Court shall hear evidence, and may make a new order sustaining the former allowance, modify or vacate the same, and from such order, error may be prosecuted, or an appeal may be taken as in civil actions. If the judgment be not appealed from, or error prosecuted, or if appealed or error prosecuted, and the judgment of the Juvenile Court be sustained or affirmed, the person filing such motion shall pay all the costs incident to the hearing of such motion.

DUTY OF COMMISSIONERS TO PROVIDE FUNDS

It is hereby made the duty of the county commissioners to provide out of the money in the county treasury, such sum each year thereafter as will meet the requirements of the court in these proceedings. To provide the same they shall levy a tax not to exceed one-tenth of a mill on the dollar valuation of the taxable property of the county. The county treasurer shall pay such allowance upon order signed by the Juvenile judge.

---

3. Mothers' aid viewed as subsidy for rearing children, Massachusetts, 1913

Massachusetts Commission on the Support of Dependent Minor Children of Widowed Mothers, *Report* (Boston, 1913), pp. 12–13, 31–32.

Massachusetts enacted a mothers' aid law in 1913.

It has long been the practice of charitable agencies in Massachusetts, as elsewhere, to separate children from their mothers when circumstances of whatever kind have made it appear that the members of the family would then be better off. In itself separation is not held to be desirable, and there is little doubt that today it is resorted to with much less readiness than was the case in the earlier period, and that very careful discrimination has come to be employed by the well-managed agencies. Separation takes place for a variety of causes, mainly reducible to two: the mother's unfitness or incapacity for

her role, and her economic disabilities. The two causes may, of course, be present together.

Your commission has sought especially to discover how frequent were the cases of economic disability. To this end it requested virtually all the important child-helping agencies of the Commonwealth to report the causes of separation for all new instances arising in the six months' period, Jan. 1 to June 30, 1912, and for all the other active cases of that period . . .

Returns were secured for 754 children not living with widowed mothers in the six months' period. In the cases of 328, or 43.3 per cent, of these children, removal was reported to have taken place because of the bad conduct of the child or — much oftener — the immorality or other unfitness of the mother. In the cases of 426, or 56.7 per cent, of the children, such causes were not reported to be involved. In a clear majority of the 426 cases economic causes determined separation . . .

.   .   .   .   .

The commission believes . . . that the widow without children or with children grown up is in a situation that she can generally manage. It believes that aid should be given only where there are young children in a good family, and then only in respect of them.

The commission rejects the principle of payment by way of indemnity for loss. It proposes the principle of payment by way of subsidy for the rearing of children. The terms "pension," "indemnity" and "compensation" are irrelevant, but the term "subsidy" implies that a condition exists which, aided, will result in positive good for the State. Subsidy makes it feasible that children should stay with their worthy mothers in the most normal relation still possible when the father has been removed by death. It is intended not primarily for those with least adequate incomes under the present system of aid, but for the fit and worthy poor. What a good mother can do for her own children no other woman can do, and no different device can do . . .

The commission believes that no aid can be given, except under the poor-law and by private societies, to widows unfit to spend money for the improvements of their families. Aid may have to be given them hesitatingly, without assurance, and under abundant supervision. When even then family life is not really maintained, separation of the children may be resorted to as being genuinely in their interests. Whether it is then best that they be boarded out or placed in institutions must depend on a variety of circumstances.

It seems not undesirable to create in the community a distinction between subsidy and relief. The family receiving the former may desire to live up to the special confidence reposed in it. Its income is regular and adequate. Supervision is less frequent than with other families. Detection of real misuse of the subsidy compels its cessation and reduces the family to the position of the incompetent poor. On the other hand, a family declared ineligible for subsidy may often, through the friendly offices of philanthropic societies, be trained to later eligibility.

---

4. Ten years of mothers' aid, 1921

Emma O. Lundberg, "Aid to Mothers with Dependent Children," *The Annals* of the American Academy of Political and Social Science, XCVIII (November, 1921), 97–105.

Miss Lundberg was director, Social Service Division of the Children's Bureau.

It may fairly be said that the principle of home care for dependent children is generally accepted in this country, but the ten years' experiment does not by any means indicate that the problem has been met. In two states laws have been inoperative because of defects; in several others, practically no use has been made of the legal provision; and in many states

where splendid work has been done in some localities, in other communities the intent of the law has been ignored or the provisions made have been so inadequate as to be of little avail.

.   .   .   .   .

The experimental character of much of this legislation, due largely to the haste with which the idea was adopted, is seen in the revisions and numerous amendments found necessary as the laws were put into operation . . . the majority of these amendments have been for the purpose of improving the administration, making the application more inclusive and increasing the amount of the grant or of the total appropriation available. The earliest Arizona law was in 1916 declared unconstitutional,[1] and another act passed in 1917 was also found to be unworkable; a new law was passed in 1921. Because of a defect in the appropriation section, the Maryland law of 1916 has been inoperative. In a few other states, while the validity of the laws has not been questioned, they have been largely ineffective because of failure to make the necessary funds available.

APPLICATION OF THE LAW

The central idea in the propaganda, and the most common inclusion in the earlier laws, was aid to widows. Gradually this conception has widened, until now only six states of the forty limit the grant to children of widows, though all states include widows directly or by implication . . . In seventeen states children of deserted mothers may be granted aid, and in six states, children of divorced mothers. Families where the father is totally incapacitated may be helped in eighteen states; fifteen states permit aid if the father is in an institution for the insane or is feeble-minded, and twenty states if

1. For a 1917 decision affirming the constitutionality of Utah's mothers' aid law, see Denver and Rio Grande Railroad Company *v.* Grand County, 51 Utah 294, reprinted in Grace Abbott, *The Child and the State*, II, 276–279.

the father is in a state penal institution. A few states gave assistance to relatives or guardians, other than parents, having custody of a dependent child. The whole trend appears to be toward giving the benefit of such aid to a larger group of children in their own homes. In Washington, the law is applicable to any "mothers who are needy"; in Maine and Massachusetts, to mothers with dependent children; in New Hampshire, to mothers dependent on their own efforts to support their children; and in North Dakota, to any woman who has one or more children dependent on her for support. Michigan and Nebraska specifically include unmarried mothers, while in some other states the law can be so applied.[2]

. . . . .

CAUSES OF DEPENDENCY

Any attempt to analyze the character of the disabilities that cause families to become applicants for this form of public assistance, must take into account variations of practice, due largely to the inadequacy of the funds and, perhaps, in lesser degree, to the differences in administrative rulings in states and localities operating under apparently similar legal provisions . . .

. . . It is probably true that the percentages of families in which the father was incapacitated physically or mentally, or in which divorce, desertion or imprisonment of the father were the causes of dependency, are lower than they would be in actual fact if the limitation of funds did not stand in the way. At any rate, the 25 per cent in which the death of the father was not the occasion for aid shows the necessity for a more general application of this form of assistance to children than was at first recognized.

. . . . .

2. See *ibid.*, pp. 306–307 for the exclusion of unwed mothers from the Wisconsin law. The law was amended in 1919 to bring these mothers under its provisions.

CHILDREN AIDED

Data on the number of children toward whose support in their own homes public grants are made, are available only to a limited extent. For a number of states and cities the proportion of children granted allowances to the total population under fifteen years of age, ranges from one-tenth of one per cent to 1.9 per cent. If similar conditions prevailed in the remaining states, it is estimated that the total number of children to receive such aid in the United States would approximate 200,000. If, on the other hand, the estimate were based on the proportion of children found to be in need of such aid in the communities where this assistance seems to be given on a fairly adequate basis both as to inclusion and amount of grants, the total number of children in the United States for whom aid should be granted in their own homes would be closer to 350,000 or 400,000 — and probably beyond even this estimate if all types of more or less permanent family disability were included. The situation that now appears to exist, in which there are proportionately almost twenty times as many families granted aid in one community as in another, probably does not imply a higher economic level in the former, but may instead indicate an absence of proper provision. Mothers' pension administration offers perhaps the most obvious arguments as to the futility, not to say actual detriment, of placing laws on the statute books but failing to make them practically effective through adequate appropriations and proper administration.

. . . . .

REASONS FOR DISCONTINUANCE OF AID

An analysis of the reasons for discontinuing aid, as given in the reports of six states and five counties containing large cities, for a total of 7,480 cases, indicates to some extent the complexity of the problem, and the necessity for keeping constantly in touch with conditions in the home if the assistance intended for the children is to be well applied. In only 44 per cent of the cases was aid discontinued because it was no longer required; most frequently, no doubt, this meant that a child began to work, or that the mother's earnings increased or that relatives or others came to the assistance of the family. Too often the mother finds it impossible to maintain her family on the allowance granted, and elects to dispense with both the aid and the regulations that accompany it, undertaking employment that necessitates either neglecting the home or making provision for the care of the children elsewhere. In truth, because of the very common inadequacy of the aid, no reliable economic interpretation can be given these figures. The reason for discontinuance, reported as next in frequency, was the remarriage of the mother — 16 per cent. In 11 per cent of the cases in which aid had been granted, it was later discontinued because the home was found unsatisfactory, the mother proved unfit to care for the children properly, or for a similar reason. In another 11 per cent the aid was discontinued because the mother or the child for whose benefit the grant was made had died, because the mother or the child was taken into an institution, the mother ceased maintaining a home, or the family left the county or state. In the states giving aid to families of fathers in prison or deserting, a small proportion were no longer aided because the fathers were released or had returned to their families.

INCREASE OF EXPENDITURES

When appropriations were first made for the aid of dependent children in their homes, there was little actual knowledge in regard to the extent of the need to be met. As experience was gained, the funds available were increased. But a study of the situation in perhaps the majority of localities will show that the amounts appropriated for grants to mothers of dependent children are still far below what is needed to carry out the spirit of these laws. In states where

there is some form of supervision by the state authorities, and in counties and cities where "case work" methods prevail, there is usually an effort to utilize the funds available in such a way that the families accepted for grants will receive the necessary amount of assistance, even though a considerable number of mothers with dependent children cannot be given aid. In one of our large cities the total state and county appropriation available for mothers' aid makes it possible to care fairly adequately for about one thousand families, leaving a waiting list that for the past two or three years has approximated eight hundred families who are under the terms of the law entitled to receive aid but who cannot be supplied. And this in spite of the fact that appropriations in this state and county have doubled and trebled during the past few years!

INADEQUACY OF GRANTS

Amounts paid for the care of children in boarding homes by private child-caring agencies in 1920 approximately averaged $4.50 a week per child; for three children, this would be approximately $60 a month. For the states in which a legal allowance is specified, the maximum grants for three dependent children in their own home are as follows: $19 to $20, seven states; $22 to $29, nine states; $30 to $39, eight states; $40 to $49, four states; $50 to $55, four states.

.   .   .   .   .

In boarding homes the family would necessarily have some other income; the families granted mothers' pensions are much less likely to have other resources. Yet the standard set in mothers' pension laws is approximately from one-third to two-thirds the amount found requisite by agencies for boarding children in family homes. Again it should be emphasized that even the inadequate maximum permitted by the terms of the law is seldom granted. Local economy and inadequate appropriations set a minimum entirely insufficient for the proper maintenance and safeguarding of the children who are by this legislation recognized as being in special need of aid and protection by the state.

The more closely the administration of aid to dependent children in their own homes approximates the methods used in good "family case work," the more nearly does the allowance approach the needs of the family and the assistance conserve the welfare of the children. Not infrequently the public funds known to be required must be supplemented by private charity or ordinary poor relief grants. Or, as seems to be the situation in a very considerable proportion of localities, the allowances must be eked out by the mothers' earnings. If proper arrangements can be made for the care and safeguarding of the children while the mother is away from the home, this may work out satisfactorily. But it requires very careful attention to the situation in each home aided to make sure that the assistance given is such that the welfare of the children is conserved.

.   .   .   .   .

State appropriations to supplement those made locally have proved an important factor in encouraging local grants and in raising the standards of relief. Twelve of the forty states are authorized to share with the counties or municipalities the cost of administration or of aid. States in which the application of mothers' pension laws was originally left to the initiative of local officials have frequently found it desirable to amend laws so as to make appropriations mandatory instead of permissive, and to supply some form of assistance or supervisory authority by the state, in order to carry out the intent of the laws.

The question of effective administration of mothers' pensions has been well summarized in the Standards agreed upon by the Conference on Child Welfare held under the auspices of the Federal Children's Bureau in 1919:

The policy of assistance to mothers who are competent to care for their own children is now well established. It is generally recognized that the amount provided should be sufficient to enable the mother to maintain her children suitably in her own home, without resorting to such outside employment as will necessitate leaving her children without proper care and oversight; but in many states the allowances are still entirely inadequate to secure this result under present living costs. The amount required can be determined only by careful and competent case study, which must be renewed from time to time to meet changing conditions.

---

5. A progress report, 1931

United States Children's Bureau, *Mothers' Aid, 1931,* Pub. No. 220 (Washington, D.C., 1933), pp. 6–24.

GROWTH IN MOTHERS' AID

Progress in the different States in the development of administrative units and in the number of families benefiting from mothers' aid is shown [in the following table[1]] which summarizes the findings of two surveys of mothers' aid administration made by the Children's Bureau in 1921 and 1931 . . .

The first country-wide survey of the extent to which mothers' aid had been made available was undertaken by the Children's Bureau in 1921 and 1922. By the end of 1921, 40 States had mothers' aid laws. At the time of the 1921 survey the laws in the different States had been in operation 1 to 10 years. Because of the inadequacy of the records, it was impossible at the time of this survey to get accurate figures from many counties as to the number of children in the families aided, but it was estimated

1. Adapted from Table 1 in United States Children's Bureau, *Mothers' Aid, 1931,* Pub. No. 220, pp. 8–9.

State	Date of passage of the first mothers' aid law	Number of families receiving aid	
		1921–22	Specified date, 1931
Maine	1917	638	608
New Hampshire	1913	144	175
Vermont	1917	43	90
Massachusetts	1913	3,391	2,817
Rhode Island	1923	—	388
Connecticut	1919	603	959
New York	1915	12,542	18,423
New Jersey	1913	2,472	7,000 (est.)
Pennsylvania	1913	2,494	6,066
Ohio	1913	5,763	7,708
Indiana	1919	114	1,083
Illinois	1911	2,500	6,087
Michigan	1913	2,072	6,555
Wisconsin	1913	3,284	7,052
Minnesota	1913	2,265	3,455
Iowa	1913	1,299	3,242 (est.)
Missouri	1917	227	307
North Dakota	1915	608	978
South Dakota	1913	423	1,290
Nebraska	1913	349	1,453
Kansas	1915	430	342
Delaware	1917	167	314
Maryland	1916	—	121
D.C.	1926	—	161
Virginia	1918	—	110
West Virginia	1915	162	334
North Carolina	1923	—	433
South Carolina	No mothers' aid law, June 30, 1931		
Georgia	No mothers' aid law, June 30, 1931		
Florida	1919	168	2,298 (est.)
Kentucky	1928	—	117
Tennessee	1915	—	190
Alabama	No mothers' aid law, June 30, 1931		
Mississippi	1928	—	45
Arkansas	1917	136	131
Louisiana	1920	—	69
Oklahoma	1915	758	1,896
Texas	1917	109	475
Montana	1915	567	839
Idaho	1913	229	230 (est.)
Wyoming	1915	95	95
Colorado	1913	428	650
New Mexico	1931	Mothers' aid law not operative	
Arizona	1914	—	131
Utah	1913	341	628
Nevada	1913	102	167
Washington	1913	527	2,517
Oregon	1913	375	862
California	1913	—	4,729
Total		45,825	93,620

that approximately 120,000 children were receiving aid on any given date. The questionnaires returned by many of the counties in some States indicated that the agencies in these counties, had little understanding of what mothers' aid was, and it is probable that many of the families reported were actually receiving poor relief only. No information as to mothers' aid could be obtained from 6 states at that time (1921–22).

In order to measure the progress made in mothers' aid administration, information was obtained in 1931 as to the situation at that time.

. . . . .

The 242 counties from which no reports were received in 1931 were scattered through 17 States, more than half of them, however, being located in Louisiana, Missouri, and Texas. Many of these counties probably were not granting aid, but some may have merely failed to report. Reports from 903 counties and cities in 32 States definitely stated that no mothers' aid was being granted. More than one fifth of these counties were in Kentucky and Mississippi, which did not enact mothers' aid laws until 1928, and in Maryland, which passed its State-wide law in 1929. The remaining counties and cities were in States that had authorized mothers' aid for a period of from 8 to 20 years.

. . . . .

The great increase in the number of families aided — 93,620 in 1931 as compared with 45,825 in 1921 — is due primarily to the increase in the number of counties granting aid and to the increase in the number of families aided in counties already granting aid in 1921 rather than to the addition of Kentucky, Mississippi, North Carolina, Rhode Island, and the District of Columbia, which passed mothers' aid laws between 1921 and 1931. Reports obtained from these States and the District of Columbia show that only 1,144 families having 3,824 children were receiving aid in these areas in 1931. In addition to the extension in the number of

counties and cities granting aid, more generous financal provisions by the local units or by the State, more liberal administrative policies, growth in population, and movement of population to the larger urban areas where mothers' aid was being granted, have all contributed to this increase.

The increase in number of families aided was not great in most of those States in which aid was being granted throughout the State in 1921. In three of these, Maine, New Hampshire, and Massachusetts, the number of families aided remained about the same or actually decreased. In contrast to this, New Jersey, one of this group, shows a steadily increasing use of public aid to children in their own homes as a method of providing for dependent children. Although the largest percentage of increase is usually found in those States in which there has been great growth in the number of administrative units granting aid, some States, for example, New York, Ohio, and Wisconsin, show a marked increase in families aided and a relatively small addition to the number of administrative units granting aid. In those States in which some of the counties failed to distinguish between mothers' aid and poor relief, it is difficult to measure progress, since the 1921 figures probably included many families that were actually receiving poor relief. In these States some of the counties reporting aid in 1921 were not the same as those reporting aid in 1931.

Increase in the number of families aided in a State should be accompanied by provision of funds sufficiently large to make possible adequate standards of living for all families. Unfortunately, comparable statistics as to expenditures in 1921 and 1931 are not available.

TYPES OF FAMILIES AIDED

Persons Caring for Children
and Status of Fathers

Information as to the persons caring for children receiving mothers' aid and as to the status of the fathers was obtained for the majority of families reported by 38 States and the District of Columbia . . .

Mothers' aid is still limited largely to families of widows . . .

Families for which status of father was reported	
Father dead	
Number	49,477
Per cent	82
Father deserting	3,296
Parents divorced	1,369
Father disabled physically	2,325
Father disabled mentally	1,984
Father imprisoned	1,596
Mother unmarried	55
Other status	17
Total	60,119

An interesting development, when studied in the light of legal limitations on eligibility, is the freedom with which some administrative agencies have come to interpret mothers' aid laws and provide aid for some mothers not strictly eligible for assistance. Experience has shown that in the metropolitan centers where other agencies are available and mothers' aid is administered by a special staff, the eligibility of the mother under the law is considered of primary importance in awarding a grant. In the smaller counties, however, lack of other agencies, ignorance of the law, or extreme liberality in its interpretation have placed families on the mothers' aid list for other reasons. It is probable also that because records were obtained in many localities from the county clerk, who also kept records of families receiving poor relief, the failure to discriminate between these two forms of relief resulted in the inclusion of families actually receiving poor relief. Although there are special administrative problems connected with the extension of this form of aid, the need of the security of income provided by mothers' aid is just as important for families deprived of the breadwinner for causes other than death as it is for the universally accepted one of widowhood. The need for further ex-

pansion in the types of families aided by mothers' assistance laws is evident.

In 5 of the 10 States that do not provide in the statutes for assistance to deserted mothers, a few such mothers were nevertheless reported to be receiving aid. Of the 22 States making no provision for mothers who are divorced, 12 reported aid given by some counties to divorced mothers. It is possible that in some of these States mothers who had been deserted before applying for a divorce were considered eligible on the ground of desertion. No provision is made in 8 States for families in which the father has been imprisoned; in 3 of these, however, aid was being granted to a few families of prisoners. With the exception of Connecticut and Utah, which provide for widows only, the needs of families in which the father is permanently disabled physically or mentally have been recognized in all States; in some of these, however, provision for the family is made only under particular conditions or for special handicaps. Michigan, Nebraska, and Tennessee have made specific provision in their statutes for granting aid to unmarried mothers, and 31 of the 55 unmarried mothers reported to have been granted aid were from these States. Although mothers' aid has not been extended to the children of the unemployed by statute in any State (except in New Hampshire as an emergency measure), in the reports received it was definitely stated in a few cases that the reason for the grant was that the father was unemployed. This is another illustration of the occasional inclusion of families receiving general relief in those reported as receiving mothers' aid.

In 23 States and in the District of Columbia a total of 1,012 persons other than the mothers were caring for dependent children and receiving mothers' aid for their support. Nearly two thirds (646) of these family groups were reported by New York State, which makes legal provision for aid to such groups. Thirteen States that had made no provision in the statutes for aid to such families reported scattering numbers under care.

Even when the statutory provision is liberal,

it is the willingness of the community or its administrative agency to provide, through mothers' aid, for families with different types of problems that influences the number of such families aided. The cases reported by administrative agencies in 17 States and the District of Columbia having liberal laws showed that in many localities widows constitute a large majority of the mothers aided. In these States the percentage of the families in which the father was dead varied from 54 in Washington to 93 in New Hampshire. Much difference is found in the willingness of agencies in different States to provide for families in which the father has deserted or has been divorced. In 5 States (Colorado, Florida, Kansas, Nebraska, and Washington) from 21 to 35 per cent of the families assisted had needed aid because of desertion or divorce, whereas in 5 other States (Missouri, Nevada, New Hampshire, North Carolina, and Rhode Island) less than 10 per cent of the families aided presented these domestic difficulties. In States having legal provisions allowing aid to deserted but not divorced mothers the number of deserted families receiving aid varied from 2 per cent of the families in New York to 13 per cent of the families in Wyoming. The percentage of mothers aided who were deserted by the fathers seems little affected by the specific provisions (which are found in 10 States) as to the length of time the father must have been away from the family before aid is granted.

The proportion of families aided in which the father was unable to support his family by reason of his imprisonment or physical or mental disability was usually small, but in 6 States (Arkansas, Massachusetts, Michigan, Minnesota, Missouri, and North Carolina) and the District of Columbia, from 15 to 22 per cent of the families belonged in these groups. In North Carolina the State appropriation has been divided so that a special fund has been made available for assistance to prisoners' families. Proportionately the State fund for prisoners' families was much more liberal than the State grant for other mothers' aid cases, which

probably accounts for the large percentage of prisoners' families reported for this State. The laws of Utah and Connecticut make no provision for grants to families in which the father is mentally or physically disabled. In addition, Idaho, Oklahoma, Pennsylvania, and Texas make no provision for families in which the father is physically handicapped, and provide for mental cases only when the father is under care in an institution. Iowa restricts its assistance to families in which the mentally or physically disabled father is in a State institution. New York and Michigan provide for families in which the father is receiving hospital care and for those in which a tuberculous father under adequate medical care remains in the home. In the other States any family in which the father is disabled may receive aid, especially if he is receiving hospital care. Analysis of the reports received showed that 1,076 or almost half of the 2,325 fathers who were physically incapacitated, but only 53 of the 1,984 who were mentally incapacitated, were living in the home.

RACE OF MOTHERS

Information as to the race of the mothers aided was obtained from all reporting agencies in 18 States and the District of Columbia, but from only a part of those in 20 States. No information on race of mother was available for 6 States. Of the total number of families (46,597), 96 per cent were white, 3 per cent were Negro, and 1 per cent belonged to other races. About half of the Negro families aided were reported by counties in Ohio and Pennsylvania.

Comparison of the percentage of Negro families in the total population of the counties reporting race, with the percentage of the families aided that were Negro, shows that provision for Negro families was limited in a number of States. The disproportion between probable need and provision is even greater when the lower income level of Negro families is taken into consideration.

.   .   .   .   .   .

During the year ended June 30, 1931, $33,-885,487.36 was expended for grants to mothers in the 44 States and the District of Columbia reporting to the Children's Bureau. This amount is an understatement of what was actually spent in grants in aid, as complete figures were not available for California and New Jersey, and no information was received from a few localities known to be granting aid.

During the year covered by the survey the increasing need for assistance to families because of the depression was bringing a large number of applicants for mothers' aid in some localities. At the same time appropriations were being curtailed or entirely withdrawn because of greatly reduced public revenues. Twenty-one of the 101 counties in four States — Arkansas, Oklahoma, Texas, and West Virginia — reporting on mothers' aid stated that aid had been discontinued during the year, or that the number of families had been reduced because of lack of public funds. Inability to collect taxes was given as the cause of such decrease in some of the counties. In one of these States only 13 of the 75 counties in the State had been giving aid, and 4 of these counties discontinued such grants before June 1931 because their funds had been exhausted. Instances of similar limitations in funds were reported from other States. The reports of most localities showed, however, that increasing need had been met by larger appropriations from local and State funds. Comparison of expenditures for mothers' aid for the year ended June 30, 1931, with those for the year ended on the same date in 1930 shows that in 23 of the 30 States for which information was available, expenditures had increased.

.   .   .   .   .   .

The amounts provided from tax sources for the care of dependent children in their own homes in different parts of the country varied widely. Average annual expenditures in the different States for all administrative areas granting mothers' aid ranged from 3 cents to 82 cents per capita. In individual counties or cities annual expenditures ranged from less than one half cent to as much as $2.61 per capita.

In a large proportion of the administrative units that reported figures, funds were too limited to provide adequately for all the families made eligible for assistance by the statutes. In localities in which standards of administration were high and in which other agencies were available to care for dependent families, there was a definite tendency, under these circumstances, to limit the number of families accepted for care, in order that allowances for families should not fall below an amount necessary to assure normal and satisfactory development for the children for whom the public had accepted responsibility. Average monthly grants for all administrative areas in the different States varied from $4.33 to $69.31. With average monthly grants in 21 States falling below the median grant of $21.78 per family, it is evident that allowances in many localities had been affected by the attempt to divide limited funds among many families. Such allowances bear no relation to the actual needs of the families. Mothers' aid is not an emergency measure. It is a long-time program to prevent the breaking up of families and to assure care for dependent children in their own homes, often during the most formative years of their lives. Every effort should be made to provide allowances that will maintain a satisfactory standard of living in these families.

III Issues in Child Care

A. SUBSIDIES AND SUPERVISION

Despite the growth of mother's aid, the United States continued to rely on institutions and foster homes for the care of most of its dependent children. Dependency statistics for this period suggest rather than define the actual situation. Especially in the earlier years, accurate records were a rarity. Confusion of terms, not only among child-caring organizations, but also from one census to the next, further invalidates the findings. The figures for 1930, obtained from those state

Per cent of dependent children receiving specified types of care away from own homes[a]

	Dec. 31, 1910	Feb. 1, 1923	July 1, 1930
In institutions	77	66	58
In foster homes	15	30	39
Awaiting placement in receiving or boarding homes	2	3	—
Elsewhere	6	1	3

[a] Compiled from U.S. Bureau of the Census, *Benevolent Institutions, 1910* (Washington, D.C., 1913), pp. 28, 37; U.S. Bureau of the Census, *Children Under Institutional Care, 1923* (Washington, D.C., 1927), pp. 32, 38; and Emma O. Lundberg, *Child Dependency in the United States* (New York, 1933), p. 118. In *Children Under Institutional Care, 1923*, p. 30, the Bureau of the Census estimated that on a given day in 1923, 121,000 children were receiving care in their own homes under mothers' aid programs, a figure approaching the 138,760 in institutions.

welfare boards which required reports from all institutions and agencies, reflect a greater degree of precision than the census figures for 1910 and 1923. Yet, at best, a comparison can do no more than hint at general trends.

The New York charities controversy, 1914–1917

During the administration of John Purroy Mitchel, mayor of New York City from 1914 to 1918, a heated controversy arose regarding supervision of private child-caring institutions which received subsidies from city funds. Mitchel's commissioner of public charities, John A. Kingsbury, opened the debate by attacking scandalous conditions in the institutions and by charging the State Board of Charities with failure to enforce rules and laxity in issuing certificates of compliance to institutions. The dispute was a factor in the defeat of the Mitchel administration in the election of 1917. A general account of the controversy may be found in David M. Schneider and Albert Deutsch, *The History of Public Welfare in New York State, 1867–1940* (Chicago, 1941), pp. 142–155. For a more detailed analysis see Arnold S. Rosenberg, Social work and Politics: John Adams Kingsbury and the Struggle for Social Justice in New York City, 1914–1918, unpublished Ph.D. thesis, New York University, 1968.

398

1. Municipal inspection and supervision of private institutions, 1914

"Report of the Commissioner [John A. Kingsbury]," in New York City, Department of Public Charities, *Annual Report for 1914* (New York, 1914), pp. 14–15.

Before becoming commissioner of public charities in 1914 Kingsbury had been field agent of the National Association for the Study and Prevention of Tuberculosis and secretary of the New York Association for Improving the Condition of the Poor.

Conspicuous among the result of the year's work has been setting up of definite standards and ideals to be obtained by the various private institutions which care for charges of the City. To these institutions the City is now appropriating annually a sum exceeding $5,000,000 which is paid on a per capita basis when cases have been accepted as proper public charges by the Department of Public Charities. The magnitude of this appropriation and the quality and amount of the work performed by these institutions constitutes, therefore, one of the largest problems of the Department.

In dealing with these private institutions we realize fully that we are facing a condition and not a theory. Whatever may be our personal views with regard to the principle of disbursing public moneys through private corporations, we are appreciative of the fact that existing conditions make such a system for the time being inevitable. It is our purpose, therefore, to make the best of conditions as we find them and to secure the maximum results from the system as it exists. It is our aim to strengthen those institutions which are striving to improve their work and at the same time to deal vigorously with those institutions which in the presence of undesirable conditions are making no effort to remedy them.

There have been institutions which have sought earnestly to assist us in establishing and maintaining a high standard for the care of dependent children. These institutions we have aimed to encourage and support in their work, at the same time refusing to commit the City's wards to the custody of the most undeserving institutions. This is the first time in the history of the City, so far as I am aware, that the Department itself has attempted to exercise definite supervision over these private institutions under private management, which receive public funds.

It has been the custom in the past for the Department to receive and accept the reports of the State Board of Charities on these various institutions, without making any inquiry itself as to the kind of care afforded the children for whose support it is paying. During the year 1914, however, we found that the conditions in some of these institutions bearing the certificate of approval of the State Board of Charities were such as to be little less than a public scandal and disgrace. The agents of the Board, presumably without the full knowledge of all the members of that body, had apparently gone through their inspection of these institutions with both eyes closed or with one auspicious and one drooping eye. Naturally when we found on the certified lists of the State Board, institutions in which the beds were alive with vermin, in which the heads of boys and girls were itching with uncleanliness, in which antiquated methods of punishment prevailed, and in which the children were disgracefully overworked and underfed, we found it necessary to decline to commit children to those institutions, and to decline to accept as reliable the official reports of the State Board of Charities. It is obvious that it should not be necessary for the City to duplicate in expense and effort the work intended to be performed by an already existing public agency. The conditions which make necessary this wasteful duplication of effort, it seems to us, would warrant a special inquiry into the methods of this branch of the State government by the Governor or by the State Legislature.[1]

1. Mayor Mitchel forwarded Kingsbury's report to Governor Charles S. Whitman, who appointed Charles H. Strong to investigate. For Strong's report see doc. 4 below.

We have, during the past year, instituted and put into effective operation a plan for the rigid inspection and supervision by experts of national reputation of every home or asylum which houses a dependent person who is a City charge. It seemed to us that in sending large numbers of persons, especially children who would remain in orphan asylums for a long period of years, to these private institutions, we were exercising an extremely serious responsibility and ought to exercise it with the fullest knowledge of all that it involved.

It was for this reason that we determined to try an experiment, which we believe is somewhat unique in this country, of employing a small committee composed of men actively engaged in the conduct of children's institutions and recognized as experts in child-caring work to systematically inspect and supervise the work of the private institutions receiving public charges. I chose for this important task Dr. Ludwig B. Bernstein, Superintendent of the Hebrew Sheltering Guardian Society; Dr. R. R. Reeder, Superintendent of the New York Orphan Asylum, and Rev. Brother Barnabas, who is the head of the country branch of the Catholic Protectory located at Lincolndale, New York. The Department deeply regretted that Brother Barnabas found it impossible to serve for more than a brief period on this committee. These three men represent successful institutions of the leading religious denominations. It was arranged that they, together with Deputy Commissioner William J. Doherty, for many years the executive of the Catholic Home Bureau for Dependent Children, should in person, accompanied by their staff of nurses and doctors, visit the private child-caring institutions one by one, going over them carefully, and in a perfectly friendly spirit ascertain under what conditions the City's dependent children were being brought up. As a result of these visits and inquiries I am glad to report that a number of the institutions which house the City's wards, some by coercion but most of them voluntarily, have elevated their standards and ideals to the

positions which we demand they must maintain so long as they continue to receive City funds. Many of them have improved their dietaries, developed their educational work, and established cleanliness and order.

2. Conditions reported by inspectors, 1914

"Report of the Second Deputy Commissioner [William J. Doherty]," in New York City, Department of Public Charities, *Annual Report for 1914,* pp. 49–55.

MEDICAL SERVICE

The amount and character of the medical service rendered children varies greatly. In some institutions the attending physician makes a daily visit, in others, the physician calls but once a month, while, in one institution, caring for more than three hundred children, the attending physician makes a professional visit only when summoned. Among the institutions visited only once a month by the attending physician, one has a census of four hundred children and another a population of more than five hundred. On no institutional staff, thus far visited, is an orthopedic surgeon listed though the necessity was quite apparent in some institutions. In one institution the Board of Health physicians reported that 64 of the 200 children under care were in need of tonsil operation, yet no record could be found tending to show that any effort had been made by the institutional authorities to remedy this serious condition. Perhaps the explanation will be apparent, when it is stated that this institution, thus far, has not perceived the necessity of employing a nose and throat specialist.

.   .   .   .   .

BATHING

Some institutions have yet failed to grasp the idea that proper and frequent bathing of children is one means of helping to ward off disease. The bathing facilities in some of the institutions are extremely crude and antiquated. In one institution, some thirty or more boys are compelled to bathe at one time in a tank three feet deep. On entering the water, each child is supplied with a nail brush and a piece of soap which he hands over to his neighbor when leaving the tank, and so the exchange goes merrily on until the last child is bathed. In another institution, it is the custom to bathe the nursery children two at a time in a tub. In a number of institutions, children are required to wash their hands but once each day . . . In some places a common wash cloth was used by a number of children. While individual towels are quite generally supplied in all institutions, the evidences in some cases indicated promiscuous use.

SUPPLY OF TOILET ARTICLES

Individual combs and brushes were found provided in but few of the institutions visited. For the use of one hundred children in a certain institution visited, only four combs and brushes were supplied. In one institution, in which combs and brushes were viewed as useless impedimenta because the hair of the children was usually clipped, four fine combs constituted the sole supply, for nearly three hundred children. When the inspector reported that the heads of the greater number of these poor children were in a frightfully filthy condition, the cause was not difficult to ascertain. No tooth brushes were supplied for two hundred children in one institution. The person in charge explained their absence by stating that they had been discarded because the children could not be taught to use them. The racks in the bath room of one institution contained an extra supply of tooth brushes. When the inspector, a trifle surprised, made inquiry concerning the over-supply, she was informed that the tooth brushes of children discharged were disinfected and placed in the racks ready for the use of newcomers.

FOOD

An analysis of the dietaries furnished in a number of the institutions showed that, in many instances, the food served was not at all adapted to the needs of growing children and not calculated to develop muscle and bone. Tea and coffee, generally admitted to be most harmful to the nervous system undergoing development, were served in a number of institutions, sometimes as frequently as twice a day. Milk seldom is given to children in certain institutions. In one institution milk is such a scarce article, that it is served only to sick children.

In one institution visited, the dinner served to little children consisted of frankfurters, cabbage and watermelon. In many of the institutions the supper served children usually consists of bread and molasses, or bread and jelly. Cocoa, made with water, is the usual beverage served.

An examination of copies of the menus furnished by certain institutions showed the same combination of food served at meals recurring over and over again. There is little variety from day to day. In general, fruit is provided only on certain festive occasions.

DINING ROOMS AND SERVICE

Though it had been thought that it was quite generally understood that backless seats and benches were injurious to the spine of the growing child, their use is still maintained in the dining rooms of certain institutions. Bare board tables, likewise, are not uncommon and neither are dishes of agate and tinware. The use of table linen and napkins is religiously tabooed in some of the institutions visited. Dreary silence, during meal time, is compulsory in certain institutions though, in one institution, whispering is permitted.

CLUBS AND ENTERTAINMENTS

While literary, dramatic, debating, athletic and game clubs exist and are encouraged in some institutions, in the majority of the orphanages visited, these opportunities so essential for the happiness of the children, are conspicuous for their absence. No provision is made to permit the children to exercise initiative in their own affairs, team work is discouraged and no means employed to develop leadership among the boys and girls.

In most instances, meagre provision is made for the entertainment of the children. While certain institutions are notable exceptions to this rule, the majority do not think it should form any part of their curriculum. In one institution visited, the authorities spoke of having provided two or three lectures for the children last year.

The playrooms, too frequently, were found painfully clean and practically barren save for the presence of a number of backless benches. Dolls and toys usually are brought out upon the scene around Christmas time and sometimes during vacation. In some institutions, while games and toys were said to be supplied the children, they were found new and fresh, securely locked away in closets. In one institution, where no games could be discovered, the attendant stated that there was a big supply kept in the closet. Of course, the closet was locked but when the inspector insisted upon having it opened, the only games found included a brand new set of the Encyclopedia Britannica, some reports of conferences of charities, some sheets of music and old copies of the Saturday Evening Post. The children certainly must have had much enjoyment playing these games.

OUTDOOR PLAYGROUND

An outdoor playground, fenced in like a chicken coop in some places, with scarcely el-

bow room for one-half the children compelled to make use of it, surely is a dreary place in which to spend so many hours. Yet, such obsolete conditions exist in a number of institutions of the present day. The children may feast their eyes upon the green lawns fronting the building but to them is reserved the use of dreary, bleak looking rear playgrounds, devoid, in many instances, of proper play facilities. While, in one instance, a playground director visits the institution to teach the children folk dancing and to help them in their play, in the majority of the institutions visited no one was found whose business it was to direct the play activities of the children.

MILITARY DRILL

In some institutions, great stress is laid upon the importance of military drills. Even were it likely to convince one that it is possible for the children to derive a good deal of fun from these military drills, the frequency of the performance robs it of the charm of novelty. In addition it must be hard on the little fellows of eight and nine to march and manoeuvre with boys of fourteen.

. . . . .

Many of the institution schools, thus far inspected, get nowhere in particular with their pupils. The result of the inspections went far to indicate that most institutions merely provided schooling for their wards. In the majority of the schools examined the fact was painfully apparent that no particular aims, goals or standards were set up and efforts made to attain them. There was an utter absence of inducements to secondary or higher education to arouse the ambition of bright or gifted pupils. Apparently, the limit upward for all pupils is the end of the elementary course. Children of higher educational promise push their heads against this low roof in vain. It was not surprising to find that, as a natural result of such conditions, a very large percentage of retardation existed among institution pupils. In many of the class rooms inspected more than half the pupils were found over age for their grade. While, perhaps, it may be true that many of the pupils, because of poverty, misfortune and adverse family home conditions, already are retarded when they enter the institution, yet, after making all due allowances for these, it has been demonstrated, that there is a great increase in retardation after admission to the institution, and, as has been found, many of the children retarded practically have spent all of their school life in the institution.

Doubtless it will be granted that every institution caring for a hundred or more children, retaining them as wards until from fourteen to sixteen years of age, should have a number of high school pupils. Unfortunately, however, not one institution in ten caring for several hundred wards sends any pupils to the high school. In one institution school, the reason given for not promoting pupils was lack of class room accommodations in the higher grades. These upper grades, therefore, were sitting on the heads of those below, holding them down until older pupils were discharged to make room for their promotion. This form of cruelty is as real as that of stunting the physical growth of the child by underfeeding or limiting his stature by a Procrustean bedstead. It can only result in both individual and social waste. Instead of helping to eliminate it tends, in great measure, to repeat the dreary round of dependency in succeeding generations.

VOCATIONAL TRAINING

With respect to vocational training, the larger number of the institutions inspected showed a lack of proper understanding of the real meaning of the term vocational training. In most instances, the equipment provided is distinctly primitive and the instruction crude and valueless. In but few institutions did there exist any clearly defined policy to outline and govern a systematic and progressive course of instruc-

tion. As a rule, under the guise of vocational training, the work carried on was purely utilitarian in character, lacking even the very elementary essentials of real vocational training. In very few instances was it found that the bulk of the boys and girls over the age of twelve years were receiving the benefits of a well-balanced vocational course. Compared with the total number of children in the care of institutions, the proportion receiving vocational instruction was insignificant. Relatively, a very small number of the girls receive instruction in sewing, millinery, embroidery and domestic science. The number of boys receiving instruction in woodwork is very, very small. In one institution, the teacher in charge of the vocational training, originally was the institution's tailor. Now, he is engaged as instructor in shoemaking and woodwork. In this institution, only five boys receive instruction in woodwork and in the shoeshop, whereas twenty-eight, eighteen of whom are little chaps, ten or eleven years, were found working the tailor shop.

CHILD LABOR

In certain institutions for the care of girls, what was termed vocational training, practically amounted to exploiting and overworking children who had no redress. Try to conceive of a girl being compelled to go to work at a wash tub at five o'clock in the morning there to remain until the dinner bell sounded at noon when respite was had, and have such brutal procedure styled "vocational training." Yet such was actually the condition found existing in one institution, the managers of which roundly scored the inspectors as drastic and over-oppressive because they dared to brand their so-called "home" as worse than a penal institution.

In another institution, the authorities were strongly directed to abolish immediately the deplorable practice of exacting cheap labor from a group of defenceless girls, fourteen years of age and over, who were found rendering from eight to nine hours of hard service, with no compensation whatever. It was pointed out very plainly that, under no circumstances, could the board and lodging received by these girls at the hands of the institutional authorities, be considered a quid pro quo for the labor and service rendered. If the service these girls were compelled to render had in it any real educational value, it would not be so objectionable, but, to keep girls of fourteen years of age busy carrying clothes from the laundry to the linen room, scarcely could be said to constitute a proper preparation for after life.

---

3. Sociology versus religion

Paul L. Blakely, S.J., "Paganizing Charity," in *A Campaign of Calumny; the New York Charities Investigation* (New York, ca. 1915), pp. 64–68.

Although the city investigators condemned fourteen Protestant institutions along with a dozen Catholic ones, and although Mayor Mitchel and Assistant Commissioner Doherty were Roman Catholic, a group of priests felt that the city government and the Strong Commission were seeking to undermine Catholic charities. In a series of pamphlets distributed at neighborhood parishes, the priests attempted to refute charges made against Catholic orphanages, and accused city officials of complicity, unfairness, and perjury. The following article from one of the Catholic pamphlets expresses the fear which motivated the Catholic protest against increased governmental supervision.

To the omnipotent State the philosophy of revolt has extended the right of life and death over the private institution of charity. The cup of cold water may indeed be given, but only after investigation, and only in the name of the State. For modern sociology has arisen to teach that the whole system of charity, individual and collective, founded on the precepts and example of Jesus Christ, and elaborated through the centuries by the Catholic Church, is essentially wrong. And why? The reason is at hand. Every human being is a ward of the State. The physical and mental welfare of the individual is the exclusive concern of the State. Therefore, if in need, he must be succored by the State, nor may any aid be given, without the consent of a strictly-supervising State.

Further, the private charity, especially as fostered and governed by the Catholic Church, is anti-social, since it will not recognize the complete supremacy of the State. It resolutely opposes race-suicide, divorce, lawless marriages, sterilization, and such-like evils, suggested by modern sociology to the consideration of man's supreme guardian, the State. In other words, the Catholic Church insists on the inclusion of God and His law in the consideration of every phase of life. Modern sociology regards this insistence as a relic of superstition, akin to the tabu of Tahiti.

It is true that certain private charities may, in the opinion of modern sociologists, be permitted a temporary existence, provided that they engage in work which, for the present, the State cannot conveniently assume, and provided further, that they act purely as agents of the State. This however, argues no right of existence for the private institution, but merely the toleration of the civil authority . . . Modern sociology proposes to suppress legitimate individuality, by merging, as far as human nature will allow, all activities in the State . . . We Catholics must arouse ourselves to the importance of employing every legitimate means to overthrow this return of paganism, if we wish to remain secure in the exercise of our right to conduct institutions of education, charity, and reform . . .

Our enemies are many; their methods, as recent events in New York have proved, are dark, devious and unscrupulous. Possibly the following suggestions may pave the way for a more effective program of "preparedness":

(1) Let no calumny against our Catholic institutions remain unanswered. Unless dealt

with summarily, the modern sociologist will set no bounds to his policy of lying. (2) Every legitimate means must be used to prevent the appointment or election of pagan sociologists to public offices exercising supervision over institutions of charity and reform. This is no question of petty politics. It is a question of whether paganism which regards man as a ward of the Caesarized State, or Christianity which holds that he is made to God's image, shall prevail in this country. (3) Catholics must show a deeper practical interest in the local institutions, by visiting them and learning of their splendid work. The religious men and women who conduct these homes of mercy have given up all to follow Christ, but they are still human. Intelligent interest on the part of Catholics will stimulate them to even greater efforts. (4) Few if any Catholic institutions are endowed . . . The Catholic flock is not wise in the wisdom of this world, but it has a heart for giving, when its attention is properly directed. Are you going to do your share, contributing in full measure . . . to the poor and afflicted who represent Jesus Christ Himself . . . as did your forefathers in the country? "Suffer the little children to come unto me and forbid them not; for such is the kingdom of God." This is the issue at stake.

There can be no doubt as to the answer. We have our traitors and our weak-kneed brethren, who with a penny's worth of help or none at all, contribute volumes of criticism. Happily, these are few, and some of them are now known. But measured in legal tender, how much is your undoubted sympathy for the calumniated Catholic institutions worth? The destiny of immortal souls, for whom Christ died, may hang on your answer.

---

4. The Strong Report, 1916

Charles H. Strong, "Report of Commissioner to Examine into the Management and Affairs of the State Board of Charities . . . to Governor Whitiman" (1916), in Abbott, *The Child and the State,* II, 116–122.

Strong was a prominent attorney long active in municipal reform movements in New York City.

The question remaining for consideration is, how has the State Board of Charities discharged its duty under the Constitution and the laws toward the private child-caring institutions in New York City . . .

First, as to the rules. It is suggestive of the general attitude of the State Board that its rules were adopted after conferences with the representatives of the institutions which were to be subjected to them and with their approval and consent . . .

Oddly, the State Charities Law since 1895 has required industrial training in the institutions, but there was no mention of it in the rules until 1910.

The President said he thought the board had once adopted a rule against corporal punishment. It met with a storm of disapproval. It was repealed. The rules now call for a record of punishment authorized, but are silent as to punishment actually employed . . .

Secondly, as to visitation, inspection and enforcement. The State Board's staff of paid inspectors grew from 3 in 1896 to 21 in 1915, falling to 19 in 1916; but of these only 8 inspect private institutions, and of these 8, only 3 or 4 are available regularly for children's institutions in New York City. Eight inspectors are relied upon to inspect 640 institutions once a year, 364 of which, including dispensaries, are in or near New York City . . .

.　　.　　.　　.　　.

I find that the State Board of Charities was censurable for failure to issue certificates of non-compliance with its rules, or for failure to withhold certificates of compliance therewith, when and as often as they should have been issued or withheld, as to every one of the twenty-four institutions on the City's controverted list . . .

I find it is beyond question that such vigorous, yet reasonable and just, action as the State Board might have taken from time to time prior to 1914 relative to these institutions, would have resulted in such improved conditions as would have made unnecessary or futile the City's investigation in 1914 and 1915 . . .

The City has proved its case against the State Board out of the pages of the State Board's own inspection reports . . .

From 1895 to date, the board has once, and only once, issued a certificate of non-compliance with its rules, and this was in July, 1910, one day after the date of a report of inspectors of the Department of Finance in New York City reflecting most seriously upon an institution in Brooklyn. This institution is not one of those upon which the City's investigators reported adversely in 1914 or 1915. The record does not show what reason was given by the State Board for issuing this certificate of non-compliance . . .

When the City's investigating activities became fully apparent in 1915, 50 certificates on 37 institutions were withheld by the State Board. The Board had withheld the certificate as to only 8 out of the 24 institutions on the controverted list prior to the city's investigation . . .

The board has never once resorted to its power under the State Charities Law to issue an order upon court approval directed to an institution when, upon an investigation of an institution, it appears that "inadequate provision" is made for "a condition necessary to their wellbeing" (which would seem to cover industrial and educational training as required by law). The State Board is empowered to issue this order on approval of the Supreme Court, after notice to the institution to apply such remedy as the board shall specify in the order. Disobedience of such order is a misdemeanor . . .

Even in a case where cruel and inhuman punishment in the form of shackles and chains was discovered by the State Board in an investigation of a private institution in Westchester County in 1895, the order was not issued and not even was the certificate withheld, as far as the record shows . . .

The question naturally arises, what did the State Board do to enforce compliance? . . .

It sent its reports of inspection to the boards of managers . . . There was a table of "Needs and Defects" in each report. But important criticisms continued in the body of the report were often not included in the list of "Needs and Defects." This in and of itself was not calculated to impress the managers. A number of "Needs and Defects" were carried in the reports from year to year in precisely the same language. This also was not a particularly incisive method of getting the managers to take notice. It wrote letters. It has several forms, printed or partly printed, to fit various sets of circumstances . . . The President and Secretary in numberless instances followed this up by more letters in cases where institutions did not respond satisfactorily. Sometimes improvements were secured; sometimes, as I have said, the same list of "Needs and Defects" persisted in the reports year after year . . .

Patient persuasion is the avowed policy of the State Board. Never go to court; only once in 21 years directly interfere with commitments; rarely delay the institution in getting its money from the City; never make public any criticism of any abuse . . .

We have seen what are the methods of the State Board in enforcing its recommendations. They may be contrasted with those of the [City] Department of Public Charities.

1. The Department sent the reports of the advisory committee to superintendents as well as to the managers of each of the affected institutions (the State Board sends only to the mnaagers) . . .

2. It sent the reports to the State Board . . .

3. It ceased commitments to 15 of the 24 institutions, and at the close of the hearings it had not resumed in 8 cases. Ceasing to commit was a spur to institution improvements because

the per capita cost of maintenance goes up as the number of inmates goes down.

4. It refused in some cases to certify the monthly bills of the institution against the City. This served the same purposes.

5. It resorted to publicity in the newspapers. In Mr. Doherty's address before the Baltimore Conference in May, 1915, some of the reports containing serious criticisms of institutions were made public. In that address, Mr. Doherty apportioned the blame for conditions among the boards of managers, the [New York City] Department of Public Charities and the State Board of Charities.

6. It issued a document consisting of standards for inspectors, called "The Questionnaire" . . .

It is my view that, in the last analysis, the City's investigation of 1914 and 1915, over and above all the resentments that have been aroused, has been of incalculable value to the children in the institutions. Evidences of this multiply . . . The [New York City] Department of Public Charities has organized its first Bureau for Child Placing. The Association of Catholic Charities has announced that it would "appoint an auxiliary to follow the inspections of the authorities in the attacked institutions . . ."

But it is also my view . . . that under the constitution and the laws, we . . . must continue to look, to the State Board of Charities, with its rule-making power, to establish and enforce reasonable and enlightened standards for the private institutions. Its duty of inspection and supervision is primary, is superior. It *must* inspect. The City *may*. If institutions with their self-perpetuating boards of managers are left without a spur, it is not surprising that they follow the easy path, that they are content with the old methods, content to furnish perhaps the best of bodily care and fail to grapple with the more difficult questions of education and training . . .

The persistent explanation or excuse of the State Board throughout the inquiry for failure to enforce upon the institutions full and reasonably prompt observation of its own rules . . . was that the institutions had not the money, that the City will not give it, and that to close the institutions would leave the City in a quandary . . . The State of New York has deliberately thrown the care of dependent children upon the cities. If the City chooses to aid private institutions . . . then the State Board must fix the standards and the City and the institutions must pay the price . . .

I do not share the aversion with which the State Board shrinks from publicity as a method of enforcement of its recommendations to end abuses. I cannot comprehend it. Publicity, in the relation between a state department and a private institution holding any religious faith is essential. This is one of the few instances where church and state come into contact. In this country, there may not be permitted to grow up any subservience of the state to the church. I concur in the view that the state must always dominate the partnership between it and the private institutions . . .

---

5. State Board defends its records and policies, 1916

New York State. State Board of Charities, *Fiftieth Annual Report, 1916,* I (Albany, 1917), 42–49, 89–100.

Attention has been called by Commissioner Strong, in his report, to the meaning of the constitutional terms, "Visitation and Inspection," and he reads into them a large measure of actual control . . .

The State Board of Charities can counsel, guide and assist in the development of institutional activities, but neither the Constitution nor statutes intimate that it was organized to discharge the duty of management, and the weakness of any argument which contends that supervision implies control is shown by the fact that boards, commissions, or other administrators cannot make dispassionate and judicial criticisms of their own work. This applies to the State institutions where the statutes place the responsibility of administration upon boards of managers, leaving supervision to the State Board, and in this way providing for oversight which should prevent abuses, and promote efficiency.

.   .   .   .   .

It is unfortunate that the Commissioner did not fully acquaint himself with all the facts in this case before taking this position. We agree that it is not necessary to provide by fines and other punishments for the coercion of members of Boards of Managers . . . Compliance with recommendations made by the State Board of Charities must be obtained otherwise. In the opinion of the Board, its recommendations must commend themselves to the mature judgment of the managers, which is based upon experience and careful study of conditions, and in the last analysis this is invariably found to be the result.

—————   .   .   .   .   .

Through all these years the State Board of Charities was building up these institutions by the process of demanding and obtaining from them every improvement in their management that was permitted by their means. It early adopted a system of classification as to the private institutions under its supervision. No. 1 indicated the highest condition, No. 2 a condition that would be deemed satisfactory under the laws of the State, and No. 3, a condition which required improvement.

From the outset all the institutions were desirous of complying with the recommendations of the Board, but many of them were absolutely unable to do so, owing to their financial conditions, and some of the recommendations made by the Board to particular institutions were in many instances not complied with for a considerable period, and in some cases even for a long time, by reason of their financial condition,

but by degrees substantial improvement was obtained in all the institutions.

From time to time the rules of the Board were amended or altered to suit conditions as they were found to exist in the gradual development of the work of the institutions. More was required of the institutions and very much more was recommended by the Board, but had it at the outset expressly required the manual and industrial training and recreation facilities later largely required and given, it would have met with failure.

In 1899 a large majority of the child-care institutions were without provisions for industrial training except so far as necessary for the maintenance of the institutions. The children were usually considered reasonably well trained if given an opportunity to do the various household tasks, and boys given special training in gardening or farming were deemed fortunate.

The standards of child training in public schools and institutions generally have made a marked advancement during the past twenty years, and particularly during the past decade. Of this the Board has taken cognizance, and its reports to the Legislature have from time to time recommended higher standards for the institutions of the State. The Board called into conference with it the representatives from the institutions to be affected by its rules, and at all times sought the cooperation of the institutions, and regrets that the Commissioner does not approve such action.

.   .   .   .   .

The effect of the supervision by the State Board of Charities of private institutions of all classes has been to improve methods and conditions with the result that whereas the large majority of them in 1906 were poor, judged by present standards, this is now true of only a small number. The modification of the Board's rules which became effective January 1, 1911, was only an added step in the plans of the Board for a higher standard of care and training of children in institutions and for the improvement of the general administration.

The Board found that its classifications of the institutions contributed to the improvement of their management. Those rated two or three were anxious to get a higher rating, and those holding the highest rating were anxious to maintain it. It is also the fact that when institutions neglected to comply with the requirements of the Board that were by it deemed of serious moment, the Board declined to accept the statement of the officials of the institutions that its rules had been complied with and certificates were withheld until conditions were improved, if deemed immediately necessary, or were in progress.

The withholding of such certificates always resulted in correspondence and conferences with the institutions and further inspections to note corrections claimed to have been made, and ultimately in almost all cases the issuance of the certificates followed . . .

The Commissioner, in criticising the Board for not withholding certificates when reasonable efforts were being made by the institutions to comply with its requirements, forgot that discretion must be exercised by the supervising power in this matter, especially when there is every reason to believe that the desired improvements are in progress; withholding the moneys due might make it impossible for the institution to pay its bills to the merchants from whom it purchased supplies and the employees whose services it had received, and also prevent the making of desired improvements and thus embarrass many innocent persons. It would hinder compliance with the requirements and suggestions of the Board, and therefore withholding of certificates has occurred only when all other means have been exhausted.

. . . . .

Concerning the criticism that the Board should have compelled the closing of some or all of the institutions attacked by the city we submit to your Excellency that it would have found great difficulty in doing so. If the Board had attempted to avail of the provisions of section 14 of the State Charities Law the Board must have satisfied a justice of the Supreme Court that the inmates of the institution were cruelly, negligently or improperly treated, or that inadequate provision was made for their sustenance, clothing and care, or for other conditions necessary to their comfort and well-being. This no judge would have found, and moreover while the conditions in some of the institutions were unsatisfactory, they were being corrected at the time the city commenced its inspections.

. . . . .

The high standards of modern child-care institutions which are desirable were repeatedly recommended in the reports of this Board, but could not form the basis of any procedure against any institution. That procedure must be based upon the requirements of the State as to education, food and clothing, or a finding that inmates are cruelly, negligently and improperly treated, or that inadequate provision is made for their sustenance, clothing and care, or that other conditions necessary to their comfort and well-being are not maintained.

It is doubtless true that housekeeping conditions in any institution in the State can at times be criticized. In an institution with many children of immature years as inmates, some of whom may be feeble-minded, and others delinquent, housekeeping conditions will frequently be found which can be described in decidedly unpleasant language. More particularly was it so in the case where evidence was tendered, in the hearing before Commissioner Strong, that such conditions existed in parts of the building closed from use, or which were being repaired; or, where a catch-basin in a room containing 78 overhead showers is described as a "bathing plunge." Such evidence presented concerning conditions in seven of the twenty-four institutions in question may have made them appear to the Commissioner as just a little less than "public scandal and disgrace," and yet they may have been based upon housekeeping conditions which could be remedied, even though they may have appeared to the

Commissioner to justify the language ascribed. They might not have so appeared if the City of New York had been contesting an application by the State Board of Charities for an order closing the institutions.

.   .   .   .   .

In justice to the inspectors of the State Board of Charities, it should be said that they have performed their duties in a thoroughly satisfactory manner in the numerous child-care institutions under the supervision of the State Board of Charities. The inspectors of this Board are men and women of high character, good judgment, wide experience and in nearly every instance of broad education, many being college graduates and experienced teachers, which enables them to understand the grave problems presented by the dependent wards of the State. They have never been charged with lack of courage in the performance of duty, nor has it heretofore been alleged that they were not alert in its performance. Not one of them is a "time-server," nor can they be influenced to make reports which do not state the truth. It is but simple justice to these faithful agents of the State, whose duty is so important, that the State Board of Charities should resent any imputation upon their integrity, ability or efficiency, which the "closed," "auspicious" and "drooping eye" implies.

Raising the standards of child welfare

In the two decades following the organization of the Children's Bureau, the drive to safeguard dependent children through increased state regulation continued. State boards of charities received increasing responsibilities, and in some instances, began to share the work of coordination and supervision with county child welfare boards.[1] The federal Children's Bureau conducted studies of the administration of child care programs in various states, offering constructive suggestions for improvement. The second and third White House Conferences formulated and publicized standards by which states could measure their progress. By 1930 the problem was no longer, as in 1909, whether there should be state supervisory boards, but whether those boards would be adequately financed and professionally staffed. As the standards of institutions and placing-out societies improved, social workers began to focus on the prevention as well as the alleviation of dependency. Despite these advances, weaknesses in the states' programs presented serious difficulties when the Depression diminished financial resources and accelerated the incidence of dependency.

---

1. White House Conference sets minimum standards, 1919

United States Children's Bureau, *Standards of Child Welfare: A Report of the Children's Bureau Conference, 1919,* Pub. No. 60 (Washington, D.C., 1919), pp. 440–442.

For the work of the Second White House Conference, see also below, Part Six, Chap. I, sec. B.

MINIMUM STANDARDS FOR THE PROTECTION OF CHILDREN IN NEED OF SPECIAL CARE

1. General statement

Every child should have normal home life, an opportunity for education, recreation, vo-

1. See below, Part Six, Chap. II.

cational preparation for life, and for moral and spiritual development in harmony with American ideals and the educational and spiritual agencies by which these rights of the child are normally safeguarded. The Conference recognizes the fundamental rôle of home, religion, and education in the development of childhood.

Aside from the general fundamental duty of the State toward children in normal social conditions, ultimate responsibility for children who, on account of improper home conditions, physical handicap, or delinquency, are in need of special care devolves upon the State. Particular legislation is required for children in need of such care, the aim of which should be the nearest approach to normal development. Laws enacted by the several States for these purposes should be coordinated as far as practicable in view of conditions in the several States, and in line with national ideals.

2. Home care

The aim of all provision for children in need of special care necessitating removals from their own homes, should be to secure for each child home life as nearly normal as possible, to safeguard his health, and provide opportunities for education, recreation, vocational preparation, and moral and spiritual development. To a much larger degree than at present, family homes may be used to advantage in the care of special classes of children.

3. Adequate income

Home life, which is, in the words of the Conclusions of the White House Conference, "the highest and finest product of civilization," cannot be provided except upon the basis of an adequate income for each family, and hence private and governmental agencies charged with the responsibility for the welfare of children in need of special care should be urged to supplement the resources of the family wherever the income is insufficient, in such measure that the family budget conforms to the average standard of the community.

4. Incorporation, licensing, and supervision

A State board of charities, or a similar supervisory body, should be held responsible for the regular inspection and licensing of every institution, agency, or association, public or private, incorporated or otherwise, that receives or cares for children who suffer from physical handicaps, or who are delinquent, dependent, or without suitable parental care.

This supervision should be conceived and exercised in harmony with democratic ideals which invite and encourage the service of efficient, altruistic forces of society in the common welfare. The incorporation of such institutions, agencies, and associations should be required, and should be subject to the approval of the State board of charities or similar body.

5. Removal of children from their homes

Unless unusual conditions exist, the child's welfare is best promoted by keeping him in his own home. No child should be removed from his home unless it is impossible so to reconstruct family conditions or build and supplement family resources as to make the home safe for the child, or so to supervise the child as to make his continued presence safe for the community.

6. Principles governing child placing

This Conference reaffirms in all essentials the resolutions of the White House Conference of 1909 on the Care of Dependent Children. We believe they have been guides for communities and States that have sought to reshape their plans for children in need of special care. We commend them for consideration to all communities whose standards do not as yet conform to them, so that such standards may be translated into practice in the various States.

Before a child is placed in other than a temporary foster home adequate consideration should be given to his health, mentality, character, and family history and circumstances. Remediable physical defects should be corrected.

Complete records of every child under care are necessary to a proper understanding of the child's heredity, development, and progress while under the care of the agency.

Careful and wise investigation of foster homes is prerequisite to the placing of children. Adequate standards should be required of the foster families as to character, intelligence, experience, training, ability, income, and environment.

A complete record should be kept of each foster home, giving the information on which approval was based. The records should also show the agency's contacts with the family from time to time for the purpose of indicating the care it gave to the child entrusted to it. In this way special abilities in the families will be developed and conserved for children.

Supervision of children placed in foster homes should include adequate visits by properly qualified and well-trained visitors and constant watchfulness over the child's health, education, and moral and spiritual development. Supervision of children in boarding homes should also involve the careful training of the foster parents in their task. Supervision is not a substitute for the responsibilities which properly rest with the foster family.

---

2. Subsidies and supervision in 1929

C. C. Carstens, "Dependent and Neglected Children," *Social Work Yearbook, 1929* (New York, 1929), pp. 130–131.

At present only three states — Mississippi, Nevada, and Utah — are without supervisory boards or departments of public welfare, although they differ greatly in their functions as they relate to child care . . . Massachusetts has an extensive program of direct child care with very limited powers for the supervision of private agencies and institutions, and New York has a limited program of direct child care with extensive powers for supervision of private agencies and institutions, while Alabama has extensive programs in both fields.

The supervision of private child care agencies, when fully developed, generally includes the approval of petitions for incorporation of institutions or agencies both as to need and adequacy, their annual licensing, and their periodical inspection, including a financial audit unless this has already been made by some competent person or agency. There is a tendency at present to emphasize the importance of control at the time of incorporation and an educational inspection each year, but to lay less stress on licensing when there is periodical inspection.

In the older states especially, private agencies and institutions for the care of children preceded the development of public systems whether by the state, county, or municipal government. When the question of support for these agencies became a pressing one, many asked the public authorities to provide a part of the cost. These institutions or agencies generally have reputable and influential men and women on their boards of managers whose services express devotion if not always special knowledge and skill. The general hesitation of citizens to trust public authorities with social service has led to an extensive development of public support of private agencies or subsidies, the extent of whose use and influence in America has never been completely fathomed. Such subsidies to children's organizations are very numerous. They are of two forms, the payment per capita for services rendered, as in New York and California, and the payment of lump sums to the organizations' budgets, as in Maryland and Pennsylvania. While in the second form of payment the amount is supposed to approximate the cost of service rendered, it is not actually in proportion to the number of children previously aided or to be aided in the current year.

There is available testimony that would seem to show that either form of subsidy is apt to lead to influences being used in the legislature or body appropriating the funds which have no bearing upon the need for the agency or the quality of service rendered by it. It has also been observed in certain instances that subsidies to private children's agencies have led them to be less ready to act as friendly but fearless critics of governmental action where the protection of children is involved, for fear that by voicing frank criticisms appropriations may be endangered.

---

3. "A broad program designed to safeguard children," 1930

White House Conference on Child Health and Protection, *Addresses and Abstracts of Committee Reports* (New York, 1931), pp. 331–336.

On the third White House Conference, see also below, Part Six, Chap. I, sec. B.

CAUSES OF CHILD DEPENDENCY

Among the major causes of child dependency . . . are sickness, mental disturbances, accidents, premature death, irregular employment, unemployment, and insufficient income when employed.

Sickness. An estimate in 1928 of the costs of illness to the people of the United States, including loss of wage during illness (but not including future net earnings lost on account of premature death) gave an average of $31.08 for every person, or $134.88 for each family per annum. This amount would mean, in countless instances, a deficit in what otherwise might be a satifactory family budget for the year.

The social loss is not susceptible of like measurement, but is obviously very serious. The ill mother, whatever her courage and de-

votion, cannot provide for her children all that constant watchfulness and unceasing solicitude which tax to its utmost the resourcefulness of the mother whose health is unimpaired.

Mental Disturbances. Based on the latest data available, there were in hospitals for the insane in the United States, 338,251 persons. Almost all of these were adults. The actual age distribution is not available, but tremendous numbers of them are of the age periods at which the men would normally be supporting families and the women caring for households.

If the mother be sent to a hospital for mental patients, some makeshift must be resorted to. In many cases, the home is broken up temporarily or permanently. If the father is the victim of mental disturbance, the income of the family is abruptly cut off. In many instances the children are sent to the care of others, and long-range planning is impossible. If one could look into the family groups from which this army of more than 300,000 mental patients came, an amazing volume of child dependency and neglect would inevitably be disclosed.

We are just beginning to realize that probably the total volume of responsibility placed upon society by mental disease and defects is about equal to that of all other disease and defects put together, not including those acute situations that lead to institutional care.

Loss through Accidents. The number of persons injured or killed in accidents in this country each year exceeds the total casualties sustained by the American forces during the whole period of the World War. Although the exact number of those injured or killed at work is not known, estimates based on available data place the number at over 2,000,000 each year.

In spite of a declining accident rate in certain industries, there has been in industry as a whole an increase both in the number and severity of accidents, and there has been a tremendous increase in automobile accidents. The present method of dealing with accidents cannot, therefore, be considered satisfactory.

The American accident table shows that for every 100,000 industrial accidents, 762 are fatal, and of those who die, 279 leave 709 dependent children. Consequently, there are over 14,000 children who are orphaned annually by fathers dying from accidents met while engaged in earning a livelihood for their families.

At present, all but four states have some type of workmen's compensation legislation and approximately $150,000,000 is expended annually in awards and medical benefits. However, many thousands of employees are not protected, as these laws do not cover certain occupations. Railway workers engaged in interstate commerce are a notable example. In this occupation there were almost 1,700 deaths from accidents in 1927. Most of the laws exempt agricultural, domestic, and casual employment; twelve states exclude non-hazardous employments; and twenty-three states exempt employers of less than a stipulated number of employees. Occupational diseases are compensable in only a few instances.

The many restrictions and qualifications in the compensation laws have resulted in the injured workers bearing about 50 per cent of the burden of accidents in states having the most favorable legislation, while in the other states their share is from 65 to 80 per cent.

Compensation benefits must in many cases be supplemented by public or private relief. According to the latest reports of four state industrial commissions, over one-half the injured workers earned thirty dollars a week or less. It is apparent that any interruption or reduction of income will work hardship on their dependents.

Besides the industrial accidents and the 31,000 automobile fatalities and 23,000 public accidents, there are 23,000 domestic fatalities, all of which affect the lives of children.

Premature Death. The deaths that disrupt families and create dependency are primarily those between the ages of twenty and fifty. On the last date for which figures are now available, the three largest causes of deaths among women in the entire registration area of the United States between the ages of fifteen and forty-five were the following:

Tuberculosis	122	per 100,000
Childbirth	70	per 100,000
Heart disease, organic	35	per 100,000

Among men from twenty to fifty-five years of age, the four leading causes of death in the United States registration area in 1926 were in the following order:

Death by violence (excluding suicide)
Tuberculosis
Pneumonia
Heart disease

These four causes accounted for considerably more than half the total number of deaths of males of these ages and are, therefore, the chief factors which sent widows to the offices of the mothers' aid officials, and to many other family and child-caring agencies of the country. A study by this Committee revealed that in 9,471 families receiving mothers' aid in 1930, over 71 per cent of the fathers died before reaching the age of forty-five years.

Irregular Employment and Unemployment. Seasonal activities, a failure to adjust supply to changing demands, and an excessive number of workers accustomed to a particular occupation, deprive many thousands of families, most of them in the lower wage groups, where at best the regular wage barely suffices to meet the current needs, of that regular income which is essential to the maintenance of a normal standard of living. In addition, the displacement of labor by the invention of new machinery or the improvement of technical processes produces at all times a substantial amount of unemployment of persons, who, at best, can only gradually find places in other occupations.

In addition to this, business cycles and obscure factors of a social, economic, and political character, create business depressions which cause huge volumes of unemployment for shorter or longer periods.

These various types of irregular employment and indefinite unemployment are a major factor in privation and want among children.

Unemployment bears most heavily on families of fathers in the lower income levels. They attempt to meet it by exhausting their savings, and the mother and the older children who are taken out of school seek employment. When their earnings are not sufficient, credit becomes exhausted, and the result is a dangerous saving on food, clothing, and fuel. The Children's Bureau study of the effects of unemployment on 366 families in two cities where the fathers had been unemployed in 1921–22 reported that children's earnings supplemented the reduced wages of the father in 20 per cent of the group; the mother's earnings in 32 per cent; 43 per cent used their savings; credit and loans were secured by 90 per cent; and charitable aid by 52 per cent. Communities where charitable aid is available for special unemployment crises cannot wholly prevent its devastating effects on children. It means in many cases removal of children from parental care. In families that manage to keep together, the loss of family morale, discouragement of parents, the extra strain on the mother, have a direct and disastrous result on the welfare of children.

FAMILY INCOME AND THE CHILD'S SECURITY

Economic security or continuous ability to provide adequate food, clothing, housing, leisure for recreation, medical care, and some surplus for temporary incapacity to earn, and for the waning productivity of old age, is a fundamental requisite to wholesome family life. The normal and socially desirable situation is one in which the infant is born into a family in which a mother is continuously present during his period of helplessness to attend to his needs, and where a father is at work and earns enough to provide the necessities of life. Whether a father works, where he works, and what he earns, are factors of the first importance to all who are dependent on him.

We have now reached the point where those interested in child welfare must advance on a broad program designed to safeguard children through the medium of greater economic protection for their parents, or commit themselves irrevocably to the prospect of receiving endless thousands of children into foster care in the years to come.

The first test of adequate income is the pay envelope measured against the cost of living. Child-caring agencies and institutions are generally not asked to accept into care children of families which for any considerable time have had an appreciable surplus above their necessary living expenses. Experts, as a result of extensive research, are in general agreement that in cities, at this time, an ordinary family cannot maintain a reasonable standard of family life for less than from $1,600 to $1,800 per annum . . .

In a comparison of the wage figures for the industry employing the largest number of workers in each of twelve groups covered by the United States Bureau of Labor Statistics for 1928, one finds only three industries reaching or exceeding a minimum wage level of $1,700 a year. Two industries fall short of the minimum standard by over $800.

Studies of the distribution of income in the United States show that the majority of families in this country are living close to the margin of economic want. The experience of social agencies shows that there is always a group living below this margin. These figures, which are presented only as illustrative material, throw considerable doubt upon the ability of large numbers of male wage-earners to earn enough to support a family at current wages even if steadily employed.

There is no certainty, then, that many wage-earners will earn enough to support a normal family even when steadily employed. When the hazards of unemployment, illness, and accident are taken into account, in many cases all hope of their doing so vanishes.

Persons of low income make up practically the entire group coming to social agencies, and consequently, since most of our organized social effort is carried on in cities, such agencies are intimately concerned in the problems of the lower ranges of the wage-earning class. Their problems are of paramount importance, since neither the individual nor his family can control the purely economic features of his environment.

---

4. Depression necessitates replanning of children's work

C. W. Areson, "Status of Children's Work in the United States," *Proceedings* of the National Conference of Social Work (1933), 91–103

After the World War this country flamed with determination that the horrors of war should no longer be visited on children. Our citizens by the thousands poured into Europe a golden flood of succor to save the future citizens of other lands. Our government appropriated millions. In our own country the Federal Children's Bureau led a great movement to save our underprivileged children from neglect. There was a second White House Conference, and three years ago a third. It seemed that we were committed to real opportunity as the birthright of every child, at least within our borders.

But in the darkness of the depression years we seem to have lost sight of this goal. Our efforts are confused. For example, it is tragic that even today, in the fourth depression year, we do not know the extent of need among neglected and potentially dependent children. Every one of the many correspondents who contributed to this paper stated that need outruns services. And yet not one gave any hint that his community had devised a way to learn the full effect of the disaster upon the children. Concern for children must again be raised above the threshold of public consciousness.

At the National Conference in Providence in 1922, when we were emerging from a milder depression, Miss Grace Abbott said: "We all know that the problem of unemployment is in its last analysis a child welfare problem. In the past and at present a large burden of unemployment has fallen, not on industry and not on the community, but on the backs of little children. These children, passing through any particular stage of life, lose forever those benefits, which come from having enough to eat and a happy home, free from that harrowing anxiety of not knowing how food and clothes are to be secured. No child should suffer this anxiety in the United States." That these words are again applicable is little short of a national disgrace. Has not the time come to lift from children the horrors of the depression?

One fact alone seems to me to mitigate the situation. There is the Federal Children's Bureau, and in a great many of the states there are state departments or bureaus whose business it is to know about children and to develop services for them. To the extent that these departments are efficient and continue to be supported they can be spokesmen for the children. It is therefore of the utmost importance that they continue at the top of their efficiency and that all social forces combine to guard their services from the raids of false economy.

To a certain degree it would appear that services to children are in somewhat the position that the services to families were a few years ago. I refer to those days, now so remote, when officialdom, big business, and the leaders we were then expected to heed were telling us that unemployment-relief need was not as great as we thought, that there were yet local resources to be tapped, that charitable people would come forward in the American manner to support their stricken neighbors — in a word, that the situation need not be squarely faced for the major disaster that it is. In the family-relief field this stage is history, the need is acknowledged, and no responsible official or leader of opinion is using the discredited phrases current less than three years ago.

In the greater complexity of the children's field, not a few communities are still in the stage of uncertainty as to whether child need too must be faced as something unprecedented, or instead as something that does not require for its solution the strong forces of government, but may be left to the responsibility of community chests, churches, groups, localities of voters, etc.

All available data show a tremendous rise in foster-home care, more particularly in boarding-homes; static or even declining populations in institutions; and these trends seem to hold generally for the various sections of the country represented in the statistics. That foster-home care should have been capable of such great expansion as the depression demands rose higher and higher is an interesting commentary on the flexibility of community provisions already existing, and also an indorsement of the practicability of the program as well as of its appeal to thousands of families whose personal participation in it alone make it possible. If reasonable standards bay be maintained to safeguard both the foster-families and the children placed with them, there should result from this experience a wider understanding both of the numbers of children who have to be cared for and of their essential likeness to all other children. The "orphan" of other days ought to be even less a representative symbol.

At the same time there is some evidence of makeshift procedure, highly dangerous to the children and devoid of almost any consideration of their personal fortunes. For example, a member of the Child Welfare League of America reports the following: "The county authori-ties have been doing more child-placing them-selves, either boarding children in needy families in lieu of relief orders, placing them through an agency outside the county which makes free home placements, or placing them in boarding-homes of their own selection so as to feel free to remove them to free homes if any become available."

One hopes that this may be an isolated in-stance, yet it does not stand entirely alone. In one large city, family-agency workers have felt obliged by the restrictions on intake in the chil-dren's agencies to place neglected children from relief families informally with other relief families or with relatives receiving relief. In this instance the family agency is protesting that its workers should not be forced to these unsatis-factory measures. From another large city comes a guarded statement that there seemed to be some tendency in that city for family agencies "to enter fields which have hitherto been regarded as the jurisdiction of child-care agencies."

Over against this should be set evidence that children's agencies in some communities have expanded their functions to undertake giving relief to families whose children they are super-vising either in the absence of adequate relief service or by agreement with such agencies. In several places family agencies are giving relief in the homes of children under the supervision of children's agencies while the latter continue to carry case-work responsibility. In one city the Welfare Department pays board for chil-dren for whom it asks the services of the chil-dren's agency.

Undoubtedly the availability of funds for one particular type of work or another greatly influences arrangements in some places, with the restriction of federal aid almost exclusively to family relief playing a prominent part. Prob-ably the following statement or some variant of it would describe the situation in a great many places: "Demand on private family agencies has absorbed private funds, and ability of children's agency to accept children for care is limited.

Need for food and shelter has diverted municipal funds from child care." In quite another manner finance is hampering normal work for children in a county where "more families have been referred to us for clothing because of increases in applications but decrease in service of Poor Board"; or in a midwestern city where an institution finds "we are handling cases which in normal times would be cared for by a family agency"; of where, family service being inadequate, "more families are applying for care of children where lack of income is the major difficulty."

Confusion of function is thus aggravated not only by pre-existing status of one or another type of service, but also, more evidently, by the adequacy or inadequacy of general relief programs. The rôle of the relief program is well illustrated in two large eastern states adjacent to each other, in one of which a very efficient relief program was organized early in the depression while in the other the organization was much delayed and the program has not yet become adequate.

.   .   .   .   .

Children's services, other than simple care for children, are undoubtedly suffering. Probably most of us have heard a board member, or public official, or budget committee suggest that protective and preventive work should or must give way in favor of payment for the board of children. A state-wide protective agency has noted an appreciable increase in calls in each of several years past. Set over against the impossibility of increasing staff, this has produced unreasonably large case loads. Perhaps the opinion of the executive of this organization might express the experience of many in this aspect of child care. He says, "While unemployment might be expected to increase dependency it should not necessarily increase neglect. However, our agencies have noted that family tensions have developed or been intensified by reason of unemployment of husbands and fathers, with consequent breakdown in

family morale, and abuse and neglect of children. In fact, the depression has very evidently increased our work. We have noted, also, that minimum standards of family life and child care have fallen during this period. Public opinion, as expressed through the judiciary, is somewhat tolerant toward neglectful parents who plead unemployment and lack of family resources." . . .

In the May 15 *News Letter* of the Child Welfare League of America it is stated that about one-third of the one hundred member agencies answering a questionnaire indicated lessened or inadequate community services for children in various special groupings. Among the correspondents who assisted with information for this paper a considerable number referred to decreased intake, smaller numbers accepted for care, and cuts in service because of decreased income. Such reports would seem to contradict the large increase in the number of children in care shown by the statistics of the Federal Children's Bureau. In certain urban communities, however, the contradiction is more apparent than real. A great number of agencies are leaving children in doubtful homes from which they would have been removed in more settled times. Where this is accompanied by adequate service it may not in the end be entirely unfortunate.

But there is evidence, on many hands, that service is not available and that in many places something not far short of abandonment is taking place. Of the one hundred agencies referred to, eleven reported complete closing of intake and forty-six a partial closing, for rather long periods of time. The condition is frequently complicated, too, by the necessity of providing means of exploitation—"Children are being exploited as in the old days of indenture placement" is the statement.

But black is not the only color. For example, exceptionally well-trained and vigorous leadership in the sectarian work in a certain large city is shown in a 20 per cent increase of children at board; only a small reduction in salaries and boarding rates; a perceptible increase in medical and psychiatric service; and a determined effort to work out a method of caring for all of the older children who are in need. A state-wide agency reports that community-chest failures and other similar happenings have furthered the merging of its casework service with institutional programs to the advantage of several smaller cities.

Redistribution of services upon a planned basis is going forward. In one or two cities children's services are being separated from their former family-agency connections to become self-contained children's aid services. In one of them this includes the merging of certain institutional facilities that had hitherto remained more or less unconnected with the case-work program of the community—a much-improved arrangement. In certain states where governors or state departments of welfare, or both, have been alert, social work is being implanted in areas heretofore barren of such services. It would seem probable that the new administration of federal aid would definitely accelerate this development.

.   .   .   .   .

I have attempted to point out that we are facing something of a collapse in public concern for children, sharply at variance with our national traditions; that no reliable method of ascertaining their need exists, while at the same time there is widespread evidence of tremendous unmet needs. Through the federal and state departments and the national agencies we ought, however, to be able to make a successful drive to return attention to children. Care must be exercised neither to destroy private initiative nor to make private agencies mere parasites on public money. Organization must be sound, both for the protection of the children and because child care is a long-time program. Partial services, public or private or both, cannot be satisfactory, but there is real opportunity to formulate co-ordinated programs.

B. RESEARCH AND DEMONSTRATION

Studies of institutions and placing-out societies

---

1. Boston Children's Aid Society
evaluates its work, 1915

Ruth W. Lawton and J. Prentice Murphy, "A Study of Results of a Child-Placing Society," *Proceedings* of the National Conference of Charities and Correction (1915), 164–174.

We began our study with the idea that the many thousands of families that had come to the society during, say, the ten years previous to 1913, and certainly the two thousand and odd children who had been received into care during the same period, presented in their varied and tragic needs an array of ills and results which, if once focused, would produce one or many social documents of very great value . . . To our great surprise and disappointment we found in 1913, after superficial examination, that our histories as written records were of little value; that, although they represented many evidences of good and bad work, there were too few facts on which sound, wise studies could be based.

.   .   .   .   .

There is, even now, much that we do not know about the children or their families, and which we can never ascertain; yet the 129 children included in the study, coming from 117 families, had involved up to October, 1913, an expense approximating $100,000. In spite of all that has been said on the value of careful initial reception inquiries, many of these children were taken on meagre information, often engaging us in the task of fitting round pegs to square holes, and in some cases exposing communities to great dangers from the acts of exceedingly difficult children.

．　　．　　．　　．　　．

On the reception-inquiry side we found that we had accepted children in very critical need of special kinds of care without knowing the particular defects in heredity which made certain of our treatments unwise or dangerous. For example, we had one exceedingly nervous girl in charge for several years before we discovered that she had an insane grandmother; that her father and mother had both died insane, and that this strain of insanity explained certain characteristics which we had most incorrectly interpreted. We also discovered during the study that another, none too robust, girl suffering with congenital syphilis had three generations of ancestors with almshouse records, a grandmother who was insane and at one time a state ward, and a mother who was both epileptic and an imbecile. The need of a most protective kind of care, expressed in quietness, careful medical supervision and freedom from strain were indicated as clear essentials; yet in one instance we were planning to put the child under very great discipline because she seemed stubborn.

We also discovered, purely by chance, through one of the visitors . . . that one of our wards, a nervous, sensitive girl of great refinement, had a heredity strain of appalling extent, going back three generations, and showing that nineteen of her immediate ancestors had been alcoholic, epileptic, neurotic and sexually promiscuous. These facts were only meagrely known to us when we began our long, expensive, and what now promises to be successful service.

．　　．　　．　　．　　．

In 1912 we received a boy, then fourteen years of age, whose father had been cruelly abusive to him. The boy indicated no marked objectionable tendencies and was supposedly progressing in one of our families. Coincident with the charge that he was showing precocious sexual habits, involving girls in the school he attended, we learned that sexual perversity had been a prominent family characteristic for over two generations . . . With such a background it was dangerous for us to have placed this boy except with a foster mother and under a visitor completely informed.

In no instance would it have been easy for us to have secured all this information when the children were first received; but that we learned much of it years afterwards is proof that in some cases we could, and should, have had it from the start.

．　　．　　．　　．　　．

In the matter of applications made for the children involved in the study, we discovered that 30 per cent of the families involved made two or more applications before we took action . . . it will be of value to study this further in comparing the family home type of care with the institutional type of care, because the institution may accept a child at once, whereas in difficult cases some time is required for the family agencies to find the home that exactly fits the child. It should be remembered in this connection that no one institution would have been able to receive all the varied types included in this study.

During the time the children were in care up to October, 1913, the general physical condition of 91 of them averaged good or excellent; for 38 the average was fair or below. A total of 440 visits each year from physicians are recorded for the period studied, less than one-third of these visits being by local physicians. The general tendency was for the children longest in care to show the highest health averages. It is against our credit that only 37 general physical examinations and 4 mental examinations were made for these 129 children before they were first placed. Two, and probably three, girls out of the 60 in the group, one-half of whom were over twelve years of age when received, contracted gonorrhea while in our care, and two became pregnant while in our care; one of these two became pregnant twice.

We ascertained, on the mental side, that 26 had been examined; for the other cases we are giving the visitors' estimates. One hundred and three children were considered normal, six backward, twenty subnormal and defective.

At the date of the study, October 1, 1913, 45 of the 69 boys and 25 of the 60 girls were attending school . . . During placements the children attended a total of 194 different public schools, 163 of which were studied. All but 5.5 per cent of these schools were standard graded schools; 113 were within one-half mile of the children's homes and a total of 139 within a mile. It is of value to have this information respecting the schools because fears have often been expressed that we, along with many other placing-out societies, were sending most of our children to ungraded schools located at great distances from the children's homes, and thus offering them school services far below those offered to them in their own city schools. Of the 73 children in school the greatest number were fourteen years of age or under; 24 were attending high or normal schools. The children were on the whole about a year behind the average grade per age for children living in their own homes — which indicates nothing for our children except that

they started under handicaps which do not hold for most children.

. . . . .

The material gathered during the study with reference to our use of foster homes and the supervision of our children in these homes does seem of very special value. We found that up to October, 1913, these 129 children had been cared for in a total of 498 homes or families, this being an average of almost four homes for each child. This, of course, includes the homes selected for temporary care as well as the home selected for permanent care. For the 498 homes there were 528 placements, which is an average of more than four placements for a child. Thirty-seven per cent of all the placements were temporary, which may indicate one weakness in our family plan.

. . . . .

It is our purpose to select our families so carefully, and with such concern for the special fitness of the particular children to the particular homes selected that the caring families, under the oversight of our visitors, will be generally responsible for the training of the children received. It is necessary, of course, for our visitors to make certain visits to these families from time to time. This is another point for which the family plan agencies are criticised; namely, that their supervision is not close or adequate enough. It can not be stated too strongly that numbers of visits alone are no indication of supervision efficiency. Days may be spent in finding a home with the right training adjustments for a child, and by very reason of the care exercised at the start there can safely be fewer supervision visits than in the case of a child hurriedly placed in a home possessing no special qualifications.

. . . . .

Our visitors in considering the children studied agreed that out of the total 129 involved, only 70 had been truly and adequately supervised throughout the whole period; 14 were inadequately supervised for only part of the time and 42 inadequately supervised for practically all of the time. When we say that only 70 out of the 129 children were considered to have been adequately supervised over the whole period, we do not mean that the remainder have all necessarily suffered through inadequate oversight, because the majority of the remainder have been, and are, doing very well in the homes to which they have gone; but their progress is something for which we can not ask praise because of what we have done. Adequate supervision calls for intimate and continuous oversight and knowledge of the children and the homes under care.

The reasons given for the inadequate supervision of 42 of the children noted were as follows: too many cases assigned a new visitor during her first year; too many cases assigned to a visitor throughout her whole term of service; ineffectiveness of a visitor as to training and personality; too frequent change of visitors; changing of visitors at a critical time when the child would not accept the new authority; too long lapses between visits of two different visitors; inadequate and insufficient reception inquiries so that the placing visitors had no information with which to do their work; case work handicapped because of reorganization in the office; too frequent change of homes and too distant placements; vocation plan for and preparation of child neglected; visiting sufficiently frequent but careless in interpretation; frequent visiting but insufficient for certain difficult children; conflict of authority in the minds of foster parents because the authority of previous visitor who had retained guardianship was held above that of the new visitor; placing undue confidence in the foster home and thus visiting less frequently than later results indicated to be wise; interference of child's family with the work of the society; failure to recognize mental defects and less difficult cases overshadowed by more difficult sisters or brothers.

We found that the average period a child was under one visitor was one year, six months and fifteen days, so that every one of these children had a change of visitor every year and a half. This, of course, as every placing-out worker knows, is a very serious condition of affairs, because the supervision visitors for placing-out societies hold a control and a knowledge of the children and their special families that can not be passed on to other people with ease, or with any degree of certainty. The continuity of service for visitors of a placing-out society for at least five-year periods is an absolute essential. We found that the mere fact of visitors leaving our staff for the purpose of getting higher salaries with other agencies was responsible for 122 out of a total of 230 transfers of children from one home to another . . .

These results as submitted challenge the services of every child-placing organization. If, with an average of 45 children per visitor for most of the period studied, we are forced to report such findings for our own society, what must conditions be with organizations averaging from one to two hundred for each visitor.

---

2. A follow-up study of foster children, New York, 1924

Sophie Van Senden Theis, "How Foster Children Turn Out," *Proceedings* of the National Conference of Social Work (1924), 121–124.

A complete account of this investigation may be found in the same author's *How Foster Children Turn Out: A Study by the State Charities Aid Association* (New York, 1924). For an earlier follow-up study of foster children see Massachusetts State Board of Charity, "After Careers of Minor Wards of the Massachusetts State Board of Charity," *Thirty-Second Annual Report, 1910* (Boston, 1910), pp. 119–136.

How foster children turn out is a question which has been asked by social workers, scientists, and everyone interested in dependent children. What are these children who are adopted in babyhood like, later in life? How do the children and foster-parents who have gone through periods of difficult adjustments feel when the children have grown up? What do they think about it? Is the effort which goes into giving the children who start life handicapped and have difficulties of temperament and behavior which sometimes seem insuperable, worth while?

Thus, the primary object of our critical study and analysis was to find out what had become of a group of such children; into what sort of adults they had developed, and to what extent they had adapted themselves to the good standards of the communities in which they were living. The group which was studied intensively consisted of 910 individuals, all those of the 3,600 placed in free foster homes by the State Charities Aid Association since 1898, who on January 1, 1922, were eighteen years of age or more and who had been under the care of the Association for a minimum period of one year.

It is essential to describe briefly this group of 910 children who were placed in foster homes. There are about 150 more girls than boys in the study group. Thirty-four per cent were under five years of age at placement in their first foster homes, 21 per cent between five and ten, and 45 per cent over ten years of age; in other words, a little more than half were under ten, and slightly less than half over ten years of age when first placed. Practically all of the children were American born, and relatively few had foreign parents.

About a fourth of them were foundlings — babies picked up in hallways or from park benches, whose own families and homes were entirely unknown. For 149 other children there was not enough information on which to base a judgment of the intelligence, health, habits, or occupation of the parents. There was, however, available enough information about the

homes and family background of 544 children to make some classification possible. Our analysis of these showed that approximately 80 per cent of the children came from a background which in so far as known was predominantly bad, about 8 per cent from predominantly good, and 12 per cent from a mixed background. The classifications were based on the plain man's opinion about family background; that is, the original recording of information and the basis of classification were made from a human and social point of view and not from any one specialist's angle. The findings regarding the family background became more significant when considered in relation to the length of time that the children lived in the environment created by their families. Nearly one-half of the 910 children stayed with their own families for five years or more.

Slightly more than 1,600 homes were used for these 910 children in the process of fitting together the right child and right home. Our analysis of these foster homes showed that the great majority—73 per cent of them—belonged to the average middle group; they were the people of moderate income, offering homes of average comfort—the self-respecting, self-supporting, kindly families who make up the large part of every community. About 15 per cent of the families offered opportunities above the average, mostly in the way of unusual cultural and educational advantages. About 12 per cent were distinctly mediocre, that is, people of very limited intelligence and moderate ability offering very few opportunities. A minimum standard was required of all homes. The families had to have an income adequate to maintain the family with an additional member, healthful living conditions, moral character above reproach, and good reputation. The child taken into the household had to be regarded as a member of the family.

We have told briefly something of the children and something of the foster homes and what they offered. That serves as a background. The objective of our study was an analysis of the present situation of these 910 children who have reached an age of maturity. This was the primary purpose of our inquiry. First—where are they? Thirty-five per cent of those whose present situation is known are still in their foster homes; 31 per cent are married and have their own homes; 24 per cent are working away from home; 25 of them are now living with their own relatives; 22 are in institutions receiving correctional physical or mental treatment or custodial care, and 28 are dead.

But more important than this external fact of where these children are, is the question: "Did these 910 subjects succeed or fail in meeting the responsibilities of adult life?" Success and failure are obviously relative and hard to define, but clearly some standard of measurement had to be applied. "Is the subject capable of managing himself and his affairs with ordinary prudence?" was the question which served as a means of judging the subject's adaptation to life. Rated by this standard it was found that 615 subjects are law-abiding and manage their affairs with good sense; are capable of self-support, and are living in accordance with the good moral standards of their communities. Of those who were rated as "incapable," 89 are irresponsible or shiftless persons of limited capacity or inferior character, or are partially incapacitated mentally or physically; 26 are persons who because of some previous offense against society still need supervision, and their future development is uncertain; 20 are in correctional or custodial institutions, and 47 are definitely harmful, that is, in conflict with accepted standards of morality or law. Thus we found 77.2 per cent of the subjects decent, law-abiding citizens, respected in their communities; 22.8 per cent ranging from those who are harmless to those actively harmful, incapable of meeting the ordinary demands of self-support and personal and community obligations.

The question which arises is: Why did these particular 615 subjects succeed and the 182 fail in the ordeal of adjusting to life? Were there any common elements running through

one group distinguishing it from the other group, which might explain why one group was more successful in development than the other? The family background of the children is very much the same for the two groups. The incapable children did not come in a significantly larger proportion from bad backgrounds. Our classifications showed no difference in the types of foster homes used for the two groups. The proportion of superior, good, and mediocre foster homes in which the children who proved to be incapable were placed was almost identically the same as that of the capable group. It was in the age at which the child was placed in his foster home where the most significant difference was found. Throughout our whole study it was clear that children placed when less than five years of age showed a marked superiority in development over the group older at placement. A large proportion of the younger group have proved to be competent, well-adapted, happy individuals. They are in a larger proportion law-abiding and steady. They were given a better education and had the advantage of more sympathetic and understanding care from their foster parents.

The facts considered in determining a subject's capability or incapability of managing himself and his affairs with ordinary prudence were his personal characteristics and traits and habits, his health, his occupation, his degree of self-support, school and work record, and his general reputation, and place in his family and community. These topics were carefully and separately studied, but there is no time to give a detailed report on our findings. It will have to suffice here to state that the schooling received by these foster children compares favorably with that given the children of the general population. There is no outstanding observation to report about their occupations, their health, their degree of adaptation, their habits and behavior, unless the fact that there is no outstanding observation to report is in itself significant. The majority are working steadily at the kind of jobs which keep most people busy. In so far as it was possible to tell by lay judgments, the group showed no prevalence of any special type of disease or physical defect. How these children compare with the average population we do not know. Too little is known about human beings and their development and the "average" population to tell with any exactness how this group compares with them.

It seemed to us that the human relationship which developed between individuals mattered far more than the material surroundings in which the child was placed. It is impossible to express anything so subtle as human relationships in terms of statistics with any degree of mathematical accuracy. Because of this our classifications should be taken as suggestive only. About 60 per cent of the children had a satisfactory relationship with their foster parents and formed a tie which was firm and lasting. In many instances, particularly in the case of the child who was placed young, the relationship appeared to be a complete substitution for the natural parent-child relationship. For 25 per cent the relationship was temporarily satisfactory; that is, the children were reasonably contented while they were in their foster homes, and their foster parents were reasonably satisfied with them. For 15 per cent the foster home offered little more than food and shelter, and in some instances aroused in the children antagonism and a spirit of rebellion.

We pass now to the consideration of clarifying the theory and harmonizing the practice of child-placing agencies. This must start with such societies as are represented at this Conference, which realize that the science of adoption is thus far a very inexact one. Most of the theories and conclusions in this field are assumptions.

Our study as a whole, our analysis of special groups, and perhaps even more strikingly, our study of individual children, gave us the distinct impression that an immense power of growth and adaptation was shown among these 910 children. A consideration of this group gave one the sense that there are latent powers within individuals awaiting development, and

that under favorable conditions these powers may be developed and directed toward accomplishment. We would not say that anything could be made of any child, but rather that there are potentialities which may be developed and directed, and that these potentialities appear to reveal themselves only under certain conditions.

Our findings and impressions should be taken as showing tendencies rather than as conclusions, for all but 150 of the group are as yet less than twenty-five years old. Nevertheless, there is unquestionably real significance in the fact that up to this time so large a proportion of the children have "made good." It is of positive value to us social workers to know that so many of these dependent children, without homes of their own, who started life seriously handicapped, have found in their foster families the close human relationships which have satisfied one of their deepest human needs. The majority of them are reasonably happy, are maintaining themselves well, and are taking in an adequate way their share of the community's work. The foster parents, according to their own testimony, have gained, and in so far as every decent, self-sustaining citizen is an asset to society, the community has gained. It seems to us that we have reason to believe that social work in behalf of these 910 children has been worth while.

3. Need for institutions questioned, 1924

Stuart A. Queen, "Are Orphan Asylums Necessary?" *The Journal of Social Forces,* II (1924), 384–388. By permission of the University of North Carolina Press.

Queen was professor of sociology at the University of Kansas and author of *Social Work in the Light of History* (Philadelphia, 1922).

In the winter and spring of 1923, a study was made, by the writer, of four children's institutions in a middle western state. While the intention was to make an efficiency study rather than anything else, the findings led almost inevitably to the question—are these institutions needed at all? To indicate some of the facts which led to this skeptical attitude, a brief summary will be offered of the conditions discovered in this group of four institutions.

Most significant were the statistics assembled from such records as these institutions possessed. First, as to the family statistics of the children, it was found that only 7 out of 212 studied were known to be full orphans; 68 were half orphans, while the remainder represented various types of broken families. Reduced to percentages, 3.3 per cent were whole orphans, 32.5 per cent were half orphans, while 64.2 per cent were believed to have both parents living. Because the data were so very meager in the records of these institutions, the nature of the family difficulties could not always be determined with much accuracy. However, so nearly as it was possible to determine, 23 children were in the institution because parents were divorced, 49 because they were "separated," 37 appeared to have been deserted by at least one parent, and others seemed to be in the institution because of rather temporary emergencies due to sickness in the home, or imprisonment of the father.

Although these institutions are known as orphanages, they seem to be used very largely as receiving homes. Out of 151 children who left the institutions during one year, 51 had remained less than a month, and 33 one month but less than three months. Stated in terms of cumulative percentages, 33 per cent remained less than a month, 51 per cent remained less than three months, and 69 per cent remained less than six months. This may be much better than if the children remained longer, but it should not be imagined that these institutions are places from which children go out into supervised homes. On the contrary, the great

majority of them return to their parents and that too without evidence of any constructive work being done.

Of 120 children whose disposition could be determined from the records, 64 returned to their mothers, 19 to their fathers, 6 to both parents, and 12 to other relatives. Reduced to percentages, this means that 74 per cent were discharged to the care of one or both parents, 10 per cent to other relatives, and only 16 per cent had to be otherwise disposed of.

.　　.　　.　　.　　.

From the data assembled it was frankly not possible to say conclusively that all four of these institutions should be closed, but it would seem quite within the limits of safety and truth to insist that *not one of the institutions had demonstrated that it was really needed.* After presenting some of these facts and the conclusions based upon them to a Parent-Teachers' Association I was interested to clip from the local newspaper the following Sunday, the communication which I quote here because it illustrates so well the usual sentimental attitude toward orphan asylums, and the utter failure to get the point of my remarks. This communication was signed by the matron of one of the institutions, the judge and probation officer of the juvenile court, police matron, and municipal welfare officer.

"The question has been asked: 'Do we need orphan homes in —— because only seven real orphans have been found out of 212 that were in the orphanages last year. I would like to give you a few facts in regard to this.

"In the last fifteen years, I have had under my care over 1,300 children and if it had not been for the orphan home, many of these would have been out on the street, and God only knows what would have become of them. A number of their mothers have died, and the little children have been left without care. Also there are some cases where their fathers have died, and the poor mother is left without a home or means to provide for her little flock.

"What can she do? She does not wish to

part with her children forever, so she is compelled to work. She goes out to find a place for her children, but although she tramps the city over till she is worn and tired, no place can she find for her little ones. No private family wishes to be bothered with her children and if she should find someone that would take them, they would ask from $5 to $6 a week for their board, and she cannot pay, as she only gets $12 and has her own board and room rent to pay.

"With a sad heart she goes to her room. The rent is up and her money gone, so she must seek shelter for her babies somewhere else.

"She goes to the police matron or welfare board and tells her story. After listening to it the officers tell her there is an orphan home, where she can put her children and they will be cared for, and she will have the privilege of going and seeing them. How glad she is. What a load has been lifted from her heart.

.   .   .   .   .   .

"If —— had as many more homes as they have, they would all be filled to overflowing. Not long ago a father came to our home and wished to leave his little 11-year-old girl, whose mother was dead. He had tried to get her in a private home, but couldn't find any one who would take her in. When told that we were full, and didn't see how we could take her in he said, 'Well I just don't know what to do. I suppose I can do as one man did, throw my daughter in the river.' We felt very sorry indeed for the father and said that we would crowd up and take the little girl in. How glad the father was. We could tell of a good many children that have been sent to the home by the welfare board, police matron, associated charities and juvenile court. Many children that have been found by the police are brought to the home in the middle of the night. Those children did not have a place to lay their heads, and were turned out into the cold. What would become of them, if it had not been for the orphan homes? And if the 212 children that were in the orphan homes of —— had been

turned out, they would have been on the streets without shelter and food. Who would have taken them in?"

In the face of this situation it seemed wise to make the following recommendations to this group of institutions and to the Community Chest from which three of them received a portion of their funds. The first recommendation was that there be established a central agency whose duties should be: (1) To investigate all applications for admission to these children's institutions. (2) To undertake the rehabilitation of the families to which these children belonged, in coöperation with other interested organizations. (3) To investigate homes before children are discharged, and to follow up children after they leave the institutions. (4) To find foster homes for children who can be better cared for thus than in institutions. (5) To supervise such foster homes in coöperation with other organizations.

The second recommendation was that the existing institutions should be classified and institute a division of labor. It was suggested that one should serve as a receiving home, one as a day nursery, one as a home for low grade children, and one as a school for older children difficult to place in foster homes. Other recommendations had to do with the improvement of the present staffs, installment of a uniform accounting system, study of feeding by a competent dietitian, use of a Confidential Exchange, and the securing of mothers' pensions wherever these might seem advisable.

Rural and urban dependency

1. Caring for dependents in West Virginia, 1922

Sara A. Brown, "Rural Child Dependency, Neglect and Delinquency," in National

Child Labor Committee, *Rural Child Welfare* (New York, 1922), pp. 176–218 *passim*.

The information for this study was gathered from twenty-three rural counties containing 270 children from broken homes.

With Relatives. Rural folk generally are alike in the warmth of their hospitality toward homeless children though frequently they do not work harmoniously together for any common economic interest in their neighborhood. The relatives — "kinsfolk" — are first to receive children who for any reason are separated from their own parents. Whether they live in the neighborhood or far away, children are taken into their homes without question of conditions, size of family, financial ability to assume the additional burden, or the fitness of either the children for the homes or the homes for the children. The matter of blood relationship is the determining factor and overrides every other consideration. If there are no relatives, neighbors open their homes, again without question, and for so long a time as the children choose to remain. One hundred and forty children of 86 families are living with relatives in 97 homes. Girls outnumber boys by four. Grandparents are caring for by far the largest number, or 67 per cent; aunts for 15 per cent; uncles, 14 per cent, and cousins, 4 per cent. The spirit through them all is typified in the story of Maxine's "Grandpap."

"That's where *my* grandpap lives and my poppy run'd away with a married woman, he did," said little Maxine, age 7, as we met her on the road from school and inquired the way to what chanced to be her grandfather's home, two miles from the county seat. We found a picturesque, one-room log cabin, about 12 by 18 feet, with a lean-to kitchen and a loft. The friendly warmth from the big, open hearth shed a soft light on what seemed a myriad of faces gathered about. We counted eight children and three adults, 11 in all; five children under seven years whose mother died of tuberculosis three years ago and whose father, one year later, deserted; their mother's sister, in an advanced stage of tuberculosis, who with her two children, six and eight years, came home for care; and another sister, 16 years, who spends much of her time with her invalid, aged, paternal grandparents in a cabin nearby. These, with Maxine's grandfather and grandmother, make up the group of 11. The grandfather, able-bodied, alert, is deeply devoted to his kinsfolk. The grandmother, paralyzed, is unable to leave her chair. The little home provides four double beds, two in the living room and two in the loft. Water is carried from a spring several yards from the house. The sole support is derived from the 80-acre mountain farm and an old gas lease. The adults can barely read and write, but talk intelligently of preventing the spread of disease. They are confident "the children's father will some day come back, will want his kids and won't git 'em!"

In Foster Homes. From interviews with foster fathers and mothers caring for children in no way related to them, we find that the circumstances under which the children are received are large factors in shaping plans for them. Homes which take children on definite arrangement from those legally charged with their custody and which plan for legal adoption or for rearing them as members of the family without adoption, we refer to as "foster homes."

· · · ·

Children in foster homes show something of the extent to which agencies outside the family are reaching rural children and taking responsibility for placing them in farm homes. A larger number of children than in any other group were taken at the request of those not akin. Out of 81 children, 12 were taken at the request of a private home-finding society; 12 at the request of the state; 7 of an orphanage; 15 at the request of the mother; 5 each at the request of the father, the court, and overseer of the poor; 4 at the request of a probation officer; 6 are unknown; 3 each were taken at the request of a friend, a club woman and a mission; and one at the request of a justice of the peace. Doubtless these agencies account for the definite arrangement and plans in many instances. Those long experienced in home-finding confirm our observations that families more quickly accept the responsibility for children who are without homes than for those who have already been transferred to a receiving home or to an orphanage. The appeals of mothers or of neighbors to take helpless children and rear them as their own are not easily ignored, and agreements to care for them frequently prove as binding as an order of court.

. . . . .

We found 49 children representing 24 families in 46 hit-or-miss homes.

A large number, no one knows how many, drift from one home to another, no one assuming responsibility for permanent care, while many children tramp for weeks or even months at a time — not for the sake of adventure — but because they have no home. Tramp children are not at all uncommon in the rural communities covered in this study.

Annie, age 14, is typical of a distressingly large number of such children. In March we found her at Grapevine attending school for the first time in her life. She lives with Granny McCauley a mile and a half up the hollow. As we walked home with her after school, her story ran something like this: with three younger sisters, she lived in a one-room mountain cabin; the mother died a year ago; the father, never a good provider, frequently deserted during the lifetime of the mother. Just before last Christmas he left early one morning, presumably for the village nine miles away, and did not return. The supply of food became exhausted. The fuel gave out and the children gathered more from the mountain side. Meanwhile, a heavy snow had fallen. Rather reluctantly, Annie admitted she *was* afraid because there were so many lonely graves scattered about, but did not dare let her sisters *think so*. At the end of the fourth day,

she took the children to a neighbor where they stayed a couple of days, while the man of the house made inquiry regarding her father. Hearing nothing, Annie returned to the cabin, rolled their meager supply of clothing together and started with her three little sisters over the mountain to a friend of the mother. It was nearly dark when they arrived at the friend's cabin, only to find the doors locked, no fire and no tracks on the fresh snow. They trudged on about half a mile and spent the night with a neighbor. For three weeks they tramped, never staying more than one night in any place. Annie had no definite point in mind but a very clearly defined idea that she was responsible for finding a home where they could stay together. They drifted into a neighboring county where a man put them on the train with tickets to their own county seat. They arrived about 9:30 at night; the conductor left them in charge of the station master and sent for the sheriff who took them to the jail for the night. The following day, he sent word to the county probation officer nine miles in the country. They stayed with the sheriff three or four days, while the women of the town provided them with new clothing, the sheriff and prosecuting attorney searched for the father, and the kindly probation officer found them homes, as he said, "so they wouldn't have to go to no orphan asylum."

. . . . .

[*Home conditions*]

One foster mother who recently took the third child from a home-finding society and said she wanted another, may be a good mother but showed poor judgment in at least one respect. During our conversation in her "settin' room," little dark-haired, dark-eyed Virginia, age nine, came home from school. The foster mother remarked, "This is the little orphan we got last time. We wanted a boy, but Mr. Blank didn't have one so we took this 'un, and I told him if I *had* to take a girl I wanted one with light hair and blue eyes so I could dress her up pretty, and this is what I got." Virginia dropped into a little rocking chair at the farthest side of the room, her large eyes questioning, pleading, and watching every move her new-found mother made.

Out of 63 foster parents, 37 are farm owners, 14 renters and 12 squatters; 26 of their houses are built of logs, 28 are frame, 4 log and frame, 4 brick, and one is a slab shack. The number of rooms to a family averages five, the number of persons to a family 5.1. Water supply is obtained for 38 families from wells; 22 from springs; and 3 from streams; 3 have water piped into the house. Toilet accommodations are provided on 43 farms and on 20 no provision is made. Forty-eight households are presided over by man and wife, 16 of whom are classed as aged couples; 15 are homes of widows, 10 of them were classed as aged. In 36 homes reading matter of some description is found . . . and 12 have sufficient number of books to be called a library. In 27 homes there is nothing to read. In answer to our inquiry as to what the children had to read, one foster father of two boys remarked, "Sometimes I get a funny paper a purpose for 'em." An old woman, commonly called "Granny," laboriously climbed a ladder to the loft, and brought down a large volume of "The New Knowledge Library," for which she paid $6.50, saying proudly, "When the boys learn everything in this book, they'll know a heap, won't they?" Four orphans stand to her credit for she "never turns an orphan away."

.   .   .   .   .

[*In almshouses*]

Sentiment against keeping children in almshouses has crystallized in a very positive demand that all normal children be removed, and no new cases of child dependency be accepted. This demand has penetrated into some of the most rural counties; as one keeper said regarding normal children, "We have had none here for over a year and the most we ever had at one time was nine, two years ago." Another reported 28 children at one time during the winter of 1919 and 1920, with 19 attending district school. While it is not a general practice to house children there, they nevertheless are found in almshouses. Seventeen counties out of 23 receive and care for normal children, and three counties with thriving, wide-awake cities as seats of government are the most serious offenders.

We visited 58 children in 19 almshouses, 40 of whom are recognized as normal and 18 mentally defective. We found records of 24 but recently removed, nine of whom had been placed in foster homes and 15 just dismissed. In each instance, children associate with old men and women, with the feeble-minded and sypilitic inmates, and with two exceptions occupy the same sleeping rooms, use the same toilets and eat in the same dining rooms with the inmates. With two exceptions, they attend free school in the neighborhood. One county conducts a private school on the farm, and the other has never sent the children to school.

.   .   .   .   .

In [one] county with an active department of poor relief, a juvenile court, and probation officer, the almshouse has been designated as juvenile detention home, and the keeper named as superintendent, but he should not be required to carry responsibility for children in addition to managing the large farm, and caring for the aged and sick residents of a county home.

At the time of our visit there were eight boys present, only one of whom is considered deficient. With the exception of a baby born in the almshouse in June, 1920, the boys sleep in the old men's department in the first room adjoining the family quarters. The room has bare walls, windows and floor. Double beds with mattresses and badly worn blankets are the only furnishings. The boys use the same stairs, toilet and bathroom, and eat in the same dining-room as the old men. They care for their own room under the direction of the kindly housewife and assist with the work about the house and farm yard. On the day of our visit,

Up the Rigging.

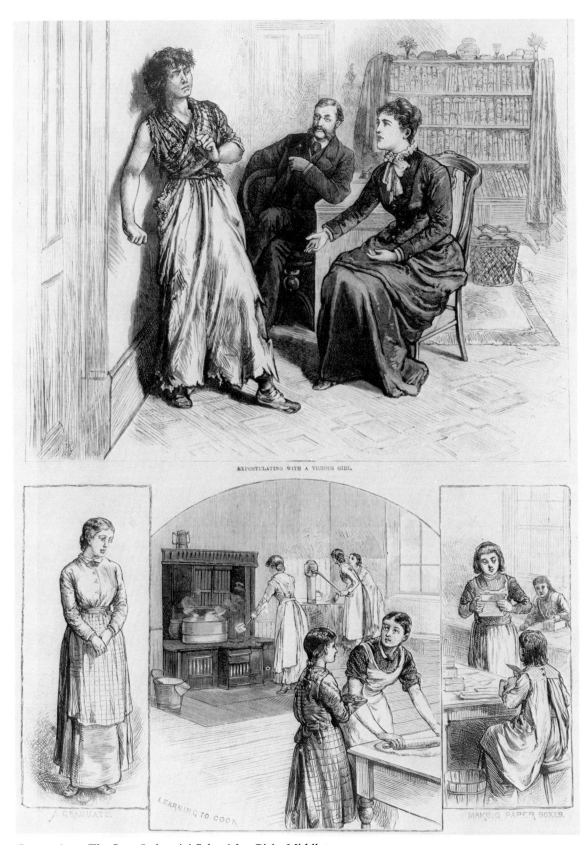

EXPOSTULATING WITH A VICIOUS GIRL.

GRADUATE.

LEARNING TO COOK.

MAKING PAPER BOXES.

Connecticut: The State Industrial School for Girls, Middletown.

a nine-year-old boy carried dinner trays to men in the hospital some distance removed from the house; when he entered "old Bill's room" the child found him dead. During the afternoon the child's cheeks were flushed, his hands trembled, yet no one comforted him or helped adjust him to the unusual and distressing experience.

Children were helping in the one kitchen where all food was prepared, along with a woman who within the week had been diagnosed as an open case of syphilis by two physicians. Ugly sores were on her face. A girl, 13, recently returned from the State Industrial School because afflicted with venereal disease, had proven uncontrollable, and was being detained in the county jail for treatment; when staying at the almshouse as a detention home, she lived in the women's section, associating with feeble-minded and decrepit old women.

.   .   .   .   .

What are the outstanding conclusions with regard to rural dependency as covered by this study of conditions? One of the most striking is that there is universal indifference to the rights of dependent children, indifference on the part of public officials, and indifference on the part of private citizens, who, although familiar with conditions surrounding a child or a family of children, dismiss all responsibility for providing for their needs. The generally accepted standards for the care of dependent children are not applied in the case of rural children, because of the lack of understanding of rural folk, lack of vision, lack of knowledge, and lack of means of transportation.

Counteracting this spirit of indifference is the hospitable response made to the appeal of mothers, or the appeal of children, whom families receive into their homes, unwilling as they say "to turn any orphan away." This hospitality, however, is seldom accompanied by full understanding of the responsibility involved or by a sense of what is or what is not for the children's best interests. It is folly to believe that any home, just because it is in the open country, is a good home for any dependent child. It depends on the home and on the child. Rural folk may be kind, they may be hospitable and fond of children, yet in no sense be the best folk available for raising dependent children.

Perhaps the most urgent need of rural dependent children is at least one person in every county, capable, accessible, and vested with authority to befriend every dependent child and, in cooperation with all other child-protecting factors in the county and state, responsible for the best available care for every child according to his need. Such an agent, public or private or both, must be accessible, which means that he must be provided with the most rapid means of transportation practicable in his county; in some counties it may mean an auto; in others, a saddle horse; but accessible he must be. It is folly to expect an officer, however socially minded he may be, to remain at the county seat and know conditions surrounding children in the open country. Until he goes into the country and makes careful and thorough investigations there, he is not qualified to determine plans for the children's future.

It is very obvious that leadership technically trained for child-caring work is not now available to rural children in many counties. However, it is a fact that in practically every county there is living at least one person, in most cases a woman, who understands children, understands family problems and human nature, and is willing to undertake, with the tactful counsel of a well-trained state supervisor, the responsibility of developing a county-wide program for the care of all rural dependent children. Everywhere the need for her services is urgent.

---

2. Cleveland attacks the causes of dependency, 1925

United States Children's Bureau, *The*

Children's Bureau of Cleveland, Pub. No. 177 (Washington, D.C., 1927), pp. 85–87.

The Cleveland Children's Bureau, established in 1921, served as a central clearing agency for dependent children admitted to the city's institutions and placing-out societies.

Already the children's bureau and other child-welfare agencies of Cleveland are aware of the outstanding forces destroying children's homes and are formulating policies as to how best to meet the needs of children with whom these forces have played such havoc, but much more research must be done to know the subtler forces causing dependency. The extensive knowledge of causes of dependency has been made possible only by the uniform and thorough investigation of applications for the admission of children to institutions made by the Children's Bureau of Cleveland and of applications for foster-home care of children made by the Cleveland Humane Society.

The data indicate that illness of father or mother, chiefly of mother, was the first great cause of dependency of children in Cleveland; that divorce, separation, and desertion constituted the second greatest cause; and that death of one or both parents, but usually death of the mother, was the third.

From one point of view the increase in the number of children in need of community care due to illness of the mother is one of the most hopeful indications of the new sense of responsibility that is awakening in the community. The influence that health centers and hospital clinics have had in promoting better health for mothers and babies is shown in the greater demand for hospital care during illness, particularly during confinement. With the completion of a new maternity hospital in connection with Western Reserve University in Cleveland, it is expected that the need for temporary institutional care of children whose mothers are confined in the hospital rather than at home will be increased. Better health facilities have had

a direct influence on the population of children's institutions and agencies — temporary care of children during illness of mother becoming more extensive.

Separation, divorce, and desertion are the most baffling of all causes of dependency. It is hardly possible to speak of them as causes, since they are in reality symptoms of other conditions such as unemployment, ill health, mental defect, and difficult personality traits that are destroying the structure of the home. No other problem related to the dependency of children is so great a tax on the financial resources and on the skill of the staffs of social-welfare agencies as that of divorce, separation, and desertion. The difficulties in families broken by divorce or desertion are so complex that the work of medical and social agencies of a community must be well coordinated in order to salvage as many of these wrecked families as possible. This coordination of the agencies in Cleveland has been one of the distinct services of the children's bureau.

Death, usually of one parent but not often of both, as cause of dependency, though still a serious problem in planning for the care of children, is no longer so difficult to meet as formerly. The emphasis on better health, its promotion by local health authorities through clinics and by national organizations through educational propaganda, and the provision for aid to children in their own homes have accomplished much in the preservation of family ties. Cleveland unfortunately has not had a sufficient appropriation for the mothers' pensions department of the juvenile court to make it a real asset in the care of Cleveland families where the death or incapacity of the father has occurred. The result has been that the greatest number of these families have been carried by the Cleveland Associated Charities, which receives its support from the public at large through subscription to the Community Fund. The appropriation of an adequate amount of money to carry on the work of the mothers' pensions department would release the funds now used by the associated charities for care of widowed families, and then these funds might be used for the development of foster-home care of children through the Cleveland Humane Society, which has been hampered greatly through lack of funds. No entirely satisfactory method of providing for the widowers' families without placing the children away from their fathers has been evolved, but much attention is now being given to this problem.

Psychological approaches to child welfare

1. A training home for problem children, 1928

Elizabeth E. Bissell, "The Effect of Foster Home Placement on the Personality of Children," *The Family,* IX (1928), 157–162. By permission of the Family Service Association of America.

Elizabeth Bissell was director of the department of foster home care, New England Home for Little Wanderers, Boston.

The very flexibility of the system of foster home care works against the principle which we all know is fundamental, and that is consistent living and training for the child. In spite of the fact that we have tried to adhere to the principle of taking plenty of time in the beginning, knowing our child thoroughly and selecting the foster home which will be best adapted to his needs both as to physical environment and emotional factors, we do have too much change and too many upheavals. Foster mothers and fathers are not trained to understand and deal with the more intricate mechanisms of behavior in the children whom we are now placing. We have thought we could educate them to the job, and perhaps we could

do more satisfactory work along this line if the case load per visitor could be considerably reduced, but I am interested in the question of how many foster mothers and fathers really and truly take advice from their visitors and act on it. How many of us like to act on other people's counsel? And when it comes to the question of training children we see very few foster parents who are willing to adopt other ideas than those they have carried for years.

.   .   .   .   .

What is needed is a more professional attitude on the part of people who deal with our children day by day: An attitude of trying to find a way around each difficulty that arises, a warm interest in children and yet a scientific spirit that is interested in working out new methods and principles. Our diagnostic methods are good; our day-by-day training is poor. We have a great opportunity to contribute much to the body of knowledge on the subject of method if people with training and insight would go into the job of taking children, and if child-placing agencies would recognize the need of small training homes where adults with training have actual charge of the children — adults whose motive is first and foremost re-educating the child to be a socially effective person; adults who understand what is behind the unacceptable behavior and deal with it in a sincere, honest, courageous manner.

Such a training home does exist. It is conducted by a social worker who understands the children placed with her and whose technique in method is developing continually through her experience. I should like to tell you about Agnes, fourteen years old, who has been in this training home for nearly two years. Agnes was a very disturbed personality when her problem was first known to the children's society. She is the eldest of three children (the other two are boys — one ten and the other eight). At the time of placement the mother had gone to the state hospital on a voluntary commitment. She had become increasingly seclusive and ingrowing and unnaturally hard in her attitude toward the children. She had been a school teacher and had married late in life. The father had been her pupil in high school and was thirteen years her junior. He had always retained the pupil attitude through the years of their living together, and the mother the teacher attitude, decidedly dominating the situation. Her one insistent ambition seemed to be to have her children develop into models of scholarship. At the time of her mental breakdown, Agnes was not able to live up to her mother's excessive ambition for her and had ceased making an effort. She was extremely shy and withdrawn and had developed very little social feeling. Due to the mother's seclusiveness the child had had no chance to make contacts outside the home. She showed little spontaneity and had no interest in her youngest brother, the baby of the family; in fact, she said she hated him. Agnes came to the training home with a great burden of family disruption and discord upon her, and the task of her re-education began.

The first phase of shyness soon wore off. As soon as the repressions of her own home were lifted, she reacted to the opposite extreme and became quite a "rowdy." She desired always to be the center of attention. She developed a strident voice and a rather swaggering manner and was aggressive and over-affectionate and very selfish. The foster mother tried to understand this phase of behavior — difficult though it was. Knowing how little the child had felt she counted as a real person in her own home, she tried to give her opportunities to count in worthwhile ways and to give her real recognition for what she did in a helpful way. She gave logical explanations for everything that was required of the child and when it was necessary to give punishment, planned it so that only Agnes was inconvenienced. Recreational activities were planned for her and the neighborhood children invited in for Friday frolics.

In school the child felt competition keenly and would not try, believing always that she was bound to fail. She was kept at home and tutored for some weeks, and in the quiet, non-competitive atmosphere of the home this tension less-

ened and Agnes gradually found that she could progress little by little if she tried. Recognition was given for each accomplishment, not over-praise but recognition commensurate with the progress. She was gradually learning that one does not always need to be in the limelight in order to be noticed; that some good honest effort on her part brings its own satisfaction. Thus she was encouraged to test herself still further. Gradually she began to do some helpful things for the foster mother unasked, and to get a bit of the co-operative spirit on which the training home is organized. She began to show a sense of humor and gradually the foster mother found that she could point out the funny side of some failures to the child and she would even laugh at herself and say, "Gee, wasn't I a goop?" She longed to be athletic so skis were purchased for her and the foster mother found teaching possibilities in this project, and opportunities for the child to develop courage and good sportsmanship. At the end of three months she visited her own home. Her mother had returned for a visit though still under the supervision of the hospital. She found Agnes alive and bubbling with excitement, a real contrast to her former repression.

The next phase of behavior which we find developing is jealousy of another girl of her own age who was placed in the training home. To help meet this problem, the foster mother explained a little of each girl's situation to the other and tried through clear explanation to have them understand each other. Agnes is jealous of Helen's greater popularity and easy way of making friends, so the foster mother points out to Agnes her own assets and successes and tells her that just as she overcame her difficulties in scholarship so can she overcome her difficulties in her disposition, her tendency to have a chip on her shoulder and to expect friends to come crowding round her instead of doing something herself to win friends. Each girl has her place in the foster mother's affections and comparisons are never made between the two girls.

It is a slow process but there is steady growth

in dependability and effective social co-operation. The child understands her relationship to the foster mother and to the home. She knows she will always have a square deal from the foster mother and will be dealt with frankly and truthfully. There is no mystery to be feared. In this warm atmosphere of interest and understanding and equal give and take, she is learning what interesting things there are to do in the world besides being bound up in one's own selfish desires and expecting the world to come to one's feet. The training home is demonstrating a true experiment in social living.

The reason the problem child can be re-educated more effectively in this sort of home is that the home really has to revolve about the child for a time until some of the rough corners are smoothed down and the personality conforms a bit more to the normal. A foster mother, with her own family problems and worries, finds it very difficult so to organize her affairs that the environment for the foster child is softened and moulded to meet his particular difficulty while he is learning to stand on his own feet and face things squarely. The trained worker can safely know every scrap of history and use it wisely and can interpret the child's family to him and the child to the family, for through visits and contacts the director at the home is helping the members of the family as well as the child to modify their attitudes.

I believe that the organization of such training homes is the next progressive step toward the effective re-education of problem children who have seriously deviated from the normal line of development.

2. Changing psychological premises, 1918–1930

Jessie Taft, "A Changing Psychology in Child Welfare," *The Annals* of the American Academy of Political and Social Science, CLI (1930), 122–128.

Dr. Taft worked with the Children's Aid Society of Pennsylvania and directed the Department of Child Study, Seybert Institution, Philadelphia.

In 1918, children placed in foster homes by the agency in question were understood almost entirely in behavioristic terms . . . We saw only what the child did. If what he did was acceptable to foster parents and community, we heaved a sigh of relief; good children were never conceivably in need of understanding. If he stood out in the foster home as too peculiar, too different, we took him to the neurologist; if he was actively disturbing and antisocial, we joined with the foster parents in devising punishments and correctives, or we sided with the child against the foster parents and got him a new home, where he would get better treatment. The child whom no punishment cured and no foster parent would endure, ended in some institution.

But already in 1918, psychology and psychiatry were upon us . . . The influences were apparent at first in the growing consciousness of a need to control processes, and in the belief that such control could be attained only through the discovery of causal connections. If we could find what caused the behavior which was so destructive, perhaps we might do something about it — perhaps we could learn to know in advance whether or not a given placement would be successful, or how to alter habits which the parents could not endure and punishment failed to correct.

Heredity offered the first clue, and we have the eugenics field worker to thank for our beginning interest in a history of the child's family background . . . We were eager to find the cause of stealing, or sex interest, in the similar tendencies of parents, siblings, or relatives further removed; but this proved too sterile a solution.

For the case worker whose interest is therapy

and not theory, and who lives to see a child successfully placed in a foster home, the uselessness of heredity to do anything but explain and excuse, its finality for the unhappy child who happens to have a bad history, and the impossibility of utilizing it in a constructive treatment process, soon led to the abandonment of that trail. However, the emphasis on constitutional factors was not without its reward for the child placing agency, for soon afterwards came the psychometric test as a diagnostic agent, more reliable than the uncertain family tree, and promising some immediate practical estimate of the kind of child to be placed, at least in so far as his native mental equipment was concerned.

.   .   .   .   .

The failure of the psychometric test to solve the whole problem of behavior rapidly led to a discrimination between the emotional and the intellectual factors, between innate ability and adjustment, and thus, for the first time, to the comprehension of child placing as a psychological as well as a practical problem, in which there is no short cut, no possible avoidance of the effort to understand personality in its emotional and impulsive aspects.

It is interesting to note the two general directions in which our necessity to understand has led us — the one towards the search for causal connections, no longer in heredity, but in genetic developmental history and immediate family relationships; the other towards the describing, the measuring, the gauging, the seeing of the child as he is presented to us at the moment.

The belief that the facts of a social and developmental history were important, and somehow held curative powers, has been with us from the first. For a long time we accumulated elaborate statements of facts which gave us comfort but which we sometimes confessed to ourselves seemed of very little practical significance.

.   .   .   .   .

Despite this confusion of theory and practice, children were helped; transformations occurred; the child who had been a devil in one home was seen to grow into an angel in another, and vice versa. We saw something happening, but we did not know exactly how or why. We explained to foster parents, and at the same time to ourselves, why this particular child was exhibiting these particular symptoms. Sometimes we even explained it to the child. We thought that if we could give causal explanations, cure would follow, and sometimes it did — not because of the explanation, for we now know how little factual knowledge has to do with emotional reality, but because somehow through our efforts to understand, both we and the foster parents were able to identify with the child despite his behavior, and in the change of attitude thus produced, the child found release.

This hodgepodge of theory without consistency, and with a therapy whose basis we did not clearly see, was drawn into an ordered whole of consistent, thoroughgoing, psychological interpretation, with treatment logically based on actual findings, for the first time, about 1926, by Dr. Marion Kenworthy, in what her students have learned to know as the ego-libido method.

.   .   .   .

This point of view differentiates the love interest (libido) from the ego or self-maximation interest, and clearly recognizes that an individual may find satisfaction for either need in experiences which tend to hinder normal growth. This permits us to see such a habit as enuresis, for example, in several aspects — as satisfying to a libidinal need, dissatisfying to ego pride, and, on the whole, destructive to both love and ego growth.

This analysis and evaluation of experiences is applicable to parents as well as to children, to foster parents as well as to real parents, and gives a basis for interpreting the immediate present relationships as existing in the family . . .

Moreover, after every detail known to us in

the life history has been weighed, we should be in a position to see, almost on a quantitative basis, where treatment lies — whether the destructive development has been primarily on the ego or libidinal side, what there is of constructive experience to build on, and what type of constructive satisfying experiences are needed to even the imbalance or to release the infantile individual for growth towards maturity in the socially acceptable way.

. . . . .

To describe the present situation, psychologically speaking, as it exists in the agency with which the writer is most familiar, is no easy task. Certain shifts in emphasis are very apparent. The child is no longer the target for direct attack, either by psychologist or case worker. He is to be understood either in terms of his developmental experiences, or through direct observation of his present patterns as they come out in the various contacts in which the worker can get first-hand information.

In foster-home supervision, the worker now accepts her function as largely confined to the foster parents, to whom she leaves all intimate contacts with the child, and whose relation to the child she tries to observe directly. She understands much better than she once did that if the placement is to become permanent, it will do so only as the foster parents take over full responsibility for the child, who will look to them, and not to the worker, for his security. She has learned not to be disturbed by symptoms, and to recognize even sex manifestations as largely symptomatic.

The worker's effort is not so much to suggest correctives or interpret behavior, as to reassure foster parents through her own attitude, and to bring into the situation a tolerance and a freedom from fear which may alter the interplay of forces lying back of the symptoms. She recognizes *her* relation to the foster parents as the therapeutic agent, in so far as there is one. If they can become aware of some of their problems, and get release from fear, irritation, or guilt through her understanding and acceptance of them, the whole situation may improve. If they cannot, no direct treatment of the child, whose problem is in relation to them, seems likely to help very much.

. . . . .

The worker who approaches her task in this spirit is expressing a profound change in the psychological basis on which she works. Once, knowledge was enough. Once, we were satisfied to understand intellectually the life experiences of child and foster parent, to set them down in black and white and figure out in advance just what each combination ought to produce in the way of results. Now, we know that such exact one-to-one correspondence of psychological factors in living situations does not necessarily work out as planned by us. These paper causes and effects have a way of taking on an independent life when let loose in immediate dynamic relationships. We have become much more humble in laying down complete plans for other people, much less glib in handing out rationalized formulae as cures. We are more ready now to admit that we deal with human emotions and human wills first-hand, not only in our clients but also in ourselves; that no developmental history can substitute for the living present, and no past cause can be recreated to control an immediate situation.

We have talked for a decade about individualizing the child, but it has been largely a literary individualization. The period of description, of intellectual acceptance, seems to be passing. As we approach the child today there is a genuine respect for his pattern; a profound realization that any vital change will come from within through his own choice and determination. We no longer set ourselves to alter his make-up, mold his will, or weigh and measure the exact amount of security or satisfaction we have decided he needs. Rather, we are more willing to admit from the beginning that he is already an individual whose make-up we are bound to accept, and that at best our function is limited. We are fortunate, indeed, if our understanding of his personality enables us to select a home in which he will realize some measure of freedom to be himself — to develop not merely in resistance or submission, but positively, according to his own nature.

Part Four Juvenile Delinquency

During the second half of the nineteenth century, the number and variety of reform schools for juvenile delinquents increased greatly but so too did the severity of institutional problems. Outside of the deep South, where few provisions were made for delinquents until after 1900, state governments established separate reform schools for boys and girls and separate reformatories for young men and women, ages sixteen to thirty, who were first-time offenders. Beginning with the Elmira, New York, Reformatory (1869), these institutions utilized the indeterminate sentence and the mark system (institutional rewards for good behavior). According to penologist Frederick Wines, "the methods adopted resembled those which had long been in use in institutions for the reformation of juvenile offenders." [1]

Following the Civil War, welfare services of individual states expanded greatly and the consequent demand upon state revenue forced reform schools and other penal institutions to place increased emphasis upon earning part of their own income by contracting the labor of inmates to local manufacturers. This development hindered further growth of genuine farm reform schools such as those begun in the 1850's in Ohio and Massachusetts and even led to the conversion of some farm schools (the New Jersey reform school at Jamesburg, for instance) into traditional institutions with congregate workshops.[2] As a rule, manufacturers controlled the children during work hours and instances of exploitation and brutality were not uncommon. "I have seen boys punished for not completing their tasks, so that blood ran down into their boots," reported a former employee of the New York House of Refuge in 1871.[3] Occasionally the children retaliated. Rioting, incendiarism, and even murder marked the history of nearly every institution. In 1877, for example, Superintendent Loring Lathrop of the Massachusetts girls' reform school reported, "House No. 3, an old building . . . replete with interesting associations, was burned to the ground, having been set on fire by two of our inmates." [4] There seems little reason to doubt the wider applicability of James Leiby's characterization of the New Jersey state reform school as "not a family, nor a reformatory, but a boys' prison." [5]

Concerned citizens and elected officials recognized the failure of reform schools and made efforts both to improve institutional life and to prevent children from being incarcerated in the first place. Special state legislative committees investigated abuses in the contract labor system in New York (1871) and Pennsylvania (1876) and, with the establishment of state boards of charity in most states, reform schools like other public institutions were subjected to annual inspections by an outside regulatory agency. In 1884, William Pryor Letchworth, president of the New York State Board of Charity, influenced the legislature to outlaw contract labor in reform schools and, the next year, was instrumental in gaining state support to introduce, at

1. Frederick Wines, *Punishment and Reformation* (New York, 1918), pp. 207–208.

2. On the origin of farm schools, see Volume One, pp. 705–708, 726–728.

3. New York State Assembly, "Report of the Commission on Prison Labor," Doc. 18, *Documents, 1871,* IV, (Albany, 1871), 181.

4. Massachusets State Industrial School for Girls at Lancaster, *Twenty-Second Annual Report, 1877* (Boston, 1878), p. 16.

5. James Leiby, *Charities and Correction in New Jersey* (New Brunswick, 1967), p. 82.

the Western House of Refuge (Rochester), the first comprehensive plan of vocational education.

Improved reform schools, however, developed slowly or often not at all and, as a result of the mood of futility associated with their work, different kinds of private institutions, designed to save semi-delinquent children from reform schools as well as from crime, were established. The Burnham Industrial Farm (1887) sought to recapture the ideal of agrarian reform schools by implementing an authentic cottage system and farm routine while the George Junior Republic (1895) emphasized juvenile self-government as a means of reformation and improvement. Women's organizations in a number of states, beginning with Illinois (1879), established industrial schools for troublesome girls who needed "to be kept safe for a year or two." [6]

Distrust of reform schools also manifested itself in the combined activities of charitable organizations and state legislatures and the skeptical attitude of the law. Some states authorized children's aid societies to represent delinquents in court or to receive them prior to trial and to supervise their probation. Massachusetts (1869) and Michigan (1873) even provided state probation agents for delinquent children. Several legal decisions, but especially People v. Turner [55 Illinois 280 (1870)] challenged the parental role of the state (*parens patriae*) as it was exercised by reform schools. Under this doctrine, institutions detained their youthful inmates, some of whom were merely orphans or vagrants, by presuming to educate and protect them instead of punishing them. The Illinois court concluded to the contrary that the reform school boy was ". . . a prisoner made subject to the will of others" and reasoned therefore that he at least ought to have the same legal rights as an adult convict.[7]

The development of the juvenile court represented the culmination of various efforts to reform children without committing them to reform schools. The Illinois juvenile court law (1899), first of its kind, combined the concept of probation as developed in Massachusetts with several New York laws providing for special trial sessions for and detention of delinquents. There was, however, no provision for paying probation officers, a deliberate omission based upon the belief that officers appointed through political influence "would render the law useless and inoperative." [8] In order to sustain the state's right to assume parental power over children, the new court was explicitly designated a chancery or non-criminal court of equity which, by definition, assumed that disposition of juvenile cases would be in the best interests of the child and need not be overly concerned with the child's legal rights.

The founders of the juvenile court succeeded in their purposes. By 1912 twenty-two states had passed juvenile court legislation; in 1932 every state in the country, except Maine and Wyoming, had juvenile courts organized under special laws and Maine had provisions for probation and separate hearings of children's cases in regular courts. More important, the legality of the juvenile court was upheld in a number of decisions. The chancery nature of its proceedings rendered the court impregnable, for the time being, to the charge that it deprived children of their legal rights.

The growth and systemization of the juvenile court also led to an expansion of court services. Probation could no longer be entrusted to irregular voluntary agents, but became the work of civil service professionals trained in the art of social investigation at the new schools of social work. Family or domestic relations courts, deal-

6. Hastings H. Hart, *Preventive Treatment of Neglected Children* (New York, 1910), p. 72.
7. Subsequent decisions took issue with People v. Turner, and defined reform schools as non-penal and therefore did not allow juvenile offenders the legal safeguards supposedly accorded adults. See, for example, *Ex parte* Ah Peen, 51 Cal. 280 (1876); *In the matter* of Ferrier, 103 Ill. 367 (1882); Milwaukee Industrial School v. The Supervisors of Milwaukee County, 40 Wisc. 328 (1876) and Rule v. Geddes, 23 App. D.C. 31 (1904). These and similar decisions cited *Ex parte* Crouse, 4 Wharton 9 (Pa., 1838), discussed in Vol. I, pp. 671–672, 691–693.
8. *Charities*, X (Jan. 3, 1903), 14–15.

ing with cases of non-support and desertion as well as juvenile delinquency, augmented the work of juvenile courts. Buffalo established the first domestic relations court in 1910. In 1914, Judge Charles W. Hoffman of Cincinnati defined the family court as the product of "increasing the jurisdiction of the juvenile court and designating it by the more comprehensive term . . ." [9] Other courts such as the Chicago Boy's Court (1914) extended the juvenile court procedures to adolescents over juvenile court age (generally 16–21 years of age).

Juvenile courts enjoyed widespread but not unanimous support. Immigrant and minority groups occasionally saw the court and its probation staff as wolves in sheeps' clothing — benevolent guises designed to steal their children under the rationale of *parens patriae*. Other critics believed that the court had grown beyond its means and, in the words of sociologist Thomas D. Eliot, "became a sort of 'department of maladjusted children'." [10] The expanding bureaucracy of juvenile justice and

9. Charles W. Hoffman, "Social Aspects of the Family Court," *Journal of Criminal Law and Criminology,* X (November 1919), 409–422.

10. Thomas D. Eliot, *The Juvenile Court and the Community* (New York, 1914), p. 17.

the proliferation of detention homes connected with juvenile courts led, contrary to the original intention of the juvenile court movement, to increased commitments to reform schools. To counter these trends, Eliot and other commentators recommended that public school systems take over most of the functions of the juvenile court.

Whatever the value of the juvenile court as a reformatory agency, it did prove important as a repository of the social and psychological histories of individual delinquents. The court's administrative power and generally urban location — where case histories were available and delinquents themselves could be studied — allowed it to serve as a laboratory for the professional study of delinquency. By studying the mental problems of children in the Chicago and Boston juvenile courts, psychologist William Healy overturned the traditional scientific explanations of delinquency as being related to bodily form or defective ancestry. Sociologists and ecologists at the University of Chicago also used the records of the Chicago court to study the poverty and social disorganization which shaped the delinquent careers of children in the urban slums.

I. Delinquency in the Late Nineteenth Century

A. JUVENILE DELINQUENCY IN THE SOUTH

Children in jail

Conditions in Southern prisons were so bad that younger offenders were often pardoned.

Blacks, often put in jail or leased on contract to railroad companies for committing minor offenses, constituted the bulk of the prison population.

1. Negro children in the Mississippi State Penitentiary

a. Mississippi House of Representatives, *Journal, 1873* (Jackson, 1873), pp. 573, 580.

Name	County	Crime	Term	Expiration of sentence	Age	Height (ft., in.)	Description
Day, Robert	Amite	Murder	Life		12	4-9	Complexion black, hair and eyes black, scar from dog-bite on calf of right leg, scar on left arm, dim scar corner left eye.
Harrington, Jas	Yazoo	Burglary with intent to rape	Ten years	October 27, 1880	13	5-1	Complexion black, hair and eyes black, second small toe on each foot deformed.

b. Mississippi. *Biennial Report of the Superintendent, Physician and Chaplain of the Mississippi Penitentiary, 1878–1879* (Jackson, 1880), pp. 15, 50.

Name	County	Crime	Term	Expiration of sentence	Age	Height (ft., in.)	Description
Brown, Adaline	Yalobusha	Mingling poison with milk	Five years	May 30, 1883	14	5-2	Black, hair and eyes black, woman.
Hale, Moses	Washington	Murder	Life		13	5-8	Black, hair and eyes black, mole on back of neck.

2. A Negro boy in the South Carolina State Penitentiary, 1880

Rupert Sargeant Holland, ed., *Letters and Diary of Laura M. Towne* (Cambridge, Mass., 1912), p. 302.

Laura M. Towne (1835–1901) was a Boston-born abolitionist who devoted her life to the education and care of the freedmen of St. Helena, one of the South Carolina Sea Islands.

May 23, 1880   Evening

Rina and Ellen are all excitement about the sermon of today.[1] The young minister, who has been to Columbia to a theological school, went to the penitentiary to see some people he knew, and the description he gives of the convicts is too horrible to tell. He says "the Democrats must think there is no hell for bad people, for they make a hell of that prison." Men are there chained with their necks in an iron collar and joined to ankle chains. They never take these off. A young boy of fourteen, sentenced to five years for only *being in* a whiskey shop where a man was killed, wears hand cuffs, and the poor fellow . . . prays night and day that God will let him die. The irons have cut into his wrists. The beds are rotten straw, full of vermin.

The keeper said to Ishmael Williams (the minister) when he paid his entrance fee, "you have come, I suppose, to see how we take niggers down. I'll show you." Then he began with the treatment, in which he said they soon took the stiffness and strength out of the new-comers. I can't tell you all, but the whole church broke out with groans, and the elders

1. Rina was the chief household servant at Frogmore, Miss Towne's plantation. Ellen Murray was Miss Towne's friend and co-worker for many years.

cried and shook their heads and wiped their faces as if every one had a friend there.

3. Executive clemency for Georgia children, 1895

Georgia House of Representatives, *Journal, 1895* (Atlanta, 1895), pp. 78–79, 82.

The pardons were granted by William Yates Atkinson (1855–1899), Governor of Georgia 1894–1898.

William Whitlock. — Convicted of misdemeanor, county court of Elbert county, August, 1894; sentence, twelve months in chain-gang. Pardoned in consideration of the fact that the defendant is quite a youth, about thirteen years of age, that he pleaded guilty to the offense, and that he is a simple, weak-minded boy.

.   .   .   .   .

Hardy Bragg. — Convicted of arson, May term, 1894, Screven county; sentence, three years. October the time offense was committed. Bragg was only twelve years of age and he was induced to commit it by an adult relative. Petition indorsed by judge, solicitor-general, and a large number of citizens.

.   .   .   .   .

Wade Hampton. — Convicted of burglary, October term, 1893, Fulton county; sentence, five years. At time of his conviction was a mere child, and since confinement has lost a leg. Application for pardon indorsed by judge and several of the county officers. Pardoned after serving one half of his sentence.

Institutions for delinquents

Institutions for juvenile delinquents were established in the border states, but children in the deep South continued to be treated as adult criminals.

---

1. Cause and cure of delinquency among Negroes, 1900

John Henry Smyth, "Negro Criminality," *The Southern Workman and Farm School Record,* XXIX (1900), 630–631.

John Henry Smyth (1844–1908), a free-born Negro, was educated at the Pennsylvania Academy of Fine Arts. In 1872, after teaching in Pennsylvania public schools, he graduated from the Howard University Law School. In 1878 President Hayes appointed him minister to Liberia, a post he held until 1885 when he became editor of the Richmond, Virginia, *Reformer.* His crusade to remove delinquent Negro boys from Virginia jails was realized with the establishment in 1897 of the Virginia Manual Labor School, a private institution financed in part by the railroad magnate, Collis P. Huntington.

Negro parents who were themselves victims of oppression as well as those who were born under the benign influences of freedom, have crude and unwise notions about the duty of requiring their children to do some kind of work. Too many Negro children are guarded from soiling their hands and developing their muscles with necessary and useful toil. The struggling, industrious widow as well as the well-conditioned housewife whose husband has a good home and makes a good living, seeks to relieve her children of work. This encouragment of

laziness can have but one outcome — the living in the sweat of others' faces than their own. Under conditions such as these, parents possessed of radically ignorant and wrong notions about rearing their children, unconsciously cultivate tendencies which lead to criminality. To the extent that a child's mind becomes familiar with higher conditions and mind-work, to that degree does physical exertion in the way of mere muscle-work become distasteful, and as a result the child becomes less efficient as a mere breadwinner by the sweat of his brow. Education is chargeable with producing a condition for which parents and not school-teachers are responsible. Complete and entire reform in our system of home-training of our boys and girls will go far to relieve youthful Negroes of just censure for ill-breeding. How far all these reflections are applicable to the rearing and training of white children is for white parents to consider.

·   ·   ·   ·

What are the remedies for existing criminality, and how may its increase be checked? Popular secular education for whites and blacks, compulsory, if possible, erected on a broad basis of Christianity, is the only safe, enduring, moral, and economic remedy. Mere secular education may not be relied upon to restrain crime, and we must honestly own that our only hope is in the diffusion of true religion . . . If the Holy Scriptures be not the basis of all worthy knowledge our civilization is a fraud. Individual philanthropy has done much towards aiding in the matter of education, particularly so-called higher education. May not individual wealth help to minimize ignorance, dissipate poverty, help the feeble in mind and morals of the race to robust Christian manhood? . . .

The reform schools for juveniles throughout the North and West, and those in Virginia, represent Christian agencies for the reduction and destruction of crime in its germinal state, and are a display of wise and humane statesmanship on the part of legislators. The white people of Virginia, ever responsive to appeals in behalf of human need, made possible the Virginia Manual Labor School at Broad Neck Farm, Hanover, Va. It was this sentiment in behalf of moral reform among Negro children and youths that brought to the aid of this institution the interested concern of a man of wealth and national influence, whose sympathy for the poor and ignorant of his countrymen, white and black, is as broad and far-reaching as ignorance and human suffering. This reformatory, opened September 12, 1899, and aided by the state February 5, 1900, began with a nucleus of five Negro boys, and has now under its guardianship fifty-two children. It has thus early demonstrated conclusively that saving and redemptive elements of character exist in Negro children no less than in those of other races; also that for tractableness and responsiveness to kindly influences, delinquent Negro children show themselves of legitimate kinship to that race among whom, as the classic writer tells us, "the gods delighted to disport themselves — the gentle Ethiopians."

---

2. Governor Jeff Davis of Arkansas proposes an institution for black and white juvenile offenders, 1905

Arkansas House of Representatives, *Journal, 1905* (Hot Springs, 1905), pp. 31–32.

Jeff Davis (1862–1913), governor of Arkansas from 1901 to 1907 and United States Senator from 1907 to 1913, made his reputation as a vigorous opponent of trusts and as a demagogic orator who catered to the prejudices of rural voters. As governor, he urged more liberal appropriations for state charitable institutions and larger pensions for the veterans of the Confederate army.

". . . I have laid special stress upon the need for a reform school in this state . . . It has been my policy, in order to bring about a public discussion of this subject and force a public knowledge of the necessity of this institution, to pardon all white boys under the age of eighteen confined in the penitentiary, regardless of the crime they had committed . . . In all preceding sessions of the Legislature . . . the argument has been made that there are too many negroes under this age confined in the penitentiary, and that the institution would amount in fact to an institution for the correction of negro juvenile offenders: that the proportion of white boys under this age that are sent to the penitentiary, as compared to the negroes, is so small that we had better suffer the ills of the white boys being confined than to populate an institution of this kind largely with negroes. With this sentiment I do not agree. If we can but save one white boy . . . we will have accomplished more of real good for the State than such an institution would cost us. But the facts and figures since I have been your Governor do not bear out the contention of the obstructionists in this direction. During the four years I have been Governor there have been confined in all 115 white boys under the age of eighteen . . . During the same period there have been confined 217 negroes under this age . . . The suggestion that I would make along this line and which would earnestly impress upon you is this: Authorize the Governor to appoint three discreet citizens as a committee to buy a cheap piece of land somewhere adjacent to Little Rock, say 160 acres, costing not over $2,000 or $3,000, upon which fair crops might be raised . . . where white boys might be taught some useful occupation and the negro boys compelled to work and support the institution while it is being done. This would prove a blessing, not only to the white boy, but to the negro boy as well . . .

---

3. Dormitory paid for by labor of reform school boys, Kentucky, 1907

"Annual Report of the Kentucky House of Reform, 1907" in Kentucky *Documents, 1906–1907* (Louisville, 1908), pp. 4–5.

When the control of this Institution passed to the Board of Penitentiary Commissioners in March, 1906, we found but one dormitory for white boys and this was so crowded that the youthful inmates were required to sleep two in a single bed and many others were confined in the jails in the State, because the facilities in the Institution for caring for more were inadequate. There were some instances in which children under sentence for some petty crime, were confined in the county jail in the county of their conviction for as long as eight months before room could be made for them at the House of Reform. Notwithstanding the improvements that the Board and Superintendents have made at the Institution, for the accommodation of a greater number of inmates at the Institution, the condition in the State is now nearly as bad, and in many jails in the State there are inmates under sentence waiting to be conveyed to the School of Reform when room can be made for them.

Since the passage of the Juvenile Court Act in 1906, the population of this Institution has increased from three hundred to about four hundred and fifty. The Board realizing the very crowded condition of the Institution, made a contract with the Ford & Johnson Co., by which that company erected two dormitories, one being now used for white boys and the other for colored boys, the cost of the two being $10,189.64 without the furnishings or heating; the Ford & Johnson Company paying for the buildings and being repaid by the Board in the labor of the inmates over fourteen years of age, who work four and one half hours a day in the construction of reed chairs and other reed work. The price paid by the Ford & Johnson Company for the labor of these boys is at the rate of thirty cents per day. Since the contract has gone into effect, the labor of the inmates has extinguished the indebtedness of the Board to the Ford & Johnson Company,

on account of the erection of the two dormitories, to the extent of $4,221.79. Much is necessary to be done to make the Institution a creditable one to the State, and a habitable one for the inmates, and we must earnestly call your attention to, and request you to call the attention of the Legislature to the needs of the Institution.

4. A reform school for "juvenile negro law breakers," Alabama, 1911

"An act to create and establish a reform school for the training of juvenile negro law breakers . . . ," 1911 — ch. 336. *General Laws of Alabama, 1911* (Montgomery, 1911), 678–680.

There is hereby created and established at Mont Meigs, Montgomery county, Alabama, a reform school for educating and training juvenile negro law-breakers, to be governed and controlled by a board of trustees, composed of the governor, the superintendent of education, and seven other trustees, five of whom may be negro women who are interested in the proper education and training of juvenile negro law-breakers, to be appointed by the governor by and with the advice and consent of the senate.

．　　．　　．　　．　　．

The school is established for the proper education and training of juvenile negro law-breakers, as may be lawfully committed to it. The course of instruction in the school shall include a common school education, with a thorough training in agriculture and industries, and giving special attention to moral training so as to make him a self respecting, industrious, good citizen. Provided, that no criminal over the age of fifteen years shall be admitted to said institution.

The board of trustees accept land and building at Mount Meigs where the reformatory is now located, and known as the "reformatory for negro boys," under the management of the State federation of colored women's clubs, incorporated under the laws of Alabama. The board of trustees shall take charge of the property and school and manage and control it under this act . . . If any trustees should die, or resign the governor shall appoint a successor to hold for the unexpired term. All trustees for the school shall be appointed by the governor by and with the consent and advice of the senate.

. . . . . .

The authorities of the school shall receive every negro boy who may be committed to it by an order or judgment of any court of record to the State of Alabama, and support, govern and teach the boy until he shall be of the age of eighteen years or legally discharged from the school.

. . . . . .

For the support and maintenance of the school there is hereby appropriated the sum of one dollar and seventy-five cents per week for every boy lawfully attending and being instructed in the school, which shall be paid monthly upon the sworn statement of the president of the school and approved by the governor, out of the State treasury. The expense for transporting such boys, including the expenses of one guard, shall be paid out of the State treasury upon the sworn statement of the president of the school and approved by the governor.

B. REFORM SCHOOLS

School ships

of ship school reformatories in New York and San Francisco.

1. The Massachusetts Nautical Reform School, 1860–1870

Enoch C. Wines and Theodore W. Dwight, *Report on the Prisons and Reformatories of the United States and Canada* (Albany, 1867), pp. 353–358.

The Massachusetts Ship School, established in 1860, was intended both to reform delinquents and to contribute well-trained seamen to the merchant marine. It was abandoned in 1872 as a result of serious disciplinary problems, heavy operating expenses, and economic depressions which put adult seamen out of work and made further job competition unwelcome. Similar factors explain the demise

Massachusetts boasts one institution for youthful offenders quite unique in its character — the Nautical Branch of the State Reform School. The inmates of this institution, to the number of 160, were accommodated, when we visited it, in the Ship *Massachusetts,* of 650 tons burthen, then lying in Boston harbor. Another ship, considerably larger and capable of receiving 200 pupils with their officers, was then fitting up, and nearly ready for occupancy. It has been now, for a year or more, fulfilling the noble purpose to which it is destined so long as it shall be fit for use at all. These two ships, it will be seen, are capable of affording accommodations for 360 juvenile delinquents, who may have been committed to them by the proper authorities. One of them is stationed in Boston harbor, and the other in the harbor of New Bedford; but both spend a good part of the summer in cruising about the waters of Massachusetts, and visiting its various seaport towns.

The limit of age at which boys are excluded from the reform school at Westborough is 14; but they can be received into the school-ships up to the age of 18. The superintendent of the *Massachusetts,* when we visited her, was Capt. Richard Matthews, and the teacher, Mr. Martin L. Eldridge. Both of these gentlemen seemed to us eminently adapted to their work, and they were zealously devoted to it, even to enthusiasm. The boys were divided into equal sections. The members of each section were in school every other day. For our gratification, Mr. Eldridge put them through various exercises, the subjects of examination being arithmetic, geography, history, and especially navigation, on which latter branch the instruction seemed to have been particularly thorough. All the questions put were answered with the utmost alacrity, and with a promptness and accuracy which were surprising. They also sang a number of sailors' songs with a spirit and fervor, which showed that their soul was in the exercise. The section not engaged in lesson learning were on duty in cleansing the ship, cooking the meals, setting and clearing the tables, and other domestic employments; in repairing sails and rigging; in going through every variety of nautical evolution; in gaining a knowledge of sheet and halyard, brace and clewline, and the technical language of sailors; in short, in becoming practical seamen. A ready comprehension and rapid execution of orders, the dextrous handling of rope and oar, and the ability to climb the rigging with ease and rapidity, are thus acquired. The summer cruises are anticipated with eagerness, and enjoyed with a keen relish by the boys; and they serve at once to develop and to test their seamanship.

.   .   .   .   .

One hundred and seventy-two boys were sentenced to the ship in 1865. As showing the character of these youths, Capt. Matthews reports that of this number there were committed for assault and battery, two; assault with intent to rob, two; breaking and entering to steal, 32; idle and disorderly, one; incendiary, two; larceny, 70; malicious mischief, two; stubbornness, 44; vagrancy, two; returned from probation, seven; transferred from state reform school, eight. It is a sad view of the case of these boys that nearly two-thirds of them had lost one or both of their parents. Fifty-five had been arrested once previously; twenty-four, twice; eight, three times; two, four times; and two, five or six times. Thirty-one were habitual drinkers of ardent spirits, and ninety-five were in the constant use of tobacco. Their ages were as follows: Seven were 12 years old; seven, 13; thirty-eight, 14; fifty-three, 15; twenty-seven, 16; and forty, 17 — the average of their ages being about 15 years. Of the 172 received, two did not know the alphabet; seven could not read at all; 34 could read a little in the first reader; 75 could read in the second reader; 40 could read in the third reader, and only 16 in the fourth; 23 could not write; 41 had not studied arithmetic; 65 had studied mental arithmetic, and 66 had studied written arithmetic more or less. The average length of time during which the boys had not attended school prior to their commitment, exceeded twenty months. Of course, they had forgotten much which they had previously learned.

Captain Matthews makes the following interesting statements in his report:

.   .   .   .   .

"The graduates from this institution, so far as heard from, have generally done well; some, as might be expected, have lapsed into the pursuit of evil courses, but a great majority are doing well, and giving evidence of thorough reform. The fidelity and devotion of those who have served their country during the war, in the navy and army, is very gratifying, and will ever be a source of just pride in the institution which in part, at least, prepared their hearts to love and hands to defend the land of their birth.

"Many interesting letters have been received from boys who have been in the navy and army, giving very clear and truthful accounts of engagements by sea and land.

.   .   .   .   .

"The close of the war, and the consequent discharge of so many seamen from the navy, has so increased the number of men seeking voyages, and so reduced the rates of wages as to make the demand for boys much less than during the three years previous. You will observe by reference to Table 1, that fewer boys have been sent on voyages at sea this past year, than for two or three years before.

"This, however, I do not consider a misfortune, by any means, as the length of time which the boys have heretofore spent in the institution has been too short for thoroughness either in reform or instruction.

"With the increased facilities for the accommodation of boys, we shall not only be able to give instruction upon a broader system, but by having a greater range of selection, shall be prepared to give better satisfaction than ever before, by offering only boys whose characters and capabilities have been tested by a long residence in the school.

"Religious exercises have been regularly attended on the Sabbath, when the boys have been addressed by gentlemen representing the different religious denominations and the various callings in life. By this means the interest of the boys has been kept up, and doubtless many good resolutions have been formed and kept."

---

2. New York City school ship, 1869

"The School-Ship Mercury," *Frank Leslie's Illustrated Newspaper,* XXIX (December 4, 1869), 191–192.

With all the efforts of philanthropists to ameliorate the condition of outcast and destitute children in the metropolis, and provide for their education, it has been extremely difficult to prevent their going back to the streets. However kind and attentive their instructors may be, the boys seem unable to resist a frolic on the streets, which not infrequently results in the arrest and imprisonment on Blackwell's Island of some of their number. That large numbers of children who were the beneficiaries of our model institutions have relapsed into vicious courses, and become active participants in crime, is a fact that cannot be gainsaid, and one that brings sore disappointment to the large-hearted gentlemen and ladies who have eagerly watched an improved condition of this class of unfortunates.

The Commissioners of Public Charities and Correction have, we think, taken a step in the right direction. They purchased the clipper *Mercury,* formerly a Havre packet, and converted it into a school-ship, to which the boys from Blackwell's and Hart's Islands have been transferred. There, it is hoped, they will receive a good education, and become hardy and useful seamen. There they will be removed from scenes of vice, and with strict but kindly-enforced discipline their evil propensities may be overcome, and the germs of honorable manhood planted in their young hearts.

The *Mercury,* which is temporarily anchored off the Battery, is a noble vessel, 200 feet in length, 40 feet beam, and 21 feet in depth, and about 1,600 tons register. Her dimensions between decks are 7½ feet. Her accommodations and fitting up in cabins, storerooms, etc., are perfection. She has been arranged for 300 boys, though at present there are only 114 on board. The yards are so heavy, that to fill all the stations in man-of-war style, it requires 300 boys, and this number will be on board as soon as the uniforms, which are being made at one of the public institutions, are completed.

The boys are divided into starboard and port watches, in naval style, and are well and warmly clothed in naval uniforms, having round their blue cap a ribbon with "Mercury" in golden letters. They rise at half-past five (at five A.M. in summer), stow away their hammocks and wash the decks, clean the brace-work, and make things ship-shape until half-past seven, when they have breakfast. Then half of each watch goes to school, and the other half goes on deck, loosing and reefing sails, learning seamanship, exercising with the two brass six-pounders they have on board, and making all kinds of sennit [plaited rope] to noon, when there is a spell for dinner and recreation until one. At that hour, work of the same kind recommences until five P.M., when comes supper and freedom until half-past seven. At that hour they sing hymns and strong, hearty songs, which they give with immense gusto. Then comes the *viva voce* recitation of the Lord's Prayer, then five minutes' silent prayer, and then hammocks are piped down, and in a few moments the embryo tars are in the soundest of slumbers.

Their dietary is ample, generous, splendid. Fresh meat four times a week, salt twice, fish, fresh or salt, on Fridays, with an abundance of fresh mixed vegetables, and puddings every day, of Indian meal or flour, with plums (the traditional plum duff), is the dinner. The breakfast and supper are tea, coffee, or cocoa, with biscuit and butter, and, in harbor, soft bread, with molasses or apple-sauce, and twice a week boiled rice.

.   .   .   .   .

Admiral Porter has informed General Bowen, one of the Commissioners of Public Charities, that he is highly in favor of the institution, and believes it will prove a valuable nursery for our naval forces. Everything is done in man-of-war style, and the boys, quick and impressionable, have caught the feeling, and nine-tenths of them declare that, when they are fit, they will join the naval service.

But the desire of the boys to be thorough seamen is not feigned. It is earnest and true. They stand occasional rough weather in their trips of fifteen or sixteen days with actual complacency,

and go aloft, reef, furl and secure sails and rigging with rapidity and in good style. In their practice, short-handed as they are, they have furled and loosed sails in fourteen minutes, although from their scant numbers there are no boys to fill the stations of the lower sails. The interest of the officers is equally great; they are as desirous to teach as the boys to learn. There is the utmost harmony and good-feeling among them, and there can be little doubt that we have at last discovered the real way to utilize our juvenile delinquents.

3. Failure of school ships to discipline and train

Massachusetts Board of State Charities, *Eighth Annual Report, 1871* (Boston, 1872), pp. xxxviii–xxxix.

All the various violations of wise principles of juvenile reformation to be found in the different institutions which attempt to do their work by wholesale, and which aggregate the vicious material for the sake of handling it more cheaply, are necessarily combined when the youth are packed together in ship, and then set afloat, dissevering all the wholesome daily ties with earth. The packing is more close; the depraving contact more continuous; the evil communications are more corrupting; the lack of family influence, of female society, of variety in occupation and of amusement, are necessarily felt more keenly than in land reformatories.

The zeal of the friends of the School Ship, and the anxious care and constant vigilance of officers and teachers, have done all that could be expected from men resolutely engaged in such uphill work. They have not been able, however, to do an amount of good equivalent to the outlay of time and of money; nor to prevent the conviction that the same means, more wisely directed, would produce more abundant and more satisfactory results. Hence the ready acquiesence in the sale of one ship, and the complacent reception of the idea of disposing of the other.

The Report of last year states the average number of boys during the year to be one hundred and fifty-nine, and the cost of the institution, $31,419.40, or $3.80 per head, as against $3.04, the average cost in the two land reformatories.

That the reformatory effects of the nautical discipline were unsatisfactory, appears from the statement of Superintendent Evans of the Reform School at Westborough, to whose charge were transferred forty-five boys upon the sale of their ship, the *Massachusetts*. He says the "forty-five boys received from the School Ship have a demoralizing effect upon the rest of the school. They introduced disgusting habits among the boys, from which we have not as yet fully recovered. They were clannish and did not readily assimilate with the other boys. They were destitute of industrious habits."

There is some force in the remarks of the superintendent of the nautical branch, that of late a larger number of boys, older in years and in crime, have been committed to the ship than was formerly done. This, however, does not explain the difference satisfactorily. The boys come from the same class of society, and have been subjected to the same demoralizing influences.

Moreover, the School Ships have failed to meet the expectations of those who hoped that they would considerably increase the supply of seamen for our merchant marine. Good seamen are made only out of those who have a natural taste for salt water. The growth cannot be forced, especially out of unfavorable material. Comparatively few graduates of the School Ship ever become good sailors. Besides, as the Secretary well remarks, "juvenile reformatories are established to make of boys good men, and not to replenish any branch of industry supposed to be languishing."

Life in the reform schools

1. In the Chicago House of Correction, 1870's

Eddie Guerin, *I Was a Bandit* (New York: Doubleday, 1929), pp. 5–13.

Guerin (b. 1860) won international notoriety for his daring bank robberies in the United Sates and France and for his escape from the penal colony in French Guiana.

The Chicago of the 'seventies was a wild and woolly affair. Public houses and pool rooms, gambling establishments of all kinds, red-light houses kept by foreign women, were open all night long, and with no one to exercise any control over my habits I drifted into the pool rooms at a time when I should have been home in bed. I was only fourteen years of age when I obtained a job as a cash boy in the Marshall Field store in Chicago, the same place where Mr. Gordon Selfridge made his beginning. Well, if I had stuck to my work there is no saying that I, too, might not have become a millionaire like Mr. Selfridge. The opportunity was there, but I could not see it.

Running about with money appealed to me well enough, though I could not earn sufficient to satisfy myself. Seven or eight months I lasted in the store, and then I became a Western Union telegraph boy, delivering telegrams about the city. But here again the pay did not come up to my requirements. Night after night I would be playing pool and gambling in dollars, until I began to look round for ways and means of raising more money. The only opportunity I could see of getting any was to steal. Delivering telegrams as I was to all sorts of private houses and business establishments, I found there were plenty of chances of pilfering small articles. These I used to sell, and for a time played pool to my heart's content.

However, this sort of thing could not continue indefinitely. I was only just fifteen years of age when the police took me into custody for stealing a box of cutlery from a place to which I had been sent. They threw me into a cell with a collection of tramps and old-timers who seemed to be much amused at my boyish tears at being locked up.

"Cheer up, kiddo," they all said to me, "it won't be long before you're used to it. Keep smiling and you'll be all right."

I shall never forget my first taste of prison life. They put me in what was known as the House of Correction and I went numb with horror at the sights I saw. There were blacks and whites of all ages and sizes, and the place stunk like a sewer. Men were lying about the floors smoking, spitting, cursing, idling away the time until they were dealt with. They laughed when they saw me, asked me what I had done, and amusedly poked each other in the ribs when I said I was in for nicking a box of cutlery.

Night time came, and with it no hope of my release. The big Irish policeman who had arrested me good-naturedly said he would let my mother know and see if she could not do something for me. But I am afraid I had long ago estranged any sympathy at home. A warder came along and hustled me into a cell, rudely requested me to stop blubbing, and left me locked up feeling as miserable as it was possible for any boy to feel. I got nothing to eat all night. In the morning a trusty came along, shoved some bread and coffee inside the cell, winked at me, and left me to my wretched thoughts until ten o'clock, when I was taken to the police court and charged.

There was quite a bunch of us to be dealt with. Chicago was full of criminals then, as it is now. I was taken to the court, heard as in a dream the evidence that was given against me, and just dimly remembered being informed by the jailer that I would go to the Sessions for trial.

What a tragical farce! Fifteen years of age, barely old enough to know better, flung like a dog into a filthy prison crowded with all the thugs and thieves in Chicago. Regularly night after night while awaiting trial I cried myself to sleep, bitterly promising myself that I would never do anything wrong again. Most of my fellow prisoners were kind enough. They gave me food to supplement the mush, a sort of porridge we had for breakfast, slung me pieces of meat to eke out the scanty diet, and asked me if I would like a chew. Boylike, I tried to masticate some tobacco, but it only made me feel worse than ever. I went about hardly knowing what I was doing until the time came, a fortnight later, to appear at Sessions.

I had nobody to defend me. My poor mother would have nothing to do with me, so, taking the advice of the men in the prison, I pleaded guilty and was sentenced by the Judge to nine months' imprisonment. I hardly heard what he said. I had been in a trance from the moment the police arrested me, and I was still bereft of my senses when they took me back to the prison and shoved me into a cell about four feet wide and seven feet long. My mother, broken-hearted, would not come to see me, and the only people to whom I could turn for any sympathy were the other men in the jail.

For more than a week I lay there without any exercise whatever. I asked the trusty who came round with the food what I could do about it.

"Say you want to see the Captain," he advised me. "But mind you be mighty civil to him, kid, or else he will jump on your toes. He's a pretty slick customer if you start sassin' him."

I did not feel in the mood to "sass" anyone, and I must say it was in a very humble tone that I asked one of the warders for permission to see the boss.

"What do you want him for?" demanded the fellow suspiciously. "Ain't you satisfied with what you've got?"

"It isn't that, sir," I replied meekly. "I want to know if I can't have something to do."

"You stop where you are and don't make a

nuisance of yourself," snarled the warder, banging the door, "or else I'll give you something to remember. Who do you think you are, saying you want to see the Captain? You wait until the Captain wants to see you."

I did not know what was going to happen to me then. I expected to be put on bread and water or suffer some other dire fate. At night the prison was a place of horror. I could hear the Negroes wailing in their cells, occasionally a foul-mouthed burst from some irate prisoner demanding something he couldn't get. But about eleven o'clock the following morning the bolts on my cell door clanged and I saw the Warden, a big, full-blooded Irishman, in company with a couple of warders.

"Stand to attention!" rapped one of them.

"Well, what's the matter with you?" inquired the Warden, scowling at me. "What do you mean by sending for me?"

My heart dropped right into my boots and for a time I could only stutter.

"Please, s-s-s-sir, couldn't you give me something to do?"

"Do!"

"Yes, s-s-sir," still more meekly.

"Huh! So you're starting to make trouble already? What is it you want to do?"

I explained as best I could that I must do something or I would go mad.

"Oh, give him something," grunted the Warden, moving away.

I discovered then the foolishness of making yourself known in prison. It is far better to say nothing and do nothing — just let them do what they like with you. In that way you don't get singled out.

A few days after seeing the Warden — I found out that his name was Captain Mack — I was put to work in a sort of factory where they knitted stockings. I couldn't knit, and the warder who had charge of the place couldn't teach me, so he made me a sort of dispatch clerk. I had to pack the stockings in a box to be sent away to be sold, and it was not long before the idea came to my mind of trying to

make my escape. Even in those early days I had no inclination to remain in prison any longer than was absolutely necessary. I used to lie awake at night thinking how I could get out, and it occurred to me that the long boxes in which I packed the stockings might provide the means.

A pretty daring scheme for a boy of fifteen, if you like! By keeping close observation every day I soon discovered that the boxes were taken out of the prison as soon as we came back from our midday meal. The plan I had in mind was nothing less than to be carried out myself in place of the usual consignment of stockings.

But I had to get someone to help me. "Little Eddie," as everybody termed me, was quite well liked, and I fastened upon a man named George O'Donnell, who seemed quite friendly toward me, as my accomplice. His eyes glistened as I told him of my scheme.

"My God, kid!" he exclaimed admiringly, "you've sure got some gumption. But, tell me, how are you thinking of getting out of the box? It'll have to be nailed down."

"I've thought of all that," I said. "If we get a set of false nails and just get the box lightly nailed down I can burst the top off as soon as I get down to the depot."

I wanted O'Donnell's help to hammer the false nails down, and of course I had to trust him. I got the nails all right, and everything was fixed for me to get into the box and be carried out of the prison, put on the express wagon, and taken outside the gates. The time came to put my plan into execution, but just as the very last moment when I was ready to climb into the box O'Donnell came over to me and whispered:

"I can't do it, Eddie, I'll sure be copped. You'll have to find someone else."

"You dirty skunk!" I hissed back at him. "Are you going to snitch?"

"Not me," said George. "But it's no good, Ed. They'll be sure to get you."

There was no help for it. I had no stockings to put in the box, and it had to go out empty.

The following day it reached its destination and then, by Jove, wasn't there a hullabaloo! The next thing I heard was that Captain Mack wanted me, and I knew that I was in for trouble. He had me down to the office, closely guarded by a couple of men three times my size.

"Ah!" he cried the moment he saw me, "so now I know why you wanted some work. What have you got to say for yourself?"

"I don't know what you're talking about," I replied, looking him full in the face.

"You don't, hey?"

"No, sir."

"I'll tell you," he bawled at me angrily. "You sent an empty box out of the prison yesterday. You thought you were going in it, didn't you?"

"But I'm sure I don't know anything about it, sir," I said as boldly as I could, though I could feel the blood draining from my face. I had a premonition then that someone had given me away and I made a mental vow that whoever the snitch was he would pay for his treachery.

The Captain did not waste much time questioning me.

"Call up O'Donnell," he ordered brusquely.

One look at my confederate was quite enough. The dirty dog would not meet my eye.

"What do you know about this affair, O'Donnell?" asked the Captain. "You're in this, and if you don't spill the whole story I'll give you something you'll remember to your dying day."

O'Donnell didn't need much urging. Then and there he snitched, put everything on me, and was then hustled out of the room, leaving me to be dealt with.

"Now, then, you," said the Captain, fixing me with a liverish eye, "what do you think is going to happen to you?"

"I can't say, sir," I replied, quite truthfully for once.

"But I can," the Captain shouted. "What you'll get is a first-class beating up. I'll teach you to break out of prison. By the time I'm finished with you you'll wish you were dead."

He was almost as good as his word. The warders took me away and put me into a solitary cell where they could keep a close watch on me. I got nothing but bread and water to eat, no books to read, nobody to whom I could talk. I could see them on the qui vive for something they could find to punish me. The week I remained in that silent cell brought home to me as nothing else could have done the awful precariousness of crime.

The beating-up I expected didn't come, and I fondly hoped the Captain had forgotten all about it. But, alas! one morning a couple of warders came along, unceremoniously yanked me out of the cell, and pulled me along to a place where there was an iron register over the stairs going up to the first terrace of cells. Hanging over it was a pulley with a long rope. Miserably wondering what was going to take place next, I saw the Warden come along.

"Get hold of him," he ordered the two warders. They put a pair of handcuffs on my wrists, put a hook between them, and then pulled me up the stairs and dropped me down again until I almost fainted. For something like ten minutes they kept on with the torture. Up and down I went, screaming blue murder and calling Mack and the warders all the names I could think of. I was on the verge of unconsciousness when they finally hauled me up, took the handcuffs off my wrists, and flung me into a dungeon, with a basin of water and a lump of bread to keep me alive. Nobody came near me. My wrists were lacerated, my head almost bursting with pain. But I stuck my tongue between my cheeks, resolved to show no fear. Twenty-four hours elapsed, when the warders came again, told me to get up, and escorted me to one of the punishment cells on the first range, where they kept me without exercise of any kind for three whole months.

This is the plain, undeniable truth. Just imagine a boy fifteen years of age being subjected to torture for the perfectly natural desire of wanting to escape! No one came near me except the man who put the food in my cell and occasionally a hypocritical, sniveling old chaplain who besought me to give up my evil ways and lead an honest life. I rudely told him to go to the devil, for which he promised to report me to the Warden.

2. The New York Catholic Protectory, 1876

William P. Letchworth, "Orphan Asylums and Other Institutions for the Care of Children," in *Ninth Annual Report of the New York State Board of Charities* (Albany, 1876), pp. 264–274.

The Protectory, founded in 1863, was the largest institution for delinquent, para-delinquent, and neglected children in the United States.

The object of this society is "to provide for the education and support of such idle, truant, vicious, or homeless children of both sexes, from seven to fourteen years, as may be properly surrendered to its protection, or committed to its custody by the order of any magistrate of New York, or by the Commissioners of Public Charities and Correction." In addition to the class of children sent to the Protectory under commitment, the officers are allowed to take children who may be intrusted to them by their parents.

.   .   .   .   .   .

The Protectory is located in the town of Westchester, in Westchester county, eleven miles from the City Hall in New York. Its post-office is Westchester. The institution may be reached by a short ride upon the Harlem Railroad, leaving the train at Tremont station. A ride of about two miles from the depot brings one to the extensive group of large buildings which comprise the Protectory establishment. Prominent among these, and first arresting the attention, is the boys' department, an imposing brick structure, four stories high, with basement and mansard roof, having a central tower containing a fine tower clock. The architectural design of the tower, as well as of the entire building, is quite elaborate, the whole presenting a stately appearance. The edifice is situated in the midst of extensive grounds, which are being improved. The site is an eligible one, the land in front gently sloping away from the main building. The soil is desirable for agricultural purposes, and the location is healthful.

A visitation with Commissioner Hoguet was made to this institution October 15, on which occasion the boys' department was found to be under the care of Brother Teliow, assisted by thirty of the Roman Catholic Order of Christian Brothers, and the girls' department under the charge of Sister Helena, with twenty-two other Sisters of Charity of Mt. St. Vincent associated with her in the work.

Although it will be difficult to convey to the reader, in the short space allotted to it in this report, an adequate idea of the system and arrangement of this immense establishment, yet a brief sketch of its noteworthy features which came under our observation will be attempted. The various parts of the institution were visited in the following order, beginning with the

Boys' department. — There were here at the date of visitation about thirteen hundred and forty boys. In the large printing room there were between seventy and eighty, under the supervision of a foreman, himself once an inmate, but now a superior workman. In this room are three steam-power presses. Stereotyping is carried on to an extent enabling the establishment to make all the castings used in its printing. About fifty-five boys were setting type, whose ages averaged about fourteen, and twenty little fellows were folding paper, none of whom were older than eleven years. There were also ten, between fourteen and eighteen years of age, working at the presses.

In the tailoring department were about thirty boys sitting cross-legged on a platform, like tailors, and very busy at work; others were operating sewing machines, in all about sixty boys. The boys make every thing they wear, and in addition do a great deal of work for employers.

In the room appropriated to the boys' clothing are cases containing fourteen hundred small compartments, one of which is allotted to each boy. These are numbered, and the clothes that are in them are also numbered to correspond. The garments are of a warm woolen material, and of various colors. The President remarked: "I will not permit the boys to wear uniform clothes. I never buy two pieces of cloth alike."

In the shoemaking department there were nearly four hundred boys, ranging in ages from eleven to seventeen years. There are two shops in this department, one for making nailed and the other for making sewed shoes. The work is done largely by machinery. The boys wrought with alacrity, and seemed cheerful and attentive to their duties. The Brother says: "They have stated hours for labor and for education, and a given space of time for recreation. They have certain tasks to do, and when these are done they can go and play."

It is gratifying to state that the system of letting out the services of the boys to contractors at a fixed price per day is not in practice here. On this point the President of the Protectory remarks: "The boys do not work on contracts. We make a shoe and sell it for as much as we can. We are training boys to be shoemakers. We are working this institution for the benefit of the State. We are taking the raw material and trying to make out of it self-sustaining men. If in the process we can save a few dollars so much the better, but that is not our primary aim. We have conducted this department for years without making a shilling. Last year we made money; this year we lose."

About two hundred boys were employed in the cane-seating department, their ages varying from nine to eleven years. The work here seemed to be well done, and the boys' movements were brisk and orderly.

In a room in the basement were found about four hundred boys engaged, some in blocking out soles, and all working with a will.

The laundry contains four steam washing machines. The washing for the institution is all done by the boys, under the supervision of one of the Brothers and an assistant.

In the cabinet making department the boys were engaged in making bureaus, chests of drawers, wash-stands, etc. Many creditable specimens of their handiwork were there for inspection. Attached to the establishment is a blacksmith's shop, a wheelwright's shop, a horse-shoeing and a wagon-making department, and a machine shop, in which the machinery is repaired. The iron bedsteads used in the establishment are also made here. Bedsteads are likewise made to supply outside orders.

In the box-making department the boxes for packing shoes are made. All the carpentry about the institution, the Brother says, is done by the boys, and two buildings have been put up by them. In addition to the trades taught in all the departments named, the boys are instructed in gardening and farming. About seventy-eight were engaged in this kind of work.

A good working Fire Company has been organized among the boys, which is equipped with engine and hose cart. The Company does good service, not only in the institution, but in the neighborhood, having laid residents in the vicinity under obligations to them in several instances by putting out their fires, and thus saving their houses.

There is also a fine Cornet Band, composed of the boys who have a talent for music. This was organized by one of the Brothers. They wear a blue uniform. This band, the Brother informed us, attend the Jerome Park races regularly, and get thirty dollars a day for their services.

One of the large yards containing swings, etc., for the boys' recreation, was at the time of our visit filled with juveniles, who were here allowed to pursue their sports, and to indulge their boisterous propensities, to their hearts' content. The Brother said: "We have three hundred boys unemployed, simply because there is no money to put up workshops for them."

The steam engine in use on the premises is from forty to fifty horse power. The steam from several large steam boilers heats the building, and affords steam for cooking. A spring supplies the house with water, which is gathered in a reservoir, and carried through the building in pipes.

Thirty-five cows are kept on the place. All their milk is used in the institution, but even this, we were informed, is insufficient for the inmates. All the vegetables used are raised in the extensive gardens of the Protectory, except a full supply of potatoes. The lands of the institution cover one hundred and forty-seven acres. One hundred and thirty-five acres are under cultivation, twenty acres being laid out in garden.

The domestic part of the house is on the same large plan as the industrial. The kitchen, with its huge caldrons and polished boilers for coffee and tea, and with its other appurtenances, is on a scale commensurate with the requirements for feeding fifteen hundred mouths at a single meal, and is suggestive of the hospitality of baronial times.

The refectory is capable of accommodating eleven hundred boys at a sitting. In addition to these, a considerable number of the foremen sit here on a dais at one end of the room, and eat with them. A smaller refectory for the little boys could seat about three hundred. A Brother sat at one end, and the clerks and foremen of departments at the other. The boys were well supplied with a meat stew, bread, turnips, potatoes and apples. Before eating, the form of grace usual in Roman Catholic Asylums was repeated, and after the meal thanks were in like manner returned.

Beeves are butchered on the place to supply meat for the table. A very large and well-constructed slaughter-house, furnished with all the necessary conveniences for butchering the animals required for the sustenance of the children, has been erected during the year.

The dietary is as follows:

For ordinary days: Breakfast — Coffee, bread, butter and meat.

Dinner — Soup, meat, vegetables, bread and fruit in its season.

Supper — Bread, butter, tea and dessert.

For Fridays: Breakfast — Coffee, bread, butter and cakes.

Dinner — Soup, fish, potatoes, bread and coffee.

Supper — Bread, butter, tea and biscuits.

In the Junior Department meat is served but once a day; and as a substitute gruel of Indian or oaten meal, rice, etc., is given in the morning.

The dormitories are very large, containing about three hundred and fifty beds each, and are all similarly furnished. They are lighted on four sides. The windows are large and mullioned. In an alcove off each room, and separated from it by curtains, are beds for three of the Brothers. The boys' bedsteads are of iron, single, two feet four inches wide, having head and foot rails. Straw beds are used; the straw being changed every three months; the pillows are some of husks, some of sponge and some of hair. The beds were square and regularly made; they were very thick, the depth of straw in the ticks being fully fourteen inches. The Brother remarked on this point: "It pays us to buy straw to make decent beds for the boys. As soon as it becomes broken and inelastic we send it off and use it in the stables." Each bed had two sheets, two blankets and a coverlet. The covering is increased as the weather becomes colder. The rooms are lighted by gas. A spacious gas-house, with all its necessary dependencies, retorts, iron receivers, tank, storehouse for coal, and full complement of service pipes for all buildings of the institution, has been constructed.

Night closets adjoin each dormitory.

The chapel is of old Saxon-Gothic architecture, and has a capacity for seating fifteen hundred. It contains a large central altar, a confessional at each end, a gallery and a piano. The piano when used is accompanied by music upon stringed instruments.

The infirmary is on the same floor as the chapel. There was here one inmate, suffering from consumption; another from pneumonia; and a third from a swollen foot. This department is in charge of a Brother, and contains twenty beds. In connection with it is an apothecary shop. A large gas jet is kept burning in a flue in the center of the infirmary, for the purpose of ventilation.

The halls of the Protectory are ten feet wide, and extend through the whole length of the building. In addition to the central staircase are four other flights of stairs, rendering easy egress from the building in case of fire. Each floor has a water-pipe and a number of leather buckets ready for use in case of fire.

.   .   .   .   .

Girls' Department. — The spacious and tasteful edifice, formerly occupied by the girls, was burned down and its contents destroyed, July 25, 1872, causing much inconvenience to the institution. This building had been erected at a cost of about $165,000, mainly from the proceeds of a single fair. In the interval, between its destruction and the partial completion of the new building, temporary structures on the grounds were improvised. These were still in partial use on the day of visitation.

A new engine and boiler house is in progress of construction for the female department, and the managers are making arrangements for the introduction of steam power into a part of the temporary wooden buildings, which are being converted into a large workshop, in which the business of silk-winding will be conducted, under a contract recently entered into by the managers with well-known silk manufacturers.

.   .   .   .   .

. . . The number of girls on the day of visitation was six hundred and one, their ages ranging between seven and sixteen years. They were dressed neatly and differently, the Sisters preferring variety in color and material as a matter of taste. The girls' hair was mostly tied up with ribbons, and their faces looked clean and bright.

Care is taken in the arrangements for ablutions. Each inmate has her own towel. This is numbered with her own number. Every girl in the house, Sister Helena informed us, has a number, and this number is on her clothes, her books, and every thing allotted to her, and each is held responsible for her own. In this way an opportunity is more readily afforded for observing and rewarding those who show the most neatness in the care of what belongs to them.

The school comprises ten classes of about fifty each in the primary departments, and sixty or seventy in the classes of the older pupils. The rooms are furnished with patent desks and all modern appliances. The personal cleanliness of the inmates was marked. The Sister says: "The mornings and evenings are devoted to the school, and the afternoons to work. Young children of either sex are not expected to work. Their day is divided between the school and the play-ground. Special pains is taken to give young girls ample out-door recreation. About three hundred and seven girls, comprising all of the junior classes, are kept in school five hours per day. Those girls who are engaged in the industrial departments during part of the day, are kept in school two hours in the morning, and those employed in house labor are kept in school two and one-half hours in the afternoon."

In one of the classes we found about sixty-eight girls engaged in finishing off shirts. In the "operating room" there were sixty-two machines, all worked by girls, who are paid according to their capacity. The following figures will better explain the extent of the industrial features of this department: About ninety-six girls are engaged at shoe-fitting, about one hundred and seventy-six in plain sewing, and about twenty-five in house-work.

The average annual cost for the maintenance of each girl is stated to be $115.31. Regarding the value of the labor, it is said that "$5,000 in cash has been paid into the treasury in 1875, from the proceeds of their labor in 1874; and the inventories of the female industrial department just made show profits of nearly $14,000 for the year just closed." It is further asserted that "a continuance of results such as these, together with a total cessation of building, would, in the course of a few years, materially decrease the share of the present floating debt justly chargeable to the female division of the Protectory."

The room intended for school purposes is now used as a dormitory. It is furnished with single iron bedsteads, two feet three inches wide. The beds are of straw and very thick.

The house was found to be very clean and tidily kept and the order prevalent throughout in all the housekeeping as well as industrial departments, it would seem, must have a beneficial effect upon the children, many of whom, before coming here, were brought up in the utmost neglect, and left to habits of heedlessness. The demeanor of the Sisters appeared to be that of earnest women, engaged in a work undertaken as a duty, investing them with a dignity that seemed to inspire respect among the children.

The whole number of children, both boys and girls, in the Protectory at the date of October 1, 1875, was 1,944. Of these, 538 were orphans, 1,021 half-orphans, and 365 had both parents living. There were of native parentage, 147, and of foreign parentage, 1,797. Of the entire number, fifty-three were partially supported by parents or friends. The number of children transferred from Randall's Island Nursery and the county poor-house of Westchester at the time the system of rearing children in these institutions was broken up, was 108. The whole number of children received during the year was 941; the number discharged, 839. Of the latter, 84 were indentured, 643 returned to parents or guardians, 79 left without permission, 19 were transferred to other institutions, and 14 died.

A new feature relating to the disposition of the children in the Protectory is thus outlined by its Rector: "We hope soon to have agencies established throughout the State, by means of which the institution can be relieved, its objects extended, and the State in general benefited. Through these agencies, it is the intention to locate boys in self-sustaining positions with farmers and mechanics, thus making room for others in the Protectory, and benefiting the community by furnishing well-tutored and reliable youths to mechanical, agricultural and general commercial pursuits."

---

3. A Pennsylvania reform school, ca. 1886

Josiah Flynt, *My Life* (New York, 1908), pp. 86–96.

Josiah Flint Willard (1869–1907), a nephew of temperance leader Francis E. Willard, wrote on vagrancy and criminology under the pen name, Josiah Flynt. After an unhappy childhood, he ran away and became a tramp. When about sixteen, he was caught horsestealing and committed to the Pennsylvania Western House of Refuge.

If some one could only tell us exactly what should, and should not, be done in a reform school a great advance would be achieved in penology, which at present is about as much of a science as is sociology. Both — and criminology can be thrown in, too — always reminded me of a cat after a good sousing — they are quite as much in earnest in shaking off what does not agree with them, or what they think does not agree with them, as is the cat in drying itself; but again, like the cat, the shaking often seems to make them look more ragged than ever.

The most that I can attempt to do here is to describe the Reform School I learned to know in Pennsylvania, and tell what it accomplished and failed to accomplish in my case.

The superintendent was the brother of one of the most astute politicians and officeholders this country has produced. He held his position largely through his brother's influence, and might just as well have been given any other "job," so far as his particular fitness for public office was concerned. In spite of all this, however, he was a fairly kind and just man, and probably did right according to his light and leading.

The institution sheltered some three hundred boys and girls, the latter being officially separated from the boys; the "safeties," however, the boys who had the run of the farm, saw not a little of them. The place was arranged on the cottage plan — the boys of a certain *size* being toed off to a certain cottage. For instance, I was placed with lads much younger and far more inexperienced than I was simply because I was their height. It struck me at the time — and I am even more impressed to-day — that this was a very peculiar way of classifying prisoners, particularly boys. Far more important, it seems to me, is a classification based on age, training, experience, disposition and temperament. But the great State which had taken me in charge practically overlooked all of these matters in locating us boys in the different homes. Who was to blame for this I cannot tell, but one would think that the superintendent would have thought out something better than the system we had to live under. Right here is the trouble in so many penal and reformatory institutions — what other superintendents and wardens have found "good enough," their latest successor also finds "good enough"; the wheels and cogs have been kept going on the old basis, and the new-comer is afraid to "monkey" with them during his term of office. Many a prison in this country merits a good overhauling, and while exposure of misuse of public funds is the order of the day, and new blood is being called for in so many quarters, it might not be a bad plan to examine carefully into the management of our penitentiaries, workhouses, reform schools and jails.

There was no wall around the school to which I had been committed, a fact which I noted immediately on my arrival. In place of a wall, and as supposed safeguards against escapes, the superintendent had a shrieking whistle for both day and night, and a huge, flaming natural gas-light, more particularly for night, although the miserable thing, as I considered it, burned the entire twenty-four hours. There were five divisions, or cottages, for the boys, including the main building, which could hardly be called a cottage. Unless my memory plays me false, I was in Division G, next to that of the "biggest" boys, yet I was considerably older and certainly more traveled and "schooled" than many of the latter. Theoretically each inmate was to remain in the school until twenty-one, unless relatives or friends took him away after he had earned the requisite number of good-conduct marks. Ten was the maximum daily number, and five thousand were required before good conduct was considered established and a release permissible. The day was about equally divided between study and work, but being outclassed for study in Division G, I was allowed to work all day in the brush factory. Punishment was measured according to the offense, sometimes also according to the number of marks a boy had and the proximity of his release. But in general these rules prevailed: For minor offenses, "standing in line" — a sentence involving loss of the privilege of play and the necessity of toeing a mark with other victims during recesses; for serious offenses, a prescribed number of lashes with a leather strap, a reduction in the boy's marks, and imprisonment in a cell on bread and water. Some boys had long since earned their five thousand marks, and were theoretically — there is so much that is theoretical in *State* institutions — entitled to their freedom. But no relatives, friends or employers coming forward to vouch for their safe-keeping "outside," they were compelled to stay on until somebody came to their rescue.

The word "outside" characterized a great deal of the life in the school. Used originally exclusively in penitentiaries, the boys had appropriated the word for their own use as well, although there was no wall, and the "outside" was as plainly visible as the "inside." Under restraint and kept within bounds we certainly were, but it was considered smart and "wise" to use the prison expression. Consequently every boy with any gumption in him was continually thinking about what he would do when free again, when the great "outside" would be open territory once more.

We also had an institutional lingo, or slang, patterned as much as possible after the dialect used by "the real thing," the crooks in the "Pen." Guards became "screws," bread and water "wind pudding," detectives "elbows," and so on. When among ourselves, in shop, schoolroom or at play, aping "the real thing," the crooks, and their mannerisms, or what we took to be such — and nearly all the boys had had preliminary jail experiences and had associated with crooks — was a constant amusement for all, and with many a serious study. This posing was one of the worst things taught and learned in the school. Originally intended to be very humanitarian and modern in purpose and organization, to be a disciplinary home rather than a mere place of incarceration — witness the absence of a wall and the cottage system of housing — the boys themselves were defeating these ends with their prison conversations, things they had learned at the taxpayers' expense in various county jails.

Speaking generally, the boys were divided into two sets or rings — the "stand-patters" and the "softies." The former were the boys of spirit and adventure, the principal winners in their classes as well as on the playground; the latter were the tale-bearers, the mouthy ones — "lungers" was also a good name for them — who split on the "stand-patters" when "lunging it" promised to gain favors for them. Whatever else I did or did not do while in the school, I fought very shy of all officers who tried to get me to "peach" on my companions. This may not have been a virtue, but it secured good standing for me among the boys of spirit and enterprise, and I think that any boy wanting agreeable companionship in such a place would naturally turn to the "stand-patters." Of course, my selection of cronies was watched by the officers and made a mental note of to be used later on, either for or against my record, as it suited the

purposes of the observing overseer, as were many other things that I did or failed to do. In general the officers were fair-minded and reasonable, but thinking them over now, with the exception of one or two, they were not particularly adapted for reform-school work; they were mainly men who had drifted into the life accidentally, and had clung to it for want of something better to do. They were judged by the boys according to their varying abilities in wielding the strap. Some were strong and heavy, and were called "sockdologers"; others, not so effective physically, were dubbed "lightweights." At night we slept in dormitories, leaving all our clothes except our shirts in the basement, an arrangement which made night escapes difficult. In the main the dormitory life was clean and correct, indeed very much cleaner than cell life in many of our prisons and jails. The daily programme, as I recall it now, began at five-thirty in the morning in summer and at six in the winter. The great whistle started the day, and we all had to jump out of our beds, make them, and then in single file march to the basement, where we washed and dressed. Soon after came the molasses-and-tea breakfast, after which we had a half-hour or so on the playground. Recreation over, we were toed off into two squads, one for the schoolroom and the other for the factory. There were also "detail" boys, inmates of long standing who could be trusted as messengers, in the bakery, plumbing shop, and at different occupations in the cottages and on the farm. I made a bold and early bid for a "detail" job, but with no success. The superintendent told me that only those boys of whom he was sure received such positions, and I retired with the knowledge that he was not sure of me, and the determination to make him keep on guessing about me indefinitely. At noon sharp, came dinner, followed by another half-hour of recreation, when school and factory started again. Six o'clock saw us all at supper, and nine in bed, the intervening time being spent in the playground and in the schoolroom.

One day there was a revolution in the factory. One of the older boys had thrown a

"Who are we?"

Prisoners.

Judge Stubbs Talking to Boys in the Indianapolis Court.

Playground in a Mill Village. Photograph by Lewis W. Hine, n.d.

wrench at a brow-beating guard, and had been well beaten for his disobedience — beaten and hit with the man's fist, the boy claimed. At recess there was a hurried consultation among the "stand-patters."

"Let's hike it to the Super's office and complain," some one suggested, and before we had half seriously considered what we were doing, away we scampered to the superintendent's office in the main building, the officer to be complained about following leisurely after us. It was as clear a case of mob insanity as I have ever seen; the battered and bloody face of our companion so incensed us that rules and regulations were thrown to the winds. Indeed, if all of us had kept on going, so fleet were our feet, probably half could have gotten away for keeps then and there. But escape was not in our minds. We wanted, and were going to demand, if possible, the dismissal of the overbearing guard. At first, as is the case with nearly all mobs, the various boys wanted to talk at once, and the superintendent had considerable difficulty in getting our side of the story. We were then ordered to the schoolroom of our division, the superintendent desiring to interview the guard alone. The upshot of the affair was that the guard resigned and each boy received fifteen lashes with the strap. The superintendent personally attended the thrashing. Our first officer, a mild-mannered, much bewhiskered man, who had always treated me very considerately, was the first to wield the strap. We boys sat in our seats with folded arms, awaiting our turns. Finally mine came. The officer looked at me disappointedly; he did not seem to want to punish me. He had to obey orders, however, just as we boys did, and I received my fifteen lashes. During each "whaling" the other victims looked on intently, like children about to sit down at a Thanksgiving dinner; they wanted to see if the "whaled" one would "squeal." Excepting a more or less half-witted lad, who had run with the rest of us for no other reason than that he "saw us going and thought we were playing follow the leader," none of us whimpered. The first officer gave out completely after ten boys

had been punished, and a substitute — the school carpenter — took his place. I remember how glad I was that my turn came under the first officer's régime, and when he had begun to wobble.

Although the much-disliked factory guard had disappeared, the revolt and "whaling" set the escape thoughts going in the minds of four boys at a very much accelerated speed. Such thoughts are always on top, as it were, wherever human beings are shut up — even in hospitals; but the four lads — I was one of them — put their heads together and plotted as never before. A fight, and a subsequent order to stand "in line," sent my desire for freedom soaring uncommonly high. One of the "softies" and I had clashed for some reason or other, and a "whaling" at night, besides "standing in line," stared us in the face. Throughout the afternoon I pondered over ways and means to reach the great "outside," taking four trusted "stand-patters" into my confidence; they also wanted to go. For different reasons punishment of some kind awaited all of us, and as I was almost sure of a thrashing for fighting, I concluded that, if caught, I might as well make it do duty for trying to escape as well. All the boys calculated on such lines very nicely.

It was finally decided that the most practicable plan was to jump from the schoolroom window, when we were marching in line to the basement, to undress for the night. The distance to the ground was perhaps twenty feet, but during the afternoon we studied very carefully the probable spot we should land on, and all felt equal to the adventure. We should have to make the escape in bare feet, and without coats, but we decided that we didn't want the tell-tale jackets anyhow, and we thought we could smuggle our socks and caps into the schoolroom without detection.

That last evening in the schoolroom was a very nervous one, for four boys at least. From time to time, when the officer was not looking, we exchanged significant glances to make sure that there had been no defection in our ranks. Our caps and socks were hidden in our clothing. At last the whistle blew, books were put away, and the order to form line was given. My mind was firmly made up. Even if the other boys weakened I was going through the open window and on to the "outside." For some reason I felt as if success awaited me, and barring the drop from the window and a possible immediate capture, I feared very little. I was the first to take the drop. Suddenly I fell out of line, scrambled over the sill, and — dropped into the darkness. Whether the other three followed my example or not I do not know; probably not, because my disappearance made the officer reach threateningly for his revolver, as I was able to see while going over the sill. Once on the ground I waited for nobody, but went tearing over the lawn, barefooted and bareheaded, in the direction of the railroad track at the foot of the slope. There I concealed myself under a fence, and in a moment the great whistle told the surrounding country, with long blasts, that a "Ref" boy had escaped, while the flaring light lit up the lawn and assisted the officers in their search. Pretty soon I heard their voices and hurrying footsteps all about me, but they never came quite close enough to uncover my hiding place. I must have remained under the fence two good hours before I dared to proceed. This was about the conventional time given to a search, and I remained silent as the grave until all was quiet. Then, crawling rather than walking, I made my way to the railroad bridge, crossed it cat-like, and proceeded boldly toward the wooded hills opposite the school — the hills that I had so often looked at longingly, and wondered whether I should ever be able to cross without being captured. The underbrush and fallen twigs and branches must have hurt my feet, but the scratches and bruises were hardly noticed in the excitement of getting away. And although the night had become fairly cool, and I had nothing but shirt and trousers to cover me, I was literally in a violent perspiration when I reached the top of the first hill, and looked back on the school and the flaming light.

"Good-bye, brush factory and strap," I murmured. "May we never meet again."

The value and values of reform schools debated

---

1. An optimistic view of reformatories, 1875

U.S. Bureau of Education, *Circulars of Information, Number 6* (Washington, D.C., 1875), pp. 42–45, 49–50.

This report was written by Mrs. S. A. Martha Canfield, foundress of the Canfield Home for Colored Orphans, Memphis, Tennessee.

It is now fifty years since the first house of refuge was established in the United States, and however sanguine may have been the founders as to the result of such establishments, it is believed that their estimate of good to be done hardly reached what has been actually accomplished. There is now no doubt of the capability of these institutions to effect the purpose designed, and every succeeding year has strengthened the conviction. The system has undergone various changes and modifications and still is by no means regarded as complete in all its methods. The public mind, until within a few years, seemed impressed with the idea that if a person committed a crime he was truly depraved, and no hope remained for his reformation. The time of such ignorance is passed. An effort towards reformation, and not severe punishment, is more in accordance with the principles of Christianity and philanthropy, and after trial it has been found more successful than any other treatment, and far less expensive.

To place the erring youth where he cannot commit depredations; to teach him to restrain his passions; to show him the sure penalty that a course of crime will bring upon him; to speak kindly to him, and tell him how he can be useful and happy; to kindle in his soul the spark of manhood that has been long latent; to stir up the feeling of self-respect that has too often been crushed by the treatment of others; to find that tender place in his heart; that moral principle which has been so nearly extinct — to do all this is the mission of the reform-school; and statistics show that 75 per cent of all the youths sent to these institutions have been reclaimed and restored to society, clothed and in their right minds. It is to be remembered that many of these unfortunates are simply delinquents, neglected or wronged children, who of themselves have offended neither the public law nor the public morals.

For these at least it would seem right to provide favorable chances for bettering their condition. They are the unhappy, perhaps erring, members of a large community of children, who, not being cared for by their natural guardians, have become the wards of the public, and who, brought under enlightened tutelage, should repay this public, by future well-doing and prosperity, for her expenditure of beneficence and means in their behalf.

LABOR AS A MEANS OF REFORMATION

Disciplined physical employment is one of the most effective curatives as a moral agent, without which there can be no such thing as a successful reformation. Labor is the remedy that God ordained to restore the fallen, and the remedy admits of no substitute.

The formation of the habit of labor, of constant, continued effort in any one direction, is a most difficult part of education; it is rendered doubly difficult by the almost inconquerable aversion to any kind of patient industry, which is manifested by this class of children. This impatience of steady employment is always accompanied by the temptation to obtain property by dishonest means; therefore, if we would

make these children honest, we must make them industrious; inculcate in them a habit of labor by affording the means of steady employment, and furnish a purpose by exciting a laudable ambition to excel in all that requires mechanical skill.

A greater variety of trades or mechanical pursuits than are now taught in reformatories would be desirable. Skilled mechanics are needed, and the supply might be increased by introducing the various mechanical pursuits that might profitably be engaged in, and the boys thoroughly instructed in such trades as are best suited to their tastes or inclinations, so that when they were released they might find remunerative employment, become honest as well as industrious citizens, and rise to a respectable position in society.

MENTAL AND MORAL DISCIPLINE ALSO NECESSARY

The mind, however, must have its proper culture by well-drilled training, more fully to insure that subordination, intellectual improvement, and moral progress, which can give a hope of success to any system. The vagrant mind needs the habit of concentration and exercise of methodic study, as much as the vagrant body requires physical restraint and a rightly-directed exterior.

If it is needful to rightly occupy the body and the mind, it is no less an emphatic and accepted truth that the heart should be moved and the conscience awakened by appropriate religious instruction — Sunday observances statedly performed, the practical truths of the Bible taught, and serious appeals made to the better inner nature.

PHYSICAL TREATMENT CALLED FOR

Much of the so-called moral turpitude of humanity is the result of physical ailment. This may be inherited or acquired. In either case, it demands treatment skillfully applied and faithfully administered. The feelings and thoughts, and consequently the words and acts, are all modified and characterized by the condition of the physical system.

We may, with as much reason, look for pure water from an impure fountain, as to expect a consistent daily life in one whose system is diseased from the crown of the head to the sole of the foot.

The nervous system cannot fail to transfer its nervous action to the mind and the life. The thoughts generated in the brain through which scrofulous blood flows must be sordid and gross. Cutaneous irritability cannot fail to produce mental irritability and corresponding action.

There must, hence, be a system of medical and hygienic regimen adopted in connection with the other means of good referred to. The services of a skillful and experienced physician must combine with those of a judicious housemother for the restoration of a healthful circulation and a proper digestion of the food; for only as health comes to a diseased and irritated system can there be tranquil mental action and thorough openness to moral influences for reform.

.   .   .   .   .

The Industrial School for Boys in Wisconsin has opened a correction-house for the larger and more refractory boys. In this department, work takes the place of play. The boys are given three sessions to work and one in school, studying their lessons during the interval. The correction-house is the last resort for persistent disobedience, and its utility has been fully demonstrated and its results most favorable. Two or three months of this needful discipline has in most cases been all that was necessary to bring the boy into a better state of mind, and it is seldom that a boy is returned for a second trial.

The superintendent of the Wisconsin school proposes a theory, one on which he has ex-pended much thought and made limited experiments. It is as follows:

"A system of compensation or pay to all inmates, after reaching certain limits of age and good conduct, for all the service rendered in the institution, and a charge for all which they receive — a system of debt and credit with each. If this could be so nicely adjusted that a boy, by commendable exertion and diligence, could make a small saving each week over and above his expenditures, it would furnish a motive to action not usually felt by inmates in institutions of this kind. As things are now done, we have little opportunity to cultivate economy. The boy is now fed and clothed whether he works well or not. He learns from the book that ten dimes make one dollar; still he has little idea of its value, and less judgment how to expend it judiciously. In vain he is told the cost and importance of food, clothes, and home. He gets them free, and, like the air and the sun-light, he presumes that they, as a matter of course, are a part of his inheritance. All children are liable to this delusion; the children of the State preeminently so. This is seen in the destruction of books and tools. Take the book as an illustration. If the boy is charged seventy-five cents for a reader to-day, and he knows that when he is ready, say in six months, to be promoted or leave the school the value of the book then will pass to his credit, it presents a motive to care for it. The same of tools, clothes, &c. Another most valuable purpose would be saved. When a boy escaped, the cost of his return could be met by the use of his funds and an assessment on the funds of those who were accessory. This would furnish a leverage to find out all who were involved, embracing in certain instances a large portion of the members of a family or shop. A careful examination of the feasibility of this suggestion is solicited."

An odium rests upon the character of *all* children confined in a house of refuge. Many of them unquestionably need the high walls and the invariable key for their restraint and for an evidence of sure means to control and punish. But there are others, and those not a few, who become demoralized by the very precautions which are adopted to reform them, and being prisoners in fact become worthy of the infliction *in their own idea,* and thus a hindrance to self-respect and moral amendment is perniciously interposed.

It is advised that there be established a department in such institutions to which any child may be graduated by a course of good conduct and faithful and ingenuous observance of such salutary rules as the managers may propose, and that then the child may have the liberty of passing beyond the inclosures, to take service in the shop of the artisan, or the office of the merchant, or any other desirable place for its day's duty, returning to the refuge at its close. The night-school would then be employed for its intellectual instruction, the tone of the institution would be greatly improved, encouragement would take the place of frequent depression, and an aim would be presented to the inmates perfectly legitimate and entirely within their possible reach, which would stimulate their very best qualities to a healthy development. And for such inmates there might be a possible relaxation of the penal discipline and incarceration, which does not now discriminate in such respects in behalf of any.

THE FAMILY-SYSTEM OF REFORM

In several institutions the "family-system" has been adopted with great success. The children are regarded as subjects of restraint, but not subject to penal infliction or punishment. Walls, bolts, and bars, and all prison-appliances, of whatever description, are dispensed with, and a home and school established for the proper care, training, and education of wayward and neglected children. From these schools the pupils can go forth into the world, prepared for its duties and responsibilities, with no stigma attached to their names, and be received by the community with trust and confidence.

In the "family-system" natural laws are rec-ognized and acted upon by natural principles. The family is a divine institution, and the Creator has so arranged it that every human being is influenced more for good in the family than by any other influence in social life. This influence is indefinable, and runs through the whole social organization; it appeals to our individual self-respect, and addresses our hopes by opening to our vision fair prospects in life. The nearer the approach to the home and the family in the system adopted, the greater will be the power exerted on the hearts and lives of those placed under its influence.

.   .   .   .

There are some boys who, recreant to all the advantages of a good home and culture, rush thoughtlessly into an evil and criminal life, but, subjected to reformatory discipline and treatment, give but little trouble and are considered hopeful cases. Friendless and dependent boys, compelled at a tender age to earn a living, failing to find a home and employment, or a place to learn a trade, become discouraged, and in an evil hour fall from their integrity and are sent to a reformatory, where for the first time in their lives they find a good home with the discipline and training necessary to prepare them to earn honest bread and the confidence of the public.

Boys are sometimes sent to the reformatories ragged, filthy, and in irons. This is a great wrong inflicted on the poor boy, and whoever has the power or interest to send him to the institution should see that he be sent neat and clean in his apparel and person, that on his arrival he may be received and welcomed into the family designated as his future home without showing any outward evidence of his previous life or personal appearance. An unhappy, discontented boy is not in a condition favorable to reformation and improvement. To change a bad boy into a good one, the proper agencies must be adopted and employed. In his new home, he comes under the rulings of the law of kindness and of love. Here the work of reformation is fairly inaugurated, and in a few days the home-feeling is produced and its power realized. His character must be studied, his wants known, and his personal peculiarities ascertained; then reach to him the helping hand of sympathy and encouragement, bring to bear upon his thoughtless mind and stubborn will the power of moral truth and the authority of law, reach his heart through his understanding, let him feel and realize that his recovery from the power of evil is possible, and that by the divine blessing he may become his own deliverer. His dormant energies must be aroused and directed; his purpose to attain a better life must be fixed and avowed; then trust him, and give him the opportunity and the encouragement to do well. This he can enjoy in the schoolroom and chapel, on the fields and in the shops, in his family and on the play-ground. Some boys are weak and helpless at the beginning of their struggles; but, the intellect aroused, the hand employed, and the heart cheered, a beginning is made, the point of indifference is passed, and, step by step, progress in the right direction is made, the careless become thoughtful, idleness is changed for industry, rebellion for obedience, truth for falsehood, and virtue for vice.

Where the reformatory is a good home, and not a cheerless, gloomy prison; its buildings commodious, light, and airy; its surroundings attractive; its pervading influence elevating, at the very beginning a deep and favorable impression will be produced upon the mind and heart of the new-comer, and he submits cheerfully and hopefully to the authoritative guardianship over and around him. Such a home and such a system of treatment form a wall higher and stronger than granite and iron. It is a better preventive to escapes than cells and manacles. Well fed, comfortably lodged and clothed, taught habits of personal neatness and cleanliness, the boy is ready to take hold of every duty, and his state of mind is favorable to receive moral and religious instruction.

The modes of punishment and the certainty of their infliction should be well known and appreciated by the inmates. The law of punishment is a terror to evil-doers, and, properly used, is an accepted element of power in the discipline of the institution. Slight offenses should receive light punishments, but in cases of grievous transgressions the offenders should know that there exists a power in reserve ready to be used when occasion demands it.

In most cases, kindness is a more effective means of reforming boys than punishment; no boy can be reformed without winning his confidence, and that cannot be won by harsh treatment or force.

---

2. Mary Carpenter attacks the congregate system, 1875

Proceedings of the Conference of Charities held in connection with the General Meeting of the American Social Science Association (1875), 67–69.

Mary Carpenter (1807–1877), English philanthropist, established a reformatory school for boys at Kingswood in 1852 and one for girls at Bristol in 1854. She influenced passage of the Youthful Offenders Act of 1854 and Industrial Schools Act of 1857. This paper was prepared by Miss Carpenter and read by William P. Letchworth of New York.

During the visit which I made to this country in the summer of 1873, my time and attention were especially devoted to the study of the prisons and reformatory institutions of those cities through which I passed. My object was to study the principles on which these were established and the results of the working of those principles. I availed myself, on all occasions, of the opinions and experience of persons who had studied the subject, and had acquired practical experience of the working of different systems.

.   .   .   .   .   .

In all cases, it appears to me, and this is the view now generally adopted in Great Britain, that up to the age of fourteen the child who has not such a home as will prepare him to take his proper place in society, and is deprived, whether by the course of nature or by human laws, of parental control, should be placed by the State, representing society, in a condition as nearly as possible representing *a good home*. Hence, in all cases, I object to large institutions for children, where individuality is destroyed, and where there cannot be any home influence. The family system should be represented as completely as circumstances will permit, the parental control and authority being delegated by the State to the managers of the institution, and the loving spirit of a family being infused by the resident officials and by voluntary benevolent effort. The surroundings of the young persons thus brought into an artificial atmosphere should correspond with their natural mode of life, as far as is compatible with sanitary conditions, order and propriety; while the educational and industrial learning should be such as to prepare them to discharge well the duties of the condition of life which they may be expected to fill.

Such will be generally found to be the accepted ideas in the development of English protestant reformatories and industrial schools. The older reformatory schools in New York and Philadelphia were established on the congregate system. That at Westboro', in Massachusetts, was established later, but the family system was never fully adopted in it, and the various serious catastrophes which have befallen it indicate an entire want of the family spirit. From all I heard it was rather a juvenile gaol. Shortly before my arrival about eighty boys had absconded. I was not invited to visit the place, and did not believe that I should gain much by going there. I carefully visited the New York Reform School, on Randall's Island, and the pauper schools on the same island. The former is a splendid institution, and managed with great care and effort; but it is carried on, it appears to me, on a false principle. There is no natural life or freedom; young men of an age to have very large experience of vice are associated

with young boys; all arrangements are artificial; instead of the cultivation of the land, which would prepare the youth to seek a sphere far from the danger of large cities, the boys and young men were being taught trades, which would confine them to the great centres of an overcrowded population. The girls were being carefully taught, and even too much attention was paid to their personal comfort; *but they were prisoners; they were not being prepared for a home life, which is the best life of the woman, and could not be so under existing circumstances,* which were perfectly artificial, and, as it appeared to me, calculated to engender vanity and self-consideration. The same tendencies were more strikingly developed at the Lancaster [Massachusetts] Girls' Reformatory.

In Philadelphia the same remarks must be applied to the large, prison-like buildings both for boys and for girls. Hundreds of youths were there congregated under lock and key, and, however good were the arrangements, they entirely failed to convince me that the principle was good on which the institutions were founded.

---

3. Exploitation of reformatory children, 1882

William Pryor Letchworth, *Labor of Children in Reform Schools* (New York, 1882), pp. 3–7.

Letchworth, a commissioner of the New York State Board of Charities, offered his testimony in support of a New York State bill forbidding the employment of refuge and reformatory children by contract. The 1882 bill was vetoed but similar legislation became law in 1884. See *Laws of the State of New York, 1884* (Albany, 1884), p. 540.

Mr. Chairman and Gentlemen. — I appear before you unofficially — simply as a citizen of the State of New York, deeply interested in the welfare of our public institutions, and especially so in the reformation of the class of children to whom the provisions of this bill refer. I desire to be understood as not directing my remarks to any particular institutions or their boards of managers, with many of whose members I am personally acquainted, and for whom, as well as for the superintendents, I entertain great respect. I simply wish to speak of the contract system as affecting children in our State reform schools.

.   .   .   .   .

The following appears to me to be forcible reasons why statutory enactment for the further protection and reformation of children committed to our reform schools must be regarded as eminently proper:

Under the contract system the reformation and improvement of the child is subordinated to the interest of the contractor.

It is for the interest of the contractor to so subdivide the labor on each article manufactured, that the boy learns but one process in the operation, and leaves the institution unable to compete with those who have learned a trade.

It is for the interest of the contractor to exact the largest possible amount of work from the boy. The latter is, therefore, put on task work, and his task is increased as his capacity develops, until there is danger of overtaxing the boy's strength.

The contractor's foremen, to gain personal credit by showing large products, or to promote their own ease, have been known to influence the keepers of the shops by making them presents, thus converting them from being servants of the institution into agents of the contractors, leaving the children without protection from mercenary greed.

Under the contract system boys are supplied surreptitiously with tobacco by contractor's agents in order to stimulate them to the performance of greater tasks than is proper, and in this way an objectionable and expensive life-long habit is acquired.

It is for the interest of the contractor to hire such instructors for the boys as will most promote his pecuniary interests, without reference to moral qualifications or fitness to associate with youth. The influence of such men upon the boys is often pernicious, and their passing several times daily in and out of the shops affords opportunity for illicit traffic with the outside world, damaging to the cause of reform.

It is for the interest of the contractor to protract to the fullest extent the hours of labor in order to meet his fixed daily expenses, and the desire of managers to keep on good terms with profitable contractors may induce them to extend the working hours, encroaching on those which should be devoted to school and recreation.

When the demand for his goods is large, the contractor is disposed to engage the labor of very young children, who are thus subjected to rules and discipline too severe for their tender years.

Children under sixteen years of age, when subjected to long hours of labor, in irksome positions, under a task contract system, are likely to be retarded in their development, and fagged out at the end of their long confinement, are too weary to derive due advantage from the teachings imparted in the evening school.

While flogging has long been abolished in the Navy and the use of the "cat" in the State Prisons, it is still thought necessary, in order to realize a fair pecuniary return from the children's labor, for the contractor to inflict severe corporal punishment for deficiency in imposed tasks. One institution in the State, in order to meet the expectation of contractors, was forced in a single year to inflict on the boys employed, upon the direct complaint of contractors, their superintendent, overseer and employes, corporal punishments *two thousand two hundred and sixty-three times*. This was administered with a strap or rattan on the hand, or on the posterior bare or covered, as the gravity of the case demanded. During the same period the punishments in school, in order as it was said, to "wake up" their already overtaxed attention, was so considerable as to swell up the aggregate punishments for the year to the magnitude of *ten thousand*.

The tendency of the contract system in reformatory institutions for boys, is to retain as long as possible those who are most valuable to the contractor, and as these generally belong to the most dutiful class and consequently entitled to an early discharge, a great injustice is done, which sometimes drives boys to desperation. On the other hand, the intent of the contractor being to rid himself of the unskillful and careless workers, there is danger of a premature discharge of such before the work of reformation is completed.

Were the contract system abolished, the children could be placed entirely under the training of those carefully selected by the managers as specially fitted for the work, and an elevating moral influence thereby exerted.

The children could be taught such industries as the managers deemed would best enable them to earn an honest livelihood after leaving the institution, and could be taught the whole of a trade instead of a part.

The abolishing of the contract system need not embarrass the officials in finding suitable employment for the children; the products of their labor are always marketable. The work being wholly directed by the officers of the institution, elevating influences would be exerted.

A scheme of employment adapted to adult convicts in a penal establishment, is not suited to a reform school for children, where a home atmosphere should prevail, and where encouragement, sympathy and the inculcation of self-respect by association with disinterested teachers, should be characteristic features.

The impression produced upon the mind of the boy, under the contract system, that he is part of a scheme for making money for the institution which maintains him, interferes with that trustfulness which is one of the first essentials in operating a reform.

The system of contracting *per diem* for the labor of children is almost obsolete in America, while in Germany, France, Switzerland and England, where reformatory schools have been so successful, such a system would be looked upon as mercenary, unwise and destructive of the very ends sought.

Keeping in mind that the primary aim in dealing with juvenile offenders is their *reformation,* whatever method will most effectually reach this end is the cheapest.

---

4. Value of "technologic training" for reform school boys, 1884

J. D. Runkle to William P. Letchworth, Feb. 16, 1884, in William P. Letchworth, *Technologic Training in Reform Schools* (Buffalo, 1884), pp. 25–27.

John Daniel Runkle (1822–1902), mathematician, was president of Massachusetts Institute of Technology from 1870 to 1878. Impressed by the Centennial Exposition exhibit of the Imperial Technical School of Moscow, Runkle personally investigated technological schools in Europe and helped to establish a program of mechanical arts at M.I.T.

MY DEAR SIR:

Our experience is, that boys of twelve have sufficient strength to take up courses of instruction in woodworking, but cannot make as rapid progress as older boys. From twelve to eighteen, boys can be taught a variety of processes which apply in wood and metal constructions, and at the same time carry on the studies of a common education to advantage.

One lesson a day in shop instruction is ample, and this lesson should not exceed three hours. We have found that two hours make too short and four too long a lesson. It takes some time to get a class at work, as the explanations and general directions must be given first, and at the end the tools must be put in place, with washing and change of clothing in most courses. If you have a large number of boys to teach, it is best to begin with as many shops as possible, in order to diversify the instruction and enable each boy to work in the direction which his taste or capacity dictates. For this purpose each boy should be given a short elementary course in each shop, and then devote his time more especially upon that department in which he has shown the most capacity and interest.

In this way a boy (say from ten to seventeen years of age) who has any capacity for hand work can, in two or three years, fit himself to enter some establishment and apply his knowledge and skill to the mutual advantage of his employer and himself. Such a boy is vastly better off than an ordinary apprentice of the same length of service, because he has been taught a much wider range of processes or arts. His ordinary education has also been continued. If you can give me some idea of the average age and number of boys in the institution in which you would like to make an experiment of this kind (or rather introduce this kind of education, for I do not regard the matter as in the experimental stage), I will gladly do what I can to aid you in arranging the details of the shop instructions adapted to the case. If you can so educate the boys in your charge as to make them conscious of the ability to help themselves, I am sure that you will do more for their future than by any other course.

When boys are once in a reformatory, all the money needed to reform them will be well spent — the only better way of spending it is by keeping them out of the reformatory. It does seem to me that if our education could better develop the special aptitudes and tastes of each child, and lead all in a clear path to some useful pursuit, we should have less reform work to do.

Very truly yours,

J. D. RUNKLE.

---

5. Homer Folks of the Children's Aid Society

of Pennsylvania lists the shortcomings of the refromatory system, 1891

Homer Folks, "The Care of Delinquent Children," *Proceedings* of the National Conference of Charities and Correction (1891), 137–139.

---

1. The temptation it offers to parents and guardians to throw off their most sacred responsibilities. Abundant evidence that this is frequently done has come under our immediate observation. A woman called at our office not long since to ask how she could secure admission for her son to the Huntingdon Reformatory, stating incidentally that she had sent both her daughters to be educated in the House of Refuge, but was inclined to prefer an institution in the country for her son. We could multiply such instances almost indefinitely. Within two months our agent has found in the county prisons, awaiting trial, two young men who were at an early age sent to a reformatory for a home and to be educated . . . We would . . . call attention to the fact that in proportion as the educational and industrial features of these institutions are perfected this temptation is increased . . .

2. The contaminating influence of association. It is certainly unjust to crowd into one building the good and the bad, the innocent and depraved, the homeless boy and the juvenile criminal. Is it not just as unwise to put under one roof numbers of children who are equally depraved and criminal? Cut off from the infinite diversity of interests of ordinary life, will they not inevitably dwell on the evils which led to their commitment, and tell over to each other the story of their lives, and teach each other whatever cunning device they may have known? Probably nothing has done more to emphasize the hereditary aspect of crime than the little volume entitled "The Jukes." Considering that heredity is often reckoned as an argument for the reformatory, is it not strange that the same research which gave to the world the story of the Jukes family led its author to

declare that "prisons and houses of refuge are the nurseries, not the reformatories, of crime," and to denounce the congregate system, which he declares allows abundant opportunity for criminal training?

3. The enduring stigma which the fact of having been committed to such an institution fastens upon the child. The reformatory is, first and foremost, a place to which criminal children are sent to be reformed; and the implication is, in the case of every child thus committed, that the community was obliged in self-defence to place it behind bars. Just as the criminal discharged from prison finds it difficult or impossible to reinstate himself in society, so the boy discharged from the reformatory finds himself branded with the trademark of crime. This perpetuates the evil of association, since the discharged boy seeks as his companions those who by similar discipline and education have the same interests and sympathies.

4. Such a system renders impossible the study and treatment of each child as an individual. As we shall show later on, we fail to find any common traits running through this mass of children by virtue of which they require the same treatment. On the contrary, each child who has fallen into the hands of the law has done so through a perfectly definite series of facts, and has individual characteristics and peculiarities. Moral infirmities require as careful diagnosis as physical, and to treat all practically alike seems to us as wild as for a physician to prescribe one sort of medicine for all diseases.

5. The great dissimilarity between life in an institution and life outside. How great the change the day the boy steps from the institution to family life! His temptation has been reduced to a minimum. Perhaps committed for larceny, he has had no chance to commit larceny since. Now he is thrown into the midst of temptations, doubly powerful because of novelty. Just at this moment the strict discipline must be withdrawn. The routine of life by which he has been carried along is removed. To-day he must decide for himself a hundred matters which yesterday were decided for him. All these make new and large demands for individuality and self-control, and a knowledge of the affairs of ordinary life. Of the ninety-five children readmitted to the [Philadelphia] House of Refuge in 1890, 43 or 45 per cent had been discharged less than three months.

C. NEW INSTITUTIONS FOR DELINQUENTS AND UNRULY CHILDREN

In the late nineteenth century a variety of institutions were founded in an attempt to reform children whose misbehavior had not yet become serious enough to require incarceration in state institutions. Industrial schools were originally intended to save semi-delinquent girls from the odium of the reform school, while military schools — particularly those established in the Northern states — relieved middle-class parents of the responsibility of bringing up obstreperous sons.

Private reformatories

1. Industrial schools for girls, Illinois

"An act to aid industrial schools for girls," *Laws of the State of Illinois, 1879* (Springfield, 1879), pp. 309–313.

Be it enacted by the People of the State of Illinois, represented in the General Assembly, That any seven or more persons, residents of this State, a majority of whom are women, who may organize, or have organized, under the general laws of the State, relating to corporations, for the purpose of establishing, maintaining and carrying on an Industrial School for Girls, shall have under the corporate names assumed, all the powers, rights and privileges of corporations of this State, not for pecuniary profit, and shall be, and hereby are exempted from all State and local taxes: *provided however,* that any persons organized, or who may hereafter organize as above set forth, desiring to avail themselves of the provisions of this act, shall first obtain the consent of the Governor thereto, in writing, which consent must be filed in the office of the Secretary of State.

The object of Industrial Schools for Girls shall be to provide a home and proper training school for such girls as may be committed to their charge; and they shall be maintained by voluntary contributions, excepting as hereinafter provided.

Any responsible person who has been a resident of any county in this State, one year next preceding the time at which the petition is presented, may petition the county court of said county to inquire into the alleged dependency of any female infant then within the county, and every female infant who comes within the following descriptions shall be considered a dependent girl, viz:

Every female infant who begs or receives alms while actually selling, or pretending to sell any article in public; or who frequents any street, alley or other place, for the purpose of begging or receiving alms; or, who having no permanent place of abode, proper parental care, or guardianship, or sufficient means of subsistence, or who for other cause is a wanderer through streets and alleys, and in other public places; or, who lives with, or frequents the company of, or consorts with reputed thieves, or other vicious persons; or who is found in a house of ill-fame, or in a poor house.

The petition shall also state the name of the father of the infant, if living, or if dead, the name of the mother; and if neither the father nor mother of the infant be living, or to be found in the county, then the name of the guardian, if there be one. If there be a parent living, or guardian, the petition shall set forth not only the dependency of the infant, but shall also show that the parent or guardian is not a fit person to have the custody of such infant. Such petition shall be verified by oath, and upon being filed, the judge of said court shall have the female infant, named in the petition, brought before him for the purpose of determining the application in said petition contained, and for the hearing of such petitions the county court shall be considered always open.

Upon the filing of such petition, the clerk of the court shall issue a writ to the sheriff of the county, directing him to bring such infant before the court to order a jury of six to be summoned, to ascertain whether such infant is a dependent, as alleged in such petition, and also to find if the other allegations are true, and if found to be such, they shall also find her age in their verdict, and when such infant shall be without counsel, it shall be the duty of the court to assign counsel for her; and if the jury finds that the infant named in the petition is a dependent girl, and that the other material facts set forth in the petition are true, and if, in the opinion of the judge, she is a fit person to be sent to an Industrial School for Girls, the judge shall enter an order that such infant be committed to an Industrial School for Girls in the county, if there be such school in the county; but if there be no such school in the county, then to any Industrial School for Girls, elsewhere in the State, to be in such school kept and maintained until she arrives at the age of eighteen years, unless sooner discharged therefrom in the manner hereinafter provided. Before the hearing aforesaid, notice shall be given to the parent or guardian of the infant, if to be found in the county, of the proceedings about to be instituted, and they may appear and resist the same.

If the court finds as in the preceding section, it shall further order of record, that such infant has no guardian; or that her guardian or parent is not a fit person to have the custody of such infant, as the case may be, and the court may thereupon appoint the president or any one of the vice-presidents of such Industrial School the lawful guardian of such infant, and no bond shall be required of such guardian, and such guardian shall permit such infant to be placed under the care and in the custody of such Industrial School for Girls as hereinafter provided.

.   .   .   .   .   .

The fees for conveying a dependent girl to an Industrial School for Girls, shall be the same as conveying a juvenile offender to the Reform School for Juvenile Offenders, at Pontiac, in this State, and they shall be paid by the counties from which such dependent girls are sent, unless they are paid by the parent or guardian.

It shall be the duty of the county judge to see that every dependent girl committed by him to an Industrial School for Girls, shall, at the time she is conveyed to the school, be furnished with three chemises, three pairs of woolen stockings, one pair of shoes, two woolen petticoats or skirts, three good dresses, a cloak or shawl, and a suitable bonnet. The expense of said clothing shall be paid out of the county treasurer upon the certificate of the county judge. But if the dependent girl have a parent or guardian, the court shall render judgment against him for the amount to be paid the county for such clothing, together with cost of collection; and if such expenses and cost of collection are recovered the money shall be paid into the county treasury. For the tuition, maintenance and care of dependent girls, the county from which they are sent shall pay to the Industrial School for Girls to which they may be committed, as follows:

For each dependent girl under the age of ten years; ten dollars per month.

For each dependent girl ten years and under fourteen years of age, ten dollars per month.

For each dependent girl fourteen and under eighteen years of age, ten dollars per month. And upon the proper officer rendering proper accounts therefor, quarterly, the county board shall allow and order the same paid out of the county treasury: *Provided,* that no charge shall be made against any county by any Industrial School for Girls on account of any dependent girl in the care thereof who has been by said school put out to a trade or employment in the manner hereinafter provided.

The officers and trustees of any Industrial School for Girls in this State, shall receive into such school all girls committed thereto under the provisions of this act, and shall have the exclusive custody, care and guardianship of such girls. They shall provide for their support and comfort; instruct them in such branches of useful knowledge as may be suited to their years and capacities, and shall cause them to be taught in domestic avocations, such as sewing, knitting, and housekeeping in all its departments. And for the purpose of their education and training, and that they may assist in their own support, they shall be required to pursue such tasks suitable to their years and sex, as may be prescribed by such officers and trustees.

Any girl committed under the provisions of this act to an Industrial School for Girls, may by the officers and trustees of said school be placed in the home of any good citizen upon such terms and for such purpose and time as may be agreed upon, or she may be given to any suitable person of good character who will adopt her, or she may be bound to any reputable citizen as an apprentice to learn any trade, or as a servant to follow any employment which, in the judgment of said officers and trustees, will be for her advantage . . . *Provided,* that any disposition made of any girl under this section shall not bind her beyond her minority; *And, provided, further,* that such officers and trustees shall have a supervising care over such girl to see that she is properly treated and cared for; and in case such girl is cruelly treated, or is neglected, or the terms upon which she was committed to the care and protection of any person are not observed, or in case such care and protection of any person are not observed, or in case such care and protection shall for any reason cease, then it shall be the duty of such officers and trustees to take and receive such girl again into the custody, care and protection of said industrial school.

No imbecile, or idiotic girl, or one incapacitated for labor, nor any girl having any infectious, contagious, or incurable disease, shall be committed or received into any Industrial School for Girls in this State.

Any girl committed to an Industrial School for Girls, under the provisions of this act, may be discharged therefrom at any time, in accordance with the rules thereof, when in the judgment of the officers and trustees, the good of the girl or good of the school, would be promoted by such discharge, and the Governor may at any time order the discharge of any girl committed to an industrial school under the provisions of this act.

All Industrial Schools for Girls in this State, shall be subject to the same visitation, inspection and supervision of the Board of State Commissioners of Public Charities, as the charitable and penal institutions of the State, and avoiding as far as practicable, sectarianism; suitable provisions shall be made for the moral and religious instruction of the inmates of all Industrial Schools for Girls in this State. But no such industrial school shall receive an appropriation from the State for any purpose, and any school receiving an appropriation from the State shall not have the benefit of the provisions of this act.

---

2. The Burnham Industrial Farm, New York

W. M. F. Round to Rutherford B. Hayes, enclosure, Dec. 1, 1887, Rutherford B. Hayes Papers (Hayes Library, Fremont, Ohio). By permission of the Rutherford B. Hayes Library.

William Marshall Fitts Round (1845–1906),

a social reformer and journalist in New York and Boston, became a member of the executive committee of the Prison Association of New York in 1881. His work brought him to the attention of Frederick G. Burnham, a wealthy New York lawyer, who wanted to develop his large farm into an effective reformatory for New York City boys. Round, believing that the cottage system, as originally applied in Europe, had not received a fair trial in the United States, carefully supervised its adoption at the Burnham Industrial Farm. The name was changed to the Berkshire Industrial Farm in 1896.

Former President Rutherford B. Hayes (1822–1893) had an active interest in prison reform and was president of the National Prison Association in 1883.

The chief source from which the criminal classes are recruited is the large number of boys who grow up without industrial training, and without the moral influences of home. Long experience has shown that this training and these influences cannot be fully replaced by any system which keeps together large communities of boys in Asylums and Refuges, especially in great cities; and while some of these institutions do an excellent work, they greatly need to be supplemented by others which provide for a more natural and healthful life. The plan found most effectual is that practiced for many years with eminent success at Mettray, in France, and at the Rauhe Haus, near Hamburg. Here the boys are distributed in cottage families, not more than fifteen or twenty under one roof, and, under careful personal supervision, are trained in the labor to which their capacities are adapted, with as much as possible of the social and moral influences of home, until they are fitted to be self-supporting citizens. The great majority of those who have been gathered into these institutions, out of the vagabond class, have been permanently saved to society.

The Burnham Industrial Farm, of nearly six hundred acres, beautifully situated in Columbia

County, New York, has been given by Mr. and Mrs. Frederick G. Burnham to a Board of Trustees, incorporated by a law of New York for this purpose. The land is fertile and diversified, the air is pure, the scenery charming, and the buildings, long the home of an industrial Shaker community, are well fitted for the beginning of the enterprise. Early in 1887 the trustees placed upon the farm an excellent superintendent and an experienced matron, and began carefully to select and receive boys from a vast number of candidates for admission. Under the charter the corporation may obtain the custody of boys by surrender on the part of parents or guardians, by the sentence of a committing magistrate for vagrancy, or by transfer from other charitable institutions. They must be between seven and sixteen years of age when received, and may be retained until bound out as apprentices or servants, or adopted into families, or until they attain their majority.

Thirty boys have been received and gradually incorporated in the life of the farm, and the results have been most encouraging. The rapid improvement of the pupils in health, industry and morals, their loyalty to the institution, and their attachment to their officers, show that the system meets their needs, and prove that the useful work of the farm is only limited by its resources. These are as yet small. It is not endowed, and the trustees are firmly convinced that its independence and Christian character will be best secured by maintaining it as a private charity, not by appealing for aid to the State. But now that its experimental stage is passed, and that hundreds of boys, on the way to ruin, are waiting to be rescued by it, they are confident that the situation needs only to be known in order to bring it, from a philanthropic public, all requisite support. Every subscription shall be applied, with the utmost care and economy, to increase the extent and efficiency of the work, and the trustees believe that there is no direction in which Christian philanthropy can accomplish so much good with so moderate an expenditure.

Boarding and military schools

1. Should I send my boy to a boarding school?

J. M. Buckley, "About Sending Boys to Boarding-School," in *Catalogue of the Bordentown Military Institute, Bordentown, N.J., 1893–1894* (Philadelphia, 1894), pp. 31–32.

James Monroe Buckley (1836–1920) was a well-known Methodist clergyman and, from 1880 to 1912, editor of his denomination's leading periodical, the *Christian Advocate*. Buckley wrote and spoke frequently on the evils of theater going and the difficulties of disciplining young men.

The question, What shall I do with my boy? constantly arises in the minds of parents, and resolves itself into the alternatives, Shall we keep him at home, or send him to boarding-school?

Much may be said on both sides. Doubtless there are cases that settle themselves without much consideration. A boy is doing so well at home and has such exceptional facilities that no one thinks of sending him away; or, he is doing so ill at home, or has such unsatisfactory opportunities, that no one thinks of keeping him there. These cases, we think, are comparatively few in number. Many boys are doing neither well nor ill at home, but are somewhat sluggish, little inclined to study, and are to some extent under the influence of other boys, and while there is no occasion for serious disquietude of mind concerning them, the question arises whether a change would not be better. Some, too, appear to have reached the highest point which the home influences can give.

.   .   .   .   .

The question often comes up, Which class of boys on the average is the more moral, those that stay at home, or those that are sent a portion of the time to boarding-school? Many years ago we thought that those who stayed at home were more likely to grow up moral and religious than those who go to boarding-school. More extended observation has convinced us that a very large proportion of the boys living at home in cities do not do as well as the average of those sent to good Christian schools. The proportion of young men converted in the boarding-school is much larger than the proportion of those who do not go.

It is true that boys who have been sent to the very best schools often tell to their younger brothers and playmates, and even to their parents, the most startling accounts of the escapades in which they have engaged, and of the ingenious but not ingenuous manner in which they deceived the Faculty. But two things should be remembered: One is that there is often much exaggeration about these tales. The other is boys *living* at *home* do *not* give account to their parents, or to others, so that their parents can hear of them of the wrong actions which they do. So that the reports from the schools are often worse than the facts, while the *appearance* at home is often below the reality. Of course, these remarks do not apply to the best boys either at home or away at school. But to average boys both recollection and observation compel us to believe that they do apply.

Thousands of young men owe their hope of heaven and their religious character to the influence exerted upon them in the schools, sustained by the respective denominations to which their parents belong. There are some exceptions where the spirit of schools is irreligious, where doubt fills the atmosphere. The number of these under Methodist auspices is very small.

Boys must leave home some time. It is certainly better for them to begin the experiment under the care of intelligent, educated men and women than to thrust them out from home without any previous preparation.

Boys at home often fail to appreciate the kindness of parents, the comforts of home and its opportunities as they should. When they are sent away to school, even to the best schools, it has been observed that their love of home and parents frequently greatly increases. We have seen a letter from such a boy, who was always considered a good boy at home, loving and grateful, in which this passage occurred: "O, father, I never knew what a home I had until I went away to school." It was a somewhat pathetic little note that a boy put away to boarding school sent to his father. He was a little homesick, and said, "Dear father: Life is short, let us spend it together. Your affectionate son."

---

2. The "aim and scope" of the Culver Military Academy, 1897

Catalogue of the Culver Military Academy (Culver, Ind., 1897), pp. 26–29.

Culver Military Academy was founded in 1894 by H. H. Culver, a wealthy citizen of St. Louis, Missouri. It was a private school charging tuition.

The critical years of every boy's life are those between twelve and twenty. Home influence begins to lose its hold, and the restlessness and lawlessness of young manhood to assert itself even in the noblest and most generous natures. Many a parent, feeling that his boy was growing too large for his control, or painfully conscious of wild and reckless impulses and energies in his hitherto docile child, acting as he thinks for the best, has sent him to college or university. There, with his mind unawakened and his moral nature undisciplined, he has fallen an easy victim to vicious companions or to the evil influences to which he must needs be exposed.

We owe it to our boys to shield them in every

possible manner in this period of greatest danger. How is this to be done?

MENTAL TRAINING

Can do much, and upon this idea alone the college or university is based. The mind is awaking, and seizes upon new ideas, or seeks knowledge with as keen a relish as the hungry boy devours food. And every teacher knows that the eager student is far less open to every form of temptation, is far apter to occupy a higher moral plane than his less interested companion.

But this is not all. The very activity of his mind is often a severe tax upon his physical strength, and many of the most successful students spend the best years of their early manhood in recovering from the evil effects of overwork, or the direct violation of nature's laws during their college course.

ATHLETIC SPORTS

Form an excellent outlet for the energies. But these must be wisely directed and judiciously used, for the boy is not the wisest judge of what is best in these sports.

Who are the boys who usually succeed best at college? Those to whom poverty teaches the stern lessons of self-denial and self-control, from which those who are able gladly shield their children for a longer period. And they do so wisely, if they can at the same time procure for them a discipline which will take the place in part of the severer discipline of life. This is the claim made for the

CULVER MILITARY ACADEMY

It is proposed to keep the Cadets fully occupied; to stimulate mental activity and promote intellectual growth by all means in the power of the best teachers; to preserve a careful oversight of the physical health; to encourage all gymnastic and athletic sports. Above all, it is believed that in the

MILITARY FEATURE

of this school is offered the wisest solution of the even more important question of the development of a character based upon right principles, without which all else is vain. By this feature, so fascinating to every boy's natural taste, there can be exercised over him a restraint under which he would surely chafe if it came from any outside source. He is bound by every noble impulse and by every incentive of honor and ambition to learn first the self-control and implicit obedience to orders, by which alone he can prepare himself in turn to command and control others.

The George Junior Republic

William R. George (1866–1936) was born near Ithaca, New York, but as a young man moved to New York City where he prospered in the export business. In 1890, he opened a fresh air camp for Manhattan street children in Freeville, New York, not far from his boyhood home. After a few years, George became convinced that the children were being pauperized by the summer outings. To discourage this tendency and to promote self-reliance, he began to require that everything be paid for by labor and that the children elect their own representatives to administer the routine of the camp. The George Junior Republic, which was established in 1895 on a year-'round basis, grew out of "Daddy" George's belief that dependent and delinquent children could teach themselves the virtues of good government and self-support.

A private corporation, it served as a model for other Junior Republics throughout the United States. Many institutions for juvenile delinquents adopted some form of inmate self-government.

---

1. "Daddy" George discusses the origin and purpose of his Republic

Radio speech by William R. George (1925?), Box 47, George Junior Republic Papers, Cornell University. By permission of Cornell University, Ithaca, N.Y.

The Junior Republic was started July 10, 1895. Its object was to instill in the lives of young people, the virtues of self-support and self-government. This could only be done by direct application. To accomplish that end the customary form of controling and directing youth by the institution method was renounced. Instead of constructing an institution, a village similar in all essentials to a village of grown-ups was built and put in operation. The young people residing in this village were its voting citizens. They faced the same social, civic, and economic problems that the voting citizens of any other American community confront. These issues they heroically confronted with a forti-tude and intelligence equal to that of the adult. Nothing Without Labor was their motto. The economic condition of earning both necessities and luxuries by hard work was a wholesome tonic. Thus they realized the value of civic laws to protect their property.

Theoretical instruction or class room lecture to teach the values of laws and property rights to them was simply infantile. In their daily life of practical experience they did the real thing. No idle play was their court of justice operated by their judge, attorneys and jurors; their jail and its warden; their police force with its phys-ically fit "cops"; their town meeting where they enacted their own laws; their president who made these laws enforceable by his signa-ture; their bank; their store; their employment at trades for which they received payment based on the value of the labor they performed. In plain words it was conditions and not theo-ries that daily confronted them. Backbone be-gan to develop here and there in individuals where previously it had seemed to be non-exist-ent.

The unique and picturesque life of the Junior Republic was quick to bring visitors by the hun-dreds to observe the self-governing colony. Not only the curious surveyed it but educators and government representatives from all parts of the world were frequent visitors.

In the first years of its life it was a favorite subject for magazine articles, newspapers, and educational conferences. Various attempts were made to establish other Junior Republics but consummate success to the mind of the founder was not achieved because all too often some of the underlying basic principles involving self-government and self-support were either mod-ified or entirely withheld. However it started a wave of self-government in schools, clubs, and other assemblies of young people throughout the United States and somewhat abroad. In the meantime the Republic at Freeville progressed and developed a still wider field of usefulness.

For the first years of its history its citizen-ship, with some exceptions, was boys and girls from poor and neglected homes in New York City. Sometime during that period an interest-ing phenomenon blazed forth; many of the boys, who before entering the Republic had been excelling in delinquencies in their city haunts, were upon arrival at the Republic regu-lated with neatness and dispatch by their fellow citizens. Straight way after release from their incarceration in the jail, they joined the ranks of good citizenship and became valiant support-ers of law and order. The fact their peers had locked them up because they couldn't trust them had taken all the romance out of wrong doing. This condition was so noticeable that for a time we announced that general badness, so far as boys were concerned, was a special qualification for admittance to the little colony. This move on our part met with two reactions, one good for it demonstrated the efficacy of self-government and self-support as a reforming agency, the other bad for this procedure instantly caused the public to regard the Junior Republic as useful only in the service it rendered as a regulator of delinquent youth. However, during this early period we also had a number of youthful citizens who had entered the little colony without any reproach attached to their personal history. These of course had no occasion to anticipate disciplinary regulation by their fellow citizens. They didn't come to the Junior Republic to be "saved" speaking in the sense of rescue from delinquency. But the economic and civic training which they received in the little colony could not be excelled. Careful observation of this group demonstrated conclusively that the economic and civic responsibilities which these normal youngsters tackled developed them rapidly in these imperative essentials.

Encouraged by the value of the economic and civic reactions upon youth both good and bad when given so large a measure of individual responsibility, we determined to stand by our findings in the experiment — which had really ceased to be an experiment — and give all youth the opportunity of citizenship so far as our limited geographical area would permit. So we threw down the gauntlet and declared that we did not care whether the young citizens came from the city or the country, from rich homes or poor homes or no homes at all, whether they were Catholics or Protestants or Jews, whether previous to their arrival in the colony they had been very very good or very very bad so long as they were very very something. And so it came to pass that the Junior Republic during its latter years has had heterogeneous representation to verify this policy and it has worked successfully. In this connection it has been interesting to note how readily all normal youth rise to emergencies when confronted with actual responsibilities. Especially is it interesting to note what a small factor

previous "class condition" plays. The official currency of the Junior Republic, token money, is a principle factor in economic adjustment. A lad who has come from a poor home or no home at all may, through thrift, acquire a substantial bank account and the rating of a millionaire in its Junior Republic appelation, while a youngster who has come from a home of wealth may, at the beginning of his career, scorn the idea of working for his food with the result that he lands in the jail for vagrancy; for it is a fact that no matter how wealthy his father may be and how much he may pay in gold for the privilege of his son being in the Junior Republic, the young gentleman does not receive a mouthful of food until he works for it. Sooner or later he adjusts himself to the slogan of Nothing Without Labor and thereafter all goes well. In the Junior Republic it is not what you were before you became a citizen of the little colony; it's what you are after confronting the unerring laws of political economy and the civic responsibilities which follow in their wake.

---

2. "Go to work, Kid"

Box 47, George Junior Republic Papers.

This and the following document are examples of promotional literature issued by the George Junior Republic.

Billie Smith arrived at the George Junior Republic a husky boy of sixteen. He had never known responsibility, and had given little thought to the why or the wherefore of things that came to him in life. His path had not been exactly a primrose one, yet he had known few disappointments, and very few inconveniences. For Billie things had always "Just happened."

Self-government, self-support, economic and civic duties were all things he had heard about in a hazy way, but never given serious thought to. He was what would be called an average boy. Not bad, yet not particularly good. He liked to play and he disliked work, and studies to him were nothing but boredom.

Being captain of his own soul was a new experience, and he immediately decided that as he was to guide his own destiny he was going to make it as pleasant as possible. With this determination he stretched luxuriously in bed in the morning and watched other fellows, who were foolish enough to do so, hustle out to a quick breakfast and work.

When the time came to pay his board and lodging, and a few incidental bills were presented to him, he calmly exchanged some of the American money given him on leaving home for Junior Republic currency, paid his bills, and then sat down and wrote home for more money. Then came his first surprise, he was not allowed to receive any money that he had not worked for. This upset his scheme of things very much. He complained bitterly to several citizens, and even to Daddy George himself. But the answer was always the same: "Go to work."

But going to work didn't suit him. He had enough money to carry him through another week, so he paid up, and kept his credit good. But when Saturday came around again he was broke. However, he had plenty of things he could sell at a fair price, so he commenced selling first one article then another. Finally he came to a point where he had nothing more to sell, except things that he considered were necessities. Yet he could not bring himself to take a job.

When he couldn't pay his board he had to leave his boarding house, and take up quarters in a less desirable lodging. Next he fell into the habit of borrowing. He readily found a number of industrious citizens who had money and were willing to lend it for interest, provided there was good security back of it. Finally Billie had mortgaged everything he possessed, even to the watch given him on his last birthday, which he was so very proud of.

His notes fell due and he could not meet them, nor could he pay a premium to have them renewed. The holders foreclosed, and the court ordered an auction sale of all of Billie's belongings. Here was a lesson in law with a vengeance.

Billie stood with breaking heart while one by one his treasures passed into the hands of fellows who had worked and saved their money. When the watch was sold and its new owner proudly put it in his pocket Billie could stand no more, and the tears he had been bravely holding back came in a flood.

After the creditors had been paid Billie was handed enough money to last him a little over a week. "Go to work, Kid, and earn your stuff back," advised the auctioneer.

That seemed the best thing to do, and the next day Billie was up early hunting a job. He set his jaw, and tackled the uninteresting work given him with a dogged determination. Slowly he rose to a post of trust in the Republic. With the possession of property that he had worked for he developed an interest in civics and economics. He ran for and was elected to various offices, till in his last year he was president. Meanwhile he had bought back most of his treasures, and when he went home for the Christmas holidays he was able to wear his watch again, but then it held a greater value than it had ever held.

---

3. Hustlers, 1896–1897

Box 2, George Junior Republic Papers.

"APPRECIATED" CURRENCY

A great deal of interest is always manifested by the citizens of the G.J.R. whenever mysterious boxes or barrels arrive at the Republic and are placed before its store.

They understand that without doubt these packages contain goods that can be purchased with the J.R. currency. No Fifth Avenue belle or dude could be more interested in the Spring Opening of a popular store than these young hopefuls. Their pleasure is considerably intensified if they have the privilege of seeing the barrel heads and box covers removed, and the goods conveyed to the shelves and counter of the store.

The other day, a great big dry goods case, that nearly filled the truck arrived at the store. It was sent by the many friends of the Republic in Germantown Pa. The citizens at once discovered that it was about to be opened. First the idle drew near, then those working at odd jobs, then the public officials, then the industrious workmen, and last the contractors. As the cover was knocked off, a lot of new clothing was revealed to view.

"That's a beauty sweater, just my size," said No. 51 enthusiastically "but pshaw, haint got no money ceptin that money what I deposited for bail on L.K."

"All right B" (No. 51) "I've got the chink, you can watch me while I wear it," said No. 110.

A few layers of clothing were removed by the storekeeper, and a large quantity of new shirts came into view.

Chorus — "Oh, aint those daisies."

"Sure there's enough for every fellow on the place," said No. 28.

"Yes, if they got the dough to buy them, which I haint," said No. 91, philosophically.

"Aw, if you hustled more, you'd have enough to buy things," said 79 scornfully.

Chorus of citizens "That's no lie either, W — " (91).

Just at this moment the storekeeper turned up a large package of brand new knee pants.

"Nothin second hand about those" cried 114. "Sure, I got some money too, but it's in the same place with B's (No. 51). All in on bail for L.K."

At this juncture 51 edges around to 114 and whispers, "Tell you what D," (114) "let's withdraw our bail on L.K."

"I'll see yer about that just a little later" said 114. "It's a rank shame, we should be dished out of buying these things just because L.K. was fool enough not to behave himself, and get jugged."

The storekeeper had just struck a strata of shoes, "Ray" shouts 71. "I'll give $3.00 for those tans, hey storekeeper, will you sell 'em to me for that?"

"I'll go him a half dollar better" cries 69.

"I'll give $4.00," shouts 80, "only I hain't got it."

"Ray, storekeeper, open up right away will yer?"

Storekeeper — "Think I'll just wait a little while, we'll open it up pretty soon however."

Chorus — "That's right" as they run back pell mell to their work.

"Hey F." cries 80, "you'se want to hustle around now, and get that half dollar, I loaned you the other day, for I'll need it in the store."

"I'll try S.," said F. seriously.

"Sure that's what yer promised me forty times before, but I haint seen it yet." (Aside to fellow citizens, " 'fraid I won't either but I tell you what I will do, I'll sue him and if I get the case, I'll seize those felt boots he's wearing.")

A few minutes later, 114 — 51 — and 28 were observed counselling together. It was only for a brief period, then in a body they moved to the police station. They had not been gone long, when suddenly, "Woodsie" (the cop) came flying out of the door, and marched straight to where L.K. was working as enthusiastically as a boy or man for that matter could possibly work. He was whistling cheerily and seemed to be far removed from care of any kind. All this was brought to a sudden end, by Woodsie, the cop.

"Hey L.K. you've got to go back in the jug."

L.K. starts, drops his broom, looks up with mingled surprise and apprehension — "What's up, Woodsie."

"Oh, B.(51), D.(114), and W.(28) have withdrawn their bail they put on you; they want to use the money in the store, so you'll have to go back and be locked up till yer can find some one else to go it, or stay in till yer trial. Of course you know all that it won't be necessary for me to waste time giving you descriptions."

L.K. burst into tears. "A ———— that's what I call a dirty mean trick" said he between his sobs, "don't you think so Woodsie?"

"Perhaps, but then you shouldn't have given them occasion to be obliged to put money up on you in the first place. How's that."

"Well, I suppose there is something in that," said L.K. wiping his tear-stained face on the sleeve of his coat; "but it's mighty tough."

L.K. was lodged in jail. His friends were notified of the condition of affairs, and they at once scurried about to secure new bondsmen but the economic conditions produced by the large box of clothing that was about to be placed on sale in the store seemed likely to prove disastrous to L.K. His friends discovered that holders of money were anxious to retain their money for bargains in the store.

Late in the day however, they succeeded in finding one who was philanthropic enough to pledge the necessary bonds, and L.K. again secured his liberty until the day of the trial.

---

4. The worth of citizens, 1898

Record Book of Citizens, Box 2, George Junior Republic Papers.

Name	Occupation	Age	In Junior Republic (years, mos.)		Wealth in cash	Bank account	Loaned	Personal property	Indebtedness	Total wealth	Former residence
Anderson, Arthur	Publishing house	13	2½		60¢	No	1.60	15.00	No	17.20	N.Y. City
Borton, Clarence	Publishing house, hotel servant	12		2	10¢	No	2.00	1.50	None	3.60	Moorestown, N.Y.
Graff, Jno.	Kitchen and publishing house	16	1½		4.50	No	No	1.50	No	6.00	N.Y. City
Jackson, Gilbert	Hotel keeper and publishing house	14	2½		No	16.00	13.25	2.50	None	31.75	N.Y. City
Kary, Edward	Kitchen and police officer	17	2		6.26	None	None	1.00	None	7.26	N.Y. City
Young, Leonard	High school	17	1	7	2.00	None	None	30.00	None	32.00	N.Y. City
Montgomery, R.	Publishing house	8		6	None	None	None	None	None	Nothing	Rochester
Bannon, Mamie	Senator helper in kitchen and publishing house	15	1	7	4.76	None	.40	2.00	7.90	7.16	N.Y. City
Meade, Ella	Dining room and publishing house	16	1		None	None	None	None	.40	Behind	Syracuse

D. SPECIAL LEGAL PROVISIONS FOR CHILDREN PRIOR TO THE ESTABLISHMENT OF THE JUVENILE COURT

Parens patriae *versus the natural parent*

---

1. "The State has no power to imprison a child, who has committed no crime . . . ," Illinois, 1870

The People *v.* Turner, 55 Ill. 280.

Michael O'Connell sought a writ of *habeas corpus* to release his son, Daniel, from the Chicago Reform School. The boy had been confined under a law of 1863 which provided that children under sixteen found to be "vagrant . . . destitute of proper parental care or . . . growing up in mendicancy, ignorance, idleness or vice" should be committed to the reform school until reformed or until the age of twenty-one.

Mr. Justice Thornton delievered the opinion of the court

.   .   .   .   .

The warrant of commitment does not indicate that the arrest was made for a criminal offense. Hence, we conclude that it was issued under the general grant of power, to arrest and confine for misfortune.

The contingencies enumerated, upon the happening of either of which the power may be exercised, are vagrancy, destitution of proper parental care, mendicancy, ignorance, idleness or vice. Upon proof of any one, the child is deprived of home, and parents, and friends, and confined for more than half of an ordinary life. It is claimed, that the law is administered for the moral welfare and intellectual improvement of the minor, and the good of society. From the record before us, we know nothing of the management. We are only informed that a father desires the custody of his child; and that he is restrained of his liberty. Therefore, we can only look at the language of the law, and the power granted.

What is proper parental care? The best and kindest parents would differ, in the attempt to solve the question. No two scarcely agree; and when we consider the watchful supervision, which is so unremitting over the domestic affairs of others, the conclusion is forced upon us, that there is not a child in the land who could not be proved, by two or more witnesses, to be in this sad condition. Ignorance, idleness, vice, are relative terms. Ignorance is always preferable to error, but, at most, is only venial. It may be general or it may be limited. Though it is sometimes said, that "idleness is the parent of vice," yet the former may exist without the latter. It is strictly an abstinence from labor or employment. If the child perform all its duties to parents and to society, the State has no right to compel it to labor. Vice is a very comprehensive term. Acts, wholly innocent in the estimation of many good men, would, according to the code of ethics of others, show fearful depravity. What is the standard to be? What extent of enlightenment, what amount of industry, what degree of virtue, will save from the threatened imprisonment? In our solicitude to form youth for the duties of civil life, we should not forget the rights which inhere both in parents and children. The principle of the absorption of the child in, and its complete subjection to the despotism of, the State, is wholly inadmissible in the modern civilized world.

The parent has the right to the care, custody and assistance of his child. The duty to maintain and protect it, is a principle of natural law. He may even justify an assault and battery, in the defense of his children, and uphold them in their law suits. Thus the law recognizes the power of parental affection, and excuses acts which, in the absence of such a relation, would be punished. Another branch of parental duty, strongly inculcated by writers on natural law, is the education of children. To aid in the performance of these duties, and enforce obedience, parents have authority over them. The municipal law should not disturb this relation, except for the strongest reasons. The ease with which it may be disrupted under the laws in question; the slight evidence required, and the informal mode of procedure, make them conflict with the natural right of the parent. Before any abridgment of the right, gross misconduct or almost total unfitness on the part of the parent, should be clearly proved. This power is an emanation from God, and every attempt to infringe upon it, except from dire necessity, should be resisted in all well governed States. "In this country, the hope of the child, in respect to its education and future advancement, is mainly dependent upon the father; for this he struggles and toils through life; the desire of its accomplishment operating as one of the most powerful incentives to industry and thrift. The violent abruption of this relation would not only tend to wither these motives to action, but necessarily in time, alienate the father's natural affections."

But even the power of the parent must be exercised with moderation. He may use correction and restraint, but in a reasonable manner. He has the right to enforce only such discipline, as may be necessary to the discharge of his sacred trust; only moderate correction and temporary confinement. We are not governed by the twelve tables, which formed the Roman law. The fourth table gave fathers the power of life and death, and of sale, over their children. In this age and country, such provisions would be atrocious. If a father confined or imprisoned his child for one year, the majesty of the law would frown upon the unnatural act, and every tender mother and kind father would rise up in arms against such monstrous inhumanity. Can the State, as *parens patriae,* exceed the power

of the natural parent, except in punishing crime?

These laws provide for the "safe keeping" of the child; they direct his "commitment," and only a "ticket of leave," or the uncontrolled discretion of a board of guardians, will permit the imprisoned boy to breathe the pure air of heaven outside his prison walls, and to feel the instincts of manhood by contact with the busy world. The mittimus terms him "a proper subject for commitment;" directs the superintendent to "take his body," and the sheriff endorses upon it, "executed by delivering the body of the within named prisoner." The confinement may be from one to fifteen years, according to the age of the child. Executive clemency can not open the prison doors, for no offense has been committed. The writ of *habeas corpus,* a writ for the security of liberty, can afford no relief, for the sovereign power of the State, as *parens patriae,* has determined the imprisonment beyond recall. Such a restraint upon natural liberty is tyranny and oppression. If, without crime, without the conviction of any offense, the children of the State are to be thus confined for the "good of society," then society had better be reduced to its original elements, and free government acknowledged a failure.

In cases of writs of *habeas corpus* to bring up infants, there are other rights beside the rights of the father. If improperly or illegally restrained, it is our duty, *ex debito justitiae,* to liberate. The welfare and rights of the child are also to be considered. The disability of minors does not make slaves or criminals of them. They are entitled to legal rights, and are under legal liabilities. An implied contract for necessaries is binding on them. The only act which they are under a legal incapacity to perform, is the appointment of an attorney. All their other acts are merely voidable or confirmable. They are liable for torts, and punishable for crime. Lord Kenyon said, "If an infant commit an assault, or utter slander, God forbid that he should not be answerable for it, in a court of justice." Every child over ten years of age may be found guilty of crime. For robbery, burglary or arson, any minor may be sent to the penitentiary. Minors are bound to pay taxes for the support of the government, and constitute a part of the militia, and are compelled to endure the hardship and privation of a soldier's life, in defense of the constitution and the laws; and yet it is assumed, that to them, liberty is a mere chimera. It is something of which they may have dreamed, but have never enjoyed the fruition.

Can we hold children responsible for crime; liable for their torts; impose onerous burdens upon them, and yet deprive them of the enjoyment of liberty, without charge or conviction of crime? The bill of rights declares, that "all men are, by nature, free and independent, and have certain inherent and inalienable rights — among these are life, liberty, and the pursuit of happiness." This language is not restrictive; it is broad and comprehensive, and declares a grand truth, that "all men," all people, everywhere, have the inherent and inalienable right to liberty. Shall we say to the children of the State, you shall not enjoy this right — a right independent of all human laws and regulations? It is declared in the constitution; is higher than constitution and law, and should be held forever sacred.

Even criminals can not be convicted and imprisoned without due proces of law — without a regular trial, according to the course of the common law. Why should minors be imprisoned for misfortune? Destitution of proper parental care, ignorance, idleness and vice, are misfortunes, not crimes. In all criminal prosecutions against minors, for grave and heinous offenses, they have the right to demand the nature and cause of the accusation, and a speedy public trial by an impartial jury. All this must precede the final commitment to prison. Why should children, only guilty of misfortune, be deprived of liberty without "due process of law?"

It can not be said, that in this case, there is no imprisonment. This boy is deprived of a father's care; bereft of home influences; has no freedom of action; is committed for an uncertain time; is branded as a prisoner; made subject to the will of others, and thus feels that he is a slave. Nothing could more contribute to paralyze the youthful energies, crush all noble aspirations, and unfit him for the duties of manhood. Other means of a milder character; other influences of a more kindly nature; other laws less in restraint of liberty, would better accomplish the reformation of the depraved, and infringe less upon inalienable rights.

It is a grave responsibility to pronounce upon the acts of the legislative department. It is, however, the solemn duty of the courts to adjudge the law, and guard, when assailed, the liberty of the citizen. The constitution is the highest law; it commands and protects all. Its declaration of rights is an express limitation of legislative power, and as the laws under which the detention is had, are in conflict with its provisions, we must so declare.

It is therefore ordered, that Daniel O'Connell be discharged from custody.

---

2. The commitment of Ah Peen, California, 1876

Ex parte Ah Peen, 51 Cal. 280.

Application to the supreme court to be discharged on *habeas corpus*.

By the Court:

It appears by the return to the writ that in August last the police judge of the city and county of San Francisco, upon application and complaint made to him in that behalf by two citizens of the State, residents of the city and county, alleging that Ah Peen, the legality of whose detention is in question here, is a minor child, of the age of sixteen years, leading an idle and dissolute life in said city and county, and not subject to any parental control whatever —

his parents being unknown — caused the said Ah Peen to be brought before him for examination touching the said several matters alleged, and that upon the appearance of the said minor child, the said several matters alleged were proven to be true in point of fact to the satisfaction of the police judge, who thereupon committed him to the custody of the authorities of the Industrial School, in accordance with the provisions of the act of April 15, 1858.

It is now claimed on the part of the minor that the proceedings resulting in his detention were contrary to the third section of Article I of the Constitution, which provides that the right of trial by jury shall be secured to all; and to the eighth section of the same article, which provides that no person shall be deprived of his liberty without due process of law.

It is obvious that these provisions of the Constitution have no application whatever to the case of this minor child. The action of the police judge here in question did not amount to a criminal prosecution, nor to proceedings against the minor according to the course of the common law, in which the right of trial by jury is guaranteed. The purpose in view is not punishment for offenses done, but reformation and training of the child to habits of industry, with a view to his future usefulness when he shall have been reclaimed to society, or shall have attained his majority. Having been abandoned by his parents, the State, as *parens patriæ,* has succeeded to his control, and stands *in loco parentis* to him. The restraint imposed upon him by public authority is in its nature and purpose the same which, under other conditions, is habitually imposed by parents, guardians of the person, and others exercising supervision and control over the conduct of those who are by reason of infancy, lunacy, or otherwise, incapable of properly controlling themselves.

It is, therefore, ordered that the said Ah Peen be, and he is hereby remanded to the custody of the Superintendent of the Industrial School, to be by him detained as directed in the warrant of the police judge of the city and county of San Francisco.

3. An industrial school is not a prison, Illinois, 1882

In the Matter of Ferrier, 103 Ill. 367.

Appeal from the County Court of Cook county; the Hon. Mason B. Loomis, Judge, presiding.

Appellee filed a petition in the county court of Cook county, under section 3 of "An act to aid industrial schools for girls," approved May 29, 1879. (Laws 1879, p. 309.) The petition set forth that Winifred Breen, the appellant, was a girl nine years old; had repeatedly been picked up by the police and others while wandering about the streets at night; was a truant from school, and had not proper parental care, and was in imminent danger of ruin and harm, etc.

Three witnesses testified as to the character and habits of the girl, Winifred Breen, stating that she was without proper parental care; that she wandered upon the streets of Chicago at all hours of the day and night; that she had been frequently picked up by the policemen of the city, late at night and miles away from her usual place of abode, and had been confined all night in police stations; that she kept bad company, and was in great danger of being ruined; that the mother of the child is weak-minded, and at times insane, having on one occasion attempted to hang Winifred; that she was unfit to have the control of the child, and incapable of managing her; that the step-father is poor and an invalid, earning only a small salary, and is compelled to be absent from his home the entire day, and he found it impossible to control the girl, and that she had been guilty of thefts and falsehood. The fourth witness, Mrs. Beveridge, stated that she was president of the Industrial School for Girls; that the school is situated in Evanston, in Cook county, on a five-acre tract of beautiful rolling ground, over which the inmates have free range as a play-ground; that there is no more restraint upon their liberty than that imposed upon children in an ordinary family or institution of learning; that they are taught ordinary household duties, sewing, and the ordinary branches of English education; that parents are permitted to visit their children when they desire, and that children are given places in private families whenever suitable places can be procured, but not without their and their parents' consent . . .

The jury returned a verdict that Winifred Breen was a dependent girl, and that the facts set forth in the petition were true, and thereupon the county judge entered an order that said Winifred should be committed to said Industrial School for Girls, and appointed Mrs. Ellen Woodward, one of the vice-presidents of the school, guardian of the child, in accordance with a provision of the act. The county attorney, whom the court had appointed counsel for the girl, and who appeared for her, took an appeal to this court.

.   .   .   .   .

Mr. Justice Sheldon delivered the opinion of the Court:

It is insisted that the law under which the proceeding was had is unconstitutional — first, as being violation of the Bill of Rights as to personal liberty, in respect of the provision that no person shall be deprived of life, liberty or property without due process of law, and *The People* v. *Turner,* 55 Ill. 280, is relied upon as being a decisive authority in favor of appellant in this respect.

In the statute now under consideration, anxious provision is made for the due protection of all just rights. To begin, there must be the petition of a responsible person, verified by oath, setting forth the facts, and if there be a parent or a guardian, it must also show that the parent or guardian is not a fit person to have the custody of the infant, there must be notice to the parents, the child must be brought before the court, there is a trial as to the facts by six jurymen, defence by counsel is provided, proof is made before a court of record of the facts alleged, there is the verdict of a jury of six men, and if, by the 4th section, after the verdict of the jury the judge is of the opinion that the girl

should be sent to the industrial school, then he may order that she be committed there. Provision is made for a discharge from the school, when proper, through the managers, and the Governor may at any time order a discharge. This institution is not a prison, but it is a school, and the sending of a young female child there to be taken care of, who is uncared for, and with no one to care for her, we do not regard imprisonment. We perceive hardly any more restraint of liberty than is found in any well regulated school. Such a degree of restraint is essential in the proper education of a child, and it is in no just sense an infringement of the inherent and inalienable right to personal liberty so much dwelt upon in the argument.

We find here no more than such proper restraint which the child's welfare and the good of the community manifestly require, and which rightly pertains to the relations above named, and find no such invasion of the right to personal liberty as requires us to pronounce this statute to be unconstitutional. The decision in 55 Ill. as to the reform school, we do not think should be applied to this industrial school.

The judgment of the county court will be affirmed.

Judgment affirmed.

Legal rights of minor offenders

1. An unfair trial, 1880

Angelo *v.* The People, 96 Ill. 209.

Mr. Justice Walker delivered the opinion of the Court:

At the August term, 1878, of the Morgan circuit court, the grand jury presented an indictment against John Angelo, then about seventy-eight years of age, and his son, Theodore Angelo, about eleven years of age, for the murder of Isaac Hammill. A trial was had at the following November term of the court, resulting in the acquittal of John, on the ground of insanity, and the conviction of Theodore of manslaughter, and the jury fixed the term of his imprisonment in the penitentiary at six years. A motion for a new trial by Theodore was entered, but over-ruled by the court, and he was sentenced to the Reform School for four years; and he prose-cutes error, and brings the record to this court, and urges a reversal, on several grounds.

The statute has provided, by section 282 of the Criminal Code, that a person shall be con-sidered of sound mind who is neither an idiot nor lunatic, nor affected with insanity, and who has arrived at the age of fourteen, or before that age if such person knows the distinction be-tween good and evil. The 283d section provides that an infant under ten years of age shall not be found guilty of any crime or misdemeanor.

In Great Britain the lowest possible period fixed by law at which an infant could be con-victed for a crime, was seven, whilst our statute has fixed the period at ten years. In both coun-tries fourteen is the period after which the law presumes capacity, without proof of knowledge of good and evil.

.   .   .   .   .

There is uncontradicted evidence in the rec-ord that plaintiff in error was little more than eleven years of age when the homicide was committed . . . If this was true, and the evi-dence tended to prove it, the rule required evi-dence strong and clear beyond all doubt and contradiction, that he was capable of discerning between good and evil; and the legal presump-tion being that he was incapable of committing the crime, for want of such knowledge, it de-volved on the People to make the strong and clear proof of capacity, before they could be entitled to a conviction. This record may be searched in vain to find any such proof. There was no witness examined on that question, nor did any one refer to it. There is simply evidence as to his age. For aught that appears, he may have been dull, weak, and wholly incapable of knowing good from evil. It does not appear, from even the circumstances in evidence, that he may not have been mentally weak for his age, or that he may not have even approached idiocy.

The law presumes that he lacked mental ca-pacity at his age, and that presumption has not been overcome by the requisite proof, or, in fact, any proof. The court below should there-fore have granted a new trial, and erred in re-fusing it.

Again, the jury were not clearly and fully in-structed on this question. Several instructions given for the People omitted this rule, when they should have been qualified by informing the jury that proof, and clear proof, of capacity must be given. In such a case the mere an-nouncement of the rule in general terms, as was done in the eighth of the People's instructions, was not sufficient. The jury may have been mis-led by the instructions that should have been qualified.

It is to be regretted that counsel who assisted the prosecuting attorney referred, as he did in his argument to the jury, to the fact that plain-tiff in error was not placed on the stand as a witness, as one of the reasons why he should be convicted. It is true, that when stopped by the court, he said it was inadvertently done, and the jury were directed by the court to disregard that portion of his argument. Notwithstanding what he said, and the direction of the court to disre-gard it, who can know what effect it may have had on the jury in forming their verdict? Such comments are prohibited by the statute, and it is strange that any attorney should so far forget the rights of the accused, and his professional duty, for a moment, even in the heat of discus-sion; but he said it was inadvert, and we are loth to believe that any attorney would inten-tionally act so unfairly and unprofessionally. We can not conceive that any member of the bar could deliberately seek by such means to wrongfully procure a conviction and the execu-tion of a fellow being, when his highest profes-sional duty to his client only requires him to see that there is a fair trial according to the law and the evidence. Where such things are done, whether intentionally or inadvertently, it may make an impression on the minds of the jury that nothing can remove. And who can say that this inadvertence may not have produced the verdict of guilty?

We think plaintiff in error has not had a fair trial, and the judgment of the court below must be reversed and the cause remanded.

---

2. A delinquent may not be committed to a reformatory by a grand jury, California, 1897

Ex parte Becknell, 51 Pac. Rep. 692.

Appeal from superior court, Los Angeles county.

Proceeding upon presentment of the grand jury, for the commitment of Jonie Becknell, a minor, to the Whittier School. From an order of commitment, the father appeals, and petitions for a writ of habeas corpus. Granted.

Beatty, C. J. By section 13 of the act of March 23, 1893, relating to the Whittier State School (St. 1893, p. 332), section 17 of the original act was amended so as to read as follows: "If any accusation of the commission of any crime shall be made against any minor, under the age of eighteen years; before any grand jury, and the charge appears to be supported by evidence sufficient to put the accused upon trial, the grand jury may, in their discretion, instead of finding an indictment against the accused, return to the superior court that it appears to them that the accused is a suitable person to be committed to the care and guardianship of said institution. The court may thereupon order such commitment, if satisfied from the evidence that such commitment ought to be made, which examination may be waived by the parent or guardian of such minor." Acting under this provision of the statute, the grand jury of Merced county made a presentment to the superior court as follows: "To the Judge of the Superior Court of the County of Merced, State

of California: An accusation against Jonie Becknell, a minor under the age of eighteen years, to wit, of the age of thirteen years, charging the said Jonie Becknell with the crime of burglary, committed in Merced county, state of California, on or about the first day of August, 1897, and the charge appearing to the grand jury to be supported by evidence sufficient to put the said Jonie Becknell upon his trial therefor, and it appearing to said grand jury that the accused is a suitable person to be committed to the care and guardianship of the reform school for juvenile offenders at Whittier, the grand jury therefore recommend that said Jonie Becknell be committed to the care and guardianship of said institution." Thereupon the court directed the said Jonie Becknell to be brought into court, and against his special protest and objection, on the ground that the court had no jurisdiction to act in the matter, proceeded to take testimony for the purpose of determining whether said Jonie Becknell was a suitable person to be committed to the Whittier State School. Upon the testimony so taken, and without any other proceeding or any trial by jury, the court did adjudge the said Jonie Becknell to be a suitable person to be committed to the Whittier State School until he should reach his majority, and made an order accordingly, under which he is now held in the custody of the superintendent of the school. The boy is under 14 years of age. His father and mother are residents of Merced county, and are able and willing to provide for his support and education.

Upon this state of facts appearing on the return to the writ of habeas corpus, issued upon petition of the boy's father, we are asked to discharge him from custody. The petition must be granted. As a judgment of imprisonment, the order of the superior court is void. The boy cannot be imprisoned as a criminal without a trial by jury. As an award of guardianship it is equally void, for his parents — his natural guardians — cannot be deprived of their right to his care, custody, society, and services except by a proceeding to which they are made parties, and in which it is shown that they are unfit or unwilling or unable to perform their parental duties. All the cases cited by counsel are consistent with, and several of them sustain, these views. The minor is discharged from the custody of the superintendent, and restored to the custody of the petitioner.

Probation and supervision of juvenile delinquents

1. Massachusetts establishes office of visiting agent, 1869

"An Act in Addition to an Act to Establish the Board of State Charities," ch. 453 — 1869 in Abbott, *The Child and the State*, II, 366–368.

A similar agency was established in Michigan in 1873.

SECTION 1. The governor, with the advice and consent of the council, shall appoint an agent to visit all children maintained wholly or in part by the Commonwealth, or who have been indentured, given in adoption or placed in the charge of any family or person by the authorities of any state institution, or under any provision of this act.

He shall hold his office for one year, subject to removal by the governor and council, and shall receive an annual salary of twenty-five hundred dollars; and, with the approval of the board of state charities, he may employ such assistants and incur such expenses as may be necessary for the discharge of his official duties.

SEC. 2. It shall be his duty to visit the children aforesaid, or cause them to be visited, at least once in three months, to inquire into their treatment, their health and their associations, and especially to ascertain whether their legal rights have been invaded, and whether all contracts or stipulations made in their behalf have been duly observed, and to collect such other information respecting them as the board of state charities may direct; and, for this purpose, he shall have the right to hold private interviews with the children, whenever he may deem it advisable.

SEC. 3. All applications to take any of the children above specified, by indenture, adoption or any other method fixed by law, shall be referred to the aforesaid agent, who shall investigate the character of each applicant, and the expediency of so disposing of the child applied for, and report the result to the board or magistrate having jurisdiction over the child, and no such child shall be indentured or otherwise disposed of until such report is received; and in case any child shall be placed in a home which the said agent may deem unsuitable, he shall forthwith report the facts to the board of state charities for their action thereon, and the governor and council may at any time annul any indenture by which such child may be held.

SEC. 4. Whenever application is made for the commitment of any child to any reformatory maintained by the Commonwealth, the magistrate before whom the hearing is to be held shall duly notify the visiting agent of the time and place of hearing, by written notice mailed one week at least before the time of hearing, and directed to said agent at the state house, and the agent shall attend at said hearing in person or by deputy, in behalf of the child; and if it shall appear to the said magistrate that the interests of the child will be promoted by placing him in a suitable family, he may, instead of committing him to a reformatory, authorize the board of state charities to indenture the child during the whole or a portion of his minority, or to place him in such family. And the board of state charities is hereby authorized to provide for the maintenance of any child placed in a family as aforesaid at an expense not exceeding the average cost of the support of such child in any of the state reformatories. And it shall be the duty of said agent to seek out families willing and suitable to receive such children, and furnish the names and places of residence of the same to the boards or magistrates who are to provide for the commitment or indenture of a child under this act: *provided,* that the provisions of this section so far as they require notice to the visiting agent shall not apply to the superior court.

SEC. 5. The visiting agent shall make a monthly report to the board of state charities of all his proceedings, especially concerning children placed in families under the fourth section of this act, and any person aggrieved by his action shall have the right of appeal to the board or magistrate having original jurisdiction of the child.

SEC. 6. The duties required in sections three and four of this act shall, in case of the industrial school for girls, be performed by the officers of that institution under the supervision of the board of state charities.

---

2. Massachusetts visiting agent explains his work

Gardiner Tufts, "Family Visitation of the Wards of the State as Practised in Massachusetts" in Enoch C. Wines, ed., *Transactions* of National Congress on Penitentiary and Reformatory Discipline (1871), 360, 368–369.

The duties of the agency are wholly in connection with juveniles, and those of two classes, viz., the wards of the state and those liable to become such. The wards of the state are the children in the public correctional or reformatory institutions and the primary school, and also those placed out therefrom not discharged from custody, and those received by the visiting agent from the courts and placed out by the board of state charities, without having entered any institution. Those liable to become wards of the State are boys and girls under sixteen years of age, arraigned before the courts for any offence not punishable by imprisonment for life, except offences against city ordinances or town by-laws. This latter class comes under the cognizance of the agency by an official notice from the magistrate the moment complaint is entered against them. These classes include boys and girls, offenders and dependents.

The business of the agency relates almost wholly to children outside of the institutions, and never to those inside, except upon propositions for their removal therefrom. It is essentially an out-of-door agency.

.   .   .   .   .

By the attendance of the agent or his assistant upon the courts, there is secured for each child arraigned a full hearing; the acquittal of some who would otherwise be punished; the probation of many who would otherwise be committed; homes for many who have none either in fact or name, and who, but for the intervention of the visiting agent, from the mere absence of homes, would be inmates of public reformatory institutions during minority, or successful candidates for houses of correction and jails.

One hundred and three such children have been placed in families direct from the courts since the agency commenced its work; only eight have gone beyond its control, and they have not again troubled the officers of the law, and five were subsequently committed to reformatory institutions; the remainder are doing well. Children taken direct from the courts and placed in families do as well as those placed out from the institutions.

Under the law of 1869, thirty cases a month, on an average, arose before the courts, of which the visiting agent had notice. Under the present law the average is about one hundred and fifty; from one-fourth to one-fifth of this number are committed to public institutions; one-seventh are taken by the agent, and the balance are put on probation or discharged.

During the term of our office 799 complaints have been made against juveniles before the courts, of which the agency had notice; 86 of the arraigned were sent to the nautical school; 90 to the state reform school; 42 to the industrial school for girls; 135 were put in charge of the visiting agent of the board of state charities; 171 were put on probation; 149 were discharged; 52 were fined; 43 entered private or local institutions; and 31 failed to appear at the hearings.

The result of the present system of "seeking out persons to take" charge of children is the procurement of a better class of persons.

The result of the present plan of "investigating applications for indenture, adoption, release and discharge," is a more complete knowledge of the character and surroundings of the applicants, and, consequently, better means for discreet action in the disposal of children.

The result of the system of "visitation" is a comprehensive knowledge of, and a thorough acquaintance with, the condition, wants and progress of our children, and the effect which the reformatory appliances and methods have had and are having. The work which the agency does in obtaining a history of results we deem very important, as such data must afford the wisest rules for future action.

By the visitation, already made, the result of the reformatory methods of the state, in the cases of 2,316 children who had been in the public institutions, has been shown, covering a period of seven years. Of that number, 1,171 were found doing well; 838 were found *not* doing well. Of this latter number 118 have been, or are now, in correctional institutions; 67 are again in reformatory institutions, and 40 in charitable ones; 67 of the boys entered the army and navy during the war; and the remainder of the 2,316 are dead, or gone beyond the knowledge of the state.

The "visitation" keeps those placed out from absconding by increasing the means of recovery; impresses them with the uselessness and disadvantage of escape; corrects grievances; and regulates the disturbing forces. Every day's experience makes more firm the belief that visitation is an effective measure in the reformatory scheme. The more frequent the visits, the more effectual will be the work.

3. A friend in court for delinquent children, Ohio, 1892

Ohio, *General and Local Acts, 1892* (Columbus, 1892), LXXXIX, 161.

It shall be the duty of the probate judge or other officer in each county, whenever proceedings are instituted before him to commit a child under sixteen years of age to the boys' industrial school at Lancaster, or the girls' industrial home at Delaware, to have notice of such proceedings given to the board of county visitors of such county, whose duty it shall be to attend such proceedings, either as a body or by a committee, and protect the interests of such child.

Special trials for children

1. Massachusetts, 1870

"An act relating to the state visiting agency and juvenile offenders," 1870 — ch. 359. Massachusetts, *Acts and Resolves* (Boston, 1870), p. 262.

When a boy or girl, except in the county of Suffolk, is brought before a trial justice, police or municipal court, on complaint for any offence not punishable by imprisonment for life, except for an offence against a town or city by-law or ordinance, and, in said county of Suffolk, is so brought for any offence first described, but not now within the final jurisdiction of any police or municipal court therein, and it appears at or before the trial, that such boy or girl is under the age of sixteen years, the justice or court shall make an endorsement of the fact upon the original warrant, and the officer who served said warrant, or any other officer qualified to serve the same, shall take said boy or girl with said warrant and the complaint before the judge of the probate court, who shall have jurisdiction thereof in like manner as if originally brought before him. And in the county of Suffolk, all boys and girls under sixteen years of age, complained of for any offence before any police or municipal court, shall have the complaints against them heard and determined, by themselves, separate from the general and ordinary criminal business of said courts.

2. New York, 1892

"An act to amend section two hundred and ninety-one, of the Penal Code, relative to criminal charges against children," 1892 — ch. 217. *Laws of the State of New York, 1892* (Albany, 1892), I, 459–460.

Any magistrate having criminal jurisdiction may commit, temporarily, to an institution authorized by law to receive children on final commitment, and to have compensation therefor from the city or county authorities, any child under the age of sixteen years, who is held for trial on a criminal charge; and may, in like manner, so commit any such child held as a witness to appear on the trial of any criminal case; which institution shall thereupon receive the same, and be entitled to the like compensation proportionally therefor as on final commitment, but subject to the order of the court as to the time of detention and discharge of the child. Any such child convicted of any misdemeanor shall be finally committed to some such institution, and not to any prison or jail, or penitentiary, longer than is necessary for its transfer thereto. No child under restraint or conviction, actually or apparently under the age of sixteen years, shall be placed in any prison or place of confinement, or in any court-room, or in any

vehicle for transportation in company with adults charged with or convicted of crime.

All cases involving the commitment or trial of children for any violation of the Penal Code, in any police court or court of special sessions, may be heard and determined by such court, at suitable times to be designated therefor by it, separate and apart from the trial of other criminal cases, of which session a separate docket and record shall be kept.

3. Rhode Island, 1898

"An act relating to juvenile offenders," 1898 — ch. 581. *Acts and Resolves of the State of Rhode Island and Providence Plantations, 1898* (Providence, 1898), pp. 40–41.

Whenever a minor under the age of sixteen years shall be brought before any court in the counties of Providence and Newport in this state, charged with any crime or misdemeanor, said minor shall be arraigned and tried separate and apart from the arraignment and trial of other cases; but the provisions of this section, or of the following sections, shall not apply to any minor jointly charged or in any way connected with an older person or persons in the commission of any crime or misdemeanor.

Said courts in said counties shall designate suitable times for the trial of such cases, to be called "The Session for Juvenile Offenders," and of these sessions a separate docket and record shall be kept.

It shall be the duty of the agent of the board of state charities and corrections, or such other person as they may appoint, or of the agent of the Rhode Island Society for the Prevention of Cruelty to Children, or the agent of the Saint Vincent de Paul Society, upon receiving notice thereof to be given by order of said court, to be present at the arraignment and trial of such juvenile offenders; to secure the services of counsel in their behalf, by and with the authority of the court; to learn all that is possible regarding said children for the purpose of aiding said court, and, generally, to take care of the interests of said children.

.   .   .   .   .   .

Whenever any child under thirteen years of age is held by any court for examination or trial, and said child is unable to furnish bail for such examination or trial, such court shall commit said child to the custody of said agent of the board of state charities and corrections, or to the agent of the Society for the Prevention of Cruelty to Children, or to the agent of the Saint Vincent de Paul Society, and said agent is hereby authorized to make all proper provisions for the safe keeping of said child and for his presence at the examination or trial for which he is held, and said court, upon motion of said agent (or either of them), made at any time before sentence, may provisionally place any juvenile offender under his control and supervision until the further order of said court.

No court shall commit any child under thirteen years of age to a jail or to the state prison in default of bail, for non-payment of fine or costs, or both, or for any punishment for any offence not punishable by imprisonment for life, of which said child may have been adjudged guilty, but such commitment shall be to the Sockanosset school for boys or the Oaklawn school for girls.

Juveniles when placed under arrest shall not be confined in any apartment in any police station with other offenders not juveniles.

Commitment of delinquents to charitable institutions

1. California, 1883

"An act . . . to provide for the probationary treatment of juvenile delinquents," 1833 — ch.

91. *The Statutes of California, 1883* (Sacramento, 1883), pp. 377–378.

Final judgment may be suspended on any conviction, charge, or prosecution for misdemeanor, or felony, wherein the judgment of the Court in which such proceeding is pending there is a reasonable ground to believe that such minor may be reformed, and that a commitment to prison would work manifest injury in the premises. Such suspension may be for as long a period as the circumstances of the case may seem to warrant, and subject to the following further provisions: During the period of such suspension, or of any extension thereof, the Court or Judge may, under such limitations as may seem advisable, commit such minor to the custody of the officers or managers of any strictly non-sectarian charitable corporation conducted for the purpose of reclaiming criminal minors. Such corporation, by its officers or managers, may accept the custody of such minor for a period of two months (to be further extended by the Court or Judge should it be deemed advisable), and should said minor be found incorrigible and incapable of reformation, he may be returned before the Court for final judgment for his misdemeanor. Such charitable corporation shall accept custody of said minor as aforesaid upon the distinct agreement that it and its officers shall use all reasonable means to effect the reformation of such minor, and provide him with a home and instruction. No application for guardianship of such minor by any person, parent, or friend shall be entertained by any Court during the period of such suspension and custody, save upon recommendation of the Court before which the criminal proceedings are pending first obtained. Such Court may further, in its discretion, direct the payment of the expenses of the maintenance of such minor during such period of two months, not to exceed, in the aggregate, the sum of $25 (twenty-five dollars), which sum shall include board, clothing, transportation, and all other expenses, to be paid by the county where such criminal proceeding is pending, or direct action to be instituted for the recovery thereof out of the estate of said minor, or from his parents. Such Court may also revoke such order of suspension at any time.

2. New York, 1884

"An act to amend the Penal Code," 1884 — ch. 46. *Laws of the State of New York, 1884* (Albany, 1884), p. 47.

When a person under the age of sixteen is convicted of a crime, he may, in the discretion of the court, instead of being sentenced to fine or imprisonment, be placed in charge of any suitable person or institution willing to receive him, and be thereafter, until majority or for a shorter term, subjected to such discipline and control of the person or institution receiving him as a parent or guardian may lawfully exercise over a minor. A child under sixteen years of age committed for misdemeanor, under any provision of this code, must be committed to some reformatory, charitable or other institution authorized by law to receive and take charge of minors. And when any such child is committed to an institution it shall, when practicable, be committed to an institution governed by persons of the same religious faith as the parents of such child.

Placing delinquents with families

Homer Folks, "The Care of Delinquent Children," *Proceedings* of the National Conference of Charities and Correction (1891), 136–144.

In the nine years since its organization the Children's Aid Society of Pennsylvania has made provision for 3,927 children. At first considerable use was made of various institutions for the temporary care of children; but every step taken since its organization, after a careful study of the work, has been toward a more exclusive use of the family plan. Its first efforts were in behalf of destitute children, but it soon came to find that there were no hard-and-fast lines separating children into classes. Many of these children received from the almshouse or from destitute families proved themselves, in one way or another, troublesome, and the Society found the whole problem of delinquent children continually forced upon its consideration. At nearly every meeting the question arose, Is it best to place this troublesome child in a reformatory or in a carefully selected private family? Very naturally, both methods were tried and the results studied. It is to be a fact of tremendous significance that after eight years of such experience the Society determined not only to provide for the delinquent children whom it might thus find in its charge, but to make a special effort for the rescue of the younger children who had found their way to the police stations and criminal courts.

.   .   .   .   .

We have tried in earnest the bold experiment of placing such children in families. Deciding about a year ago to extend our work in this line, we gave notice through the press that we would receive such children. We established friendly relations with the police headquarters. We sent a circular letter to the magistrates and judges, explaining our methods and offering to receive delinquent children under fourteen years of age. We have gone to the county prison, where boys were awaiting trial on various charges, and, after inquiring into their history, have received them from the judge of the criminal court, after a verdict of guilty had been pronounced.

Since June, 1890, we have received from these sources forty-one such children, who belong unquestionably to the so-called delinquent class, and who but for our special effort would have been committed to reformatory institutions. The charges against these children were as follows: vagrancy, six; immoral tendencies, five; forgery, one; runaways, six; larceny, eleven; ill-tempered and unmanageable, twelve. The disposition made of the children is as follows: Of the six vagrants, two received under protest, on account of their age, were placed for wages near the city, and disappeared at the close of the first month; one was returned to parents; three confirmed vagrants were placed with families at a distance from the city, where they remain and show most encouraging signs of improvement. The five girls with immoral tendencies were placed at a distance, and all give evidence of decided improvement. Also the forger, a girl of fourteen. Of the six runaways, two disappeared in the city before their antecedents could be traced; the other four were found to have both parents living. Three were returned to their homes: the fourth was left in the Society's care, his home being such as to justify his departure. The eleven boys convicted of larceny were all placed at a distance from the city, and with two exceptions have remained where placed, with decided improvement; and, of the twelve ill-tempered and unmanageable, seven were thus placed, all with excellent results. Of the four who remained in the city, two show slight improvement and two were returned to their parents unimproved, one of whom had spent two years in a reformatory, and one was recalled by his people, who were not willing that he should be sent to a distance. To summarize, then, of the twenty-eight over whom the Society had sufficient control to remove them from the city, twenty-six have remained as first placed, unless changed by the Society, and show decided improvement. The two exceptions repeated their offence and returned to the city very soon after their removal, but were recovered and placed in another part of the State, and have remained six and three months in their places. One shows decided improvement, the other doubtful.

These results have been more encouraging than most of us had dared to hope. We have sometimes left our wards in their homes with fear and trembling, and returned half expecting the next mail to announce their evil-doing and disappearance. But we have been happily surprised as weeks passed by and all the reports were hopeful. Later visits were full of encouragement. The old life and associations have, for a time at least, been forgotten. Among the hopeful signs are, in most cases, greatly improved physical health, a quickening of the mental faculties by regular attendance at school and a multitude of new associations and interests, a growth of the moral sense, especially in regard to the right of property, more self-control and submission to discipline, and the recognition of religious obligations and privileges.

A few words as to the methods by which these results have been secured. I can readily conceive of certain conditions under which the result would have been far different. If, sitting in our office, we had counted these boys out like articles of merchandise to those who might happen to come to us for the purpose of securing a cheap service, without careful study of each child, and careful investigation of every family proposing to undertake their training; if we had placed these boys near the city, where "taking children" is a recognized method of lessening the expenditure for hired help, and where the alternative of a return to the old associations is continually presented; if we had insisted that the city boy, going to the country with absolutely no knowledge of farm life and duties, must be self-supporting from the first; and if, further, we had "bound out" the boy to serve his master until he had reached a certain age, and to receive no compensation whatever until the end of this period, — under these circumstances it would have required no prophet to assure us of the hopeless failure of our experiment.

The first step when the child is received, or before, if possible, is a careful study of his antecedents, his home life, and his companions. Such an investigation often throws a flood of light upon the causes of the delinquency, and is invaluable in determining what new environment will most counteract these forces making for evil, and develop new interests along those lines in which the child may have natural abilities or tastes.

As a rule, these children are sent a considerable distance from any large city, — usually from 250 to 300 miles from Philadelphia. In finding homes for these children, we do not rely upon the natural demand for servants. We discard all applications like the following, which is a true copy: "I desire to adopt a little girl about fifteen years of age. I intend to raise her in the nurture and admonition of the Lord, therefore she must be of good disposition, and not too small in stature." We usually advertise for families willing to board a boy and give attention to his moral training. Among the answers to such an advertisement are nearly always several from the best families of the neighborhood. The other applications are discarded. Having made sure, by a system of references and personal visitation, which homes are desirable, it still remains to decide which family can do most for the individual child under consideration . . . It is not easy to explain the care with which each child is fitted into his new surroundings; and the best results often seem to come from a sort of intuition, — an intuition born, however, of years of experience in placing children in families. Another consideration of importance is that very few of these children are expected to be self-supporting from the start. The city boy is a total stranger to country life and work, and must receive careful instruction. After the novelty passes away, he inevitably becomes, at times, impatient of its monotony, and feels a peculiar and powerful yearning for the excitement of the city. He has days when he is restless, impatient, impudent. All this requires an amount of patience and intelligent training which we cannot secure without remuneration; nor have we any right, on purely business principles, to expect it. We therefore pay for their training, education, and maintenance, usually at the rate of $2.00 per week. The greater control which the Society retains over the boarding child, the difference in the standing of the child in the community, the higher grade of homes which can be obtained, the necessity of tiding over these outbursts of temper, which would otherwise result in the return of the child, — all these emphasize the importance of this remuneration. This expense is entirely justifiable; for, if the same children had been placed in reformatories, they would have cost the community from $150 to $200 per year. Is there any reason why the community should not pay the country farmer or tradesmen the same amount, if necessary, provided he secures for them equally good or better results? However, a study of the comparative costs of the different methods . . . shows a difference in the yearly cost of from $50 to $100 per capita in favor of the family plan.

What do we seem to have learned from this year's work? First, we have a clearer idea as to who compose this class of delinquent children. It is very easy to speak of these as "the children of criminals," or "the offspring of the slums," and the fact of heredity in crime is unquestioned. Such children there are in the number; but to infer that all, or nearly all, belong to this class, is a most unwarranted and unjustifiable assumption. While statistics as to this point are very incomplete, they are highly suggestive. 400 boys were admitted to the State Industrial School of New York (formerly the Western House of Refuge) during the past year; of only 61 had either parent been arrested. Of 460 inmates received at the Huntingdon Reformatory, the taint of crime could be found in the parentage of only 19; the parentage of 441 being, as far as could be ascertained, respectable as against 19 criminal. Of our own children the parents of 24 are eminently respectable and law-abiding; of 12, disreputable.

We are willing to go a step farther, and assert our belief that not only are many of these children of respectable parentage, but that a considerable portion are themselves very little different from ordinary children. The readiness with which these children have responded to their new environments and have formed new attachments, and their submission to the regulations of the household, all seem to indicate that they are not so very different from ordinary children as to require that heroic treatment which may be necessary for adult criminals. To what, then, shall this large share of juvenile delinquency be attributed? To a thousand different causes, which can be decided in each case only by careful study, but which can in a majority of cases be traced to a lack of parental oversight, due to the loss of one or both parents. The death of a father or mother leaves too heavy a burden on the surviving parent, and the children suffer, receiving their training in the street, not in the home. While we have no statistics as to the proportion of orphan children in the community, it is evidently not large. The records, however, show that about half of the children committed to reformatories are orphans or half-orphans.

Of the children committed to the Philadelphia House of Refuge in 1889, 57 per cent were orphans or half-orphans; of those committed in 1890, 50 per cent; of children committed to the Morganza [Pa.] Reform School in 1889, 48 per cent; in 1890, 50 per cent; of those committed to the State Industrial School of New York in 1890, 40 per cent; to the Cincinnati House of Refuge, 45 per cent.

In a few cases the root of the trouble lies in some physical weakness or defect which renders the child ill-tempered and troublesome, — which is, being interpreted, incorrigible. In several of our cases, improved health, due to mountain air and country life, has solved the problem. How unwise to place such children in a large institution, where the chances for good health are, at least, not above the average!

The runaways are a peculiarly interesting and difficult class. It is an established custom among them to insist that they are orphans and homeless. To win their confidence and learn the true story of their wanderings is a task requiring the greatest delicacy and tact. Perhaps the necessity for painstaking study of each individual is nowhere more apparent than in dealing with this class.

We have also learned that homes of high grade can be secured for this work. Our worst children are trained by the very best families in the community. Several of our boys are in charge of men whom their fellow-citizens have honored with positions of trust.

We have proven, too, that we can hold the children by our methods. The fear that they would run away, which harassed us when we began the work, we have seen to be largely ill-founded. We have learned that boys, incorrigible boys, may be kept in their places by other means than stone walls. This fact is fast being recognized within institutions as well as out. The last report of a well-known institution remarks upon the significance of the fact that "boys sent out of the city upon their honor disdain to take advantage of the trust imposed in them, and yet sometimes the same boys will attempt to scale the walls and thus escape, selecting the very highest place for their attempt."

While, of course, it is too soon to say that we have reformed these boys, recognizing ourselves that our work is still largely of the nature of an experiment, we are able to say that, with the two exceptions noted, we have kept these children from committing farther crime; and, considering the nature of the offences for which they were received, this is a most encouraging fact. We can say farther that in nearly every case there is a marked improvement in lines already indicated, which, unless there are some sudden and radical disturbances of which we see no indication, must lead ultimately to reformation and good citizenship.

I shall not consider the objections which might be urged against this method as regards its effect upon the children themselves, as I have already anticipated them in my explanation of the work. There remains to be considered one other objection. We are continually being told that our method is dangerous to the community, and in saving one child we corrupt ten others. We reply that this is an entirely gratuitous assumption regarding what is a matter of fact, not of opinion; that we continually have this consideration in our minds, and endeavor to reduce such danger to a minimum by placing our children in families of adults; that many of these children are not the depraved creatures often supposed; that much of their former life seems to have been laid aside and superseded by new interests; and that we have failed to see any specific instances of such contamination. That there may be a certain amount of undesirable knowledge communicated we would not deny; but is this not inevitable under any system? Does not depravity propagate itself in the reformatory as well as out, in the city as well as in the country?

The chief magistrate of this nation said in a speech a few days since: "The American home is the one thing we cannot afford to lose out of American life. As long as we have pure homes, and God-fearing, order-loving fathers and mothers to rear the children that are given to them, and to make these homes the abodes of order, cleanliness, piety, and intelligence, American society and the American Union are safe." It is this sort of home life that we would bring to bear upon each separate unit of the delinquent class. In this moral infirmary we believe that ignorance, injustice, vice, and hatred are to be cured by their opposites, — knowledge, justice, purity, and love, to be administered in large quantities.

II The Juvenile Court

A. THE FIRST COURTS

Chicago

---

1. "Brutal treatment brutalizes"

John Peter Altgeld, *Our Penal Machinery and Its Victims* (Chicago, 1886), pp. 31–32.

As governor of Illinois from 1893 to 1897, Altgeld (1847–1902) sympathized with reformers and organized labor. His pardon of three Haymarket anarchists in 1893 and his reluctance to call federal troops during the Pullman strike of 1894 led to attacks on him as a radical and defender of crime.

What effect does arrest and imprisonment have on those arrested, more particularly on the young?

Considering the great number annually arrested and imprisoned, the facts that the great majority of all these are under twenty-six years of age, that a very large proportion of them are under twenty years of age, and that in some instances one-fifth of them are females; and, still further, the fact that almost all of them are of the poor — of the class that needs encouragement more than almost anything else, — this is a most important question, especially as our present system of treating offenders does not seem to be a success. However great an improvement it may be on the past (and nobody disputes that it is) still it is not a success.

Turning now again to the Report of the Chief of Police of Chicago, we find that of the 32,800 arrested, 10,743 were discharged by the police magistrates, to say nothing of those that were bound over to the grand jury and then discharged. So that during the one year there were in that one city upwards of 10,000 young persons given a regular criminal experience without having committed any crime. Think of this a moment. And if so many in one city, what a multitude must there be throughout the land! Mind, these were not even offenders. But what was the treatment they received? Why, precisely the same as if they had been criminals. They were arrested, some of them clubbed, some of them handcuffed, marched through the streets in charge of officers, treated gruffly, jostled around. At the police station the name and a complete description of the person of each was written on the prison records, there to remain. Some of them were bailed out, while the remainder were shoved into cells and forced to spend a night and sometimes a week there, forced to stand around with criminals, before they were discharged. Now, what effect will this treatment have on them? Will not every one of them feel the indignity to which he or she was subjected, while life lasts? Will they not abhor the men who perpetrated what is felt to be an outrage? Will they not look on this whole machinery as their enemy, and take a secret delight in seeing it thwarted? Will they not almost unconsciously sympathize with those who defy this whole system, and are they not thus suddenly brought a whole length nearer crime than they were before? And will not those who were already weak, and having a hard struggle for existence, be farther weakened, and therefore more liable soon to become actual offenders than they otherwise would have been? Remember, *brutal treatment brutalizes* and thus prepares for crime.

---

2. The baby crook, Chicago, 1898

Horace Fletcher, *That Last Waif or Social Quarantine* (Chicago, 1898), pp. 22–28.

Horace Fletcher (1849–1919) wrote and lectured on nutrition and other subjects such as the need to introduce free kindergartens into the public school system. The following anecdote intended to support the kindergarten movement in Chicago was widely discussed at the Illinois Conference of Charities in 1898. This meeting was devoted entirely to the problems of public care of dependent and delinquent children, and served as a catalyst for many of the ideas which were incorporated the following year into the first juvenile court law in the country.

Under the shadow of the portal of the Pullman Building, which serves as general offices of the Pullman's Palace Car Company, we met an adventure that showed an appalling contrast to the patriotic enthusiasm that blared in the thoroughfares we had just quitted. We were arrested by the plaintive voice of a child in the toils of a six-foot policeman.

"Please, mister," wailed the child, "lemme go. I didn't swipe none ov dem cakes; 'twas me brudder and de odder kids dat swiped 'em; I ain't done nothin', and I won't do nothin' no more if you'll only let me slide; I won't never come out annudder night — honest I won't — if you'll let me go. Me brudder an' de udder kids 'll go home widout me an' I don't know de way. Please, mister cop, lemme go; please! please!! — "

The child could not have been more than four years of age, but his small vocabulary was as full of the slang of the slums as it was deficient in the terms of childhood and innocence. The policeman was kindly disposed, but felt compelled to administer some sort of correction, and this is how he did it: His reproof was well meant, but oh! how evil was it in its suggestions to a soul just receiving its first impressions of life, and of the world, out of which to build a character.

"What's the use of your lyin' to me, yer little monkey? You know you're a thief and the kid of thieves. The gang you trains wid is the toughest in town. Every mother's brat of you'll deckerate a halter one of those days — sooner or later anyhow, an' probably sooner. You're born to it an' can't help it, I s'pose, but if I catches yer 'round here again I'll thump yer on the head wid my club and you'll find that'll hurt wurser'n a lickin'. — Where does yer live, anyhow?"

The child answered, giving an indefinite address on the West Side that was undoubtedly false, as charged by the officer, but which was as glibly given as a parrot's favorite phrase.

"Oh! I knows you're a-lyin', but I knows yer gang just the same; it's the rottenist in the city and turns out more thieves and murderers than all the rest of town put together. Well! yer h'aint got much show to be different; and (turning to us, who had stopped to listen) — I don't s'pose the kid's ter blame for doin' what all the people he knows does all the time and thinks it's workin'. I s'pose his father and mother sends him out to steal; that is, if he's got a father — which 'aint likely. There's a gang of about fifty of 'em that works my beat and durin' these excitin' times when there's big crowds on the streets and plenty of hayseeds in town they give a pile of trouble. They hangs around and swipes anything they can get hold of. The little rascals knows that we 'aint got no place to jug 'em 'cept in the regler coolers and as there 'aint no more'n enough room in them for the big crooks we has to let 'em go, and the little cusses knows that as well as we does. They knows a trick or two besides; fer instance, they rushes a fruit stand or a bakery in a gang, carryin' the babies along wid 'em. The big fellers — the biggest of 'em 'aint more'n about ten — is all as spry as cats and darts in and collars the plunder and then out again into the crowd in a jiffy, leavin' the babies to be scooped by the shop people and turned over to us. This satisfies the shop people all right and the real thieves escapes. We take the little cusses in charge an' have to do something wid 'em, so we takes 'em round a corner, lectures 'em and lets 'em go. That's all we can do an' as the kids knows it, it's a part of their game."

Turning again to the boy, who all the time had been begging to be allowed to go, the officer said, "Who's them kids on the other side of the street — your brudders, is they? Well, you tell 'em when you sees 'em that if I ever catches 'em on my beat again I'll brudder them so 't they won't ferget it. I'll learn 'em to dance the shuffle as a defi' to me. An' if you git into my hands again I'll cut your ears off close ter yer head, and I'll sew yer mouth up so's yer can't eat no cakes, an' then I guess yer won't want ter steal 'em. Now git yer little bastard, and *ter hell wid you!*"

The baby "crook," scampered across the street to where his companions were waiting for him. All the boys put their thumbs to their noses in the direction of the officer, screamed a derisive yell, and disappeared around the corner to "work some other beat" or seek some further amusing adventure.

---

3. Julia Lathrop on the origin of the Illinois juvenile court

Julia C. Lathrop, "The Background of the Juvenile Court in Illinois," in *The Child, the Clinic and the Court* (New York: New Republic, 1925), pp. 290–295.

The belief that childhood is the period for education and should be spent neither in idleness nor in labor was haltingly expressing itself in our child-labor laws and school laws. But a more baffling problem presented itself. It applied not to all children but only to a neglected minority—those who committed or were charged with offenses against the law. Their sufferings made an appeal to both common-sense and pity, while their menace to the order of the society which disregarded them could not permanently be ignored.

In Illinois the popular confidence in institutional care for children was still great and institutions providing care for orphans and homeless children were fairly adequate. The industrial schools for dependent boys and for girls were obliged to receive many neglected children whose experiences had been so nearly criminal that their mingling with innocent children was undesirable; yet they necessarily mingled in these institutions. This was because offenses were minimized by the courts in order to commit to industrial schools and thus save the child from the sure demoralization of imprisonment.

Another miscarriage of justice was obvious and it was also unavoidable without great changes in the treatment of delinquent children. Children over ten years of age were arrested, held in the police stations, tried in the police courts. If convicted they were usually fined and if the fine was not paid sent to the city prison. But often they were let off because often justices could neither tolerate sending children to the bridewell nor bear to be themselves guilty of the harsh folly of compelling poverty-stricken parents to pay fines. No exchange of court records existed and the same children could be in and out of various police stations an indefinite number of times, more hardened and more skillful with each experience.

Into this situation came a body of women, many of unusual cultivation and public spirit, who had given earnest study and hard personal work to the social and civic problems of their city — The Chicago Woman's Club. Other clubs of women, other organizations, civic and philanthropic, were helpful; but I select this body as a type because its effective work is recognized, its activities have been carefully recorded and were of basic importance.

In the special field of our present discussion it is noteworthy that from 1883 the Chicago Woman's Club committees had done much to improve the decency of the police stations and the jail. They secured women matrons; they maintained for years, until taken over by the county, a school for boys awaiting trial or serving sentence in the jail. They urged a truant school and supported compulsory education. They were deeply concerned by the official indifference which made the John Worthy School a disappointment to those who hoped it would aid in wiser treatment of juvenile delinquents. They protested against the presence of children in the Cook County Poorhouse and did much to reduce their number.

As far back as 1892, a juvenile court had been suggested to the club by its Jail Committee, "that these boys might be saved from contamination of association with older criminals." If justification of this recommendation was needed it was to be found in the Club's record of a report of the teacher of the jail school describing the excitable condition of her pupils owing to an execution held in the jail. "Conversation for two weeks had been chiefly of its harrowing details and the boys suffered either from nervousness and horror or were brutalized, according to their age and temperament."

The attention of the Club was also drawn to the working-out of the law regarding so-called dependent children and industrial schools. Under it, the county or probate judge who heard dependent cases had no discretion. If the child was declared dependent, he or she must be committed to one of the industrial schools which was made, in effect, guardian during minority. The schools could discharge at will, place out or retain until of age. The counties paid a fixed monthly amount for each child so committed and although every school was obliged to seek further funds for its maintenance from charitable givers, the counties sometimes had a policy expressed in an old story ascribed to a county judge. When asked to commit some neglected children to an industrial school he said, "Oh, that will cost the county too much. Let them run another year and you can send them to the state school [for delinquents] and that will not cost the county anything."

In 1895 a bill was drafted at the instance of the Chicago Woman's Club providing for a separate court for children and a probation staff; but the project was abandoned because the Club's legal advisers doubted the constitutionality of the proposed measure. However, interest was only stimulated by defeat. The concern became more general. Judges and prison wardens and other officials, public-spirited physicians, lawyers and clergymen, settlements, the State Board of Charities, the State Federation of Clubs, the principal child-caring societies, the Bar Association, showed a common desire to help. For some years the State Board of Charities had been accumulating first-hand information as to the conditions of children throughout the state who were in poorhouses or otherwise neglected.

When the annual session of the Illinois State Conference of Charities was held in November, 1898, with the Rev. Jenkin Lloyd Jones as president, the entire program was devoted to one topic — "The Children of the State." The papers were given by authorities of national standing. Members of the Chicago Woman's Club, notably Mrs. Lucy L. Flower and Miss Mary M. Bartelme, shared in the discussions, as did Dr. F. H. Wines, who said: "We ought to have a children's court in Chicago and we ought to have a children's judge." Dr. H. H. Hart said, "Now if we can all get together and agree upon what shall be the future policy of the state, we shall accomplish something."

It was plain that various state organizations were considering legislative proposals for the benefit of differing types of child. Mutual good-will animated the occasion and a resolution was adopted that: "The Committee on Legislation to be appointed by the Conference take steps to bring about an early meeting of the other committees of the state dealing with the subject, and endeavor to agree upon the scope and form of the bills proposed to be submitted to the Legislature."

From this Conference emerged the committee which drafted the Illinois Juvenile Court Act. Too many of those whose wisdom gave form and substance to that measure are no longer living. But I think all who were associated in any way with the period during which the act was drafted would agree that though others gave much aid two great figures stand forth, Mrs. Lucy L. Flower and Judge Harvey B. Hurd. They worked together with perfect accord, yet in their respective fields. Mrs. Flower was a leader in the Chicago Woman's Club, the Every Day Club and in many other civic, philanthropic and educational activities. Judge Hurd was a jurist of distinction. His fairness and skill are illustrated by the ingenuity with which, in writing the bill, he was able to overcome the constitutional difficulty which earlier had appeared to others to be insuperable.

After the bill was drawn its passage through the legislature required authoritative support and here undoubtedly no other single influence aided so much as that of the Chicago Bar Association. Upon the request of Mr. Ephraim Banning, a member of the State Board of Charities and also of the Bar Association, a Bar Committee was appointed, whose support of the bill was convincing to the legislature, the press and the general public.

If there were dissensions at any point in securing the passage of the bill, time has amiably obliterated them from my mind and I recall only an extraordinary degree of that coöperative work in a good cause, for which the men and women of Chicago have long been distinguished.

The law was secured because of a great, though slowly developed, popular interest in the protection of helpless children. The title of the original act is, "An act to regulate the treatment and control of dependent, neglected and delinquent children." These words show the broad purpose to protect neglected childhood and indicate the various angles from which, as I have tried to show above, the matter was considered in preparing the bill. Within this great purpose the separate juvenile court was conceived as a protecting expedient, to which resort could be had when needful.

Men and women worked together to secure the law. Court officers and volunteers have worked and sacrificed to carry on the Court in Chicago. It is plainly impossible to mention individually, or even to know, all the persons and associations contributing to the growth of opinion which crystallized in this act. Inevitably I have omitted much that is of interest. But I believe the foregoing brief outline suggests the modernizing influences which led to the making of the Juvenile Court.

---

4. The country's first juvenile court law, Illinois, 1899

"An act to regulate the treatment and control of dependent, neglected and delinquent children," 1899 — ch. 23. *Revised Statutes of the State of Illinois, 1899* (Chicago, 1899), pp. 255–259.

Sec. 1. *Be it enacted by the People of the State of Illinois represented in the General Assembly:* This act shall apply only to children under the age of 16 years not now or hereafter inmates of a State institution, or any training school for boys or industrial school for girls or some institution incorporated under the laws of this State, except as provided in section twelve (12) and eighteen (18). For the purposes of this Act the words dependent child and neglected child shall mean any child who for any reason is destitute or homeless or abandoned; or dependent upon the public for support; or has not proper parental care or guardianship; or who habitually begs or receives alms; or who is found living in any house of ill fame or with any vicious or disreputable person; or whose home, by reason of neglect, cruelty or depravity on the part of its parents, guardian or other person in whose care it may be, is an unfit place for such a child; and any child under the age of 8 years who is found peddling or selling any article or singing or playing any musical instrument upon the street or giving any public entertainment.

The words delinquent child shall include any child under the age of 16 years who violates any law of this State or any City or Village ordinance.

The word child or children may mean one or more children and the word parent or parents may be held to mean one or both parents when consistent with the intent of this Act.

The word association shall include any corporation which includes in its purposes the care or disposition of children coming within the meaning of this Act.

Sec. 2. The circuit and county courts of the several counties in this State, shall have original jurisdiction in all cases coming within the terms of this act. In all trials under this act any person interested therein may demand a jury of six or the Judge of his own motion may order a jury of the same number to try the case.

Sec. 3. In counties having over 500,000 population, the judges of the circuit court shall, at such times as they shall determine, designate one or more of their number, whose duty it shall be to hear all cases coming under this act. A special court room to be designated as the juvenile court room, shall be provided for the hearing of such cases, and the findings of the court shall be entered in a book or books to be kept for that purpose, and known as the "Juvenile Record," and the court may for convenience be called the "Juvenile Court."

Sec. 4. Any reputable person being resident in the county, having knowledge of a child in his county who appears to be either neglected, dependent or delinquent, may file with the clerk of a court having jurisdiction in the matter, a petition in writing, setting forth the facts, verified by affidavit. It shall be sufficient that the affidavit is upon information and belief.

Sec. 5. Upon the filing of the petition a summons shall issue requiring the person having custody or control of the child or with whom the child may be, to appear with the child at a place and time stated in the summons, which time shall be not less than 24 hours after service. The parents of the child, if living, and their residence is known, or its legal guardian, if one there be, or if there is neither parent or guardian or if his or her residence is not known, then some relative, if there be one, and his residence is known, shall be notified of the proceedings and in any case the judge may appoint some suitable person to act in behalf of the child. If the person summoned as herein provided shall fail without reasonable cause to appear and abide the order of the court, or to bring the child, he may be proceeded against as in case of contempt of court. In case the summons can not be served or the party served fails to obey the same, and in any case when it shall be made to appear to the court that such summons will be ineffectual, a warrant may issue on the order of the court, either against the parent or guardian or the person having custody of the child or with whom the child may be or against the child itself. On the return of the summons or other process, or as soon thereafter as may be, the court shall proceed to hear and dispose of the case in a summary manner. Pending the final disposition of any case, the child may be retained in the possession of the person having the charge of same, or may be kept in some suitable place provided by the City or County Authorities.

Sec. 6. The Court shall have authority to appoint or designate one or more discreet persons of good character to serve as probation officers, during the pleasure of the court; said probation officers to receive no compensation from the public treasury. In case a probation officer shall be appointed by any court, it shall be the duty of the clerk of the court, if practicable, to notify the said probation officer in advance when any child is to be brought before the said court; it shall be the duty of the said probation officer to make such investigation as may be required by the court; to be present in court in order to represent the interests of the child when the case is heard; to furnish to the court such information and assistance as the judge may require; and to take such charge of any child before and after trial as may be directed by the court.

Sec. 7. When any child under the age of sixteen (16) years shall be found to be dependent or neglected within the meaning of this act, the court may make an order committing the child to the care of some suitable State institution or to the care of some reputable citizen of good moral character, or to the care of some training school or an industrial school, as provided by law, or to the care of some association willing to receive it, embracing in its objects the purpose of caring or obtaining homes for dependent or neglected children, which association shall have been accredited as hereinafter provided.

Sec. 8. In any case where the court shall award a child to the care of any association or individual in accordance with the provisions of this act, the child shall, unless otherwise ordered, become a ward, and be subject to the guardianship of the association or individual to whose care it is committed. Such association or individual shall have authority to place such child in a family home, with or without indenture, and may be made party to any proceeding for the legal adoption of the child, and may by its or his attorney or agent appear in any court where such proceedings are pending and assent to such adoption. And such assent shall be sufficient to authorize the court to enter the proper order or decree of adoption. Such guardianship shall not include the guardianship of any estate of the child.

Sec. 9. In the case of a delinquent child, the court may continue the hearing, from time to time, and may commit the child to the care and guardianship of a probation officer duly appointed by the court, and may allow said child to remain in its own home, subject to the visitation of the probation officer; such child to report to the probation officer as often as may be required, and subject to be returned to the court for further proceedings, whenever such action may appear to be necessary; or the court may commit the child to the care and guardianship of the probation officer to be placed in a suitable family home, subject to the friendly supervision of such probation officer; or it may authorize the said probation officer to board out the said child in some suitable family home, in case provision is made by voluntary contribution or otherwise for the payment of the board of such child until a suitable provision may be made for the child in a home without such payment, or the court may commit the child, if a boy, to a training school for boys, or if a girl, to an industrial school for girls. Or if the child is found guilty of any criminal offense and the judge is of the opinion that the best interest requires it, the court may commit the child to any institution within said county incorporated under the laws of this State for the care of delinquent children, or provided by a city for the care of such offenders, or may commit the child, if a boy, over the age of ten years to the State reformatory, or if a girl over the age of ten years to the State home for juvenile female offenders. In no case shall a child be committed beyond his or her minority. A child committed to such institution shall be subject to the control of the board of managers thereof, and the said board shall have power to parole such child on such conditions as it may prescribe, and the court shall, on the recommendation of the board, have power to discharge such child from custody, whenever in the judgment of the court, his or her reformation shall be complete; or the court may commit the child to the care and custody of some association that will receive it, embracing in its objects the care of neglected and dependent children, and that has been duly accredited as hereinafter provided.

Sec. 10. When, in any county where a court is held as provided in section three of this act, a child under the age of 16 years is arrested with or without warrant, such child, may instead of being taken before a justice of the peace or police magistrate, be taken directly before such court, or if the child is taken before a justice of the peace or police magistrate, it shall be the duty of such justice of the peace or police magistrate to transfer the care to such court, and the officer having the child in charge to take such child before that court, and in any such case, the court may proceed to hear and dispose of the case in the same manner as if the child had been brought before the court upon petition as herein provided. In any case the court shall require notice to be given and investigation to be made as in other cases under this act, and may adjourn the hearing from time to time for the purpose.

Sec. 11. No court or magistrate shall commit a child under twelve (12) years of age to a jail or police station, but if such child is unable to give bail, it may be committed to the care of the sheriff, police officer or probation officer, who shall keep such child in some suitable place provided by the City or County outside of the inclosure of any jail or police station. When any child shall be sentenced to confinement in any institution to which adult convicts are sentenced, it shall be unlawful to confine such child in the same building with such adult convicts, or to confine such child in the same yard or inclosure with such adult convicts, or to bring such child into any yard or building in which such adult convicts may be present.

Sec. 12. It shall be the duty of the Superintendent of the State Reformatory at Pontiac

and the board of managers of the State Home for Juvenile Female Offenders at Geneva, and the board of managers of any other institution to which juvenile delinquents may be committed by the courts, to maintain an agent of such institution, whose duty it shall be to examine the homes of children paroled from such institution, for the purpose of ascertaining and reporting to said court whether they are suitable homes; to assist children paroled or discharged from such institution in finding suitable employment, and to maintain a friendly supervision over paroled inmates during the continuance of their parole; such agents shall hold office subject to the pleasure of the board making the appointment, and shall receive such compensation as such board may determine out of any funds appropriated for such institution applicable thereto.

Sec. 13. All associations receiving children under this act shall be subject to the same visitation, inspection and supervision of the board of State commissioners of public charities as the public charitable institutions of this State. The judges of the courts hereinbefore mentioned may require such information and statistics from associations desiring to have children committed to their care under the provisions of this act as said judges deem necessary, in order to enable them to exercise a wise discretion in dealing with children. Every such association shall file with the board of State commissioners of public charities an annual printed or written report, which shall include a statement of the number of children cared for during the year, the number received, the number placed in homes, the number died, the number returned to friends; also a financial statement showing the receipts and disbursements of the associations. The statement of receipts shall indicate the amount received from public funds, the amount received from donations and the amount received from other sources, specifying the several sources. The statement of disbursements shall show the amount expended for salaries and other expenses, specifying the same, the amount expended for lands, buildings and investments. The secretary of the board of public charities shall furnish to the judge of each of the county courts a list of associations filing such annual reports, and no child shall be committed to the care of any association which shall not have filed a report for the fiscal year last preceding with the State board of commissioners of public charities.

Sec. 14. No association whose objects may embrace the caring for dependent, neglected or delinquent children shall hereafter be incorporated unless the proposed articles of incorporation shall first have been submitted to the examination of the board of State commissioners of public charities, and the Secretary of State shall not issue a certificate of incorporation unless there shall first be filed in his office the certificate of said board of State commissioners of public charities that said board has examined the said articles of incorporation and that, in its judgment, the incorporators are reputable and responsible persons, the proposed work is needed, and the incorporation of such association is desirable and for the public good; amendments proposed to the articles of incorporation or association having as an object the care and disposal of dependent, neglected or delinquent children shall be submitted in like manner to the board of State Commissioners of public charities, and the Secretary of State shall not record such amendment or issue his certificate therefor unless there shall first be filed in his office the certificate of said board of State commissioners of public charities that they have examined the said amendment, that the association in question is, in their judgment, performing in good faith the work undertaken by it, and that the said amendment is, in their judgment, a proper one and for the public good.

Sec. 15. It shall be lawful for the parents, parent, guardian or other person having the right to dispose of a dependent or neglected child to enter into an agreement with any association or institution incorporated under any public or private law of this State for the purpose of aiding, caring for or placing in homes such children, and being approved as herein provided, for the surrender of such child to such association or institution, to be taken and cared for by such association or institution or put into a family home. Such agreement may contain any and all proper stipulations to that end, and may authorize the association or institution, by its attorney or agent, to appear in any proceeding for the legal adoption of such child, and consent to its adoption, and the order of the court made upon such consent shall be binding upon the child and its parents or guardian or other person the same as if such parents or guardian or other person were personally in court and consenting thereto, whether made party to the proceeding or not.

.   .   .   .   .

Sec. 18. The county judge of each county may appoint a board of six reputable inhabitants who will serve without compensation to constitute a board of visitation whose duty it shall be to visit as often as once a year, all institutions, societies and associations receiving children under this act; said visits shall be made by not less than two of the members of the board who shall go together or make a joint report; the said board of visitors shall report to the court, from time to time, the condition of children received by, or in the charge of such associations and institutions, and shall make an annual report to the board of State commissioners of public charities, in such form as the board may prescribe. The county board may, at their discretion, make appropriations for the payment of the actual and necessary expenses incurred by the visitors in the discharge of their official duties.

Sec. 19. The powers and duties herein provided to be exercised by the county court or the judges thereof, may, in counties having over 500,000 population, be exercised by the circuit courts and their judges as hereinbefore provided for.

Sec. 20. Nothing in this act shall be construed to repeal any portion of the act to aid industrial schools for girls, the act to provide for and aid training schools for boys, the act to establish the Illinois State Reformatory or the act to provide for a State Home for Juvenile Female Offenders. And in all commitments to said institutions the acts in reference to said institutions shall govern the same.

Sec. 21. This act shall be liberally construed to the end that its purpose may be carried out, to-wit: That the care, custody and discipline of a child shall approximate as nearly as may be that which should be given by its parents, and in all cases where it can properly be done, the child be placed in an improved family home and become a member of the family by legal adoption or otherwise.

---

5. Detention home of the Chicago
Juvenile Court

Mrs. Joseph T. Bowen, "The Early Days of the Juvenile Court," in *The Child, the Clinic and the Court,* pp. 300–305.

Louise DeKoven Bowen was president of the Chicago Juvenile Court Committee, a voluntary organization of philanthropic citizens and representatives of women's clubs which was formed to support the auxiliary services of the Chicago court in its early days.

I have said that we had no place to confine children pending their hearing. They could not be kept in the jails or the police stations so we took an old house on West Adams Street which had been fitted up as a Detention Home and run by the Illinois Industrial Association. They could not support it, so it was taken over by the Juvenile Court Committee. The girls and the dependent children were kept in the house, which was a very simple homelike place. Behind it was a large, two-story building which had been used as a stable. We fitted this up,

using the first floor as a kitchen and sitting room and the second floor as sleeping quarters. It contained fifty beds for the boys who were confined there. We maintained this house for seven years in coöperation with the city and county, from twenty-six to twenty-eight hundred children passing through it yearly. The city allowed us eleven cents a day for food for each child and the county gave us certain things, among others the services of the county physician, transportation to and from the Court, etc. During these seven years the institution was never quarantined on account of contagious diseases. When a child was ill the county physician was immediately called and if the child had a contagious disease he was at once removed to what, I think, was the contagious ward in the County Hospital.

This Detention Home was under the charge of one of the members of our committee, now Mrs. Harry Hart. She was at the Home every day and looked after every detail, using the greatest economy in purchasing. It was owing to her good management that we were able to maintain the Home for so long a period.

We had, at that time, a fine body of men and women who were most anxious for the success of the Court and for the good of the children, and we finally secured the passage of a law which provided that probation officers be placed on the payroll of the county. I well remember how that law was passed, because it gave me a feeling of great uneasiness that it was so easy to accomplish. I happened to know at that time a noted Illinois politician. I asked him to my house and told him I wanted to get this law passed at once. The legislature was in session; he went to the telephone in my library, called up one of the bosses in the Senate and one in the House and said to each one, "There is a bill, number so and so, which I want passed; see that it is done at once." One of the men whom he called evidently said, "What is there in it?" and the reply was, "There is nothing in it, but a woman I know wants it passed"—and it was passed. I thought with horror at the time, Supposing it had been a bad bill, it would have been passed in exactly the same way.

The Juvenile Court Committee was at that time made up of women delegates from the various clubs. These clubs took a great interest in the Home: they visited it frequently; they pulled down the covers of the beds to see if they were clean; they tasted the food to see if it was good. Seldom a day passed without a visitor from one of these organizations and it certainly tended to keep us alert and active on the job. I remember at one time we were summoned into court charged with having served worms to the children in their soup. When we responded to the summons and listened to the evidence, it was found that one of the parents of the children had seen vermicelli in the soup and thought it was worms. Another time we were berated by a club because we only had one sheet on the beds. It was difficult for us to get the boys to use sheets at all or even to undress or take off their shoes. They would strip the clean sheets off the beds, saying they could not bear to get them dirty, and one of their favorite tricks (smoking was not allowed) was to take the shoe strings out of their shoes to bed with them and smoke them in comfort until the guard for those fifty boys smelt the burning strings and hastened to confiscate them. We had a teacher from the Board of Education who was excellent with the boys and kept them occupied—the great secret of keeping boys out of mischief. She was very proud of her class and the boys themselves were proud of their progress.

I suppose boys were very much then as they are now and yet we had almost no trouble with them. Our superintendent was a little old woman, I should say over seventy years of age, but there was nothing about children she did not know. On one occasion when I was at the Home, she came in from the stable quite irate at the boys, as they had been acting badly, she said. I asked her what they were doing and she said, "Oh, I thought something was wrong and went out there and found they had their guard on the floor, bound; and they were all

sitting on him, jabbing his head with his own revolver." When I asked her if she called the police, she said, "No, indeed, why should I call the police? I told them to get up and unbind the guard and apologize at once." "Did they do it?" I asked, and she replied, "Why, of course." That, as far as I remember, was the only outbreak we ever had.

On one occasion one of our best boys escaped from the Home. We were rather unhappy about it because we had given him certain privileges and he seemed a reliable boy. He returned at the end of the day, very triumphant, carrying in each hand several chickens tied by the legs, and he said, "I felt so sorry for you ladies. You seemed to have such a hard time raising money to feed us kids that I just went out to Mrs. Story's chicken yard and got these chickens for you." He was very much upset, and we felt almost apologetic, to take the chickens away from him and return them to the rightful owner.

It was very difficult to get the city or the county authorities to give us any money or necessary equipment for the Home. The county had given us an old omnibus, drawn by a very small horse, which struggled painfully to drag the omnibus between the Court and the Home. The old vehicle grew older and older and became very rickety, and one day the driver came to say that some of the boards had fallen out of the bottom and he had nearly dropped the children on the street. The omnibus could not be repaired, so I went to the county for relief and was told that this was a city matter and I must go to the chief of police. I went to his office and stood up against the wall all day; the office was full of expectorating gentlemen who occupied chairs and were rather amused at a woman wanting to see the chief of police. When I went to luncheon Miss Lathrop took my place in holding up the wall and we spun the day out that way, until the chief left by a back door when it was dark. Next day I was in my place again and this time saw him. He said he had nothing to do with the matter and referred me to the repair department; they said the omnibus could not be repaired and referred me to the construction department. The construction department could do nothing about it unless it was O.K.'d by the mayor, who referred me to the county commissioners, who referred me to another department.

After six weeks of seeing one man and then another, in desperation the Juvenile Court Committee bought a new omnibus. It was too heavy for the little horse to pull, so I went all over the ground again, to get another horse. Finally, after having been referred to the fire department, I was informed that there was a horse out on a farm that had been laid off because he was lame, but perhaps he could draw the omnibus. He was brought to the city and proved to be a large, husky animal. He was harnessed to the omnibus with the little horse, but evidently thought he was going to a fire and rushed down the street so rapidly that the driver had to stop him, as the pony was nearly strangled from having been lifted off its feet.

We then bought a pair of horses and the city gave us a barn four miles from the Home. We were told several days later by the driver that the stalls in the barn were so small that the horses had not been able to lie down for four days and nights. Finding we could not do anything about the matter, we rented a stable ourselves and tried to get the city to provide us with food for the horses. We even let them go three days without food, hoping in this way to force the city to provide for them. The whole thing ended in the committee buying its own omnibus, its own horses, renting its own stable and furnishing its own horse-feed.

Some of the children who were brought into the Detention Home in these early days were pitiful objects. I remember two children, a boy and a girl, who had been found in a pigpen; their mother and father must have been out of their minds because they had kept the children in with the animals, wearing no clothes and eating only the food furnished the pigs. They did not know how to talk and jabbered like little animals.

6. The juvenile court and the delinquent family

Sophonisba P. Breckinridge and Edith Abbott, *The Delinquent Child and the Home* (New York, 1912), pp. 170–174.

Miss Breckinridge (1866–1948) and Miss Abbott (1876–1957) were directors of the Department of Social Investigation in the Chicago School of Civics and Philanthropy, predecessor of the School of Social Service Administration, University of Chicago.

Looking at these "delinquent" families from the point of view of the court they fall into several classes. There are first, those in which the conditions within the home are favorable and in which the parents understand the child's delinquency and either appeal to the court to support their authority or, when they do not take the initiative themselves by bringing the child into court, are quite willing to co-operate in the measures taken for his welfare. This is a hopeful and fortunately a numerous class so far as delinquent boys are concerned; and it includes homes from every economic stratum. In these families over and over again the mother's comment to the investigator was that little Bill or John had not been "really bad" and that "getting into court gave him such a scare that he straightened up at once and the officer did not have to come very long." It is clear that in cases like this where the home is good and the parents merely need to have their own policy with regard to the child given the temporary support of a coercive authority, there is no "family problem" before the court. The family becomes only a most valuable co-operating agency.

In a different class, however, are those homes in which the parents wish to co-operate, but in which the conditions in the home or the neighborhood make co-operation impossible. The figure of the widowed or deserted mother who goes out to work looms large in this group. Although she is intelligent enough to know what a good home is and does her best to maintain one, the condition of her misfortune renders her most strenuous efforts futile. In the families in this group, the spiritual power is greater than the pecuniary resources. They are poor because the breadwinner may have been disabled or because there may have been illness or accident or other misfortune. In these homes the ideals are good, but misfortune leading often to economic pressure seems to necessitate the sacrifice of the children. This class presents a difficult problem to the court and one that can never be adequately dealt with except by such effective co-operation between the court and the organized public and private charity of the city as will keep the competent working mother at home, lighten the economic pressure that is exploiting the child, improve the neighborhood conditions that are promoting delinquency, or move the family to safer quarters. Until this co-operation is perfected the court must remain handicapped.

There are many cases in which the court, recognizing the good intentions of the family, puts the child on probation without having the resources to alter the conditions which are really responsible for the child's presence before the judge. Sooner or later, however, because of these conditions, the child is returned to the court and committed to an institution, while the family circumstances remain unchanged. After a brief time he is returned to the delinquency-promoting conditions from which he originally came, is later returned again to the court, returned to an institution, returned again to his family, and then the vicious circle begins all over, not only for the boy but for his younger brothers and sisters. The court returns the child to the home, because the essential rightness of the intentions of the family is recognized and because the only alternative to the home is an overcrowded institution, which may soon turn the child out to make room for the "next case." It is not a choice between the poor home and the ideal institution, but between the home that seems bad and the institution that is surely worse.

In a third class of families, which presents a still more difficult problem to the court, there is no question of economic pressure or unlooked-for misfortune. In these families the child is being sacrificed or exploited because his needs either are not properly understood or are wilfully disregarded. Unlike the families in the first class, these neither seek nor welcome but rather resent the relationship of the court to the child; unlike the second class, the spiritual rather than the material conditions are unfavorable. The father while not "brutal" is often extremely severe, the mother too little concerned with the care or training of the children. Here the sense of parental right is strong and the court is regarded as a trespasser and interloper. In dealing with families of this type, the coercive power of the court is exercised over the parents rather than over the child. While no poverty exists, there are often crowded conditions of living because lodgers are taken either to share the rent or to add to the fund for purchasing the house. In short, homes of this type are uncomfortable for the child and often unsafe. Here the chief function of the probation officer is to expound to the parents the standard to be maintained for the child and if possible to enforce that standard.

A fourth class, though not a large one, is interesting and should be noticed. It includes families again not poor nor outwardly degraded, whose homes seem comfortable, so that it is not easy for the court to contemplate removing the child. There often are marital difficulties, — occasionally divorce; or a diseased spot in the family life may be discovered; but sometimes the character of the delinquency and the fact that none of the children — or none of the girls in one case — escape the taint, is the chief evidence of a degeneracy evidently far gone in the family life, which is like a fruit of fair exterior but rotten at the core. For children from homes such as these little can be done except to place them in institutions and postpone the day of their complete undoing. In the treatment of such cases, until further light is thrown on the subject by the researches in biological and psychological laboratories, the court must act feebly and on the whole blindly.

Finally there remains the class in which are found only the dregs of family life, and here action must be sure as it should be swift. For here are found drunkenness, immorality, crime, filthy and degraded homes — homes below any acceptable standards of cleanliness, of decency, and of competence. In these homes the court finds only opposition in the intentions of the family and insurmountable difficulties in the way of maintaining right conditions of living. Here the right of family life has been forfeited and that privilege should be denied by the court. As a major operation is undertaken by a surgeon, amputation should be resorted to in these cases and the child promptly and permanently removed from the contaminating influences.

Thus it may be said that so far as the family problem before the court is concerned, the homes fall, broadly speaking, into two large divisions, the one containing those homes in which the care of the court can be exercised in co-operation with the family, the other those in which it can be exercised only in opposition to the wishes of the family, and in which the family is antagonistic to the standards that the community has set for its children.

From this it is evident that there must be developed a much finer discrimination in judging of the rights of parents. To the competent parent all aid should be given; of the competent parent the efficient performance of parental duties should be demanded. Over the inefficient, careful supervision should be exercised. To the well-intentioned, aid should be rendered by the use of such agencies as the school nurse, the visiting housekeeper, the truant officer, and the sanitary inspector; to the degraded parent no concessions should be made.

When there are evidences of drunkenness or vicious and immoral living, complete separation is probably the only safeguard. To accomplish this, the machinery of the court for dealing with dependent children should be rendered strong enough and skillful enough to discover conditions unfavorable to child life at a very early period, and the staff of probation officers should be efficient, well equipped, and thoroughly grounded in the principles of relief and of sound family life.

Denver

Benjamin Barr Lindsey (1869–1943) was born in Tennessee, moved to Denver in 1885, and was admitted to the Colorado Bar in 1894. From 1900 to 1927 he used his position as judge of the County Court of Arapahoe County, Colorado (Denver), to promote the juvenile court movement.

---

1. Ben Lindsey's first juvenile case, 1894

Benjamin B. Lindsey and Rube Borough, *The Dangerous Life* (New York: Horace Liveright, 1931), pp. 49–53.

The clerk gave me the numbers of the cases. I got the pleadings and went into the old West Side jail to see my clients. The Warden smiled when I told him their names. I followed him through clanging iron doors with their rattling bolts and bars to the back part of the building.

At the end of a corridor I came in front of a cage on the floor of which were two small boys engaged in gambling with two grown men who had been brought in from some outlying section of Arapahoe county, a sparsely settled empire that then ran clear to the eastern state line.

I found that these boys had already been in jail more than 60 days and had learned to play poker from their older cell mates, a safe cracker and a horse thief, upon whom they had come to look as great heroes.

My first thought was that the judge in assigning me to defend two such men from serious crimes had given me a pretty tough job but my concern was soon relieved as the Warden explained:

"It's the kids the judge wants you to look after. He was over here the other day and he didn't like it very much that they're still here. He said he knew a young fellow who was just the one to look after the case. I guess it must be you."

"Then," I asked, to make doubly sure, "it's not those two men who are my clients?"

"No," he drawled. "Those guys have got two real lawyers to defend 'em."

"But," I persisted, "I am appointed to defend two burglars."

The kids looked like such real boys that in my confusion I had been unable to visualize them as criminals — my mind just refused to work that way.

"Sure you are," said the Warden, "but them's the burglars."

A number of things shot through my mind as this first step in my difficulties cleared up. One was that it, perhaps, took "two burglars" like these boys to make "one burglar." And so my pride that had soared from the flattery of two assignments when any young fellow would have been tickled to death with one was a bit humbled.

My first task — that was afterward to become my task in so many thousands of cases that I then little knew were to follow — was to get acquainted with the prisoners. It was my first appearance before the bench of youth but its lesson was to stay with me even in the days when I had long ceased to be a lawyer and had become a judge. For there by those bars that would have shamed the King Tiger of the Jungle I was able to begin a lasting friendship with the little prisoners.

They were typical boys from the realm of Gangville, as I was to come to know it so well. They were about twelve years of age.

The one that impressed me most was a little freckle-faced Irish lad with a sense of humor. He was charged with having gone into a railroad section house and taken a lot of tools.

"Sonny," I said, "you are charged with burglary."

"I ain't no burglary," he countered.

"I guess you don't know what burglary means," I ventured. And I explained to him that the long rigamarole in the complaint papers meant to charge him with breaking and entering a tool house and THAT constituted burglary.

"I never stole 'em, I just took 'em," he answered heatedly. "So I ain't done no burglary — I ain't done nothin'."

"Well, one thing you can't deny," I went on, getting chummy with my client. "You've got the dirtiest face I ever saw on a kid."

" 'Tain't my fault," he shot back with a grin. "A guy threw water on me and the dust settled on it."

When I protested to the Warden against this good-natured boy being held in jail with two hardened old criminals, he admitted it was "a damned outrage."

"How many boys are there in jail?" I asked.

"Oh, quite a number," he answered. "Most of them don't stay so long as these two boys — they're waiting for the fall term of court. Their families couldn't afford to put up bonds."

"But why do you put them in with that horse thief and safe cracker?"

"The jail is crowded," he said. And he gave various other excuses.

Well, in answering the charge against those kids, I did a thing that was perhaps purely artless, the direct reaction from my rage complexes, my indignation at injustice.

I prepared an answer that was an indictment against the state of Colorado for its crime against those two boys. The thing got a lot of public discussion and raised quite a furor.

Here were two boys, neither of them serious

enemies of society, who were about to be convicted of burglary and have felony records standing against them for the remainder of their lives. And, pending the decision of their cases, they were associating generally with criminals and particularly with a horse thief and a safe cracker. The state was sending them to a school for crime — deliberately teaching them to be horse thieves and safe crackers. It was outrageous — and absurd.

My first fight then was with the state of Colorado. I was determined that those boys should have their chance. I saw only vaguely then what afterward became clearer to me — that my first fight with the state was not just for those two boys but for millions like them. Even then, however, — before I had formulated any plan to change the things that were or had written any of the hundreds of laws I afterward wrote for my own and other states and foreign countries — I had made up my mind to smash the system that meant so much injustice to youth.

Although I did not know it, I was well on the road to "The Dangerous Life," with its sorrow and disappointment, and its satisfaction in achievements marred by the consciousness of a goal never fully reached.

How little the judge knew the real size of that first little case to which, in a whimsical moment, he had assigned me!

I went back to him. I talked and he listened. I found him in a measure sympathetic, though he did not fully share my indignation over the situation and warned me against taking it too seriously.

However, he gave me to understand that he would not be bound too much by rule and rote, technicality and precedent, but would cooperate with me as far as he could to do what was "best for the boys" even though, according to the conventions of that time, it might not seem to be the "best for the state." (Of course, I was to know in time that, when properly understood, whatever is "best for the child" is really "best for the state.")

He was not just sure that he had authority to do what he thought he ought to do. But he finally agreed I might continue the case from time to time that we might spare these boys from the blight of conviction for felony and its drag and handicap in after years — provided I would look after them in the meantime.

And, of course, I agreed to that.

I became the Juvenile Judge and Probation Officer.

Such was my first juvenile case.

---

2. Letters of Charles Wise, an inmate at the State Industrial School for Boys, Golden, Colorado, to Judge Ben Lindsey

Benjamin B. Lindsey Papers, Library of Congress, Box 1.

December 17, 1902

My dear friend,

I would like to know how you are.

I read your last letter.

I was very glad to hear that you were comming.

There are fifty seven in company B.

I am very sory but I have got the sixth badge.

We are requested to say that no visitors will be allowed up here on Christmas day.

Your loving friend
Charlie Wise

January 1, 1903

My Dear friend

I would like to know how you are.

I receive your last letter.

I had a good time Christmas.

I had a box of candy and a orange.

And a box of popcorn.

I thought I would write a few lines.

Mr. Laughlin company command of C company quit.

We got a sack of penuts.

> Your loving friend
> Charlie Wise

April 8, 1903
My Dear Friend; I would like to know you are. I am in the third grade. I have got the fourth badge . . . The last two times I wrote to Mrs. Willard and didn't get any answer. So I felt like writing and see if I could get an answer but I am writing to you. I am going to straiten up.

> Charles Wise

---

3. "The larger fight"

Ben B. Lindsey, "My Lesson from the Juvenile Court," *The Survey,* XXIII (February 5, 1910), 652–656.

We are now in our tenth year of Juvenile Court work, and it is my purpose not to deal so much with the law or the work directly done by the court. Our chief work during those years of struggle for the children has been to secure very important palliatives. I do not wish to underestimate their importance; I wish rather to sound a note of warning against placing our reliance too much upon them.

When I first became interested in the Juvenile Court my enthusiasm was limited to public playgrounds, detention schools, public baths, probation system, summer outings, fresh air camps, day nurseries, laws changing the methods of procedure from that of criminal courts to that of chancery courts, to applying the rules of equity rather than those of the criminal code, etc. That was all very important. And the changes we set out to make, the equipment we set out to obtain, have all come about. The achievements in this direction are really more than we hoped for. They have made the ten years more than worth while. We got these things largely through presenting facts and educating the people. We created public sentiment. That sentiment in time demanded justice for the child, and in that work we are proud of the part played by the Juvenile Court.

But what began to loom upon me almost to oppress me, was the injustice in our social and economic system that made most of these palliatives necessary. I began to see more than I ever saw in my life how the foundation of the republic is the home, and the hope of the republic is in the child that comes from the home, and that there can be no real protection, no real justice for the child, until justice is done the home. More than through books I saw through the tears and misfortune of these children, the defects and injustice in our social, political and economic conditions, and I have to thank the child for my education. After ten years I owe more to the children than they owe to me. They have helped me be a better man and, I am sure, a more useful and serviceable one. I had learned to love to work with them and for them in the boys' clubs, the recreation centers, through the court and probation work and in other ways, and when I began to see, as I thought I saw, some of the causes of poverty, misfortune, misery, and crime, I began to question myself. Could I help do real justice to the child unless I could help smash some of these causes that were smashing the homes, crippling the parents and robbing the child of his birthright?

.   .   .   .   .

A heart-broken mother whose child was becoming dependent can tell her own story: "My husband, judge, is a good man; he was steady at his employment as structural iron worker until recently. Now he is neglecting his home and his work. As soon as he quits work he goes down to the gambling house and there he is being ruined. He used to go to mass with me on Sunday, and he was so good and loving to us all. Now he is indifferent, gloomy and melancholy. I am without clothes and the children have no shoes. He has gambled away two hundred dollars of the money that belongs to his union, for he was highly respected and elected its treasurer. I gave him fifty dollars to pay the chattel mortgage on our furniture, and I did not know that he had gambled it away until the chattel mortgage man came and threatened to take the stove and furniture out of the house. I went to police headquarters and they were rude and insulting to me. But one of the officers came up to me and whispered confidentially to me that if I would go to the Juvenile Court they might help me out of my troubles."

Of course the "big business" men who commercialize political parties had little concern about their part in the ruin of that home and in the dependency and delinquency of that child. I sent for their political partner, the gambler who conducted the hell that was burning up that home. He admitted it all. I told him I would make a noise if he did not pay back that money to the poor mother. He paid it back. It would have been useless to talk about arrest and prosecution, for the public offiical of that period would do neither.

I saw how the "System" was debauching the homes of the city. It was also bringing the church and religion into contempt. Other cases deeply affected me. Through injustice to the home I saw the cause of much child crime and poverty. The twelve-year-old boy was beyond the control of his mother. He was delinquent and a subject for the court. The agent for the Humane Society had suggested it would be necessary to take the smaller children away from the mother. It was suspected, he said, that the moral conditions of the home were not as they should be. There was a "boarder" in the two or three rooms of the miserable little shack. The husband and father had been blown up in the gas works. The mother was forced, she said, into immorality. The boarder helped provide. (He became the husband, not through love but economic necessity.) I had seen an officer of that company stand with folded arms in court and smile into the faces of young men who had

been compelled to use fake tax receipts and fraudulently vote at an election to enable it to obtain franchises worth millions of dollars. Some of the young men had refused to testify lest it incriminate them. Others had, to the degradation of their homes and their manhood, calmly committed perjury to protect the franchise grabs of the rich criminal. I had seen corporation lawyers rush into courts and promptly receive any kind of a writ they asked for to keep that rich criminal out of jail. This child was going to jail and to hell for the crimes of some men like that. I had seen a man like that give money for the boys' club and the day nursery, and then direct the lobby in the legislature to defeat an employer's compensation or liability law designed to compel him and those like him to share the risk and hazard under which that father had labored. If we had a law requiring the public, the employer and the employe to create a fund to compensate such mothers (and there are hundreds of thousands like them), they could take care of their own homes and their own children and spare the state the burden. They need not live in shacks down by the railroad tracks . . .

Of what wealth is the child robbed when the father goes to work at 6 A.M. and gets home worn out at 7 P.M.? There was not much in the home to make life worth while. The boy did not like the home — he preferred to steal. He hardly knew father or mother. They were more than half dead to him. He was robbed of a mother's love and a father's firm and guiding hand. It is not orphans who need parents most.

And there were no playgrounds in the congested districts in which they lived. The millions taken from the people in the theft of their streets would have provided recreation centers, and better pay for teachers, and helpers for the helpless home. But that child was robbed of his heritage in the very streets. I had seen it done. And I had been shocked by the defense of the street boy of his right to gamble and steal because he knew that the police protected men in such lawlessness to "help business." Every politician knew that the three or four men who controlled the utility corporations and owned the political parties could close those gambling hells any minute, and they also knew that they seldom closed them except for business and political purposes. The partnership between "big business," vice and injustice was real and from that the child suffered most.

The child's crime was frequently its appeal for justice. Kindness alone was not what the child and the home wanted. It wanted justice. There is no real kindness without justice, and justice is the highest type of kindness.

Thus I found I could make no real fight for the child without opposition, unless I consented to shut my eyes to the political, business and social crimes about me. These crimes involved public gambling, grafting by public officials, stuffing of ballot boxes to gain special privileges and indecent millions, and the spreading of political poison that was debauching the manhood of the state, hurting the home and the child, denying economic justice and robbing the people of their liberties. No man could honestly make a real fight for childhood — for the home — unless he fought these evils. At least it was so in my own small experience, and I have no apologies for our part in the larger fight. There we shall find the way out.

A judge explains his court, Boston, 1910

Harvey H. Baker, "Procedure of the Boston Juvenile Court," *The Survey,* XXIII (February 5, 1910), 643–650.

In 1906 Harvey Humphrey Baker (1869–1915), a bachelor from a well-to-do Brookline, Massachusetts, family, was appointed the first judge of the Juvenile Court of Boston. Baker emphasized close co-operation with the many social agencies of the city and urged the creation of a clinic to study difficult children individually. Following his death in 1915, friends and associates endowed the Judge Baker Foundation which opened in 1917.[1]

The Boston Juvenile Court is administered on the assumption that the fundamental function of a Juvenile Court is to put each child who comes before it in a normal relation to society as promptly and as permanently as possible, and that while punishment is not by any means to be dispensed with, it is to be made subsidiary and subordinate to that function.

The officials of the court believe it is helpful to think of themselves as physicians in a dispensary. The quarters of the court are well adapted in location and arrangement for carrying out that conception. Although they are in the main court house of the city, they are adjacent to the quarters of the Supreme Judicial Court and the Probate Court, in the portion of the building most remote from the criminal court. They are in a quiet corner overlooking an interior quadrangle quite away from the notice of passers on the street or persons in the court house on other business. They comprise a large waiting room, 37 by 25½ feet, where offenders and all other persons attending the court wait for the cases to be called, and the judge's small private room, 17½ by 12½ feet, where all cases are heard. There is no regular dock or detention enclosure connected with the general waiting room and the children usually sit with their parents in chairs placed along the sides of the room. Occasionally a boy who is under arrest and likely to yield to the temptation to leave without permission is placed behind the railing which keeps the general public at a proper distance from the clerk and his papers, or a girl is placed with the stenographer in the probation officer's record room. There are no uniformed officials.

The statute establishing the court provides that "so far as possible the court shall hear all cases in chambers" . . . *i.e.,* in the judge's private room. The judge's room cannot com-

1. On the Judge Baker Foundation see below, Chap. III, sec. A, Psychological study of delinquents, doc. 6.

fortably hold more than a dozen persons, and there are seldom that many in it together. It is entirely without decorations or objects which might distract the attention of a child. The presence of the clerk and stenographer is dispensed with, and the probation officer is the only court attendant ever in the room. With the exception that the judge sits on a platform about six inches high, much like a school teacher's platform, there is no more formality of arrangement or attendance than there is in a physician's examination room.

The statute establishing the court also provides that "all persons whose presence, in the opinion of the court, is not necessary shall be excluded from the room" . . . Acting under this provision the judge excludes all newspaper reporters and all other persons having only a general interest in the proceedings. The sheltered location of the room, the absence of decoration, the dispensing with attendants and the exclusion of outsiders give the simplicity which is necessary to gain the undivided attention of the child, and give the quiet which is indispensable for hearing clearly what the child says and speaking to him in the calmest tone.

When the judge is ready to hear a case the probation officer brings in the child from the waiting room. The child does not stand in front of the desk, because that would prevent the judge from seeing the whole of him, and the way a child stands and even the condition of his shoes are often useful aids to a proper diagnosis of the case. The child stands at the end of the platform where the judge can see him from top to toe, and the judge sits near the end, so he is close to the child and can reassure him if necessary by a friendly hand on the shoulder. The platform is just high enough to bring the average child's eye about on a level with the eye of the judge.

If it seems likely that the child will be inclined to hold back the truth about the affair which has brought him to court, the judge sometimes talks with him entirely alone, and frequently talks with him in the presence of no one but the probation officer. This is done to relieve the child of the embarrassment, and indeed the fear, which he often feels in speaking the truth in the presence of his parents.

The judge always has the formal papers of the case in his hand, but, except in the few cases where a fine is likely to be imposed, there is no formal reading of the complaint, and the child is not required to make any formal answer such as pleading "guilty" or "not guilty." The examination varies in its details according to the nature of the case and the character of the child, but the following will give a general idea of the usual examination and adjudication:

"John, do you know what you have been brought to court for?"

"I suppose it is about Mrs. Doe's money."

"What have you got to say about it?"

"I took it, but it was the first time," etc.

The attendance of at least one parent at court at the beginning of the case is of course always insisted on, and after the above conversation the parents and the police officer in charge of the case, and sometimes the aggrieved parties, are brought into the room, if they were not admitted with the boy, and the judge says:

"John says it is true that he took Mrs. Doe's money and I adjudge him delinquent, and he has the right to appeal."

The police officer is then dismissed, the child sent out of the room and the judge talks over the case with the parents and the probation officer; and the parents can thus be admonished, if admonishment is necessary, without the risks of lowering them in the estimation of the child and thereby further impairing their already insufficient control. Then the child is brought back and informed of the disposition of his case, with such comments on his past behavior and such admonition or encouragement as seem appropriate.

If the child denies the truth of the charge against him, the judge sometimes talks with him at considerable length, reasoning with him, but never threatening him or offering inducements to him directly or indirectly, or asking him to inform on other children unless they are much older than he. The child is told in the course of a free conversation between him and the judge that in this court there is only one thing worse than stealing (or whatever the child is supposed to have done), and that is not telling the truth about it afterwards; that children often keep back the truth because they are afraid, but nothing worse can happen to him if he tells the truth himself than will happen to him if the judge believes the officer and witnesses and gets the truth from them. He is asked if he is not keeping back the truth in the hope that so long as he denies it himself, his parents may refuse to believe the witnesses, and he may thus escape a whipping. He is asked (if he appears pretty intelligent) if he were the judge which he would believe, the witnesses or the boy, if the grown-up witnesses said one thing and the boy another. He is asked if his story seems to be reasonable; if the court is not treating him squarely to give him so full an opportunity to tell his story, and whether he is sure he is treating the court fairly. He is asked if the boys don't say: "Never confess when you are caught and the judge may be in doubt and let you off." He usually admits that that is the case, and he is told that it is true that he may get off that way this time, but that he cannot always succeed, and if later a court finds him acting that way in a case, it will go much harder with him.

All these pains are taken to get the boy to tell the truth himself because it greatly enhances the efficacy of the subsequent treatment of the case, first, because the child is much more receptive to the advances of the judge and probation officers after he has confided in them, and second, because his parents are much more ready to accept the intervention of the judge and probation officers and co-operate with them when the child admits his fault, for they are apt to be quite unwilling to accept the statements of the witnesses against the child's denial, and so long as they believe in the child they regard the judge as a tyrant and the probation officer as an intruder.

If the child persists in denying his delinquency, his parents and the police officer are brought in, and the case is heard in the ordinary way (except that only one witness is in the room at a time), but at a hearing conducted under such circumstances as those described above shy children talk more freely than in public and bold children cannot pose as heroes.

It should be added that offenders brought before the Juvenile Court have just as much right to be represented by counsel as offenders brought before any other court. This right is fully recognized, and when counsel has entered an appearance no step is taken without consulting him, and he may conduct the case in the same way in which he would conduct it in any other court, although in most instances even counsel who are the most technical in other courts actually co-operate with the judge of the Juvenile Court in trying to make parents understand that the court is only seeking to do what is for the best interest of the child in the long run, and in persuading them to submit to the orders of the court.

In determining the disposition to be made of the case the procedure of the physician is very closely followed. The probation officer investigates the case and reports to the judge all available information about the family and other features of the environment of the boy, the boy's personal history at home, in school, at work, and on the street, and the circumstances attending the particular outbreak which got him into court. The boy himself is scrutinized for indications of feeble-mindedness or physical defects, such as poor eyesight, deafness, adenoids. The judge and probation officer consider together, like a physician and his junior, whether the outbreak which resulted in the arrest of the child was largely accidental, or whether it is habitual or likely to be so; whether it is due chiefly to some inherent physical or moral defect of the child, or whether some feature of his environment is an important factor; and then they address themselves to the question of how permanently to prevent the recurrence. If there is any reason to believe the child is feeble minded, he is submitted to a specialist; if there are indications of physical defects, he is taken to a dispensary; if the environment seems to be at fault, a change is secured through the parents by making them realize that the child will be taken from them if they do not make the change, or where the parents are unable to make the change or are themselves the disturbing factor the child is taken away by the court. Of course the court does not confine its attention to just the particular offence which brought the child to its notice. For example, a boy who comes to court for some such trifle as failing to wear his badge when selling papers may be held on probation for months because of difficulties at school; and a boy who comes in for playing ball in the street may (after the court has caused more serious charges to be preferred against him) be committed to a reform school because he is found to have habits of loafing, stealing or gambling which cannot be corrected outside.

Only a very small portion of the children are committed to institutions, and in the treatment of the very large number who are suffered to remain at home the procedure of the physician is again closely followed. If the child's fault is not due to any deep seated difficulty and is trifling in its character, such as throwing stones in the street, he may be sent home to copy an eight-page pamphlet containing extracts from the ordinances regulating the use of streets and laws which children are likely to violate, and the judge sees him only once more, to examine him on his work when it is finished, just as a physician might do in the case of a burn or a bruise. If the offence is serious and likely to be repeated or the conditions surrounding the boy are such that he is liable to have a serious breakdown or if the cause of the difficulty is obscure, he is seen by the judge at frequent intervals, monthly, weekly, or sometimes even daily, just as with patient and the physician in case of tuberculosis or typhoid.

.   .   .   .   .

The cases of girls are handled from the very beginning by women and the men probation officers have nothing to do with them, except to make sure in cases of arrest that the girls are promptly turned over to an accredited woman agent or their parents. If a girl is arrested, a woman is at once called by the probation officer to the police station to take her in charge, unless her parents arrive promptly and are considered fit to hold her until court opens again. When she comes into the judge's chamber she is attended by a woman, who remains constantly in attendance throughout the examination. The judge never talks with girls alone as he sometimes does with boys. If a girl is committed to an institution she is taken by a woman. The court has no women probation officers and all the services in the girls' cases are performed by the woman agents of the Massachusetts Society for the Prevention of Cruelty to Children, the Boston Children's Aid Society, the Council of Jewish Women, the St. Vincent De Paul Society and the Boston Italian Immigrant Society. After a girl's case has been heard she is kept away from the court as much as possible, and is not brought to court to report during a term of probation except in cases of conduct requiring very serious admonition.

B. JUVENILE COURT ISSUES

Legal issues

---

1. The juvenile court legally sustained, Pennsylvania, 1905

Commonwealth *v.* Fisher, 213 Pa. 48.

Opinion by Mr. Justice Brown, October 9, 1905:

In a proceeding conducted in the court of quarter sessions of the county of Philadelphia under the provisions of the Act of April 23, 1903, *P.L.* 274, Frank Fisher, the appellant, was committed by that court to the House of Refuge. From the order so committing him an appeal was taken to the Superior Court, which affirmed it: *Commonwealth* v. *Fisher,* 27 Pa. Superior Ct. 175. The constitutionality of the act of 1903 was the sole question before the court in that case, and is renewed here. The objections of the appellant to the constitutionality of the act, as presented by counsel, are: (*a*) Under its provisions the defendant was not taken into court by due process of law; (*b*) he was denied his right of trial before a jury on the charge of the felony for which he had been arrested; (*c*) the tribunal before which he appeared and which heard the case and committed him to the house of refuge was an unconstitutional body and without jurisdiction; (*d*) the act provides different punishments for the same offense by a classification of individuals according to age; (*e*) the act contains more subjects than one, some of which are not expressed in the title. In considering these objections the order in which they are made will not be followed.

The act is entitled: "An act defining the powers of the several courts of quarter sessions of the peace, within this commonwealth, with reference to the care, treatment and control of dependent, neglected, incorrigible and delinquent children, under the age of sixteen years, and providing for the means in which such power may be exercised." By this title notice of the purpose of the act is distinctly given. It is a single one. It is to define what powers the state, as the general guardian of all of its children, commits to the several courts of quarter sessions in exercising special guardianship over children under the age of sixteen years needing the substitution of its guardianship for that of parents or others. This purpose is expressed in the title in as few words as are consistent with clearness. No one from reading the title can possibly misunderstand the purpose of the act that follows, and Art. III, sec. 3, of the constitution is not offended, if, in passing to the body of the act, nothing is there found but this one single purpose. The preamble to it is a recital that, as the welfare of the state requires that children should be guarded from association and contact with crime and criminals, and as those who, from want of proper parental care or guardianship, may become liable to penalties which ought not to be imposed upon them, it is important that the powers of the court, in respect to the care, treatment and control of dependent, neglected, delinquent and incorrigible children should be clearly distinguished from those exercised by it in the administration of the criminal law. After defining the powers of the court the act proceeds to direct how they are to be exercised in giving effect to its purpose. Nothing in the first nine sections can be read as relating or germane to any other purpose than the one named; and there can be no surer test than this of compliance with the constitutional requirement of the singleness of purpose of an act of assembly.

The objection that "the act offends against a constitutional provision in creating, by its terms, different punishments for the same offense by a classification of individuals," overlooks the fact, hereafter to be noticed, that it is not for the punishment of offenders, but for the salvation of children, and points out the way by which the state undertakes to save, not particular children of a special class, but all children under a certain age, whose salvation may become the duty of the state in the absence of proper parental care or disregard of it by wayward children. No child under the age of sixteen years is excluded from its beneficent provisions. Its protecting arm is for all who have not attained that age and who may need its protection. It is for all children of the same class. That minors may be classified for their best interests and the public welfare, has never been questioned in the legislation relating to them . . .

No new court is created by the act under consideration. In its title it is called an act to define the powers of an already existing and ancient court. In caring for the neglected or unfortunate children of the commonwealth, and in defining the powers to be exercised by that court in connection with these children, recognized by the state as its wards requiring its care and protection, jurisdiction is conferred upon that court as the appropriate one, and not upon a new one created by the act. The court of quarter sessions is not simply a criminal court. The constitution recognizes it, but says nothing as to its jurisdiction. Its existence antedates our colonial times, and, by the common law and statutes, both here and in England, it has for generations been a court of broad general police powers in no way connected with its criminal jurisdiction. Innumerable statutes upon our own books during the last two centuries attest this. With its jurisdiction unrestricted by the constitution, it is for the legislature to declare what shall be exercised by it as a general police court, and instead of creating a distinctively new court, the act of 1903 does nothing more than confer additional powers upon the old court and clearly define them . . . The court of quarter sessions has for many years exercised jurisdiction over the settlement of paupers, over the relation of a man to his wife and children in desertion cases, in surety of the peace cases, in the granting of liquor licenses, and in very many of the ways in which the public welfare is involved, where there is neither indictment nor trial by jury . . . It is a mere convenient designation of the court of quarter sessions to call it, when caring for children, a juvenile court, but no such court, as an independent tribunal, is created. It is still the court of quarter sessions before which the proceedings are conducted, and though that court, in so conducting them, is to be known as the juvenile court, the records are still those of the court of quarter sessions . . .

To save a child from becoming a criminal, or from continuing in a career of crime, to end in maturer years in public punishment and disgrace, the legislature surely may provide for the salvation of such a child, if its parents or guardian be unable or unwilling to do so, by bringing it into one of the courts of the state without any process at all, for the purpose of subjecting it to the state's guardianship and protection . . . The act simply provides how children who ought to be saved may reach the court to be saved. If experience should show that there ought to be other ways for it to get there, the legislature can, and undoubtedly will, adopt them, and they will never be regarded as undue processes for depriving a child of its liberty or property as a penalty for crime committed.

The last reason to be noticed why the act should be declared unconstitutional is that it denies the appellant a trial by jury. Here again is the fallacy, that he was tried by the court for any offense. "The right of trial by jury shall remain inviolate," are the words of the bill of rights, and no act of the legislature can deny this right to any citizen, young or old, minor or adult, if he is to be tried for a crime against the commonwealth. But there is no trial for any crime here, and the act is operative only when there is to be no trial. The very purpose of the act is to prevent a trial . . . The court passes upon nothing but the propriety of an effort to save it; and if a worthy subject for an effort of salvation, that effort is made in the way directed by the act. The act is but an exercise by the state of its supreme power over the welfare of its children, a power under which it can take a child from its father, and let it go where it will, without committing it to any guardianship or any institution, if the welfare of the child, taking its age into consideration, can be thus best promoted . . .

None of the objections urged against the constitutionality of the act can prevail. The assignments of error are, therefore, all overruled and the order of the Superior Court, affirming the commitment below, is affirmed.

---

2. Juvenile court must find parents incapable before committing their children, California, 1917

In the Matter of David Brodie, 33 Cal. App. 751.

The Juvenile Act provides that it shall be made to apply to certain persons under the age of twenty-one years. A description of such persons is found in thirteen subdivisions which immediately follow. Subdivision 13 declares that a person within the age mentioned, "who violates any law of this state or any ordinance of any town, city, county, or city and county of this state defining crime," shall be subject to the provisions of the act. Procedure for the issuance of a citation to the parent and guardian, requiring the production of a minor complained against, follows. A hearing is provided to be had and authority is given to the judge of the juvenile court to declare a minor complained against to be a ward of the court. Section 8 of the act provides that when a person is so adjudged to be such ward, he may be committed to a home or to some reputable person, society, or corporation, or to the care of a probation officer. Subdivision "e" of section 8 provides that the court may, if the ward be a boy and over the age of sixteen years, commit him to the Preston School of Industry for the period of his minority. It is further provided that in lieu of such commitment, the court may admonish the person and dismiss the petition. Section 9b of the act provides as follows: "No ward of the juvenile court as defined in this act shall be taken from the custody of his parent or legal guardian, without the consent of such parent or guardian unless the court shall find such parent or guardian to be incapable of providing or to have failed or neglected to provide proper maintenance, training and education for said person; or unless said person has been tried on probation in said custody and has failed to reform or unless said person has been convicted of crime by a jury, or unless the court shall find that the welfare of said person requires that his custody be taken from said parent or guardian."

It will be noted by the provisions of this section that where the parent or guardian of a minor is deprived of his or her custody, certain findings must be made by the juvenile court. It is complained on this appeal that the court made no finding sufficient to satisfy either of the conditions enumerated in the section, and we think that the appellant is correct in that assertion. We have examined the record diligently, which covers the entire proceedings, both as to the documents filed, the records prepared, and testimony heard. As we view the provisions of the act, it is essential that the court make such findings as are required by section 9b and in writing. In section 16 of the same act it is provided: "The orders and findings, if any, of the superior court in all cases coming under the provisions of this act, shall be entered in a suitable book or books or other form of written record, to be kept for that purpose, and known as the 'juvenile court record,' and the court, when acting under this act, shall be called the 'juvenile court.' " The attorney-general concedes that if the proceeding under the Juvenile Act is to be regarded as criminal and the commitment of the minor is to be regarded as punishment for an offense, then there would be no escape from the first proposition made by appellant that the constitutional right to a trial by jury would be violated. However, the attorney-general's position (to which we agree) is that a formal guardianship by the state is provided for only. That being the true construction, the provisions of section 9b above quoted are harmonious to that end. In other words, there would be no excuse or reason for depriving a natural guardian, capable, able, and willing to train, care for, and educate the minor, of the custody of the minor, unless the court should determine that the welfare of the person required that his custody be taken away from the parent or guardian. The making of such a finding, we think, was essential to sustain a valid order of commitment, and that because of its absence the judgment should be reversed.

The judgment is reversed and the matter remanded to the juvenile court for rehearing.

Probation

1. Juvenile probation in Buffalo, 1902

Frederic Almy, "Juvenile Courts in Buffalo," *The Annals* of the American Academy of Political and Social Science, XX (July 1902), 279–284.

Frederic Almy was the secretary and treasurer of the Charity Organization Society, Buffalo.

On February 26, 1900, the Buffalo Charity Organization Society appointed a committee on probation which held several meetings, but found that nothing could be done without legislation, which it was then too late to procure. A law passed May 1, 1901, through the efforts of

this committee, allowed the Buffalo police justice to suspend sentence with juvenile delinquents, and place them under probation for a term not exceeding three months. The act allowed him to appoint five unsalaried probation officers, and provided that when practicable the probation officer should be of the same faith as the child placed in his care. The court opened July 1, 1901. By an amendment passed in February, 1902, the number of probation officers, still unpaid, was increased to ten, and authority was given to extend the probation for additional terms of three months in the discretion of the judge. A state probation law was also passed in 1901, but was so amended that it applied only to those over sixteen years of age. Consequently in New York State, outside of Buffalo, a chance is given to adult delinquents which is denied to little children.

. . . . .

Judge Murphy, of the Buffalo Police Court, was an active member of the committee of the Charity Organization Society which procured the probation law. Although the law was permissive only, he at once put it into effect, and also on his own motion transferred all his juvenile cases to a separate building, several blocks distant from the police court, where he holds his juvenile court on Tuesday and Friday afternoons. The great success of the court in Buffalo is chiefly due to his interest. Where for any reason a good judge is not available a juvenile court must suffer, for probation gives many opportunities for favoritism to both the judge and the probation officers. It is hardly too much to say that the character of the court will be the same as the character of the judge.

Of the ten probation officers in Buffalo all are unpaid for this special work, but two are truant officers, two are officers of the Charity Organization Society, and one is the head worker of Welcome Hall, a leading settlement. The city is divided into two districts, in each of which there are a Catholic and a Protestant female officer for the girls and the younger boys, and a Catholic and a Protestant male officer for the older boys. There are a Jewish officer and a Polish officer for the city at large.

.   .   .   .   .

The Buffalo juvenile court has not quite completed its first year, and no definite records have been compiled, but two results are already notable — the decrease in the number of commitments to the truant school and to reformatories, and the increase in the number of children arrested. The first result was expected, for many children are now cared for in their homes under probation who would otherwise have to be sent to the public truant school or to a reformatory. The second result was not anticipated, but is in this way excellent. Much juvenile lawlessness formerly ran riot without arrest because the officers knew that the judge would not send a child away for petty offenses, and mere rebuke meant so little that the child fresh from court would jeer at the officer who had arrested him. With probation an arrest is taken more seriously by the children. At a recent session of the court Judge Murphy called attention to this increase in the number of arrests, and recommended legislation which should make convictions in the juvenile court inadmissible as evidence of character in either civil or criminal actions, so that mere juvenile peccadilloes could not constitute a criminal record.

The economy of probation greatly reinforces the support of the system on ethical grounds. It is not often that a measure of social reform makes an immediate appeal to the taxpayer, but probation relieves him from the public maintenance of many delinquents who under this plan are maintained at home at their parents' charge . . . On the side of morality the saving is still greater, though less definite. If this saving of character could be translated into dollars and cents the cash gain to the state through the diminution of crime would be seen to be even greater than the saving in maintenance.

Again, the presence daily in the court of a group of disinterested men and women of char-acter helps to maintain the moral tone of the court. They sometimes see things which the court unaided might not see. More than once in Buffalo pettifogging lawyers, who have been reaping fees from parents on the pretence that their services caused the judge to put children on probation instead of sending them away, have been excluded from the court on report of the probation officers as to their practices.

The teachers usually co-operate willingly in filling out the weekly cards which show the behavior and the attendance of a child while on probation, and they use their influence to hold children to their best. Some have spoken with wonder of the favorable effect of probation on the school work.

.   .   .   .   .

Criminal law has relied too much upon confinement and compulsion, both of which involve cost to the state and rancor and sullenness in the individual. The features of probation are first, the retention of natural conditions, in the home, if it is at all fit, and second, loving, patient, personal service. Instead of withdrawing the child from the environment in which it lives, it tries to assist that environment. It is possible to draw many analogies. In medicine we now give fewer drugs and rely on the natural powers of the body with the personal service of trained nurses. In charity we give fewer alms, and rely on the natural resources of the family with the personal service of trained friendly visitors. In government we use less law, but rely on natural forces with the aid of the Church, the school and other instruments of social reform.

With children the question of reformation is especially important. The chief cause of crime has been said to be neither intemperance, nor avarice, nor lust, but neglected childhood, for neglected childhood means neglected character, and at an age when character is still plastic. Children under arrest for the first time are more peculiarly susceptible to influence than even other children, and the impressions made at this crisis go far to fix their lives. If you catch character young, and at the right moments, you can do almost anything with it. It is even possible to confine the baser parts of a child's life, as the Chinese do the feet of their children, so that the development of these baser parts will be permanently stunted. Swaddling environments, continued for years, can do much to form character by compulsion, so to speak, and to thwart the growth of what is undesirable. This exclusion of evil is the method of the military school and of the reformatory of the military type. There is something unnatural about it, but there is no doubt that in this way habits can be formed; and there is an inertia of character which makes good habits difficult to break as well as bad ones.

The other method is to leave the natural conditions with as little disarrangement as possible; to let the feet grow and become a support for the whole body; to take the activity which might become crime and turn it into industry; to take the affection which might become lust and turn it into love; and to do all this as far as possible under natural conditions. It is possible to do this, not by a high wall which wards off all contamination but casts a shadow on the young life within, but by applying some antiseptic which will make the contagions of daily life harmless. Those of us who with Milton "cannot praise a fugitive and cloister'd vertue, unexercis'd and unbreath'd," believe that everywhere character is better formed by liberty than by force. Antiseptics against temptation are being found by modern charity. I would wish to leave a child undisturbed in its home, if the home is decent, and trust to the Church, the school, the tenement house law and the settlements, as antiseptics against contamination; next to this I would leave the child at home, but under probation; next I would seek a foster home, well chosen and well watched; next, for some children, an open reformatory of the free type exemplified in the George Junior Republic; and last, a reformatory of the more military type. In confinement a boy may find himself kindly and wisely treated, but his social side is not much considered, and this is not in keeping with modern pedagogy. Very much can be done through a boy's affections.

2. The essential factors of probation, 1906

Homer Folks, "Juvenile Probation," *Proceedings* of the National Conference of Charities and Correction (1906), 117–122.

Folks induced the New York State Charities Aid Association, of which he was secretary, to sponsor legislation organizing a permanent state Probation Commission. The commission was established in 1907 in spite of bitter opposition from politically appointed probation officers.

Probation has to do with moral delinquency. As applied to neglected children it is, in effect, an effort to reach the parents, and to affect, for good, their attitude toward their children. It implies, in substance, a conviction. If it be not a conviction in technical terms, it implies a finding on the part of the judge that the child is in need of oversight because his morals are in danger. Probation implies, besides a finding of moral delinquency, a suspension of sentence, either in terms or by a postponement of more drastic measures. Probation does not necessarily involve the investigation of the circumstances of the case by a probation officer. In localities in which there is no other existing agency for the purpose it is undoubtedly the case that the probation officer is best fitted to perform this service, and to represent the interests of the child in court, but it is quite possible for all of that work to be done by other agencies and still to have an effective probation system, the work of the probation officer not beginning until after the court has reached its findings.

The fact that the child has been brought into

court is, in itself, a valuable factor, both as regards the child and the parents. The proceedings of the court, and especially the admonition of the judge, are important facts in the probation system. The continuing possibility of further proceedings and of more drastic measures, without any further conviction for a new offence, is still more important. Most important of all, however, is the probation officer. In fact, it is not too much to say that all the factors previously mentioned simply provide favorable conditions under which the probation officer may do effective work. It is the personal influence of the probation officer, going into the child's home, studying the surroundings and influences that are shaping the child's career, discovering the processes which have been exercising an unwholesome influence, and, so far as possible, remedying these conditions, — this is the very essence of the probation system. The friendly side of the probation officer's work is its important side. His duty is by no means simply that of securing information for the court as to the child's conduct, but that of securing reformation. He is not to be a dispassionate observer but an active influence. Without such work on the part of probation officers, without probation officers qualified to conduct such work and to carry it on consistently and without intermission, the court is practically helpless.

It is but natural, perhaps, that in some cases the court should overestimate the value of those factors in probation with which it has most immediate concern and most direct knowledge, — the court proceedings, the suspended sentence, and the admonition and counsel bestowed by the judge. We would not omit any of these things, but it is, perhaps, time to say plainly that these things alone are not probation. It is easy to overestimate the effectiveness of the court proceedings, and even the fatherly admonitions of the judge. In fact, the impression is produced upon the minds of some, who have observed the proceedings of juvenile courts, that the admonition of the judge, while taken seriously by him, is not regarded so

seriously by any of the other parties in interest. If the idea goes into circulation in the community that being placed on probation is a "soft snap," that you can do what you like without being found out, and that this suspended sentence is in fact an unconditional discharge, the warnings and admonitions of the court will not carry far beyond the doors of the court room.

Probation is not simply an act of clemency on the part of the judge. It is not primarily a personal relation between the judge and the probationer, though these things are desirable features of probation. The probation system is really a new way of treating offenders. It provides a new kind of reformatory, without walls and without much of coercion, but nevertheless seeking to bring to bear upon each child the influences which will make for his betterment, and seeking to provide for him, so far as possible in his own home, opportunities and facilities for education and discipline, which we have heretofore provided only in an institution.

It is a truism, that although any offender, child or adult, is brought into court for some particular act, the community is really dealing with him, not so much because of this particular act, but because of the long train of influences and factors, personal and social, which have exercised an unfavorable influence upon him. The institutional method of dealing with offenders recognizes only the individual element in wrong doing. It removes the individual from his surroundings in order that it may concentrate upon him uplifting influences and opportunities, believing that, when he is released, he, himself, will be so changed that he will resist the tendencies in his surroundings which at an earlier date led him astray. The probation system, with, it seems to me, a truer estimate of all the circumstances, takes into account both the individual and his surroundings, regards his offence as the joint product of his individuality and his environment, and seeks to influence both factors so that they shall work together for good and not for evil. The work of the probation officers must, therefore, begin, if it does not begin earlier, the very moment the child leaves the court. It must utilize to the fullest degree whatever advantages there are in the shock caused by apprehension of the child, by the court proceedings and the judge's counsel. It must, by force of personal influence, and in whatever ways may be possible, build up a strong influence in the home of the child.

We are told that no two children and no two families being alike, probation work cannot be and must not be organized, and that if organized it would lose all of its spirit and value. Is that the case? On the contrary, it seems to me that the fact that probation work must be carried on in the homes of a community, out from under the eyes of the judge and the court, the fact that no hard and fast rules can be laid down for the treatment of individual cases, makes it all the more necessary that an adequate and effective plan for securing probation officers, for instructing them in their duties, for holding them responsible for the proper performance of their duties, should be organized.

Probation work is not after all so very different from several other things that we are quite familiar with. We used to think we could only send out a gentleman to place out children and tell him to do the best he could. Now, we all know the results of placing out children on that sort of plan and method, we know the progress that has been made in the last two or three decades. All this has grown step by step with the development of a logical, practical, careful plan, whereby the selection of homes has been carefully and systematically done and a plan devised for visiting the children and keeping track of them.

Probation work is not unlike friendly visiting. It is not unlike the work of the district committee of the charity organization society. But who would suggest there must be no well-knit scheme for the oversight of the work of the agents of the charity organization society. Let us speak frankly. We all know perfectly well that it is just the kind of work that, without the most careful oversight, is liable, nay, is sure to be superficial and ineffective; that our own minds are so constituted that it is the easiest thing in the world for us to believe that because we have the names of certain families before us and because we plan to visit them from time to time, we are doing something when we are really doing nothing effective.

We must have a well-knit plan for the selection of our probation officers, for instructing them in their duties, for holding them responsible, for knowing what they really do, for interviewing them in regard to their work from time to time, and for bringing actual results, not the intended or supposed results, but the actual results to a knowledge of the court and community.

How shall we work by organization? That brings me to a point on which I speak with some hesitancy, because the conclusion I have reached upon it is wholly different from that I expected to reach when I began to study the subject. In the first place it becomes painfully evident to any one who attends the sessions of the juvenile court in a large city that it is physically impossible for the presiding judge himself to discharge the duties of his position and at the same time be the superintendent of a large force of probation officers. There are not enough hours in the day. There is not enough strength in any one person to discharge these two obligations. There must be built up then a probation system, for the direction, organization and control of the probation work done in the court.

But further than that, and this, I think, lies at the bottom of the question, I am led to believe that the oversight and direction of the work of probation officers from day to day and from week to week, perfecting their plans, their methods and holding them to their duty is not necessarily, is not preferably a judicial but is an executive function, just as much so as the administration of the reformatory institutions to which those same children might and recently would have been committed. The judicial frame of mind is that of taking up case by case, eliminating all other considerations and all other facts, and centering the attention for the time upon the law and the facts in that one individual case, then to pass on to another, and to another and to another. Doesn't that tend to build up a machine — I don't mean a political machine but an administrative machine? It is one and one and one and one. In the consideration of each of these it is inherently important that all the others should be left aside. Now then, the work of the probation officer is inherently and essentially that of keeping all of these under his care and in his mind continually. It is that of perfecting, step by step, an organized plan by which he knows all the time what is going on about all of these children.

The judge has no deputy. The court is not organized in this way, it has no administrative department. The actual administration of probation work is not necessarily, and in great cities to my mind is not preferably, a part of the work of the judiciary. Now what is essential? We have before us in any one of our large cities where the probation system is in effect, several hundreds of children who we have decided are in need of oversight, care, assistance, direction and whatever we can do for them. If we were dealing with them by any other plan what would we have? We would have, in the first place, a chief executive officer, some one person responsible for directing all the assistants and agents and subordinates and holding them to their responsibilities and making sure that they perform their duties. In a reformatory there would be a superintendent; in a charity organization society, a general secretary; some one person in whom is placed continual responsibility for all that is done. And then, secondly, we would have a board of directors, by whatever name they may be known, a group of citizens willing to give their names and their reputations to probation work in that locality, willing to stand for it and to secure funds for its maintenance, to share in the responsibility for its successful administration. In some fashion we must have a chief executive officer and in some fashion we must have persons to discharge the essential duties of a board of directors.

I have realized since coming to this conference as I did not before, the extent to which we have these committees, juvenile court committee, probation committee in nearly all of our cities. We have a committee, which unofficially and without legal sanction, has performed substantially those duties of selecting probation officers and directing their work, or securing this effect and all standing sponsor for it. Now, I think we shall need to go a step further and make that a recognized part of the machinery of government for the reformation of the juvenile offenders and for improving the conditions of neglected children placed on probation. The committee may be appointed by the judiciary, if circumstances are such that there is some one judge or one court clearly indicated as being the proper court for the appointment of such a board. But if the probation work is scattered through a number of courts in the city, then it seems to me entirely proper and desirable that the board should be appointed by the chief executive officer of the city, viz., the mayor.

---

3. The probation officer as "missing link"

Julian W. Mack, "Prevention and Probation," *Proceedings* of the National Prison Association (1907), 27–28, 32.

Mack (1866–1943) received his law degree from Harvard in 1887 and taught law at Northwestern University and the University of Chicago. He was elected judge of the Circuit Court of Cook County in 1903 and, in 1905, was assigned to the juvenile court. He later served with distinction as a federal jurist and as a leader of American and World Jewry.

Probation for the child has been established wherever the juvenile court laws have been passed. Without it there would not be much to juvenile court legislation. If all that we could do were to put the child into a school instead of a prison, we would not have reached a very much higher plane than that on which we stood before; but we have adopted as a fundamental principle the doctrine that there is some latent good in every child that ought to be brought out; that the place for a child is a home, and not an institution, and that the best place, if it be at all possible, is the child's own home. Therefore, as long as it can be done with safety to society and with helpfulness to the child, the child is sent back to its own home. But it is not sent back with merely a word of good advice. If the child has reached a stage of delinquency which has compelled the notice of public officials, evidently it has gotten out of harmony with society and something more is needed to bring it back into its true relation. The probation officer aims to supply this missing link. The probation officer aims to act not merely as the representative of the court, to enforce the rules that the court may lay down, but as the representative of the parental power of the State, seeking to stimulate the child, to supply that friendly interest, that parental feeling, of which the child may be in need.

Obviously the probation officer needs training, to be able to perform these all-important duties, and one of the difficult problems in this work is to secure the proper probation officers. We are trying to get them in Illinois through the civil service law, and I believe we shall secure as good officers as could be obtained through any other feasible method of selection. There are now in New York, Boston, St. Louis, Chicago and possibly elsewhere, schools of philanthropy which aim among other things to train men and women to perform the difficult duties that attend the position of probation officer.

We are but in the commencement of the work today and cannot as yet give any very definite figures as to results. But this much is certain — the former methods produced no good. To throw a boy into jail, to contaminate him by contact with the criminal adult, was found to make him worse. Possibly in many cases probation has not succeeded in doing all that its friends hoped for, but certainly it has not made the boys worse.

.   .   .   .   .

Now let me say just a word about the adult. If probation is a good thing for the child, if the child can be kept from becoming a criminal by being given a chance under proper supervision, notwithstanding the fact that it has gone wrong, why cannot a great many of our first offenders be dealt with in the same way? Why must we take them away from their families and lock them up in a cell and degrade them in their own sight and in the sight of their fellowmen, without any consideration of the influence of their environments, of the conditions material, mental and physical that caused the crime? Why must we continue to ask merely, what has the man done? Why should we not begin to ask in addition, what is this man and how has he become what he is? Why should we not entrust to our judges the power and the duty not merely of sentencing the convicted prisoner, but of determining from all the surrounding circumstances, including the entire life history of the wrong-doer, whether it would not be best both in the interest of society and of the offender, particularly the first and the youthful offender, to place him on probation?

---

4. "Probation as a Reconstructive Force," 1914

Bernard Flexner and Roger N. Baldwin, *Juvenile Courts and Probation* (New York, 1914), pp. 81–86.

Bernard Flexner (1865–1945) and Roger

Nash Baldwin (b. 1884) were closely associated with the origin of juvenile courts and probation systems in their home cities, Louisville and St. Louis. Flexner later became a leading figure in American Zionism. Baldwin was the first director of the American Civil Liberties Union.

The whole function of the probation and supervision of delinquent and neglected children is coming to be recognized as a positive method of treatment, as an active, constructive force in the lives of the children under its influence. Probation is regarded less and less as a form of discharge, of "letting children off easy," an idea surviving with that of punishment. Delinquent children are put on probation because it is the most suitable educational influence for them.

The period of probation should always be indeterminate, in the same way as all commitments to institutions. Judges cannot possibly fix the period of treatment in advance. The probation officer must ordinarily be the judge of the proper time to recommend the termination of probation.

This conception of probation as a vital, active force, naturally carries with it the requirement that those who exercise this function — the probation officers — should be trained, sympathetic, and experienced men and women. They must measure up to high standards of character, personality and ability; they must know child life, the problems of the family, local social conditions, and the use of social agencies. The probation officer must bring home to every child a feeling of the directing force of probation. The old type of loose and lifeless supervision which passed under the name of probation — permitting a boy to go for weeks without seeing his probation officer, to fail in his reports without being looked up — is being rapidly displaced by this positive conception of probation as a vital, adjusting, educational force.

.   .   .   .   .   .

THE JUDGE'S RELATION TO PROBATION

Probation is not a judicial function. It is executive, similar to the administration of a reformatory institution. It is wholly unlike the judicial function. The primary function of the judge is to hear the evidence, pass upon the investigations and to enter judgment. Following up the treatment of children who are made wards of the court is a secondary and quite different function. *As a general rule the judge should keep in close touch with the probation work, as well as with the institutions to which the court commits.* This contact helps the judge in his work on the bench, it increases the efficiency of the probation officers and it helps the children.

In a separate juvenile court, presided over by a judge with no other duties, the judge may even take an active part in the probation work. He often keeps in close personal touch with probation and is at once judge and chief probation officer.

When the court is a division of an existing court, as is most frequently the case, the judge's service is usually limited, or much of his time taken up with other work. It is manifestly impossible for a judge so limited to do any satisfactory probation work. *But many judges sitting in courts of this kind, attempt to supervise children on probation by requiring them to report in court at stated intervals.* This practice has little, if any, value. It is not possible for the judge to establish close personal relations with many children, and the quality and quantity of the work is necessarily limited. It is also open to the serious objection of compelling the child's frequent attendance in court. Mere reports are of little value in working out children's problems. *It is the visit to the child's home and school, the knowledge of his family, his friends and neighbors that tell most in the reconstructive process.*

As a general rule, therefore, reports to the judge by probationers are valuable only in those juvenile courts where the judge has ample time for juvenile court work. In courts where he has little time, the judge's chief contribution to the probationary process, is in taking up difficult cases with probation officers, and checking up the work done by them.

PROBATION BY TRAINED PROBATION OFFICERS

No probation work can be really effective unless done by or under direction of regular probation officers, devoting their entire time to the work. The service requires training, undivided attention, and interest in its problems. The courts are coming to require more generally this type of service from officers paid out of public funds.

In the earlier days of the juvenile court, many officers were paid out of private funds. Some gave the whole, others only part of their time to the work. In some very large cities, numbers of probation officers are still paid entirely from private sources. Some of them are agents of children's societies appointed as probation officers by the court. Others are paid by emergency citizens' committees, organized to perform a public function until the State by legislation and appropriation takes it over. In some cities, officers of the court, such as the sheriff or clerk, are appointed to exercise the function of probation, and in others police officers are appointed for that service. Many courts utilize so-called volunteer probation officers, men or women, who give a small portion of their time from business and private affairs to looking after a few children assigned them by the court.

A classification of the various persons exercising the function of probation shows the following groups:

1. *Persons giving their whole time to probation work.*

(a) Those paid from the public funds either as regularly employed probation officers or as officers from other departments detailed as probation officers (chiefly the police and truant officers).

(b) Those paid from private funds either as special agents or as paid agents of some children's society detailed to this work.

(c) In exceptional cases, some volunteers who give their whole time without remuneration.

2. *Persons giving only part of their time to the work of probation.*

(a) Agents of private societies who do probation work in addition to their other duties.

(b) Court officers giving part time to probation work.

(c) Part-time volunteer probation officers.

It is clear from the previous statement of the function of probation that many of the arrangements outlined above are mere make-shifts, tolerable only until such time as the court can secure its own paid officers. The difficulty of controlling the work of officers appointed by agencies other than the court must be apparent.

Several courts using large numbers of volunteer officers have advanced the belief that "the volunteer is a better worker with the child than a paid officer" on the ground that the paid officer becomes impersonal and professional and lacks the human interest and fresh touch of the volunteer. If that distinction is true anywhere, it is due not to the merits of volunteers as opposed to paid officers, but to the personalities and qualifications of individuals.

As a general proposition, the function of probation is such a delicate and continuous service that only persons who give their whole time to it can be expected to influence effectually the lives of the children committed to their care. It is just as necessary to have paid probation officers giving their whole time as it is to have paid employees in institutions caring for children, or paid teachers in the schools. The process is not one that can be undertaken intermittently, as is frequently the case when a volunteer engaged actively in some other business undertakes to care for a child on probation. The most effective probation officers are those who are able to establish close, natural relationships with the children and families with whom they deal.

Evaluation of detention homes, 1930

William Healy and Augusta Bronner, "Juvenile Detention Homes," *The Annals* of the American Academy of Political and Social Sciences, CLI (September, 1930), 180–193.

On Healy and Bronner's work with delinquents see below Chap. III, sec. A, Psychological study of delinquents.

Our ideas and our concern about detention homes for juveniles are based on long experience. We have worked for years with young people in an office within a detention home, and also in a large city which gets along very well without such an institution. Besides this, we have had opportunity to observe many other detention homes, large and small, and often have had direct contact with those who are or who have been inmates. Consequently, we can very well sum up the administrative advantages of detention and, on the other hand, through direct knowledge we are well acquainted with the great disadvantages that accrue to individuals through detention.

In considering what can be said for or against the building and the utilization of detention homes, we stand face to face with the question of what society is attempting to do when in any way it lays its hands through the law upon the human individual. In this specific matter we must ask, To what purpose is detention directed? And we must ask for sincerity and honesty in the answer. The purpose of detention is certainly not the protection of society, primarily and immediately, as it is with older offenders who are jailed and then sentenced for a period of segregation. At least, only in very rare cases is this the immediate purpose and aim of detention.

Is detention, then, a process carried out in order to render court procedure easier, so that the boys and girls shall be on hand when their cases are called in the juvenile court? This seems to be one of the main reasons for it, but we find that the court hearing, which obviously with better methods might come vastly sooner, is sometimes so delayed that the average period of waiting under detention ranges in several large jurisdictions from ten to over thirty days.

Is the detention of juveniles often a matter of police convenience — the youngster being locked up until the police or probation officers can decide or care to decide what to do about the case? This is common practice, we know. In some places, a large proportion of the individuals detained are allowed to go home without any court hearing.

Is detention necessary in order to prevent escape of young delinquents? In rare cases this is necessary, for example, when the delinquent is a runaway from some other part of the country; but the problem of escape very seldom enters into the cases of young offenders who live at home.

Is detention regarded as punishment of a milder sort, or as a measure of warning? This can be answered in the affirmative, for some police and probation officers hold strongly to the idea that a taste of segregation will turn a trick that no amount of talking to a boy or girl will effect. From our experience we should say that occasionally this measure does work out as intended, but that in the vast number of cases there are no such results. Statistics of recidivism as it applies to juvenile detention homes easily disprove that detention can be regarded as an effective deterrent measure.

The accessory advantages of detention, particularly the opportunity which it affords for study of the young individual, are only in some cases and in some places the real reasons for detention. To be sure, in a few detention homes, actual medical, surgical, or dental work is carried on, but this is not at all general. As a matter of fact, the most important studies, namely psychological, psychiatric, and social, can be undertaken as well, and in many instances much more auspiciously, when a young person is seen in an office that is not in a detention home. We believe we have much evidence to support this conclusion.

It is perfectly true, of course, that the local geographical situation and the size of the jurisdiction of any given juvenile court bears greatly upon the local needs and the advantages of detention, including the study or the medical treatment of a case. It would be almost impossible, for example, for the juvenile court in Cook County, Illinois, to function if there were not in Chicago a large detention home to which youngsters from that immense area could be sent and held. But this is far from saying or proving that the best interests of these young persons, and consequently some vastly important interests of the community, are not jeopardized by such detention.

The origin of the juvenile detention home, together with that of the juvenile court itself, was entirely humanitarian — it was conceived to be utterly wrong for a child to be held in a police station or a jail to witness the miserable scenes that so frequently are enacted there. It goes without saying that this desire for better treatment of our youth was fine and right, just as was the conception of the unrighteousness of handling juveniles in court under the procedure of the criminal law. But our knowledge of what actually occurs very frequently when juvenile offenders are herded together — and even when dependents are placed in groups under detention — throws new light upon the most practical matters that pertain to the detention of juveniles.

The whole subject may best be considered first from the standpoint of the theory of handling juvenile offenders under the juvenile court law. This standpoint is certainly not that of the criminal law, which considers as of foremost importance the protection of society, whether through segregation or some other form of punishment that may prove to be reformative or deterrent — and more recently through adult probation. The basic idea of the juvenile court is that it shall function as a wise parent in rela-

tion to the young individual. The juvenile offender is to be treated in terms of reëducation, and through meeting his needs in sufficient measure. Considerations pertaining to the protection of society rule in the cases of adult offenders and there is very little thought about what is really done personally to the criminal by imprisonment and other forms of punishment; but in the case of the juvenile court, the consideration, above everything else, must be the effect upon the young individual of any form of dealing with him that is undertaken.

We may pertinently here review some of our own observations about detention, not alone in terms of the above general philosophy, but rather with our attention centered on specific and readily ascertainable facts.

The first observation that any one can readily make with regard to juvenile detention homes is that inevitably there is an unfortunate mixing of inmates. This occurs not only in the larger detention homes, but is as manifest when even four or five youngsters are held together. The significance of this does not lie in the age mixture of older and younger delinquent individuals; age divisions, even when enforced, by no means separate those who are farther advanced in the development of antisocial tendencies from those who are less experienced. In some cases, a young boy or girl may have more deeply set tendencies towards bad conduct than the average run of those who are years older.

It is well recognized that the possibility of contamination in matters of vice and criminalism is very real, but all too little attention is paid to this possibility in committing to, or in managing, juvenile detention homes. Much has been made of the evil influence of bad adults upon children, and we hear of this constantly whenever there is consideration of children being held even for a few hours in a jail or a police station; but the fact seems to be that what most often gets under the skin during child life is bad teaching and bad suggestion received from other individuals of about the same age or at most a little older. In studying the causes of antisocial conduct, we have the very definite finding that what is learned from bad companionship is one of the greatest factors in the production of delinquent trends. These observations hold true whether for children and young people in their ordinary social relationships or as they may have been held under detention. We have known an extraordinary number of cases where the individuals have given us pretty certain evidence that the worst they have ever learned, or the greatest influences that have ever set them towards delinquency, have come through being thrown among other offenders. This is as true of girls as it is of boys.

It is a very curious fact that in a given group, at least in any group of young people who are segregated in an atmosphere that reeks with delinquency, the worst things that the worst individual knows are likely to permeate the ideational lives of members of that group more quickly and more virulently than anything else will do. On a number of occasions we have seen three or four boys under very good physical surroundings in a detention home, though not under close supervision, gathered together, listening to what the worst boy of the group had to offer. We could give much illustrative material bearing on this matter of moral contamination in detention homes. It forms a point for the most earnest consideration, because it is through such development of delinquent ideation that so many delinquent careers are formed.

We have also observed much hardening directly ensuing from detention. A youngster definitely says, "Oh, I don't mind this. It isn't half so bad as I thought." Or, "I am not so bad; I find here a lot of others that are much worse." Or, and we have heard this a number of times, "They sent me here to teach me to be good, did they? Well, they couldn't have sent me to a place where I could have learned more that was bad." Even if detention has not been met in quite this spirit, still there may have been a hardening process through the boy or girl becoming indignant at being held, or through learning how to lie, or how to appeal to another court in states where this is possible. All these

things develop disrespect for the law through direct contact with what is done under the law, and lead the individual to become scornful of the whole procedure.

Again, harmful companionships are not infrequently made that develop into delinquent friendships on the outside.

It is through review of what we have learned from cases studied that we are forced to the conclusion that the detention of juveniles is very frequently inimical to the interests of society and to the fundamental intentions of a good juvenile court procedure. Very few youngsters are held long enough under good treatment to bring about reconstruction of behavior trends. In general, we believe, nothing of the sort is expected. Very frequently a detention home is merely a dumping place for the police; or children are held for long periods because court arrangements do not admit an early hearing, or because probation officers who do investigatory field work are overloaded with work. In any case, there is a large chance of the young individual being sacrificed.

. . . . .

Only those should be detained who cannot be held at home and induced to keep appointments as directed by the court or probation officer. If a court area is unwieldy because the distances to be traversed are too great, then the court itself should be split up into divisions and smaller detention homes established if necessary; but with courts more contiguous to home districts, less detention will always be necessary.

Our sole plea in all this matter is for the intelligent protection of childhood as part of efficient community service.

Criticism of the court

1. Juvenile courts must observe legal procedures

Timothy D. Hurley, "Necessity for the Lawyer in the Juvenile Court," *Proceedings* of the National Conference of Charities and Correction (1905), 173–177.

Hurley was President of the Chicago Visitation and Aid Society, a Catholic charitable organization whose influence was important in the establishment of the Chicago Juvenile Court. He was also editor of the *Juvenile Court Record,* which published news about the juvenile courts and other matters relating to dependent and delinquent children.

In the past the person of the child was not taken cognizance of by the court unless there was an estate, and then the court very guardedly cared for the maintenance and education and welfare of the child. Property seems to have been uppermost in the minds of all law makers throughout the entire country. Thousands of volumes of legal lore have been written on the property rights of the child, but little, if anything, is said of the person of the child.

.   .   .   .   .

The law has definitely fixed the definition of truancy, dependency and delinquency; and unless one or more of these causes is alleged and proven the child cannot be adjudicated a dependent or delinquent. Proof without allegation will not suffice any more than averment without proof. Children and parents have constitutional rights and they must be observed. We have on the Illinois statute books 70 pages of laws relating to children. Industrial school laws; manual training school laws; parental school laws; juvenile court laws; state training school for girls' laws; training school for boys' laws; laws relating to apprenticeship, adoption, various criminal sections, and others too numerous to mention. No doubt similar laws exist in practically every state of the Union.

The contention has been made from time to time that a lawyer should not appear to plead the case. The fact remains that the Juvenile Court law is the result of mature thought on the part of a lawyer. The general idea of the law may have been prompted by public opinion, but it remained for a lawyer to draft the law, and after it became a law to put it in force and effect. No person not a lawyer would pretend to manage or conduct a minor's estate, either in the Probate Court or a court of chancery; no matter how small the estate may be letters of guardianship must be prepared by the legal adviser. Bonds must be secured; reports made; accounts required. Final settlements are provided for by the statute in the interests of the child's property, on the theory that by preserving the child's property suitable provision may be made therefrom for the care of the person and education of the child. Such care being required by the statute in reference to the child's property, is it not reasonable to ask, "Why should not like care be required in reference to the person of the child?"

The proceedings of the Juvenile Court, in many cases may fix the status of the child for life, and certainly they should follow the forms required by law. How can the statute be complied with and requirements of the law fulfilled, by a person — though a probation officer if you will, prompted by highest of motives, interested solely in the welfare of the child, looking only for the interests of the child and the parent, but having no legal conception of the statute, who has never read law, who cannot point out the difference between the various acts relating to children?

.   .   .   .   .

There has been a popular outcry throughout the country, insisting that the proceedings in the Juvenile Court should be informal. Such is the wording of the Juvenile Court laws of various states, however, this idea should not be carried too far. God, in his goodness and mercy, blessed parents with children and before the court severs the relations of parent and child, take the child from its home, and transfer it to a foster home or to an institution, greatest care should be exercised.

In conclusion, I contend that the same care,

the same attention, the same consideration should be accorded the person of the child as is accorded the child's property. There is more at stake when the child is taken from its parents, taken from its own relatives, than when the property of the child is affected. If a lawyer is essential in the care of a child's property, then the lawyer is doubly essential in the care of the person of the child.

---

2. Juvenile courts are "all things to all men," 1914

Thomas D. Eliot, *The Juvenile Court and the Community* (New York, 1914), pp. 13–16.

Eliot was secretary of the Pacific Coast office of the American Social Hygiene Association (1914–1916) and professor of sociology at Northwestern University.

When probation officers first began to grapple with cases, they found that every child brought in represented the failure of one or more other social agencies to reach the child in time. Nay, they often found that the agency which should have kept the child normal simply did not exist. Juvenile delinquency is a sort of precipitate of all such forms of maladjustment. The probation officer was forced to become a Jack-of-all-trades or first-aid man. He secured for the child shoes, job, club, book, medicine as the case demanded, in addition to supplying the primary need of moral education. Usually he had no time or thought to go deeper than the immediate need. Most probation officers still take their work in this way.

Wherever a community is especially lacking or inefficient in its child-caring equipment of a certain sort, whether institutional or legal, children needing that kind of care are likely to get into trouble in large numbers. Many a court, alert to such a pressing need, has at once undertaken to meet the emergency with special funds or facilities for the purpose.

Among these extra activities undertaken by juvenile courts in connection with the probation office are employment bureaus, recreational facilities, placing-out departments, widows' pension offices, and neighborhood "preventive work" by the regular staff. In some cases, work of these and other kinds is turned over to a greater or less extent to an auxiliary organization, usually closely identified with the court, but legally separate. Of these, the Juvenile Protective Association of Chicago is the most active.

Another phase of juvenile court work which has developed spontaneously and almost universally is the extra-legal handling of children "out of court" by the probation office. Children are given treatment or placed under supervision by common consent, without trial. Several courts handle as many or more cases in this way than through the regular channels. This is partly to reduce the volume of business, partly to avoid the stigma of trial in the milder cases of delinquency.

In these cases it is the children and parents who are free from legal compulsion. Many courts have also established or coöperated with volunteer probation officers' associations, composed of persons who offer themselves for the supervision of such of the courts' wards as are assigned to them. In this case it is the volunteer worker who is ordinarily not subject to legal compulsion, and has no legal authority; and experience has almost universally proved the system a failure in the long run, if not from the start.

The activities so far described include most of the kinds of work undertaken by juvenile courts through the probation office. The judge himself sometimes undertakes to perform some work which properly belongs to the probation office. Ordinarily, however, he confines himself to the examination and adjudication of cases.

The nucleus of the ordinary business of a juvenile court is composed of cases of delinquency. Most courts also handle dependents. The laws allow some courts to handle truancy cases as such, and intrust to others the issuance or review of child-labor permits, or even the enforcement of the child labor law.

It is obviously impossible for every court and probation office to attempt to undertake all these functions. In most cases the special activities have been the response to some crying need, along lines of least resistance and local expediency, without a clear-cut plan or theory as to the juvenile court's real function in our social economy. Juvenile courts were supposed to fill every gap in the child-caring system. Assuming the premises that probation belonged to the juvenile court, and should meet all needs of the abnormal child, the above is the logical proceeding. However, if this be granted, no line can be drawn short of a court administering all the children's charities. It would become a sort of "department of maladjusted children" — many of whom might have been kept normal had the community shouldered the task in time. Some courts actually state this as their ideal: they are all things to all men. But the theory leads in practice to makeshifts, overlapping, and friction, and to inefficiency because of the natural limits of money, staff, time, and strength.

---

3. The mechanical progress of the juvenile court, 1925

Miriam Van Waters, "The Juvenile Court from a Child's Point of View," in Lathrop *et al., The Child, the Clinic and the Court,* pp. 243–237.

On Miriam Van Waters' work with delinquents see below The federal government and juvenile offenders, doc. 3 and Chap. III, sec. B.

If we study the progress made by the juvenile court we find that it has been chiefly along the line of organization. We have taken great strides in material efficiency; to-day there are far more bricks, stones, desks, filing cabinets and records than there were at the beginning. That is to say, our progress has been along mechanical lines, those things which lie furthermost from the spirit of the child. Have we not burdened ourselves with too many forms? Are we not unduly hampered by the very efficiency of our organization? On the one hand, we must struggle with what we have inherited from the law itself — a number of legalistic atavisms and rudimentary organs, hoary with age; such as warrants, bonds, fines and the use of criminalistic words and procedure, etc. — and on the other hand, the newer, but no less burdensome, machinery of science, and of business efficiency.

It must be the task of the social worker in the court to win back to simplicity for the sake of the child. For the judge, on viewing the inexorable severities of the intelligence quotient and the blood Wassermann, is likely to wish to brush them aside and treat the child as if he never had had a mental test or a physical examination. But the judge is solicitous if anything threatens the sanctity of legal tradition; whereas the doctor frequenlty criticizes courts, judges, lawyers and jury, but is exceedingly punctilious about the rules of his own game. To the social worker belongs this delicate matter of adjustment in the court between form and content, structure and use.

To our critics who say the court has been too parental, we say boldly, "The thing is imposible; we have not been parental enough." To those other critics who say our work should be done by the school, the police, the protective agency, or what not, we say, "You, like the home, have the child first. Do what lies in your power. Try to persuade the child to live aright; to leave off bad company; but when it will not, do not threaten the child with the court, nor foster by word, or deed, the criminal concept that prevents, wherever it exists, the saving work the court was created to do." Social workers, no less than the general public, must be educated to see the court as the only *force* that can be substituted legally for weakening parental control.

What then can we reasonably and faithfully expect of the future? "Those who cannot remember the past are condemned to repeat it," said an American philosopher. For this reason we hold anniversaries.

If we can read the signs of the times, the future development of the juvenile court does not lie along the line of better organization. For busines efficiency, when it entered the court, quickly took possession of its allotted territory.

Our chief goal should be the establishment of personal relationships with the child. We must grasp him with heart and mind, vividly and clearly, as our own flesh and blood in distress. To gain this position only two things are necessary, simplicity and sincerity. Our emphasis must therefore be on better personnel. The next task of the juvenile court movement is to secure to it service in every capacity, from probation officer to judge and psychiatrist, those men and women with the finest intellects and with well-developed personalities. Some communities have already established traditions of this sort concerning their judges. It is my firm conviction that no juvenile court system can do its work well unless the judge assumes leadership and responsibility for the entire situation: court, probation work, detention and treatment. The judge must interpret the work of the court to the community. Not only should judges be chosen for their special fitness: their wisdom, insight, and integrity; but all workers under the judge who deal with the child should at least be worthy of imitation by the child.

The boy who was asked by his probation officer, "Do you wish to become a regular crook like this fellow here, or would you like to grow up to be a man like me?" and who replied, "I don't care to be like either of you," spoke accurately and profoundly.

In conclusion: for twenty-five years we have been busy establishing, elaborating, refining, and extending our organizations. The work was necessary. In innumerable communities there are yet, truly speaking, no juvenile courts — and all the country must have juvenile courts. But when the court is organized we possess only the framework. It must be built up literally of adequate personalities within clear ideas, with good-will, and the right attitude toward the child.

We must return occasionally to the original source for guidance and a fresh definition of our goal. The original idea was to so protect childhood that no child would ever undergo a *criminal procedure,* and that no child would ever be placed in jail. We may differ as to whether childhood ends at sixteen, seventeen, eighteen or twenty-one, but it may be presumed we all agree on the fundamental idea.

It is important for us to remember that it was a small group of people that created the juvenile court movement. In every community it is still a small group who are steadfast and clear-headed enough to keep juvenile court machinery from stamping out juvenile court ideas.

Three points are to be emphasized for our future journey:

First, a sincerity of purpose which is best known and fostered by *simplicity.* "Only children are childlike enough for children," wrote a great educator. But all good courts are conducted with an intimacy and simplicity which goes straight to the being of a child. Second, emphasis on personnel. Nohing else is so important.

Third, a widespread education about juvenile delinquency throughout our communities. Never before in America was this so sorely needed; a respect for the rights of childhood; the fundamental difference between child and adult, in particular his almost unlimited, unexplored capacity for spiritual growth, for modification, in the right soil, with the right person taking an interest in him — an attitude which, without relaxing its parental solicitude for the offending child, places the burden of delinquency and the responsibility for its treatment upon the adult world.

Relationship of juvenile courts to family courts

1. Juvenile courts become family courts, New Jersey, 1912

"An act providing for the hearing and determination of disputes or matters affecting the domestic relation, and conferring jurisdiction upon the county juvenile courts," 1912 — ch. 360. *Acts of the State of New Jersey, 1912* (Trenton, 1912), pp. 630–632.

Be it enacted by the Senate and General Assembly of the State of New Jersey:

1. In all counties of this State where there is or may hereafter be established a county juvenile court, said court is hereby vested with jurisdiction to hear and determine all disputes involving the domestic relation, the jurisdiction over which is now or may hereafter be by law vested in any court of this State except the Court of Chancery and the Orphans' Court.

2. By "disputes involving the domestic relation" is meant all complaints . . . where the gravamen of the complaint is the failure or neglect of one member of a family to satisfy or discharge his legal obligations to another member or members of the family; and all charges against any persons for abandonment or non-support of wives, or children, or poor relatives, under any provision of law; and all prosecutions instituted by the poormaster of any municipality, based upon or arising out of the marirage state; *provided, however,* that nothing in this act shall be construed to confer upon such court jurisdiction to hear and determine any criminal complaint for the violation of any law of this State denominating any such conduct a crime or misdemeanor, except as provided by law.

3. The jurisdictions of courts now authorized by law to hear and determine any of the matters herein referred to shall not be curtailed or affected by the passage of this act, but the county juvenile court shall have jurisdiction in such cases concurrent with such courts; *provided, however,* that any such cases pending in any other court, excepting the Court of Chancery or the Orphans' Court, may be transferred to the county juvenile court by the order of the judge of such court having first obtained jurisdiction, or said cause may be transferred to the county juvenile court upon the application of any party complainant or defendant, provided such application is approved by the judge of the county juvenile court, which approval shall be certified by a written order signed by the judge of such county juvenile court.

4. In all cases coming before the county juvenile court under or by virtue of the provisions of this act, said court shall be vested with all the powers, rights and privileges incident to the hearing, determination and final disposition of such cases, and the process to secure the appearance of parties and witnesses shall be, as nearly as may be, such process as is required to secure the presence thereof in the other courts of this State having jurisdiction of such matters, and process may be served in the same manner as provided for the service of process in other cases in which the juvenile court has jurisdiction.

5. No compensation shall be allowed to any public officer or official for any service performed under and by virtue of the provisions of this act, except as expressly provided for by law.

2. Juvenile court an integral part of family court, 1918

Charles W. Hoffman, "Courts of Domestic Relations," *Proceedings* of the National Conference of Social Work (1918), 125–126.

Hoffman, judge of the Court of Domestic Relations, Cincinnati, was chairman of the

National Probation Association committee on domestic courts which issued this report.

The family court is not intended to limit or restrict the jurisdiction incident to juvenile courts. In fact, the juvenile court will become an integral part, or division, of the family court. By reason of the organization of family courts, we believe that the administration of the juvenile court will become more effective and significant and better understood, not only by those connected with the juvenile court, but by the public generally. There is need for publicity on this point.

The juvenile courts were founded and organized not as criminal courts, but as child saving instituitons from which were to be excluded all semblances of criminal procedure and penal methods. In many localities the interest of social workers in these courts has decreased, because they have become no more than police courts where children are "tried." The idea of saving the child has been lost, and the instances are altogether too frequent when the judge in the spirit of semivindictiveness, such as the populace sometimes exercises, commits the child to a semi-penal institution as punishment. And, strange as it may appear, beating, lashes and whipping posts are sometimes covertly suggested, if not actually used.

There is a misapprehension in some jurisdictions as to the function of these courts . . . It is not a court in which the child should be tried for the commission of an offence; in fact, in a number of the states of the Union it is specifically enjoined upon the judge not to try a child for the commission of an offence, but to transfer the guardianship of the child from the parents to the court, as the representative of the state, and save the child for the benefit and welfare of the state. The misconception of the juvenile court that exists in some localities deserves investigation.

It is the duty of the juvenile court to save the child by whatever means it may have at its command. If the child be feebleminded, it should be sent to an institution for the feeble-minded to ascertain the extent of its feeble-mindedness and the chances of its being educated, so that it may be released without danger to the community. If the child cannot be educated or returned safely to society, it should be permanently segregated in order that it may not propagate its kind, or commit devastating offences. If the child comes into court by reason of social influences, such influences should be removed.

If a child, who is mentally normal, comes into court with a mind bent upon the commission of some offence, he should be sent to a special school, having for its purpose the education of such children. This is one of the great problems for the schoolmen to solve. There is a strong probability, amounting almost to certainty, that a normal child, having a tendency to commit anti-social offences, can be cured by means of proper education and treatment . . . Let the great departments of psychology and sociology of our colleges and universities devise a course of instruction and education that will reclaim a juvenile delinquent, who is mentally and physically sound. If they can accomplish this, thousands of boys and girls, who annually pass through the juvenile courts, will be redeemed.

These brief comments on the juvenile court are made in this report, because of the obvious connection of the juvenile court with the family courts. It is clear . . . that the principle of the juvenile court is the foundation upon which the family court must be constructed.

The boys' court

---

1. Special provisions for dealing with boys over juvenile-court age in the United States, 1930

Dorothy Williams Burke, *Youth and Crime: A Study of the Prevalence and Treatment of Delinquency among Boys over Juvenile-Court Age in Chicago,* United States Children's Bureau Pub. No. 196 (Washington, D.C., 1930), pp. 18–21.

It is a generally accepted principle that offenders under 16 years of age should be dealt with by courts as wards of the State rather than as criminals. All but two States (Maine and Wyoming) have juvenile-court laws providing such treatment for children under that age, with exceptions in some States in cases of serious crimes. For young persons above this age court treatment varies. The feeling is developing that treatment different from the usual criminal procedure should be extended to young people of the next age group. This tendency shows itself principally in two ways: First, the extension of juvenile-court jurisdiction to higher ages; and, second, the assignment of cases involving these young persons to other specialized courts.

The committee on juvenile-court standards appointed by the Children's Bureau recommended an age limit under which the court might obtain jurisdiction in children's cases not lower than 18 years. Nearly half the States meet or exceed this standard in regard to boys, with certain exceptions . . .

State laws in Massachusetts, Missouri, New Mexico, New York, and Pennsylvania have made some provision for specialized treatment of minors over juvenile-court age by courts other than juvenile courts. In Boston and Springfield, Mass., and in Buffalo, N.Y., certain cases of minors are heard in domestic-relations branches of municipal courts. In Pittsburgh, Pa., cases of persons between 16 and 21 years of age, whether they be complainants or defendants, are dealt with by the morals court. The juvenile court of Waterbury, Conn., which is an independent court presided over by judges of the city court and served by the same clerk and probation officers as that court, has juris-diction over children under 16 years of age. Cases of young defendants above that age in the city court are heard in the court room used for juvenile cases. The boys' court branch of the municipal court of Chicago has jurisdiction over all types of cases except indicted felonies involving boys between 17 and 21 years of age.

In 1923 the New York Legislature passed a law outlining procedure regarding girls between the ages of 16 and 21 who might be deemed "wayward minors." In 1925 boys of similar ages were included, and a fifth clause was added to the definition of wayward minors. The present law defines as a wayward minor any person —

. . . between the ages of 16 and 21 who either (1) is habitually addicted to the use of drugs or the intemperate use of intoxicating liquors, or (2) habitually associates with dissolute persons, or (3) is found of his or her own free will and knowledge in a house of prostitution or assignation or ill fame, or (4) habitually associates with thieves, prostitutes, pimps or procurers, or disorderly persons, or (5) is wilfully disobedient to the reasonable and lawful commands of parent, guardian, or other custodian and is morally depraved or is in danger of becoming morally depraved.

Such cases, involving offenses less than felonies or misdemeanors, are brought before the magistrates' courts. The law provides that a wayward minor "before commitment to an institution shall, so far as practicable, be placed upon probation for a period not to exceed two years," or if not a fit subject for probation shall be committed to a reformative institution for an indeterminate period not to exceed three years. In Buffalo cases of wayward minors are heard by the domestic-relations division of the city court. Elsewhere they are disposed of by the lower criminal courts.

The misdemeanants' division of the municipal court of Philadelphia, established in 1915, hears cases of incorrigible, runaway, and vagrant boys and girls between 16 and 21 years of age, of women street walkers regardless of age, and of men pandering in the streets. The Pennsylvania law relating to wayward minors, as amended in 1917, provides that the municipal court of Philadelphia shall have exclusive jurisdiction in "all proceedings concerning, or trials of charges brought against all minors between 16 and 21 years who shall disobey their parents' commands, or be found idle in the streets, and against all disorderly children," and defines as disorderly "all children not under the age of 16 years deserting their homes without good and sufficient cause, or keeping company with dissolute or vicious persons, against the lawful commands of their fathers, mothers, or guardians, or other person standing in the place of a parent."

Massachusetts courts have jurisdiction over "stubborn children" under 21 years of age, derived from an old law applying to rogues and vagabonds, stubborn children, runaways, "common drunkards," and a number of other classes of persons. Such persons may be punished by commitment to a State reformatory or farm or to a house of correction or workhouse, fined, or discharged on entering into a recognizance, with surety, for good behavior. The form of indictment for a stubborn child, as specified in the law, is as follows: "That A. B., a minor, during the three months next before the making of this complaint, was a stubborn child and stubbornly refused to submit to the lawful and reasonable commands of C. D., whose commands said A. B. was bound to obey." In the central district of Boston and in Springfield such cases are heard by domestic-relations courts. Elsewhere they are disposed of by the ordinary courts of inferior criminal jurisdiction.

In Missouri minors between 17 and 21 who commit acts that would constitute delinquency if committed by a minor under 17 (including serious offenses) may be tried for misdemeanor in any court of record, including the juvenile court. A New Mexico law of 1919 gives the district court exclusive jurisdiction over girls between 16 and 18 years of age accused of felonies less than murder or of misdemeanors, but in 1929 certain offenses specified in the 1919 law were in effect placed under the jurisdiction of the juvenile courts.

CHICAGO PLAN FOR DEALING WITH BOYS
OVER JUVENILE-COURT AGE

The Chicago juvenile court, which has jurisdiction over delinquent boys under the age of 17 years, was the pioneer juvenile court in the United States. Chicago has also been a pioneer in the development of specialized court treatment of boys from 17 to 20 years of age, inclusive. The municipal court act of 1905 centralized in one court, with various branches, inferior civil and criminal jurisdiction throughout the city. A boys' court branch was established by rule of court in 1914. Its creation is an example of what can be accomplished without special legislation in reform of judicial organization.

---

2. Juvenile and adolescent offenders, New York City, 1931

Harry M. Shulman, *The Youthful Offender: A Statistical Study of Crime among the 16–20 Year Age Group in New York City,* Report of the Subcommission on Causes and Effects of Crime, New York State Crime Commission (Albany: J. B. Lyon, 1931), pp. 150–152.

The sharp distinction in the criminal law between children over sixteen and those under sixteen is well illustrated in New York City, where the Children's Court is under equity proceedings. A child under sixteen, since 1925, may not be charged with a criminal act. In all breaches of the peace, save for a capital offense, he becomes the ward of the court, rather than its prisoner. He is not arraigned as a criminal, although his breach of peace would be classed as a criminal act had it been committed by an adult. The fact of his arraignment and of its disposition does not appear on the criminal records of the adult courts and of the police, nor is he fingerprinted or otherwise classified for purposes of criminal identification.

Not only is the juvenile court in New York City completely a civil court, but its procedures are radically different from those of the criminal courts. He may not be detained in a jail or detention prison used for adults but is detained in a special children's detention building, in character more like a school than a jail. His trial is informal, departing radically from the conventional criminal trial. His case is heard by a single judge, usually without counsel, either for the court or for defense, and there is no jury. The function of the judge is not primarily to direct the trial, and lead to a verdict of guilt or innocence, but to determine whether the child is in a condition of delinquency, apart from the specific complaint that led to his arraignment. To aid the judge in determining the condition of the child, an elaborate investigating personnel exists in the Probation Department, which is charged with examining the entire past background of the child, and of reporting in an outline social history the outstanding facts of that background. Further, for children who show some signs of deviation from the normal, the services of physicians, psychiatrists and of psychologists are sometimes provided, to assist the judge in determining treatment.

If supervision is decided upon, the probation department, aided by voluntary associations of case workers, supervises the child's subsequent behavior for a specific period of time. If a commitment is ordered, the child goes to a juvenile institution.

If, however, a child is above the age of sixteen, by as much as a single day, he is subject to all of the rigors of the adult courts; of police arrest, of jail detention, of arraignment before a trial judge in a formal courtroom filled with spectators, of contact with criminal lawyers and legal tactics, such as adjournments, changes in plea, and pleas to lesser offenses, and, in many instances, of sentence as a felon to a reformatory or state prison where he mingles with hardened adult criminals.

The tremendous cleavage of the civil law from the criminal law in the treatment of the adolescent has no discernible historical basis in the theories of criminal law or of criminology, save that criminal behavior, which was regarded as a matter of choice, could be imputed to a child who was old enough to understand, verbally at least, the code of his superiors. The gradual loss of influence of superstition and of medieval beliefs as to personal responsibility for every aspect of behavior seems to have led to a gradual amelioration of the lot of the child under the criminal law, without, however, a counterpart appearing in its theory. The growth of sociology and psychology have done a great deal to acquaint us with the limitations of childhood capacities, and with the nature of individual differences, as well as with the nature of environmental influences that affect and control conduct.

But neither of these sciences has been able as yet to tell the law-makers at what point adult responsibility begins. Nor is there any prospect that such an answer will be forthcoming in the near future from experimental sciences.

The paradox in this situation has been apparent to many for a long while. From a remedial point of view, in light of the abuses to which adolescents are subject, when in contact with the criminal law, a practical solution can probably be arrived at sooner than a scientific one. The tendency, therefore, has been to seek relief, not in an appeal to scientific inquiry, but in an appeal to law itself, to modify the harshness of the criminal law in its relation to adolescent offenders.

The federal government and juvenile offenders

1. A debate on the education of delinquent children, Washington, D.C., 1916

Congressional Record, 64 Cong., 1 Sess. (1916), LIII, Pt. 7, p. 6745.

In 1916 a bipartisan Congressional coalition attempted to amend the juvenile court law of the District of Columbia, with the aim of eliminating punitive trial and sentencing procedures and replacing them with provisions for educating delinquent children at the National Training School (the District's reform school). Southern Congressmen, opposing the benefits which this change would bring to the large Negro population of the District, fought this measure and postponed its passage until 1938.

Mr. Howard.[1] A good many gentlemen from some sections of the country are always ready and glad to criticize the section from which I come on the subject of crime, when if you will go to your court records here you will find that 75 per cent of the crimes of all kinds committed in the District of Columbia are committed by one-third of the population, although they are in an environment and they are aforded all the facilities to train this class of our citizens, to advance them in civilization, to teach them to become law-abiding citizens, to teach them to be better and more helpful citizens. In this District, where the Government of the United States with generous hand has dealt with them, we find that the cold records of the courts show that 75 per cent of all crimes, including felonies, are committed by a little less than one-third of the population of this city. Seventy-five per cent of the time of this juvenile court will be consumed in the trial of cases concerning one class of citizens in this District.

Mr. Madden.[2] How many classes of citizens have we in the United States?

Mr. Howard. Two.

Mr. Madden. I thought we had only one.

Mr. Howard. In what State?

Mr. Madden. In the United States.

Mr. Howard. Oh, I mean white and black,

if the gentleman wants to know. That is what I am talking about. I am comparing the negro and the white man. Why, take the great Federal prison in Atlanta. The number has been reduced now, thank God, but formerly we got a great number of them sent to that prison from the District of Columbia. At one time all of that class from the District of Columbia were dumped into that one prison. Now they divide them up, and Fort Leavenworth is getting some of them. The negroes of the District reduced the "good-conduct" records in these institutions 25 per cent. And I want to call your attention to the national training school out here on which we expend thousands of dollars annually, and to the girls' training school on which we are spending thousands of dollars annually. You go out there and see who is there.

Mr. Madden. Will the gentleman yield for a question?

Mr. Howard. In just a minute. I am not jealous of the expenditure of this money. If you can reform them, for God's sake double the sum, but you can not "make a silk purse out of a sow's ear."

Mr. Madden. I wanted to ask the gentleman whether he was opposed to the education of American citizens?

Mr. Howard. Not at all. I am very heartily in favor of it; but I am opposed to taxing my people in Georgia to give all sorts of hifaluting curleycues in the way of education to a crowd of Washington niggers that is of no benefit to them. That is what I am opposed to.

Mr. Tribble.[3] I should like to say to the gentleman from Georgia that since the war there has been no distinction made between white and black as to the public fund appropriated for the education of the citizens of the State of Georgia.

Mr. Howard. Of course not; but I am just bringing this matter home.

Mr. Madden. I was not raising any question about Georgia.

Mr. Howard. When it comes to exempting

1. William S. Howard (Dem. — Ga.).
2. Martin B. Madden (Rep. — Ill.).

3. Samuel J. Tribble (Dem. — Ga.).

a 17-year-old young nigger buck from prosecution for criminal assault in the District of Columbia I will sit here till the ants drag me out before I will vote for such a bill.

Mr. TOWNER.[4] Will the gentleman yield for a question?

Mr. HOWARD. Yes.

Mr. TOWNER. Is it not the policy of the gentleman's own State and of all the better elements of the South that the more you can educate and improve the condition of the black race the better it is for society in general?

Mr. HOWARD. And we are doing it, and 375,000 of them this very minute are in the public schools of Georgia, and 95 per cent of the taxes are borne by the white citizens of that State. [Applause.] I am getting tired ——

Mr. TOWNER. I am glad that that is true, and I want the gentleman to help here in the District of Columbia just as much as his own people are helping down in Georgia.

Mr. HOWARD. I am helping here. I get ashamed that I do help to the extent that the money is being wasted in the District of Columbia upon certain lines of education inaugurated by a crowd of fanatics. What you want here, as elsewhere, is to teach negroes and white folks, too, to learn to work their hands as well as their heads.

. . . . . .

Mr. TOWNER. Mr. Chairman, there is, as it seems to me, no point, no strength of argument in the remarks of the gentleman from Georgia unless it shall be this, that inherently the black man is incapable of improvement and education, and therefore what we do for him is money thrown away. Now, he does not mean that, because his own action, his own conduct, the action of the people of his own State has been directly contrary to that proposition. They understand that if the black man is educated he will make a better citizen than uneducated. They understand that if the black man is sober he will make a better citizen than if he is

4. Horace M. Towner (Rep. — Iowa).

drunken. They understand that everything that is done to improve the intelligence, elevate the character, Christianize the colored man is just as much an improvement to him as it is to the white man.

If money is wasted in the District of Columbia for any purpose, we ought to see to it that no waste occurs. It is not a legitimate argument to make that because we do expend money for the education and improvement of the colored man in the District of Columbia that that money is thrown away unless you take this absolutely indefensible position that to improve the colored man is not to improve his condition or make him a better member of society.

---

2. Juvenile offenders against federal laws, 1922

Ruth Bloodgood, *The Federal Courts and the Delinquent Child,* United States Children's Bureau Pub. No. 103 (Washington, D.C., 1922), pp. 1–3, 64–68.

A phase of the problem of juvenile delinquency not heretofore given special consideration is that of the children who violate Federal laws and are taken before United States district courts. Attention has centered on the number of children coming before State courts and on the progress these courts have made in affording special treatment of children's cases. That there are considerable numbers of juveniles arrested and tried on Federal charges is shown in the reports of the Attorney General for the last two years, which give a total of 1,038 persons under 20 years of age committed to institutions for violations of Federal laws by United States district courts; figures are not available for the total number under 20 years of age before these courts.

The attention of the United States Children's

Bureau had been called to the problem of children violating Federal laws by several persons in different parts of the country. In one instance a member of a grand jury to which several children's cases had been presented felt very keenly that young children should not be subjected to the formal procedure and limited facilities for treatment in the Federal courts. It seemed particularly appropriate that the Children's Bureau, a Federal agency concerned in raising the standards of child protection and child care, should interest itself in the methods employed by the Federal Government in dealing with children violating the laws of the United States. For these reasons an inquiry was undertaken covering, so far as the information was available, the numbers of children violating Federal laws in 1918 and 1919, their ages, the types of offenses committed, the methods of procedure, the dispositions made, and to a limited extent the home conditions and social histories of the children.

The Department of Justice and the Post Office Department were most helpful in making available the data upon which the inquiry is based.

Records of the chief inspector of the Post Office Department relating to offenders against postal laws were the first sources of information. Data were obtained on all such offenders under 18 years of age arrested throughout the United States during the calendar years 1918 and 1919.

As the National Training School for Boys in the District of Columbia is the institution to which the largest number of boys under 18 years of age are committed for all types of Federal offenses, the records of this institution were consulted, information being obtained in regard to all children sent to this institution for offenses against Federal laws committed during the years selected. Besides this Federal institution, two State institutions were included in the study — the New York State Reformatory at Elmira and the Iowa State Reformatory at Anamosa. These institutions, located in different parts of the country, are among those with

which the Government contracts to receive Federal commitments.

The information from the National Training School for Boys and the Post Office Department furnished the basis for selection of the eight United States courts chosen for special study, namely, the Supreme Court of the District of Columbia and seven United States district courts (Illinois, northern district; Indiana; Maryland; Massachusetts; New York, eastern and southern districts; and Pennsylvania, eastern district). Juvenile and other State courts in these districts were visited for the purpose of obtaining information with regard to any Federal cases which were referred to them.

·   ·   ·   ·   ·

This study has shown that throughout the United States during a two-year period 1,145 children under 18 years of age were arrested for violation of postal laws. From the eight districts and the three institutions visited, 211 children were reported arrested during the same period for other Federal offenses — a number which undoubtedly represents only a small proportion of the total arrests for such offenses in the United States. During the two-year period, the yearly average number of children included in the two groups was 678; if complete data were available for the entire country the total yearly average under 18 years of age would without doubt be found to be nearly 1,000 and might exceed that figure. Of these, it appears that the majority are under the age of 16 years and that some are under 10 years of age.

·   ·   ·   ·   ·

Of the 1,356 cases included in this study, 121 were reported only by the National Training School for Boys or by the New York and Iowa State reformatories, and all these were tried by United States district courts or by courts in the District of Columbia. Of the remaining 1,235 cases, 758, or 61.3 per cent, were tried by United States district courts; 375, or 30.4 per cent, were taken before juvenile and other State courts; 8 cases were tried first by United States district courts and were then transferred to juvenile courts; court action was not reported in 15 cases; and in 79 cases no court action was taken.

The fundamental concept of the juvenile-court movement is that children should not be held criminally responsible for their misconduct, but that they should be afforded protection, care, and training, within or outside an institution and should be safeguarded from contact with adult offenders. This principle has not been applied in the Federal courts, in which the chancery procedure has not been substituted for the criminal in children's cases, nor the criminal procedure modified. Thus, the proceedings are formal and frequently include several preliminary hearings followed by grand-jury action and public trial, while long delays are often occasioned by crowded calendars, absence of continuous session, and the distance of the court from the child's place of residence. Further difficulties are found in lack of facilities for discovering what kind of child is being dealt with, his past experience and his possibilities of development, and in the inability of the court to suspend sentence, place on probation, and supervise the child in the community. During the long periods frequently occurring between the apprehension of the children and the disposition of their cases, the children must often be kept in detention — and jail detention is the form most frequently used by Federal courts. Holding children of tender years in jail, where they are terrified by the experience and subjected to contact with adult criminals, leaves an impression not conducive to normal development or good citizenship, that is difficult if not impossible to eradicate.

Moreover, the Federal courts are at present limited with reference to the institutions to which they may commit children. The national training schools for boys and girls, in the District of Columbia, are the only Federal institutions especially adapted to the care of delinquent children. Federal authorities in distant States are frequently reluctant to send children so far away from home, such a disposition often inflicting great suffering on both parents and child. On the other hand, the institutions nearer home with which the United States Government has made arrangements for the care of Federal offenders are frequently institutions designed primarily for adult offenders and are conducted as prisons with cell blocks and prison discipline. The younger children committed to these institutions are subjected to a program not adapted to their training and are in contact with older offenders. The officials sometimes make an effort to modify the régime in favor of a young child — keeping him in the office of the institution during the day, for instance — but such practices can be only sporadic and of doubtful success.

An essential feature of the juvenile-court system is that a finding of delinquency does not constitute a conviction of crime, and that juvenile records, therefore, do not stand as criminal records. In the Federal courts the children found to have committed the offenses with which they are charged thereby stand convicted of crime, and suffer throughout life from the disqualifications consequent upon a criminal record.

Many judges, commissioners, attorneys, and post-office inspectors were found who recognized that the usual procedure was not adapted to the handling of children's cases; and, moreover, the statement was sometimes made that grand juries were very unwilling to return indictments in these cases. Under a more or less rigid legal system, when there exist in any particular case unusual circumstances, such as the extreme youth of the offender, one of three courses may be followed: (1) The imposition of the penalty fixed by law, sometimes in spite of doubt in the minds of the authorities as to whether such disposition is in accord with real justice; (2) the dismissing or nol-prossing of the case or refusal to indict, the authorities taking no steps to correct the offender or to safeguard society; and (3) the use of various expedients not specifically provided by law, which it is hoped will more nearly achieve justice, the correction and training of the offender, and the protection of the community. Many instances of the adoption of such expedients have been cited in this report. They range from immediate reference of the case to juvenile courts by post-office inspectors and United States attorneys to the use of informal probation by the Federal authorities themselves, prior to the hearing or pending continuance on condition of good behavior. They also include short-term jail sentences and such nominal sentences as small fines and sentences to one day in the custody of the United States marshal. Except the reference to juvenile courts, none of these methods of handling children's cases is satisfactory, because the authorities have no facilities for ascertaining the necessary facts about the child and his environment, nor the means for the intensive supervision and reconstructive work essential to treatment of delinquents in the community.

Following is a comparison of the usual procedure in a well-organized juvenile court and in a United States district court, leaving out of consideration expedients sometimes used by Federal authorities:

Juvenile-Court Procedure	United States District-Court Procedure
1. Initiation of case.	
Complaint and summons, except in cases of summary arrest.	Arrest upon warrant, or summary arrest. (In some cases arrest follows instead of preceding indictment.)
2. Period between initiation and court action.	
Prompt court action (within a few days or a week).	Frequently weeks or months elapse before final court action.
3. Care pending court action.	
Release to parents on personal recognizance, or detention in detention home for children.	Release on bond or detention in jail.
4. Preliminary investigation	

Thorough investigation including:
    Physical examination.
    Mental examination.
    Personal history (schooling, recreation, habits, companions, etc.).
    Home conditions.
    Family history.
	Investigation confined mainly to ascertaining whether or not child committed the offense.

5. Court action.	
Hearing — private, informal, without jury.	Preliminary hearing before commissioner. Presentment to grand jury, or direct to court on information filed. Trial — public, formal, often with jury.

6. *Disposition of case.*

Dismissed or filed, if child not in need of protection or discipline, *or*	Dismissed, or nol-prossed, *or*
Probation, *or*	Fine, *or*
Placement in care of child-placing agency, *or*	Jail sentence, *or*
Commitment to special institution for care of juvenile delinquents.	Commitment to National Training School (District of Columbia), *or*
	Sentence to reformatory or penitentiary (State or private institutions for delinquent children are available to a few United States courts).

7. *Follow-up care.*

For children on probation by trained probation staff.	No provision.

8. *Effect of adjudication.*

Juvenile-court record does not constitute a criminal record.	Conviction of crime.

---

3. Juvenile offenders against federal
laws, 1931

Miriam Van Waters, "Problems Presented to the Federal System of Justice by the Child Offender" in National Commission on Law Observance and Enforcement, *Report* (Washington, D. C., 1931), pp. 21–23.

In 1922 Miriam Van Waters surveyed girls' reform schools for Chicago philanthropist Ethel S. Dummer and, from 1927 to 1929, studied juvenile courts in Massachusetts for the Boston Crime Survey (conducted by the Harvard Law School). In 1929 Dr. Van Waters was appointed consultant to the National Commission on Law Observance and Enforcement (The Wickersham Commission).

The child offender under the judicial code of the United States is on the same footing as the adult. The Federal penal code makes no definition of juvenile delinquency. To the substantive law which concerns itself with the statement of legal rights and duties the age of an offender presents no problem.

It is on the administrative side of the law that problems due to age arise. Administrative law states the means by which governmental agencies enforce the laws, and has to do with the performance of such tasks as detection, arrest, prosecution, and detention of offenders, the organization and procedure of courts, and the management of penal institutions. The Department of Justice is the central administrative agency affected by problems presented by child offenders; the Bureau of Investigation and the Bureau of Prisons are the principal divisions concerned.

Many of the problems of dealing with youthful offenders are found in adult cases also. Modifications of court procedure and penal administration occur by sheer pressure of necessity when the accused is under handicap, as for example, dangerously ill, or ill of a contagious disease, insane, imbecile, or deaf and dumb, etc. Women may present separate problems; so do the extremely aged. The child's problems, however, fall into unique classification, apparent to "common sense," but not readily capable of definition. Recognition of child's claim to some distinctive method of handling is found throughout the Federal administrative process; police, marshals, commissioners, district attorneys, judges, jailers, wardens, and superintendents of penal institutions, express awareness of it in various ways, which may be summarized in the question, "what shall we do with these children?"

The age distribution to which the administrative process makes some kind of concession includes the total period of minority. Practical problems range from the care of infants born to mothers serving sentence in correctional institutions to the requirement of youths under 21 who can not submit to necessary surgical operations until a guardian is appointed to give consent. Some children below 7 years of age are detained in jail awaiting the outcome of cases of their parents charged with violations of the immigration laws. Theoretically there is no age limit below which a child may not be prosecuted under Federal statutes; in practice it is evident very young children are otherwise disposed of. Census of the present population made by our field workers of Federal offenders in correctional institutions shows no child committed under 9 years of age. Children under 7, however, have been brought before United States commissioners.

Geographical distribution of Federal cases adds to their difficulty. The major factors in the decision as to place of commitment are the types of institutions available and the extent to which they are already overcrowded. A secondary consideration may be the distance between the place of trial and the receiving institution. Cases of violations of the national motor vehicle theft act and the white slave traffic act are by definition interstate matters; the offenders are in transit and the place of trial is distant from the legal residence. A survey of population in correctional institutions shows minors from Alaska, China, the Hawaiian Islands, Philippines, and Porto Rico serving sentences in various parts of the United States. Children from the Atlantic seaboard are found in the institutions of the Northwest and Pacific coast; children from the Pacific seaboard and the South may be sent to institutions in Washington, D. C. Among the problems presented by the extensive geographical range are adjustment to radical climatic changes, different customs of living, and the severing of family and community relationships.

When we deal with children we encounter human needs centered in homes, schools, churches, and neighborhoods. The assumption at the root of the application of modern science to the treatment of the child is that normal social development is conditioned by family relationships; when these are broken the child is dependent upon near-by substitutes, foster-homes, or local institutions maintained by schools, churches, social agencies, etc. It may be inferred that the farther we travel from these community structures the greater is the child's handicap.

The institutional problems presented by juvenile offenders are distinct from those of adults. Diet should be adapted to various growth periods. Health supervision is more urgent since childhood and adolescence show an increased liability to certain infectious and contagious diseases. Periods of rest and physical exercise are required at intervals that vary with age. The amount of sleep needed to maintain health varies with childhood, puberty, adolescence, and maturity. The entire physical regimen should be more flexible in the interests of normal development. These requirements are met with difficulty in institutions especially designed for children; they are not met at all where individuals of all ages are subjected to the same program.

Problems in providing education for minors, habit training, recreation, character development, discipline, vocational training, religious education, have been assumed by the penal administration of the Federal Government. The question arises whether its facilities can or should be further developed to treat juvenile offenders adequately, or in certain instances can some of these tasks be intrusted to the States.

III Modern Theories and Studies of Juvenile Delinquency

A. DELINQUENCY AS PHYSICAL AND MENTAL DISEASE

Defective delinquents

1. The inheritance of delinquency

Richard Louis Dugdale, *The Jukes: A Study in Crime, Pauperism, Disease and Heredity* [*and*] *Further Studies of Criminals* (New York, 1877), pp. 9–10, 98–100.

Richard Louis Dugdale (1841–1883) emigrated to the United States when he was ten years old. He attended Cooper Institute in New York City and in the late 1860's became active in the Prison Association of New York. *The Jukes,* orginally published in 1875, was based on his investigation, sponsored by the Prison Association, of the family backgrounds of inmates of county jails.

In July, 1874, having been appointed a committee to visit thirteen of the jails of this State and report thereupon, I made a tour of inspection in pursuance of that appointment. No specially striking cases of criminal careers, traceable through several generations, presented themselves till ——— county was reached. Here, however, were found six persons, under four family names, who turned out to be blood relations in some degree. The oldest, a man of fifty-five, was waiting trial for receiving stolen goods; his daughter, aged eighteen, held as witness against him; her uncle, aged forty-two, burglary in the first degree; the illegitimate daughter of the latter's wife, aged twelve years, upon which child the latter had attempted rape, to be sent to the reformatory for vagrancy; and two brothers, aged respectively nineteen and fourteen, accused of an assault with intent to kill, they having pushed a child over a high cliff and nearly killed him. Upon trial the oldest was acquitted though the goods stolen were found in his house, his previous good character saving him; the guilt belonged to his brother-in-law, the man aged forty-two, above mentioned, who was living in the house. This brother-in-law is an illegitimate child, an habitual criminal and the son of an unpunished and cautious thief. He had two brothers and one sister, all of whom are thieves, the sister being the contriver of crime, they its executers. The daughter of this woman, the girl aged eighteen above mentioned, testified at the trial which resulted in convicting her uncle and procuring his sentence for twenty years to State prison, that she was forced to join him in his last foray; that he loaded her with the booty, and beat her on the journey home, over two miles, because she lagged under the load. When this girl was released, her family in jail and thus left without a home, she was forced to make her lodging

555

in a brothel on the outskirts of the city. Next morning she applied to the judge to be recommitted to prison "for protection," stating she had been obliged to submit to nine men the night previous. She has since been sent to the house of refuge. Of the two boys, one was discharged by the Grand Jury; the other was tried and received five years' imprisonment in Sing Sing.

These six persons belonged to a long lineage, reaching back to some of the early colonists, who had intermarried so slightly with the emigrant population of the old world that they may be called a strictly American family. They had lived in the same locality for generations, and were so despised by the reputable community that their family name *had come to be used generically as a term of reproach.*

.   .   .   .   .

[Two case histories]

T. H——n, aged 21½; robbery, 4 years. He is an illegitimate child, his mother probably a prostitute, intemperate, and negligent of her children, of whom she has had four living. Knows nothing of his father. He has had two brothers, one of them was sent to the house of refuge in 1863, and subsequently to Sing Sing for ten years, but died before the expiration of his sentence. Timothy's temperament is nervous bilious, active and excitable, vitality average, health good, head undersized, narrow and low, eyes light hazel and bloodshot. He is shrewd, ignorant, has a weak moral sense about some things, partly from education received in reformatory, but no moral balance, and is plucky and vain. His case is an illustration of the bad effects of prolonged institution life. At 7 years stole from his mother, at 8 ran away from home and "knocked about," at 10 was sent to house of refuge for vagrancy, was a bad boy when in refuge, very mischievous and insubordinate, stayed 6 years and 4 months and was discharged. At 17 again in house of refuge, where he remained 1 year and 8 months. He then became one of the ringlead-

ers in a plot to escape from the refuge, and it was he who forged pikes and knife blades which were to be used to carry the gates by storm. In consequence of the plot being discovered, he was, at 19, sent to the Rochester work-house for one year; at 20 committed to Buffalo work-house six months for petit laceny, and, at the expiration of that time, was sent to Auburn, for robbery and assault, four years. In the last eleven years and a-half he has received ten years and a-half of imprisonment, has committed fifteen offenses and been arrested four times. It will now be very difficult to reform him, but not impossible, and even the want of self-reliance, which institution life has now made constitutional, could be turned to advantage. What he needs is to be taken charge of by some person for whom he has formed a strong personal attachment — something analogous to that of a dog for his master — a man who knows how to judiciously enlist his vanity in a line of conduct which will gradually, and by successive degrees, organize steadiness of character and self-reliance. For occupation he should be employed where there is some adventure, physical activity not too continuous, and the opportunity for display of pluck such as would be needed on the water, but he would not make a sailor.

.   .   .   .   .

Chas. P——n, aged 21; petit larceny from person; second offense; one year. His father was murdered when this boy was only one month old. His mother, 38 years of age, has been three times married, is intemperate, a pauper, a criminal and a harlot, keeping a brothel, in which may be found her daughters and stepdaughters, some of whom have been driven out of various towns for their vileness. His head is average size, well proportioned, with a wide base. He is of a hopeful disposition, vain and quarrelsome. He claims to be temperate. At 14, committed to Lockport jail ten days for assault and battery; at 15, burglary and larceny; Rochester house of refuge one year; at 21, petit larceny; Buffalo work-house three months, and, on conviction of petit larceny, second offense, to Auburn State prison one year. When in the refuge he is reported as behaving well. In this case we have a convict with strong pauper alliances in several branches of the family, and although there is no long lineage of habitual crime, it does begin in the previous generation in the person of his mother, while the environments, both at home and at work on the canal, have been destructive. The difficulties to be met with in dealing with the mingled complications of neglect, bad inheritance and worse associations, would be very great if an effort were made to reform this boy, and yet he is by no means a hopeless case, for he possesses average intelligence and sufficient vanity to make him tractable under a judicious adviser. The greatest difficulty would be to get him to work steadily at any thing. The order of management requires a correction of hereditary tendencies, to be induced mainly by industrial training, and, on liberation, to be settled away from his family with some employer who will have the tact and will to hold him steady. For this case, however, with iron uniformity, the State has provided the lockstep, and the ephemeral imprisonment which, last November, turned him loose to return to the brothel home which has already done so much to bring him to the cell. As a set-off, however, the prison doors are ever ready to swallow him again.

---

2. Institutions for treating "moral insanity," 1879

Josephine Shaw Lowell, "One Means of Preventing Pauperism," in William Rhinelander Stewart, *The Philanthropic Work of Josephine Shaw Lowell* (New York, 1911), pp. 96–100.

On Mrs. Lowell see above Part Three, Chap. II, sec A, Philanthropic Experiments, 1893–1910, doc. 2. This paper was prepared as the result of her investigation of the antecedents of inmates in the county poorhouses of New York State. Mrs. Lowell was particularly concerned about "Women who from early girlhood have been tossed from poorhouse to jail and from jail to poorhouse . . ." As the result of her suggestion, the Newark Asylum at Newark, New York, was incorporated in 1885 as a separate institution for the reception of feebleminded women of childbearing age.

These women and their children, and hundreds more like them, costing the hardworking inhabitants of the State annually thousands of dollars for their maintenance, corrupting those who are thrown into companionship with them, and sowing disease and death among the people, are the direct outcome of our system. The community itself is responsible for the existence of such miserable, wrecked specimens of humanity. These mothers who began life as their own children have begun it, inheriting strong passions and weak wills, born and bred in a poorhouse, taught to be wicked before they could speak plainly, all the strong evil in the nature strengthened by their surroundings and the weak good crushed and trampled out of life, hunted and hounded, perhaps committed to jail while their tender youth had yet some germs of virtue remaining, dragged through the mire, exposed to the wickedness of wicked men and women whose pleasure it is to sully and drag down whatever is more innocent than themselves, in the power of brutal officials, — what hope could there be for them? And how shall we cast a stone at them, whom we ourselves have, by the strong arm of the law, thrust into the direst temptation? To begin at the beginning, what right had we to permit them to be born of parents who were depraved in body and mind? What right have we today to allow men and women who are diseased and vicious to reproduce their kind, and bring into the world beings whose existence must be one long misery to themselves and others? We do not hesitate to cut off, where it is possible, the entail of insanity by incarcerating for life the incurably insane; why should we not also prevent the transmission of moral insanity, as fatal as that of the mind?

These men and women are now constantly maintained by the public, sometimes for years at a time in the same institution, sometimes continually changing from one to another, but never failing to demand support from their fellows. Why, then, should they not be maintained in institutions fitted to save them from their own weaknesses and vices, where in due time they may be formed anew in body and mind, and be ready to enter the ranks of the free and intelligent men and women? . . .

In the present paper, I speak chiefly of women, because they form the visible links in the direful chain of hereditary pauperism and disease, but it must not be forgotten that the treatment here prescribed for them should also be applied to the reformation of the men whose evil propensities may be likewise handed down from one generation to another.

.   .   .   .   .

The presence of these women in the poorhouses, penitentiaries and jails, under the circumstances, renders it certain that they have less than the average self-control. They have entered on the downward course. In neither jail, poorhouse nor penitentiary, will they find anything to help them turn back; on the contrary, all the surroundings will force them lower, and this would be the case, were they much more able to resist than they are. In the jail and penitentiary every door to virtue is closed, and every avenue to vice and crime is open. In the poorhouse they find others like themselves, and although the degrading influences may not be so strong as in jails and penitentiaries, they are there, and strong enough to prevent any chance of rescue. Having an inherited and deep-seated repugnance to labor, these women, both in the poorhouse and jail, are supported in absolute idleness, without even the bodily exercise which is necessary for health. They are shut up in poisonous air, suffering a physical degeneration only to be compared with the ruin wrought at the same time in their minds and souls.

To rescue these unfortunate beings and to save the industrious part of the community from the burden of their support, reformatories should be established to which all women under thirty, when arrested for misdemeanors, or upon the birth of a second illegitimate child, should be committed for very long periods, not as a punishment, but for the same reason that the insane are sent to an asylum, and where they should be subject to such physical, moral and intellectual training as would re-create them. Such training would be no child's play; since the very character of the women must be changed, and every good and healthy influence would be rendered useless without the one element of time. It is education in every sense which they need, and education is a long process, tedious and wearing, requiring unfaltering hope and unfailing patience on the part of teacher and pupil. Consequently these reformatories must not be prisons which would crush out the life from those unfortunate enough to be cast into them; they must be homes, — homes where a tender care shall surround the weak and fallen creatures who are placed under their shelter, where a homelike feeling may be engendered, and where, if necessary, they may spend years. The unhappy beings we are speaking of need, first of all, to be taught to be women; they must be induced to love that which is good and pure, and to wish to resemble it; they must learn all household duties; they must learn to enjoy work; they must have a future to look forward to; and they must be cured, both body and soul, before they can be safely trusted to face the world again.

---

3. A plea for the "indeterminate sequestration" of defective delinquents, 1890

Isaac N. Kerlin, "The Moral Imbecile," *Proceedings* of the National Conference of Charities and Correction (1890), 244–245, 248–249.

Isaac Newton Kerlin (1834–1893), pioneer psychiatrist, became superintendent of the Pennsylvania Training School for Feebleminded Children at Elwyn in 1864 following a year's service with the United States Sanitary Commission. In 1883 he introduced the cottage plan in order to separate teachable from unteachable children. His belief that children who disrupted the routine of the institution needed separate and special care laid the basis for the concept of the defective delinquent.

An experience of thirty years in the care and training of feebleminded children has brought to my observation a group of cases quite distinct in their symptoms of derangement, and requiring forms of discipline quite unusual as compared with those applicable to the children ordinarily recognized as idiotic. Two of these, studied twenty-five years ago, have been followed by experiences with others, so that now in a population of 740 inmates we differentiate 16 as belonging to this special group and 90 others who merge into it.

Besides these who have been under daily study and discipline, many more have been brought to our knowledge through correspondence, — a correspondence revealing the agony and unrest of as many homes, caused by the baneful and incomprehensible misconduct of certain children in whose interest the most pathetic appeals have been made.

The symptoms marking the diseased lives of these scores of children have been confined either mainly or entirely to aberration of the "moral sense," with either no deterioration of the intellect or, if slight, such as could be considered secondary only. These phenomenal disorders have dated from temper explosions, night terrors, and most remarkable obstacles observed in infancy and early childhood, or may have originated in a marked and well-remembered febrile attack, associated with some infantile disease and accompanied perhaps with convulsions, or, more rarely, may have followed a markedly nervous and precocious youthhood too suddenly reaching a serious climax at puberty. The fundamental disorder is manifested in derangement of the moral perceptions or emotional nature rather than in the intellectual life, which not infrequently is precocious. Unaccountable and unreasonable frenzies, long periods of sulks, and comfort in sulking; motiveless and persistent lying; thieving, generally without acquisitiveness; a blind and headlong impulse toward arson; delight in cruelty, first toward domestic pets, and later toward helpless or young companions; self-inflicted violence, even to pain and the drawing of blood; occasionally, delight in the sight of blood; habitual willfulness and defiance, even in the face of certain punishment; a singular tolerance to surgical pain and hebetude or insensibility under disciplinary inflictions, — these are some of the forms in which the congenital deficiency of the moral sense evidences itself. It is hard to answer, "What is there in all this to distinguish from simple wickedness or badness?" unless the answer is contained in the persistency of the trait and the utter destitution of any reason for it, as is indicated in the confessed helplessness of the child to do differently. As a further aid to the diagnosis, we may refer to the fact that in one class of these cases the conduct is the reverse of what might be expected from the environment in which the child has developed; or, on the other hand, the ancestral and prenatal history of the child is such as to project a strong light for the interpretation of this condition as that of a neurotic inheritance.

Of the several children observed at Elwyn, quite frequently they are of faulty stock, presenting the gravest statistics of inebriety, epilepsy, acknowledged insanity, and in some instances even crime.

During the thirty years' contemplation of the subject, a marked change in professional opinion has been noted, so that it is no longer hazardous to reputation to believe in the existence of a condition termed "moral insanity" nor to refer to it as of commonly congenital origin, and hence better denominated "moral imbecility."

.   .   .   .   .

Ladies and gentlemen, if we could come to the conclusion that we have a class of little children whose heredity and aberrations are such as to make them the predestined inmates of our insane hospitals and jails, what an advance we would make in the diminution of crime and lunacy by a methodized registration and training of such children, or, these failing, by their early and entire withdrawal from the community!

Instead of so much interest being centered about the seventy-five per cent who are discharged annually from your refuges, alleged to be reformed and fit for society, a no less interest would be displayed in the black residuum of twenty-five per cent who are also discharged, to be as yet unaccounted for in the statistics of reformatory work, but, pariah-like, to add a contribution of evil to society which will shadow, if not eclipse, the accredited value of our whole reformatory work.

Cannot an almost unerring decision be made by the trained and humane experts of our asylums, jails, and reformatories, by which the indeterminate sequestration, under the best conditions for their moral and physical welfare, shall be the practice of those who are congenitally unfit to mingle their lives and blood with the general community?

4. Defective delinquents in Kansas, 1897

F. W. Blackmar, "The Smoky Pilgrims," *American Journal of Sociology*, II (June, 1897), 490–495, 499–500.

Frank Wilson Blackmar (1854–1931) re-

ceived his Ph.D. from Johns Hopkins in 1889 and taught economics, history, and sociology at the University of Kansas from 1889 until his retirement. He was dean of the graduate school from 1896 to 1922.

In a sparsely settled portion of L———, Kansas, dwells, or stays, a family for more than twenty years well known to the benevolent people of the town. The house is made of loose boards and scraps of tin and sheet iron rudely patched together. In summer it is a hot and uncomfortable shed, in winter a cold and dreary hut. The main room or living room, 14 x 16, contains a meager supply of scanty furniture and soiled and even filthy bedding. A small shed or "lean-to" attached to this room serves as kitchen, storeroom and chicken house. One small window allows the light to show the scanty furniture of the room and to exhibit its untidy appearance. The walls of the room are decorated with cheap pictures and bits of bright-colored papers. Among the larger pictures is that of Abraham Lincoln, which makes one pause for reflection, as his benign countenance beams upon the observer in these unpleasant surroundings. This small house is, or rather was until the number was increased as stated below, the home of seven individuals. For the use of the land on which the house stands they pay a nominal rental of twenty-five cents per month.

Another habitation used by a branch of the family is situated on P——— street. It is a board house of a single room 12 x 14, which is the home of three persons. This single room serves as living room, sleeping and cooking room, and for the entertainment of guests. The same scanty and cheap furniture is here as in the other habitation, and squalor and filth abound. The evidences of poverty and wretchedness characterize the surroundings. The rental paid for this habitation is $1.25 per month. It protects from the heat of summer and the cold of winter somewhat better than does habitation No. 1, but otherwise it has much the same appearance in the interior. The difference in rent is an economic problem not completely solved. There is no drainage connection with either habitation, and no water supply. But of water the occupants apparently have little need. Between these two homes the various members of the two families pass daily to and fro.

To the family, now numbering but ten persons, living in these two habitations the name "Smoky Pilgrims" has been given; chiefly on account of their dusky color and their smoky and begrimed appearance. Possibly the sickly yellow color, on account of the negro blood in the veins of part of the family, may have suggested the name. By this name they are known to the people of the town. They represent a family or tribal group with loose habits of family association. They are known as people seeking odd jobs of work, with an air of fear lest possibly they may find them; as petty thieves, beggars, in part as prostitutes, and in general as shiftless, helpless, and beyond hope of reform.

. . . . . .

The mother of the tribe, whom we will call "T—," has industrious habits and still retains industrious notions. She still has an idea of giving something in return for what she receives. Since coming to L——— she has worked at odd jobs, principally washing, housekeeping, and cleaning. At one time she was called to care for a sick woman who subsequently died. After the death "T—" took charge of the home and cared for the husband of the deceased and subsequently married him. He was shiftless and improvident, and finally died and was buried at the expense of the county. At another time "T—" found a home for a time at the county poor farm, but preferring her present mode of existence she left the home prepared for the needy. At present she is just recovering from protracted sickness, and is too weak for any work. It is pitiable to think of a person confined to a bed of sickness for months in such a rude hovel, but it is the life she prefers rather than the one which a

county provides for her. Were the other members of the tribe as much inclined to industry as this one, there might be some hope of bringing them back into the ranks of industrial society. "T—" deplores her present condition and considers her life a chain of misfortunes.

. . . . . .

The eldest daughter, "A—," is between thirty-six and forty years of age . . . she shows marked weakness of character, with low order of physical structure, decidedly weak mentality, and lack of energy of any kind. She constitutes an organization of low order due rather to habits of life and social environment than to natal characteristics. Her face is ugly and repulsive, and her whole demeanor shows under-vitalization and degeneration on account of her mode of life. Some years ago she married a colored man named "B—," who subsequently died. She has four children, one white and three colored, each one having a different father. The oldest was born a long time before her marriage. The woman works a little, does considerable foraging and tramps the street much of the time, but is considered a harmless creature so far as social order is concerned. With her, as with all of the remainder, sexual relations are irregular.

"N—," the oldest son of "A—," is about eighteen years of age, and has a fair degree of physical strength. He is not much at home but remains most of the time in the portion of the town known as "the bad lands." Several times he has been apprehended for stealing. More recently he has done a little work. He has intellect enough and sufficient physical endurance to become a criminal if his mode of life is not changed. "N—" is supposed to be always "finding work."

"S—," the second child, is also a colored boy, about fourteen years of age. He is inclined to stupidity, but shows extreme good nature and is perfectly contented with a happy-go-lucky life. When questioned he shows a disposition to do something if he had a chance. But with a real test he is inclined to succumb to the influences of his home life. He has attended school but little and is now out "doin' nothin'," as he says. His schooling has been so irregular as to be of little service to him. Begging and idling in the streets is his occupation most of the time. His cousin goes with him to act as spokesman for the twain. They indulge in light pilfering and foraging, and have been before the police court for stealing.

.   .   .   .   .   .

It will appear evident that no reform of any permanent character can obtain in this tribe without a change in their present mode of habitation. The home must be improved or entirely broken up. It is impossible to reorganize a group of this kind so long as they live in dirty hovels and lead a semi-gypsy life. The adults should be sent to the county poor farm and there be forced to earn a living. Unfortunately this is not easy, on account of the loose methods of administration of county almshouses, and from lack of compulsory acts to force unwilling inmates to remain. The older children should be sent to the reform school. This statement is met with two difficulties. The first, that a person can be committed to the Kansas reform school only upon sentence by the judge of a competent court on some specific charge. This is a difficult thing to obtain. Secondly, at present the reform school of Kansas is overcrowded, and if a person were committed he would be obliged to remain in a county jail until there was room for him. This would be worse than the present mode of existence, for our county jails are at present the most prolific breeders of crime in the land.

It is seen at once that families of this class, although not considered particularly dangerous to a community, are the most difficult to deal with, because they have no place in the social life, and it is very difficult to make a place for them. Their influence can be bad in a general way only. However, with the concerted action of citizens much could be done to relieve the situation. In fact, since this investigation began there are some marks of improvement in

the children of this group. They have attended school more regularly and seem inclined to be free from thieving. But let it be repeated, better home influences, which means a breaking up of the family group, steady enforced employment until the habits of life are changed and become fixed, are indispensable means of permanent improvement. The difficulty of the task appears when we consider that these people must be taught not only to earn money but to spend it properly; they must be taught to change their ideals of life as well as their practices. The arts of civilization must begin from the foundation. The warp and the woof of the whole fabric must be constructed. Their desires for a better life are not sufficiently persistent to make a foundation for individual and social reform. How difficult the task to create new desires in the minds of people of this nature! Considered in themselves, from the standpoint of individual improvement, they seem scarcely worth saving. But from social considerations it is necessary to save such people, that society may be perpetuated. The principle of social evolution is to make the strong stronger that the purposes of social life may be conserved, but to do this the weak must be cared for or they will eventually destroy or counteract the efforts of the strong. We need social sanitation, which is the ultimate aim of the study of social pathology.

---

5. A proposed study of the physical and mental characteristics of delinquents, 1908

Arthur MacDonald, *Juvenile Crime and Reformation, Including Stigmata of Degeneration,* 60 Cong., 1 Sess. (1908), Senate Doc. 532 (Washington, D.C., 1908), pp. 16–17.

Arthur MacDonald (1856–1936) studied psychology under G. Stanley Hall at Johns Hopkins in 1883 and then toured Europe where he collected the works of Cesare Lombroso and other criminologists of the positivist school. In 1897, as an employee of the U.S. Bureau of Education, he published in the Bureau's Annual Report writings of European criminologists as well as the results of anthropometrical experiments conducted upon American and Canadian school children by Henry P. Bowditch, Franz Boas, and William Townsend Porter. In the present document MacDonald drew upon his earlier work in an unsuccessful appeal to Congress for funds to establish a laboratory conducting anthropometrical measurements of juvenile delinquents.

In the study of man the individuals themselves must be investigated. As the seeds of evil are usually sown in childhood and youth, it is here that all inquiry should commence, for there is little hope of making the world better if we do not seek the causes of social evils at their beginnings.

Much money has been given and great interest manifested for the discovery of new chemical elements or the search for unknown planets. We erect statues and found art galleries at great expense. These things may not all be immediately useful. Indeed, the highest art spurns even the idea of utility; and yet when it is proposed to study a child thoroughly to gain an insight into its nature, to find the causes of its defects, so that we may protect it and help it to become a good citizen, the utilitarian cry is heard. The time has come when it is important to study a child with as much exactness as we investigate the chemical elements of a stone or measure the mountains on the moon.

If facts about children, whether immediately useful or not, are not important, we desire to ask what is important in life?

As an illustration of such investigation I give the following plan: To study 1,000 boys in industrial schools, ages from 6 to 15; 1,000 boys in reformatories, ages from 15 to 30; this investigation to consist in a physical, mental, moral, anthropological, social, and medico-social study of each boy, including such data as

are deemed most important from these several points of view. The general plan would be to employ specialists in psychology, medicine, and anthropology, the work of the director being in the main to conduct the plan and give the results and their import. Just what data would be taken would depend in part on the views of each specialist, but probably among these would be: Age, date of birth, height, weight, sitting height; color of hair, eyes, skin; first born, second born, or later born; strength of hand grasp, left handed; length, width, and circumference of head; distance between zygomatic arches, corners of eyes; length and width of ears, hands, and mouth; thickness of lips, measurements of sensibility to heat and pain; examination of lungs, eyes, pulse, and respiration; nationality, occupation, education, and social condition of parents; whether one or both are dead or drunkards; stepchildren or not, hereditary taint, stigmata of degeneration. All data gathered by the institutions as history and conduct of inmates might be utilized.

---

6. "Twenty-five per cent of delinquents are mentally defective"

Henry H. Goddard, "The Treatment of the Mental Defective who is also Delinquent," *Proceedings* of the National Conference of Charities and Correction (1911), 64–65.

Goddard (1866–1957) was the director of psychological research at the Vineland, New Jersey, Training School for mental defectives from 1906 to 1918. He was professor of abnormal and clinical psychology at Ohio State University from 1922 to 1938.

Twenty-five per cent of delinquents are mentally defective. While we have no absolute statistics, there are many indications that this is a safe estimate. All mental defectives would be delinquents in the very nature of the case, did not some one exercise some care over them.

There is only one possible answer to the question, "What is to be done with the feeble-minded person who is delinquent?" He must be cared for, but he must be cared for in a place where we care for irresponsibles. The jail or prison or reformatory, is not for him, neither must he be turned loose on the streets or sent back to the home and environment in which he has already become a delinquent.

In the present state of our laws and customs, delinquency is the one means by which we are able to get hold of a certain type of mental defective and provide for him as he should be provided for. Many of these feebleminded of the moron type come from homes or have attained to such an age or position that we have no way of getting hold of them until they do some wrong and come under the head of delinquents. But when that has happened and we have them where we can prescribe for them, it is worse than folly for us to let them go and turn them back into their former environments where they must only repeat the offense or even commit a worse one.

We must have enough institutions or colonies for the feebleminded to care for all the feeble-minded delinquents at least. As it is today, even under the best conditions, many a judge recognizes mental defects in the cases that come before him and would gladly send the child to an institution for the feebleminded, but there is no room, and so he is compelled to utilize some makeshift which oftentimes is worse than nothing at all.

But the broadest treatment of this topic must go farther back than the question of what to do with these feebleminded persons who have already become delinquent. We must consider the cause here as we are trying to do everywhere in modern methods, and treat the cause rather than trying to cure. In other words, the feebleminded person should be taken care of before he becomes a delinquent. Here the first problem is diagnosis. How shall we recognize this feeble-minded child of high type, this moron grade, as we now call them?

Until recently we have been more or less helpless in this matter, but now we may say with perfect assurance that the Binet tests of intelligence are entirely satisfactory and can be relied upon to pick out the mental defective at least up to the age of twelve years. The public schools will be the clearing house for all these cases; they may there be tested and their mental condition found, and they can then be cared for as condition leads. We have too long attempted to treat all children alike, whether in the public school or before the courts. When we have learned to discriminate and recognize the ability of each child and place upon him such burdens and responsibilities only as he is able to bear, then we shall have largely solved the problem of delinquency.

Psychological study of delinquents

William Healy (1869–1963), a psychologist, was primarily responsible for reorienting scientific study of delinquency toward the examination of mental processes instead of bodily form or defective ancestry. As director of the Juvenile Psychopathic Institute (Chicago), 1909–1917, and the Judge Baker Foundation (Boston), 1917–1946, Healy and Augusta F. Bronner, his second wife, examined repeated juvenile court offenders for psychiatric as well as physical defects. Their work stimulated establishment of similar clinics, organized initially in association with juvenile courts, but later founded in connection with hospitals, schools and community agencies.

---

1. Healy outlines a plan of study, Chicago, 1909

William Healy to Julia Lathrop, April 4, 1909, Foster 578, Dummer Papers, Schlesinger Library, Radcliffe College.

Julia Lathrop was heading a committee from Hull House and the (Chicago) Juvenile Protective Association seeking to establish a clinic to study repeated offenders in the Chicago Juvenile Court. This clinic was established in 1909 and financed for five years by Chicago philanthropist Ethel Sturges Dummer (1860–1954).

Dear Miss Lathrop:

.   .   .   .   .

The need . . . is for work, extensive, solid work, to be done in determining as much as possible the causation of delinquency and other mental unfitness, in deciphering for diagnosis the proper values of the various physical and mental stigmata which we know exist in most of these cases, in developing a classification of the individuals according to their needs, in estimating results obtained in the various private and public schools for defectives which are now on the veriest experimental basis. With the spread of well-grounded information much practical good will be derived from education of physician, layman and legislator.

You ask for a plan of work. In general . . . the details could only be completely developed as the work went along. I believe that what I know is needed can only be accomplished by a thoroughly experienced and unbiased man working with the best medical and psychological technique over a prolonged period. No commanding results can be obtained with less expenditure of effort. The literature must be thoroughly culled, statistics studied, institutions at home and, perhaps abroad, visited all to gain the strongest possible point of view. Then a very large series of cases must be investigated — probably in some measure all by the same man in order to get the best values for comparison. Taking, for instance, at least 500 cases of really delinquents from the Juvenile Court and as many patients as possible from the clinics and private practice — you know the latter are perhaps not found in the Juvenile Court merely on account of home custodianship — and other cases from various institutions, one could then and then only, get reliable conclusions. The examination would have to involve all possible facts about heredity, environment, antenatal and postnatal history, etc. You have already in your work on old Juvenile Court cases surely collected much that would bear on these points. The main worker would have to have some assistance, how much I am not sure, in examining ordinary physical functions, and also particularly in studying families and their histories when possible at first hand. You can realize that this is a big bit of work to devolve mostly on one person. You ask how long an examination of a delinquent is necessary. Well, most of the cases would certainly require at least one to two hours for complete tests and I believe very much of value for developing a classical work on the subject would be lost if they were not all examined by the same person. If less than the work I have outlined were undertaken I feel sure that we should stand just about where we do now, and only another bit of slip-shod social work would have been compiled with no great credit to American scholarship.

It is a task for four or five years, I should judge, to get anything like complete or commanding results out of this problem, although, of course, stimulating and educative papers could be presented to both physicians and the laity in less time.

I have been over the field fairly thoroughly and I am convinced of the need for a work that may be as classical as that of Lombroso, that may be much more scientifically founded and a thousand times more practically beneficial. But it can only be accomplished by long labor in competent hands.

Faithfully yours,
— William Healy.

2. The case study approach, Chicago, 1914

William Healy, *The Individual Delinquent* (Boston, 1915), pp. 3, 250–253, 278–280, 398–399.

Healy gathered the material for this book from his experiences treating children at the Juvenile Psychopathic Institute.

Out of deep consideration of hard-won facts this work is produced. In view of the failure of the past and the present effectively to handle anti-social conduct, and in the light of the enormous expense of criminality, standing in striking contrast to recent progress in many other fields of human endeavor, there seems the utmost justification for research work in the underlying causations of delinquency.

It has been called to our attention again and again that there is astonishingly little in the literature of criminology which is directly helpful to those who have to deal practically with offenders. Of general theory there is no lack, but when we come to that study of the individual which leads to clear understanding and scientific treatment, there is almost no guidance. The field covered by this volume, which is developed from the findings in many well-rounded case-studies, has only been touched heretofore in spots. Pioneering has stimulated deepest endeavor, but pleasure in it is tempered by the realization that fewer mistakes might have been made had there been more scientific foundations upon which to build. Through appreciation expressed, we know that some service has been rendered by our development of mental tests and methods of case study, and it is hoped that the present elaboration of the whole subject will prove of much further value.

.   .   .   .   .   .

Case 22. — Maria X. This girl of 12 1-2 years was brought to us by her straightforward New England parents. They were intensely disturbed about her delinquency, and blamed themselves for not having been foresighted enough to have prevented it. They are both healthy. We obtained at that time no facts of significance in regard to heredity. The last two children were twins, and one of them was the subject of our study. The girl has been all her life in a lively manufacturing town. Her developmental history is said to have been absolutely normal and free from illness, except for the fact that she has twice had convulsions. The first attack came when she was 9 and the second when she was 10 1-2 yrs. During her recent years she has been notably larger, stronger and better developed than her twin sister. She menstruated when she was just 12. Her sister has not yet done so. There is a difference between them also on the mental side, but this is much in favor of the sister, who is a full grade higher, and seems considerably brighter. (As we observed this sister, she is a typically slim and physically unattractive girl, quite normal for her age.) The parents tell us that Maria has been discovered to have been long engaged in sex delinquencies with young men.

On the physical side we found an extremely well-nourished girl of 4 ft., 11 in. In general sex characteristics she is astonishingly developed; attitude and bearing strong and upright; well-muscled arms. We also noted that she had a pleasant face, good features, beautiful skin, and the broad hips and prominent bust of a well-developed young woman. One observer states that the girl has the most beautiful neck and shoulders she had ever seen in a young girl. Vision slightly defective. Speech rather hesitating, with a hardly perceptible stutter at times. Tonsils and adenoids had been removed. Other examination negative.

The summary of our psychological findings is that the girl showed a good deal of mental irregularity and lack of control. To be sure she was under some emotional strain, but, even so, her ability could hardly be called better than poor. After we heard the story of her delinquencies we were inclined to believe that perhaps she might be dull by reason of excessive sex practices, or at least that her mental processes were under poor control for that reason. Even more noteworthy than the result on performance tests, was her absurdly small range of information. She was not sure who was the president of the United States, and did not know what the Fourth of July celebrated. When telling us her story, we found her attention had to be frequently called to the matter in hand, although we observed nothing definitely like *petit mal*.[1]

Of course Maria's mental condition as well as her physical make-up was a matter of grave interest and importance for prognosis and treatment. She was reported thoroughly dutiful, and a good worker at home. Sometimes she tells fanciful stories for the sake of deceiving others, but is not a great liar. The mother says the girl seems almost to wander in her mind at times, but after we heard of her behavior we did not wonder at this. We felt, too, that her habits might account for the fact that she had not yet passed into 5th grade, in spite of having gone to school between 7 and 8 years.

The freely told history of delinquency revealed to us the most extensive amount of sex indulgence with others that we have ever heard of from a child, except in the case of some feeble-minded girl. For two years, between school and home, she has been engaging in sex misconduct with various boys and young men. On account of her charms she has even posed for pictures of the nude. She wrote suggestive notes to boys in school.

The most remarkable social feature of this case is the fact that the twin sister had accompanied this girl back and forth from school, but had taken no interest in what was definitely going on between her sister and members of the opposite sex, and seems to have been in no moral danger at any time. She had simply waited for her in this or that place, and either did not wish to tell tales, or did not concern herself enough to inform her parents.

We never felt certain of the diagnosis in this case, especially in regard to abnormal psycho-logical features. But the physiological aspects stand out in great prominence, especially in comparison to the make-up of her sister. The social bearings of her unusual development are obvious. It was evident that Maria needed the utmost protection and control, and her parents now realized this. Our card of causation as ascertained at this time runs as follows:

Over-development and premature puberty.   Case 22.
      Remarkably attractive   Girl, age 12 yrs.
      physically.
Mentality: Dull, perhaps from epilepsy, or
      sex practices.
   Parental neglect—unwitting.

                           Mentality:
Sex + + +   Dull as above.

The parents soon decided it was impossible for them to properly control this girl on account of the extreme tendencies she had developed. They placed her in an institution. A year or so later she returned home. Recently we have again been consulted about her. It seems that after a few months at home she again became a sex delinquent. Study of her case now shows that she has frequent attacks of *petit mal*. They are described by Maria herself, and have been observed by her parents and others. There is no longer any doubt of her being an epileptic. The family now give a history of epilepsy in a maternal great-uncle to Maria, of fainting attacks in Maria's maternal aunts; also a paternal uncle had convulsive seizures following an accident. At 16 Maria is no longer so disproportionately over-developed, and shows little of her old attractiveness. Again we find it necessary to recommend an institution.

This case illustrates two of the points we have elsewhere made in regard to over-development. Premature development and over-development are found with astonishing frequency in cases of epilepsy. Secondly, early over-development does not always mean great size later.

.   .   .   .   .

It might be a difficult matter to show how even the most excessive use of tea and coffee

---

1. *Petit mal* describes a form of epilepsy characterized by mild convulsions with brief clouding of consciousness.

could cause criminalism in an adult, but the relationship of anti-social tendencies in a child to the overuse of these stimulants is quite clear. They cause an amount of excitation and unsteadiness of the nervous system, and a general restlessness which makes the individual unable to comfortably maintain school life. Truancy is the natural reaction, and from this arises the usual range of temptations and undesirable tendencies. The same is true of life in the home. With an excessive use of stimulants there is very apt to be irritability, disobedience, and family friction. These in turn may induce anti-social reactions. In a considerable number of cases we have noted this. For instance, in the following:

Case 35. — Boy, 10 years, 9 months. Weight 55 lbs., height 4 ft. 2 in. General and neurologic examination negative, except that right pupil is twice as large as left. Two years ago he fell from a second story, striking the back of his head, and rendering him unconscious. Bled from ears and nose. Eyes said to have crossed at that time. Was in the hospital for 3 weeks. Nowadays complains of many headaches, mostly on one side. Is a weak and irritable type.

Mentally we find him to be about fair in native ability. He is only in second grade, but has been out of school much. We regard him as perhaps being somewhat dull from physical causes. He gets into much trouble in the schoolroom on account of recalcitrancy.

This boy comes from a family which shows many peculiarities. The father was a hard drinker, once sentenced for disorderly conduct, later committed suicide. An older brother was earlier a delinquent, but later made good. One sister attempted suicide.

This boy has been found very difficult to handle through his stubbornness. There has been lack of home control on account of the mother being away working. He has been accustomed to get up early in the morning for his coffee, go back to bed, and get up later to make more coffee when his mother had gone away. He began it very early. She states that they could not afford to have meat, and so they had to have coffee. He has been accustomed to drinking about 7 cups of coffee and 2 of tea in a day.

Seen 4 years later, we still note his poor development. Now at almost 15 years he weighs only 53 lbs., height 4 ft. 7 1-4 in. He is a restless, repressed type, with overuse of the facial muscles. The pupils are still unequal. Vision slightly defective in one eye. Other examination negative, except that we note his club-shaped finger tips. He speaks in staccato voice, is nervous and furtive. His people at home say he is not right mentally and that they can do nothing with him. As a matter of fact they abuse him. Home conditions bad in many ways. A man in the same house has recently committed suicide.

The boy has been stealing and in a burglary. He has only reached 3d grade. In spite of his terrifically poor school record we find him to have good ability in many ways. He does a number of our difficult tests very well indeed, showing good powers of reasoning and mental representation. Evidently he has paid very little attention to reading for he does about 2d grade work in it. Is known in his neighborhood to have a good deal of mechanical ability. Has made a machine-like contrivance. This boy still uses tea and coffee at the rate of about 6 cups a day, and our impression is that much of his trouble still arises from that cause. A good proof was that when placed out in the country and deprived of these stimulants he began to improve immediately on the physical side.

The standard rule in pharmacy is that the effect of a drug is proportionate to the weight of the individual. If this is true for tea and coffee, as it probably is, one can best think of the result upon this small boy in terms of what a proportionate amount would do to an adult.

It is unnecessary to give other examples, because all cases of this kind read alike. It is perfectly clear that the unsettling of the nervous system which occurs in young people by the excessive use of these stimulants is a direct factor making in many environments for delinquency.

.   .   .   .   .

Case 74. — This was a little girl of 12 who had been given a very black name by certain institutional people and others on account of alleged exceedingly bad behavior; in fact, reformatory treatment was demanded for her. Not only was it said that she was a delinquent, but that she was also a mental defective, on account of apparently proved inability to grasp school work.

We found a rather poorly nourished little girl who was suffering frequently of late from headaches. These, she told us, sometimes lasted for hours and were accompanied by curious sensations of lights in her eyes. Different colors appear, and the lights seem like snakes coming from all directions, while perhaps she cannot see anything at all for a time. She bites her nails much. Both vision and hearing were slightly defective, the latter on account of a previous middle-ear infection. On the mental side it was a matter of only a few minutes to prove that she was anything but a mental defective, indeed we graded her as being well up to the ordinary in ability and information.

We could learn from the father nothing of significance in the family or developmental history. None in the family of either parent is known to be epileptic or insane, nor can we hear of any migraine. The mother died of cancer four years previously, and the father was previously alcoholic, although for some time now he has not been drinking hard. The whole story centers about the fact that this child's older sisters, after the mother's death, considered the father as unworthy, and some six months prior to the time we saw her, practically kidnapped the girl from home. There was no statement that he had ever mistreated the child in any way. She was not said to be delinquent before then, and she had been doing well in the 5th grade at school. Up to that time she says she had suffered from headache perhaps only a couple of times.

The little girl readily acknowledged her misbehavior, which consisted, according to the institutional people with whom she was placed, in running away (it seems she once got as far as the railroad station in an endeavor to get back to her father), in clandestine correspondence, lying, and refractoriness in the schoolroom. Besides this she was found "mentally queer, dazed and stupid-looking at times. She once threatened to kill herself."

From the girl herself we get an account of terrific loneliness, with whole days of distress, although she has been away months from her father. "I'm not happy. He was always good to me. I've written for him to come, but they got the letters first. I'll sit there and not know what I'm doing, I'll be biting my finger nails and everything. My sisters think my father is mean, but he treats me nice. I never ran away except from this here Home. They treat me all right. My heart hurts me. Only one thing, I didn't want to go to a Home."

The father's sympathy and love were really proved in this case by his quick response when he knew that the child wanted him.

Here was an aspect of child life totally overlooked and misunderstood by people dealing constantly with children, as well as by some court authorities. For us the point is not only this, but also the details of the physical and mental conditions and the delinquent reactions which have arisen psychogenetically, namely, from the repression and ferment in the mind. Even the first analysis of the case brought out the fact that she thought homesickness was all that was the matter, although she had never intimated to others any explanation of her conduct. How much of the emotion and connecting links of reaction were subconscious it would be difficult to say. With return to her home, defective though it was, came cessation of headaches, and of her delinquencies, and gain of weight.

3. Demonstration clinics to prevent
delinquency, 1925

Joint Committee on Methods of Preventing
Delinquency, *Commonwealth Fund Program
for the Prevention of Delinquency:
Progress Report* (New York: The
Commonwealth Fund, 1925), pp. 14–18.

In 1921 the Commonwealth Fund
inaugurated a program "to promote
community services for the understanding and
guidance of behavior problem children."
In addition to supporting demonstrations of
psychiatric clinics, the program provided
funds to familiarize social workers and
visiting teachers with the psychiatric
approach toward delinquency.

This Division has been primarily engaged in
conducting demonstration child guidance clinics
in cities which desire to establish under local
auspices permanent child guidance clinics to
serve the public schools, the social agencies, the
juvenile court, and parents in dealing with children presenting problems of adjustment to
home, school, or community. The purpose of
the demonstration is not only to show the contribution psychiatric study can make to the
treatment of behavior difficulties in children
but to work out the functional relationships of
a child guidance clinic to those other agencies
in the community, medical, educational, and
social, on whose cooperation the effectiveness
of the clinic's work must largely depend. In
addition to its demonstration work, the Division provides consultant service to communities prepared to undertake on their own initiative and resources the establishment of child
guidance clinics.

At first the work . . . was concerned
mainly with the study and treatment of children
already under supervision of the juvenile courts.
By properly directed methods of treatment it
was believed that the social rehabilitation of
such children and the consequent reduction of

delinquency in the community could be definitely advanced. In practice, however, it soon
became evident that work with children who
present behavior problems would be more effective if the problem were recognized and dealt
with before the behavior had become so serious
as to necessitate some form of court action. This
meant that it became increasingly necessary for
the demonstration clinics to establish direct
contacts with the public schools, with social
agencies, and with homes.

In the light of experience, then, the objectives
of this part of the Program have been broad-
ened to cover a more general type of clinical
service to the children of the community. This
new emphasis on the constructive aspects of the
mental hygiene of childhood implies no abandonment of the specific aim of preventing delinquency but rather the recognition that the
best preventive technique is a broad and positive effort to redirect the energies of maladjusted children before they become problems in
the community.

The boys and girls who need and receive the
services of a child guidance clinic do not fall
into fixed classifications of those who will inevitably develop delinquency or mental disease,
and those who will not. The actual records of
children studied during the past two years show
that the demonstration clinics are helping many
youngsters of whom it could hardly be said that
without the aid of the clinic they would become
either criminal or insane. What would happen
in many such cases is that without early recognition and correction of the difficulty, the child
would carry along habits and attitudes tending
toward an unnecessarily unhappy and ineffective adult life. From neither the administrative
nor the broad human standpoint is it wise to
attempt the organization of a clinical service
which shall neglect the needs of such children
while dealing with the graver cases. A competent agency must reach and guide those dealing
with the child by throwing the clearest possible
light on every factor in his problem, be it physical, mental, or social; and this agency should
stand open to all unhappy or maladjusted

youngsters, regardless of the degree of intensity of the problem.

The staffs of the demonstration clinics have been enlarged to meet the greater demands arising out of this broadening of the scope of the work with its emphasis upon the treatment of the individual child and upon the coordination of clinic activities with those of other social agencies in the community. The average staff of a demonstration clinic comprises the director (a psychiatrist), a chief of staff (also a psychiatrist), a fellow in psychiatry, two psychologists, six psychiatric social workers, a statistical recorder, a secretary, an office assistant, and four stenographers. In addition to its paid staff the clinic usually has the services of trained workers loaned for stated periods of active work under close supervision; these are placed in the clinic by local agencies which, in the interest of a more effective future cooperation, desire to secure in this way a working knowledge of the clinic's point of view and methods.

Several important considerations govern the choice of the city in which the demonstration clinic is placed. One of these is the evidence of an intention to establish at the close of the demonstration a permanent clinic with a budget sufficient to insure adequate staff and good standards of work. Equally vital in selecting a city is the question of how progressive the social agencies, the school system, the medical clinics, etc., of the community are and how well-coordinated a plan of cooperation between these and the clinic can be formulated.

The exceptional importance of this feature of cooperation from community agencies has been made amply clear since the demonstrations began. Success cannot be expected if the demonstration clinics are limited to their own efforts and resources. It is a slow and difficult task to fit the clinic whose work is at first little understood into the existing network of social, medical, educational, and recreational agencies of a community so that the new child guidance activities will be effectively and smoothly coordinated with old established community processes. It was soon evident that the demonstra-

tion periods would have to be increased from six months to one year, and the demonstrations now in progress have been planned for two-year periods.

Study of the past work of the Division and plans for its future activities indicate three major objectives which must be attained by each demonstration child guidance clinic if the subsequent permanent clinics are to be successful from the beginning. These objectives may be summarized under the headings of demonstration, education, and research.

In the first place, the clinic must provide a convincing demonstration of methods of study and treatment of behavior problems. This involves the actual study and treatment of a sufficient number of cases by the clinic alone or in cooperation with other agencies, and the communication of methods and technique to trained workers from other fields who are enrolled as volunteer members of the clinical staff for varying periods of time.

Secondly, the demonstration must undertake educational work in the community in the field of mental hygiene and the application of psychiatric methods to problems of behavior. A comprehensive scheme of educational effort involves, first, lectures and publicity for the community in general regarding the work of the clinic, to arouse interest and insure community backing and cooperation. Special lectures and case discussions in psychiatry and psychology are given for social workers in various fields. Parents and school teachers are reached by lectures and articles and by direct contact, so that they may come to understand how the home and the school sometimes contribute to behavior disturbances. Arrangements also are made for courses in psychiatry, abnormal psychology, and psychiatric social work for students in colleges and professional schools.

The third objective, research into causes and treatment, involves critical analysis of the work of the clinic itself and development of better methods of study and treatment of behavior problems in the light of accumulating experience.

None of these objectives can be ignored if a demonstration is to be effective. They vary somewhat in importance, however, and require different stress in different communities. In all cases, the main goal is that of establishing the clinic firmly as an integral part of the socially organized community, giving and receiving service in smooth and effective working relations with all other community agencies.

---

4. An evaluation of the Boston Juvenile Court and the Judge Baker Foundation, 1934

Sheldon and Eleanor T. Glueck, *One Thousand Juvenile Delinquents* (Cambridge, Mass.: Harvard University Press, 1934), pp. 228–233. Copyright, 1934, by the President and Fellows of Harvard College; 1962 by Sheldon Glueck and Eleanor Touroff Glueck.

Sheldon Glueck (b. 1896) and his wife Eleanor (b. 1898), Harvard criminologists, conducted this study as part of the Harvard Law School's Survey of Crime and Criminal Justice in Boston. The institutional records, upon which their findings were based, covered the period 1917–1922.

Who are delinquents? The available evidence is now before us. Out of the mass of facts, figures, and inferences presented in the preceding chapters, certain major findings call for emphasis before we consider possible improvements in the existing practices. First let us renew our acquaintance with the delinquents and their background. In broad strokes, the picture of the boys who passed in and out of the Boston Juvenile Court and the Judge Baker Foundation is the following.

To a larger extent than the general population, they are the native-born sons of foreign-born parents, a situation likely to make for cultural friction. Their parents have had a very meager education. The boys are members of un-usually large families, which even in happier economic times would continually be on the ragged edge of poverty. These families have disintegrated early; often the parents have become separated or divorced, or are unduly quarrelsome, and the home life has been distorted by inadequate care and discipline of the children. The standards of the parents, as interpreted through evidences of thrift, temperance, and moral decency, are very low, and criminality on the part of the parents, brothers, and sisters of our young delinquents is an all too frequent phenomenon.

It is therefore not surprising that the boys with whom the court and clinic have had to deal were retarded in school; that they were compelled to leave school at an early age, usually because of economic necessity; that they began their industrial careers in the street trades. Nor is it cause for great wonderment that many of these boys spent part of their childhood in foster-homes and in non-penal and correctional institutions, even preceding their appearance before the Boston Juvenile Court. As we should expect, life in the crowded city streets engaged their leisure hours. Very few of them had ever been members of wholesome, supervised play-groups or clubs. In large measure they had truanted from school or had "bunked out," such behavior reaching back to their early childhood. As a rule, they had been arrested (and usually placed on probation) more than once prior to the arrest which brought them into the Boston Juvenile Court and the J. B. F. clinic. Most of them were under twelve when first apprehended, an age still plastic enough to justify the utmost rehabilitative efforts. Yet an appreciable time had elapsed between the first manifestations of their antisocial conduct and their examination at the clinic. To a great extent our delinquent boys were brought into the Boston Juvenile Court for larceny or burglary, offenses which they had in large measure committed with one or more companions.

Our delinquents were found to be in good physical condition when examined at the clinic. Many of them, however, were either of subnormal intelligence or burdened with marked emotional and personality handicaps and defects.

The picture that we have sketched is a composite one, and is therefore naturally somewhat marred by distortions of perspective and arrangement. But for the present purpose it is sufficiently clear to reveal to us a class that is biologically and economically handicapped.

.   .   .   .   .

What the clinic recommended. It should be recalled that the clinic as a rule had but one contact with a delinquent boy and with the members of his family. Its work was limited to examining him, securing the necessary information from some member of his family, and sending to the court a summary of its findings and its recommendations for treatment. The clinic had no part in the actual carrying out of the treatment; that was left to the court, the probation officers, institutional authorities, and those social workers who were called upon by the probation officers for assistance.

What kind of prescriptions did the clinic send to the court? Let us first recall its recommendations as to the basic problem of where the delinquent should reside. Most frequently the clinic recommended that the boys be kept in their own homes under such oversight as could be given by a probation officer; but in an appreciable number of cases it advised placement in the country, or in a foster-home, or sentence to a correctional school; the bottles in the clinic's medicine-chest were few in number. As a rule the clinic made two or three additional suggestions for treatment; these usually dealt with improvement of health, educational needs, and vocational adjustments, and with a miscellaneous assortment of matters designated as "other constructive supervision." Though, as we have already seen, our young delinquents were in great need of wholesome recreational outlets, it was the exception rather than the rule for the clinic to make any suggestions in this regard.

What the court and others concerned did. To what extent were the clinical prescriptions put into effect? In a fifth of the cases, the *place-of-living recommendation* was not followed at all; in more than an additional third the recommended treatment was in effect for six months or less—hardly a sufficient time in which to bring about enduring transformations in habits and attitudes. If we consider a period longer than six months as indispensable to a deep-seated adjustment, two-fifths of the young offenders were under treatment for an adequate period of time, two-fifths were not, and one-fifth were not treated at all. Least often carried out by the court were the recommendations for placement of the boys in a foster-home, with relatives, in the country, or in a school for the feebleminded; most often followed were those dealing with residence at home under probationary oversight and with sentence to correctional institutions.

The recommendations pertaining to *other matters* than where the boy should live were not followed at all in two-fifths of the cases and fully carried out in but a fifth, while in the remaining two-fifths they were only partially put into effect. Least often carried out were the recommendations dealing with the recreational needs of the boys, with improvement of their family and living conditions, with the advisability of further clinical examination, and with attention to health matters. Most often put into effect were the recommendations concerning vocational and school adjustments, and problems of discipline.

Of the total of 2246 clinical recommendations made in these cases, over half were not carried out at all and only three-tenths were fully executed within the treatment period. In only 195 of the thousand cases were all of the clinical recommendations followed.

The principal reasons for non-compliance with, or modification of, the clinical recommendations appear to have been these: (1) Various unrecorded differences of opinion between the Judge and clinical experts; (2) legal or administrative obstacles; (3) lack of cooperation by parents; (4) non-cooperation of the delinquents; (5) refusal or inability of various social agencies to assist the court in the placement of delinquents; (6) refusal or inability of public institutions and authorities to aid the court in carrying out the recommendations; (7) the limited understanding and skill of certain probation officers and social workers; (8) paucity of community facilities needed for coping with delinquency; (9) the experimental or unrealistic nature of some of the clinical recommendations; and (10) in certain cases, rapid transformations of the original delinquency and family situations, resulting in the obsolescence of the recommendations.

These findings lead to the conclusions that the working relationship between clinic and court might be considerably improved; that the success of both institutions is greatly dependent upon the adequate collaboration of other social agencies; that the work of all organizations concerned with various aspects of the prevention and treatment of delinquency needs to be effectively integrated; that additional specialized community facilities for coping with delinquency are necessary; and that the court needs to have greater power over the families of delinquents.

Recidivism following treatment. What was the conduct of our boys in the five-year post-treatment period? *Eighty-eight per cent of them continued their delinquencies during this period.* They were arrested on the average of 3.6 times each. Nor were the arrests of our youths essentially for petty offenses; two-thirds of the entire group of 905 boys whose post-treatment conduct was determinable committed serious offenses, largely felonies.

The major conclusion is inescapable, then, that *the treatment carried out by clinic, court, and associated community facilities had very little effect in preventing recidivism.*

---

5. "New orientations" on delinquency

William Healy and Augusta F. Bronner, *New*

Light on Delinquency and Its Treatment (New Haven: Yale University Press, 1936), pp. 8–13.

This study was initiated in 1928 under the Institute of Human Relations of Yale University. Healy and Bronner compared delinquent and non-delinquent children in the same families in three cities: New Haven, Boston, and Detroit.

. . . how does it happen that some young people living in the same family environment as the delinquent, with the desires common to youth, with the same social pressures, and always with ideas of delinquency easily obtainable, are able to refrain from antisocial conduct? We have often turned to consideration of the non-delinquent with the thought that it is more astonishing to discover that they have refrained from delinquency than that a brother or sister has developed antisocial behavior. It has been part of our task to study the personalities and lives of these non-delinquents for comparative purposes. In endeavoring to answer the question why ideas of delinquency have never been considered, or if considered why they have been rejected, we have had to take account of various differences in personality characteristics but in the main we have found the behavior derivatives of emotional satisfactions to be the answer. When there have been no intense feelings of deprivations, inadequacies, or thwartings as related to either ego-impulses or desires for affection, the individual has been able readily to find sufficient satisfactions in socially acceptable behavior. Our comparative studies of two children in the same family bring this out clearly and especially our studies of twins, one of whom was delinquent and one not delinquent.

As cause and effect most closely linked to the deeper satisfactions and dissatisfactions of children are the behavior attitudes of those in contact with the children. This stands out very plainly as we have compared the emotional lives of the delinquents with a brother or sister who has avoided delinquency. Many of the families from which the delinquents came lived in situations that could be considered thoroughly inimical for the upbringing of a child, yet even under these conditions it was clear that the non-delinquents had distinctly more satisfactory human relationships than had the delinquents.

It would be easy to generalize that parents through their own dissatisfactions arising from discrepancies between cultural or economic desires and the realities of their life situations could reasonably be expected to display asocial attitudes, even as exhibited in their behavior toward their children. But for our research it was most enlightening to uncover the additional fact that there had been great differences in their feelings and behavior toward their different children — more sympathetic understanding, more fulfillment of fundamental needs, less inconsistent treatment very frequently indeed having been exhibited from early years toward one child as compared to another.

As investigators of the stream of life's activities we are led to wonder why at various points there have not been dams or barriers which might have prevented the current from flowing in the direction of delinquency. We can readily understand that when a channel has been formed by habits of thought or by established social contacts the difficulties of checking the flow of activities are great. How often we have heard, "I got in the habit of stealing," or, "I couldn't stop going with those fellows!" Some more introspective youngsters have related to us their story of how thoughts, once started in this direction, returned again and again in idle or half-waking moments to ideas of delinquency — they had nothing else to absorb their interest, nothing else that gave them commanding satisfactions.

But aside from this matter of the strength of habit formation there remains the question why the delinquent early or later did not find in himself inhibiting forces strong enough to check delinquent impulses. As we looked into the lives of these young people, it was clear, for one thing, that social restraints and inhibitions were in many instances absent because of poor for-

mation of what is so aptly termed an ego-ideal. There had been no strong emotional tie-up to anyone who presented a pattern of satisfactory social behavior. To put it in another way, the child had never had an affectional identification with one who seemed to him a good parent. The father or mother either had not played a rôle that was admired by the child or else on account of the lack of a deep love relationship was not accepted as an ideal.

We have found it impossible to present the above fact statistically for our series of cases, because it would have required a tremendous amount of time to analyze the emotional lives of the delinquents in order to gain subjective evidence that ego-ideals had not been an influence in their personality development; but the objective facts are plain enough. If from nowhere else, it would have been made clear to us from our present comparative studies that the effectiveness of moral teaching and of good example is dependent on emotional values attached to them by the child. The feeling tone about right conduct derives most powerfully from the emotional side of human relationships. Ethical concepts that have no personification have little force in the lives of young people.

But in contrast, when studying the non-delinquents we came across many striking evidences of influential ties to some person, nearly always a parent — sometimes an unworthy parent though not felt as such by the child — whose esteem was desired and was obtained and retained if the child remained non-delinquent. The importance of building up standards through such personal relationship can hardly be overstated.

We might go a step further in inquiring why the young individual finds in himself no barriers preventing his ideas and activities from flowing in channels of delinquent conduct. In particular we may ask, why has the delinquent in and of himself, arising from his own sense of what is right and wrong, no strong feeling about the wrongfulness of delinquency? Now it is very true that we constantly find the delinquent fully able to express his conscious belief that delinquency represents wrong conduct, but evidently his *feeling* about its wrongfulness has not been sufficiently strong to function as a preventive. How then does it happen, that the delinquent's personality is possessed of such an impotent categorical imperative, conscience, or superego? Why, for example, has "Thou shalt not steal" no strong sanctions for him?

To be sure, we have partly covered this point in the preceding discussion. We know that the introjection, as the analysts phrase it, of parental prohibitions, the absorption of parental ideas of right and wrong, is the anchorage of conscience long before the principles of good conduct are taught by church or school. Through the earliest prohibitions, even with regard to bodily functions, family possessions, or behavior in the family circle, the child develops a conscience or superego long before it comes to any question of social behavior outside the family. This is obvious, but it leaves the whole matter of the growth of the sense of right and wrong an extremely complicated problem.

The fact seems to be clear that the barrier which we call conscience or the superego is universally found, but in different individuals plays various and partial rôles in determining or motivating behavior. Hence conscience may cover only certain areas in the field of conduct. In one case of our series a young boy evidently had a strong conscience about being mannerly and doing his school work well, while stealing seemed really to mean nothing to him except as he might be caught for it. And we have noted in some instances that lying was quite condoned by conscience while stealing was a sin, and that in other cases this was exactly reversed.

A final consideration in this discussion of the development of delinquency as one special manifestation of behavior is the origins of the attitudes and beliefs of parents — just because these have so much to do with the development of conduct trends in their children. Quite apart from the knowledge we gained of the parents' scale of values resulting, more or less unconsciously, from the influences of their own early lives, there is another matter of vast import to general social welfare. Though we made no special study of this, it often cropped out that certain undesirable attitudes and behavior tendencies exhibited by parents were related, sometimes vaguely and sometimes explicitly, to prevalent asocial ideologies. Our population in general is well acquainted with the exploitations, unfairnesses, and dishonesties which are current in many spheres of activity. From this it follows that parents who feel deprivations and discomforts and who have not ideals that prevent can readily rationalize the situation. They may easily persuade themselves that, such being the state of things, the sensible behavior is to get what one can by whatever means are available, to consider one's own personal advantage at the expense of anything else, to enjoy oneself as best one can. It goes without saying that these sentiments based on current ideologies of self-considering individualism militate against the proper upbringing of children and specifically tend to pervade the household, spreading — though, for various reasons, differentially — from parents to members of the younger generation.

B. THE CULTURE OF DELINQUENCY

The Chicago School

Under the leadership of Albion W. Small (1854–1926) and Ernest W. Burgess (1886– 1966), the Department of Sociology at the University of Chicago became preeminent in the systematic and first hand investigation of urban life. To these sociologists, juvenile delinquency was one of several pathological signs which characterized life in those areas of the city which were physically deteriorating and without rehabilitating community organizations. Frederic Thrasher (1892–1962) described delinquency as the normal type of group or gang activity in slum areas while Clifford Shaw (1896–1963) investigated in detail the individual careers of delinquent boys in order to show the debasing effect of life in their social environment. William I. Thomas (1863–1947) studied Polish immigrant life in Chicago from the same point of view.

---

1. Gangland is an interstitial area

Frederic M. Thrasher, *The Gang: A Study of 1,313 Gangs in Chicago,* 2nd rev. ed. (Chicago: University of Chicago Press, 1936), pp. 5–7, 22–25. First published in 1927.

No less than 1,313 gangs have been discovered in Chicago and its environs! A conservative estimate of 25,000 members — boys and young men — is probably an understatement, for the census taken in connection with this study is not exhaustive.

It must be remembered in reading the following description of gangland that the writer is presenting only one phase of the life of these communities. There are churches, schools, clubs, banks, and the usual list of wholesome institutions in these areas as well as gangs. The gangs and the type of life described here may not even be apparent to the average citizen of the district, who is chiefly occupied in his own pursuits.

The reader should also bear in mind that the gang is a protean manifestation: no two gangs are just alike; some are good; some are bad; and each has to be considered on its own merits. Many of the gangs mentioned by name in the following account are delinquent groups, for they are usually of the picturesque sort, attracting more attention and receiving names more readily than other types.

THE EMPIRE OF GANGLAND

The broad expanse of gangland with its intricate tribal and intertribal relationships is medieval and feudal in its organization rather than modern and urban.

The feudal warfare of youthful gangs is carried on more or less continuously. Their disorder and violence, escaping the ordinary controls of the police and other social agencies of the community, are so pronounced as to give the impression that they are almost beyond the pale of civil society. In some respects these regions of conflict are like a frontier; in others, like a "no man's land," lawless, godless, wild.

In Chicago the empire of the gang divides into three great domains, each of which in turn breaks up into smaller kingdoms. They are natural areas, differentiated in the processes of human interaction, and having their own characteristic place in the mosaic of the city's life.

The first of these we may call the "North Side jungles"; the second, the "West Side wilderness"; and the third, the "South Side badlands" — names which well characterize the regions so far as gang life is concerned. Gangland stretches in a broad semicircular zone about the central business district (the Loop) and in general forms a sort of *interstitial* barrier between the Loop and the better residential areas.

*   *   *   *   *

GANGLAND IS AN INTERSTITIAL AREA

The most important conclusion suggested by a study of the location and distribution of the 1,313 gangs investigated in Chicago is that *gangland represents a geographically and socially interstitial area in the city.* Probably the most significant concept of the study is the term *interstitial* — that is, pertaining to spaces that intervene between one thing and another. *In nature foreign matter tends to collect and cake in every crack, crevice, and cranny — interstices. There are also fissures and breaks in the structure of social organization. The gang may be regarded as an interstitial element in the framework of society, and gangland as an interstitial region in the layout of the city.*

The gang is almost invariably characteristic of regions that are interstitial to the more settled, more stable, and better organized portions of the city. The central tripartite empire of the gang occupies what is often called "the poverty belt" — a region characterized by deteriorating neighborhoods, shifting populations, and the mobility and disorganization of the slum.

Abandoned by those seeking homes in the better residential districts, encroached upon by business and industry, this zone is a distinctly interstitial phase of the city's growth. It is to a large extent isolated from the wider culture of the larger community by the processes of competition and conflict which have resulted in the selection of its population. Gangland is a phenomenon of human ecology. As better residential districts recede before the encroachments of business and industry, the gang develops as one manifestation of the economic, moral, and cultural frontier which marks the interstice.

This process is seen, too, in the way in which a business street, stream, canal, or railroad

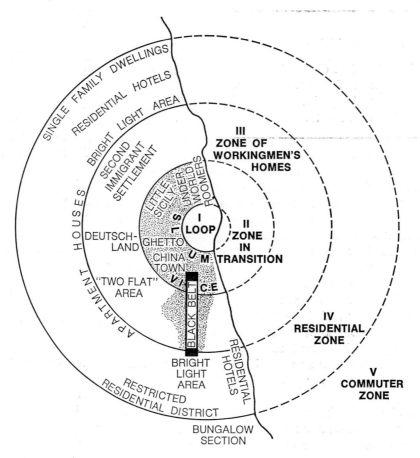

The place of Chicago's gangland in the urban ecology. The shaded portion indicates the approximate location of the central empire of gangland, which has been superimposed upon E. W. Burgess' chart showing urban areas in the development of the city. (See E. W. Burgess, "The Growth of the City," in Robert E. Park, *et al., The City* [Chicago, 1925], p. 55.)

track running through a residential area tends to become a "finger" of the slum and an extension of gangland. Borderlands and boundary lines between residential and manufacturing or business areas, between immigrant or racial colonies, between city and country or city and suburb, and between contiguous towns — all tend to assume the character of the intramural frontier. County towns and industrial suburbs which escape the administrative control and protection of the city government and whose conditions of life are disorganized, as in the case of West-Town, develop into appended ganglands. The roadhouses fringing the city, and those occupying positions between its straggling suburbs, represent an escape from society and become important factors in maintaining the power and activities of the gang. The region of 155th Street and South Halsted has been representative of these conditions in the southern part of Cook County.

The city has been only vaguely aware of this great stir of activity in its poorly organized areas. Gang conflict and gang crime occasionally thrust themselves into the public consciousness, but the hidden sources from which they spring have not yet been understood or regulated. Although their importance in the life of the boy has sometimes been pointed out, the literature of the subject has been meager and general. This region of life is in a real sense an *underworld,* through whose exploration the sociologist may learn how the gang begins and how it develops, what it is and what it does, the conditions which produce it and the problems which it creates, and ultimately he may be able to suggest methods for dealing with it in a practical way.

---

2. The Dirty Dozen, a Chicago gang

Thrasher, *The Gang,* pp. 46–50.

The Dirty Dozen began merely as the result of a dozen or more fellows (from sixteen to twenty-two years of age) meeting casually on a street corner at the entrance of one of Chicago's parks and later on in "Mike's" poolroom a short distance away. Most of the boys were loafers, who spent their time swimming, playing baseball and football, shooting craps, or sitting around and talking. They liked brawls and fights, and the gang helped to satisfy these wants with less personal discomfort than might occur if one fellow alone started hostilities or tried to steal something. Of their various activities, some form of conflict seems to have been the chief.

There was war between the gang and the police, for even though the latter did not always have any particular offense for which the fellows were wanted, they did try to break up the group whenever it congregated on the corner.

The gang as a whole often came into direct conflict with other gangs. One night at the old Imperial Theater, the Dirty Dozen found themselves seated opposite the "Chi" gang, their rival in football and baseball. During the show, which was poor vaudeville, the fellows started to hurl remarks at each other. The verbal conflict grew into a near-riot, which continued until the police came.

The Dirty Dozen, however, was capable of collective action against other enemies than rival gangs. One night while the race riots of 1919 were at their height, the gang, armed with revolvers, blackjacks, and knives, started out to get the "niggers."

At Thirty-fifth and State streets, five miles or more from their own territory, and after some preliminary skirmishes, "Shaggy" Martin threw the trolley of a street car filled with colored people. The rest of the gang, which had increased to about twenty by this time, piled on. "Shaggy," who was left alone at the back to hold the trolley-rope, was standing there with it in one hand and a billy in the other when a colored woman slashed him across the heart with a razor. Then someone hit her, and another fellow "got" her husband.

Shaggy died in the patrol on the way to the hospital. "Swede" Carlson, the only fellow the police caught at that time, said that his last words were, "What will mother say?" The gang took up a collection for flowers, but the direct result of the episode was a desire for revenge. They killed two negroes and "beat up" five more after the death of Shaggy.

The standing of each fellow in the gang was determined by competition and conflict within the group itself. Each member was trying to outdo the others in football and everything else. There was always a struggle for the leadership, which usually went to the best fighters.

"Slicker" Charlie and Ellman were for some reason or other "on the outs," and a fight was arranged to see who was better. The encounter came off in the park. Each fellow had his second, and the time of the rounds was set just as if it were a regular prize fight. Ellman, who won, mauled Charlie severely, and the latter fell into disgrace, at least in his own opinion.

This feeling of his own belittlement caused Charlie much resentment toward the victor and led to another fight in which Charlie struck Ellman with a lead pipe. The blood shot out of a big gash in his head. After they had taken him to the emergency hospital, a cop came in and wanted to know how it had happened, but Ellman would say nothing except that he had fallen and his head hit a rock. The code of the gang was that honor forbade squealing. With this incident the feud came to an end.

An example of conflict of the play type, which had a very tragic outcome, occurred one day in the park. About eight of the fellows went to the lagoon and piled into two tiny rowboats. It was a warm summer evening, and the bunch was feeling pretty good, so they decided to have a battle. Splashing soon led to striking with oars. The battle was raging when one of the boats went over. In it was a fellow called "Steam," who could not swim. The others struck out for the shore, but Steam went down. As soon as they discovered that he was gone, they went out and dived for him until one of them succeeded in getting the body. The fire department came and a pulmotor was used, but to no avail. Before the funeral a collection was taken up, and an expensive floral piece was purchased. The gang turned to the good for one day, and every member went to the church. Steam was never spoken of afterward, for each one of them felt a little bit responsible for his death.

Members of the gang often engaged in shady exploits as individuals or in pairs. Ellman and "Dago" were always managing to make some money in one way or another. At one time Ellman told me of the "booze" ring, for which he and Dago did the delivering. Where they got the booze I never found out, but they made $25 or $30 apiece for a night's work and gambled it away at a place which was a regular Monte Carlo, with tables for crap-shooting, and caller's chips which were purchased from the cashier.

The same pair were involved in the robbery of a golf shelter. Owing to Ellman's carelessness, he was followed and arrested. He was convicted of petty larceny and put on probation, but the police could not make him reveal the name of his pal. By keeping mum he saved Dago a lot of trouble.

The gang also enjoyed many quiet evenings. It was the rule for the fellows to meet at Mike's on winter nights to shoot pool and talk. In the summer their hang-out was on the corner at the entrance to the park. There was a tendency to stick together at all times in play, just as in other activities. They often went swimming. Every year they played football, for which they tried to keep in training, and they developed a good team. The older fellows were the leaders in their athletic activities.

One of the exploits of the gang was a migration from Chicago to Detroit when high wages were being paid to automobile-workers. They rented a house there and the whole gang lived together. Even though they were making fabulous wages, they did not save a cent, and finally came back to Chicago — broke. It was this Detroit adventure that made bums out of most of them. They had drinking orgies almost every night at their house, and the crap games took their money.

The gang controlled its individual members, particularly when the group was together. As individuals, and in other group relationships they were not so bad, but in the gang they tried to act as tough as possible. The man who danced, who went out with girls, or who was well-mannered was ostracized. Charlie used to act hard-boiled, and he even wore his cap so that it made him look tough. Ellman, who liked to give the impression that he was a ruffian, was going with a girl on the sly. When he was with the gang he was one of the meanest fellows in it, but when he went out with his girl he was very courteous, quitting his loud talk and dropping his braggadocian air.

In the last few years the gang has disintegrated. There has been a tendency for its members to be incorporated into the more conventional activities of society. The majority of them seem to have become more settled in their mode of life. Some have moved away. Even the fellows who have changed, however, are still pretty low under the polished surface. Gang habits and influences still persist.

---

3. Stanley, the Jack-Roller

Clifford R. Shaw, *The Jack-Roller: A Delinquent Boy's Own Story* (Chicago: University of Chicago Press, 1930), pp. 47–53, 65–70, 84–86, 95–100. Reprinted by permission of University of Chicago Press.

STARTING DOWN GRADE[1]

To start out in life, everyone has his chances —some good and some very bad. Some are born with fortunes, beautiful homes, good and educated parents; while others are born in ignorance, poverty, and crime. In other words, Fate begins to guide our lives even before we are born and continues to do so throughout life. My start was handicapped by a no-good, ignorant, and selfish stepmother, who thought only of herself and her own children.[2]

As far back as I can remember, my life was filled with sorrow and misery. The cause was my stepmother, who nagged me, beat me, insulted me, and drove me out of my own home. My mother died when I was four years old, so I never knew a real mother's affection. My father remarried when I was five years of age. The stepmother who was to take the place of my real mother was a rawboned woman, devoid of features as well as emotions. She was of Polish stock, and had the habits and customs of the people of the Old World. She came to America when about thirty years old; was married at the time, and had seven children. Her husband was in ill health and he died soon after arriving in Chicago. After burying her husband, she found herself without financial resources for herself and children. Realizing her predicament

1. This is the first chapter of Stanley's "own story" of his experiences in truancy and delinquency. Aside from a number of corrections in punctuation, the story is presented precisely as it was written by the boy. He is also entirely responsible for the organization of the material into chapters, and suggested all of the chapter headings with the exception of that of Chapter X. The sincerity of the story cannot be questioned. Through our numerous personal contacts with Stanley during the last five years we are convinced that the story reveals his fundamental attitudes and typical reactions to the various situations in which he has lived. Furthermore, the events described in the story are confirmed throughout by official records and by information secured directly from persons who had contact with Stanley during the period in which his delinquencies occurred. The story should be read with a view to getting insight into the boy's attitudes, typical reactions, and the social and moral world in which he lived. From this standpoint, as previously indicated, rationalizations, prejudices, exaggerations are quite as valuable as objective description. [All notes in this document are in Shaw.]

2. This introductory paragraph is typical of Stanley's self-justificatory attitude toward his own problems and situations. In this paragraph and throughout the entire document, he makes a rather definite attempt to place the responsibility for his misconduct upon fate, circumstances, and other persons, particularly his stepmother. Regardless of the justifiability of his attitude, it reflects a fundamental aspect of his personality.

and the necessity of immediate action, she ventured out to find a husband, a man to support herself and her seven children; literally to slave and labor and bring home the bacon. Her venture was not so successful at first. Men were not wont to fall for her precious few charms. And, besides, did she not have seven children as an added burden?

My father was in a similar predicament, my mother having died and left three children. His thoughts went in quest of a woman to be his wife and a mother to his children. So it happened that Fate brought about a meeting of the two. A hasty courtship ensued, and in a short time they were married. My father worked for the Gas Company, and my stepmother proceeded to establish a home.

To this day I wonder how my father could have picked out such a woman for a wife. My conclusion is that she, in her desperation, used all her charm and coercion to get a man — any man who was able and inclined to work. My father, being fond of his whiskey and beer, and being in need of a mistress, became intoxicated and, thus blinded to her nature and circumstances, yielded to her coercion.

.   .   .   .   .

The stepmother favored her own children in every way. They received what luxuries were to be had, while my brother and sister and I had crumbs to pick off the table. She let her children eat at the table, and made us wait. Whenever one of her children would do a wrong they would tell her that I did it, and then I, instead of the culprit, would get the beating. My father couldn't interfere, because if he did the stepmother would threaten to leave. That would have been the best thing for his children, but of course he didn't want her to go.

Things went on this way. We fought with her because she favored her children at meals and beat us for their misdemeanors. Hard indeed it was for me to get enough to eat. Often when I would go to the store to buy food for the family, I would take a little biscuit or anything I could without my stepmother knowing it. So that much was I ahead when I got my portion at mealtime. My father worked steady and received good wages, so there was no good reason why we could not have enough to eat. But the stepmother was saving and fed her own children and let us go starved and half-naked on the street.

The stepmother also made us (brother, sister, and myself) do all the hard work in the house. And then she would beat us if we complained. That is what embittered me against her and her children. I developed a hatred against her that still lasts; a hatred that was so burning that when she would look into my eyes she would read it there, and in that way she knew my feeling. The Lord knows I tried to love her, but my nature could not stand her caresses in one of those sympathetic moods which she seldom had. Occasionally she would seem to feel sorry for her abuses and cruelty, and would ask me to kiss her; but my feelings protested. My fear and hatred made me avoid her and resent her caresses. Then she would get angry and beat me.

So I grew old enough to go out on the street. The life in the streets and alleys became fascinating and enticing. I had two close companions that I looked up to with childish admiration and awe. One was William, my stepbrother. The other one was Tony, a dear friend of my stepbrother, William. They were close friends, four years older than me and well versed in the art of stealing.

To my child-seeing eyes, I visioned Tony as a great leader in the neighborhood, and he directed his gang around with much bravado. He and William were always stealing and talking about stealing and I fell in with them as soon as I began to play around in the neighborhood.

Tony was a squatty boy, rough features, closely set eyes, and a body that bespoke strength and ruggedness. With his strength and fighting ability, he maintained leadership over his gang. He was also daring and courageous. I remember vividly how awed I was by his daring in stealing and fighting. These things made him a guy to be looked up to and respected in the neighborhood.

Tony liked his whiskey and in our neighborhood one could find as many as four or five saloons in one block in those days. He would dare me to drink and I would, although it burned my throat. I was what they call "game" and I just swallowed it without a word, to maintain that high distinction which I was openly proud of.

Tony had two sisters who always played with us and went on our stealing adventures. They could steal as good as any boy. Also they had sex relations openly with all the boys in the neighborhood. I remember how the boys boasted that they had had sex relations with each of them. All the boys talked about it and the girls didn't care; they seemed to be proud of it and expect it. The funny thing about it was that Tony knew all about his sisters and their behavior and only made merry about it.

The boys in the gang teased me about Tony's sisters, asking me how many times I had had sex relations with them. Even the girls would talk to me about sex things, put their arms around me, and touch my body. At first I was too young to know what it all meant, but I soon learned and developed many sex habits, like masturbation and playing with girls.

Tony didn't work, but made his money by stealing, and he made lots of it for a boy of his age.

My stepmother sent me out with William (my stepbrother) to pick rags and bottles in the alleys. She said that would pay for my board and make me more useful than fretting and sulking at home. I did not mind that in the least. In fact, I enjoyed it, because I was at least out of the old lady's reach. I began to have a great time exploring the whole neighborhood — romping and playing in the alleys and "prairies," gathering rags, bones, and iron, and selling them to rag peddlers. This romping and roaming became fascinating and appealed to my curiosity, because it was freedom and adventure. We played "Indian" and other games in the alleys, running through the old sheds and vacant houses. Then we gathered cigarette "buttses" along the street and took them to the shed, where we smoked and planned adventure. I was little and young, but I fell in with the older guys. Outside, in the neighborhood, life was full of pleasure and excitement, but at home it was dull and drab and full of nagging, quarreling, and beating, and stuffy and crowded besides.

.   .   .   .

One day my stepmother told William to take me to the railroad yard to break into box-cars. William always led the way and made the plans. He would open the cars, and I would crawl in and hand out the merchandise. In the cars were foodstuffs, exactly the things my stepmother wanted. We filled our cart, which we had made for this purpose, and proceeded toward home. After we arrived home with our ill-gotten goods, my stepmother would meet us and pat me on the back and say that I was a good boy and that I would be rewarded. Rewarded, bah! Rewarded with kicks and cuffs.

After a year of breaking into box-cars and stealing from stores, my stepmother realized that she could send me to the market to steal vegetables for her. My stealing had proved to be very profitable to her, so why not make it even more profitable? I knew it was for my own good to do what she wanted me to do. I was so afraid of her that I couldn't do anything but obey. Anyway, I didn't mind stealing, because William always went with me, and that made me feel proud of myself, and it gave me a chance to get away from home.

.   .   .   .   .

[Stanley ran away from home repeatedly and, after numerous commitments to the Chicago Parental School and the Juvenile Detention Home, he was finally sent to the St. Charles School for Boys in Kane County, Illinois. He was not yet ten years old.]

I was awed by the sight of the St. Charles School for Boys,[3] for it is a beautiful landscape

3. In view of Stanley's personality, we would scarcely anticipate a favorable reaction to the formal

to gaze upon from the outside. But it is quite a different place on the inside, as I learned during fifty months of incarceration there. My formal entry consisted of a few questions regarding my birth, age, nationality, religion, and so on. At the receiving cottage I was directed to remove my clothes, which consisted of a pair of pants and a blouse — no shoes, underwear, or cap did I wear. I was so scared that I couldn't remove my scant attire, but a little help from the rough hands of a boy guard caused me to get them off in a hurry. After a bath, I received my prison suit of overalls, blouse, hard shoes, and white cap.

The institution is built or designed à la military syle,[4] so that strict observance of the

rules was necessary or punishment was due as sure as rain. Of course I knew I was in a reform school and expected discipline, having been in Chicago Parental School. But the discipline was so strict that inwardly I harbored rebellion.

For making even a little noise or even talking out loud, you would get a beating. The first night I thought I could never stand it. I got so lonesome for the city and my old pals that I couldn't sleep and cried most of the night. Everything was under pressure and forbidden.

The boys were not allowed to talk in the cottage, either at the table or in the reading room.[5] So they slipped around in their soft house-slippers, quietly and weirdly. They reminded me of dumb mutes. This everlasting quietness, without any talking from my fellow-prisoners, gave me a creepy, clammy feeling and almost drove me crazy for a few weeks.

It was soon impressed upon my mind that life in this institution was a matter of survival of the fittest, and it was hard enough for the fittest. Secretly, most of the boys stuck together against the official and against the boy captain and other boy officers. The boys had a code which is found throughout the criminal world; it is, "To squawk on a fellow-prisoner is an unpardonable sin and only the lowest characters will squawk." But there were boys who would squawk and they would usually become boy officers, so we did not trust them but harbored hatred toward them. They were not fit to be associated with decent boys. The boys had to have a secret code there to protect themselves from the guards, boy captains, and other

---

regime in St. Charles. Mr. M. H. Cone, who has been a St. Charles parole officer in the Chicago district for many years and who was responsible for the supervision of Stanley, gives the following description of the institution:

"The institution at the present time covers a tract of land of twelve hundred acres in Kane County in the Fox River Valley, one of the most picturesque regions in Illinois, being located thirty-eight miles west of Chicago on the Lincoln Highway. It is nationally known for its perfection of beauty in arrangement and equipment, being one of the show spots of the State, having a property valuation of $1,250,000.00.

"The State gives a most careful study to all beneficial factors which may enter into the moral, physical and intellectual betterment of the youth, whose attitude, in the opinion of the Court, is beyond the normal restraint of parental control. Most all forms of healthy outdoor exercise are allowed and encouraged. School and industrial training form the important part of the daily routine. The closest possible kindly supervision by night as well as by day, controls the life in every cottage. The result of this effect is shown in the co-operative activity throughout the School on the part of all interested in it or connected with it through commitment.

"In this institution Stanley served three terms, covering periods altogether of some fifty months, before he was sixteen years old. At the close of his first term, because of unsuitable conditions for a successful parole in his own home, he was given a trial on an outside farm. Here he remained but a few days. As the only recourse left, he was given a chance with his step-mother. But after a brief stay with her, he reported to me in rags, saying: 'She give me de gate.' He claimed, with good reason, 'that even the street was better than living with one who was always hollerin.'"

4. Quoting again from Mr. Cone: "The two out-

standing features at the St. Charles School are order and obedience. Because it teaches obedience and promotes discipline, military training is a necessity, being carried on to a high point of efficiency. With this training goes an appeal to all that is best in the future citizen. He is taught reverence and respect for the flag of his country so that his conduct may be in accord with its ideals."

5. Quoting again from Mr. Cone's record: "In order to avoid unnecessary noise and confusion in a cottage, where as many as fifty or sixty boys are housed, conversation is prohibited. Also this restriction is a means of establishing habits of obedience and order in the boys who are so much in need of proper discipline and restraint."

officials. A squawker is usually a goodie-good boy and finds life miserable, for he is maligned by the other boys until he turns to their desires or he gets protection from the house father and becomes a boy officer.

.   .   .   .   .

The institution has too much discipline. Every time you turn around you break a rule. So you are always in fear of doing something wrong, of breaking a rule and then getting a bawling out or some form of punishment. I was punished many times, often for trivial things, and many times because I wouldn't squawk, and there grew up in me a hatred against these enemies; a hatred that still burns. I still remember the times that I was kicked and cuffed, and these memories shall always live with me.

The different forms of punishment were beatings, bawling out, being deprived of food and sleep, muscle grinders, squats, haunches, benders, etc. In muscle grinders the victim gets down, stretches out his toes and hands, and then goes up and down for an hour. It soon tires one out. In squats you put your hands behind the neck, then raise and lower yourself, bending the knees. An hour of this will leave anyone exhausted. In haunches, you stand on tiptoes, arms outstretched, and raise and lower the body. Ten minutes of this and you'll do anything to be relieved. In benders you touch the floor with tips of fingers, without bending knees. One hour of this will cure any disease. Polishing the floor for hours while you are resting the weight of the body on the tips of the toes is another form of punishment. All of these are often accompanied with clouts and general razzing.

.   .   .   .   .

There was lots of sex perversions in the form of masturbation and sodomy committed in one of the cottages. The bullies would attack the younger boys in the dormitories and force them to have relations. Some of the boys caught venereal diseases and had to be treated. That was very easy in a place like that, where there were a lot of boys living together in close quarters, especially where the older boys mingle with the younger ones. The younger ones get all the bad habits of the older boys, and sex habits are very common in every institution where the boys or men are confined. I've seen lots of it. I knew little boys who had sex relations with four or five older boys every night. It was easy in the dormitory to slip into another boy's bunk. They separate the boys by their weight, and that puts young fellows in with oldtimers, who are little but well educated in crime. The oldtimer stands as a hero and impresses his superiority on the younger boys, who are always ready to admire a brave crook. As a child in St. Charles, I looked up to the fellows who had done deeds of daring in a criminal line. I wanted to go out and do something worthy of commendation too. While in my cottage I met young crooks and old crooks, and began to think I was a pretty wise crook and began to tell lies about my exploits to make a good impression on my fellow-prisoners.

.   .   .   .   .

[After being released from St. Charles the third time, Stanley worked in a factory for a short time but soon, in his own words, "was down and out again." Ed.]

I began to look shabby and dirty, so I went to the Working Boys' Home and told them my story. They took pity on me and took me in and told me I could live there, and they got me a job the next morning. I worked at this job just one week. I had the habit of going to poolrooms at night and staying quite late. That was contrary to the rules of the Home, so they bawled me out and I resented it. They bawled me out twice, and at the end of the week I drew my check, quit my job, and ran away from the Home.

I went immediately to the News Alley, and there met an old pal that I had become acquainted with in St. Charles. I showed him the bank roll, and that strengthened our friendship considerably. So we started to blow it in. I was lord of all for a few days. We had our "wild women," went to movies, and had plenty to eat. We also shot crap, which is the term of the underworld vernacular, and in a few days the dough was gone. This little spurt of fortune and adventure had turned my head. Now I wanted a good time. I had tasted the life and found it sweet. But I was in a predicament, for I had no money, and you can't enjoy life without dough. My buddy, being an old "jackroller," suggested "jack-rolling" as a way out of the delima. So we started out to "put the strong arm" on drunks. We sometimes stunned the drunks by "giving them the club" in a dark place near a lonely alley. It was bloody work, but necessity demanded it — we had to live.

As I'd walk along Madison Street there'd always be some man to stop me and coax me into having sex relations with him. My friend and I used this little scheme to entice men into a room to rob them. This very day a fellow stopped me and asked for a match. I accommodated him, and he started a conversation. He was about eight years my senior, and big and husky. He said he was a foreman in a machine shop, and when I said I was out of work, he promised to get a job for me at his shop. He invited me to have supper with him up in his room, which was built for light housekeeping. He was a kind guy, with a smile and a winning way, so I went up to have supper on his invitation. We ate, and then he edged up close to me and put his arm around me and told me how much I appealed to his passions. He put his hand on my leg and caressed me gently, while he talked softly to me.

I had to wait a few minutes for my buddy to come to help put the strong arm on this man. I couldn't do it alone. My buddy had followed us all the time and was only waiting for a chance to come to my rescue. Finally, he came and we sprang into the fellow with fury. He started to grab me and my buddy dealt him a heavy blow.

We found thirteen dollars in his pockets.

Since he had tried to ensnare me I figured I was justified in relieving him of his thirteen bucks. Besides, was he not a low degenerate, and wouldn't he use the money only to harm himself further?

.   .   .   .   .

Necessity drove me to look for work, which I found in a restaurant on West Madison Street, near Halsted. I had to wash dishes from 7 A.M. until 9 P.M., with only a few hours of rest. It was hard work and poor pay, but I had to do it or beg (I was too proud to beg as a profession), borrow, or steal, and I choose the safest way, at first. I worked for four weeks at this place, and became sick. I was weak and had spells of nervousness and depression and long severe headaches. I got so weak that I had to be sent to the Cook County Hospital for a week. The doctor said I needed a rest, and that I was too young and frail to work such long hours. I was despondent and longed to die and get out of my misery. The doctor had given me a prescription, but I was too poor to have it filled — not having a cent in my pocket. Going back to Madison Street I found that my old job was taken, so I began to hang out at a poolroom with a bunch of crooks. These crooks were young boys like myself, fifteen and sixteen years old, but they were more wise to the world and tougher. There were four of us who hung around together. The other three had been in St. Charles School for Boys while I was there, and that strengthened our faith in each other. I was looked up to as the hero of the quartet because I had done fifty-six months in St. Charles, more than all the others put together. They naturally thought I was one who had a vast experience and was regarded as one might regard the big social hit of society.

These lads had been "jack-rolling" bums on West Madison Street and burglarizing homes on the North Side of the city. Knowing of my long record, they asked me to join them, so I fell in with them. We formed "The United Quartet Corporation," and started to "strong arm" "live ones" (drunks with money) and to burglarize homes.

My fellow-workers were fast guys and good pals. We were like brothers and would stick by each other through thick and thin. We cheered each other in our troubles and loaned each other dough. A mutual understanding developed, and nothing could break our confidence in each other. "Patty" was a short, sawed-off Irish lad — big, strong, and heavy. He had served two terms in St. Charles. "Maloney" was another Irish lad, big and strong, with a sunny disposition and a happy outlook on life. He had done one term in St. Charles and had already been in the County Jail. Tony was an Italian lad, fine-looking and daring. He had been arrested several times, served one term in St. Charles, and was now away from home because of a hard-boiled stepfather. We might have been young, but we sure did pull off our game in a slick way.

So we plied our trade with a howling success for two months. Sometimes we made as much as two hundred dollars in a single day. But I had a weakness for gambling, so I was always broke. West Madison Street and vicinity was a rather dark section of the city, so it was easy to strong arm the "scofflaws." There were a lot of homosexuals and we played our game on them. We would let them approach one of us, usually me, because I was so little and they like little fellows, and then I'd follow him to his room or to a vacant house to do the act. My pals would follow us to our destination, and then we'd all rob him. We made that part of our regular business. Two or three times a week we would pull off a burglary on the North Side or on the South Side.

It was springtime and we would go out to Grant Park during the day and lounge around and plan our burglaries. We always planned very carefully, and each pal had to do a certain thing. It was our absolute rule that if any pal did shrink from his part in the deal he would be branded and put out of "The United Quartet Corporation." We had a common fund

for overhead expenses. If a pal had to take a bum to dinner so he could find out if he was "ripe" (had dough) or if a pal had to rent a room to take a bum into, supposedly for homosexual purposes but really to rob him, the expenses came out of the funds.[6]

One day we were strolling along West Madison Street "taking in the sights," or, in other words, looking for "live ones." At the corner of Madison and Desplaines we saw a drunk who was talking volubly about how rich he was and that the suitcase he had in his hand was full of money. We were too wise to believe that, but we thought he might have a little money, so we would try. We tried to lure him into an alley to rob him, but he was sagacious even if he was drunk. He wanted to take me up to a room for an immoral purpose, but we decided that was too dangerous, so we let him go his way and then shadowed him.

He went on his aimless way for a long time, and we followed him, wherever he went. He finally went into a hotel and registered for a room. I saw his room number and then registered for a room on the same floor. Then we went up and worked our plans. It was not safe for all of us to go to his room, for that would arouse suspicion. One man could do the job and the others would stand by because they might be needed. But who would do the job? . . .

Putting on a bold front, I stepped into the hall and surveyed the field. Then I went to the drunk's door, my spinal nerves cold as ice. I tried the door and it was open, and that saved

6. This is an interesting illustration of an organized delinquent gang. It not only functioned according to the code of the criminal world, but developed definite techniques which were adapted to the particular delinquency in which the group specialized. These techniques usually vary with different types of offenses. For example, the techniques employed in "jack-rolling" will be quite different from those used in burglary. It should be noted that these techniques are transmitted from one person to another or from one group to another, in much the same manner that any cultural element is disseminated through society.

me a lot of work and nerve. The occupant was snoring, dead drunk, so the way was clear. I had a "sop" (blackjack) with me to take care of him if he woke up. I rifled the room, picked his pockets, and took the suitcase to our room. With great impatience we ripped it open, only to stare at a bachelor's wardrobe. That was quite a blow to our expectations, but we dragged everything out, and at the bottom our labor was rewarded by finding a twenty-dollar bill. With the thirteen dollars I had found on his person and the twenty-dollar bill, we had thirty-three dollars — eight dollars and twenty-five cents apiece. We debated what to do. Since the job would be found out and suspicion would be directed toward us, it was decided to separate for a day or two, then we would not be caught in a bunch. We divvied up the clothes. I got a pair of pants and some other small articles. Then we separated.

I got a room in a hotel on Halsted Street. The next evening while sitting in my room reading a novel, there was a loud rap on the door. Not being suspicious, I opened the door, and "a very well-known friend" greeted me with a gun in his hand. He was a policeman and ordered me to go down to the street with him, even without giving me time to get my money on the dresser. Who did I see on the street but the bum we had robbed the day before. He recognized his pants which I was wearing, and also he remotely recognized me from the day before. The policeman, being convinced that I was one of the guilty party, called the "patty wagon" and took me and the bum to the police station. Here the bum filed a complaint against me.

At the police station I was ordered to give the names of my partners. Of course I refused and said I didn't have any partners. For this remark I received a clout on the ear, and then a general beating and razzing. It was a terrible ordeal of razzing and cussing and making threats, but nothing could make me squawk on my partners. I would die first. My belief in the code was unbreakable. The code is considered by all criminals a standard to live up to, and

it is an unpardonable sin to violate this code by squawking. Once a criminal violates it by turning against his partners in crime, he is branded as a rat by the underworld. One must learn to keep his mouth shut concerning other individuals when being questioned by the police or while doing time. A "rat" has been the cause of many a crook's downfall. Therefore he is the crook's worst enemy, not barring the police. I had learned when a child and in St. Charles to live up to this code. I regarded the "rat" as a snake in the grass. I was limp from the awful ordeal and filled with hatred. Seeing that I could not be forced to squawk, the guard threw me into a cell, with the parting remark, "Stay in there awhile, damn you, and you'll be glad to talk."

I lay in the dirty old cell for three or four days, harboring a peculiar revenge. I became sullen and finally became indifferent. There was no hope for me, so I just as well take things as they come, so I thought. Jail had ceased to hold any fears for me, for I was used to it. Inwardly, I felt like a hero who had won a battle single-handed. I thought I had done a great thing by stealing and standing up for my pals and therefore I was one of the going-to-be gunmen. I felt hard and began to wear a sneer on my face, and was always murmuring to myself, "To hell with the world, I should worry about a little thing like being in jail." My cell mates and the other prisoners called me the "baby bandit," and that set me up not a little.

So my trial came up in the Boys' Court. I was glad to be brought to the Boys' Court because I thought if I was to go back to the "bandhouse" I'd rather have some new scenery. I was awed by the ceremony and inwardly scared. The judge asked if the complainant was in court. He was not; in my bewilderment I lost my head and pleaded guilty. That was a great mistake, because I would have gone free otherwise, because the complainant was not there. The judge deliberated a moment and then uttered the condemning words which branded me as a convict. My "rap" was one year in the Illinois State Reformatory and a fine of one dollar.

---

4. Juvenile delinquency among Polish-American children in Chicago, 1918

William I. Thomas and Florian Znaniecki, *The Polish Peasant in Europe and America,* 2nd ed. (New York: Alfred A. Knopf, 1927), pp. 1776–1782, 1792–1797, 1800–1803, 1806–1808, 1819–1821.

. . . in so far as the child of the immigrant has any life-organization socially implanted in him in this country, this organization, while differing with regard to its practical schemes, from the traditional one and usually less complete and strong, is nevertheless still essentially identical with the latter in its most important social and moral principles. Demoralization in the proper sense of the term, *i.e.,* the decay of this life-organization, is therefore similar in its general outlines whether the individual whose moral system is decaying was brought up exclusively in the old country or partly or wholly in a Polish-American community. The process of social disorganization is continuous and increases in intensity rather than changes in character when passing from the first to the half-second and second generations.

But an entirely new side of the whole question is disclosed when we ask ourselves not how the young generation loses a life-organization that it has acquired but how it ever acquires a life-organization at all. For then it proves that, while in relatively organized and isolated Polish-American communities — particularly in provincial towns — the economically most settled and socially most active part of the population can still impart to the growing youth a certain minimum of normal and vital

principles of behavior, there is a large proportion of immigrant children — particularly in large cities — whose home and community conditions are such that their behavior is never socially regulated, no life-organization worthy of the name is ever imposed upon them. Their status is, exactly speaking, not that of demoralization — for demoralization presupposes the loss of a moral system and they never had any moral system to lose — it is simple and plain "a-morality." If personal character is the product of social education acting upon a given temperamental foundation, such individuals in the most radical cases have no character, good or bad. They are originally in a condition similar to that which, as we saw in the preceding chapter, even socially formed individuals can reach if left outside of any organized social group and subjected to destructive influences — a condition of passive or active wildness in which behavior is not controlled by social customs and beliefs but directly conditioned by temperamental tendencies and swayed by momentary moods.

Such is the fundamental significance of the cases which we are to investigate in this and the following chapter. When we have to deal with an individual who evidently had no social education and therefore no moral status to lose, our problem is not what were the negative influences which led him astray and demoralized him. Such a way of putting the problem is very common, but it implicitly rests upon the false presupposition that man has an innate system of morality which would make him socially normal if he were not subjected to external demoralizing forces. Our problem will be just the opposite, namely, given an a-moral individual following merely his impulses, what are the socially constructive influences which tend to develop in him a normal life-organization and why do they fail or succeed.[1]

1. We may, indeed, meet cases where, judging from the social conditions in which the individual has been reared, it seems as if he should have had a morality to start with. In these cases we must

92. *John Falarski.*[2] John was 13 years old when his mother died March 8th, 1915. There were 4 younger children. Mr. Falarski remarried a few weeks later but after 2 weeks his wife left him. She had him arrested for nonsupport. She said that 2 weeks after their marriage he wanted her to go out to work and she would never live with him again. He had been out of work 8 months. His brother-in-law complained that he neglected the children, did not give them the proper food and that he had seen him with other women. The father said he had a housekeeper now, so the judge gave children to him on probation. In the beginning of October the Juvenile Protective Association was notified that John was sleeping on the prairie. The visitor "found that John had been away from the house for about a week but was lurking in the neighborhood and had twice met his sisters on their way to school and had asked them to bring him food . . . [His sister wrote] 'Dear Sir: Will you pleas tire to get my brother that ran away from home. He says very bad wrods on the lady [housekeeper]. He says that he don't want to see our father any more. The lady was calling him but did not want to come. He wants to broke all the windows and doors. He digs a hole under the house and get in. He took 11 cents from me. He took my and sister's lunches and when we go to school he hits us. He takes my little brother and learns to bum. To Mr. House, From the dare little girl Sophie Falarski.' Called at home. Saw Frank. Found rooms clean. Housekeeper said other children were at school. John was away for a week on a bum but returned Sunday, Oct. 17th . . . John back again in the 7th grade and doing nicely . . .

"November 27, 1915, saw father and all of the children except John at home. The father said that he had been without a housekeeper about 2 weeks but was trying to get another. John had been gone 3 days . . . December 30, case in court . . . Last week he was picked up by the police. The day before he was picked up . . . he took a dollar from a boy on the street . . . [John said] 'I don't like to go to school; it is too hard. History I can't remember' . . . Paroled to live with father. [Good reports for some time, but then again John left home. Was rough and abusive to his sisters.] . . .

"June 13, 1916, in court. [Complaint.] . . . 'This boy stole a bicycle from a little boy in March. He also stole some bread . . . This boy is always running away from home and in winter time he sleeps in chicken coops . . . The father is a peculiar man. He is a capable man. He makes $28 a week.' Judge: 'This boy is an exceptionally bright boy' . . . [John said he made $5 when he was away. Slept 'in some hall of under steps,' lost his job because he was sent with a bundle and lost it in the car.] 'I was passing through and I knew that boy, but I did not know his name. He had a bicycle. I asked him for a ride and I had a bicycle bell and he gave me a ride for it. I took a ride and he forgot to take the bicycle and when we came back it was gone.

"Judge: Where did you put the bicycle?

"A. In front of his house . . . [Placed in the Working Boys' Home.]

"Oct. 20, 1916, in court. Officer: 'This boy set fire to his father's new building in the basement flat and burned a hole in one of the bedrooms' . . . John: 'I had trouble with my stepmother.' [Stayed only 4 days with Father Leddy. Father married again.] The first [second] wife, it developed, had been previously married . . . I understand the present stepmother goes away for 2 or 3 weeks at a time and then comes back. They used to lock the other [youngest] boy in the house and leave him alone. The stepmother refused to talk to any one when she was in here." Committed to St. Charles.

---

evidently investigate whether this presumption is justified, and if so consider the problem of the breakdown of this morality. [Notes from Thomas and Znaniecki.]

2. The names of delinquent boys and girls are fictitious.

From the *Records of the Juvenile Court of Cook County.*

93. *Joe and John Kasperek.* Mr. and Mrs. Kasperek were married in Galicia and came to Chicago in 1902. John was born 1903, Joe in 1905, Mary 1908 and Stanley 1910. Mrs. Kasperek died in 1911 and Kasperek married again in 1912. A girl was born in 1913. In July, 1913, John and Joe left home separately. After 8 days John was picked up by an officer, but Joe was gone 5 weeks. Joe had a record for repeatedly running away during the last 2 years. Once he had taken his little sister and kept her 4 days. They slept in sheds and under sidewalks. The truant officer said he had had trouble with the boys for years but would not bring them to Court because their father was too anxious to have them placed in an institution. Father and stepmother both worked, the latter leaving at 5.30 A.M., and returning at 7 P.M. The children were locked in the dirty, miserable house. She did not stay home when ordered to by the Court, but continued to work, saying she had no money for food. The officer wrote: "I always find the 2 youngest children sitting on a bench, never talk, appear frightened." John frequently stayed home and looked after the younger children, but Joe was wilder and was soon sent to an institution. The father was ordered to pay $5 a month board. This he never did and when arrested always claimed he was out of work. John was picked up later and sent to the Parental School also. The parents did not go to see the children or send them any clothes, though ordered to do so by the court. The father pretended he did not know where they were. When they were released Joe and another boy broke into a dry-goods store and stole some things. Joe skipped out of the State, but was brought back and sent to St. Charles School. John about the same time was arrested for stealing $1 from his father and leaving home.

Neighbors complained that the stepmother was neglecting the children and even mistreating them, made them all sleep on the floor, and that the house was a rendezvous for drinking people, as both father and stepmother were heavy drinkers. Joe and John were found stealing potatoes from the railroad. Dr. Healy reported Joe in general poor physical condition, enlarged tonsils and defective vision. He had run away from his father while leaving court and told the judge he did it to escape a whipping. The father said: "I do not whip him so bad." Father made $1.75 a day working in a box-factory. Mother said she worked to help pay off debts. Both boys were again paroled to their parents. The Parental School refused to receive Joe back saying he didn't need "correction," only "permanent care" and it must have been by mistake he was sent there in the first place. The family was entirely indifferent to him, neither visited him, nor provided him with anything.

Joe and John both disappeared soon. Once in mother's absence they entered house through pantry-window and took 60 cents. A man reported that he had picked up Joe, given him clean clothes and offered him a home, but he had run away again. Officer called at home one Monday: "I found Mr. Kasperek at home playing the accordion to his wife (he was perfectly sober but very sentimental). Said he worked all day Sunday so was entitled to stay home Monday." Soon he was out of work and Mrs. Kasperek was picking potatoes off the railroad tracks. The landlady said she beats her children. "There was a girl's new bicycle in the bedroom. She said he had bought it. I doubt this very much . . . Her own girl was well dressed. I censured her for not putting more clothing on the other children.

"Joe was picked up in front of Detention Home . . . had slept for 3 nights in a wagon almost in front of Detention Home. When found was almost starved, dirty and with a very sore foot. Was kept in bed for a week or 10 days. This child had a good record at the Detention Home [always behaved well when there]. Asked him why he will not stay home. He says he does not get breakfast at home.

Talked to father and mother. Both . . . have tried to do better and in a measure have succeeded, but for some reason their boys won't stay home."

John was not yet 14 years old and was sent back to Public School. He attended regularly except when it was stormy, "he had a very long walk and was always poorly clothed." Joe was released and went to school regularly too for awhile. The family moved to better rooms. Joe soon disappeared. The stepmother developed tuberculosis. At first she refused treatment but was soon so ill that she was taken to the County Hospital, where she died. John and Joe were sent to St. Charles School.

.   .   .   .   .

The documents, as we see, corroborate our assumption that in studying the delinquency of children there is no need to ask what are the factors of demoralization, for there is no morality to start with . . . A well furnished and cleanly kept house — a point on which much stress is now being laid by American social agencies — shows a certain economic stability and an interest of the woman in housekeeping but does not permit us to conclude that vital moral traditions or active educatory interests are present in the parents, nor even that strong bonds unite the marriage-group. Even the preservation of active solidarity between husband and wife does not necessarily argue in favor of their ability or willingness to educate their children. Assumptions of this kind are based upon the mistaken idea that the family (by which always the marriage-group is here meant) is by its very existence a constructive social agency and bound to have a positive educatory influence if only the parents are not completely demoralized and do not actually teach the children evil ways. In fact, the marriage-group organization is a good instrument for imparting to the young generation schemes of behavior with the help of which their life-organization can be built; but this instrument is worthless unless properly

used, *i.e.,* unless the parents have a well ordered set of schemes of behavior to impart and know how to do it. And these are precisely the weak points in an average immigrant family.

We must realize that in Polish peasant life the educatory rôle of the marriage-group was something entirely different, much richer in content and better ordered than it is here. The marriage-group was an integral part of the wider social milieu and shared its stock of traditions and schemes of behavior. The children were early made to participate in all the activities of the parents — economic, hedonistic, social, religious—and thus unreflectively absorbed and imitated their entire life-organization. Further, the parents gradually, without effort or reflection, introduced the children into the accumulated body of traditions of the community and into the present active life of the latter and thus prepared them to supplement later from the principles and examples offered by the community whatever deficiencies there might have been in their early education. The parents did not need to be expert educators nor even to be conscious of their moral standards and planfully follow an educational system. All they had to do was to act themselves in accordance with the morality of their social milieu and to mediate between the traditions and social opinion of the community and the consciousness of their children.

All this is radically changed in America. The children no longer take part in the activities of their parents. They go to school or run the streets while the parents work, or play in their own separate milieux. There is still some community of interests and occupation left between the girl and her mother but the boy has very little in common with his father. Education by action is no longer possible. And even if the boy had any opportunities of participating in his father's activities he would not gain much by it for these activities have little social meaning left in them — unless, of course, the father is one of the active builders of the Polish-American social system. Furthermore, the marriage-group is no longer the medium through which the child is introduced into the social life of his wider milieu. On the contrary, not only are his contacts with this milieu for the most part direct and independent of the selective control of his elders but he is often called to mediate between his parents and American institutions whose real meaning he may not understand any better than they, but with which he has a better superficial acquaintance. Any authority which the parents might claim as bearers of the social traditions of the wider milieu is thus definitely undermined.

Under these circumstances the immigrant's home could acquire an educatory influence only if the older generation were trained in moral ideals, if their intellectual horizon were widened, if they were taught how to follow a system of rational education and were willing to do it. In other words, reflective, voluntary, planful educational methods would have to be substituted in each home for the unreflective, spontaneous "natural" ways by which social education successfully proceeded in the Polish peasant life. But this is clearly, at the present stage of development of the lower classes in all countries and under the present economic and social conditions, for the immense majority of mankind, an unattainable aim. The immigrant would have an incomparably more difficult task in this respect than the average native American who has still a large stock of traditions and whose old unreflective educational methods still work. How large is the proportion of intelligent American homes where these traditional methods are supplemented or supplanted by a new, rational, planfully organized system of education?

If now a practically a-moral boy who has no efficient life-organization inculcated in him is put in contact with the complex life of an American city, it is only natural if he simply follows his instincts and moods, and it depends on the nature of these instincts and moods and on the values which happen to come within his reach whether he will approximately "behave himself," *i.e.,* do things which usually do not fall under the attention of the agencies maintaining public order, or will "misbehave," *i.e.,* transgress the limits of the permissible imposed by law and police ordinances and earn a reputation for wildness or even viciousness. Regular work in school or shop is not a form of life which would temperamentally appeal to him any more than to anybody else, for the habit of work requires a control over temperamental impulses which can be only implanted by social training. He may be frightened into it, if temperamentally cowardly or passive, by continuous threats of punishment, but if he thinks that he can avoid punishment it is only natural that he should be a truant during his school years and later leave every "job" after its novelty has worn off. If his home is associated with unpleasant experiences — lack of freedom, penalties deserved or undeserved, uncongenial family atmosphere — it is not strange that he should run away from home and try to avoid these unpleasant experiences, for filial love and obedience and even ordinary foresight, which would make him prefer the smaller evils at home to the greater evils awaiting him outside, are institutional, not temperamental attitudes. If he sees things which he covets displayed in shopwindows or pleasures which he enjoys to be obtained with a little money, it is perfectly natural for him to steal, burglarize or rob, since respect for property is not a matter of instinct but of long and complex social education. If he is of a fighting or revengeful disposition, there is nothing to prevent him from fighting or even killing except compassion and fear which may depend on the mood of the moment and in general require an active, socially trained imagination. If the spirit of adventure stirs in him, with or without the cooperation of dime novels and moving pictures, there is no reason in his eyes why he should not launch into the wide unknown world, full of new and marvelous experiences. There is from the standpoint of his own consciousness nothing immoral in whatever he may do, for he knows only conflicts between momentarily opposing wishes but no moral conflicts between a wish and a general norm of behavior voluntarily accepted as binding.

Of course, usually such an a-moral boy, if his temperamental impulses are not particularly strong, becomes step by step adapted to the practical conditions of life by the mere pressure of the social machinery which forces him to develop a minimum of foresight, to choose the lesser evil of work rather than the worse evil of prison or hunger, to keep away from too dangerous adventures, to imitate the example or to obey the will of other, already settled, members of society and thus to acquire a set of habits just sufficient to keep him floating with the current of social life. He does not become thereby any less a-moral, only learns to remain within the limits of the legally permitted, or more exactly, unlearns to transgress these limits. This kind of passive adaptation is prevalent among the second generation. It produces a large mass of individuals who from the social standpoint are not definitely negative, since they do not actively disturb the social order, but are simply worthless.

.   .   .   .   .

The position of a girl in an immigrant family differs from that of a boy in the fact that the claims which the family puts upon her are greater. She is supposed to be under stricter control even after school-age. She is expected to help in housework if she does not work outside, and to turn all of her earnings into the home. Moreover, the old rule prohibiting sexual relations before marriage is still enforced upon her. Thus a few remnants of the traditional life-organization are preserved for her benefit; her rearing is on the average not as a-moral as that of a boy.

But there are many exceptions. When the parents themselves are demoralized sexually the traditional rule, of course, cannot be efficiently enforced and cases are not rare when the girl is actually pushed into sexual demoralization by her parents. And even when the marriage-group keeps a minimum of respectability and the parents wish the girl to remain "straight," applying to her the old social schemes, the latter have little if any educational value, for the social meaning which they had in the old country is lost in the new conditions and the schemes are empty forms with no vital power of regulating conduct. The participation of the girl in the household activities of her mother has no constructive influence because . . . these activities have no longer the same positive significance for the mother herself that they had in the old country and because the feeling of familial solidarity which made individual cooperation in family affairs interesting has for the most part disappeared. Therefore also the claim of the parents to the girl's earnings seems no longer socially justified and is apt to appear to the girl's individualized consciousness as unjust exploitation. It was perfectly normal for a girl in the old country to turn over all her earnings to her father or mother, but then she knew that these earnings went toward her future dowry or marriage outfit, and even if the family was too poor to give her a dowry — it was never too poor to make an outfit — she was positively interested in keeping its economic standing above the level of misery, for its standing was her own standing as well. All this is lost here. Finally, the demand of sexual purity was there really a demand of the most vital importance. A girl who lost her "virginal wreath" discredited for ever herself and to a certain degree also her family in the eyes of the community and impaired or even destroyed her chances of marriage, i.e., the only possible form of normal life in her own eyes and in those of her relatives and acquaintances. The possibility of her actions remaining a secret was exceedingly small, and she knew it. The only course left to her under normal conditions was to leave for the city or for a foreign country, which meant breaking all the strongest and most deeply implanted social ties. Whereas here the weakness of social control, the feeling of personal independence early developed by the numerous contacts outside of home, the innumerable suggestions of sexual life pervading the city atmosphere and — perhaps most of all — the looseness of sexual mores in the immigrant community, all cooperate in depriving sexual relations before marriage not only of most of their traditional social "badness" but even of any really deep personal importance. The whole matter acquires the character of an incident, important only when either resulting in pregnancy and childbirth or when leading to a more or less lasting life-policy — concubinage, with possible marriage later, or a prostitute's career.

Under these circumstances the rulings to which the girl is subjected at home — and which are certainly neither rationally explained to her nor tactfully suggested — appear often arbitrary and tyrannical, and not infrequently, instead of helping to restrain her instincts, stir her to a more radical revolt and from merely a-moral make her distinctly anti-moral.

99. Stella Kurowska. Stella was 15 years old when she told this story to the Juvenile Court: "On the night of June 7, 1916, about 8 o'clock Helen Sikowska and I were standing at the corner . . . Mike and Tomczak and another Mike came along in an automobile and Helen asked them for a ride. We went quite a ways, and then Tomczak said he wanted to [have intercourse with] me. He said if we did not do it he would not take us home . . . They drove up in front of a saloon and all three of the fellows went in the saloon and stayed there about one hour. Helen and I sat in the car and waited for them. They came out and we started back for home. We drove for a ways, and when we came to a place where there was no houses they stopped the machine and said it was broke. Tomczak went to sleep. Mike, the driver of the car, got out and took me with him and walked me over the prairie. There he knocked me down and . . . did something bad to me . . . Then they took us back home."

Mike was a chauffeur, 19 years old. His parents had died when he was young and a friend, a married woman, had cared for him since. She stated that he had never been in any sort of trouble before and was always a good boy. Others corroborated this.

Shortly after Helen Sikowska, who was 18 years old, ran away from home sending word to her mother that she would not return. The home conditions were excellent and the mother said that Helen had always been a good girl until she met Stella.

.   .   .   .

102. Marien Stepanek. Marien was arrested for acting "obstreperous" with another girl in a railway waiting room. She had no underclothing on when arrested [in June]. She was 16 years old, had left home before Easter and had been going much to shows and moving picture theaters. She told a police woman that she had been drugged on the North side and carried to a room by two men on different nights. She had been in the habit of receiving mail at the General Delivery and frequented the Boston Store with a man about 45 years of age whom she claimed was her husband.

Marien said she had "no fault to find" with her home, her father and mother were kind to her but she met a lady by the name of Le Mar and told her she lived in Milwaukee. "And she asked me to live with her, said she was getting a divorce from her husband, and I stayed with her for awhile . . . assisted her with the work." When asked where she met her girl friend she said: "Met her at the Boston Store and did not want to talk to her. And she came up to me and she wanted me to fix it up for her. Said she wanted to get away from home and said I should call up her mother and tell her that she was doing housework and told me to talk as if I was an elderly lady, and I went and did that."

The following letter was received from her while she was away: "Dear Mother, I am feeling fine. Everything is all right, don't worry about me. I am leading high life because I am an actress. I got swell clothes and everything, you wouldn't know me. I had Clara down town one day I was out with the manager.

She had a nice time . . . I never had just nice times in all my life. Everybody says that I am pretty. I paid 65 dollars for my suit and 5 dollars had [hat], 6 dollars shoe 3 gloves 2 dollar underwar 5 dollar corest. Know I have hundred dollars in the bank but I want you to write a letter and say youll forgive me for not telling the truht but I will explain better when I see you and will return home for the sake of the little ones. I will bring a hundred dollars home to you and will come home very time I can its to expensive to liv at a hotel now sent the letter to me this way Genarel Devilery Miss Marion Stephan."

Her father testified: "After Easter got a letter from her something like that one only more in it. She was rich and everything else, which is not so. So she says answer me quick as you can because I go to Milwaukee tomorrow. And I answer it right away to come home as soon as possible. Thought maybe the letter would reach her and heard nothing more until 3 weeks ago and then this letter come and I begging her to come home and be a good girl. She come home and asked if wanted to stay home now and she feel very happy that she is home and thought maybe she would behave . . . Next day she said she was going for her clothes . . . and I says I go with you. And I could not go and left my boy and girl to go with her Sunday. And she left them in the park and did not come home. Then she was back again Tuesday and in the evening when I come home from work she was not there . . ."

Marien said she kept company with men for quite awhile, giving three names, but she denied immoral relations with any of them. She said she had been going out with another fellow "but he is a gentleman in every way."

"Court: With whom have you had immoral relations?

"A. Cannot remember.

"Q. Have you been to a hotel at any time since you have been away?

"A. Been to a hotel one time with Helen . . . and a girl, Freda Jones. She lives under a different name, Freda Jarvis . . .

"Q. Did you hear anybody offer $2 at this hotel?

"A. I heard that what Freda said. She was kind of sore . . . She said about it: "What they think I am anyhow, stingy fools. Think I am doing anything for $2 . . . Helen and I laughed at her . . .

"Q. What did you understand by that?

"A. I understood what she meant by it . . .

"Q. What did you mean by the statement that you are leading a 'high life'?

"A. Meant had been to cabarets and dance halls. Been going to Morrison Ball room . . . and I went to the 'Booster's Club,' that's the old Morrison place."

Marien was sent to the reform school in Geneva but released in September, as her home conditions were good.

.   .   .   .   .

The conclusion as to the significance of sexual immorality in girls of the second generation is perfectly obvious. Illicit sexual tendencies are simply a component — sometimes predominant, oftener subordinate — of a powerful desire for new experience and for general excitement which under the given conditions cannot be satisfied in socially permitted ways. It depends in some measure on individual temperament whether in a given case this desire for new experience will be successfully counteracted by a desire for security which tends to make the girl stay in the beaten path and follow the rules laid down by society. But this depends also, perhaps in a still larger measure, on the question what attractions are offered by society to those who stay in the beaten path. And these attractions are certainly neither many nor strong for the daughter of a Polish immigrant. First school, which to her mind does not lead anywhere, is not a means to any definite end. Then dependent and meaningless housework at home or tiresome shopwork with no profit to herself. Later marriage and, after a few short new experiences, continuation of the same meaningless work from day to day without any new outlook for the future, with children as the only important genuine interest — and this has to be bought at the cost of pain, ceaseless toil, increased poverty and diminished chances for personal pleasure. There is little response at any period of her life from parents, husband or children, little recognition, for in a loose community recognition does not come as a reward of "sterling moral qualities" and "honest labor" but goes to all kinds of superficial brilliancy and show.

Perhaps the girl would settle down unrevoltingly to this steady life, however dull, if the apparent possibilities of an entirely different life, full of excitement, pleasure, luxury and showing-off were not continually displayed before her eyes in an American city. Shop windows, theaters, the press, street life with its display of wealth, beauty and fashion, all this forms too striking a contrast to the monotony of the prospect which awaits her if she remains a "good girl." If she felt definitely and irremediably shut off from this "high life" by practically impassable class barriers, as a peasant girl in Europe feels, she might look at all this show of luxury as upon an interesting spectacle with no dream of playing a rôle in it herself. But even aside from the idea of democracy — which though it does not mean much to her politically, teaches her to think that the only social differences between people are differences of wealth — she feels that some small part at last of this gorgeousness actually is within her reach, and her imagination pictures to her indefinite possibilities of further advance in the future. Sooner or later, of course, she will be forced back into her destined channel by society, by the state, by economic conditions, will be forcibly "reformed" and settled, not into a satisfied, positively moral course of life but to a more or less dissatisfied acceptance of the necessary practical limitations of her desires and of the more or less superficial rules of *decorum*. But before her dreams are dispelled she tries to realize them as far as she can. We have here, of course, only one specification of the unrest which characterizes America and American women.

Miriam Van Waters

In 1920 Miriam Van Waters (b. 1887) was appointed first superintendent of El Retiro School for Girls, a Los Angeles County home for semi-delinquent girls. There she created a "society of inmates" by emphasizing group participation in government and self-expression through plays, essays, and a school newspaper.

---

1. Delinquent girls talk about their problems, 1926

Letters to Miriam Van Waters from girls in the El Retiro School, 1926, Van Waters Papers, Schlesinger Library, Radcliffe College.

[Dear Dr. Van Waters]

If I express my opinions about the things going on in this world. The first thing I would like to say is something about the schools and other reformatories for boys and girls. I think that boys and girls should not be taken away from their mothers and fathers so frequently as they are being taken. Especially boys and girls that have no fathers. Their poor mothers left to grieve. I think that nine out of ten would do right if they were given more chances for their mothers sake. And I do not think they should be *put* in schools or other reformatories for every little thing they do. I think we the boys and girls of America should have at least one chance and if that is taken advantage of then it is different according to home conditions. Our mothers suffered for us. Why must we be taken away. My own mother has suffered *hell* and no doubt many others have. On account of courts, always courts. I think that if

America is a *free* country lets have *Liberty absolutely.*

.   .   .   .   .

[Dear Dr. Van Waters]

There are a great many things that go to make up the unhappinesses of the young boy and girl of today.

First: children born out of wedlock is caused by the wrong kind of company and the wrong environment. The girl of today is usually led into trouble by bad companions and this is caused by sometimes the mistrust of the parents in the child. When a child knows they are not trusted they will naturally do the wrong thing.

When a boy or girl is (penned up) as you might call it, they are inclined to want worldly things and will toy to get them honorably or dishonorably.

When the parents of a girl will not permit their girl to have company at the house she will naturally meet them on corners and sneak out, whereas if the girl was allowed to have her company at home she would meet the right sort.

When a girl meets her company on the corner it usually ends up that the girl has gotten into trouble and the first thing asked of her by the parents is, Well whose fault is it? In a case like this it is the parents fault but many people never look at it this way but is talked about and when her parents try to do something about it her name is dragged down and the newspapers get hold of it and the readers class the girl as an outcast and is no good and she pays for the rest of her life. The ways this sort of thing may be prevented are: more trust in the child and the parents should be more of a companion to the children. If a girl likes to dance her mother or a good chaperon should take the girl to the best and cleanest place to dance.

There are plenty of good clean amusements to be found everywhere. The girl should be allowed to go to the place suitable to her age.

Second: Young Marriages

Girls should not marry ranging from the ages of 15 to 20 then they know more of what they are doing, that is if she has reached the age of 19 or 20. Usually the girl who gets married around that age leaves school without an education and know how to do nothing worth while in case they have to help make a living.

Usually young marriages end up with a divorce and if not they do not get along together and when children come they are usually not wanted and are sometimes neglected because of the mother having to work. And then the children will grow up not having an education and are usually nothing but street urchins because the mother and father did not have an education themselves and did not know the value of it until too late.

If these things are to be prevented their should be more knowledge given on the value of education. Young marriages should also be prevented if possible by keeping the girl and boy interested in the school, and to keep them amused in other ways besides dances and all night parties — etc, and also not to intermarry.

---

2. Culture for delinquent youths

Miriam Van Waters, *Youth in Conflict* (New York: New Republic, 1925), pp. 140, 144–145.

To-day the some two hundred thousand delinquent boys and girls in correctional schools, hundreds of thousands before courts and social agencies, know little about religion, art and science. The young people in dance-halls, cabarets, resorts, millions who throng city streets in a ceaseless, unhappy quest for "something to do" have certainly not been reached by any valid adventure of the spirit.

.   .   .   .   .

If any one doubts that subject matter and attitudes of religion, art and science are almost unknown to average youth, let him try the experiment of making a list of questions for boys and girls of average intelligence:

"What are the lessons of the Sermon on the Mount?"

"Of what spiritual meaning is baptism, marriage, a funeral service, Easter, Christmas?"

"Explain: 'Blessed are the pure in heart for they shall see God.' "

"What did Christ mean when he said: 'Unless ye become as little children ye cannot enter the kingdom of Heaven.' "

" 'He that is without sin among you let him cast the first stone.' "

"Name a symphony you have heard."

"Name one great composer of music (who did not write jazz)."

"Tell the story of the love of Dante for Beatrice."

"Why was Hamlet unhappy?"

"What did Thomas Jefferson say about rebellion and conflicts in American public life?"

"Why are plants green?"

"Name one star, besides Venus and Mars."

"How can we be called children of the sun?"

"How is human life reproduced?"

Let each one collect these answers for himself, and make others, far simpler questions. He will be surprised, even stunned at the result.

On the other hand do not attribute it to dullness of the children. Let them prepare a list for you:

"Who won the last automobile championship race?"

"Who are the five most married moving picture stars?"

"Who wrote the Love Bird?"

"Name the eight best jazz orchestras in town."

"What is the income of Rudolf Valentino?" And so on.

Clearly certain sections of community thought and action get themselves expressed to youth far better than others. Culture and virtue among adults are paying too high a price for their distinction, their isolation. Unless means of communication are found for opinions and ideas of creators among the human race, modern youth will adopt the religion of paganism, and moral codes of the daily press.

Part Five   Child Labor

"There is scarcely one subject in the whole range of social reform more important than that of child labor," wrote W. D. P. Bliss in the *Encyclopedia of Social Reform* (New York, 1898). In retrospect much of the history of modern American reform can be written in terms of the struggle to curb child labor. The movement held the attention of Americans from the 1880's to the depression of the 1930's, when emphasis shifted from ending child labor to securing youth employment.

Until the 1880's child labor was considered both economically and ethically valuable. Such child labor laws as existed stemmed from the efforts of educational reformers who sought to strike a balance between work and education in order to prevent pauperism and crime. The focus of the legislation was on the schooling of working children rather than on protecting them from industrial hazards and exploitation. Nevertheless, as early as the 1860's it was recognized that school attendance laws then on the books were unenforceable.

Rapid industrialization after the Civil War increased the child labor force, introduced new occupations for children, and spread child labor into new parts of the nation, especially the South. By 1900 one-third of the workers in southern mills were children. More than half of them were between ten and thirteen years of age; and many were under ten. In the absence of legislative restrictions the South repeated the experience of New England in its early period of industrialization.

The nation-wide extent of child labor became visible in 1870 when the Census Bureau established a separate category of the gainfully employed who were from ten to fifteen years of age. According to the 1870 census about one out of every eight children were employed. By 1900 approximately 1,750,000 children, or one out of six, were gainfully employed. Sixty per cent were agricultural workers; of the 40 per cent in industry over half were children of immigrant families.

Bureaus of labor statistics, founded in many states after establishment of the Massachusetts' bureau in 1869, increased information available on child labor. Despite reluctance of employers to provide information, the bureaus kept the public aware of the extent and hazards of child labor. Their influence re-enforced the popular tendency to consider child labor as an industrial problem even though most employed children worked in agriculture.

By 1899 twenty-eight states had passed some legislation regulating child labor. The laws ordinarily applied only to manufacturing and generally set the minimum age limit at twelve. A few states, however, had raised the working age to thirteen or fourteen.

The attack on child labor at the turn of the century was part of a general protest against exploitation of the working class, industrial hazards, and involuntary poverty. Robert Hunter, a New York settlement worker described a vicious circle of deprivation: poverty of parents, premature employment of children, and the children's poverty in maturity. The Roman Catholic economist, John A. Ryan, declared in 1902 that if fathers received a living wage no child under sixteen would have to work except possibly during school vacations.[1] Meanwhile a growing volume of periodical literature asserted

1. John A. Ryan, "What Wage Is a Living Wage," *Catholic World*, 75 (April 1902), 8.

that the working child was a victim rather than a self-reliant little man. Countless articles told consumers how their luxury items were manufactured. Accounts of the "slaughter of the innocents," "child slavery," and "cannibalism" in American factories pricked the conscience of the middle class.

Reformers also examined child labor from the standpoint of new biological and educational theories which held that prolongation and protection of childhood was essential to human progress. Using such ideas reformers argued that exploitation of the young undermined their biological potential as parents. In the Progressive era, this view carried special weight because of fear of race suicide. Applying the principle of evolution to child development, G. Stanley Hall defined distinct periods of growth, each with its own needs and potentials. Hall warned that outside pressures and interference with the child's natural development would not only stunt the individual but arrest the evolution of society. In 1900 the United States Census Bureau applied Hall's model to the age classification of child laborers:

"In the age period ten to fifteen occurs the transition from childhood to adolescence and normally each year included in that period marks important changes in the child's growth and development; hence in any question relating to the education and welfare of the child, a difference of only one year is significant." [2]

The "new psychology" stressed the physiological and psychological importance of play in child development just when social reformers discovered that premature toil and the absence of playgrounds deprived the children of the poor of the opportunity to play. Child labor reform and the playground movement, therefore, became two aspects of the same campaign, and both dramatized the failure of urban America to meet the needs of childhood. In *Poverty* (1904) Robert Hunter warned: "You cannot rob children of their play any more than

you can forget and neglect the children at their play, as we now do in the tenement district, without at the same time paying the penalty. When children are robbed of playtime, they too often reassert their right to it in manhood, as vagabonds, criminals, and prostitutes." [3]

John Dewey made the realization of childhood's potential a basic goal of a democratic society. Florence Kelley, secretary of the National Consumers' League, applying Dewey's concept to her campaign for the abolition of child labor, asserted that the right to childhood "follows in the existence of the Republic." [4] The argument for a decent childhood as a basic requirement of democracy appealed especially to those concerned with preservation of the nation's natural resources. Thus when Theodore Roosevelt attacked child labor in 1912, he emphasized need for "conservation" of childhood.

As the twentieth century opened, opposition to child labor became an organized crusade. Social workers, political economists, constitutional lawyers, and disinterested industrialists came together in tightly-organized state committees supported by consumers' leagues and women's clubs. In true Progressive spirit the reformers relied on exposure to arouse the public conscience, and on the leadership of informed citizen's groups to point the way to corrective legislation and effective enforcement. These attitudes were manifested by the Alabama and New York child labor committees which were formed independently of each other within the space of one year. Reverend Edgar Gardner Murphy, an Episcopalian clergyman, organized the Alabama Child Labor Committee in 1901 to mobilize public support for a bill then pending in the state legislature. The New York Child Labor Committee stemmed from a meeting of representatives of thirty-two settlement houses in New York City in 1902. The meeting, called by Lillian Wald and Florence Kelley, decided to found an organization to in-

---

2. U.S. Department of Commerce and Labor, Bureau of the Census, *Bulletin* 69 (Washington, D.C., 1907), p. 7.

3. Robert Hunter, *Poverty* (New York, 1904), p. 223.
4. Florence Kelley, *Some Ethical Gains Through Legislation* (New York, 1905), pp. 3–4.

vestigate and expose child labor conditions. The Committee succeeded in enlisting both the moral and financial support of wealthy New Yorkers. It launched the first extensive investigation into working conditions in New York City, agitated for and secured passage of the stronger child labor law of 1903 which included regulation of the street trades, launched an ambitious program of scholarships for working children, and in 1909 obtained enactment of a dangerous trades act.

The campaign for child labor reform assumed broader scope in 1904 with the organization of the National Child Labor Committee. The board of the National Committee was headed by Felix Adler and included Florence Kelley, Jane Addams, Lillian Wald, Edgar G. Murphy, Edward T. Devine, Robert W. D. De Forest, and Homer Folks. The Committee's triple goals were nation-wide investigation, campaigns for more stringent legislation, and enforcement of existing laws. From headquarters in New York City the Committee directed a national campaign with Alexander McKelway acting as special field representative for the South and Owen Lovejoy for the North. Within several years of its existence the Committee had secured the organization of local committees in every state with a child labor problem, and was cooperating with state committees as a propaganda agency and clearing house for child labor campaigns. In addition to its own pamphlets and *Child Labor Bulletin,* the Committee obtained publication outlets in *Survey, The Outlook, Arena,* and *The Annals* of the American Academy of Political and Social Science and in newspapers throughout the country. It held traveling exhibits and was the first organized reform movement to make wide use of photographic propaganda.

Until 1914, although "national" in organization, the Committee devoted its activities to reform at the state level. Aiming at uniform state laws, the Committee set up legislative standards for a minimum age of fourteen in manufacturing and sixteen in mining, documentary proof of age, a maximum eight-hour work day, and prohibition of night work. At the time of the

Committee's organization in 1904 no state had legislation meeting all these standards. By 1914 thirty-five states had a fourteen-year age limit and an eight-hour day for workers under sixteen; thirty-four states prohibited night work under age sixteen, and thirty-six states had appointed factory inspectors to enforce the laws.

Despite these legislative gains child labor remained a serious national problem because of loopholes in the laws or lapses in their enforcement. Agricultural labor was still unregulated; canneries obtained exclusion from child labor laws; domestic service, street trades, and sweat shop labor escaped regulation; and exemption clauses for children of widows and poor parents robbed southern laws of their effectiveness. In 1914, summing up a decade of the National Child Labor Committee's work, Owen Lovejoy concluded, "We have been disillusioned. More has been done than seemed possible within the period, but the field is immensely larger than was supposed." [5]

In 1914 the Committee, previously divided on the need and desirability of federal legislation, decided that the only way to obtain uniform national standards was through federal child labor legislation. After 1914, therefore, the Committee joined forces with the United States Children's Bureau and acted as an effective lobby for a national child labor law. In 1915 at the peak of the campaign for passage of the federal child labor bill the Committee used 416 newspapers and distributed more than four million pages of propaganda materials.

Passage of the Keating-Owen Act in 1916 marked the greatest triumph of the Progressive campaign against child labor. Rejection of the proposed constitutional amendment in the 1920's marked the movement's worst defeat. The story of these episodes can be followed in the documents. Here it is necessary only to point out the irony, which was not lost on the reformers, that the major reform efforts were directed toward a minority of the child labor force: children in factories and mines.

5. Owen R. Lovejoy, Annual Report for 1914, *Child Labor Bulletin,* III (November 1914), p. 9.

As already noted, agricultural workers, domestic servants, child laborers in sweat shops, and children in the street trades were overlooked by both state and federal laws. Perhaps that is why the proposed child labor amendment, which would have permitted broader and more stringent regulation than was attempted in the federal child labor laws of 1916 and 1919, encountered such fierce opposition.

One of the major difficulties of child labor reform in the early twentieth century was the cultural and economic gap between middle-class reformers and working-class parents. The reformers, in their zeal to refute the stereotype of the poor widow dependent on her little boy's earnings, may have underestimated the economic necessity of child labor among large segments of the working class. On the other hand, the support Homer Folks, Lillian Wald, Florence Kelley, and Jane Addams gave to such causes as mothers' aid, workmen's compensation, minimum wage laws, health insurance, and scholarships for poor children proved that they recognized child labor could not be ended without finding means to supplement family income. The attack on child labor was one of the converging lines of reform which, even before the Great Depression, led to realization that solving problems of childhood required comprehensive efforts to promote economic security for families.

I The Working Force

A. EXTENT AND VARIETY OF CHILD LABOR

Estimates of the number of child laborers, 1870–1930

1. The increase of child labor, 1870–1900

H. L. Bliss, "Census Statistics of Child Labor," *Journal of Political Economy*, XIII (1904–1905), 246.

Bliss pointed out that comparative census statistics on child labor for 1870–1900 were unreliable owing to variations in methods of enumeration. Since the census figures of 1890 excluded children from fourteen and one-half to sixteen years who had been included in previous censuses, there actually was an increase of child labor in 1890 instead of a decrease as shown. The figures for 1900 should also be revised upward, because enumerators for that year, unlike previous years, excluded all children who worked less than one-half time.

Number and percentage of children at work during the four census years 1870, 1880, 1890, and 1900.

Census years and classification of ages	Males	Females	Total
1870			
Total children, 10 to 15 years, inclusive	2,840,200	2,764,169	5,604,369
Number of above at work	548,064	191,100	739,164
Percentage of above at work	19.30	6.91	13.16
1880			
Total children, 10 to 15 years, inclusive	3,376,114	3,273,369	6,649,483
Number of above at work	825,187	293,169	1,118,356
Percentage of above at work	24.44	8.96	16.82
1890			
Total children, 10 to 14 years, inclusive	3,574,787	3,458,722	7,033,509
Number of above at work	400,586	202,427	603,013
Percentage of above at work	11.21	5.85	8.57
1900			
Total children, 10 to 15 years, inclusive	4,852,427	4,760,825	9,613,252
Number of above at work	1,264,411	485,767	1,750,178
Percentage of above at work	26.05	10.23	18.25

2. The extent of child labor, 1900–1930

Grace Abbott, *The Child and the State* (Chicago: University of Chicago Press, 1938), I, 265–267.

With the organization of the National Child Labor Committee in 1904, many state laws were greatly improved in the first decade of the twentieth century. But in spite of the new legislation the number of working children was very large. Considering only those employed in nonagricultural occupations, the census enumeration of 1900 showed 186,358 children between ten and thirteen years of age and 501,849 fourteen and fifteen years of age. In 1910 the number of children so employed who were ten to thirteen years of age was 98,525, while there were 466,338 fourteen and fifteen years of age.

While there was a decrease in the number of children employed in nonagricultural occupations, toward which the laws were directed, a large number ten to fourteen years of age were still reported employed in 1910. Child labor reformers were discouraged by the showing made, particularly as the method by which the facts are secured from parents by temporary and usually untrained census enumerators results in an understatement of the number of employed children.

.   .   .   .   .   .

By 1920 the number of children reported to the census enumerators as gainfully employed in occupations other than those connected with agriculture was 49,766 in the ten- to thirteen-year group and 366,918 fourteen and fifteen years of age.

The decline continued during the next decade. The census report for 1930 showed 29,765 children ten to thirteen years of age in nonagricultural occupations and 167,856 fourteen and fifteen years of age. This meant that the number of children gainfully employed, including those in agriculture per 1,000 of the total num-

ber of children ten to thirteen years of age had dropped from 121 in 1900 to 24 in 1930, and of those fourteen and fifteen years of age from 309 to 92 per 1,000 of that age group. While for the reason previously given the census reports give an understatement of the number of working children, they probably accurately reflect the trend. That child labor is numerically a much less serious problem in the United States than in Great Britain both the school and census returns bear evidence.

3. Children employed in manufacturing, 1920

Adapted from United States Children's Bureau, *Child Labor Facts and Figures,* Pub. No. 197 (Washington, D.C., 1930), p. 18.

Children 10 to 15 years of age, inclusive, employed as laborers and semiskilled operatives in manufacturing and mechanical industries, 1920

(all branches of the textile industry grouped together).

Textiles	54,840
Iron and steel	12,904
Clothing	11,767
Lumber and furniture	10,535
Food	9,934
Shoe	7,645
Building[a]	7,478
Clay, glass, stone	4,968
Cigar and tobacco	4,938
Printing and publishing	4,028
Chemical	2,153
Rubber	2,106
Electrical supply	1,892
Paper box	1,790
Paper pulp	1,273
Tanneries	781
Other metal	3,766
All other industries	21,519

[a] In addition 6,980 apprentices are reported in this industry. [Note in *Child Labor Facts and Figures.*]

4. Prevalence of child labor by region, 1920

Testimony of Grace Abbott at U.S. Congress, Senate Hearings before a Subcommittee

of the Committee on the Judiciary, *Child Labor Amendment,* 67 Cong., 1 Sess. (1923), pp. 31–32.

Prevalence of child labor by region, 1920.

Region[a]	Total	Children 10 to 15 years of age, inclusive						
		Engaged in gainful occupations						
				Agricultural		All other		
		Number	Per cent	Number	Per cent	Number	Per cent	
United States	12,502,582	1,060,858	8.5	647,309	5.2	413,549	3.3	
New England	768,131	59,239	7.7	3,053	.4	56,186	7.3	
Middle Atlantic	2,397,736	131,541	5.5	8,922	0.4	122,619	5.1	
East North Central	2,312,711	100,801	4.4	23,425	1.0	77,376	3.3	
West North Central	1,477,363	57,906	3.9	29,722	2.0	28,184	1.9	
South Atlantic	1,911,574	273,981	14.3	214,906	11.2	59,075	3.1	
East South Central	1,267,275	221,342	17.5	196,620	15.5	24,722	2.0	
West South Central	1,449,764	184,267	12.7	158,187	10.9	26,080	1.8	
Mountain	393,563	15,612	4.0	8,950	2.3	6,662	1.7	
Pacific	524,465	16,169	3.1	3,524	.7	12,645	2.4	

[a] The regions break down as follows: New England — Maine, New Hampshire, Vermont, Massachusetts, Rhode Island, Connecticut; Middle Atlantic — New York, New Jersey, Pennsylvania; East North Central — Ohio, Indiana, Illinois, Michigan, Wisconsin; West North Central — Minnesota, Iowa, Missouri, North Dakota, South Dakota, Nebraska, Kansas; South Atlantic — Delaware, Maryland, D.C., Virginia, West Virginia, North Carolina, South Carolina, Georgia, Florida; East South Central — Kentucky, Tennessee, Alabama, Mississippi; West South Central — Arkansas, Louisiana, Oklahoma, Texas; Mountain — Montana, Idaho, Wyoming, Colorado, New Mexico, Arizona, Utah, Nevada; Pacific — Washington, Oregon, California.

5. Comparative census statistics of child labor, 1910–1930

U.S. Bureau of the Census, *Sixteenth*

Census of the United States: 1940. Population. Comparative Occupation Statistics for the U.S. 1870 to 1940 (Washington, 1943), pp. 73–78.

	1910	1920	1930
Total child population 10–13	7,259,018	8,594,872	9,622,492
Total gainfully employed	895,976	378,063	235,328
Percentage of total population gainfully employed	12.3	4.4	2.4

Occupations	Total	Per cent of total working force	Total	Per cent of total working force	Total	Per cent of total working force
Agriculture	798,543	89[a]	328,297	90	205,563	90
Total nonagricultural	97,433	11	49,766	10	29,765	10
Forestry and fishing	947	–	385	–	222	–
Extraction of minerals	2,358	–	647	–	137	–
Manufacturing and mechanical industries	33,391	–	9,733	–	4,761	–
Transportation and communication	2,679	–	1,899	–	583	–
Trade	17,540	–	17,333	–	14,746	–
Public service	63	–	153	–	143	–
Professional service	578	–	637	–	969	–
Domestic and personal service	32,635	–	12,172	–	7,501	–
Clerical occupations	7,242	–	6,807	–	703	–

[a] Approximate percentage.

Apprenticeship under the Black Codes

1. South Carolina, 1865

"An Act to Establish and Regulate the Domestic Relations of Persons of Color . . . ," *Statutes at Large of South Carolina,* XIII (Columbia, 1866), 291–295.

XV. A child, over the age of two years, born of a colored parent, may be bound by the father, if he be living in the District, or in case of his death, or absence from the District, by the mother, as an apprentice, to any respectable white or colored person, who is competent to make a contract; a male until he shall attain the age of twenty-one years, and a female until she shall attain the age of eighteen years.

XVI. Illegitimate children, within the ages above specified, may be bound by the mother.

XVII. Colored children, between the ages mentioned, who have neither father nor mother living in the District in which they are found, or whose parents are paupers, or unable to afford to them maintenance, or whose parents are not teaching them habits of industry and honesty, or are persons of notoriously bad character, or are vagrants, or have been, either of them, convicted of an infamous offence, may be bound as apprentices by the District Judge, or one of the Magistrates, for the aforesaid term.

XVIII. Males of the age of twelve years, and females of the age of ten years, shall sign the indenture of apprenticeship, and be bound thereby.

XIX. When the apprentice is under these ages, and in all cases of compulsory apprenticeship, where the infant refuses assent, his signature shall not be necessary to the validity of the apprenticeship. The master's obligation of apprenticeship, in all cases of compulsory apprenticeship, and cases where the father or mother does not bind a child, shall be executed in the presence of the District Judge, or one of the Magistrates, certified by him, and filed in the office of the Clerk of the District Court.

.   .   .   .   .

XXII. The master or mistress shall teach the apprentice the business of husbandry, or some other useful trade or business, which shall be specified in the instrument of apprenticeship; shall furnish him wholesome food and suitable clothing; teach him habits of industry, honesty and morality; govern and treat him with humanity; and if there be a school within a convenient distance, in which colored children are taught, shall send him to school at least six weeks in every year of his apprenticeship, after he shall be of the age of ten years: *Provided,* That the teacher of such school shall have the license of the District Judge to establish the same.

XXIII. The master shall have authority to inflict moderate chastisement and impose reasonable restraint upon his apprentice, and to recapture him if he depart from his service.

XXIV. The master shall receive to his own use the profits of the labor of his apprentice. The relation of master and apprentice shall be dissolved by the death of the master, except where the apprentice is engaged in husbandry, and may be dissolved by order of the District Judge, when both parties consent, or it shall appear to be seriously detrimental to either party. In the excepted case, it shall terminate at the end of the year in which the master died.

XXV. In cases of the habitual violation or neglect of the duties herein imposed on the master, and whenever the apprentice is in danger of moral contamination by the vicious conduct of the master, the relation of master and apprentice may be dissolved by the order of the District Judge; and any person shall have the right to complain to the District Judge that the master does not exercise proper discipline over his apprentice, to the injury of his neighbors; and if upon investigation, it shall be so found, the relation between the parties shall be dissolved.

XXVI. In cases of alleged violation of duty, or of misconduct on the part of the master or apprentice, either party may make complaint to a Magistrate, who shall summon the parties before him, inquire into the causes of complaint, and make such order as shall be meet, not extending to the dissolution of the relation of the parties; and if the master be found to be in default, he shall be fined not exceeding twenty dollars and costs; and if the apprentice be in default, he may be corrected in such manner as the Magistrate shall order. A frivolous complaint made by either party shall be regarded as a default.

XXVII. In cases in which the District Judge shall order the apprentice to be discharged for immoderate correction, or unlawful restraint of the apprentice, the master shall be liable to indictment, and, on conviction, to fine and imprisonment, at the discretion of the Court, not exceeding a fine of fifty dollars, and imprisonment of thirty days; and, also, to an action for damages, by the apprentice.

---

2. Former owners of slave children given preference in their apprenticeship, Alabama, 1866

A. J. Walker, ed., *Revised Code of Alabama* (Montgomery, 1867), p. 347.

Sheriffs, justices of the peace, and all other civil officers of the several counties in this state, must report to the probate courts of their respective counties, at any time, all minors under the age of eighteen years, within their respective counties, beats, or districts, who are orphans without visible means of support, or whose parents have not the means, or who refuse to provide for and support such minors; and thereupon such probate court must apprentice such minor to some suitable and competent person, on such terms as the court may prescribe, having a particular care to the interest of such minor; but if such minor be a child of a freedman, the former owner of such minor shall have the preference, when proof is made that he is a suitable person for that purpose, and such judge of probate must make a record of all the proceedings in such case, for which he shall be entitled to a compensation of one dollar, to be paid by the master.

3. Maryland

"Laws in Relation to Freedmen Compiled by Command of Major General O. O. Howard, Commissioner, Bureau of Refugees, Freedmen and Abandoned Lands" in U.S. Senate, *Executive Document No. 6,* 39th Cong. 2d Sess. (Washington, 1867), pp. 187–188.

Sec. 31. The several orphans' courts of this State shall, upon information being given to them, summon before them the child of any free negro, and if it shall appear upon examination before such court that it would be better for the habits and comfort of such child that it should be bound as an apprentice to some white person, if a male till he is of the age of twenty-one years, or if a female till she is of the age of eighteen years.

Sec. 32. The sheriff or any constable of the county or city shall serve any process issued by the orphans' court to bring the child of any free negro before the court, and, in the service of such process, shall arrest and carry such child before the court, on the day therein named.

Sec. 33. No negro child shall be bound under this article if the parent or parents have the means and are willing to support such child, and keep the same employed, so as to teach habits of industry; and the parent or parents shall be summoned to be present at such binding.

Sec. 34. In binding such children the orphans' court shall give preference to those persons who may be selected by the parents, if there be any, and if not, by the children, if the person selected by them be approved by the court.

Sec. 35. Every such indenture of apprenticeship shall state the name and age of the child bound, and the name of the master, and shall be recorded in the office of the register of wills of said county, at the expense of the master, within one month after the making of the same; and no indenture under this section shall be invalid for want of form, if it contains the name of the master, and the name and age of the apprentice.

Sec. 36. It shall not be necessary in any such indenture, or in any indenture of a negro made by the trustees of the poor, to require that any education shall be given to such negro apprentice.

Sec. 37. The master of any negro apprentice, or the executor or assignee of such, may, with the assent of the orphans' court, to be entered on the minutes, assign and transfer such apprentice to any other person residing in the same county.

Sec. 38. Upon the death of the master, or his assignee, of any negro apprentice, the property and interest of the master and assignee shall pass to the widow, if there be a widow, of such deceased master or assignee, and if no widow, then to the executor of said master or assignee.

Sec. 39. If any negro, or other person, shall entice or persuade any negro apprentice to run away or abscond from the service of the master, or person entitled to his or her service, such negro or other person so offending shall, upon conviction in the circuit court of the county, or the criminal court of Baltimore, be subject to fine and imprisonment, as for a misdemeanor, or, at the discretion of the court, be confined in the penitentiary house of this State for not more than four years, nor less than eighteen months.

Sec. 40. If any negro apprentice abscond, or run away, the orphans' court of the county where he may have been bound shall have full power to adjudge and order such apprentice to serve such further time, after the expiration of the period for which such apprentice may be bound, as will compensate the master or person entitled to the service for all loss occasioned by such running away, including expenses of recapture; and the said court shall have full power to authorize the master of such absconding apprentice to sell such apprentice, and for the whole period he may have to serve, to any person within this State: *Provided,* The said court shall be satisfied that such apprentice was not induced to run away by the ill treatment, or fraud, or contrivance of the master.

4. United States Circuit Court holds that Maryland apprenticeship statute for black children violates the Civil Rights Act, 1867

In re Turner, 24 Fed. Cas. 337

Justice Salmon P. Chase maintained that the Maryland act created an unconstitutional distinction among different classes of citizens.

CHASE, Circuit Justice. The petitioner in this case seeks relief from restraint and detention by Philemon T. Hambleton, of Talbot county, in Maryland, in alleged contravention of the constitution and laws of the United States. The facts, as they appear from the return made by Mr. Hambleton to the writ, and by his verbal statement made in court, and admitted as part of the return, are substantially as follows:

The petitioner, Elizabeth Turner, a young person of color, and her mother, were, prior to the adoption of the Maryland constitution of 1864, slaves of the respondent. That constitution went into operation on November 1, 1864, and prohibited slavery. Almost immediately thereafter many of the freed people of Talbot county were collected together under some local authority, the nature of which does not clearly appear, and the younger persons were bound as apprentices, usually, if not always, to their late masters. Among others, Elizabeth, the petitioner, was indentured to Hambleton by an indenture dated November 3, two days after the new constitution went into operation.

Upon comparing the terms of this indenture (which is claimed to have been executed under the laws of Maryland relating to negro apprentices) with those required by the law of Maryland in the indentures for the apprenticeship of white persons, the variance is manifest. The petitioner, under this indenture, is not entitled to any education; a white apprentice must be taught reading, writing, and arithmetic. The petitioner is liable to be assigned and transferred at the will of the master to any person in the same county; the white apprentice is not so liable. The authority of the master over the peti-

tioner is described in the law as a "property and interest"; no such description is applied to authority over a white apprentice. It is unnecessary to mention other particulars.

. . . The following propositions, then, seem to me to be sound law, and they decide the case:

1. The first clause of the thirteenth amendment to the constitution of the United States interdicts slavery and involuntary servitude, except as a punishment for crime, and establishes freedom as the constitutional right of all persons in the United States.

2. The alleged apprenticeship in the present case is involuntary servitude, within the meaning of these words in the amendment.

3. If this were otherwise, the indenture set forth in the return does not contain important provisions for the security and benefit of the apprentice which are required by the laws of Maryland in indenture of white apprentices, and is, therefore, in contravention of that clause of the first section of the civil rights law enacted by congress on April 9, 1866, which assures to all citizens without regard to race or color, "full and equal benefit of all laws and proceedings for the security of persons and property as is enjoyed by white citizens."

4. This law having been enacted under the second clause of the thirteenth amendment, in enforcement of the first clause of the same amendment, is constitutional, and applies to all conditions prohibited by it, whether originating in transactions before or since its enactment.

5. Colored persons equally with white persons are citizens of the United States.

The petitioner, therefore, must be discharged from restraint by the respondent.

Kinds and conditions of child labor

1. The experiences of Chicago's working children

Florence Kelley and Alzina P. Stevens,
"Wage-Earning Children," in Residents of
Hull House, eds., *Hull House Maps and Papers*
(New York, 1895), pp. 49, 52, 54–58.

Florence Kelley (1859–1932), daughter of
a Republican congressman from Pennsylvania,
was a licensed attorney. She became a resident
of Hull House in 1891 and with fellow
resident Alzina Stevens conducted an
investigation of women and children in sweated
industry which led to the passage of the
Illinois eight-hour law of 1893. Under this
law she was chief inspector of factories from
1893 to 1897. From 1899 until her death
she was general secretary of the
National Consumers' League.

In a discussion of child-labor in Chicago, it
may simplify matters to point out, at the outset,
what things are not to be looked for. Thus,
there is in Chicago virtually no textile industry;
and the cotton-mill child of Massachusetts, or
the carpet-mill child of Philadelphia, has no
counterpart here. There is no industry in which,
as in the spinning and weaving of silk, the deft
fingers of young children have been for generations regarded as essential. With the large exception of the cigar, tobacco, and paper trades
(including both the manufacture of paper boxes
and the printing and binding industries), and
with the further exception of the utterly disorganized and demoralized garment trades, the
industries of Illinois are essentially men's trades.
The wood, metal, and food industries employ a
heavy majority of men. The vast army of fathers employed in transportation and in the
building-trades demand, and as a rule obtain,
wages sufficient to support their young children, who are therefore not crowded into factories . . .

.   .   .   .   .

THE WORKING CHILD OF THE NINETEENTH WARD

The Nineteenth Ward of Chicago is perhaps
the best district in all Illinois for a detailed
study of child-labor, both because it contains
many factories in which children are employed,
and because it is the dwelling-place of wage-
earning children engaged in all lines of activity.

The Ewing Street Italian colony furnishes a
large contingent to the army of bootblacks and
newsboys; lads who leave home at 2.30 A.M. to
secure the first edition of the morning paper,
selling each edition as it appears, and filling the
intervals with blacking boots and tossing pennies, until, in the winter half of the year, they
gather in the Polk Street Night-School, to doze
in the warmth, or torture the teacher with the
gamin tricks acquired by day. For them, school
is "a lark," or a peaceful retreat from parental
beatings and shrieking juniors at home during
the bitter nights of the Chicago winter.

There is no body of self-supporting children
more in need of effective care than these newsboys and bootblacks. They are ill-fed, ill-
housed, ill-clothed, illiterate, and wholly untrained and unfitted for any occupation. The
only useful thing they learn at their work in
common with the children who learn in school,
is the rapid calculation of small sums in making
change; and this does not go far enough to be
of any practical value. In the absence of an
effective compulsory school-attendance law,
they should at least be required to obtain a license from the city; and the granting of this
license should be in the hands of the Board of
Education, and contingent upon a certain
amount of day-school attendance accomplished.

In this ward dwells, also, a large body of
cash-children, boys and girls.[1] Their situation is
illustrated by the Christmas experience of one
of their number. A little girl, thirteen years of
age, saw in an evening paper of December 23d
last, an advertisement for six girls to work in
one of the best-known candy stores, candidates
to apply at seven o'clock the next morning, at a
branch store on the West Side, one and a half
miles from the child's home. To reach the place
in time, she spent five cents of her lunch money

1. Before the invention of pneumatic tubes, children were employed to carry customers' money to
the cashier to be changed.

for car-fare. Arriving, she found other children, while but one was wanted. She was engaged as the brightest of the group, and sent to a downtown branch of the establishment, at a distance of two and a quarter miles. This time she walked; then worked till midnight, paying for her dinner, and going without supper. She was paid fifty cents, and discharged with the explanation that she was only required for one day. No cars were running at that hour, and the little girl walked across the worst district of Chicago, to reach her home and her terrified mother at one o'clock on Christmas morning.[2] No law was violated in this transaction, as mercantile establishments are not yet subject to the provisions of the factory act.

Fortunately the development of the pneumatic tube has begun to supersede the cash-children in the more respectable of the retail stores; and a movement for extending the workshop law to the mercantile establishments would, therefore, meet with less opposition now than at any previous time. The need for this legislation will be acknowledged by every person who will stand on any one of the main thoroughfares of Chicago on a morning between 6.30 and 7.30 o'clock, and watch the processions of puny children filing into the drygoods emporiums to run, during nine or ten hours, and in holiday seasons twelve and thirteen hours, a day to the cry, "Cash!"

In the stores on the West Side, large numbers of young girls are employed thirteen hours a day throughout the week, and fifteen hours on Saturday; and all efforts of the clothing-clerks to shorten the working-time by trade-union methods have hitherto availed but little. While the feeble unions of garment-makers have addressed themselves to the legislature, and obtained a valuable initial measure of protection for the young garment-workers, the retail-clerks, depending upon public opinion and local ordinances, have accomplished little on behalf of the younger clothing-sellers.

2. Incidentally it is of interest that this firm was one of the most liberal givers of Christmas candy to the poor. [Note in *Hull House Maps and Papers*.]

In dealing with newsboys, bootblacks, and cash-children, we have been concerned with those who live in the nineteenth ward, and work perhaps there or perhaps elsewhere. We come now to the children who work in the factories of the nineteenth ward.

The largest number of children to be found in any one factory in Chicago is in a caramel works in this ward, where there are from one hundred and ten to two hundred little girls, four to twelve boys, and seventy to one hundred adults, according to the season of the year. The building is a six-story brick, well lighted, with good plumbing and fair ventilation. It has, however, no fire-escape, and a single wooden stair leading from floor to floor. In case of fire the inevitable fate of the children working on the two upper floors is too horrible to contemplate. The box factory is on the fifth floor, and the heaviest pressure of steam used in boiling the caramels is all on the top floor. The little girls sit closely packed at long tables, wrapping and packing the caramels. They are paid by the piece, and the number of pennies per thousand paid is just enough to attract the most ignorant and helpless children in the city. Previous to the passage of the factory law of 1893, it was the rule of this factory to work the children, for several weeks before the Christmas holidays, from 7 A.M. to 9 P.M., with twenty-minutes for lunch, and no supper, a working week of eighty-two hours. As this overtime season coincided with the first term of the night-school, the children lost their one opportunity. Since the enactment of the factory law, their working week has consisted of six days of eight hours each; a reduction of thirty-four hours a week.

2. Children in textile factories

a. Children in southern cotton mills

Irene M. Ashby, "Child-Labor in Southern Cotton Mills," *World's Work*, II (1901), 1290–1295.

Irene Ashby's report is the result of the first extensive investigation of cotton mills in the South. Miss Ashby, a young English reformer, came to the United States in 1900. Samuel Gompers sent her to Alabama in 1901 as representative of the American Federation of Labor to launch a campaign for child labor legislation. While the legislature was in recess she visited twenty mills. She found ten mills operated by northern capital which employed 4,400 operatives of whom 215 were children, and thirteen mills operated by southern capital which employed 1,968 operatives of whom 115 were children under twelve.

During the latter half of December, 1900, and the first half of January, 1901, I visited twenty-four cotton mills in sixteen cities and villages of Alabama. I chose Alabama because the industry, although comparatively new there (only four out of the twenty-four mills I went through averaging more than five years' existence), is in an active stage of growth, and a child-labor bill had been pending before the Legislature.

I was prepared to find child-labor, for wherever easily manipulated machinery takes the place of human muscles the child is inevitably drawn into the labor market, unless there are laws to protect it. But one could hardly be prepared to find in America today white children, six and seven years of age, working for twelve hours a day — aroused before daybreak and toiling, till long after sundown in winter, with only half an hour for rest and refreshment. When the mills are tempted by pressure of work they make the same old mistakes of their industrial ancestry. Some of them run the machinery at night, and little children are called on to endure the strain of all-night work — and are sometimes kept awake by the vigilant superintendent with cold water dashed into their faces. I should hardly have believed it had I not seen these things myself.

One evening in December I stumbled through a totally unlighted mill village, falling by the way into ditches and deep ruts, and knocked at the door of one of the wooden huts where I saw a light. I asked the woman who opened it if I might come in. Assenting, she ushered me in. She was surrounded by a brood of very small boys, and her consumptive husband sat beside the fire. The smallest child, a poor little fellow that looked to be about six years old, nestled up to me as I talked to them. All worked in the mill, except the mother, they told me.

"Not this one!" I exclaimed, looking down at the wee, thin boy beside me.

"Why, yes." He had worked for about a year; last year he worked forty nights; he was nearly eight years old now. They left that mill because the night work was too hard on the children.

In answer to a query from me, the child said that he could scarcely sleep at all in the day time.

At one place I heard of children, working on the night shift, turned out for some fault at two o'clock in the morning, allowed by a compassionate clerk to go to sleep on a bench in the office, as they were afraid to go home. Ladies told me, too, of a common sight in the mill cottages: children lying face downward on the bed sleeping with exhaustion, just as they had come in from the night shift, too utterly weary even to remove their clothes.

The long day work for children prevailed in every mill that I visited: in six of these night work had been or was still the custom.

.   .   .   .

Often the whole family, except the baby actually in the cradle, is in the mill. Two or three of eight years or older might be on the pay-roll, but the youngest paid worker can get through her "side" — at ten cents a day — with more ease if she has her little brother of six to help her. I have seen a boy under four beginning his life of drudgery by pulling the yarn off bobbins to make bands. A manager courteously conducting me through the mill would often explain — at some exclamation from me — "These very little ones are not working; they are only helping their brothers and sisters." I accepted the explanation until it dawned on me how numerous were these wee unpaid assistants.

. . . . .

In spite of the excellent system of ventilation adopted in most of these factories by which the atmosphere is rendered bearable, a very little inquiry shows that it is by no means as healthy as one would be led to believe from the eulogies of those who are seldom in it. The flying lint often brings on throat and lung trouble, while pneumonia resulting from the sudden change from the hot factory to the early morning and the late evening mists is not uncommon . . .

In one factory I found a little girl aged ten, in the "drawing in" room, where every individual thread of the warp is drawn through the "harness" of the weaving loom. She could earn as much sometimes as 75 cents a day, though alas, at the expense of the beautiful blue eyes she turned up to me as I spoke to her. Her mother told me that she brought her youngest daughter, aged seven, into the mill with her, and although urged to allow her to work, there being many as small in the mill, she would not allow it. Yet without doing any work the child had lost in weight in a year through confinement in the mill atmosphere. Over and over again I was told that the mill was a "playground."

"If anyone tells you that," said a superintendent to me with concentrated scorn, "he either doesn't know what he's talking about, or he's telling a downright lie. I've been in the mill since I was eight years old myself, and I know. We're no charity institution."

"What do you do when you are very tired?" I asked a little girl, putting my mouth close to her ear to make myself heard. "I cry," she said, shyly. She would make no reply when I asked her what happened then, but another child, who

had literally poked her head into the conversation, put in tersely, "The boss tells her to go on with her work."

. . . . .

This is not an isolated instance. Much of the opposition to the passage of a protective law through the Southern legislatures is made by the representatives of Northern corporations, who are taking full advantage of the possibility of child-labor. In eleven mills I visited, owned by Northern capital, there were twice as many children under twelve as in thirteen owned by Southern capital. The total number of children under twelve in the mills of Alabama (including the unpaid "helpers")[1] I computed to be about 1,200. This number is not stationary or diminishing; on the contrary, it is steadily increasing, and the experience of the other Southern States proves that it must be so. In one of the older mills, they told me that the children were younger and more numerous than they had ever had them before . . .

Statistics are scanty and difficult to obtain, but there are some established facts which are significant enough.

In Alabama the proportion of such young children to grown workers is between six and seven percent, or between 500 and 600 in the twenty-four mills I visited. In Augusta, Ga., a count was made in June, 1900, through eight mills, and 556 children under twelve were found working. In South Carolina Mr. John B. Cleveland, president of the Whitney mills, giving evidence before the legislature, stated that thirty per cent of the operatives in the Whitney mills were under twelve, and Mr. James L. Orr, president of the Piedmont mills, South Carolina, that twenty-five per cent of his machinery was run by such children. The statement sometimes made that the number of children affected is so small that it is not worth public attention is not borne out by these figures, nor by the fact that

1. For a more detailed explanation of the helper system, see below Chap. II, sec. A, Problems of enforcement, doc. 8.

in Georgia as many as thirty mill presidents appeared before the legislature to defeat the child-labor bill there.

b. Why families go to the mills, ca. 1906

August Kohn, *The Cotton Mills of South Carolina* (Columbia, S.C., 1907), pp. 30–31.

This document was a handbill circulated by a cotton mill in the Piedmont section and distributed around Clyde, North Carolina.

Three years ago I owned a little mountain farm of two hundred acres. I had two good horses, two good cows, plenty of hogs, sheep and several calves. I had three girls and two boys; ages run from 11 to 21. On my little farm I raised about four hundred bushels of corn, thirty to forty bushels of wheat, two hundred to three hundred dozen oats, and cut from four to eight stacks of hay during the summer. After I clothed my family, fed all my stock during the winter, I had only enough provisions and feed to carry me through making another crop, and no profit left. I sold my farm and stock, paid up all my debts and moved my family to a cotton mill. At that time green hands had to work for nothing til they learned their job, about one month, but now my youngest daughter, only 14 years old, is making $6 per week, my other two are making $7.50 each per week and my two boys are making $8 per week and I am making $4.50 per week; a total of $166 per month. My provisions average $30, house rent $2, coal and wood, $4, total $36; leaving a balance of $130, to buy clothes and desposit in the bank.

My experience is that, while you are on the farm toiling in rain and snow, feeding away what you have made during the summer and making wood to keep fires to keep your family from freezing, you could at the same time be in a cotton mill and in a good, comfortable room, making more than you can make in the summer time on the farm, and there is no stock to eat up what you make. At the mills, children over 12 years old, after they learn their job, can make more than men can make on farms. It is not every family that can do as well as the above family, but it only shows what a family can do that will try and work. Most any family can do half as well — so divide the above number of workers' wages by two and see if you would not still be doing well.

Give this matter your careful thought.

c. In the mule-room, ca. 1895

Al Priddy, *Through the Mill* (Norwood, Mass., 1911), pp. 167–178.

Frederick K. Brown, who wrote under the name Al Priddy, was born in northern England in 1882. He came to America with his uncle's family at age eleven and settled in New Bedford, Massachusetts. He was soon initiated into picking wood and coal in the Charles Street dumping ground. At age thirteen, he went to the "Mill School" — a department of the Common Schools especially for boys and girls planning to enter the mill as soon as they fulfilled their legal education requirements.[1]

My work in the spinning-room, in comparison with my new work in the mule-room, had been mere child's play. At last the terror of the mill began to blacken my life. The romance, the glamour, and the charm were gone by this only a daily dull, animal-like submission to hard tasks had hold of me now.

Five days of the week, at the outer edge of winter, I never stood out in the daylight. I was a human mole, going to work while the stars were out and returning home under the stars. I

1. According to the Massachusetts compulsory attendance law of 1867, every child had to attend school for the equivalent of three months each year.

saw none of the world by daylight, except the staring walls, high picket-fences, and drab tenements of that immediate locality. The sun rose and set on the wide world outside, rose and set five times a week, but I might as well have been in a grave; there was no exploration abroad.

The mule-room atmosphere was kept at from eighty-five to ninety degrees of heat. The hardwood floor burned by bare feet. I had to gasp quick, short gasps to get air into my lungs at all. My face seemed swathed in continual fire. The tobacco chewers expectorated on the floor, and left little pools for me to wade through. Oil and hot grease dripped down behind the mules, sometimes falling on my scalp or making yellow splotches on my overalls or feet. Under the excessive heat my body was like a soft sponge in the fingers of a giant; perspiration oozed from me until it seemed inevitable that I should melt away at last. To open a window was a great crime, as the cotton fiber was so sensitive to wind that it would spoil. (Poor cotton fiber!) When the mill was working, the air in the mule-room was filled with a swirling, almost invisible cloud of lint, which settled on floor, machinery, and employees, as snow falls in winter. I breathed it down my nostrils ten and a half hours a day; it worked into my hair, and was gulped down my throat. This lint was laden with dust, dust of every conceivable sort, and not friendly at all to lungs.

There are few prison rules more stringent than the rules I worked under in that mule room. There are few prisoners watched with sterner guards than were the bosses who watched and ordered me from this task to that.

There was a rule against looking out of a window. The cotton mills did not have opaque glass or whitewashed windows, then. There was a rule against reading during work-hours. There was a rule preventing us from talking to one another. There was a rule prohibiting us from leaving the mill during work-hours. We were not supposed to sit down, even though we had caught up with our work. We were never supposed to stop work, even when we could. There was a rule that anyone coming to work a minute late would lose his work. The outside watchman always closed the gate the instant the starting whistle sounded, so that anyone unfortunate enough to be outside had to go around to the office, lose time, and find a stranger on his job, with the prospect of being out of work for some time to come.

For the protection of minors like myself, two notices were posted in the room, and in every room of the mill. They were rules that represented what had been done in public agitation for the protection of such as I: rules which, if carried out, would have taken much of the danger and the despair from my mill life. They read:

"The cleaning of machinery while it is in motion is positively forbidden!"

"All Minors are hereby prohibited from working during the regular stopping hours!"

If I had insisted on keeping the first law, I should not have held my position in the mule room more than two days. The mule-spinners were on piece work, and their wages depended upon their keeping the mules in motion, consequently the back-boy was *expected,* by a sort of unwritten understanding, to do all the cleaning he could, either while the machines were in motion or during the hours when they were stopped, as during the noon-hour or before the mill started in the morning. If a back-boy asked for the mules to be stopped while he did the cleaning, he was laughed at, and told to go to a very hot place along with his "nerve." I should have been deemed incapable had I demanded that the machinery be stopped for me. The spinner would have merely said, "Wait till dinner time!"

Not choosing to work during the stopping hour, I should merely have been asked to quit work, for the spinner could have made it impossible for me to retain my position.

So I just adapted myself to conditions as they were, and broke the rules without compunction. I had to clean fallers, which, like teeth, chopped down on one's hand, unless great speed and precautions were used. I stuck a hand-brush into swift-turning pulleys, and brushed the cotton off; I dodged past the mules and the iron posts they met, just in time to avoid being crushed. Alfred Skinner, a close friend of mine, had his body pinned and crushed badly. I also tried to clean the small wheels which ran on tracks while they were in motion, and, in doing so, I had to crawl under the frame and follow the carriage as it went slowly forward, and dodge back rapidly as the carriage came back on the jump. In cleaning these wheels, the cotton waste would lump, and in the mad scramble not to have the wheels run over it to lift the carriage and do great damage to the threads, I would risk my life and fingers to extract the waste in time. One day the wheel nipped off the end of my little finger, though that was nothing at all in comparison to what occurred to some of my back-boy friends in other mills. Jimmy Hendricks to-day is a dwarfed cripple from such an accident. Hern Hanscom has two fingers missing, Earl Rogers had his back broken horribly. Yet the notices always were posted, the company was never liable, and the back-boy had no one but himself to blame; yet he could not be a back-boy without taking the risk, which shows how much humanity there can be in law.

Legally I worked ten and a half hours, though actually the hours were very much longer. The machinery I could not clean while in motion, and which the spinner would not stop for me during work-hours, I had to leave until noon or early morning. Then, too, the spinner I worked for paid me to take over some of his work that could be done during the stopping hours, so that there was a premium on those valuable hours, and I got very little time out of doors or at rest. There were generally from three to four days in the week when I worked thirteen and thirteen hours and a half a day, in order to catch up with the amount of work that I had to do to retain my position.

In all, at this time I had five men over me who had the right to boss me. They were: two spinners, the overseer, second hand, and third hand. One of the spinners was a kindly man, very considerate of my strength and time, while the other was the most drunken and violent-tempered man in the room.

.   .   .   .

But day after day I had to face the thousands of bobbins I had in charge and keep them moving. Thousands of things turning, turning, turning, emptying, emptying, emptying, and requiring quick fingers to keep moving. A fight with a machine is the most cunning torture man can face — when the odds are in favor of the machine. There are no mistaken calculations, no chances with a machine except a break now and then of no great consequence. A machine never tires, is never hungry, has no heart to make it suffer. It never sleeps, and has no ears to listen to that appeal for "mercy," which is sent to it. A machine is like Fate. It is Fate, itself. On, on, on, on it clicks, relentlessly, insistently, to the end, in the set time, in the set way! It neither goes one grain too fast or too slow. Once started, it must go on, and on, and on, to the end of the task. Such was the machine against which I wrestled — in vain. It was feeding Cerebus, with its insatiable appetite. The frames were ever hungry; there was always a task ahead, yes, a dozen tasks ahead, even after I had worked, exerted myself to the uttermost. I never had the consolation of knowing that I had done my work. *The machine always won.*

I did take a rest. I had to steal it, just as a slave would. I had to let the machine go on, and on, and on without me sometimes, while I took a rest and let the tasks multiply. That meant double effort after I got up, getting in the mill a little earlier on the morrow, a shorter time for dinner at noon. The tasks had to be done in the end, but I took some rest. I hid from the eyes of the overseer, the second hand, the third hand, and the spinners, behind waste boxes and posts, and had spare minutes with a book I had brought in and hidden under some cotton, or with dreaming about "making something of myself, some day." If I let myself dream beyond the minute, a vile oath would seek me out, and I would hear my Jamaica-

ginger-drinking-spinner sneering, "You filthy
———! Get that oiling done!"

---

d. Employees of a California jute mill,
1889–1890

California, Bureau of Labor Statistics,
Fourth Annual Report, 1889–1890
(Sacramento, 1890), p. 31.

The mill situated in East Oakland was
founded in 1865 as a cotton mill and
changed to a jute mill in 1869. Jute was
used for burlap sacking and twine.

THE BOYS IN THE JUTE MILL

The boys employed are a mixture of races —
white, black, and yellow. Their ages are from
ten to sixteen years. Until the law went into
effect prohibiting the employment of children
under ten years, there were children working in
the mill as low as eight years of age. The majority of the boys and girls are from Portugal
or the Azores Islands. Their work consists in
removing empty bobbins from the spinning
frames and replacing them with full ones. They
have to be very quick at the business, for the
machinery has to stop while they are doing this.
Older hands cannot do this work so well, for
it requires small, deft fingers to get in between
the narrow spaces in the machinery. Few of
these children have received any education
whatever. Their parents are very poor and illiterate. The mothers, and, in some cases, the
fathers of these children, work in the mill, and
I have been credibly informed that some of the
unnatural parents live off the earnings of these
little overworked toilers. Girls are chiefly employed in bag sewing and piling. In the latter
they earn 40 cents a day.

---

3. The stockyards

a. Boy butchers

Illinois, Inspectors of Factory,
Third Annual Report, 1895
(Springfield, 1896), pp. 10–11.

The total number of children is 242 this
year compared with 320 in 1894; the number
of girls having fallen from 18 to 5, and the
number of boys being 65 less than last year.
There is reason to suppose that this decrease of
78 children is due, in some measure, to frequent
inspection and to the successful prosecution of
eight of the thirteen managers of these firms
upon charges of employing twenty-nine children, either under 14 years of age or without
affidavits under 16 years of age.

There is no improvement in the conditions
under which the children work. Some of the
boys act as butchers, sticking sheep, lambs and
swine; others cut the hide from the quivering
flesh of freshly stunned cattle; still others sort
entrails, pack meat, and make the tin cans in
which goods are shipped. In several places a
boy has been found at work at a dangerous
machine, *because his father had been disabled
by it,* and keeping the place pending recovery
depended upon the boy's doing the work during
the father's absence.

---

b. Setting lard-cans

Upton Sinclair, *The Jungle* (New York,
1906), pp. 84–85.

Upton Sinclair used the form of the novel
for his exposé of the exploitation of Polish
immigrants in the Chicago stockyards.

Meantime Teta Elzbieta had taken Stanislovas to the priest and gotten a certificate to the

effect that he was two years older than he was; and with it the little boy now sallied forth to make his fortune in the world. It chanced that Duraham had just put in a wonderful new lard-machine, and when the special policeman in front of the time-station saw Stanislovas and his document, he smiled to himself and told him to go — "Czia! Czia!" pointing. And so Stanislovas went down a long stone corridor, and up a flight of stairs, which took him into a room lighted by electricity, with the new machines for filling lard-cans at work in it. The lard was finished on the floor above, and it came in little jets, like beautiful, wriggling, snow-white snakes of unpleasant odor. There were several kinds and sizes of jets, and after a certain precise quantity had come out, each stopped automatically, and the wonderful machine made a turn, and took the can under another jet, and so on, until it was filled neatly to the brim, and pressed tightly, and smoothed off. To attend to all this and fill several hundred cans of lard per hour, there were necessary two human creatures, one of whom knew how to place an empty lard-can on a certain spot every few seconds, and the other of whom knew how to take a full lard-can off a certain spot every few seconds and set it upon a tray.

And so, after little Stanislovas had stood gazing timidly about him for a few minutes, a man approached him, and asked what he wanted, to which Stanislovas said, "Job." Then the man said "How old?" and Stanislovas answered, "Sixtin." Once or twice every year a state inspector would come wandering through the packing-plants, asking a child here and there how old he was; and so the packers were very careful to comply with the law, which cost them as much trouble as was now involved in the boss's taking the document from the little boy, and glancing at it, and then sending it to the office to be filed away. Then he set some one else at a different job, and showed the lad how to place a lard-can every time the empty arm of the remorseless machine came to him; and so was decided the place in the universe of little Stanislovas, and his destiny till the end of his

days. Hour after hour, day after day, year after year, it was fated that he should stand upon a certain square foot of floor from seven in the morning until noon, and again from half-past twelve till half-past five, making never a motion and thinking never a thought, save for the setting of lard-cans. In summer the stench of the warm lard would be nauseating, and in winter the cans would all but freeze to his naked little fingers in the unheated cellar. Half the year it would be dark as night when he went in to work, and dark as night again when he came out, and so he would never know what the sun looked like on week-days. And for this, at the end of the week, he would carry home three dollars to his family, being his pay at the rate of five cents per hour — just about his proper share of the total earnings of the million and three-quarters of children who are now engaged in earning their livings in the United States.

---

4. The glass industry — boys on the night shift

John Spargo, *The Bitter Cry of the Children* (New York, 1906), pp. 155–159.

I shall never forget my first visit to a glass factory at night. It was a big wooden structure, so loosely built that it afforded little protection from draughts, surrounded by a high fence with several rows of barbed wire stretched across the top. I went with the foreman of the factory and he explained to me the reason for the stockade-like fence. "It keeps the young imps inside once we've got 'em for the night shift," he said. The "young imps" were, of course, the boys employed, about forty in number, at least ten of whom were less than twelve years of age. It was a cheap bottle factory, and the proportion of boys to men was larger than is usual in the higher grades of manufacture. Cheapness and child labor go together, — the cheaper the grade of manufacture, as a rule, the cheaper the labor employed. The hours of labor for the "night shift" were from 5.30 P.M. to 3.30 A.M. I stayed and watched the boys at their work for several hours, and when their tasks were done saw them disappear into the darkness and storm of the night . . .

In the middle of the room was a large round furnace with a number of small doors, three or four feet from the ground, forming a sort of belt around the furnace. In front of these doors the glass-blowers were working. With long wrought-iron blowpipes the blowers deftly took from the furnace little wads of waxlike molten "metal" which they blew into balls and then rolled on their rolling boards. These elongated rolls they dropped into moulds and then blew again, harder than before, to force the half-shaped mass into its proper form. With a sharp, clicking sound they broke their pipes away and repeated the whole process . . .

Then began the work of the boys. By the side of each mould sat a "take-out boy," who, with tongs, took the half-finished bottles — not yet provided with necks — out of the moulds. Then other boys, called "snapper-ups," took these bodies of bottles in their tongs and put the small ends into gas-heated moulds till they were red hot. Then the boys took them out with almost incredible quickness and passed them to other men, "finishers," who shaped the necks of the bottles into their final form. Then the "carrying-in boys," sometimes called "carrier pigeons," took the red-hot bottles from the benches, three or four at a time, upon big asbestos shovels to the annealing oven, where they are gradually cooled off to insure even contraction and to prevent breaking in consequence of too rapid cooling. The work of these "carrying-in boys," several of whom were less than twelve years old, was by far the hardest of all. They were kept on a slow run all the time from the benches to the annealing oven and back again. I can readily believe what many manufacturers assert, that it is difficult to get men to do this work, because men cannot stand the pace and get tired too quickly. It is a fact, however, that in many factories men are employed

to do this work, especially at night. In other, more up-to-date factories it is done by automatic machinery. I did not measure the distance from the benches to the annealing oven, nor did I count the number of trips made by the boys, but my friend, Mr. Owen R. Lovejoy,[1] has done so in a typical factory and very kindly furnished me with the results of his calculation. The distance to the annealing oven in the factory in question was one hundred feet, and the boys made seventy-two trips per hour, making the distance travelled in eight hours nearly twenty-two miles. Over a half of this distance the boys were carrying their hot loads to the oven. The pay of these boys varies from sixty cents to a dollar for eight hours' work. About a year ago I gathered particulars of the pay of 257 boys in New Jersey and Pennsylvania; the lowest pay was forty cents per night and the highest a dollar and ten cents, while the average was seventy-two cents.

---

5. Children in southern oyster canneries

Lewis W. Hine, "Baltimore to Biloxi and Back," *Survey,* XXX (May 3, 1913), 167–172.

Born in Oshkosh, Wisconsin, in 1874, Lewis Hine came to New York City in 1901. In 1908 he resigned from his job as a teacher and devoted his full career to photography. As a crusader for social reform, Hine exposed the record of suffering and poverty in America's industrial life. As a reporter for the National Child Labor Committee he followed working children to cranberry bogs, canneries, coal mines, sweatshops, and tenements, recording their labor in 5,000 photographs.

When we speak of child labor in oyster canning, we refer to the cooked or "cove" oysters,

1. Lovejoy was an officer of the National Child Labor Committee.

not to the raw ones. Children are not used in opening raw oysters for the sole reason that their fingers are not strong enough. Occasionally one finds young boys at work on the boats dredging for the oysters, but not many children work on the boats, for that is a man's job.

.   .   .   .   .

Come out with me to one of these canneries at three o'clock some morning. Here is the crude shed-like building, with a long dock at which the oyster boats unload their cargoes. Near the dock is the ever present shell pile, a monument of mute testimony to the patient toil of little fingers. It is cold, damp, dark. The whistle blew some time ago, and the young workers slipped into their meager garments, snatched a bite to eat and hurried to the shucking shed. The padrone told me "Ef dey don't git up, I go and *git 'em up.*" See those little ones over there stumbling through the dark over the shell piles, munching a piece of bread, and rubbing their heavy eyes. Boys and girls, six seven and eight years of age, take their places with the adults and work all day.

The cars are ready for them with their loads of dirty, rough clusters of shells, and as these shells accumulate under foot in irregular piles, they soon make the mere matter of standing one of physical strain. Notice the uncertain footing, and the dilapidated foot-wear of that little girl, and opposite is one with cloth fingers to protect herself from the jagged shells — they call them "finger-stalls." Their fingers are often sore in spite of this precaution.

When they are picking shrimps, their fingers and even their shoes are attacked by a corrosive substance in the shrimp that is strong enough to eat the tin cans into which they are put. The day's work on shrimp is much shorter than on oysters as the fingers of the worker give out in spite of the fact that they are compelled to harden them in an alum solution at the end of the day. Moreover, the shrimp are packed in ice, and a few hours handling of these icy things is dangerous for any child. Then, too, the mornings, and many of the days, are cold, foggy and damp.

The workers are thinly clad, but, like the fabled ostrich, cover their heads and imagine they are warm. If a child is sick, it gets a vacation, and wanders around to kill time.

The youngest of all shift for themselves at a very early age. One father told me that they brought their baby, two months old, down to the shucking-shed at four o'clock every morning and kept it there all day. Another told me that they locked a baby of six months in the shack when they went away in the morning, and left it until noon, then left it alone again all the afternoon. A baby carriage with its occupant half smothered under piles of blankets is a common sight. Snuggled up against a steam box you find many a youngster asleep on a cold morning. As soon as they can toddle, they hang around the older members of the family, something of a nuisance, of course, and very early they learn to amuse themselves. For hours at a time, they play with the dirty shells, imitating the work of the grown-ups. They toddle around the shed, and out on to the docks at the risk of their lives.

.   .   .   .   .

As soon as they can handle the oysters and shrimps, they are "allowed to help."

The mother often says, "Sure. I'm learnin' her de trade," and you see many youngsters beginning to help at a very early age. Standing on a box in order to reach the table, little Olga, five years old, was picking shrimps for her mother at the cannery I visited. Later in the day, I found her at home worn out with the work she had been doing, but the mother complained that Olga was "ugly." Little sympathy they get when they most need it! Four-year-old Mary was working irregularly through the day shucking about two pots of oysters. The mother is the fastest shucker in the place, and the boss said,

"Mary will work *steady* next year." The most excitement that many of them get from one month to another is that of being dressed up in their Sunday best to spend the day seeing the sights of the settlement.

Now we all know that the amount of work these little ones can do is not much, and yet I have been surprised and horrified at the number of hours a day a six or a seven year old will stay at work, and this with the willing and eager consent of the parents. "Freckled Bill," a bright lad of five years, told me that he worked, and his mother added reproachfully,

"He kin make fifteen cents any day he wants to work, but he won't do it steady."

Annie, seven years old, is a steady worker. The mother said, for her benefit, of course, "She kin beat me shuckin', an' she's mighty good at housework too, but I mustn't praise her too much right before her."

This is only one of the means used to keep the children at work. Another method is to tell the neighbors that Annie can shuck eight pots a day. Then some other child beats the record, and so the interest is kept up, and incidentally the work is done and the family income enlarged. Can we call that motherhood? Compared with real maternity, it is a distorted perversion, a travesty. The baby at Ellis Island little dreams what is in store for him.

Hundreds of these children from four to twelve years of age are regularly employed, often as helpers, for the greater part of the six months if it is a good season. At three and four years of age they play around and help a little, "learnin' de trade." At five and six years of age they work more regularly, and at seven and eight years, they put in long hours every working day. This is the regular program for these children day after day, week after week for the six months of their alleged — "outing down South."

---

6. Sweatshops

Elizabeth Shepley Sergeant, "Toilers of the Tenements Where the Beautiful Things of the Great Shops are Made," *McClure's Magazine,* XXXV (July 1910), 231–232.

Articles of fashionable women's dress, such as artificial flowers, feathers, lace, and embroidery were usually partially made at home by tenement families. The Italian family in the following document made artificial flowers.

. . . Mrs. Rapallo, a woman of thirty, of the striking South Italian type, and her five eldest children, were gathered closely around the table, working on the flowers, while two babies were playing with the finished bunches of violets on the floor. The mother and the two older children, Michele, a boy of fourteen, and Maria, a girl of twelve, were fitting the petals to the stems with a bit of paste from a glass, by a deft turn of the finger. Pietro and Camilla, the younger children, were engaged in the simpler task of winding stems with green tape; while Antoinette, an undersized child of nine, under the mother's direction made the flowers and leaves into a "corsage bouquet." Such a bouquet sells in the shops for about a dollar and a half.

All the family looked happy except Michele, who bent over his work with a scowling face. I hoped to find out what was the matter by asking him how soon he would graduate from school. He pulled his cap over his eyes and did not reply.

"Mike no like school," explained Mrs. Rapallo; "he want to work out, but he has one hundred and thirty days of school to make up yet."

"Do you like to work at home better than to go to school?" I asked.

"Tired of flowers," he muttered, and dropped his head lower.

"But he have to help me all the same," continued his mother severely. "My old man he no good — no work for two years; all them children must help me."

"Mother, you speak to Camilla," interrupted Maria shrilly. "She isn't doing anything."

"Isn't she rather young to work after school?" I inquired, sorry to see Camilla's gaiety repressed by a slap.

"She too young for school," Mrs. Rapallo replied. "She can't do anything, only help me with flowers all day. We get fifteen cents a bunch for this kind of flowers," she went on, "and we can make five bunches a day if they all work. But seventy-five cents a day's not much, with rent eleven dollars a month, and seven children who always want to eat."

Four dollars and fifty cents a week was the wage for the united labor of a woman and five children. All the children but Camilla looked listless and weary as the excitement of my arrival wore off . . . The floor was dirty, and one of the babies who sat there sucking a violet with very purple lips, had sore eyes. All the children's fingers were stained green and purple. I had been told that the dye was poisonous, and I asked Mrs. Rapallo if it hurt the children. She shook her head philosophically.

"The doctor say it may be the dye when Pietro have his pains in his stomach. But what can I do?"

---

7. Breaker boys in the coal regions

Francis H. Nichols, "Children of the Coal Shadow," *McClure's Magazine,* XX (February 1903), 435–444.

This report is typical of a variety of expositions of child labor conditions in the periodical press. The occasion of the article was the strike of over 50 thousand anthracite coal miners enrolled in the United Mine Workers, demanding a 10 to 20 per cent increase in pay.

The nine "hard coal counties" of Pennsylvania are Susquehanna, Lackawanna, Luzerne, Carbon, Schuylkill, Columbia, Sullivan, Northumberland, and Dauphin. A community of interests and the ties of labor unions have so bound the counties together that they constitute a sort of separate and distinct state, called by its inhabitants "Anthracite." Practically the whole population of the nine counties is discontented. Nearly every man has a grievance, and lives in a state of protest, and in this protesting wives and mothers join; with their husbands and sons they share a deep sense of wrong and injustice.

·   ·   ·   ·   ·

The School of the "Breaker"

The company's nurseries for boys of the coal shadow are the grim black buildings called breakers, where the lump coal from the blast is crushed into marketable sizes.

In speaking of the events of his childhood, the average man is far more apt to refer to the time "when I was working in the breaker" than to any occurrence of his school-days. After being ground in heavy machinery in the cupola of the breaker, the broken coal flows down a series of chutes to the ground floor, where it is loaded on freight cars waiting to receive it. The chutes zigzag through the building, about three feet apart. Between them, in tiers, are nailed a series of planks; these serve as seats for the "slate-pickers." Mixed with the coal are pieces of slate rock which it is the duty of the slate-picker to detect as they pass him, and to throw into another chute which passes to the refuse heap below. A few of the slate-pickers are white-haired old men, superannuated or crippled miners who are no longer able to blast coal below ground, and who for the sake of a dollar a day pass their last years in the breaker; but an overwhelming majority in all the breakers are boys. All day long their little fingers dip into the unending grimy stream that rolls past them.

Dangers and Hardships of the Work

The coal so closely resembles slate that it can be detected only by the closest scrutiny, and the childish faces are compelled to bend so low over the chutes that prematurely round shoulders and narrow chests are the inevitable result. In front of the chutes is an open space reserved for the "breaker boss," who watches the boys as intently as they watch the coal.

The boss is armed with a stick, with which he occasionally raps on the head and shoulders a boy who betrays lack of zeal. The breakers are supposed to be heated in winter, and a steam pipe winds up the wall; but in cold weather every pound of steam is needed in the mines, so that the amount of heat that radiates from the steam pipe is not sufficient to be taken seriously by any of the breakers' toilers. From November until May a breaker boy always wears a cap and tippet, and overcoat if he possesses one, but because he has to rely largely upon the sense of touch, he cannot cover his finger-tips with mittens or gloves; from the chafing of the coal his fingers sometimes bleed, and his nails are worn down to the quick. The hours of toil for slate-pickers are supposed to be from seven in the morning until noon, and from one to six in the afternoon; but when the colliery is running on "full capacity orders," the noon recess is reduced to half an hour, and the good-night whistle does not blow until half-past six. For his eleven hours' work the breaker boy gets no more pay than for ten.

The wages of breaker boys are about the same all over the coal regions. When he begins to work at slate picking a boy receives forty cents a day, and as he becomes more expert the amount is increased until at the end of, say, his fourth year in the breaker, his daily wage may have reached ninety cents. This is the maximum for an especially industrious and skillful boy. The average is about seventy cents a day. From the ranks of the older breaker boys are chosen door-boys and runners, who work in the mines below ground.

The number of boys who work in hard coal mines is imperfectly realized in the rest of the United States. According to the report of the Bureau of Mines of Pennsylvania for 1901, 147,651 persons were employed "inside and outside the mines of the anthracite region." Of these, 19,564 were classified as slate-pickers,

3,148 as door-boys and helpers, and 10,894 as drivers and runners.

The report makes no classification of miners by their ages, but I am convinced that 90 per cent of the slate-pickers, 30 per cent of the drivers and runners, and all of the door-boys and helpers are boys. In other words, a total of 24,023, or nearly one-sixth of all the employees of the anthracite coal mines, are children.

Age Certificates and What They Amount To

According to the mining laws of Pennsylvania, "no boy under the age of fourteen shall be employed in a mine, nor shall a boy under the age of twelve be employed in or about the outside structures or workings of a colliery" (*i.e.,* in a breaker). Yet no one who stands by the side of a breaker boss and looks up at the tiers of benches that rise from the floor to the coal-begrimed roof can believe for a minute that the law has been complied with in the case of one in ten of the tiny figures in blue jumpers and overalls bending over the chutes. The mine inspector and the breaker boss will explain that "these boys look younger than their ages is," and that a sworn certificate setting forth the age of every boy is on file in the office.

Children's age certificates are a criminal institution. When a father wishes to place his son in a breaker, he obtains an "age blank" from a mine inspector, and in its spaces he has inserted some age at which it is legal for a boy to work. He carries the certificate to a notary public or justice of the peace, who, in consideration of a fee of twenty-five cents, administers oath to the parent and affixes a notarial seal to the certificate.

Justifiable and Unjustifiable Perjury

According to the ethics of the coal fields, it is not wrong for a minor or his family to lie or to practise any form of deceit in dealing with coal-mine operators or owners. A parent is justified in perjuring himself as to his son's age on a certificate that will be filed with the mine superintendent, but any statement made to a representative of the union must be absolutely truthful. For this reason my inquiries of mine boys as to their work and ages were always conducted under the sacred auspices of the union.

Testimony "On the Level"

The interrogative colloquy was invariably something like this:

"How old are you?"

Boy: "Thirteen; going on fourteen."

Secretary of the Local: "On the level now, this is union business. You can speak free, understand."

Boy: "Oh, dat's a diffurnt t'ing altogether. I'm nine years old. I've been working since me fadder got hurted in th' explosion in No. 17 a year ago last October."

---

8. Street trades

a. Street work, New York

Ernest Poole, "Waifs of the Street," *McClure's Magazine,* XXI (May 1903), 40–44.

Poole (1880–1950) lived at the University Settlement in New York from 1902 to 1905. During this period he wrote numerous articles for muckraking magazines as well as a pamphlet on tuberculosis in tenement districts. In the following study, he traced the life histories of newsboys and dispelled the myth that they grew up to be successful capitalists.

We all glance in passing at the shrewd little newsboys, peddlers, messengers, and bootblacks that swarm by day and night through every crowded street of busy New York. We catch only a glimpse. The paper is sold in a twinkling, and like a flash the little urchin is off through the crowd. We admire his tense energy, his shrewd, bright self-reliance. We hear of newsboys who in later life have risen high; and we think of street work, if we think of it at all, as a capital school for industry and enterprise. Those who follow deeper are forced to a directly opposite conclusion. The homeless, the most illiterate, the most dishonest, the most impure — these are the finished products of child street work. They are the minority of its workers. But this is only because the greater number stay but a few years, and so leave before thoroughly trained to the service. It is of the finished products that I wish mainly to write. They poison the rest, for in the street morals spread, like a new slang word, with amazing rapidity. And what is true of hundreds applies in some degree to most of the recruits around them.

The main characteristic of street work is its unwholesome irregularity. The work is almost wholly dependent on the crowds in the street, and is shaped to meet their irregular tastes and habits. The crowd pays best, and pays most carelessly, at night. In cold or rainy weather business drops almost to the vanishing point. It comes up with a rush in every time of excitement, for excitement, good or bad, is what street work is built on. This is especially true of the messenger service. Messenger boys are the most irregular of all street workers. One of the large New York companies employs one thousand boys at a time, but employs six thousand during the year. The night shift seems generally the most popular. Night messengers do all-night work between all-night houses and all-night people — some every week, some alternate weeks, some in four-hour shifts, and some twelve hours at a stretch. In one office of nineteen boys the oldest was sixteen, the youngest looked barely twelve. They went on at eight o'clock at night, and I found them still there at ten the next morning. It is the business of their manager to employ just enough boys to keep them all on the street all through the night.

For many this nervous irregular life is sustained and poisoned by hastily bolted meals, with often double a man's portion of coffee, cigars, and cigarettes . . . .

Smoking is almost universal, and coffee is used to an amazing excess. I know over a hundred boys who average at least three huge bowls each night, and some who often drink six at supper. In thousands of cases, too, the work makes the sleep irregular. Several hundred at least sleep all night on the streets, in stables, condemned buildings, and halls of tenements, waiting until after midnight when the lights are all out . . .

Irregular work brings irregular pay. Newsboys get their papers on credit, are not forced to save for the next day's business, and so keep in debt most of the time. Messenger boys do a large side business in tips. The peddlers and bootblacks are paid on the spot. All classes have ready money — some in copper, some in silver — and reckless spending is a most natural result . . .

The street's improvidence is a natural result of its irregularity. Gambling and improvidence go together. Most street workers are inveterate players at the game of "craps." This whiles away the time between the irregular working periods, and often runs well up into the dollars. In one of the large messenger offices on Broadway it is common for boys to lose the entire week's earnings in the hall and stairway before reaching the street.

.   .   .   .   .

On all the freedom and irregularity of street life leave their marks in some degree. At one large department store I found that of sixty-two cash boys nineteen had been messengers or newsboys, but only three of these had been there over two months. Seven had been both messengers and newsboys. One had served as bootblack, messenger, newsboy, and peddler; later as assistant to a junkman, next to a dentist, and now at seventeen he was cash boy at $2.50 a week. He had held the position ten days. It is the same constant thirst for change that Mr. Heig has combated so long and so well at the Newsboys' Home down near Newspaper Row. Most of his boys have formerly been street workers, but by untiring effort he

has secured for most of them other employment. Thirty per cent of these lose their places almost immediately, while the majority of the rest are frequently changing. They have always their old street work to fall back on. Their average age is seventeen; their average wages, four dollars a week.

.   .   .   .   .

To offset this extreme irregularity street work gives no useful training for later trade or business. Out of the thousands of messenger boys only a very small per cent become operators. Few bootblacks come to have stands of their own. All are constantly pushed on by the thousands of new-comers, and the street gives later work to only a small per cent of these thousands. Newsboys do not become reporters. An editor of one large New York daily told me he knew of not a single instance. Some of the brightest win good positions in the newspaper delivery departments, others on wagons, in factories, and in the markets. Many become office boys and some find the excitement they love in the Fire Department, while others appease their restlessness as traveling salesmen. The messenger boys often find congenial employment as drivers of "night hawks." The best of them end as messengers on Wall Street. But even there it is rare to find one working up.

.   .   .   .   .

Street work saps the strength of home influence. In some it wholly destroys this influence. In all it is a constant impelling force. For its earnings first induce parents to send boys out on the streets, and later these same earnings give boys access to the gambling, cheap pleasures, and vice that make home seem so dull and slow by comparison. Child street work soon implants that amazing precocity and independence which is often so attractive, and which yet leads to so much harm. I heard it briefly expressed once by a youngster of twelve. He had made trouble at school, and his teacher threatened to report him to his parents "Aw go on wid yer reportin' to me parents!" he indignantly rejoined. "I'm supportin' 'em bot'." On inquiry his importance was found to be hugely exaggerated. And this exaggeration is common. Upon it is built the popular notion that every street worker represents a starving, widowed mother. In reality it has been found by closer study that these earnings are not generally the essential part of the family income. No doubt they do often help considerably, but this help is terribly paid for by the complete ruin which child street work brings to hundreds of its workers. Often the "supportin'" grows irksome, and starts the common process by which a boy becomes wholly estranged from his home. First gambling eats into his earnings. He begins to lie to his parents about the amount. When this keeps on, they forbid him to come home without money. Then comes the first night out. A beating follows, and makes it only easier to stay out again. In summer this becomes a comfortable habit. When winter arrives, the majority take to sleeping at home again; but always with some the seeming freedom has become an iron habit, for which even the slight restraints of the lodging house are too severe. So the habit grows, and the summer's recruits move slowly up to the head of the profession. For them child work in the streets is an enemy to all home influence. It is the more an enemy because at first it seemed a friend.

b. Newsboys

Myron E. Adams, "Children in American Street Trades," *The Annals* of the American Academy of Political and Social Science, XXV (May 1905), 23–30, 43–44.

Adams (1876–1930), a social worker and Baptist minister, was associated with the West Side Neighborhood House in New York from 1904 until 1906.

The newsboy has become a part of our city environment. A familiar figure, rather undersized as we know him best, flipping the street cars, or standing on street corners holding his stock in trade under his arm. A veritable merchant of the street, who scans each passer-by as a possible customer. Quick of wit and intent upon his trade he reads their peculiarities at a glance, and makes the most of their weaknesses. The public sees him at his best and neglects him at his worst. He is not considered in the problem of child labor, because he works in the open and is seemingly apart from the associations which are so hostile to the health and happiness of the factory child.

It seems the part of the iconoclast to controvert the popular conception of the newsboy. His energy and enthusiasm in the few hours when his work is at its best add to the picturesque in the city's life; his sacrifice and his service have always been the peculiar field of the melodrama or the boy's story book. It is very hard to throw these early impressions ruthlessly aside. This class of boys have the ability to do things which attract and to conceal those things which repel.

Undoubtedly in the early days of paper selling and before the child of foreign parents secured such a monopoly of street trades, there were some features of paper selling which were more attractive than they are to-day. With the changing character of the street there has also come the realization that the ordinary boy has little or no future there. The opportunity for him in the business of the paper is small. In fact the uncertainty and license of the street provides but a poor education for any occupation which requires either regular or persistent effort.

.   .   .   .   .

In the early phases of newspaper selling the street corner in the downtown district was the scene of physical battles for supremacy. For many years the Irish lad held absolute possession. With strong fist and ready tongue, backed by many friends, he seemed almost invincible, but back of it all there was a certain lack of persistence that proved to be his undoing. The Jewish boy came next. He would not fight the Irish lad with the weapons of his choosing, he knew a better way. Every day he was at his post, in winter and summer, in good weather and bad, the customer could depend on his appearance with the paper. So his trade increased, and at last he gained a monopoly of the corner. In turn he fell, and the Italian, the prince of street venders, because he possessed both of the strong points of his predecessors, secured the monopoly of most of the good corners. He was both a ready fighter and a persistent worker.

Meanwhile the circulation managers of the newspapers came into the field with assurance of assistance to him who possessed the corner. The corner, which had been merely a prize for a physical contest, now came to have a quasi-legal position that implied pecuniary value. Its value was so great that it could not pass unnoticed by the circulation managers, and protection of some sort seemed necessary. The social privilege must have a more stable backing than merely the "good will" of the street. Protection finally came from the newspaper in the form of a card bearing the name of the dealer and the position of his corner, with the condition that no one could buy early papers without presenting this card . . .

. . . The dealers are empowered by the papers to arrange the territory each boy is to cover. Some of these boys receive a small salary from the newspapers, others are dependent upon the small sum which they derive from sub-letting of their districts, and they manage to earn a very fair salary when they combine the actual selling of papers with their other duties. Among the men and boys who own corners outside the downtown district there is a great divergence, both in age and nationality,

but the boy finally chosen as overseer is usually the best representative of the district in which he lives.

In addition to this selling on the street corner many of the older boys have established regular routes, which often require the delivery of five or six hundred papers each day. One young man who has a route of this kind has been able to secure an education by means of selling papers. He finally graduated from high school and from a medical college, received a degree, and practiced medicine for two years, yet he still continued with the old route and depended upon it chiefly for support. Many instances came to the notice of investigators of persons who had in this way earned a living while pursuing a scientific or professional course.

. . . . . .

The small boy, under ten years of age, is on the ragged edge of the newspaper business. He may aid the corner dealer somewhat, and serves his purposes very well, but he is not a necessary part of the circulation system. His absence would not materially affect the general sale of the papers, since there are news stands in charge of older boys on practically every corner, but would preserve the small boy from the temptations which easily lead to a system of begging. The younger boy seems to learn early the strategic way of disposing of his wares. Three boys were found begging on State street between eleven and twelve o'clock one night. Each boy carried a paper under his arm, but made no attempt to sell it. They would watch each passerby and without exception select a man accompanied by a lady. As soon as the man's attention was attracted by the paper the boy would ask for money, and continue to do so until he either received the money or had been refused many times. One boy (T.P.), received fifteen cents in less than a half hour. When questioned, he stated that all the younger boys remaining on the street after ten o'clock did the same thing.

9. Children on strike

a. Children's unions in the coal counties
of Pennsylvania, 1902

Nichols, "Children of the Coal Shadow,"
441–444.

The boys worked as breakers in the coal
mines while the girls were employed in the
textile mills which utilized the female labor
force of miners' families. The fact that boys
constituted 20 per cent of the membership
of the United Mine Workers of America
was a sore point with the President's
Commission investigating the Anthracite
Coal Strike of 1902. The Commission felt
that it was "unwise and impolitic to permit
boys of immature age and judgment to
participate in deciding the policy . . .
of a labor union," especially since the boy
delegates often held the balance of power
in union meetings.[1]

. . . The children have their unions as well
as the grown folk. Almost as soon as the
breaker boy's certificate is accepted and placed
on file in the colliery office he makes application to become a member of the "Junior
Local," the members of which are all boys
under sixteen. Their weekly meetings take
place at night, and are conducted with the
utmost secrecy, the members being admitted
only by password. The monthly dues range
from ten to twenty-five cents, in accordance
with the wages received by the members.

.   .   .   .   .

At Harwood, a village about four miles from
Hazleton, I attended a meeting of a Junior
Local. Promptly at eight o'clock the boys,
about fifty in number, gathered in the school-

house. Their oily caps and grimy overalls gave
evidence of their having only recently left their
day's toil in the mines and breakers. After the
blinds had been drawn, and the door locked,
the president mounted the teacher's platform
and called the meeting to order by pounding
on the desk with his fist. On the front row of
benches sat the vice-president, treasurer, and
secretary. Comparatively few of the members
who filled the benches in the room would have
been pronounced by any observer of ordinary
perspicacity outside the perjured world of
Anthracite as being more than ten years of age.
"How old are you?" I asked the assembled
meeting, and the answer came back in a grand
chorus, "Thirteen." An accord of ideas, as well
as ages, worthy of a union.

Mill and factory girls are as zealous as their
brothers in forming and maintaining unions.
The employees of knitting mills are members
of the Textile Workers' Union of America.
Silk workers have a union, and girls who make
squibs belong to the United Powder and High
Explosive Workers of America. The weekly
meeting of the union is the great event in the
life of every child in the coal fields. When attending meetings members of girls' unions
are required to wear "the same clothes that
they would in church." The debates relate to
grievances, and they are always of a serious
and sometimes of a strenuous character.

Before a local can be taken seriously it must
have wrung some concession from the boss. Its
members must have gone through at least one
strike before the district organizer will point to
them with pride and will say, "They are all
right. They know how to assert their manhood."
This is one of the technical phrases of labor
leaders, and is always used in the generic sense.
Pale-faced little girls "assert their manhood"
quite as often and as rigorously as do stalwart
coal-begrimed miners.

.   .   .   .   .

Puerile, and almost amusing, as are children's unions, they have in some instances met

1. U.S. Anthracite Coal Strike Commission, *Report to the President on the Anthracite Coal Strike
of May–October, 1902.* 58 Cong., Spec. Sess., Doc.
6 (1903), I, 65.

with success in advancing wages and in shortening hours of labor . . .

.   .   .   .   .

It is, however, a peculiarity of children's unions that they not infrequently declare a strike because of a grievance that has nothing directly to do with hours or wages. The child of the Coal Shadow submits uncomplainingly to a habitual treatment which in a country like China would be considered cruel and intolerable. But when extra pressure is so brought to bear upon the little human machine that it is strained to the breaking point: when the child's very life is threatened; then, as a last resort, he turns for protection to the union, composed of children like himself, who share his sorrows and who can appreciate his sufferings. The seventeen-year-old girl president of a union told me this story of the latest victory of her District Local:

In the performance of certain work in the factory a little girl was employed to operate a treadle.

"She had to work all day long, and as she was growing pretty fast, she began to get kind of crippled-like. She was lame in one leg, and she was lop-sided, one shoulder being higher than the other. By and by she got so bad that she had to lay off for a week and go to bed. While she was away the boss hired a big boy to work the treadle, and paid him, of course, considerable more than she was getting. But when she came back to work, he fired the boy and put her on the treadle again. Our Grievance Committee waited on the boss and asked him polite, as a favor, to give her an easier job, because she was getting deformed. But he said that he wouldn't have no interference with his business. He was an American citizen, and no one could dictate to him. Then I called a meeting of our Local.

"'Girls,' I says, addressing them from the chair, 'shall we stand for it — we, that believes in the rights of man? Shall we stand for seeing her growing up a cripple and the union not doing nothing nor reaching out no hand for to help? I know that it's tough to strike now, because some of us is supporting our families, whose fathers is striking. Shall we stand for it?' They voted unanimous to strike if she wasn't took off the treadle. We had the resolution wrote out nice on a typewriter. The Grievance Committee handed it to the boss. He thought it over for two days, and then he give in. The boy is working the treadle yet, and the girl is at the bench."

---

b. Child paper-workers on strike in New York, 1904

William English Walling, "A Children's Strike on the East Side," *Charities,* XIII (1904–1905), 305.

William Walling was secretary of the Woman's Trade Union League which sponsored this strike.

The strike of 125 employees of the Cohen paper box factory, at 84 Bowery, has aroused the interest of the East Side as no other strike since the great conflict in the garment trades last summer. A large majority of the strikers are girls and of these most are very young, many being mere children of fourteen and fifteen years.

These young people have been out for eight weeks living on the pittance which the Hebrew Trades Council has raised from small contributions of sympathetic working people of the East Side. So strong is the feeling against their employer that they are willing to fight it out indefinitely as long as they are provided with the five or ten cents necessary for each meal.

The Hebrew Trades Council, by means of popular concerts and direct contributions by the unions, has furnished about $700 to the strikers, whose local and national organization is without funds.

The socialist Jewish paper, *Vorwarts*,[1] has also raised money in the strikers' behalf and aroused a general public interest in the strike.

The struggle of these young girls to better their conditions was laid before the Woman's Trade Union League a few days ago, and the league, after considerable investigation, has decided to take up the case of the strikers, raise funds for them, give publicity to the facts, and urge a settlement on the employers.

The strike was caused by a proposed reduction of wages amounting to ten per cent. Before the cut the girls were getting three dollars a thousand boxes. There was no union at the time, but one was formed for the purpose of resisting the reduction. Already the employer has offered to take some of the employees back at the old wages. There is no doubt that he needs them, for he has used every effort to persuade them to leave their organization and is said even to have visited some of their homes. The season for the making of cigarette boxes, which is the business of this factory, will soon reach its height, and experienced workers are difficult to obtain.

An extraordinary and deplorable feature of the strike has been the arrest of a number of the small girls on charges of assault. The youth and gentleness of these girls seem to make it most unlikely that they are guilty of the disorderly conduct with which they are charged. In each case the girls have been dismissed, but the small sums of money the strikers have been able to get together have been almost instantly disbursed by the arrests and fines levied against the men of the union who have been endeavoring to put their case before the new employees hired by Mr. Cohen. The strikers charge that the arrests are illegal and absolutely without cause.

The Woman's Trade Union League intends to get to the bottom of these arrests and to watch closely those that are made in the future. It has also directed the attention of the daily

1. The Jewish Daily *Forward* was the largest Jewish newspaper in America. It was published in Yiddish under the editorship of Abraham Cahan.

press to the strike and hopes that the pressure of public opinion will have some influence on the employer.

.   .   .   .   .

The youth of the employees as well as their sex makes it necessary that they should secure public support if they are to win their struggle.

---

10. Rural child labor

a. Cotton pickers in Texas

Lewis W. Hine, "Children or Cotton?" *Survey*, XXXI (February 7, 1914), 589–590.

The motions are simple and easily learned. After that it is a question of nimble fingers and endurance. Pick, — pick, — pick, — pick, — drop into the bag, a step forward. Pick — pick — drop into the bag — step forward; one hundred bolls a minute — six thousand an hour — seventy-five thousand a day. This for six days in the week, five months in the year, under a relentless sun. And they speed each other up to stimulate the numb fingers and aching backs.

.   .   .   .   .

. . . Come out with me at "sun-up" and see [the children] trooping into the fields with their parents and neighbors. At first the morning will be fresh, and nature full of beauty. You will see kiddies four or five years old picking as though it were a game of imitation and considering it great fun, and you will think (perhaps) that it is a wholesome task, a manifestation of a kind Providence. But watch them picking through all the length of a hot summer day, and the mere sight of their monotonous repetition of a simple task will tire you out long before they stop. Their working day follows the sun and not until sun-down do they leave the fields for the night. Then turn to the "older" children of six and seven, who are considered steady workers, and responsible for a share of the output, and you will realize that for them even in the beauty of the early morning the fun has quite lost its savor.

Millie, aged four, was picking eight pounds a day when I saw her, and Mellie, her sister, five years old, thirty pounds a day. Ruby, a seven-year-old girl on another farm stopped picking long enough to say, as I stood by her, "I works from sun-up to sun-down, an' picks thirty-five pounds a day." I did not see any of the champion child pickers with records of two hundred and three hundred pounds a day, whose achievements are so often recorded in the daily papers . . . But when we think how many light and feathery bolls little hands must pick to turn the scale at thirty pounds, these common daily averages are sufficiently appalling!

---

b. Migrant workers in the Northwest

Sara A. Brown, "Neglected Children of Migrant Workers," *The Missionary Review of the World*, XLVI (July 1923), 515–520.

Large armies of boys and girls, with their parents, migrate annually to the open country to do hand work in specified farm crops, in truck gardens and small fruit areas; without regulation as to age, daily working hours, kind of labor required its conflict with their attendance upon school, and other factors affecting their development. These children do not belong to the "tramp family" . . . nor the "crop follower," leading a nomadic life with little or no desire for a permanent home. They belong to the high-type laborer family, unafraid of adventure, unafraid of hard toil or of life in the open.

East, west, mid-west, north, and south, they are to be found in all parts of the United States.

Two widely different groups furnish illustration of what in general seems to be the experience of all. They are the children of native born parents who migrated from rural and urban districts in 1922 to the "onion-marshes" of Ohio; migrated largely from urban centers, to the "sugar-beet fields" of Michigan . . .

The children are largely American born. In crops depending almost exclusively on contract labor recruited from immigrant sections of large cities, the children are predominately American born . . .

Parents take children of all ages to the country, though the largest number are from five to sixteen and most of them work. Little "tots" under five go with their mothers into the fields or remain at the house in charge of another child acting as "little mother."

The major reason families migrate to the open country is work; work with its contribution to the family income; work without restriction for all members of the household, young and small, old and large. Unhesitatingly, fathers say they would not go without the children to do the work: "In the city jes me and the woman works, chillins' go to school; in the country chillins' work too, more money, go to school jest after work." Mothers after many years as migrants frequently say, "me no more come to fields mit the kids when they is big enough to work in the city." The work children may do in factories and mills is regulated by school and child labor laws, not so for children of migrant workers.

.   .   .   .   .

As soon as the work is done in the fall, the family is ready to move again, usually at the end of five or six months. About twenty-five per cent stay in the country. They come to the fields and marshes early in the spring, often six weeks or more before they begin work. Families of 199 contract beet laborers, who migrated from urban centers, arrived twenty-three days before they began work the first of June. Many were still in the fields after the middle of November. They have been doing this year after year from five to ten years in succession. Movements of the "onion workers" are very much the same.

The hand-work done by children, generally, is weeding, hoeing, harvesting or gathering in the crop. It is estimated that a child topping beets[1] handles on an average between two and three tons daily. As in other farm work during any season, the work day is from "light to dark." For 276 children in the onions, it ranges from ten to four hours, with more than half working ten hours or more.

.   .   .   .   .

Work goes on in all kinds of weather, in the hot sun, hot winds, dust storms, in rain, snow, cold winds, and freezing temperature. A family of six children from seven to fifteen years of age, and three adults (including the mother with a baby) worked 111 acres of beets. Allowing 37 acres for the adults, the children earned two-thirds of the $1,198.00 income for seven months of the year . . .

The matter of suitable living quarters is always difficult. Every available shelter is used, good farm houses, others long since discarded, barns, garages, shanties, shacks, and "company houses." Many are unpainted and unkempt, with leaking roofs; more than half without screened doors; more than two-fifths without water at the same place as the house; nearly two-thirds without garden space enough to supply the major part of the family including vegetables.

The most deadening influences are, however, found in the life of the family and the uncertain place it holds in the neighborhood. The family has no sense of belonging to the community, no interest, no responsibility, no part in its government. Residents of the community hold the migrant worker in scorn. He and his children are dubbed "hunkies" and the like. His position is menial. Nothing in the com-

munity belongs to him. A fifteen-year-old girl for nine years migrating to the beet fields, begged her father not to contract again for she said "What chance have I ever to be anything but a 'beet hunkie'? What else can I ever know? What can I ever do but marry a 'beet hunkie' and be a 'hunkie' all my life?" Never, in the nine years, did the family have a neighborly neighbor.

Children of migrant families are deprived of essentials for proper development: First by being set apart from natural community associations of home, of church and school; by being cut off from participation in and responsibility for things pertaining to their own and their neighbor's welfare. It is little wonder that children and their parents develop bitter feelings of hatred; that many believe every man's hand is against them, except for what he can get out of them.

Second, they are deprived of opportunity to attend school and of educational training. Those migrating from cities leave six or eight weeks before schools close in the spring and do not enter rural schools. The majority return eight or twelve weeks after schools open in the fall. At least twenty-five per cent do not attend rural schools at any time. This means each child misses four or five months of school every year. School attendance is affected by migration and it is not the matter of one or two years, for these families have been migrants an average of six years, many as long as twelve and fourteen. Irregular attendance, among other things, contributed to retardation . . .

Why children worked

---

1. Children support their families

Kelley and Stevens, "Wage-Earning Children," p. 72.

---

1. Cutting off the leafy tops of beets with a long hooked knife.

It has been found in the case of the cutlery and stamping works that some of the children working for wages are orphans and half-orphans, but a large majority are the children of men employed in industries without strong labor organizations, such as laborers, lumbershovers, or employees in the garment trades. In an incredibly large proportion of cases, the fathers of young wage-earning children not only do not support the family, but are themselves supported by it, being superannuated early in the forties by the exhaustion characteristic of the garment trades, or the rheumatism of the ditcher and sewer-digger, and various other sorts of out-door workers; or by that loss of a limb which is regarded as a regular risk in the building-trades and among railroad hands. Long years of consumption make hundreds of fathers burdens on their younger children. Some of the children, however, principally Italians, Bohemians, and Germans, are sent to work by their parents out of sheer excess of thrift, perhaps in order to pay off a mortgage upon some tenement house. In hundreds of cases during 1893–1894 the children left school and went to work because the father, previously the sole support of the family, was now among the unemployed. This is a lasting injury wrought by every industrial crisis; for the children so withdrawn from school are ashamed to return, after prolonged absence, to a lower class; and, having tasted the excitement of factory-life and partial self-support, are unfitted for anything else . . .

---

2. Children work for reasons other than necessity

Spargo, *Bitter Cry of the Children,* pp. 210–216.

In the hope that I might be able to gather sufficient accurate data to warrant some fairly definite conclusions upon this point, I spent several weeks making careful personal investigations into the matter in four states, New York, New Jersey, Pennsylvania, and Massachusetts. I made inquiries into 213 cases, first getting the children's stories and then carefully investigating them. The results are clearly set forth in the accompanying schedule, but explanation of a few points may be helpful to the reader.

In choosing a wage standard to represent the primary poverty line, I somewhat arbitrarily fixed upon $10 per week. In either of the four states named, such a wage must mean poverty and lead to the employment of children at the earliest possible moment. Intemperance appears in four cases, but that does not mean that it did not enter into other cases at all. In the four cases noted the fathers were earning from $12 to $18 per week, and while it is possible that with such wages they might be honestly and honorably poor, since even $18 is not a very princely wage, it is a fact that their expenditures upon drink constituted the real cause of the poverty which forced their children to work. On the other hand, I do not suppose that all the cases of child labor due to the primary poverty of their families are noted. In the last column several cases are given of children who were "sick when attending school," or who "could not get on at school." For reasons given in an earlier chapter, I am inclined to believe that these cases would have to be transferred to the other column if it were only possible to investigate them more fully.

. . . The number of cases investigated [here] is too small to give the results more than suggestive value. Personally, I believe that the cases given are fairly typical, and that is the opinion also of some of the leading authorities upon the subject to whom I have submitted the table . . .

.   .   .   .   .   .

The table shows more than mere poverty. First of all there is the senseless, feverish, natural ambition of the immigrant to save

Table showing reasons for the employment of 213 children.

No. of children	Occupations	Reasons given which indicate primary poverty		Reasons given other than apparent primary poverty	
Boys, 34	Glass factory workers	Wages of father less than $10 per week	9	Parents saving money to buy their homes, etc.	8
		Father sick or injured	5	Children working to keep father who is able to work but won't	2
		Father dead	2		
		Father unemployed	1		
		Father in prison	1	Not determined	6
Boys, 23 Girls, 57	Textile mill workers	Wages of father less than $10 per week	14	Tired of school	13
		Father unemployed	6	Discouraged by being "put back" at school every time family moved	6
		Father dead	5		
		Father sick or injured	6	Parents saving the money	5
		Father deserted family	2	Because companions went to work	9
		Father drunkard	1	To get better clothes	4
				Not determined	9
Boys, 33 Girls, 22	Cigarette, cigar, and tobacco workers	Father's wage less than $10 per week	14	Because friends worked	6
		Father dead	3	Tired of school	5
		Father sick or injured	4	Parents saving money	4
		Father unemployed	4	To get better clothes	3
		Father drunkard	3	Sick while at school	2
				Not determined	7
Boys, 18 Girls, 26	Delivery wagon boys 4 Match packers 12 Candy factory girls 10 Wire factory workers 7 Rubber factory workers 11	Wages of father less than $10 per week	15	Couldn't get on at school	4
		Father dead	2	To get better clothes	6
		Father sick or injured	4	Because friends went to work	3
		Father unemployed	2	Sick while at school	3
		Father deserted family	2	Not determined	3

Total no. of children	Occupations	Summary of causes in primary poverty group		Summary of causes other than primary poverty	
Boys, 108 Girls, 105		Low wages	52	School difficulties	30
		Unemployment	13	Because friends went to work	18
		Father's death	12	To get better clothes	11
		Father's sickness	19	To enable parents to save	17
		Father's desertion of family	4	Sickness of child while at school	5
		Father's intemperance	4	Father's laziness	2
		Father in prison	1	Not determined	25
Total, 213		Total, 105 = 49.30%		Total, 108 = 50.70%	

money, to be rich. "Ma boy getta much mona — I get richa man," said one of the Italians included in the first line of the fourth column of the foregoing table. How often I have heard that speech! Not always in the broken music of Italian-English, but in the many-toned, curious English of Bohemian, Lithuanian, Scandinavian, Russian, Pole, and Greek — all drawn by the same powerful magnet of wealth — all sacrificing, ignorantly and blindly, the lives of themselves and their children in their fevered quest . . .

The virtual breakdown of our school system is one of the gravest problems indicated by the table and enforced by general observation. The children who go to work in factories and mines because they are "tired of school," or "because they could not learn," are, it is to be feared, not always but too often, the victims of undernutrition. The school spends all its energies in the vain attempt to educate wasting minds in starving bodies, and then the child, already physically and mentally ruined, goes to the mine or the factory, there to linger on as half-starved plants in arid soil sometimes linger, or to fade away as a summer flower fades in a day. Poverty began the ruin of the child by denying it proper nourishment, and ignorance and greed combine to complete the ruin by sending the child in its weakness forth to labor.

---

3. Father killed at work, 1906–1907

Crystal Eastman, *Work Accidents and the Law* (New York, 1910), pp. 137–142.

Miss Eastman investigated the causes and consequences of 526 fatal work accidents occurring in Allegheny County, Pennsylvania, between July 1, 1906, and June 30, 1907.

Mrs. August Stanley, widow of a Pennsylvania Railroad brakeman, who was struck by an engine in the yards at night while on his way to the bunk room after work, has four children, the oldest 14, and all in school. As a brakeman her husband earned from $20 to $22 a week, and they paid $10 a month rent. Up to seven months after the accident they were living in the same place. The expenses of the accident were not heavy. She spent $155 on the funeral, of which sum the company paid $141. Mrs. Stanley makes $3.00 or $4.00 a week by washing and sewing, and her thirteen-year-old boy carries papers before and after school, earning $2.00 a week. Thus with the $750 from the Relief Association to which her husband paid $2.75 a month dues, and $13.50 from the Brotherhood, they will get along for a while, if no more disasters befall them. But it will mean a pinching economy for a family accustomed to a $20 income.

.   .   .   .   .

Patrick Feenan, a laborer, killed at Jones and Laughlin's after 19 years' service there, left a wife and five children under fourteen. The company paid the funeral expenses and gave the oldest boy a job. He is thirteen, and earns $6.00 a week. An old uncle of Mrs. Feenan lives with them, and his earnings with those of the boy made up the family income until the hard times came, when both were thrown out of work.

Thomas J. Barton, employe of Jones and Laughlin, working at night with a wrecking train, was run down and killed. This man was fifty-one, and earned $9.50 a week. He had two sons working, one an electrician and one a machinist, besides five younger children in school. They owned their own house of six rooms and had but $1,000 more to pay on it, but they carried no insurance. Mrs. Barton did not try to get money from the company, — even for funeral expenses, which were $195, — and they did not offer her anything. The oldest son soon married. This left the family dependent on an eighteen-year-old machinist making $12 a week. So the next boy, aged sixteen, left school and became an apprentice, adding $4.50 to the weekly income; and finally the fourteen-year-old boy left school and brought in $3.60 a week as a special messenger.

.   .   .   .   .

Albert Owen was a car repairer on the Pennsylvania Railroad, making $12 a week. On October 5, 1906, he was jerked off the footboard of an engine and run over. Owen was insured in the relief association for $500. For some time after the accident Mrs. Owen and the three boys, twelve, ten, and four, lived on this sum with great economy. The oldest boy is lame and very small for his age. Some one from the railroad company promised to give him a job as messenger, but when he appeared at the office he was told that he could not pass the physical examination. Finally, after more than a year, through the efforts of a minister, he got a job as messenger boy in an electrical company and earns $4.00 a week. This lame, undersized boy, not yet fourteen, is bringing in the family's only income.

.   .   .   .   .

William Evans, miner for the Pittsburgh Coal Company, was a widower. When he was killed, there was left a family of six, his oldest daughter with a baby, a boy of sixteen who had been Evans' helper in the mine, a girl of thirteen, and two boys eleven and eight. There was nothing for this family to do but scatter. The sixteen-year-old boy went off and took care of himself by working in a glass factory. The grown daughter took her baby and youngest brother and went to live with a sister. This left the two children of thirteen and eleven, for the grandparents, Evans' father and mother-in-law, to take care of. They lived in a small house, and were supported by an unmarried son of twenty-three, a miner earning $15 a week. The old man is crippled with rheumatism, and his wife who is sixty-two, after a long hard life, had given up going out to work, and settled down to look after her husband and

son. When the two children came back upon her, she began again going out by the day to do washing for her neighbors. After the first winter the little girl, then nearly fourteen, got a place to work in a family for her "keep." This made things easier for the grandmother. (In this coal company there is a relief association. The men pay 40 cents a month and this provides $75 benefits if one is killed. To this the company adds $75, making $150. In Evans' case $90 was used in the funeral.) As a result of this one accident, then, we have the standard of living of one family lowered by the addition of three dependent members, we have a boy of sixteen left to look out for himself, a girl barely fourteen gone out to service for her "keep," and an old grandmother doing other people's washing.

---

4. Children contribute to the upward mobility of the family

U.S. Department of Commerce and Labor, *Report on Condition of Woman and Child Wage-Earners in the United States,* I (Washington, D.C., 1910), 120–123.[1]

. . . Thus in New England, of the operatives reported, only 27.3 per cent had spent their early childhood on farms, while 44.5 per cent were brought up in cities, as against 75.8 per cent in the southern group from farms and only 4 per cent from cities. The 20.2 per cent whose childhood was spent in villages were largely the children of cotton-mill operatives who had moved from farms to cotton-mill villages.

Some of those who reported that their early childhood was spent on a farm came from small farms in the mountains of Virginia, North Caro-

1. For fuller details on this investigation see below Chap. II, sec. B, Investigation of child labor by the federal government.

lina, and Tennessee. The exact proportion of those coming from the mountains was not secured, and the proportion varies greatly in different sections. Taking the mill population as a whole, for the mills visited during this investigation the percentage of such operatives was very much smaller than the percentage of those who come from the lowland farms surrounding the cotton-mill villages.

For varying reasons the small farmers leave the farm and move to the mill village. Some have been unsuccessful as farmers. Some have been disheartened by poor crops or low prices. Others have, perhaps, been moderately successful but hope for a more comfortable life, with a larger remuneration, at the cotton mill. Whatever discontent with their conditions or desire for improvement exists is fostered by the labor agent, who is usually the head of a family which has been successful at the mill and who canvasses the country thoroughly and frequently.

When the mill needs workers, one of the plans used to obtain them, as outlined by the secretary of one of the mills, is to select a day when there is a circus, show, or celebration in town, which will assemble many farmers from the surrounding country. "Dodgers," setting forth the benefit to be derived from cotton-mill work and the amounts paid to children and adults, with a few attractive statements as to what can be earned by a family of so many workers, etc., are gotten out, and not given to the farmers, but dropped into their wagons where they will be sure to find them when they get home. Letters are received in reply to these, and many families are obtained. Another plan is to post similar dodgers in small stations.

The personnel of the family often accounts for migration from the farm to the cotton mill. The widow with children too young for farm work readily seizes the opportunity for her children to help in the support of the family at lighter work. The father who is disabled is also easily induced to bring his family from the farm to the mill, where he can get the benefit of his children's labor.

Fathers whose only disablement is laziness are also easily induced to bring their families to the mill village for the same reasons, but the percentage of fathers of this kind found during this investigation was very small and leads to the conclusion that the extent to which these cases exist in southern mill villages has been very much exaggerated.

. . . . .

Another type of family attracted to the cotton mill is that which has a predominance of females. Necessity may compel the women and girls to assist in the support of the family, and while the farm work is not suited to their strength the work at the mill, which is lighter and unaffected by the vicissitudes of the weather, is attractive to them.

Some of the larger mills have sent agents into the mountains and secured a goodly number of the mountain farmers. Aside from these, however, except in the mills located near the foothills or in the mountains, there is only a sprinkling of mountain families. Mills in western North Carolina, mills at Spartanburg, Greenville, and other large mill towns in upper South Carolina, and mills in northern Georgia and northeastern Alabama were found to have many mountain people among their employees. Mountaineers were not found at any great distance from the mountains, however, except occasionally among migratory families.

. . . . .

. . . The people who have lived in the mountainous section are quite likely to go back to the mountains during the heated months. Doubtless a large percentage never return to the farm or mountains, and of those who do it is not probable that any large percentage remain away permanently from the cotton mills after having once worked in them. The father and mother may tire of the excitement of the mill village and wish to return to the quiet of the farm or mountains, but the children are usually unwilling to leave the associations of the mill village.

A particular study was made in the mountain

region from which a part of the labor force of the cotton mills has been recruited as to the conditions of life among the class from which this labor comes. Among the poorer classes of farmers in the more remote mountain districts much extreme poverty and hard conditions of life were found. Living isolated in mountain coves, eking out in many cases a wretched existence from small and barren patches of land, with either no facilities or scant facilities for either the education of their children or anything approaching an opportunity for a normal social development, the comfort of this class and the opportunity for the education of their children could not fail to be improved by their migration to industrial communities . . .

5. Children necessary for parents' employment

U.S. Department of Commerce and Labor, *Report on Condition of Woman and Child Wage Earners in the United States,* III (Washington, D.C., 1911), 158–159.

Agents of the Bureau of Labor investigated 179 establishments manufacturing glass, which comprised 75 per cent of the glass industry in 1908. The following states were represented: Massachusetts, Connecticut, New York, New Jersey, Pennsylvania, Ohio, Indiana, Illinois, Wisconsin, Missouri, Kansas, West Virginia, Maryland, Virginia, Tennessee, Georgia, and South Carolina. The establishments investigated employed a total of 109,-928 workers, of whom 5,705 were children under sixteen. Of these children only 583 were female.[1]

Apart from the importation of such families, there is a very well defined attitude on the part

1. U.S. Department of Labor, Bureau of Labor and Statistics, *Bulletin No. 175,* "Summary of the Report on Condition of Woman and Child Wage Earners in the United States" (Washington, D.C., 1916), pp. 117–118.

of a large number of manufacturers to compel their unskilled and semiskilled workmen to put their children in the factory as soon as they become of legal working age, or in some cases, before legal age is actually reached. No instances of specific written agreement on the part of workmen to put their children into the factory were developed by the investigation, but a number of manufacturers stated frankly that such an understanding was usually had when an unskilled laborer was employed, while in other cases there was merely a tacit understanding that the men who would be retained by the company in case it became necessary to reduce the force were the men who had sons in the factory. An excellent illustration of this is afforded by the case of a large bottle factory in which it became necessary during the financial depression of 1908 to lay off about two hundred unskilled laborers. Of the ten who were heard to ask the superintendent to be retained only one spoke of his own efficiency, all the others basing their claim to a job on the assertion that they had kept one or more sons in the factory throughout the winter. All were refused, and one of the men in the office said when one threatened to remove the boys, "It's a sure thing he won't; he'll have a hard time keeping that big family of his for the next six months even with his kids in the factory."

6. The desire for independence

Mother's letter to the advice column, *Jewish Daily Forward,* March 23, 1920.

The *Jewish Daily Forward,* a socialist paper founded in 1897, was the largest foreign language paper in the United States. Its daily circulation in the 1920's was approximately 155,000.

I have a fifteen-year-old boy. Last September, when the schools opened after summer vacation, my boy declared that he would not go to school. He would work instead. He still had one year till graduation.

My husband was content to let him work. "Since he does not want to study," my husband said, "we need not force him." But I wanted very badly that my boy should finish school, and tried to persuade him with kind words. I warned him that later in life he would not regret having attended school. My boy is good. He listened to my advice and agreed to go on. He went to school every day and studied well. He brought good report cards.

One day last week he left for school as usual, but did not come home.

.   .   .   .   .

The next day the principal told me that my boy had appeared with a strange man, whom he introduced as his boss, and asked for a work permit. The principal refused to grant such a permit, insisting that the boy return with his father.

Several days later we received a letter from my boy. He wrote that he was in a town near Maine and that he worked in a print shop. He asked us not to try to find him, because he was pleased with his job. He said he would return to us when he is grown up and will have saved enough.

My husband argues that because of my insistence on the school I have driven our child from home. Had I permitted my son to work here he would not have run away to the corner of the earth . . .

Our friends and neighbors side with my husband's view. So, it turns out that I have committed a crime by trying to coax my boy into school, and now my conscience tortures me. I am at fault for this trouble.

Dear Editor, what shall we do. If we try to find him and return him home, he will run away again and will not disclose his location. But to leave a young boy alone in a strange town without supervision, we fear that this will not bring much good.

The desperate mother.

[Editor's reply:]

It is ridiculous to blame the mother. She had the best intentions for her child, and the husband is committing a sin in reproaching her.

As to whether the parents should force him to return: According to the law they could do it. But there is truth in the opinion of their friends that he might run away again. The desire to work is very much developed in him. And if they will force him to go to school, he will surely run away again.

It is therefore advisable that one should persuade him to come home out of his free accord and permit him to work here. Then he would surely want to stay with his parents.

Hazards of the job

1. The price of child labor

Spargo, *Bitter Cry of the Children,* pp. 175–180.

It is a sorry but indisputable fact that where children are employed, the most unhealthful work is generally given them. In the spinning and carding rooms of cotton and woollen mills, where large numbers of children are employed, clouds of lint-dust fill the lungs and menace the health. The children have often a distressing cough, caused by the irritation of the throat, and many are hoarse from the same cause. In bottle factories and other branches of glass manufacture, the atmosphere is constantly charged with microscopic particles of glass. In the wood-working industries, such as the manufacture of cheap furniture and wooden boxes, and packing cases, the air is laden with fine sawdust. Children employed in soap and soap-powder factories work, many of them, in clouds of alkaline dust which inflames the eyelids and nostrils. Boys employed in filling boxes of soap-powder work all day long with handkerchiefs tied over their mouths. In the coal-mines the breaker boys breathe air that is heavy and thick with particles of coal, and their lungs become black in consequence. In the manufacture of felt hats, little girls are often employed at the machines which tear the fur from the skins of rabbits and other animals. Recently, I stood and watched a young girl working at such a machine; she wore a newspaper pinned over her head and a handkerchief tied over her mouth. She was white with dust from head to feet, and when she stooped to pick anything from the floor the dust would fall from her paper head-covering in little heaps. About seven feet from the mouth of the machine was a window through which poured thick volumes of dust as it was belched out from the machine. I placed a sheet of paper on the inner sill of the window and in twenty minutes it was covered with a layer of fine dust, half an inch deep. Yet that girl works midway between the window and the machine, in the very centre of the volume of dust, sixty hours a week. These are a few of the occupations in which the dangers arise from the forced inhalation of dust.

In some occupations, such as silk-winding, flax-spinning, and various processes in the manufacture of felt hats, it is necessary, or believed to be necessary, to keep the atmosphere quite moist. The result of working in a close, heated factory, where the air is artificially moistened, in summer time, can be better imagined than described. So long as enough girls can be kept working, and only a few of them faint, the mills are kept going; but when faintings are so many and so frequent that it does not pay to keep going, the mills are closed. The children who work in the dye rooms and print-shops of textile factories, and the color rooms of factories where the materials for making artificial flowers are manufactured, are subject to contact with poisonous dyes, and the results are often terrible. Very frequently they are dyed in parts of their bodies as literally as the fabrics are dyed. One little fellow, who was employed in a Pennsylvania carpet factory, opened his shirt one day and showed me his chest and stomach

dyed a deep, rich crimson. I mentioned the incident to a local physician, and was told that such cases were common. "They are simply saturated with the dye," he said. "The results are extremely severe, though very often slow and, for a long time, almost imperceptible. If they should cut or scratch themselves where they are so thoroughly dyed, it might mean death." In Yonkers, N.Y., are some of the largest carpet factories in the United States, and many children are employed in them. Some of the smallest children are employed in the "drum room," or print-shop, where the yarns are "printed" or dyed. Small boys mostly Slavs and Hungarians, push the trucks containing boxes of liquid dye from place to place, and get it all over their clothing. They can be seen coming out of the mills at night literally soaked to the skin with dye of various colors. In the winter time, after a fall of snow, it is possible to track them to their homes, not only by their colored footprints, but by the drippings from their clothing. The snow becomes dotted with red, blue, and green, as though some one had sprinkled the colors for the sake of the variegated effect.

Children employed as varnishers in cheap furniture factories inhale poisonous fumes all day long and suffer from a variety of intestinal troubles in consequence. The gilding of picture frames produces a stiffening of the fingers. The children who are employed in the manufacture of wall papers and poisonous paints suffer from slow poisoning. The naphtha fumes in the manufacture of rubber goods produce paralysis and premature decay. Children employed in morocco leather works are often nauseated and fall easy victims to consumption. The little boys who make matches, and the little girls who pack them in boxes, suffer from phosphorous necrosis, or "phossy-jaw," a gangrene of the lower jaw due to phosphor poisoning. Boys employed in type foundries and stereotyping establishments are employed on the most dangerous part of the work, namely, rubbing the types and the plates, and lead poisoning is excessively prevalent among them as a result. Little girls who work in the hosiery mills and carry heavy baskets from one floor to another, and their sisters who run machines by foot-power, suffer all through their after life as a result of their employment. Girls who work in factories where caramels and other kinds of candies are made are constantly passing from the refrigerating department, where the temperature is perhaps 20 degrees Fahr., to other departments with temperatures as high as 80 or 90 degrees. As a result, they suffer from bronchial troubles.

.   .   .   .   .   .

No combination of figures can give any idea of that price. Statistics cannot express the withering of child lips in the poisoned air of factories; the tired, strained look of child eyes . . .

---

2. Illness, death, and mutilation

Kelley and Stevens, "Wage-Earning Children," pp. 58–68.

. . . Among the occupations in which children are most employed in Chicago, and which most endanger the health, are: The tobacco trade, nicotine poisoning finding as many victims among factory children as among the boys who are voluntary devotees of the weed, consumers of the deadly cigarette included; frame gilding, in which work a child's fingers are stiffened and throat disease is contracted; buttonholing, machine-stitching, and hand-work in tailor or sweat shops, the machine-work producing spinal curvature, and for girls pelvic disorders also, while the unsanitary condition of the shops makes even hand-sewing dangerous; bakeries, where children slowly roast before the ovens; binderies, paper-box and paint factories, where arsenical paper, rotting paste, and the poison of the paints are injurious; boilerplate works, cutlery works, and metal-stamping works, where the dust produces lung disease; the handling of hot metal, accidents; the hammering of plate, deafness. In addition to diseases incidental to trades, there are the conditions of bad sanitation and long hours, almost universal in the factories where children are employed.

.   .   .   .   .

Of the reckless employment of children in injurious occupations the following are examples: —

.   .   .   .   .

Joseph Poderovsky, aged fourteen years, was found by a deputy inspector running a heavy buttonhole machine by foot-power at 204 West Taylor Street, in the shop of Michael Freeman. The child was required to report for examination, and pronounced by the examining physician, rachitic, and afflicted with a double lateral curvature of the spine.[1] He was ordered discharged, and prohibited from working in any tailor-shop. A few days later he was found at work at the same machine. A warrant was sworn out for the arrest of the employer; but before it could be served the man left the State. This boy has a father in comfortable circumstances, and two adult able-bodied brothers.

Bennie Kelman, Russian Jew, four years in Chicago, was found running a heavy sewing-machine by foot-power in a sweat-shop of the nineteenth ward where knee-pants are made. A health certificate was required, and the medical examination revealed a severe rupture. Careful questioning of the boy and his mother elicited the fact that he had been put to work in a boiler factory two years before, when just thirteen years old, and had injured himself lifting heavy masses of iron. Nothing had been done for the case; no one in the family spoke any English, or knew how help could be obtained. The sight test showed that the boy did not know his letters in English, though he said that he could read Jewish jargon. He was sent

1. According to the Illinois Workshops and Factories Act of 1893, a factory inspector could demand a certificate of physical fitness for a child who looked too sickly to work. These were often issued to unfit children by unscrupulous physicians for a small fee.

to the College of Physicians and Surgeons for treatment, and forbidden work.

If health certificates are granted to wage-earning children merely *pro forma,* upon the representation of the employer or the child, the object of the law is nullified. The physician who grasps the situation, and appreciates the humane intent of the law, will always find time to visit the factory and see under what conditions the child is working. Otherwise his certificate may be worse than valueless, and work a positive injury to a child whom the inspectors are trying to save from an injurious occupation. Thus, a healthy child may wish to enter a cracker bakery; and unless the physician visits it, and sees the dwarfish boys slowly roasting before the ovens, in the midst of unguarded belting and shafting, a danger to health which men refuse to incur, he may be inclined to grant the certificate, and thereby deprive the child of the only safeguard to health which the State affords him. Similar danger exists in regard to tobacco, picture-frame, box, metal-stamping, and wood-working factories.

.   .   .   .   .   .

. . . If [a health] certificate formally meets the requirement of the law, the child must be left at work, no matter what the effect upon its health, present and future. The same is true where inspectors have tried to save children from danger to life and limb, by requiring health certificates for them when found working amidst dangerous machinery. There is in the Illinois law no provision for the safeguarding of machinery; and if a physician issues a certificate to a child merely because it is for the moment in good health, with no knowledge of the dangerous occupation of the child, the inspector, under the present law, is powerless. An example is afforded by a stamping-factory of this ward. The inspector called the attention of the head of the firm to the danger to which employees were subjected, because of unguarded shafting and machinery, and required a health certificate for every minor employed there. A week later a deputy inspector went to this factory, and

found twenty-five health certificates, in proper form, on file. One of these certificates was already superfluous. The boy for whom it had been obtained had been killed in the factory the day before. Within two years two boys have been killed outright, and several mutilated in this factory. The last boy killed had lost three fingers at his machine only a few months before his death.

One machine used in the stamping-works consists of an endless chain revolving over a trough filled with melted solder. In this trough cans are kept moving in unbroken procession, revolving as they go. At each end of the trough stands a boy with a little iron poker, made for the purpose of keeping the cans in their places and pulling them out at the end. But the poker is not always quick enough, and the boy's hand is apt to get into contact with the melting fluid. In preparation for this danger the lads wrap their hands before beginning work; but this precaution is only good for minor burns, and the real danger to the child is that he may lose a hand outright. This machine has been superseded in the stamping-works of more progressive manufacturers by a self-actor, which may be made free from danger to an employee; but this is expensive, and children of the class employed at the stamping-works are so thoroughly defenseless by reason of poverty and ignorance of the laws and language of the country, that the company finds it cheaper to use the old-fashioned machine, and take the risk of damage suits, than to pay for the more modern solderer. The metal-stamping trade, like the candy, paper-box, and garment trades, is without organization, and the children employed in it suffer accordingly. This company employs a large body of recently immigrated Russian and Bohemian men, boys, and girls, many of whom are wholly illiterate; and even if they can read their own language, this is of little avail for reading the terms of the contract, printed in English, under which they are employed, or the card of directions which each one is required to carry in his or her pocket, in order that the company may prove, in case of injury to an employee, that notice of the danger had been given, and that the injury was therefore no fault of the company, but solely due to the recklessness of the boy or girl.

Of the rules printed on these cards, one reads as follows: —

11. All employees are strictly forbidden placing their hands under the dies; and all employees, other than those whose duty it is to repair or clean machines, are strictly forbidden to place their hands or any part of their body in contact with or within reach of those portions of the machinery intended to be in motion when the machinery is in operation, or in contact with, or in reach of the shafting; and this applies to machinery in operation and not in operation. It is dangerous to disobey this rule.

For middle-aged men, self-possessed and cautious, able to read these rules and ponder them, it would still be a grewsome thought that the penalty of violation may be instant death; but where the employees are growing lads, many of them unable to read at all, and all at the age when risk is enticing, and the most urgent warning is often a stimulus to wayward acts, what excuse can be offered for supplying machinery lacking in any most trifling essential of safeguard? Yet these rules themselves announce that the surroundings of these boys are so fraught with danger, that a whole code of fourteen rules and regulations is needful to protect the pockets of the company in the probable event of injury to the children. There are other wealthy corporations and firms in Chicago today holding contracts with the parents or guardians of employed children, and with casualty insurance companies, releasing the employers from liability in case of accident to the child. Does any one suppose that an employer would hold such contracts unless accidents to children in his employ were numerous, and might be made costly?

Ingenious safeguards are a part of the construction of machinery in modern plants; but many factories are operated without such im-

provements, and expose employees, old and young, to constant danger of death or mutilation. Even where the latest patents in safeguarding are found, accidents are possible if operators are careless. In a factory where accidents are of almost daily occurrence among the children employed, we are told, "They never get hurt till they get careless" . . .

---

3. Parents release employers of responsibility for industrial accidents

Illinois, Inspectors of Factory, *Third Annual Report, 1895* (Springfield, 1896), pp. 35–37.

ILLINOIS STEEL COMPANY

I, ——— of ——— my minor son, who is of the age of ——— years, hereby make application to the Illinois Steel Company to receive, upon the following terms, and continue in its employ the said ——— at the ——— Works of said company upon the following conditions:

I, ——— parent, as aforesaid, fully recognize the hazardous nature of the employment in which my said son is about to engage and to continue in; but, nevertheless, I, the said parent, desire his employment as aforesaid in such departments and occupations as the said company may from time to time designate; and I hereby consent to such employment of said minor, and in consideration thereof and for the further consideration of one dollar to me in hand paid, the receipt whereof from said company I hereby acknowledge, I do hereby release and forever discharge the Illinois Steel Company of and from all claims and demands for loss of service of said ——— minor, on account of any personal injuries he may sustain while in the employ of said company in any of its departments; and I do hereby emancipate the said minor, and I agree that any and all time, salary or wages that may be due him for work or labor performed by him for said company, shall be entered to his credit and paid to him direct by the treasurer or paymaster of said company; and I hereby authorize such payments and agree that his receipt therefor shall be binding upon me; and I release and discharge said company from all liability whatsoever for the value of his services during his minority. Said ——— was born at ——— on ——— day of ——— 18 —

The above was read to and signed by the said ——— in our presence at ——— the ——— day of ——— 189 —

WITNESS my hand and seal at ——— Illinois, this ——— day of ——— 189 —

——— (Seal)

Note — The above release is in all cases to be executed by the father, if living, in the presence of two witnesses; if the father is dead, it is to be executed by the mother, and the fact of the death of the father must be noted across the face of the release in ink, as follows, to-wit: "Father is dead."

.   .   .   .   .

CHICAGO DROP FORGE AND FOUNDRY CO.

"We hereby certify that our son, Axel Swanson, was born on the 29th day of June, 1878; and that we consent to his employment at grinding, heating, carrying stock, and trimming, by the Drop Forge & Foundry Co.; and in consideration of such employment do hereby release said employers from any and all claims or demands that we either of us may have as parents of said minor, growing out of any personal injury that may accrue to him while so employed.

(Signed)

E. W. SWANSON,
MRS. SWANSON"

4. Overwork and accident in a steel factory, 1909

Inland Steel Company *v.* Yedinak, 172 Indiana 423.

The appeal of the Inland Steel Company on a judgment against it in favor of thirteen-year-old John Yedinak was unsuccessful. The Company's defense was Yedinak's contributory negligence, but the Court of Appeals upheld the previous judgment that the boy had been employed at an age beneath the legal minimum and for hours in excess of the maximum number allowed by the law.

Action by John Yedinak, by his next friend, against the Inland Steel Company. From a judgment for the plaintiff for $2,000 defendant appeals . . .

MONTGOMERY, J. . .

[The employer] was, at and before the time of the happening of the grievances complained of, a corporation engaged in the manufacture of iron and steel. [Yedinak] . . . a minor under the age of sixteen years, was employed by Inland Steel in its rolling-mill, and was required to work for twelve hours each night for six nights in each week. For more than a week prior to the time of receiving his injuries he had been compelled to and did work, under his employment, fourteen hours each night . . . Under his employment [Yedinak] was required to and did open and hold open the doors of certain furnaces, while iron was being placed therein or taken therefrom, when requested to do so by [his employer] or by workmen whose duty it was to perform such work. Iron was placed in [the] furnaces every half hour, and during the intervals [Yedinak] had no duty to perform except to wait in [the] mill, and be ready to open and hold [the] doors when so directed. [The employer] furnished [Yedinak] no place in which to wait when not actively engaged, but directed him to wait in [the] rolling-mill.

At 5 o'clock P.M. on October 5, 1903, [Yedinak] went to work, and was required to and did remain continuously at [his] work until 4 o'clock A.M. of the following day, and was then in the performance of [the] work under his employment. He was then but thirteen years of age, and became weary and exhausted from exertion and loss of sleep, caused by his continuous work in his . . . employment, and, having no duty to perform except to wait in attendance, sat down upon an iron door in [the] mill, four feet distant from and elevated two feet above, a certain railroad track used by appellant to convey iron in cars to the furnaces, and for no other purpose.

.   .   .   .   .

[Yedinak] had not been instructed nor notified to any danger in sitting near [the] track, and, by reason of his youth, inexperience, exhaustion and sleepiness, he was incapable of appreciating any danger . . . Upon sitting down upon the iron door, because of such exhaustion and sleepiness, he immediately and involuntarily fell asleep and became unconscious, and while so asleep, his foot and leg were involuntarily placed upon the rail of [the] track, and while so on [the] track, and before the iron in [the] furnaces had been removed . . . [the employer] caused a car loaded with iron to be moved along the track, over the rail and over Yedinak's foot and leg, thereby crushing the bones, muscles and flesh . . . and producing the injuries of which he complains.

.   .   .   .   .

. . . In answer to interrogatories the jury found that [Yedinak] was born January 20, 1890, was employed by [Inland Steel] May 6, and injured October 6, 1903. That during the two nights immediately preceding the time of receiving his injury he had worked twenty-two and one-half hours. It thus appears that he was under fourteen years of age, and the evidence warranted this finding. During an intermission in his active work he left the place he occupied when operating the furnace doors and went a distance of fifty feet or more and sat down near one of the furnaces. He was asked why he sat down there, and responded in a characteristic way as follows: "Kind of chilly that night, and I didn't have nothin' to do for that twenty minutes or so, and I sat down there, and I was so sleepy I couldn't — I don't know — I didn't go over to sit down, but I just sat down there to take a rest while they were gone — then they would go to feed ore again — I sat down to take a rest, and before I knew it I was dreaming — almost fell asleep, and I heard the cars coming, but I couldn't get up; it was just like dreaming; I tried to get up but I couldn't; I was dreaming like — so sleepy." He had sat down with his legs doubled up and his hands clasped about his knees, and said further: "I was sitting down, that is all; I know I had my feet up when I sat down, and all at once — I don't know how the car happened to get it — I saw two cars go past me, and then the third one happened — my leg was under the third one, that is all I know."

—————————————

5. Minors killed at work, Pittsburgh, 1906–1907

Eastman, *Work Accidents and the Law*, pp. 80, 88–89.

Eighty-two or 16 per cent of 526 fatal work accidents investigated by Miss Eastman (see above sec. A, Why children worked, doc. 3) involved youths under twenty-one years of age.

—————————————

Elevators seem to offer a peculiar temptation to recklessness; 14 of . . . 19 [elevator] accidents involved carelessness. Here are a few instances. An errand boy poked his head through a small window in a shaft and was killed by the descending elevator. An elevator boy put his head over the gate after he had started the elevator upward, and was caught.

One of the janitors in an office building, in a hurry to get his work done, attempted, against the rules of the building, to run an elevator and was killed. A seventeen-year-old dressmaker in a department store, running for an elevator that had started upward, slipped and fell through the opening.

.   .   .   .   .

Thirteen of the 132 who were in a measure responsible for their own deaths, were not men but boys. A fourteen-year-old assistant chemist was run over by an engine in the yards of a steel mill at night. A thirteen-year-old boy tried to pull up a freight elevator because one of the girls in the shop asked him if he could. It came up suddenly and fast, and struck him while he was leaning over. Two sixteen-year-old boys were killed while meddling with elevators. A newly landed Croatian lad of seventeen was killed by fooling with a switch with wet gloves on, watching the sparks fly.

In all these cases it could be said that there was no excuse. There was a path outside the tracks where the little chemist should have walked. The Croatian had been warned to keep away from the switch. The others had no business trying to run the elevators. It is all true, but they were children. We are too likely to think that a laborer must be grown up. We might expect that ten hours' work a day would take the nonsense out of any boy, but it doesn't. These very boys, full of mischief and daring in dangerous workshops, the boys who get hurt, are first cousins to the boys who, notwithstanding all the trouble they make, are most prized and most loved in the schools.

Two boys were killed in the Homestead steel works while they were asleep. Both accidents happened at 1:30 in the morning. One boy was a "pull-up," fifteen years old, who had worked eight hours out of a thirteen-hour night turn. He had a few minutes to rest, and went back of the furnace to lie down in a wheelbarrow. He fell asleep and was struck and killed by the extending arm of a ladle which the crane man was bringing back to the pit.[1] The other was an eighteen-year-old "hook-on" who, after seven hours of his working night had passed, climbed into a buggy and went to sleep. The crane man, not knowing this, lowered an iron bucket on the buggy and killed him.

Many kinds of carelessness which we should heartily condemn in a grown man, must be expected in a boy. For this reason we class these 13 cases with the 22 cases of ignorance.

---

6. Occupational injuries of young boys

Report of investigation sponsored by National Child Labor Committee, 1913, Box 3, National Child Labor Committee Papers, Library of Congress.

Guilford Avenue Plant. Inquiries received by boys working at Crown Cork & Seal Company — Testimony.

. . . Witness Abraham Henderson says he has known several boys who had their fingers amputated and one boy his arm broken who got caught in machinery. Witness also was cut on the hands. Witness claims that they even refuse to give them dressings for cut fingers. Company does not allow wages when boy remaining at home from injuries. When hurt, if boy loses an hour from injuries, he is docked for loss of time. Witness worked for Company four months. He claims that there is constant danger of being cut by the crown making machines and also from hanging up the tin

1. In a later reference (pp. 142–143) to this case Miss Eastman reported: "Joseph Koprivia, one of the boys killed in the Homestead works at night while asleep, although only fifteen, was earning as much as his father, a laborer of fifty. The mother is nearly blind, and there is a sister unmarried, and a boy of five, in the family. They still owe $400 on their house, and they are anxious about the future. They counted on Joseph's help. The Carnegie Steel Company gave the boy's mother $100, which she spent on the funeral."

sheets. Wages cut from $5.50 to $4.60 per week.

.   .   .   .   .

Joseph Alski, aged 14, injured at Jane Mills Fruit Packing Co. Injured while coring apples. The knife slipped and stuck him in the eye. The accident caused complete blindness, also affecting sight of the other eye. He lost two months and about $24 pay. No financial relief was given. May 17, 1913.

.   .   .   .   .

Frank Bauer . . . Worked in cork cutting department. Witness complains that the dust was unbearable and irritated his air passages so much that his parents made him stop work. Witness says boy by name of John Hind had his finger tip cut off. Dust caused much coughing among the boys employed.

Benjamin Lesius . . . Worked for American Tobacco Company, tin cutting department. Had ulcer of nasal cavity, fumes from stamping of hot tin. Witness claims that he knows several boys that had their fingers cut off by tin cutting machine. Also had fingers mashed by pressing machines. Witness had his fingers cut and exhibited scars of same.

.   .   .   .   .

David M. Foreman, employed at Crown Cork & Seal, Melting Department. His face was burned by splattering of hot wax, while employed at the wax machine. Lost seven days. Wages were paid, but boy was obliged to be present at factory every day and was docked 6 hours the day he had been treated by physician. March 12, 1913.

.   .   .   .   .

Elmer Preston, aged 14, employed at A. Hoen Lithographing and working in bronze. Worked in bronze used in coloring pictures on labels; took sheets out of machine and straightened them out. Hands were smeared with bronze, chapped and sore. Boy was discharged when he stayed home from work one day. April 16, 1913.

B. THE PROGRESSIVE ATTACK ON CHILD LABOR

Arguments of ethics and evolution

---

1. What child labor involves

Jane Addams, "Evils of Child Labor," in *Register* (New Haven, Conn.), Oct. 25, 1903.

Miss Addams' letter was printed in newspapers throughout the country.

. . . We may trace a connection between child labor and pauperism, not only for the child and his own family, bringing on premature old age and laying aside able-bodied men and women in the noon-tide of their years; but also the grievous charge is true that it pauperizes the community itself. I should also add that it debauches our moral sentiment, it confuses our sense of values, so that we learn to think that a bale of cheap cotton is more to be prized than a child properly nourished, educated and prepared to take his place in life. Let us stand up to the obligations of our own age. Let us watch that we do not discount the future and cripple the next generation because we were too indolent. I was going to say because we were too dull to see all that it involves, when we use the labor of little children.

2. The natural right to a long infancy

F. A. Verplanck, "Shortening the Period of Infancy," *Education Review*, XXVII (April 1904), 406–409.

A supervising principal in the school of South Manchester, Connecticut, Verplanck applied the theories of evolution and G. Stanley Hall's definitions of adolescence to the child labor problem.

The late John Fiske contributed a part to the generally accepted theory of evolution. His part was the portion which deals with the prolongation of infancy. In brief, the theory is something as follows. Those animals which at birth are nearly fully developed, and are able to care for themselves independent of parental assistance, are capable of little change and do change but little from generation to generation. On the other hand, those animals which at birth are well-nigh helpless and which remain for a time in this state, being dependent upon parental help, are capable of change and of education. That is, those animals which have had a short period of infancy have been capable of very little development from generation to generation. Those animals, which have had a long period of infancy have developed more rapidly from generation to generation. Man stands at the head of the animal kingdom. The period of infancy with man is the longest of any of the animals. He is, therefore, the most capable of education.

This part of the theory of evolution is of the greatest importance to parents, to teachers, and to all who are thoughtfully interested in the welfare of the human race. For whatever in our system of civilization tends to lengthen the period of infancy should tend to the advancement of the race as a whole. Whatever tends to shorten the period of infancy must subtract something from the sum total of advancement.

How long is the period of infancy? Among the lower animals, the period of infancy ends when the young animal is able to procure for itself food and shelter, and has the power to protect itself against its enemies. Our modern community life does not require the young *genus homo* to expend much energy in protecting himself against his enemies. It will be shown that in his case the period of infancy is often very much prolonged, but yet ends when he is capable of procuring his own food and shelter. In the case of certain favored individuals, the period is now longer probably than at any other time in the world's history. For instance, a boy completes his elementary education at the age of fourteen years. He leaves the high school at eighteen and graduates from college at the age of twenty-two years. He now spends two years in the medical school and then, after two years of hospital work, at the age of twenty-six years, may hope, if fortunate, soon to be self-supporting. The detailed reports of child labor in Southern cotton mills, or the work of the breaker boys in Northern coal mines, gives instances of the length of the period of infancy at the other extreme of a long and varying series of individuals and occupations.

In the good old days in New England, a boy worked for his father until he was twenty-one years of age. If he did not work at home, his father was entitled to collect his wages and usually did so. The young man, on reaching his twenty-first birthday, was given his freedom suit and was hereafter entitled to all the fruits of his own labor. The girl usually remained an inmate of her father's house, and her time and energy were expended for the welfare of the family until her wedding day. In general, a boy was an infant until he became of age, a girl until she married. They were under the influence of home and home training, until they had passed the period of adolescence and were really young men and young women.

This long period of parental influence has passed away. The scene has changed from the farm to the village or city. The stimulating outdoor life of the farm; filled with duties and responsibilities, has been replaced by the enervating routine of life in store, office, or factory. Together with this loss has come a still greater loss in the diminution of the length of time that the child is under the restraint and guidance of his parents.

The conditions in Connecticut are equal, at least, to those which generally obtain in the Northern States. Under the Connecticut law, a teacher upon application gives to each pupil who has passed his fourteenth birthday a certificate which permits him to go to work. In a short time he receives his wages and has money in his pocket . . .

Having money to spend has a wonderful effect on character. From the standpoint of many children money cannot be pleasurably expended in the home. The spending of it takes the child out of the house. The streets of many of our towns and cities are filled on summer evenings or Sunday afternoons with well-dressed young people, many of whom have not reached their majority. They have asserted their independence. Home no longer seriously restrains them. They earn their own money and spend it. They go where they wish. They choose their own associates, and make their own decisions in many of the most important and vital affairs of life.

Modern educational philosophy seems to teach that the period of adolescence is often the time of danger for the future man or woman. Then, if ever, he or she should be under the wise guidance of a watchful guardian. It would seem that our modern system, which allows a boy or girl to throw off all the restraints of home so early in the period of adolescence, is a direct violation of the principle. If we are shortening the period of infancy, if we are violating one of nature's laws, we must pay the penalty. It is already said that the second generation of those who come to us from foreign shores are interpreting the word freedom to mean license. It is said that it is difficult to make young people assume responsibility.

The reason is not far to find. The character-forming agencies of the past have been the school, the home, and the Church. The work of the school now ceases for many children at the age of fourteen years. The training of the Church and the home becomes optional, and is often disregarded by many children soon after this age. Children are becoming men and women too early. If the principle laid down at the beginning of this paper is correct, this means retrogression.

. . . The obvious answer is to prolong the period of infancy, which, in many cases, means lengthen the time that the child shall remain in school. It may be argued that many parents must take their children from school at the age of fourteen years. True, but many children leave school at the age of fourteen who could remain. When times are good, and work easily obtained, children leave school. When times are hard, children remain in school. Often, the welfare of the child is not the consideration which governs. The consideration which leads many children to leave school is to them of a practical nature. A bicycle, better clothing, money to spend are some of the inducing motives. These desires can be quickly satisfied by working. The remedy for our troubles in many cases must be such as will reach the child and which can be applied by the teacher.

---

3. Biology and ethics require abolition of child labor, 1905

Felix Adler, "Child Labor in the United States," in National Child Labor Committee, *Addresses at the Annual Meeting Held in New York City, February 14 to 16, 1905* (New York, 1905), pp. 14–16.

Felix Adler (1851–1933), professor of political and social ethics at Columbia University, was founder of the Ethical Culture Society and chairman of the National Child Labor Committee. He delivered this address at the first annual meeting of the Committee in 1905.

. . . I should like in approaching the close

of my address to present the grand positive reason why child servitude should be abolished throughout the length and breadth of this land. The battle is sometimes put on what are called sentimental grounds. Any one who has children of his own cannot help enduring a certain anguish in thinking of such cases as those of the little children treading up and down those stairs of the inferno of the English coal mines with buckets of coal on their backs, or of the little children in the mills returning to their squalid homes at 2.30 in the morning, or of the little boy rolling "tobies" in the dark and ill-ventilated room for fourteen mortal hours, coughing, with a pain "here and there." And when we picture these things and realize what they mean we are apt to cry out in a sort of wild indignation, saying: "These things must stop; we will not permit them to go on." In other words, we think of the individual children; and as we are men and women capable of sympathetic feeling, our hearts bleed for them.

But in addition we must never forget that beyond the individual interest there is a vast social interest at stake, the interest of American civilization, of human civilization, of all those generations that are to succeed us. The reason why child labor must be abolished, apart from the sufferings of individuals, is one which biology and ethics combine to enforce upon us. The higher the type of living being the finer the organism, the longer the period of time required for its maturing. The young of birds and of the lower animals are full grown after a few days or a few weeks. They acquire with incredible rapidity the use of inherited instincts, and after the shortest infancy are ready to take up the struggle for existence after the fashion of their species. The human being requires a period of preparation extending over years before he is ready to take up the struggle for existence after the human fashion. First infancy, then childhood, then early youth; and during all that period he must remain dependent on the protection and the nurture of adult kinsfolk. If that period is curtailed the end of Nature

in this highest type of living being — man — is thwarted. It is for this reason that premature toil is such a curse. The child must develop physically, and to do so it must play; the child must develop mentally, and to do so it must be sent to school; the child must develop morally, and to do so it must be kept within the guarded precincts of the home.

The physical effects of precocious childhood are arrest of growth, puny, stunted stature, anaemia, thin, emaciated limbs, sunken cheeks and hollow eyes; and diseases of all kinds — of the lungs, of the joints, of the spine — for arrest of development does not mean mere arrest, but means malformation.

The mental effects of precocity labor are likewise arrest of mental development; and this, too, means not only a stopping short but a development in the wrong direction. The brilliant but short-lived intelligence of many newsboys, their high-strung excitability, their sinister anticipation of world knowledge, followed often by torpor and mental exhaustion later on are an instance in point. We laugh at and applaud their sallies of wit, their quick repartee, their seeming ability to play the game of life on a par with adults; we do not look beyond the moment, nor count the cost they pay.

And the moral effects, as is to be expected, are of the same sort: loosening of family ties, roving the streets, familiarity with vice and the haunts of vice, a startling independence before the moral nature is fit to maintain independence, a process of selection so trying that while sometimes it leads those subjected to it to distinguished achievement, more often it leads to ruin.

The finer the type the longer the period needed for the maturing of it. In the case of youths dedicated to the professions, the period of preparation at present extends far into the twenties. In the case of all who are to be component members of this American nation, to carry on its great traditions and help in solving its tremendous problems, the period of preparation should not be cut short below the sixteenth year. This is the standard toward which we are working, toward which we hope to approximate — more rapidly in the older communities, more patiently and with a due regard to all the interests involved in the less advanced communities. But we look forward to the day when the standard shall be adopted in all the American Commonwealths, and the total abolition of child labor in every form shall be the honorable achievement of the entire American people.

The emancipation of childhood from economic servitude is a social reform of the first magnitude. It is also one upon which we can all unite. There are so many proposed reforms upon which it is impossible to secure agreement, different minds, though alike honest, inevitably differing with regard to them. But here is a reform upon which we can agree, which must appeal to every right thinking person, and which is urgent. And one particular advantage of it I should like to point out, namely, that it is calculated to be the best induction into the right spirit of social reform, that it will attune the community in which it is achieved to a favorable reception of sane and sound social reforms generally. Because if once it comes to be an understood thing that a certain sacredness "doth hedge around" a child, that a child is industrially taboo, that to violate its rights is to touch profanely a holy thing, that it has a soul which must not be blighted for the prospect of mere gain; if this be once generally conceded with regard to the child the same essential reasoning will be found to apply also to the adult workers; they, too, will not be looked upon as mere commodities, as mere instruments for the accumulation of riches; to them also a certain sacredness will be seen to attach, and certain human rights to belong, which may not be infringed. I have great hopes for the adjustment of our labor difficulties on a higher plane, if once we can gain the initial victory of inculcating regard for the higher human nature that is present potentially in the child.

4. Protect the children for the sake of the future

Theodore Roosevelt, "The Conservation of Childhood," in National Child Labor Committee, *Pamphlet No. 163* (New York, 1911), pp. 2, 4–5, 8.

Roosevelt delivered this speech at the Seventh Annual Conference on Child Labor held at Birmingham, Alabama, March 3–12, 1911.

Friends, Men and Women of Alabama, My Fellow Americans: I come this evening to speak to you on one of the great, fundamental questions of our citizenship in this republic.

I make an appeal for limiting by law the age under which children shall not be allowed to work, an appeal for limiting by law the hours that they shall be allowed to work in the daytime, and an appeal absolutely to prohibit by law working them at night.

.   .   .   .

I wish to see the new South go forward. I take the greatest pride and exultation in every particle of your industrial success. I am glad to see the spirit of the new South, embodied as it is here in your marvelous city, but I want you to keep the power of idealism of the old South.

.   .   .   .

. . . I ask you to remember that great though the importance of developing the mine, the mill, the factory, the railroad, great though the importance of developing all that tends to make for industrial supremacy, it is still more important to develop the right kind of citizenship.

I want you to take pride in getting the very best machinery . . . In the same way it is even more important to have the right kind of man behind the machine than it is to have the right machine. And you can not have the right kind of man unless you have the child trained in the right way, unless you have the child brought up amid right conditions.

How do you want your children brought up? You mothers and fathers who are fortunate enough to be able to decide for yourselves how your children shall be brought up, think of how you wish it done, and then see to it that the state provides that as far as possible the children in less fortunate conditions shall at least approximate in their bringing up to what you demand for your own children. Now is not that a common-sense demand? . . .

It ought not to be necessary to make very much of an appeal. You have done a great deal in Alabama to improve your stock, to improve your breeds of horses and of cattle. You use horses and mules for ploughing; sometimes oxen. How far would you get in a stock farm if you plowed with your colts? Put a couple of calves to a plow, and see what kind of oxen they will make.

.   .   .   .   .

Remember, that the human being is the most important of all products to turn out. I am eagerly anxious to do everything I can to wake up our people to the need of protecting the soil, protecting the forests, protecting the water; but first and foremost, protect the people. If you do not have the right kind of citizens in the future, you cannot make any use of the natural resources. Protect the children — protect the boys; still more, protect the girls; because the greatest duty of this generation is to see to it that the next generation is of the proper kind to continue the work of this nation.

The economic argument against child labor

1. A child learns only a fractional part of a trade

Testimony of P. H. McLogan, printer in Chicago, representative of Chicago Assembly in the Federation of Trades Unions, in U.S. Senate Committee on Education and Labor, *The Relations Between Labor and Capital,* I (Washington, D.C., 1885), 568.

A. We find that in the various wood-working departments of trade there are thousands of children employed. Take cabinet-making for instance. Formerly a boy went into a cabinet-maker's shop and learned the trade, but since the introduction of labor-saving machinery the cabinet-makers will take boys from twelve to sixteen years of age, and will put them into the cabinet shop to do a certain part of the work that they can easily learn to do in a short time. Take a bureau, for example; these boys will learn to make, say, one twenty-third part of a bureau; that is, they learn to do a certain little piece of the work by means of labor-saving machinery, and there they remain from year to year making that same little piece, and then all the pieces are put together, and the bureau is made. The same rule applies in other trades, in fact in almost all the other branches of mechanical industry, so that it is very difficult now for a boy to learn a trade at all.

Q. You mean that they learn the one twenty-third or some other fractional part of a trade, but not the whole trade? — A. That is just about it.

2. Effects of child labor on the economic development of the South

Irene M. Ashby [McFadyen], "The Last Stronghold of Infant Mill Slavery," *Social Service,* IV (December 1901), 204–205.

Irene Ashby's[1] denunciation contains all the arguments in the protest literature on child slavery in the South. Her articles achieved wide circulation and served as standard sources for Robert Hunter, John Spargo, and members of the National Child Labor Committee.

The folly and wrong of thus deliberately repeating the economic errors of past generations cannot be too strongly stated. The Southerners are new to commercial enterprise, but many of the mills are run by Northern managers and a larger number owned by Northern capital. Northerners at least should know better than to think, as they allege, that the long hours (eleven or twelve per day), cheap labor and employment of children are the determining factors in making competition with the North possible . . .

The absence of any child labor law encourages the parents in idleness, and it is not uncommon for quite young children to be supporting the family to the detriment of their health and education. Yet it is to the intelligence of the operatives that the South must look for successful competition. For the coarse goods now manufactured formidable competition is being prepared in other parts of the world. In India, China and Egypt cotton mills are already at work, and on the west coast of Africa cotton is being grown equal to that of the Southern States, whiles hordes of laborers, capable of manipulating coarse goods only, await the arrival of the industry. The competition of the Southern States will then be shifted to fine goods and her hope for success will lie in the resource and technical skill of her operatives. In what plight will she be then, if she continues to force compulsory ignorance, ill health, and mental paralysis on her future operatives in their infancy? Never in the world's history have economic sins been visited more quickly with less time for repentance and re-

1. Miss Ashby was married in late 1901 to an Englishman, McFadyen.

pair. No country can afford now to blunder on as did the old countries.

---

3. Child labor pauperizes the nation

Addams, "Evils of Child Labor," in *Register* (New Haven, Conn.), Oct. 25, 1903.

What connection do we find between child labor and pauperism? One of the first causes of pauperism is non-employment. Those who are first to lose their places in an industrial crises are those who have never had sufficient training and who curiously lack strength and vigor. In our municipal lodging-house in Chicago it is surprising to find how many tramps are tired to death with labor and begin to tramp in order to get away from it. This inordinate desire to get away from work seems to be connected with the fact that the men have started to work very early, before they had the physique to stand up to it, or the mental vigor with which to overcome its difficulties, or the moral stamina which makes a man stick to his work whether he likes it or not.

Another cause of pauperism is illness. A potent cause of disease is due to the breaking down of the organs which were subjected to abnormal uses before they were ready to bear it. I recall a tailor for whom the residents of Hull-House tried to get medical assistance. He died at the age of 33, and his death certificate bore the record of "premature senility" due to the fact that he had run a sewing machine since he was 6 years old. It is no figment of the imagination to say that the human system breaks down when it is put to monotonous work before it is ready to stand up to that work, and that general debility and many diseases may be traced to premature labor. No horse trainer would permit his colts to be so broken down.

Then we have the pauperizing effect of child

labor on the parents. Many of our European immigrants resent the monotonous petty work of the factory, but their children become adapted to it, and you get the curious result of the parent of the household being more or less dependent upon the earnings of the child. This tends to break down the normal relation between parents and children.

The pauperization of society itself is another serious charge.

When an industry depends upon the labor of boys and girls it takes them at a time when they ought to be at school. The wages paid to them are wages of mere subsistence. In almost all factories the work at which the children are employed leads to no trade. By the time they are old enough to receive adult wages they are often sick of the whole business. Such an industry is parasitic on the future of the community.

from the well-known fact that the labor of children is constantly in competition with the labor of their elders. In most cases it means that the child displaces the adult . . . The children displace the men, and the younger children displace the older children. This widespread economic effect of the employment of children is perhaps more important than any other. Child labor, wherever it exists, must be counted as one of the important causes of unemployment among adults. Of course, the lower wages at which children may be hired is the greatest inducement for their employment. The competition of children with adults in the labor market can hardly fail to have the effect of reducing the wages paid to the latter, and it has been found by actual investigation that where child labor is most common the earnings of the children are at least partly offset by a corresponding loss in the earnings of the adults.

---

4. Child labor retards industrial progress

Hunter, *Poverty,* pp. 244–246.

These injuries which child labor inflicts upon the children are terrible; but they are, perhaps, no more important than the injuries child labor inflicts on society. As a matter of fact, child labor often retards industrial progress. Through cheap labor, manufacturers are often able to retain and perpetuate methods of manufacture which are unnecessary and antiquated. The so-called belated industries, like the sweating system, are made possible only through the cheapness of child and woman labor. Greed for profits alone makes it necessary for children of six years to carry the newly blown glass bottles from hot ovens to a place for cooling. The same thing can be done by mechanical means. Mechanical ingenuity and inventive skill are enabled to lie dormant because the labor of children and women is cheap and plentiful . . .

Another evil of economic importance results

5. Child labor means less earning power as adult

S. W. Woodward, "A Businessman's View of Child Labor," *Charities and the Commons,* XV (1905–1906), 800–801.

. . . It may be stated as a safe proposition that for every dollar earned by a child under fourteen years of age tenfold will be taken from its earning capacity in later years. Lest it be said the statement is too strong, the writer hastens to say that he is perfectly familiar with instances, from Alexander Hamilton to Andrew Carnegie and many others of personal knowledge, who were compelled to begin life's work at the age of thirteen and whose success would seem to disprove the statement. One of the most successful merchants in Boston today was forced at nine years of age, on account of his father's death, to assist a widowed mother in the support of three younger children.

But exceptions only prove the rule, and it is

only necessary to point to the large number of children under sixteen years of age who for greater or less misdemeanors have become public charges upon the state and are compelled a few years later to go into life's work with not only little education to help them, but an experience which will tend to degrade them, to show the necessity for wise legislation in the matter.

6. The employment of children is an economic error

A. J. McKelway, "Child Labor in the Southern Cotton Mills," *Proceedings* of the National Child Labor Committee (New York, 1906), pp. 8–9.

McKelway, assistance secretary of the National Child Labor Committee, attacked the Southern argument that cheap labor was essential for the competition of Southern cotton products with those of New England.

The employment of children is an economic error in that it tends to lower the standard of efficiency in industry and to use up the labor supply in exactly the same way that the putting of colts to the plough would do in agricultural communities . . . The New England mills that are prospering the most have thrown their old machinery upon the scrap pile and have ceased competition with the South by manufacturing the finer goods, in which there is the greater margin of profit. Mills for the manufacture of these finer goods are now being erected in the South, but the demand goes up from them for a better class of labor, and it is another economic truth that the child laborer does not ordinarily develop into a skilled laborer . . . What a short-sighted policy it is, for the profit of the moment, to be wasting the opportunity for building up at the South an industry that shall be distinguished from the same industry

in both New England and Old England, by being free at once from the long hours and the low wages and the infant labor that have been the curse of the cotton mill for a hundred years, and are chiefly now the curse of the Southern cotton mills.

The social consequences of child labor

1. Child labor creates a self-perpetuating factory population

Edgar Gardner Murphy, *Problems of the Present South* (New York, 1904), p. 106.

Edgar Gardner Murphy (1869–1913), Episcopal minister in Montgomery, Alabama, became committed to child labor reform after he met Irene Ashby McFadyen on her investigation trip in 1900. Murphy organized the Alabama Child Labor Committee and became one of the most influential publicists of child labor conditions. He was the leading spirit in the creation of the National Child Labor Committee in 1904.

The more important factories are now seldom found without the factory school, where — in spite of the many calls to the mill, to meet the exigencies of "rush orders" — the children, or a fraction of them, are given an elementary training in "the three R's." When the more ambitious boy or the more capable girl is advanced to "piece-work," the result of an active day is often a gratifying wage. But the period of satisfactory earning power reaches its maximum at about the eighteenth or nineteenth year, and the operative is held by the rewards of the industry at the only time when another career might seem possible and practicable. When it is clearly perceived that the strain of the long factory hours does not bring a really satisfactory adult wage, it is too late to change; and the few who pass upward in the mill are but a small proportion of the mass. These, under the pressure of the economic situation just suggested, yield to that class tendency which is just as active among the poor as among the rich. The forces of a common origin, of neighborhood life, of a social experience shut in by the factory enclosure, — with no opportunity for the home, that best basis of social differentiation, — all conspire to emphasize the distinctions and the barriers of caste, and we find in process of creation a "factory people" . . . There will be found among them, in frequent and appalling evidence, two symbols of a low industrial life, — the idle father and the working child.

2. Moral dangers of child labor

Spargo, *Bitter Cry of the Children*, pp. 181–182, 184–185.

The moral ills resulting from child labor are numerous and far-reaching. When children become wage-earners and are thrown into constant association with adult workers, they develop prematurely an adult consciousness and view of life. About the first consequence of their employment is that they cease almost at once to be children. They lose their respect for parental authority, in many cases, and become arrogant, wayward, and defiant. There is always a tendency in their homes to regard them as men and women as soon as they become wage-earners. Discipline is at once relaxed, at the very time when it is most necessary. When children who have just entered upon that most critical period of life, adolescence, are associated with adults in factories, are driven to their tasks with curses, and hear continually the unrestrained conversation, often coarse and

foul, of the adults, the psychological effect cannot be other than bad . . .

No writer dare write, and no publisher dare publish, a truthful description of the moral atmosphere of hundreds of places where children are employed, — a description truthful in the sense of telling the whole truth. No publisher would dare print the language current in an average factory. Our most "realistic" writers must exercise stern artistic reticence, and tone down or evade the truth. No normal boy or girl would think of repeating to father or mother the language heard in the mill — language which the children begin before long to use occasionally, to *think* oftener still . . . for the plastic and impressionable mind of a child the moral atmosphere of the average factory is exceedingly bad.

.   .   .   .   .

[A] physician, in Lancaster, [Pennsylvania] is quoted as saying that he had "treated boys of ten years old and upwards for venereal affections which they had contracted." In upwards of a score of factory towns I have had very similar testimony given to me by physicians and others. The proprietor of a large drug store in a New England factory town told me that he had never known a place where the demand for cheap remedies for venereal diseases was so great, and *that many of those who bought them were boys under fifteen.*

Nor is it only in factories that these grosser forms of immorality flourish. They are even more prevalent among the children of the street trades, newsboys, bootblacks, messengers, and the like. The proportion of newsboys who suffer from venereal diseases is alarmingly great . . .

The messenger boys and the American District Telegraph boys are frequently found in the worst resorts of the "red-light" districts of our cities. In New York there are hundreds of such boys, ranging in age from twelve to fifteen, who know many of the prostitutes of the Tenderloin by name. Sad to relate, boys like to be employed in the "red-light" districts. They like it, not because they are bad or depraved, but for the very natural reason that they make more money there, receiving larger and more numerous tips.

---

3. Child labor upsets the racial balance in the South

Congressional Record, 59 Cong., 2 Sess. (1907), XLI, Part 2, p. 1821.

This argument presented by Senator Albert Beveridge of Indiana in a speech in the Senate was most popular among southern child labor reformers, such as Alexander McKelway. Theodore Roosevelt and Samuel Gompers picked it up and frequently used it in their denunciations of child destruction in the South.

Mr. BEVERIDGE. If there is any person on this floor, including the Senators from the South, who has a greater affection than I for that section of the country, from which I draw my own blood, I do not know it. And now I want to give a solemn warning to my brothers of the South.

I have had some conversation with my friends upon the other side who come from the South. There is one thing which I want to call to your attention — I do not know whether your attention has been called to it or not: certainly mine would not have been if I had not carefully studied the question. It is a serious question.

We have had much of this session taken up with a discussion of the race question. We have had the assertion of the superiority of the white race made time and time again; that the white race would never yield to the black race.

Yet the children who are at work in the southern cotton mills are from the white working class of the South; and this terrible situation stares the South in the face that, *whereas the children of the white working people of the*

South are going to the mill and to decay, the negro children are going to school and improvement.

I am glad to see the negro children going to school, but it is enough to wring the heart to think that day by day you are permitting a system to go on which is steadily weakening the white race for the future and steadily strengthening the black race for the future.

It is not in the power of any man to keep "superior" by *asserting* superiority. The truth of it is the South is face to face with the situation of their white children in the mills and their black children in the schools.

---

4. Illiteracy and child labor

Alexander J. McKelway, "The Needs of the Cotton Mill Operatives," address delivered at Rome, Georgia, March 29, 1909, Box 3, National Child Labor Committee Papers.

Alexander J. McKelway (1866–1918) was Presbyterian minister of Charlotte, North Carolina, and editor of the *Presbyterian Standard* and the Charlotte *News.* He became interested in child labor through his work for the *Standard* in 1902. Two years later he gave up his newspaper work to become secretary for southern states for the National Child Labor Committee.

The statistics show that in Georgia and the two Carolinas, the centre of the cotton mill industry in the South, one cotton mill operative out of three was from ten to fifteen years of age. For these three States 997 children under ten were reported by the enumerators as at work in the mills, though their instructions did not call for such reports. In the Northern States, the proportion of children workers to adults was one to ten. The *Blue Book,* a textile directory corrected annually, showed in 1907,

209,000 operatives. Thirty per cent of this number would be 62,700! When the absence of birth records are considered, the desire of parents to put their children to work that they "may subsist by the oppression of their off-spring," the demand for labor in the mills that has often rendered it impossible to secure sufficient adult help, and the complaisance of factory superintendents at admitting children under age when their parents say that they are over the legal age, it is certainly within the bounds of probability that there are sixty thousand children under fourteen years of age. A recent investigation of over half the cotton mills of Mississippi disclosed the fact that on a most conservative estimate twenty-five per cent of the operatives were under fourteen. In one mill the percentage was as high as forty per cent. A recent most friendly investigation of South Carolina mills showed 1,500 children employed under twelve years of age.

.   .   .   .   .

The census figures show that in North Carolina the general white illiteracy for children from ten to fourteen years of age is 16.6 per cent. But the illiteracy of the factory children between these ages is 50 per cent. In South Carolina the corresponding figures are 14.8 per cent and 48.5 per cent. In Georgia, 10.4 per cent and 44 per cent. That is, the illiteracy of the children from ten to fourteen years of age in the factory families is from three to four times as great as the illiteracy of the white children in the State at large. Moreover, the general percentage of illiteracy includes that of the mill villages. Considering the numbers of the children now gathered at the factories it is hardly too much to say that the problem of white illiteracy could be solved for our generation if the children of the factories were sent to school. In the investigation just mentioned of the cotton mills of Mississippi, in 1907, fifty per cent of the children were found to be illiterate.

I visited a typical country cotton mill in Georgia before the enactment of the Georgia child labor law. The school had been built by the corporation and a large part of the teachers' salaries was paid from the corporation's funds. The enrollment was found to be ninety. The attendance averaged about thirty. The average age of the children was nine years. Twenty-two children had left the school for the mill during the session and eight of the thirty children then attending school had been at work in the mill. Of those who had left the school for the mill one was seven, five were eight, two were nine, three were ten, four were eleven and two were twelve years of age.

It is asserted that the children of the mills have come from districts where they had no school advantages and that their illiteracy should not be charged to the mills. But these are children between the ages of ten and fifteen and one year of schooling would enable them to read "See the old hen," and prevent their being classed as illiterates! It is a painful fact to record in this connection, that when the Georgia Legislature was considering, in 1906, the present child labor bill, the Georgia Industrial Association made its main attack upon the provision requiring children under eighteen to attend school three months of one year as a prerequisite to employment the following years, and the same body of manufacturers asked the Attorney-General for an opinion whether instruction in a night school would be a compliance with this provision of the law as passed. The Attorney-General made answer that in his opinion the Legislature was aiming at the protection of the children, not their destruction, and he considered that the requirement that the children attend school at night after working twelve hours a day tended to their destruction.

It should be said in justice that a few conspicuous mills are encouraging the education of children by all the means in their power, and that the manuafcturers of North and South Carolina have advocated compulsory education up to twelve years of age. But the very fact that these few mills are always mentioned in the apologies for the child labor evil is proof that they are exceptional. And while North Carolina has passed a compulsory education law by means of which any school district may vote to come under the operation of the law, I have yet to hear of any mill district so voting, and that could be easily accomplished if the mill management desired to exert its influence in that direction.

---

5. Child labor disintegrates the family

Alexander J. McKelway, "The Needs of the Cotton Mill Operatives," March 29, 1909, Box 3, National Child Labor Committee Papers.

Through the long ages of human history the family as the social unit has been developing motherhood, fatherhood, brotherhood, patriotism, philanthropy. It is one of the commonplaces of social science that child labor disintegrates the family. That very dependence of the child which has been the main instrumentality in the development of the social virtues is changed into unnatural independence. The duty of the father is relegated to the child, that of earning bread. The child becomes an asset instead of an incumbrance. The child in the labor market depresses wages to the child-standard and by competition with the father absolutely prevents the possibility of his efficiency as food-provider. The system perpetuates itself through the resulting poverty and the ignorance that comes from this perversion of childhood to the function of bread-winning. The child, having to fulfill the duties of manhood, feels the right to its privileges, and early marriages with the consequence of degenerate offspring are the rule. The manufacturers of Tennessee and of South Carolina have been most earnest in their effort to forbid these early marriages by law, apparently failing to recognize that child labor itself is the root of the evil that must first be cut. Even before marriage the bread-winning child finding him-

self necessary to the support of the family, becomes independent of all parental restraint, and the ranks of our criminal class are being constantly recruited from the army of child laborers. I need not . . . adduce the proof of these statements. They are well-known facts.

The case of the girls is even more pitiable. While the boy grows up ignorant of the duties of citizenship, the girl is without knowledge of the ordinary duties of home-making. In those industries that are cursed with child labor and therefore with long hours and low wages, the marriage of the girl does not take her from her task of bread winning. The duties of wifehood and motherhood are complicated with the unending task of providing food. The children born into such homes must soon, how soon sometimes is almost incredible, add their pittance of wages to the family support. Is not the home, the American home, destroyed?

Organized labor recommends age and hour limits for working children, 1881–1894

In 1881 the first convention of the Federation of Organized Trades adopted a resolution favoring state regulation of child labor. This organization, which in 1886 became the American Federation of Labor, endorsed an eight hour day for women and children at its 1894 convention. The Federation took a strong interest in state child labor legislation and sponsored several investigations including that of Irene Ashby McFadyen in Alabama in 1901. It was divided over the desirability of federal legislation in 1906, but supported the Palmer-Owen bill in 1914.

---

1. Resolutions and debate on compulsory education and child labor laws, 1881

Proceedings of the Convention of the Federation of Organized Trades and Labor Unions (1881), pp. 3, 18–19.

Resolved, . . .

2. That we are in favor of the passage of such Legislative enactments as will enforce, by compulsion, the education of children; that if the State has the right to exact certain compliance with its demands, then it is also the right of the State to educate its people to the proper understanding of such demands.

3. That we are in favor of the passage of laws in the several States forbidding the employment of children under the age of fourteen years in any capacity, under penalty of fine and imprisonment.

.   .   .   .   .

The preamble and resolutions Nos. 1 and 2 were adopted without discussion. No. 3, having reference to the employment of children, was opposed by Mr. Brennan, of Pittsburg, on the ground that its enforcement would be an interference with individual rights.

Mr. Powers: I want this plank to go through this meeting with all the force that can be given it. With hundreds of examples under my own observation in Chicago, I say that there is no crime greater under the heavens than that of employing child labor in mills, factories, and industrial establishments. Chicago is raising up an army of criminals by this very thing. Children from the tender age of ten up to fourteen are driven into factories by brutal fathers that they may earn a livelihood for them. Boys are training for criminals and girls for prostitutes. See what I have seen of the gigantic evils of this, and if you had a hundred votes you would cast them for this resolution.

Mr. Dwyer: I want to raise my voice in favor of giving this resolution to the world as the sentiment of the Labor Congress. I, too, have seen the effects of this curse. I know of little children that support families, their drunken fathers and elder brothers, by the toil of their little hands. Before they have the chance of rudimentary education they are put out to labor for the support of lazy, drunken fathers. I am the father of fifteen children, yet I would work till my fingers were worn to the bone before I would allow one of my little ones to go forth and toil day by day as some I have seen.

Mr. Michels: The employment of children under fourteen years of age is prohibited in many States by statute, but is not always enforced. What do the law-makers care for the children of the masses? What care they for the hordes of boys and girls at work that should be at school? John B. Gough has said that the saddest thing he ever saw was a little child with an old face. Oh, I have seen them by hundreds — seen them in mills and factories. I want these law-makers, who protect the capitalist to know, like Napoleon, that they must heed the mutterings of the masses. By all means set this resolution before the world as our sentiment — as our demand. Blazon it high up, where all may see and read what we think of the employment of children in any capacity of work.

Mr. Gompers: Not long since I was on a committee appointed to visit the tenement cigar shops. I saw there on that visit scenes that sickened me. I saw little children, six and seven and eight years of age, seated in the middle of a room on the floor, in all the dirt and dust, stripping tobacco. Little pale-faced children, with a look of care upon their faces, toiling with their tiny hands from dawn till dark; aye, and late into the night, to help to keep the wolf from the door. I asked them how long they worked, but they did not, could not understand. In the simplest way I talked to them, and learned that they began before daylight, and worked till long after dark. Often they would be overcome with weariness and want of sleep, and fall over upon the tobacco heap. Shame upon such crimes; shame upon us if we do not raise our voices against it.

The resolution was passed unanimously.

2. Samuel Gompers condemns child labor, 1888

Proceedings of the Convention of the American Federation of Labor (1888), pp. 12–13.

In 1887 Gompers (1850–1924), president of the A.F.L., denounced the employment of women and children as tending to reduce the wages and displace the labor of men. In his presidential report at the 1888 convention he attacked child labor on humanitarian grounds.

So far as the labor of children is concerned, it is the same sad story; the exploitation of the tender and young, drawn into the factory, into the shop, into the mill, into the mine, and the stores by the drag-net of modern capitalism, frequently to supplant the labor of their parents; robbed in their infancy of the means of an education, dwarfed both in mind and body, what may we expect of the future manhood and womanhood of America? Apart from all material considerations, humanity and patriotism crys aloud against this great wrong of our time. I am conscious of the fact that the general Government under present condition, can do very little towards bringing about a change in this deplorable state of affairs; but I urge upon you, as I do upon all the working people of our country, to do all that lies in your power in the various states to see that a law shall be passed, absolutely prohibiting the employment of any child in any occupation until it shall have arrived at least, at the age of fourteen years. I repeat what I said one year ago, "children must be protected alike from the ignorance and greed of their parents, as well as the rapacious avarice of their employers."

3. Eight-hour day for women and children, 1894

Proceedings of the Convention of the American Federation of Labor (1894), 45.

WHEREAS, Improved machinery, which is now the chief factor in the production of all branches of manufacture, has brought about the displacement of men's labor by that of women and children; and

WHEREAS, The health of these women and children is ruined by long hours of toil; and — even worse than this — the overtaxing of the strength of the girls of today threatens to destroy the generations to come; and

WHEREAS, The American Federation of Labor, believing in the eight-hour day for all workers of both sexes, is pledged to the support of all measures tending to that end; therefore

RESOLVED, That we believe there should be a uniform limit to the hours of labor for women and children in all manufacturing establishments; and this limit should be secured by legislative enactment; and that such legislation should be based upon the best law yet enacted; and

RESOLVED, That the eight hour limit to the working day of females prescribed by the Illinois Workshop and Factories law should be extended to the women and minors in all the states; and

RESOLVED, That we recommend that a bill to secure this eight-hour law for all women and children be introduced by the various affiliated bodies in every State Legislature meeting this winter.

Muckraking child labor

1. Must practical barbarism be made compulsory for the child worker?

Helen Campbell, "White Child Slavery," *The Arena*, I (1889–1890), 591.

In 1887 Helen Campbell (1839–1918), a forerunner of the muckrakers, wrote an exposé of depressed wages in sweated industry which led to the formation of consumers' leagues. A regular contributor to *The Arena*, a magazine devoted to social problems, she pointed out the physical and moral toll of child factory labor.

It is this phase that is even more fatal than the disintegration of the family which is the result of mother and children being absorbed by factory life. What type of citizen for the State can come from a parentage in which every fibre, mental, physical, and moral, is either inert or diseased? Our enormous insane, idiot, and other asylums are the answer, and as their numbers swell, the cry is still for more and more. It would seem as if society had organized deliberately to fill them to overflowing. Every factory in the land where child-labor is permitted, turns out two products, one for the consumer of goods, another for hospital, asylum or prison, and at last the grave, the best place of deposit if such a product is inevitable, but from which will spring growth even more poisonous than has filled it.

Is this the inevitable order of modern progression? Is our complex civilization to give more and more to the highest and take more and more from the lowest? Must practical barbarism be made compulsory for the child worker, and the shadow of death hang over every loom run by child-labor? Never! Such labor has no right or place in a State whose mission is to give the largest opportunity to the individual, and develop a citizen whose life shall be part of its own progress and value.

A world of thought and action is already given to the rescue of children from the slums. Let it reach one step further and rescue them with no less eagerness and determination from the factory. If present methods of production cannot go on without them, alter the methods. The loss on one side will be more than balanced by a lessening rate in our asylums, and a gradual lowering of the tax for their support,

paid now with a cheerfulness which may well be transferred to another form of loss, loss today, perhaps, but gain for all days to come. We expend money for foreign missions while the heathen are here at our own doors. Out from the child faces, preternaturally aged, brutalized, and defrauded of all that belongs to childhood, look eyes that hold unconscious appeal for that justice which is the birthright of every soul born to the Republic. Ignore it, deny it, and the time comes when the old words sound again, and we hear the judgment: "Whosoever shall offend one of these little ones that believe in me, it is better for him that a millstone were hanged about his neck and he were cast into the sea."

---

2. Sacrifice of children in factory, store, and shop

Edwin Markham, "The Grind Behind the Holidays," *Cosmopolitan*, XLII (December 1906), 143, 144.

This was one of a series of articles on child labor which the poet Markham contributed to *Cosmopolitan* in 1906 and 1907 under the general title, "The Hoe-Man in the Making."

. . . Yet the mysterious and awful mandate of some Power has gone out over our own land, summoning our little ones from shelter and play and study, summoning them to a destruction less swift, less picturesque, less heroic, but hardly less fatal, than that medieval destruction. Greed and Gain, grim guardians of the great god Mammon, continually cry in the ears of the poor, "Give us your little ones!" And forever do the poor push out their little ones at the imperious ukase, feeding the children to a blind Hunger that is never filled. And the spell of material things is so heavy on the hearts of all of us that scarce a protest goes up against this betrayal of youth, this sacrifice of the children in factory, store, and shop.

.   .   .   .   .

"Small" children are wanted, you will notice, not "young" children; for the inconvenient law declares, in some quarters, that young children shall not be drawn into these devouring doors. "Small" children are called for; and who can deny the factory pasha's right to fix the stature of his workers? Can it be possible that "small" children mean small wages and large profits? And at Christmas time — "the children's time," as we call it in our soft rhetoric — the march of this army of little workers is heaviest; it is then that the feet falter most wearily. You cannot, in any city, at *any* season, go upon the streets too early nor too late to miss the tired recruits of this children's army. Between seven and eight in the morning, and between six and seven in the evening, you see them sprinkling the ways of traffic, flying to or from their work. But at Christmas time this army of little conscripts suddenly increases. On the streets; in halls and elevators; in offices, stores, and cellars; in workshops and factories — in almost every industry we have built for luxury or utility, thousands of little feet and hands and brains are there to serve and suffer.

II State and Federal Regulation of Child Labor

A. STATE CHILD LABOR LEGISLATION

Regulation of child labor by the states

---

1. Outline of legislation, 1830–1929

United States Children's Bureau, *Child Labor Facts and Figures,* Pub. No. 197 (Washington, D.C., 1930), pp. 4–8.

1830–1860

1. Early legislative efforts, as in England, failed to establish adequate standards or to make necessary provisions for enforcement. Prior to 1830 no effective regulation of child labor was accomplished.

2. The lack of education among working children was the first evil to be recognized and the first for which legislative remedies were sought.

  (a) Connecticut, in 1813, passed a law providing for the education of working children by the proprietors of manufacturing establishments in which children were employed.

  (b) Massachusetts, in 1836, provided that children under 15 employed in manufacturing should attend school at least three months a year.

  (c) Prior to 1860 at least four other States (Rhode Island, Maine, New Hampshire, and Pennsylvania) had passed similar laws.

3. The regulation of hours of work was the next step in child labor legislation.

  (a) In 1842 Connecticut and Massachusetts passed laws restricting the employment of young children to 10 hours a day in certain manufacturing establishments.

  (b) Prior to 1860 similar legislation was passed in New Hampshire, Maine, Rhode Island, Pennsylvania, New Jersey, and Ohio.

4. Commencing about the middle of the century, legislation began to be passed prohibiting the employment in manufacturing industries of children under certain ages in Pennsylvania (12 and 13 years), Rhode Island (12 years), Connecticut (9 and 10 years), and New Jersey (10 years).

5. By 1860 some public recognition of the abuses resulting from early child labor and of the right of the State to correct these abuses by legislation had developed in the industrial States of the North. Only a few laws had as yet been passed, however, for the purpose of correcting and regulating these abuses, and these were for the most part found to contain inadequate provision for enforcement.

1860–1929

1. Laws prohibiting the employment of children below certain specified ages have gradually been extended in these years to include at least factories and in many cases a large number of other occupations in almost all States,

666

while the specified age minima have gradually been raised from 10 to 12 to 14, and in a few States to 15 and 16 years.

(a) In 1887 and 1889, respectively, Colorado and New York passed the first laws providing for a 14-year minimum for both boys and girls (manufacturing).

(b) While the child-labor laws of the greater number of States to-day provide for a 14-year minimum for general industrial employment, most States have established higher age minima for employment in mines and at other occupations regarded as especially hazardous.

(c) The trend of legislation is at present toward the establishment of 15 and 16 year age minima for all gainful occupations.

2. Further restrictions on the employment of young children have been effected in this period through legislation requiring certain educational qualifications for admission to employment.

(a) The earliest form of this regulation required a definite period of schooling each year during the child's employment until he had reached a certain age, or in the year immediately preceding his first employment.

(b) The ability to to read and write simple English sentences was another early requirement.

(c) The completion of a specified school grade was a requirement introduced in later legislation and is generally regarded as the most definite and satisfactory form of regulation.

(d) At the present time 38 States restrict child labor directly through requiring some kind of educational qualification of children entering employment, 31 of them requiring the completion of a specified school grade.

3. Within comparatively recent years a further restriction on the numbers of children entering employment has been effected through the requirement of certain minimum conditions of health and physical development.

(a) The earliest form of such regulation was effected through conferring on the factory inspector authority to exclude from employment working children who were found, on physical examination, to be physically unfit to perform the work they were engaged upon.

(b) Other comparatively early laws required that the officers issuing work permits, or employment certificates, should have examined by a physician all children about whose physical condition they were in doubt.

(c) The most recent and satisfactory type of legislation requires that each child desiring to enter employment shall be examined by a public medical officer and shall not be permitted to work unless he is found to be of normal physical development, in sound health, and physically fit to perform the work which he is expecting to do.

(d) At the present time physical requirements for the issuance of regular employment certificates are contained in the child-labor laws of 33 States, in 25 of which an examination by a physician is compulsory.

4. During these years legislation extending the age of compulsory full-time school attendance and providing for the compulsory attendance of working children at continuation schools has been another important indirect means of restricting the numbers of child workers.

5. Laws regulating the hours of children's work have been enacted in practically all industrial States. At the same time the working day has been gradually shortened, so that the 8-hour day or the 44 or 48 hour week for children under 16 is now found in 36 States.

(a) The earliest laws provided for a 10-hour day and a 60, 58, 56, or 55 hour week.

(b) The first 54-hour-week law for children under 14 was passed in Michigan in 1889.

(c) The first 8-hour laws for children under 16 were passed in Illinois (any gainful occupation) and in Colorado (manufacturing) in 1903.[1]

---

1. In 1887 Alabama passed an eight-hour law for children under fourteen, but it was repealed in 1894.

6. Since 1860 legal prohibitions of the employment of children under 16 years of age at night have extended to 43 States.

7. Special protection against dangerous, hazardous, or unhealthful occupations is a logical development. The first legislation of this sort is found in provisions of the penal codes of many of the States which make the employment of children in "vocations injurious to health or dangerous to life or limb" a misdemeanor.[2] Transferring this prohibition to the labor law and making the factory inspector responsible for its enforcement was the next step. Though the language of these early provisions was so broad that it would seem to have included the employment of children under the prohibited age in occupations in which they were exposed to dangerous gases, poisons, and other health hazards, it was generally narrowly interpreted so as to include only immoral exhibitions, acrobatic performances, and occupations usually described as vicious in themselves. About 1900 the policy of including in the child-labor laws lists of prohibited machines and unhealthful occupations was begun.

8. Adequate legal provisions for the enforcement of child-labor laws have been established only comparatively recently. These consist of —

(a) Factory inspection.

(b) Requirement of a work permit, or employment certificate. This measure is of more recent development, but such a working paper, guaranteeing the eligibility of children entering employment, is now required in all except three States.

---

2. The goal of an advanced reformer, 1903

Florence Kelley, "An Effective Child-Labor

2. New York, *Acts of 1876*, ch. 122; Wisconsin, *Acts of 1880*, ch. 239.

Law," *The Annals* of the American Academy of Political and Social Science (May 1903), XXI, 438–445.

The legislation proposed by Miss Kelley was substantially that endorsed by the National Child Labor Committee at the time of its organization in 1904. For a later model child labor law prepared by the National Committee see Owen R. Lovejoy, *Uniform Child Labor Laws* (New York, 1911).

First among all the aims to be striven for is uniformity among the states on the basis of the best that has already been accomplished in the most enlightened states . . .

.   .   .   .

Effective legislation dealing with child-labor involves many differing elements including the child, the parent, the employer, the officials charged with the duty of enforcing the statutes, and finally the community which enacts laws, provides schools for the children when they are prohibited from working, supports and authorizes officers for the enforcement of the laws, prescribes penalties for their violation, assists dependent families in which the children are below the legal age for work. In the long run, the effectiveness of the law depends upon the conscience of the community as a whole far more than upon the parent and the employer acting together.

With the foregoing reservations and qualifications duly emphasized, the following schedules are believed to outline the substance of the effective legislation which it seems reasonable to try to secure in the present and the immediate future. They deal only with provisions for the child as a child, taking for granted the provision for fire-escapes, safeguards for machines, toilet facilities and all those things which the child shares with the adult worker.

An effective child-labor law rests primarily upon certain definite prohibitions among which are the following:

LABOR IS PROHIBITED

(1) for all children under the age of fourteen years,

(2) for all children under sixteen years of age who do not measure sixty inches and weigh eighty pounds,

(3) for all children under sixteen years of age who cannot read fluently and write legibly simple sentences in the English language.

(4) for all children under the age of sixteen years, between the hours of 7 P.M. and 7 A.M., or longer than eight hours in any twenty-four hours.

(5) for all children under the age of sixteen years in occupations designated as dangerous by certain responsible officials.

Of the foregoing prohibitions Number 1 is in force in a number of states so far as work in factories, stores, offices, laundries, etc., is concerned. In New York and Massachusetts recent statutes restrict, though they do not yet prohibit outright, work in the street occupations for children under the age of fourteen years. The movement in this direction gained marked headway during the past winter. Number 2 is not yet embraced in any statute, but is vigorously advocated by many physicians and others practically acquainted with working children. Number 3 has long been the law in New York State, and is of the highest value to the immigrant children so far as it is enforced. Number 4 is in force in Ohio. Number 5 is in force in Massachusetts.

THE CHILD

Effective legislation requires that before going to work the child satisfy a competent officer appointed for the purpose, that it

(1) is fourteen years of age, and

(2) is in good health, and

(3) measures at least sixty inches and weighs eighty pounds, and

(4) is able to read fluently and write legibly simple sentences in the English language, and

(5) has attended school a full school year during the twelve months next preceding going to work.

THE PARENT

Effective child-labor requires that the parent

(1) keep the child in school to the age of fourteen years, and

(2) take oath as to the exact age of the child before letting it begin to work, and

(3) substantiate the oath by producing a transcript of the official record of the birth of the child, or the record of its baptism, or some other religious record of the time of the birth of the child, and must

(4) produce the record of the child's school attendance, signed by the principal of the school which the child last attended.

THE EMPLOYER

Effective child-labor legislation requires that the employer before letting the child begin to work,

(1) obtain and place on file ready for official inspection papers showing

(a) the place and date of birth of the child substantiated by

(b) the oath of the parent corroborated by

(c) a transcript of the official register of births, or by a transcript of the record of baptism, or other religious record of the birth of the child, and by

(d) the school record signed by the principal of the school which the child last attended, and by

(e) the statement of the officer of the Board of Education designated for the purpose, that he has approved the papers and examined the child.

(2) After permitting the child to begin to work, the employer is required to produce the

foregoing papers on demand of the school-attendance officer, the health officer and the factory inspectors.

(3) In case the child cease to work, the employer must restore to the child the papers enumerated above.

(4) During the time that the child is at work, the employer must provide suitable seats, and permit their use so far as the nature of the work allows; and must

(5) post and keep posted in a conspicuous place, the hours for beginning work in the morning, and for stopping work in the middle of the day; the hours for resuming work and for stopping at the close of the day; and all work done at any time not specified in such posted notice constitutes a violation of the law. The total number of hours must not exceed eight in any one day or forty-eight in one week.

and requiring the consecutive attendance of all the children to the age of fourteen years. It is never certain that children are not at work, if they are out of school. In order to keep the children, however, it is not enough to compel attendance, — the schools must be modified and adapted to the needs of the recent immigrants in the North and of the poor whites in the South, affording instruction which appeals to the parents as worth having, in lieu of the wages which the children are forbidden to earn, and appeals to the children as interesting and attractive. These requirements are so insufficiently met in the great manufacturing centres of the North, that truancy is in several of them, at present, an insoluble problem. No system of child-labor legislation can be regarded as effective which does not face and deal with these facts.

THE OFFICIALS

Effective legislation for the protection of children requires that the officials entrusted with the duty of enforcing it

(1) give their whole time, not less than eight hours of every working day, to the performance of their duties, making night inspections whenever this may be necessary to insure that children are not working during the prohibited hours; and

(2) treat all employers alike, irrespective of political considerations, of race, religion or power in a community;

(3) prosecute all violations of the law;

(4) keep records complete and intelligible enough to facilitate the enactment of legislation suitable to the changing conditions of industry.

THE SCHOOL

The best child-labor law is a compulsory education law covering forty weeks of the year

3. Volume and provisions of state child labor legislation, 1903–1915

Elizabeth Sands Johnson, "Child Labor Legislation," in John R. Commons et al., *History of Labor in the United States* (New York: The Macmillan Company, 1918–1935), III, 403–456.

The volume of legislative achievement in the states in the years from 1902 to the time of the passage of the first federal child labor law in 1916 was tremendous. In the one year of 1903, 11 states passed comprehensive child labor laws. Five of these were southern states, which had previously had no child labor laws whatever. From 1902 to 1909, 43 states enacted significant child labor legislation, either wholly new laws or far-reaching amendments. In 1900 there were still 24 states and the District of Columbia in which there was no minimum age for employment in factories. In 1909 there were only six states without such a standard. As in other fields of labor legislation, the peak years in the enactment of child labor laws were 1911 and 1913 when 30 and 31 states respectively, enacted such measures. In 1915, 25 states took some action in this field.

.   .   .   .   .   .

Child labor legislation at the end of the nineteenth century contained most of the elementary principles of modern child labor laws; i.e., regulations affecting the minimum age for employment, the maximum hours of work, and the health, safety, and education of employed children. The task of the first years of the twentieth century was to devise specific standards and methods of administration to translate these principles into actualities. The development of standards proceeded along these lines: (1) provisions for evidence of age that could withstand the circumventions of employers or parents; (2) hour provisions that should bear some relation to the amount of work that children could do with a reasonable degree of safety to their health and welfare; (3) educational provisions that really protected normal children from reaching adulthood handicapped by a lack of the fundamentals of an education; (4) provisions that excluded children from specific occupations in which they would be unreasonably exposed to risk of accident, occupational disease, or to immoral influences; and (5) health provisions that prevented children from engaging in the kinds of work that might undermine their health and physical fitness. Another significant development was the building of a system of official supervision over working children, whereby the qualifications of all children seeking employment were systematically ascertained, and whereby all children were accounted for and none might escape the protection intended for them — that is, the employment certificate system. More important even than a system of employment certificates in bringing about effective enforcement of child labor standards was compulsory school attendance.

Problems of enforcement

---

1. Difficulties in enforcing the Massachusetts education laws, 1868

Massachusetts, Senate, "Report of the Honorable Henry K. Oliver, Deputy State Constable," Doc. 44, *Documents, 1869* (Boston, 1869), pp. 14–15, 20–21.

Massachusetts prohibited the employment of children under ten years of age in any manufacturing establishment and permitted the employment of children between ten and fifteen only if they had attended school for three months prior to their employment and for three months of each year. As deputy state constable and, after 1869, as commissioner of the Massachusetts Bureau of Statistics and Labor, Henry K. Oliver (1800–1885) reported widespread evasion of the laws.

There is no power conferred whereby the party detailed to attempt its execution can determinately secure satisfactory evidence of its having been violated . . .

No power to enter any such establishment, in order to learn of any overt act under the law, is conferred upon any party whatever . . .

No provision is made for the manner of prosecution, nor is any form of indictment prescribed, nor any court named before which parties charged with violation of the statute, shall be summoned for trial.

The law is unbending, and yields nothing in any cases whatever, not even in those, and many such there be, where its rigid enforcement would be not only needless, but positively injurious to all parties concerned.

Its own phraseology is not prohibitory, in certain cases, of violations of its own provisions.

.   .   .   .   .   .

It provides no system of documentary papers, by the use of which information in the premises can be obtained . . .

It provides for no forms of certificates, — and these should be uniform throughout the State, — nor for other necessary papers to be used in determining either the age of a child employed, or the school attendance of such child, or length of time of employment in mill or elsewhere. It provides for no methods or books of registration to be kept by employers, setting forth the age and birthplace of the several children employed, the dates at which they commenced work, the amount of annual schooling, etc., etc., all of which, and many more, are essential to a perfect working of an exact and practical statute.

It makes it "the duty of the constable of the Commonwealth to detail ONE of his deputies" to see to compliance with the provision of the Act. In my former Report, I have attempted to show that, under my experience, *one man* is wholly insufficient for the perfect fulfillment of duties involving the great and severely important matters contemplated under this statute.

. . . . . .

It will be made manifest by this condition of things, that two very powerful obstacles are at work impeding the education of these factory children, — one of them the personal self-interest of an unscrupulous employer, and the other, the poverty of the employed; and this appealing to the sympathy of such employer, puts him in possession of an argument by means of which he may appear to be influenced by compassionate motives, while in reality he is but sustaining his own advantage, under this plea of bowels of mercy.

The fault, however, is not wholly with employers. The necessities, or the selfishness of parents, will frequently lead them to place their children at work, in violation of the law, and to the ruin of their education, and often of their character and morals. And it is this last-named fact which makes it so difficult to carry out any law which may be passed on the subject. The pressure of poverty will induce acts which may relieve the present pressing necessity, but yet leave things worse for the future. Even ignorant and unthinking parents wish their children to be instructed, and know that they will be the better for it in after years; but they will not always, and sometimes they cannot, postpone the wants of the moment to those of the future.

There is still another difficulty in the way of accomplishing the object of the law . . .

If a child, at the end of three months, comes back, and *says he has attended school* during that period, or if his parents say so, the employer is not, under our statute, provided he believes the statement, prohibited from re-employing him. *No certificate of schooling is required,* nor does the law give any methods of detail by which any facts in the premises can be made known to the employer. It is a *law of words and threats and penalties,* and by the insertion therein of the word "KNOWINGLY," there is loop-hole of retreat ample enough for any transgressor to escape with very little effort at shrinkage and small amount of friction.

2. Pragmatism in the enforcement of the Pennsylvania child labor law, 1893

Pennsylvania, Factory Inspector, *Fourth Annual Report, 1893* (Philadelphia, 1894), pp. 7–8.

EMPLOYMENT OF CHILDREN

On June 3, 1893, there were employed in the various establishments which were amendable to the Factory Law, about 5,000 children under thirteen years of age, all in possession of certificates, stating the time and place of birth respectively.[1] A very large number of people supposed that these children would all be discharged under the amended Factory Law, but I did not deem it wise or prudent to take any such radical step, nor did I believe that the Legislature had any such intention. To have peremptorily discharged this large number of children would have done an injustice to those who had already provided themselves with certificates, as required by Section 2 of the Act of 1889. It would also have worked great injury to the silk and woolen manufacturers who employ fully 75 per cent. of these children. I therefore instructed the members of the Department to permit all children under 13 years of age, lawfully employed prior to June 3, 1893, to remain at work, but to prohibit the employment of any child under 13 years of age after that date, and I am satisfied that by June 3, 1894, there will not be any child under 13 years of age employed in the establishments which are amendable to the Factory Act. We shall, therefore, have reached a very desirable result without having caused a harsh shock to any branch of industry, and without doing injustice to any of the 5,000 children involved. There is required the greatest amount of vigilance, on the part of the entire force, to prevent violations of the law in this respect, for it is a lamentable fact that there is a disposition on the part of certain manufacturers to employ children regardless of age, because they work more cheaply than adults.

---

3. Florence Kelley, Illinois Factory Inspector, recommends prosecution of derelict parents, 1894

Illinois, Factory Inspectors, *Second Annual Report for the Year Ending December 15, 1894* (Springfield, 1895), pp. 12–24.

---

1. The Pennsylvania law of 1893 changed the minimum age in manufacturing and mercantile establishments from twelve to thirteen.

Although the law prohibits absolutely the employment of any child under 14 years of age in manufacture, yet the children under 14 years can never be wholly kept out of the factories and workshops until they are kept in school. At present the school attendance law is almost useless, at least in Chicago, where the largest number of children have been found at work. Although the Chicago Board of Education employs attendance agents, yet children leave school to sell papers; to carry cash in stores and telegrams and messages in streets; to peddle, black boots, "tend the baby," or merely to idle about. Unruly children are expelled from school to suit the convenience of teachers. Principals of schools have sent to the inspectors children 11 years old, with the written request that permits be granted to enable the children to go to work (in violation of the factory law) because in each case the child is "incorrigible." As no factory can be a better place for a child 11 years old than a reasonably good school, this request voices the desire of the principal to be relieved of the trouble of the child. For all these various reasons, and perhaps also because of the want of sufficient school accommodations, children are freed from school attendance at such a rate that the last school census, 1894, shows 6,887 children between the ages of 7 and 14 years, in Chicago alone, who attend no school.

Of these thousands, hundreds are seeking work in shops and factories, and when they find work and the laws of the state are thereby violated, the task of prosecution, which should fall in part at least on the Board of Education of Chicago, devolves upon the State Factory Inspectors alone.

Co-operation with the Chicago Board of Education. — In three months, September, Ocber and November this department forwarded to the compulsory attendance department of the Chicago Board of Education, the names and addresses of 76 children under 14 years of age who were found by inspectors during these months at work, in violation of Section 4 of the Factory and Workshop law; also the names and addresses of 27 other children who, in these three months, applied at the office for permission to go to work in violation of the law, and to whom we refused age affidavits because they were not yet 14 years old.

These 103 children under 14 years of age, found at work or seeking work since the present school year began, have all been seen and talked with by one or more inspectors of this department, and we therefore speak with knowledge of each case, when we say that none of these children has yet mastered the teachings of a primary school; a large number cannot yet write their own names; and some of them cannot yet speak the English language.

As to the environment in which the 76 children were found working, 30 were in sweat shops, 6 in cigar factories and 15 at the stock yards; leaving only 25 of the 76 in occupations relatively harmless.

To rescue in three months 51 children under 14 years of age from nicotine poisoning, from the miasma of the stock yards, and from the horrible conditions of the sweat shops is to accomplish something worth doing, — if we could be certain that the rescue would result in added school life and opportunities for normal growth and development for the children. Unfortunately our experience has convinced us that we may find the child discharged today at work tomorrow, or next week, in some other shop or factory.

The State inspectors having obtained the conviction of 25 employers upon 33 charges of having in their factories or workshops children under 14 years of age, while no parent has been prosecuted under the school laws, it is manifest that parents are going unpunished who share the responsibility for their children's unlawful employment.

The Board of Education has kindly furnished us a report of the disposition made of such of the children reported by us as received the attention of its attendance agents during September and October. This report shows that the officers placed in school 31 children out of 64 investigated by them; a little less than one-half. Upon the remaining 33 cases the report shows that several children were not found by the attendance agents; a few were given permits to work in stores; some were dropped with the remark that the children were "incorrigible;" and in 15 cases the mere statement of the parent that the child was over 14 was received by the compulsory department as sufficient reason for dropping the case, although in each such case the parent declined, in dealing with us, to make affidavit to show the child to be more than 14 years old.

Nullification of Section 4. — The humane intent of the first clause of Section 4 of the workshop and factory law is obvious: that the child under 14 years is to be safeguarded by the State against employment injurious to it. This intent is nullified if the child is not kept in school, but drifts from one workshop into another, or from the factories into the streets.

We therefore recommend that the legislature make the prosecution of derelict parents not as it now is, merely discretionary with the local school boards, but mandatory upon them; as the prosecution of manufacturers is made mandatory upon them; as the prosecution of manufacturers is made mandatory upon the factory inspectors by Section 9 of the factory law.

---

4. Parents and notaries connive at the employment of children, New York

"Report and Testimony Taken Before the Special Committee of the Assembly Appointed to Investigate the Condition of Female Labor in the City of New York," *New York Assembly Documents, 1896,* XXIII, No. 97, Part I, pp. 5, 6–8.

At the time of this investigation, the minimum age for work in manufacturing establishments was fourteen. The Reinhard Committee, named after its chairman, Philip W. Reinhard, recommended that a work certificate for every child be issued by the Board of Health on evidence of legal age and good health. These recommendations were followed in the New York law of 1903.

The opinion of the committee presented in its preliminary report, that large numbers of children were employed in manufacturing places contrary to law, has been amply confirmed by its further and fuller investigations. The committee stamps the employment of child labor under the statutory age as one of the most extensive evils now existing in the city of New York, and an evil which is a constant and grave menace to the welfare of its people. Many children were found by the diligent efforts of the committee's subpoena servers and brought before the committee, who were under the requisite age, and many others were seen by members of the committee upon their investigation tours. These children were undersized, poorly clad and dolefully ignorant, unacquainted with the simplest rudiments of a common school education, having no knowledge of the simplest figures and unable in many cases to write their own names in the native or any other language.

.   .   .   .   .   .

Fannie Harris, who earned two dollars per week, of which her mother allowed her two cents a week for spending money, testified:

Q. Now, have you been to school in this country? *A.* No.

Q. Can you read? *A.* I can read a little, not much.

Q. What can you read — can you read "dog?" *A.* No, sir.

Q. Do you know how to spell dog? *A.* I went to night school.

Q. Do you know how to spell dog? *A.* I have forgotten it since night school stopped.

Q. Can you spell "cat?" *A.* Yes, sir.

Q. How do you spell it? *A.* I have forgot.

Q. When did you have a birthday; did you have a birthday lately? *A.* No, sir.

Q. Did you ever have a birthday? *A.* No, sir.

Q. You know what a birthday is, don't you Fannie? *A.* Yes, sir.

Q. What is that? *A.* The day that you were born.

Q. Now, didn't you have a birthday? *A.* I never had a birthday because we have not any money to make a birthday.

Q. That is, you never had a little party? *A.* No, sir.

Q. A birthday is a day when you have a little party, is it not? *A.* Yes, sir.

Q. Does your mamma work? *A.* Now she ain't working, because I am working, but before, when I didn't work, she worked.

Q. Your mamma is not sick, is she? *A.* No, sir.

Q. And your mamma wants you to go to work? *A.* Yes, sir; sure she does; and I want to go to work myself.

Q. And if you don't go to work then your mamma will have to go to work? *A.* Sure.

Q. Now, Fannie, when will you be 15 years of age? *A.* I don't know.

Q. Are you 15 now? *A.* No, sir.

Q. And this paper (showing age certificate) your mamma gave you, did she?

A. I went to a lawyer and paid twenty-five cents and he gave me it . . .

Parents and mercenary and corrupt notaries alike connive at the employment of children under the statutory age. A parent who is willing to permit its child to work in a factory at an age under 14 is ordinarily just as willing to perjure himself as to the age of the child. To carry out his purpose he has little difficulty in obtaining the assistance of a notary, who is willing, for the illegal fee of twenty-five cents, to be a party to the crime. While the legal fee of a notary for taking the affidavit is twelve and one-half cents, many of the notaries have charged twenty-five cents upon the specious plea that the labor of filling out the blank spaces in the age certificate is worth the additional twelve and one-half cents. The committee discovered that the taking of affidavits of the age of children was engaged in by notaries public as a business . . .

---

5. Self-regulation as a substitute for child labor legislation, 1901

Samuel Gompers, "Subterfuge and Greed in North Carolina," *American Federationist,* VIII (May 1901), 163.

The *Federationist* reported that one hundred cotton mill owners and managers in North Carolina had adopted the following resolutions:

"We, the undersigned, cotton mill owners and managers, agree to the following, taking effect March 1, 1901:

"(1) That one week's work shall not exceed 66 hours.

"(2) That no children less than 12 years' old shall work in a cotton mill during the term of an available public school.

"*Provided,* this shall not apply to children of widows or physically disabled parents; *provided further,* that 10 years shall be the lowest limit at which children may be worked under any circumstances.

"(3) That we will co-operate with any feasible plan to promote the education of working people in the State, and will cheerfully submit to our part of the burdens and labors to advance the cause of general education.

"(4) On the basis of the above agreements of the cotton mill owners and managers, we hereby petition the legislature not to pass any labor laws at this session of the legislature."

In the following article, Gompers denounced the resolutions as frauds.

First. They offer *an eleven hour day for working children.*

Second. They propose that no child under twelve years of age shall work in a cotton mill during the term of an *available* public school.

In the annals of child labor there is never an "available" school when the employer is made the judge of that point or when the "available" school would take from him the labor of the children which he thinks profitable. The employers evidently propose to work the children any number of hours they choose when the school is not available.

Third. The employers will co-operate with any "feasible" plan to promote the education of working people and "will cheerfully submit to their part of the burdens and labors to advance the cause of general education."

The latter phrase is what a popular writer recently termed a "weasel" sentence. It looks well and sounds well, and means — nothing. Of course all citizens have to bear their share of the expenses and burdens of general education, the wage-workers quite as much as their employers. Employers are accepting no new responsibility in making this promise.

But the real point of this third section lies in the word "feasible." No employer who utilizes child labor finds it "feasible" to promote the education of working people and thereby make them intelligent and prosperous enough to keep their children out of the factory. It is perfectly safe to promise education with the "feasible" proviso.

For fear this should not leave loop holes enough, the employers provide that children of widows or physically disabled parents shall not share in these advantages. The orphan or child of disabled parents may be employed at the tender age of ten, and as many hours and under whatever circumstances his employer desires. Verily will the children of the unfortunate receive consideration from the philanthropic employers of North Carolina.

---

6. Enforcement problems in Missouri, 1906

"Report of the Missouri Child Labor Committee at the Third Annual Convention of the National Child Labor Committee, 1906," *The Annals* of the American Academy of Political and Social Science, XXIX (1907), 148–149.

Missouri prohibited employment of children under fourteen in factories and mines. But as the Missouri Child Labor Committee complained, the provisions for inspection of factories and prosecution of offenders were especially weak.

. . . In the first place, the financial provision for the factory inspection department is entirely inadequate and not in proportion to the size and industrial productivity of the state. Consequently, not enough inspectors can be employed to do more, for the most part, than make routine inspections twice a year, or less often, along regular and carefully mapped routes. Consequently managers and foremen often know pretty well when inspectors may be looked for, and can be ready to hurry suspiciously young-looking children out of the way before the official eye falls upon them. In the second place, even this insufficient appropriation for inspection is required to be collected by the inspectors themselves in the form of one dollar fees; this has the effect of largely converting what is supposed to be an inspection bureau into a collection bureau; about half the time of the chief inspector and of his office staff is taken up in correspondence and bookkeeping necessitated by this duty, incongruously laid upon him, of providing the revenue for the payment of the salaries and expenses of himself and his assistants. And when an inspector does, in spite of these hindrances, succeed in discovering young children actually at work in a prohibited industry, his troubles have only begun. For, first, in the absence of the requirement of an employment certificate, there rests upon the inspector the burden of proving by legal evidence that the child is actually under age; and this he often or usually

must do in the face of parental prevarication or perjury. Second, if he can get enough such evidence to warrant carrying the case into court, he is likely to be confronted with a plea for exemption under the extreme poverty clause of the law.[1] And the St. Louis courts, at least, have shown a tendency to find extreme destitution in the circumstances of most parents who care to represent themselves in that light . . . In view of all these difficulties, it is, perhaps, not greatly surprising that informations for violations of the child labor laws were filed by the factory inspector during the past twelve months in only twenty-two cases. Warrants were issued in sixteen of these cases. Twelve of the cases resulted in convictions, with fines aggregating $150; in two other cases a general continuance was ordered, and one case is still pending.

But the worst deficiency of the Missouri provisions for factory inspection has yet to be mentioned; namely, the fact that the jurisdiction of the state factory inspector extends only to cities having more than thirty thousand inhabitants. This singular feature was incorporated in the law by an amendment passed in 1903. Missouri has a large number of small manufacturing cities and towns; in none of these is there any practical restriction whatever upon the employment of children of any age, at any hour of day or night, in any industry. The enormous loophole thus deliberately put into the law is rapidly growing bigger and more serious because of the increasing tendency of certain classes of manufacturing establishments to remove from the large cities to smaller places . . .

7. Objective tests of the enforcement of state laws, 1907

1. As did many other southern states, Missouri exempted from the operation of its child labor laws children who could prove that their families were dependent on their support.

Florence Kelley, "Obstacles to the Enforcement of Child Labor Legislation," *Child Labor and the Republic* (New York, 1907), pp. 51–53.

There are three objective tests of the enforcement of our laws. One is the presence of children in school. This is now being shown in an interesting exhibit of industrial conditions in Philadelphia. There is a chart showing the attendance of the children of Chicago at school in the year 1902. A small block symbolizes the attendance in that year. For the following year the same block repeated symbolizes the attendance; but the next year, 1904, when the present drastic child labor law of Illinois had taken effect, the enrollment in the Chicago schools of the children of compulsory school age trebled.[1] It required three times the original block to indicate the school attendance in the year after that new law took effect and was enforced. That statute carried a thousand children out of the stockyards in a single week; and later it carried 2,200 children out of the mines of Illinois in another week, following the decision of the enlightened judge of the Peoria district. And the increased school enrolment showed whither the children went.

The second objective test of the enforcement of child labor laws is prosecution. The child labor law is enforced in Illinois by persistent prosecution. Hundreds of employers have paid thousands of dollars in fines, and the visible result of the success of those prosecutions is the presence of the children of compulsory school age in school. That is an infallible test of the effectiveness of the enforcement of the law which prohibits children working throughout the period of compulsory school attendance.

South of Baltimore — south of Louisville —

there are no prosecutions; there is no compulsory school attendance. In any southern state to-day school attendance does not serve as a test of the efficiency of the protection of the children, because there are not schools enough to enroll the children if they were all dismissed from the mills. The test of the presence of the children in the schools works only when there are schools enough to enroll the children. We enroll our children in New York City. I wish I might say that we kept them in school . . . Even where there are not schools enough to admit the children, we can at least enroll them so that we may know where they are, and the opportunity to enroll them depends largely upon the efficiency of the prosecutions carried out by the factory inspectors.

The enforcement of the law depends not only on the quality of the men to whom the work of enforcing it is entrusted; it depends far more largely on the quality of the community in which those men hold office. There are few blacker chapters in the history of this republic than the ever-recurring story of removal of efficient officers because they have attempted to enforce child labor laws in communities which were willing to have those laws on the statute books so long as they were not enforced, but either repealed the statutes or removed the officers as soon as there was any effective prosecution.

There is a brilliant example of this in the history of the City of New York. The mercantile employees' law, when first drafted, provided that the same officer who enforced the law in factories should enforce it in the stores. But the Retail Dealers' Association of New York City objected, and prevented the enactment of the statute until a compromise was achieved. That was in the days when we had a very efficient inspector in office . . . A compromise was achieved, and the enforcement of the law in stores was left to local boards of health. The Retail Dealers' Association highly approved the appointment of a leading philanthropic merchant of New York to the position

1. This was a 1903 amendment to an 1897 law which made it mandatory that children between seven and fourteen attend school for its entire session of 110 days.

of commissioner of health.[2] This gentleman said quite frankly when he took office that he did not mean to hold it long, that he had only two aims which he wished to achieve. One aim was to get free sterilized and pasteurized milk for the children of the tenements; the other aim was to cut out of the municipal budget the appropriation for local inspectors to enforce the child labor laws in stores. He achieved both these ends; he cut out the municipal appropriation for the enforcement of the law in stores, and he established pasteurized milk for children in tenements. Then he resigned. His successor cut out the pasteurized milk; and then we had neither mercantile inspection nor pasteurized milk. And to this day the child labor law has never been enforced in stores. Notice is served upon the incoming commissioner of health by the secretary of the Retail Dealers' Association that they do not consider it desirable that the law should be enforced in stores with the same rigor with which it is enforced in factories.

Two years ago I saw one hundred and fifty children working illegally at twenty minutes past ten o'clock at night in a perfectly reputable dry goods store in the City of New York on the Saturday night before Christmas. If one of those children had stolen any small article, a doll or a penknife, the heavy hand of the law would have carried that child promptly into the juvenile court. But one hundred and fifty children were robbed of sleep in violation of the law; and the merchant, their employer who robbed them, has never been prosecuted to this day, and will never be prosecuted. The community does not insist that the great in New York City shall obey the law for the protection of the children; and no commissioner of health has had the moral courage to do that which his community does not wish done.

2. Nathan Straus (1848–1931), an owner of R. H. Macy and Company, was president of the New York City Board of Health in 1898. For Straus's role in the pure milk movement see below Part Seven, Chap. I, sec. D, Clean milk, doc. 2.

8. Evasion of child labor laws in the South, 1910

U.S. Department of Commerce and Labor, *Report on Condition of Woman and Child Wage-Earners in the United States,* 61 Cong., 2 Sess. (1910), I, 188–190, 193–196.

By the time of this investigation Virginia, North Carolina, South Carolina, Georgia, and Alabama had established twelve years as the legal minimum working age. Mississippi had not yet enacted a minimum age law.

In Mississippi every establishment investigated employed children under 12 years of age. This was not true of any other State. In 1 establishment . . . such children constituted 15.87 per cent of all employees, a higher percentage than in any other establishment investigated. Of the total employees in the establishment visited, children under 12 constituted 5 per cent, a much higher proportion than in any other State.

In the 5 States having child-labor laws, 753 out of 9,126 children, or 8.3 per cent, were found to be under the legal age. If those under 12, but legally excepted are added, the total is 836, or 9.2 per cent. In each of the 9 establishments investigated in Mississippi, more than 10 per cent of all children were under 12 years of age, and in all but 1, more than 15 per cent. In the 9 establishments, 113 of the 539 children, or 21 per cent, were under 12 years of age. This again is a much higher proportion than in any other State.

It appears, therefore, that although the child-labor laws were found to be flagrantly violated in all Southern States visited having such laws and particularly in North Carolina and South Carolina, yet these laws have had no little effect in reducing the number of child employees under 12 years of age. The industry in Mississippi is newer than in the other States and this would account in part for the higher proportion of children. The difference, however, was too great to be accounted for in this way and was without doubt due to the absence of law on the subject in Mississippi. At the same time it should be noted that a few mills in North Carolina and South Carolina had practically as high a proportion of children under 12 as any in Mississippi and that many had a higher proportion than the average for that State.

.   .   .   .   .

Of the 753 children illegally at work in the establishments investigated, the names of 592 appeared upon the pay rolls of the establishments employing them and the names of 161 were omitted therefrom. The wages of these 161 children were included with those of some other member of the family, and they were what are commonly known in southern cotton mills as "helpers."

The term "helper" when applied to a child at work in a cotton mill . . . does not mean a person who occasionally assists another, nor does it necessarily mean a person who regularly does so. In a few cases . . . the entry "not on pay roll," which is synonymous with the term "helper," may include children who assist some member of the family only before and after school and on Saturdays. In a few cases it may include a child who merely lightens the labor of another member of the family. Ordinarily, however, the children tabulated above as "not on pay roll," are employees who work as regularly as other workers and who are relied upon to do their share of work the same as are other employees. Because they are unquestionably under the legal age, however, and are admitted so to be, the employer refuses to place their names upon the books of the company, but raises no objection, and does not refuse to give them work, if some other member of the family can be induced to carry the "helper's" wages home.

In other words, the helper system ordinarily is merely a subterfuge whereby a law which prohibits the employment of children under a certain age is evaded. If the name is omitted from the pay roll, the employer argues that he is not "employing" the child . . .

That so-called helpers ordinarily are in fact regular employees is shown by a few concrete examples. When a certain family at a mill in North Carolina was visited it was found that two sisters, aged 9 and 11, worked regularly in the mill. Their names could not be found on the payroll. The parents explained that an older brother was a spinner tending 5 sides. The two sisters tended 5 more, and the brother was paid for tending 10 sides.

At another mill in North Carolina was a spinner tending 6 sides, but for some time her sister, aged 11 years, had been helping her and together they had tended 8 sides, and the older sister had received payment for tending 8 sides. At an establishment in Georgia a woman reported that her little daughter 10 years old worked every day helping her two sisters. The child quit for a while, but the overseer said to the mother, "Bring her in; the two girls can not tend those machines without her." The mother asked that the child be given work by herself, but the overseer replied that the law would not permit it.

.   .   .   .   .

. . . This custom of indirectly employing children under the legal age has been so well recognized that according to a labor agent in North Carolina families on farms or in the mountains have commonly been assured that under the helper system all of their children may work in the mill and earn wages

.   .   .   .   .

In at least 10 other mills, 3 in North Carolina, 6 in South Carolina, and 1 in Georgia, deliberate and determined efforts were made by mill officials to cover up the actual conditions in regard to child labor. Children were discharged temporarily, sent home for a few hours or a few days, or hidden in entries, in water closets, or in waste boxes, anywhere so that they would not be discovered by the agent when going through the mill. Of these facts proof was obtained in every case. In 9 of these 10 mills statements of persons acquainted with the facts were taken in the presence of two agents of the Bureau. In each of these cases the report of these statements was signed by both agents, and in 6 cases both of them made affidavit that the conversations were correctly reported. In some of the first mills in which fraud of this character was discovered the agents reporting the attempts at deception were not required to make special affidavit as to the truth of their reports.

The children or other persons who furnished information concerning the hiding or sending out of children were not placed under oath because it was very evident that this procedure would have frightened them into silence. As it was, they spoke with great reluctance, for they apparently feared that they would be discharged if the employers learned of what they were doing. The statements of children who were hurried away and of adult witnesses were so clear and convincing, however, and agreed even as to details with such surprising harmony as to leave no doubt as to their accuracy. In each case, furthermore, it clearly appeared that the deception was practised at the instance of some one in authority, the president, manager, or superintendent.

.   .   .   .   .

At a mill in North Carolina a woman reported that she saw a little girl running toward home "fit to kill." She asked what was the matter, and the child told her she was "running from that woman in the mill who was trying to make all the children go to school." The child did not stop running, the informant said, until she reached home. This little girl, when interviewed, said that the overseer sent her and five others out and "told us all to come back after dinner as soon as you had gone." This was on the occasion of the agent's first visit to the mill. At the second visit (as information gathered later established) the mill was again thoroughly prepared for an inspection. One boy was locked in the supply room, but beat the door with a piece of iron until the overseer had to let him out. Others of the children refused to hide, and the overseer (as was reported independently by several employees) was angry and cursed and scolded them. He sent several home, and one little boy 10 years old who refused to go was locked in the broom closet. Others were hidden under burlap. All of these efforts at deception proved to be unnecessary on that day, however, for the agent, all unaware of what was taking place, remained in the mill office copying wage data from the pay roll.

.   .   .   .   .

When attempts were made to ascertain, independently of mill officials, the extent of the illegal employment of children, the agents were confronted with new difficulties. No proof of age was on file in the mill office. There was no register of births with city or town officials which could be consulted. Little or no use could be made of school enumerations or teachers' records, partly because they had not been compiled or kept with care and partly because of the migratory character of employees. In some cases where school children had been transferred from one room to another there was as much as two years' difference in the ages recorded. Ordinarily a visit to the family was the only method by which the true ages of children could be obtained.

Time did not permit the agent to visit all families, and the truth was not always obtained in those families which were visited. There were many reasons why parents would try to deceive the agent concerning the ages of their children. They had perhaps misstated the ages to the mill superintendent in order to secure work for them. They would be inclined to make a similar misstatement to an agent investigating the mill. Again, the idea that the agent had the authority to forbid the employment of children under the legal age and that the purpose of his visit was to do so prevailed in practically every mill village which was visited. In some cases this idea was disseminated by the mill officials.

As a consequence, parents frequently believed that if they admitted the truth concerning the ages of some of their children their incomes would be diminished by the loss of the child's earnings.

This misapprehension and frequently many other vague but harmful ideas concerning the object of the investigation had to be overcome before inquiry could be made concerning ages. Even then it was frequently discovered that some parents did not know the ages of their children.

State child labor laws in the courts

1. Child labor legislation is within the police power of the state, 1904

City of New York v. Chelsea Jute Mills, 88 N.Y. Supp. 1085.

This decision upheld the New York law of 1903 which prohibited the employment of children under fourteen during school hours and provided that employers keep a certificate of the child's age on file.

ROESCH, J. This is an action to recover a a statutory penalty. As it is a test case, upon the outcome of which many others depend, and is the first of its kind in this state, a full examination of the questions involved will be attemped . . .

The salient facts are not disputed. Annie Ventre resides with her parents in this city, borough of Brooklyn, in which the defendant, a domestic corporation organized under the laws of our state, transacts its business of manufacturing and selling seamless jute bags and other jute fabrics. She was but 12 years of age on July 29, 1903. She began to work in the factory of the defendant on April 7, 1903, and

continued until the day preceding the trial. She worked at emptying "bobbins," beginning her labors at 7 o'clock A.M., and stopping at 6:15 o'clock P.M., with an intermission from noon until 12:45 o'clock for lunch, except that on Saturdays, with the same hours otherwise, she ceased work at 2:15 o'clock P.M. When she applied for work on April 7, 1903, she stated she was "sixteen passed," and gave the forelady an affidavit, signed and sworn to by her father on April 6, 1903, before a commissioner of deeds, to the effect that she was born "on April 4, 1887, and that she was sixteen years old on April 4, 1903." The father testified that the affidavit was not in fact true, but that July 29, 1903, was her twelfth birthday. The mother testified positively that her daughter was 12 years old on July 29, 1903 . . .

The statute is assailed for unconstitutionality. No particular provision of the state or federal Constitution is assigned. It is claimed to be "an unwarranted, illegal, and unconstitutional deprivation of the liberties of the defendant." The defendant also urges immunity from the penalty on account of the alleged "good faith, absence of intent to violate the statute, nonemployment of Annie Ventre since her age was established in court." The integrity of the statute is upheld under the police power of the state. A statute should not be declared unconstitutional unless required by the most cogent reasons, or compelled by unanswerable grounds . . . Every presumption is in favor of the constitutionality of a statute . . . It is difficult to satisfactorily define the police power to cover every case. But it includes such legislative measures as promote the health, safety, or morals of the community . . . It is true that the Legislature must respect freedom of contract, and the right to live and work where and how one will . . . Yet the weal of the people is the supreme law. The Legislature may not disregard it; private interests are subordinated to the public good, and even a statute opposed to natural justice and equity, requiring vigilance or causing vexation or annoyance, will be upheld if within constitutional limitations . . . Much more potent, if possible, is a statute seeking the protection of children. They are the wards of the state, which is particularly interested in their well-being as future members of the body politic, and has an inherent right to protect itself and them against the baneful effects of ignorance, infirmity, or danger to life and limb . . . Legislation is replete with enactments of such a character. We have a most enlightened Code for the prevention of cruelty to children.

.   .   .   .   .

The test of such legislation is to determine whether on its face it serves a public purpose, reaches all persons of a reasonably ascertained class indiscriminately, and is cognate to the objects it proposes to subserve. Unless these questions are negative, the court must declare the act constitutional . . .

The statute under consideration does not discriminate, is auxiliary to the primary purpose to enforce education and elevate future citizenship, is not arbitrary, puts no unnecessary restriction upon freedom of action, and resorts to no unnecessary rigor, because it would be impossible, otherwise than by an absolute prohibition of employment of all children under 14 years of age, to accomplish its beneficent ends. Nor does it constitute any improper infringement of any right a parent may have in a child or to its labor, or a child may have to labor.

.   .   .   .   .

It is further objected that the section under consideration is foreign to the scope of the school law, in no way aids the school authorities in their work, and has no legitimate place in that statute. The objection is not tenable. The provisions of the child labor law must be read in connection with the section in question, which is complementary to and a necessary concomitant of the former. They but emphasize the intent of the Legislature to prohibit the labor and enforce the education of children under the stated age. In no other way could its salutary purpose have been more effectually encompassed . . .

So here the section is not invalidated merely because embodied in the school law. The Legislature thus reaffirmed its mandate against child labor to foster education, upon the benign theory that representative government can be safe only when future suffrage is enlightened by education. Legislation providing for compulsory education of children has been specifically held valid in other states under the general police power . . . From the foregoing the conclusion is irresistible that the section assailed is a just and valid exercise of the police power of the state.

Nor may the defendant assert exemption from liability on account of "good faith, want of intent to violate the statute, and nonemployment of the child since the trial." Assuredly the last ground is not seriously urged.

.   .   .   .   .

The present statute is absolute. It must necessarily be so to accomplish its object. The employer acts at his peril. The fact of employment makes him liable. The contention of the defendant would require judicial legislation and render the statute nugatory, for good faith could easily be alleged and seldom disproved. It would, furthermore, put a premium on perjury to obtain employment. The decisions are adverse to the position of the defendant.

.   .   .   .   .

The Legislature must be presumed to have had such lessons in mind, and to have deliberately passed an act that would not nullify itself. If this law be declared invalid, the door will be thrown wide open to the most noxious kinds of child labor . . .

Judgment for plaintiff for the penalty of $50, together with costs and disbursements.

---

2. Regulation of children's work hours constitutional, Oregon, 1906

State *v.* Shorey, 48 Ore. 396.

MR. JUSTICE BEAN: The defendant was accused by information of the crime of employing a minor under the age of 16 years for a greater period than 10 hours a day, in violation of Section 5 of the child labor law of 1905, which reads as follows:

No child under sixteen years of age shall be employed at any work before the hour of seven in the morning, or after the hour of six at night, nor employed for longer than ten hours for any one day, nor more than six days in any one week; and every such child, under sixteen years of age, shall be entitled to not less than thirty minutes for meal time at noon, but such meal time shall not be included as part of the work hours of the day; and every employer shall post in a conspicuous place where such minors are employed, a printed notice stating the maximum work hours required in one week and in every day of the week, from such minors.

1. A demurrer to the information was overruled, and he entered a plea of not guilty. Upon the trial it was stipulated that the averments of the information were true, and he was thereupon adjudged guilty and sentenced to pay a fine and costs. From this judgment he appeals, claiming that the law which he is accused of violating is unconstitutional and void because in conflict with the Fourteenth Amendment to the Constitution of the United States, which provides that no state shall "deprive any person of life, liberty or property without due process of law," and of Section 1 of Article I of the Constitution of Oregon, which reads: "We declare that all men, when they form a social compact, are equal in rights."

These constitutional provisions do not limit the power of the state to interfere with the parental control of minors, or to regulate the right of a minor to contract, or of others to contract with him. It is competent for the state to forbid the employment of children in certain callings merely because it believes such prohibition to be for their best interest, although the prohibited employment does not involve a direct danger to morals, decency, or of life or limb. Such legislation is not an unlawful interference with the parents' control over the child or right to its labor, nor with the liberty of the child . . .

2. . . . laws regulating the right of minors to contract do not come within the principle [of the Fourteenth Amendment]. They are not *sui juris* and can only contract to a limited extent. They are wards of the state and subject to its control. As to them, the state stands in the position of *parens patriae,* and may exercise unlimited supervision and control over their contracts, occupation and conduct, and the liberty and right of those who assume to deal with them. This is a power which inheres in the government for its own preservation and for the protection of the life, person, health and morals of its future citizens . . .

The supervision and control of minors is a subject which has always been regarded as within the province of legislative authority. How far it shall be exercised is a question of expediency and propriety which it is the sole province of the legislature to determine. The judiciary has no authority to interfere with the legislature's judgment on that subject, unless perhaps, its enactments are so manifestly unreasonable and arbitrary as to be invalid on that account. It is not a question of constitutional power . . . Mr. Freund, in his work on *Police Power,* says: "The constitutionality of legislation for the protection of children or minors is rarely questioned; and the legislature is conceded a wide discretion in creating restraints" . . .

3. We are of the opinion, therefore, that the law prohibiting the employment of a child under 16 years of age for longer than 10 hours in any one day is a valid exercise of legislative power. It is argued, however, that the provisions of the statute forbidding the employment of such a child at any work before the hour of 7 in the morning or after the hour of 6 at night, is so manifestly unreasonable and arbitrary as to be void on that account. The defendant is not accused nor was he convicted of violating this provision of the statute, and is therefore

not in a position to raise the question suggested.

It follows that the judgment of the court below must be affirmed, and it is so ordered.

---

3. Review of court decisions involving damages or compensation for children injured on the job, 1915–1917

Theresa Wolfson, "How Our Courts Interpret Child Labor Laws," *The American Child,* I (August 1919), 133–136.

This summary is based on twenty representative cases involving the interpretation of state child labor laws from 1915 to 1917 as reported by the United States Department of Labor.

The United States Department of Labor issues each year a compilation of the decisions of courts affecting labor. These are the decisions of higher courts — courts of last resort for cases on appeal. Twenty representative cases involving the interpretation of the child labor laws of various states, and covering a period of three years — from 1915 to 1917 inclusive, were used as the basis of this article.

The uniform child labor law fixes the age at which a child may be employed and the hours of labor, and makes special provisions for employment in dangerous occupations. These three phases furnish the points of contention for the majority of cases brought to court. Eight out of 20 cases were concerned with working children below the legal age who had received injuries of some sort while thus illegally employed.

Fifteen year old Fannie A. brought action against a New York laundry for the loss of her right hand through an injury received while in the employ of the company. She was placing a napkin in a steam mangle, the article being first placed upon a convex brass table and pushed under a felt-covered roller two inches in diameter whence it emerged to be taken up by the ironing rollers. The felt roller revolved so as to carry the napkin forward between the ironing rollers. The general manager testified that the purpose of the smaller roller was that of guard. The court held that the roller was only incidentally if at all intended as guard and that it was not a proper guard under the statute. The local court awarded the girl $12,000 but the higher court reduced the amount to $9,000 because of the fact that the girl had only been earning $4.50 a week.

In this case the girl was working illegally at dangerous machinery, since the minimum age in New York at which a girl may work in such hazardous occupation is 16 years.

Another suit involving similar points of contention was brought up in Pennsylvania. A coal company brought action against an insurance company for the amount paid by the former as damages to an injured minor. The latter company made answer that the injury was caused by a minor under 18, employed contrary to the statute which forbids the employment of such minors at switch tending, and as brakemen, engineers and motormen upon railroads. The coal company contended that the boy was injured while working on a private narrow gauge railroad, not a public carrier. The lower court rendered a decision in favor of the insuring company. The higher court upheld this decision, the interpretation being, "the legislative thought was to protect minors under 18 years of age against dangers incident to switch tending and the operating of engines on railroads."

All of the eight final decisions were in favor of the minors involved. Several were reversals from the decisions of the lower courts. One reduced the amount of damages awarded.

COMPENSATION

Under the problem of compensation for injuries received, two factors are considered, first, the question of the application of workmen's compensation, second, the right of the parents to sue for the loss of the child's earnings. Nine cases involving compensation were among the decisions studied. One, involving a question of validity of contract between an employer and an injured minor, 13 years of age, was decided in the lower court of New Jersey in favor of the child. An appeal to a higher court reversed this decision by declaring that the workmen's compensation provision could not apply when the child was employed in violation of the law regulating the employment of children. The boy was given the right to sue through his guardian for damages.

Another suit involved the legal employment of a 14-year old boy who was injured while doing work of a hazardous nature for which he had not been engaged. It was held that the boy could assume the risk of employment.

The Wisconsin Court decided that a boy legally employed and injured at that occupation could not bring liability action against his employer. "He is considered competent to contract as regards subjecting himself to the provisions of the workmen's compensation law, as fully as an adult person."

The Supreme Court of New Jersey affirmed a compensation decision in favor of the company. An injured minor brought suit to recover damages for personal injuries. The defense set up was that the compensation provisions are applicable unless there is a written statement to the contrary in the contract or notice has been given by or to the parent or guardian of the minor employed. On behalf of the plaintiff it was argued that this provision sought to bind minors without their consent, and is invalid in denying them the equal protection of the law. Judgment in the Supreme Court had been for the company, and this was affirmed by the Court of Appeals.

A somewhat similar action with a contrary decision comes from the same state. A minor brought action for personal injuries due to the company's negligence. The company answered upon the ground that the matter was governed by the compensation act. It developed that it had printed on the boy's pay envelope a warning that the provisions of the compensation act were not intended to apply to him. The envelope was handed over to the boy's father. This acted as the written notice of election to avoid the compensation act — therefore, the minor had the right to sue at common law.

Six of these cases were decided in favor of the minor and awards made.

HOURS OF LABOR

Only one case involved the factor of illegal hours of labor. A suit was brought against a cotton oil company of Oklahoma by a 15-year old lad, who was injured while adjusting the belt of one of the machines. The occupation which was in itself illegal because of the hazardous nature was further complicated by the charge of "negligence contributing to the injury." The boy was employed from 7 p. m. to 6 a. m. making 12 hours of night work. The company alleged in defense that it was misled as to his age, since at the time of the boy's employment his mother stated that he was over 16. The trial rendered judgment for the plaintiff which was affirmed by the Supreme Court in a statement that "negligence upon the part of the employer is not sufficient. The statutes prohibiting the act from being done, must be complied with strictly, and if violated the same constitutes negligence upon the part of the employer." The employment of a child under 16 in a factory to do work in violation of the provisions of the statute, was held to be evidence of negligence.

MISCELLANEOUS

A series of miscellaneous cases in which two of the decisions were adverse to the claimant and two in favor are next considered. In one a 16-year old boy employed as water boy had his right hand caught in the gears of a stone crusher. Compensation was paid him for several months. He then returned to work at his regular wages of $9 a week. The Massachusetts

Taken at 2 A.M., Feb. 10, 1903, near a Stable.

The Basket Kid. Photograph by
Arnold Genthe, n.d.

Boy Workers in a Coal Sorting Shed. Photograph by Lewis W. Hine, n.d.

Child Labor on the Farm. Photograph by Lewis W. Hine, 1930.

687] Federal Legislation

court found that his right hand was permanently disabled and awarded compensation accordingly. Later the decree granting compensation for total disability was reversed, with instructions that the boy did not suffer a total loss of wage-earning ability and should therefore be given an opportunity for further hearing for such compensation as he was legally entitled to.

Another suit upheld the right of a father to sue for loss of income of a minor son who had been injured. The Nebraska Court sustained an award made to an injured minor who after having his foot crushed received compensation. During the period of convalescence he attended business school. He returned to work with the same company and was able to command a higher salary. At the time of hearing he was earning $15 a week which was $8 more than he received when injured. The award was made upon the basis of the former salary.

B. FEDERAL CHILD LABOR LEGISLATION

Investigation of child labor by the federal government

1. Roosevelt proposes an investigation to rouse the public conscience

Theodore Roosevelt, "Sixth Annual Message, December 3, 1906," in *The Works of Theodore Roosevelt,* XVII: *State Papers as Governor and President, 1899–1909* (New York: Charles Scribner's Sons, 1925), 421–422.

Roosevelt first recommended a national investigation of child labor in his annual message of 1904; he repeated the recommendation in 1905 and 1906. Congress authorized the investigation in 1907.

More and more our people are growing to recognize the fact that the questions which are not merely of industrial but of social importance outweigh all others; and these two questions most emphatically come in the category of those which affect in the most far-reaching way the home life of the nation. The horrors incident to the employment of young children in factories or at work anywhere are a blot on our civilization. It is true that each State must ultimately settle the question in its own way; but

a thorough official investigation of the matter, with the results published broadcast, would greatly help toward arousing the public conscience and securing unity of State action in the matter. There is, however, one law on the subject which should be enacted immediately, because there is no need for an investigation in reference thereto, and the failure to enact it is discreditable to the National Government. A drastic and thoroughgoing child-labor law should be enacted for the District of Columbia and the Territories.

2. Sectional and partisan considerations

Curtis Guild to Theodore Roosevelt, Jan. 28, 1905, Theodore Roosevelt Papers, Manuscript Division, Library of Congress. Reprinted with permission of the Massachusetts Historical Society.

Guild (1860–1915), a Boston newspaper owner, was lieutenant governor of Massachusetts, 1902–1905, and governor, 1906–1909. He proposed that Roosevelt order the Department of Commerce to investigate child labor.

. . . the matter is of such great importance that I cannot but feel that I wish you to take the matter up personally. I have already written to Cabot Lodge. He agrees with me and has urged me to write to you directly. The real cause of the depression in our cotton mill industry in all New England is the employment of child labor at long hours in the southern states . . . The next step planned by the Democratic Party is a bill *already introduced by a Democratic Congressman* asking for a national investigation by Congress of Child Labor with the object of a uniform law by the states or for a national law as the commission . . . may recommend. I have been preaching against Child Labor all my life . . . It is perfectly possible not only for us to get the credit of this reform but for us to effect therefrom much more quickly than it can be done by Congress . . . In the case of Child Labor . . . you will have not only labor with you but you will also have capital on your side in every state except North Carolina, South Carolina, Georgia, and Alabama where the hideous abuse of little children is generally carried on . . . If the Republican Party can take up this great cause as it should . . . by an executive order for investigation from you *and the fact that you have ordered an investigation can be made public* we, Republicans, who have always stood against Child Labor, can be made to appear in our own clothes before the Democratic Party can steal them from us. As you know the restriction of Child Labor is severest in Massachusetts.

Henry Cabot Lodge to Curtis Guild, Dec. 8, 1905, Lodge Papers, Massachusetts Historical Society. Reprinted with permission of the Massachusetts Historical Society.

It will be a very good thing if we could get a proper law applying to the District, because the example of the national government in legislation for the District would have a very powerful influence everywhere else.[1] You remember, of course, what a fight was made on the stopping of the slave trade in the District of Columbia merely on account of its moral effect, and the passage of a child labor bill for the District would have the same result. I am very anxious that Gardner's[2] bill for an enquiry should be brought to a vote, because my own belief is that we should have much resistance to it from the South, and that would enable us to develop and make clear to our people the source of opposition to this important legislation. I am heartily in sympathy with you as you know in this matter, and you have had a very great share and taken the principal part in bringing about this agitation, which I am sure will bear fruit.

---

3. Roosevelt wants the investigation conducted by the Bureau of Labor

Theodore Roosevelt to Victor H. Metcalf, May 12, 1906, in Elting E. Morison, ed., *Letters of Theodore Roosevelt,* V (Cambridge, Mass.: Harvard University Press, 1952), 269.

Metcalf (1853–1936) was secretary of the Department of Commerce and Labor, 1904–1906. Neill (1865–1942) was commissioner of labor, 1905–1913. At the time of this letter the Census Bureau had not yet published the statistics on child labor of the census of 1900.

I am anxious that the various Departments shall cooperate and of course the same thing is necessary of the bureaus within the Departments. I have recommended that the Bureau of Labor be empowered to undertake an investiga-

1. The D.C. act was passed in 1908. See *Acts of U.S. Congress, 1907–08,* chapter 209.
2. August Peabody Gardner (1865–1918) was Lodge's son-in-law. A Republican, he served in the House of Representatives, 1902–1917.

tion into the conditions of labor of women and children. I am informed that some representative of the Census Bureau has told Members of Congress that it is unnecessary to pass this bill because the Census Bureau has done, or can do, the work in question. I should like the attention of the Census Bureau called to this matter and that it be directed to investigate and find out if any employee of that Bureau has made such a statement and to report the facts to me. The Census Bureau is not the proper Bureau to do the kind of work I desire to have done. Mr. [Charles P.] Neill is peculiarly fitted to do it through his Bureau, and I desire to have the work undertaken by him if Congress will authorize it.[1] *Sincerely yours*

---

4. The authorization of an investigation of women and child wage earners, 1907

U.S. Statutes at Large, 59 Cong., 2 Sess. (1907), p. 866.

The Report on the Condition of Woman and Child Wage Earners in the U.S. was published in nineteen volumes between 1910 and 1913.

CHAP. 432. — An Act to authorize the Secretary of Commerce and Labor to investigate and report upon the industrial, social, moral, educational, and physical condition of woman and child workers in the United States.

Be it enacted by the Senate and House of

1. Crumpacker of Indiana, opposing Roosevelt's recommendation, had quoted on the floor of the House a memorandum by Joseph A. Hill, a division chief in the Census Bureau, dealing with a proposed report by that bureau on the conditions of labor of women and children. The Census Bureau had not actually begun an investigation, nor did it undertake one, but the bill empowering the Bureau of Labor to conduct an investigation did not come to a vote in the 59th Congress. The next Congress, however, passed the enabling legislation Roosevelt had requested. [Note in Morison, ed., *Letters of Theodore Roosevelt*.]

Representatives of the United States of America in Congress assembled, That the Secretary of Commerce and Labor be, and he is hereby, authorized and directed to investigate and report on the industrial, social, moral, educational, and physical condition of woman and child workers in the United States wherever employed, with special reference to their age, hours of labor, term of employment, health, illiteracy, sanitary and other conditions surrounding their occupation, and the means employed for the protection of their health, person, and morals.

Sec. 2. And for the purposes of this Act the Secretary of Commerce and Labor is hereby directed to utilize in so far as they may be adequate the forces of the Bureau of Labor and Bureau of Census.

Sec. 3. That this Act shall take effect immediately.

Approved, January 29, 1907.

The first attempt at federal legislation

---

1. The Beveridge-Parsons bill, 1906–1907

"A Bill to Prevent the Employment of Children in Factories and Mines," S. 6562 and H.R. 21404 (1906), reprinted in Abbott, *The Child and the State,* I, 472–473.

Senator Albert J. Beveridge (1862–1927) of Indiana introduced the bill in the Senate on December 5, 1906. The next day Representative Herbert Parsons (1869–1925) of New York introduced it in the House. Both men were Republicans. Beveridge's bill was referred to the Senate Committee on Education and Labor, while in the House, Parson's bill was sent to the Committee on Interstate and Foreign Commerce. Both committees pigeonholed the bills.

. . . Six months from and after the passage of this act no carrier of interstate commerce shall transport or accept for transportation the products of any factory or mine in which children under fourteen years of age are employed or permitted to work, which products are offered to said interstate carrier by the firm, person, or corporation owning or operating said factory or mine, or any officer or agent or servant thereof, for transportation into any other state or territory than the one in which said factory is located.

SEC. 2. That no carrier of interstate commerce shall transport or accept for transportation the products of any factory or mine offered it for transportation by any person, firm, or corporation which owns or operates such factory or mine, or any officer, agent, or servant of such person, firm, or corporation, until the president or secretary or general manager of such corporation or a member of such firm or the person owning or operating such factory or mine shall file with said carrier an affidavit to the effect that children under fourteen years of age are not employed in such factory or mine.

SEC. 3. That the form of said affidavit shall be prescribed by the Secretary of the Department of Commerce and Labor. After the first affidavit is filed a like affidavit shall be filed, on or before July first and on or before December thirty-first of each year, with the interstate carrier to which such factory or mine offers its products for transportation; and after the first affidavit subsequent affidavits shall also state that no children under fourteen years of age are employed or permitted to work in said factory or mine or have been employed or permitted to work in said factory or mine at any time during the preceding six months.

SEC. 4. That any officer or agent of a carrier of interstate commerce who is a party to any violation of this act or who knowingly violates any of the provisions of this Act shall be punished for each offense by a fine of not more than ten thousand dollars nor less than one thousand dollars or by imprisonment for not more than six months nor less than one month or by both

said fine and imprisonment, in the discretion of the court. Any person by this act required to file the affidavit herein provided for who fails or refuses to file such affidavit or who shall make a false statement in said affidavit, shall be punished by a fine not exceeding twenty thousand dollars nor less than five thousand dollars or by imprisonment not exceeding one year nor less than three months, or by both said fine and imprisonment, in the discretion of the court.

---

2. Senator Beveridge declares federal legislation imperative, 1907

Congressional Record, 59 Cong., 2 Sess. (1907), XLI, Part 2, 1807–1808.

In January 1907 Beveridge, in an effort to get his bill before the Senate, offered it as an amendment to a bill to regulate child labor in the District of Columbia. The following address, delivered on January 29, was part of a three-day presentation of evidence on the abuse of child labor and failure of state regulation.

Beveridge, an insurgent in the Taft administration, was defeated for re-election in 1911.

Mr. President, it has got to stop. I infer from what I have heard here in the interruptions that everybody agrees it has got to stop. As a matter of fact, I have never seen any human reform proposed in this Senate that everybody was not "for" it, but most were against any effective *means* of accomplishing it. We are confronted now with a proposition. I have heard it whispered about the corridors, and so have other Senators, that we must not go "too fast"; that we are bound to have an "investigation."

Oh, no; let us not go "too fast." The evidence is before the Senate of the slow murder of these children, not by tens or hundreds, but by the thousands. But let us not "hasten" to their relief "too fast." Let us "investigate," just as the manufacturers of England asked when they were confronted with the same kind of a reform. "Why not investigate?" said they.

Now, Mr. President, it has got to be stopped and *stopped now*. We all agree upon that — anyhow, everybody says that he agrees it must be stopped; "only," says some, "let us be careful about the Constitution." The Constitution, it appears, is a very mysterious instrument. But never mind; child labor has got to be stopped. How? The States can not stop it. At the beginning of the discussion of the State part of this matter I wish the Senator from South Carolina and the other Senators who apparently intend to oppose this bill to end the evil in their sections of the country, as well as in the North, were here.

I hear that "States rights" is to be used as the excuse for killing this bill. I say there are no "States rights" involved in this bill . . .

Mr. President, something has been said more or less all along about "States rights." But suppose States rights were involved a little bit. Last year we passed the quarantine law. For a hundred years the subject of quarantine has been universally recognized to be exclusively within the province of the States. The effect of the law last year was to make it a national quarantine system. There was not a bit of resistance to it. The people were not willing to quibble; the people were not willing to make a strained construction of the Constitution when yellow fever was knocking at the gates. There was no resistance in the Senate. There was some resistance in the House, made purely upon the "States rights" proposition that it was the province of the State, and that the National Government was taking the right to quarantine from the States.

.   .   .   .   .   .

Mr. President, why is it that the States can not stop this evil? In the first place . . . If one State passes good laws and enforces them and another State does not, then the business men in the former State are at a business disadvantage with the business men in the latter State.

The business man in the State that has the good laws suffers from the very righteousness of that State's laws, and the business man in the State that has bad laws profits by the very wickedness of that State's laws.

.   .   .   .   .   .

Mr. President, the next reason why the States can not adequately handle this question is because neither in this nor in any other important question have the States ever succeeded in having uniform laws; and it is clear that this evil can not be remedied unless there *are uniform laws upon it.*

Suppose, for example, that Ohio passes an excellent child labor law and my State repeals ours, instantly every manufacturing establishment in my State would drain the child labor from Ohio to us, because it is cheaper and more profitable, and the manufacturers of Ohio would be at a disadvantage with the manufacturers of Indiana.

Not only that, but if every single State in the Union but one were to enact a good law and execute it (and I will show you in a minute that they do not and that they can not — and I will show you why they do not and can not), nevertheless the one State that did not and that continued to permit the infamy that exists in many of the States now that I have referred to today would be ruining citizens not of that State only, but citizens of the Nation also.

A child that grows up in New York and becomes a citizen is not alone a citizen of New York. He is a citizen of the Republic as well. He does not vote exclusively if he is in North Carolina for North Carolina candidates. He votes for the President of the Republic; he votes for members of the legislature that elect a United States Senator; he votes for a Congressman. He is as much a citizen of the Nation as he is a citizen of the State, and when any system of labor or of lack of education ruins him for citizenship in the State he is ruined for citizenship in the Nation.

So not only, Mr. President, is there inequality of business opportunities, but by that inequality the ruin of citizens in any one State, the murder of the innocents in any one Commonwealth, affects the entire Republic as much as it affects that State.

Senators who are sincerely anxious about the question of the rights and the dignity of the States must not also forget the rights and the dignity and the future of the Nation. We have not any right to permit any State to produce in this Republic a degenerate class unfit for citizenship beneath the flag, because they vote at National ballot boxes as well as State ballot boxes, if any exercise of our power under the Constitution can prevent it.

Now, Mr. President, there can not be any uniformity. There is not. Here is an abstract of the State laws upon the subject of child labor. There are not six of them alike. Some have no child-labor laws at all; others are worse than any laws, because they are pretenses at labor legislation which make the people and the country think that something has been done, when, as a matter of fact, nothing has been done, and the ruin that went on before without the sanction of the law continues under the sanction of the law.

National Child Labor Committee met with Senator Beveridge to discuss endorsement of his federal child labor bill. A dissenting letter from Robert De Forest (1848–1931), a New York corporation lawyer and former president of the National Conference of Charities and Corrections, was read to the meeting, but all trustees present except one endorsed the bill. This decision marked a departure from the Committee's original aim. Soon after the endorsement, southerner Edgar Gardner Murphy resigned from the National Child Labor Committee, and opposition began to deepen. Lindsay, who had changed his mind and now felt that federal legislation was necessary, volunteered his reasons in a letter to George Foster Peabody (1852–1938), a banker, philanthropist, and prominent Democrat. But he was in the minority, along with Homer Folks, Lillian Wald, and Florence Kelley. Rather than have the Committee split over this issue, the trustees voted on October 25 and again on November 26, 1907, not to endorse the Beveridge bill. Instead, they decided to devote their energies to state legislation and the establishment of a Children's Bureau.

The national child labor committee's stand on federal legislation, 1905–1907

On February 14, 1905, in the opening address at the first meeting of the National Child Labor Committee, the presiding officer, Samuel McCune Lindsay, stated that the purpose of the Committee was to foster state and local child labor legislation. Lindsay (1869–1959) was professor of sociology at the University of Pennsylvania and, after 1907, professor of social legislation at Columbia University.

On December 6, 1906, the trustees of the

1. Lindsay outlines the goals of the Committee, 1905

"Proceedings of the Annual Meeting of the National Child Labor Committee, February 14–16, 1905," in National Child Labor Committee, *Child Labor* (New York, 1905), pp. 160–161.

The National Child Labor Committee has been organized but a very short time. The meeting for the purpose of organization was held in New York City last April, and several months elapsed before an executive office could be established and the machinery for practical work set in motion. Therefore we have been at work practically only three or four months, gathering data from all parts of the country, collecting literature and information concerning the laws, the economic and industrial conditions together with the sentiment prevailing in the different communities with respect to the protection of children.

.   .   .   .   .   .

. . . The committee was not organized with the intention of supplanting or taking the place of the local efforts made in the various parts of the country to do this work, but rather to co-operate with and to strengthen the hands of the bodies organized for this work, or those making this a special feature of the work of their organization . . . Our committee has not been organized to take the place of any other existing committee or any other organizations established for securing more adequate laws or better enforcement of existing legislation; nor was it organized for the purpose of securing national legislation, for we are far removed from the point where we can deal with this matter legislatively in a national way. Our chief purpose is to develop a national sentiment for the protection of children and to make the power of public sentiment felt in all localities, to raise the standard gradually in the different communities, and to have a standard established where none exists at present; to meet industrial and economic conditions in this country in the way acknowledged as best by those who know those conditions best . . .

2. Robert De Forest opposes endorsement of the Beveridge bill

Robert de Forest to Paul Warburg, Dec. 6, 1906, Box 6, National Child Labor Committee Papers.

I should like to be recorded at the meeting this evening as opposed to any endorsement by our National Child Labor Committee of Senator Beveridge's bill. Reflection has only confirmed the opinion I sought to express the other evening. I welcomed the introduction of the bill because it called public attention to this important subject. I am opposed to having our National Committee endorse it for the following reasons amongst others.

The field in which we wish to lay the emphasis of our work is in the South. Public sentiment in the North and West can be relied upon to secure state legislation there. Not so to the same degree in the South. We are succeeding reasonably well in the South with the process of state legislation. We have sought to dissipate Southern prejudice against our organization, in which Northern influence predominates, by some measure of assurance that we would not attempt to secure Federal legislation to directly affect state action. I think our influence in the South would be seriously impaired by giving our official approval to a measure which many Southerners will think of the Force Bill variety.

This objection on my part would be removed if our representative Southern members were of a contrary opinion. Failing such an affirmative expression of opinion however, it would be controlling upon me. Moreover, I think giving our support to this particular measure might weaken our influence for other measures. I notice Senator Lodge has introduced a bill, and President Roosevelt's recommendations, which seem to me admirable, are also before the people. However much we may be ready to endorse Federal legislation, I think it would weaken our influence to endorse this particular legislation at this time, when the field is open and when other proposals may be made with which we may find ourselves in closer sympathy.

Moreover, there is grave doubt about the constitutionality of this bill. Personally I do not think it constitutional. For us to put ourselves behind a bill of doubtful constitutionality seems to me to weaken our influence for the cause.

It is not now a question whether we as a

body favor Federal legislation, academically considered. The only question as I understand relates to this particular bill.

Further, I think the bill would be futile and ineffective, and I think this would be the opinion of any man experienced in business affairs and at all familiar with the practical results of such legislation. Nothing short of Federal inspection could make such legislation effective. Practically, every employer would make a certificate, and every carrier would carry, and conditions would remain the same, except that our whole cause in that section of the country which we seek to influence most would be prejudiced by the claim that we were endeavoring by Federal legislation to interfere with a proper subject of local regulation.

. . . . .

This is far from meaning that I would have our Committee oppose Senator Beveridge's bill. We have all the sentimentalists of the country with us. We want the support of practical business men. It will tend to alienate that support to have us tie our fortunes to a particular bill so open to constitutional and home rule objections and so futile in any promise of practical accomplishment. We have ample justification for neutrality in the degree of assurance we have given to those who have joined our movement on the faith of our declaration against Federal interference which most people consider state issues.

3. Lindsay supports federal legislation

"Samuel McCune Lindsay to George Foster Peabody, January 25, 1907," in John Braeman, "Beveridge and the First National Child Labor Bill," *Indiana Magazine of History,* LX (March 1964), 21.

. . . . States seem to be impotent to enforce their child labor legislation. This is true—both North and South, of all the States, with very few exceptions. The reason for this impotency is largely attributable to the opposition of manufacturers who fear inter-State competition, and in part is due to the poverty of the States in supplying the necessary machinery, such as factory inspection, to carry out legislation of this kind. The Federal Government, on the contrary, can establish a national uniform standard which equalizes competitive conditions, and the Federal Department of Justice has ample resources in backing up, inquiring into, and prosecuting any reports of violation.

4. The National Child Labor Committee does not endorse the Beveridge bill

Minutes of the Board of Trustees, Nov. 26, 1907, Box 6, National Child Labor Committee Papers.

WHEREAS, Wide divergence of opinion exists among those who favor the abolition of child labor as to the desirability of federal regulation, and

WHEREAS, On February 19, 1907, Congress authorized a federal investigation of the subject of child labor under the direction of the United States Bureau of Labor, and the results of such investigation may more clearly define the need for federal legislation or indicate other means better adapted to the regulation of child labor; and

WHEREAS, It is reasonable to expect that a more thorough examination and discussion of the questions constitutional, political and ethical involved in the relation of the federal and the State Governments, respectively, to social legislation will lead to increased clarification and unification on this vital issue;

THEREFORE RESOLVED, That the National Child Labor Committee will for the present take no further action with reference to National legislation until the results of the National investigation are available and the results of a more searching consideration of the whole subject point the way to action upon which we can hope to unite all forces now devoted to the cause of child labor reform; and

BE IT FURTHER RESOLVED, That we concentrate our efforts for the winter of 1907–8 upon the formulation and active support of wise State and local legislation and other measures for the suppression of child labor, including efforts to secure a Children's Bureau in Washington.

The first federal child labor law

1. The National Child Labor Committee and the Palmer-Owen bill, 1914

Owen R. Lovejoy, "Federal Government and Child Labor," *Child Labor Bulletin,* II, (February 1914), 19, 20–22, 23.

In 1908 the committee opened a Washington, D.C., office under the direction of Alexander J. McKelway. A bill drafted by the Committee served as the basis for the Palmer-Owen bill of 1914 and the Keating-Owen Act of 1916. It was prepared with the assistance of officials of the Children's Bureau, constitutional lawyers, and members of Congress. William Draper Lewis, dean of the University of Pennsylvania Law School, and Charles P. Neill, former commissioner of labor who had been in charge of the *Report on Women and Child Wage Earners,* were chiefly responsible for its contents and form. Representative A. Mitchell Palmer of Pennsylvania introduced it in the House on January 16, 1914, and Senator Robert L. Owen of Oklahoma introduced it in the Senate on February 21, 1914.[1] Both were Democrats.

1. 63 Cong., 2 Sess., H.R. 12292 and S. 4571. On the history of the Bill see Stephen Wood, *Constitutional Politics in the Progressive Era* (Chicago, 1969), chaps. 2 and 3.

The introduction of the Palmer Child Labor Bill in Congress on January 26th marks a new stage in the campaign for child labor reform in America. This bill, drawn by the National Child Labor Committee, is the result of careful and mature deliberation by the Committee and of extensive correspondence with prominent lawyers, state and federal officials and others interested in this great problem.

The National Child Labor Committee has been from time to time solicited to give its endorsement to various pending child labor bills, but on careful analysis it has been unable to do so either on account of their limited scope or because they did not seem designed to control the situation in the most effective way.

The two considerations that most directly affected the Committee in drafting this bill were the questions of constitutionality and of effectiveness. On the question of constitutionality it is believed that a clear line of Supreme Court decisions dating from the early history of the Republic down to the recent decisions in the Mann White Slave Act definitely lay upon Congress the responsibility for discouraging by the power of federal law interstate traffic in the lives and health of little children. It is realized by the Committee that no conclusion on the question of constitutionality can be reached at the present time. Constitutional lawyers of the highest reputation differ in their judgment and one Congressman significantly remarked—"You never can tell until it comes before the court of last conjecture."

The National Child Labor Committee has, from the beginning, worked in close co-operation with departments of factory inspection in the various states and in order to test the attitude of these officials toward this proposition an inquiry has been conducted for the past year to learn whether in their judgment the enactment of such a law would prove effective in reducing the evils of child labor in their respective states, whether the presence of federal authority would duplicate the work of state officials, and if so, whether this would tend to discourage or to stimulate and standardize the work of state departments. It is encouraging to the friends of federal legislation, as well as significant of the broad-minded spirit in which these officials view the responsibilities resting upon them, to record that with very few exceptions state labor commissioners, factory inspectors and other officials charged with the enforcement of child labor laws look upon legislation by Congress as a definite step in advance. It is the general opinion that under the provisions of this bill a large force of factory inspectors will not be required; but although in some instances the work of the state and federal authorities may duplicate, even in such instances the presence of federal officials and the power of a federal law will directly stimulate and encourage state inspection and law enforcement.

This bill differs from bills already pending in Congress in many respects. It is much broader in scope than the bills which provide only for regulation of employment of children under 14 years of age. The National Child Labor Committee's bill seeks to forbid the employment of children under 16 years in mines and quarries and under 14 years in manufacturing establishments and also to forbid employment of children under 16 years of age for more than eight hours a day or at night. It also differs from other bills in constituting a permanent board of the heads of three administrative departments on the same plan as that provided for administration of the Food and Drugs Law. It does not seek to penalize the interstate carrier, but attempts to place responsibility upon the real offender, i.e., "the person, partnership, association or corporation or any agent thereof" producing the goods.

Its penalty provisions are also adjusted to meet varying situations. As expressed by ex-United States Commissioner Charles P. Neill "It is not our design to confiscate the property of a man who through some accident or oversight permits a child to be employed in violation of the law. We have therefore made the penalty light enough to work no hardship on first offenders, but by providing that every delivery for shipment shall constitute a separate offense, we make it possible for the Federal Government to give the incorrigible offender all the punishment he wants."

The Palmer bill offers better protection for the children than another pending bill that expressly exempts from its regulation shipments from states which have laws prohibiting "anti-social child labor." The Committee does not believe that any state in the Union should be exempt from the operation of this law simply because there happens to be on its statute books a law providing the same standards. One of the chief scandals in connection with this whole national abuse is the presence of state laws in commonwealths that have either nullified their law by failing to appropriate funds for its administration, or have so tied the hands of officials by political obligations that effective administration becomes impossible . . .

One bill which the Committee could not endorse provides that in order to violate the law it must be done "knowingly." Since it is impossible for any official to determine what is in the mind of an exploiter of little children or to discover whether he actually knows that he is reaping profits from the illegal labor of such a child, the Committee believes it preferable to provide a light minimum penalty so as not to work an injustice upon an employer who commits this misdemeanor through accident or oversight; but it cannot agree that the prosecution of an offense under this law should be compelled to prove that the offender knew he was violating it.

•   •   •   •   •

Members of the National Child Labor Committee who wish to aid in promoting this legislation should write at once to the members of the [House] Committee on Labor urging that their early and favorable consideration be given the bill. Also write your Congressman urging him to lend his support when the bill is reported out of committee.

2. Federal child labor legislation is unjust and unconstitutional

U.S. Congress, Senate, *Hearings on H.R. 8234, Child Labor Bill,* 64 Cong., 1 Sess. (1916), pp. 5–6, 11–13, 140–141, 154, 157–159, 172–173.

The Keating-Owen bill was identical with the Palmer-Owen bill. Senator Owen reintroduced the bill in the Senate on December 7, 1915, and Representative Edward Keating, a Colorado Democrat, introduced it in the House on January 7, 1916. During the Palmer-Owen hearings, opposition to federal child labor standards had been voiced ineffectually. But two years later, David Clark, publisher of the *Southern Textile Bulletin,* had organized southern cotton manufacturers into an "Executive Committee," the purpose of which was to oppose federal child labor legislation. Clark employed William Kitchin (1866–1924), a former governor of North Carolina, to represent the Committee at the Keating-Owen hearings. These two men were joined by James Emery (1876–1955), the general counsel of the National Association of Manufacturers. The southerners emphasized the negative consequences of the bill and the positive aspects of state regulation. Emery conjured up the menace of federal regulation in every sphere of life.

["WORK IN THE MILLS NOT AS INJURIOUS AS WORK ON THE FARMS"]

Mr. CLARK . . . The proposition of the National Child Labor Committee is that the cotton mill boys and girls are injured by working in the mills. That is the basis of their claim, as I understand it. They also claim that the second generation is going to show the effect of that injury. Now, as a matter of fact, the second generation of the cotton-mill people in the South are better physically, better looking people, than the first generation that came from the mountains. I have here a few photographs which I desire to pass around among the members of the committee, showing some of the children of the operatives.

Mr. LONDON. Does that apply to both men and women—that they are better looking?

Mr. CLARK. Yes, sir. A number of years ago we had no law that prohibited work of children 8 or 9 years of age. Now, the children of those who worked at 8 or 9 years of age are shown in these pictures. That is the way they are today. I want you to look at these pictures so that you can see whether they compare physically with other children in other places.

Mr. KEATING. It is your belief, Mr. Clark, that putting children in the cotton mills in the South when they are 8 or 9 years old and subjecting them to the rigorous treatment there, performing a day's work, will not have any bad effect upon the children?

Mr. CLARK. I did not state that.

Mr. KEATING. Well, according to your pictures, you would demonstrate, without any statement from you, using the pictures as evidence, that the working of children in the past in the South at so early an age as 8 or 9 years, would not have a bad effect upon those children?

Mr. CLARK. No, sir; because of the fact that before they came to the mills they had worked on the farms, where they had worked longer and harder hours.

Mr. KEATING. Do you mean to say that before they went to work in the mills they had served an apprenticeship on the farm?

Mr. CLARK. No; I mean the parents of those children had worked on the farms before they came there to the mills.

Mr. KEATING. Then your idea is that the parents having worked on the farms and having secured an excellent constitution in that way, their children are able to endure the work in the mills?

Mr. CLARK. No, sir. My theory is that the work in the mills is not as hard or as injurious as the work on the farms. The promoters of this bill have not the nerve to include the farms or even to refer to the farms. . .

[THIS LEGISLATION WILL PUT 25,000 BOYS AND GIRLS OUT OF WORK]

Mr. KEATING. You say that this legislation will put 25,000 boys and girls out of employment in the mills of the South.

Mr. CLARK. Practically so.

Mr. KEATING. Now, it would be necessary for the mill owners to employ substitutes for those 25,000 employees.

Mr. CLARK. Yes, sir.

Mr. KEATING. And they would be compelled to employ adults.

Mr. CLARK. They would have to employ operatives over 16; yes.

Mr. KEATING. Now, in what particular would the mill owner be injured? Would he be compelled to pay higher wages?

Mr. CLARK. The mill itself would not be so greatly injured. The operative is going to feel it more than the mill. The greatest opposition to this bill is from the operatives.

Mr. KEATING. Then, as I understand you, you are not speaking in behalf of the owners of the mills, but on behalf of those who work in the mills.

Mr. CLARK. I am speaking on behalf of both of them. I deal with both of them. As editor of the Textile Bulletin I come in contact with both the owners and operatives.

Mr. KEATING. But you do not feel that it would injure the mills?

Mr. CLARK. Well, it would injure them to some extent, because naturally they will have to reorganize their employees and it will injure them for a while.

Mr. KEATING. The principal thought is to safeguard the interest of the children?

Mr. CLARK. It is not a question of safeguarding interests. The mill people need employment, and what are you going to offer them? They have not money enough to seek education. What are you going to do for them when you turn them out of the mills?

Mr. KEATING. Of course, that is a question that I do not expect to answer. I merely wanted to get at the motives of those who are opposing this legislation. I wanted to make it clear whether they were antagonizing this legislation on the ground that it would injure the business interests of the South, or whether they thought this legislation would oppress the children who are employed in the mills.

Mr. CLARK. It will injure the business interests to a certain extent and also turn out of employment a large class of people who need employment.

.   .   .   .   .

We all know how kind your intentions are. If you drive these children out of the mills, they have to go on earning money, they must exist. You do not drive them into the schools. Some of them would probably loaf around. Some of them, of course, would go back to the farms, where they would eke out probably a scanty living, but without the same advantages. You do not get all your education from books — from going to school. So far as intelligence and getting information is concerned, one boy in an ordinary cotton-mill village will learn better how to take care of himself, acquit himself in company, to be a good man and a good citizen, in 12 months than out on some lonely mountain farm in two or three years.

You can not appreciate that. You gentlemen who live in great cities and in thickly populated communities, can not understand the lonesome life that many people in our agricultural communities endure.

[THE STATES HAVE BEEN MAKING RAPID PROGRESS]

[Mr. CLARK] . . . We insist that the children of the South, many of them, must labor. It is not a question of desire upon their part. It is a question of necessity. They must work. There are orphans, children of widows, and dependents who must work in order to live. Now, how to exclude them is a question for the State, because that class should be excluded from the operation of a law of this kind. But if you say that a child under 14 or under 16 must work — and you can not deny it if you are acquainted with southern conditions — then we insist that a cotton mill pays him more wages than he can get anywhere else in the South; that the conditions under which he works are better than those of any other industry — I do not except farms; that his educational opportunities and religious opportunities are equal, if not superior, to those he can get anywhere else; that he lives in a better home, has better clothing and better food in 99 cases out of 100 than he had before his parents came to the mill, or than he would have if he was driven from the mills by this bill.

Now, those are the cold facts surrounding conditions under which the child works — wages, health, sanitation, etc. Then we insist that the mills themselves have shown a greater interest in the development and improvement of the conditions of labor than this Congress can ever show. We propose to show by witnesses that in the last 20 years there has been almost a revolution in the mill conditions in the Southern States. We want you to consider that in the last 15 years these same Southern States have greatly improved their labor laws. They are not yet what we want, but the States have been making such rapid progress that they are now in touch with the situation and know the conditions, and the people of North Carolina are just as humane — North Carolina, South Carolina, Mississippi, Alabama, and Georgia — and think as much of those children as any member of this committee. They are making such rapid progress that we think this committee ought to be encouraged to leave this matter to the States themselves.

[THE RIGHTFUL AUTHORITY OF CONGRESS IS LIMITED TO THE QUALITY AND CONDITION OF THE ARTICLE]

[Mr. KITCHIN] The preamble of the Constitution says that one of the purposes of organizing this Government was to secure liberty for ourselves and our posterity. Securing that liberty did not mean obtaining it, as I contend. The States had it then, but it was to secure it, to make it firm, and undoubted for the future. As I proceed you will, I trust, discover that a law of this character will infringe upon that liberty which the Constitution intended to secure. When the Constitution says that life, liberty, and property of the citizen shall not be taken from him without due process of law it means that Congress itself can not do it and the States can not do it. If a man has property there is no power in this Republic that can deprive him of it without due process of law, and an act of Congress such as the bill proposed is not due process of law.

The distinguished chairman of this committee, in his report, made a statement with which I thoroughly concur. He said, in substance, that it is from the Federal Constitution that we derive our right to interstate commerce except in deleterious substances. That is sound. Except I would say instead of from the Constitution we derive our rights to interstate commerce, it is rather by the Constitution our rights in interstate commerce are guaranteed. It does guarantee them, because we had the right to engage in interstate commerce before the constitution was formed. It is one of the rights akin to the right to the product of your own labor. No law gave it to you. The God that endowed you with intelligence and gave you the muscle gave you the right to exercise it in all just and lawful ways.

The CHAIRMAN. Will you pardon this suggestion? The Constitution conferred a much higher right of interstate commerce than existed before, did it not?

Mr. KITCHIN. I am coming to that. You are right in that. Now, it is one of these rights to own property and to dispose of it, to buy and sell, and travel — go from one State to another. It was a right which every Amercian had before the Constitution, and that right was guaranteed by the Constitution when it said they could not take life, liberty, or property without due process of law.

The CHAIRMAN. Do you not think the right was a very deficient one when each State could impose tariff restrictions and embargoes?

Mr. KITCHIN. I understand that. And that was the great reason the Constitution was formed — to forbid shutting the goods of any State up within its borders.

It was for the purpose of preventing restraints by States upon the free transportation of goods from one State to another. If Virginia or North Carolina had a right to forbid goods from another State coming in, and they did have it, that great right the States surrendered.

You search in vain, Mr. Chairman, with all due respect, to find one single instance in all our country's history, State or national, where a law has ever been sustained that undertook to prevent a sound and healthful product from transportation into another State.

. . . Congress, under the commerce clause, can not constitutionally look backward into the conditions of manufacture and say whether or not those conditions meet its approval. The rightful authority of Congress is limited to the quality and condition of the article when it first becomes a part of the interstate commerce. It can ascertain at that time whether it is spurious, or adulterated, or impure, or immoral, or is to be used to the injury of the health or morals of the State into which it is to be shipped, and if so, it can forbid its transportation in interstate commerce.

[THE FEDERAL GOVERNMENT
BECOMES A DESPOT]

I realize that when a manufacturer or his representative appears before a committee of this character he is embarrassed by possibly the suspicion or suggestion that, because he is opposed to the subject matter of the regulation, or any regulation of the subject itself whatever. The National Association of Manufacturers has been at no time opposed to the regulation of child labor. It has never appeared in any State, so far as I know, in opposition to or criticism of the radical regulation of child labor.

Let me say first, if I may, parenthetically, that if I discuss this bill from the standpoint of the right of a State to regulate its internal affairs and the right of a citizen of that State to be regulated or controlled by his local government in those matters which are purely domestic I am not asserting an imaginary or obstructive state right, but a very real one that is essential to the maintenance of the integrity of our form of government itself — not in my opinion, but in the opinion of every commentator not only upon the Constitution but upon our peculiar form of government.

Now, if this legislation is placed upon our statute books, you will immediately encounter a demand in Congress for legislation against the shipment of goods of all kinds in interstate commerce. You would probably hear of a very strong idea that the workers of this country ought not to receive less than $3, $4, or $5 a day. If this law was passed, Congress could be asked to prevent the shipment of any goods in interstate commerce produced by men who worked more than eight hours a day, or who received less than $3 a day. Or the requirement might be that the men who produced the goods should be able to speak 300 words in the English language, or 200 or 100. You could apply a literacy test precisely the same as that which was vetoed by President Wilson in the last immigration bill, which passed the Sixty-third Congress. If the Congress, in its plenary power, can attack such conditions as are named in the bill now before the committee to the shipment of goods in interstate commerce, where will it lead to? With continual restrictions placed upon the shipment of goods in interstate commerce, Congress, instead of keeping commerce free, would lay new burdens upon it.

. . . With 90 per cent of the commerce of this country sold in places outside of the State in which it is produced, if Congress fixed the conditions under which production is to be had, then the whole police power of the State is an empty thing; then the State government passes away, and the Federal Government becomes a despot, possessing and exercising the powers of the State with respect to the supervision and control of the production of the goods which are essential to the public welfare. If a proposition such as is now before the committee can be seriously considered, however meritorious its purpose may be, and however sympathetic we may be with its object, it means that there is practically no regulation of production of a fairly reasonable nature by Congress that would be imposing unreasonable burdens upon commerce and substituting its views and its judgment — the judgment of about 400 men — in place of the views of representative men of the different States in which local conditions are sought to be remedied . . .

---

3. The child labor question in party platforms, 1912–1916

Kirk H. Porter, comp., *National Party Platforms* (New York: The Macmillan Company, 1924), pp. 334, 383, 402.

PROGRESSIVE PARTY PLATFORM OF 1912

The supreme duty of the Nation is the conservation of human resources though an enlightened measure of social and industrial justice. We pledge ourselves to work unceasingly in State and Nation for:

Effective legislation looking to the prevention of industrial accidents, occupational diseases, overwork, involuntary unemployment, and other injurous effects incident to modern industry;

The fixing of minimum safety and health standards for the various occupations, and the exercise of the public authority of State and Nation, including the Federal Control over interstate commerce, and the taxing power, to maintain such standards;

The prohibition of child labor;

Minumum wage standards for working women, to provide a "living wage" in all industrial occupations;

The general prohibition of night work for women and the establishment of an eight hour day for women and young persons;

One day's rest in seven for all wage workers;

The eight hour day in continuous twenty-four-hour industries;

DEMOCRATIC PLATFORM OF 1916

We favor the speedy enactment of an effective Federal Child Labor Law and the regulation of the shipment of prison-made goods in interstate commerce.

REPUBLICAN PLATFORM OF 1916

We pledge the Republican party to the faithful enforcement of all Federal laws passed for the protection of labor. We favor vocational education, the enactment and rigid enforcement of a Federal child labor law; the enactment of a generous and comprehensive workmen's compensation law, within the commerce power of Congress, and an accident compensation law covering all Government employees . . .

---

4. Steering the child labor bill through Congress

Edward Keating, *The Gentleman from Colorado; A Memoir* (Denver: Sage Books, 1964), pp. 347–353. Reprinted with permission of Mrs. Edward Keating.

Edward Keating chanced upon the Palmer-Owen bill after he had been appointed to the House of Representatives Committee on Labor, one of the least important committees. He decided to sponsor the bill because he felt it was a potentially significant and timely issue.

It was December of 1914 . . .

Palmer had been defeated for senator in

Pennsylvania. Democrats didn't have much chance in the Keystone State in those days . . .

I was startled one day when he stopped me in the Speaker's Lobby and said: "I believe you are interested in child labor legislation" . . .

"Well," he continued, "the National Child Labor Committee asked me to suggest someone to handle its bill in the next Congress and I have told the committee you are the man."

I thanked him with very genuine sincerity. When the 64th Congress convened, I decided to rush the legislation through the House as soon as possible. The National Child Labor Committee, headed by Owen Lovejoy, provided me with able and devoted helpers, including Dr. McKelway . . .

The constitutionality of the bill was vigorously challenged and as I had never opened a law book, I had to have a competent legal adviser. The National Child Labor Committee engaged a brilliant youngster, Tommy Parkinson. He did a magnificent job before congressional committees and later, when the entire issue was thrashed out in the Supreme Court, he made the principal argument . . .

With the aid of Davy Lewis and Johnny Nolan, I succeeded in expediting the hearings and secured a favorable report, despite the opposition of the Southerners, led by a gracious gentleman from Virginia, Congressman Watson . . .

I knew the Rules Committee would not grant me a rule and that my only hope was to get the bill before the House on "Calendar Wednesday." I told Watson if I delayed reporting my bill, the Labor Committee might be called and passed. In that event, it might be six months or more before our committee would be called again.

Watson made light of this, pointing out that there were many committees ahead of the Labor Committee and that our committee could not hope to be reached for weeks. I respected Watson, but I had a "hunch" that delay might prove fatal. Events demonstrated I was right.

On the first "Calendar Wednesday" the Clerk of the House ran through the list of committees and found that few of them had any legislation ready to report. Then he called the Labor Committee and Davy Lewis claimed the floor and called up by bill. *The Labor Committee wasn't called again for about a year.*

We experienced comparatively smooth sailing in the House. Public sentiment had been aroused on the child labor issue. Democrats and Republicans from the North and West were a unit for my bill. Several Southerners advocated it including . . . Swager Sherley from Louisville, Kentucky . . . He made a curious speech. In the beginning, he said, he thought the bill unconstitutional and prepared to discuss it from that point of view. However, as he went into the precedents, he changed his mind, determined it was constitutional and said so on the floor of the House.

A little later I had occasion to discuss the measure with President Woodrow Wilson. He wasn't enthusiastic. He raised the constitutional question. I told him a member of his Cabinet, Franklin K. Lane, brilliant Secretary of the Interior, had gone into the matter thoroughly and had assured me the bill was constitutional.

Wilson smiled and replied: "Perhaps Lane is right, but once upon a time I was paid to teach constitutional law."

Well, we got the bill through the House and Senator Robert L. Owen of Oklahoma was supposed to look after it in the Senate, but Owen, like myself, had a one-track mind. At the moment he was deeply involved in other legislation of the first importance. I felt confident he couldn't spare the time needed to make a fight for the Child Labor bill. I knew powerful Southern senators would endeavor to defeat it and would resort to a filibuster, if necessary.

I looked around for help and I had another "hunch." Senator Joe Robinson of Arkansas also boarded at the Congress Hall Hotel. He had served in the House for a number of years, but had just entered the senate. I had observed that Robinson was passionately fond of children. If a toddler came into the lobby of the hotel, the senator would turn aside from the most distinguished visitor to play with the little one.

So, one evening I sat down with Robinson and explained my dilemma and asked him to lead the fight in the Senate. He filled my heart with joy by accepting the task without hesitation. He knew Owen and was confident he could work with him, and he did, carrying ninety per cent of the load.

Just as I had anticipated, certain Southern senators stalled for time. It was a presidential year — 1916. Congress would adjourn early for the primaries and conventions. One night the Democratic leaders of the Senate cruised down the Potomac and agreed on a program. The Southerners said they would go along if the Child Labor bill could be pushed aside.

The moment he got to Washington Senator John W. Kern, then Democratic floor leader in the Senate, told me what had happened. The next day I rushed to the White House. The President said he couldn't intervene. Congress must adjourn! Apparently my Child Labor bill was ditched.

Fortunately, the Republicans secured the details of the Democratic program, and Senator Gallinger of New Hampshire, then Republican floor leader, led an effective assault on the Democratic position.

He emphasized that, in their eagerness to start the hunt for votes, the Democrats were willing to sacrifice *even* child labor legislation; furthermore, that they were doing this at the command of Southern senators, who spoke for the textile interests.

A day or two later my secretary burst into my office exclaiming: "Do you know what's happened? President Wilson is on Capitol Hill, demanding the Senate pass your Child Labor bill!"

I couldn't believe it — I still remembered Wilson's statement that the legislation was unconstitutional — but the story was true. At that moment, the President was on the Senate side of the Capitol, conferring with the Democratic leaders, and an hour or two later it was announced that Congress would not adjourn until it had acted on the Child Labor bill.

The next day I went to the White House to thank the President. "Don't thank me," he said. "I still fear the bill is unconstitutional, although I am in complete sympathy with the principle. However, there was nothing we could do after Gallinger made his attack. Rejection of the Child Labor bill might prove a serious matter in the coming campaign."

---

5. The Keating-Owen Act, 1916

"An Act to Prevent Interstate Commerce in the Products of Child Labor, and for Other Purposes," 1916 — ch. 432, *U.S. Statutes at Large,* XXXIX, Part I, pp. 675–676.

As indicated in section 7, the Act, passed on September 1, 1916, was to go into effect on September 1, 1917.

Be it enacted by the Senate and House of Representatives of the United States of America in Congress assembled, That no producer, manufacturer, or dealer shall ship or deliver for shipment in interstate or foreign commerce any article or commodity the product of any mine or quarry, situated in the United States, in which within thirty days prior to the time of the removal of such product therefrom children under the age of sixteen years have been employed or permitted to work, or any article or commodity the product of any mill, cannery, workshop, factory, or manufacturing establishment, situated in the United States, in which within thirty days prior to the removal of such product therefrom children under the age of fourteen years have been employed or permitted to work, or children between the ages of fourteen years and sixteen years have been employed or permitted to work more than eight hours in any day, or more than six days in any week, or after the hour of seven o'clock postmeridian, or before the hour of six o'clock antemeridian: *Provided,* That a prosecution and conviction of a defendant for the shipment or delivery for shipment of any article or commodity under the conditions herein prohibited shall be a bar to any further prosecution against the same defendant for shipments or deliveries for shipment of any such article or commodity before the beginning of said prosecution.

SEC. 2. That the Attorney General, the Secretary of Commerce, and the Secretary of Labor shall constitute a board to make and publish from time to time uniform rules and regulations for carrying out the provisions of this Act.

SEC. 3. That for the purpose of securing proper enforcement of this Act the Secretary of Labor, or any person duly authorized by him, shall have authority to enter and inspect at any time mines, quarries, mills, canneries, workshops, factories, manufacturing establishments, and other places in which goods are produced or held for interstate commerce; and the Secretary of Labor shall have authority to employ such assistance for the purposes of this Act as may from time to time be authorized by appropriation or other law.

SEC. 4. That it shall be the duty of each district attorney to whom the Secretary of Labor shall report any violation of this Act, or to whom any State factory or mining or quarry inspector, commissioner of labor, State medical inspector, or school-attendance officer, or any other person shall present satisfactory evidence of any such violation to cause appropriate proceedings to be commenced and prosecuted in the proper courts of the United States without delay for the enforcement of the penalties in such cases herein provided: *Provided,* That nothing in this act shall be construed to apply to bona fide boys' and girls' canning clubs recognized by the Agricultural Department of the several States and of the United States.

SEC. 5. That any person who violates any of the provisions of section one of this Act, or who refuses or obstructs entry or inspection authorized by section three of this Act, shall for each offense prior to the first conviction of such person under the provisions of this Act, be punished by a fine of not more than $200, and shall for each offense subsequent to such conviction be punished by a fine of not more than $1,000, nor less than $100, or by imprisonment for not more than three months, or by both such fine and imprisonment, in the discretion of the court: *Provided,* That no dealer shall be prosecuted under the provisions of this Act for a shipment, delivery for shipment, or transportation who establishes a guaranty issued by the person by whom the goods shipped or delivered for shipment or transportation were manufactured or produced, resident in the United States, to the effect that such goods were produced or manufactured in a mine or quarry in which within thirty days prior to their removal therefrom no children under the age of sixteen years were employed or permitted to work, or in a mill, cannery, workshop, factory, or manufacturing establishment, in which within thirty days prior to the removal of such goods therefrom no children under the age of fourteen years were employed or permitted to work, nor children between the ages of fourteen years and sixteen years employed or permitted to work more than eight hours in any day or more than six days in any week or after the hour of seven o'clock postmeridian or before the hour of six o'clock antemeridian; and in such event, if the guaranty contains any false statement of a material fact, the guarantor shall be amenable to prosecution and to the fine or imprisonment provided by this section for violation of the provisions of this Act. Said guaranty, to afford the protection above provided, shall contain the name and address of the person giving the same: *And provided further,* That no producer, manufacturer, or dealer shall be prosecuted under this Act for the shipment, delivery for shipment, or transportation of a product of any mine, quarry, mill, cannery, workshop, factory, or manufacturing establishment, if the only employment therein, within thirty days prior to the removal of such product therefrom, of a child under the age of sixteen years has been that of a child as to whom the producer or manufacturer has in good faith procured, at the time of employing such child, and has since in good faith relied upon and kept on file a certificate, issued in such form, under such conditions, and by such persons as may be prescribed by the board, showing the child to be of such an age that the shipment, delivery for shipment, or transportation was not prohibited by this Act. Any person who knowingly makes a false statement or presents false evidence in or in relation to any such certificate or application therefor shall be amenable to prosecution and to the fine or imprisonment provided by this section for violations of this Act. In any State designated by the board, an employment certificate or other similar paper as to the age of the child, issued under the laws of that State and not inconsistent with the provisions of this Act, shall have the same force and effect as a certificate herein provided for.

SEC. 6. That the word "person" as used in this Act shall be construed to include any individual or corporation or the members of any partnership or other unincorporated association. The term "ship or deliver for shipment in interstate or foreign commerce" as used in this Act means to transport or to ship or deliver for shipment from any State or Territory or the District of Columbia to or through any other State or Territory or the District of Columbia or to any foreign country; and in the case of a dealer means only to transport or to ship or deliver for shipment from the State, Territory, or district of manufacture or production.

SEC. 7. That this Act shall take effect from and after one year from the date of its passage. Approved, September 1, 1916.

---

6. The federal child labor law is the beginning — not the end

Owen R. Lovejoy, "What Remains of Child Labor," *New Republic,* IX (November 11, 1916), 39.

. . . Is not the task achieved? Is not the yoke of industrial bondage lifted? Have not the children been set free? No. Our work has been a failure if American intelligence thinks it finished. It has only begun. What has been accomplished is rudimentary. Here is the beginning of the chapter — not the end. How does it read?

First: A written law is a prescription, not a recovery. Congress has not abolished child labor but only made it possible for you to do so. Responsibility is laid on you, on every citizen, to see that this law is enforced in your community. It is a duty you cannot delegate. The public-spirited man of business who has been annoyed by the guerilla warfare of his unscrupulous competitor may now defend himself. The citizen who has found local administration of the child-labor law bound by graft and politics may now bring his complaint before the United States Department of Labor. The discouraged factory inspector whose faithful attempts to prosecute have been paralyzed by petty courts dominated by powerful local interests will now lay his case before a Federal Grand Jury. These are your weapons.

Second: Assuming that this law is effectively enforced, how far does it reach? Only 150,000 children will be affected. The other 1,850,000 children are left untouched. No federal law can reach them. They are the wards of the several states: the young hawkers of news and chewing-gum on our city streets; the truck-garden conscripts of Pennsylvania, New Jersey, Ohio, Colorado and Maryland; the sweating cotton-pickers of Mississippi, Oklahoma and Texas; the 90,000 domestic servants under 16 years of age in our American homes; the cash-girls in our department stores.

Only one state has thus far passed an adequate law to regulate street trades. The delusion that every small street peddler is supporting a widowed mother dies hard. Street trading in our large cities is the primary department in the school of vice. That school must be closed. The place to begin is in your city.

From the sugar-beet fields of Colorado, from the berry fields of New Jersey, Maryland and Delaware, from the onion beds of Ohio, from the tobacco fields of Kentucky and from the hot cotton fields of Oklahoma and Texas, the cry of the children ought to make itself heard. But they are mute. They have not tasted liberty. Without complaint they step into the ranks of the 5,000,000 illiterates to grope blindly through a land of plenty.

---

7. Administration of the first federal child labor law

Grace Abbott, *Administration of the First Federal Child Labor Law,* United States Children's Bureau Pub. No. 78 (Washington, D.C., 1921), in Abbott, *The Child and the State,* I, 486–495.

Grace Abbott (1878–1939) was appointed director of the Child Labor Division of the Children's Bureau in charge of the administration of the new law. The act was in effect for 275 days — September 1, 1917, until June 3, 1918 — when the Supreme Court declared it unconstitutional.

A basis for co-operation between the Federal and State Governments was provided in the act. The Child Labor Division [of the Chil-

dren's Bureau] laid out its plans on the theory that the successful and economical administration of the measure required that this co-operation should be developed into a genuine working relationship[1] . . .

Plans for the issuance of certificates of age were made on the theory that the successful enforcement of the law depended primarily upon a well-administered certificating system. State experience had demonstrated that only if no child is employed without a certificate, and if no certificate is issued except upon reliable evidence that the child is legally qualified to work, will the age, education, and physical standards of a child labor law be evenly and uniformly enforced. With a good certificating system, inspection serves as little more than a reenforcement of respect for the certificate by both employer and child. If, however, certificates are issued on inadequate evidence or a careless canvass of the facts, official approval of the employment of children who are below the legal age is sure to be given by the issuing officer. This places a very heavy burden on the inspection department, as under such circumstances the inspector must determine the ages of all children employed, whether with or without certificates . . .

Unlike State child labor laws, the Federal act did not penalize the employer covered by the terms of the act if he did not keep on file certificates of age for all children within prescribed ages in his employ. It did provide that if certificates were procured in good faith by an employer and the children proved to be under the legal age, he was protected against prosecution for shipment of his products in interstate or foreign commerce. Two kinds of certificates would afford this protection under the terms of the Federal act: (1) Those issued by Federal agents under the regulations laid down by the Child Labor Board; and (2) age, employment or working certificates, or papers

1. The Bureau of Chemistry had a similar problem in the administration of the Food and Drug Act, and its experience was utilized by the division. [Notes 1–3 in Abbott, *Administration.*]

issued under State authority in States designated by the board.

To avoid the expense and inconvenience to the child, the employer, and the Government of a double certificating system it was important that, so far as the State laws and administrative practices made it possible, State certificates should be accepted for the purposes of the Federal act. In a number of States, radical amendment of the State law was necessary before a reasonably satisfactory certificating system could be assured . . .

The regulation finally adopted by the board with reference to designation of States was as follows:

Regulation 3 — Authorization of acceptance of State certificates. — States in which the age, employment, or working certificates, permits, or papers are issued under State authority substantially in accord with the requirements of the act may be designated as States in which certificates issued under State authority shall have the same force and effect as those issued under the direct authority of this act, . . .

In accordance with this regulation . . . 39 States and the District of Columbia were designated on August 15 by the board, the designation to take effect on September 1, for a six-months period.

. . . . . .

On March 1, 1918, the designation of all these States expired. At this time 13 States were redesignated for a period of 12 months; and 22 States and the District of Columbia were redesignated for a period of 6 months.

The redesignation of Virginia and West Virginia was limited to a period of three months.

The evidence of age required by the Virginia law was below the Federal standard, and the certificates were issued by notaries public. . . . It was to be expected that under such a system results would be entirely unsatisfactory. Investigations and inspections made in Virginia showed that the notaries were making a general practice of issuing when the only

proof of age presented was a parent's affidavit, although documentary evidence required by law was easily obtainable. At the time when the first designation of six months expired (Mar. 1, 1918), legislation was pending which if passed would have made it possible to continue to accept the Virginia certificates. The measure finally adopted required better proof of age, but the issuing of the certificates was still left to the notaries public. It was therefore considered necessary to begin the issuance of Federal certificates in Virginia.

The question of the redesignation of Indiana and West Virginia was pending at the time the law was declared unconstitutional . . .

The principal difficulty in deciding as to the designation of many of the States was that the certificating was done well in one town and very poorly in another. In a few States — for example, Connecticut, New Hampshire, and Wisconsin — the work was under State control; but in most States the authority to issue certificates was given to the local superintendent of schools. The work requires careful attention to administrative details. This kind of attention, as the inspections made clearly show, will usually not be given by busy school or other local officers unless the value of it is clearly and frequently indicated by State officers . . .

Federal certificates of age were issued first in North Carolina, South Carolina, Georgia, and Mississippi, and later in Virginia, because the certificating requirements of their State child labor laws were far below the standards set by the Federal rules and regulations.

. . . . .

In North Carolina, Georgia, and Mississippi, employers, parents, children, and public officials were quite unfamiliar with a State certificating system, and the State child labor standards were lower in every particular than those established by the Federal act . . . What was more serious, no provision had been made in North Carolina for State enforcement of even these low standards. The State commissioner of labor and printing had no funds for inspection and no legal right of entry if he were given funds . . .

In South Carolina the situation was better. The minimum age standard had been recently raised, and certificates were required for all children between 14 and 16 years of age employed in factories. The legal working day and the regulation of night work were substantially the same as in North Carolina. But in South Carolina the enforcement of the law was lodged with the State commissioner of commerce, agriculture, and industries. He had done much to acquaint manufacturers with the provisions of the State law and the Federal act; inspections had been made regularly, and violations of the State law had been prosecuted . . .

Inspections under the Child Labor Act of 1916. — Inspections under the child labor act began as soon as the law went into effect, but, owing to a postponement of the civil service examinations, the full staff of inspectors was not available until several months later, so that this work was hardly under way before the law was declared unconstitutional.

Relation between federal and state inspectors. — The first consideration in planning the inspections was the work already being done by the various State departments of labor or of factory inspection in the enforcement of State child labor laws. The Children's Bureau was convinced that the full value of a national minimum for the protection of children would never be secured except through a genuine working relationship between Federal and State officials. The resources of both were inadequate for the task before them. It was important that needless Federal inspections should be avoided, and that so far as they were made they should result in a strengthening of respect for both State and Federal laws — that, so far as possible, experience and interest should be pooled. With this in view a conference of State officials was called by the Secretary of Labor on July 27, 1917, so that the committee composed of the Secretaries of Labor, Commerce, and the Attorney General might have the benefit of the advice of State officials before the rules and regulations were adopted, and the Child Labor Division, the opportunity for a more detailed discussion of what were the common problems of State and Federal officers . . .

The State commissioners and chief factory inspectors who came from these States voted that they desired to have formal recognition by the Federal Government, and in accordance with their vote all State officers charged by statute with the enforcement of a State child labor law were commissioned by the Secretary of Labor to assist in the enforcement of the Federal act. In commissioning them, attention was called to the fact that inspections would be made by the Child Labor Division in any State either upon its own initiative, upon complaints of violations, or upon the request of State officials.

The help given by the State officials in the enforcement of the Federal act was substantial. It began in some States before the law went into effect, with an educational campaign to acquaint employers and parents with the provisions of the act. In a number of States in which children between 14 and 16 years of age were allowed under the State law to work more than eight hours a day, State inspectors checked time records in the course of their regular inspections to see whether the Federal eight-hour standard was being violated and called the attention of the employers to the fact that their products could not be shipped in interstate or foreign commerce if the Federal standard was not observed.

An inspector of the Child Labor Division was assigned the special duty of co-operating with State officials, and joint inspections with State inspectors were tried out in a number of localities. These were useful in acquainting Federal and State inspectors with the methods followed by each and in impressing employers with the fact that Federal and State officials were working together. It was felt, however, that if long continued, joint inspections would be wasteful, as the time of two sets of inspectors was consumed for work which could be done by one. A regular exchange of information was probably what each needed from the other, and with this end in view, arrangements were made by the Child Labor Division to send to the State a summary of the findings of its inspectors, as well as all "Opinions of General Interest" and "Announcements of Judgments," which were published from time to time.

On the basis of their child labor legislation the States could be classified roughly into three groups — (1) a number which had enacted child labor laws with standards higher than those of the Federal law; (2) a much larger number whose age and hour standards were the same; and (3) a smaller number with lower standards. The differences in administration were much more difficult to classify. In some the appropriation given the State factory-inspection department was altogether inadequate; in some, conviction of violations of the law were very difficult to secure because of local prejudice; in some, a combination of political and economic conditions kept a department impotent.

REPORTS OF INSPECTIONS UNDER CHILD LABOR ACT OF 1916

General. — Before the act was declared unconstitutional inspections had been made of 689 establishments situated in 24 States and the District of Columbia, and of 28 mines situated in 4 States.

Violations of the law were found in 293 of the 689 mills, factories etc., inspected — there were 385 children under 14 years of age found employed; and 978 children between 14 and 16 years of age were working more than 8 hours a day, 3 more than 6 days a week, and 116 between 7 P.M. and 6 A.M., in mills, factories, etc., which were regularly shipping in interstate or foreign commerce . . .

Before the act was declared unconstitutional 8 employers had pleaded guilty and fines had been imposed as follows.[2] One, $50; 3, $100; 1, $150; 2, $160; and 1, $300; 17 cases were pending at the time the law was declared unconstitutional; 21 others had been sent to the Department of Justice recommending prosecution. The others were in preparation for transmission by the law officer of the division or were awaiting some further reports . . .

Pennsylvania (mines). — Prior to 1909 Pennsylvania had prohibited the employment of children under 16 years of age in the mines, but the only kind of certificate required was the parent's affidavit, and in consequence the law did not keep children under that age out of the mines. In 1909 the law was amended so as to require documentary proof of the child's age, but it is reported that "through an unfortunate error in drafting the bill"[3] the minimum age was reduced to 14 years for employment inside the anthracite mines. This was amended in 1915, so that at the time the Federal law went into effect no minor under 16 years of age could be legally employed or permitted to work "in any anthracite or bituminous coal mine or in any other mine" . . .

Under the interpretation of the State law, followed by the State officials, children between 14 and 16 years of age were permitted to work on breakers, but they could not be legally so employed more than 51 hours in any one week, or more than 9 hours in any one day, or before 6 in the morning or after 8 in the evening. . . . The breaker children frequently worked until late at night "recleaning" coal that had been condemned. The inspector found one boy who stated that he had been so employed until

2. One of the eight pleaded guilty the day before the law was declared unconstitutional. In two cases complaint was lodged by the State factory inspector of Oregon.

3. Owen R. Lovejoy, "The Coal Mines of Pennsylvania," *Uniform Child Labor Laws, Proceedings of the Seventh Annual Conference on Child Labor, 1911* (New York: National Child Labor Committee, 1911), p. 135.

2:30 in the morning, and the pay check of a 13-year-old breaker boy showed 128 hours of work for the first half of March . . .

There were no certificates on file for 30.4 per cent of the children under 16 years of age employed about these mines in Pennsylvania, and of those on file 20 per cent had been so irregularly issued that they constituted a protection to employers in the violation of the law. For example, in one town visited, a superintendent of schools who had recently been removed had made a practice of selling certificates to under-age children, and certificates issued by him were found both inside and outside the district in which he had taught. Most of these children were two years younger than the age given on the certificate. In another town parents, most of them Polish and Slovak immigrants, made affidavit that they had paid fees to secure certificates from the superintendent. Thus, the parents of a boy of 12 paid only 50 cents for a certificate showing him to be 14 years of age while for another 12-year-old boy a fee of $5 had been collected. In another family the payment had been $1 for a vacation permit and $2 for a general certificate. Apparently the theory of the principal was to charge all that the traffic would bear. A supervising principal who had 32 widely scattered schools in his district was a justice of the peace and notary public as well. He had an office in the rear room of a saloon which he used for issuing certificates and transacting his business as justice of the peace. The room was very dirty and the records in great confusion. What he described as baptismal certificates had been accepted for a considerable number of children, although, as the certificates presented clearly stated, they were in fact merely the parent's statement of the child's age to the priest . . .

Such disregard of the State law was not found in all the mining towns visited . . .

West Virginia (*mines*). — Eight of the nine coal mines inspected in West Virginia were violating the Federal standards. There were 15 children under 16 years of age working inside the mines as trapper boys (opening and closing doors), and in tending switches, coupling cars, and even as miners, picking out coal and loading cars. While the inspectors were at work in the State a boy was seriously crippled in one mine, and another a colored trapper boy — who was in fact 15 years old, but whose mother had made affidavit that he was 16 years of age — was run over by a car. . . The boy did not live long, and one of the officials, taking advantage of the "Fuel will win the war" slogan, said: "The boy has died for his country" . . .

Constitutionality of the Keating-Owen Act

1. Strategy for testing the Act

"Letter to the Editor," *Southern Textile Bulletin,* Aug. 24, 1916, p. 10.

Immediately after passage of the Keating-Owen Act the Executive Committee of Southern Cotton Manufacturers solicited advice on procedures for testing the law in the courts. The Committee had been founded in 1915 to oppose federal child labor legislation. The anonymous letter from a lawyer outlines the strategy that the Committee followed in the selection and preparation of the Dagenhart case.

No legal proceedings will lie until the bill is in operation. Some action must be taken under some provision of the bill so that a real and not moot question is raised. A court, in order to pass upon any phase of it, must have before it an actual case, and if the measure is to be contested the case should not only be carefully selected in order that the constitutional principle desired to be raised may be clearly presented, but I believe then that when the issue is raised, if possible, a judicial district should be selected in which the judge is a man of known courage. This is no case to try before a weak character.

It is very difficult to say how long it will take to bring this question to the Supreme Court of the United States. It would depend upon the circumstances of the case. The facts might present an issue that admitted of an extraordinary remedy that could be taken by the shortest process to the Supreme Court. Thus the issue might be raised by the refusal to permit an inspector of the Department of Labor to enter a factory for the purpose of discharging the duty laid upon him under the bill, or it might be raised by the arrest of a factory manager or corporation officer, or the issue might possibly be raised on behalf of an operative threatened with discharge although this is a delicate and somewhat complex question. If the question went up to the Supreme Court on appeal from a conviction in a lower court, it might take from a year to two years, all depending upon the congestion of the calendar. If raised on an application for a writ to restrain an officer from entering a factory there might be [a] somewhat shorter proceeding. But it is almost impossible to say how long it would take to bring the matter to a final issue, for that is something that is not in the control of litigants or their counsel. The case, however, will be one of such extraordinary importance that the utmost care should be taken in choosing the circumstances and locality of jurisdiction.

2. Background of the Dagenhart case

Thomas I. Parkinson, "The Federal Child Labor Law," *Child Labor Bulletin*, VII, No. 2 (August 1918), 89–90.

Thomas Parkinson, director of the Legislative Drafting Bureau at Columbia University, had assisted the National Child Labor Committee in drafting the Keating-Owen bill and had defended its constitutionality before the Senate and House committees in 1916. In 1917, following the plea of the National Child Labor Committee, Parkinson was appointed special assistant attorney general for the Dagenhart case.

Because of the differences of opinion as to the constitutionality of the [Keating-Owen Act], it was expected that one of the first prosecutions for its violation would be carried to the Supreme Court as a test case; but this test was not permitted to await the beginning of a prosecution by the government. In August, 1917, one Dagenhart, the father of two boys, one under 16 and the other under 14, employed in a North Carolina cotton mill, applied to the Federal District Court for an injunction to restrain the enforcement of the act. His claim to this extraordinary remedy was based on the allegation that if the act went into operation in accordance with its terms, the employer of the boys, rather than stand the chance of a prosecution, would discharge them. Therefore the father alleged that the effect of the act, which he asserted was unconstitutional and void, would be to deprive the boys of their right to pursue the occupation which they and he had selected for their life work and to deprive him of their earnings. In order to hasten the decision in the lower court and to avoid all questions of fact and technicalities of procedure it was agreed by counsel that the argument and decision of the case should be narrowed to the single issue of the constitutionality of the act. After hearing the argument, Judge Boyd in a brief oral opinion held the act unconstitutional and issued an injunction restraining its enforcement in the Western District of North Carolina. Meanwhile the act was in force in all parts of the United States outside of this District.

The government immediately appealed this decision to the Supreme Court of the United States, and the case was argued before that court in April of this year. The argument in support of the act before the Supreme Court was made by Mr. Solicitor-General Davis of the Department of Justice. The decision rendered on June 3 by a divided court — four out of the nine justices dissenting — affirmed the judgment of the District Court. The number of justices dissenting, coupled with the emphatic tone of their dissent, gave rise to the hope that the case might be reargued and reconsidered. On June 10th, Mr. Davis moved for leave to apply for a reargument, but this motion was subsequently abandoned. A reargument in the near future could not reasonably be expected to produce a change in the decision. It may be assumed that Mr. Justice Holmes and those justices who concurred in his vigorous dissent urged their views upon their associates quite as persuasively as counsel for the government could be expected to do on reargument; and if they were unable to win over one of the majority, it is unlikely that counsel could succeed in doing so.

---

3. U.S. Supreme Court declares the Act unconstitutional, 1918

Hammer v. Dagenhart, 247 U.S. 251, 268–281.

Opinion of the Court, delivered by MR. JUSTICE DAY, as follows:

A bill was filed in the United States District Court for the Western District of North Carolina by a father in his own behalf and as next friend of his two minor sons, one under the age of fourteen years and the other between the ages of fourteen and sixteen years, employees in a cotton mill at Charlotte, North Carolina, to enjoin the enforcement of the act of Congress intended to prevent interstate commerce in the products of child labor . . .

The District Court held the act unconstitu-

tional and entered a decree enjoining its enforcement. This appeal brings the case here.

.   .   .   .

The controlling question for decision is: Is it within the authority of Congress in regulating commerce among the States to prohibit the transportation in interstate commerce of manufactured goods, the product of a factory in which, within thirty days prior to their removal therefrom, children under the age of fourteen have been employed or permitted to work, or children between the ages of fourteen and sixteen years have been employed or permitted to work more than eight hours in any day, or more than six days in any week, or after the hour of seven o'clock P.M. or before the hour of six o'clock A.M.?

The power essential to the passage of this act, the Government contends, is found in the commerce clause of the Constitution which authorizes Congress to regulate commerce with foreign nations and among the States.

.   .   .   .

The first of these cases is *Champion* v. *Ames,* 188 U.S. 321, the so-called *Lottery Case,* in which it was held that Congress might pass a law having the effect to keep the channels of commerce free from use in the transportation of tickets used in the promotion of lottery schemes. In *Hipolite Egg Co.* v. *United States,* 220 U.S. 45, this court sustained the power of Congress to pass the Pure Food and Drug Act which prohibited the introduction into the States by means of interstate commerce of impure foods and drugs. In *Hoke* v. *United States,* 227 U.S. 308, this court sustained the constitutionality of the so-called "White Slave Traffic Act" whereby the transportation of a woman in interstate commerce for the purpose of prostitution was forbidden.

.   .   .   .

In each of these instances the use of interstate transportation was necessary to the accomplishment of harmful results. In other words, although the power over interstate transportation was to regulate, that could only be accomplished by prohibiting the use of the facilities of interstate commerce to effect the evil intended.

This element is wanting in the present case. The thing intended to be accomplished by this statute is the denial of the facilities of interstate commerce to those manufacturers in the States who employ children within the prohibited ages. The act in its effect does not regulate transportation among the States, but aims to standardize the ages at which children may be employed in mining and manufacturing within the States. The goods shipped are of themselves harmless.

.   .   .   .   .

That there should be limitations upon the right to employ children in mines and factories in the interest of their own and the public welfare, all will admit. That such employment is generally deemed to require regulation is shown by the fact that the brief of counsel states that every State in the Union has a law upon the subject, limiting the right to thus employ children. In North Carolina, the State wherein is located the factory in which the employment was had in the present case, no child under twelve years of age is permitted to work.

It may be desirable that such laws be uniform, but our Federal Government is one of enumerated powers; "this principle," declared Chief Justice Marshall in *McCulloch* v. *Maryland,* 4 Wheat. 316, "is universally admitted."

A statute must be judged by its natural and reasonable effect. *Collins* v. *New Hampshire,* 171 U.S., 30, 33, 34. The control by Congress over interstate commerce cannot authorize the exercise of authority not entrusted to it by the Constitution. *Pipe Line Cases,* 234 U.S. 548, 560. The maintenance of the authority of the States over matters purely local is as essential to the preservation of our institutions as is the conservation of the supremacy of the federal power in all matters entrusted to the Nation by the Federal Constitution.

In interpreting the Constitution it must never be forgotten that the Nation is made up of States to which are entrusted the powers of local government. And to them and to the people the powers not expressly delegated to the National Government are reserved. *Lane County* v. *Oregon,* 7 Wall. 71, 76. The power of the States to regulate their purely internal affairs by such laws as seem wise to the local authority is inherent and has never been surrendered to the general government. *New York* v. *Miln,* 11 Pet. 102, 139; *Slaughter House Cases,* 16 Wall. 36, 63; *Kidd* v. *Pearson, supra.* To sustain this statute would not be in our judgment a recognition of the lawful exertion of congressional authority over interstate commerce, but would sanction an invasion by the federal power of the control of a matter purely local in its character, and over which no authority has been delegated to Congress in conferring the power to regulate commerce among the States.

We have neither authority nor disposition to question the motives of Congress in enacting this legislation. The purposes intended must be attained consistently with constitutional limitations and not by an invasion of the powers of the States. This court has no more important function than that which devolves upon it the obligation to preserve inviolate the constitutional limitations upon the exercise of authority, federal and state, to the end that each may continue to discharge, harmoniously with the other, the duties entrusted to it by the Constitution.

In our view the necessary effect of this act is, by means of a prohibition against the movement in interstate commerce of ordinary commercial commodities, to regulate the hours of labor of children in factories and mines within the States, a purely state authority. Thus the act in a twofold sense is repugnant to the Constitution. It not only transcends the authority delegated to Congress over commerce but also exerts a power as to a purely local matter to which the federal authority does not extend. The far reaching result of upholding the act cannot be more plainly indicated than by pointing out that if Congress can thus regulate matters entrusted to local authority by prohibition of the movement of commodities in interstate commerce, all freedom of commerce will be at an end, and the power of the States over local matters may be eliminated, and thus our system of government be practically destroyed.

For these reasons we hold that this law exceeds the constitutional authority of Congress. It follows that the decree of the District Court must be affirmed.

MR. JUSTICE HOLMES, dissenting: The single question in this case is whether Congress has power to prohibit the shipment in interstate or foreign commerce of any product of a cotton mill situated in the United States, in which within thirty days before the removal of the product children under fourteen have been employed, or children between fourteen and sixteen have been employed more than eight hours in a day, or more than six days in any week, or between seven in the evening and six in the morning. The objection urged against the power is that the States have exclusive control over their methods of production and that Congress cannot meddle with them, and taking the proposition in the sense of direct intermeddling I agree to it and suppose that no one denies it. But if an act is within the powers specifically conferred upon Congress, it seems to me that it is not made any less constitutional because of the indirect effects that it may have, however obvious it may be that it will have those effects, and that we are not at liberty upon such grounds to hold it void.

The first step in my argument is to make plain what no one is likely to dispute — that the statute in question is within the power expressly given to Congress if considered only as to its immediate effects and that if invalid it is so only upon some collateral ground. The statute confines itself to prohibiting the carriage of certain goods in interstate or foreign commerce. Congress is given power to regulate such commerce in unqualified terms. It would not be argued today that the power to regulate does not include the power to prohibit. Regulation

means the prohibition of something, and when interstate commerce is the matter to be regulated I cannot doubt that the regulation may prohibit any part of such commerce that Congress sees fit to forbid. At all events it is established by the *Lottery Case* and others that have followed it that a law is not beyond the regulative power of Congress merely because it prohibits certain transportation out and out. *Champion v. Ames,* 188 U.S., 321, 355, 359, *et seq.* So I repeat that this statute in its immediate operation is clearly within the Congress's constitutional power.

The question then is narrowed to whether the exercise of its otherwise constitutional power by Congress can be pronounced unconstitutional because of its possible reaction upon the conduct of the States in a matter upon which I have admitted that they are free from direct control. I should have thought that that matter had been disposed of so fully as to leave no room for doubt. I should have thought that the most conspicuous decisions of this Court had made it clear that the power to regulate commerce and other constitutional powers could not be cut down or qualified by the fact that it might interfere with the carrying out of the domestic policy of any State.

The manufacture of oleomargarine is as much a matter of state regulation as the manufacture of cotton cloth. Congress levied a tax upon the compound when colored so as to resemble butter that was so great as obviously to prohibit the manufacture and sale. In a very elaborate discussion the present Chief Justice excluded any inquiry into the purpose of an act which apart from that purpose was within the power of Congress. *McCray* v. *United States,* 195 U.S. 27. As to foreign commerce see *Weber* v. *Freed,* 239 U.S. 325, 329; *Brolan* v. *United States,* 236 U.S. 216, 217; *Buttfield* v. *Stranahan,* 192 U.S. 470. Fifty years ago a tax on state banks, the obvious purpose and actual effect of which was to drive them, or at least their circulation, out of existence, was sustained, although the result was one that Congress had no constitutional power to require. The Court made short work of the argument as to the purpose of the act. "The judicial cannot prescribe to the legislative department of the government limitations upon the exercise of its acknowledged powers." *Veazie Bank* v. *Fenno,* 8 Wall, 533. So it well might have been argued that the corporation tax was intended under the guise of a revenue measure to secure a control not otherwise belonging to Congress, but the tax was sustained, and the objection so far as noticed was disposed of by citing *McCray* v. *United States. Flint* v. *Stone Tracy Co.,* 220 U.S. 107. And to come to cases upon interstate commerce, notwithstanding *United States* v. *E. C. Knight Co.* 156 U.S. 1, the Sherman Act has been made an instrument for breaking up of combinations in restraint of trade and monopolies, using the power to regulate commerce as a foothold, but not proceeding because that commerce was the end actually in mind. The objection that the control of the States over production was interfered with was urged again and again but always in vain. *Standard Oil* v. *United States,* 221 U.S. 1, 68, 69. *United States* v. *American Tobacco Co.,* 221 U.S. 106, 184. *Hoke* v. *United States,* 227 U.S. 308, 321, 322. See finally and especially *Seven Cases of Eckman's Alterative* v. *United States,* 239 U.S. 510, 514, 515.

The Pure Food and Drug Act which was sustained in *Hipolite Egg Co.* v. *United States, . . .* applies not merely to articles that the changing opinions of the time condemn as intrinsically harmful but to others innocent in themselves, simply on the ground that the order for them was induced by a preliminary fraud. *Weeks* v. *United States,* 245 U.S. 618. It does not matter whether the supposed evil precedes or follows the transportation. It is enough that in the opinion of Congress the transportation encourages the evil . . .

The notion that prohibition is any less prohibition when applied to things now thought evil I do not understand. But if there is any matter upon which civilized countries have agreed — far more unanimously than they have with regard to intoxicants and some other matters over

which this country is now emotionally aroused — it is the evil of premature and excessive child labor. I should have thought that if we were to introduce our own moral conceptions where in my opinion they do not belong, this was preeminently a case for upholding the exercise of all its powers by the United States.

But I had thought that the propriety of the exercise of a power admitted to exist in some cases was for the consideration of Congress alone and that this Court always had disavowed the right to intrude its judgment upon questions of policy or morals. It is not for this Court to pronounce when prohibition is necessary to regulation if it ever may be necessary — to say that it is permissible as against strong drink but not as against the product of ruined lives.

The act does not meddle with anything belonging to the States. They may regulate their internal affairs and their domestic commerce as they like. But when they seek to send their products across the state line they are no longer within their rights. If there were no Constitution and no Congress their power to cross the line would depend upon their neighbors. Under the Constitution such commerce belongs not to the States but to Congress to regulate. It may carry out its views of public policy whatever indirect effect they may have upon the activities of the States. Instead of being encountered by a prohibitive tariff at her boundaries the State encounters the public policy of the United States which it is for Congress to express. The public policy of the United States is shaped with a view to the benefit of the nation as a whole. If, as has been the case within the memory of men still living, a State should take a different view of the propriety of sustaining a lottery from that which generally prevails, I cannot believe that the fact would require a different decision from that reached in *Champion* v. *Ames.* Yet in that case it would be said with quite as much force as in this that Congress was attempting to intermeddle with the State's domestic affairs. The national welfare as understood by Congress may require a different attitude within its sphere from that of some self-seeking State. It seems to me entirely constitutional for Congress to enforce its understanding by all the means at its command.

MR. JUSTICE MCKENNA, MR. JUSTICE BRANDEIS and MR. JUSTICE CLARKE concur in this opinion.

---

4. The Dagenharts in 1924

Lowell Mellett, "The Sequel of the Dagenhart Case," *The American Child,* VI (January 1924), 3.

This is the story of an ungrateful child. The story of a lad for whom all the machinery of the American judiciary was turned to preserve his constitutional rights and who, after six years, has not yet brought himself to give thanks.

The boy is Reuben Dagenhart, of Charlotte, N.C.

Six years ago, Federal Judge James E. Boyd, of the western North Carolina district, interposed the majesty of the law in Reuben's behalf. Some months later Chief Justice White and Justices Day, Van Devanter, McReynolds and Pitney did the same. They declared — and they made it stick — that the Congress of the United States could not take away from young Reuben Dagenhart his "constitutional" right to work more hours every day than a boy of 14 ought to work.

There may be another ungrateful boy in the picture — John Dagenhart. John, aged 12, had his constitutional rights defended by the same courts to the extent that he was allowed to go on working in a cotton mill at an age when no boy should work at all in a cotton mill. But two days' roving through the cotton mill towns around Charlotte last week failed to find John, and readers will have to be content with the story of Reuben. This leaves out, also, the story of Roland H. Dagenhart, father of the boys, whose constitutional right to put them to work in the mills and to receive their wages each

Saturday was upheld by the same upright judges . . .

And should not the Dagenhart boys be grateful for that?

Well, Reuben isn't.

I found him at his home in Charlotte. He is about the size of the office boy — weighs 105 pounds, he told me. But he is a married man with a child. He is 20 years old.

"What benefit," I asked him, "did you get out of the suit which you won in the United States Supreme Court?"

"You mean the suit the Fidelity Manufacturing Company won? (It was the Fidelity Company for which the Dagenharts were working.) I don't see that I got any benefit. I guess I'd been a lot better off if they hadn't won it.

"Look at me! A hundred and five pounds, a grown man and no education. I may be mistaken, but I think the years I've put in in the cotton mills have stunted my growth. They kept me from getting any schooling. I had to stop school after the third grade and now I need the education I didn't get."

"How was your growth stunted?"

"I don't know — the dust and the lint, maybe. But from 12 years old on, I was working 12 hours a day — from 6 in the morning till 7 at night, with time out for meals. And sometimes I worked nights besides. Lifting a hundred pounds and I only weighed 65 pounds myself."

He explained that he and his sister worked together, "on section," spinning. They each made about a dollar a day, though later he worked up to where he could make $2. His father made $15 a week and infant John, at the time the suit was brought, was making close to $1 a day.

"Just what did you and John get out of that suit, then?" was asked.

"Why, we got some automobile rides when them big lawyers from the North was down here. Oh, yes, and they bought both of us a coca-cola! That's all we got out of it."

"What did you tell the judge when you were in court?"

"Oh, John and me never was in court! Just Paw was there. John and me was just little kids in short pants. I guess we wouldn't have looked like much in court. We were working in the mill while the case was going on. But Paw went up to Washington."

Reuben hasn't been to school, but his mind has not been idle.

"It would have been a good thing for all the kids in this state if that law they passed had been kept. Of course, they do better now than they used to. You don't see so many babies working in the factories, but you see a lot of them that ought to be going to school."

"What about John? Is he satisfied with the way things turned out?"

"I don't know. Prob'ly not. He's not much bigger than me and he's got flat feet."

"How about your father?"

"Oh, he's satisfied, I guess. But I know one thing. I ain't going to let them put my kid sister in the mill, like he's thinking of doing! She's only 15 and she's crippled and I bet I stop that!"

The second federal child labor law

1. Alternatives to the Keating-Owen Act

Thomas I. Parkinson, "The Federal Child Labor Law Decision," *Child Labor Bulletin,* VII (August 1918), 94–96.

Many suggestions have been made for legislative or administrative action by the federal government to replace the act which the decision annulled. The War Labor Policies Board has requested employers to refrain from using child labor contrary to the standards prescribed by the act and is preparing for insertion in all government contracts a clause prohibiting such child labor. Undoubtedly, a number of employers will heed the request of the Board, and if to their number be added those government contractors who would be subject to the proposed contract clause a considerable reduction would be affected in the number of employers as to whom restrictive legislation would be necessary.

Bills have been introduced in Congress proposing a tax on employers of child labor or its products. The Ways and Means Committee in the course of the preparation of the new revenue bill has rejected a proposal that all plants employing child labor should pay a 10 per cent tax on gross annual sales. These prohibitive taxes used for regulatory purposes find precedents in the oleomargarine tax which was upheld by the Supreme Court and in the more recent phosphorus match tax and cotton futures tax. While the use of the taxing power as a substitute for the commerce power to enable the federal government to restrict child labor should receive serious consideration, it must be remembered that from the point of view of securing the enactment of such a tax many persons in and out of Congress do not like to see the taxing power used for such purposes, and from the point of view of permanent legislation there is real danger that the Supreme Court will hesitate to extend its decision upholding the oleomargarine tax. This is especially true since it has taken the position in the child labor case that the commerce power cannot be used to control local conditions of production.

A bill is pending in Congress applying to child labor products the principle of the Webb-Kenyon law which deprived interstate shipments of intoxicating liquors of their interstate character, thereby subjecting them to the laws of the state of consignment. But to make this principle applicable would require the enactment by the states of laws prohibiting the sale of child labor products. Variations of the Webb-Kenyon law have been suggested but have not yet been worked out in detail. In considering the various possibilities of this suggestion it must be remembered that at the conclusion of its opinion upholding the Webb-Kenyon law the Supreme Court expressly warned that its decision was based on the "exceptional nature of the subject" there regulated, that is, intoxicating liquors; and there is little reason for hoping that the principle of that case would be extended to the products of child labor by the court which has refused to extend to such products the principle of the Lottery case.

Another pending bill withdraws the privileges of the United States mails from employers of child labor. Mail matter addressed to persons whom the labor department certifies to be employers of such labor is required to be returned to the sender. This follows a recent enactment requiring the return of mail addressed to persons who violate the espionage act. Irrespective of the question of the constitutionality of such a provision or the possibility of administering it, the opposition to such use of the control of the mails would probably prevent its adoption.

More radical proposals to overcome the effects of the decision involve either administrative or legislative action. It has been suggested that the railroad administration refuse the facilities of railroads under government control to employers of child labor; that the fuel administrator refuse them fuel; or even — and this suggestion illustrates the wealth of indirect federal power — that they be declared alien enemies. Dean Pound, of Harvard Law School, has suggested that the act of 1916 be reenacted in its original form and phraseology, except that it be introduced by a declaration that the states are powerless to forbid the sale within their borders of child labor products brought from other states, and concluded with a declaration that it is not the intent of Congress by this prohibition of interstate commerce to interfere with local conditions.

2. The War Labor Policies Board exercises emergency powers to stem increase of wartime child labor

Raymond G. Fuller, "A National Children's

Policy," *Child Labor Bulletin,* VII, (Nov., 1918), 199–200.

The War Labor Policies Board on July 12, 1918 ordered that the following clause be included in all federal government war contracts: "The contractor shall not directly or indirectly employ in the performance of this contract any minor under the age of 14 years, or permit any minor between the ages of 14 and 16 years to work more than 8 hours in any one day, more than 6 days in any one week, or before 6 a.m. or after 7 p.m." Fuller was director of publicity for the National Child Labor Committee.

Here in the United States, the public has been slowly waking up to the national menace of the great decrease in school attendance and the great increase in the amount of child labor. Fortunately there exists in Washington a definite, genuine policy in respect to the wartime welfare of American children. It is a policy that looks not only to the present but to the future. This national policy of the national government already deserves much credit for achievement, though its full benefits will not accrue until later. Let us hope that the policy itself will continue after the war.

Upon our entry into the world war a disposition was manifested in some of the states to relax protective labor standards generally and, in a few instances, the legislature empowered the governor to suspend the labor laws in case of demand from the Council of National Defense, which, seemingly in its haste, had suggested such authorization. Miss Julia C. Lathrop, Chief of the Federal Children's Bureau, protested against this letting-down of the bars and received from the Council the following assurance:

"The Council of National Defense is very desirous of maintaining existing standards as to labor. Furthermore, the labor laws as to which the power to suspend was asked to be given to the governers, were intended to be only those relating to the adult male labor engaged in war

One Reason for the Child Labor Problem.

"Mr. President, we don't want anything. We just want to grow up." Drawing by
William H. Walker, 1913.

Drawn by John Sloan, June 1913

Race Superiority

work. The Council of National Defense therefore unites with the Children's Bureau in urging that the laws relating to the hours and conditions of labor of women and children should be rigorously enforced."

It should be noted, perhaps, that no governor has yet been asked by the Council of Defense to suspend any of the labor laws of his state. On the contrary the Council has actively cooperated in carrying out the Government's policy for the protection and education of the children. It is not improbable that the Defense Council, in making its original request, was actuated by the desire to keep the suspension of labor laws in its own safe hands.

On several occassions the President has personally given expression to the Government's policy. For instance, he wrote a year ago: "As the labor situation created by the war develops, I am more interested than ever, if that were possible, in throwing all the safeguards possible around the labor of women and children in order that no intolerable or injurious burden may be placed upon them. I am therefore very glad indeed that the National Child Labor Committee is diligently continuing its labors and extending its vigilance in this important matter. By so doing it, is contributing to efficiency and economy of production, as well as to the preservation of life and health."

The Secretary of War, the Secretary of the Navy and the Secretary of Labor, as executive officers of the Government, have also taken a decided stand against the plea that the employment of children in industry is a war necessity. In conjunction with other Cabinet members they declared last spring that "no emergency exists which justifies proposing any relaxation of the laws safeguarding the working conditions of young people." On October 1, this position was publicly reaffirmed by Sceretary Wilson when he said, "I have no objection to having a child do what will not injure his strength and development, but industry is too exacting. It is absolutely imperative that we preserve at least minimum standards under which children are admitted into industry.

3. Hope for war profits increases child labor

New York Times, Nov. 24, 1918.

In those industries not directly bearing upon the war the Government, even if it would, cannot bring the offender to justice. The revocation of the child labor law of 1916 made that impossible.

.   .   .   .   .

In Texas . . . the Superintendent of the schools of the city of Dallas recently announced that the State compulsory education law would be suspended in Dallas until Jan. 1. The Fall session of the school term began Sept. 11. The attendance, it can readily be understood, was not very large. The *Dallas Despatch* naively mentioned the fact in its columns, stating that beginning Jan. 1 the State school law would apply to children between the ages of eight and fourteen for the remainder of the school year, adding that the School Board had decided upon this course on account of war conditions and because more children were needed for work in the Fall months than in the Winter months.

In Massachusetts the school enrollment this year has been 14 per cent below normal. Fifty thousand children in that State have during the last year been sucked up into the industries of that section of the country. In Philadelphia, it was found necessary by the Bureau of Compulsory Education to inaugurate a city-wide raid in order to bring back to school 2,000 school delinquents who were found working illegally, that is, without the necessary papers.

Here in our own city, the number of children between 14 and 16 years old who have taken out working papers this year is more than 10 per cent above that of last year. On July 1, 1917, the records showed that 42,145 children had received permission to go into industries. On Aug. 2 of this year the figures were 45,887. These of course are entirely apart from the numbers of children who are working without legal papers.

An item in the news column of *The Lexington Leader* in Kentucky openly comes out with the fact that the industries in that section of the country are draining the schools with the full permission of the educational authorities. It reads as follows:

"If business men and others who want to employ boys within the provisions of the child labor law will send their needs in writing to Attendance Officer J. Sherman Porter, McClelland Building, he will recommend boys for such places. All boys who want to work this year who are under 16 years of age and over 14, and through the fifth year of the public schools, will be given certificates if they ask for them."

The opening of the schools for the Fall term gave the Children's Bureau an opportunity to find out to just what extent children were leaving school prematurely, whether those who had worked on vacation permits had returned, and in general, the conditions among working children. A series of inquiries were made to typical industrial and commercial centres to throw light on these and other questions. The cities studied included New York, Philapdelphia, Chicago, Boston, Baltimore, Pittsburgh, Washington, Wilmington, St. Louis, Cincinnati, Louisville, and several other cities. In Washington, it was found that this year 1,095 permits to work either outside of school hours or full time had been granted under the law which permits children of 12 or 13 to work if in the opinion of the Juvenile Court the poverty of the family justifies it. In 1916–1917 only 277 such permits were issued. This is a gain of 295 per cent. In Wilmington 61 per cent more children have taken out permits this year than last. Practically all of this 61 per cent have definitely left school to enter industry on full time.

Reports of greatly increased shifting from job to job seem to indicate that the child is not finding in his work a steadily progressing training. The figures do not show that children are staying at their jobs because of higher wages or that they are staying long enough to gain from their industrial training experience which will make them increasingly useful.

The attitude taken by all those industrial heads of the country who have been engaged in this exploitation of child labor is that it is a war measure, or, now that the war has ended, a necessary reconstruction measure; that in order to meet the requirements made upon them they must employ children.

4. The Senate adopts an amendment to the War Revenue bill, December 1918

New York Times, Dec. 19, 1918.

The adoption of a committee amendment imposing a 10 per cent tax on profits from child labor products entering interstate commerce was the only action taken by the Senate today on the War Revenue bill. The vote on the amendment was 50 to 12, with Democrats casting all the negative votes.

Debate on this contested provision and two hours' unexpected discussion of other subjects delayed progress on the bill, but leaders still hope for its passage by next Monday, with a view to securing an extended recess over the holidays.

.   .   .   .   .

The child labor amendment, drafted jointly by the Senators Pomerene of Ohio, Lenroot of Wisconsin, and Kenyon of Iowa, is designed to replace the child labor law declared unconstitutional by the Supreme Court. Senators Hardwick of Georgia and Overman of North Carolina led the fight on it, and on the roll call these Senators voted against its adoption:

Bankhead of Alabama, Beckham of Kentucky, Hardwick of Georgia, Martin of Kentucky, Overman of North Carolina, Pollock of South Carolina, Simmons of North Carolina, Smith of Georgia, Smith of South Carolina, Thomas of Colorado, Underwood of Alabama, and Williams of Mississippi.

The amendment, which will go to conference

when the Senate passes the Revenue bill, is said to have President Wilson's approval.

Constitutional questions principally were raised by the Senators who spoke against the amendment. They also said that its primary purpose was not to raise revenue, but to meet the decision of the Supreme Court in holding the former Child Labor act unconstitutional.

Advocates of the legislation, including its authors, said that Congress had the right to use its taxing power to deal with other subjects and confidently predicted that the amendment would be sustained by the Supreme Court.

As retained in the bill, the amendment imposes the 10 per cent tax on profits from products entering interstate commerce from mines and quarries employing children under 16 years of age, and from mills, factories, and similar industrial establishments employing children under 14 years, or those between 14 and 16 for more than eight hours daily.

---

5. The child labor tax

Tax on Employment of Child Labor: Title XII of "An Act to Provide Revenue, and for Other Purposes," approved Feb. 24, 1919, *U.S. Statutes at Large,* XL, Part I, chap. 18, p. 1138.

This measure, more comprehensive than the Keating-Owen Act, applied to every "mine, mill, cannery, workshop, factory or manufacturing establishment." It was based on a draft submitted to Senator Atlee Pomerene by the National Child Labor Committee, but modified by him without consulting the Committee or the Children's Bureau. While the National Child Labor Committee's version vested the administration of the law in the Children's Bureau, Pomerene assigned its administration to the Office of Internal Revenue, Treasury

Department. The law was in effect from April 25, 1919, until May 15, 1922.

SEC. 1200. That every person (other than a bona fide boys' or girls' canning club recognized by the Agricultural Department of a State and of the United States) operating (*a*) any mine or quarry situated in the United States in which children under the age of sixteen years have been employed or permitted to work during any portion of the taxable year; or (*b*) any mill, cannery, workshop, factory, or manufacturing establishment situated in the United States in which children under the age of fourteen years have been employed or permitted to work, or children between the ages of fourteen and sixteen have been employed or permitted to work more than eight hours in any day or more than six days in any week, or after the hour of seven o'clock post meridian, or before the hour of six o'clock ante meridian, during any portion of the taxable year, shall pay for each taxable year, in addition to all other taxes imposed by law, an excise tax equivalent to 10 per centum of the entire net profits received or accrued for such year from the sale or disposition of the product of such mine, quarry, mill, cannery, workshop, factory, or manufacturing establishment.

.   .   .   .   .

SEC. 1203. (*a*) That no person subject to the provisions of this title shall be liable for the tax herein imposed if the only employment or permission to work, which but for this section would subject him to the tax, has been of a child as to whom such person has in good faith procured at the time of employing such child or permitting him to work, and has since in good faith relied upon and kept on file a certificate, issued in such form, under such conditions and by such persons as may be prescribed by a board consisting of the Secretary, the Commissioner, and the Secretary of Labor, showing the child to be of such age as not to subject such person to the tax imposed by this title. Any person who knowingly makes a false statement or presents false evidence in or in relation to any such certificate or application therefor shall be punished by a fine of not less than $100, nor more than $1,000, or by imprisonment for not more than three months, or by both such fine and imprisonment, in the discretion of the court.

.   .   .   .   .   .

Sec. 1206. That for the purposes of this Act the Commissioner, or any other person duly authorized by him, shall have authority to enter and inspect at any time any mine, quarry, mill, cannery, workshop, factory, or manufacturing establishment. The Secertary of Labor, or any person authorized by him, shall, for the purpose of complying with a request of the Commissioner to make such inspection, have like authority, and shall make report to the Commissioner of inspections made under such authority in such form as may be prescribed by the Commissioner with the approval of the Secretary of the Treasury.

6. The administration of the child labor tax

U.S. Treasury, Commissioner of Internal Revenue, *Annual Report* (Washington, D. C., 1920), pp. 19–21.

The section of the act levying tax upon the employment of child labor became effective April 25, 1919, two months before the beginning of the fiscal year. Consequently, the first full year of the operation of this law is now completed. The law, however, was so drawn that it did not permit taxation until the company subject to the tax completed its fiscal year, with an additional 60 days for filing returns.

The basis for the tax is employment in a mine or quarry of a child under 16 years of age; or in a mill, cannery, workshop, factory, or manufacturing establishment of a child under 14 years of age; or of a child between 14 and 16 for more than eight hours in a day or more than six days a week, or before 6 o'clock in the morning or after 7 in the evening.

The amount of tax imposed for nonobservance of these standards is 10 per cent of the annual net profits of the taxpayer. An establishment secures immunity from tax, however, by procuring, prior to employing or permitting a child to work, a certificate in which the child's age has been authoritatively established, and by observing the time limitations as stated.

During the past year Federal age certificates were issued by child-labor tax officers in five States. The issuance continued throughout the year in four States; in the fifth, certification was not begun until March 15, 1920. In a sixth State Federal age certificates were issued during the year by school authorities.

There were reported from these States 32,207 applications for age certificates. Of 18,715 cases definitely disposed of, 15,810 children, or 84.5 per cent, received certificates; and 2,905 children, or 15.5 per cent, were refused because applicants had not attained the prescribed age. The remaining applications were temporarily continued until adequate proof of age could be obtained, dropped because not prosecuted further, or are still under investigation.

The original methods of issuing certificates have been greatly improved. The influence of compulsory school laws is reflected by the sudden reduction in the number of applications at the beginning of the school term and the immediate increase when the compulsory period ends.

An employment certificate or other similar document attesting the age of a child, issued under State child-labor laws, is accepted by the Bureau in 37 States, designated by the Child Labor Tax Boards as having the same force and effect as a Federal age certificate. A careful study must be made of State laws on child labor and education, of their administration, and of the forms and methods of certification before the designation of a State can be considered.

In addition, an intensive field study has been made of the certification in two States, and a more or less detailed study in three other States. From time to time instances of faulty certification practices have been referred to the proper authorities for correction.

Probably the most important piece of work undertaken was the collection by deputy collectors throughout the country of a child-labor tax information return. Questionnaires bearing upon liability to tax for the first taxable year and requiring answer under oath were submitted on this form to establishments employing children under 17 years of age. Thousands of these questionnaires have been collected, thus spreading a knowledge of the law and bringing to the Bureau much valuable data for future use. The educational value of this distribution and its effect on the law's observance can not be overestimated.

Some employers have been misled by the fact that State child-labor laws and the Federal taxing law differ in essentials. Under the laws of some States 10 hours of employment for children instead of 8 are permitted; the time in others is extended beyond 8 hours for five days in order to provide a short working day, or perhaps a holiday, on the sixth day of the week; some States do not prohibit child labor before 6 o'clock in the morning or after 7 at night; and others do not count the time the child spends in vocational schools as part of the hours of labor. Many employers who observed every feature of the State law found themselves subject to the Federal tax law. As a consequence of the differences being called to their attention through the circulation of the information return many employers have taken the necessary steps to avoid taxation under the Federal law.

The general correspondence of the division indicates that employers are becoming better informed as to the child-labor tax law. Early in the year the questions asked often betrayed ignorance of the law. Later correspondence indicates a broader knowledge of the technical phases of the law and regulations, and the information sought is on the points of application.

Knowledge of tax liability is obtained through the activity of special inspectors, the cooperative action of State officials engaged in enforcing State child-labor laws, and inspections made by internal-revenue collectors. Child-welfare agencies also frequently report cases, and the information returns above referred to often reveal liability to tax.

During the year liability to tax has been established in the following States: Arizona, California, Delaware, Georgia, Illinois, Indiana, Louisiana, Maryland, Michigan, Mississippi, New Jersey, New York, North Carolina, Ohio, Oklahoma, Pennsylvania, South Carolina, Tennessee, Texas, Virginia, and Washington. In most cases showing nonobservance of the law initial action has been taken for the collection of tax.

Little tax could be collected during 1920, as the law provides that the taxpayer shall be given two months after the completion of his business year in which to make a return of the amount of tax due. Furthermore, an audit of the return is necessary in every instance.

The Child Labor Tax Division has an office force of 18 employees, and a field force of 12 age-certificating agents and 15 inspectors and assistant inspectors. The services of deputy collectors in the different districts are utilized for inspection, and a special force of field auditors, directed by the Supervisor of Collectors' Offices, is to be utilized for verifying and auditing the returns upon which tax is to be assessed. In districts where child labor is most common deputy collectors have received much information and a valuable training through working with expert child-labor inspectors sent out by the division. This experience will prove valuable, since it follows that within a short time every collector will have his own corps of specially qualified men for child-labor tax work.

This division is completely organized and may be said to be on a permanent basis. Its forces are well trained, and its work is on a current basis in so far as the provisions of the act permit.

---

7. The tax on employment of children is declared unconstitutional, 1922

Bailey, Collector of Internal Revenue, *v.* Drexel Furniture Company, 259 *U.S. Reports* 20, 34-44.

MR. CHIEF JUSTICE TAFT delivered the opinion of the court.

This case presents the question of the constitutional validity of the Child Labor Tax Law. The plaintiff below, the Drexel Furniture Company, is engaged in the manufacture of furniture in the Western District of North Carolina. On September 20, 1921, it received a notice from Bailey, United States Collector of Internal Revenue for the District, that it had been assessed $6,312.79 for having during the taxable year 1919 employed and permitted to work in its factory a boy under fourteen years of age, thus incurring the tax of ten per cent on its net profits for that year. The Company paid the tax under protest, and after rejection of its claim for a refund, brought this suit. On demurrer to an amended complaint, judgment was entered for the Company against the Collector for the full amount with interest. The writ of error is prosecuted by the Collector direct from the District Court under sec. 238 of the Judicial Code . . .

The law is attacked on the ground that it is a regulation of the employment of child labor in the States — an exclusively state function under the Federal Constitution and within the reservations of the Tenth Amendment. It is defended on the ground that it is a mere excise tax levied by the Congress of the United States under its broad power of taxation conferred by sec. 8, Article I, of the Federal Constitution. We must construe the law and interpret the intent and meaning of Congress from the language of the act. The words are to be given their ordinary meaning unless the context shows that they are differently used. Does this law impose a tax with only that incidental restraint and regulation which a tax must inevitably involve? Or does it regulate by the use of the so-called tax as a penalty? If a tax, it is clearly an excise. If it were an excise on a commodity or other thing of value we might not be permitted under previous decisions of this court to infer solely from its heavy burden that the act intends a prohibition instead of a tax. But this act is more. It provides a heavy exaction for a departure from a detailed and specified course of conduct in business. That course of business is that employers shall employ in mines and quarries, children of an age greater than sixteen years; in mills and factories, children of an age greater than fourteen years, and shall prevent children of less than sixteen years in mills and factories from working more then eight hours a day or six days in the week. If an employer departs from this prescribed course of business, he is to pay to the Government one-tenth of his entire net income in the business for a full year. The amount is not to be proportioned in any degree to the extent or frequency of the departures, but is to be paid by the employer in full measure whether he employs five hundred children for a year, or employs only one for a day. Moreover, if he does not know the child is within the named age limit, he is not to pay; that is to say, it is only where he knowingly departs from the prescribed course that payment is to be exacted . . .

Out of a proper respect for the acts of a coordinate branch of the Government, this court has gone far to sustain taxing acts as such, even though there has been ground for suspecting from the weight of the tax it was intended to destroy its subject. But, in the act before us, the presumption of validity cannot prevail, because the proof of the contrary is found on the very face of its provisions. Grant the validity of this law, and all that Congress would need to do, hereafter, in seeking to take over to its control any one of the great number of subjects of public interest, jurisdiction of which the States have never parted with, and which are reserved to them by the Tenth Amendment, would be to enact a detailed measure of complete regulation of the subject and enforce it by a so-called tax upon departures from it. To give such magic to the word "tax" would be to break down all constitutional limitation of the powers of Congress and completely wipe out the sovereignty of the States . . .

Although Congress does not invalidate the contract of employment or expressly declare that the employment within the mentioned ages is illegal, it does exhibit its intent practically to achieve the latter result by adopting the criteria of wrong-doing and imposing its principal consequence on those who transgress its standard.

.   .   .   .   .

The analogy of the *Dagenhart Case* is clear. The congressional power over interstate commerce is, within its proper scope, just as complete and unlimited as the congressional power to tax, and the legislative motive in its exercise is just as free from judicial suspicion and inquiry. Yet when Congress threatened to stop interstate commerce in ordinary and necessary commodities, unobjectionable as subjects of transportation, and to deny the same to the people of a State in order to coerce them into

compliance with Congress's regulation of state concerns, the court said this was not in fact regulation of interstate commerce, but rather that of State concerns and was invalid. So here the so-called tax is a penalty to coerce people of a State to act as Congress wishes them to act in respect of a matter completely the business of the state government under the Federal Constitution . . .

But it is pressed upon us that this court has gone so far in sustaining taxing measures the effect or tendency of which was to accomplish purposes not directly within congressional power that we are bound by authority to maintain this law.

.   .   .   .   .

The court said that the [Narcotic Drug] act could not be declared invalid just because another motive than taxation, not shown on the face of the act, might have contributed to its passage. This case does not militate against the conclusion we have reached in respect of the law now before us. The court, there, made manifest its view that the provisions of the so-called taxing act must be naturally and reasonably adapted to the collection of the tax and not solely to the achievement of some other purpose plainly within state power.

For the reasons given, we must hold the Child Labor Tax Law invalid and the judgment of the District Court is affirmed.

MR. JUSTICE CLARKE dissents.

C. THE CHILD LABOR AMENDMENT

The call for an amendment

―――――――――――――――――――

1. The trustees of the National Child Labor Committee consider an amendment

Letter from Samuel McCune Lindsay to Owen Lovejoy quoted in minutes of Board of Trustees, May 29, 1922, National Child Labor Committee Papers, Library of Congress.

―――――――――――――――――――

. . . I may say that Dr. [William D.] Lewis

and I favor a broad constitutional amendment which would delegate to the Federal Government power to deal not only with child labor but with the National aspects of other labor and industrial problems but we both realize that it would not be politically expedient to propose such an amendment at the present time. We do think, however, that immediate action ought to be taken while the public interest in the failure of the Federal Child Labor Tax Law is aroused to press for some such simple amendment covering the child labor matter as that proposed in the H. J. Resolution 327 introduced May 17th in the House of Representatives by Congressman Fitzgerald of Ohio which proposed a new article as an amendment to the Constitution to read as follows:

> The Congress shall have power to regulate throughout the United States the employment of persons under 18 years of age.

Col. [F. G.] Caffey dissents from this view and is, I believe, opposed to any constitutional amendment dealing with this matter on the principle that it is the wrong method of approach. He think something could be done through the treaty-making power to lay the basis for a national regulation of child labor and the maintenance of national standards through legislation by Congress in carrying out the provisions of a treaty.

.   .   .   .   .   .

[Julia Lathrop's comments on the amendment]

Julia Lathrop: I agree with you that the first effort must be for "vigorous state action, both for local work and national membership." This is an unfavorable time to launch a movement for a constitutional amendment centralizing law enforcement. I have been astonished to find the popular distaste for governmental activity in this part of the country and I suspect it is typical. My first impression is that the committee should make its state and local work as intensive as possible, centering on enforcement where there is good law and on securing state legislation where that is needed. I fear that a campaign for a constitutional amendment would not be favorably launched at the present time. Would a Fabian policy be advisable for the present?

Minutes of Board of Trustees, May 31, 1922, National Child Labor Committee Papers.

The secretary presented the invitation extended to him to represent the Comm. at the conference in Wash on June 1st called by the Amer. Fed. of Lab. to consider a proposed const'l amend . . .

It was voted to send the sec'y to the Conf. w/ the following instructions. The National Child Labor Committee is in favor of such federal action as will tend to eliminate the evils of child labor & we are prepared to endorse a proposed const'l amendmt unless some method offering more immediate & effective relief is proposed. We have not yet had oppor. for sufficient consid. of the subject to be quite sure what the form or language shld be. In so doing we do not suggest this as an alternative to state action but believe & urge that everyone shld join in promoting very vigorously state action ind. of what may happen to a const'l amendment.

---

2. The American Federation of Labor calls for an amendment

New York Times, June 2, 1922.

On June 1, 1922, Samuel Gompers called together numerous labor, religious, and women's organizations to form the Permanent Committee for the Abolition of Child Labor which called for a constitutional amendment.

WASHINGTON, June 1. — A permanent organization to work for "absolute abolition of child labor in the United States" was formed here today by representatives of a number of national associations called into conference on the subject by Samuel Gompers, President of the American Federation of Labor. The meeting was arranged by Mr. Gompers following the recent decision of the United States Supreme Court holding that special excise taxes on the product of minor labor were invalid.

Spokesmen for the new organization, after a conference at the American Federation of Labor headquarters, appeared before the House Judiciary Committee to urge legislation prohibiting or regulating employment of children in mines, factories and similar arduous occupations. Representative Chandler, Republican, of New York, said it was the opinion of himself and other members of the committee that the Supreme Court's ruling had made it impossible to accomplish anything by legislative regulation unless and until a constitutional amendment had been adopted.

The organization formed today to institute a campaign for such an amendment will be known as "the permanent conference for the abolition of child labor." Mr. Gompers accepted the post of permanent Chairman. A committee of ten was appointed to draft a constitutional amendment and "the best form of law" to meet the situation.

.   .   .   .   .

Saying he did not wish to criticise the recent decision of the Supreme Court nor set up his judgment against that of the Court, Mr. Gompers insisted that significance should attach to its previous decision upholding the match tax to protect the health of labor against harmful sulphurous fumes. He also suggested that the decision of the Supreme Court holding constitutional the oleomargarine law provided a precedent for finding the child labor tax law constitutional and expressed the opinion that the Sixteenth Amendment authorizing a tax on income from whatever source derived, warranted a special tax on incomes derived from child labor.

3. National Consumers' League urges an amendment

Florence Kelley, "Industrial Conditions as a Community Problem With Particular Reference to Child Labor," *The Annals* of the American Academy of Political and Social Science, CIII (1922), 60–64.

When the United States Supreme Court held the first federal child-labor law contrary to the Constitution and therefore void, children whose names had been listed in advance were called into cotton mills and tobacco factories, canneries and glass works, on that same day. They began to work on the following morning as their elder brothers and sisters had done before the law was passed. The Supreme Court has now held the second child-labor law unconstitutional, and again the young children have gone back to work in the mills. Soon they will again be working in factories, workshops, mines and quarries. Yet the arguments in favor of the passage of the first bill still hold. And every fact which led Congress to pass the second bill calls, as urgently as it did then, for the strong hand of the government to guard equally in every part of the country the children who are the nation of tomorrow. This Republic is One.

.   .   .   .   .

Before attempting to get a federal measure, state laws had been tried for more than eighty years and found wanting. A crazy quilt of them almost covered the country. In general the better and more widespread the good state laws, the greater the injustice to the unprotected child toilers in the backward states. How can a vast democratic, industrial Republic be expected to live, if its children are treated according to forty-eight different standards? . . .

Without reasonably uniform justice and cherishing, the children cannot thrive, or later serve the Republic. For this the one indispensable requisite is a federal law based upon an amendment to the federal Constitution. If, as interpreted by eight Justices, the Constitution makes the federal law impossible today, if it serves as a pretext for restoring young children to their exploiters, and gives federal sanction to overwork of older children, clearly that Constitution, 143 years old, must be modernized. No ancient instrument is *sacrosanct* which imperils the nation by imperiling its youth. The Constitution adopted in 1789 is older than the earliest American textile mill.

No theory of the distribution of powers of government is sound, which ignores injury to boys and girls, such as the textile, tobacco factories, canneries and glass factories have inflicted continuously, except during the brief period of federal safeguarding now ended by the decision of May 15.

. . . . .

Secretary Hoover recommended to the National Conference of Social Work at Providence on June 27, 1922, that they make one more combined effort to deal with child labor state by state. Then after another demonstrable failure a Constitutional amendment should be tried. This idea is utterly immoral and wrong. The children, according to this, are to go back to their slavery while our nation makes further effort to do the impossible, — to assure to them the equal protection of the law under forty-eight divergent legislatures. After it is conclusively shown that they are again suffering stupefaction and physical injury, the slow task of amending the Constitution may be undertaken.

Morons are now authoritatively described as persons incapable of learning from experience. Should we not show ourselves to be a nation of morons if, after eighty years of effort which we definitely abandoned in 1906 when we introduced the federal child labor bill into Congress, we should now return to that fundamentally discredited method?

The time to save the working children of the United States is now. Underlying everything is the wanton, wholesale sacrifice of their bread-winners. For it is still the rule that fathers maintain their children.

While we enact the amendment we must strive also to remove the evils sketched above. And may we be forgiven if we reiterate the ungracious query: Where have the social workers been throughout the long struggle to compel the guarding of life, limb and health in industry? Who have helped except the American Association for Labor Legislation, the Consumers' League, the Child-Labor Committee, and the labor organizations?

The possibilities of state regulation were exhausted before the federal laws were passed. The possibilities of federal regulation appear to have been, for the present, exhausted. To solve this grievous moral problem, what remains is, therefore, to enact a federal child-labor amendment. With voting mothers and teachers added to the men who elected the Congress which passed the federal child-labor laws, it is reasonable to hope that the achievement of this amendment may be speedy.

If with the passage of time, and the unimaginable changes in American industry since 1789, the Constitution has become an obstacle to righteousness, as it was once held to be the bulwark of chattel slavery, let us profit by the tragic teaching of the Civil War, and mend our ways and our fundamental law before it is again too late.

4. A summons to the League of Women Voters

Felix Frankfurter, "Child Labor and the Court," *New Republic,* XXXI (July 26, 1922), 248–250.

The recent decision of the Supreme Court, invalidating the Federal Child Labor Tax Law, raises two wholly different questions, each of very serious public importance. The first involves judgment upon the Supreme Court's action, and to that extent is part of a process of continuing critique of the functioning of the Supreme Court in our national life. A totally different, and immediately practical, issue is presented by the consequences of the Supreme Court's decision; in other words, what are we going to do about child labor?

.   .   .   .   .

The door to the Federal action having now been twice shut, what are we to do about child labor, particularly in the stubborn black spots of the South? In my judgment further Federal legislation, under the existing Constitution, is unavailing and any such proposal as requiring the products of child labor to be branded as a means of notice to the consumer, before acceptance for interstate shipment, would be as futile as, under Hammer v. Dagenhart, it is clearly unconstitutional. Naturally, therefore, in and out of Congress, the friends of the child labor movement are pressing for a constitutional amendment. But a whole brood of questions at once demands attention as to the form of such an amendment. Should the amendment deal with children alone, or should Congress be given power to deal with industrial relations? If the amendment concern itself wholly with the prohibition of child labor what means of enforcement should be provided — what power or what duty of enforcement should be lodged in the States? Prohibition of child labor presents different elements from prohibition of liquor; nevertheless, the eighteenth amendment has taught us something as to the limits of effective Federal enforcement. At least it has taught us that there *are* limits. These are questions that call for the most mature consideration, and should enlist, for their wise solution, not merely devoted humanitarians, but legal specialists equally zealous to abolish the plague spots of child labor, but also alive to the delicacies of American constitutional law and to the inherent difficulties of law enforcement.

One even ventures to express serious doubt of the wisdom of a constitutional amendment, rather than, as Secretary Hoover urges, a re-newed energetic movement to rouse the States to action. Such an attitude, I am well aware, will be received with impatience and disdain by those who see nothing but the cruel evils of child labor to the exclusion of all else. But the method of dealing with this ancient enemy does present difficulties perhaps as important as the evil itself. Nothing less seems to be involved than the fashioning of responsible citizenship. It is too easy to look to Washington and a centralized administration for the correction of all our national shortcomings. I do not speak from any regard for traditional states' rights, nor as the exponent of any theory of political science, but as one with some knowledge of the functioning of the Federal machinery and its power further to absorb and discharge effectively nation-wide duties, especially duties of intimate local concern, affected by local conditions of great variety throughout the country.

Of course child labor is of national concern, and some benefits will accrue from national action. But this is true of many other fields which we have not turned over to Washington, because such concentration would be self-defeating in its execution and make for a corresponding paralysis of local responsibility.

Withdrawing children from shop and mine is not enough, unless provision is made to put the children into schools. Today no State can plead financial want, or the need for aid to discharge these duties. If these rudimentary tasks are not fulfilled by the States, the fact shows that there is not enough civic understanding and will, among a sufficiently large number of people, to bring to pass a decent level of citizenship. The deeper statesmanship may well be not to attempt removal from the remote centre of this or that glaring evil, but to awaken the community to the need of its removal, for only by such vigorous civic education will an informed public opinion, essential to the enforcement of decent standards, be secured and sustained. Only thus will the national aspirations be translated from mere negative prohibitions into affirmatively good lives of men and women. The mere fact that progress through the States in the past has been slow — which, naturally, tries the devotion of such noble champions of children's lives as Mrs. Florence Kelley — need be no measure of future progress. For a new political instrument is now available — the women's vote. Why should not the League of Women Voters in every state make it the order of the day to put a wise child labor law upon the statute books of every State and — what is almost everywhere forgotten — an adequate and efficient corps of inspectors for enforcement? What possible competition for the women's interest *in action* can there be to that of securing a wholesome and just child life? If it be said that the women are least organized in those States where the evil of child labor is the most flagrant the simple answer is that nothing will furnish such a stimulant to the cohesive organization of women, for the exercise of their political power, as the procurement of fit lives for children. If the women will it, not only would child labor be prohibited by paper legislation but the enforcement of such laws, and an environment fit for children to be born into and to grow up in, will quickly become the possession of every State in the Union. Indeed, the States would furnish competition not in child labor, but in child welfare.

The amendment takes shape, 1923–1924

1. Chief of Children's Bureau on need for a national minimum standard

Testimony of Grace Abbott, Jan. 10, 1923, U.S. Congress, Senate, *Hearings before the Committee on the Judiciary, Child Labor Amendment,* 67 Cong., 4 Sess. (1923), p. 48.

I feel . . . very strongly, that we should have a Federal minimum standard for the protection of children, and that without that, if we wait for the time to come when it will be brought up to any particular standard, we may have to wait for a whole generation for the protection which science indicates is needed at the present time. And if we enact — phrase it how you will — an amendment which establishes a minimum standard, and allows the State to establish higher and not lower standards, we shall be giving to the children the real advantages of our Federal form of government, and higher local protection.

I can not see why any State wants to ask to be able to exploit its children, or why it should claim that its rights have been infringed if that is denied them. And we do have throughout the country, changing from time to time, a certain concensus of opinion as to what is the minimum standard. It was that which led Congress to enact the law of 1916. At that time the 14 year age limit set a new standard, almost, in the world. There were only two or three countries that had ever attempted it. At the present time practically every civilized country has come up to that standard. The few States that did not establish that standard here in the United States now ought to be compared with China and Japan, Persia and the Orient in the protection which they afford their children, and not with Europe. And the standard, which was a sort of an American standard, not observed throughout, but which Congress by very large majorities established in 1916 and 1918, is now a world standard in civilized countries. Whether the next one will be an age minimum of 15 years, or whether it will be the requirement of an educational or physical test I am not prepared to foretell, but I do feel very strongly that it is not a departure from the real purposes of our Government to afford to the children of the country a minimum standard, allowing to the several States a right which I never want to see taken away from them, of giving them more protection and better care than the Federal minimum gives them.

---

2. Organized labor endorses the proposed amendment, 1923

Testimony of Samuel Gompers, Jan. 15, 1923, U.S. Congress, Senate, *Hearings before Committee on the Judiciary, Child Labor Amendment,* pp. 70–71.

I have lived rather a long life and have had some experience and have had the desire to observe, and I know the difference in the conditions between the industrial conditions of my early boyhood and young manhood to what they are to-day. We have advanced. It is a calumny and it is a libel upon our intelligence and upon those who have gone before to say that we have not made some advances, that we have not progressed. It is not true. But it is equally true that we have not kept pace with the tremendous industrial struggle, and that we have not gone as far as it is necessary that we should go in order to meet the development in industry.

In a modern industrial plant you will scarcely find 2, 3, or 5 per cent of men who are capable of knowing how to produce an entire article. With the inventions of machines and improvements in tools of labor, with concentrated industry, with the new propelling powers that drive machines, in the modern factory a workman performs one infinitesimal thing over and over and over again, thousands upon thousands of times a day, until the monotony of it is enough to drive a man mad. In boyhood, girlhood, into a factory, into a mill, into a mine, into a modern plant, without the opportunity of an education, working, working from 6, 7, 8, 9, 10, 15 years at one of those monotonous pieces of work, is it any wonder that when the draft was held in our country

for the needs of our country for men in the Army and the Navy that so many of them failed to meet the physical and mental requirements; that more than one-third were rejected? Why? Why were they rejected? They were the boys of the factory and the mills and the mines. Dwarfed in body and mind. Children now from 10 to 15 years, a million of them — the turnover has already been referred to — but as these children grow up to 21 and more they are the voters of our country, they are the future citizens of our country, and they are the future men and women upon whom our country must depend in any emergency which may arise.

Yes; I am deeply touched by the humanitarian consideration of this problem. But I can not drive from my mind the facts of life also. It is inhuman and it is uneconomic to have children in the factories and workshops, mills, and mines engaged in all these gainful occupations. It is uneconomic. In industry it does not pay. That may seem presumptuous on the part of one who is not an employer of labor, but it is uneconomic, and the manufacturer who in the long run employs adult labor finds that it is more profitable and advantageous than the employment of children. If in this competition between rivals, the question of cutting here, clipping here, instead of these so-called economies being practiced in order to drive the life-blood out of the children, if that was applied to more intelligent management we would find much greater economy, greater profit, greater product, better things for all the people of our country and for our standing.

.   .   .   .   .

The need is great, and I believe that it requires the potential power and influence of our Federal Government to see to it that this great wrong is righted . . . I believe that the opportunity should be given to the people of the country, and as soon as possible, to express themselves by the arrangement now prevailing; not to weight it down by another proposition which may arouse additional antagonism, but the simple proposition of saving child life, that it may be submitted by the Congress to the States under the present régime and provisions for amending the Constitution, so that we may soon have a decision upon this problem for the abolition of child labor.

3. The House reports favorably on the proposed amendment

Report of the Committee on the Judiciary, U.S. House of Representatives, on the Child-Labor Amendment to the Constitution of the United States to Accompany H. J. Res. 184, House Report No. 395, 68 Cong., 1 Sess. (1924), pp. 16–19.

THE ADVOCATES OF A CHILD LABOR MOVEMENT

In the course of the hearings representatives of the following national organizations urged favorable action on the amendment: American Association of University Women, American Federation of Labor, American Federation of Teachers, American Home Economics Association, Commission on the Church and Social Service, Federal Council of the Churches of Christ in America, Democratic National Committee, General Federation of Women's Clubs, Girls' Friendly Society in America, National Child Labor Committee, National Council of Catholic Women, National Council of Jewish Women, National Council of Mothers and Parent-Teacher Associations, National Council of Women, National Education Association, National Federation of Business and Professional Women's Clubs, National League of Women Voters, National Woman's Christian Temperance Union, National Women's Trade Union League, Republican National Committee, Service Star Legion, Young Women's Christian Association.

The State legislatures of six States — California, Massachusetts, Nevada, North Dakota, Washington, and Wisconsin — have petitioned Congress to submit an amendment.

It will be remembered that President Harding and President Coolidge have both recommended to Congress the submission of a child-labor amendment to the States, the former in his message of December 9, 1922, the latter on December 6, 1923. The late President Wilson was an enthusiastic supporter of the principle of Federal regulation and personally urged its importance on both Congress and the country as a whole. The platform of the National Republican Party for 1920 contains the following clause:

The Republican Party stands for a Federal child labor law and for its rigid enforcement. If the present law is found unconstitutional or ineffective, we shall seek other means to enable Congress to prevent the evils of child labor.

The National Democratic Party in that year made the following declaration:

We urge cooperation with the States for the protection of child life through infancy and maternity care, in the prohibition of child labor, and by adequate appropriations for the Children's Bureau and the Women's Bureau in the Department of Labor.

THE OPPONENTS OF A CHILD LABOR AMENDMENT

The principal opposition to the amendment came from the National Manufacturers' Association, the Pennsylvania Manufacturers' Association, the *Southern Textile Bulletin,* the Sentinels of the Republic, the Moderation League of Pennsylvania, the Women's Constitutional League of Maryland, an organization with 50 active members formed to oppose the maternity and infancy act, and the Woman Patriot Publishing Co., first established as the organ of the Antisuffrage Association. Some of these representatives deplored any amendment to the Constitution since the first 10; some opposed particularly the eighteenth amendment, and were in consequence opposed to any further "tampering with the Constitution;" some opposed any amendment to the Constitution except one as to the method of amendment. Officers of the Child Welfare Board of North Carolina reported the decision of the board that the interests of the children of North Carolina can be cared for best by North Carolina. Many of those appearing against the amendment indicated their disapproval not only of Federal regulation of child labor but of any regulation or prohibition of child labor, whether State or National.

THE REASONS WHY FEDERAL ACTION IS CONSIDERED NECESSARY

It is believed that little weight will be given to the argument for a return to the conditions of a hundred years ago when there was complete freedom in the employment of children. The case against child labor has been made. That it creates a vicious circle of poverty, ignorance, and poor physical development has been scientifically established. The question of interest at the present time is whether the Federal Government should cooperate with the States in eradicating the evils which flow from the premature employment of children. The reasons why Federal legislation in this field was first sought were: First, because in some States a single industry was so powerful as to prevent the passage of a reasonable child labor law or the enforcement of one after it was passed; second, because consumers had come to feel a moral repugnance to the use of the products of child labor; third, because manufacturers objected to the competition of those who relied upon the low wages of children as the basis of their profits; and, finally, because States found themselves unable to protect not only their consumers and the manufacturers but their citizenship. For after all, children who suffered from the educational, physical, and spiritual losses which premature child labor brings could migrate to any State, so that the citizenship of no State was secure against the neglect of another State.

A new need for Federal regulation has recently been emphasized by disclosures regarding the sweat-shop labor of young children in their homes on work sent in from other States. A recent investigation of home work by children in Jersey City disclosed the fact that more than 1,000 children, the great majority of whom were under the age of 14, were doing sweat-shop work in their homes under dangerously insanitary conditions. Wages were very small, families of three and four working long hours earning as little as $3 and $5 a week.

It was brought out in the testimony given in connection with these inquiries that a considerable amount of the tenement home work done by the New Jersey children was distributed from factories in neighboring States. Thus, New York manufacturers, who were sending their work to Jersey City to escape the New York regulations against tenement home work, were not subject to the penalties imposed by the New Jersey laws. In this way they succeeded in successfully dodging State laws.

Child workers themselves cross the State lines also and create special local problems. The importation of workers to one State from another is a particular feature of the canning industry. According to the findings of the Bureau of Labor Statistics investigation, the condition of woman and child wage earners in canneries —

As the industry has shifted to the Southern States the difficulty of securing an adequate labor supply has led to a system of importing help from northern cities, principally Baltimore and New York, for the season and returning there when they are no longer needed. When this is done there is a tendency to select "family help," that is, the employers hire heads of families with the understanding that wives and children are to be brought also.

A Children's Bureau study in 1919 of child labor in canneries on the Gulf coast showed that large numbers of families were still going from northern cities, principally Baltimore, for work in the canneries of Mississippi, Alabama, Florida, and Louisiana. It was estimated at that time by the assistant general passenger agent of the railroad which usually carries the migrating families from Baltimore to the Gulf coast that in normal years from 3,000 to 3,500 workers go South annually from Baltimore alone to work in the oyster and shrimp canneries. In 88 of these families included in the Children's Bureau study 105 children from 6 to 14 years of age worked in the canneries. Inspections of fruit and vegetable canneries made by the Children's Bureau in Maryland showed that many of the larger canning factories import their labor from Philadelphia as well as from various parts of Maryland. Some of these families, it was found, follow cannery work throughout the year, working in the Maryland fruit and vegetable canneries in summer, and going South to the oyster and shrimp canneries in winter. Because of this nomadic life and the fact that the communities where they lived and worked temporarily did not regard themselves as responsible for their education or general protection, some of the children interviewed had never attended school, and others were barely able to read and write. Child labor is thus not only a matter of national importance because of the numbers involved and the geographical distribution of working children or because of the present serious inequalities in State legislation which hamper effective action in every State, but it has also an interstate aspect for which local control is difficult or impossible . . .

THE FORM OF THE AMENDMENT

It has been generally agreed by those favoring an amendment that it should be so worded as to give to Congress the power to regulate and prohibit the labor of children and young persons and at the same time reserve to the individual States the right to legislate with reference to such labor. This conclusion has been reached because it is believed (1) that legislation enacted by Congress, in the event that the amendment is adopted, will doubtless establish what would be in effect a national minimum standard of protection, and that many States may desire to enact higher stanadrds; (2) that it is desirable that State laws and State machinery for the enforcement of State laws even in States whose child-labor standards may be lower than the standards which Congress may from time to time enact should continue to function, and that only when the State law would through some requirement, which, of course, would usually be an affirmative one, conflict with the Federal law, should the State law be suspended, and then only so far as that particular requirement is concerned. Finally, it has been agreed that since the amendment is a grant of power to Congress it should be generally and broadly inclusive in terms. What occupations a statute would include, what age and hour regulations would be adopted, would be for Congress to determine from time to time, in the light of what it finds is for the welfare of the children . . .

---

4. The child labor amendment, 1924

U.S. Statutes at Large, XLIII, Part I, p. 670.

The amendment, sponsored by the American Federation of Labor, the National Child Labor Committee, and the Consumers' League was originally drafted by Edward P. Costigan (1874–1939), a member of the United States Tariff Commission and Democratic Senator from Colarado from 1931 to 1937. It was introduced as a joint resolution by Senator Medill McCormick of Illinois and Congressman Israel M. Foster of Ohio. After some changes in wording the resolution was approved by a vote of 297 to 69 in the House (April 26, 1924) and 61 to 23 in the Senate (June 2, 1924).

Resolved by the Senate and House of Representatives of the United States of America in Congress assembled (two-thirds of each House concurring therein), That the following article is proposed as an amendment to the Constitution of the United States, which, when ratified by the legislatures of three-fourths of the several States, shall be valid to all intents and purposes as a part of the Constitution:

"ARTICLE ———.

"SEC. 1. The Congress shall have power to limit, regulate, and prohibit the labor of persons under eighteen years of age.

"SEC. 2. The power of the several States is unimpaired by this article except that the operation of State laws shall be suspended to the extent necessary to give effect to legislation enacted by the Congress."

Opposition to the amendment

The joint resolution proposing the amendment passed both houses of Congress by large majorities but powerful opposition to ratification soon manifested itself in the states. During 1924 the legislatures of Georgia and Louisiana refused to adopt the amendment and the voters of Massachusetts rejected it in a popular referendum.

———

1. The amendment called a communist plot hatched by "Pacifist internationalist Federal Children's Bureau"

Petition of Woman Patriot Publishing Company, May 31, 1924, *Congressional Record*, 68 Cong., 1 Sess. (1923–1924), LXV, Pt. 10, pp. 9962–9964.

The Woman Patriot Publishing Company, originally an anti-woman's-suffrage organization, opposed the Children's Bureau, the Sheppard-Towner Act, and the child labor amendment. The following petition was presented a few days before the Senate adopted the McCormick resolution.

———

Gentlemen: The board of directors of the Woman Patriot Publishing Co. is unanimously opposed to the child labor amendment.

A hearing before the Senate Judiciary Subcommittee on Child Labor having been denied us, we therefore respectfully petition the honorable Members of the United States Senate:

First. That the improperly termed "child" labor amendment be rejected for the following reasons:

The youth of the Nation up to 18 years would be outrageously wronged by national prohibitions of the right to work for their parents or for their own self-support and higher education.

The youthful poor of the Nation, if forbidden to work up to 18 by the Government, with the alternative of obeying the law or of starving, would be driven to work underground, in sweat shops, where there is much more danger of exploitation than in open, inspected factories, and there would result all the evils of bootleg child labor, followed by vicious espionage and invasion of the homes of the people in violation of Article IV of the Bill of Rights by swarms of bureaucrats from Washington with inquisitorial powers. It is absurd to pretend that these salaried professional humanitarians would have the interest of the youth of distant States as much at heart as the mothers who bore them or the communities in which they live.

This benign-looking amendment, drawn and promoted principally by an American Socialist leader (Mrs. Florence Kelley, translator of Karl Marx and friend of Frederich Engels, who instructed her how to introduce socialism "into the flesh and blood" of Americans), is a straight Socialist measure. It is also promoted under direct orders from Moscow. (Documentary evidence on the above is submitted in detail hereafter.)

The spearhead of the communist campaign in the United States is the joint promotion of two congressional measures — of this amendment, to prohibit the labor of all youth, making Government financial support (doles for children) a necessity, and of the Sterling-Reed Federal education bill, engineered by the self-same groups to obtain central control of the minds of American youth, to destroy their love of country and willingness to defend her by means of doctored textbooks, prepared in the interlocked interests of socialism, pacifism, internationalism, and bureaucracy.

The youth of the Nation up to 18 years can not be placed under the guardianship of the pacifist internationalist Federal Children's Bureau without endangering America's future means of national defense.

Second. That if the Congress shall deem it necessary to propose an amendment to nationalize legislation for youth, that the proposal, affecting the future rights and liberties of every father, mother, and child in the United States, shall be submitted for ratification to conventions of delegates elected on this issue in each State, in accordance with the provisions of Article V and in accordance with the manner in which the Constitution itself was submitted to the people, through conventions, by unanimous resolve of the framers, in 1787.

.   .   .   .   .   .

That this amendment is also a reversal of our dual form of government — which leaves local and domestic affairs to the administration of the States, where they are most efficiently and democratically adjusted by the people in their local communities — is so self-evident that it is not discussed further in this memorandum.

Your petitioners, however, respectfully record themselves as not only in favor of regulation of child labor by the States, but as firm believers that only by State regulation, with opportunity for changes dictated by local ex-

perience, can the problem of child labor ever be dealt with successfully.

.   .   .   .   .

That the demand for this amendment does not spring from the people, but is a stimulated propaganda by groups of self-interested proponents, is shown by the general attitude of the American people on child-labor legislation, as well as by the duplicity and exaggerations and self-contradictions resorted to to promote this amendment's passage, shown hereafter.

.   .   .   .   .

Four self-interested groups are proponents of this amendment:

1. Certain employers in States having highly restrictive child labor laws, who favor this amendment, believing a uniform national law would eliminate competition with States having less stringent laws.

.   .   .   .

2. Leaders of the American Federation of Labor, who advocate this amendment not only in the belief of its benefits to the child but also because they believe (mistakenly, in our opinion) that its adoption would eliminate the competition of unorganized child workers with organized adult labor.

.   .   .   .

3. Job hunters and bureaucrats seeking to create new jobs in defiance of public demand for reduction of bureaucracy, both because of its cost and of its political machine power.

4. Communists and socialists striving to establish governmental control and support of the entire youth of the Nation, which is the basic tenet of communism.

---

2. Manufacturers' journals denounce the amendment

a. "It is Russian in origin"

"What the Child Labor Amendment Means," *Manufacturers' Record* (Baltimore), Sept. 4, 1924.

Because the Child Labor Amendment in reality is not legislation in the interest of children but legislation which would mean the destruction of manhood and womanhood through the destruction of the boys and girls of the country, the *Manufacturers' Record* has been giving much attention to the discussion of the subject, and will continue to do so . . .

This proposed amendment is fathered by Socialists, Communists and Bolshevists. They are the active workers in its favor. They look forward to its adoption as giving them the power to nationalize the children of the land and bring about in this country the exact conditions which prevail in Russia. These people are the active workers back of this undertaking, but many patriotic men and women without at all realizing the seriousness of this proposition, thinking only of it as an effort to lessen child labor in factories, are giving countenance to it.

If adopted, this amendment would be the greatest thing ever done in America in behalf of the activities of Hell. It would make millions of young people under 18 years of age idlers in brain and body, and thus make them the devil's best workshop. It would destroy the initiative and self-reliance and manhood and womanhood of all the coming generations.

A solemn responsibility to this country and to all future generations rests upon every man and woman who understands this situation to fight, and fight unceasingly, to make the facts known to their acquaintances everywhere. Aggressive work is needed. It would be worse than folly for people who realize the danger of this situation to rest content under the belief that the Amendment cannot become a part of our Constitution. The only thing that can prevent its adoption will be active, untiring work on the part of every man and woman who appreciates its destructive power and who

wants to save the young people of all future generations from moral and physical decay under the domination of the devil himself.

b. "It will give employment to government parasites"

"High Cost of Government," *Manufacturers' News* (Chicago), Oct. 3, 1925.

Office holding parasites want to prohibit work by all minors under 18. Why? So they can put to work several thousand inspectors to see that the youth of the land are properly idle. Too much sociology. Too much bureaucracy. Too many payrollers. Too many drones in the hive.

c. "Parental rights and the amendment"

The Manufacturers' Record, Sept. 11, 1924.

You must bear in mind that this Amendment takes entirely from the parents the right to have their children, sons or daughters, do any work of any kind so long as they are under 18 years of age. Those who are backing this amendment distinctly state that the intention of the bill is to prevent the employment, for instance, of any boy under 18 years of age in any farm work of any kind. It was specifically stated by one of the most active promoters of this scheme that this was intended to keep boys under 18 years of age from driving up the cows, or hoeing the vegetables, or doing any work of the character even for their own parents. Under that bill the mother would have no right to teach her daughter to do any housework whatsoever, whether it be the sweeping of floors or the washing of dishes.

.   .   .   .   .

The adoption of this amendment, I believe, would mean the complete destruction — and I say this fully appreciating the meaning of my words — of the manhood and womanhood of this country.

Every vote that is given for the adoption of this amendment is a vote for the destruction of the moral and physical character of all coming generations.

.   .   .   .   .

It carries the limit of 18 years, before which no youth, male or female, can work at home, on the farm, or in the factory or the office.

I do most earnestly protest in the name of the coming generations against an effort to pauperize in thought and in act every boy and girl under 18 years of age and to give the devil full sway in utter destruction of these young people while living in idleness when they should be at work.

---

3. A child welfare reformer opposes the amendment

Joseph Lee, letter to the editor, *Boston Transcript,* Oct. 14, 1924.

Lee (1862–1937), a Boston philanthropist, was promoter of the playground movement and president of the Playground and Recreation Association of America.

Letters to the Editor

CHILD LABOR AND LOCAL RESPONSIBILITY

To the Editor of the Transcript: —

I am opposed to the child labor amendment because I am and always have been in favor of the regulation of child labor, and because I believe that national legislation upon the subject will in the end largely supersede legislation by the several States, while itself necessarily lacking in that local support and that adaptation to local conditions upon which the effectiveness of all such measures must depend.

Child labor, as both the supporters and opponents of the amendment are agreed, is primarily an educational undertaking. It cannot be successfully carried out except in close co-operation with the public school and with the home. To exclude a child from work without at the same time providing him with a school is to decree that he shall grow up in enforced idleness, a prey to evil influence. To determine the sort of schooling that shall be provided, moreover, and the ages at which it shall be provided for different kinds of children, is far from being a simple matter. Some children, for instance, can get very little benefit from schooling after their fourteenth year and none at all unless they also have the experience of actual work. For others the limit is fifteen years, for others sixteen, for others twenty, twenty-two, or twenty-seven. For some the best kind of education outside of the home is through that form of part-time schooling in which two boys occupy one work-bench in the factory and one seat in the school, changing positions like Box and Cox at the beginning of each month. In other cases the best plan is that of the continuation school — say for from eight to twelve hours a week. In others the evening school will be sufficient. So that to work effectively a child labor law must be accompanied by a corresponding school law and also by the provision of especial educational opportunities in local industries for certain classes of children. The working out of such a system is an intricate piece of business, its successful development depending very much on local conditions. In order to be accomplished satisfactorily it must be a matter of growth and adjustment, not of national legislative fiat applying to all parts of the country at the same time.

Under the proposed amendment Congress would indeed have the power to decree what sort of schooling should be provided in the several States to fit in with the labor legislation it might adopt. But no constitutional amendment can give to Congress the power of understanding local conditions and of carrying local opinion along with it, nor the power of adapting its legislation in each State to the particular conditions obtaining in that State, such as our State Legislatures possess. A law suited to Massachusetts might not fit Arizona; one adapted to the conditions in a Southern State like Georgia might not be the best for Wyoming. It is true that the States affected by a national law might of their own voluntary action organize their schools and other educational provisions to conform to it so far as possible. But the purpose of this amendment is to enforce child labor legislation upon States who do not want it now, and it is not certain that they will be eager, when a law is thus forced upon them, to extend their educational system to correspond.

There must also be co-ordination between child labor legislation and the home. The child excluded from work may be the family breadwinner. It is often desirable that he should nevertheless be so excluded, but it is not desirable that in that case the family should starve. The State is a much more appropriate, and in the long run more efficient, body to control the matter of poor relief within its own borders than officials appointed from Washington can ever be.

The greatest objection, however, to national legislation upon this subject is that by lessening the responsibility of the States for dealing with the matter, it will inevitably weaken the effect of local agitation and the corresponding development of that local public sentiment upon which the effectiveness of all laws must ultimately depend. Without national legislation our laws regulating child labor in the several States have rapidly advanced. They will continue to do so if this amendment is not passed, and they will in that case retain the advantage of being effectively enforced. This amendment tends to dry up at their source the springs of public opinion from which in the long run all progressive legislation must proceed.

---

4. Archbishop of Boston opposes ratification, Boston, 1924

Circular Letter, William Cardinal O'Connell to all churches in the Archdiocese of Boston, October 1, 1924, in Vincent A. McQuade, *The American Catholic Attitude on Child Labor Since 1891* (Washington, D.C., 1938), p. 97.

The Archbishop's letter appeared in *The Pilot* (Boston, October 4, 1924). The referendum was defeated by a 3 to 1 margin.

. . . I would recommend that you bring to the attention of your parishioners at all the Masses on Sunday, October 5th, the dangers hidden in the proposed Child Labor Amendment and the necessity of their registering during the week and of their voting on election to protect the interests of their children.

(Signed) William Cardinal O'Connell, October 1, 1924.   Archbishop of Boston

Defense of the amendment

---

1. The scope and limitation of the amendment

National Child Labor Committee, *Dean Roscoe Pound of Harvard Law School writes on Child Labor Amendment,* Pub. No. 322 (New York, 1924), n.p.

Pound (1870–1964) was dean of Harvard Law School, 1916–1936.

Dear Mr. Lovejoy: —

1. Will the Bill of Rights be abrogated if the child labor amendment is ratified? This seems to me the most absurd bogey that ever was conjured up. Let me give you an example of the way lawyers can argue on such points. Probably there is no better authority on law in the country than Mr. Hughes. When the income tax amendment was under consideration he urged strongly that the result of it would be to allow the national government to tax state and municipal securities out of existence. Certainly the language of the amendment was very strong — income "from whatever source derived." Nevertheless the Supreme Court of the United States has held that the amendment did not have any such destructive effect. Now take the present case. The argument is that a power of prohibition and regulation is conferred, and that there are no limits upon that prohibition or regulation. But the amendment is meant to fit into the Constitution as a whole, and the Bill of Rights provides that the federal government shall not deprive any person of life, liberty or property without due process of law. Therefore any unreasonable means of regulation, and anything arbitrary or unreasonable in the carrying out of the prohibition would be subject to the limitation that applies to all Congressional exercise of powers given by the Constitution. The Supreme Court of the United States has never manifested any inclination to give free rein to social legislation. On the contrary, it has always scrutinized it very jealously. I see no reason to suppose that it would allow legislation under this amendment to run wild. If it is said that we may presently get a radical court, my answer would be that when we get such a court, it won't need constitutional amendments to enable it to sanction Congressional dealing with the subject of child labor. It will simply overrule the first child labor decision and let the matter go at that.

2. You ask whether the Supreme Court will allow educational control to be implied from the amendment. Here again, I can only say that the Supreme Court has shown no inclination to allow wide latitude for social legislation. Why it should be supposed that this amendment will bring about an entire change of front in the attitude of the court I cannot perceive. The amendment says nothing whatever about education. What it says is that Congress may regulate and prohibit child labor. Under the tenth amendment "the powers not delegated to the United States by the Constitution nor prohibited by it to the states are reserved to the states respectively or to the people." This seems to me to settle the matter. There being nothing whatever in the Constitution about education, it is committed to the states respectively where it stands now. If certain children are not permitted to be employed in labor, and therefore it is deemed they ought to be educated, the matter of educating them rests with the state exactly as the matter of protecting them from being run over by automobiles in the streets does.

3. You ask will the amendment give Congress a power more extensive than that now possessed by the states? I suppose the states have power to deal with the matter of child labor up to the age of twenty-one. Very likely regulations of labor above twenty-one would be said not to be due process of law. If that is the case the power given by this amendment is less than the power actually possessed by every state in the Union at present. It should be borne in mind that the Supreme Court of the United States has expressly decided that the states may enact child labor legislation. What this amendment does is to give to Congress a power to deal uniformly with the whole country in a matter with respect to which each state now has greater powers than those which this amendment proposes to confer upon Congress.

Let me say one thing more. I have read attentively the voluminous literature which has come out upon this subject recently in which some very good lawyers (obviously retained for the purpose) have expended the resources of ingenious advocacy in conjuring up bogies in this connection. It should be remembered that excellent lawyers have always done this with respect to every important measure in our history. We certainly have never had a greater lawyer in this country than James Kent. But he thundered against the Louisiana purchase as unconstitutional, revolutionary and subversive of American institutions. Nothing that I have read about the child labor amendment paints a gloomier picture for the future than that which this eminent lawyer painted in his opposition to acquisition by the United States of a territory which would make it an American empire.

Yours very truly,
(Signed) Roscoe Pound

2. A reporter supports the amendment

Henry F. Pringle, "If this be treason," *New York World,* Jan. 27, 1925, in Grace Abbott, "Federal Regulation of Child Labor, 1906–38," *Social Service Review,* XIII (September 1939), 421–422.

Pringle (1897–1958), reporter for several New York newspapers, wrote a Pulitzer-Prize-winning biography of Theodore Roosevelt and a biography of William Howard Taft.

To the Editor of *New York World:*

It is wtih considerable hesitation that I ask an opportunity to point out a few of the reasons why — despite the opposition of the *World* — I still believe in the Child Labor Amendment. Reporters, of course, are not supposed to have opinions. Their task is to present the facts.

But my interest in this subject is peculiarly personal. Something over a year ago I was assigned, as a member of the staff of the *World,* to obtain the facts with reference to child labor. Resolutions for an amendment were pending in Congress. Were the various States, enjoying full control, taking care of the children? Were children still at work?

It wasn't at all difficult to find them at work. The harrowing conditions of twenty years ago had passed, it was true. But during the course of a 6,000-mile trip, from Colorado to the Atlantic Coast and from Michigan to Louisiana, boys and girls as young as five and six years old were discovered working. The articles that I wrote as published in the *World,* were naturally a plea for Federal control. Now I find myself in the strange position of a reporter whose facts were not emphatic enough . . . to win over his own paper.

The *World* believes the problem is one for the States to solve, that the situation is not serious enough to justify further invasion of States' rights. You admit the "serious evils" of the present time, but you think that the States will take proper steps if sufficient pressure is brought to bear upon them.

With all due humility, I don't think that the editor of the *World* would have very much faith in some of the States if he had been with me on portions of my trip . . .

The *World* suggests that the District of Columbia enact an ideal Labor Law and that this be held up to the States as a model. But the District of Columbia has no cotton-mills. It has no beet fields and no oyster and shrimp canneries. Surely it is the height of optimism to believe that the ten and eleven hour cotton-mill day — for boys and girls between fourteen and sixteen in the South — will be shortened because of any law in the District of Columbia. Many mill-owners told me that it was necessary to get "mill-workers while they're young." Otherwise these children might learn of a world, more bright and cheerful, beyond the horizon of the mill town.

The fact of the matter is that I haven't much faith in the States. I don't think they are entitled to their "rights" when they fail to exercise them. So I hope the Twentieth Amendment passes and that the *World* loses. "If this be treason." —

---

3. Senator Walsh answers opponents of the amendment

Congressional Record, 68 Cong., 2 Sess. (1924–1925), LXVI, Pt. 2, pp. 1438, 1442–1443, 1445–1446.

Thomas James Walsh (1859–1933), senator from Montana from 1913 to 1933, was in charge of the investigation of the leasing of naval oil reserves at Teapot Dome, Wyoming, and Elk Hills, California. A Democrat and Roman Catholic, Walsh was an expert in constitutional law. His speech was delivered on January 8, 1925.

Mr. WALSH of Montana. Mr. President, it has become evident that a well-organized and liberally financed movement has been launched to defeat the ratification of the child labor amendment to the Constitution . . . It has been ratified by the Legislature of the State of Arkansas, rejected by the law-making bodies of Georgia and Louisiana, and defeated in a referendum in the State of Massachusetts, advisory in character, and will presumably be under consideration before the legislative assemblies of 38 of the States, including Massachusetts, convening during this month of January.

The result of the test vote in Massachusetts has emboldened the enemies of the reform to such an extent that it has been followed by a surprising quantity of press matter in denunciation of the proposed amendment along the line of what passed for argument in the campaign in that State. Much of this is so irrelevant to the issue, more of it so perfectly puerile, that it was never uttered in the debates in Congress.

Not a little of it consists of such palpable misrepresentation, such obvious appeals to passion induced thereby that a cautious campaigner might reasonably expect that before any intelligent audience it would defeat its purpose. The revoltingly sordid motives back of much of the effort to accomplish the defeat of the amendment can not be concealed. Of that later. For the present I shall review the objections in the main urged against it on the assumption that they are put forth in the utmost good faith however their shallowness may induce suspicion with reference thereto. No doubt they have been accepted by many honest, well-meaning people who are entitled to a respectful consideration of the reasons which have impelled them to that course . . .

One of the stock arguments is that, as expressed in an editorial in the Florida Times-Union, gravely reproduced in the Washington Post of December 22, 1924, the whole movement is a "communist plot," it having been "discovered that the proponents are closely allied with the Russian Soviet." It can not have escaped the notice of the most casual reader that latterly every piece of legislation, every proposed change of policy, evoking the antagonism of big business is denounced as socialistic, communistic, bolshevistic, inspired if not directed from Moscow. The farm relief legislation that occupied so much of the thought of Congress in recent sessions, the provision for the publication of the list of income-tax payers and the amounts paid by them, the income tax itself, the farm loan law, the proposal that the Government operate its $150,000,000 plant at Muscle Shoals, as provided in the Norris bill and conditionally in the Underwood bill, indorsed by the President of the United States, these all like the child labor amendment, are not the product of American statesmanship or American economic thought, but have their origin, a credulous public is told, in the brains of the coterie of conspirators who rule and have nigh ruined Russia.

.   .   .   .   .

THE SANCTITY OF THE HOME
AND INTERFERENCE WITH PARENTAL
AUTHORITY

. . . It is indisputable that the movement to prevent by law the exploitation of children in industry is world-wide, long antedating in its origin the rise of communism in Russia, and in full flower and fruitage before the spread of its pernicious doctrines alarmed timid souls or afforded talking matter to hidebound reactionaries in America. That phase of the question was thus dwelt upon because it is intimately related to another line of argument much relied upon, namely, that by the policy proposed the sanctity of the home is invaded, the State displaces parents in the natural right, duty, and privilege of rearing their children; that if the policy was not inspired from Moscow it is in harmony with, or at least in embryo emulates, that said to be taught, if not practiced there, namely, that the rearing of children is and should be a function of the state. Thus, Dr. Nicholas Murray Butler, stubborn reactionary, who has never become reconciled to the adoption of the eighteenth amendment and who lent no aid to, if he did not actually oppose, both the sixteenth and the seventeenth, registering his opposition to the proposed amendment in a letter addressed to the Sentinels of the Republic, whose president is Louis A. Coolidge, treasurer of the United Shoe Machinery Corporation, says:

> Surely no true friend of childhood can wish to support a measure which will make possible the substitution of congressional control of childhood and youth for the natural relationship of parent and guardian.

It was along this line in the main that the campaign against the amendment, under the direction of Cardinal William O'Connell, was prosecuted in connection with the Massachusetts referendum. One of his subordinates, the Rt. Rev. M. J. Splaine, D.D., expressed himself on the subject thus —

> There never was a more radical or revolutionary measure proposed for the consideration of the American people than this so-called child labor amendment that at one stroke of the pen would set aside the fundamental American principle of State rights, and at the same time would destroy parental control over children and commit this country forever to the communistic system of the nationalization of her children.

In an editorial in the Boston Pilot, organ of the cardinal, of October 4, 1924, is the following:

> For the parental control over children it would substitute the will of Congress and the dictate of a centralized bureaucracy, more in keeping with Soviet Russia than with the fundamental principles of American Government.

.   .   .   .   .

The trouble with that argument is that it comes nearly a century too late. The cardinal, whose priestly office, as well as his high character, forbids the belief that he is consciously playing the game of sordid and mercenary employers, is apparently unconscious that he is not arguing against Federal control over child labor but against any governmental control whatever, either State or national. For undeniably, if congressional legislation dealing with that subject, prohibiting child labor, restricting or regulating it, is an unwarrantable interference with parental control, an invasion of the sanctity of the home, equally so legislation by the State must be. If fundamental rights are disregarded when a heartless employer or an unfeeling parent is haled into a Federal court, the one for hiring and the other for permitting a child of tender years to work in a sweatshop 10 hours a day, they are equally trampled upon when such delinquents are brought to trial in a State court.

So far as the family relation is concerned, it is immaterial whether the law emanates from the State or from the Federal Government. There may be political reasons why such control as is to be exercised, if any, should be lodged in the State governments rather than in the Federal authority, but those reasons are of no especial concern to Cardinal O'Connell in his clerical functions. If the power is to be exercised at all, it is a matter of indifference to him ecclesiastically, however it may be to him as a plain citizen of the Republic, in which sovereignty it is to be lodged or whether it shall be exercised concurrently.

Doctor Butler avoids this pitfall by advancing that "congressional control of childhood and youth" would be a substitution "for the natural relationship of parent and guardian." So also to the same extent would unlimited State control of childhood and youth be a substitution for the natural relationship of parent and guardian. So long as congressional legislation goes no further than State legislation, the one is no more of a substitution for parental control than the other.

The answer to the argument being combated is that the whole civilized world has arrived at the conviction that child labor laws constitute no unjust interference with parental rights, no invasion of the sanctity of the home, that they bear no relation to the nationalization of children, if that is the proper term to designate the policy of committing to the State (using the term in its general not its specific significance) through its appropriate agencies, the rearing of children, implying all necessary provision for their existence and development, physical and intellectual, the spiritual being ignored as unessential.

It is too late to enter upon a discussion of the wisdom or the necessity of child-labor legislation. It is justified by the enlightened opinion of the world, however it be a reproach to recreant parenthood or heartless greed.

. . . . . .

CLAIM THAT AMENDMENT AUTHORIZES FEDERAL CONTROL OF EDUCATION

Quite akin to the contention that the sanctity of the home is invaded or that parental authority is displaced by the amendment, perhaps embraced within that claim, is the far-fetched argument that the education of children in some manner passes by it within the field of Federal legislation.

In a communication to the Journal of Commerce, one George Steward Brown, on the Massachusetts referendum, refers to the amendment as one "granting power to Congress to limit, regulate, or prohibit the 'labor' — which by necessary implication carries with it implied Federal power over education as well — of all persons under 18 years of age." This opinion has been dignified by being quoted in certain religious journals strongly antagonistic to Federal control of education. The author got the rise for which he baited.

The relevant section of the amendment reads: "The Congress shall have power to limit, regulate, and prohibit the labor of persons under 18 years of age."

The inquiry is propounded as to whether the word "labor" does not include intellectual as well as physical labor. The whole history of the child-labor movement answers that it does not. The context answers that it does not — that is, except in the most limited sense. In determining what Congress meant by the language it used and what the people of the country mean by the terminology employed in the amendment should it be ratified through the action of their representatives in the State legislatures, regard must be had to the evil to be met and remedied. Indisputably, undeniably, it was to save children from the evil effects of undue physical toil or physical toil under conditions inimical to health and normal growth. Public attention has been called to the case of infant prodigies or other very young children of unusual talents who were permitted or required for profit publicly to exhibit their gifts or attainments to an extent perilous to their physical growth or possibly their normal intellectual development. And it may be that some child labor laws have attempted to meet such cases, but disregarding such exceptional conditions, they have uniformly been addressed to the physical labor of the child. Even in the exceptional cases referred to the physical effort was to be repressed though the supposed injury was due to the accompanying extraordinary mental exertion.

The conclusion to which a consideration of the evil to be remedied, as that subject is illuminated by the history of the child-labor movement, necessarily impels is enforced by the very language of the amendment which gives Congress authority to "limit," to "regulate," and to "prohibit" the labor of persons under 18 years of age. Would it not be perfectly absurd to imagine that the people intend to authorize Congress to prohibit the intellectual labor of such persons and thus prevent them from getting an education at all? Yet to this conclusion we are driven if we conceive that either the words "limit" or "regulate" are to be held to apply to such labor. It will scarcely be argued that the power to "limit" would authorize the entry of the nation upon the task of educating children and certainly the power to "prohibit" would not. When the Congress and the people conclude to vest the National Government with the authority to take over the enormous task of public instruction, the education of the youth of the Nation, some less equivocal language will doubtless be used and must be used to satisfy any sensible court of that purpose.

Authority as well as reason impels to the conclusion that the fears entertained in some quarters that the Federal Government would, in some wise, under the amendment control education are without foundation.

.   .   .   .   .

WHY FEDERAL LEGISLATION IS NECESSARY

The only legitimate ground of discussion of the amendment before us is as to the wisdom of reposing in the Federal Government the same power now intrusted to the State governments, the two to deal with the subject concurrently. There is nothing new or startling in such common authority. Story divides the powers of Congress into those which are exclusive and those which are concurrent, the former to be exercised by Congress only, the latter by

it and by the States respectively as well. That question is fairly debatable and to it and to it alone the discussion must be confined by all who care honestly to canvass it. I shall spend little time upon it, conceiving as I do that the sentiment of the country has been repeatedly and authoritatively declared in the most unmistakable way, a sentiment that rests upon grounds that are well understood. I have called attention to the overwhelming vote by which the act of 1916 and again the act of 1919 passed both Houses of Congress, and the decisive vote on the resolution to submit the amendment for ratification, as well as to the formal declarations of the two great political parties in their platforms of 1916 and 1920. Thus the American people have eloquently expressed the view that the welfare of the children of the Nation and of the Nation itself requires that the Federal power be exercised in their behalf.

The necessity arises from the fact that 11 States allow children under 16 to be worked from 9 to 14 hours a day. One State puts no limit whatsoever on children's hours of labor. Four States say nothing about night labor for children under 16. Thirty-five States fail to require so much as a common-school education for children between 14 and 16. Thirty-five States do not carry their restrictions on dangerous occupations up to the 18-year standard. Fourteen States do not reach the 16-year standard. Five States say nothing about children in dangerous occupations. Twenty-three States with nominal 14-year age limits allow so many exemptions as to practically nullify the law.

.   .   .   .   .

Reference has been made to the effort to standardize the labor laws of the various nations, and particularly the child labor laws, that one country having or disposed to have humane and liberal regulations might not be compelled to meet the competition in industry of other countries content with a lower standard, the tendency being inevitably to the latter. In the same way it is eminently unjust that a

State, moved to the adoption and enforcement of child labor laws of high character, should be required to encounter the rivalry in industry of another State which either makes no adequate provision in the laws to prevent the exploitation of children or allows them to remain practically a dead letter. Justice requires that a common standard be established.

It is advanced, however, that the occasion has gone by when Federal interposition was necessary or advisable. It is true that public sentiment on the subject has advanced and with it an advance has been made both in the standard established by the laws and in the enforcement of the same. That advance has characterized the whole history of the movement from its inception. A gratifying decrease is noted in the number of children between 10 and 15 years employed in gainful occupations as shown by the census of 1920 as compared with the census of 1910. How much of this is due to the agitation for and the enactment of the two Federal statutes held unconstitutional it is impossible to say, but presumably those influences were profound. Laggard States, apprehensive of Federal action, were spurred to avert that event. It is asserted that there was an access in the number of children employed as factory hands in each instance of the annulment of the Federal law by the Supreme Court, but authentic figures are lacking. So, likewise, are reliable statistics showing any material alteration in the conditions exhibited by the census returns. In any case the necessity for a common standard is constant.

STATE RIGHTS

I notice now the States rights argument. Philippics are thundered against anyone who would entrench upon that sacred doctrine — with few exceptions the fulminations of individuals who for some other reason are opposed to the amendment. I have yet to learn of anyone whose opposition to the amendment rests solely upon his attachment to the principle of States rights. A close scrutiny usually reveals that some other consideration is the impelling motive for his attitude.

The doctrine is a salutary one that no power ever ought to be reposed in the National Government that can as well be entrusted to the State, none to the State that can as well be exercised by the county . . . It is a sorry state of mind that, disregarding that rule, pins its faith to systems simply because they were instituted or endorsed by our forbears. They devised the institutions they handed down to us to meet conditions as they knew them and as they conceived they would arise in the future. It is found from time to time in this new world in which we live that they do not always and in every respect fit as admirably as they did in the times which saw their origin. The centralizing tendencies of the times are deplored. Much eloquence is expended in the recital of the advance in that direction and the peril involved in it. Caution ought, of course, to be exercised lest the tendency be unduly accelerated, but Mrs. Partington was no more unequal to the task she essayed than is her prototype in our day who attempts to arrest the expansion of the field of all governmental action, including that of the Federal Government. In my youth the construction and care of highways was a function of the town, later the county assumed the burden, now few States are lacking in a highway commission, and the National Government has already begun cooperation. This is a perfectly natural development. A similar evolution has taken place in provisions for safeguarding public health. When it took a month to travel from Boston to New Orleans and six months to go from the metropolis to San Francisco — before the daily newspaper came into practically every home on the day of its publication, or shortly thereafter — before the telegraph, the telephone, and the radio made possible instant communication between every part of our vast territory, it was unwise and unsafe to entrust to the central Government many of the broad powers it now exercises wisely and to the promotion of the public weal. I have the most profound respect for the men who framed our Constitution. No panegyrist has to my mind, ever exceeded their deserts in his encomiums on their wisdom, sagacity, and prescience. But they were not omniscient, and it is no impeachment of them, either their foresight or their profundity, that they did not anticipate the industrial development of our day, or of the evils inseparably incident thereto, or the necessity of safeguarding the dearest asset of any nation — its children — from exploitation in connection therewith. I have endeavored in brief in what has been said to indicate why, by reason of the changed conditions, of which they could have had no just conception, the Federal Government should lend its aid in that cause. It seems to me a feeble answer to say that our forefathers thought such governmental control as ought to be exercised might wisely be left to the States.

The failure of ratification

1. National Child Labor Committee appraises situation, 1925

Memorandum from Samuel McCune Lindsay to Owen Lovejoy re Federal Child Labor Amendment, 84th Meeting of the Board of Trustees, March 13, 1925, National Child Labor Committee Collection, Library of Congress

The summary of your reports on legislation clearly indicates the present popular tide against the Child Labor Amendment. Without admitting defeat, we are forced to recognize the fact that for at least two years, and probably four years, there is no possibility of ratification.

Meantime, the policy of the National Child Labor Committee as summarized in its "pur-pose and scope" must not be frustrated by delay. In fact, it appears that the widespread opposition to the Amendment has given our work unprecedented publicity which should be turned to the immediate advantage of the children . . .

My suggestions to you are therefore as follows:

(1) Continue to give our associates in Washington and local and state groups everywhere such cooperation as your office is able, in developing the strategy of the campaign for final victory of the Amendment . . .

(2) Accept every opening that offers to assist the people or officials of any state in bringing their own laws up to standard. Your attention is called to the fact that proponents of the Constitutional Amendment base much of their argument for its necessity upon the fact that only thirteen states measured up to the standards specified in the first and second federal laws and only eighteen approximated those standards.

(3) Continue the present work of analyzing every state law and its system of administration so as to have available for immediate use a memorandum of practical suggestions for our co-laborers in the various states.

(4) Wherever possible have bills introduced in state legislatures this season as soon as the Amendment is disposed of, whether favorably or otherwise. This plan is vital as it forces the opposition to prove their willingness to take care of their own problems or else acknowledges the need of a national standard . . .

(5) Wherever a state legislature submits the Amendment to a referendum, place your office and its facilities, as far as possible, at the disposal of proponents of the Amendment . . . However, seek to avoid a state referendum. The Constitution of the United States makes no provision for such action. It is extra legal, expensive and misleading. Wherever urged thus far it has been done by the opposition for the obvious purpose of confusing the voters . . .

Despite the apparent failure of the Amendment to meet public approval, I am confident that when its exact meaning is understood by the American people, it will be ratified, unless in the meantime all state laws and their enforcement have been brought up to such standards that federal action will no longer be necessary . . .

---

2. Factors in the defeat of the amendment and a plan for the future, 1925

Lucia Johnson Bing, "Child Labor Still a Living Issue," *The Ohio Woman Voter,* IV (December 1925), p. 2.

Rejection of the amendment in Massachusetts, New York, and Ohio made it unlikely that approval of the requisite number of states could be obtained. Supporters like Mrs. Bing, who was active in the League of Women Voters of Ohio, continued to work for passage but by 1933 only six states had ratified the amendment.

There are four things to keep in mind, beside keeping one's temper, when considering the Child Labor Amendment. First, that the average person objects to the wording of the amendment because he does not understand the language of constitutional law. Second, that through long years, the remarkableness and hence the sacredness of the Constitution has been taught by schools and politicians until most people think of it as [someone] did of the public building on which were carved the letters, A.D., as being "all done." Third, that most men believe the purpose of law and government is to protect and encourage business and not to control or curb it. Finally, that to be interested in public welfare movements is considered sentimental. According to many, sentiment may be permitted and even encouraged among women in private life, but is not to be permitted in government.

We may as well be philosophical, too, and realize that in the after-war slump from the heights of Hoover unselfishness and Wilson idealism of war days to the depths of individual anxiety over holding one's job or of securing a market for one's produce, the public mind was not favorable to restrictions on the employment of children. It could better afford to be unselfish when work was plentiful.

Recognizing these difficulties, do we want to quit? Does a woman ever want to abandon an argument when she knows she's right?

If the enemy cannot be taken by direct assault, it may be he may be overtaken by "peaceful penetration."

The place to begin is perhaps with our own boards, to make sure that every member understands the conditions of child labor and is convinced that the federal amendment is necessary. Friendly discussion should be encouraged at every board meeting with new arguments presented from time to time by the child welfare chairman.

Conferences with the officers of the Parent-Teacher Associations and the W. C. T. U. are very important, as these organizations which have worked so valiantly from their national headquarters have not yet reached and convinced their entire local membership. It may encourage them to be told that the 17th amendment was introduced 200 times, the 18th amendment 50 times, and that the 19th amendment was before Congress 46 years. It takes long, hard work and brains to convince people of the need for any change. The voter has adopted the custom of voting against what he does not understand. The task would be simpler if he voted on what he understood and left other matters alone.

Finally, since, in Ohio, ratification was defeated by farmers and farm organizations, why should we not go to them and ask whether they are content to leave conditions as they are? The well-informed person can secure their admission that conditions need improvement. Having found their objections to the present amendment, try to meet them, one by one, taking plenty of time and not trying to do it all at one sitting. Send for help, as you need it, to headquarters.

Agriculture could not be exempted in the wording of the amendment, first because the place for any exemption is in the law itself and not in the enabling act, and second, because of the growth of the factory system in agriculture where children are employed in large groups at piece work by a boss who does not own the land nor feel any concern for the children he works, as in the onion, beet and cotton fields.

Once the rural-minded person is convinced of the facts, he is generous enough to be interested. A harder task remains with the manufacturer and business-minded person.

To these it may be pointed out how much our government has already done for business.

Do they believe that the protective tariff, for instance, was unwarranted interference? Or has it, in times past, enabled certain captains of industry to build their fortunes sky-high? Was there too much government in business when national roads were built across the continent to assist men in carrying produce to market? How about the generous appropriations to the Department of Agriculture for animal husbandry, for the protection of the farm crop from boll-weevil, corn-borer, and gypsy moth?

Present business interests are apt to feel that government is establishing a new and unwarranted precedent in these latter days when it shows concern over the length of the working day, the age and the health of the worker. But in the sacred Constitution itself, we read that one of the primary concerns of government is "to promote the general welfare."

Part Six   Administration of Child Welfare Services

The following is the introduction Grace Abbott prepared for the section entitled "Organizing for Administration of Child Welfare Services" in Volume II of *The Child and the State* (Chicago, 1938). It seems appropriate to reprint Miss Abbott's introduction here because her long and distinguished career as an administrator of child welfare services gave her unique knowledge of the issues and developments treated in Part Six.

Some consideration of the general organization and administration of the public social services for children in relation to the whole welfare program is necessary in order to bring into proper focus the administrative problems to which attention has been called.

As we have seen, the state has recognized certain obligations to all its children. For example, it has expended large sums for free schools and playgrounds to aid parents in their common-law duty to educate their children. This has been done in part because collective provision is the best way to meet a universal need. But in its public-school program the state also recognized it had a responsibility for the training and protection of children, which could be met only by providing the necessary facilities for such training and insuring the use of these facilities by prohibiting the employment of children and requiring their attendance at schools. In recent years the state has likewise accepted responsibility for safeguarding the health of children — not merely to prevent sickness and death but to insure optimum physical development of the population. For those children who are wholly dependent upon the state, who are

especially handicapped by reason of birth or physical or mental defect, who are becoming delinquent or are delinquent, the state has a special responsibility. The substantive provisions of a law, the administrative organization, the personnel, and the appropriation provided to carry out the responsibility the state assumes for a group of children will determine how well their needs will be met.

Speaking of education, John Dewey said, "What the best and wisest parent wants for his own child, that must the community want for all of its children. Any other ideal for our schools is narrow and unlovely; acted upon, it destroys our democracy." [1] This is equally true with regard to our health services and especially as to the provision the state makes for the children for whom it assumes complete responsibility.

In its provision for the children in need of special care the state has, however, not acted on Mr. Dewey's theory. Generally speaking, it has undertaken to provide for their care only when the evidence of need made such action inevitable. Reluctant to undertake a clear duty, it is not surprising that legislatures have sought to provide not "what the best and wisest parent wants for his own child" but the cheapest possible care, and that law-makers have been slow to recognize that this not only violated sound humanitarian tenets but was in the long run very costly economy. Likewise, when a state gives to a department new duties and administrative responsibilities, for example, the licensing and supervision of private agencies, the

1. John Dewey, *The School and Society* (University of Chicago Press, 1899), p. 3. [Note in Abbott, *The Child and the State*.]

same false economy has often meant that inadequate funds were provided for the tasks the law imposed. When the funds are inadequate, officials often become discouraged and give up the struggle for adequate standards, with the result that the administrative performance is then not as good as the available funds make possible.

While provision for dependent and delinquent children was at first the responsibility of the local poor officials, three levels of government — federal, state, and local — now participate in the program.

The creation of the United States Children's Bureau in 1912 was the first recognition that the national government had a responsibility to promote the welfare of the children of the nation. An expression of the growing interest in child conservation, the creation of the Bureau may be said to have ushered in a new era in the child welfare movement. The plan for the Bureau followed no traditional organization of state or local government or private child welfare agency. It was to serve and evaluate agencies concerned with any aspect of child health, child labor and child welfare. It was originally wholly a research organization and information center as were the scientific bureaus in the departments of Agriculture, the Interior, and Commerce and Labor. While scientific research in animal husbandry, foods, minerals, or fish was accepted without question as a function of the government, the proposal to study the physical, mental, and social problems of childhood was opposed as socialistic. Opposition, which delayed the enactment of the law creating the Bureau for three years after it was recommended in a special message by President Roosevelt, was in part due, however, to the fact that the National Child Labor Committee urged its creation, and the issue of child labor was then highly controversial.

The Act of 1912 gave to the Children's Bureau a very broad grant of power. The whole child was made the subject of its research. The interrelated problems of child health, dependency, delinquency, and child labor were to be considered and interpreted in relation to the community program for all children. Specialists in all these fields were to work together on studies of the individual child and in the evaluation of services for children. The use of experts in several fields — medicine and law as well as social work and administration — would it was hoped give a more scientific appraisal than was possible when only one aspect of child life was considered. Julia C. Lathrop, the first chief of the Children's Bureau, had had long years of experience in public welfare as well as private social agencies. She recognized the inevitable limitations of the latter and was convinced that the state had only just begun to accept the responsibility it must finally assume for insuring minimum standards of care for all children. A democracy in her opinion must seek continually new ways of insuring the optimum growth and development of all Amercan children.

Miss Lathrop thought a social program must be built on a factual basis, and she was prepared to follow wherever investigations, carefully planned and meticulously executed, led her. The Children's Bureau began its work with a budget of approximately $25,000, but in spite of this limitation Miss Lathrop made plans for research by the Bureau so that it would meet progressively the objects for which it was created and would be able to justify on a scientific basis any recommendations made. While prevention of dependency and delinquency was a goal toward which the Bureau investigations were directed, the need of scientific treatment of those who were or would, in the future, become dependent or delinquent was recognized in the original plans made for the studies to be undertaken.

That under Miss Lathrop the Bureau gave the kind of national leadership which led to an increase in its budget and functions and promoted the welfare of children everywhere is not surprising. In later years when the Bureau was given the administration of grants-in-aid to the states, more direct participation in the development of the public child health and welfare programs became possible, and, as its appropriations increased, some research by demonstration or experiments in new types of care also have been possible.

State departments of social welfare developed in the latter half of the nineteenth century around an institutional program and until recently little effort was made in most states to have the state government assume additional responsibility or participate in any other type of care. The first forward step in improved organization for administration of the child welfare services was the establishment in the more progressive states of a children's bureau or division in the state department of public welfare. To these bureaus or divisions was given the responsibility for the administration of the laws relating to the inspection and licensing of boarding-homes, agencies, and institutions and the direct-care program for dependent children, if the state had one. Administration of the state institutions for delinquent children, clearly a function of the children's bureau or division, has too often been given to the bureau of prisons. Supervision of local public agencies for the care of children was usually made a responsibility of the state agency, but until recently authority to enforce minimum standards was lacking.

The importance of financial participation by the state government in the discharge of the responsibilities which had historically been given to local governments was little recognized until after 1920. During the period when the local governments bore all the costs of the program, progressive improvement was made in the standard care provided in most of the largest metropolitan communities where social work leadership was available and the needs of the children were dramatized by the very numbers involved, but children in the smaller cities and rural communities were greatly neglected under this system of complete local responsibility.

While there was a movement for co-ordination of the county and state welfare agencies in the latter part of the nineteenth century, it was projected on the basis of a very different program from the present one. In Indiana, under a law first enacted in 1891, nearly all the counties appointed unpaid county boards of children's guardians which were under the control of the county commissioners but had the responsibility of co-operating with the State Board of Charities in the care of dependent children. Unfortunately, reorganization in accordance with present-day thinking was delayed in Indiana because of the loyalties that had been developed to a plan that had been a forward step a generation earlier but had become an inadequate organization for administering the social services of today.

The United States Children's Bureau, by directing national attention to the defects in the old systems of administration and new types of organization that promised to improve greatly the services for children, played its part in the development of public appreciation of the importance of effective organization for the administration of the services for children. The state children's code committees or commissions also did much to promote better co-ordination and administration of children's services. Ohio appointed the first such commission in 1911, and from that time the legislatures or governors of state after state have given a selected group of citizens the responsibility of examining the state laws relating to children with a view to suggesting amendments and additions. It was inevitable that these commissions should discover that state and local administrative machinery was ill suited to provide the needed services.

As in the organization of public health services, so in the provision of child welfare services, it was clear that a larger unit for local administration than the town was necessary, and a county system or a combination of two or more counties was urged. This twentieth-century movement for county organization of health and welfare services first made progress in the southern, middle western, and far western states, in part because of the fact that historically the county was the important unit of local government in those sections.

Among the states, Minnesota and North Carolina led in 1917 in a new attack on the problem of administration, the former by definitely adopting the principle of a state-county system in the administration of its child welfare services, and the latter by providing a similar system for its general public welfare services, including those for children. Other states followed the example of these two states in passing county-organization laws, but, except in Alabama, progress in county organization was much slower than in Minnesota or North Carolina. The United States Children's Bureau adopted the policy of making currently available the facts as to the progress being made in these and other states.

While a children's program is a part of a general social service program, it is not surprising that in a number of states modern organization of the services for children antedated the reorganization of the other services. This was because a new and widespread interest in child welfare had been developed and because public sympathy for children was more easily aroused. In contrast, the long-established agencies for poor relief had been in most places uninfluenced by the great changes in social work standards, and in the East social workers, believing that reform of public relief agencies was hopeless, had sought to abolish them.

Prior to 1935 the general problem was how to induce the county boards to provide a county public welfare or child welfare department even when the law providing for its creation was mandatory. As the system of state grants-in-aid to local governments for the financing of the social service program had been developed in only a few states, the state departments had usually no financial inducement to offer the county boards. They had an argument which should have won their support — the improvement of the services for children which would follow better organization. But the boards regarded themselves as the watchdogs of the county treasury, and these theoretical advantages to children were unconvincing.

During the predepression period Alabama led the states in developing correlated state and county child welfare services. Alabama's suc-

cess was due to the skilful work of the state director and her assistants but also to the fact that a grant-in-aid by the state for the administration of the truancy law was made available to the Child Welfare Commission. This grant, available on the condition that it was matched by the county, enabled the state Child Welfare Commission to persuade the counties to provide at least one full-time trained worker for a general child welfare program in sixty-five out of the sixty-seven counties of the state. Minnesota succeeded in getting a large number of county child welfare boards created, but with only a few exceptions no paid staff was provided. North Carolina, although the Act was mandatory on the counties, made little progress until in 1931 the state adopted the Alabama plan of a state grant-in-aid for enforcement of the truancy law, available only if the county set up a county welfare department. In New York, where the State Charities Aid co-operated with the Department of Social Welfare in developing county programs, much progress was made in the local organization of care for dependent children, and other states, notably California, were also making progress in developing local county-wide services.

When the epidemic of unemployment spread throughout the country, when federal funds became available in 1932 and the states made their first appropriations for relief, emergency state relief organizations were set up in one state after another for the relief of the unemployed. While these organizations belonged in the state departments of public welfare and leaders in this field urged that they be placed there, it was probably wise that, in the existing emergency, independent organizations were created. As a result the regular work of the state departments did not have to bear the criticism to which these emergency organizations were subjected. The progress in state-wide organization for relief through the grants from the Federal Emergency Relief Administration and the financial participation of the state governments in the emergency relief programs demonstrated the need of a permanent federal and state program for the relief of the unemployed and the unemployable and the incorporation of what had been begun as an emergency program in the state and county welfare departments.

.   .   .   .   .

Children, it should be repeated, are not pocket editions of adults. Because childhood is a period of physical and mental growth and development, a period of preparation for adult responsibility in public and private life, a program for children cannot be merely an adaptation of the program for adults, nor should it be curtailed during the periods of depression or emergency expansion of other programs. Whether children remain in their own homes cared for and supported by their parents or maintained by a public agency, special provision for their needs must be made. All children are dependent, but only a relatively small number are dependent on the state. Most of them are in some degree problem children, but only a few have such serious difficulties in adjusting to their environment that the state feels obliged to assume responsibility for their care.

The line between dependency, neglect, and delinquency is less easy to draw as the causes of delinquency are better understood. That the social services provided for dependent, neglected, and delinquent children and for those born out of wedlock should be in a separate division of the state and county public welfare departments is clear. In rural counties where it may be possible to employ only a single child welfare specialist much assistance will have to be given by the experts in the child welfare division of the state department.

While organization for administration is important, success or failure of the program will be determined by the personnel employed. Fortunately, the last few years have seen a growing appreciation of the value of the trained social worker in the public social services. The adop-

tion of a special merit system for the public welfare services or of a general civil service law in an increasing number of states should, if the new systems are well administered and supported by the general public, result in great improvements in administrative practices. The civil service principle, selection of the best available person by an open competitive examination, is not self-executing. To accomplish this purpose the civil service organization must function efficiently in the detailed administrative work which is necessary. The classification of personnel, the recruitment of candidates, the setting of examinations, the method of certification of those who qualify, the length of the probation period, the promotion policy, the elimination of employees whose work falls below an acceptable standard are some of the detailed problems the solution of which will determine the effectiveness of the civil service system. But of fundamental importance is the decision as to what type of training and experience is to be considered in determining who is the best available candidate. If proper standards are not adopted, open competition will keep out the political appointee but will not insure good care for the children. In the field of child welfare the selection of the best available person by competition among those who have the basic qualification of training in social service and experience in the child welfare field is necessary to bring the public services up to the level of the best private agencies. The county and state residence requirements in many civil service laws and the almost universal veteran's preference tend to defeat the merit principle in selection of personnel.

Progress is being made, but it is discouragingly slow when one considers the wrongs that are being committed in the name of child welfare by untrained administrators whether appointed under a civil service or a spoils system.

I The Children's Bureau

A. ESTABLISHING THE BUREAU

Proposals for a Children's Bureau, 1903–1909

1. Lillian Wald suggests a national bureau for children

Lillian Wald, *The House on Henry Street* (New York, 1915), pp. 163–165. By permission of Holt, Rinehart and Winston, Inc.

Miss Wald (1867–1940), organizer of public health nursing at the Henry Street Settlement in New York, first thought of a Children's Bureau in 1903. With Edward Devine and Florence Kelley she introduced the idea into reform circles and proposed the idea to President Roosevelt.

Experience in Henry Street, and a conviction that intelligent interest in the welfare of children was becoming universal, gradually focused my mind on the necessity for a Federal Children's Bureau. Every day brought to the settlement, by mail and personal call, — as it must have brought to other people and agencies known to be interested in children, — the most varied inquiries, appeals for help and guidance, reflecting every social aspect of the question. One well-known judge of a children's court was obliged to employ a clerical staff at his own expense to reply to such inquiries. Those that came to us we answered as best we might out of our own experience or from fragmentary and incomplete data. Even the available information on this important subject was nowhere assembled in complete and practical form. The birth rate, preventable blindness, congenital and preventable disease, infant mortality, physical degeneracy, orphanage, desertion, juvenile delinquency, dangerous occupations and accidents, crimes against children, are questions of enormous national importance concerning some of which reliable information was wholly lacking.

Toward the close of President Roosevelt's administration a colleague and I called upon him to present my plea for the creation of this bureau. On that day the Secretary of Agriculture had gone South to ascertain what danger to the community lurked in the appearance of the boll weevil. This gave point to our argument that nothing that might have happened to the children of the nation could have called forth governmental inquiry.

The Federal Children's Bureau was conceived in the interest of all children; but it was fitting that the National Committee on which I serve, dedicated to working children, should have become sponsor for the necessary propaganda for its creation.

It soon became evident that the suggestion was timely. Sympathy and support came from every part of the country, from Maine to California, and from every section of society. The national sense of humor was aroused by the grim fact that whereas the Federal Government concerned itself with the conservation of material wealth, mines and forests, hogs and lobsters, and had long since established bureaus to supply information concerning them, citizens who desired instruction and guidance for the conservation and protection of the children of the nation had no responsible governmental body to which to appeal.

---

2. The necessity for more accurate and current information about the condition of children, 1906

Florence Kelley, "The Federal Government and the Working Children," *The Annals* of the American Academy of Political and Social Sciences, XXVII (1906), 289–292.

For more than a generation we have had a so-called Department of Education. It has published information so inconclusive and so belated that it is the laughing stock of Europeans interested in our educational institutions; so belated, moreover, that it is worthless for our own uses in obtaining improved legislation in this country.

Meanwhile it is left to a feeble volunteer society[1] to collect a few hundred dollars, here and there, and publish in January, every year, the new statutes which have taken effect in the twelve months next preceding. Why does not the Department of Education do this? Why has not the Department of Labor always done this? Why have they not made it a joint undertaking? What are these departments for, if they are not to furnish to the people information concerning the working children at a time when it can be used?

So far as I have been able to learn by studying the reports of these two departments, the hieroglyphics on the pyramid of Cheops are not more remote from the life of to-day than their

1. National Comsumer's League.

statistics are remote from the life of the working children of Georgia and Pennsylvania.

.   .   .   .   .

Surely it is more important that the American people should know what is really happening to its young children in industry than that we should learn at brief intervals how the young lobsters are faring on the coast of Maine and the young trout in the remote streams of Northern Wisconsin.

At last, there is a proposal that we should rise from our low position among the nations when we are ranked according to our care of our children. We are not, when graded according to our care and education of our working children, in the same class of enlightened and humane nations as England, France, Germany, Holland, Switzerland and Scandinavia.

.   .   .   .   .

It is now proposed that we should limp haltingly after those nations, though Congress may be by no means ready to legislate in a unified way for the children as it does, for instance, for the textile industry, the glass industry and the interests of agriculture.

It is proposed that there should be devoted to the children one bureau of our government, by means of which the people should be able to obtain, from month to month, recent trustworthy information concerning everything that enters into the lives of the children; everything that makes for or against their vital efficiency, their educational opportunity, their future industrial and civic value.

A bill will be presented to Congress, with the hope that there may be established a bureau of research and publicity in the interests of all the children in the Republic.

---

3. Favorable editorial comment on the first national Children's Bureau bill, 1906

"Children's Bureau and State Control,"
Providence Journal, March 18, 1906.

The first bill proposing a federal Children's
Bureau (S. 2962) was introduced in the
Senate by Senator Winthrop M. Crane of
Massachusetts on January 10, 1906; a companion bill was introduced in the House
(H.R. 19115) on May 9, 1906, by Rep.
John J. Gardner of New Jersey. The bills,
drafted by the National Child Labor Committee, proposed establishing in the Department
of the Interior "a bureau to be known as the
Children's Bureau," whose duties would be to
investigate and report on "all matters pertaining to the welfare of children and child
life," and publishing the results from time to
time. Neither the Crane nor the Gardner bill
was reported out by the committee to which it
was referred, but the proposal for establishing
the Bureau received some notice in the press.

While it is easy to recognize the almost self-
evident truth that the welfare of children is of
vital importance to the country, it is far less
easy to find methods of improving their conditions. Congress has no power to enact legislation for the States prohibiting child labor or
dealing with the problems of illiteracy, illegitimacy, juvenile crime, children's courts and
allied questions. Each State must regulate these
affairs for itself. The question, then, is far more
complicated and much more delicate than if it
could be settled by one law-making body. It
partakes of the subtle difficulties common to
many of the problems now uppermost in the
minds of thinking Americans — it belongs to
the State for solution, but it is national both in
the interest it arouses and in the danger it
threatens.

.   .   .   .   .

Fortunately it seems possible to solve the
problem of the protection of children by a
method in which the State will lose none of its
rights and the Government will lend its valuable
offices and powerful prestige.

The national child labor committee, which is
conducting the campaign in favor of national
legislation in behalf of children, asks simply for
the establishment of a children's bureau in the
Department of the Interior. The bill now before
the Senate seeking this end grants to that office
only the rights of investigation and publicity.
These rights, however, if well used, will result
in the collection of all the data the public needs
to form its opinion; and this opinion can then
easily find expression in the enlightened state
laws. May it not be that in this proposed union
of national research and publicity with State
autonomy many of the most trying of the great
modern evils will be cured? If such should be
the fortunate result, good laws would not mean
curtailing in the slightest degree the liberty of
the several States.

---

4. First White House Conference on Care of
Dependent Children publicizes the need for a
national Children's Bureau, 1909

Lillian Wald, "A Plea for the Creation of the
Children's Bureau," *Proceedings* of the White
House Conference on the Care of Dependent
Children (1909), 5–7.

In January 1909, three years after Senator
Crane had introduced the first Children's
Bureau bill, he reintroduced it in the Senate
(S. 8323). Rep. Herbert Parsons of New
York sponsored the measure in the House
(H.R. 24148). At this time preparations
were underway for the First White House
Conference on Dependent Children. Several
speakers at the Conference, held on January
25 and 26, 1909, testified in favor of the bills
at House and Senate hearings. One of the
recommendations forwarded to President
Roosevelt by the Conference called for enactment of the Children's Bureau bill.

Although the National Child Labor Committee stands sponsor for the bill introduced in

Congress for the establishment in the Department of the Interior of a Children's Bureau, the committee can no longer claim sole guardianship of this measure, nor would it indeed desire to do so.

. . . Not only have the 25,000 clergymen and their congregations shown their desire to participate in furthering this bill, but organizations of many diverse kinds have assumed a degree of sponsorship that indicates indisputably how universal has been its call to enlightened mind and heart. The national organizations of women's clubs, the consumers' leagues throughout the country, college and school alumnæ associations, societies for the promotion of special interests of children, the various state child labor committees, representing in their membership and executive committees education, labor, law, medicine, and business, have officially given indorsement.

The press, in literally every section of the country, has given the measure serious editorial discussion and approval.

Not one dissenting voice has it been possible to discover — not one utterance contradicts the principles that have been laid down by these various representatives of humanitarian thought and unselfish patriotism throughout America and which they believe the bill will advance as that within its scope of potentialities for such broadening.

.   .   .   .   .   .

What would the bureau do?

.   .   .   .   .

It would investigate legislation affecting children in the several States and Territories, and all other facts that have a bearing upon the health, the efficiency, the character, the happiness, and the training of children. Nothing would it do to duplicate any work now being done by State or Federal Government, but it would strengthen their work and bring into immediate usefulness all of the statistical facts that may lie in the treasure-house of any governmental department or any private associ-

ation. Practical cooperation of this kind, based on intelligent sympathy, has already been assured by the far-seeing Chief of the Educational Bureau and by the head of the Census Bureau. As much of the results of their researches as would enrich the Children's Bureau would be laid before it almost without the asking, and yet, important as is their information and their knowledge, it covers only a part of what pertains to the whole great question of the wisest and most enlightened guardianship of our children, the most valuable natural asset of our nation . . .

The Children's Bureau would not merely collect and classify information, but it would be prepared to furnish to every community in the land information that was needed, diffuse knowledge that had come through experts' study of facts valuable to the child and to the community. Many extraordinary valuable methods have originated in America and have been seized by communities other than our own as valuable social discoveries. Other communities have had more or less haphazard legislation and there is abundant evidence of the desire to have judicial construction to harmonize and comprehend them. As matters now are within the United States, many communities are retarded or hampered by the lack of just such information and knowledge, which, if the bureau existed, could be readily available. Some communities within the United States have been placed in most advantageous positions as regards their children, because of the accident of the presence of public-spirited individuals in their midst who have grasped the meaning of the nation's true relation to the children, and have been responsible for the creation of a public sentiment which makes high demands. But nowhere in the country does the Government, as such, provide information concerning vitally necessary measures for the children. Evils that are unknown or underestimated have the best chance for undisturbed existence and extension, and where light is most needed there is still darkness. Ours is, for instance, the only great nation which does not know how many children are born and how many die in each year within its borders; still less do we know how many die in infancy of preventable diseases; how many blind children might have seen the light, for one-fourth of the totally blind need not have been so had the science that has proved this been made known in even the remotest sections of the country.

Registration and our statistics on these matters are but partial, and their usefulness is minimized by the unavoidable passage of time before their appearance. There could be no greater aid to the reduction of infant mortality than full and current vital statistics of children, such as no one community can obtain for itself, and for want of which young lives, born to be valuable to society, are wasted. We realize only occasionally, or after the occurrence of some tragedy, how little is known of other important incidents of the children's lives. We can not say how many are in the jails or almshouses, though periodically the country is stirred by some newspaper report, such as that one of a little boy of twelve sentenced to five years in a federal penitentiary, or that of a little boy confined for some months upon a trivial charge and incarcerated with a murderer, and other evil men and women, in the cell of a county jail. Outside the few States which have juvenile courts there is chaos in the treatment and punishment of difficult children, and largely because of lack of knowledge concerning this important matter. This information can not be effectively obtained by private agencies. It is too vital to be left to that chance. Only the Federal Government can cover the whole field and tell us of the children with as much care as it tells of the trees or the fishes or the cotton crop.

.   .   .   .   .

What measures for the advantage of the child and the country would the bureau further? No direct responsibility or administrative function for furthering new measures would fall upon the experts of a children's bureau, but proceeding by the experience of other scientific bodies there would be ample justification for employing the best minds of the country for the application of the knowledge gained, by using the stimulus of suggestion and education. It takes no stretch of the imagination to believe that, with the light of knowledge turned by responsible experts upon all phases of the problem of the child, the American people could be trusted, if not with the immediate solution, then with serious consideration, for what appears to be a national apathy is not really so in fact. This conference would disprove that. What innovation in the governmental function would this introduce? This measure for the creation of a children's bureau can claim no startling originality. It would introduce no innovation, no new principle, in the functions of government. It is along the line of what we have been doing for many years to promote knowledge on other interests. On material matters look carefully into the history of the development and present scope of the various bureaus within the authority of the Government, and ample and fascinating analogies will be found.

The struggle for passage of the Children's Bureau bill, 1909–1912

1. Roosevelt urges favorable action

Theodore Roosevelt, "Special message to Congress," Feb. 15, 1909, *Proceedings* of the White House Conference on the Care of Dependent Children (1909), 6–7.

There are pending in both Houses of Congress bills for the establishment of a children's bureau, i.e., Senate bill No. 8323 and House bill No. 24148. These provide for a children's bureau in the Department of the Interior, which

shall investigate and report upon all matters pertaining to the welfare of children and child life, and shall especially investigate the questions of infant mortality, the birth rate, physical degeneracy, orphanage, juvenile delinquency and juvenile courts, desertion and illegitimacy, dangerous occupations, accidents and diseases of children of the working classes, employment, legislation affecting children in the several States and Territories, and such other facts as have a bearing upon the health, efficiency, character, and training of children.

One of the needs felt most acutely by the [White House] conference was that of accurate information concerning these questions relating to childhood. The National Government not only has the unquestioned right of research in such vital matters, but is the only agency which can effectively conduct such general inquiries as are needed for the benefit of all our citizens. In accordance with the unanimous request of the conference, I therefore most heartily urge your favorable action on these measures.

2. Majority and minority report on the Children's Bureau bill, 1909

U.S. Congress, House, *Establishment of Children's Bureau,* 60 Cong., 2 Sess. (1909), Report 2144, pp. 3–6.

H.R. 24148 was reported out of the Committee on Expenditures in the Interior Department on February 13, 1909. Despite favorable testimony from social workers attending the White House Conference the bill failed to receive a unanimously favorable report, and a minority statement was included. Although President Roosevelt endorsed the bill on February 19 and Herbert Parsons spoke eloquently on behalf of the measure on February 22, it never reached the floor of Congress.

By 1909 the main lines of opposition to the Bureau had been set. The main contention of the opposition was that the bill was not constitutional because it purported to exercise jurisdiction over state and local agencies concerned with child welfare. The opposition of the

New York Society for the Prevention of Cruelty to Children conducted mainly by its president, John Lindsay, was on this ground. A second ground for opposition was the question of bureaucratic efficiency. At various times opponents held that either the Bureau of the Census or the Bureau of Education could exercise the functions of the proposed Children's Bureau. The main source of opposition was southern opponents of child labor legislation who associated the Bureau with its sponsor, the National Child Labor Committee.

[Views of the Majority]

In pursuance to a call by the President of the United States, over 200 people, representing practically every State in the Union, and all shades of political and religious opinions, assembled at the White House, all working in harmony to devise plans that would result in the best interests of the children, unanimously adopted a resolution favorable to the passage of this bill.

The committee is in receipt of hundreds of letters, petitions, and resolutions from all parts of the country, also urging the establishment of this bureau.

No opposition to the bill appeared before the committee, but strong protest is made by John W. Lindsay, president of the New York Society for the Prevention of Cruelty to Children. The objections he makes are that these matters are exclusively of state concern, and that the subject does not properly belong to the Federal Government, except possibly for the collection of statistics, and that this can be done by the Census Bureau.

The consensus of opinion among those favoring the establishment of such a bureau was that much good would result from this legislation. In view of the fact that there are no general statistics within the country as to the subjects enumerated in the bill, the compilation, publication, and dissemination of such information is much needed in order to accomplish the desired results.

The bill has not only for its object the compiling of statistics which are needed, but also a compilation of measures adopted by the several States, and nations, such as France, Germany, England, and other countries engaged in this grand and valuable work. The object is not to duplicate the present volume of statistics which we now get in the present form from the various government bureaus, but to gather up and bring together from all possible sources all the valuable information that is now being brought out in the scientific investigations that would have a bearing on these questions, and the dissemination of this information in the form of documents and bulletins, such as are being published by the Department of Agriculture, and which is rendering so valuable a service not only to the farmers and agricultural classes of this country, but to all the people.

There seems to be a woeful lack of knowledge as to the causes of crime, diseases, and other existing evils among our children; and it is essential to have more specific information leading up to these causes, and the dissemination of this information; to have a central body, a central bureau, for research work and publicity, for the gathering of information; to get scientific data, and at actual facts, as well as the results of the best scientific treatments with regard to children; information as to wise as well as unwise legislation affecting children; not only as to legislation, but as to plans of work evolved by various individuals, organizations, and States, and as to the dangers of child life and how they may be avoided; information as to diseases.

.   .   .   .   .

. . . Not only information on diseases and those subjects enumerated herein or in the bill, but general information as affecting the children. To collect all the information just as the Bureau of Education does; to give it widespread publication all over the country for the benefit of the public, private individuals, organizations, States, and all agencies engaged in looking after the welfare not only of the dependent and destitute children and

those who need homes, but that the mother and everybody who has the welfare of the children at heart may have the benefit of the knowledge and experience of others.

The legislation affecting the children that is being enacted by many States could be wisely directed with the information that would be obtained through such a bureau. The light that would come from special investigations of these questions that come up in the treatment of the problems of childhood would enable the various private individuals, organizations, and States to multiply many fold the value of the work for the nation that is now being done by them by giving them the benefit of each other's experience and knowledge.

Each would be stimulated to better efforts. It would permit better cooperation among the various societies and States in devising ways and means to eliminate or reduce crime and, as far as possible, the causes of diseases, and would result in enlightened legislation and the betterment of the conditions surrounding many of the poor and afflicted children, and in the end we would have better men and women.

Besides the consideration given by the committee to the needs and demand for such legislation, the committee consulted the Director of the Census, the Commissioner of Labor, and the Commissioner of Education as to the best method by which the objects of this bill could be obtained — whether by the establishment of a new bureau, as provided in the bill, or the creation of a division under some other bureau. Their unanimous opinion was that a new bureau should be created.

The Director of the Census states that his bureau is purely a statistical bureau and could not make scientific investigations of causes and conditions. The Commissioner of Labor states that his duties pertain to labor conditions alone, and that with the multitude of questions to be handled by his bureau proper attention could not be directed to the proposed new work. Substantially the same contention is made by the Commissioner of Education. All, however, admitted that there would be no duplication, and that they could and would be very glad to co-operate with such a bureau, and could no doubt be of valuable assistance.

.   .   .   .   .

[Views of the Minority]

The undersigned members of the Committee on Expenditures in the Interior Department have not been able to agree with the majority in their report upon this bill, and we respect-fully submit herewith our reasons for opposing the passage of this measure:

The committee had before it a number of people favoring the bill, representing various organizations for the betterment of child life, as well as the Director of the Census and the Commissioners of Labor and Education.

.   .   .   .   .

It is clear to us that already there exists gov-ernmental departments for the gathering of all necessary information desired by the advocates of this bill; in fact, much of it is being gathered. The Census is the one great statistical bureau of the Government, and deals with infant mortal-ity and the birth rate. The Bureau of Labor, if it is doing the work it was created to do, is investigating all subjects connected with the working people, children as well as adults, in-cluding dangerous occupations, employment, and diseases of the children of the working classes. The Bureau of Education is doing work and gathering statistics as to legislation affect-ing children in the several States, and such facts as bear upon the health, character, efficiency, and training of children.

Therefore the establishment of the bureau will mean a duplication of work. In addition to all that the National Government is doing along the lines indicated, every State in the Union is engaged in identically the same work. Nothing, perhaps, affecting the people has had from the legislatures of the several States during recent years so much attention as the welfare of the children, resulting in child-labor laws, the establishment of orphanages and reforma-tories. In fact, it appears that this whole move-ment for the benefit of children had its incep-tion in States and cities. We believe this to be specifically the work of the various States and that the entrance of the National Government into this field would be followed by a loss of interest and a cessation of effort on the part of the States. The bill goes into the domain of the health and character of its citizens, a field not only belonging to the States but one with which the States are better qualified to deal, for the reason that they can follow up the work of in-vestigation with necessary legislation.

---

3. Senate debates on Children's Bureau bill, 1911–1912

Congressional Record, 62 Cong., 2 Sess. (1911–1912), XLVIII, Pt. 1, 189; Pt. 2, 1247–1250, 1252–1254.

In 1910 a third set of Children's Bureau bills was proposed. One bill managed to pass the Senate only to die in the House. This bill differed from previous ones in that the Chil-dren's Bureau was placed in the Department of Commerce and Labor instead of the De-partment of the Interior. In April 1911, Sena-tor William Borah of Idaho introduced S. 252 establishing the Bureau in the Department of Commerce and Labor. This was the bill des-tined to become law. Although there was no opposition to the measure in committee, the old arguments were repeated during debate.

[The Children's Bureau would usurp functions of the family.]

[Senator Heyburn of Idaho.] I am not going to discuss the bill at length, but I am very loath to see the matter come to a vote under the cir-cumstances. It is one of those bills whose only recommendation is its title. Such bills are not infrequent. If you introduced a measure here, "*Resolved,* That the Congress of the United States is in favor of the eternal salvation of mankind," it would doubtless be passed because people would not dare to vote against it. Introduce a bill here for the protection of the children of the country and the title is such as to warn Senators against declaring themselves as not being in favor of that kind of legislation.

I had sincerely hoped that the Senator from Texas [Bailey] would develop the ideas he suggested, because I am in accord with his views so far as he has expressed himself. Personally I did not desire to enter upon the discussion of it, not feeling quite equal to it physically, but I must be equal to the performance of a duty when it is thrust upon me.

Briefly, Mr. President, I desire to suggest that this class of legislation has been growing upon us; that is to say, the frequency of and insistence for this class of legislation seem to be growing with accelerated speed. The jurisdiction established over the children of mankind in the beginning of the human race has worked out very well. It is in accord with the rules of nature. It is based not upon duty but upon the human instinct that establishes the principle upon which all duties rest. The mother needs no admonition to care for the child, nor does the father. The exceptions to that rule are such as those to the rule against the taking of human life. We have laws providing for the punishment of those who destroy human life, but as compared with the human family the instances in which it is necessary to invoke them are rare.

This has another element wrapped up within it that we ought not to lose sight of. While upon the face of this measure it merely provides for the taking of statistics, the accumulation of knowledge, yet we know from other measures which have been introduced, some from the same source, that it contemplates the establishment of a control, through the agencies of government, over the rearing of children. There are other measures now pending in committees of this body going much further, going to the extent of interference with the control of a parent over the child. I believe I read on Saturday a bill which has been introduced that prevents the employment of any child under 16

years of age, without any accompanying provision for the maintenance of the parents who, by reason of age or infirmity, can not provide for their own wants. That is what I call a poorhouse bill. It is a bill that would result in the necessity of aged or infirm parents going to the public almshouse, notwithstanding there were strong, hustling sons 14 and 15 years of age.

These suggestions arise out of any consideration that may be given to this class of legislation. It is the class of legislation that I object to, because as yet this bill does not enter into details to an extent which would enable one to criticize it, except upon the general principle involved in it. We have sometimes an oversupply of sympathy, or that which is supposed to be based upon sympathy for our fellow kind, sympathy for the children whose condition in life is not as favorable as that of some other children. Our sympathies are human; you can not avoid them; but those clothed with the responsibility of government must be on guard against being swept away on unsafe seas in legislation.

This is not a proper subject for legislation. It is a police measure. If children are not cared for within the recognized rules of humanity, or if they are neglected in violation of provisions of law, then the police department of the Government may deal with it.

A few weeks ago I read in one of the papers of this city an account of an attempt that was made to take children away from the parents, who were recently foreigners, because the committee did not approve of the manner in which the children were being raised and cared for. The development of the facts showed that the children were being reared and cared for according to the rules that had always existed among that class of people of that nationality. And yet the old saying that old bachelors' and old maids' children are better cared for than anybody else's arose in my mind as being a suggestion worthy of some consideration.

Now, Mr. President, anxious as I am that the sense of the Senate may be tested, I sincerely hope that no final action will be taken upon this class of legislation. No one can be more sympathetic than I am with the needs, the welfare, and the comfort of the children of the country, but I am not willing to substitute any other control for that of the parent. I would control the parents, if necessary, when they would violate the recognized rules of the domestic establishment. I would control the parents, but I would do it through the police laws of the land, the local laws. This is no question for the General Government to take up; it is a question of local legislation, if it is one for legislation at all.

.   .   .   .   .

Mr. President, when this question was before the Senate for consideration a few days ago I took advantage of the opportunity to express some views that I entertained upon it, and I am not now going to enlarge to any extent upon them or attempt to delay the disposition of this bill; but when the Senate of the United States is acting responsibly upon a question that I consider to be of the first importance, I want the RECORD to indicate where I stand in regard to it.

This measure is not new. It is something after the character of the arrangement of the Greeks before our era, when the State was the nursery of the children; and they carried it to very great extremes. Finally, one crank, following in the footsteps of another, conceived the idea that the children should be so mixed and so reared that it would be impossible for any particular person to claim any particular child or any particular child to recognize any particular person as its parent. We all know from reading the history of those times how utterly destructive it was of the sentiment of the household, which is the most sacred sentiment that actuates the human family and one out of which all other worthy sentiments arise.

Such a condition arose that there was no longer any home tie among that then great nation of people. No child recognized the sovereignty or the authority of the individual par-

ent; it only knew the Government; and heroic deeds are recited that were based upon that supposed meritorious condition. It resulted in the overthrow of the Greeks; it resulted in the depreciation of the sentiment of the family among those people; and one day their eyes opened and they realized that what they lacked in Greece was the home tie, and that without it they could have no concerted patriotism.

.   .   .   .

Is it merely for the education of the persons collecting it, to swell the cost of printing each year, by telling how many children are defective and how many children are ignorant and how many children are unprovided for? No; that is not the purpose.

I have a large correspondence in regard to this matter which tells the purpose of it, because those who favor it tell in their letters what they expect to do under it. I have had time since the former discussion of this measure to correspond with some of them. They are intelligent people. I asked them specifically what their object was in supporting this measure which they insisted I should vote for. I asked them what they hoped to accomplish. Their answer, if not in uniform speech, in spirit is that they hoped to be in a position to exercise jurisdiction over children who in their judgment are not being properly cared for. They want to become substitutes for the parents. Perhaps some of them may be parents. Many of them to my knowledge are not. But they are anxious to secure an opportunity, which they have not improved on their own part, of becoming the parents in fact of other people's children.

.   .   .   .

Mr. President, we are treading on pretty dangerous ground this morning by common consent. What is anticipated by this proposition that makes it so dangerous to send out — that some Government report is going to say that John Smith and his wife are brutal to their children or starving them or not providing for them or not educating them, and leave an indelible stamp upon the history and the records of the country that will follow the children, and their children, and so on. Is that the purpose? Are we going to start out to exploit the individual judgment and idiosyncrasies of parents at public expense?

It would become a school of slander. I suppose there is no hope of getting a little stay of execution in this case until the interested party can pray and repent.

[Uses and public availability of statistics compiled by the Bureau.]

Mr. OVERMAN. [North Carolina] Mr. President, it will no doubt be remembered that four years age we appropriated $300,000 for the purpose of investigating child labor and the children of the country. With that $300,000 they sent agents all over our country, into the homes of our people — the poor people in the mountains. They sent in their reports, and here to-day, in the document room, there are 13 volumes, and there are 5 more volumes yet unpublished. I want to say here to-day upon this floor that some of those reports were so obscene and so scandalous and outrageous that the Secretary of the Department of Commerce and Labor refused to print them. He had agents to revise them, to go over them. They went all over Tennessee and South and North Carolina, Georgia, and other Southern States preparing these scandalous reports.

.   .   .   .   .   .

Mr. BORAH. There may be things in those reports that Senators ought not to read, and I hope they will not, if they ought not to read them. But the fact remains that a vast amount of the facts were based upon real investigations and brought forth a number of things which were startling to the country. I do not know whether there are things in them that are untrue or not, but I know from investigations of my own, which have resulted since I took charge of this measure, a great many of those things reported to be true are true.

And if they are true, Mr. President, there is certainly nothing that we need to know more concerning than the condition, environment, and circumstances under which the children are growing up to manhood and womanhood.

I do not propose at this time to enter into a discussion of some of those facts and some of the conditions which have been revealed in many parts of this country. I have not tried to do that in this discussion. It is not my desire ;to reflect upon any community or any part of this country in the passage of this bill. But the fact remains that conditions do exist in this country which it would be shocking for the community, indeed, to know, and the bill is pressed for the purpose of bringing to light that condition of affairs in order that those conditions may be remedied.

Mr. BAILEY. [Texas] Remedied by whom?

Mr. BORAH. Remedied by the State and the people who make laws.

Mr. BAILEY. Leave it to the States, then.

Mr. BORAH. We will leave it to the States to enact the law, because the Government of the United States has so arranged that it must be done by the States, and we are perfectly content that it shall be done by the States. In one State of this Union, where they have an efficient child-labor bureau, a representative of that bureau told me in this city day before yesterday that the demands they have from different parts of the Union for facts and for information it is beyond their power to furnish. That from all over the Union those who are engaged in bettering the condition of the children of this country are calling for information, and yet the Government of the United States locks its Treasury against furnishing the facts as to the actual condition of children. Is there anyone who does not really want to know as to the truth of the reported fearful conditions? Is there anyone who does not care to remedy them if they really exist as reported or rumored?

.   .   .   .   .   .

Mr. DIXON. [Montana] I should like to ask the Senator from North Carolina if the opposition to the reports to which he refers did not come largely from the cotton-mill employers of his State?

.　　　.　　　.　　　.　　　.

Mr. OVERMAN. There was no opposition to these reports. It was opposition to some of the agents. There was a complaint as to the agents from Florida. I remember the Senator from Florida and myself received letters from certain interests saying that these long-haired men and short-haired women were coming down there and going into their mills, and they did not like it.

.　　　.　　　.　　　.　　　.

How would the Senator from Montana have liked for a Government agent to have gone down into his father's humble home, or his grandfather's in the days of the Revolution, investigating the condition of his sacred home? That is what I object to.

[The constitutionality of the Children's Bureau.]

Mr. BAILEY. [Texas] Mr. President, I was of the opinion that the Federal Government had authority to obtain in any reasonable way information which might enable its several departments to execute their functions, but it is a novel, and, I must be permitted to say, it is a dangerous doctrine that the Federal Government has the power or that it rests under the duty to obtain information which will enable the State governments to execute their functions.

I am of the opinion that the State of Idaho ought to know just as much, and only just as much, about its own people and their conditions as it chooses to know. I do not believe that the people of Texas, acting through their Representatives in this and the other House of Congress, have any right to force upon the people of Idaho an unwelcome knowledge of their condition. I would object to that if it were purely academic, if it were a mistaken philanthropy, and proceeded upon the false notion that it was their Christian duty to enlighten their brother; but I resent it all the more when it is made apparent by specific declaration that the very purpose of this bill, and the information which it seeks to accumulate, is to force the States of this Union to legislate in a given way.

.　　　.　　　.　　　.

Mr. BORAH. Do I understand the Senator to say, to force States to legislate?

Mr. BAILEY. I do not, of course, mean physical force.

Mr. BORAH. There can be no force, Mr. President, but public opinion in this matter. There can be no force other than that which arises by reason of the people being informed as to a condition which they desire to remedy, and that is the force which causes legislation and the legislation of a State.

.　　　.　　　.

Mr. BAILEY. Mr. President, it is the worst curse of American politics to-day that the Federal Government has absolutely bribed the States into a surrender of so many of their powers. The States want something done, and they choose for the Federal Government to pay the expense, and thus they consent for the Federal Government to do it, strangely forgetful of the fact that the Federal Government never possessed a dollar that it did not either take from the people of the States before it was spent or else obtain it upon the credit of the people of the States, whose labor or property must discharge the debt.

If there was some necromancy by which the Federal Government could obtain money and spend it without the people of the States having first or last to pay it, that suggestion would appeal to many who look to the cost rather than to the political consequence; but, as a matter of fact, the States, or rather the people of the States, must pay every dollar that the Federal Government spends; and the Federal Government, be it remembered, in collecting it pursues a system of taxation that aggravates the burden of the tax; and yet we go on, the State avoiding the expense and encouraging the Federal Government to incur it. If the people of Nebraska want this information and the people of Texas think they know enough without it, the people of Texas ought not to be required to contribute to the education of the people of Nebraska.

Or if there comes a question about which our people are deeply concerned, and we want information on it, let our own taxpayers pay for it; and we have no right to ask the people of Nebraska, who, perhaps, are not interested in the question or may know all they want to know about it, to bear the expense of educating the people of the State of Texas.

Mr. DIXON. Mr. President, I hope neither one of the pending amendments[1] will prevail. I have read the bill as carefully as I could, and I confess I can, under the terms of this bill, see no danger from publicity of any facts that the Government might collect which would jeopardize or hurt anybody on earth unless it be some person who has done something to which publicity should not be given.

Mr. BAILEY. Will the Senator from Montana permit me to ask him a question?

Mr. DIXON. Very gladly.

Mr. BAILEY. The Senator is a good lawyer. I will ask him to tell me upon what provision of the Constitution he rests this authority.

Mr. DIXON. I think on the same ground ——

Mr. BAILEY. The general-welfare clause?

Mr. DIXON. I think on the same ground upon which a thousand other measures have passed this body.

Mr. BAILEY. That is no answer at all.

Mr. DIXON. We expend five times this amount every year for the publication known as Diseases of the Horse, of which each Congressman gets a thousand copies.

Mr. BAILEY. But under what provision of the Constitution is this measure proposed?

Mr. DIXON. The general-welfare clause.

Mr. BAILEY. I knew it would come to this. This bill really undertakes to excuse itself on that ground because it is entitled "A bill to col-

lect statistics for the 'welfare' of the children."

Mr. DIXON. All right.

Mr. BAILEY. The Constitution says the general welfare.

Mr. DIXON. The children are the biggest part of the general welfare of this Nation. They are the coming citizenship who are to take the place of the men and women upon the stage of action at this time.

[Mr. BAILEY]

I want to agree with the Senator from Montana this far. If that provision for the general welfare is a substantive grant of power, then what I have said on the constitutionality of this question falls utterly to the ground. But I have the Supreme Court on my side of the question, and it has said more than once that it is not a substantive grant of power. That really is connected with the question of levying taxes, and the most that can be said is that the Congress has the power to levy taxes to provide for the general welfare.

Mr. DIXON. But we are wandering away from the purpose and object of the bill. If there is one crime of which modern commercialism stands convicted in the forum of public opinion, it is the abuse of child labor.

Now, I know there are valid objections in the minds of some Senators to the constitutionality of this bill, but the overwhelming opposition to the pending bill does not arise on any ground of implied unconstitutionality. It comes from the men of this country who are employing little children in the sweatshops and factories and coal mines and in the other great centers of modern commerce and industrialism in the country.

---

1. Senator John B. Works of California proposed an amendment on January 24, 1912, that "such published matter shall be furnished to legislative bodies and boards of health and health officers, but not to the general public, except on request."

---

4. Commissioner of Education opposes creation of Children's Bureau, 1912

P. P. Claxton, Commissioner of Education, to Walter L. Fisher, Secretary of the Interior, Jan. 3, 1912, in *Congressional Record,* 62 Cong., 2 Sess. (1912), Pt. 4, 4223.

In 1909 Elmer E. Brown, commissioner of education until 1911, testified in support of the Children's Bureau bill. His successor, P. P. Claxton, a southern educator who served as commissioner of education, 1911–1921, came out against a separate Children's Bureau just when the Borah measure was coming up for debate in the Senate.

I have read carefully all the correspondence on file in this Bureau in regard to the proposed Children's Bureau, the arguments submitted at the hearing May 12, 1911, before the Committee on Labor of the House of Representatives, and the report made August 14, 1911, by Senator Borah for the Committee on Education and Labor, and I find no reason to modify the opinion expressed in my letter of December 21, 1911, to wit: That the work specified in this bill to be done by the proposed Bureau can be done more effectively and with better results in the Bureau of Education, and that, therefore, the appropriation asked for the new bureau should be made to the Bureau of Education for the creation of one or more new divisions for some portions of this work and for strengthening the divisions already engaged on important parts of it.

In Section 2 of S.252, the purposes of the proposed Bureau are set forth as follows: "The said bureau shall investigate and report upon all matters pertaining to the welfare of children and child life, and shall especially investigate the questions of infant mortality, the birth rate, orphanage, juvenile courts, desertion, dangerous occupations, accidents and diseases of children, employment, legislation affecting children in the several States and Territories, and such other facts as have a bearing upon the welfare of children. The chief of said bureau may from time to time publish the results of these investigations."

The phrase "all matters pertaining to the welfare of children and child life" would cover the greater part of the work of the Bureau of Education, and as pointed out in my letter of December twenty-first, all the items specified, with one possible exception, are either direct or indirect problems of education with which the Bureau of Education now deals or should undertake at the earliest possible moment.

Permit me to submit the following reasons for my position in this matter:

1. The Bureau of Education is already doing much of the work specified in Senate bill 252. It collects and publishes statistics of school population and school attendance, summaries of school and child labor laws, facts as to school buildings, grounds, and sanitary arrangements, and statistics in regard to schools for exceptional children, including the deaf, dumb, blind, feeble-minded, and children of criminal tendencies. In its Annual Reports and in special bulletins it has frequently dealt in a special way with various phases of the subject of child welfare. Within the last few months there has been established in this Bureau a Division of School Hygiene and Sanitation to which is allotted for annual support $5,950 exclusive of the help given by clerks in the Correspondence Division. Estimates recently submitted by me and now embodied in the estimates of the Department of the Interior include an addition of $9,300 for this division. If this appropriation is made, this division will then have a total annual fund of $15,250, and will be able to do for the health of children all that can be done with a like fund in any bureau. School sanitation necessarily includes the health of children out of school. The same individual can not be a healthy child in school and a sick, diseased, or uncared for child out of school. School hygiene necessarily takes hold of the home. It happens that the chief of this division has in the last week submitted for my approval a letter which he is preparing to send to all the state and city boards of health, offering the cooperation and services of this division of the Bureau in all matters pertaining to the health of chil-

dren. He suggests especially that help be given by making this division a clearing house for all matters pertaining to the health of children.

2. For most of its information, except such as is gathered by the Census Bureau, the proposed bureau would have to depend largely on the agencies on which the Bureau of Education depends and with which the Bureau of Education is more closely allied than the proposed bureau would be. These agencies include school boards, superintendents, and principal of schools, teachers and truant officers, and school physicians. For carrying into effect any plans for improving the condition of children the dependence would be greater still. Other agencies could and would cooperate with the Bureau of Education just as readily as with the new bureau.

3. To unite in the Bureau of Education all things which pertain to the welfare of children would aid much in giving to the people the right conception of education, which is too often supposed to be merely the results of formal lessons in school.

I therefore renew my suggestion that the appropriation asked for the establishment and maintenance of a Children's Bureau be made to the Bureau of Education for such of the purposes specified in S.252 as are not now served by this Bureau.

---

5. Why the New York Society for the Prevention of Cruelty to Children opposes passage of Children's Bureau bill, 1912

a. John Lindsay charges interference

John D. Lindsay to Hon. David J. Lewis, Feb. 13, 1913, Grace Abbott Papers, University of Chicago.

As early as 1909 John D. Lindsay, a New York lawyer and president of the New York Society for the Prevention of Cruelty to Children, opposed the creation of a Children's

Bureau on the grounds that it would "inevitably interfere with the work of our Societies wherever they exist throughout the entire United States."

The New York Society for the
Prevention of Cruelty to Children
No. 297 Fourth Avenue.

New York, Feb. 13, 1913
Hon. David J. Lewis,
House of Representatives
Washington, D.C.

Dear Sir:

This Society is opposed to Senator Borah's Bill (S. 252; S. Rep. No. 141; H.R. 4694; Rep. No. 235) to establish a Federal Children's Bureau.

The Society has not the slightest objection to the fullest examination of its affairs by those entitled to make such examination. It does, however, object, on principle, to the intrusion of strangers, just as it resisted, some years ago, the attempt made by the State Board of Charities to supervise and regulate its work, and thus to usurp the functions of the Supreme Court, which alone has power under the laws of this State to visit and inspect such institutions as ours. Referring to this power of the Supreme Court, the Court of Appeals said (161 N.Y. 247): "It is *scarcely conceivable that* it was intended to subject the defendant to two distinct and different methods of state supervision."

If this be so, upon what principle can be defended the proposition to subject our Societies to *both state and federal investigation?* Such a system would lead, inevitably to confusion, friction and collision of authority, and the serious derangement of our work.

According to the Senate Report, the proposed Bureau can gather the desired information "more effectively than the States." But the federal constitution makes no provision for a national control over matters affecting the welfare of children, and even though it were true that no power is adequate to deal with the subject other than that of the national government, that, would not justify unconstitutional legislation. "If no such power has been granted" (by the Constitution to Congress) "none can be exercised." (Kansas *v.* Colorado, 206 U.S., 46, 92).

It is not [un]likely that at the start the representatives of the Bureau would be sensible and careful; but the possession of great power begets a proneness to use it to its fullest extent. And the ability of such a Bureau to interfere directly and immediate[ly] with our work, should it after a time grow arrogant from long use of its authority, is a danger too substantial to be lightly dismissed, especially when it is perceived that the only express limitation upon the power of the Bureau's representatives is that (incorporated by Senator Culberson's amendment) which forbids them to enter over the objection of the head of the family, a house occupied exclusively for a private residence.

If there is no intention of interfering with our work, how do you suppose it came about that whereas previous bills have expressly excepted the work and archives of societies for the prevention of cruelty to children from their operation, the present bill contains no such exception?

Sincerely yours,
John D. Lindsay
President.

b. Elbridge T. Gerry raises constitutional objections

New York Times, Jan. 28, 1912, p. 14.

OPPOSED TO FEDERAL CHILDREN'S BUREAU

Proposed New Government Department Not Needed, Say Child Welfare Workers.

WOULD FURNISH SINECURES

Senator Borah's Bill an invasion of the Rights of Each State, Declares Commodore Gerry.

The bill for a Federal Children's Bureau, presented by Senator Borah of Idaho, which is to come up for final passage in the Senate at Washington on Tuesday, has developed considerable opposition to its provisions among the officials of various child protective societies in this city and elsewhere. It is attacked by some of them as unnecessary, an illegal encroachment on the police powers of the several States and likely merely to furnish sinecures for well paid but useless commissioners at Washington, who will gather statistics concerning the conditions of children throughout the country without giving power to the Federal authorities so constituted to bring about practical results on the findings of their reports.

•   •   •   •   •

Elbridge T. Gerry, founder and counsel for the New York Society for the Prevention of Cruelty to Children, declared several days ago that there is no need of the passage of such a bill, and that its enforcement is a matter belonging under the Constitution to each State.

"The scheme is a dangerous one," he said. "Practically it creates an additional department of the United States Government for the purpose of dictating to States the laws they should pass for their own government on the subject of their children. Connected with this there is a chief with a definite salary, who apparently is to advise and direct the whole subject everywhere, so that the States are to be guided and governed by this political appointee in disregard of the right of each sovereign State to regulate its own police powers by appropriate legislation within its geographical limits. To place such a power in the hands of a governmental department located at Washington, and to expect it to be enforced by a political appointee, who of necessity cannot be familiar with every statute in every part of the Union, is in reality to invade rights which have existed since the foundation of the National Government and are by its Constitution intrusted to the individual States of the United States of America.

"Centralization of power as contemplated in such a department and official would certainly be most dangerous. It would lead to discord and confusion in the administration of justice. It would open avenues of escape to those who when detected seek for loopholes in the law through which they may escape condemnation and punishment. To utilize the prevention of cruelty for political patronage and for personal capital is to lower the whole moral tone of the Nation.

"The vagueness of the terms of the bill is a fundamental difficulty. It is an attempt to build up a new system of legislation, leaving the construction of its terms either to the head of a department, which is to enforce the law, or to the courts having jurisdiction over the subjects which it affects.

"The bill seems to have been framed, unconsciously perhaps, on the Sherman anti-trust law, using vague words and leaving it to the courts to guess what those words mean, how they are to be applied and what powers are conferred by their use in the statutes using them. No provision is made for the enforcement of the act by any one.

"Apart from the salaries specified, which are susceptible to enlargement at any time by subsequent legislation, there is no provision as to who is to pay or furnish the money to pay the incidental expenses for seeking the information which it is the apparent object of the bill to obtain. Suppose, for instance, the chief of the proposed bureau in the Department of Commerce and Labor, as he is called in the bill, directs the adoption by a society of an elaborate system of bookkeeping by an expert. Is the society to be penalized, and perhaps a large amount of its funds absorbed in the expenses attending the furnishing of such accounts to the examiner? What remedy is provided for any person or so-

ciety refusing to comply with the orders of the chief, or what redress exists if unable to do so, and in what courts and by what process?"

---

c. Lillian Wald's reply to the S.P.C.C., 1912

Lillian Wald, letter to the editor, *New York Times,* Feb. 1, 1912.

February 1st, 1912.

New York Times,
    Broadway and 42nd St.,

Dear Sirs: —

The "Times" of Sunday printed a lengthy article upon Commodore Elbridge T. Gerry's and Mr. John D. Lindsay's criticisms of the proposed Federal Children's Bureau. The article is headlined " 'New Government Department Not Needed', Say Child Welfare Workers."

.   .   .   .

So far as the friends of the children have been able to discover opposition to the Bill among the children's societies has been confined to Commodore Gerry and his personal associates, and not to his society, as among its directors have been men who have worked for the creation of the Bureau.

.   .   .   .

In the "Times" of Sunday a speech made by Commodore Gerry was quoted by Mr. Lindsay in part as follows:

"Bequests now made to the Society for Prevention of Cruelty individually would instead be left to this great central National bureau, to be squandered at its pleasure [on] 'educational' work and fat salaries to the deserving. Useless statistics would be piled up by the millions and our great glorious work of rescue and prevention obscured. I cannot well conceive of a plan framed better than this to destroy our usefulness."

I cannot believe that Commodore Gerry or Mr. Lindsay have read or studied the purposes of the Bill with open minds, but they fearing some menace to the Society for which they have labored so long . . . see objections which do not exist and which could not possibly occur under the provisions of the Bill.

At least they stand opposed to the convictions of the progressive child welfare workers from Maine to California.

Very truly yours,
Lillian D. Wald

---

6. The Children's Bureau bill becomes law, 1912

U.S. *Statutes,* 62 Cong., 2 Sess. (1911–12), Pt. 1, chap. 73, pp. 79–80.

On January 31, 1912, after eight hours of debate Borah's bill passed the Senate. The vote was 54–20. Advocates of the measure believed the last-minute support of Elihu Root of New York was an important factor in the victory.[1] The bill passed the House on April 2 and President Taft signed it on April 9, 1912. The Bureau, originally placed in the Department of Commerce and Labor, was transferred to the newly formed Department of Labor in March 1913.

Be it enacted by the Senate and House of Representatives of the United States of America in Congress assembled, That there shall be established in the Department of Commerce and Labor a bureau to be known as the Childrens' Bureau.

1. "I wept (and felt like an idiot!) when Root came forward and fought for it. For I saw it meant the tide had turned and we had won." Owen R. Lovejoy to Lillian Wald, Jan. 31, 1912, Grace Abbott Papers.

SECTION 2. That the said bureau shall be under the direction of a chief, to be appointed by the President, by and with the advice and consent of the Senate, and who shall receive an annual compensation of five thousand dollars. The said bureau shall investigate and report to said department upon all matters pertaining to the welfare of children and child life among all classes of our people, and shall especially investigate the questions of infant mortality, the birth rate, orphanage, juvenile courts, desertion, dangerous occupations, accidents and diseases of children, employment, legislation affecting children in the several States and Territories. But no official, or agent, or representative of said bureau shall, over the objection of the head of the family, enter any house used exclusively as a family residence. The chief of said bureau may from time to time publish the results of these investigations in such manner and to such extent as may be prescribed by the Secretary of Commerce and Labor.

SEC. 3. That there shall be in said bureau, until otherwise provided for by law, an assistant chief, to be appointed by the Secretary of Commerce and Labor, who shall receive an annual compensation of two thousand four hundred dollars; one private secretary to the chief of the bureau, who shall receive an annual compensation of one thousand five hundred dollars; one statistical expert, at two thousand dollars; two clerks of class four; two clerks of class three; one clerk of class two; one clerk of class one; one clerk, at one thousand dollars; one copyist, at nine hundred dollars; one special agent, at one thousand four hundred dollars; one special agent, at one thousand two hundred dollars, and one messenger at eight hundred and forty dollars.

SEC. 4. That the Secretary of Commerce and Labor is hereby directed to furnish sufficient quarters for the work of this bureau at an annual rental not to exceed two thousand dollars.

SEC. 5. That this Act shall take effect and be in force from and after its passage.

B. THE CHILDREN'S BUREAU IN OPERATION

The major administrative problems facing the Children's Bureau during its first twenty years were inadequate appropriations, defining relations with other government agencies such as the Bureau of Education and the Public Health Service, and warding off efforts to remove maternal and child health functions from its jurisdiction. Materials relating to the substantive work of the Bureau are included in the sections on dependent children, child labor, juvenile delinquency, and child health.

The chiefs

1. Jane Addams and Julius Rosenwald recommend the appointment of Julia Lathrop, 1912

Telegram from Jane Addams and Julius Rosenwald to Lillian Wald, April 12, 1912, Grace Abbot Papers, University of Chicago.

As chief of the Children's Bureau from 1912 to 1921, Miss Lathrop (1858–1932) was the first woman to be appointed by the President and confirmed by the Senate as head of a statutory federal bureau. Miss Lathrop, an associate of Jane Addams at Hull House, was strongly recommended for the post by the National Child Labor Committee, whose assistance in finding a suitable person to fill the position had been solicited by Charles Nagel, secretary of the Department of Commerce and Labor. "She had statesmanlike vision, ability to work out careful plans, and the patience to carry through constructive programs." [1]

1. Edith Abbott in *Dictionary of American Biography*, XI, Supplement One, ed. Harris E. Starr (New York, 1944), p. 486.

April 12, 1912

Chicago, Ill. 12
Miss Wald 265 Henry St.
Miss Lathrop would not consider seeking the appointment but would serve if the President desired. Miss Addams feels that she is undoubtedly better equipped than any one so far suggested. We cannot conceive of a more ideal appointment considering executive ability, sympathy, deliberate, sane judgement combined of Charities with the Chicago Juvenile Court, with years of experience on the State Board and as graduate trustee of Vassar College. In our opinion, woman's ability could have no better demonstration than would result from her appointment. Please communicate this promptly to other members of the committee.

Jane Addams
Julius Rosenwald

2. Grace Abbott replaces Julia Lathrop

Harriet Taylor Upton to Warren G. Harding, Aug. 8, 1921, Harding Papers, Ohio Historical Society.

Miss Abbott (1878–1939), a Hull House resident, joined the staff of the Children's Bureau in 1917 as director of the Child Labor Division. She served as chief from 1921 to 1934. Mrs. Upton (1884–1945) was active in the woman suffrage movement and at this time served on the executive committee of the Republican National Committee.

August 8, 1921.

My dear Mr. President:
You will remember I talked with you some months ago about Miss Lathrop's successor. At that time she wanted to leave the Bureau. She has been there a long time and really wants a rest, besides she is frank enough to say that

Miss Grace Abbott can direct the work there better now than she can. I urged her not to resign at that time. She had framed the Maternity Bill and she had to be here to boost it, and she certainly has had a strenuous life with it.

Mr. Winslow, Chairman of the Interstate Commerce Committee of the House, who is dreadfully opposed to the Maternity Bill,[1] is very antagonistic toward Miss Lathrop. He cannot hold out against the pressure in the Committee and of course the Bill will go through the House if it gets by Congressman Philip Campbell of the Rules Committee.

Now, Miss Lathrop has come to me again and wants to know if it is not time for her to resign. She knows that I try to hold the Party and the women together and she naturally takes my advice. I have told her frankly that I believe this is the time. She has done all she possibly can for the Maternity Bill and if she should resign now Mr. Winslow would pretend that since she is out of the way that he would have less objection [to] the Bill. Of course this is just an excuse but we ought to take advantage of it.

Furthermore, the Secretary of Labor is ready to accept Miss Lathrop's resignation and is ready to appoint Miss Abbott, but the matter has been hanging fire so long that both of them I think wonder if you remember about it. In other words, Miss Lathrop does not want to resign unless she is sure of Miss Abbott's appointment, and, the women do not want her to resign unless Miss Abbott is sure of the appointment.

You know that I never ask you for appointments but I am sure you also know that it is my bounden duty to watch these things and I am perfectly sure that Miss Abbott is the woman for the place.

Sincerely yours,
Harriet Taylor Upton

Hon. Warren G. Harding
The White House

1. On the Sheppard-Towner Act, see below, Part Seven, Chap. III, sec C.

Appropriations

1. Crippling effect of low appropriation, 1914

Congressional Record, 63 Cong., 2 Sess. (1914), LI, Pt. 7, pp. 6710–6711.

The first appropriation for the Children's Bureau was $25,640. In 1914 the Bureau requested an increase to $165,000 to allow employment of additional personnel, printing costs, and other expenses. The Appropriations Committee denied the request and again allotted $25,640. On the House floor Rep. M. Clyde Kelly of Pennsylvania made an unsuccessful effort to obtain a larger appropriation.

Mr. KELLY of Pennsylvania . . . The Children's Bureau is absolutely crippled by the appropriation made in this act, the sum provided being so small in comparison with the work before this bureau that it is absolutely pitiful. The officials of the bureau came before the committee and showed that by reasonable computation the proper conduct of the bureau will require $165,000, and showed how it could be used. I submit, Mr. Chairman, that this question is too important to be completely ruled out by a point of order without full and fair consideration of its merits. The establishment of this Children's Bureau two years ago was the first recognition on the part of the Federal Government that the children of the Nation are worthy of attention. That, in spite of the fact that one of the reasons that caused the Pilgrim Fathers to adventure to America, was the desire to protect their little ones from grinding toil.

This reason, quoted from the memorial drawn up by these founders of a new civilization, is as follows:

That many of our children, through the extreme necessity that was upon them, although of the best disposition and graciously inclined, and willing to bear their part of their parents' burdens, were often-times so oppressed with their heavy labors that, although their spirits were free and willing, yet their bodies bowed under the weight of the same and became decrepit in their very youth, and the vigor of their strength was consumed in the very bud.

Yet its was 292 years after that time that the Nation they made possible officially discovered children and recognized them as national assets, worthy of care and protection.

Even then the Children's Bureau was not established without meeting the bitter opposition of the powers that thrive at the expense of humanity. Successfully brought into being, it has met and still meets with determined opposition, and it has been handicapped in many ways. In spite of every obstacle, however, it has done a great work, and it deserves the support of every patriotic legislator and citizen. Any attempt to impair its efficiency and mar its work by insufficient funds merits the condemnation of every American who has regard for the welfare of the Nation in the future.

Why should this bureau be so severely crippled by an appropriation of $25,000 when it is admitted that the efficient conduct of its work requires $165,000? This Congress is not wont to be so parsimonious in matters of property. Why become so economical in matters of human life? This body has already appropriated $600,000 for dealing with hog cholera. It has appropriated $400,000 to eradicate the tick among southern cattle. It has provided $375,-000 for the study of the cotton-boll weevil. This very bill carries $293,000 for the work of the Bureau of Standards.

All these concern the things of money and materials. But for the study of the things of human life, the protection of childhood, this small sum is deemed sufficient. It is less than 1 cent for every 12 children in this country under the age of 15 years. By this method of figuring a hog or a cow or a bale of cotton is more valuable than a child.

Mr. Chairman, the most priceless asset of this Nation is not its cattle nor swine nor cotton crop. It is the army of children, 30,000,000 strong, under the age of 15 years, who live in this land of ours. With them rests the future of the Republic. Their health will determine that of future generations. Their character will determine that of the American citizenship to come. Their education and their morality will set the mark for the future. The work done for the children of to-day is work done for the men and women of to-morrow.

I maintain that those who oppose granting this all-important bureau ample funds either do it through ignorance of the vital importance of its work or they are the defenders of those who profit from the exploitation of childhood in America. I submit that no quibble over the technical construction of a rule will furnish an excuse for those who would cripple this bureau when they face the aroused public conscience of this Nation.

---

2. Senate debate on Children's Bureau appropriation, 1917

Congressional Record, 64 Cong., 2 Sess. (1917), LIV, Pt. 2, pp. 1667–1668, 1672–1675, 1679–1680.

Every time the Children's Bureau appropriation was debated, southern Democrats and some New Englanders mounted an opposition to it on the grounds of constitutionality and efficiency. Its defenders were usually midwestern Progressives. In this debate, Senators William Kenyon of Iowa and William Borah of Idaho defended the Bureau against John D. Works, a California Republican and Nathan P. Bryan, Democratic senator from Florida.

[The educational campaigns of the Children's Bureau justify maintaining the appropriation]

Mr. KENYON [R–Ia.] Mr. President, I tried very briefly before adjournment on yesterday to review one branch of the work of the Children's Bureau. The only argument presented for reducing the appropriation as the committee has proposed to reduce it was that the work of the Children's Bureau duplicated the work of some of the other departments of the Government. It is perhaps true that the Health Bureau and the Educational Bureau have done some work along the same line as has the Children's Bureau, but while the Children's Bureau has dealt somewhat with the question of infant mortality and the medical relations thereto, its particular purpose seems to have been to investigate as to the social and economic questions involved, as I pointed out last night, and the relationship between poverty and low wages and infant mortality. If, however, there has been any duplication of work, the duplication comes through the action of the Bureau of Education and the Health Bureau. The particular studies along the line of infant mortality and of maternal mortality, as I understand, were practically commenced by the Children's Bureau, and subsequently these other bureaus commenced some studies along those lines. In any event, however, where there has been apparently a conflict approaching or a duplication of work there has been coordination between these different bureaus.

.   .   .   .   .

This investigation and report [C. B. Annual Rept., 1913] along these lines of maternal mortality show that the public neglect is due to ignorance, and this board is awakening a healthy public sentiment. It was stated on the floor of the other House — I do not know that I have a right to refer to that, but I refer to it in no critical way — by some Representative that mothers' clubs have been organized in his district to study these questions; that they were going directly to this bureau to secure their information; and that it had been of great help to them in an educational way.

I know, Mr. President, that it is easy to make fun of these rural studies; it is easy to laugh at old-maid experts going out to teach people how

to raise babies, and I realize that a good deal of ridicule can be heaped upon the proposition of caring for babies in this way; but if in any way by any action of the Government we can reduce this death rate by investigation, by education, or by publicity, it is a great work.

.   .   .   .   .

Out of this, too, has come what is called the "national baby week," purposed to popularize the study of these matters; and if Senators will examine the map which is in the report they will find that there were over 2,000 of these celebrations last year.

Moving pictures, lectures, competitions, in which mothers answered questions concerning the welfare of children, clubs of women, and other educational efforts along these lines have resulted in many places establishing visiting nurses, pure-milk stations, and other things conducive to the children's welfare.

.   .   .   .   .

[The Children's Bureau duplicates work done elsewhere]

Mr. WORKS [R–Cal.] Mr. President, I voted against the bill establishing the Children's Bureau because, as I believed and understood, the very work that was expected to be done by the Children's Bureau was already being done by other departments and bureaus of the Government. I think that is equally true to-day. We are constantly duplicating not only the work that is done by the departments and bureaus of the Government, but we are duplicating by the work of the Government what is being done by the States, and are spending millions of dollars unnecessarily and that might just as well be thrown away.

Perhaps I am as much interested in the welfare of the children of this country as most people. I think I recognize as fully as almost anyone the obligation that rests on the Government of the United States to protect its people in their morals, in their health, and in their social relations. Therefore I am not disposed at any time to be overeconomical when it comes to a question of this kind. But I have had something to say in the Senate very lately about the extravagance of the Government in many directions. This is one of them.

.   .   .   .   .

But what is the condition in the District of Columbia, Mr. President, with all these forces that should be at work, if they are not? We have places in the District of Columbia that are a disgrace to this country. I have called attention to it time and again, and I feel like calling attention to it whenever I have the opportunity. What are these people doing, the Children's Bureau or the Public Health Service or any of these organizations, for the children who live in those places? I believe in doing something more than merely taking and publishing statistics, making an investigation and dealing theoretically with these important questions. I believe they ought to be dealt with practically, not theoretically.

Mr. President, all this may be done, it may be capably done, it may be thoroughly and competently done, by the Children's Bureau. If so, that work should be transferred to the Children's Bureau so that it might be done by that bureau, and by it alone. There is no reason why it should be done by three different departments or bureaus of the Government, duplicating the work that is to be done. There is not any excuse for it at all.

.   .   .   .   .

I think one of the difficulties about the Children's Bureau is that it is trying to do pretty much everything else except that for which it was organized; going into the question of widow's pensions and various other things that ought to have no connection with the work of that bureau at all.

If that work could be separated, Mr. President, so that the work of the Children's Bureau could be confined to the condition of the children and to their benefit, and take it away

from other departments of the Government, then I could see why these appropriations ought to be made for the purpose of carrying on that work; but so long as at least three different bureaus are doing exactly the same thing, and appropriations are being made for all of them to triplicate the work, it seems to be unreasonable, and that it ought not to be done.

Mr. President, I have not said this in any sense in antagonism of the Children's Bureau, or in antagonism of any efforts that may be made by any bureau of the Government to better the condition of the children of this country—far from it — but the Government of the United States ought in the first instance to keep itself within its own jurisdiction and not be doing the work that belongs to the States. Then, again, it ought not to be doing it by three bureaus doing exactly the same thing, but it ought to be confined to one of them. For that reason I think it is a wise thing to begin to curtail these appropriations.

.   .   .   .   .

Mr. BRYAN [D–Fla.] Mr. President, the item under discussion reads as follows:

To investigate and report upon matters pertaining to the welfare of children and child life, and especially investigate the questions of infant mortality, $72,120.

.   .   .   .   .

Much of what has been said would lead one uninformed to believe that this appropriation was principally for the benefit in a practical way of child diseases. These people will stay right in Washington, and the clerks will be drawing clerks' salaries. I do not think it makes much difference whether that work, if it is being done at all, is being done by a set of clerks in the Public Health Service or by a set of clerks in the Children's Bureau. The work done is the publication of pamphlets.

Here [exhibiting] are some pamphlets gotten out by the Public Health Service. Let us see if there is any duplication. The Secretary of Labor says that the duplication is almost without limit. I suppose he knows as much about it as does the chief of the bureau under him. I read his own language in the time of the Senator from California [Mr. WORKS], and I will now read it again. The nature of this overlapping between the Public Health Service and the Children's Bureau "in the same fields of endeavor is of such a character that there is practically no limit to the duplication and resultant likelihood of confusion unless there is complete and harmonious adjustment of the respective activities."

.   .   .   .   .

The amount asked for in this amendment is practically to enable the Children's Bureau to double its office force and to employ people to stay here in Washington, not to go about in the country to investigate children's diseases in the homes of the children, but to write learned pamphlets upon how those diseases can be prevented.

.   .   .   .   .

[Julia Lathrop denies duplication of effort]

Mr. KENYON. Mr. President, so much has been said this afternoon about duplication that I desire to have read and placed in the RECORD a memorandum from Miss Lathrop covering, I think pretty clearly, that question. I ask the Secretary to read it.

The VICE PRESIDENT. The Secretary will read as requested.

The Secretary read as follows:

RELATION BETWEEN THE CHILDREN'S BUREAU AND OTHER GOVERNMENT BUREAUS WITH THE PUBLIC HEALTH SERVICE

When the Children's Bureau began operations in the autumn of 1912, I called upon the head of the Public Health Service to make sure that there was no duplication of work on the part of the Children's Bureau. I explained the bureau's purpose to undertake a study of the social and economic factors surrounding infant mortality. I was assured by the head of the Public Health Service that such a study had never been made, and that it would be valuable, and that the Public Health Service had no purpose to undertake it. It was also fully explained in the beginning to the Public Health Service that the bureau purposed publishing a series of popular pamphlets upon the care of children, beginning with one upon prenatal care. It was my distinct understanding that into this field of popular instruction the Public Health Service had no purpose to enter and cordially approved the work of the Children's Bureau. Cooperation was offered, and the pamphlet upon prenatal care profited by the advice of the Public Health Service.

.   .   .   .   .

A year later I learned by chance that the Public Health Service had in proof a popular pamphlet upon the care of babies. As the pamphlet of the Children's Bureau on infant care was then well under way, was much fuller than that of the Public Health Service, differed in presentation, and formed part of the series originally discussed with the Public Health Service, it was published as planned.

As a matter of fact, the call for this type of literature is so great that the Children's Bureau publications, and those of the Public Health Service jointly, are not sufficient to meet the demand. The regrettable circumstances is that it should be made to appear that the Children's Bureau deliberately duplicated work undertaken by the Public Health Service, when in fact, although the subject was especially assigned to it by law, the Children's Bureau undertook no work without the fullest consultation with the Public Health Service, and the assurance that the Public Health Service had not done and did not purpose to do the same work.

WITH THE PUBLIC HEALTH SERVICE AND THE BUREAU OF EDUCATION

It should be noted, however, that a successful piece of cooperation had been carried on between the Public Health Service, the Bureau of Education, and the Children's Bureau. In a study of the feeble-minded in Delaware, in which the three bureaus have joined with the Delaware educational authorities, the Children's Bureau has made the social and family studies of the feeble-minded. The Public Health Service has furnished an expert for the mental examinations. I can not see how work could be more economically done. The Children's Bureau has never attempted to establish a service of medical experts upon feeble-mindedness. On the other hand it has a competent service of field agents. In this connection I inclose a preliminary summary of part of the Deleware report.

WITH THE CENSUS BUREAU

The special statistical inquiries of the Children's Bureau are necessarily based upon census figures, and the bureau is under great obligation to the census authorities for invaluable cooperation. At the suggestion of Dr. Wilbur, vital statistician of the Census Bureau, the Children's Bureau has carried on in cooperation with the census for the last three years a continuous campaign for better birth registration in which thousands of volunteers have helped.

WITH THE DEPARTMENT OF AGRICULTURE

The bureau has furnished large numbers of publications on the care of children for circulation by the county agents of the Department of Agriculture.

Functions

1. Program and achievements of the Children's Bureau, 1912–1922

Grace Abbott, *Ten Years' Work for Children* (Washington, D.C., 1923), pp. 2–10.

[Infant mortality studies]

In her first annual report Miss Lathrop pointed out that it is the "final purpose of the bureau to serve all children, to try to work out the standards of care and protection which shall give to every child his fair chance in the world." This meant that, in addition to consideration of the problems of the various agencies that specialized in the care of those unfortunate groups of children which are found in every community — the neglected, dependent, delinquent, and defective — there must be a working relationship with the child-caring agencies and also with the great groups of people in the country who are concerned with the community problems of child care, and the still larger numbers of individual parents who are asking for help in the problems connected with their own children.

The subject of infant mortality was selected for the bureau's initial inquiry because it was of fundamental social importance and of popular interest, and could be made in small units and the conclusions given to the public as each unit was completed. It was determined that this inquiry should reverse the usual method of studying infant mortality from the death records; that it should begin with birth records and follow each child through the first year of his life, or such part of the first year as he lived. A schedule was prepared for this inquiry which would give a picture of the social, civic, and industrial conditions of the families studied, together with a careful history of the baby's growth with special attention to feeding. As the questions were necessarily intimate and difficult, only women agents were employed in securing the replies. The first study was made in Johnstown, Pa., and subsequently in nine other industrial towns and cities, including Baltimore, Md., and Gary, Ind. Studies of the care available to mothers and infants in typical rural communities of 12 States of the South, Middle West, and West were also made.

The coincidence of a high infant mortality rate with low earnings, poor housing, the employment of the mother outside the home, and large families was indicated in all these studies. They all showed that there is great variation in the infant-mortality rates, not only in different parts of the United States but in different parts of the same State and the same city, town, or rural disrict. These differences were found to be caused by different population elements, widely varying social and economic conditions, and differences in appreciation of good prenatal and infant care and the facilities available for such care.

Evidence of the methods used in successful efforts to reduce infant mortality was also assembled. The instruction of mothers through infant-welfare centers, public-health nurses, and popular bulletins as to the proper care of children, the value of breast-feeding, the importance of consulting a doctor upon the first evidence of disease, everywhere brought substantial decreases in deaths.

Along with these first studies of infant mortality, popular bulletins on prenatal care, infant care, and child care were published. Popular bulletins on other subjects have also been published from time to time, but these three were not only immediately useful but the demand for them has increased each year. Since July 1, 1922, more than 600,000 of these bulletins were distributed, although many requests can not be filled.

In the period from 1915 to 1921, there was a substantial reduction in the infant-mortality rate in the birth-registration area of the United States, but five nations still had lower rates than the American. A study of vital statistics showed that little progress was being made in reducing the deaths in early infancy, including deaths caused by premature birth, congenital debility, and injuries at birth, which all have maternal causes. Consideration of infant mortality therefore inevitably led to the question of the care

mothers are receiving before, during, and after childbirth. Unfortunately, the maternal death rate in the United States has increased rather than decreased, so that the American rate for 1920 is the highest among all the nations for which recent statistics are available. With an annual loss of approximately 200,000 babies and 20,000 mothers, the need of extending on a national scale the successful local efforts to provide better care for mothers and infants was obvious.

[Responsibilities under Sheppard-Towner Act, 1921]

In her annual report for 1917, Miss Lathrop called attention to the method of cooperation between the national and local government adopted by Great Britain in the so-called grants in aid for maternity and infant welfare work, and suggested that the United States should use the well-established principle of Federal aid as a basis of National and State cooperation in reducing the unnecessarily high death rate among mothers and babies in the United States. The Sheppard-Towner Act for the promotion of the welfare and hygiene of maternity and infancy, which became a law on November 23, 1921, is in all essentials the same as the plan for the "public protection of maternity and infancy" submitted by Miss Lathrop in 1917. This act authorizes an annual appropriation of $1,240,000 for a five-year period, of which not to exceed $50,000 may be expended by the Children's Bureau for administrative purposes and for the investigation of maternal and infant mortality, the balance to be divided among the States accepting the act as follows: $5,000 unmatched to each State, and an additional $5,000 to each State if matched; the balance to be allotted among the several States on the basis of population, and granted if matched.

The act intends that the plan of work shall originate in the State and be carried out by the State. A Federal Board of Maternity and Infant Hygiene, composed of the Chief of the Children's Bureau, the Surgeon General of the United States Public Health Service, and the United States Commissioner of Education, may approve or disapprove State plans, but the act provides that the plans must be approved by the Federal board if "reasonably appropriate and adequate to carry out its purposes." The national administration of the act is immediately in charge of the maternity and infancy division of the Children's Bureau, of which Dr. Anna E. Rude is director.

Forty States have by legislative action accepted the terms of the act — all except Maine, Vermont, Massachusetts, Connecticut, Rhode Island, Illinois, Kansas, and Louisiana. With this very general approval of the measure, there was also some opposition. Suits were brought by the State of Massachusetts, and by a taxpayer to test the constitutionality of the measure. A decision handed down by the United States Supreme Court in June, 1923, to which there was not a dissenting vote, has ended this controversy, so the work can be pushed without danger of its suddenly coming to an end on the ground of its unconstitutionality.

The plans under which the States are operating under this act vary greatly, but everywhere, as a result of the widespread discussion of the whole question of maternity and child care and of the measures initiated in the States, real progress is being made.

[Child labor and related activities]

In addition to the maternity and infancy division, the bureau has a child hygiene division, an industrial division, and a division of social service, whose field of research includes the children in need of special care, the dependent, neglected, and delinquent children; a statistical division which is in charge of the statistical work of the bureau and also makes investigations which are primarily statistical; an editorial division; and the beginnings of a recreation division.

It is not possible to enumerate all the work done by these divisions, but some examples will indicate the type of studies that have been made in these four or five categories. In addition to its investigations of infant mortality in selected areas in the United States, the bureau has investigated the health problems of children of preschool age, their physical status, mental habits, nutrition, and community methods used for improving the care of these young children. The methods of child care in New Zealand, which has the enviable record of the lowest infant-mortality rate, have been investigated. The laws relating to child labor, juvenile courts, mothers' pensions, children born out of wedlock, have been analyzed and published in tabular form; those on sex offenses against children, importation and exportation of children, and adoption will appear shortly. In the field of child labor the most important studies include the industrial home work of children, child labor and the work of mothers in oyster and shrimp canning communities on the Gulf coast, and child labor in an anthracite coal community. A series of studies of rural child labor, particularly with reference to its effect on school attendance, is now being published. In this series work in the sugar-beet and tobacco fields, at cotton picking, in the truck gardens of the East, in the corn and wheat belt, and in hop picking on the Pacific coast, will be included. A report on vocational guidance and another on children in street trades will shortly be issued.

Studies of juvenile delinquency and juvenile courts, of illegitimacy as a problem in child welfare, of the methods of administering so-called mothers' pensions laws, and of the care of dependent children, have also been published. Most of these are schedule studies of individual children, but some are analyses by experts in their respective fields of methods used in various communities.

The Children's Bureau has had the responsibility for one piece of administrative work in addition to the administration of the maternity and infancy act to which reference has already been made. This was the first Federal child labor law, passed in 1916, 10 years after it was first introduced in Congress.[1]

. . . . .

In the course of the inspections and issuance of work permits much material of general social interest was discovered, which demonstrated the vicious circle of child labor, illiteracy, bodily feebleness, and poverty, as almost never before.

[Birth registration, Baby Week, and Children's Year]

From the beginning, the bureau has had the cooperation of the great national women's organizations of the country, as well as the professional organizations in the field of child care. Several very important pieces of work have been undertaken, either in cooperation with the women or at their request. The first piece of work of this sort was a campaign for birth registration.

The annual reports of the bureau record the progress of this cooperation. In 1900, 1,500 club women in 17 States were reported to be helping. In the report of 1915, the chief of the bureau recorded 222 committees formed in 24 States. In 1916, this movement was expanded into National Baby Week campaigns, the plans for which were worked out with the General Federation of Women's Clubs with the idea of making the week a period of education and demonstration which would lead to the initiation of permanent health activities.

1. This act prohibited the shipment in interstate or foreign commerce of the products of (1) a mine or quarry in which, within 30 days prior to the removal of said products therefrom, children under 16 years of age had been employed or permitted to work; and (2) a mill, cannery, factory, workshop, or manufacturing establishment in which, within 30 days prior to the removal of the products therefrom, children under 14 years of age had been employed, or children between 14 and 16 years of age had been employed, or permitted to work more than 8 hours a day, or 6 days a week, or before 6 A.M. or after 7 P.M. It became effective Sept. 1, 1917. [Note in Abbott, *Ten Years' Work*.]

During the year 1916, 257 communities were organized in 24 States. In 1916 there were 2,083 Baby Weeks celebrated and every State in the Union took part in the movement.

In 1917, the clubs had many permanent results to report. The following year, when the United States was faced with the problems which came with the war, and when, through the women's committee of the Council of National Defense, State and local committees were being organized throughout the country, the Children's Bureau was asked to cooperate in a child-welfare program. It was decided to call the second year of this country's participation in the war Children's Year, and to set forth a simple national program of child welfare. Four items were included in the program: Public protection of maternity and infancy; mother's care for older children; enforcement of all child-labor laws and full schooling for all children of school age; and recreation. In order to make the movement educational and at the same time furnish a basis for a practical follow-up program in child health, it was decided to conduct a weighing and measuring test for children of preschool age. It was thought that the undertaking could be considered successful if, through the interest aroused by the women's committees, several hundred thousand children were weighed and measured. But in three months the first edition of 500,000 record cards had to be increased to 6,000,000. All but two States finally participated in the Children's Year program, in connection with which the Council of National Defense estimated that at least 17,000 committees were formed with a total membership of 11,000,000 women. More than 16,500 cities, towns, villages, and rural communities conducted weighing and measuring tests.

[Summary]

It is difficult to summarize the results of the activities of the Children's Bureau. Since its creation, it has worked side by side with other agencies, public or private, in the promotion of child welfare, and the advancement made has been the result of many forces. Ten years ago the birth-registration area had not been established by the Division of Vital Statistics of the Bureau of the Census, and facts were in consequence not available as a basis for community action. Now the birth-registration area includes 30 States and the District of Columbia — 72.2 per cent of the population. The number of States which have special bureaus or divisions dealing with child health has increased from 1 to 46; 40 States have availed themselves of the benefits which the maternity and infancy act of 1921 offers. More than half the States have created commissions to make comprehensive inquiries into all aspects of child welfare, with a view to a recodification of existing laws and such improvements in law and administration as are found to be needed to bring the State's care of its children up to standard. In more than half the States, bureaus or divisions dealing especially with dependent, neglected, or delinquent children have been organized either as independent administrative units or in the State departments of public welfare or charities. The number of States which provide, through so-called mothers' pensions, public aid for dependent children in their own homes has increased from 2 to 42. There has been an increasing appreciation of the importance of scientific research and good administrative technique in the field of child care; of linking up the State with the local administrative machinery and of including in the field of interest all the children in the community. The medical profession is giving more consideration to the social and economic aspects of child health, and the social workers have learned the importance of a physical diagnosis before determining social treatment. The Children's Bureau does not claim credit for these changes. It can, however, be said that its investigations furnished the facts on which action was frequently based, and through the coop-

eration of experts in child-welfare, public and private child-caring agencies, and women's organizations, the bureau has been able to focus national attention on some of the most important aspects of child care.

---

2. Information bureau

Mrs. ——— ———, San Antonio, Texas, to Children Bureau, Washington, D.C., March 1, 1928, Children's Bureau Records, National Archives.

In the 1920's the Children's Bureau received and answered numerous letters from parents requesting advice on rickets, feeding, crying, bedwetting, and other problems of child rearing.

San Antonio, Texas
March 1st 1928

Children Bureau,
    Washington, D.C.

Gentlemen: —

Please be so kind as to send me the three pamphlets entitling, "Prenatal Care," Pre-School age" and "Infant Care" and could you tell me what could I do as to gain the sleep which my 3 and ½ months baby lost since she was born?

As this is my first baby I did not know nothing about babies and my neighbors would come when the baby was 3 or 4 days old and would keep her awake so as to get a habit I suppose, because she never does sleep 3 or 4 hours without waking, she sleeps ½ an hour or ¾ of an hour and her eyes are wide open and is nothing but misery because she crys and naturally I have to be carring her and cannot do a thing.

Thanking you,
Mrs. ——— ———

March 7, 1928.

Mrs. ——— ———,
San Antonio, Texas.

My dear Mrs. ———:

Your letter of March 1 is acknowledged. There will go forward to you in another envelope, as you request, our publications on prenatal and child care.

From your description, we should think that your baby has become a little spoiled and she probably cries because she knows that she will be picked up which she enjoys. The baby should be fed regularly by the clock and, after she has been changed, put into her bed to sleep. Even though she may wake up and lie awake, it does not mean that she has to be picked up. If she does wake up and cry, and she is dry and comfortable, she should be allowed to cry it out once or twice. This may be difficult for you but it is the quickest and easiest way to teach her to sleep. She may cry quite a long time until she learns that she will not be picked up.

It may be a good idea to have your doctor examine the baby to be sure that she is perfectly all right physically before you begin to train her.

In your State Board of Health at Austin there is a Bureau of Child Hygiene of which Dr. H. N. Barnett is the director. If you will communicate with him you may receive additional information.

Very truly yours,
Viola Russell Anderson, M.D.,
Division of Maternity and Infant Hygiene.

The Children's Bureau and the White House Conference of 1930

In July 1929 President Hoover issued a call for a White House Conference on Child Health and Protection "To study the present status of the health and well-being of the children of the United States and its possessions; to report what is being done; to recommend what ought to be done and how to do it." The Conference met on November 19–22, 1930, under the chairmanship of Roy Lyman Wilbur (1875–1949) secretary of interior in the Hoover administration. Approximately 3,000 leaders in the fields of child health, education, and social work attended the Conference.

1. Lillian Wald defends the policy of viewing the child as a whole, 1930

Lillian Wald, "Shall We Dismember the Child," *Survey,* LXIII (1929–1930), 458.

In the late 1920's the complaint was again raised that the Children's Bureau was duplicating the health activities of the Public Health Service. A Massachusetts congressman introduced a bill in 1927 to transfer the health activities of the Children's Bureau to the Public Health Service and an Ohio congressman proposed in 1929 that the Sheppard-Towner administrative board be chaired by the surgeon general of the Public Health Service rather than the chief of the Children's Bureau.[1] Neither of these bills was reported out of committee, but the friends of the Children's Bureau were fearful that a reorganization was imminent.

Perhaps Solomon the Wise had specialists in mind when he tested the love for a child by the unwillingness to have it dismembered. Certainly the studies of the specialists themselves constantly are showing that to understand fully the kinds of trouble into which people fall — sickness, poverty, difficulties in home or job —

1. The board was composed of the chief of the Children's Bureau, the surgeon general, and the commissioner of education.

we need to know all the factors that affect their lives. This understanding is especially imperative in the case of children who necessarily are governed to a far greater degree than adults by conditions about them over which they have no control.

For this reason there is ground for rejoicing among friends of the federal Children's Bureau that President Hoover has set his seal of approval on one of its major activities in public health in his annual message to Congress — the activities administered by the bureau under funds available through the Sheppard-Towner Act to promote the welfare and hygiene of maternity and infancy. The President recommends that the purpose of the act be continued under the Children's Bureau for a limited period. We hope that Congress will speedily enact the necessary legislation.[2]

On the broad question of the bureau's continuing place in federal health work there was interesting testimony at a hearing held in February, 1927, on a bill to provide coordination of pubic health activities of the government, when the surgeon-general, Dr. Hugh S. Cumming, pointed out that it "would be unfortunate if the President or anybody should attempt to transfer to the Public Health Service all the medical activities of the government . . . A few of them might be, but others are inseparably connected with the major activities in their respective bureaus," and he cited the Children's Bureau as an instance of these latter. Yet the friends of the bureau find some reason for misgiving in Mr. Hoover's message, which raises the fear of a reorganization of the government departments in which federal activities in public health might possibly be taken from the various services and bureaus to which they

are now delegated and grouped under an assistant secretary.

In common with many friends and admirers of the Children's Bureau, I believe that the interests that we have most deeply at heart — the development of children as healthy, happy, well-educated and self-supporting citizens — can best be served by the present plan of organization. Despite relatively meager limits in budget, the bureau has shown its efficiency in considering the child as a whole and very human being, not merely as an actual or potential victim of malaria or hookworm, or of the many other adverse social conditions which can be considered *en masse*. Of course at any time the Children's Bureau should continue to work, as it always has worked, in the closest cooperation with the various special services, standing behind the social measures which they find efficacious and relaying their aid to parents.

.   .   .   .   .

During the past seventeen years the bureau has rolled up an impressive record of research, education, legislature and administrative achievement in these many fields. But its outstanding contribution has been the test of a unified approach to the problems of childhood. The staff of physicians, scientists, lawyers, psychologists, and statisticians have studied together the problems of child welfare and have fully demonstrated the effectiveness of a single agency dealing with childhood as a whole to bring home to the individual community and the individual parent the results of its scientific research. Our Children's Bureau remains unique in the combination of scientific research and popular publication.

Its studies on family income and infant mortality reveal the forces moving through whole communities, family by family, determining how many babies will have a chance to live. Its research into children on the street trades show why children are at work, what that work means in terms of their health and progress in school, how a community may set and hold

2. The Sheppard-Towner Act, under which the Children's Bureau administered federal grants-in-aid to the states for infant and maternal health, lapsed in 1929. Measures to restore the program were introduced in each session of Congress after 1928 and eventually were included as Titles V and VI of the Social Security Act of 1935. Edward R. Schlesinger, M.D., "The Sheppard-Towner Era: A Prototype Case Study in Federal-State Relationships," *American Journal of Public Health*, LVII (1967), 1034–1040.

standards for the development of children. The attitudes of juvenile and domestic relations courts disclose in the broadest outlines the factors of family and community which seem to work toward delinquency.

In all . . . spheres, it is essential that knowledge available on all aspects of a child's and a community's life be centered and interpreted if we are to attack the problems of the present in a sure and intelligent fashion. This is just the approach of the newer educational currents in the universities, such as the Institute of Human Relations at Yale for the study of man in his entirety. It is the approach that the settlements have tested for years in considering their neighbors not only as collective groups but also as individuals — and for both individual and group, life is made up by the related power of all the forces that give it strength and beauty — health, recreation, music, employment, vocational guidance, advice in trouble, education.

To many of us this approach seems so wholly wise and necessary that we should consider with great disquietude any plan for governmental reorganization that threatens the unity of the Children's Bureau, wherein as a government and as workers in many fields we pool our knowledge, love and efforts for all the children of America.

2. Preliminary report recommends transfer of health activities of Children's Bureau to Public Health Service

White House Conference on Child Health and Protection, *Preliminary Committee Reports* (New York, 1930), pp. 72–73, 79–80.

The preliminary report, distributed to conferees in advance of the Conference, was in book form and copyrighted but was marked *"Confidential — not for publication."* The

following is from the report of Committee A, Public Health Organization of Section II, Public Healh Service and Administration. The chairman of the Committe was E. L. Bishop, M.D., commissioner of the Tennessee State Health Department, 1924–1935; Hugh S. Cumming, M.D., surgeon general of the United States Public Health Service, 1920–1936, was chairman of Section II. Grace Abbott's minority report, opposing transfer of Children's Bureau health activities to the Public Health Service, was not printed.

DECLARATION OF PRINCIPLES
AND POLICIES

1. The organized promotion of child health in the future will depend as it has in the past upon the quality of trained professional leadership for, and the organization and financial support of, full-time administrative health services provided to benefit all the persons old and young, and of both sexes, in each community in our nation.

2. The health interests of the child as an individual, and as a member of the family, and of the community, are inseparable from those of adults, both men and women.

3. Public health organization throughout the world, and in particular in the States, counties and municipalities of this country, has recognized the wisdom of including its administrative resources for health under one direction and for a common purpose, whatever be the particular problem of preventive medicine uppermost in the public mind at the present moment, or however great the immediate needs of a limited age or sex group in the community for which additional efforts or resources are required.

4. The problems of health protection of the child show in common with those of the adult a great complexity of origins, consequently it is only through a centralized authority, trained in the medical and biological sciences and with

understanding of the fields of economics and sociology, that we may expect to obtain comprehensive and enduring results.

5. No public health organization, federal, state or local which lacks provision of expert, specially trained direction for child health can be considered adequate for the needs of American families today.

6. The committee believes that the best health service to the child is to be accomplished by inclusion of child health within a program of general health service applicable according to age and condition to all members of the community.

7. The services which government should provide for the children of the nation fall logically for purposes of administration into three groups: (a) Health, (b) Education, (c) Social Welfare.

8. It is desirable for the federal government to develop and extend its interest in the health of children and of the population as a whole. Methods by which it can constitutionally promote the public health include:

(a) Studies and investigation for purposes of extending scientific information and perfecting more effective methods for application of present knowledge for the prevention and control of disease.

(b) The perfection and extension of facilities for disseminating scientific information concerning the prevention and control of disease.

(c) Professional advice and assistance to communities and States by competent experts in the several special phases of public health.

(d) Financial assistance in the further development of efficient local and state health services; this assistance having for its primary object the stimulation of a larger sense of local responsibility for public health and the provision of inspiration and example for a higher grade and more adequate volume of health work appropriate to local needs.

9. The principle of federal aid for many community activities has been accepted as a governmental policy under various acts of Congress over a period of a generation. In no phase of community welfare is there a greater need for federal assistance than in public health.

.   .   .   .   .

RECOMMENDATIONS

1. That federal grants in aid of health be continued and increased by specific Congressional act, and that any such legislation which may be enacted by the Congress be administered under the joint supervision and control of the Public Health Service and the State Health authorities, and through no other channels, in the interest of effectiveness, simplicity and economy of administration within the Federal, State and local governments.

Such federal aid granted in the interest of the health of children should be devoted primarily to building up more effective local health services as a part of a general health program, particularly in those areas and population groups most in need of health services, as determined by federal and State Health authorities and not solely or mainly on the numerical basis of population distribution.

2. That through a continuation and expansion of present federal activity in the field of public health research, and in increasing the number of scientific personnel specially trained in the various administrative problems of public health, marked progress can be made in improving the health of children and of the population as a whole.

3. That consolidation of federal health activities be provided for by Congressional act, specifically authorizing the transfer of the functions together with the personnel and necessary appropriations for their support, of the Division of Vital Statistics of the Bureau of the Census to the Public Health Service, and the health activities of the Divisions of Child Hygiene and of Maternity and Infancy of the Children's Bureau to the Public Health Service, except so far as these latter are concerned with health

studies inseparable from and indispensable to the functions of this Bureau in the field of welfare of women and children.

4. That the coordination of federal health activities other than those of the central federal health agency, the Public Health Service be extended by the use of existing Congressional authority for the assignment of personnel from the Public Health Service to them, as may be required.

5. That cooperation between federal agencies for the better administration of educational efforts and researches in the various borderlands of health, and in the ancillary sciences be required through executive direction by the President and members of his Cabinet.

6. That the creation of a Department of Public Health under the direction of a Cabinet Officer, in the Federal Government is not essential to the accomplishment of the desired objectives.

---

3. Dissension at the Conference

"Child Parley Split over Bureau Shift,"
New York Times, Nov. 21, 1930.

Washington, November 20. — Controversy over the proposed transfer of child health activities from the Children's Bureau to the Public Health Service occasioned today the first wide disagreement in the sessions of the White House conference on child health and protection.

The opening gun of the opposition to the proposed transfer was fired this morning by James J. Davis, the Secretary of Labor, who, in his opening address as vice chairman of the conference, appealed instead for an expansion of the Children's Bureau and the assembly thereunder of "scattered child welfare which bureaus charged with other major responsibilities are now attempting to perform."

Then, in a meeting of the Committee on Federal Health Activities, Miss Grace Abbott,

chief of the Children's Bureau, dissented from the majority report, read by Dr. Haven Emerson of Columbia University, recommending the shifting of child health, maternity and infancy work. Miss Abbott was strongly backed by women delegates in insisting upon keeping the bureau unified and intact.

.   .   .   .

Secretary Davis, in his address told the delegates that all the volumes of their conclusions, unless translated into action, would be only of interest to social historians.

"If we could put into practice what is now known about safeguarding the health of children, preventing dependency and delinquency, providing opportunities for wholesome group activities," he said, "we could in a single generation profoundly improve the whole character of our national life.

.   .   .   .

"The Labor Department and labor generally, believe in specialists for jobs that require specialists. It does not engage a plumber to assist in lowering our maternal mortality rate nor an electrician to study delinquency. It recognizes and respects the special contribution of these experts to our national life, but it also utilizes the medical and social sciences, the law and the science of public welfare administration in the fields where their expert assistance is of value.

The Children's Bureau has on its staff specialists in all these fields, and we have been especially grateful for the great service which has been rendered by the distinguished pediatricians, obstetricians, lawyers and social scientists who have served on its advisory committees.

"This conference has been possible because of the collaboration of specialists in all these fields. That specialists disagree is axiomatic, but, I am sure, we shall have at this conference sufficient agreement to advance the cause of children as did the conference of 1909 and that of 1919.

"At any rate, I can pledge you on behalf of

the Department of Labor and the Children's Bureau that we shall leave nothing undone that will promote or make more effective our future cooperation with all the agencies assembled in this conference on the health and protection of American children."

.   .   .   .   .   .

MISS ABBOTT AGAINST BUREAU SPLIT

Secretary Davis's plea to keep the Children's Bureau intact was parallelled in the minority report of Miss Grace Abbott, chief of the bureau, dissenting from the report of the Conference Committee on Federal Health Activities. Addressing the morning session of the committee, of which she is a member, Miss Abbott said:

"It is necessary that the records of the conference show that I do not concur in all the conclusions of the committee and especially in the recommendation that the child health and maternity and infancy work of the Children's Bureau should be transferred to the Public Health Service.

"The conception of the unity of the child and the value of having the disciplines and techniques of the social, medical, statistical and other related sciences associated in the scientific study was advocated by the conference in 1909 and enthusiastically approved by President Roosevelt and, in turn, by Congress.

"There is ample evidence that this plan of unified approach has greatly increased public interest in all the problems of children and child life. To remove the health work from the Children's Bureau would not merely remove one section of the bureau's activities, it would destroy it as a children's bureau."

WOMEN SUPPORT MISS ABBOTT

In support of the opposition of Secretary Davis and Miss Abbott, to the change in the Children's Bureau, a resolution adopted by twelve national organizations of women was presented by Miss Marguerite M. Wells, acting president of the National League of Women Voters, and telegrams from several prominent physicians in the country were read by Miss Lillian D. Wald of New York City.

The women in the crowded session room were apparently a unit in opposition to the adoption of the recommendation by the conference.

In the interest of harmony, Miss Abbott urged the elimination from the report of the disputed paragraphs and their further consideration at future meetings of the committee.

―――――――――――――――

4. Dissatisfaction at a "managed" Conference

J. Prentice Murphy, "When Doctors Disagreed," *The Survey*, LXV (1930–1931), 311, 314, 315, 348.

―――――――――――――――

"You see, this is a health conference."

"You are wrong; this is a general child-welfare conference."

"No, you are mistaken; non-health agencies have been invited because they are needed in the development and execution of any sound child-health program."

"Well, that's news to me!"

The above is part of a conversation which took place at one of the many luncheons held in connection with the White House Conference on Child Health and Protection. It is perhaps a key to one of the most amazing gatherings ever held in this country. It may explain a number of confusing situations and supply the answer to many questions which hampered the activities and effectiveness of the outstanding child-welfare event of the year. It may be the reason for some of the strongly expressed and carefully phrased conflicting points of view as to administrative procedure. It may account for the fact that some committees seemed to look upon the Washington meetings as places where reports were to be calmly accepted as presented — these reports, in certain instances, being the final recommendations of experts who were not looking for votes of approval from members of other sections or even other committees of their own section. It may help in interpreting fairly the reaction of some of these experts when they found that even the several thousand general delegates who had never served on committees could not be prevented from asserting their right to express an opinion where they felt qualified, especially as to administrative procedure. It may also account for a conference which began on a plane of high expectancy and ended in a hastily prepared final statement which was confusing, discouraging, and infinitely narrower than other celebrated conference pronouncements made ten and twenty years ago. Viewed as a skeletonized health statement, a different judgment might be rendered by some.

. . . . .

The conferences of 1909 and 1919 were deliberative, democratic affairs. The members as a whole — as in the first one or in three sections in the second — created, perfected, and after careful consideration, ratified their pronouncements.

It cannot be said that the final chapter of this third conference was built on similar lines. The publication, in advance, of a cloth-bound, copyrighted volume containing summaries of numerous committee reports, section by section, aroused much uneasiness among many committee members who read it. This volume had every air of permanence. It was a matter of gossip at the conference, later commented on in the press, that a large number of copies had been or were about to be sent to libraries throughout the United States. That it was the well-laid plan of some to have its contents approved and ratified as thus submitted, becomes increasingly evident as one reviews the whole course of this further venture in child wel-

fare. That whoever so planned made a serious mistake, is equally clear.

. . . The error in including the seemingly unanimous specific recommendations of the Section on Public Health restricting the future powers and usefulness of the federal Children's Bureau in favor of the United States Public Health Service, but omitting Miss Abbott's minority report, became a blessing in disguise . . .

The controversy as to the Children's Bureau was recognized by the press as involving a really vital question. That it beclouded other issues is doubtful, for reasons which were inherent in the way in which this Conference was organized.

. . . . .

. . . What the Conference did was to invite a great host of the Bureau's supporters to Washington and then ask them to agree to a plan which later on might be cited in Congress as a reason for reducing its sphere of usefulness. Naturally, such a plan could not be accepted.

The controversy did not represent a contest between the medical and social-work groups as such, although there were some who so thought. It brought out one curious quality of this conference, however; namely, the many walls which separated the thinking of different groups. It showed that the philosophies embodied in the specializations which hold in the various fields of public health — medical care, education, and social welfare — need a vast amount of integration. Perhaps this is to be one of the main tasks of the continued Conference meetings which are to come. It also showed wherein the fields of medicine and nursing interact on each other and the relative parts they are going to play in the next ten years.

The discussions as to the proposed change in the Children's Bureau assumed for a time the aspects of an issue between men and women, but the number of men who upheld the Bureau's side ultimately disposed of that thought. However, they clearly revealed the need for closer exchange of ideas between the fine group of physicians who are viewing the future in terms of public health and those who in social work are concerned with a more inclusive program of social welfare. Already strong groups within the field of medicine are working in complete harmony with social workers in developing the outlines of mutually related fields. Public health and welfare services in the United States include many strong units. Organizations such as the National League of Women Voters, National Consumers' League, American Federation of Labor, and other bodies which have watched and supported the Children's Bureau in its development and knew its strength, showed a practical grasp from which they refused to be swerved by coercion or criticism or by views which seemed incomplete.

.   .   .   .   .

That the support of the Children's Bureau was widespread appears in the resolutions favoring a renewal of federal maternity and infancy support under the Children's Bureau and continuance of its child-hygiene work as an integral part of its program . . .

5. No report from the Committee on Public Health Organization

White House Conference on Child Health and Protection, *White House Conference, 1930: Addresses and Abstracts of Committee Reports* (New York, 1931), p. 113.

PUBLIC HEALTH ORGANIZATION

Section II — Committee A

In this brief transcript of the Conference proceedings it has been deemed advisable to omit the report of the Committee on Public Health Organization, because in some of its aspects the report touches controversial points which require further consideration.[1]

6. Children's Bureau commended by Committee on Prenatal and Maternal Care

White House Conference on Child Health and Protection, *White House Conference 1930: Addresses and Abstracts of Committee Reports*, pp. 89–90.

Fred L. Adair, M.D., was chairman of the Committee on Prenatal and Maternal Care.

The interest and zeal of the Children's Bureau of the Department of Labor and the Census Bureau have been of invaluable aid in the collection and correlation of statistical data on factors causing maternal mortality. The Children's Bureau has given valuable service in the direction of the administration of the Federal Maternity and Infancy Act and in other demonstrations, in addition to the publication of many bulletins of educational and practical value dealing with maternal and infant and child welfare.

Children's Bureau in the Depression

The Children's Bureau was the sole government agency that published relief statistics

1. After the Conference, Florence Kelley wrote: "The dominant interest of this year's conference was the overwhelming protest of the delegates against the committee recommendation that all medical work of the federal Children's Bureau be transferred to the United States Public Health Service. The recommendation split the conference on Thursday morning, November 20, and there was no subsequent reconciliation. On Saturday morning, the closing day, Secretary Wilbur announced that the recommendation would not be further discussed, but would go to a Continuation Committee to be appointed by President Hoover." "Save the Children," *The Nation* CXXXI (December 10, 1930), 643–644.

during the Hoover administration and the first administration of Franklin D. Roosevelt. Beginning in July 1930 the Bureau published monthly relief statistics for all cities of 5,000 or over as well as in rural areas. In addition the Bureau cooperated with the American Friends Service Committee in the extension of relief to depressed coal mining areas. Senators Robert La Follette and Edward P. Costigan proposed in 1931 that the Children's Bureau administer unemployment relief but their relief bills were defeated in 1932.

---

1. Rural relief surveys in coal-mining communities, 1931

U.S. Dept. of Labor, *Report of the Chief, Children's Bureau, 1931* (Washington, D.C., 1932), p. 4.

In last year's report reference was made to the fact that at the request of the President's Emergency Committee for Employment surveys of the extent of the need and the available resources for local relief were made in certain coal-mining counties in Pennsylvania, West Virginia, and Kentucky. During the past year coal-mining counties in the following States were included in the survey: Alabama, Arkansas, Illinois, Indiana, Kansas, Missouri, Oklahoma, and Tennessee. Communities in the lumber areas of Michigan and Mississippi were also visited. The counties selected in all these States were, in general, those in which unemployment had been reported to be especially serious and relief inadequate, although there were other counties in each State in which there was little reason to believe that conditions were much better.

The information which formed the basis of the report submitted to the President's committee by the bureau was obtained by interviews with public and private relief officials, superintendents of mines, union officials, school principals and teachers, health officers, priests and ministers of local churches, the neighborhood grocers and milk companies, and anyone else who could give information as to conditions among the unemployed. As the first draft of the report for each State was prepared, it was made available promptly to the President's committee and to State welfare officials, chairmen of State employment committees, and executives of private agencies who were interested in relieving conditions and expressed a desire to see the reports.

The county studies presented variations of the same story of general unemployment and underemployment, of reluctance of the miners to report their need of assistance, of quite inadequate resources for public aid, of private relief agencies unable to meet the needs of those who were dependent in the cities or largest towns and able to give little or no assistance to the small mining towns or camps. Undernourishment among children was widespread. In many communities the school principals and teachers had taken the leadership in organizing some relief for the children. Out of their own salaries and such other contributions as they were able to collect, lunches had been provided at many schools, and the teachers were also collecting and distributing clothing.

---

2. Cooperation with the American Friends Service Committee in relief activities, 1931

U.S. Dept. of Labor, *Report of the Chief, Children's Bureau, 1931*, p. 5.

In the autumn of 1931 the American Friends (Quakers) Service Committee undertook to provide food and clothing for children and clothes and garden seeds for adults in a number of coal-mining communities. They were enabled to do this through a grant of $225,000 by the American Relief Administration and through contributions of clothing, food, and money by members of the organization and interested individuals and firms. At the request of this committee the Children's Bureau lent the services of two members of its staff for limited periods to assist in getting the work started. By March, 1932, the Friends were feeding approximately 24,000 school children in 6 States and furnishing milk to 3,174 preschool children and expectant mothers; the largest number of children being fed through the public schools between September, 1931, and August, 1932, was 40,000, living in 38 counties of Maryland, Kentucky, Tennessee, Illinois, Pennsylvania, and West Virginia. Everywhere the addition of carefully selected lunches served to the school children resulted in prompt improvement in their appearance and mental alertness, and the morale of the miners was greatly strengthened by the interest and assistance of the Friends. Early in July, because of exhaustion of funds, the child-feeding program was given up, except for the distribution of such supplies as were already on hand. At no time, the Friends report, were they able, in cooperation with existing local agencies, to meet even the most pressing needs of the unemployed miners' families. State and Federal assistance were needed to provide immediate relief and to work out some plan for the re-employment of the fathers of these children.

3. La Follette and Costigan propose a relief bill, 1931

U.S. Congress, Senate Committee on Manufactures, *Hearings on S. 174 and S. 262, Unemployment Relief*, 72 Cong., 1 Sess. (1931–1932), pp. 1–2.

A BILL to provide for cooperation by the Federal Government with the several States in relieving the hardship and suffering caused by unemployment, and for other purposes

Be it enacted by the Senate and House of Representatives of the United States of America in Congress assembled,

That (a) for the purpose of cooperating with the several States in relieving the hardship and suffering caused by unemployment there is hereby authorized to be appropriated the sum of $125,000,000 for the fiscal year ending June 30, 1932, and $250,000,000 for the fiscal year ending June 30, 1933 . . .

Sec. 2 (a) There is hereby created a Federal board for unemployment relief (hereinafter referred to as the "board"), which shall consist of the Chief of the Children's Bureau in the Department of Labor, the Director of Extension Work in the Department of Agriculture, and the Chief of the Vocational Rehabilitation Service of the Federal Board for Vocational Education. The board shall elect its own chairman and shall prescribe rules and regulations for the administration of this act and exercise the functions provided for in this act. The board shall cease to exist on June 30, 1934, and all unexpended moneys held by it shall be covered into the Treasury as miscellaneous receipts.

(b) The Children's Bureau shall be charged with the administration of this act, except as otherwise provided, and the Chief of the Children's Bureau shall be the executive officer of the board. It shall be the duty of the Children's Bureau to make or cause to be made such studies, investigations, and reports as will promote the efficient administration of this act.

. . . . .

Sec. 4. In order to obtain the benefits of the appropriations authorized in section 1 of this act a State shall, through its legislative authority, (1) accept the provisions of this act, (2) create or designate or authorize the creation or designation of a State agency to cooperate with the Children's Bureau in accordance with the provisions and purposes of this act; . . .

Sec. 5. Within twenty days after an appropriation has been made under authority of this act, the Children's Bureau shall make the apportionment on the basis of population provided in this act, shall certify to the Secretary of the Treasury and to the treasurers of the several States the amount apportioned to each State on the basis of population for the fiscal year for which the appropriation has been made, and shall certify to the Secretary of the Treasury the amount estimated by the bureau, with the approval of the board, to be necessary for administering the provisions of this act.

II State and County Child Welfare Agencies

A. INNOVATIONS IN ADMINISTRATION

Boards of guardians and code commissions

---

1. County Boards of Children's Guardians established, Indiana, 1891

"An act to amend an act entitled 'An Act to establish a Board of Child Guardians in townships,'" *Laws of the State of Indiana . . . 1891* (Indianapolis, 1891), pp. 365–367.

Under this law, nearly all the counties appointed unpaid county boards which were under the control of the county commissioners but cooperated with the state Board of Charities in the care of dependent children.

Sec. 1. *Be it enacted by the General Assembly of the State of Indiana . . .* . That in all counties of this State which have a population of more than seventy-five thousand inhabitants, as shown by the United States census for the year 1890, there shall be created a Board composed of six persons, three of whom shall be women, which Board shall be a body politic and corporate, known as the Board of Children's Guardians of ———— County, and in such name may sue and be

sued. The members of such Board shall be appointed by the Circuit Court of the county in which such townships are situated, and shall serve without compensation . . .

[Sec. 2.] . . . Whenever said Board shall have probable cause to believe that any child under fifteen years of age is abandoned, neglected or cruelly treated by its parent or parents, or its custodians, or is habitually sent out or permitted to beg upon the streets, or is an habitual truant from school, in idle and vicious association, or that the parent of any child is in constant habits of drunkenness and blasphemy, or of low and gross debauchery, or that the associations of such child are such as tend to its corruption or contamination, or that such child is known by language and life to be vicious or incorrigible, such Board shall file a petition in the office of the Clerk of the Circuit Court of the county setting forth such facts in regard to such child, and thereupon the Clerk shall issue a writ for the custody of such child, which shall be served upon the parent or person having actual custody or control of said child, or if such child is under no actual parental custody or control, then upon the child itself, and thereupon said Board shall take and keep said child at the temporary home of said Board until the final order of the Circuit Court or Judge thereof . . . An appeal from the decision of the Circuit Court and the Judge thereof, sitting in vacation, may be taken to the Supreme Court as in civil causes, but such appeal shall not stay the order of said Court as to the custody of said child, which shall remain in the custody of said Board until such appeal shall be finally disposed of; and all children committed to the custody and control of said Board of Children's Guardians shall be under the supervision and control of such Board in the manner provided in this act until such children shall become of age.

SEC. 3. In all cases where there is no children's home in the county or township in which such Board shall be appointed, the Board of County Commissioners shall provide, either by purchase or lease, a house of suitable size and convenience for the accommodation of the children placed under the custody and control of such Board; shall pay a Matron, to be appointed by said Board of Children's Guardians, and shall pay thirty cents per day for each child under the care of such Board of Children's Guardians kept in said House, or maintained outside of said house.

---

2. A state board of children's guardians, New Jersey, 1899

"An Act for the creation of a state board of children's guardians," 1899 — ch. 165, *Acts of the . . . State of New Jersey, 1899* (Trenton, 1899), pp. 362–365.

BE IT ENACTED *by the Senate and General Assembly of the State of New Jersey:*

1. There shall be appointed by the governor seven persons, two of whom shall be women, who shall be known as the state board of children's guardians, two of whom shall hold office for two years, two for four years and three for six years, as shall be indicated by the governor on making their appointment, and thereafter all appointments, except to fill vacancies in the

said board, shall be for six years, and shall be made by the governor; said board shall receive no compensation for their time or services but the actual and necessary expenses of each of them while engaged in the performance of the duties of his or her office.

2. In case of the death or resignation of any member, or in case any member ceases to be a resident or citizen of this state, it shall be the duty of the governor to fill such vacancy for the unexpired term only, and any member may be removed by the governor for cause.

3. Said board of children's guardians shall have and it is hereby vested with power to adopt a seal and reasonable rules and regulations; said board of children's guardians shall have the care of and maintain a general supervision over all indigent, helpless, dependent, abandoned, friendless and poor children who may now be or who may hereafter become public charges; and said board shall have the care of and maintain supervision over all children adjudged public charges, who may now be in the charge, custody and control of any county asylum, county home, almshouse, poorhouse, charitable institution, home or family to which such child or children may be or have been committed, confined, adopted, apprenticed, indentured or bound out; said board shall have and is hereby vested with power to appoint such agents, one being a woman, and other subordinate officers as it may deem necessary; said board shall fix their compensation, subject to the approval of the governor, and the amount paid for compensation of such agents and other officers shall not exceed the sum appropriated by the legislature for the purpose.

4. It shall be the duty of the state board of children's guardians, upon receiving notice of the commitment of any child as a public charge, to place such child in the care of some family within this state, with or without the payment of board, and with or without indenture; and it shall further be the duty of such state board of children's guardians to place such child in

the care of a family of the religious faith of the parent or parents of such child, and during the period in which the state board of children's guardians is seeking such family for such child, and until such family is secured as hereinbefore provided, it shall be the duty of the state board of children's guardians to place such child in the custody and care of an institution in this state for the care of children; *provided,* that the institution in which the child is placed shall be one maintained for children of the religious faith of the parent or parents of such child when such an institution exists therein; in case no institutions of such religious faith exists in this state, then the said board of children's guardians shall use its discretion in providing an institution for the care of such child until a family has been secured; . . .

5. It shall be the duty of the state board of children's guardians to visit, by its agent or agents, quarterly, all children who may be committed under this act, and also any home, asylum, institution or private family where any such child or children may be placed; said board shall report from time to time to the governor, and make a yearly report to the governor and legislature of the state, showing in detail the work of said board for that time.

6. The county board of chosen freeholders of the respective counties of this state shall annually hereafter provide sufficient funds for the objects of this act in their respective counties for the support, care and education and maintenance of any child or children adjudged to be a public charge.

.   .   .   .   .   .

9. It shall be the duty of the state board of children's guardians, upon receipt of the notice of the commitment of any child as hereinbefore provided, to place such child or children in the manner hereinbefore provided as soon as possible thereafter; and in no case shall said child or children who may hereafter be committed as public charges, who may be over the age of twelve months, be confined in such almshouse for a longer period than thirty days, and the keeper of such almshouse shall surrender such child or children to the care and custody of the state board of children's guardians at any time within thirty days, when surrender is demanded.

10. The state board of children's guardians may, in its discretion, return any child or children becoming wards of said state board to the parent or parents or other relative agreeing to assume the care and maintenance of such child or children or of sufficient ability to do so.

.   .   .   .   .   .

12. The state board of children's guardians shall remain the guardians of all children indentured, bound out or put forth, who may now be or may hereafter become public charges.

13. This act shall be construed liberally and for the benefit of any child or children so becoming ward or wards of such state board of children's guardians as aforesaid.

---

3. The first children's code commission, Ohio, 1911

"An act to provide for the appointment of a commission to revise . . . the statute laws . . . which pertain to children," *Legislature Acts . . . of the State of Ohio, 1911* (Springfield, 1911), pp. 123–124.

State children's code commissions, beginning with that of Ohio, sought to coordinate administration of children's laws and suggest new ones. By 1929 thirty-four states had created children's code commissions.

Be it enacted by the General Assembly of the State of Ohio:

SECTION 1. That the governor be, and is

hereby, authorized and required to appoint two (2) competent commissioners to revise, consolidate and suggest amendments and additions to the statute laws of the state of Ohio which pertain to children, and which may be in force at the time such commissioners shall make their report; and in case a vacancy shall occur in such commission by reason of death or resignation the governor is hereby authorized to fill such vacancy.

The commissioners shall be appointed and commence the discharge of their duties not later than the first day of July, 1911, and shall report to the governor not later than the first day of July, 1912. Such report shall be transmitted by the governor to the general assembly next following.

SECTION 2. That in performing this duty such commissioners shall unify the present laws pertaining to illegitimate, defective, neglected, dependent and delinquent children, and to their treatment, care, maintenance, custody, control, protection and reformation; and shall suggest such amendments and additions as to them may seem best calculated to bring the statute law of this state into harmony with the best thought on this subject. They shall arrange their report with head-notes briefly expressive of the matters contained therein, and with marginal notes of the contents of each section and with reference to the original act from which it is compiled. They shall provide, by an index, for an easy reference to every portion of their report, and shall designate such statutes and parts of statutes as, in their judgment, ought to be repealed, with the reasons for such recommendation.

SECTION 4. That such commissioners shall serve without compensation, but shall render an account to the governor of the clerical and expert service rendered and the expense of the same, together with all incidental expenses incurred by such commission, including their own expenses.

Minnesota revises laws concerning children, 1917

1. The recommendations of the children's code commission

United States Children's Bureau, *State Commissions for the Study and Revision of Child-welfare Laws,* Pub. No. 131 (Washington, D.C., 1924), pp. 49–51.

[A] *Child-Welfare Commission,* consisting of 12 members, was appointed by the governor, August, 1916, to revise and codify the laws of the State relating to children.

No appropriation was made by the State, but private funds were secured, and an executive secretary was employed. The personnel of the commission included nine men and three women, their interests being defined as follows: "Of the men three were judges — two members of the district bench, assigned to the juvenile court, and the third a former justice of the supreme court; two were members of the legislature, one from each house; and the remaining four were an assistant secretary of a civic and commerce association of long professional training in philanthropic work, a member of the State board of control, which manages the institutions of the State, the superintendent of the State school for dependent children, and a Jewish rabbi who had taken an active interest in civic affairs. Of the women, one was active in the management of a social settlement in the largest city of the State, another was the director of the bureau of women and children of the State labor department, and the third was a woman of broad civic interests." The executive secretary was a lawyer.

The study undertaken by the commission was divided as follows:

1. Defective children, with reference to the blind, the deaf, the crippled, and deformed, the feeble-minded and epileptic, and — as related

matter — the protection of children from transmissible disease and the regulation of marriage.

2. Dependent and neglected children, touching upon courts, and procedure, illegitimacy, adoption, public relief at home, maternity hospitals, lying-in places, baby farms, placing-out agencies, institutional homes, abandonment, and desertion.

3. Delinquent children, including courts and procedure, correctional institutions, moral safeguards, and adults contributing to delinquency.

4. General child welfare, including birth registration, vital statistics, regulation of midwives, school attendance, regulation of employment, and crimes against children.

Four committees were appointed to cover the subjects as outlined, and to report their findings to the whole commission. After six months of work the commission submitted its report to the governor, 43 bills being proposed. The secretary states:

The findings of the commission were adopted in almost every instance by a unanimous vote of that body. Where there was a division, a substantial majority had approved.

The legislature passed a resolution (Laws 1917, p. 874, Resolution No. 1) authorizing the appointment of a special committee of seven members of the house and five of the senate to consider the bills to be recommended by the child-welfare commission and other bills introduced that concerned child welfare. This joint committee was authorized to hold public hearings and "introduce and recommend to the house and senate such bills as in its judgment will bring about the proper revision of the laws of this State relating to children." Of the 43 measures recommended to the legislature, 35 were enacted into law. These 35 measures repealed 114 sections and amended 60 sections of previously existing law.

The bills recommended to the legislature, with synopses of changes from the existing law, were published in the report of the Minnesota Child-Welfare Commission, 1917 . . . The results attained through the work of the commission have been summarized by the executive secretary in the article previously cited. He states that "time did not permit the assembling of these measures in such a way as to make possible their passage as a code rather than as individual laws, but the existing statutes are now for the most part coherent, consistent, and interdependent. They seek to express the State's responsibility for its handicapped children as far as it seems possible to go at this time." One of the new laws centralized in the State board of control the administration of all laws for the care and protection of children and authorized the creation of a special division of the board for this purpose and the organization of county child-welfare boards.

The gains through the passage of laws recommended by the commission were summarized by the executive secretary as follows:

There has been created as a bureau of the board of control a regularly organized State agency charged with the fulfillment of the State's obligation to all children in need of care and guardianship, with special reference to the illegitimate child. The laws relating to illegitimacy have been revised, and the father of a child born out of wedlock is subject to the same degree of responsibility as though the child were legitimate. Supplementary to this, it has been made a felony to abscond where issue is born of fornication. Safeguards have been thrown about the adoption and placing out of children; lying-in hospitals must now be properly licensed and subjected to wise regulation. The law relating to abandonment and nonsupport has been revised and strengthened. The so-called mother's pension law was rewritten, its provisions enlarged, and standards of administration established in the light of the experience of our own and other States. The juvenile-court law has likewise undergone a thorough process of recasting at the hands of persons intimately acquainted with juvenile-court problems. The scope of the law, the machinery of its procedure, and the spirit of its text have been put on a sound and liberal foundation.

2. The creation of county child welfare boards

"An act to . . . provide for child welfare boards in the several counties of the state,"

1917 — ch. 194, *Session Laws of the State of Minnesota, 1917* (Minneapolis, 1917), p. 280.

This law, which was recommended by the children's code commission, also gave the state board of control the duties of protecting delinquent and dependent children and acting as children's guardians.

.   .   .   .   .

Sec. 4. County child welfare boards. — Appointment of agents. — The state board of control may when requested so to do by the county board appoint in each county three persons resident therein, at least two of whom shall be women, who shall serve without compensation and hold office during the pleasure of the board, and who, together with a member to be designated by the county board from their own number and the county superintend-

ent of schools, shall constitute a child welfare board for the county, which shall select its own chairman; provided that in any county containing a city of the first class five members shall be appointed by the state board of control. The child welfare board shall perform such duties as may be required of it by the said board of control in furtherance of the purposes of this act; and may appoint a secretary and all necessary assistants, who shall receive from the county such salaries as may be fixed by the child welfare board with the approval of the county board. Persons thus appointed shall be the executive agents of the child welfare board.

Sec. 5. Agents where no child welfare board. — In counties where no child welfare board exists the judge of the juvenile court may appoint a local agent to co-operate with the state board of control in furtherance of the purpose of this act, who shall receive from the county such salary as may be fixed by the judge with the approval of the county board.

B. STANDARDIZATION IN ADMINISTRATION

State and local units of service

1. A plea for standardization at the White House Conference of 1919

C. C. Carstens, "The Method of Procedure," in *Standards of Child Welfare,* United States Children's Bureau Pub. No. 60 (Washington, D.C., 1919), pp. 416–419.

Diversities of race, of language, and of political development in our various States have led to a complicated divergence in chil-

dren's laws and in the organizations which care for the various groups that are the subject of our interest. In Michigan, Minnesota, Massachusetts, and certain other States a clear recognition that the State has a central responsibility for its wards is shown in the development of its institutions. In Pennsylvania, Connecticut, and many other States the State as a unit of administration gives little if any indication of the assumption of such responsibility, while New York, Ohio, and Indiana seem to lie between the two extremes. The fact of such diversity, which is recognized by all of us, is not to be lamented so much in itself as in the fact that it connotes a lack of clear thinking, of the proper adaptation of our institutions to our needs, and of such a minimum uniformity as is after all needed between States.

The Federal Government is giving increasing recognition to the social welfare of the people of this country. This has been evidenced in various ways, and in children's work particularly by the establishment of the Federal Children's Bureau and by the passage of a Federal law protecting children from exploitation through labor. But for the proper development of child-welfare standards and child-welfare institutions, the United States is still very largely in the position of a group of forty-eight little republics each of which may learn from its neighbor but none of which needs modify its plans because of the existence of a better procedure in a neighboring State.

The task before any group who are urging the standardization of children's laws throughout the Nation resolves itself in large part into an effort to inspire groups in the various States to study good methods in children's work, to learn the weaknesses of the plans of their own State, and to work for the adoption of a new children's code, or to discover the next logical steps to take in the development of the State's child-welfare institutions. The method which has been pursued by several States with the greatest success has consisted in obtaining the appointment of State commissions by the governor, either with or without legislative sanction. Such commissions generally consist of a group of citizens interested in various forms of child welfare. An executive secretary is appointed to undertake the secretarial work and the direction of the various investigations that are needed. The Federal Children's Bureau has given great aid by providing not only an index of child-welfare legislation in the particular State, but also digests of certain types of laws in force in the various States. If a State cannot convince its governor or its legislature that a commission to revise and codify children's laws is desirable, a group of citizens who have become convinced of this need can make at least a preliminary investigation and can

generally bring about the appointment of a commission at a later date, or can draft laws to submit to the legislature without the assistance of a commission.

The procedure of any such State commission may be outlined as follows: At the beginning it should determine how broad its field of work shall be. For instance, shall it deal with the needs of the various classes of handicapped children only? Or shall it concern itself with all children, and so include for instance the welfare responsibilities of the school, such as medical inspection, physical education, vocational guidance, continuation schools, and various other subjects that have such a large part in the life of the child and his training for the world's work? Then the field chosen must be carefully studied. There are in all our States at the present time colleges and universities, members of whose staffs are ready to take their share in making and directing investigations. Civic leagues; bureaus of research and child welfare; and family, neighborhood, and industrial agencies are also ready to help. The coordination of these various resources provides a means for making field and library investigations of great value. The Federal Children's Bureau has made important investigations, enunciated important principles and standards, and is becoming increasingly valuable in child-welfare work. In the gathering together of facts many different agencies can contribute, but in studying the results of the investigation and making recommendations for changes, the commission must become a well-organized body in order to coordinate these recommendations with each other and with the body of child-welfare law already in existence in its State. When the law recommendations have been decided upon, there comes the important procedure of drafting the code or the separate bills. This is a service which law schools like to share with drafting departments of the universities of our various States.

There are certain clearly marked tendencies in the development of child-welfare legislation in our various States. While there are now but few States in the Union, where a central board, such as a board of charity or a board of children's guardians, has assumed responsibility for the care of the children of that State, sentiment is growing in favor of legislation to establish such a body. Under whatever name such powers may be administered, it is essential that States should have such a board with State-wide power and responsibility. This body should be charged not only with the State's responsibility for the handicapped groups, but should consider also the welfare of the hundred per cent of children, and should be required to investigate untoward conditions and propose to the legislature needed changes in legislation without waiting to be specifically asked to do so.

Along with the development of such a central body there grows increasingly a sense of the need of a well-organized local public-service unit. In most parts of the United States this unit should cover the area of the county in which it would perform the various social functions in connection with probation, parole, recreation, protective, and other child-caring work. Although the county shows here and there a backward development, it offers the largest opportunities of usefulness. Some of our States have begun to organize county boards of public welfare. Missouri, Kansas, and North Carolina will shortly have lessons to teach us in this field, and Dutchess County, New York, has been carrying on an interesting experiment in developing a county social-welfare unit.

The importance of these two, the State and local units of service, and their interrelation, will become increasingly appreciated as we come to add varying forms of social service. The lack of them has already led to the development of unrelated boards or the addition of administrative functions to juvenile courts in many States and cities.

Much of the impetus for new boards to administer mothers' pensions, industrial schools, probation, and such activities, has come because of the revolt against the word "charity" and the bald facts of charitable administration. A board of children's guardians avoids this objection and may easily undertake a variety of functions that are at foundation closely interrelated.

The scheme of having forty-eight individual republics independent as far as State and local legislation is concerned, has some very decided advantages when once we have grasped certain national ideals in social service and education. In the different States it is possible to experiment with various forms of administration while the subject is still in the experimental stage.

.   .   .   .   .   .

The interrelation of public and private child-welfare service is not one of the least important questions to be determined by a children's code commission, especially in all the eastern States. Upon the expression of that relationship will depend, on the one hand, the progressive development of the State's functions in child welfare, and, on the other hand, the encouragement of private effort and association in such a way that it will never hamper the public as it does now in certain States, but will remain as a friendly critic, a guide for greater public effort, and an anchor for good public service.

These are but a few of the many subjects that must have the consideration of a child-welfare commission. The drive is on. Minnesota has set the pace; Kansas and Missouri have gained part of their programs and are making another attempt; Indiana sends word that a commission has been authorized; in Pennsylvania a bill for a commission has been presented; what new State is sufficiently interested in its children's problems to be the next? Uniformity we shall probably never have. That is not our goal. But we would that certain national ideals in child welfare might be clearly enunciated and become the warp and woof of our child-welfare legislation in the various States.

2. A Children's Bureau Survey of County Child Welfare Administration, 1922

United States Children's Bureau, *County Organization for Child Care and Protection,* Pub. No. 107 (Washington, D.C., 1922), pp. 1–2, 4–7.

The Children's Bureau was anxious to publicize successful child welfare administration in various states. In addition to this report, the Bureau published two other studies on the county as an administrative unit, one in 1926 (No. 169) and one in 1933 (No. 224).

County organization . . . does not deal entirely, or even mainly, with rural conditions. The principles of coordination of effort, socialization of the work of public agencies, and cooperation with a central State body are applicable to counties containing largely urban populations, as well as to those that are sparsely settled. But in the larger cities, and in counties containing such cities as centers, the establishment of "boards of public welfare" has pertained mainly to the reorganization and development of work already being done in some manner. Among the more scattered populations, on the other hand, county organization must originate work of care and protection. It implies uncovering neglected social needs and building up means of dealing with them constructively. In most counties there has existed some form of "poor relief," either care in almshouses or county homes, or scanty doles to families; but child-welfare activities in behalf of the 49 per cent of the children of this country who are living in rural communities have been largely neglected. It is, therefore, on child welfare and on reconstructive work with families that the emphasis has been placed in the movement for organization of county activities.

The impetus to the movement for unifying and socializing local activities which has come from the development of State supervisory and administrative work in the care and pro-tection of handicapped children and adults, has been due to increasing recognition of the needs and rights of the individuals concerned. This individualizing of "charities and corrections" has led rapidly to search for causes and preventive measures. Prevention and reconstruction call for local action. The county and community must function here; the State can go no further than to point out the obvious results of neglected social problems.

The methods of social case work are being applied by public as well as by private agencies, and are mainly responsible for the changing emphasis. Home care for dependent children has become a recognized principle, with the emphasis on the prevention of child dependency through constructive aid in preserving the child's own home whenever possible. In the care and training of deaf and of crippled children progress has been in the direction of supplying corrective treatment through clinics and the necessary equipment for training in local public schools, so that the handicapped child, while remaining a member of his own group, may be helped to gain a normal relation to the community. Likewise for children who have committed offenses against the law, supervision has largely taken the place of commitment to institutions, and such children are more and more coming to be considered as in need of special care and guidance, while custodial care is used only as a final resort.

This ideal of prevention and reconstruction is an outstanding feature of the plans of work of the county organizations usually given such titles as "county board of child welfare," or "county board of public welfare."

It is difficult to define categorically the types of county organization that have developed so rapidly within recent years. Many of them, as pointed out above, have resulted directly from the efforts of State boards to secure local attention to the causes and the treatment of dependency and delinquency. Frequently the change has come about through local effort to combine modern principles of social work with business methods. The State's function has been educational and has been directed toward bringing into cooperation the various county agencies in the interest of better standards of work.

The fundamental differences in the several States and their various needs—inherent either in basic conditions or in local preferences for certain methods of handling situations—are indicated by the fact that in no two States are the plans of county organization exactly similar, even though they may follow the same general trend. It is, indeed, doubtful if the methods of work undertaken in any two counties of the same State are identical. Probably no State will find it practicable to follow in detail the plans adopted by any other State, however successful they may have proved. The material presented in this publication in regard to the methods of organization and the work undertaken by county units in various States indicates certain fundamental principles as a guide for the development of similar activities. In their application they must be made to fit local conditions and requirements.

In general, the forms of county organization as they exist to-day in different parts of the country may be divided into three groups: First, those represented in this publication by Minnesota, North Carolina, and California, the county organizations provided for by the Arkansas and Virginia laws and the duties designated for county superintendents of public welfare in Missouri. In these States the county work is public, is in direct cooperation with the State board of charities or a similar department, and includes varied programs of child care and protection, relief of dependent families, probation and parole, enforcement of social legislation, and other forms of assistance and of reconstructive and preventive effort. The work in Alabama, Pennsylvania, and South Carolina also belongs in this class of organization.

The second type of public county organization is concerned mainly with the care of de-pendent children. It is found in Indiana and Arizona, in the permissive law passed in Ohio in 1921, in the two New York counties of Dutchess and Suffolk, and in the provisions of the general law passed in New York State in 1922.

The third type of county organization is that under private auspices, and directed to the development of either a broad program or work with a specific group. The county activities undertaken in the States of New York, New Jersey, and Florida are examples of this type.

From the standpoint of the future development of constructive county-wide work, the most significant form of county organization is that represented by Minnesota and North Carolina.

.   .   .   .   .

The Minnesota . . . law relative to the appointment of county boards by the State board do[es] not specify in detail the work of the local board, but merely designate[s] that they shall perform such duties as may be required of them by the State board. In Minnesota, the law states that the executive agents and assistants appointed by the county child-welfare boards "may also, when so directed by the county board, perform the duties of probation and school attendance officers, and may aid in the investigation and supervision of county allow-ances to mothers." The duties delegated to the county boards by the State board of control . . . relate mainly to investigation of proposed adoptions, supervision of placed-out children, protection of the interests of children born out of wedlock and supervision of feeble-minded children.

The varied duties that have been placed upon the county superintendents of public welfare of North Carolina, include enforcing school attendance, poor relief, aftercare of persons released from hospitals or institutions, parole, probation, preventing juvenile delinquency, promoting wholesome recreation, supervising children placed in family homes, finding employment, enforcing the child labor law, inspecting county institutions, acting as agent of the State board "in relation to any work to be done by the State board in the county," and, as a general provision, ascertaining conditions and causes of poverty and distress in the county . . .

Proposed standards for state child welfare departments

1. Recommendations of White House Conference, 1930

White House Conference on Child Health and Protection, *Preliminary Committee Reports* (New York, 1930), pp. 417–421.

Some States may provide service to children in more than one department, as welfare, education, health, probation, or mental hygiene, but, wherever responsibility may be lodged, the activities must be coordinated and certain essentials for state welfare work for children must be considered. Some of these essentials are as follows:

1. Every State should furnish leadership in work being done for dependent, neglected, delinquent, physically and mentally handicapped children, and should set standards, promote social work programs, and stimulate protective work for children.

2. Every State should make provision for the care of delinquent and of mentally handicapped children needing institutional treatment, and assure adequate supervision of those children who remain in the community.

3. Every State should secure for physically handicapped children — the blind, deaf and crippled — the medical care, education, and social service that their handicaps require, and should regulate the standards of their care.

4. Appropriations for the state's child welfare activities should be adequate in order to make social legislation effective since mere legislative enactment is not sufficient.

5. A state department should maintain adequate standards in reference to qualifications and size of its staff, in relation to the work undertaken, and to the quality of its service.

6. The state child welfare program should be free from domination by partisan politics.

These requirements involve important relationships of state departments of welfare to other departments in the state government; to local public and private welfare organizations, to the welfare authorities of the federal government and of other States; to the legislature; and to the general public. These relationships should be thoughtfully worked out.

.   .   .   .   .

A state welfare department should have supervision of all child caring organizations within the State, and articles of incorporation of new child caring organizations should be granted only upon its approval.

The purpose of state supervision is to assure the establishment and maintenance of good standards of work, the setting up of progressive programs, and the protection of the interests of children under care. Most States now have laws providing some form of state supervision or direction of local public and private child caring organizations, but the extent and methods of their supervision vary. The fact that they have such statutes does not imply that they are effective nor that adequate appropriations have been made to permit the enforcement of the existing laws.

All child caring work, whether publicly or privately supported, including public officials and county or local boards dealing with children, should be under the supervision of the State. Where juvenile courts act as general child caring units in addition to their judicial functions, the state welfare department should be given authority to establish for them standards of case work on the same level that is required of other child caring organizations.

The methods of state supervision fall into two general classes: licensing, approval or certification; inspection or visitation. The choice between these methods is relatively unimportant, but it is imperative that the department have sufficient legal powers to make its supervision effective. The leadership and educational duties of the State are, however, more important than the exercise of arbitrary authority.

Many States have felt that they can best meet their responsibilities through the method of inspection and visitation. This requires careful study at first hand of physical plants, methods of administration, and policies of child care in reference to standards set by the department, followed by discussion of the findings with the organizations' representatives. Such a system may be effective in the long run, but leaves much to be desired in the way of quick and decisive action, unless the state department is given authority to make and enforce orders for the correction of unsatisfactory conditions, which will be available in case of emergency and useful where persuasion and recommendations fail.

Other States attempt to exercise their supervisory powers through a licensing system. The issuance of a license must rest upon minimum standards clearly set forth in the regulations of the department rather than upon detailed requirements set by the statute. This method gives an adequate means of controlling child caring activities, provided it also includes the right to close an organization which definitely refuses or neglects to bring its work up to reasonable standards.

Whatever system is established, it is not sufficient unless it includes an additional program in which the voluntary cooperation of child caring groups is obtained. It must also be safeguarded from possible abuse by allowing for appeal and judicial review of a department's decisions.

There seems to be general agreement in reference to the necessity of some control of maternity homes and hospitals, because of the delicacy of the problems with which such organizations deal and the danger of commercialization in their work. An increasing number of States require licensing of child placing societies. An interesting, new and sound development is found also in those States which require in adoption cases some method of investigation and approval by the department.

The incorporation of all child caring organizations which assume the custody of children is desirable. The requirement that articles of incorporation be granted only with the approval of the department which will supervise their work should prevent the establishment of unneeded organizations.

Every state welfare department should contain a division authorized and equipped to handle all cases of an interstate character, especially those which require agreements with other States in reference to the treatment of children who are to be either returned to or recovered by the state authorities. Greater advances have been made in agreements between States over the care of non-resident mental patients than of other non-resident dependents. This is due largely to the fact that most States have a centralized method of handling the mentally handicapped, but have not developed similar centralization in dealing with other classes of dependents.

These interstate questions of responsibility for support are determined by laws covering settlement which, being part of the poor law or similar statutes, are likely to place emphasis on the protection of the community rather than on the protection of those in need of care. State statutes are sharply at variance with one another and these statutes are often at variance with the interests of the children concerned. This is repeatedly illustrated in cases of migratory families and of children about whose settlements there is disagreement between States. The lack, too, of any "national minimum" of child welfare work, or even of a minimum standard of well-being for all children, makes interstate problems peculiarly difficult of adjustment. The care of migratory families should be the responsibility of the State rather than of the local unit. Until some far-reaching method of interstate care has been worked out the principles of human welfare should be applied in larger measure than now prevails in certain States.

No far-reaching improvement can come until a uniform settlement law, similarly administered in the several States, is adopted throughout the country, or some federal assistance in dealing with the problem is made available. Certainly sound case work principles must be the basis for treating cases of children about whose settlement there is dispute. These principles involve careful investigation, adequate treatment according to the needs discovered, and a universal acceptance and utilization of some form of transportation agreement, such as has been applied by a limited number of public and private agencies since 1902.

It is recommended that the voluntary association of public officials, organized on a national basis, should consider the problems involved in these interstate relations and should take action looking towards their solution.

Thirty States now have statutes regulating the placement in foster families of children from outside the State. These laws, primarily intended to protect the States against children who may become public charges through mental defect, disease, or for other reasons, have also provided some protection for the children themselves. Many States now have statutes regulating the placement of their own children, requiring certain methods, standards of work, and reports. Much is needed along these lines to extend to non-resident children the same methods of protection and supervision which are becoming more generally available for resident children.

States that have statutes designed to safeguard children, brought in from other States and placed in family homes, often do not enforce those statutes because of the demands of other duties upon their staffs, and possibly through lack of interest in the problem.

---

2. American Legion promotes improvements in child welfare administration, 1932

"Report of the Chairman of the Legislative Committee of the National Child Welfare Committee," The American Legion, *Fourteenth Annual Convention, 1932* (Portland, 1932), p. 23.

The National Child Welfare Committee of the American Legion was founded in 1925. It sought to organize the Legion's strength in each state in the interest of child welfare. Milt D. Campbell of Ohio was chairman of the Legislative Committee.

To conform with the various resolutions as adopted by national conventions and by meetings of the National Child Welfare Committee of The American Legion, the National Child Welfare Division has set up a minimum program of legislation for the departments to foster in their respective states. This can not, of course, be accomplished except through an intensive educational campaign among the members of the Legion and the Auxiliary, and by co-operation with existing and efficient social welfare and relief organizations in the various states. The following is the minimum program recommended to the departments:

MINIMUM PROGRAM

1. A good family desertion and non-support law under which a deserting father can be easily extradited if he goes into other states.

2. A widowed mothers' allowance law

which will allow help to keep children in their own homes.

3. Provisions for the appointment of an unpaid county child welfare board of three or more members in each county to advise with the county attorney, probation officers, judges and public charities on individual cases.

4. A state children's bureau with a director in charge who shall have the duty of appointing and advising the county child welfare boards and supervising the general administration of the law with regard to dependent, neglected and defective children. (If the state has a State Board of Charities, State Board of Corrections or Board of Control, or Department of Public Welfare, this bureau may be made a part of the same, but a special director trained in child welfare should be assigned to the work.)

5. "A public health record for every child."

6. Importance of co-ordination of county child welfare activity looking toward county unit co-operation and clearance between all forms of county and state aid, including soldiers' relief to dependents of veterans.

7. Aid for the care of dependent children in homes with relatives or persons who stand in the relationship of parents.

8. It is recommended to the departments to co-operate with all the other organizations and agencies in strengthening child labor laws.

9. So long as the federal government continues its practice of encouraging state activity by Federal aid to states, it is recommended that measures providing such Federal aid for the physical rehabilitation, education, vocational guidance, and vocational education of physically-handicapped children and their placement and follow up in employment be given the support of The American Legion.

10. It is recommended to the departments that the question of dealing with the juvenile offender be given special attention and that every effort be made to attain adequate standards for the state in juvenile court administration and juvenile detention homes and juvenile correctional care.

General: States that have not progressed to including in their child welfare provisions the facilities stated in the minimum program, and that do not now have a state child welfare commission or committee, should persuade the governor to help intelligent action by requesting him to appoint a state child welfare commission of interested persons to study and formulate the recommendation of a group of practical child welfare laws. No authority from the legislature is necessary for the appointment of such a commission; said commission to serve without pay. The commission's report should be printed for the purpose of circulation to interested persons.